Homeland and National Security Law and Policy

Homeland and National Security Law and Policy

Cases and Materials

Matt C. Pinsker

CRIMINAL DEFENSE ATTORNEY AND ADJUNCT PROFESSOR
VIRGINIA COMMONWEALTH UNIVERSITY

R. James Orr III

ASSOCIATE PROFESSOR OF NATIONAL SECURITY STRATEGY
NATIONAL WAR COLLEGE

CAROLINA ACADEMIC PRESS
Durham, North Carolina

Copyright © 2017
Carolina Academic Press, LLC
All Rights Reserved

ISBN: 978-1-61163-748-9
eISBN: 978-1-53100-328-9

Library of Congress Cataloging-in-Publication Data

Names: Pinsker, Matt C., author. | Orr, R. James, III, author.
Title: Homeland and national security law and policy : cases and materials / Matt C. Pinsker and R. James Orr III.
Description: Durham, North Carolina : Carolina Academic Press, [2017] | Includes bibliographical references and index.
Identifiers: LCCN 2017024283 | ISBN 9781611637489 (alk. paper)
Subjects: LCSH: National security--Law and legislation--United States. | Internal security--Law and legislation--United States. | Security classification (Government documents)--United States. | Official secrets--United States. | National security--Law and legislation.
Classification: LCC KF4850 .P56 2017 | DDC 343.73/01--dc23
LC record available at https://lccn.loc.gov/2017024283

The material presented in this text is the product of the authors and does not necessarily represent the positions of the U.S. Department of Defense or the United States Government.

Carolina Academic Press, LLC
700 Kent Street
Durham, North Carolina 27701
Telephone (919) 489-7486
Fax (919) 493-5668
www.cap-press.com

Printed in the United States of America

Contents

Introduction	xi
Chapter 1 · The Constitutional Framework	3
Overview	3
Judicial Review	6
Marbury v. Madison, 5 U.S. 137 (1803)	8
McCulloch v. Maryland, 17 U.S. 4 Wheat. 316 (1819)	15
The Extent of a President's Executive Authority	25
Chapter 2 · Criminal Procedure and Homeland/National Security	
Part One: An Introduction to Fourth Amendment Law	35
Overview	35
The Fourth Amendment	36
Reasonableness	39
Searches Not Requiring a Warrant	41
Terry v. Ohio, 392 U.S. 1 (1968)	46
Protecting against Unreasonable Searches — The Exclusionary Rule	57
Mapp v. Ohio, 367 U.S. 643 (1961)	58
Chapter 3 · Criminal Procedure and Homeland/National Security	
Part 2: Fifth and Sixth Amendments — Due Process, Self-Incrimination, and the Right to Counsel	69
Overview	69
Miranda v. Arizona, 384 U.S. 436 (1966)	72
Brewer v. Williams, 430 U.S. 387 (1977)	86
Public Safety Exception	95
New York v. Quarles, 467 U.S. 649 (1984)	95
Application of the *Quarles* Public Safety Exception to Terrorism Cases	101
Impact of *Miranda* Warnings, Waiver, and Interrogation Tactics	102
Chapter 4 · Search and Seizure Law and Technology	109
Overview	109
Olmstead v. United States, 277 U.S. 438 (1928)	110
The Right To Privacy	114
Katz v. United States, 389 U.S. 347 (1967)	119
The Plain View Doctrine	124
The Third-Party Doctrine	126

United States v. Miller, 425 U.S. 435 (1976) 127
Smith v. Maryland, 442 U.S. 735 (1979) 130
Statutory Protections of Privacy 134
Expanding Technology and Privacy Implications 137
Kyllo v. United States, 533 U.S. 27 (2001) 138
The Emerging "Mosaic Theory" of Surveillance Law 144
United States v. Jones, 132 S. Ct. 945 (2012) 146
Florida v. Jardines, 569 U.S. (2013) 156

Chapter 5 · Foreign Surveillance, Searches, and Seizure 167
Overview 167
No National Security Exception to the Constitution 167
United States v. U.S. District Court (Keith), 407 U.S. 297 (1972) 168
Foreign Intelligence Surveillance 176
United States v. Truong Dinh Hung, 629 F.2d 908 (1980) 178
The Foreign Intelligence Surveillance Act 183
Who Can Be Targeted by a FISA Order? 185
United States v. Steven J. Rosen, Keith Weissman,
447 F. Supp. 2d 538 (2006) 186
FISA and the First Amendment 195
United States v. Rosen, 445 F. Supp. 2d 602 (2006) 196
Prosecuting with FISA Evidence 199
The "Wall" between Intelligence and Law Enforcement 200
In re: Sealed Cases Nos. 02-001, 02-002, 310 F.3d 717 (2002) 202
Foreign Searches and Seizures 209
Foreign Searches of Non-Citizens 210
United States v. Verdugo-Urquidez, 494 U.S. 259 (1990) 210
Foreign Searches of U.S. Citizens 217
In re Terrorist Bombings of U.S. Embassies in East Africa,
552 F.3d 157 (2008) 217
Reasonableness of Foreign Searches of U.S. Citizens 223
Cross-Border Actions 226

Chapter 6 · National Security Information
*Classified Information, State Secrets, and Other Issues of Litigating
National Security* 231
Overview 231
Protection of Classified Information from Disclosure 233
18 U.S. Code § 798—Disclosure of classified information 234
Executive Order 13526: Classified National Security Information
(Dec. 29, 2009) 234
New York Times Co. v. United States, 403 U.S. 713 (1971) 240
Open Government and Access to Government Information 244
The Privacy Act 244
The Freedom of Information Act 245
Litigating Cases involving Classified Information 246

Protecting Classified Information in Criminal Cases:
    The Classified Information Procedures Act   247
    2054. Synopsis Of Classified Information Procedures Act (CIPA)   248
    United States v. Richard Craig Smith, 780 F.2d 1102 (1985)   253
Protecting Classified Information in Civil Cases:
    The State Secrets Doctrine   260
    Cases where the Subject of the Case Is Classified —
        The *Totten* Bar   262
    Totten v. United States, 92 U.S. 105 (1876)   262
    Protecting Classified Evidence in Civil Lawsuits —
        The *Reynolds* Privilege   264
    United States v. Reynolds, 345 U.S. 1 (1953)   265
    Mohamed v. Jeppesen Dataplan, 614 F.3d 1070 (2010)   270

Chapter 7 · Bars to Litigating National Security Matters   287
  Overview   287
  Political Questions   288
    El-Shifa Pharmaceutical Industries Co. v. United States,
        607 F.3d 836 (2010)   289
    Lowry v. Reagan, 676 F. Supp. 333 (1987)   298
    Schneider v. Kissinger, 412 F.3d 190 (2005)   302
  Standing   309
    Campbell v. Clinton, 203 F.3d 19 (2000)   310
  Ripeness   313
    Dellums v. Bush, 752 F. Supp. 1141 (1990)   315

Chapter 8 · National Emergencies and Domestic Preparedness   327
  Overview   327
  The Police Power of the Government   328
    Gibbons v. Ogden, 22 U.S. 9 Wheat. 1 (1824)   328
    Jacobson v. Massachusetts, 197 U.S. 11 (1905)   332
    Smith v. Avino, 91 F.3d 105 (11th Cir. 1996)   340
  A Short History of Disaster and Emergency Preparedness   343
  Emergency Preparedness and Response Statutes   352
    Statutory Provisions In General   352
        Excerpts from Title 42 — Public Health and Welfare   354
  Presidential Directives Regarding Emergency Preparedness
    and Response   369
    HSPD-5 — Management of Domestic Incidents   369
    HSPD-7 — Critical Infrastructure Identification, Prioritization,
        and Protection   370
    HSPD-8 — National Preparedness   371
    PPD-8: National Preparedness   371
        Presidential Policy Directive / PPD-8: National Preparedness   372
  Use of the Military in Disaster Response   376
    Title 18 U.S. Code — Crimes and Criminal Procedure   377

Title 10 U.S. Code — Armed Forces	377
Excerpts from 10 U.S. Code Ch. 18 — Military Support for Civilian Law Enforcement Agencies	378
Bissonette v. Haig, 776 F.2d 1384 (1985), affirmed 485 U.S. 264 (1988)	381

Chapter 9 · War Powers 391

Overview	391
Orlando v. Laird, 443 F.2d 1039 (1971)	397
The Prize Cases, 67 U.S. 635 (1863)	401
Durand v. Hollins, 8 F. Cas. 111 (C.C. S.D. N.Y. 1860)	407
Little v. Barreme, 6 U.S. 170 (1804)	411
Youngstown Sheet & Tube Co. v. Sawyer, 343 U.S. 579 (1952)	414
The War Powers Resolution	428
Text of Public Law 93-148	429
R.M. Nixon memorandum of 24 October 1973 to House of Representatives	431
Office of Legal Counsel Opinion dated 1 April 2011 (Applicability of WPR to military operations in Libya)	435
Memorandum Opinion for the Attorney General, April 1, 2011	435

Chapter 10 · International Law and National Security 449

Overview	449
The Paquete Habana, 175 U.S. 677 (1900)	452
Roper v. Simmons, 543 U.S. 551 (2005)	457
When Domestic Law Conflicts with International Law	459
Al-Bihani v. Obama, 590 F.3d 866 (2010)	459
Enforcing International Human Rights Law in U.S. Courts	464
Filartiga v. Pena-Irala, 630 F.2d 876 (1980)	467
Sosa v. Alvarez-Machain, 542 U.S. 692 (2004)	472
Kiobel v. Royal Dutch Petroleum Co., 133 S.Ct. 1659 (2013)	478
Treaties in the U.S. Legal System	484
Foster & Elam v. Neilson, 27 U.S. (2 Pet.) 253 (1829)	486
Whitney v. Robertson, 124 U.S. 190 (1888)	487

Chapter 11 · International Law and Federalism 493

Overview	493
Missouri v. Holland, 252 U.S. 416 (1920)	495
Asakura v. Seattle, 265 U.S. 332 (1924)	497
Crosby v. National Foreign Trade Council, 530 U.S. 363 (2000)	500
Medellin v. Texas, 552 U.S. 491 (2008)	505
Extradition	512
Terlinden v. Ames, 184 U.S. 270 (1902)	512
Collins v. Loisel, 259 U.S. 309 (1922)	515
Lo Duca v. United States, 93 F.3d 1100 (2d Cir., 1996)	518
Ntakirutimana v. Reno, 184 F.3d 419 (5th Cir., 1999)	523
United States v. Alvarez-Machain, 504 U.S. 655 (1992)	528

Chapter 12 · Detention and National Security — 535
Overview — 535
Ex Parte Merryman, 17 F. Cas. 144 (C.C.D. Md., 1861) — 540
Ex Parte Milligan, 71 U.S. 2 (1866) — 547
Ex Parte Quirin, 317 U.S. 1 (1942) — 555
Military Detention and Trial after 9/11 — 565
Johnson v. Eisentrager, 339 U.S. 763 (1950) — 566
Hamdi v. Rumsfeld, 542 U.S. 507 (2004) — 574
Rasul v. Bush, 542 U.S. 466 (2004) — 584
Hamdan v. Rumsfeld, 548 U.S. 557 (2006) — 588
Boumediene v. Bush, 553 U.S. 723 (2008) — 593

Chapter 13 · Military Justice — 607
Overview — 607
Reid v. Covert, 354 U.S. 1, 1957 — 608
Purpose of the Military Justice System — 611
Criminal and Disciplinary Processes — 615
Due Process and Civil Rights of Service Members — 620
Improper Command Influence — 620
U.S. v. Baldwin, 54 M.J. 308 (2001) — 621
Miranda Rights and the Military — 623
U.S. v. Loukas, 29 M.J. 385 (1990) — 625
Searches and Inspections — 630
U.S. v. Campbell, 41 M.J. 177 (1994) — 631
Free Speech in the Military — 636
U.S. v. Howe, 37 C.M.R. 429 (1967) — 637
Uniquely Military Offenses — 640
AWOL and Desertion — 640
U.S. v. Mackey, 46 C.M.R. 754 (1972) — 642
The General Article — 643
Conduct Unbecoming — 645
Parker v. Levy, 417 U.S. 733 (1974) — 645
Dereliction of Duty — 653
U.S. v. Allen Lawson, 33 M.J. 946 (1988) — 653
Abu Ghraib, Dereliction of Duty, and Maltreatment — 655
U.S. v. Harmon, 66 M.J. 710 (2008) — 655

Chapter 14 · Other Civil Rights Issues in Homeland and National Security Law — 663
Overview — 663
National Security and the First Amendment — 663
Brandenburg v. Ohio, 395 U.S. 444 (1969) — 665
Solicitation and Conspiracy — 668
U.S. v. Rahman, 189 F.3d 88 (1999) — 669
Material Support of Terrorism — 675
Holder v. Humanitarian Law Project, 561 U.S. 1 (2010) — 675

Civil Liberties Issues and Profiling ... 682
   Farag v. U.S., 587 F. Supp. 2d 436 (2008) ... 683
   Internment of Japanese-Americans during World War II ... 696
     Korematsu v. United States, 323 U.S. 214 (1944) ... 696
Extrajudicial Killings ... 704
   Al-Aulaqi v. Obama, 727 F. Supp. 2d 1 (2010) ... 706
Voluntary Searches and the Right to Travel ... 716
   MacWade v. Kelly, 460 F.3d 260 (2006) ... 717
   Gilmore v. Gonzales, 435 F.3d 1125 (2006) ... 726
   U.S. v. Arnold, 533 F.3d 1003 (2008) ... 730

Concluding Thoughts ... 737
Glossary ... 739
Index ... 745

Introduction

Thank you for your purchase of *Homeland and National Security Law and Policy: Cases and Materials*. If you are reading this, there is a good chance you are an undergraduate or graduate student taking a class in national security law or a related subject. This book has been specifically written for individuals like you who have no formal legal training or education beyond what you learned in high school government or social studies classes and, perhaps, similar courses earlier in college.

Overview

This book is intended to expose you to the highly diverse range of legal issues tackled by national security professionals. The topics covered by this book include but are not limited to the following: criminal procedure, interrogation, stop-and-frisk, warrants, electronic surveillance, domestic surveillance, foreign surveillance, foreign searches, state secrets, classified information, war powers, litigation, civil rights, free speech, military justice, international law, detainees, drones, military justice, rules of engagement, and much more.

Although this book is a mile wide in terms of the subjects covered, it is only an inch deep in the depth given to each topic. Each of the subjects touched upon in this book can be (in fact, often are) the subject of much more detailed and specialized texts. But the approach we have taken in writing this book is to provide a survey of the field in a manner that makes this text an excellent source from which to learn the basic principles of national security law. This book is intended for a wide variety of audiences including aspiring law enforcement, diplomats, intelligence analysts, military officers, civil rights advocates, and others who simply want to know more about the issues in the news every day. It is very possible you are a student in one of the following disciplines: criminal justice, homeland/national/international security, prelaw, international relations, political science, intelligence studies, or public policy to name but a few. Or maybe you are taking a class in national security because the class you really wanted was full and this was the only one you could fit in your schedule. Whatever your aspiring path or discipline may be, this book will give you the basics of the legal issues in homeland and national security.

Now, the definitions of homeland security and national security tend to be difficult to pin down. Those who have looked at the issue have found as many as seven different definitions in the guidelines of different agencies. For our purposes here, we will rely on the vision of homeland security that is used by the Department of Homeland Security:

> A homeland that is safe, secure, and resilient against terrorism and other hazards, where American interests, aspirations, and way of life can thrive.[1]

Compare this to the definition of homeland security provided by the Department of Defense:

> A concerted national effort to prevent terrorist attacks within the United States; reduce America's vulnerability to terrorism, major disasters, and other emergencies; and minimize the damage and recover from attacks, major disasters, and other emergencies that occur.[2]

National security is defined in the same document as:

> A collective term encompassing both national defense and foreign relations of the United States with the purpose of gaining: a. A military or defense advantage over any foreign nation or group of nations; b. A favorable foreign relations position; or c. A defense posture capable of successfully resisting hostile or destructive action from within or without, overt or covert.[3]

You can see there is a fair bit of overlap in the terms, and so this one text is designed to give you a sense of the law and, in some cases, the policies that provide a framework for authorities to seek these goals.

How This Book Works

Each chapter of this book introduces you to legal issues and concepts which are summarized and explained. Excerpts of relevant statutes, directives, and case law are provided. In this text, more so than in many undergraduate texts, we provide you edited versions of the governing court decisions and opinions rather than relying on a summary or analysis of those opinions. The analysis will come out as you discuss the cases with each other, in class or out.

Now, many of the cases we include are very long, in some cases more than a hundred pages in length. In addition, some of the writing of the cases may be difficult to understand, with arcane legal language and lists of in-text citations. In an effort to make the cases shorter and more easily read, we have tried to paraphrase parts of the decisions that may be difficult for undergraduate students to understand, and we have edited out parts of the cases that do not bear directly on the issues we are highlighting in the text. We've also eliminated many of the in-text references, quotation marks, and other aspects that we think would just confuse the reader. Now, you may want to read the case as originally written, so we have provided the accurate case title and source. That way you can look up the full text of the case if you wish.

---

1. Department of Homeland Security, *The 2014 Quadrennial Homeland Security Review*, p. 14.
2. Joint Publication 1-02, Department of Defense Dictionary of Military and Associated Terms.
3. Id.

We will spend a bit more time on the law regarding search and seizure and due process than you might find in other textbooks on homeland security law or national security law. Because much of the effort to protect our nation from terrorist attacks is actually good police work, it is important to have a good foundation in these areas of the law. Terrorism is a crime that presents certain challenges often not found in the more common crimes our authorities deal with. The need to act in a way that catches these perpetrators before they commit their acts is so much more important, the laws regarding surveillance and searches, detention and use of force, have been applied by the authorities and considered by the courts in new and complicated ways.

We also spend a chapter talking about the laws that apply to disaster relief. Our nation has long recognized that the effect on the nation and its people from large-scale attack is, in many ways, similar to the effects from natural disasters like hurricanes, wildfires, and floods. So some laws have been written in ways to allow first-responders at the federal, state, local, and tribal levels to work together.

While we include portions or summaries of some key statutes, regulations, and policies, most of this book uses the case law and opinions of the U.S. Supreme Court and other federal and state courts to discuss what the law is.

Now, you may be wondering just what are "case law" and "opinions"? Case law is law that is written and explained by judges. As you learned in high school government, the legislature makes the law, and the judges interpret the law. Often, disputes arise as to how the law, which may not be very precise, applies in a particular case or controversy. When that happens, it is up to the judges to interpret and clarify the law and apply it to the specific facts before them. When judges do this, they write an opinion to explain their interpretation of the law and how it applies to a particular case. These opinions are in turn considered and relied on by other judges in cases that arise under slightly different facts. The opinions are also relied on by attorneys, law enforcement officers, and other individuals. When this is done, the case law is referred to as "precedent." Because the facts of every case are slightly different, it is important that the reasoning of the court be explained so that the actual decision can be understood and applied as precedent in the best possible manner. The opinions, in other words, provide the "why" of the law's development as much as the "what."

In an opinion, the judges give you the facts and events that led to the case and legal issue in question, and then lead you through a discussion of the legal issues and the applicable law. In this discussion, the judges explain how the law applies to the facts before them and how that analysis leads them to an eventual legal conclusion. The law and reasoning the judges give in an opinion for one case will be applied in the future to other cases which raise similar (but often slightly different) legal or factual issues.

The challenge in dealing with case law is that the opinions are often written in a manner difficult to understand, especially for those who have not handled case law before. The judges who write case law are among the most experienced, brilliant, and respected attorneys in the country. Unfortunately, they write at a level beyond the education and experience of the average individual, especially those who are untrained in the law, using advanced legal terminology, Latin phrases, and a vocabulary beyond that of the average individual.

What the authors of this book have done is edit the opinions written by judges in matters concerning national security. In preparing the opinions you read in this book, we have removed some of the complicated legal jargon, extensive footnotes and references, obscure Latin phrases, and discussions of topics other than those that apply to the concepts we are trying to help you understand, leaving only the part of the decision that addresses the national security issues on which you should be focusing. Essentially, the authors have abridged the cases to make them more friendly and understandable for an undergraduate audience without any legal training. In some cases you will see parts of decisions are underlined or in bold print. The authors have added these in order to make sure you see a key point made in the decision. All this has been done to make the judicial opinions not only readable, but more easily understood by a non-lawyer like you. If you are interested in reading the unedited versions of these cases, most are publicly available and can be found online with a simple Google search.

Some Cautions

It is common for anyone interested in a particular field to watch television shows, read novels, or see movies related to your interest. That is fine, so long as you remember that what you are watching or reading is entertainment and not information. Even those shows that are "documentaries," "docudramas," "inspired by a true story," or "based on the events of . . ." will be extremely inaccurate and can give you the wrong ideas about the subject. They have been written and edited to entertain, not to inform.

This is especially true when these shows get into a field as complex and as necessarily precise as the law. These shows often get more wrong about the law than they get right. Just as you would not try to learn physics from watching *Star Trek* and science fiction, do not try to learn the law by watching these shows or other legal fiction. After you complete this class, the next time you watch a police drama or movie involving national security or the law, you will have a completely different outlook.

Be warned, the knowledge you gain from this book just might ruin your enjoyment of those shows!

Next, we ask you to be careful of bias or preconceived ideas about the law that block your learning. As a free people, we have many disputes over what the law is or what the law should be. Reasonable minds can disagree as to what should be legal or how the U.S. Constitution should be interpreted. For example, there is considerable controversy in the U.S. over the meaning of the Second Amendment and the right to keep and bear arms. It is likely that you have your own opinion as to how the Second Amendment should be interpreted. But how you think this law *should* be applied may be different than the way the law *is* applied. Both are useful and valuable, but it is important to know the difference.

The Latin terms for this distinction are *lex lata* (what the law is) and *lege ferenda* (what the law should be, or how the law should develop). You will need to know the difference and be able to distinguish between the two. Here is an easy test—*lex lata* is contained in the words of the Constitution, a treaty, or a statute, and in the majority (deciding) opinion of a court case (usually the Supreme Court). If you are reading a scholarly article, a newspaper account, or someone else's analysis of the law, you are very possibly reading what that writer thinks the law *ought* to be (*lege ferenda*).

As much as possible, this book seeks to refrain from offering an opinion as to what the law should be, focusing on what the law is as interpreted by the courts. Unless it specifically states otherwise, this textbook seeks to present the law as it is and explains why it is a certain way, informing the reader as to the debates which occur in society concerning these issues. That is why most of the textbook consists of actual court decisions and the language of the statutes, and not a summary or analysis provided by the authors. It is up to you, the reader, to decide for yourself whether the law is proper or right, or should be changed. You are more than welcome to disagree with the laws of this country. In fact, throughout this book you will encounter laws and decisions you not only disagree with, but which you may also find odious to civil liberties, laws which you believe actually endanger national security, or which simply do not make sense. Just remember, no matter how much you disagree with a law, it is still the law unless and until it is changed by a court decision or legislation.

Finally, in this field perhaps more so than in any other, the law changes, and in some respects changes quickly. A president may issue an order that changes how a law is applied, or Congress may pass a law responding to a Supreme Court decision. The laws we include in this book have been chosen to ensure you understand the concepts and principles, but no textbook can be fully up to date in this day and age. So make sure that you learn how to find the law from outside sources to keep up with it as it evolves.

Sources of Law

So what are the sources of law contained in this book?

First we will discuss the U.S. Constitution. It is, as most of us know from grade school, the founding document on which our system of government and its laws are based. The Constitution controls the government by providing express and implied powers for the branches of the federal government, by limiting the powers of the federal government, and by protecting individual rights from infringement by the government. The Constitution also provides for the federalist system we have in the United States, with different roles for the federal and for state governments. It provides, as we'll discuss later, for international law—treaties and other international agreements—to be a part of our law. The Constitution, as we will explain in the next chapter, established the legislative, executive, and judicial branches of government. "The law" can be found in official documents and decisions that flow from each of these. In fact, the Constitution itself tells us what the law is in Article VI:

> This Constitution, and the laws of the United States which shall be made in pursuance thereof; and all treaties made, or which shall be made, under the authority of the United States, shall be the supreme law of the land

Often, when people think of "the law" they are thinking about the statutes that Congress passes. Congress may pass laws that establish the law's content (such as laws that prohibit certain behavior, such as human trafficking or torture) or laws that establish procedures (such as the Foreign Intelligence Surveillance Act), providing guidance to the executive branch on how things should be done. Law is established through executive regulations that the president or individual federal agencies issue pursuant to inherent Constitutional authority or through a statutory grant of authority. In the case of executive action involving national security, these regulations can take the form of an executive order (such as E.O. 12333 that regulates the intelligence community by prohibiting assassinations), or through National Security Decision documents that may or may not be classified. Finally, law is established through decisions of the U.S. Supreme Court and the subordinate courts, giving us interpretations of the Constitution, statutes, and regulations as they apply to specific cases and controversies arise.

Other sources of the law we will discuss in this text include treaties and other international agreements, as well as the statutes, court decisions, and regulations enacted by the states, territories, and tribal authorities in the U.S. We will talk about HOW the courts use these treaties and agreements to tell us what the law is. It's not an automatic process, as you will come to see.

All of these sources together provide "the law." But even then, in our system, "the law" is sometimes established by custom and practice. This is often the case because the legislature or the courts have not acted. In the field of national security more so than in any other, understanding the law often requires an understanding of history and what the president has done in the absence of (or sometimes in disagreement with) actions and decisions of Congress or the courts. When Congress or the courts then act (if they do), the law changes. What "the law" is, then, can shift as each of these actors (Congress, the president, agencies, courts, states) takes a turn pronouncing the law. And it is important to understand that this shifting, this interplay between the different branches of government, is not a flaw in our system, but is in fact exactly how our system was designed to work.

So, for example, the president may act pursuant to what he considers his inherent authority as commander-in-chief — say by directing certain surveillance of individuals considered threats to the nation. And, pursuant to that, he issues an executive order to the Department of Defense. That order would apply only to the executive branch (in this case the Department of Defense) and affects only how they do their business. This is just like any boss telling a subordinate office what to do. From the perspective of that agency (or the executive branch as a whole), that executive order has "the force of law." In other words, they have to follow it.

Now, the courts may get a complaint in the form of a case from a person claiming that this surveillance constitutes an illegal search and violates the Fourth Amendment.

A scholarly article published in a law journal, tracing the history of search and seizure law and concluding that the case has merit, is NOT the law. It might be convincing, and may or may not convince the president's lawyers, but they are not obliged to follow the law review article's analysis. On the other hand, if the case does go to court, and the courts agree with the complainant, then that court decision IS the law, and the president, and his subordinate agencies will have to change their behavior to comply with the court decision.

Now, let's say that Congress thinks that, while the Supreme Court had some valid points, the need exists for this type of surveillance to be conducted. So Congress passes a law providing some guidelines. Based on that law, the president revises his executive order, and the Department of Homeland Security and Justice Department issue regulations telling federal agents how to obey the president and Congress. Each of these—the court decision, the statute, the revised (or new) regulation—is a part of understanding what the law is at this point in time.

In making the regulations, the executive branch may be guided by the Administrative Procedure Act,[4] which in many cases requires that proposed regulations be issued in draft form and published, so that the public has notice and an opportunity to comment on the proposed rule. The agency is then required to consider that comment before writing and issuing the final regulation. This is intended to ensure that the public is aware of what the government is doing when rules are made. There are some circumstances where this procedure is not necessary, but in most cases it is.

In the court decision, the majority opinion establishes what the legal ruling is—what the law is, as applied to the specific case before it. Other opinions, concurring or dissenting with the majority opinion, are not the law but often provide valuable insight into how the law is developing or point out ways that the next case ought to frame an issue. So, in reading court decisions, reading the concurring and dissenting opinions are important, but it is also important to keep in mind the limited role these other opinions play.

In addition to federal laws (from whatever source) are state laws. Each state has its own constitution, which cannot conflict with the U.S. Constitution, federal statute, or (by extension of federal statute) administrative laws. Within a state, no state law can conflict with the state's constitution. Finally, there are municipal laws. These are local ordinances passed by cities and counties.

The paragraphs above show that the sources of law can be presented in the following hierarchical structure:

1. The Constitution
2. Federal statutes and treaties
3. Federal executive decisions: administrative law and executive agreements

---

4. The Administrative Procedure Act (APA), Pub.L. 79–404, 60 Stat. 237, enacted June 11, 1946, is the federal statute that governs the way in which administrative agencies of the federal government of the United States may propose and establish regulations.

4. State constitution, state statutes, and state common law
5. Municipal law (cities and counties)

Case law (or judge-made law) is not included in this list because judges do not make laws in the same manner, by simply creating a new law or regulation. Instead, judges, as we have said before, interpret the laws that already exist and apply them to the cases and controversies that come before them.

However, the reality is that judges do in fact "make law" when they write their opinions. This is because these decisions provide a level of detail and specific guidance that might not exist in the text of the Constitution, or in the statute, treaty, or regulation being applied. Another way that judges "make law" through deciding cases is by balancing provisions of the law that seem to contradict each other or serve contradicting values (such as liberty and security). And, in making these judgments, the courts change how we understand and apply the law.

For example, nowhere does the U.S. Constitution specifically require a person who is being arrested be informed of the right to remain silent and the right to an attorney before being interrogated. However, the U.S. Supreme Court, in applying the rights protected by the Fifth and Sixth Amendment to police interrogations, shaped a rule that requires law enforcement to do just that. That rule, now a part of the law, is known as the Miranda Warning.

Using the example from above involving Miranda, the U.S. Constitution has always included the right of a suspect to remain silent and to have the assistance of legal counsel. To give that preexisting civil right substance and prevent its abuse or avoidance by law enforcement, the Supreme Court added the requirement of a Miranda Warning in 1966. In fact, the Supreme Court actually did not order law enforcement to read people their rights prior to being interrogated when in custody. It merely created a rule making statements made without such a warning inadmissible because they presumably violate the Fifth and Sixth Amendments.

The Federal Court System

Article III of the U.S. Constitution vests the judicial power in "one Supreme Court, and in such inferior courts as the Congress may from time to time establish." Let's provide a little background on the federal judiciary in this country. Instead of starting at the top with the U.S. Supreme Court and going down, though, let's start at the bottom and work our way up.

All over the country, we have federal judicial district courts, which are presided over by district judges. There are 94 federal judicial districts, including at least one district in each state, the District of Columbia and Puerto Rico. Three territories of the United States — the Virgin Islands, Guam, and the Northern Mariana Islands — have district courts that hear federal cases, including bankruptcy cases. In total, there are over 670 federal district judges in the nation. The United States district courts are the trial courts of the federal court system. Within limits set by Congress and the Constitution, the district courts have jurisdiction to hear nearly all categories of federal cases—both civil and criminal matters.

Criminal law is where the government brings charges against and prosecutes a person. For example, if Harry shoots and kills Bob, the government would prosecute Harry for murder. Some of the cases you will be reading came out of criminal prosecutions. Civil law, in this context, describes all law which is not criminal. Most commonly, this is where one party (which can be the government, a corporation, an individual, or any other entity) sues another person, government, corporation, or entity. In the lawsuit, the entity can ask for money, a court order (often one known as an "injunction"), or some other form of relief. For example, in a case that might be entitled "ACLU v. NSA," the ACLU would be suing the NSA, as part of the government, seeking a court order, or an injunction, which would order the NSA to halt surveillance of U.S. citizens on the grounds that such surveillance violates the U.S. Constitution. In a case that arose after the Civil War known as *Totten v. U.S.* (we will read this case later in the text), a former spy sued the U.S. government for money he said he had been promised in a contract. Many cases in this text arose from civil law suits. Decisions that are handed down by a federal district court judge are binding only within that district and not in others.

The 94 U.S. judicial districts are organized into 12 regional circuits, each of which has a United States court of appeals. A court of appeals hears appeals from the district courts located within its circuit, as well as appeals from decisions of federal administrative agencies. Although over a dozen judges will sit on a circuit court, the judges will typically hear appeals in a panel of 3 judges, who then give an opinion. If the person who is appealing, known as the "appellant," does not like the decision, he or she can appeal again, and all of the judges from the court would hear the case. When this happens, it is known as the court sitting "en banc." Any decisions issued from these circuit judges are binding upon the districts courts within their circuit, but not those that lie outside of their circuits. These circuit courts are named by number: The First Circuit Court of Appeals, the Second Circuit Court of Appeals, and so on. The only federal circuit courts without a number are the D.C. Circuit Court of Appeals and the Federal Circuit Court of Appeals.

In theory, all circuit courts are equally important and no circuit court outranks another. However, the D.C. Circuit Court of Appeals most commonly handles cases involving national security, often some of the most complex and interesting cases.

And finally, at the top of the federal judiciary hierarchy is the highest court in the land, and it is the U.S. Supreme Court. Any judgments made by the U.S. Supreme Court are final. If the case involves interpretation of a statute or regulation, the statute or regulation must be changed or the court opinion will control. Alternatively, the decision can be overturned or changed by either a new Supreme Court opinion or a change to the Constitution.

Now, this pattern is repeated in slightly different ways in each of the state court systems. Keep in mind that the state court system is much more a parallel to the federal system than a subordinate system. In the case of applying federal law—including the federal Constitution—the decisions of the federal courts are supreme. In the case of state law and the application of state constitutions, the state courts have the last word—at least up to the point where state law involves federal constitutional rights.

How to Study Court Opinions

Taking notes in a legal class that relies on case law or judicial opinions is different than taking notes in other subjects such as government or history. Although this class is reading comprehension intensive and involves many historic and governmental issues, do not approach this text as if it is a political science textbook, simply reading the material for a general comprehension. Because law appears, on the surface, to be similar to government, history, or a related social science, many students make this mistake and subsequently struggle with the material. Interestingly, students of math or physics tend to do well at law. Although physics and law are very different, the process of studying and preparing is very similar, focusing on analysis rather than simple memorization. Just as you would do with mathematics or physics, you should read and familiarize yourself with the material and then try to apply the concepts to a new set of facts. In this text we provide practice problems where you apply the material to reinforce your understanding.

Performing an IRAC Analysis

As a student of the law, the way to read and familiarize yourself with the material (prior to doing practice problems) is by briefing a case. Briefing a case is how lawyers take notes on case law and certain items of information. This method, which is more or less common to all law schools, is to draft a short one- or two-page summary of the case while focusing on the following topics: Facts (including the procedural history), Issue, Rule, Analysis or Application, and Conclusion. Below is an explanation of how you should brief the cases in this book.

Prior to reading a case, it helps to prepare a document with the following items listed:

Facts:

Procedural History:

Issue:

Rule:

Application and Analysis:

Conclusion:

As you read each case, you should fill out each item with the information you learn from the case. This means in each part you would write out:

Facts: What events transpired in the real world that led to this case?

Procedural History: Prior to getting to this court, how did this case work its way through the legal system? What did the lower courts decide?

Issue: What is the underlying question that the case grapples with?

Rule: What is the specific rule of law the judges rely on in making a decision?

Holding: How did the court decide, and who does the court rule in favor for?

Reasoning: Why did the court decide the way it did?

Application and Analysis: How does the rule apply to the facts of this particular case? What is the reasoning of the judges? Why does prior law apply, or why is this case decided differently than prior law might suggest? Explain thoroughly.

Conclusion: What is the legal conclusion reached by the judges?

To demonstrate, let's write a case brief of the famous children's book, Green Eggs and Ham:

Facts: Despite Sam-I-Am's urging and pressure, unnamed person (P) will not try green eggs and ham, claiming he does not like them. (What facts led to this issue entering the courts)

Procedural History: Sam-I-Am asks P to try green eggs and ham in different areas and under different circumstances: here and there, moves on to foxes and boxes, and concludes on a boat where, out of a sense of fatigue, P tries them. (Which courts, how they ruled, what they ruled on)

Issue: Whether it is worth trying new things. (What it's about)

Rule: Be open to try new things. (How to act when facing this issue)

Holding: Green eggs and ham are good. (The court's decision)

Reasoning: If another person is very insistent that "you may like it," you may, in fact, like it. When they say "try it you will see," it is, perhaps, worth trying. New things might taste good. (Why it reached this decision)

Application: In trying green eggs and ham, P learned he likes a new food and will eat them anywhere. (What happens when the rule is applied to the facts)

Conclusion: As green eggs and ham tasted good, despite one's initial bias, new things should be tried in other situations. (Similar to holding)

This method of briefing a case is how you learn the fundamental concepts of law and legal reasoning. In this textbook, you learn how to apply the law by doing practice problems that provide a hypothetical fact pattern based on real world events and end with a legal question for you to solve. In solving the legal question, you will have to apply what you learned from reading the applicable statutes and case law and then try to solve the question very much the same way you might solve an equation or puzzle. Many of the hypotheticals you will be asked to solve involve national security issues actually handled by professionals in the field.

You have to solve these situations by going through the formula discussed above (commonly called "IRAC"). First, read the fact pattern and try to spot the underlying legal issue. You should then state the rule, or the law, which applies to the type of legal issue raised in the fact pattern. Then, you should apply the rule to the specific facts of your hypothetical situation. When you do this successfully, you will reach the proper legal conclusion. Let's apply this to the pretend case law of Green Eggs and Ham to the following fact pattern.

> Lisa is three years old and has never gone down the slide at the playground. It looks tall and scary. Other children on the playground, who are themselves going down the slide, urge her to try, indicating she will enjoy it. Use the IRAC approach to decide what Lisa should do, applying the "legal" precedent established in Green Eggs and Ham.
>
> **Issue**: Whether Lisa should try going down the slide.
>
> **Rule**: People should try new things because they might enjoy them.
>
> **Application**: If Lisa goes down the slide, she might find it fun and not at all scary. She sees others trying it, and they are not scared; in fact, they are safe and having fun.
>
> **Conclusion**: Lisa should try going down the slide.

You will have noticed that this Issue, Rule, Application, and Conclusion (IRAC) approach you use to answer the hypothetical are the same components as in a case brief. This is no accident. Applying the "IRAC" approach is a fundamental tool of the practice of law.

One reason the study of law is more like studying mathematics and less like government or history, is that, just like briefing a case, the process of learning to IRAC is a skill acquired over time. When you first started doing long division, someone initially explained the concept to you, just like in this book, where case law written by judges explain a legal concept to you. Once the concept of long division was demonstrated to you, you completed many practice problems. The more you did long division, the easier it got. You must do the same with law. Just like long division, there is a learning curve, but the more you do it, the easier it gets.

Another way math and law are similar is that in math, you do not memorize every equation or numerical sequences that might exist. Instead, you learn concepts and procedures that apply to many different situations. If you learn the concepts of long division, such as how to divide 9 into 687, then you can work through the same procedures to divide 7 into 1,049.

Let's start out with a very easy IRAC for you to solve. Suppose Congress passed a law, which the president signed, forbidding the practice and observance of Buddhism in America. Laura, a practicing Buddhist, is arrested for practicing Buddhism as she meditates in her bedroom. The American Civil Liberties Union (ACLU) sues the government, charging that Lisa's arrest was unconstitutional and the law should be struck down. Use the IRAC process to determine how the judge should rule.

Based on what you know from high school government, you should be able to solve this problem. You know that in America, people have the right to freely practice their religion. But how would you answer this question in an IRAC format? On the left hand margin of your own word document, write

Issue:

Rule:

Application:

Conclusion:

Now that you have written out the components of IRAC, try to fill in the blanks with what you think the ISSUE is in the problem, write out the RULE that applies to the situation here, APPLY the law to the facts in this hypothetical, and, in the end, give the appropriate legal CONCLUSION as to just how the judge should rule. Be advised, there can be more than one correct way to write the Issue.

Issue: Whether the act in question is Constitutional.

Rule: The First Amendment of the U.S. Constitution prohibits Congress from passing laws that interfere with the right to the exercise (free practice) of religion.

Application: This law forbids Laura's freedom to practice her religion.

Conclusion: The law violates the First Amendment, is unconstitutional, and should be struck down.

Let's get started now by reading a couple of court opinions. We will start with the 1957 Supreme Court decision *Reid v. Covert*. This is a good case for this subject because it covers a number of different issues involving criminal procedure, international law, civil rights, and military justice. As you read the opinion, try to brief the case by identifying the Facts, Procedural History, Issue, Rule, Holding, Reasoning, Application, and Conclusion.

Reid v. Covert, 354 U.S. 1 (1957)[*]

This opinion addresses two cases which raise basic constitutional issues of the utmost concern. They call into question the role of the military under our system of government. They involve the power of Congress to expose civilians to trial by military tribunals under military rules and regulations, for offenses against the United States, thereby depriving them of trial in civilian courts, under civilian laws and procedures and with all the safeguards of the Bill of Rights. These cases are particularly significant because, for the first time since the adoption of the Constitution wives of soldiers have been denied trial by jury in a court of law and forced to trial before courts-martial.

Mrs. Clarice Covert killed her husband, a sergeant in the United States Air Force, at an airbase in England. Mrs. Covert, who was not a member of the armed services, was residing on the base with her husband at the time. She was tried by a court-martial for murder under the Uniform Code of Military Justice (UCMJ).

Counsel for Mrs. Covert contended that she was insane at the time she killed her husband, but the military tribunal found her guilty of murder and sentenced her to

---

[*] The case has been heavily edited and paraphrased by the authors for clarity. See disclaimer in introduction.

life imprisonment. Her counsel petitioned the Federal District Court for a writ of habeas corpus, which is where a person is brought before a court to determine whether or not that person is being lawfully held. Her lawyer asked that the court set her free on the ground that the Constitution forbade her trial by military authorities. Interpreting the U.S. Supreme Court's past decision in a prior opinion stating that "a civilian is entitled to a civilian trial," the District Court held that Mrs. Covert could not be tried by court-martial, and ordered her released from custody. The Government appealed directly to the U.S. Supreme Court.

Mrs. Dorothy Smith killed her husband, an Army officer, at a post in Japan where she was living with him. She was tried for murder by a court-martial and, despite considerable evidence that she was insane, was found guilty and sentenced to life imprisonment. Mrs. Smith was then confined in a federal penitentiary in West Virginia. Her father filed a petition for habeas corpus in a Federal District Court. The petition charged that the court-martial was without jurisdiction because Article 2(11) of the UCMJ was unconstitutional insofar as it authorized the trial of civilian dependents accompanying servicemen overseas. Unlike with Mrs. Covert, the District Court refused to issue the writ of habeas corpus. The appeal went to this court and it is our holding that Mrs. Smith and Mrs. Covert could not constitutionally be tried by military authorities.

At the beginning, we reject the idea that, when the United States acts against citizens abroad, it can do so free of the Bill of Rights. The United States is entirely a creature of the Constitution. Its power and authority have no other source. It can only act in accordance with all the limitations imposed by the Constitution. When the Government reaches out to punish a citizen who is abroad, the shield which the Bill of Rights and other parts of the Constitution provide to protect his life and liberty should not be stripped away just because he happens to be in another land.

Among those provisions, Art. III, § 2 and the Fifth and Sixth Amendments are directly relevant to these cases. Article III, § 2 lays down the rule that:

> The Trial of all Crimes, except in Cases of Impeachment, shall be by Jury, and such Trial shall be held in the State where the said Crimes shall have been committed; but when not committed within any State, the Trial shall be at such Place or Places as the Congress may by Law have directed.

The Fifth Amendment declares:

> No person shall be held to answer for a capital, or otherwise infamous crime, unless on a presentment or indictment of a Grand Jury, except in cases arising in the land or naval forces, or in the Militia, when in actual service in time of War or public danger; . . .

And the Sixth Amendment provides:

> In all criminal prosecutions, the accused shall enjoy the right to a speedy and public trial, by an impartial jury of the State and district wherein the crime shall have been committed. . . .

The language of Article III, §2 manifests that constitutional protections for the individual were designed to restrict the United States Government when it acts outside of this country, as well as here at home. After declaring that all criminal trials must be by jury, the section states that, when a crime is "not committed within any State, the Trial shall be at such Place or Places as the Congress may by Law have directed." If this language is permitted to have its obvious meaning, §2 is applicable to criminal trials outside of the States as a group without regard to where the offense is committed or the trial held. From the very first Congress, federal statutes have implemented the provisions of §2 by providing for trial of murder and other crimes committed outside the jurisdiction of any State "in the district where the offender is apprehended, or into which he may first be brought." The Fifth and Sixth Amendments, like Art. III, §2, are also all inclusive with their sweeping references to "no person" and to "all criminal prosecutions."

This Court and other federal courts have held or asserted that various constitutional limitations apply to the Government when it acts outside the continental United States. While it has been suggested that only those constitutional rights which are "fundamental" protect Americans abroad, we can find no warrant, in logic or otherwise, for picking and choosing among the remarkable collection of "Thou shalt nots" which were explicitly fastened on all departments and agencies of the Federal Government by the Constitution and its Amendments. Moreover, in view of our heritage and the history of the adoption of the Constitution and the Bill of Rights, it seems peculiarly anomalous to say that trial before a civilian judge and by an independent jury picked from the common citizenry is not a fundamental right. As the famous English judge Blackstone wrote in his Commentaries:

> ... the trial by jury ever has been, and I trust ever will be, looked upon as the glory of the English law. And if it has so great an advantage over others in regulating civil property, how much must that advantage be heightened when it is applied to criminal cases! ... [I]t is the most transcendent privilege which any subject can enjoy, or wish for, that he cannot be affected either in his property, his liberty, or his person, but by the unanimous consent of twelve of his neighbours and equals.

Trial by jury in a court of law and in accordance with traditional modes of procedure after an indictment by grand jury has served and remains one of our most vital barriers to governmental arbitrariness. These elemental procedural safeguards were embedded in our Constitution to secure their inviolateness and sanctity against the passing demands of expediency or convenience.

II

At the time of Mrs. Covert's alleged offense, an executive agreement was in effect between the United States and Great Britain which permitted United States' military courts to exercise exclusive jurisdiction over offenses committed in Great Britain by American servicemen or their dependents. For its part, the United States agreed that these military courts would be willing and able to try and to punish all offenses against the laws of Great Britain by such persons. In all material respects, the same situation existed in Japan when Mrs. Smith killed her husband. Even though a court-martial does not give an accused trial by jury and other Bill of Rights protections, the Government contends that Art. 2 (11) of the UCMJ, insofar as it provides for the military trial of dependents accompanying the armed forces in Great Britain and Japan, can be sustained as legislation which is necessary and proper to carry out the United States' obligations under the international agreements made with those countries. The obvious and decisive answer to this, of course, is that no agreement with a foreign nation can confer power on the Congress, or on any other branch of Government, which is free from the restraints of the Constitution.

Article VI, the Supremacy Clause of the Constitution, declares:

> This Constitution, and the Laws of the United States which shall be made in Pursuance thereof, and all Treaties made, or which shall be made, under the Authority of the United States, shall be the supreme Law of the Land; . . .

There is nothing in this language which intimates that treaties and laws enacted pursuant to them do not have to comply with the provisions of the Constitution. Nor is there anything in the debates which accompanied the drafting and ratification of the Constitution which even suggests such a result. It would be manifestly contrary to the objectives of those who created the Constitution, as well as those who were responsible for the Bill of Rights—let alone alien to our entire constitutional history and tradition—to construe Article VI as permitting the United States to exercise power under an international agreement without observing constitutional prohibitions. In effect, such construction would permit amendment of that document in a manner not sanctioned by Article V. The prohibitions of the Constitution were designed to apply to all branches of the National Government, and they cannot be nullified by the Executive or by the Executive and the Senate combined.

There is nothing new or unique about what we say here. This Court has regularly and uniformly recognized the supremacy of the Constitution over a treaty. For example, in *Geofroy v. Riggs*, it declared:

> The treaty power, as expressed in the Constitution, is in terms unlimited except by those restraints which are found in that instrument against the action of the government or of its departments, and those arising from the nature of the government itself and of that of the States. It would not be contended that it extends so far as to authorize what the Constitution forbids, or a change in the character of the government, or in that of one of the States, or a cession of any portion of the territory of the latter, without its consent.

This Court has also repeatedly taken the position that an Act of Congress, which must comply with the Constitution, is on a full parity with a treaty, and that, when a statute which is subsequent in time is inconsistent with a treaty, the statute to the extent of conflict renders the treaty null. It would be completely anomalous to say that a treaty need not comply with the Constitution when such an agreement can be overridden by a statute that must conform to that instrument.

In summary, we conclude that the Constitution in its entirety applied to the trials of Mrs. Smith and Mrs. Covert. Since their court-martial did not meet the requirements of Art. III, §2 or the Fifth and Sixth Amendments, we are compelled to determine if there is anything within the Constitution which authorizes the military trial of dependents accompanying the armed forces overseas.

III

Article I, §8, cl. 14 empowers Congress "To make Rules for the Government and Regulation of the land and naval Forces." It has been held that this creates an exception to the normal method of trial in civilian courts as provided by the Constitution, and permits Congress to authorize military trial of members of the armed services without all the safeguards given an accused by Article III and the Bill of Rights. But if the language of Clause 14 is given its natural meaning, the power granted does not extend to civilians—even though they may be dependents living with servicemen on a military base. The term "land and naval Forces" refers to persons who are members of the armed services and not to their civilian wives, children and other dependents. It seems inconceivable that Mrs. Covert or Mrs. Smith could have been tried by military authorities as members of the "land and naval Forces" had they been living on a military post in this country. Yet this constitutional term surely has the same meaning everywhere. The wives of servicemen are no more members of the "land and naval Forces" when living at a military post in England or Japan than when living at a base in this country or in Hawaii or Alaska.

The tradition of keeping the military subordinate to civilian authority may not be so strong in the minds of this generation as it was in the minds of those who wrote the Constitution. The idea that the relatives of soldiers could be denied a jury trial in a court of law, and instead be tried by court-martial under the guise of regulating the armed forces, would have seemed incredible to those men, in whose lifetime the right of the military to try soldiers for any offenses in time of peace had only been grudgingly conceded. The Founders envisioned the army as a necessary institution, but one dangerous to liberty if not confined within its essential bounds. Their fears were rooted in history. They knew that ancient republics had been overthrown by their military leaders. They were familiar with the history of Seventeenth Century England, where Charles I tried to govern through the army and without Parliament. During this attempt, contrary to the Common Law, he used courts-martial to try soldiers for certain non-military offenses. This court-martialing of soldiers in peacetime evoked strong protests from Parliament. The reign of Charles I was followed by the rigorous military rule of Oliver Cromwell. Later, James II used the Army in his fight against Parliament and the people. He promulgated Articles of War authorizing the trial of soldiers for non-military crimes by courts-martial. This action hastened the revolution that brought William and Mary to the throne upon their agreement to abide by a Bill of Rights which, among other things, protected the right of trial by jury. It was against this general background that two of the greatest English jurists, Lord Chief Justice Hale and Sir William Blackstone—men who exerted considerable influence on the Founders—expressed sharp hostility to any expansion of the jurisdiction of military courts. For instance, Blackstone went so far as to assert:

> For martial law, which is built upon no settled principles, but is entirely arbitrary in its decisions, is, as Sir Matthew Hale observes, in truth and reality no law, but something indulged, rather than allowed as a law. The necessity of order and discipline in an army is the only thing which can give it countenance; and therefore it ought not to be permitted in time of peace, when the king's courts are open for all persons to receive justice according to the laws of the land.

The generation that adopted the Constitution did not distrust the military because of past history alone. Within their own lives, they had seen royal governors sometimes resort to military rule. British troops were quartered in Boston at various times from 1768 until the outbreak of the Revolutionary War to support unpopular royal governors and to intimidate the local populace. The trial of soldiers by courts-martial and the interference of the military with the civil courts aroused great anxiety and antagonism not only in Massachusetts, but throughout the colonies. For example, Samuel Adams in 1768 wrote:

> ... Is it not enough for us to have seen soldiers and mariners forejudged of life, and executed within the body of the county by martial law? Are citizens to be called upon, threatened, ill-used at the will of the soldiery, and put under arrest, by pretext of the law military, in breach of the fundamental rights of subjects, and contrary to the law and franchise of the land? Will the spirits of people as yet unsubdued by tyranny, unawed by the menaces of arbitrary power, submit to be governed by military force? No, Let us rouse our attention to the common law—which is our birthright, our great security against all kinds of insult and oppression. ...

Colonials had also seen the right to trial by jury subverted by acts of Parliament which authorized courts of admiralty to try alleged violations of the unpopular "Molasses" and "Navigation" Acts. This gave the admiralty courts jurisdiction over offenses historically triable only by a jury in a court of law, and aroused great resentment throughout the colonies. As early as 1765, delegates from nine colonies meeting in New York asserted in a "Declaration of Rights" that trial by jury was the "inherent and invaluable" right of every citizen in the colonies.

With this background, it is not surprising that the Declaration of Independence protested that George III had "affected to render the Military independent of and superior to the Civil Power," and that Americans had been deprived in many cases of "the benefits of Trial by Jury." And those who adopted the Constitution embodied their profound fear and distrust of military power, as well as their determination to protect trial by jury, in the Constitution and its Amendments. Perhaps they were aware that memories fade, and hoped that, in this way, they could keep the people of this Nation from having to fight again and again the same old battles for individual freedom.

In light of this history, it seems clear that the Founders had no intention to permit the trial of civilians in military courts, where they would be denied jury trials and other constitutional protections. There is no indication that the Founders contemplated setting up a rival system of military courts to compete with civilian courts for jurisdiction over civilians who might have some contact or relationship with the armed forces. Courts-martial were not to have concurrent jurisdiction with courts of law over nonmilitary America.

On several occasions, this Court has been faced with an attempted expansion of the jurisdiction of military courts. *Ex parte Milligan*, one of the great landmarks in this Court's history, held that military authorities were without power to try civilians not in the military or naval service by declaring martial law in an area where the civil administration was not deposed and the courts were not closed. In a stirring passage, the Court proclaimed:

> Another guarantee of freedom was broken when Milligan was denied a trial by jury. The great minds of the country have differed on the correct interpretation to be given to various provisions of the Federal Constitution, and judicial decision has been often invoked to settle their true meaning; but, until recently, no one ever doubted that the right of trial by jury was fortified in the organic law against the power of attack. It is now assailed; but if ideas can be expressed in words, and language has any meaning, this right—one of the most valuable in a free country—is preserved to everyone accused of crime who is not attached to the army, or navy, or militia in actual service.

Because it violates the U.S. Constitution for the wives, who were not members of the military thus had all of the constitutional protections of U.S. civilians, to be tried by courts-martial, these convictions must be overturned.

END OF OPINION

Discussion:

Reid v. Covert touches on a number of legal issues. It may be one of the most frequently published cases, appearing in many textbooks because it contains information relevant to many different areas of the law, including national security, military justice, criminal procedure, international law, and constitutional law. For now, let's just focus on the main issue, which is why the court ruled that their conviction was unlawful. Hopefully you briefed the case while reading it. Below is a sample brief of the case that the reader can use to check your own effort. Do not to skip the mechanical effort of briefing cases, just looking at the answer. Learning to brief and IRAC a case takes practice. The more it is done, the easier it gets.

- Facts: Mrs. Covert, the wife of a service member stationed overseas, killed her husband and was tried at court-martial. This practice was consistent with how serious offenses committed by family members accompanying their military spouses were handled, and the statute authorizing this was enacted by Congress pursuant to an agreement between the U.S. government and the government of the countries in which they lived.
- Issue: Does the practice of trying civilians at courts-martial comply with the Constitution?

- Rule: U.S. citizens outside the U.S. are still protected by the Constitution. The U.S. Constitution is the highest legal authority, and no other law can violate its terms. The Sixth Amendment to the U.S. Constitution guarantees the accused the right in a criminal prosecution to a trial in a district court by a jury.

- Application: Courts-martial are not the same as federal district courts. In trying the wives by courts-martial, the wives were denied the fundamental right provided by the Sixth Amendment of a jury of their peers. The Constitution is the highest authority in the land, and it cannot be undermined by any statute, treaty, or executive agreement.

- Conclusion: The convictions were invalid.

Reid v. Covert is an important case. It is a reminder that, even though there may be entirely valid *policy* reasons to take an action, no law or act of a federal government entity or agent can contradict the U.S. Constitution. All U.S. citizens and any person subject to U.S. jurisdiction are protected by the Constitution. No one can make any law, rule, or regulation that takes away the protections you have under the Constitution. In *Reid v. Covert*, the protection provided by the Sixth and Fifth Amendments was under threat. At other times in history, government action was taken that risked diminishing other constitutional protections such as the right to free speech (First Amendment) and the right to be free from unreasonable government searches (Fourth Amendment). You will be reading cases in future chapters where the courts heard cases concerning these matters.

Review Problems

Now, let's apply what was learned in briefing *Reid v. Covert* to some hypothetical fact patterns. First, another example. Read the following fact pattern:

> The U.S. Senate ratifies a treaty sponsored by the United Nations and is joined in signing and ratifying the treaty by every other country on Earth. The treaty bans the private ownership of firearms anywhere in the world. Congress enacts a law to fulfill the requirements of the treaty. Jack owns a gun store in Texas and refuses to get rid of his guns. He is arrested by the local police and prosecuted for owning a firearm, in violation of the statute and Treaty.[5] Jack asks a federal judge to dismiss the case against him. To support his request, Jack points out the Second Amendment of the U.S. Constitution, which guarantees the right to keep and bear arms. The local prosecuting attorney makes his case by pointing out that there is a treaty banning private ownership of firearms and Congress was supporting this treaty when it passed its law banning all private possession of firearms. Go through the IRAC analysis to determine how the judge should rule.

---

5. At a later point we'll discuss how a treaty may or may not be enforced as part of our laws, but for now just assume the local policeman wants to comply with the treaty, and makes the arrest on that basis.

Now, here is an example of an IRAC analysis of that fact pattern:

Issue: Whether a treaty that outlaws private firearm ownership can be constitutionally enforced.

Rule: No treaty, statute, or any other law can violate the Constitution. (Reid v. Covert)

Application: Here, the treaty conflicts with the Second Amendment of the Constitution. But the treaty applies to relations between nations, not situations between a nation and its citizens. Applying the provision of the treaty to citizens of the United States would violate the Constitutional right to keep and bear arms under the Second Amendment. Even if Congress passed a law enacting the treaty as federal law, this statute also would violate the Second Amendment.

Conclusion: Although the treaty seems to be invalid because it violates the Second Amendment of the U.S. Constitution, treaties only govern relations between nations, not individuals. However, when Congress passed a law, and then when the local police and district attorney tried to prosecute a person for owning a firearm, that prosecution was unconstitutional. Jack's arrest was unlawful.

Notice that "Reid v. Covert" was written in parentheses after the Rule. This is what is known as "citing your authority." Whenever a memorandum or other document makes a claim of law, the document should also provide some reference to the source of that legal authority. The source can be a case, a statute, the U.S. Constitution, a regulation, or any other source that serves as the legal authority relied upon. Citing the source of a rule offers "proof" that the rule asserted is in fact the law, and that the writer did not make it up. Get in the habit of citing authority.

Now, consider a second hypothetical set of facts and perform an IRAC analysis:

American tourists are getting a bad reputation overseas. Many Americans go into other countries and, proclaiming America to be the greatest country on the planet, start insulting the country they are visiting. This is generating international ill-will towards America. To stop this from happening, Congress passes a law which prohibits an American overseas from criticizing the country he or she is visiting. Soon after this law is signed by the President, a U.S. citizen named Jill is visiting France and she criticizes the French as a bunch of "smelly, cheese eating, chain smoking, surrender-monkeys." Once she is back in the United States, she is arrested and prosecuted for insulting the French. Jill says she was simply engaged in free speech, which is protected by the First Amendment of the Constitution, but the government says that does not apply because she was overseas. Chart out your IRAC analysis of how the judge should rule in this dispute. Do not let the fact that she was in France affect your decision in this case. For purposes of this hypothetical, you can assume that the fact that she is a U.S. citizen means that she is always subject to U.S. laws.

Be aware that, although the American Congress cannot pass a law limiting Jill's right to free speech without violating the Second Amendment, France can always pass its own laws concerning speech. Americans who are in another country are subject to that nation's laws, just as much as foreigners in the U.S. are subject to U.S. laws. You should also be aware that the U.S. can pass laws governing the conduct of its citizens overseas. For example, under the statutes which have been enacted, if an American goes abroad and engages in child sex tourism, the American can still be prosecuted upon return to the U.S., even though the conduct took place in a foreign country.

Let's move on to another legal issue and another case involving the right to privacy. Now, this is a book about national security law, yet it contains many cases which themselves are completely unrelated to national security. The case of *Griswold v. Connecticut* is one of those cases. *Griswold* involved a challenge to a law which prohibited people from using "any drug, medicinal article or instrument for the purpose of preventing conception." Essentially, it outlawed all forms of birth control.

Obviously, issues like the legality of using condoms are far removed from national security law. Although this case itself is not about national security, it does discuss legal issues which are relevant to national security, specifically, the right to privacy. This illustrates another important concept to remember about the law and court opinions. The rules which Courts establish will have effect, as precedent, on a wide variety of cases beyond the specific one involved in the decision. Similarly, quite a few of the cases in this book, which themselves are not about national security, establish legal precedents and rules that have a profound influence on national security law.

Griswold v. Connecticut is very important to national security law because, over the years since 9/11, many Americans have claimed that their right to privacy is being violated in the name of keeping us safe. If one reads the U.S. Constitution, there is nothing explicitly stating that "we the people" have a right to privacy. How can it be that even though the U.S. Constitution does not say we have a right to privacy, the idea that such a right exists is well entrenched in the American mind-set? Studying *Griswold v. Connecticut* helps that answer to emerge, that even though the Constitution does not directly say individuals have a right to privacy, as a matter of Constitutional *law*, they do have this right.

Griswold v. Connecticut, 381 U.S. 479 (1965)[*]

Appellant Griswold is Executive Director of the Planned Parenthood League of Connecticut. The other appellant, Buxton, is a licensed physician and a professor at the Yale Medical School who served as Medical Director for the League at its Center in New Haven—a center open and operating from November 1 to November 10, 1961, when appellants were arrested.

---

[*] The case has been heavily edited and paraphrased by the authors for clarity. See disclaimer in introduction.

They gave information, instruction, and medical advice to married persons as to the means of preventing conception. They examined the wife and prescribed the best contraceptive device or material for her use. Fees were usually charged, although some couples were serviced for free.

The statutes whose constitutionality is involved in this appeal are §§ 53-32 and 54-196 of the General Statutes of Connecticut. § 53-32 states:

> Any person who uses any drug, medicinal article or instrument for the purpose of preventing conception shall be fined not less than fifty dollars or imprisoned not less than sixty days nor more than one year or be both fined and imprisoned.

Section 54-196 provides:

> Any person who assists, abets, counsels, causes, hires or commands another to commit any offense may be prosecuted and punished as if he were the principal offender.

The appellants were found guilty for violating these statutes and helping others violate them as well. They were fined $100 each. The legality of these laws has come before this Court.

The U.S. Supreme Court does not sit as a super-legislature to determine the wisdom, need, and propriety of laws that touch economic problems, business affairs, or social conditions. This law, however, operates directly on an intimate relation of husband and wife and their physician's role in one aspect of that relation. The association of people is not mentioned in the Constitution nor in the Bill of Rights. The right to educate a child in a school of the parents' choice—whether public or private or parochial—is also not mentioned. Nor is the right to study any particular subject or any foreign language. Yet the First Amendment has been construed to include some of those rights.

By *Pierce v. Society of Sisters*, the right to educate one's children as one chooses is made applicable to the States by the force of the First and Fourteenth Amendments. By *Meyer v. Nebraska*, the same dignity is given the right to study the German language in a private school. In other words, the State may not, consistently with the spirit of the First Amendment, contract the spectrum of available knowledge. The right of freedom of speech and press includes not only the right to utter or to print, but the right to distribute, the right to receive, the right to read and freedom of inquiry, freedom of thought, and freedom to teach—indeed, the freedom of the entire university community. Without those peripheral rights, the specific rights would be less secure.

In *NAACP v. Alabama*, we protected the "freedom to associate and privacy in one's associations," noting that freedom of association was a peripheral First Amendment right. Disclosure of membership lists of a constitutionally valid association, we held, was invalid as entailing the likelihood of a substantial restraint upon the exercise by petitioner's members of their right to freedom of association. In other words, the First Amendment has a penumbra where privacy is protected from governmental intrusion. In like context, we have protected forms of "association" that are not political in the customary sense, but pertain to the social, legal, and economic benefit of the members. In *Schware v. Board of Bar Examiners*, we held it not permissible to bar a lawyer from practice because he had once been a member of the Communist Party. The man's "association with that Party" was not shown to be "anything more than a political faith in a political party", and was not action of a kind proving bad moral character.

Those cases involved more than the "right of assembly"—a right that extends to all, irrespective of their race or ideology. The right of "association," like the right of belief, is more than the right to attend a meeting; it includes the right to express one's attitudes or philosophies by membership in a group or by affiliation with it or by other lawful means. Association in that context is a form of expression of opinion, and, while it is not expressly included in the First Amendment, its existence is necessary in making the express guarantees fully meaningful.

The foregoing cases suggest that specific guarantees in the Bill of Rights have penumbras, formed by emanations from those guarantees that help give them life and substance. Various guarantees create zones of privacy. The right of association contained in the penumbra of the First Amendment is one, as we have seen. The Third Amendment, in its prohibition against the quartering of soldiers "in any house" in time of peace without the consent of the owner, is another facet of that privacy. The Fourth Amendment explicitly affirms the "right of the people to be secure in their persons, houses, papers, and effects, against unreasonable searches and seizures." The Fifth Amendment, in its Self-Incrimination Clause, enables the citizen to create a zone of privacy which government may not force him to surrender to his detriment. The Ninth Amendment provides: "The enumeration in the Constitution, of certain rights, shall not be construed to deny or disparage others retained by the people."

The Fourth and Fifth Amendments were described in *Boyd v. United States*, as protection against all governmental invasions "of the sanctity of a man's home and the privacies of life." We recently referred in *Mapp v. Ohio* to the Fourth Amendment as creating a "right to privacy, no less important than any other right carefully an particularly reserved to the people." We have had many controversies over these penumbral rights of "privacy and repose." These cases bear witness that the right of privacy which presses for recognition here is a legitimate one.

The present case, then, concerns a relationship lying within the zone of privacy created by several fundamental constitutional guarantees. And it concerns a law which, in forbidding the use of contraceptives, rather than regulating their manufacture or sale, seeks to achieve its goals by means having a maximum destructive impact upon that relationship. Such a law cannot stand in light of the familiar principle, so often applied by this Court, that a governmental purpose to control or prevent activities constitutionally subject to state regulation may not be achieved by means which sweep unnecessarily broadly and thereby invade the area of protected freedoms.

Would we allow the police to search the sacred precincts of marital bedrooms for telltale signs of the use of contraceptives? The very idea is repulsive to the notions of privacy surrounding the marriage relationship.

We deal with a right of privacy older than the Bill of Rights—older than our political parties, older than our school system. Marriage is a coming together for better or for worse, hopefully enduring, and intimate to the degree of being sacred. It is an association that promotes a way of life, not causes; a harmony in living, not political faiths; a bilateral loyalty, not commercial or social projects. Yet it is an association for as noble a purpose as any involved in our prior decisions.

END OF OPINION

In this case the U.S. Supreme Court recognized that nowhere in the Constitution is there any specific statement that establishes a right to privacy. Nevertheless, the Court points out that many of the rights that are specifically guaranteed under the Constitution, when read together, create a general principle against government intrusions on people's private lives, thus creating the legal concept that in America the people have a constitutional right to privacy. As you read on in other chapters, this concept will come into play in a number of situations.

Majority, Concurring, and Dissenting Opinions

When *Griswold v. Connecticut* was decided, 7 of the 9 judges on the U.S. Supreme Court thought the law should be declared unconstitutional. It takes a simple majority of the justices (5 of 9) to reach a decision. That leads many to focus simply on the opinion written by the majority. Sometimes, however, not all of the judges will agree on how a case should be decided. Sometimes, individual justices agree with the outcome reached by the majority, but for a different reason. Those justices may write out their own reason and analysis in what is known as a *concurring opinion*. It is called a "concurring opinion" because, although the justice writing the decision agrees with the outcome of the case, meaning that he or she "concurs," his or her reasoning is different than that of one or more of the other justices. Other times, justices disagree with the majority, and vote another way on who wins a case. In layman's terms, these are the "losers" in the case as they were outvoted by the other justices. Sometimes justices vote with the losing minority, and still write an opinion as to why the majority decided the case incorrectly and why their own (losing) decision should be the correct one. This is what is known as the *dissenting opinion*. In *Griswold v. Connecticut*, Justice Stewart dissented and argued that the law should be upheld. Although he expressed the opinion that "this is an uncommonly silly law" (Yes, he really did write that!), Justice Stewart did not think that the law was unconstitutional.

Because the cases decided by the Supreme Court are often extremely difficult ones that have (at least before the decision) no clear answer, it is often important to read the concurring and dissenting opinions to fully understand the law involved. Although not binding law, concurring and dissenting opinions are very important and can still potentially be highly influential, especially in future cases. For example, in the 1896 case *Plessy v. Ferguson*, the U.S. Supreme Court, in a 7-1 vote, upheld segregation under the idea of "separate but equal." The one vote against it was by Justice Harlan, who wrote a famous dissent where he argued:

> Our constitution is colorblind, and neither knows nor tolerates classes among citizens. In respect of civil rights, all citizens are equal before the law. The humblest is the peer of the most powerful... The arbitrary separation of citizens on the basis of race, while they are on a public highway, is a badge of servitude wholly inconsistent with the civil freedom and the equality before the law established by the Constitution. It cannot be justified upon any legal grounds.

In the 1954 Supreme Court case *Brown v. Board of Education*, which declared segregation illegal, the Court cited Justice Harlan's dissenting opinion from *Plessy v. Ferguson*, adopting his reasoning as it overturned that 1896 opinion.

In the field of national security law, no court decision is more important than the decision called "The Steel Seizures case" which you will read in the next chapter and again later in the book. While that case ruled a particular action taken by President Truman to be unconstitutional, the case is best known for the concurrence written by Justice Robert Jackson. Jackson's "three-part test" for assessing the legitimacy of Presidential action is critically important.

For the sake of brevity and to help you focus on the law, many of the concurrences and dissents have been omitted from this textbook. Where we have left them in, it is because the reasoning used by the judges or justices is important for you to understand the issues addressed in the case or as they developed later. Should you be interested in getting a more complete picture of any case or a different perspective on a case, you should go online and find the full written decision along with the concurring and dissenting opinions, especially if you personally disagree with the majority opinion.

Finally, we want to emphasize again the importance of reading these opinions, not just to get the answer but also to see how the courts analyzed the issue. Remember, just as in physics or mathematics, it is the process of analysis that is most important — not just the answer. As you read these opinions, you will see how many issues that seem new to us now have, in fact, been considered before. Understanding that will give you a better understanding as to the "why" of the law as well as the "what."

By this point, you are ready to truly begin learning national security law. Good luck with the rest of this book.

Further Reading

Current policies of the United States (last accessed December 1, 2016), could be found in documents such as the following:

a. The National Security Strategy of the United States (2015), available at https://obamawhitehouse.archives.gov/sites/default/files/docs/2015_national_security_strategy.pdf

b. The Quadrennial Homeland Security Review, available at http://www.dhs.gov/quadrennial-homeland-security-review

c. The National Strategy for Counterterrorism (2011), available at https://www.whitehouse.gov/sites/default/files/counterterrorism_strategy.pdf

In addition, you may find useful information on sites such as these:

- U.S. Department of Justice Division of National Security (http://www.justice.gov/nsd)
- FBI website on terrorism (https://www.fbi.gov/about-us/investigate/terrorism)
- Department of Homeland Security (www.dhs.gov)
- State offices of homeland security, such as these for Maryland (http://gohs.maryland.gov/), Virginia (https://pshs.virginia.gov/), and New York (http://www.dhses.ny.gov/oct/)

Up-to-date commentary and analysis is increasingly available through online journals and blogs such as these:

- LAWFARE—Hard National Security Choices. http://www.lawfareblog.com/
- Just Security. https://www.justsecurity.org/
- Homeland Security Affairs Journal published by the Naval Postgraduate School Center for Homeland Defense and Security. https://www.hsaj.org/
- National Security Law Journal, published by George Mason University Law School. http://www.law.gmu.edu/students/orgs/nslj

Homeland and National Security Law and Policy

Chapter 1

The Constitutional Framework

Overview

The legal, policy, and ethical issues connected with homeland and national security are among the most challenging for our nation as well as for individuals working in the field. As we discussed in the previous chapter, homeland security implicates all aspects of our system of government. All three branches of government—Congress, the presidency, and the judiciary—hold different yet at times overlapping responsibilities in preserving national security. In addition, although homeland and national security involve key interests of the nation, protecting the homeland from both natural and man-made threats also implicates the rights and interests of individuals, businesses, and organizations. Not just the rights of citizens, but also the rights of non-citizens who reside in the United States, and even foreign interests, might be affected.

Equally important, and in some ways more complex, is the role of federalism in distinguishing responsibility between the federal government and the states when it comes to homeland security. Finally, in a globalized world where even threats to small communities and isolated localities have an international impact, what one nation does can have ramifications upon the rest of the world. We live in an international community where each sovereign nation has its allies and adversaries, each with its own interests, laws, and culture, adding to the complexity of homeland security. To understand homeland security, one must understand the system of checks and balances our founders wrote into the U.S. Constitution.

This chapter is designed to provide an overview of the Constitutional framework that applies to homeland and national security law. Some of the cases discussed will also be considered in later chapters. Much of this chapter, though, will focus on history, as our Constitution did not originate in nor does it exist in a vacuum. The U.S. Constitution is the result of the ideas and experiences of many individuals. Relative to the constitutions of many other nations, it is a very brief document and filled with ambiguities. This is no accident, but a deliberate decision on the part of the founding fathers.

Black's Law Dictionary, a leading legal dictionary, defines a "constitution" as

> 1. The fundamental and organic law of a nation or state that establishes the institutions and apparatus of government, defines the scope of governmental sovereign powers, and guarantees individual civil rights and liberties. 2. The

written instrument embodying this fundamental law, together with any formal amendments.[1]

In the case of the United States, the constitutional principle that stands out among all others is that of "limiting government," meaning the placement of restrictions on power. While the need for a strong national government, created by discarding the Articles of Confederation and drafting the Constitution, is unquestioned, the framework which resulted is unique primarily because of the system of checks and balances, of shared responsibility and power, found in its text.

The present U.S. Constitution grew out of problems with the Articles of Confederation, a document which established only "a league of friendship" between the states to better fight the Revolutionary War, vesting most federal power in a Congress. This power was, however, extremely limited—the central government conducted diplomacy and made war, set weights and measures, and was the final arbiter of disputes between the states. The federal Congress, though, could not itself raise any funds, and was entirely dependent on the states for the money necessary to operate. Each state sent a delegation of between two and seven members to the Congress. Delegations voted as a bloc with each state getting one vote. Any decision of consequence required unanimity. As a result, the federal government was often paralyzed and ineffectual.[2]

A movement to reform the Articles began, and, in May of 1787, delegates from 12 of the 13 states (Rhode Island sent no representatives) convened in Philadelphia to begin the work of redesigning government.[3] What this Convention designed, and what was enacted by the States, was a system of government that, though by no means perfect, has stood the test of time by providing a framework that is both flexible and stable.

The framework of our government is set out in the Constitution through the powers and checks contained in it. Article I deals with the powers, both express and implied, granted to the legislature (meaning Congress). Article II vests the powers of the executive in the president and his agents. Article III provides an independent judiciary. The legislature is created in two houses, the House of Representatives tied closely to the people through frequent elections and short, two-year terms, and the Senate with its six-year terms that provide greater freedom for the Senators to act in accordance with their judgment rather than public opinion. The Tenth Amendment guarantees the states retain a certain amount of sovereignty in purely local matters. Above all, the election of representatives by the people allowed for ultimate sovereign power to remain with the people.

This system of checks and balances, of divided yet shared powers, allowed the nation to create a strong federal government able to act as needed, but also remain responsive to the public. It was this system, one of purposefully intended inefficiency,

---

1. Black's Law Dictionary (10th Edition), Thomson West (2014).
2. Constitution of the United States: A History. http://www.archives.gov/exhibits/charters/constitution_history.html.
3. The Constitution. http://www.whitehouse.gov/our-government/the-constitution.

which James Madison and others in The Federalist papers saw as the greatest protection of liberty provided for by the Constitution.[4]

The allocation of powers was done in subtle as well as direct ways. Each branch of government is given its own Article—Article I sets forth the legislative power, Article II that of the executive, and Art III the judiciary. It is through these three articles most of the checks and balances are established. The first ten amendments to the Constitution, known as the Bill of Rights, were part of the deal struck at the Convention, included to protect the rights that Thomas Jefferson called "inalienable" when he wrote the Declaration of Independence.

Now, it is worth emphasizing that, as in all aspects of the law, words are important. In studying the law, you should pay close and particular attention to the language used. It is one thing to say that the Constitution provides for limited government, but how this is done depends on a close reading of the words.

The language of the first sentences of Article I and Article II are instructive in this regard.

Article I, section 1 reads:

> All legislative powers herein granted shall be vested in a Congress of the United States, which shall consist of a Senate and House of Representatives.

Article II, section 1 reads

> The executive power shall be vested in a President of the United States of America.

Note the absence of the words "herein granted" from the vesting of executive authority in Article II. This was not accidental, but rather demonstrated that, in those powers discussed in Article II, the executive was "vested" with all necessary powers, while the legislature's ability to act in these fields was limited to those powers "herein granted." There has been a lot of controversy over the decades about this balance between legislative and executive power. To some, the legislature is the voice of the people and has supremacy in most situations. To others, the need for quick action and a single voice in areas like foreign relations and command of the military demands that the executive branch take supremacy. Much of the case law you will read in this chapter and throughout the book, for that matter, reflects this tension.

To be sure, the legislature's authority is broad—not limited to those powers listed expressly in Article I and elsewhere through the document, but also to the ability

> To make all laws which shall be necessary and proper for carrying into execution the foregoing powers, and all other powers vested by this Constitution in the government of the United States, or in any department or officer thereof.[5]

Much of the development of constitutional law as it applies to national security has occurred as a result of the actions of the president and Congress through the years,

---

4. Federalist No. 47.
5. Constitution, Article I, Section 8, Clause 18.

acting to expand or contract the exercise of power as these two articles permit. But the making of law by any legislature often takes time and is always "after the fact"—passed in response to a crisis or challenge that has already arisen, or responding to action that has already been taken. As a result, presidents have, from the very beginning of the nation, seen the need to act in the face of crisis, even when it is possible or even likely that Congress (or the court) will act or rule differently.

So the president, by issuing direction to the military, to the Departments of Justice, State, or Homeland Security, to the CIA or even to the Treasury, "makes law" by issuing those orders. That, as we'll see in the cases we read, puts the burden on Congress to act in support of the president's policies, to act to undo the policies, or Congress may choose to not act, in which case the decisions of the president become part of our common law. In one respect, though, it should be noted that Congress has ultimate power over actions of the president and executive branch—the power of the purse. In Article I, Section 9, the Constitution provides:

> No Money shall be drawn from the Treasury, but in Consequence of Appropriations made by law;

Congress can direct the president to spend money in certain ways, and Congress can tell the president that money may *not* be spent in certain ways. This power was used, for example, to end the Vietnam War by telling the president that no money (and this includes salaries of military personnel) could be spent in Vietnam on military operations. Similarly, Congress has for many years told the President that money could not be spent to bring detainees from the facility in Guantanamo Bay to the United States for trial and imprisonment.

Judicial Review

So there is, in our system, a tension of shared powers and of checks and balances between the executive and legislative branches that affect how the law is made. More than anything else, though, it is the concept of judicial review that breathes life and gives real meaning to the Constitution, "making their words more than mere maxims of morality," as one scholar put it.[6] The power of the federal court system is itself, of course, governed by the Constitution through Article III. For purposes of this text, let's focus a bit on Section 2 of Article III:

> The judicial power shall extend to all cases, in law and equity, arising under this Constitution, the laws of the United States, and treaties made, or which shall be made, under their authority;—to all cases affecting ambassadors, other public ministers and consuls;—to all cases of admiralty and maritime jurisdiction;—to controversies to which the United States shall be a party;—to controversies between two or more states;—between a state and citizens

---

6. Bernard Schwartz, *Constitutional Law: A Textbook* (2d ed.) Macmillan, New York (1979), pp. 2–4.

of another state;—between citizens of different states;—between citizens of the same state claiming lands under grants of different states, and between a state, or the citizens thereof, and foreign states, citizens or subjects.

Note that the jurisdiction of the courts extends only to "cases" and "controversies." This means that the courts may not issue rulings on hypothetical legal questions, nor may they issue advisory opinions on current events. *They are limited to waiting for an actual case to come before them.* This provision provides for the concept of judicial restraint, a perspective that the courts leave most of the work balancing competing philosophies or concerns to the political branches of the executive and the legislature. Only when one of the political branches have acted, and an actual case or controversy arises and is brought before a judge, would a court have jurisdiction.

However, even if there is a case or controversy, courts may not be allowed to act, as there are other mechanisms by which our courts are required to exercise judicial restraint. Disputes in which the complaining parties are seeking the court's action in a matter in which the parties involved in the case have suffered no actual harm or there is no identifiable interest in the outcome may find that they are barred as not having "standing."[7] If complaining parties seek to bring a case before an actual controversy arises, they may find their case dismissed because the matter is not yet "ripe."[8] If their particular case has been resolved through settlement or some other action or outside even, even if the underlying legal issue has not been resolved, the case may be ruled "moot"[9] and so dismissed on those grounds. These and related concepts form the basis for the doctrine of judicial restraint. Many issues of judicial restraint are complex and will be further explored later, but for the moment, it is important to realize that they exist and may be mentioned in the decisions you read throughout this course.

The case of *Marbury v. Madison*, 5 U.S. (1 Cranch) 137 (1803), is the seminal case on the doctrine of judicial review. As such, it is essential reading for anyone studying law. The history surrounding the case is important to understand. The election of 1800 resulted in the newly organized Democratic-Republican party of Thomas Jefferson defeating the Federalist party of John Adams. This upset the Federalists; so in the final days of his presidency, John Adams appointed a large number of justices of peace for the District of Columbia. The commissions appointing the justices of the peace were approved by the Senate, signed by the president, and affixed with the official seal of the government. The commissions were not delivered, however, before Adams left office. When President Jefferson assumed office in March 1801, he ordered James Madison, his Secretary of State, to not deliver the commissions to prevent the Federalist-leaning justices of the peace from assuming office. William Marbury, one of the appointees, then petitioned the Supreme Court for a writ of mandamus, or legal order, compelling Madison to show cause for why he should not receive his commission.

---

7. *County of Riverside v. McLaughlin*, 500 U.S. 44 (1991).
8. *Abbott Laboratories v. Gardner*, 387 U.S. 136 (1967).
9. *Mills v. Green*, 159 U.S. 651 (1895).

The case may be difficult to read, but it is a foundational decision that enshrined the concept of an independent judiciary, co-equal with the other branches of government. Take the time to work through the language and look for the key points of decision.

Marbury v. Madison, 5 U.S. 137 (1803)*

Mr. Chief Justice MARSHALL delivered the opinion of the Court.

The Secretary of State is required to show why this court should not issue an order directing him to deliver to William Marbury his commission as a justice of the peace for the county of Washington, in the District of Columbia.

This is a delicate case with novel circumstances. To understand the opinion of this court, one must review the principles on which this Court is founded.

In the order in which the Court has viewed this subject, the following questions have been considered and decided.

1. Has the applicant a right to the commission he demands?

2. If he has a right, and that right has been violated, do the laws of his country afford him a remedy?

3. If they do afford him a remedy, is it a mandamus issuing from this court?

The first object of inquiry is:

1. Has the applicant a right to the commission he demands?

Marbury's right originates in an act of Congress passed in February, 1801, which authorizes the President to appoint justices of the peace for the District of Columbia.

In compliance with this law, a commission for William Marbury as a justice of peace was signed by John Adams, then President of the United States, after which the seal of the United States was affixed to it. However, the document containing this commission never reached William Marbury.

In order to determine whether Marbury is entitled to this commission, it becomes necessary to inquire whether he has been appointed to the office.

The second section of the second article of the Constitution declares,

> The President shall nominate, and, by and with the advice and consent of the Senate, shall appoint ambassadors, other public ministers and consuls, and all other officers of the United States, whose appointments are not otherwise provided for.

The third section declares, that "He shall commission all the officers of the United States."

An act of Congress directs the Secretary of State to keep the seal of the United States,

---

* The case has been heavily edited and paraphrased by the authors for clarity. See disclaimer in introduction.

to make out and record, and affix the said seal to all civil commissions to officers of the United States to be appointed by the President, by and with the consent of the Senate, or by the President alone; provided that the said seal shall not be affixed to any commission before the same shall have been signed by the President of the United States.

These are the clauses of the Constitution and laws of the United States which affect this part of the case. They seem to contemplate three distinct operations:

1. The nomination. This is the sole act of the President, and is completely voluntary.

2. The appointment. This is also the act of the President, and is also a voluntary act, though it can only be performed by and with the advice and consent of the Senate.

3. The commission. To grant a commission to a person appointed might perhaps be deemed a duty enjoined by the Constitution. "He shall," says that instrument, "commission all the officers of the United States."

The acts of appointing to office and commissioning the person appointed can scarcely be considered as one and the same, since the power to perform them is given in two separate and distinct sections of the Constitution. The distinction between the appointment and the commission will be rendered more apparent by adverting to that provision in the second section of the second article of the Constitution which authorizes Congress

> to vest by law the appointment of such inferior officers as they think proper in the President alone, in the Courts of law, or in the heads of departments;

thus contemplating cases where the law may direct the President to commission an officer appointed by the Courts or by the heads of departments. In such a case, to issue a commission would be apparently a duty distinct from the appointment, the performance of which perhaps could not legally be refused.

Although that clause of the Constitution which requires the President to commission all the officers of the United States may never have been applied to officers appointed otherwise than by himself, yet it would be difficult to deny the legislative power to apply it to such cases. Of consequence, the constitutional distinction between the appointment to an office and the commission of an officer who has been appointed remains the same as if in practice the President had commissioned officers appointed by an authority other than his own.

It is therefore decidedly the opinion of the Court that, when a commission has been signed by the President, the appointment is made, and that the commission is complete when the seal of the United States has been affixed to it by the Secretary of State.

Where an officer is removable at the will of the Executive, the circumstance which completes his appointment is of no concern, because the act is at any time revocable, and the commission may be arrested if still in the office. But when the officer is not removable at the will of the Executive, the appointment is not revocable, and cannot be annulled. It has conferred legal rights which cannot be resumed.

The discretion of the Executive is to be exercised until the appointment has been made. But having once made the appointment, his power over the office is terminated in all cases, where by law the officer is not removable by him. The right to the office is then in the person appointed, and he has the absolute, unconditional power of accepting or rejecting it.

Mr. Marbury, then, since his commission was signed by the President and sealed by the Secretary of State, was appointed, and as the law creating the office gave the officer a right to hold for five years independent of the Executive, the appointment was not revocable, but vested in the officer legal rights which are protected by the laws of his country.

To withhold the commission, therefore, is an act deemed by the Court not warranted by law, but violative of a vested legal right.

This brings us to the second inquiry, which is:

2. If he has a right, and that right has been violated, do the laws of his country afford him a remedy?

An aspect of liberty is the right of every individual to claim the protection of the laws whenever he receives an injury. One of the first duties of government is to afford that protection. There is a famous quote that:

> it is a general and indisputable rule that where there is a legal right, there is also a legal remedy by suit or action wherever that right is invaded.

It is then the opinion of the Court:

1. That, by signing the commission of Mr. Marbury, the President of the United States appointed him a justice of peace for the County of Washington in the District of Columbia, and that the seal of the United States, affixed thereto by the Secretary of State, is conclusive testimony of the verity of the signature, and of the completion of the appointment, and that the appointment conferred on him a legal right to the office for the space of five years.

2. Even though Marbury has a legal right to this office, the next question we must consider is if this court, under its powers as authorized under the U.S. Constitution, has the power to issue the order, known as a "mandamus," to order the President to deliver the commission? As explained below, the Court does not have that power.

A mandamus was

> a command issued in the King's name from the Court of King's Bench, and directed to any person, corporation, or inferior court of judicature within the King's dominions requiring them to do some particular thing therein specified which appertains to their office and duty, and which the Court of King's Bench has previously determined, or at least supposes, to be consonant to right and justice.

This writ, if awarded, would be directed to an officer of government, and its mandate to him would be to do a particular thing therein specified, which appertains to his office and duty and which the Court has previously determined or at least supposes to be consonant to right and justice."

Although we have held that Marbury has a right to the office, what is being asked for is a mandamus that the Court order the performance of the Executive to deliver the commission. Congress is silent as to the delivery of the commission. It has already been stated that the applicant has, to that commission, a vested legal right of which the Executive cannot deprive him. He has been appointed to an office from which he is not removable at the will of the Executive, and, being so appointed, he has a right to the commission which the Secretary has received from the President for his use. The act of Congress does not, indeed, order the Secretary of State to send it to him, but it is placed in his hands for the person entitled to it, and cannot be more lawfully withheld by him than by another person.

It was at first doubted whether the legal action taken by Marbury was not a specific legal remedy for the commission which has been withheld from Mr. Marbury, in which case a mandamus would be improper. But this doubt has yielded to the consideration that the judgment sought by Marbury is for the thing itself, or its value. The value of a public office not to be sold is incapable of being ascertained, and the applicant has a right to the office itself, or to nothing. He will obtain the office by obtaining the commission or a copy of it from the record.

This, then, is a plain case of a mandamus, either to deliver the commission or a copy of it from the record, and it only remains to be inquired: Whether such a mandamus can be issued from this Court.

The act to establish the judicial courts of the United States authorizes the Supreme Court

> to issue writs of mandamus, in cases warranted by the principles and usages of law, to any courts appointed, or persons holding office, under the authority of the United States.

The Secretary of State, being a person, holding an office under the authority of the United States, is precisely within the letter of the description, and if this Court is not authorized to issue a writ of mandamus to such an officer, it must be because the law is unconstitutional, and therefore absolutely incapable of conferring the authority and assigning the duties which its words purport to confer and assign.

The Constitution vests the whole judicial power of the United States in one Supreme Court, and such inferior courts as Congress shall, from time to time, ordain and establish. This power is expressly extended to all cases arising under the laws of the United States; and consequently, in some form, may be exercised over the present case, because the right claimed is given by a law of the United States.

In the distribution of this power, it is declared that

> The Supreme Court shall have original jurisdiction in all cases affecting ambassadors, other public ministers and consuls, and those in which a state shall be a party. In all other cases, the Supreme Court shall have appellate jurisdiction.

It has been insisted at the bar, that, as the original grant of jurisdiction to the Supreme and inferior courts is general, and the clause assigning original jurisdiction to the Supreme Court contains no negative or restrictive words, the power remains to the Legislature to assign original jurisdiction to that Court in other cases than those specified in the article which has been recited, provided those cases belong to the judicial power of the United States.

If it had been intended to leave it in the discretion of the Legislature to apportion the judicial power between the Supreme and inferior courts according to the will of that body, it would certainly have been useless to have proceeded further than to have defined the judicial power and the tribunals in which it should be vested. The subsequent part of the section is entirely without meaning—if such is to be the construction. If Congress remains at liberty to give this court appellate jurisdiction where the Constitution has declared their jurisdiction shall be original, and original jurisdiction where the Constitution has declared it shall be appellate, the distribution of jurisdiction made in the Constitution, is form without substance.

When an instrument organizing fundamentally a judicial system divides it into one Supreme and so many inferior courts as the Legislature may ordain and establish, then enumerates its powers, and proceeds so far to distribute them as to define the jurisdiction of the Supreme Court by declaring the cases in which it shall take original jurisdiction, and that in others it shall take appellate jurisdiction, the plain import of the words seems to be that, in one class of cases, its jurisdiction is original, and not appellate; in the other, it is appellate, and not original. If any other construction would render the clause inoperative, that is an additional reason for rejecting such other construction, and for adhering to the obvious meaning.

To enable this court then to issue a mandamus, it must be shown to be an exercise of appellate jurisdiction, or to be necessary to enable them to exercise appellate jurisdiction.

It has been stated at the bar that the appellate jurisdiction may be exercised in a variety of forms, and that, if it be the will of the Legislature that a mandamus should be used for that purpose, that will must be obeyed. This is true; yet the jurisdiction must be appellate, not original.

It is the essential criterion of appellate jurisdiction that it revises and corrects the proceedings in a cause already instituted, and does not create that case. Although, therefore, a mandamus may be directed to courts, yet to issue such a writ to an officer for the delivery of a paper is, in effect, the same as to sustain an original action for that paper, and therefore seems not to belong to appellate, but to original jurisdiction. Neither is it necessary in such a case as this to enable the Court to exercise its appellate jurisdiction.

The authority, therefore, given to the Supreme Court by the act establishing the judicial courts of the United States to issue writs of mandamus to public officers appears not to be authorized by the Constitution, and it becomes necessary to inquire whether a jurisdiction so conferred can be exercised.

The question whether an act repugnant to the Constitution can become the law of the land is a question deeply interesting to the United States, but, happily, not of an intricacy proportioned to its interest. It seems only necessary to recognise certain principles, supposed to have been long and well established, to decide it.

That the people have an original right to establish for their future government such principles as, in their opinion, shall most conduce to their own happiness is the basis on which the whole American fabric has been erected. The exercise of this original right is a very great exertion; nor can it nor ought it to be frequently repeated. The principles, therefore, so established are deemed fundamental. And as the authority from which they proceed, is supreme, and can seldom act, they are designed to be permanent.

This original and supreme will organizes the government and assigns to different departments their respective powers. It may either stop here or establish certain limits not to be transcended by those departments.

The Government of the United States is of the latter description. The powers of the Legislature are defined and limited; and that those limits may not be mistaken or forgotten, the Constitution is written. To what purpose are powers limited, and to what purpose is that limitation committed to writing, if these limits may at any time be passed by those intended to be restrained? The distinction between a government with limited and unlimited powers is abolished if those limits do not confine the persons on whom they are imposed, and if acts prohibited and acts allowed are of equal obligation. It is a proposition too plain to be contested that the Constitution controls any legislative act repugnant to it, or that the Legislature may alter the Constitution by an ordinary act.

Between these alternatives there is no middle ground. The Constitution is either a superior, paramount law, unchangeable by ordinary means, or it is on a level with ordinary legislative acts, and, like other acts, is alterable when the legislature shall please to alter it. If the former part of the alternative be true, then a legislative act contrary to the Constitution is not law; if the latter part be true, then written Constitutions are absurd attempts on the part of the people to limit a power in its own nature illimitable.

Certainly all those who have framed written Constitutions contemplate them as forming the fundamental and paramount law of the nation, and consequently the theory of every such government must be that an act of the Legislature repugnant to the Constitution is void. This theory is essentially attached to a written Constitution, and is consequently to be considered by this Court as one of the fundamental principles of our society. It is not, therefore, to be lost sight of in the further consideration of this subject.

If an act of the Legislature repugnant to the Constitution is void, does it, notwithstanding its invalidity, bind the Courts and oblige them to give it effect? Or, in other words, though it be not law, does it constitute a rule as operative as if it was a law? This would be to overthrow in fact what was established in theory, and would seem, at first view, an absurdity too gross to be insisted on. It shall, however, receive a more attentive consideration.

It is emphatically the province and duty of the Judicial Department to say what the law is. Those who apply the rule to particular cases must, of necessity, expound and interpret that rule. If two laws conflict with each other, the Courts must decide on the operation of each.

So, if a law be in opposition to the Constitution, if both the law and the Constitution apply to a particular case, so that the Court must either decide that case conformably to the law, disregarding the Constitution, or conformably to the Constitution, disregarding the law, the Court must determine which of these conflicting rules governs the case. This is of the very essence of judicial duty. If, then, the Courts are to regard the Constitution, and the Constitution is superior to any ordinary act of the Legislature, the Constitution, and not such ordinary act, must govern the case to which they both apply.

Those, then, who controvert the principle that the Constitution is to be considered in court as a paramount law are reduced to the necessity of maintaining that courts must close their eyes on the Constitution, and see only the law. This doctrine would subvert the very foundation of all written Constitutions. It would declare that an act which, according to the principles and theory of our government, is entirely void, is yet, in practice, completely obligatory. It would declare that, if the Legislature shall do what is expressly forbidden, such act, notwithstanding the express prohibition, is in reality effectual. It would be giving to the Legislature a practical and real omnipotence with the same breath which professes to restrict their powers within narrow limits. It is prescribing limits, and declaring that those limits may be passed at pleasure.

That it thus reduces to nothing what we have deemed the greatest improvement on political institutions—a written Constitution, would of itself be sufficient, in America where written Constitutions have been viewed with so much reverence, for rejecting the construction. But the peculiar expressions of the Constitution of the United States furnish additional arguments in favour of its rejection.

The judicial power of the United States is extended to all cases arising under the Constitution. Could it be the intention of those who gave this power to say that, in using it, the Constitution should not be looked into? That a case arising under the Constitution should be decided without examining the instrument under which it arises? This is too extravagant to be maintained.

In some cases then, the Constitution must be looked into by the judges. And if they can open it at all, what part of it are they forbidden to read or to obey?

The oath of office, too, imposed by the Legislature, is completely demonstrative of the legislative opinion on this subject. It is in these words:

> I do solemnly swear that I will administer justice without respect to persons, and do equal right to the poor and to the rich; and that I will faithfully and impartially discharge all the duties incumbent on me as according to the best

of my abilities and understanding, agreeably to the Constitution and laws of the United States.

Why does a judge swear to discharge his duties agreeably to the Constitution of the United States if that Constitution forms no rule for his government? if it is closed upon him and cannot be inspected by him?

If such be the real state of things, this is worse than solemn mockery. To prescribe or to take this oath becomes equally a crime.

It is also not entirely unworthy of observation that, in declaring what shall be the supreme law of the land, the Constitution itself is first mentioned, and not the laws of the United States generally, but those only which shall be made in pursuance of the Constitution, have that rank.

Thus, the particular phraseology of the Constitution of the United States confirms and strengthens the principle, supposed to be essential to all written Constitutions, that a law repugnant to the Constitution is void, and that courts, as well as other departments, are bound by that instrument.

The rule must be discharged.

END OF DECISION

Review Questions

1. Perform an IRAC brief of the case.

2. What was the actual ruling—who won? How does the outcome of the case (who won or lost) affect the rule that the case has come to symbolize? What does the opinion in this case suggest about the method of writing judicial opinions? What source does the Justice rely upon?

While *Marbury v. Madison* establishes the authority of the judicial branch in a very practical way, the case that laid the foundation regarding the authority of Congress came shortly thereafter, in the case of *McCulloch v. Maryland*.

McCulloch v. Maryland, 17 U.S. 4 Wheat. 316 (1819)[*]

MARSHALL, Chief Justice, delivered the opinion of the Court.

In the case now to be determined, the defendant, a sovereign State, denies the obligation of a law enacted by the legislature of the Union, and the plaintiff, on his part, contests the validity of an act which has been passed by the legislature of that State. The Constitution of our country, in its most interesting and vital parts, is to be considered, the conflicting powers of the Government of the Union and of its member states, as marked in that Constitution, are to be discussed, and an opinion given which may essentially influence the great operations of the Government. No tribunal can approach such a question without a deep sense of its importance,

---

[*] The case has been heavily edited and paraphrased by the authors for clarity. See disclaimer in introduction.

and of the awful responsibility involved in its decision. But it must be decided peacefully, or remain a source of hostile legislation, perhaps, of hostility of a still more serious nature; and if it is to be so decided, by this tribunal alone can the decision be made. On the Supreme Court of the United States has the Constitution of our country devolved this important duty.

The first question made in the cause is—has Congress power to incorporate a bank?

It has been truly said that this can scarcely be considered as an open question entirely unprejudiced by the former proceedings of the Nation respecting it. The principle now contested was introduced at a very early period of our history, has been recognized by many successive legislatures, and has been acted upon by the Judicial Department, in cases of peculiar delicacy, as a law of undoubted obligation.

It will not be denied that a bold and daring usurpation might be resisted after an acquiescence still longer and more complete than this. But it is conceived that a doubtful question, one on which human reason may pause and the human judgment be suspended, in the decision of which the great principles of liberty are not concerned, but the respective powers of those who are equally the representatives of the people, are to be adjusted, if not put at rest by the practice of the Government, ought to receive a considerable impression from that practice. An exposition of the Constitution, deliberately established by legislative acts, on the faith of which an immense property has been advanced, ought not to be lightly disregarded.

The power now contested was exercised by the first Congress elected under the present Constitution.

The bill for incorporating the Bank of the United States did not steal upon an unsuspecting legislature and pass unobserved. Its principle was completely understood, and was opposed with equal zeal and ability. After being resisted first in the fair and open field of debate, and afterwards in the executive cabinet, with as much persevering talent as any measure has ever experienced, and being supported by arguments which convinced minds as pure and as intelligent as this country can boast, it became a law. The original act was permitted to expire, but a short experience of the embarrassments to which the refusal to revive it exposed the Government convinced those who were most prejudiced against the measure of its necessity, and induced the passage of the present law. It would require no ordinary share of intrepidity to assert that a measure adopted under these circumstances was a bold and plain usurpation to which the Constitution gave no countenance. These observations belong to the cause; but they are not made under the impression that, were the question entirely new, the law would be found irreconcilable with the Constitution.

In discussing this question, the counsel for the State of Maryland have deemed it of some importance, in the construction of the Constitution, to consider that instrument not as emanating from the people, but as the act of sovereign and independent States. The powers of the General Government, it has been said, are delegated by the States, who alone are truly sovereign, and must be exercised in subordination to the States, who alone possess supreme dominion.

It would be difficult to sustain this proposition. The convention which framed the Constitution was indeed elected by the State legislatures. But the instrument, when it came from their hands, was a mere proposal, without obligation or pretensions to it. It was reported to the then existing Congress of the United States with a request that it might be submitted to a convention of delegates, chosen in each State by the people thereof, under the recommendation of its legislature, for their assent and ratification.

This mode of proceeding was adopted, and by the convention, by Congress, and by the State legislatures, the instrument was submitted to the people. They acted upon it in the only manner in which they can act safely, effectively and wisely, on such a subject—by assembling in convention. It is true, they assembled in their several States—and where else should they have assembled? No political dreamer was ever wild enough to think of breaking down the lines which separate the States, and of compounding the American people into one common mass. Of consequence, when they act, they act in their States. But the measures they adopt do not, on that account, cease to be the measures of the people themselves, or become the measures of the State governments.

From these conventions the Constitution derives its whole authority. The government proceeds directly from the people; is "ordained and established" in the name of the people, and is declared to be ordained,

> "in order to form a more perfect union, establish justice, insure domestic tranquillity, and secure the blessings of liberty to themselves and to their posterity."

The assent of the States in their sovereign capacity is implied in calling a convention, and thus submitting that instrument to the people. But the people were at perfect liberty to accept or reject it, and their act was final. It required not the affirmance, and could not be negatived, by the State Governments. The Constitution, when thus adopted, was of complete obligation, and bound the State sovereignties.

It has been said that the people had already surrendered all their powers to the State sovereignties, and had nothing more to give. But surely the question whether they may resume and modify the powers granted to Government does not remain to be settled in this country. Much more might the legitimacy of the General Government be doubted had it been created by the States. The powers delegated to the State sovereignties were to be exercised by themselves, not by a distinct and independent sovereignty created by themselves. To the formation of a league such as was the Confederation, the State sovereignties were certainly competent. But when, "in order to form a more perfect union," it was deemed necessary to change this alliance into an effective Government, possessing great and sovereign powers and acting directly on the people, the necessity of referring it to the people, and of deriving its powers directly from them, was felt and acknowledged by all. The Government of the Union then (whatever may be the influence of this fact on the case) is, emphatically and truly, a Government of the people. In form and in substance, it emanates from them. Its powers are granted by them, and are to be exercised directly on them, and for their benefit.

This Government is acknowledged by all to be one of enumerated powers. The principle that it can exercise only the powers granted to it would seem too apparent to have required to be enforced by all those arguments which its enlightened friends, while it was depending before the people, found it necessary to urge; that principle is now universally admitted. But the question respecting the extent of the powers actually granted is perpetually arising, and will probably continue to arise so long as our system shall exist. In discussing these questions, the conflicting powers of the General and State Governments must be brought into view, and the supremacy of their respective laws, when they are in opposition, must be settled.

If any one proposition could command the universal assent of mankind, we might expect it would be this—that the Government of the Union, though limited in its powers, is supreme within its sphere of action. This would seem to result necessarily from its nature. It is the Government of all; its powers are delegated by all; it represents all, and acts for all. Though any one State may be willing to control its operations, no State is willing to allow others to control them. The nation, on those subjects on which it can act, must necessarily bind its component parts. But this question is not left to mere reason; the people have, in express terms, decided it by saying,

> "this Constitution, and the laws of the United States, which shall be made in pursuance thereof," "shall be the supreme law of the land," and by requiring that the members of the State legislatures and the officers of the executive and judicial departments of the States shall take the oath of fidelity to it. The Government of the United States, then, though limited in its powers, is supreme, and its laws, when made in pursuance of the Constitution, form the supreme law of the land, "anything in the Constitution or laws of any State to the contrary notwithstanding."

Among the enumerated powers, we do not find that of establishing a bank or creating a corporation. But there is no phrase in the instrument which, like the Articles of Confederation, excludes incidental or implied powers and which requires that everything granted shall be expressly and minutely described. Even the 10th Amendment, which was framed for the purpose of quieting the excessive jealousies which had been excited, omits the word "expressly," and declares only that the powers "not delegated to the United States, nor prohibited to the States, are reserved to the States or to the people," thus leaving the question whether the particular power which may become the subject of contest has been delegated to the one Government, or prohibited to the other, to depend on a fair construction of the whole instrument. The men who drew and adopted this amendment had experienced the embarrassments resulting from the insertion of this word in the Articles of Confederation, and probably omitted it to avoid those embarrassments. A Constitution, to contain an accurate detail of all the subdivisions of which its great powers will admit, and of all the means by which they may be carried into execution, would partake in such a lengthy and extensive legal code, and could scarcely be embraced by the human mind. It would probably never be understood by the public. Its nature, therefore, requires that only its great outlines should be marked, its important objects designated, and the minor ingredients which compose those objects be deduced from the nature of the objects themselves. That this idea was entertained by the framers of the American Constitution is not only to be inferred from the nature of the instrument, but from the language. Why else were some of the limitations found in the 9th section of the 1st article introduced? It is also in some degree warranted by their having omitted to use any restrictive term which might prevent its receiving a fair and just interpretation. In considering this question, then, we must never forget that it is *a Constitution* we are expounding.

Although, among the enumerated powers of Government, we do not find the word "bank" or "incorporation," we find the great powers, to lay and collect taxes; to borrow money; to regulate commerce; to declare and conduct a war; and to raise and support armies and navies. The sword and the purse, all the external relations, and no inconsiderable portion of the industry of the nation are entrusted to its Government. It can never be pretended that these vast powers draw after them others of inferior importance merely because they are inferior. Such an idea can never be advanced. But it may with great reason be contended that a Government entrusted with such ample powers, on the due execution of which the happiness and prosperity of the Nation so vitally depends, must also be entrusted with ample means for their execution. The power being given, it is the interest of the Nation to facilitate its execution. It can never be their interest, and cannot be presumed to have been their intention, to clog and embarrass its execution by withholding the most appropriate means.

It is not denied that the powers given to the Government imply the ordinary means of execution. That, for example, of raising revenue and applying it to national purposes is admitted to imply the power of conveying money from place to place as the exigencies of the Nation may require, and of employing the usual means of conveyance. But it is denied that the Government has its choice of means, or that it may employ the most convenient means if, to employ them, it be necessary to erect a corporation. On what foundation does this argument rest? On this alone: the power of creating a corporation is one appertaining to sovereignty, and is not expressly conferred on Congress. This is true. But all legislative powers appertain to sovereignty. The original power of giving the law on any subject whatever is a sovereign power, and if the Government of the Union is restrained from creating a corporation as a means for performing its functions, on the single reason that the creation of a corporation is an act of sovereignty, if the sufficiency of this reason be acknowledged, there would be some difficulty in sustaining the authority of Congress to pass other laws for the accomplishment of the same objects. The Government which has a right to do an act and has imposed on it the duty of performing that act must, according to the dictates of reason, be allowed to select the means, and those who contend that it may not select any appropriate means that one particular mode of effecting the object is excepted take upon themselves the burden of establishing that exception.

The creation of a corporation, it is said, appertains to sovereignty. This is admitted. But to what portion of sovereignty does it appertain? Does it belong to one more than to another? In America, the powers of sovereignty are divided between the Government of the Union and those of the States. They are each sovereign with respect to the objects committed to it, and neither sovereign with respect to the objects committed to the other. We cannot comprehend that train of reasoning, which would maintain that the extent of power granted by the people is to be ascertained not by the nature and terms of the grant, but by its date. Some State Constitutions were formed before, some since, that of the United States. We cannot believe that their relation to each other is in any degree dependent upon this circumstance. Their respective powers must, we think, be precisely the same as if they had been formed at the same time. Had they been formed at the same time, and had the people conferred on the General Government the power contained in the Constitution, and on the States the whole residuum of power, would it have been asserted that the Government of the Union was not sovereign, with respect to those objects which were entrusted to it, in relation to which its laws were declared to be supreme? If this could not have been asserted, we cannot well comprehend the process of reasoning which maintains that a power appertaining to sovereignty cannot be connected with that vast portion of it which is granted to the General Government, so far as it is calculated to subserve the legitimate objects of that Government. The power of creating a corporation, though appertaining to sovereignty, is not, like the power of making war or levying taxes or of regulating commerce, a great substantive and independent power which cannot be implied as incidental to other powers or used as a means of executing them. It is never the end for which other powers are exercised, but a means by which other objects are accomplished. No contributions are made to charity for the sake of an incorporation, but a corporation is created to administer the charity; no seminary of learning is instituted in order to be incorporated, but the corporate character is conferred to subserve the purposes of education. No city was ever built with the sole object of being incorporated, but is incorporated as affording the best means of being well governed. The power of creating a corporation is never used for its own sake, but for the purpose of effecting something else. No sufficient reason is therefore perceived why it may not pass as incidental to those powers which are expressly given if it be a direct mode of executing them.

But the Constitution of the United States has not left the right of Congress to employ the necessary means for the execution of the powers conferred on the Government to general reasoning. To its enumeration of powers is added that of making

> all laws which shall be necessary and proper for carrying into execution the foregoing powers, and all other powers vested by this Constitution in the Government of the United States or in any department thereof.

The counsel for the State of Maryland have urged various arguments to prove that this clause, though in terms a grant of power, is not so in effect, but is really restrictive of the general right which might otherwise be implied of selecting means for executing the enumerated powers. In support of this proposition, they have found it necessary to contend that this clause was inserted for the purpose of conferring on Congress the power of making laws. That, without it, doubts might be entertained whether Congress could exercise its powers in the form of legislation.

But could this be the object for which it was inserted? A Government is created by the people having legislative, executive and judicial powers. Its legislative powers are vested in a Congress, which is to consist of a senate and house of representatives. Each house may determine the rule of its proceedings, and it is declared that every bill which shall have passed both houses shall, before it becomes a law, be presented to the President of the United States. The 7th section describes the course of proceedings by which a bill shall become a law, and then the 8th section enumerates the powers of Congress. Could it be necessary to say that a legislature should exercise legislative powers, in the shape of legislation? After allowing each house to prescribe its own course of proceeding, after describing the manner in which a bill should become a law, would it have entered into the mind of a single member of the convention that an express power to make laws was necessary to enable the legislature to make them? That a legislature, endowed with legislative powers, can legislate is a proposition too self-evident to have been questioned.

But the argument on which most reliance is placed is drawn from that peculiar language of this clause. Congress is not empowered by it to make all laws which may have relation to the powers conferred on the Government, but such only as may be "necessary and proper" for carrying them into execution. The word "necessary" is considered as controlling the whole sentence, and as limiting the right to pass laws for the execution of the granted powers to such as are indispensable, and without which the power would be nugatory. That it excludes the choice of means, and leaves to Congress in each case that only which is most direct and simple.

Is it true that this is the sense in which the word "necessary" is always used? Does it always import an absolute physical necessity so strong that one thing to which another may be termed necessary cannot exist without that other? We think it does not. If reference be had to its use in the common affairs of the world or in approved authors, we find that it frequently imports no more than that one thing is convenient, or useful, or essential to another. To employ the means necessary to an end is generally understood as employing any means calculated to produce the end, and not as being confined to those single means without which the end would be entirely unattainable. Such is the character of human language that no word conveys to the mind in all situations one single definite idea, and nothing is more common than to use words in a figurative sense. Almost all compositions contain words which, taken in their rigorous sense, would convey a meaning different from that which is obviously intended. It is essential to just construction that many words which import something excessive should be understood in a more mitigated sense—in that sense which common usage justifies. The word "necessary" is of this description. It has not a fixed character peculiar to itself. It admits of all degrees of comparison, and is often connected with other words which increase or diminish the impression the mind receives of the urgency it imports. A thing may be necessary, very necessary, absolutely or indispensably necessary. To no mind would the same idea be conveyed by these several phrases. The comment on the word is well illustrated by the passage cited at the bar from the 10th section of the 1st article of the Constitution. It is, we think, impossible to compare the sentence which prohibits a State from laying "imposts, or duties on imports or exports, except what may be absolutely necessary for executing its inspection laws," with that which authorizes Congress "to make all laws which shall be necessary and proper for carrying into execution" the powers of the General Government without feeling a conviction that the convention understood itself to change materially the meaning of the word "necessary," by prefixing the word "absolutely." This word, then, like others, is used in various senses, and, in its construction, the subject, the context, the intention of the person using them are all to be taken into view.

Let this be done in the case under consideration. The subject is the execution of those great powers on which the welfare of a Nation essentially depends. It must have been the intention of those who gave these powers to insure, so far as human prudence could insure, their beneficial execution. This could not be done by confiding the choice of means to such narrow limits as not to leave it in the power of Congress to adopt any which might be appropriate, and which were conducive to the end. This provision is made in a Constitution intended to endure for ages to come, and consequently to be adapted to the various crises of human affairs. To have prescribed the means by which Government should, in all future time, execute its powers would have been to change entirely the character of the instrument and give it the properties of a legal code. It would have been an unwise attempt to provide by immutable rules for exigencies which, if foreseen at all, must have been seen dimly, and which can be best provided for as they occur. To have declared that the best means shall not be used, but those alone without which the power given would be nugatory, would have been to deprive the legislature of the capacity to avail itself of experience, to exercise its reason, and to accommodate its legislation to circumstances.

If we apply this principle of construction to any of the powers of the Government, we shall find it so pernicious in its operation that we shall be compelled to discard it. The powers vested in Congress may certainly be carried into execution, without prescribing an oath of office. The power to exact this security for the faithful performance of duty is not given, nor is it indispensably necessary. The different departments may be established; taxes may be imposed and collected; armies and navies may be raised and maintained; and money may be borrowed, without requiring an oath of office. It might be argued with as much plausibility as other incidental powers have been assailed that the convention was not unmindful of this subject. The oath which might be exacted — that of fidelity to the Constitution — is prescribed, and no other can be required. Yet he would be charged with insanity who should contend that the legislature might not add to the oath directed by the Constitution such other oath of office as its wisdom might suggest.

So, with respect to the whole penal code of the United States, whence arises the power to punish in cases not prescribed by the Constitution? All admit that the Government may legitimately punish any violation of its laws, and yet this is not among the enumerated powers of Congress. The right to enforce the observance of law by punishing its infraction might be denied with the more plausibility because it is expressly given in some cases.

Congress is empowered "to provide for the punishment of counterfeiting the securities and current coin of the United States," and "to define and punish piracies and felonies committed on the high seas, and offences against the law of nations." The several powers of Congress may exist in a very imperfect State, to be sure, but they may exist and be carried into execution, although no punishment should be inflicted, in cases where the right to punish is not expressly given.

Take, for example, the power "to establish post-offices and post-roads." This power is executed by the single act of making the establishment. But from this has been inferred the power and duty of carrying the mail along the post road from one post office to another. And from this implied power has again been inferred the right to punish those who steal letters from the post office, or rob the mail. It may be said with some plausibility that the right to carry the mail, and to punish those who rob it, is not indispensably necessary to the establishment of a post office and post road. This right is indeed essential to the beneficial exercise of the power, but not indispensably necessary to its existence. So, of the punishment of the crimes of stealing or falsifying a record or process of a Court of the United States, or of perjury in such Court. To punish these offences is certainly conducive to the due administration of justice. But Courts may exist, and may decide the causes brought before them, though such crimes escape punishment.

The baneful influence of this narrow construction on all the operations of the Government, and the absolute impracticability of maintaining it without rendering the Government incompetent to its great objects, might be illustrated by numerous examples drawn from the Constitution and from our laws. The good sense of the public has pronounced without hesitation that the power of punishment appertains to sovereignty, and may be exercised, whenever the sovereign has a right to act, as incidental to his Constitutional powers. It is a means for carrying into execution all sovereign powers, and may be used although not indispensably necessary. It is a right incidental to the power, and conducive to its beneficial exercise.

If this limited construction of the word "necessary" must be abandoned in order to punish, whence is derived the rule which would reinstate it when the Government would carry its powers into execution by means not vindictive in their nature? If the word "necessary" means "needful," "requisite," "essential," "conducive to," in order to let in the power of punishment for the infraction of law, why is it not equally comprehensive when required to authorize the use of means which facilitate the execution of the powers of Government, without the infliction of punishment?

In ascertaining the sense in which the word "necessary" is used in this clause of the Constitution, we may derive some aid from that with which it is associated. Congress shall have power "to make all laws which shall be necessary and proper to carry into execution" the powers of the Government. If the word "necessary" was used in that strict and rigorous sense for which the counsel for the State of Maryland contend, it would be an extraordinary departure from the usual course of the human mind, as exhibited in composition, to add a word the only possible effect of which is to qualify that strict and rigorous meaning, to present to the mind the idea of some choice of means of legislation not strained and compressed within the narrow limits for which gentlemen contend.

But the argument which most conclusively demonstrates the error of the construction contended for by the counsel for the State of Maryland is founded on the intention of the convention as manifested in the whole clause. To waste time and argument in proving that, without it, Congress might carry its powers into execution would be not much less idle than to hold a lighted taper to the sun. As little can it be required to prove that, in the absence of this clause, Congress would have some choice of means. That it might employ those which, in its judgment, would most advantageously effect the object to be accomplished. That any means adapted to the end, any means which tended directly to the execution of the Constitutional powers of the Government, were in themselves Constitutional. This clause, as construed by the State of Maryland, would abridge, and almost annihilate, this useful and necessary right of the legislature to select its means. That this could not be intended is, we should think, had it not been already controverted, too apparent for controversy.

We think so for the following reasons:

1st. The clause is placed among the powers of Congress, not among the limitations on those powers.

2d. Its terms purport to enlarge, not to diminish, the powers vested in the Government. It purports to be an additional power, not a restriction on those already granted. No reason has been or can be assigned for thus concealing an intention to narrow the discretion of the National Legislature under words which purport to enlarge it. The framers of the Constitution wished its adoption, and well knew that it would be endangered by its strength, not by its weakness. Had they been capable of using language which would convey to the eye one idea and, after deep reflection, impress on the mind another, they would rather have disguised the grant of power than its limitation. If, then, their intention had been, by this clause, to restrain the free use of means which might otherwise have been implied, that intention would have been inserted in another place, and would have been expressed in terms resembling these. "In carrying into execution the foregoing powers, and all others," &c., "no laws shall be passed but such as are necessary and proper." Had the intention been to make this clause restrictive, it would unquestionably have been so in form, as well as in effect.

After this declaration, it can scarcely be necessary to say that the existence of State banks can have no possible influence on the question. No trace is to be found in the Constitution of an intention to create a dependence of the Government of the Union on those of the States, for the execution of the great powers assigned to it. Its means are adequate to its ends, and on those means alone was it expected to rely for the accomplishment of its ends. To impose on it the necessity of resorting to means which it cannot control, which another Government may furnish or withhold, would render its course precarious, the result of its measures uncertain, and create a dependence on other Governments which might disappoint its most important designs, and is incompatible with the language of the Constitution. But were it otherwise, the choice of means implies a right to choose a national bank in preference to State banks, and Congress alone can make the election.

After the most deliberate consideration, it is the unanimous and decided opinion of this Court that the act to incorporate the Bank of the United States is a law made in pursuance of the Constitution, and is a part of the supreme law of the land.

The branches, proceeding from the same stock and being conducive to the complete accomplishment of the object, are equally constitutional. It would have been unwise to locate them in the charter, and it would be unnecessarily inconvenient to employ the legislative power in making those subordinate arrangements. The great duties of the bank are prescribed; those duties require branches; and the bank itself may, we think, be safely trusted with the selection of places where those branches shall be fixed, reserving always to the Government the right to require that a branch shall be located where it may be deemed necessary.

It being the opinion of the Court that the act incorporating the bank is constitutional, and that the power of establishing a branch in the State of Maryland might be properly exercised by the bank itself, we proceed to inquire:

JUDGMENT. This cause came on to be heard, on the transcript of the record of the Court of Appeals of the State of Maryland, and was argued by counsel; on consideration whereof, it is the opinion of this Court that the act of the Legislature of Maryland is contrary to the Constitution of the United States, and void, and therefore that the said Court of Appeals of the State of Maryland erred, in affirming the judgment of the Baltimore County Court, in which judgment was rendered against James W. McCulloch; but that the said Court of Appeals of Maryland ought to have reversed the said judgment of the said Baltimore County Court, and ought to have given judgment for the said appellant, McCulloch. It is, therefore, adjudged and ordered that the said judgment of the said Court of Appeals of the State of Maryland in this case be, and the same hereby is, reversed and annulled. And this Court, proceeding to render such judgment as the said Court of Appeals should have rendered, it is further adjudged and ordered that the judgment of the said Baltimore County Court be reversed and annulled, and that judgment be entered in the said Baltimore County Court for the said James W. McCulloch.

END OF DECISION

The Extent of a President's Executive Authority

In the context of this book, the decisions of the Supreme Court in several other cases are especially noteworthy. Each case illustrates both the need to consider court decisions in understanding national security law as well as the manner in which the Court, as a branch of government, has shaped the roles of the other two branches of government and the separation of powers. While we will read longer excerpts from the decisions at later points in the text, the materials that follow provide a glimpse into principles which are important to consider at this early stage of the course.

In the case of *Totten v. United States,* 92 U.S. 105 (1875), the Constitutional authority of the President to undertake intelligence activity was recognized as an inherent exercise of the commander-in-chief power:

> We have no difficulty as to the authority of the President in the matter. He was undoubtedly authorized during the war, as commander-in-chief of the armies of the United States, to employ secret agents to enter the rebel lines and obtain information respecting the strength, resources, and movements of the enemy, and contracts to compensate such agents are so far binding upon the government as to render it lawful for the President to direct payment of the amount stipulated out of the contingent fund under his control.[10]

In the case of *United States v. Curtiss-Wright Export Corp.,* 299 U.S. 304 (1936), the Curtiss-Wright Export Corporation was charged with conspiring to sell fifteen machine guns to Bolivia, which was engaged in an armed conflict in the Chaco. This sale violated a Joint Resolution of Congress and a proclamation issued by President Roosevelt. The company argued that when Congress voted on a resolution that gave the president the ability to outlaw the sale of munitions to certain foreign nations, Congress had unconstitutionally delegated its legislative authority to the president.

Now, while there are many congressional powers granted in the U.S. Constitution that Congress may not delegate to the president, in this instance, the Court found no constitutional violation. Making an important distinction between internal and foreign affairs, Justice Sutherland argued that "the President alone has the power to speak or listen as a representative of the nation" when it comes to foreign affairs. It is worth reading the language of the Court here:

> "The broad statement that the Federal Government can exercise no powers except those specifically enumerated in the Constitution, and such implied powers as are necessary and proper to carry into effect the enumerated powers, is categorically true only in respect of our internal affairs. In that field, the primary purpose of the Constitution was to carve from the general mass of legislative powers then possessed by the States such portions as it was thought desirable to vest in the Federal Government, leaving those not included in the enumeration still in the States . . . [11]

> . . .

> The investment of the federal government with the powers of external sovereignty did not depend upon the affirmative grants of the Constitution. The powers to declare and wage war, to conclude peace, to make treaties, to maintain diplomatic relations with other sovereignties, if they had never been mentioned in the Constitution, would have vested in the federal government as necessary concomitants of nationality.[12]

> . . .

---

10. 92 U.S. 105 at 106.
11. 299 U.S. 304 at 317.
12. Id. at 318.

This view of the court in *Curtiss-Wright* was shared by the Senate early in its history. On February 15, 1816, the Senate Committee on Foreign Relations, reported to the Senate, among other things, as follows:

"The President is the constitutional representative of the United States with regard to foreign nations. He manages our concerns with foreign nations, and must necessarily be most competent to determine when, how, and upon what subjects negotiation may be urged with the greatest prospect of success. For his conduct, he is responsible to the Constitution. The committee considers this responsibility the surest pledge for the faithful discharge of his duty. They think the interference of the Senate in the direction of foreign negotiations calculated to diminish that responsibility, and thereby to impair the best security for the national safety. The nature of transactions with foreign nations, moreover, requires caution and unity of design, and their success frequently depends on secrecy and dispatch."

It is important to bear in mind that we are here dealing not alone with an authority vested in the President by an exertion of legislative power, but with such an authority plus the very delicate, plenary and exclusive power of the President as the sole organ of the federal government in the field of international relations—a power which does not require as a basis for its exercise an act of Congress but which, of course, like every other governmental power, must be exercised in subordination to the applicable provisions of the Constitution.[13]

The next important case to be noted in this context is *Youngstown Sheet & Tube v. Sawyer*, 343 U.S. 549 (1952). No other decision of the Supreme Court has had as much influence on national security law as this one. In April of 1952, during the Korean War, President Truman issued an executive order directing the Secretary of Commerce to seize and operate most of the nation's steel mills in order to avoid the expected effects of a strike by the United Steelworkers of America. As you can imagine, the production of steel was essential to the American effort in the Korean War.

Unlike the *Curtiss-Wright* case, where the president's authority was upheld, the Court in this case held that the president did not have the authority to issue such an order. The Court held that the president's military power as commander in chief of the Armed Forces did not extend to labor disputes and, since there was no congressional statute that authorized the president to take possession of private property in a situation such as that presented by the case, his order was unlawful. While the actual ruling of the Court was of course important, it is the concurring opinion written by Justice Robert Jackson that has become the important part of the opinion.

Jackson noted that the balance of presidential and congressional power could be evaluated so as to fall into one of three categories:

1. When the president acts pursuant to an express or implied authorization of Congress, his authority is at its maximum, for it includes all that he possesses in his own

---

13. Id. at 319–320.

right under the U.S. Constitution plus all that Congress can delegate. In these circumstances, and in these only, may he be said to personify the federal sovereignty. A seizure executed by the president pursuant to an act of Congress would be supported by the strongest of presumptions and the widest latitude of judicial interpretation, and the burden of persuasion would rest heavily upon any who might attack it. In the unlikely event that a court holds unconstitutional the actions of a President, acting pursuant to Congressional authorization, then would likely be because it is an action which the federal government is prohibited from doing.

2. When the president acts in the absence of either a congressional grant or denial of authority, he can only rely upon his own independent powers. But there is a zone of twilight in which he and Congress may have concurrent authority, or in which its distribution is uncertain. Therefore, congressional inertia, indifference or inactivity may sometimes, at least as a practical matter, enable, if not invite, measures on independent presidential responsibility. In this area, any actual test of power is likely to depend on the imperatives of events and contemporary imponderables, rather than on abstract theories of law.

3. When the president takes measures incompatible with the expressed or implied will of Congress, his power is at its lowest ebb, for then he can rely only upon his own constitutional powers minus any constitutional powers of Congress over the matter. Courts can sustain exclusive presidential control in such a case only by disabling the Congress from acting upon the subject. Presidential claim to a power at once so conclusive and preclusive must be scrutinized with caution, for what is at stake is the equilibrium established by our constitutional system.[14]

It is important to see here that Jackson does not suggest the president has <u>no</u> power unless Congress acts in concert with him, or that an act of Congress <u>erases</u> the power of the president. As noted above, the president's authority in Article II of the Constitution is inherent in the very office of the president. Now, to be sure, there is still a great deal of concern whenever a president states that an action is being taken pursuant to the "inherent" Constitutional authority provided by Article II of the Constitution, and Congress will, on occasion, weigh in to limit or direct the executive. Unfortunately, at times there are cases where Congress chooses to complain about action taken by a president, but fails to either constrain or to affirm the action. And, in the absence of Congressional action, the president's action remains, for all practical purposes, a statement of law. Nevertheless, when Congress and the president act *together*, the constitutional balance and legitimacy is strongest.

These cases provide important guidance on not simply the role of the different branches of government, but they reaffirm and give guidance in the application of the principle of a strong government, strong despite (or perhaps because of) the shared and divided nature of authority.[15]

---

14. 343 U.S. 579 at 636–638.
15. An excellent analysis of this case is contained in *National Security Law: Principles and Policy* by Geoff Corn, Eric Jensen, Peter Marulies, and Jimmy Gurule (Wolters Kluwer, 2015) at 14–25.

The Constitutional framework in place provides for a division of responsibilities between the federal government and the states. This division is most evident in the series of laws and policies designed to address disaster response and relief. Most notably, the Robert T. Stafford Disaster Relief and Emergency Assistance Act (Stafford Act) is a federal law designed to bring an orderly and systemic means of federal natural disaster assistance for state and local governments in carrying out their responsibilities to aid citizens. Through this law, states and localities are encouraged to develop comprehensive disaster preparedness plans, to better intergovernmental coordination at the federal, state, local, and tribal level in the face of a disaster, and to establish procedures for the provision of federal assistance both to respond to disasters and to compensate for losses due to a disaster.[16]

The conduct of national security functions (and the part of homeland security functions relating to counter-terrorism) depends upon the effectiveness of the intelligence community. Here, too, an understanding of the role and authority of the government requires looking not simply to the text of the document and to enabling statutes, but to an extensive body of case law.

One example of the Court limiting the power of the federal government even when Congress and the executive have acted together involves the issue of surveillance. As we will discuss in the next chapter, the Fourth Amendment guarantees protection against unreasonable searches and seizures, and requires that warrants be based on probable cause. A vast amount of case law has addressed the scope of this limit on government intrusiveness, even where national security is claimed as the justification.

In *United States v. United States District Court*, 407 U.S. 297 (1972), three defendants were convicted based on wiretap evidence gathered not after the issuance of a warrant, but instead based on the assertion by the Attorney General that he had approved the wiretaps for the purpose of gathering intelligence information deemed necessary to protect the nation from attempts of domestic organizations to attack and subvert the existing structure of the government. The government claimed that the surveillance, though warrantless, was lawful as a reasonable exercise of presidential power to protect the national security, and asserted that this was recognized by language in Title III of the Omnibus Crime Control and Safe Streets Act, the statutory authority for court-approved electronic surveillance, that nothing in that law limits the president's constitutional power to protect against the overthrow of the government or against "any other clear and present danger to the structure or existence of the government."

The Court disagreed, holding that the aforementioned law was merely a disclaimer of congressional intent to define presidential powers in matters affecting national security, not a grant of authority to conduct warrantless national security surveillances. The court ruled that the freedoms of the Fourth Amendment cannot properly be guaranteed if domestic surveillance, even those conducted for the purposes of national security, are conducted solely within the discretion of the executive

---

16. Robert T. Stafford Disaster Relief and Emergency Assistance Act (Public Law 93-288) as amended. See the text and discussion at http://www.fema.gov/robert-t-stafford-disaster-relief-and-emergency-assistance-act-public-law-93-288-amended.

branch, without the detached judgment of a neutral magistrate. The Fourth Amendment requires prior judicial approval for the type of domestic security surveillance involved in this case.[17]

The disclosure of broad electronic surveillance by the National Security Agency, surveillance that is not targeted at American citizens yet still involves vast amounts of electronic communication by both citizens and non-citizens, has raised a significant debate within the United States regarding the limits of Fourth Amendment protections.[18]

Constitutional guarantees of due process, and of freedom of expression, have also affected decisions on the detention of terror suspects[19] and their trial by military commission as opposed to the usual federal court system.[20]

Finally, as we mentioned in the opening chapter of the book, international law and its relationship to other sources of the law is a part of the Constitutional framework of national security law. Article VI of the Constitution states that

> This Constitution, and the laws of the United States which shall be made in pursuance thereof; and all treaties made, or which shall be made, under the authority of the United States, shall be the supreme law of the land; and the judges in every state shall be bound thereby, anything in the Constitution or laws of any State to the contrary notwithstanding.

So not only are the statutes passed by the Congress part of our body of law, but international law plays a role as well. How and to what extent this is the case, though, is often debated.[21]

International law is developed through a number of sources[22]: *jus cogens* or general principles of law established over history, treaties, and other international agreements, customary international rules established by state practice, and secondary sources of the law such as judicial decisions (normally those of international tribunals but also in some cases of national courts).

In most situations, international law is considered not to be binding on any internal decisions of the United States government, binding it only in its relations with other nations.[23] Recently, however, the force of international law, especially international human rights law and international humanitarian law, has been held to bind the federal government.[24] In future chapters we will examine these issues in more detail as well.

---

17. 407 U.S. 297 at 316–318.
18. Laura K. Donohue, "Bulk Metadata Collection: Statutory and Constitutional Considerations," 37 Harv. J.L. & Pub. Pol'y 757–900 (2014).
19. *Hamdi v. Rumsfeld*, 542 U.S. 507 (2004); *Boumediene v. Bush*, 553 U.S. 723 (2008).
20. *Hamdan v. Rumsfeld*, 548 U.S. 557 (2006).
21. We return in more depth to this subject in Chapter 10. Probably the best single resource on this issue is Curtis Bradley's book *International Law in the U.S. Legal System* (Oxford University Press, 2013).
22. Article 38 of the Statute of the International Court of Justice.
23. *United States v. Alvarez-Machain*, 504 U.S. 655 (1992).
24. *Hamdan v. Rumsfeld*, 548 U.S. 557 (2006).

Finally, to return to a point made earlier in this chapter: The authority of the president to "faithfully execute" the laws of the United States has been interpreted to give the president the ability to act even in cases where there is no express permission granted under the Constitution or by statute. This is why Justice Jackson in the *Steel Seizure* case speaks of the authority of the president to act in the absence, or even contrary to, the will of Congress. And recall that Article VI of the Constitution speaks to the Constitution, federal statutes, and treaties as being the supreme law of the land—superior to state and local law. Any question as to the applicability of federal constitutional law to the states was resolved with the enactment of the Fourteenth Amendment. The Supreme Court has, over time, held that most provisions of the Bill of Rights apply to the states through the due process clause of the Fourteenth Amendment under a doctrine called "incorporation."

In issues of homeland and national security, it is important to keep in mind that there will be both federal and state/local aspects of the issue. In our system of government, while the state retains a great deal of police power, there is an aspect of authority that the federal government holds as supreme authority. A case illustrating this tension is the Supreme Court decision *In re Neagle*, 135 U.S. 1 (1890).

David Neagle, a deputy marshal of the United States for the District of California, was brought by writ of habeas corpus before the Circuit Court of that District, upon the allegation that he was held in imprisonment by the sheriff of San Joaquin County, California, on a charge of the murder of David S. Terry. Neagle alleged that the killing of Terry by him was done in pursuance of his duty as deputy marshal in defending the life of Mr. Justice Field, while in discharge of his duties as Circuit judge of the ninth circuit. The local sheriff arrested Neagle, claiming that his position of U.S. Marshal gave him no immunity from state or local criminal law.

The courts in this case held that an assault upon a judge of a court of the United States, while in discharge of his official duties, is a breach of the peace of the United States, distinguished from the peace of the state in which the assault takes place. Since, under the provisions of Rev.Stat. § 788, it is the duty of marshals and their deputies in each state to exercise authority keeping the peace of the United States, exercising the powers given to the sheriffs of the State for keeping the peace of the State; and a deputy marshal of the United States, specially charged with the duty of protecting and guarding a judge of a court of the United States, has imposed upon him the duty of doing whatever may be necessary for that purpose, even the use of deadly force.

Accordingly, the Circuit Court of Appeals found that Neagle was in custody for an act done in pursuance of a law of the United States, and was therefore imprisoned in violation of the Constitution and laws of the United States. The Supreme Court concluded that there was a conspiracy to murder Justice Field on his official visit to California in the summer of 1889, that the existence of the conspiracy became well known, which resulted in Neagle being appointed deputy marshal for the express purpose of guarding Justice Field against an attack; that such an attack did take place; that Neagle had just reason to believe that the attack would result in the death of Justice Field unless he interfered, and his shooting of Terry while in the act of assaulting

Mr. Justice Field was justified. The Court further concluded that, in so doing, he acted in discharge of his duty as an officer of the United States and so could not be guilty of murder under the laws of California, nor held to answer to its courts for an act for which he had the authority of the laws of the United States.

Now for our purposes in this course, it is important to note that the court decided, while there was at the time no express statute authorizing the appointment of a deputy marshal, or any other officer, to accompany a judge of the Supreme Court when traveling, to protect him against assaults or other injury, the general obligation imposed upon the president of the United States by the Constitution to see that the laws be faithfully executed, impose upon the executive department the duty of protecting a justice or judge of any of the courts of the United States, when there is just reason to believe that he will be in personal danger while executing the duties of his office. We'll look at the federal/state authority issue in more detail in the chapters on disaster response and foreign relations law.

Supreme Court Justice Oliver Wendall Holmes is quoted as saying "... the provisions of the Constitution are not mathematical formulas having their essence in their form; they are organic living institutions ... Their significance is vital, not formal; it is to be gathered not simply by taking the words and a dictionary, but by considering their origin and the line of their growth."[25] So, then, all of these together—the text of the Constitution, its historic background as illuminated by documents such as the Federalist Papers, the statutes enacted and treaties entered into, and finally the vast amount of case law—give full meaning to the U.S. Constitution. Let's now begin to look at some specific applications of the law within this framework.

Review Questions

1. Presidents Washington, Jefferson, Madison, and Lincoln are among those who "made law" by taking action that was either not directly authorized by Congress or even went against the will of Congress. Find an example and consider— what would have been the implications of the president NOT acting?

2. While there are no actual records of the discussions that took place when the Constitution was drafted, *The Federalist Papers*, a series of "op-ed" like essays written by James Madison, Alexander Hamilton, and John Jay, provide the best insight into the debates that led to the text of the Constitution. These can be found in a number of locations online. Look in particular at Papers 49, 70, and 72 for discussions relating to national security and the authority of the executive. There were a series of articles written that argued against adopting the Constitution as well, known as "The Anti-Federalist Papers." Finally, you might want to find and read James Madison's Speech in 1789 on Establishing a Department of Foreign Affairs and the Pacificus/Helvidius Exchange (another set of op-ed-like papers) between Hamilton and Madison. How do the concerns and positions expressed at the time of the founding of the nation fare in today's environment?

---

25. *Gompers v. United States*, 233 U.S. 604, 610 (1914).

Key Terms

Constitution—The fundamental and organic law of a nation or state that establishes the institutions and apparatus of government, defines the scope of governmental sovereign powers, and guarantees individual civil rights and liberties.

Express powers, or enumerated powers—Those powers of the federal government that are expressly set forth (or "enumerated") in the text of the Constitution. A list of items found in Article I, Section 8 of the U.S. Constitution set forth the authority of Congress. In summary, Congress (and the other branches of the government) may exercise the powers that the Constitution grants, subject to the individual rights listed elsewhere in the Constitution and in the Bill of Rights.

Implied powers—Authoritative actions that aren't specifically granted to Congress and the other branches of government in the Constitution but are considered necessary to fulfill governmental duties. The implied powers allow Congress to draft new laws at will, especially if the legislation protects the general populace or is considered crucial for upholding laws defined by the expressed powers. The founding fathers were in favor of this policy and wanted to ensure that the federal government could adapt its powers to changing needs and take action to address unforeseen problems. However, the vague definition of the implied powers has created controversy.

Judicial review—The idea, fundamental to the U.S. system of government, that the actions of the executive and legislative branches of government are subject to **review** and possible invalidation by the **judicial** branch.

Original jurisdiction—The power to hear a case for the first time, as opposed to appellate jurisdiction, when a higher court has the power to review a lower court's decision. The original jurisdiction of the U.S. Supreme Court is set forth in Article III of the U.S. Constitution and in 28 U.S. Code § 1251.

Separation of powers—The original premise of the framers of the Constitution that the way to safeguard against tyranny is to separate the powers of government among three branches of government so that each branch checks the other two.

Writ of mandamus—A formal command issued by a court directed to an officer of the government or to any person, corporation, or inferior court, requiring them to do some particular thing which pertains to their office and duty, which the court has decided is necessary in the interest of justice.

Further Reading

Geoffrey Corn, Jimmy Gurule, Eric Jensen and Peter Margulies, *National Security Law; Principles and Policy.* New York: Wolters Kluwer, 2015.

Donohue, Laura K., *Bulk Metadata Collection: Statutory and Constitutional Considerations,* 37 Harv. J.L. & Pub. Pol'y 757–900 (2014).

Powell, H. Jefferson. *Targeting Americans: The Constitutionality of the U.S. Drone War.* New York: Oxford, 2016.

Chapter 2

Criminal Procedure and Homeland/National Security

Part One: An Introduction to Fourth Amendment Law

Overview

Whether you are dealing with ordinary criminals who are robbing liquor stores or you are dealing with terrorists who are trying to blow up airplanes, many of the rules of criminal procedure are the same. For example, if the government wants to search a person's house because they believe a bomb is being built inside, or because they believe there is a meth lab in the basement, the police must be prepared to handle many of the same Fourth Amendment issues concerning searches and seizures. Similarly, if a person is arrested and subsequently interrogated for stealing a candy bar or for going on a shooting spree at a Jewish synagogue, the Fifth Amendment, the requirement to provide *Miranda* rights, and limits on coercive techniques still apply for interrogation. The point of these examples, and of this chapter, is that it is impossible to successfully go after terrorists who threaten national security if you do not know the basic rules of criminal procedure that apply to petty criminals What you will learn in this chapter is how law enforcement officials lawfully do their jobs to ensure that as much evidence as possible is admissible in court for a defendant's prosecution.

Now, it goes without saying that the threat posed by terrorism is different than that of ordinary criminal activity. The potential for harm is greater, and there is a trans-national aspect in many (not all) cases of terrorism that is different than what is experienced in more routine law enforcement situations. But for the great majority of cases addressed by those working in homeland and national security, our system of laws begins with basic criminal procedure as its foundation. The specific challenges posed by terrorism and other national security cases are then addressed by laws that build on that foundation.

The basis of criminal procedure law in America is found in the Fourth, Fifth, and Sixth Amendments of the U.S. Constitution and in state law. Historically, most criminal law, and most of the common law rules affecting policing, originated at the state and local level because police power was originally seen as a state right under the Constitution. It was only after adoption of the Fourteenth Amendment, and application of the due process and equal protection clauses of the Fourteenth Amendment to apply the Bill of Rights to the states, that U.S. constitutional limits began to be applied to state and local police.[1] This chapter provides an introduction to search and seizure law under the Fourth Amendment, while the next chapter deals with concepts of due process and the protection against self-incrimination covered by the Fifth, Sixth, and Fourteenth Amendments.

The safeguards built into our Constitution were based on legal concepts going back through the ages as well as the experiences of the founders during the colonial period and the Revolutionary War. At its most basic level, all criminal procedure law is based on the belief that the government may not interfere with a person's life, liberty, or property except in accordance with principles of due process of law—safeguards intended to ensure the fundamental fairness of an investigation and judicial proceeding. This begins with the presumption of innocence, the concept that every person is *presumed* to be innocent of wrongdoing unless sufficient proof of guilt is presented in accordance with the law. In other words, the police who search a home must presume that all within are innocent. A person arrested must be presumed to be innocent. A person on trial—whether in a traditional court or in a military commission—is presumed to be innocent.

At every stage from investigation through conviction, the law places limits on what the government may do so that this presumption is respected, and sets forth the level of evidence (or intelligence) and procedures required in order to overcome the presumption. In some cases, as we'll see in the case of a *Terry* stop-and-frisk, the threshold is low, while in other cases, such as at trial itself, the procedures and standard of proof needed are significantly higher. So even Fourth Amendment law, as we'll see, is built on this concept.

The Fourth Amendment

As a practical matter, during the investigation of most crimes the Fourth Amendment to the U.S. Constitution is the one most frequently addressed by law enforcement, as the law on this amendment governs searches and seizures. The Fourth Amendment states the following:

> The right of the people to be secure in their persons, houses, papers, and effects, against unreasonable searches and seizures, shall not be violated, and no Warrants shall issue, but upon probable cause, supported by Oath or affirmation, and particularly describing the place to be searched, and the persons or things to be seized.

Put simply, the Fourth Amendment protects you and everyone else in the country from unreasonable government invasions of your privacy. It means that government officials cannot search your body, pockets, purse, backpack, cell

---

1. *Duncan v. Louisiana*, 391 U.S. 145 (1968).

phone,[2] car, home, and almost any other location unless they meet certain burdens of proof and/or procedural safeguards. It also prohibits the government from seizing, detaining, or arresting you or part of your property unless they have a legal justification and meet certain burdens of proof and/or procedural safeguards.

Although the Fourth Amendment is only a single sentence, it covers two separate and distinct aspects.

The first is:

1. "The right of the people to be secure in their persons, houses, papers, and effects, against *unreasonable* searches and seizures, shall not be violated."

The second is:

2. "*No Warrants shall issue, but upon probable cause*, supported by Oath or affirmation, and particularly describing the place to be searched, and the persons or things to be seized."

Let's start with the second part of the Fourth Amendment, which is known as the "warrant clause." A warrant is an authorization from a neutral judicial officer (usually a judge or a magistrate) for the police to do a search or seizure. The purpose of warrants is to create a check against the government's power in a criminal investigation to invade people's privacy and intrude upon the liberty of the people. The general rule is that for the government to search an individual's property or arrest a person, the government must have a warrant. However, as you will be exploring later in this chapter, there are many exceptions to this rule.

A search warrant authorizes the government to enter private property and look for evidence for a criminal investigation. It can also authorize law enforcement to search a person's belongings including purse, pockets, computer, cell phone, and wallet. Additionally, there can be search warrants issued to search inside a person! Have you ever heard of a cavity search? Examples of this might be a search warrant which authorizes a colonoscopy if a person is suspected of hiding drugs in his rectum. (Sadly, this is a lot more common than you probably realize.) When a person is "seized" pursuant to a warrant, we commonly mean that person is arrested. Items can also be seized as evidence of a crime while law enforcement officers execute a search warrant. For example, a search warrant for a suspected marijuana grow house would authorize the seizure of any marijuana plants.

Although the Fourth Amendment requires that warrants be issued upon a finding of "probable cause," the term "probable cause" does not mean the same in a court of law as it does in a math class. Mathematically, to say that something is "probable" means that there is a greater than 50% chance it will happen. However, to say in law that something requires "probable cause" means that there is a reasonable belief that a crime has been committed or that a search will turn up evidence of a crime. No mathematical probability is required—in fact, there is reason to believe that even as low as a 33% chance might be probable cause. This comes from the U.S. Supreme

---

2. *United States v. Jones*, 132 S. Ct. 945 (2012).

Court case *Maryland v. Pringle*[3] where there were three passengers in a car and, after a search of the car was conducted, one bag of cocaine was found along with hundreds of dollars in cash. All three persons were lawfully arrested and charged, even though it was argued that there could only be a one in three chance of the cocaine belonging to any individual.

Today, when the police want to arrest someone or conduct a search, they first go to a judge or magistrate who places the police officer under oath. Under oath, the police officer shows and/or tells the judicial officer the evidence of a crime, or presents the judicial officer with evidence or information why a search would yield evidence of a crime. If the judicial officer finds "probable cause," as required in the Fourth Amendment, then a warrant is issued to either arrest a person or to conduct a search.

When a warrant is issued, the warrant must state in writing what evidence is being sought, what property can be searched, and what can be seized. It is very important that a warrant be specific and its scope be narrowly tailored.

For example, if the police want to search the apartment of Monica G. because she is suspected of building a bomb, the warrant would likely include her exact address down to her apartment number. It would be insufficient for the warrant to simply state "the home of Monica G." or merely give the name of the apartment building without specifying which unit within the apartment building. The warrant to search Monica's apartment for suspected bomb-making material would also authorize law enforcement to seize any explosives or other materials used to construct a bomb. However, although law enforcement would be allowed to search Monica's underwear drawer and jewelry box for bomb-making evidence, they would not be allowed to seize items that have nothing to do with the construction of a bomb.

It is important that the incorrect persons or property are not searched or arrested pursuant to a faulty or incomplete warrant. This is why warrants should be as specific and precise as possible as to just who or what is to be searched and/or seized. If a person is to be seized, then as much identifying information as possible is necessary such as name, physical description, date of birth, and social security number. It has happened that innocent persons have been mistakenly arrested because they shared similar personal identifying information as persons who had a warrant out for their arrest. For example, in a big city such as New York, if a warrant is issued for the arrest of John Smith, then there are probably hundreds if not thousands of people in New York City with that name. For objects being seized, magistrates should try to specify which objects are to be seized. For example, if John is suspected of stealing car radios and storing them in his house, then a warrant should be issued specifically for car radios, and not just radios in general.

It is common for magistrates to categorize objects being seized into four distinct categories, which are detailed below.

---

3. 540 U.S. 366 (2003).

1. Contraband: This is anything which is inherently illegal such as marijuana, a sawed off shotgun, child pornography, or anthrax.

2. Fruits of a crime: This is what a person obtained from a crime, such as a stolen laptop, cash, or jewelry.

3. Instrumentalities of a crime: These are devices used to help someone commit a crime. Lock-picking tools are an example for burglary, and a marijuana pipe is useful for evidence of illegal drug use.

4. Evidence of a crime: This last one is a catchall, because in theory, anything could potentially be evidence of a crime. Examples include BAC, fingerprints, and GPS records to name but a few.

The Fourth Amendment of the U.S. Constitution does not say that warrants are needed for all searches. This is because, historically, warrants were only needed for a very narrow and limited field of searches. Many other searches (as well as more limited forms of inspection and arrests) do not require a warrant. These searches and arrests which required warrants were mostly limited to the following:

- Search of a person's house or place of business
- Intercepting a person's mail
- Searching a person's body
- Arrest for a misdemeanor not committed in the officer's presence

Reasonableness

As you can see from that short list above, the types of searches and arrests which require a warrant are very few and limited (even though many such searches take place). Over the years, the searches which require warrants have been expanded to include digital and electronic media (for example, a warrant is needed for the police to search your cell phone), but it is still the case that only a minority of searches require a warrant. Most searches do not require a warrant, but instead, must merely be "reasonable" (or more precisely, not be considered "unreasonable") in order to be lawful. Why is this? Re-read the first part of the Fourth Amendment and you will have your answer:

> The right of the people to be secure in their persons, houses, papers, and effects, against *unreasonable* searches and seizures, shall not be violated.

This is the "reasonableness clause" of the Fourth Amendment, and it requires that *all searches* performed by the government be reasonable. Any search performed after the authorities have properly obtained a warrant is presumed to be reasonable (although in court there is the opportunity to rebut this presumption), but there are also many other searches the government can perform without a warrant which can also be lawful so long as they are reasonable. Before we explore the types of searches which do not require a warrant, let's first define what we mean by "reasonable."

To determine whether or not a search is reasonable, the courts have applied a two-part test:

1. Was there a reasonable basis for doing a search?

and

2. Was the search conducted in a reasonable manner?

Let's examine each of these criteria.

When we ask if there was a "reasonable basis for doing a search," the courts have generally required commonsense and good judgment, taking into consideration the specific factors of any situation. Over the years, the courts have ruled on a wide variety of cases, providing guidance on what is considered reasonable or unreasonable. For example, whenever the police lawfully arrest a person (with or without a warrant), they are allowed to conduct a warrantless search on a person to ensure that he does not have any weapons or anything else dangerous on him. This is a historic practice under common law that predates the U.S. Constitution. This is considered a reasonable measure to protect police officers.

In a more modern example, let's look at the searches performed by airport security. The Transportation Security Administration (TSA) does not have a warrant to search each air passenger, nor do they need a warrant. Given the history of terrorism and hijackings on airplanes, it is considered "reasonable" for all passengers to have to consent to be searched prior to being given permission to board a plane.

The reasonableness clause of the Fourth Amendment includes "seizure" just as much as it includes a search. For example, if the police have merely a reasonable suspicion, a standard of proof that is far less than probable cause, that a person is engaged in criminal activity, the police are allowed to briefly detain a person. This is because the temporary detention is considered much less intrusive of a person's liberty than a full arrest, so less cause is required. Now, to be sure, a detention, though it is not an arrest, is a form of custody, meaning a seizure, since a person detained by the police is not free to leave for that brief period of time. In addition, when a person has been briefly detained by the police, it is also considered reasonable for the police to frisk a person for a weapon. The rationale for this is that it is reasonable for the police to want to take precautions for their own safety, as they never know if the person they have detained is someone who might act with violence. So both of these—the brief seizure or detention, and the minimally intrusive search, or frisk—are examples of lawful warrantless searches and seizures pursuant to the reasonableness clause of the Fourth Amendment.

The second part to the two-part test in determining if a search was reasonable is ascertaining if the search was performed in a reasonable manner. This looks at the police conduct in performing the search. Whenever the police perform a search with or without a warrant, they are required to execute the search in a reasonable manner.

Again, what is meant by "reasonable" depends on the circumstances—what is reasonable in one case may not be reasonable in another. If the police have a warrant to search a house they believe is being used as a meth lab and is controlled by a dangerous and well-armed gang, it would be reasonable for a SWAT team to enter the house in a forceful and violent manner for the protection of the police and to subdue the suspected gang members as quickly as possible. On the other hand, if the police plan to arrest a 90-year-old grandmother over unpaid parking tickets, it would be completely unreasonable to have a SWAT team break down her door and fire tear gas canisters inside the home.

In another example, if the police believe that Marcus is growing marijuana in his basement and get a warrant to search his house, they cannot just start breaking down walls on the mere possibility there might be evidence hidden in them. However, if the police have a warrant for the search of Marcus's house and in the process of the search they find reason to believe that Marcus has hidden something in the walls, then they could selectively start looking inside the walls.

Let's go back to TSA who can lawfully search all air passengers without a warrant. Even though TSA can search all air passengers, they are required to conduct their searches in a reasonable manner. Just what is a reasonable search of air passengers? Reasonable persons may disagree as to the answer here. Some people feel that asking travelers to take off their shoes or be subjected to x-ray machines or pat-downs is unreasonable and an invasion of not only privacy, but bodily integrity. However, given recent events involving bombs being smuggled onto airplanes and detonated while in flight, most people agree that x-raying luggage brought onto a plane is reasonable. Another aspect of reasonableness here is the fact that no one is forced, or has a constitutional right, to fly on an airplane. If you don't want to endure the searches, you can simply choose another form of transportation. Now, even that only goes so far, though, for at another extreme, having every air passenger submit to a cavity search prior to boarding would clearly be unreasonable, so such a requirement would violate the Fourth Amendment.

Here is another example of an unreasonable search: a criminal was in a shootout with the police and was shot, but managed to get away. Sometime later after the injury had healed, the police arrested the person they thought they had shot. An x-ray revealed that the suspect had a bullet still inside his body. The police wanted to get a surgeon to extract the bullet to prove it came from an officer's gun during the shootout, thus linking the suspect to the crime. The Court held that it is unreasonably invasive to perform risky surgery on a person to recover evidence.[4] However, other procedures that are far less invasive or dangerous than surgery, such as taking an x-ray, swabbing for DNA, or scraping under fingernails, are reasonable searches. If a search seems too intrusive or dangerous to a suspect, then the search is likely unconstitutional because it would be unreasonable.

Searches Not Requiring a Warrant

As stated earlier, only a few and limited number of searches or arrests require a warrant. Those were the types of searches and seizures established under common

---

4. *Winston v. Lee*, 470 U.S. 753 (1985).

law in England before the founding of the U.S. Many—perhaps even most—searches and seizures today do not require a warrant, but instead, must merely meet the test of being reasonable. Here is a partial list of some of the warrantless searches and seizures most commonly encountered.

Searches based on *consent*: This seems obvious. If I freely consent to a search, then the search must be reasonable, or I would not consent to it. Now, the key concept here is "freely consent." I have to have the actual ability and belief that I can refuse to allow the search without penalty. So a search of my bag when I am entering Disney World is reasonable—I have the choice to leave and not enter the park if I don't want my knapsack searched at the entrance. But a person who is in prison doesn't have that freedom, so proving consent would be much harder.

Administrative searches and inspections: Because they are not conducted to look for criminal evidence, but for some other reason, legally, these are not considered true "searches." Administrative searches and inspections are not performed because of any individualized suspicion that a person has committed a crime, but instead are usually a part of a general regulatory scheme to promote the health and safety of society. Here are some common examples of administrative searches:

- The health inspector does not need a warrant to go into a restaurant's kitchen. He is not looking for criminal evidence nor does he suspect anyone of being engaged in criminal conduct. Instead, his search is merely to ensure that there are no dangerous conditions that could make the public sick.

- Checkpoints to catch intoxicated drivers were upheld as lawful in the Supreme Court case *Michigan Department of State Police v. Sitz*. The Court explained that given the large number of fatalities caused each year by intoxicated drivers, the government has a substantial interest in stopping drunk driving. This substantial government interest outweighs the negligible inconvenience to drivers who are delayed only a couple of minutes. For DUI checkpoints to be legal, vehicles cannot be stopped based on a suspicion of drunk driving. Instead, the government must use a random or neutral method to decide which vehicles will be stopped. Examples would include stopping all cars or stopping every third car.

- Internal checkpoints near the borders with Canada and Mexico, or along commonly travelled highways leading to/from those countries, which stop vehicles and ask motorists if they are lawfully in the U.S. have also, albeit with some controversy, been upheld as legal. The rationale for these decisions is similar to why DUI checkpoints are lawful; the government has a substantial interest in stopping illegal immigration, the method of inspection is random or neutral, and the level of intrusion on the liberty of motorists is minimal.

- A car parked illegally can be seized as it is towed to an impound lot. This seizure is merely to remove a car from where it is not supposed to be because it is trespassing or creating an inconvenience to others, rather than a seizure as part of a criminal investigation.

- When the police impound a vehicle, they are allowed to open it and take an inventory. They have no suspicion that there is anything criminal in the vehicle, and their taking an inventory of its contents is not to look for criminal evidence, but instead to protect the police and the owner of the car from subsequent accusations of theft while the vehicle is in impound, to ensure there is nothing in the vehicle which might be dangerous, or to check if something was left in the vehicle that should be removed, such as an infant sleeping in the back seat or a live animal.

- As mentioned earlier, airport screenings are not being conducted to look for criminal evidence, but instead, are to simply make sure that no one has anything dangerous or something that poses a threat to air travel.

Even though administrative searches are not designed to look for criminal activity, any evidence of criminal activity found during an otherwise lawful administrative search is perfectly legal to use during criminal proceedings. For example, if a TSA screener who is performing checks for dangerous objects and substances finds a person is trying to smuggle cocaine, the TSA screener can alert the police and the cocaine will be admissible at a criminal prosecution. Similarly, if a health inspector who conducts a surprise inspection at a restaurant discovers marijuana is hidden in an "oregano" container, the drugs are admissible in a subsequent criminal proceeding.

In addition to administrative searches, there are other searches that, because of special circumstances, can also be performed without a warrant.

School searches: Public primary schools are considered special places with a special job of educating youths. Because the students are minors, the schools also have a role similar to that of parents in keeping students safe. For schools to do this, they must be able to maintain order and discipline among the students. Having to go to a judicial officer to get a warrant to detain or search students suspected of infractions would interfere with the ability of a school to swiftly discipline students. Think about it; can you imagine if a first grade teacher had to go to a judge to get a warrant to put an unruly student in time-out? For this reason, school officials need only a reasonable suspicion of a crime or of a violation of a school rule to search a student's belongings. Additionally, the school grounds and facilities, such as school lockers, are not the property of the student but of the school, so the privacy rights of the students are reduced.

To be clear, minors still do have constitutional rights including the protection of the Fourth Amendment. However, the Fourth Amendment protections are limited on school grounds because of the special needs of a school to maintain order and discipline.

The idea of "special needs" being used to justify warrantless searches at schools is also used in many other warrantless searches, such as in prisons.

Border searches: It is a customary principle of international law that nations have the inherent right to protect their sovereignty, which includes approving all persons and things entering its borders. For this reason, it is considered reasonable for nations to be able to search any containers, boxes, vehicles, vessels, or other objects entering the country, even if the authorities do not have any suspicion of criminal activity.

Now, although border agents do not need any individualized suspicion to search luggage, there are still some limitations on border searches. First, border searches cannot be unreasonably destructive. Border agents are not permitted to take a car apart to search for smuggled drugs unless they have a reasonable belief there are drugs being smuggled. Also, if border agents are going to perform a cavity search, a practice highly offensive to personal dignity, they must at least have a reasonable suspicion that a person has contraband in his rectum. However, an X-ray at the border of one's torso (as we encounter at the airport), a far less invasive procedure than a cavity search, does not require any suspicion.

Felony arrests outside the home: If the police have probable cause to think a person has committed a felony, they do not need a warrant to arrest that person outside of his or her home. However, if a person is inside his or her home, then the police do need a warrant to enter and arrest the person.

Misdemeanor arrests committed in an officer's presence: If a person commits a misdemeanor, which is a minor crime, in the presence of an officer, then the officer does not need to get a warrant to arrest that person. For example, the Supreme Court has upheld the arrest of a person for driving without a seatbelt when this was committed in an officer's presence.

Note: Some but not all states have enacted laws that limit the ability of law enforcement to arrest persons for certain misdemeanors, even when committed in their presence. For example, many states do not allow officers to arrest persons for simple traffic infractions and minor misdemeanors, such as fishing without a license. However, an officer is allowed to arrest the person if the person refuses to sign a summons where he or she promises to appear in court at a later date.

Search incident to arrest: When the police arrest a person, it is permissible for them to search the person, as well as the immediate vicinity of where the person was arrested. This is for officer safety, as well as to prevent any contraband from entering a jail along with the prisoner.

Exigent circumstances: This applies to circumstances where a warrant is normally required, but a delay in getting a warrant would result in either a loss of the evidence or bodily harm. Here, a police officer would act as his own magistrate and determine whether or not there is probable cause that a crime or evidence exists, or if there is a risk of a loss of evidence or bodily harm. If the officer has probable cause that a crime has been committed and reasonably believes that a delay to get a warrant would result in a loss of evidence or an injury, he is allowed to conduct a search without a warrant.

Here are some examples:

- Officer Brown is walking down the street, and he hears someone inside a house scream. He would be allowed to enter the house without a warrant to ensure that the people are safe inside.
  - Let's say Officer Brown hears a scream coming from inside a house so he immediately breaks down the door and rushes inside. It may turn out that

the scream was from the television, but while inside Officer Brown sees Dave doing cocaine. It would be lawful for him to arrest Dave and seize the cocaine because at the time he entered the house, he was legally justified in doing so.
- Mary is arrested for driving under the influence. Without a warrant, the police can get a blood sample or make her do a Breathalyzer because the body's own natural processes will destroy the evidence of the alcohol. (Note: Under a legal doctrine of "implied consent," many states allow people to refuse to give a blood or alcohol sample, in which case, a driver's license is automatically suspended for a set period of time. The premise is that if a person chooses to drive, then that person has already consented to providing a blood or alcohol sample upon arrest for drunk driving.)
- The police have a reasonable suspicion that Will is dealing drugs inside his house. Reasonable suspicion is less than probable cause, so they are unable to get a warrant to search his house. What they do instead is knock on his front door just to see if he will consent to a search or a conversation with them. Will opens the door, sees it's the police, and slams the door shut in their faces. Seconds later, the police hear the sound of a toilet flushing. This would give the police probable cause that Will is trying to destroy drugs by flushing them down the toilet, so they would be justified in entering the house without a warrant to stop him from destroying evidence.
- Drake is pulled over for speeding. As he rolls down the window, the police officer notices the smell of marijuana coming out of the car. This gives the police probable cause that marijuana is in the car. The police are allowed to detain the vehicle and its occupants while they conduct a search. Given the mobile nature of vehicles, if the police were to let Drake go while they obtained a warrant, Drake could either drive the vehicle out of the jurisdiction of these police or could take it somewhere he could clean it and remove any marijuana he has in the vehicle, thus destroying the evidence.
  ◦ This last example is known as the automobile exception. Police need only probable cause of a crime to search a vehicle. All automobiles are inherently considered to be exigent circumstances because of their mobile nature.
- In all of these examples, the key issue is a real danger that evidence will be lost, or that there is an ongoing danger to the public, and a very short period of time in which to act. What justifies the search without a warrant is evidence that a delay to get a warrant would result in real harm.

There are other searches that are allowed without a warrant, but the ones listed above are the most common. They are all based on a determination—often as a result of court opinions—that the combination of the circumstances leading the authorities to feel the search is needed, as well as the circumstances of how the search is undertaken, meets the Fourth Amendment standard of reasonableness.

One type of search that allows you to read through the analysis of the issues mentioned above is known as a "*Terry* Stop" or a "stop-and-frisk." As you will read below, if an officer has a reasonable suspicion that a person is involved in illegal conduct and that it is possible the person is armed, the police are allowed to briefly detain and frisk that individual for a weapon without a warrant. Here is the Supreme Court opinion that legalized the stop-and-frisk.

Terry v. Ohio, 392 U.S. 1 (1968)*

This case presents serious questions concerning the role of the Fourth Amendment in the confrontation on the street between the citizen and the policeman investigating suspicious circumstances.

Terry was convicted of carrying a concealed weapon and sentenced to the statutorily prescribed term of one to three years in the penitentiary. Officer McFadden testified that, while he was patrolling in plain clothes in downtown Cleveland at approximately 2:30 in the afternoon of October 31, 1963, his attention was attracted by two men, Chilton and Terry, standing on the corner of Huron Road and Euclid Avenue. He had never seen the two men before, and he was unable to say precisely what first drew his eye to them. However, he testified that he had been a policeman for 39 years and a detective for 35, and that he had been assigned to patrol this vicinity of downtown Cleveland for shoplifters and pickpockets for 30 years. He explained that he had developed routine habits of observation over the years, and that he would "stand and watch people or walk and watch people at many intervals of the day." He added: "Now, in this case, when I looked over, they didn't look right to me at the time."

His interest aroused, Officer McFadden took up a post of observation in the entrance to a store 300 to 400 feet away from the two men. "I get more purpose to watch them when I seen their movements," he testified. He saw one of the men leave the other one and walk southwest on Huron Road, past some stores. The man paused for a moment and looked in a store window, then walked on a short distance, turned around and walked back toward the corner, pausing once again to look in the same store window. He rejoined his companion at the corner, and the two conferred briefly. Then the second man went through the same series of motions, strolling down Huron Road, looking in the same window, walking on a short distance, turning back, peering in the store window again, and returning to confer with the first man at the corner. The two men repeated this ritual alternately between five and six times apiece—in all, roughly a dozen trips. At one point, while the two were standing together on the corner, a third man approached them and engaged them briefly in conversation. This man then left the two others and walked west on Euclid Avenue. Chilton and Terry resumed their measured pacing, peering, and conferring. After this had gone on for 10 to 12 minutes, the two men walked off together, heading west on Euclid Avenue, following the path taken earlier by the third man.

By this time, Officer McFadden had become thoroughly suspicious. He testified that, after observing their elaborately casual and oft-repeated reconnaissance of the store window on Huron Road, he suspected the two men of "casing a job, a stick-up,"

---

* The case has been heavily edited and paraphrased by the authors for clarity. See disclaimer in introduction.

and that he considered it his duty as a police officer to investigate further. He added that he feared "they may have a gun." Thus, Officer McFadden followed Chilton and Terry and saw them stop in front of Zucker's store to talk to the same man who had conferred with them earlier on the street corner. Deciding that the situation was ripe for direct action, Officer McFadden approached the three men, identified himself as a police officer and asked for their names. At this point, his knowledge was confined to what he had observed. He was not acquainted with any of the three men by name or by sight, and he had received no information concerning them from any other source.

When the men "mumbled something" in response to his inquiries, Officer McFadden grabbed Terry, spun him around so that they were facing the other two, with Terry between McFadden and the others, and patted down the outside of his clothing. In the left breast pocket of Terry's overcoat, Officer McFadden felt a pistol. He reached inside the overcoat pocket, but was unable to remove the gun. At this point, keeping Terry between himself and the others, the officer ordered all three men to enter Zucker's store. As they went in, he removed Terry's overcoat completely, removed a .38 caliber revolver from the pocket and ordered all three men to face the wall with their hands raised. Officer McFadden proceeded to pat down the outer clothing of Chilton and the third man, Katz. He discovered another revolver in the outer pocket of Chilton's overcoat, but no weapons were found on Katz. The officer testified that he only patted the men down to see whether they had weapons, and that he did not put his hands beneath the outer garments of either Terry or Chilton until he felt their guns. So far as appears from the record, he never placed his hands beneath Katz' outer garments. Officer McFadden seized Chilton's gun, asked the proprietor of the store to call a police wagon, and took all three men to the station, where Chilton and Terry were formally charged with carrying concealed weapons.

On the motion to suppress the guns, the prosecution took the position that they had been seized following a search incident to a lawful arrest. The trial court rejected this theory, stating that it "would be stretching the facts beyond reasonable comprehension" to find that Officer McFadden had had probable cause to arrest the men before he patted them down for weapons. However, the court denied the defendants' motion on the ground that Officer McFadden, on the basis of his experience, had reasonable cause to believe that the defendants were conducting themselves suspiciously, and some interrogation should be made of their action.

Purely for his own protection, the court held, the officer had the right to pat down the outer clothing of these men, who he had reasonable cause to believe might be armed. The court distinguished between an investigatory "stop" and an arrest, and between a "frisk" of the outer clothing for weapons and a full-blown search for evidence of crime. The frisk, it held, was essential to the proper performance of the officer's investigatory duties, for, without it, "the answer to the police officer may be a bullet, and a loaded pistol discovered during the frisk is admissible."

I

The Fourth Amendment provides that "the right of the people to be secure in their persons, houses, papers, and effects, against unreasonable searches and seizures, shall not be violated. . . ." This right of personal security belongs as much to the citizen on the streets of our cities as to the homeowner closeted in his study to dispose of his secret affairs. As this Court has always recognized, no right is held more sacred, or is more carefully guarded, by the common law than the right of every individual to the possession and control of his own person, free from all restraint or interference of others, unless by clear and unquestionable authority of law. We have recently held that "the Fourth Amendment protects people, not places," and wherever an individual may harbor a reasonable "expectation of privacy," he is entitled to be free from unreasonable governmental intrusion. Of course, the specific content and incidents of this right must be shaped by the context in which it is asserted. For "what the Constitution forbids is not all searches and seizures, but unreasonable searches and seizures." Unquestionably, petitioner was entitled to the protection of the Fourth Amendment as he walked down the street. The question is whether, in all the circumstances of this on-the-street encounter, his right to personal security was violated by an unreasonable search and seizure.

We would be less than candid if we did not acknowledge that this question thrusts to the fore difficult and troublesome issues regarding a sensitive area of police activity—issues which have never before been squarely presented to this Court. Reflective of the tensions involved are the practical and constitutional arguments pressed with great vigor on both sides of the public debate over the power of the police to "stop and frisk"—as it is sometimes euphemistically termed—suspicious persons.

On the one hand, it is frequently argued that, in dealing with the rapidly unfolding and often dangerous situations on city streets, the police are in need of an escalating set of flexible responses, graduated in relation to the amount of information they possess. For this purpose, it is urged that distinctions should be made between a "stop" and an "arrest" (or a "seizure" of a person), and between a "frisk" and a "search." Thus, it is argued, the police should be allowed to "stop" a person and detain him briefly for questioning upon suspicion that he may be connected with criminal activity. Upon suspicion that the person may be armed, the police should have the power to "frisk" him for weapons. If the "stop" and the "frisk" give rise to probable cause to believe that the suspect has committed a crime, then the police should be empowered to make a formal "arrest," and a full incident "search" of the person. This scheme is justified in part upon the notion that a "stop" and a "frisk" amount to a mere "minor inconvenience and petty indignity," which can properly be imposed upon the citizen in the interest of effective law enforcement on the basis of a police officer's suspicion.

On the other side, the argument is made that the authority of the police must be strictly circumscribed by the law of arrest and search as it has developed to date in the traditional jurisprudence of the Fourth Amendment. It is contended with some force that there is not—and cannot be—a variety of police activity which does not depend solely upon the voluntary cooperation of the citizen, and yet which stops short of an arrest based upon probable cause to make such an arrest. The heart of the Fourth Amendment, the argument runs, is a severe requirement of specific justification for any intrusion upon protected personal security, coupled with a highly developed system of judicial controls to enforce upon the agents of the State the commands of the

Constitution. Acquiescence by the courts in the compulsion inherent in the field interrogation practices at issue here, it is urged, would constitute an abdication of judicial control over, and indeed an encouragement of, substantial interference with liberty and personal security by police officers whose judgment is necessarily colored by their primary involvement in "the often competitive enterprise of ferreting out crime." This, it is argued, can only serve to exacerbate police-community tensions in the crowded centers of our Nation's cities.

In this context, we approach the issues in this case mindful of the limitations of the judicial function in controlling the myriad daily situations in which policemen and citizens confront each other on the street. The State has characterized the issue here as the right of a police officer to make an on-the-street stop, interrogate, and pat down for weapons (known in street vernacular as "stop and frisk").

II

Our first task is to establish at what point in this encounter the Fourth Amendment becomes relevant. That is, we must decide whether and when Officer McFadden "seized" Terry, and whether and when he conducted a "search." There is some suggestion in the use of such terms as "stop" and "frisk" that such police conduct is outside the purview of the Fourth Amendment because neither action rises to the level of a "search" or "seizure" within the meaning of the Constitution. We emphatically reject this notion. It is quite plain that the Fourth Amendment governs "seizures" of the person which do not eventuate in a trip to the stationhouse and prosecution for crime—"arrests" in traditional terminology. It must be recognized that, whenever a police officer accosts an individual and restrains his freedom to walk away, he has "seized" that person. And it is nothing less than sheer torture of the English language to suggest that a careful exploration of the outer surfaces of a person's clothing all over his or her body in an attempt to find weapons is not a "search." Moreover, it is simply fantastic to urge that such a procedure performed in public by a policeman while the citizen stands helpless, perhaps facing a wall with his hands raised, is a "petty indignity." It is a serious intrusion upon the sanctity of the person, which may inflict great indignity and arouse strong resentment, and it is not to be undertaken lightly.

The danger in the logic which proceeds upon distinctions between a "stop" and an "arrest," or "seizure" of the person, and between a "frisk" and a "search," is twofold. It seeks to isolate from constitutional scrutiny the initial stages of the contact between the policeman and the citizen. And, by suggesting a rigid all-or-nothing model of justification and regulation under the Amendment, it obscures the utility of limitations upon the scope, as well as the initiation, of police action as a means of constitutional regulation. This Court has held in the past that a search which is reasonable at its inception may violate the Fourth Amendment by virtue of its intolerable intensity and scope. The scope of the search must be "strictly tied to and justified by" the circumstances which rendered its initiation permissible.

The distinctions of classical "stop-and-frisk" theory thus serve to divert attention from the central inquiry under the Fourth Amendment—the reasonableness in all the circumstances of the particular governmental invasion of a citizen's personal security. "Search" and "seizure" are not talismans. We therefore reject the notions that the Fourth Amendment does not come into play at all as a limitation upon police conduct if the officers stop short of something called a "technical arrest" or a "full-blown search."

In this case, there can be no question, then, that Officer McFadden "seized" petitioner and subjected him to a "search" when he took hold of him and patted down the outer surfaces of his clothing. We must decide whether, at that point, it was reasonable for Officer McFadden to have interfered with petitioner's personal security as he did. And, in determining whether the seizure and search were "unreasonable," our inquiry is a dual one — whether the officer's action was justified at its inception, and whether it was reasonably related in scope to the circumstances which justified the interference in the first place.

III

The conduct involved in this case must be tested by the Fourth Amendment's general proscription against unreasonable searches and seizures. In order to assess the reasonableness of Officer McFadden's conduct as a general proposition, it is necessary first to focus upon the governmental interest which allegedly justifies official intrusion upon the constitutionally protected interests of the private citizen, for there is no ready test for determining reasonableness other than by balancing the need to search or seize against the invasion which the search or seizure entails. And, in justifying the particular intrusion, the police officer must be able to point to specific and articulable facts which, taken together with rational inferences from those facts, reasonably warrant that intrusion. The scheme of the Fourth Amendment becomes meaningful only when it is assured that, at some point, the conduct of those charged with enforcing the laws can be subjected to the more detached, neutral scrutiny of a judge who must evaluate the reasonableness of a particular search or seizure in light of the particular circumstances. And, in making that assessment, it is imperative that the facts be judged against an objective standard: would the facts available to the officer at the moment of the seizure or the search "warrant a man of reasonable caution in the belief" that the action taken was appropriate? Anything less would invite intrusions upon constitutionally guaranteed rights based on nothing more substantial than inarticulate hunches, a result this Court has consistently refused to sanction. And simple "good faith on the part of the arresting officer is not enough." If subjective good faith alone were the test, the protections of the Fourth Amendment would evaporate, and the people would be "secure in their persons, houses, papers, and effects," only in the discretion of the police.

Applying these principles to this case, we consider first the nature and extent of the governmental interests involved. One general interest is, of course, that of effective crime prevention and detection; it is this interest which underlies the recognition that a police officer may, in appropriate circumstances and in an appropriate manner, approach a person for purposes of investigating possibly criminal behavior even though there is no probable cause to make an arrest. It was this legitimate investigative function Officer McFadden was discharging when he decided to approach petitioner and his companions. He had observed Terry, Chilton, and Katz go through a series of acts, each of them perhaps innocent in itself, but which, taken together, warranted further investigation. There is nothing unusual in two men standing together on a street corner, perhaps waiting for someone. Nor is there anything suspicious about people in such circumstances strolling up and down the street, singly or in pairs. Store windows, moreover, are made to be looked in. But the story is quite different where, as here, two men hover about a street corner for an extended period of time, at the end of which it becomes apparent that they are not waiting for anyone or anything; where these men pace alternately along an identical route, pausing to stare in the same store window roughly 24 times; where each completion of this route is followed immediately by a conference between the two men on the corner; where they are joined in one of these conferences by a third man who leaves swiftly, and where the two men finally follow the third and rejoin him a couple of blocks away. It would have been poor police work indeed for an officer of 30 years' experience in the detection of thievery from stores in this same neighborhood to have failed to investigate this behavior further.

The crux of this case, however, is not the propriety of Officer McFadden's taking steps to investigate petitioner's suspicious behavior, but, rather, whether there was justification for McFadden's invasion of Terry's personal security by searching him for weapons in the course of that investigation. We are now concerned with more than the governmental interest in investigating crime; in addition, there is the more immediate interest of the police officer in taking steps to assure himself that the person with whom he is dealing is not armed with a weapon that could unexpectedly and fatally be used against him. Certainly it would be unreasonable to require that police officers take unnecessary risks in the performance of their duties. American criminals have a long tradition of armed violence, and every year in this country many law enforcement officers are killed in the line of duty, and thousands more are wounded. Virtually all of these deaths and a substantial portion of the injuries are inflicted with guns and knives.

In view of these facts, we cannot blind ourselves to the need for law enforcement officers to protect themselves and other prospective victims of violence in situations where they may lack probable cause for an arrest. When an officer is justified in believing that the individual whose suspicious behavior he is investigating at close range is armed and presently dangerous to the officer or to others, it would appear to be clearly unreasonable to deny the officer the power to take necessary measures to determine whether the person is, in fact, carrying a weapon and to neutralize the threat of physical harm.

We must still consider, however, the nature and quality of the intrusion on individual rights which must be accepted if police officers are to be conceded the right to search for weapons in situations where probable cause to arrest for crime is lacking. Even a limited search of the outer clothing for weapons constitutes a severe, though brief, intrusion upon cherished personal security, and it must surely be an annoying, frightening, and perhaps humiliating experience. Petitioner contends that such an intrusion is permissible only incident to a lawful arrest, either for a crime involving the possession of weapons or for a crime the commission of which led the officer to investigate in the first place. However, this argument must be closely examined.

Terry does not argue that a police officer should refrain from making any investigation of suspicious circumstances until such time as he has probable cause to make an arrest; nor does he deny that police officers, in properly discharging their investigative function, may find themselves confronting persons who might well be armed and dangerous. Moreover, he does not say that an officer is always unjustified in searching a suspect to discover weapons. Rather, he says it is unreasonable for the policeman to take that step until such time as the situation evolves to a point where there is probable cause to make an arrest. When that point has been reached, petitioner would concede the officer's right to conduct a search of the suspect for weapons, fruits or instrumentalities of the crime, or "mere" evidence, incident to the arrest.

There are two weaknesses in this line of reasoning, however. First, it fails to take account of traditional limitations upon the scope of searches, and thus recognizes no distinction in purpose, character, and extent between a search incident to an arrest and a limited search for weapons. The former, although justified in part by the acknowledged necessity to protect the arresting officer from assault with a concealed weapon, is also justified on other grounds, and can therefore involve a relatively extensive exploration of the person. A search for weapons in the absence of probable cause to arrest, however, must, like any other search, be strictly circumscribed by the exigencies which justify its initiation. Thus, it must be limited to that which is necessary for the discovery of weapons which might be used to harm the officer or others nearby, and may realistically be characterized as something less than a "full" search, even though it remains a serious intrusion.

A second, and related, objection to petitioner's argument is that it assumes that the law of arrest has already worked out the balance between the particular interests involved here—the neutralization of danger to the policeman in the investigative circumstance and the sanctity of the individual. But this is not so. An arrest is a wholly different kind of intrusion upon individual freedom from a limited search for weapons, and the interests each is designed to serve are likewise quite different. An arrest is the initial stage of a criminal prosecution. It is intended to vindicate society's interest in having its laws obeyed, and it is inevitably accompanied by future interference with the individual's freedom of movement, whether or not trial or conviction ultimately follows. The protective search for weapons, on the other hand, constitutes a brief, though far from inconsiderable, intrusion upon the sanctity of the person. It does not follow that, because an officer may lawfully arrest a person only when he is apprised of facts sufficient to warrant a belief that the person has committed or is committing a crime, the officer is equally unjustified, absent that kind of evidence, in making any intrusions short of an arrest. Moreover, a perfectly reasonable apprehension of danger may arise long before the officer is possessed of adequate information to justify taking a person into custody for the purpose of prosecuting him for a crime. Petitioner's reliance on cases which have worked out standards of reasonableness with regard to "seizures" constituting arrests and searches incident thereto is thus misplaced. It assumes that the interests sought to be vindicated and the invasions of personal security may be equated in the two cases, and thereby ignores a vital aspect of the analysis of the reasonableness of particular types of conduct under the Fourth Amendment.

Our evaluation of the proper balance that has to be struck in this type of case leads us to conclude that there must be a narrowly drawn authority to permit a reasonable search for weapons for the protection of the police officer, where he has reason to believe that he is dealing with an armed and dangerous individual, regardless of whether he has probable cause to arrest the individual for a crime. The officer need not be absolutely certain that the individual is armed; the issue is whether a reasonably prudent man, in the circumstances, would be warranted in the belief that his safety or that of others was in danger. And in determining whether the officer acted reasonably in such circumstances, due weight must be given not to his inchoate and unparticularized suspicion or "hunch," but to the specific reasonable inferences which he is entitled to draw from the facts in light of his experience.

IV

We must now examine the conduct of Officer McFadden in this case to determine whether his search and seizure of petitioner were reasonable, both at their inception and as conducted. He had observed Terry, together with Chilton and another man, acting in a manner he took to be preface to a "stick-up." We think, on the facts and circumstances Officer McFadden detailed before the trial judge, a reasonably prudent man would have been warranted in believing petitioner was armed, and thus presented a threat to the officer's safety while he was investigating his suspicious behavior. The actions of Terry and Chilton were consistent with McFadden's hypothesis that these men were contemplating a daylight robbery—which, it is reasonable to assume, would be likely to involve the use of weapons—and nothing in their conduct from the time he first noticed them until the time he confronted them and identified himself as a police officer gave him sufficient reason to negate that hypothesis. Although the trio had departed the original scene, there was nothing to indicate abandonment of an intent to commit a robbery at some point. Thus, when Officer McFadden approached the three men gathered before the display window at Zucker's store, he had observed enough to make it quite reasonable to fear that they were armed, and nothing in their response to his hailing them, identifying himself as a police officer, and asking their names served to dispel that reasonable belief. We cannot say his decision at that point to seize Terry and pat his clothing for weapons was the product of a volatile or inventive imagination, or was undertaken simply as an act of harassment; the record evidences the tempered act of a policeman who, in the course of an investigation, had to make a quick decision as to how to protect himself and others from possible danger, and took limited steps to do so.

The manner in which the seizure and search were conducted is, of course, as vital a part of the inquiry as whether they were warranted at all. The Fourth Amendment proceeds as much by limitations upon the scope of governmental action as by imposing preconditions upon its initiation. The entire deterrent purpose of the rule excluding evidence seized in violation of the Fourth Amendment rests on the assumption that "limitations upon the fruit to be gathered tend to limit the quest itself. Thus, evidence may not be introduced if it was discovered by means of a seizure and search which were not reasonably related in scope to the justification for their initiation.

We need not develop at length in this case, however, the limitations which the Fourth Amendment places upon a protective seizure and search for weapons. These limitations will have to be developed in the concrete factual circumstances of individual cases. Suffice it to note that such a search, unlike a search without a warrant incident to a lawful arrest, is not justified by any need to prevent the disappearance or destruction of evidence of crime. The sole justification of the search in the present situation is the protection of the police officer and others nearby, and it must therefore be confined in scope to an intrusion reasonably designed to discover guns, knives, clubs, or other hidden instruments for the assault of the police officer.

The scope of the search in this case presents no serious problem in light of these standards. Officer McFadden patted down the outer clothing of petitioner and his two companions. He did not place his hands in their pockets or under the outer surface of their garments until he had felt weapons, and then he merely reached for and removed the guns. He never did invade Katz' person beyond the outer surfaces of his clothes, since he discovered nothing in his pat-down which might have been a weapon. Officer McFadden confined his search strictly to what was minimally necessary to learn whether the men were armed and to disarm them once he discovered the weapons. He did not conduct a general exploratory search for whatever evidence of criminal activity he might find.

V

We conclude that the revolver seized from Terry was properly admitted in evidence against him. At the time he seized petitioner and searched him for weapons, Officer McFadden had reasonable grounds to believe that petitioner was armed and dangerous, and it was necessary for the protection of himself and others to take swift measures to discover the true facts and neutralize the threat of harm if it materialized. The policeman carefully restricted his search to what was appropriate to the discovery of the particular items which he sought. Each case of this sort will, of course, have to be decided on its own facts. We merely hold today that, where a police officer observes unusual conduct which leads him reasonably to conclude in light of his experience that criminal activity may be afoot and that the persons with whom he is dealing may be armed and presently dangerous, where, in the course of investigating this behavior, he identifies himself as a policeman and makes reasonable inquiries, and where nothing in the initial stages of the encounter serves to dispel his reasonable fear for his own or others' safety, he is entitled for the protection of himself and others in the area to conduct a carefully limited search of the outer clothing of such persons in an attempt to discover weapons which might be used to assault him. Such a search is a reasonable search under the Fourth Amendment, and any weapons seized may properly be introduced in evidence against the person from whom they were taken.

END OF OPINION

In reading this decision, note the detail the Court goes into to identify and balance the interests involved. In explaining the reasoning behind its decision, the Court tries to give as much insight as possible, anticipating objections, commenting on the concerns that each party raised, indicating as well what conduct or details might have caused the Court to come to a different decision. We will address some of these in the questions and discussion that follow.

As for the decision itself, there are two main ideas for you to take away from this opinion. First, that law enforcement need only a reasonable articulable suspicion (which is less than probable cause) of criminal conduct to briefly stop a person. This stop or detention is meant to be temporary and should last only as long as it takes for the police officer to ascertain the nature of the circumstances. The police need more than just a "hunch" to stop someone and their rationale cannot be subjectively reasonable. Instead, the police need "specific and articulable facts" to objectively give them a reasonable suspicion to detain a person. This is the "stop" part of "stop-and-frisk."

Second, once a person is detained, the police are allowed to frisk that person so long as the police have a reasonable belief that the person "may be armed and presently dangerous." When they frisk a person, the police are conducting a search over a person's clothes to feel if the person has a gun, knife, crowbar, or anything potentially dangerous that could be used against the police. The rationale for this is that the police need to be able to protect themselves. This is the "frisk" part of "stop-and-frisk." Because a frisk consists merely of patting the exterior of clothing and not reaching inside pockets or under clothes, it is not a very intrusive search. If an officer feels something resembling a weapon, then the officer can reach under clothes or into a pocket to pull it out and ascertain if it is in fact a weapon. If it is a weapon, the officer can, for his own safety, hold onto it for the duration of the detention.

What happens if the police officer, while frisking a person for a weapon, happens to feel something which is not a weapon, but turns out to be illegal? For example, let's say Officer Brown is frisking Debbie the Dealer, and while his hand is over her pocket, he feels an object which, based on his experience and training, gives him probable cause to believe is a crack pipe. The rule is that if in the course of a lawful *Terry* search an officer feels something he has probable cause to believe is illegal, he can reach into the pocket and search for it. This is how people who are stopped and frisked for one reason can be arrested for a different and unrelated reason.

There are very few circumstances where officers are not allowed to frisk a suspect who has been legally detained. With more facts, such as observing peculiar aspects of the woman's behavior once stopped, an argument might be made to justify the act of asking her to get out of the car and submit to a frisk. For example, if an officer testifies that after he stopped a speeding motorist the driver appeared extremely nervous, kept glancing at the glove compartment, wouldn't keep her hands in plain view despite being repeatedly told to do so, and kept trying to reach under a seat to grab something, then it would be reasonable for an officer to extend the detention and frisk the driver.

Stop-and-frisk has been in the news a lot lately over charges that it is a form of racial profiling. Note in the opinion of *Terry v. Ohio* that the Court makes specific mention of the fact that there was no evidence that the stop-and-frisk was made for any purpose of harassment or other improper motive on the basis of the police. So the reasonableness of the stop and frisk (as with all searches and seizures) depends on both the cause and on the manner of its execution. This issue as well as racial profiling in general will be addressed in the chapter on civil rights.

Review Questions

To better understand how stop-and-frisk works, examine the following hypothetical fact patterns and perform an IRAC analysis.

1. Officer Brown is walking down the street, and he sees Debbie hand Scott a plastic baggie containing small, brightly colored, pill-like items. Officer Brown then sees Scott hand Debbie cash. Even without using a lab to test the contents of the bag, common sense tells us that this is an illegal drug transaction. This will give Officer Brown the "reasonable suspicion of criminal activity" necessary to detain a person. Next, let's consider whether or not Debbie is armed. Given the very nature of the crime she is suspected of, illegal drug dealing which is an inherently dangerous business,[5] it is reasonable to believe that she might be armed. So, can Officer Brown stop-and-frisk Debbie?

2. With Debbie against a wall, Officer Brown frisks Debbie. As his hand goes over her left pocket the officer feels an object which, based on his experience and training, resembles a crack pipe. The officer reaches into her pocket and pulls out a crack pipe with some residue on it. The officer continues his search, and as his hand goes over the exterior of her right pocket, he feels an object which, based on his experience and training, resembles a bag of pills, much like the ones he saw Debbie sell to Scott. He reaches into her pocket and pulls out a Ziploc sandwich bag, but it does not contain pills. Instead, it contains the delicious candy M&M's. It turns out that Debbie had only sold Scott M&M's, which is obviously not a crime. A completion of the search reveals that she is completely unarmed. Given that the officer's initial reason for stopping-and-frisking Debbie, a belief that she was selling drugs, proved incorrect, was the crack pipe lawfully found, and can it be used as evidence against her for possession of drug paraphernalia?

3. It is illegal for convicted felons to be in possession of a firearm. One day, Officer Brown is walking down the street, and he sees Pete. Officer Brown knows that Pete is a dangerous felon who was recently released from prison where he had been serving time for armed robbery. Officer Brown observes Pete apparently walking in the direction of a bank. The officer also notices that although it is the middle of summer and the temperature is over 90 degrees, Pete is wearing a trench coat. Can Officer Brown stop-and-frisk Pete?

---

5. Given the facts that dealers are in possession of a valuable commodity and that their clientele are not the most upstanding citizens, many dealers live in fear of being robbed. Because their activity is illegal, if something goes wrong in the course of business, dealers are unable to go to the police for help. To protect themselves, dealers must engage in self-help remedies, such as being armed and developing fierce reputations to deter others from robbing them.

4. Officer Brown stops-and-frisks Pete, and it turns out that there is nothing under the trench coat except for flowers. Pete tells the officer that the flowers are for his mother who works in the bank. However, also during the search, Officer Brown felt an object that, based on his experience and training as a police officer, causes him to suspect a bag of crack cocaine. Officer Brown reaches into the trench coat pocket and pulls out a baggie containing crack cocaine. Was the cocaine lawfully found?

5. Joseph is playing basketball at a public park. Officer Brown is a veteran police officer with over 30 years of experience. He observes Joseph, and develops a gut feeling that Joseph is killing time and waiting on a drug deal to take place. Without warning, the police officer approaches Joseph and shoves Joseph against a wall and starts frisking him. As the officer feels over Joseph's pocket, he feels an object that resembles a crack pipe. He reaches into Joseph's pocket and pulls out a crack pipe with residue on it. Joseph is arrested for possession of drug paraphernalia. Was this a lawful search?

6. Bill is walking through a neighborhood known for having a serious crack problem. He is approached by a police officer who pushes him up against a wall and starts frisking him. As the officer feels over Bill's pocket, he feels an object that resembles a crack pipe. He reaches into Bill's pocket and pulls out a crack pipe with residue on it. Bill is arrested for possession of drug paraphernalia. Is the crack pipe admissible?

7. In her mini-van, Sally the soccer mom is driving her kids to soccer practice when she is pulled over. The officer tells her that with his radar gun, he caught her going 5 mph over the speed limit. The officer orders her to get out of the car and up against the vehicle so he can frisk her. While frisking her, he feels in her pocket an item that, based on his experience and training, resembles a crack pipe. He reaches into her pocket and pulls it out. Is this crack pipe admissible?

Protecting against Unreasonable Searches—
The Exclusionary Rule

What happens when the police violate the Fourth Amendment by not getting a warrant or when they conduct an unreasonable search or seizure? The previous hypothetical situations touched on a subject you may have heard of before, known as "the exclusionary rule." This rule provides that any evidence derived from a violation of a person's rights is not admissible in the criminal prosecution of that individual. This rule comes from the Supreme Court decision *Mapp v. Ohio*. The exclusionary rule is most commonly associated with the Fourth Amendment, but is used in cases involving other constitutional or statutory rights violations as well. As described in the case below, it is intended to impose a cost on the authorities for improper behavior.

Mapp v. Ohio, 367 U.S. 643 (1961)*

Mapp stands convicted of knowingly having had in her possession and under her control certain obscene, lewd, and lascivious books, pictures, and pornographic photographs in violation of Ohio law. The conviction was based primarily upon the introduction in evidence of lewd and lascivious books and pictures unlawfully seized during an unlawful search of defendant's home. On May 23, 1957, three Cleveland police officers arrived at appellant's residence in that city pursuant to information that a person was hiding out in the home, who was wanted for questioning in connection with a recent bombing, and that there was a large amount of policy paraphernalia being hidden in the home.

Miss Mapp and her daughter by a former marriage lived on the top floor of the two-family dwelling. Upon their arrival at that house, the officers knocked on the door and demanded entrance, but Mapp, after telephoning her attorney, refused to admit them without a search warrant. They advised their headquarters of the situation and undertook a surveillance of the house.

The officers again sought entrance some three hours later when four or more additional officers arrived on the scene. When Miss Mapp did not come to the door immediately, at least one of the several doors to the house was forcibly opened and the policemen gained admittance. Meanwhile Miss Mapp's attorney arrived, but the officers, having secured their own entry, and continuing in their defiance of the law, would permit him neither to see Miss Mapp nor to enter the house. It appears that Miss Mapp was halfway down the stairs from the upper floor to the front door when the officers, in this highhanded manner, broke into the hall. She demanded to see the search warrant. A paper, claimed to be a warrant but in reality wasn't, was held up by one of the officers. She grabbed the "warrant" and placed it in her bosom. A struggle ensued in which the officers recovered the piece of paper and as a result of which they handcuffed Mapp because she had been "belligerent" in resisting their official rescue of the "warrant" from her person. Running roughshod over Mapp, a policeman "grabbed" her, "twisted her hand," and she "yelled and pleaded with him" because "it was hurting." Mapp, in handcuffs, was then forcibly taken upstairs to her bedroom where the officers searched a dresser, a chest of drawers, a closet and some suitcases. They also looked into a photo album and through personal papers belonging to Mapp. The search spread to the rest of the second floor including the child's bedroom, the living room, the kitchen and a dinette. The basement of the building and a trunk found therein were also searched. The obscene materials for possession of which she was ultimately convicted were discovered in the course of that widespread search.

At the trial, no search warrant was produced by the prosecution, nor was the failure to produce one explained or accounted for. There is considerable doubt as to whether there ever was any warrant for the search of defendant's home. The Ohio Supreme Court believed a "reasonable argument" could be made that the conviction

---

* The case has been heavily edited and paraphrased by the authors for clarity. See disclaimer in introduction.

should be reversed "because the 'methods' employed to obtain the evidence were such as to offend "a sense of justice."

In *Boyd v. United States*, 116 U.S. 616 (1886), the Supreme Court ruled that the Fourth and Fifth Amendments apply to all invasions on the part of the government and its employees of the sanctity of a man's home and the privacies of life. It is not the breaking of his doors, and the rummaging of his drawers, that constitutes the essence of the offence; but it is the invasion of his indefeasible right of personal security, personal liberty and private property. It is the duty of courts to be watchful for the constitutional rights of the citizen, and against any stealthy encroachments thereon. In this jealous regard for maintaining the integrity of individual rights, independent tribunals of justice must resist every encroachment upon rights expressly stipulated for in the Constitution. Concluding, the Court specifically referred to the use of the evidence there seized as "unconstitutional."

Specifically dealing with the use of the evidence unconstitutionally seized, the Court concluded:

> If letters and private documents can thus be seized and held and used in evidence against a citizen accused of an offense, the protection of the Fourth Amendment declaring his right to be secure against such searches and seizures is of no value, and, so far as those thus placed are concerned, might as well be stricken from the Constitution. The efforts of the courts and their officials to bring the guilty to punishment, praiseworthy as they are, are not to be aided by the sacrifice of those great principles established by years of endeavor and suffering which have resulted in their embodiment in the fundamental law of the land.

Finally, the Court in that case clearly stated that use of the seized evidence involved "a denial of the constitutional rights of the accused." Thus, in the year 1914, in the Weeks case, this Court "for the first time" held that, "in a federal prosecution, the Fourth Amendment barred the use of evidence secured through an illegal search and seizure." This Court has ever since required of federal law officers a strict adherence to that command which this Court has held to be a clear, specific, and constitutionally required—even if judicially implied—deterrent safeguard without insistence upon which the Fourth Amendment would have been reduced to "a form of words." It meant, quite simply, that "conviction by means of unlawful seizures and enforced confessions should find no sanction in the judgments of the courts" and that such evidence "shall not be used at all."

In *Byars v. United States* (1927), a unanimous Court declared that it cannot be tolerated where evidence of a crime discovered by a federal officer in making a search without lawful warrant may be used against the victim of the unlawful search. The Court, in *Olmstead v. United States*, 277 U.S. 438 (1928), in unmistakable language restated the Weeks rule:

> The striking outcome of the Weeks case and those which followed it was the sweeping declaration that the Fourth Amendment, although not referring to or limiting the use of evidence in courts, really forbade its

introduction if obtained by government officers through a violation of the Amendment.

In *McNabb v. United States*, 318 U.S. 332 (1943), we note this statement:

> A conviction in the federal courts, the foundation of which is evidence obtained in disregard of liberties deemed fundamental by the Constitution, cannot stand. This Court has, on Constitutional grounds, set aside convictions, both in the federal and state courts, which were based upon confessions "secured by protracted and repeated questioning of ignorant and untutored persons, in whose minds the power of officers was greatly magnified" or "who have been unlawfully held incommunicado without advice of friends or counsel."

We hold that all evidence obtained by searches and seizures in violation of the Constitution is, by that same authority, inadmissible in a state court. Moreover, our holding that the exclusionary rule is an essential part of both the Fourth and Fourteenth Amendments is not only the logical dictate of prior cases, but it also makes very good sense. There is no war between the Constitution and common sense.

However much in a particular case insistence upon such rules may appear as a technicality that benefits a guilty person, the history of criminal law proves that tolerance of shortcut methods in law enforcement impairs its enduring effectiveness. There are those who say, as did Justice Cardozo, that, under our constitutional exclusionary doctrine, "the criminal is to go free because the constable has blundered." In some cases, this will undoubtedly be the result. But, as was said in Elkins, "there is another consideration—the imperative of judicial integrity." The criminal goes free, if he must, but it is the law that sets him free. Nothing can destroy a government more quickly than its failure to observe its own laws, or worse, its disregard of the charter of its own existence. As Mr. Justice Brandeis, dissenting, said in *Olmstead v. United States*, 277 U.S. 438 (1928):

> Our Government is the potent, the omnipresent teacher. For good or for ill, it teaches the whole people by its example. If the Government becomes a lawbreaker, it breeds contempt for law; it invites every man to become a law unto himself; it invites anarchy.

Nor can it lightly be assumed that, as a practical matter, adoption of the exclusionary rule unduly restricts law enforcement. Only last year, this Court expressly considered that contention and found that "pragmatic evidence of a sort" to the contrary was not wanting. The Court noted that the federal courts themselves have operated under the exclusionary rule for almost half a century; yet it has not been suggested either that the Federal Bureau of Investigation (FBI) has thereby been rendered ineffective, or that the administration of criminal justice in the federal courts has thereby been disrupted.

Having once recognized that the right to privacy embodied in the Fourth Amendment is enforceable, and that the right to be secure against rude invasions of privacy by officers is, therefore, constitutional in origin, we can no longer permit that right to remain an empty promise. Because it is enforceable in the same manner and to like effect as other basic rights secured by the Due Process Clause, we can no longer permit it to be revocable at the whim of any police officer who, in the name of law enforcement itself, chooses to suspend its enjoyment. Our decision, founded on reason and truth, gives to the individual no more than that which the Constitution guarantees him, to the police officer no less than that to which honest law enforcement is entitled, and, to the courts, that judicial integrity so necessary in the true administration of justice.

END OF OPINION

This opinion created a rule used in American courts known as the "exclusionary rule." It was based on the conclusion of the Court that admitting evidence obtained in violation of the law violated the due process clause of the Fourteenth Amendment. It applied to the state police authorities a rule which had already been adopted in the federal courts in the case of *Weeks v. United States*, 232 U.S. 383 (1914). As the Court explained, there has always been some level of problem in America where police violated people's constitutional rights in order to obtain criminal evidence, in some cases trying to do the right thing but taking shortcuts while in other cases more blatantly. The challenge was how to get police to change their behavior. The Court concluded that the best way to deter the police from violating the rights of individuals was to prohibit evidence from being used in criminal prosecutions when that evidence is obtained in violation of a person's rights. As you read on and learn more about the nuances of the exclusionary rule, it is important to remember that the reason the courts imposed it as a remedy for violations of civil rights was to deter the police from violating people's rights in the first place. There is nothing in the U.S. Constitution explicitly requiring that evidence obtained in violation of people's rights be excluded from evidence. This is a court-ordered remedy to deter police misconduct, based on the conclusion that "due process of law" requires the police to follow the law or be barred from using evidence they gathered improperly.

The exclusionary rule is simple to state, but in practice is highly nuanced. **Any evidence derived from a violation of a person's rights is not admissible in a criminal prosecution of that individual.** In the real world, what does this mean?

First, "any evidence derived" means that not only is evidence found directly as a result of a violation of a person's rights inadmissible, as well as any other evidence resulting from that initial violation. This is known as the "fruit of the poisonous tree" doctrine. Evidence is tainted if the basis for finding it was an initial violation of a person's rights.

For example, let's say the police, without a warrant and without any specific evidence of actual wrongdoing, enter the house of Ryan and conduct a search. While conducting a search of Ryan's home, they discover a journal that contains detailed records of drug transactions which have taken place in a tool shed in Ryan's backyard. The police then take the journal to a judge and use the incriminating statements in it to get a warrant to search the tool shed in Ryan's backyard, where they discover marijuana plants he is growing. Even though the plants were discovered pursuant to a search warrant, the way the police got the evidence to obtain the search warrant was by an initial violation of Ryan's rights. Therefore, any evidence derived from that initial violation of Ryan's rights will be excluded as "the fruit of the poisonous tree." The police subsequently getting a warrant for the search of the shed does not cure their earlier misconduct by wrongfully searching his home and seizing his journal.

In another hypothetical, let's say the police suspect that Connor has an illegal firearm in his house, but lack sufficient evidence to establish probable cause for a search. The police cannot illegally enter the house, search, find a gun, then go to a magistrate and report what they saw in hopes of getting a warrant to go back into the house and seize the weapon.

Second, the phrase "from a violation of a person's rights" is also significant. Many people mistakenly interpret the exclusionary rule to mean "any and all evidence obtained illegally is not admissible in any circumstance." This is not wholly accurate either. First of all, in most situations the exclusionary rule applies only to the person whose rights are violated. That means if the police violate the rights of Person A and, in the process, discover incriminating evidence against Person B, that evidence can still be used to prosecute Person B, although it cannot be used to prosecute Person A. For example, let's say the police enter the house of Phoebe without a warrant as she is throwing a party for her friends Rose and Molly, who are merely visiting and do not reside at the house. As the police enter the house, they see all three friends smoking marijuana. The exclusionary rule would apply to Phoebe because she resides in the house which was unlawfully entered, which means her rights were being violated. Rose and Molly do not reside in the house, so their rights were not violated by the warrantless entry; therefore, the evidence obtained by the police would be admissible against them, even though it would not be admissible against Phoebe.

Another limitation of the exclusionary rule is that it does not apply to evidence obtained by private individuals, not in the employ of or working directly on behalf of the government, who are engaged in unreasonable searches in seizures that, if performed by the police, would be considered a violation of a suspect's Fourth Amendment rights. The Constitution only applies to government officials so the exclusionary rule, as a constitutional principle, similarly only applies to government officials. Remember, the exclusionary rule exists to deter *government* misconduct; it has nothing to do with private parties. This means that if private actors break the law in order to obtain incriminating evidence against a person, the evidence is likely still going to be admissible in a court of law.

For example, let's say Jake the burglar has broken into Thomas's house and is looking for items to steal. During his search, Jake discovers a stash of child pornography under Thomas's bed. Even though he discovered this child pornography by breaking and entering into Thomas's house, if he turns the child pornography over to the police, it is perfectly admissible in court against Thomas. Why is this? Because Jake is a private actor and not a government official, and the exclusionary rule only applies to the government.

You may be asking, "Why doesn't the exclusionary rule apply to private actors?" There are two mutual explanations for this. First, remember that the Fourth Amendment (indeed all of the provisions of the Bill of Rights) does not apply to private actors and only limits actions of the government. The founding fathers wrote the Fourth Amendment to limit the power of the government and were not concerned with private actors. The second explanation is the Supreme Court's rationale that this rule was to deter law enforcement from violating people's rights. Obviously, when dealing with private actors, there are no law enforcement to deter. Remember, the exclusionary rule itself is not mandated by the U.S. Constitution, but it was imposed by the Court as a remedy to deter law enforcement from violating the Fourth Amendment and other civil rights.

The fact that the Fourth Amendment and the exclusionary rule do not apply to private actors is not saying that private actors are free to invade privacy and people's rights. It simply means that evidence obtained by private citizens violating the law is more likely to be admissible in criminal prosecution. The fact that the Fourth Amendment prohibition against search and seizure does not apply to private citizens also does not mean that private citizens are free to invade your privacy. For example, a burglar who invades your home could be convicted of a number of crimes, including trespassing! Trespassing is the unauthorized entry of another onto your property. The property could be your land, your house, your backpack, as well as numerous other possibilities. Trespassing is a criminal act, as well as a tort (a civil offense which people can sue one another over). Let's revisit Jake the burglar who broke into Thomas's house and reported the child pornography to the police. While the government is prosecuting Thomas for possession of child pornography, Thomas can file a lawsuit against Jake for trespassing on his property. If Thomas won that lawsuit, Jake could be ordered by a court to pay Thomas thousands of dollars for his trespass. Still, no matter how much money the court orders Jake to pay Thomas for the trespass, the evidence Jake found during his burglary of Thomas's house would still be admissible in the criminal process.

Finally, there is one more limiting factor for the exclusionary rule. The exclusionary rule applies only to criminal prosecution. There are many other forms of legal process where the exclusionary rule does not apply, such as civil law suits, parole revocation hearings, probable cause determinations for the issuance of a warrant, and grand jury indictment hearings.

For example, let's say Troy murders Michael. The police botch the investigation and fail to get a warrant prior to searching Troy's home where they recover the body and the murder weapon. Consequently, the most important pieces of evidence are inadmissible during Troy's criminal prosecution, so he is acquitted (meaning found "not guilty"). The family of Michael could, however, file a civil law suit against Troy, asking for money for the wrongful death of Michael. The evidence which was inadmissible during the criminal prosecution would be admissible during this civil law suit.

There are also exceptions to the exclusionary rule. Even in situations where the police violate a person's rights in collecting evidence, the courts have decided that, because of other factors, the interests of society justify allowing the evidence to still be admissible in criminal prosecution against that person. The most common exception is the "good faith exception." The good faith exception is where the police, acting in good faith, reasonably believe their actions to be legal, even if it turns out their actions were not lawful and violate a person's rights. Note this is a rule that applies only to the police — the rest of us don't get a "good faith exception" from obeying the law.

One example of this would be a case where a police officer is walking down the street and hears a loud noise that sounds like a fight inside the house, followed by a woman screaming in terror. The officer rushes to break down the door and enter the house, only to discover the screams came from the television, and no one is in danger. As he apologizes for the mistake, he sees a significant amount of cocaine on the living room table. Here, where the evidence shows that, at the time the officer entered the household, he had a good faith belief that there was an emergency (exigent circumstances) justifying his warrantless entry, the cocaine he sees once inside would still be admissible.

Remember, the purpose of the exclusionary rule was to deter police misconduct; so long as the police are *in fact* acting "in good faith" and are not intentionally acting to violate someone's rights, there is less reason for the court to decide that the evidence should be excluded.

In another example, let's say the police go to the magistrate and get a warrant to search Stu's house. Stu lives at 1434 Broad Street. However, the magistrate accidentally writes on the warrant "1436 Broad Street" which is where Ned lives. If the police execute the search warrant on Ned's house in good faith reliance on the defective warrant, anything they discover inside would be admissible against Ned. The police, who followed proper procedure and attempted to follow the law, should not be punished by the loss of evidence because of a mistake made by the magistrate. The magistrate is a neutral judicial officer and not a part of law enforcement. Obviously, there is no deterrent value in the exclusionary rule if the police are losing evidence because of the mistakes of a judge.

Now, as you can imagine, the key language in this exception is "good faith." That means the police will have to show they had all the intention to actually follow the law but made what the court concludes is, in fact, an honest mistake. Where the court finds evidence that the mistake was not made "in good faith," perhaps even simply because the police were careless, this exception will not apply.

One last major exception to the exclusionary rule is the "inevitable discovery rule." This is applied in cases where, even if the police violated a person's rights to get evidence, if they can later prove that the evidence was inevitably going to be lawfully discovered anyway, it can still be ruled admissible.

For example, let's say Steven rapes and kills a child in a tool shed he owns behind his house, and then leaves the body in there as he leaves town for a few days. While he is out of town, the police, without a warrant, search his tool shed and find the child's body. Normally, this would be an illegal search and the body would be inadmissible. However, let's say that Steven has a gardener who was scheduled to do some work while Steven was out of town and would have lawfully opened the tool shed to do his job, discovering the body. Because the body was going to be lawfully discovered anyway, it is still admissible at trial.

In the next chapter we will continue with our overview of criminal procedure law, looking at the issues of due process and the right to counsel addressed in the Fifth and Sixth Amendments.

Review Questions

Perform an IRAC analysis on the following sets of facts to determine if the exclusionary rule should be applied.

1. Jake works for Wal-Mart. His boss suspects that Jake is a drug dealer. One day while Jake is helping customers, the boss opens Jake's employee locker and discovers a backpack. The boss opens the backpack and digs through it until he finds numerous small bags of heroin. The boss then calls the police, and upon their arrival, the boss empties the backpack in front of them. Jake is subsequently arrested and prosecuted for heroin distribution. His lawyer argues that the heroin was discovered by a warrantless search, so it should be excluded. IRAC if his lawyer is right.

2. Bart and Arnie are roommates who do not get along. Bart wants the entire apartment to himself. He waits for Arnie to pay his half of the rent. Once Arnie has paid half the rent, Bart starts digging through Arnie's sock drawer until he finds Arnie's stash of cocaine. Bart then informs the police about the cocaine, and the police get a warrant to search the house and find Arnie's cocaine. Arnie is arrested and charged for possession of cocaine. His lawyer makes a motion to suppress the cocaine, arguing that the cocaine is inadmissible because it was found pursuant to an illegal search, a trespass, by Bart. How should the court rule?

> Note: Here you might have been tempted to apply the fruit of the poisonous tree doctrine because of Bart's trespass. However, it is important to remember that the poisonous tree doctrine and anything else involving the exclusionary rule does not apply to private actors.

3. Ross is a member of the KKK. The police hear rumors of his membership and also that he may be building bombs in the basement of his house. Based solely on these rumors, the police search his home without a warrant. During the search, though, they find the bombs as well as other details of a criminal conspiracy to bomb a predominantly African-American elementary school. Among the materials uncovered during the search is incriminating evidence against his co-conspirators, Jake and Chris. Ross, Jake, and Chris are all prosecuted for their conspiracy to blow up the school. In this case, perform an IRAC analysis and see what happens when the lawyers of both Ross and Jake (but not Chris) move to suppress the evidence discovered during the search.

4. Officer Joe, who is on patrol, sees Jason merely playing with a yo-yo and not bothering anyone or doing anything wrong or illegal. Officer Joe approaches Jason and pushes him up against a wall, handcuffs him, and starts searching through his pockets and backpack. During the course of this search, Officer Joe comes across many individual baggies of marijuana and a notebook containing a list of names, addresses, and dates of sales. IRAC if any of this material will be admissible to prosecute Jason.

5. Hamad works for American Airlines. He is normally a friendly guy, but lately he has been acting nervous, dodgy, and cagey. His supervisor suspects he is up to something. One day, his supervisor opens Hamad's locker at work and sifts through Hamad's backpack. In his backpack, the supervisor discovers that Hamad is part of an Al-Qaeda plot to blow up an airplane. The supervisor alerts the police as he hands over the backpack. The police arrest Hamad and take the backpack and its contents as evidence. While Hamad is awaiting criminal charges, he sues American Airlines for violating his privacy by searching his personal belongings. The jury finds that the supervisor violated his right to privacy and awards him $5,000 for this trespass. At Hamad's criminal trial, his lawyer tries to use the outcome of the civil trial to get the judge to rule that the evidence obtained from the backpack should be excluded from a criminal trial because it was searched in a manner which violated Hamad's right to privacy. IRAC if the evidence from the backpack is admissible.

6. Chris and Mike are members of the Richmond chapter of the Ku Klux Klan. This Easter, April 20, 2014, they have decided to bomb a black church in downtown Richmond. Chris and Mike meet at Chris's house to plan the attack. As they plan the attack, they keep careful notes on possible targets, materials needed to construct the bomb, and other matters involved in carrying out a terrorist attack.

Officer Alonzo Harris is an African-American police officer with the Richmond police department. He is well aware that Chris and Mike are members of the KKK, and he has had many heated altercations with them in the past during their frequent marches around the City of Richmond where they wear Klan robes and hold signs displaying hateful speech directed at blacks. Officer Harris's former police partner, Jake Hoyt, is white and has recently been working undercover in the Richmond KKK chapter. One morning while the two grab a cup of coffee, Officer Hoyt tells Officer Harris, "I heard a rumor that those idiots, Chris and Mike, are planning some sort of Easter surprise. I don't know what, but I'll let you know when I hear something."

This unsettles Officer Harris. Later that day, he runs into Mike and Chris who, as they often do, are marching down Main Street holding signs that say "White Power." Officer Harris is ignoring them as he walks around them, when Chris calls out to him using insults and racial epithets, saying "We've had enough marching and protests, and are planning something. We are finally going to take meaningful action to restore white America." Officer Harris keeps his cool. "What are you planning?" he asks. Chris and Mike don't answer, but instead just nastily leer at him.

This conversation, in conjunction with Officer Hoyt's information, causes Officer Harris to suspect Chris and Mike of planning something illegal and possibly violent. He goes to Chris's house. No one is home, but the door is unlocked so he enters and, as soon as he steps inside, sees the notes of the bombing Chris and Mike are planning in plain view on the kitchen table along with some explosives being used to construct the bomb. Officer Harris picks up the notes and starts reading. The notes are highly incriminating and link both Chris and Mike to the terrorist conspiracy.

Officer Harris takes the materials to a magistrate who issues a search warrant for the homes of Chris and Mike as well as a warrant for their arrest. Chris and Mike are arrested and Mirandized, but still give a full confession. Their case goes to trial where the prosecutor tries to get the evidence found inside the house admitted into evidence, while the defense attorney tries to keep the evidence out of court.

You are the judge. How do you rule? Here again, use the IRAC process to help your analysis but, in this case, do the following:

    A. Write an IRAC analysis for the use of the evidence against Mike.

    B. Write a second IRAC analysis for the use of the evidence against Chris.

Did you get a different answer? Why or why not?

7. Officer Davis is walking down the street, and he gets a report from dispatch that someone reported seeing a body lying in a pool of blood through the window of a house in the neighborhood where Officer Davis is patrolling. The house is described as a brick front with wood trimmings painted blue. Officer Davis knows that there is only one house in the neighborhood with that description, so he races over to it and busts down the locked front door. Inside he discovers a mannequin lying on the floor next to a busted container of red Gatorade which has spread around the dummy. He also observes a marijuana plant growing on a coffee table in the same room. The home's owner is arrested and charged with a drug offense. His lawyer makes a motion to suppress the marijuana, arguing that it was found pursuant to a warrantless entry. Write an IRAC analysis and state how the judge should rule.

Key Terms

Exclusionary rule—The judicial doctrine forbidding the use of evidence in a criminal trial where the evidence was obtained in violation of the defendant's constitutional rights.

Exigent circumstances—Unforeseen emergency situations that demand unusual or immediate action to prevent imminent danger to life or serious damage to property, the imminent escape of a suspect, or destruction of evidence.

Probable cause—A reasonable ground for belief in certain facts—that a crime may have been committed (for an arrest) or when evidence of the crime is present in the place to be searched (for a search).

Reasonableness standard—A two-part test in the case of a search or seizure conducted without a warrant that determines, first, whether there was a reasonable basis for doing a search, and second, whether the search was conducted in a reasonable manner.

Warrant—An authorization from a judicial officer (judge or magistrate), based upon probable cause, that allows the government to search for evidence or to seize and hold evidence or a suspect.

Further Reading

Kerr, Orin, *An Economic Understanding of Search and Seizure Law*, 164 University of Pennsylvania Law Review 591–647 (2016).

Kerr, Orin, *Katz Has Only One Step: The Irrelevance of Subjective Expectations*, 82 University of Chicago Law Review 113–134 (2015).

LaFave, Wayne R., *Search and Seizure: A Treatise on the Fourth Amendment*, WestlawNext (5th ed., 2012) (6 volumes).

Lee, Cynthia, *Searches and Seizures: The Fourth Amendment: Its Constitutional History and Contemporary Debate*, Prometheus Books (January 15, 2011).

Chapter 3

Criminal Procedure and Homeland/National Security

Part 2: Fifth and Sixth Amendments— Due Process, Self-Incrimination, and the Right to Counsel

Overview

In addition to the Fourth Amendment, the Fifth and the Sixth Amendments are two other important constitutional amendments governing criminal procedure. The Fifth Amendment states:

> No person shall be held to answer for a capital, or otherwise infamous crime, unless on a presentment or indictment of a Grand Jury, except in cases arising in the land or naval forces, or in the Militia, when in actual service in time of War or public danger; nor shall any person be subject for the same offense to be twice put in jeopardy of life or limb; nor shall be compelled in any criminal case to be a witness against himself, nor be deprived of life, liberty, or property, without due process of law; nor shall private property be taken for public use, without just compensation.

The first key clause—"nor shall be compelled in any criminal case to be a witness against himself"—establishes that compelled confessions are not permitted. The second key clause, concerning due process, we have already discussed some in the context of the exclusionary rule. We'll return to the subject and discuss other aspects of this due process requirement in other contexts later in the text; for this chapter; we will focus on the right to not be compelled to be a witness against oneself.

A dictionary definition of "compel" states "to force (someone) to do something." So the clearest application of this right is that it prevents the government from forcing someone to be a witness against themselves. In practice, this goes not just to what we normally think about as statements given under compulsion (including concerns about torture) but includes an affirmative recognition that all persons have the right to remain silent in any aspect of an investigation or trial.

This is the case, in large measure, because compelled statements are less reliable than those given voluntarily. As you can imagine, individuals who are under compulsion are more likely to say whatever they think will end the circumstances they find themselves in, whether that may be physical discomfort, emotional pressure, or other conditions. Indeed, there are a vast number of cases where evidence later disclosed that a person had confessed to a crime for which he was innocent.[1] Obviously this is a serious problem, because a false confession not only means that an innocent person (or at least a person innocent of the particular crime) may be unjustly punished, it also means that the real perpetrator has avoided arrest and conviction and remains free to commit more crime.

Prohibiting the use of compelled testimony helps us prevent police from using techniques that compel people to talk. If police are free to use whatever techniques are available to get a person to talk, they are more likely to do this instead of other investigation and, over time, will resort to harsher and harsher interrogation techniques. As with unreasonable searches, the remedy for improper or excessive interrogation techniques that render a compelled confession is to apply the exclusionary rule and prohibit the use of the testimony and any other evidence that may have come from it.

Guaranteeing the effectiveness of this right has also included the determination that if a person chooses to remain silent, the fact that he or she remains silent may not be used against him or her. In other words, the prosecuting attorney cannot comment on the fact that a defendant chose to remain silent or did not testify, or in any other way suggest that the choice to exercise the right implies guilt. After all, by making the suggestion, the prosecutor can compel the defendant to testify so as to avoid the implication of guilt. This not only protects the Fifth Amendment right against self-incrimination, but it also ensures the more general rule is followed under common law that the state has to prove guilt, not rely on the accused to prove innocence.

There is a catch; the person must affirmatively assert the right to remain silent. This can be done by simply saying "I choose to remain silent" or "I take the Fifth" or some other statement where a person clearly and unambiguously expresses the desire to remain silent. Once a person asserts the right, silence cannot be used against him. However, if a person simply does not say anything at all in the face of accusations or allegations, then that silence can be used against him.[2]

Now, the right against compelled self-incrimination is often paired with the right to counsel, found in the Sixth Amendment. The Sixth Amendment states:

> In all criminal prosecutions, the accused shall enjoy the right to a speedy and public trial, by an impartial jury of the State and district wherein the crime shall have been committed, which district shall have been previously

---

1. See, for example, Leo, Richard A., "False Confessions: Causes, Consequences and Implications" (January 1, 2009), *The Journal of the American Academy of Psychiatry and the Law*, 2009, Univ. of San Francisco Law Research Paper No. 2009-11, available at SSRN: http://ssrn.com/abstract=1328623; and Leo, Richard A. and Ofshe, Richard J., "The Social Psychology of Police Interrogation: The Theory and Classification of True and False Confessions," available at SSRN: http://ssrn.com/abstract=1141368.

2. *Salinas v. Texas*, 133 S. Ct. 2174 (2013).

ascertained by law, and to be informed of the nature and cause of the accusation; to be confronted with the witnesses against him; to have compulsory process for obtaining witnesses in his favor, and to have the Assistance of Counsel for his defence.

The phrase "have the Assistance of Counsel for his defence" means that all persons accused of a crime are allowed to have an attorney. Now, this was not always the case. In the landmark Supreme Court case *Gideon v. Wainwright*,[3] the Court held that if a person cannot afford an attorney and is facing a sentence of over one year in jail or does in fact receive a sentence which carries any jail time, the State is required to appoint an attorney, for free or at a subsidized rate. But when does this right attach? It is not only at trial, because in our system the entire process of investigation is over by then and that might be too late for a lawyer to do much good in protecting a client's rights — especially if the defendant has been held in jail pending trial.

The Fifth Amendment right not to be compelled as a witness against oneself and the right to the "Assistance of Counsel" are considered to be fundamental to a fair investigation and trial. The rights are considered to attach at a much earlier stage of investigation — as soon as a person is taken into custody. The problem, though, is that the nature of the interrogation process is such that individuals often fail to invoke them. So, as we'll read below, the Supreme Court required that law enforcement interrupt their process and give a person the chance to invoke their rights.

The right to remain silent and the right to an attorney go back to the founding of this country, but the requirement that law enforcement inform people of their rights is relatively new. Nowhere does the text of the U.S. Constitution require that law enforcement tell people they have a right to remain silent and a right to an attorney. The requirement that law enforcement inform people of their rights was a rule created, believe it or not, by the U.S. military at the early part of the 20th century and was adopted by the U.S. Supreme Court and made applicable to all law enforcement in the opinion *Arizona v. Miranda* in 1966. Indeed, there is no other aspect of criminal procedure more widely recognized than what has been come to be referred to simply as "the *Miranda* Warning."

You have probably seen a *Miranda* Warning being given on television or in the movies. A person who is being arrested is told something along the lines of "You have the right to remain silent. Anything you say can and will be used against you. You have a right to an attorney. If you cannot afford an attorney, one will be provided. Do you understand these rights?"

As you read the decision, pay attention to all of the concerns the Court felt it needed to address. Consider the reasoning used by the Court in coming to its decision.

---

3. *Gideon v. Wainwright*, 372 U.S. 335 (1963). Prior to the decision in *Gideon*, the 6th Amendment right to counsel was held to apply only to federal cases and to a select category of state criminal cases, such as capital cases. See *Betts v. Brady*, 316 U.S. 455 (1942).

Miranda v. Arizona, 384 U.S. 436 (1966)*

The cases before us raise questions which go to the roots of our concepts of American criminal jurisprudence: the restraints society must observe consistent with the Federal Constitution in prosecuting individuals for crime. More specifically, we deal with the admissibility of statements obtained from an individual who is subjected to custodial police interrogation and the necessity for procedures which assure that the individual is accorded his privilege under the Fifth Amendment to the Constitution not to be compelled to incriminate himself.

We dealt with certain phases of this problem recently in *Escobedo v. Illinois*, 378 U.S. 478 (1964). There, as in the four cases before us, law enforcement officials took the defendant into custody and interrogated him in a police station for the purpose of obtaining a confession. The police did not effectively advise him of his right to remain silent or of his right to consult with his attorney. Rather, they confronted him with an alleged accomplice who accused him of having perpetrated a murder. When the defendant denied the accusation and said "I didn't shoot Manuel, you did it," they handcuffed him and took him to an interrogation room. There, while handcuffed and standing, he was questioned for four hours until he confessed. During this interrogation, the police denied his request to speak to his attorney, and they prevented his retained attorney, who had come to the police station, from consulting with him. At his trial, the State, over his objection, introduced the confession against him. We held that the statements thus made were constitutionally inadmissible.

This case has been the subject of judicial interpretation and spirited legal debate since it was decided two years ago. Both state and federal courts, in assessing its implications, have arrived at varying conclusions. A wealth of scholarly material has been written tracing its ramifications and underpinnings. Police and prosecutor have speculated on its range and desirability. We granted review of these cases, in order to further explore some facets of the problems thus exposed of applying the privilege against self-incrimination to in-custody interrogation, and to give concrete constitutional guidelines for law enforcement agencies and courts to follow.

We start here, as we did in *Escobedo*, with the premise that our holding is not an innovation in our jurisprudence, but is an application of principles long recognized and applied in other settings. We have undertaken a thorough reexamination of the *Escobedo* decision and the principles it announced, and we reaffirm it. That case was but an explication of basic rights that are enshrined in our Constitution—that "No person... shall be compelled in any criminal case to be a witness against himself," and that "the accused shall... have the Assistance of Counsel"—rights which were put in jeopardy in that case through police overbearing. These precious rights were fixed in our Constitution only after centuries of persecution and struggle.

It was necessary in *Escobedo*, as here, to insure that what was proclaimed in the Constitution had not become but a "form of words," in the hands of government

---

* The case has been heavily edited and paraphrased by the authors for clarity. See disclaimer in introduction.

officials. . . . Our holding will be spelled out with some specificity in the pages which follow, but, briefly stated, it is this: the prosecution may not use statements, whether exculpatory or inculpatory, stemming from custodial interrogation of the defendant unless it demonstrates the use of procedural safeguards effective to secure the privilege against self-incrimination. By custodial interrogation, we mean questioning initiated by law enforcement officers after a person has been taken into custody or otherwise deprived of his freedom of action in any significant way. As for the procedural safeguards to be employed, unless other fully effective means are devised to inform accused persons of their right of silence and to assure a continuous opportunity to exercise it, the following measures are required. Prior to any custodial questioning, the person must be warned that he has a right to remain silent, that any statement he does make may be used as evidence against him, and that he has a right to the presence of an attorney, either retained or appointed. The defendant may waive effectuation of these rights, provided the waiver is made voluntarily, knowingly and intelligently. If, however, he indicates in any manner and at any stage of the process that he wishes to consult with an attorney before speaking, there can be no questioning. Likewise, if the individual is alone and indicates in any manner that he does not wish to be interrogated, the police may not question him. The mere fact that he may have answered some questions or volunteered some statements on his own does not deprive him of the right to refrain from answering any further inquiries until he has consulted with an attorney and thereafter consents to be questioned.

I

The constitutional issue we decide in each of these cases is the admissibility of statements obtained from a defendant questioned while in custody or otherwise deprived of his freedom of action in any significant way. In each, the defendant was questioned by police officers, detectives, or a prosecuting attorney in a room in which he was cut off from the outside world. In none of these cases was the defendant given a full and effective warning of his rights at the outset of the interrogation process. In all the cases, the questioning elicited oral admissions, and in three of them, signed statements as well which were admitted at their trials. They all thus share salient features—incommunicado interrogation of individuals in a police-dominated atmosphere, resulting in self-incriminating statements without full warnings of constitutional rights.

An understanding of the nature and setting of this in-custody interrogation is essential to our decisions today. The difficulty in depicting what transpires at such interrogations stems from the fact that, in this country, they have largely taken place incommunicado. From extensive factual studies undertaken in the early 1930's, including the famous Wickersham Report to Congress by a Presidential Commission, it is clear that police violence and the "third degree" flourished at that time. In a series of cases decided by this Court long after these studies, the police resorted to physical brutality—beating, hanging, whipping—and to sustained and protracted questioning incommunicado in order to extort confessions. The Commission on Civil Rights in 1961 found much evidence to indicate that "some policemen still resort to physical force to obtain confessions." The use of physical brutality and violence is not, unfortunately, relegated to the past or to any part of the country. Only recently in Kings County, New York, the police brutally beat, kicked and placed lighted cigarette butts on the back of a potential witness under interrogation for the purpose of securing a statement incriminating a third party.

The modern practice of in-custody interrogation is psychologically, rather than physically, oriented. As we have stated before, this Court has recognized that coercion can be mental as well as physical, and that the blood of the accused is not the only hallmark of an unconstitutional inquisition.

Interrogation still takes place in privacy. Privacy results in secrecy, and this, in turn, results in a gap in our knowledge as to what, in fact, goes on in the interrogation rooms. A valuable source of information about present police practices, however, may be found in various police manuals and texts which document procedures employed with success in the past, and which recommend various other effective tactics. These texts are used by law enforcement agencies themselves as guides. It should be noted that these texts professedly present the most enlightened and effective means presently used to obtain statements through custodial interrogation. By considering these texts and other data, it is possible to describe procedures observed and noted around the country.

The officers are told by the manuals that the principal psychological factor contributing to a successful interrogation is privacy—being alone with the person under interrogation. The efficacy of this tactic has been explained as follows:

> If at all practicable, the interrogation should take place in the investigator's office or at least in a room of his own choice. The subject should be deprived of every psychological advantage. In his own home, he may be confident, indignant, or recalcitrant. He is more keenly aware of his rights and more reluctant to tell of his indiscretions or criminal behavior within the walls of his home. Moreover his family and other friends are nearby, their presence lending moral support. In his own office, the investigator possesses all the advantages. The atmosphere suggests the invincibility of the forces of the law.

To highlight the isolation and unfamiliar surroundings, the manuals instruct the police to display an air of confidence in the suspect's guilt and, from outward appearance, to maintain only an interest in confirming certain details. The guilt of the subject is to be posited as a fact. The interrogator should direct his comments toward the reasons why the subject committed the act, rather than court failure by asking the subject whether he did it. Like other men, perhaps the subject has had a bad family life, had an unhappy childhood, had too much to drink, had an unrequited desire for women. The officers are instructed to minimize the moral seriousness of the offense, to cast blame on the victim or on society. These tactics are designed to put the subject in a psychological state where his story is but an elaboration of what the police purport to know already—that he is guilty. Explanations to the contrary are dismissed and discouraged.

The texts thus stress that the major qualities an interrogator should possess are patience and perseverance. One writer describes the efficacy of these characteristics in this manner:

> In the preceding paragraphs, emphasis has been placed on kindness and stratagems. The investigator will, however, encounter many situations where the sheer weight of his personality will be the deciding factor. Where emotional appeals and tricks are employed to no avail, he must rely on an oppressive atmosphere of dogged persistence. He must interrogate steadily and without relent, leaving the subject no prospect of surcease. He must dominate his subject and overwhelm him with his inexorable will to obtain the truth. He should interrogate for a spell of several hours, pausing only for the subject's necessities in acknowledgment of the need to avoid a charge of duress that can be technically substantiated. In a serious case, the interrogation may continue for days, with the required intervals for food and sleep, but with no respite from the atmosphere of domination. It is possible in this way to induce the subject to talk without resorting to duress or coercion. The method should be used only when the guilt of the subject appears highly probable.

The manuals suggest that the suspect be offered legal excuses for his actions in order to obtain an initial admission of guilt. Where there is a suspected revenge killing, for example, the interrogator may say:

> Joe, you probably didn't go out looking for this fellow with the purpose of shooting him. My guess is, however, that you expected something from him, and that's why you carried a gun — for your own protection. You knew him for what he was, no good. Then when you met him, he probably started using foul, abusive language and he gave some indication that he was about to pull a gun on you, and that's when you had to act to save your own life. That's about it, isn't it, Joe?

Having then obtained the admission of shooting, the interrogator is advised to refer to circumstantial evidence which negates the self-defense explanation. This should enable him to secure the entire story. One text notes that, even if he fails to do so, the inconsistency between the subject's original denial of the shooting and his present admission of at least doing the shooting will serve to deprive him of a self-defense "out" at the time of trial.

When the techniques described above prove unavailing, the texts recommend they be alternated with a show of some hostility. One ploy often used has been termed the "friendly-unfriendly," "good cop, bad cop," or the "Mutt and Jeff" act:

> In this technique, two agents are employed. Mutt, the relentless investigator, who knows the subject is guilty and is not going to waste any time. He's sent a dozen men away for this crime, and he's going to send the subject away for the full term. Jeff, on the other hand, is obviously a kindhearted man. He has a family himself. He has a brother who was involved in a little scrape like this. He disapproves of Mutt and his tactics, and will arrange to get him off the case if the subject will cooperate. He can't hold Mutt off for very long.

The subject would be wise to make a quick decision. The technique is applied by having both investigators present while Mutt acts out his role. Jeff may stand by quietly and demur at some of Mutt's tactics. When Jeff makes his plea for cooperation, Mutt is not present in the room.

The interrogators sometimes are instructed to induce a confession out of trickery. The technique here is quite effective in crimes which require identification or which run in series. In the identification situation, the interrogator may take a break in his questioning to place the subject among a group of men in a line-up. The witness or complainant (previously coached, if necessary) studies the line-up and confidently points out the subject as the guilty party. Then the questioning resumes "as though there were now no doubt about the guilt of the subject." A variation on this technique is called the "reverse line-up": The accused is placed in a line-up, but this time he is identified by several fictitious witnesses or victims who associated him with different offenses. It is expected that the subject will become desperate and confess to the offense under investigation in order to escape from the false accusations.

The manuals also contain instructions for police on how to handle the individual who refuses to discuss the matter entirely, or who asks for an attorney or relatives. The examiner is to concede him the right to remain silent. This usually has a very undermining effect. First of all, he is disappointed in his expectation of an unfavorable reaction on the part of the interrogator. Secondly, a concession of this right to remain silent impresses the subject with the apparent fairness of his interrogator. After this psychological conditioning, however, the officer is told to point out the incriminating significance of the suspect's refusal to talk:

> Joe, you have a right to remain silent. That's your privilege, and I'm the last person in the world who'll try to take it away from you. If that's the way you want to leave this, okay. But let me ask you this. Suppose you were in my shoes, and I were in yours, and you called me in to ask me about this, and I told you, "I don't want to answer any of your questions." You'd think I had something to hide, and you'd probably be right in thinking that. That's exactly what I'll have to think about you, and so will everybody else. So let's sit here and talk this whole thing over.

Few will persist in their initial refusal to talk, it is said, if this monologue is employed correctly. In the event that the subject wishes to speak to a relative or an attorney, the following advice is tendered:

> The interrogator should respond by suggesting that the subject first tell the truth to the interrogator himself, rather than get anyone else involved in the matter. If the request is for an attorney, the interrogator may suggest that the subject save himself or his family the expense of any such professional service, particularly if he is innocent of the offense under investigation. The interrogator may also add, "Joe, I'm only looking for the truth, and if you're telling the truth, that's it. You can handle this by yourself."

From these representative samples of interrogation techniques, the setting prescribed by the manuals and observed in practice becomes clear. In essence, it is this:

to be alone with the subject is essential to prevent distraction and to deprive him of any outside support. The aura of confidence in his guilt undermines his will to resist. He merely confirms the preconceived story the police seek to have him describe. Patience and persistence, at times relentless questioning, are employed. To obtain a confession, the interrogator must "patiently maneuver himself or his quarry into a position from which the desired objective may be attained." When normal procedures fail to produce the needed result, the police may resort to deceptive stratagems such as giving false legal advice. It is important to keep the subject off balance, for example, by trading on his insecurity about himself or his surroundings. The police then persuade, trick, or cajole him out of exercising his constitutional rights.

Even without employing brutality, the "third degree" or the specific stratagems described above, the very fact of custodial interrogation exacts a heavy toll on individual liberty, and trades on the weakness of individuals. This fact may be illustrated simply by referring to three confession cases decided by this Court in the Term immediately preceding our *Escobedo* decision. In *Townsend v. Sain*, 372 U.S. 293 (1963), the defendant was a 19-year-old heroin addict, described as a "near mental defective." The defendant in *Lynumn v. Illinois*, 372 U.S. 528 (1963), was a woman who confessed to the arresting officer after being coerced to "cooperate" in order to prevent her children from being taken by social workers. This Court, as in those cases, reversed the conviction of a defendant in *Haynes v. Washington*, 373 U.S. 503 (1963), whose persistent request during his interrogation was to phone his wife or attorney. In other settings, these individuals might have exercised their constitutional rights. In the incommunicado police-dominated atmosphere, they succumbed.

In the cases before us today, given this background, we concern ourselves primarily with this interrogation atmosphere and the evils it can bring. In No. 759, *Miranda v. Arizona*, the police arrested the defendant and took him to a special interrogation room, where they secured a confession. In No. 760, *Vignera v. New York*, the defendant made oral admissions to the police after interrogation in the afternoon, and then signed an inculpatory statement upon being questioned by an assistant district attorney later the same evening. In No. 761, *Westover v. United States,* the defendant was handed over to the Federal Bureau of Investigation by local authorities after they had detained and interrogated him for a lengthy period, both at night and the following morning. After some two hours of questioning, the federal officers had obtained signed statements from the defendant. Lastly, in No. 584, *California v. Stewart*, the local police held the defendant five days in the station and interrogated him on nine separate occasions before they secured his inculpatory statement.

In these cases, we might not find the defendants' statements to have been involuntary in traditional terms. Our concern for adequate safeguards to protect precious Fifth Amendment rights is, of course, not lessened in the slightest. In each of the cases, the defendant was thrust into an unfamiliar atmosphere and run through menacing police interrogation procedures. The potentiality for compulsion is forcefully apparent, for example, in *Miranda*, where the indigent Mexican defendant was a seriously disturbed individual with pronounced sexual fantasies, and in *Stewart*, in which the defendant was an indigent Los Angeles Negro who had dropped out of school in the sixth grade. To be sure, the records do not evince overt physical coercion or patent psychological ploys. The fact remains that in none of these cases did the officers undertake to afford appropriate safeguards at the outset of the interrogation to insure that the statements were truly the product of free choice.

It is obvious that such an interrogation environment is created for no purpose other than to subjugate the individual to the will of his examiner. This atmosphere carries its own badge of intimidation. To be sure, this is not physical intimidation, but it is equally destructive of human dignity. The current practice of incommunicado interrogation is at odds with one of our Nation's most cherished principles — that the individual may not be compelled to incriminate himself. Unless adequate protective devices are employed to dispel the compulsion inherent in custodial surroundings, no statement obtained from the defendant can truly be the product of his free choice. From the foregoing, we can readily perceive an intimate connection between the privilege against self-incrimination and police custodial questioning. It is fitting to turn to history and precedent underlying the Self-Incrimination Clause to determine its applicability in this situation.

II

All these policies point to one overriding thought: the constitutional foundation underlying the privilege is the respect a government — state or federal — must accord to the dignity and integrity of its citizens. To maintain a "fair state-individual balance," to require the government "to shoulder the entire load," to respect the inviolability of the human personality, our accusatory system of criminal justice demands that the government seeking to punish an individual produce the evidence against him by its own independent labors, rather than by the cruel, simple expedient of compelling it from his own mouth. In sum, the privilege is fulfilled only when the person is guaranteed the right "to remain silent unless he chooses to speak in the unfettered exercise of his own will."

The question in these cases is whether the privilege is fully applicable during a period of custodial interrogation. In this Court, the privilege has consistently been accorded a liberal construction. We are satisfied that all the principles embodied in the privilege apply to informal compulsion exerted by law enforcement officers during in-custody questioning. An individual swept from familiar surroundings into police custody, surrounded by antagonistic forces, and subjected to the techniques of persuasion described above cannot be otherwise than under compulsion to speak. As a practical matter, the compulsion to speak in the isolated setting of the police station may well be greater than in courts or other official investigations, where there are often impartial observers to guard against intimidation or trickery.

This question, in fact, could have been taken as settled in federal courts almost 70 years ago, when, in *Bram v. United States*, 168 U.S. 532 (1897), this Court held:

> In criminal trials, in the courts of the United States, wherever a question arises whether a confession is incompetent because not voluntary, the issue is controlled by that portion of the Fifth Amendment, commanding that no person shall be compelled in any criminal case to be a witness against himself.

In *Bram*, the Court reviewed the British and American history and case law and set down the Fifth Amendment standard for compulsion which we implement today. The Court in *Bram* explained that much confusion has arisen as to just how much evidence there must be to prove that a confession was made voluntarily or involuntarily. The rule we set forth is that it must be sufficient to establish that the making of a statement was voluntary; that is to say, that the accused was not involuntarily impelled to make a statement when, were it not for improper coercion, he otherwise would have remained silent.

The Court has adhered to this reasoning. In 1924, Mr. Justice Brandeis wrote for a unanimous Court in reversing a conviction resting on a compelled confession, *Wan v. United States*, 266 U.S. 1. He stated that voluntariness is not satisfied by establishing merely that the confession was not induced by a promise or a threat. A confession is voluntary in law if, and only if, it was voluntarily made. It is possible for a confession to be given voluntarily while a person is in the custody of police officers, but a confession obtained by compulsion must be excluded.

III

Today, then, there can be no doubt that the Fifth Amendment privilege is available outside of criminal court proceedings and serves to protect persons in all settings in which their freedom of action is curtailed in any significant way from being compelled to incriminate themselves. We have concluded that without proper safeguards the process of in-custody interrogation of persons suspected or accused of crime contains inherently compelling pressures which work to undermine the individual's will to resist and to compel him to speak where he would not otherwise do so freely. In order to combat these pressures and to permit a full opportunity to exercise the privilege against self-incrimination, the accused must be adequately and effectively apprised of his rights and the exercise of those rights must be fully honored.

At the outset, if a person in custody is to be subjected to interrogation, he must first be informed in clear and unequivocal terms that he has the right to remain silent. For those unaware of the privilege, the warning is needed simply to make them aware of it—the threshold requirement for an intelligent decision as to its exercise. More important, such a warning is an absolute prerequisite in overcoming the inherent pressures of the interrogation atmosphere. It is not just the subnormal or woefully ignorant who succumb to an interrogator's imprecations, whether implied or expressly stated, that the interrogation will continue until a confession is obtained or that silence in the face of accusation is itself damning and will bode ill when presented to a jury. Further, the warning will show the individual that his interrogators are prepared to recognize his privilege should he choose to exercise it.

The warning of the right to remain silent must be accompanied by the explanation that anything said can and will be used against the individual in court. This warning is needed in order to make him aware not only of the privilege, but also of the consequences of forgoing it. It is only through an awareness of these consequences that there can be any assurance of real understanding and intelligent exercise of the privilege. Moreover, this warning may serve to make the individual more acutely aware that he is faced with a phase of the adversary system—that he is not in the presence of persons acting solely in his interest.

The circumstances surrounding in-custody interrogation can operate very quickly to overbear the will of one merely made aware of his privilege by his interrogators. Therefore, the right to have counsel present at the interrogation is indispensable to the protection of the Fifth Amendment privilege under the system we delineate today. Our aim is to assure that the individual's right to choose between silence and speech remains unfettered throughout the interrogation process. A once-stated warning, delivered by those who will conduct the interrogation, cannot itself suffice to that end among those who most require knowledge of their rights. A mere warning given by the interrogators is not alone sufficient to accomplish that end. Prosecutors themselves claim that the admonishment of the right to remain silent without more "will benefit only the recidivist and the professional." Even preliminary advice given to the accused by his own attorney can be swiftly overcome by the secret interrogation process. Thus, the need for counsel to protect the Fifth Amendment privilege comprehends not merely a right to consult with counsel prior to questioning, but also to have counsel present during any questioning if the defendant so desires.

The presence of counsel at the interrogation may serve several significant subsidiary functions as well. If the accused decides to talk to his interrogators, the assistance of counsel can mitigate the dangers of untrustworthiness. With a lawyer present the likelihood that the police will practice coercion is reduced, and if coercion is nevertheless exercised the lawyer can testify to it in court. The presence of a lawyer can also help to guarantee that the accused gives a fully accurate statement to the police and that the statement is rightly reported by the prosecution at trial.

An individual need not make a pre-interrogation request for a lawyer. While such request affirmatively secures his right to have one, his failure to ask for a lawyer does not constitute a waiver. No effective waiver of the right to counsel during interrogation can be recognized unless specifically made after the warnings we here delineate have been given. The accused who does not know his rights and therefore does not make a request may be the person who most needs counsel. As the California Supreme Court has aptly put it:

> Finally, we must recognize that the imposition of the requirement for the request would discriminate against the defendant who does not know his rights. The defendant who does not ask for counsel is the very defendant who most needs counsel. We cannot penalize a defendant who, not understanding his constitutional rights, does not make the formal request and by such failure demonstrates his helplessness. To require the request would be to favor the defendant whose sophistication or status had fortuitously prompted him to make it.

Accordingly we hold that an individual held for interrogation must be clearly informed that he has the right to consult with a lawyer and to have the lawyer with him during interrogation under the system for protecting the privilege we delineate today. As with the warnings of the right to remain silent and that anything stated can be used in evidence against him, this warning is an absolute prerequisite to interrogation. No amount of circumstantial evidence that the person may have been aware of this right will suffice to stand in its stead: Only through such a warning is there ascertainable assurance that the accused was aware of this right.

If an individual indicates that he wishes the assistance of counsel before any interrogation occurs, the authorities cannot rationally ignore or deny his request on the basis that the individual does not have or cannot afford a retained attorney. The financial ability of the individual has no relationship to the scope of the rights involved here. The privilege against self-incrimination secured by the Constitution applies to all individuals. The need for counsel in order to protect the privilege exists for the indigent as well as the affluent. In fact, were we to limit these constitutional rights to those who can retain an attorney, our decisions today would be of little significance. The cases before us as well as the vast majority of confession cases with which we have dealt in the past involve those unable to retain counsel. While authorities are not required to relieve the accused of his poverty, they have the obligation not to take advantage of indigence in the administration of justice. Denial of counsel to the indigent at the time of interrogation while allowing an attorney to those who can afford one would be no more supportable by reason or logic than the similar situation at trial and on appeal struck down in *Gideon v. Wainwright* where we stated that at trial, all persons who are facing over 1 year of imprisonment or if any prison time is issued, an indigent defendant is entitled to counsel at the state's expense.

In order fully to apprise a person interrogated of the extent of his rights under this system then, it is necessary to warn him not only that he has the right to consult with an attorney, but also that if he is indigent a lawyer will be appointed to represent him. Without this additional warning, the admonition of the right to consult with counsel would often be understood as meaning only that he can consult with a lawyer if he has one or has the funds to obtain one. The warning of a right to counsel would be hollow if not couched in terms that would convey to the indigent — the person most often subjected to interrogation — the knowledge that he too has a right to have counsel present. As with the warnings of the right to remain silent and of the general right to counsel, only by effective and express explanation to the indigent of this right can there be assurance that he was truly in a position to exercise it.

Once warnings have been given, the subsequent procedure is clear. If the individual indicates in any manner, at any time prior to or during questioning, that he wishes to remain silent, the interrogation must cease. At this point he has shown that he intends to exercise his Fifth Amendment privilege; any statement taken after the person invokes his privilege cannot be other than the product of compulsion, subtle or otherwise. Without the right to cut off questioning, the setting of in-custody interrogation operates on the individual to overcome free choice in producing a statement after the privilege has been once invoked. If the individual states that he wants an attorney, the interrogation must cease until an attorney is present. At that time, the individual must have an opportunity to confer with the attorney and to have him present during any subsequent questioning. If the individual cannot obtain an attorney and he indicates that he wants one before speaking to police, they must respect his decision to remain silent.

This does not mean, as some have suggested, that each police station must have a "station house lawyer" present at all times to advise prisoners. It does mean, however, that if police propose to interrogate a person they must make known to him that he is entitled to a lawyer and that if he cannot afford one, a lawyer will be provided for him prior to any interrogation. If authorities conclude that they will not provide counsel during a reasonable period of time in which investigation in the field is carried out, they may refrain from doing so without violating the person's Fifth Amendment privilege so long as they do not question him during that time.

If the interrogation continues without the presence of an attorney and a statement is taken, a heavy burden rests on the government to demonstrate that the defendant knowingly and intelligently waived his privilege against self-incrimination and his right to retained or appointed counsel. This Court has always set high standards of proof for the waiver of constitutional rights, and we re-assert these standards as applied to in-custody interrogation. Since the State is responsible for establishing the isolated circumstances under which the interrogation takes place and has the only means of making available corroborated evidence of warnings given during incommunicado interrogation, the burden is rightly on its shoulders.

An express statement that the individual is willing to make a statement and does not want an attorney followed closely by a statement could constitute a waiver. But a valid waiver will not be presumed simply from the silence of the accused after warnings are given or simply from the fact that a confession was in fact eventually obtained. A statement we made in *Carnley v. Cochran*, 369 U.S. 506 (1962), is applicable here: "Presuming waiver from a silent record is impermissible. The record must show, or there must be an allegation and evidence which show, that an accused was offered counsel but intelligently and understandingly rejected the offer. Anything less is not waiver."

Moreover, where in-custody interrogation is involved, there is no room for the contention that the privilege is waived if the individual answers some questions or gives some information on his own prior to invoking his right to remain silent when interrogated. Whatever the testimony of the authorities as to waiver of rights by an accused, the fact of lengthy interrogation or incommunicado incarceration before a statement is made is strong evidence that the accused did not validly waive his rights. In these circumstances the fact that the individual eventually made a statement is consistent with the conclusion that the compelling influence of the interrogation finally forced him to do so. It is inconsistent with any notion of a voluntary relinquishment of the privilege. Moreover, any evidence that the accused was threatened, tricked, or cajoled into a waiver will, of course, show that the defendant did not voluntarily waive his privilege. The requirement of warnings and waiver of rights is a fundamental with respect to the Fifth Amendment privilege and not simply a preliminary ritual to existing methods of interrogation.

The warnings required and the waiver necessary in accordance with our opinion today are, in the absence of a fully effective equivalent, prerequisites to the admissibility of any statement made by a defendant. No distinction can be drawn between statements which are direct confessions and statements which amount to "admissions" of part or all of an offense. The privilege against self-incrimination protects the individual from being compelled to incriminate himself in any manner; it does not distinguish degrees of incrimination. Similarly, for precisely the same reason, no distinction may be drawn between inculpatory statements and statements alleged to be merely "exculpatory." If a statement made were in fact truly exculpatory it would, of course, never be used by the prosecution. In fact, statements merely intended to be exculpatory by the defendant are often used to impeach his testimony at trial or to demonstrate untruths in the statement given under interrogation and thus to prove guilt by implication. These statements are incriminating in any meaningful sense of the word and may not be used without the full warnings and effective waiver required for any other statement. In *Escobedo* itself, the defendant fully intended his accusation of another as the killer to be exculpatory as to himself.

The principles announced today deal with the protection which must be given to the privilege against self-incrimination when the individual is first subjected to police interrogation while in custody at the station or otherwise deprived of his freedom of action in any significant way. It is at this point that our adversary system of criminal proceedings commences, distinguishing itself at the outset from the inquisitorial system recognized in some countries. Under the system of warnings we delineate today or under any other system which may be devised and found effective, the safeguards to be erected about the privilege must come into play at this point.

Our decision is not intended to hamper the traditional function of police officers in investigating crime. When an individual is in custody on probable cause, the police may, of course, seek out evidence in the field to be used at trial against him. Such investigation may include inquiry of persons not under restraint. General on-the-scene questioning as to facts surrounding a crime or other general questioning of citizens in the fact-finding process is not affected by our holding. It is an act of responsible citizenship for individuals to give whatever information they may have to aid in law enforcement. In such situations the compelling atmosphere inherent in the process of in-custody interrogation is not necessarily present.

In dealing with statements obtained through interrogation, we do not purport to find all confessions inadmissible. Confessions remain a proper element in law enforcement. Any statement given freely and voluntarily without any compelling influences is, of course, admissible in evidence. The fundamental import of the privilege while an individual is in custody is not whether he is allowed to talk to the police without the benefit of warnings and counsel, but whether he can be interrogated. There is no requirement that police stop a person who enters a police station and states that he wishes to confess to a crime, or a person who calls the police to offer a confession or any other statement he desires to make. Volunteered statements of any kind are not barred by the Fifth Amendment and their admissibility is not affected by our holding today.

To summarize, we hold that when an individual is taken into custody or otherwise deprived of his freedom by the authorities in any significant way and is subjected to questioning, the privilege against self-incrimination is jeopardized. Procedural safeguards must be employed to protect the privilege, and unless other fully effective means are adopted to notify the person of his right of silence and to assure that the exercise of the right will be scrupulously honored, the following measures are required. He must be warned prior to any questioning that he has the right to remain silent, that anything he says can be used against him in a court of law, that he has the right to the presence of an attorney, and that if he cannot afford an attorney one will be appointed for him prior to any questioning if he so desires. Opportunity to exercise these rights must be afforded to him throughout the interrogation. After such warnings have been given, and such opportunity afforded him, the individual may knowingly and intelligently waive these rights and agree to answer questions or make a statement. But unless and until such warnings and waiver are demonstrated by the prosecution at trial, no evidence obtained as a result of interrogation can be used against him.

END OF OPINION

In *Miranda v. Arizona*, the Supreme Court established a rule: Prior to interrogating a person in custody, law enforcement must advise a person of his constitutional rights including:

- The right to remain silent;
- The fact that any statements made can be used against that person;
- The right to an attorney, and to have the attorney present during questioning;
- That an attorney will be appointed if he cannot afford one; and
- An affirmative obligation to check to make sure that the person understands what he has just been told and whether the individual wishes to have an attorney, or to continue the questioning without an attorney present.

After this warning is given a person can affirmatively choose to remain silent, can ask for a lawyer, or affirmatively waive the rights and choose to talk to the police.

As you read over that list, you were reading what has commonly come to be called "the *Miranda* rights." The Court created this rule, that people must be informed of their rights, because it was well documented that the nature of a custodial interrogation is inherently coercive. In some cases, law enforcement were intentionally violating people's rights and taking advantage of people who were unaware of their rights. Even where people were aware they had these rights, the police would get a rhythm going in the interrogation, such that the person being interrogated didn't feel they could stop and ask for assistance. Therefore, the *Miranda* warning exists as a prophylactic protection to help ensure that if people do have the chance to stop, think about their options, and then, if they do affirmatively waive their rights, they do so knowingly, voluntarily, and intelligently. It is a way to leave no doubt that, when people talk to the police and confess, they do not do so because of undue coercion.

To be clear, the *Miranda* opinion did not establish the right to remain silent or the right to an attorney. These rights have always existed and were always protected by the Fifth and Sixth Amendments. What *Miranda* did was establish a procedural rule where the police are required to inform people of their rights prior to custodial interrogation. The failure of the police to follow this procedural rule can result in the exclusionary rule being invoked.

Before we go further, let's consider in more detail what is meant by "custody" and "interrogation."

"Custody" is any situation where a reasonable person would not feel free to leave — a situation similar to what we think of as formal arrest. Obviously, if a person were in an interrogation room in handcuffs, that person would not feel free to leave. But a person does not have to actually be in handcuffs to not feel free to leave. A person out of handcuffs, but otherwise in an interrogation room after having been arrested, is obviously not free to leave. Similarly, if a person has voluntarily come into a police station just to "answer a few questions" and afterwards tries to leave but is told he or she may not leave and must answer more questions first, that person is in custody. Whether or not a person is in custody or not is a judgment call which one determines based on the totality of the circumstances.

On the other hand, if a person voluntarily comes down to a police station to give a statement, even to answer questions, but the circumstances are such that it is clear that the person is free to leave at any point, the person is not in custody, so no *Miranda* warning has to be given before the questioning begins. If the police briefly detain a person to conduct a *Terry* stop, and the person is not in handcuffs but merely standing on the street in front of the officer who is asking a few questions, then the person is not yet considered to be in custody and no *Miranda* warning is required. Now, it is true that a person who has been stopped by the police is not entirely free to leave, but the courts have ruled that, because the circumstances of this detention do not have the intimidating conditions that exist in a formal arrest and detention, no *Miranda* warning is required. Generally with a *Terry* stop, a person is not physically restrained, cornered, or threatened. Instead, he or she is usually out in the open, where the public can see and, importantly, where police are very unlikely to use any improperly coercive techniques to compel a statement. The person is merely verbally told he or she has to remain put. Because this is not viewed as a coercive environment, no *Miranda* warning is required prior to questioning. In some states, a person standing on the public street and in handcuffs is still not considered to be in "custody." Instead, this is referred to as merely an "investigatory detention" and does not require a Miranda Warning.

Now again, these criteria go to the issue of when the formal *Miranda* warning is issued — not when the rights attach. A person in any circumstance, regardless whether or not in custody, or whether there is zero or a lot of restraint of liberty, always has the right to remain silent. It is just that in non-coercive circumstances law enforcement do not have to go through the formal process of informing a person of the right to remain silent. Think about how when you are stopped for speeding; you are merely sitting in your car as the officer approaches. Although you are not free to leave, these circumstances are not so coercive as to require a *Miranda* warning prior to the officer speaking to you. The purpose of the warning requirement was to deter police behavior that was considered coercive. Where the nature of the questioning makes that coercion less likely, it is also less likely that the courts will rule that the *Miranda* warning is required.

A frequent tactic of officers is to ask a lot of un-Mirandized questions during the investigatory detention and, only after the person has made incriminating statements, then take the person into formal custody and issue the *Miranda* warning. Of course at this point, the person has already made admissible statements which will be highly incriminating—but they will be deemed voluntary, not compelled.

Whether or not a person's restraint of liberty is equitable to the loss of freedom associated with a formal arrest ultimately depends on the totality of the circumstances, and not simply on any formal designation. Any physical restraint, such as handcuffs, behind bars, or physically forced in a certain bodily position by law enforcement (like a head-lock or twisting an arm), are good indicators that a person is not free to leave. If the police are acting in a threatening manner, such as brandishing a weapon, a person is also likely not free to leave. If the police tell a person that he or she is not free to leave, a person may be in custody. Remember to look at the totality of the circumstances such as where the officers are positioned, where the questioning is taking place, and if the officers have given any verbal commands to the person limiting his freedom of movement. Look also to whether the police conduct in getting a person to talk can be considered "coercive." If so, then the suspect has probably been in custody.

Now let's discuss what constitutes an "interrogation." "Interrogation" is anything said or done by law enforcement calculated to elicit an incriminating response by a suspect. You probably think of interrogation as the police asking a person questions about a crime. Although this is one form of interrogation, interrogation can be much more than that. Potentially, any statements or actions made by law enforcement, even if not questions or not directed toward the suspect, can be construed as interrogation if the statements are designed to elicit an incriminating response.

Let's say the police have a suspect they know is a very religiously devout, deeply committed person. Instead of asking the suspect any questions, an officer simply starts reading a scripture passage or making comments about how "confession is good for the soul." Even though the officer is not asking any questions but is instead merely reading or talking about religion, this is legally interrogation because the officer's conduct is specifically designed to get the suspect to make an incriminating statement. To better understand what is meant by "interrogation," read the following case *Brewer v. Williams*, more famously known as "the Christian burial speech."

Brewer v. Williams, 430 U.S. 387 (1977)*

On the afternoon of December 24, 1968, a 10-year-old girl named Pamela Powers went with her family to the YMCA in Des Moines, Iowa, to watch a wrestling

---

* The case has been heavily edited and paraphrased by the authors for clarity. See disclaimer in introduction.

tournament in which her brother was participating. When she failed to return from a trip to the washroom, a search for her began. The search was unsuccessful.

Robert Williams, who had recently escaped from a mental hospital, was a resident of the YMCA. Soon after the girl's disappearance, Williams was seen in the YMCA lobby carrying some clothing and a large bundle wrapped in a blanket. He obtained help from a 14-year-old boy in opening the street door of the YMCA and the door to his automobile parked outside. When Williams placed the bundle in the front seat of his car, the boy "saw two legs in it and they were skinny and white." Before anyone could see what was in the bundle, Williams drove away. His abandoned car was found the following day in Davenport, Iowa, roughly 160 miles east of Des Moines. A warrant was then issued in Des Moines for his arrest on a charge of abduction.

On the morning of December 26, a Des Moines lawyer named Henry McKnight went to the Des Moines police station and informed the officers present that he had just received a long-distance call from Williams, and that he had advised Williams to turn himself in to the Davenport police. Williams did surrender that morning to the police in Davenport, and they booked him on the charge specified in the arrest warrant and gave him the warnings required by *Miranda v. Arizona*. The Davenport police then telephoned their counterparts in Des Moines to inform them that Williams had surrendered. McKnight, the lawyer, was still at the Des Moines police headquarters, and Williams conversed with McKnight on the telephone. In the presence of the Des Moines chief of police and a police detective named Leaming, McKnight advised Williams that Des Moines police officers would be driving to Davenport to pick him up, that the officers would not interrogate him or mistreat him, and that Williams was not to talk to the officers about Pamela Powers until after consulting with McKnight upon his return to Des Moines. As a result of these conversations, it was agreed between McKnight and the Des Moines police officials that Detective Leaming and a fellow officer would drive to Davenport to pick up Williams, that they would bring him directly back to Des Moines, and that they would not question him during the trip.

In the meantime, Williams was arraigned before a judge in Davenport on the outstanding arrest warrant. The judge advised him of his *Miranda* rights and committed him to jail. Before leaving the courtroom, Williams conferred with a lawyer named Kelly, who advised him not to make any statements until consulting with McKnight back in Des Moines.

Detective Leaming and his fellow officer arrived in Davenport about noon to pick up Williams and return him to Des Moines. Soon after their arrival, they met with Williams and Kelly, who, they understood, was acting as Williams' lawyer. Detective Leaming repeated the *Miranda* warnings, and told Williams, "We both know that you're being represented here by Mr. Kelly and you're being represented by Mr. McKnight in Des Moines, and I want you to remember this because we'll be visiting between here and Des Moines."

Williams then conferred again with Kelly alone, and, after this conference, Kelly reiterated to Detective Leaming that Williams was not to be questioned about the disappearance of Pamela Powers until after he had consulted with McKnight back in Des Moines. When Leaming expressed some reservations, Kelly firmly stated that the agreement with McKnight was to be carried out—that there was to be no interrogation of Williams during the automobile journey to Des Moines. Kelly was denied permission to ride in the police car back to Des Moines with Williams and the two officers.

The two detectives, with Williams in their charge, then set out on the 160-mile drive. At no time during the trip did Williams express a willingness to be interrogated in the absence of an attorney. Instead, he stated several times that "when I get to Des Moines and see Mr. McKnight, I am going to tell you the whole story." Detective Leaming knew that Williams was a former mental patient, and knew also that he was deeply religious.

The detective and his prisoner soon embarked on a wide-ranging conversation covering a variety of topics, including the subject of religion. Then, not long after leaving Davenport and reaching the interstate highway, Detective Leaming delivered what has been referred to in the briefs and oral arguments as the "Christian burial speech." Addressing Williams as "Reverend," the detective said:

> I want to give you something to think about while we're traveling down the road. Number one, I want you to observe the weather conditions, it's raining, it's sleeting, it's freezing, driving is very treacherous, visibility is poor, it's going to be dark early this evening. They are predicting several inches of snow for tonight, and I feel that you yourself are the only person that knows where this little girl's body is, that you yourself have only been there once, and if you get a snow on top of it you yourself may be unable to find it. And, since we will be going right past the area on the way into Des Moines, I felt that we could stop and locate the body, that the parents of this little girl should be entitled to a Christian burial for the little girl who was snatched away from them on Christmas Eve and murdered. And I feel we should stop and locate it on the way in, rather than waiting until morning and trying to come back out after a snow storm, and possibly not being able to find it at all.

Williams asked Detective Leaming why he thought their route to Des Moines would be taking them past the girl's body, and Leaming responded that he knew the body was in the area of Mitchellville—a town they would be passing on the way to Des Moines. Leaming then stated: "I do not want you to answer me. I don't want to discuss it any further. Just think about it as we're riding down the road."

As the car approached Grinnell, a town approximately 100 miles west of Davenport, Williams asked whether the police had found the victim's shoes. When Detective Leaming replied that he was unsure, Williams directed the officers to a service station where he said he had left the shoes; a search for them proved unsuccessful. As they continued towards Des Moines, Williams asked whether the police had found the blanket, and directed the officers to a rest area where he said he had disposed of the blanket. Nothing was found. The car continued towards Des Moines, and as it approached Mitchellville, Williams said that he would show the officers where the body was. He then directed the police to the body of Pamela Powers.

Williams was indicted for first-degree murder. Before trial, his counsel moved to suppress all evidence relating to or resulting from any statements Williams had made during the automobile ride from Davenport to Des Moines. After an evidentiary hearing, the trial judge denied the motion. He found that an agreement was made between defense counsel and the police officials to the effect that the Defendant was not to be questioned on the return trip to Des Moines, and that the evidence in question had been elicited from Williams during "a critical stage in the proceedings requiring the presence of counsel on his request." The judge ruled, however, that Williams had "waived his right to have an attorney present during the giving of such information."

. . .

There can be no doubt in the present case that judicial proceedings had been initiated against Williams before the start of the automobile ride from Davenport to Des Moines. A warrant had been issued for his arrest, he had been arraigned on that warrant before a judge in a Davenport courtroom, and he had been committed by the court to confinement in jail. The State does not contend otherwise.

There can be no serious doubt, either, that Detective Leaming deliberately and designedly set out to elicit information from Williams just as surely as — and perhaps more effectively than — if he had formally interrogated him. Detective Leaming was fully aware before departing for Des Moines that Williams was being represented in Davenport by Kelly and in Des Moines by McKnight. Yet he purposely sought during Williams' isolation from his lawyers to obtain as much incriminating information as possible. Indeed, Detective Leaming conceded as much when he testified at Williams' trial:

Q. In fact, Captain, whether he was a mental patient or not, you were trying to get all the information you could before he got to his lawyer, weren't you?

A. I was sure hoping to find out where that little girl was, yes, sir.

Q. Well, I'll put it this way: You were hoping to get all the information you could before Williams got back to McKnight, weren't you?

A. Yes, sir.

The state courts clearly proceeded upon the hypothesis that detective Leaming's "Christian burial speech" had been tantamount to interrogation. Both courts recognized that Williams had been entitled to the assistance of counsel at the time he made the incriminating statements. Yet no such constitutional protection would have come into play if there had been no interrogation.

The circumstances of this case are thus constitutionally indistinguishable from those presented in [the earlier case of] *Massiah v. United States*. The petitioner in that case was indicted for violating the federal narcotics law. He retained a lawyer, pleaded not guilty, and was released on bail. While he was free on bail a federal agent succeeded by surreptitious means in listening to incriminating statements made by him. Evidence of these statements was introduced against the petitioner at his trial, and he was convicted. This Court reversed the conviction, holding that the petitioner was denied the basic protections of that guarantee [the right to counsel] when there was used against him at his trial evidence of his own incriminating words, which federal agents had deliberately elicited from him after he had been indicted and in the absence of his counsel.

That the incriminating statements were elicited surreptitiously in the *Massiah* case, and otherwise here, is constitutionally irrelevant. Rather, the clear rule of *Massiah* is that, once adversary proceedings have commenced against an individual, he has a right to legal representation when the government interrogates him. It thus requires no wooden or technical application of the *Massiah* doctrine to conclude that Williams was entitled to the assistance of counsel guaranteed to him by the Sixth and Fourteenth Amendments.

The Iowa courts recognized that Williams had been denied the constitutional right to the assistance of counsel. They held, however, that he had waived that right during the course of the automobile trip from Davenport to Des Moines. The state trial court explained its determination of waiver as follows:

The time element involved on the trip, the general circumstances of it, and, more importantly, the absence on the Defendant's part of any assertion of his right or desire not to give information absent the presence of his attorney, are the main foundations for the Court's conclusion that he voluntarily waived such right.

In its lengthy opinion affirming this determination, the Iowa Supreme Court applied "the 'totality of circumstances' test for a showing of waiver of constitutionally protected rights in the absence of an express waiver," and concluded that evidence of the time element involved on the trip, the general circumstances of it, and the absence of any request or expressed desire for the aid of counsel before or at the time of giving information were sufficient to sustain a conclusion that defendant did waive his constitutional rights as alleged.

In the federal habeas corpus proceeding, the District Court, believing that the issue of waiver was not one of fact, but of federal law, held that the Iowa courts had "applied the wrong constitutional standards" in ruling that Williams had waived the protections that were his under the Constitution. The court held that it is the government which bears a heavy burden but that is the burden which explicitly was placed on Williams by the state courts.

After carefully reviewing the evidence, the District Court concluded that there is no affirmative indication that Williams did waive his rights. The state courts' emphasis on the absence of a demand for counsel was not only legally inappropriate, but factually unsupportable, as well, since Detective Leaming himself testified that Williams, on several occasions during the trip, indicated that he would talk after he saw Mr. McKnight. Both these statements and Mr. Kelly's statement to Detective Leaming that Williams would talk only after seeing Mr. McKnight in Des Moines certainly were assertions of Williams' "right or desire not to give information absent the presence of his attorney." Moreover, the statements were obtained only after Detective Leaming's use of psychology on a person whom he knew to be deeply religious and an escapee from a mental hospital—with the specific intent to elicit incriminating statements. In the face of this evidence, the State has produced no affirmative evidence whatsoever to support its claim of waiver, so it cannot be said that the State has met its "heavy burden" of showing a knowing and intelligent waiver of Sixth Amendment rights.

The Court of Appeals properly approved the reasoning of the District Court when it stated that:

> A review of the record here discloses no facts to support the conclusion of the state court that Williams had waived his constitutional rights other than that he had made incriminating statements. The District Court here properly concluded that an incorrect constitutional standard had been applied by the state court in determining the issue of waiver.
>
> The U.S. Supreme Court recently held that an accused can voluntarily, knowingly and intelligently waive his right to have counsel present at an interrogation after counsel has been appointed. The prosecution, however, has the weighty obligation to show that the waiver was knowingly and intelligently made. We quite agree that the state here failed to so show this.

The District Court and the Court of Appeals were correct in their understanding that the burden is upon the government to prove that the defendants made "an intentional relinquishment or abandonment of a known right or privilege." We have said that the right to counsel does not depend upon a request by the defendant, and that courts indulge in every reasonable presumption against waiver. This strict standard applies equally to an alleged waiver of the right to counsel whether at trial or at a critical stage of pretrial proceedings.

It is true that Williams had been informed of and appeared to understand his right to counsel. But waiver requires not merely comprehension, but relinquishment, and Williams' consistent reliance upon the advice of counsel in dealing with the authorities refutes any suggestion that he waived that right. He consulted McKnight by long-distance telephone before turning himself in. He spoke with McKnight by telephone again shortly after being booked. After he was arraigned, Williams sought out and obtained legal advice from Kelly. Williams again consulted with Kelly after Detective Leaming and his fellow officer arrived in Davenport. Throughout, Williams was advised not to make any statements before seeing McKnight in Des Moines, and was assured that the police had agreed not to question him. His statements while in the car that he would tell the whole story after seeing McKnight in Des Moines were the clearest expressions by Williams himself that he desired the presence of an attorney before any interrogation took place. But even before making these statements, Williams had effectively asserted his right to counsel by having secured attorneys at both ends of the automobile trip, both of whom, acting as his agents, had made clear to the police that no interrogation was to occur during the journey. Williams knew of that agreement and, particularly in view of his consistent reliance on counsel, there is no basis for concluding that he disavowed it.

Despite Williams' express and implicit assertions of his right to counsel, Detective Leaming proceeded to elicit incriminating statements from Williams. Leaming did not preface this effort by telling Williams that he had a right to the presence of a lawyer, and made no effort at all to ascertain whether Williams wished to relinquish that right. The circumstances of record in this case thus provide no reasonable basis for finding that Williams waived his right to the assistance of counsel.

The crime of which Williams was convicted was senseless and brutal, calling for swift and energetic action by the police to apprehend the perpetrator and gather evidence with which he could be convicted. No mission of law enforcement officials is more important. Yet disinterested zeal for the public good does not assure either wisdom or right in the methods it pursues. Although we do not lightly affirm the issuance of a writ of habeas corpus in this case, so clear a violation of the Sixth and Fourteenth Amendments as here occurred cannot be condoned. The pressures on state executive and judicial officers charged with the administration of the criminal law are great, especially when the crime is murder and the victim a small child. But it is precisely the predictability of those pressures that makes imperative a resolute loyalty to the guarantees that the Constitution extends to us all.

END OF OPINION

In this case, even though the police officer was not directly asking any questions of the accused, the "Christian burial speech" was still construed as a custodial interrogation because it was deliberately made by law enforcement with the intention of convincing a suspect, who was in custody in the back of a patrol car and who already had asserted his right to counsel and right to remain silent, to talk to the police and provide incriminating evidence. Williams had never voluntarily waived his right to an attorney or his right to remain silent, and the "Christian burial speech" was considered a way to psychologically coerce a person who had asserted those rights into talking.

This brings us back to *Miranda* warnings. When must *Miranda* warnings be issued? *Miranda* warnings must be issued whenever:

1. a person is in custody (meaning not free to leave), and

2. prior to any interrogation—including both explicit questioning as well as implicit actions designed to psychologically induce a person to provide evidence against him/herself.

Both criteria—interrogation and custody—must be present. If one or both of these criteria does not exist, then there is no requirement for law enforcement to give a person a *Miranda* warning. The mere fact that a person is being arrested does not require law enforcement to Mirandize the person; if and only if law enforcement are going to interrogate the person while that person is in custody, must law enforcement provide the *Miranda* warning.

If law enforcement interrogates a person who is in custody without giving a *Miranda* warning, it is presumed that the statements made were the product of coercion. However, if a person gives a statement after being Mirandized, and without requesting an attorney or asserting the right to remain silent, then the presumption is that the statements were made knowingly, voluntarily, and intelligibly.

Review Questions

Test your understanding by examining the following hypothetical fact patterns. In each situation, use the IRAC analysis approach to determine how much, if any, of the evidence is admissible.

1. Officer Brown hears gunfire coming from inside a house. He runs inside the house and observes Phil holding a smoking gun over the lifeless body of Helga. Officer Brown places handcuffs on Phil and leads Phil into the patrol car. Using the IRAC analysis, determine whether, while Phil is sitting in the back of the patrol car, Officer Brown must give Phil a *Miranda* warning.

2. Changing the facts slightly: This time, while driving him to the station, Officer Brown strikes up a conversation with Phil. During the conversation, Officer Brown asks, "So, mind telling me why you did it?" Phil answers, giving a full confession. Perform an IRAC analysis to determine if the confession is admissible.

3. Officer Brown hears gunfire coming from inside a house. He runs inside the house and observes Phil holding a smoking gun over the lifeless body of Helga. Officer Brown places handcuffs on Phil and leads Phil into the patrol car. While Phil is sitting in the back of the patrol car, Officer Brown says to him, "Before I can hear your side of the story, I need to give you what is called your rights warning. Now, I must advise you that you do have the right to remain silent, and anything you say can be used against you in court. You also have a right to an attorney. It is okay if you cannot afford an attorney; if that is the case, one will be appointed for you. Now, do you understand these rights as I have read them?"

Phil: Yeah, Officer, I understand these rights.

Officer Brown: Okay. Do you want to tell me your side of the story?

Phil: Yeah. The bitch attacked me.

Officer Brown: Bitches be crazy, man. Sometimes my wife does that, and I have to smack her down and show her who's boss. Especially when she won't shut up.

Phil: Tell me about it. So many times, I've had to put the bitch in her place. The bitch totally had it coming. She would not stop nagging me.

Officer Brown: My wife's the same. God, I've wanted to kill her myself so many times.

Phil: You're preaching to the choir, officer. She just wouldn't shut up tonight, and I just got tired of her yelling at me so I grabbed my gun.

Officer Brown: Yeah, I know. That's when you shot her. Right?

Phil: Yeah.

Officer Brown: While she was yelling at you?

Phil: Yeah.

Officer Brown: Was she doing anything besides yelling at the moment you shot her?

Phil: No.

Officer Brown: So you shot her when she wasn't doing anything else annoying?

Phil: Right.

Officer Brown: It was earlier that night when she came at you?

Phil: Yep.

Officer Brown: And you were pissed at her and needed to show her who the boss was?

Phil: Damn straight.

Officer Brown: So that was when you got your gun?

Phil: Right.

Officer Brown: And at that point you shot her?

Phil: Right.

IRAC if this confessions is admissible.

4. Officer Brown hears gunfire coming from inside a house. He runs inside the house and observes Phil holding a smoking gun over the lifeless body of Helga. Officer Brown places handcuffs on Phil and leads Phil into the patrol car. While Phil is sitting in the back of the patrol car, Officer Brown says to him, "Before I can hear your side of the story, I need to give you what is called your rights warning. Now, I must advise you that you do have the right to remain silent, and anything you say can be used against you in court. You also have a right to an attorney. It is okay if you cannot afford an attorney: if that is the case, one will be appointed for you. Now, do you understand these rights as I have read them?"

Phil: Yeah, Officer, I understand these rights.

Officer Brown. Okay. Do you want to tell me your side of the story?

Phil: Yeah. Bitch came at me with a knife. I had to protect myself.

Officer Brown then pulls out his gun and points it at Phil's head, and screams at him, "You lying piece of crud. Tell me the truth or I will splatter your brains across the back of my patrol car." Immediately, Phil confesses to the officer that he had in fact shot his wife because he lost his temper during an argument, and she had not come at him with a knife. Is this confession admissible?

5. Officer Brown receives a tip that Eileen is dealing marijuana, but it is not enough to get a warrant. He goes the public park where Eileen likes to play basketball and sees her sitting on the park bench. He takes a seat next to her and simply says, "Where do you keep your marijuana?" A stunned Eileen denies having any drugs, to which Officer Brown, still seated on the park bench, states, "We can either do this the easy way or the hard way. Tell me where you keep your marijuana, and I'll go easy on you." Eileen panics and tells Officer Brown that she keeps her marijuana in her gym bag, which she opens (showing him the marijuana) and hands over to him. Based on this admission, Officer Brown arrests Eileen for felony drug distribution. In a

short answer, are her confession and the evidence derived from it (fruit of the poisonous tree) admissible despite her not having received a *Miranda* warning?

6. Tommy, a known felon, is pacing in front of a liquor store, peering in the windows. Officer Swanson, an experienced police officer who recognizes Tommy as a convicted felon, observes Tommy's actions. Based on Officer Swanson's experience and training as a police officer, he develops a reasonable suspicion that Tommy is planning to rob the liquor store. Officer Swanson conducts a stop-and-frisk on Tommy and discovers a gun. He seizes the gun and places handcuffs on Tommy, arresting him for being a felon in possession of a firearm. As he leads Tommy to the patrol car, he asks, "What were you going to do with the gun?" to which Tommy responds, "I was going to rob that liquor store." Based on Tommy's statement, he is charged with attempted robbery. In his trial for attempted robbery, is Tommy's statement admissible?

7. Sandy is walking down the street when Officer Rivers steps in front of her and orders Sandy to face the wall. While Sandy is facing the wall, Officer Rivers frisks Sandy and during her search, feels an item resembling a Ziploc bag of pills inside a pocket. Officer Rivers reaches into the pocket and pulls out a Ziploc bag containing a hundred OxyContin. Officer Rivers issues Sandy a *Miranda* warning, after which Sandy affirmatively indicates that she wishes to waive her rights and talk to the police officer. "What are you going to do with all these pills?" Officer Rivers asks. "I sell them to people for $5 a pill," Sandy replies. Sandy is consequently prosecuted for drug distribution. IRAC if Sandy's confession is admissible.

Public Safety Exception

There is one notable exception to the requirement of the *Miranda* warning we want to discuss now because it has a great deal of relevance to homeland and national security cases. This is the "public safety exception." This exception applies where the interests of public safety are so compelling that the courts have determined that police can interrogate a person without first issuing a *Miranda* warning, even if the facts and circumstances otherwise would clearly meet the *Miranda* threshold of a custodial interrogation. The public safety exception is explained in the following case.

New York v. Quarles, 467 U.S. 649 (1984)*

Benjamin Quarles was charged in the New York trial court with criminal possession of a weapon. The trial court suppressed the gun in question, and a statement made by Quarles, because the statement was obtained by police before they read respondent his "*Miranda* rights." That ruling was affirmed on appeal through the New York Court of Appeals. We granted review, and we now reverse. We conclude that under the circumstances involved in this case, overriding considerations of

---

* The case has been heavily edited and paraphrased by the authors for clarity. See disclaimer in introduction.

public safety justify the officer's failure to provide *Miranda* warnings before he asked questions devoted to locating the abandoned weapon.

On September 11, 1980, at approximately 12:30 a.m., Officer Frank Kraft and Officer Sal Scarring were on road patrol in Queens, N.Y., when a young woman approached their car. She told them that she had just been raped by a black male, approximately six feet tall, who was wearing a black jacket with the name "Big Ben" printed in yellow letters on the back. She told the officers that the man had just entered an A & P supermarket located nearby and that the man was carrying a gun.

The officers drove the woman to the supermarket, and Officer Kraft entered the store while Officer Scarring radioed for assistance. Officer Kraft quickly spotted respondent, who matched the description given by the woman, approaching a checkout counter. Apparently upon seeing the officer, respondent turned and ran toward the rear of the store, and Officer Kraft pursued him with a drawn gun. When respondent turned the corner at the end of an aisle, Officer Kraft lost sight of him for several seconds, and upon regaining sight of respondent, ordered him to stop and put his hands over his head.

Although more than three other officers had arrived on the scene by that time, Officer Kraft was the first to reach respondent. He frisked him and discovered that he was wearing a shoulder holster which was then empty. After handcuffing him, Officer Kraft asked him where the gun was. Respondent nodded in the direction of some empty cartons and responded, "the gun is over there." Officer Kraft thereafter retrieved a loaded .38-caliber revolver from one of the cartons, formally placed respondent under arrest, and read him his *Miranda* rights from a printed card. Respondent indicated that he would be willing to answer questions without an attorney present. Officer Kraft then asked respondent if he owned the gun and where he had purchased it. Respondent answered that he did own it and that he had purchased it in Miami, Fla.

In the subsequent prosecution of respondent for criminal possession of a weapon, the judge excluded the statement, "the gun is over there," and the gun because the officer had not given respondent the warnings required by our decision in *Miranda v. Arizona*, before asking him where the gun was located. The judge excluded the other statements about respondent's ownership of the gun and the place of purchase, as evidence tainted by the prior *Miranda* violation. The Appellate Division of the Supreme Court of New York affirmed without opinion.

The Court of Appeals granted leave to appeal and affirmed by a 4-3 vote. It concluded that respondent was in "custody" within the meaning of *Miranda* during all questioning and rejected the State's argument that the exigencies of the situation justified Officer Kraft's failure to read respondent his *Miranda* rights until after he had located the gun. The court declined to recognize an exigency exception to the usual requirements of *Miranda* because it found no indication from Officer Kraft's testimony at the suppression hearing that his subjective motivation in asking the question was to protect his own safety or the safety of the public.

For the reasons which follow, we believe that this case presents a situation where concern for public safety must be paramount to adherence to the literal language of the prophylactic rules enunciated in *Miranda*. The Fifth Amendment guarantees that "no person . . . shall be compelled in any criminal case to be a witness against himself." In *Miranda* this Court for the first time extended the Fifth Amendment privilege against compulsory self-incrimination to individuals subjected to custodial interrogation by the police. The Fifth Amendment itself does not prohibit all incriminating admissions, for absent some officially coerced self-accusation, the Fifth Amendment privilege is not violated by even the most damning admissions. The *Miranda* Court, however, presumed that interrogation in certain custodial circumstances is inherently coercive and held that statements made under those circumstances are inadmissible unless the suspect is specifically informed of his *Miranda* rights and freely decides to forgo those rights. The prophylactic *Miranda* warnings therefore are not themselves rights protected by the Constitution but are instead measures to insure that the right against compulsory self-incrimination is protected. Requiring *Miranda* warnings before custodial interrogation provides "practical reinforcement" for the Fifth Amendment right.

In this case we have before us no claim that Quarles' statements were actually compelled by police conduct which overcame his will to resist. Thus the only issue before us is whether Officer Kraft was justified in failing to make available to respondent the procedural safeguards associated with the privilege against compulsory self-incrimination since *Miranda*.

The New York Court of Appeals was undoubtedly correct in deciding that the facts of this case come within the ambit of the *Miranda* decision as we have subsequently interpreted it. We agree that Quarles was in police custody because we have noted that "the ultimate inquiry is simply whether there is a 'formal arrest or restraint on freedom of movement' of the degree associated with a formal arrest." Here Quarles was surrounded by at least four police officers and was handcuffed when the questioning at issue took place. As the New York Court of Appeals observed, there was nothing to suggest that any of the officers were any longer concerned for their own physical safety. The New York Court of Appeals' majority declined to express an opinion as to whether there might be an exception to the *Miranda* rule if the police had been acting to protect the public, because the lower courts in New York had made no factual determination that the police had acted with that motive.

We hold that on these facts there is a "public safety" exception to the requirement that *Miranda* warnings be given before a suspect's answers may be admitted into evidence, and that the availability of that exception does not depend upon the motivation of the individual officers involved. In a kaleidoscopic situation such as the one confronting these officers, where spontaneity rather than adherence to a police manual is necessarily the order of the day, the application of the exception which we recognize today should not be made to depend on post hoc findings at a suppression hearing concerning the subjective motivation of the arresting officer.

Undoubtedly most police officers, if placed in Officer Kraft's position, would act out of a host of different, instinctive, and largely unverifiable motives—their own safety, the safety of others, and perhaps as well the desire to obtain incriminating evidence from the suspect.

Whatever the motivation of individual officers in such a situation, we do not believe that the doctrinal underpinnings of *Miranda* require that it be applied in all its rigor to a situation in which police officers ask questions reasonably prompted by a concern for the public safety. The *Miranda* decision was based in large part on this Court's view that the warnings which it required police to give to suspects in custody would reduce the likelihood that the suspects would fall victim to constitutionally impermissible practices of police interrogation in the presumptively coercive environment of the station house. The dissenters warned that the requirement of *Miranda* warnings would have the effect of decreasing the number of suspects who respond to police questioning. The *Miranda* majority, however, apparently felt that whatever the cost to society in terms of fewer convictions of guilty suspects, that cost would simply have to be borne in the interest of enlarged protection for the Fifth Amendment privilege.

The police in this case, in the very act of apprehending a suspect, were confronted with the immediate necessity of ascertaining the whereabouts of a gun which they had every reason to believe the suspect had just removed from his empty holster and discarded in the supermarket. So long as the gun was concealed somewhere in the supermarket, with its actual whereabouts unknown, it obviously posed more than one danger to the public safety: an accomplice might make use of it, a customer or employee might later come upon it.

In such a situation, if the police are required to recite the familiar *Miranda* warnings before asking the whereabouts of the gun, suspects in Quarles' position might well be deterred from responding. Procedural safeguards which deter a suspect from responding were deemed acceptable in *Miranda* in order to protect the Fifth Amendment privilege; when the primary social cost of those added protections is the possibility of fewer convictions, the *Miranda* majority was willing to bear that cost. Here, had *Miranda* warnings deterred Quarles from responding to Officer Kraft's question about the whereabouts of the gun, the cost would have been something more than merely the failure to obtain evidence useful in convicting Quarles. Officer Kraft needed an answer to his question not simply to make his case against Quarles but to insure that further danger to the public did not result from the concealment of the gun in a public area.

We conclude that the need for answers to questions in a situation posing a threat to the public safety outweighs the need for the prophylactic rule protecting the Fifth Amendment's privilege against self-incrimination. We decline to place officers such as Officer Kraft in the untenable position of having to consider, often in a matter of seconds, whether it best serves society for them to ask the necessary questions without the *Miranda* warnings and render whatever probative evidence they uncover inadmissible, or for them to give the warnings in order to preserve the admissibility of evidence they might uncover but possibly damage or destroy their ability to obtain that evidence and neutralize the volatile situation confronting them.

In recognizing a narrow exception to the *Miranda* rule in this case, we acknowledge that to some degree we lessen the desirable clarity of that rule. At least in part in order to preserve its clarity, we have over the years refused to sanction attempts to expand our *Miranda* holding. As we have in other contexts, we recognize here the importance of a workable rule "to guide police officers, who have only limited time and expertise to reflect on and balance the social and individual interests involved in the specific circumstances they confront." But as we have pointed out, we believe that the exception which we recognize today lessens the necessity of that on-the-scene balancing process. The exception will not be difficult for police officers to apply because in each case it will be circumscribed by the exigency which justifies it. We think police officers can and will distinguish almost instinctively between questions necessary to secure their own safety or the safety of the public and questions designed solely to elicit testimonial evidence from a suspect.

The facts of this case clearly demonstrate that distinction and an officer's ability to recognize it. Officer Kraft asked only the question necessary to locate the missing gun before advising Quarles of his rights. It was only after securing the loaded revolver and giving the warnings that he continued with investigatory questions about the ownership and place of purchase of the gun. The exception which we recognize today, far from complicating the thought processes and the on-the-scene judgments of police officers, will simply free them to follow their legitimate instincts when confronting situations presenting a danger to the public safety.

We hold that the Court of Appeals in this case erred in excluding the statement, "the gun is over there," and the gun because of the officer's failure to read respondent his *Miranda* rights before attempting to locate the weapon. Accordingly we hold that it also erred in excluding the subsequent statements as illegal fruits of a *Miranda* violation. We therefore reverse and remand for further proceedings not inconsistent with this opinion

END OF OPINION

In *Quarles* the U.S. Supreme Court stated that a gun lying around a grocery store where anyone could pick it up and accidentally hurt someone was a threat to public safety, so the failure to not "Mirandize" Quarles prior to asking him where the gun was located was justified. Remember, the receipt of a *Miranda* warning is not the constitutional right; it is merely a court-imposed preventative measure to minimize the likelihood of coercive behavior by police and to otherwise help individuals safeguard their constitutional rights to remain silent and to have the assistance of an attorney. It is a case of the Court balancing important legal and social interests—and in certain cases the risk to society in the facts giving rise to the public safety exception overcome the interest in making sure people have that "break" in questioning that the *Miranda* rights provide.

A confession taken in the absence of a *Miranda* warning is presumed to be coercive, but that is a presumption that can be overcome by the facts. And in this case, the facts supported a finding of voluntariness. Quarles still had his Fifth Amendment right to remain silent. He could have chosen not to answer the police officer's questions as to where the gun was located. There was no evidence that the police used any improperly coercive techniques on him (such as torture or the threat of torture)—the facts were clear that he was simply questioned. So the fact that he chose to waive that right was his decision, and not the result of undue coercion by the police, and the statement was admissible.

Now, had there been some evidence that the police used undue coercion, such as threatening him with violence unless he told them where the gun was, or used psychological incentives designed to prey on his religious beliefs, or some other tactic, then his statement would likely have been suppressed. But, so long as the facts support a finding of voluntariness free of coercion, so long as the Fifth Amendment right is not truly being violated, the courts will hold the procedural safeguard of *Miranda* secondary to any concerns about public safety.

This public safety exception is very limited, and there have only been a handful of times where it has been invoked. In *U.S. v. Talley*,[4] the police used it to question a person as to the location of a gun after seeing stray bullets. In another case, *U.S. v. Jones*,[5] a law enforcement official asked a person he was arresting, who was reported to have been carrying a gun, if the suspect had anything on him, to which the person admitted to having a gun on him. In all three of these cases, *Quarles*, *Talley*, and *Jones*, the police already had prior evidence as to the existence of a gun. This is significant because it means that the very reason they were asking questions was not a fishing expedition for criminal evidence, but because they had reason to believe that there was a dangerous object, a firearm, which was unsecured by law enforcement.

In another example, *U.S. v. Khalil*,[6] the NYPD raided an apartment and discovered pipe bombs. They questioned the suspects about the bombs including the number of bombs, how they could be detonated, and how to disarm them. This was upheld as part of the public safety exception for the police had good evidence that the bombs existed (they had seen them!), and that the questions they were asking were limited to matters involving only public safety. There is no question that possible bombs lying around are a threat to public safety.

Review Questions

Perform an IRAC analysis on some hypotheticals to test your understanding of the public safety exception.

1. Officer Brown is walking down the street as he hears gunshots coming from inside a Chipotle. Officer Brown rushes inside the Chipotle and sees a suspect fleeing into the kitchen. Officer Brown runs after the suspect, chasing him through the kitchen. The suspect slips on some guacamole on the floor and falls. Officer Brown

---

4. 275 F.3d 560 (2001).
5. USCA, DC Cir, No. 07-3070, Decided: June 9, 2009.
6. *United States v. Khalil*, 214 F.3d 111, 121–22 (2d Cir. 2000).

jumps on the suspect, immobilizing him. Officer Brown quickly places handcuffs on the suspect and then frisks him, but does not feel a gun. "Where's the gun?" Officer Brown asks. "I threw it in the trash back there," the suspect says. In court, the suspect's lawyer insists that the statement indicating the location of the gun be ruled inadmissible because it was made during custodial interrogation without him being Mirandized. How should the judge rule?

2. Officer Brown is walking down the street and as he goes past a Chipotle, he sees through the window a woman smoking a joint at her table. As soon as the woman notices the police officer watching her, she takes off running in the direction of the kitchen. Officer Brown enters the Chipotle and runs after her. She slips on some guacamole on the floor and falls. Officer Brown jumps on her, immobilizing her. Officer Brown quickly places handcuffs on the suspect and then frisks her, but does not feel anything illegal. "Where's the joint?" Officer Brown asks. The woman informs Officer Brown that she threw it in the trash bin in the kitchen. In court, the suspect's lawyer insists that the statement indicating the location of the joint be ruled inadmissible because it was made during custodial interrogation without her being Mirandized. How should the judge rule?

3. Officer Brown is walking down the street as he hears gunshots coming from inside a Chipotle. Officer Brown rushes inside the Chipotle and sees a suspect fleeing into the kitchen. Officer Brown runs after the suspect, chasing him through the kitchen. The suspect slips on some guacamole on the floor and falls. Officer Brown jumps on the suspect, immobilizing him. Officer Brown quickly places handcuffs on the suspect and then frisks him, but does not feel a gun. "Where's the gun?" Officer Brown asks. "I ain't saying nothing, pig!" the suspect screams. Officer Brown replies, "Tell me where it is, or I will taze your ass until you piss yourself." The suspect immediately tells Officer Brown where he had placed the gun. In court, will this statement be admissible?

Application of the *Quarles* Public Safety Exception to Terrorism Cases

The *Quarles* exception has recently gained new footing in dealing with terrorism suspects. Since the attacks on September 11, 2001, and the rise of transnational terror organizations such as Al-Qaeda, al Shabaab, and the so-called Islamic State (also known as Da'esh, ISIS, and ISIL), there has been an interest in being able to interrogate terrorism suspects for intelligence about other possible impending attacks, and a concern that using the standard law enforcement interrogation techniques would result in the suspect refusing to talk, with potentially disastrous results. In the weeks and months immediately following the attacks, suspects were considered detainees under the laws of armed conflict, and so outside any protection of the constitutional rights provided by the Fifth and Sixth Amendments.

Following a series of Supreme Court cases holding that suspects taken into custody and held outside of a traditional battlefield context were entitled to some level of due process, disclosure of torture and other coercive interrogation practices, and difficulties in trying terrorism suspects at military commissions, even terrorism suspects were increasingly handled using traditional law enforcement processes.[7]

In a series of cases involving an attempt to detonate a bomb onboard an airliner (the so-called "underwear bomber," Umar Farouk Abdulmutallab) and others, the practice has arisen for law enforcement to conduct an initial interrogation without providing a *Miranda* warning. The purpose of this interrogation is to ascertain whether there is any information of other imminent attacks that the suspect may be aware of. Then a new group of investigators—with no knowledge of anything the suspect may have said in the first interrogation—is brought in. A *Miranda* warning is given and a new interrogation begins. In some cases the accused has continued to talk, in others he has requested counsel and refused to talk without counsel available. Of interest, though, in all of the reported cases, the suspect has, even after having counsel present, continued to cooperate with authorities.

This practice, though successful in both gaining prosecutions and useful information, has been criticized by civil libertarians who see the process as an "end run" around the requirements of *Miranda*, and by those who simply feel that all terrorism cases should be handled outside of the law enforcement paradigm and instead as military detainees. In any case, it appears that this practice is likely to continue.[8]

Impact of *Miranda* Warnings, Waiver, and Interrogation Tactics

Whenever the police wish to question a person in custody, they must issue a *Miranda* warning. It is strongly recommended, and most jurisdictions require, that the warning not only be given orally, but also in writing with a place for suspects to sign to indicate that they wish to waive their rights to remain silent and have an attorney, and that they agree to talk to the police. That documentation makes it harder for a suspect to lie and claim the police never issued him a *Miranda* warning, or that his waiver was involuntary, when his signature is there on the written waiver.

After the warning is given, suspects will generally indicate whether or not they wish to talk. If they consent to talk, any statements they make can and will be used

---

7. More details can be found in sources such as Charlie Savage's book *Power Wars—Inside Obama's Post 9/11 Presidency*, Little, Brown and Company (November 3, 2015).

8. There are a number of articles that provide more detail about the practice, the cases in which it has been used, and the concerns from both sides of the issue. See, for example, Corn, Geoffrey S. and Jenks, Chris, "Strange Bedfellows: How Expanding the Public Safety Exception to Miranda Benefits Counterterrorism Suspects" (October 8, 2013), available at SSRN: http://ssrn.com/abstract=2337514 or http://dx.doi.org/10.2139/ssrn.2337514; Nielsen, Elizabeth, "The *Quarles* Public Safety Exception in Terrorism Cases. Reviving the Marshall Dissent," American University Criminal Law Brief 7, no. 2 (2012):19–38; and Wright, Joanna, "Applying *Miranda*'s Public Safety Exception to Dzhokhar Tsarnaev: Restricting Criminal Procedure Rights by Expanding Judicial Exceptions," (September 28, 2013), *Columbia Law Review Sidebar*, Vol. 113, p. 136, September 2013, available at SSRN: http://ssrn.com/abstract=2333989.

against them. At any point during the conversation, a suspect can choose to assert the right to remain silent or the right to an attorney. This may happen—usually too late, right after the suspect realizes they have said something incriminating. Nevertheless, if at any point during questioning the person does assert his right to remain silent or asks for an attorney, then the police must immediately cease questioning. Any further questioning by the police is not allowed, and statements derived from it are normally considered inadmissible.

Nor can the police make any other statements to try to convince a person who has asserted his rights to change his mind. Examples would be an officer saying to a person who has just asserted his right to remain silent or just made a request for an attorney, "I will respect your wish to remain silent / have an attorney. I just feel sorry for you because this makes you look guilty, and I will be unable to help you by telling the judge you were cooperative." This type of subtle coercion after a person has asserted his rights is impermissible, and any statements made afterwards would be inadmissible. However, any statements made up to that point would be admissible.

It is important to note that one's *Miranda* rights must be affirmatively asserted by suspects. If a person actually just sits in silence, it is considered a *Miranda* waiver by acquiescence, and the police can continue to ask questions. A person that wants the interrogation to stop must affirmatively state that he or she wishes to remain silent or would like an attorney present. The assertion must be clear and non-ambiguous. For example, let's say that a suspect named Burnet was arrested on suspicion of rape, and after being Mirandized, he signed a document indicating he wanted to waive his rights and then started talking to the police. As he spoke to the police, he made numerous incriminating statements. In the middle of it, he asked the police, "Do I need a lawyer?" The police immediately stopped asking him questions about the case. What the police did was responded by saying, "That is up to you." Burnet then asked the officer interrogating him, "Where do I get a lawyer?" The police told him that they did not know. Everyone in the interrogation room sat in awkward silence for a while, and eventually, Burnet told the police that he would like to continue talking to them. Before asking him any more questions, the police asked if he would re-sign the document indicating that he consented to waiving his right to remain silent and an attorney. Only after Burnet re-signed the document did the police resume asking him questions about the incident.

At trial, Burnet's lawyer challenged that the police had violated his rights when they resumed questioning after he had asked for a lawyer. The judge disagreed, pointing out that Burnet had never actually asked for a lawyer. Instead, he asked if he needed a lawyer. This is a big difference. He never affirmatively asserted his right to an attorney (or the right to remain silent), so there was no violation of his rights. For suspects to assert their rights, they must state, "I wish to remain silent," "I would like an attorney," or some other phrase or expression which makes perfectly clear without any ambiguity that the person is asserting his or her constitutional rights.

When *Miranda v. Arizona* first came out, many people were concerned that the requirement of police having to tell suspects that they have the right to remain silent and are entitled to an attorney would result in people not talking to the police, leading to fewer confessions. Confessions are an important part of the criminal process, and it was believed that this procedural hurdle would result in fewer convictions and more criminals walking free. Although there have been circumstances where this has occurred, generally, this has not been the case.

Now, when this argument was made at the Supreme Court, the justices commented that the rule had been in place in the U.S. military since about 1920, and the military seemed to be able to function just fine, so they refused to give this argument any credence.

The justices were right — the reality is that nearly EVERYONE who is taken into custody and questioned talks to the police! That's right — despite being specifically informed of a right to remain silent and the right to have an attorney present, almost everyone who is questioned waives that right and talks to the police. Many defense attorneys will tell you that over 95% of their clients spoke to the police and made incriminating comments, even after being Mirandized. Almost as many clients will also waive their Fourth Amendment right and give police permission to search their vehicle, home, or person. Surprisingly, even people who know they have illegal materials will usually consent to police requests for a search. Even lawyers and judges who should know better also often make statements, consent to searches, or fail to ask for a lawyer.

You may be wondering, why do people, especially people who have committed crimes or know that they have incriminating evidence on them, waive their constitutional rights concerning searches, silence, and an attorney? There is some significant research on this, and the researchers have concluded that there are many reasons.[9] When it comes to searches, many people mistakenly believe that the police are going to search them anyway, so they figure that they might as well be cooperative. The reality is that if the police are asking for permission to do a search, it is because they probably need permission. (Still, even if police do believe they have legal authority to do a search without permission, it is still a good idea to ask permission anyway just in case the officer is mistaken in her legal judgment.) Another reason why many people waive their rights is because they think it would look suspicious to not give the police permission to conduct a search, to assert the right to remain silent, or to ask for an attorney. This is an error, because legally, refusing to consent to a search, remaining silent, or asking for an attorney cannot be used against someone or be a cause of suspicion. The police may not use a person's assertion of his or her rights as a basis to form any suspicion. For example, if a police officer asks to search a vehicle and a person refuses, the police cannot use the refusal in determining whether or not he has probable cause to search. A judicial officer also cannot use the refusal of a person to consent to a search or talk to the police in determining if there is probable cause to issue a search or arrest warrant.

---

9. See, for example, Richard A. Leo, "Inside the Interrogation Room," 86 J. Crim. L. & Criminology 266 (1995–1996), and Richard A. Leo, *Police Interrogation and American Justice*, Harvard University Press, 2008.

Many people waive their *Miranda* rights because they believe they can talk their way out of trouble, or are anxious to learn what the police know about their crime. Sometimes, a suspect choosing to talk to the police is his way of thinking he is taking control of the situation. This almost never works. Police have special training and often years of experience at interrogations and will outmaneuver and outsmart the suspect.

Another reason why people often waive their rights is because the police have lawful ways to coerce people into waiving them. So long as the coercion is not so strong that it overrides an individual's free will (like by threats of violence or threats to split up a family), mild forms of coercion will be upheld as lawful. A popular police method used to get a suspect to waive his Fourth Amendment right is to say, "The decision is yours; we can either do this the easy way or the hard way. You can either let me search your house and I'll go easy on you, or I can come back with a warrant and search your house, and if I have to do that, I definitely will not go easy on you." It also helps that police will never refer to an interrogation as an "interrogation." Instead, they just call it an "interview" because it sounds much more pleasant for a person to be "interviewed" rather than "interrogated."

Police are also allowed to lie to suspects. During a lawful interrogation (meaning the person has either been Mirandized or the person is not in custody), the police might say to a suspect, "Just between you and me, off the record, what really happened?" The truth is that nothing said to a police officer is "off the record." Another popular police lie is, "If you just tell me where the marijuana/gun/pills are, I'll go easy on you." A variation of this lie is, "Just tell me where the marijuana/gun/pills are, and I probably won't arrest you." If the police arrest two people for a crime, they can separate them for questioning and tell both suspects, "Your friend in the next room is telling us everything and is selling you up the river. Because he has been cooperative, he'll get a good deal and you won't." Another common lie is for law enforcement to say, "I don't think you committed a crime. I just want to clear you as a possible suspect." This lie is also misleading, because no person has the burden to prove his innocence; instead, the burden is on the government to prove a person's guilt.

There are some lies which are prohibited. The lies cannot be so overwhelming so as to be unduly coercive, such as threatening to "pound you to a pulp" or "unless you cooperate, social workers will take away your kids and put them in foster homes." Threats of destruction of property or incarceration should also be avoided. Law enforcement are also prohibited from manufacturing evidence, such as making a suspect believe he is connected to a lie detector and pretending that the machine is reporting that the suspect is lying.[10]

Law enforcement can also put social pressure on suspects. People generally want to be helpful and look good in front of law enforcement. If a person does not want to waive his rights, so long as a person is not in custody, law enforcement can make

---

10. There is anecdotal evidence that, in the past in some jurisdictions, police had a tactic where they would put write the word "lie" in a copying machine and run fake wires from the machine to a suspect. They would then ask the suspect a question, and when they thought he was lying, they would hit the "copy" button which would spit out the word "lie."

comments such as "Are you actually going to be that kind of person?" or "So you don't want to be helpful and cooperate?" Putting some mild social pressure on a person is not undue coercion, which would make any waiver of rights involuntary. For example, police can encourage an individual to "man-up and take responsibility for your actions." Another police expression to pressure a person to waive right is by telling a defendant, "it does not look good for you if you don't cooperate." Legally, this is irrelevant because a refusal to waive rights cannot be held against someone.

Another trick is for law enforcement to pretend to be a sympathetic ear and on the suspect's side. As you can imagine, a suspect who thinks the police are against him is far less likely to open up and talk than a suspect who believes the police are there to help him and are on his side. For example, in a rape investigation a police officer could say something like, "I like you and want to help you. I mean, I saw that girl and she was hot. And the way she was dressed, she was just asking for it. And the way you say she was acting at the party, dancing and grinding up on people . . . I can tell she wanted it. I've heard she is a complete slut and sleeps with everyone, so I have no doubt she wanted to sleep with you and it was all consensual. I really don't think you committed any crime, but I need a record of that. I just need to get from you what happened once the two of you got back to your apartment. Once I get that information from you, I can close this case and you'll be free to go." Upon hearing that, a person who might earlier have denied having sex with an alleged rape victim might then admit to it. As the Supreme Court discussed in *Miranda*, it is a common interrogation tactic for the police officer to appear to be a friend of the suspect. Many suspects forget that the police are not there to be their friend or help them out of a legal situation; the police are there to do justice by solving a crime and help the prosecutor get a conviction.

Law enforcement also encourages people to waive their rights by telling suspects that they will put in a good word with the judge if the person cooperates. There is a lot of truth to this. In many jurisdictions, when judges sentence a person, they ask the police officers involved if the defendant had been polite, respectful, or cooperative. A police officer's input on this matter often weighs heavily with a judge in considering a sentence. Hearing that a suspect had not been rude to the police can make a major difference in the amount of a fine or time, if any, a person will spend in jail.

Despite this, no defense attorney would want a client to have spoken to the police without his permission. There are many reasons for this. First, there is the simple fact that in many cases, although cooperating with the police gets a reduced sentence, not cooperating at all would prevent a conviction in the first place! For example, if a person had not consented to a search of his vehicle, the police might have never found the drugs inside. Second, even if a person is innocent and talks to the police, the person is likely to make some small mistake or error in telling his story. Think about it; if on a Saturday morning you told your friends about a fun time you had Friday night, you would make some small error or forget something. If you tell that same story again Saturday evening, you would again make some other small error or forget something, so your story would be slightly different than what you told Saturday morning. The danger to an innocent person is that these small but natural inconsistencies will be focused on at trial as "proof" that a person is lying.

A person can be polite and respectful to the police while still asserting his rights. This can be done by a suspect telling a police officer who has asked to search his vehicle, "Officer, I respect that you are just trying to do your job, but I do not consent to any searches." Or if a person has been arrested, the suspect can say, "Officer, I would be more than happy to answer any questions you may have and assist you in your investigation. I would just like to speak with my lawyer first and assert my right to remain silent until my lawyer advises otherwise." Once a person says this, the officer cannot continue questioning and, if asked, would have to tell a judge that the person was polite and respectful. Another approach if a person is being questioned by the police is simply telling an officer, "I respectfully assert my right to remain silent." All statements should be made in a calm and polite tone. This way, when the judge asks if the person was polite and respectful, the officer would have to tell the officer he was.

Lastly, a person can always make incriminating statements against himself at a later date. The least a defendant can do is try to get a definite plea bargain in exchange for incriminating himself, rather than an abstract futuristic promise from a police officer to "go easy on him" or "put in a good word." It is much more likely that a person's attorney can get him a much better deal than anything that would result from him just talking to the police.

At this point, you have a fundamental understanding of the basics of criminal procedure in the U.S., and are prepared for a more detailed look at the Fourth Amendment and surveillance in the context of homeland and national security in the next couple of chapters.

Key Terms

Custody—Any situation where a reasonable person would not feel free to leave.

Interrogation—Asking questions, engaging in conversation, or anything said or done by law enforcement intended to elicit an incriminating response by a suspect.

Public safety exception—A situation where the interests of public safety are so compelling that the courts have determined that police can interrogate a person without first issuing a *Miranda* warning, even if the facts and circumstances otherwise would clearly meet the *Miranda* threshold of a custodial interrogation.

Further Reading

Corn, Geoffrey S. and Jenks, Chris, *Strange Bedfellows: How Expanding the Public Safety Exception to Miranda Benefits Counterterrorism Suspects* (October 8, 2013). Available at SSRN: http://ssrn.com/abstract=2337514 or http://dx.doi.org/10.2139/ssrn.2337514

Schaedig, Christopher R., *Protecting the Worst Among Us: A Narrow Quarles Public Safety Exception in the Boston Bombing and Other Terror Investigations* (July 30, 2013). Available at SSRN: http://ssrn.com/abstract=2312608 or http://dx.doi.org/10.2139/ssrn.2312608.

Chapter 4

Search and Seizure Law and Technology

Overview

In the next two chapters, we are going to examine search and seizure law in the context of homeland and national security a bit more closely. This chapter will look at the impact of technology on search and seizure law, while Chapter 5 will examine how the law applies in the context of foreign intelligence and foreign law enforcement efforts.

To start with, let's review the Fourth Amendment:

> The Right of the people to be secure in their persons, houses, papers, and effects, against unreasonable searches and seizures, shall not be violated, and no warrants shall issue, but upon probable cause, supported by oath or affirmation, and particularly describing the place to be searched, and the persons or things to be seized.

The Fourth Amendment was ratified in 1789, long before computers, cell phones, or even the telegraph. "Persons, houses, papers, and effects" pretty much covered it. Telecommunications, airborne cameras, and other forms of electronic surveillance were concepts of which the founding fathers had no idea at the time they were writing the Bill of Rights. Back then, the only way to intercept a communication was by opening someone else's mail, going through another person's files, or having a well-placed person eavesdropping on a conversation. Also in 1789, a search could only be performed by physically going through one's personal belongings (papers, purse, luggage, etc.) or physically entering one's property (house, barn, office, etc.) and looking around.

In contrast, people today communicate using landline telephones, cellular phones, email, texts, and faxes, any of which can be intercepted and permanently recorded by an expert, either one employed by the government or one working for your telecommunications service provider. In addition, people often store large quantities of highly personal information on their computers, tablets, and cell phones, and information is also stored in "cloud" electronic storage maintained by a third party. This information all can be accessed by those with the right skills and might be benevolent systems administrators, government agents, or criminals. All this can be done while the technician is located thousands of miles away and without the subject of the search ever knowing that his or her privacy was invaded.

So how does the Fourth Amendment apply in the face of this technology? Up until fairly recently, the Fourth Amendment did not apply to electronic communication at all. In 1928, in the case *Olmstead v. United States*, the Supreme Court held that the Fourth Amendment did not even apply to a wiretap, and so there was no search and seizure as far as the Constitution was concerned. As you will read below, because the communication travelled outside of the home, it was considered to be outside the protection of the Fourth Amendment.

Now, this is not true today. The decision in *Olmstead* was later overturned by another decision we'll read in this chapter, *Katz v. United States*. Nevertheless, *Olmstead* is an important piece of legal history, and this decision helped develop the framework of how we look at the Fourth Amendment and electronic surveillance. The rationale of the Court in *Olmstead* was very much the prevailing view in society, and so to understand how we got to where we are in the law (and perhaps begin thinking about how the law still needs to develop), this is an important case. Nevertheless, remember that *Olmstead* is no longer good law and does not apply today.

Olmstead v. United States, 277 U.S. 438 (1928)*

The question is whether the use of evidence of private telephone conversations between the defendants and others, intercepted by means of wiretapping, amounted to a violation of the Fourth Amendment.

The petitioners were convicted for conspiracy to violate the National Prohibition Act by unlawfully possessing, transporting and importing intoxicating liquors and maintaining nuisances, and by selling intoxicating liquors. Seventy-two others in addition to the petitioners were indicted. Some were not apprehended, some were acquitted, and others pleaded guilty.

The evidence in the records discloses a conspiracy of amazing magnitude to import, possess and sell liquor unlawfully. It involved the employment of not less than fifty persons, of two seagoing vessels for the transportation of liquor to British Columbia, of smaller vessels for coastwise transportation to the State of Washington, the purchase and use of a ranch beyond the suburban limits of Seattle, with a large underground cache for storage and a number of smaller caches in that city, the maintenance of a central office manned with operators, the employment of executives, salesmen, deliverymen, dispatchers, scouts, bookkeepers, collectors and an attorney. In a bad month, sales amounted to $176,000; the aggregate for a year must have exceeded two millions of dollars.

Olmstead was the leading conspirator and the general manager of the business. . . . Of the several offices in Seattle, the chief one was in a large office building. In this there were three telephones on three different lines. There were telephones in an office of the manager in his own home, at the homes of his associates, and at other places in the city. Communication was had frequently with Vancouver, British Columbia.

---

* The case has been heavily edited and paraphrased by the authors for clarity. See disclaimer in introduction.

Times were fixed for the deliveries of the "stuff," to places along Puget Sound near Seattle, and from there the liquor was removed and deposited in caches.

One of the chief men was always on duty at the main office to receive orders by telephones and to direct their filling by a corps of men stationed in another room— the "bull pen." The call numbers of the telephones were given to those known to be likely customers. At times, the sales amounted to 200 cases of liquor per day.

The information which led to the discovery of the conspiracy and its nature and extent was largely obtained by intercepting messages on the telephones of the conspirators by four federal prohibition officers. Small wires were inserted along the ordinary telephone wires from the residences of four of the petitioners and those leading from the chief office. The insertions were made without trespass upon any property of the defendants. They were made in the basement of the large office building. The taps from house lines were made in the streets near the houses.

The gathering of evidence continued for many months. Conversations of the conspirators, of which refreshing stenographic notes were currently made, were testified to by the government witnesses. They revealed the large business transactions of the partners and their subordinates. Men at the wires heard the orders given for liquor by customers and the acceptances; they became auditors of the conversations between the partners. All this disclosed the conspiracy charged in the indictment. Many of the intercepted conversations were not merely reports, but parts of the criminal acts. The evidence also disclosed the difficulties to which the conspirators were subjected, the reported news of the capture of vessels, the arrest of their men and the seizure of cases of liquor in garages and other places. It showed the dealing by Olmstead, the chief conspirator, with members of the Seattle police, the messages to them which secured the release of arrested members of the conspiracy, and also direct promises to officers of payments as soon as opportunity offered.

The Fourth Amendment provides—

> The right of the people to be secure in their persons, houses, papers, and effects against unreasonable searches and seizures shall not be violated, and no warrants shall issue but upon probable cause, supported by oath or affirmation and particularly describing the place to be searched and the persons or things to be seized.

The well known historical purpose of the Fourth Amendment was to prevent the use of governmental force to search a man's house, his person, his papers and his effects, and to prevent their seizure against his will. This phase of the misuse of governmental power of compulsion is the emphasis of past opinions of this court. For example, a representative of the Intelligence Department of the Army, having by stealth obtained admission to the defendant's office, seized and carried away certain private papers valuable for evidential purposes. This was held an unreasonable search and seizure within the Fourth Amendment. A stealthy entrance in such circumstances became the equivalent to an entry by force. There was actual entrance into the private quarters of defendant, and the taking away of something tangible. Here we have testimony only of voluntary conversations secretly overheard.

The Amendment itself shows that the search is to be of material things — the person, the house, his papers, or his effects. The description of the warrant necessary to make the proceeding lawful is that it must specify the place to be searched and the person or things to be seized.

The Fourth Amendment may have proper application to a sealed letter in the mail because of the constitutional provision for the Post Office Department and the relations between the Government and those who pay to secure protection of their sealed letters. The law gives Congress a monopoly in the carriage of letters and excludes from that business everyone else, and forbids any postmaster or other person to open any letter not addressed to himself. It is plainly within the words of the Amendment to say that the unlawful rifling by a government agent of a sealed letter is a search and seizure of the sender's papers or effects. The letter is a paper, an effect, and in the custody of a Government that forbids carriage except under its protection.

The United States takes no such care of telegraph or telephone messages as of mailed sealed letters. The Amendment does not forbid what was done here. There was no searching. There was no seizure. The evidence was secured by the use of the sense of hearing, and that only. There was no entry of the houses or offices of the defendants.

By the invention of the telephone fifty years ago and its application for the purpose of extending communications, one can talk with another at a far distant place. The language of the Amendment cannot be extended and expanded to include telephone wires reaching to the whole world from the defendant's house or office. The intervening wires are not part of his house or office any more than are the highways along which they are stretched.

This Court, in *Carroll v. United States* (1925) where we ruled that the police needed only probable cause and not a warrant to search an automobile, declared:

> The Fourth Amendment is to be construed in the light of what was deemed an unreasonable search and seizure when it was adopted and in a manner which will conserve public interests as well as the interests and rights of individual citizens.

Justice Bradley, in the *Boyd* case, and Justice Clark in the *Gouled* case, said that the Fifth Amendment is to be liberally construed to effect the purpose of the framers of the Constitution in the interest of liberty. But that cannot justify enlargement of the language employed beyond the possible practical meaning of houses, persons, papers, and effects, or so to apply the words search and seizure as to forbid hearing or sight.

Hester v. United States held that the testimony of two officers of the law who trespassed on the defendant's land, concealed themselves one hundred yards away from his house, and saw him come out and hand a bottle of whiskey to another was admissible. While there was a trespass, there was no search of person, house, papers or effects.

Congress may, of course, protect the secrecy of telephone messages by making them, when intercepted, inadmissible in evidence in federal criminal trials by direct legislation, and thus depart from the common law of evidence. But the courts may not adopt such a policy by attributing an enlarged and unusual meaning to the Fourth Amendment. The reasonable view is that one who installs in his house a telephone instrument with connecting wires intends to project his voice to those quite outside, and that the wires beyond his house and messages while passing over them are not within the protection of the Fourth Amendment. Here, those who intercepted the projected voices were not in the house of either party to the conversation.

Neither the cases we have cited nor any of the many federal decisions brought to our attention hold the Fourth Amendment to have been violated as against a defendant unless there has been an official search and seizure of his person, or such a seizure of his papers or his tangible material effects, or an actual physical invasion of his house "or curtilage" for the purpose of making a seizure. We think, therefore, that the wiretapping here disclosed did not amount to a search or seizure within the meaning of the Fourth Amendment.

END OF OPINION

In the *Olmstead* opinion, the U.S. Supreme Court was fixed on the idea that the Fourth Amendment only applied to physical intrusions of a person or property. The view at the time *Olmstead* was decided in 1928 was that the Fourth Amendment did not apply to telephones and telegraphs, the only publicly available electronic communications at the time, because using them to conduct surveillance did not involve a physical intrusion upon anyone's private property or a body itself. The Court's rationale was the perceived lack of trespass.

Trespass is an ancient legal doctrine that others may not intrude upon one's property. Examples would include you not allowing someone inside your apartment or on your lawn, or forbidding anyone from opening your purse or backpack. These are your personal property, and others cannot invade them without your permission. In many states, it is a crime for people to commit a trespass. In addition, in many states a person can also be sued for trespass. In the U.S., we give the utmost respect to one's right to control his or her personal property.

When the Fourth Amendment was written, it was written from the perspective of that ancient historic doctrine of trespass. It was a way to limit the power of the government by forbidding the government from committing trespasses upon the citizens' private property, bodily integrity, or papers and effects, unless certain requirements (involving a warrant or reasonable justifications) were met. Back in the 1700s, a physical trespass upon a person, property, or personal items was the only way to conduct a search.

When electronic communication such as the telegraph and telephone first emerged, it was the first time that the government was able to conduct surveillance without a physical intrusion. This challenged the notion of trespass, which had always been limited to physical intrusions of property, personal effects (papers, bags, containers, etc.), and bodily integrity. Given that the framework of the Fourth Amendment had been based in trespass which had always involved a physical intrusion, the Supreme

Court just could not see how a non-physical intrusion by electronic surveillance could violate the Fourth Amendment.

Now, even though the *Olmstead* case was based on the "trespass" approach to search and seizure law, the concept had been under consideration for several years. In fact, the first published challenge to the notion of this "trespass" or property-based approach to search and seizure law came in an article published in the Harvard Law Review in 1890. Take the time to consider how many of the concerns that Warren and Brandeis raised over a century ago still apply when we think of "the right to privacy."

The Right To Privacy

By Samuel Warren and Louis D. Brandeis

Originally published in 4 Harvard Law Review 193 (1890)

(Citations omitted)

That the individual shall have full protection in person and in property is a principle as old as the common law; but it has been found necessary from time to time to define anew the exact nature and extent of such protection. Political, social, and economic changes entail the recognition of new rights, and the common law, in its eternal youth, grows to meet the demands of society. Thus, in very early times, the law gave a remedy only for physical interference with life and property, for trespasses *vi et armis*. Then the "right to life" served only to protect the subject from battery in its various forms; liberty meant freedom from actual restraint; and the right to property secured to the individual his lands and his cattle. Later, there came a recognition of man's spiritual nature, of his feelings and his intellect. Gradually the scope of these legal rights broadened; and now the right to life has come to mean the right to enjoy life—the right to be let alone, the right to liberty secures the exercise of extensive civil privileges; and the term "property" has grown to comprise every form of possession—intangible, as well as tangible.

. . .

This development of the law was inevitable. The intense intellectual and emotional life, and the heightening of sensations which came with the advance of civilization, made it clear to man that only a part of the pain, pleasure, and profit of life lay in physical things. Thoughts, emotions, and sensations demanded legal recognition, and the beautiful capacity for growth which characterizes the common law enabled the judges to afford the requisite protection, without the interposition of the legislature.

Recent inventions and business methods call attention to the next step which must be taken for the protection of the person, and for securing to the individual what Judge Cooley calls the right "to be let alone." Instantaneous photographs and newspaper enterprise have invaded the sacred precincts of private and domestic life; and numerous mechanical devices threaten to make good the prediction that "what is whispered in the closet shall be proclaimed from the house-tops." For years there has been a feeling that the law must afford some remedy for the unauthorized circulation of portraits of private persons; and the evil of the invasion of privacy by the newspapers, long keenly felt, has been but recently discussed by an able writer. The . . . question whether our law will recognize and protect the right to privacy in this and in other respects must soon come before our courts for consideration.

Of the desirability—indeed of the necessity—of some such protection, there can, it is believed, be no doubt. The press is overstepping in every direction the obvious bounds of propriety and of decency. Gossip is no longer the resource of the idle and of the vicious, but has become a trade, which is pursued with industry as well as effrontery. To satisfy a prurient taste the details of sexual relations are spread broadcast in the columns of the daily papers. To occupy the indolent, column upon column is filled with idle gossip, which can only be procured by intrusion upon the domestic circle. The intensity and complexity of life, attendant upon advancing civilization, have rendered necessary some retreat from the world, and man, under the refining influence of culture, has become more sensitive to publicity, so that solitude and privacy have become more essential to the individual; but modern enterprise and invention have, through invasions upon his privacy, subjected him to mental pain and distress, far greater than could be inflicted by mere bodily injury. Nor is the harm wrought by such invasions confined to the suffering of those who may be made the subjects of journalistic or other enterprise.

In this, as in other branches of commerce, the supply creates the demand. Each crop of unseemly gossip, thus harvested, becomes the seed of more, and, in direct proportion to its circulation, results in a lowering of social standards and of morality. Even gossip apparently harmless, when widely and persistently circulated, is potent for evil. It both belittles and perverts. It belittles by inverting the relative importance of things, thus dwarfing the thoughts and aspirations of a people. When personal gossip attains the dignity of print, and crowds the space available for matters of real interest to the community, what wonder that the ignorant and thoughtless mistake its relative importance. Easy of comprehension, appealing to that weak side of human nature which is never wholly cast down by the misfortunes and frailties of our neighbors, no one can be surprised that it usurps the place of interest in brains capable of other things. Triviality destroys at once robustness of thought and delicacy of feeling. No enthusiasm can flourish, no generous impulse can survive under its blighting influence.

It is our purpose to consider whether the existing law affords a principle which can properly be invoked to protect the privacy of the individual; and, if it does, what the nature and extent of such protection is.

. . .

The common law secures to each individual the right of determining, ordinarily, to what extent his thoughts, sentiments, and emotions shall be communicated to others. Under our system of government, he can never be compelled to express them (except when upon the witness stand); and even if he has chosen to give them expression, he generally retains the power to fix the limits of the publicity which shall be given them.

The existence of this right does not depend upon the particular method of expression adopted. It is immaterial whether it be by word or by signs, in painting, by sculpture, or in music. Neither does the existence of the right depend upon the nature or value of the thought or emotion, nor upon the excellence of the means of expression. The same protection is accorded to a casual letter or an entry in a diary and to the most valuable poem or essay, to a botch or daub and to a masterpiece. In every such case the individual is entitled to decide whether that which is his shall be given to the public.

. . .

Although the courts have asserted that they rested their decisions on the narrow grounds of protection to property, yet there are recognitions of a more liberal doctrine. . . . If the fiction of property in a narrow sense must be preserved, it is still true that the end accomplished by the gossip-monger is attained by the use of that which is another's, the facts relating to his private life, which he has seen fit to keep private. . . . But if privacy is once recognized as a right entitled to legal protection, the interposition of the courts cannot depend on the particular nature of the injuries resulting.

. . .

The principle which protects personal writings and all other personal productions, not against theft and physical appropriation, but against publication in any form, is in reality not the principle of private property, but that of an inviolate personality.

If we are correct in this conclusion, the existing law affords a principle which may be invoked to protect the privacy of the individual from invasion either by the too enterprising press, the photographer, or the possessor of any other modern device for recording or reproducing scenes or sounds. For the protection afforded is not confined by the authorities to those cases where any particular medium or form of expression has been adopted, nor to products of the intellect. The same protection is afforded to emotions and sensations expressed in a musical composition or other work of art as to a literary composition; and words spoken, a pantomime acted, a sonata performed, is no less entitled to protection than if each had been reduced to writing. The circumstance that a thought or emotion has been recorded in a permanent form renders its identification easier, and hence may be important from the point of view of evidence, but it has no significance as a matter of substantive right. If, then, the decisions indicate a general right to privacy for thoughts, emotions, and sensations, these should receive the same protection, whether expressed in writing, or in conduct, in conversation, in attitudes, or in facial expression.

. . .

The principle which protects personal writings and any other productions of the intellect or of the emotions, is the right to privacy, and the law has no new principle to formulate when it extends this protection to the personal appearance, sayings, acts, and to personal relations, domestic or otherwise.

If the invasion of privacy constitutes a legal injuria, the elements for demanding redress exist, since already the value of mental suffering, caused by an act wrongful in itself, is recognized as a basis for compensation.

The right of one who has remained a private individual, to prevent his public portraiture, presents the simplest case for such extension; the right to protect one's self from pen portraiture, from a discussion by the press of one's private affairs, would be a more important and far-reaching one. If casual and unimportant statements in a letter, if handiwork, however inartistic and valueless, if possessions of all sorts are protected not only against reproduction, but against description and enumeration, how much more should the acts and sayings of a man in his social and domestic relations be guarded from ruthless publicity. If you may not reproduce a woman's face photographically without her consent, how much less should be tolerated the reproduction of her face, her form, and her actions, by graphic descriptions colored to suit a gross and depraved imagination.

. . .

It remains to consider what are the limitations of this right to privacy, and what remedies may be granted for the enforcement of the right. To determine in advance of experience the exact line at which the dignity and convenience of the individual must yield to the demands of the public welfare or of private justice would be a difficult task; but the more general rules are furnished by the legal analogies already developed in the law of slander and libel, and in the law of literary and artistic property.

First. The right to privacy does not prohibit any publication of matter which is of public or general interest.

. . .

The general object in view is to protect the privacy of private life, and to whatever degree and in whatever connection a man's life has ceased to be private, before the publication under consideration has been made, to that extent the protection is to be withdrawn.

. . .

Second. The right to privacy does not prohibit the communication of any matter, though in its nature private, when the publication is made under circumstances which would render it a privileged communication according to the law of slander and libel.

. . .

Third. The law would probably not grant any redress for the invasion of privacy by oral publication in the absence of special damage.

. . .

Fourth. The right to privacy ceases upon the publication of the facts by the individual, or with his consent.

. . .

Fifth. The truth of the matter published does not afford a defense.

. . .

Sixth. The absence of "malice" in the publisher does not afford a defense.

. . .

The invasion of the privacy that is to be protected is casually complete and equally injurious, whether the motives by which the speaker or writer was actuated are, taken by themselves, culpable or not; just as the damage to character, and to some extent the tendency to provoke a breach of the peace, is equally the result of defamation without regard to the motives leading to its publication. Viewed as a wrong to the individual, this rule is the same pervading the whole law of torts, by which one is held responsible for his intentional acts, even though they are committed with no sinister intent; and viewed as a wrong to society, it is the same principle adopted in a large category of statutory offenses.

. . .

It would doubtless be desirable that the privacy of the individual should receive the added protection of the criminal law, but for this, legislation would be required. Perhaps it would be deemed proper to bring the criminal liability for such publication within narrower limits; but that the community has an interest in preventing such invasions of privacy, sufficiently strong to justify the introduction of such a remedy, cannot be doubted. Still, the protection of society must come mainly through a recognition of the rights of the individual. Each man is responsible for his own acts and omissions only. If he condones what he reprobates, with a weapon at hand equal to his defense, he is responsible for the results. If he resists, public opinion will rally to his support. Has he then such a weapon? It is believed that the common law provides him with one, forged in the slow fire of the centuries, and today fitly tempered to his hand. The common law has always recognized a man's house as his castle, impregnable, often even to its own officers engaged in the execution of its commands. Shall the courts thus close the front entrance to constituted authority, and open wide the back door to idle or prurient curiosity?

COMMENT

Obviously, the arguments made by Justice Brandeis and Mr. Warren were unable to persuade the courts of this "Right to Privacy" approach to the law for a number of decades after they were written, although Justice Brandeis raised these issues when he dissented from the holding on *Olmstead*. The intellectual seeds sowed by this article did take root and, fortunately, there has since been a change in the law in how we look at the Fourth Amendment.

Today, we no longer look at the Fourth Amendment strictly from the perspective of trespass and property. Instead, we look at the Fourth Amendment as a general protection which prohibits the government from intruding upon the people's "reasonable expectation of privacy." This change of viewing the Fourth Amendment as a way to protect "reasonable expectations of privacy" and not only a prohibition against government trespass happened with the landmark Supreme Court decision in *Katz v. United States* in 1967. This is the most important case which instructs as to when the Fourth Amendment applies, and how to interpret the Fourth Amendment.

Katz v. United States, 389 U.S. 347 (1967)*

Katz was convicted for illegal gambling by telephone from Los Angeles to Miami and Boston, in violation of a federal statute. At trial, the Government was permitted, over Katz's objection, to introduce evidence of the Katz's end of telephone conversations, overheard by FBI agents who had attached an electronic listening and recording device to the outside of the public telephone booth from which he had placed his calls. In affirming his conviction, the Court of Appeals rejected the contention that the recordings had been obtained in violation of the Fourth Amendment, because "there was no physical entrance into the area occupied by the petitioner." We granted review in order to consider the constitutional questions thus presented.

Katz has phrased those questions as follows:

A. Whether a public telephone booth is a constitutionally protected area so that evidence obtained by attaching an electronic listening recording device to the top of such a booth is obtained in violation of the right to privacy of the user of the booth.

B. Whether physical penetration of a constitutionally protected area is necessary before a search and seizure can be said to be violative of the Fourth Amendment to the United States Constitution.

We decline to adopt this formulation of the issues. In the first place, the correct solution of Fourth Amendment problems is not necessarily promoted by incantation of the phrase "constitutionally protected area." Secondly, the Fourth Amendment cannot be translated into a general constitutional "right to privacy." That Amendment protects individual privacy against certain kinds of governmental intrusion, but its protections go further, and often have nothing to do with privacy at all. Other provisions of the Constitution protect personal privacy from other forms of governmental invasion. But the protection of a person's general right to privacy—his right to be let alone by other people—is, like the protection of his property and of his very life, left largely to the law of the individual States.

Because of the misleading way the issues have been formulated, the parties have attached great significance to the characterization of the telephone booth from which the petitioner placed his calls. The petitioner has strenuously argued that the booth was a "constitutionally protected area." The Government has maintained with equal vigor that it was not. But this effort to decide whether or not a given "area," viewed in the abstract, is "constitutionally protected" deflects attention from the problem presented by this case. For the Fourth Amendment protects people, not places. What a person knowingly exposes to the public, even in his own home or office, is not a subject of Fourth Amendment protection. But what he seeks to preserve as private, even in an area accessible to the public, may be constitutionally protected.

The Government stresses the fact that the telephone booth from which the petitioner made his calls was constructed partly of glass, so that he was as visible after

---

* The case has been heavily edited and paraphrased by the authors for clarity. See disclaimer in introduction.

he entered it as he would have been if he had remained outside. But what he sought to exclude when he entered the booth was not the intruding eye—it was the uninvited ear. He did not shed his right to do so simply because he made his calls from a place where he might be seen. No less than an individual in a business office, in a friend's apartment, or in a taxicab, a person in a telephone booth may rely upon the protection of the Fourth Amendment. One who occupies it, shuts the door behind him, and pays the toll that permits him to place a call is surely entitled to assume that the words he utters into the mouthpiece will not be broadcast to the world. To read the Constitution more narrowly is to ignore the vital role that the public telephone has come to play in private communication.

The Government contends, however, that the activities of its agents in this case should not be tested by Fourth Amendment requirements, for the surveillance technique they employed involved no physical penetration of the telephone booth from which the petitioner placed his calls. It is true that the absence of such penetration was at one time thought to foreclose further Fourth Amendment inquiry, *Olmstead v. United States*, for that Amendment was thought to limit only searches and seizures of tangible property. But the premise that property interests control the right of the Government to search and seize has been discredited. Thus, although a closely divided Court supposed in *Olmstead* that surveillance without any trespass and without the seizure of any material object fell outside the protections of the Constitution, we have since departed from the narrow view on which that decision rested. Indeed, we have expressly held that the Fourth Amendment governs not only the seizure of tangible items, but extends as well to the recording of oral statements, overheard without any physical trespass. Once this much is acknowledged, and once it is recognized that the Fourth Amendment protects people—and not simply "areas"—against unreasonable searches and seizures, it becomes clear that the reach of that Amendment cannot turn upon the presence or absence of a physical intrusion into any given enclosure.

We conclude that the underpinnings of *Olmstead* have been so eroded by our subsequent decisions that the "trespass" doctrine there enunciated can no longer be regarded as controlling. The Government's activities in electronically listening to and recording the petitioner's words violated the privacy upon which he justifiably relied while using the telephone booth, and thus constituted a "search and seizure" within the meaning of the Fourth Amendment. The fact that the electronic device employed to achieve that end did not happen to penetrate the wall of the booth can have no constitutional significance.

The question remaining for decision, then, is whether the search and seizure conducted in this case complied with constitutional standards. In that regard, the Government's position is that its agents acted in an entirely defensible manner: they did not begin their electronic surveillance until investigation of the petitioner's activities had established a strong probability that he was using the telephone in question to transmit gambling information to persons in other States, in violation of federal law. Moreover, the surveillance was limited, both in scope and in duration, to the specific purpose of establishing the contents of the petitioner's unlawful telephonic communications. The agents confined their surveillance to the brief periods during which he used the telephone booth, and they took great care to overhear only the conversations of the petitioner himself.

Accepting this account of the Government's actions as accurate, it is clear that this surveillance was so narrowly circumscribed that a duly authorized magistrate, properly notified of the need for such investigation, specifically informed of the basis on which it was to proceed, and clearly apprised of the precise intrusion it would entail, could constitutionally have authorized, with appropriate safeguards, the very limited search and seizure that the Government asserts, in fact, took place. Only last Term we sustained the validity of such an authorization, holding that, under sufficiently precise and discriminate circumstances, a federal court may empower government agents to employ a concealed electronic device for the narrow and particularized purpose of ascertaining the truth of the allegations of a detailed factual affidavit alleging the commission of a specific criminal offense. In *Osborn v. United States* we said that the order authorizing the use of the electronic device afforded similar protections to those of conventional warrants authorizing the seizure of tangible evidence. Through those protections, no greater invasion of privacy was permitted than was necessary under the circumstances. Here, too, a similar judicial order could have accommodated the legitimate needs of law enforcement by authorizing the carefully limited use of electronic surveillance.

The Government urges that, because its agents relied upon the decisions in *Olmstead* and *Goldman*, and because they did no more here than they might properly have done with prior judicial sanction, we should retroactively validate their conduct. That we cannot do. It is apparent that the agents in this case acted with restraint. Yet the inescapable fact is that this restraint was imposed by the agents themselves, not by a judicial officer. They were not required, before commencing the search, to present their estimate of probable cause for detached scrutiny by a neutral magistrate. They were not compelled, during the conduct of the search itself, to observe precise limits established in advance by a specific court order. Nor were they directed, after the search had been completed, to notify the authorizing magistrate in detail of all that had been seized. In the absence of such safeguards, this Court has never sustained a search upon the sole ground that officers reasonably expected to find evidence of a particular crime and voluntarily confined their activities to the least intrusive means consistent with that end. Searches conducted without warrants have been held unlawful "notwithstanding facts unquestionably showing probable cause," for the Constitution requires that the deliberate, impartial judgment of a judicial officer be interposed between the citizen and the police. Over and again, this Court has emphasized that the mandate of the Fourth Amendment requires adherence to judicial processes, and that searches conducted outside the judicial process, without prior approval by judge or magistrate, are per se unreasonable under the Fourth Amendment subject only to a few specifically established and well delineated exceptions.

It is difficult to imagine how any of those exceptions could ever apply to the sort of search and seizure involved in this case. Even electronic surveillance substantially contemporaneous with an individual's arrest could hardly be deemed an "incident" of that arrest. Nor could the use of electronic surveillance without prior authorization be justified on grounds of "hot pursuit." And, of course, the very nature of electronic surveillance precludes its use pursuant to the suspect's consent.

The Government does not question these basic principles. Rather, it urges the creation of a new exception to cover this case. It argues that surveillance of a telephone booth should be exempted from the usual requirement of advance authorization by a magistrate upon a showing of probable cause. We cannot agree. Omission of such authorization bypasses the safeguards provided by an objective predetermination of probable cause, and substitutes instead the far less reliable procedure of an after-the-event justification for the search, too likely to be subtly influenced by the familiar shortcomings of hindsight judgment. Bypassing a neutral predetermination of the scope of a search leaves individuals secure from Fourth Amendment violations "only in the discretion of the police."

These considerations do not vanish when the search in question is transferred from the setting of a home, an office, or a hotel room to that of a telephone booth. Wherever a man may be, he is entitled to know that he will remain free from unreasonable searches and seizures. The government agents here ignored "the procedure of antecedent justification . . . that is central to the Fourth Amendment," a procedure that we hold to be a constitutional precondition of the kind of electronic surveillance involved in this case. Because the surveillance here failed to meet that condition, and because it led to the petitioner's conviction, the judgment must be reversed.

It is so ordered.

MR. JUSTICE HARLAN, concurring.

I join the opinion of the Court, which I read to hold only (a) that an enclosed telephone booth is an area where, like a home, where a person has a constitutionally protected reasonable expectation of privacy; (b) that electronic, as well as physical, intrusion into a place that is in this sense private may constitute a violation of the Fourth Amendment, and (c) that the invasion of a constitutionally protected area by federal authorities is, as the Court has long held, presumptively unreasonable in the absence of a search warrant.

As the Court's opinion states, "the Fourth Amendment protects people, not places." The question, however, is what protection it affords to those people. Generally, as here, the answer to that question requires reference to a "place." My understanding of the rule that has emerged from prior decisions is that there is a twofold requirement, first that a person has exhibited an actual (subjective) expectation of privacy and, second, that the expectation be one that society is prepared to recognize as "reasonable." Thus, a man's home is, for most purposes, a place where he expects privacy, but objects, activities, or statements that he exposes to the "plain view" of outsiders are not "protected," because no intention to keep them to himself has been exhibited. On the other hand, conversations in the open would not be protected against being overheard, for the expectation of privacy under the circumstances would be unreasonable.

The critical fact in this case is, as stated by the majority opinion, that "one who occupies a telephone booth, shuts the door behind him, and pays the toll that permits him to place a call is surely entitled to assume" that his conversation is not being intercepted. The point is not that the booth is "accessible to the public" at other times, but that it is a temporarily private place whose momentary occupants' expectations of freedom from intrusion are recognized as reasonable.

Finally, I do not read the Court's opinion to declare that no interception of a conversation one-half of which occurs in a public telephone booth can be reasonable in the absence of a warrant. As elsewhere under the Fourth Amendment, warrants are the general rule, to which the legitimate needs of law enforcement may demand specific exceptions. It will be time enough to consider any such exceptions when an appropriate occasion presents itself, and I agree with the Court that this is not one.

END OF OPINION

Katz is the most important case in modern Fourth Amendment law because it determines whether or not the Fourth Amendment applies to a government intrusion of one's privacy. Today, to determine whether or not the Fourth Amendment applies, we apply the two-part test explained in Justice Harlan's concurrence. If both parts of the following test are met, then the Fourth Amendment applies and law enforcement need a warrant to conduct a search or surveillance, be it physical or electronic.

Here is the two-part test:

1. Has the person subjectively demonstrated an expectation of privacy?
2. Is society going to recognize that expectation as reasonable?

So, to review, we apply this test to the facts in the *Katz* case:

1. Here, in entering a phone booth and shutting the door, Katz was subjectively demonstrating that he expected his telephone call to remain private and not heard by a third party.
2. Society considers shutting the door to be alone in a phone booth to have a conversation to be a completely reasonable act to demonstrate an expectation of privacy.

With the two-part test being met, the police were required to get a warrant.

The shortcut to the two-part test is simply asking the following question:

Does a person have a "reasonable expectation of privacy"? If so, then it is required for the police to get a warrant for a search (or in some other fashion demonstrate that an exception to the warrant requirement applies such as public safety or exigent circumstances). This is why, when trying to determine if the police should have obtained a warrant, you should use as the general rule: "whenever the police invade an area where a person has a reasonable expectation of privacy, the Fourth Amendment applies and they need a warrant."

Review Questions

Apply the reasoning of the *Katz* decision to the questions below:

1. Jeremy is on a crowded public bus and is loudly talking to his drug dealer on his cell phone, making arrangements to buy cocaine. He happens to be sitting next to an off-duty police officer in civilian clothes who is recording the conversation on his smartphone. Once Jeremy hangs up, the officer arrests him. Jeremy protests, claiming the officer was invading his privacy by eavesdropping. Did the police officer need a warrant to record that conversation?

2. Ben is a known drug dealer and is spotted in the mall by Officer Finnegan. Officer Finnegan surreptitiously follows Ben into the restroom and as Ben goes into one bathroom stall and closes the door behind him, Officer Finnegan goes into the other bathroom stall. Like most stalls in public bathrooms, the barriers between toilets does not go all the way up to the ceiling, so while standing on the toilet seat in his stall, Officer Finnegan can peer over the barrier and look down upon Ben. He observes as Ben pulls out his I-pad and starts texting his friends. From his position, Officer Finnegan can read the texts Ben is sending and sees that Ben is arranging to sell drugs in the Gap in the mall in 15 minutes. Officer Finnegan follows Ben out of the bathroom, arranges backup, and at the moment the drug deal is going down, he and the officer arrest Ben and the buyer. At trial, Ben's lawyer asserts that the surveillance in the bathroom required a warrant. Is the lawyer right? Apply the two-part test.

In general, people have a reasonable expectation of privacy in the contents of their homes, their computers, and conversations. For this reason, warrants are usually required for the police to invade or access these. This is why the police will get a warrant to tap a phone conversation, enter a house, or search a computer. Here again, the concept originates from the property-based view of search and seizure law, as the searches required a physical invasion of property—entering the house, rummaging through papers and effects, and so forth. *Katz* shifts the discussion to where and under what circumstances a person has a "reasonable expectation of privacy" and under what circumstances the law will decide that no such reasonable expectation exists.

The Plain View Doctrine

You may have heard the term "plain view" or "plain view doctrine." The plain view doctrine is an exception to the warrant requirement which allows officers to discover and sometimes seize items which they observe and immediately recognize as evidence or contraband while they are lawfully present in an area protected by the 4th Amendment. The foundation case providing the elements of a plain view seizure as related to the plain view doctrine is *Horton v. California*, 496 U.S. 128 (1990). For the doctrine to apply for discoveries, the *Horton* decision established a three-part test. First, the officer must be lawfully present at the place where the evidence can be plainly viewed. Second, the officer must have a lawful right of access to the object. Third, the incriminating character of the object must be "immediately apparent."

Boiled down, you can see that the idea of "plain view" is exactly what it says; an object or criminal act is occurring in the open, where anyone can see it. Examples might include a marijuana plant growing in the window on the front of someone's house, or if the police are invited in someone's house, they might observe a crack-pipe lying in the open on a table (as opposed to hidden at the bottom of an underwear drawer).

This is consistent with the rule expressed in *Katz*. If a person has left something in plain view where anyone can lawfully observe it, then the person has demonstrated that he or she has no reasonable expectation of privacy in it. Think about it: it would be completely unreasonable for a person growing marijuana in the window where anyone walking by on the public sidewalk can see it to claim that he expected that marijuana plant to remain private! The plain view doctrine is an extension of *Katz*. If warrants are required for the police to invade areas people have a reasonable expectation of privacy, then logically police do not need a warrant to access areas people do not expect privacy. If something is in "plain view," obviously a person does not have an expectation of privacy, so no warrant is needed.

It is important to remember that an item which is in plain view can only be seized if the police are legally present where the item is. If police see blocks of cocaine through the window of the house, the police must go get a warrant to enter the house. However, if the police are already legally inside the house and happen to see drugs in plain view, then the police can also seize the drugs without first getting a warrant.

Review Questions

Let's do some practice problems to determine whether the Fourth Amendment applies and, if so, whether or not a warrant is needed. As always, use an IRAC analysis to help find your answers.

1. Emily is a member of the KKK and is planning a bombing of a black church. She keeps all of the plans of the bombing on her password-protected computer in her bedroom. Her roommate, Ashley, works for the NSA. Ashley suspects that Emily is planning something bad, but she doesn't know what. While at the NSA one day, she hacks Emily's computer and discovers the plans of the bombing. Was this a lawful search?

2. Emily is a member of the KKK and is planning a bombing of a black church. She does not own a computer, and instead, she keeps all of the plans of the bombing on the hard drive of a computer at the local library. On the hard drive, she has marked the folder containing the plans "PRIVATE INFORMATION, DO NOT OPEN." A police officer who has been following Emily around gets on the computer right after her and discovers the folder, opens it, and reads her plans for the bombing. He then uses this information to arrest her. IRAC if the plans discovered by the officer are admissible.

3. Jack and Jill are a married couple living inside a small house. They frequently get drunk and start screaming at each other, causing neighbors to call the police. This is one of those nights, and they are still screaming at each other as the police are walking down the public sidewalk to their house. Even while on the public sidewalk, the police can hear their screams. This time, the police hear Jill scream at Jack, "You stupid drug dealer! I want my cut of the crack you hide underneath the kitchen sink!" The police report this statement to the magistrate, who issues a warrant for a search underneath the kitchen sink. At trial, the defense attorney argues that because this argument was occurring in a private residence, it was a private conversation and the police violated their rights by listening to it. How should the judge rule?

4. Jack and Jill are a married couple living inside a home. They are quiet and dignified, and surprisingly, are members of Al-Qaeda. The police have probable cause that Jack and Jill are terrorists, but want to get enough evidence to convict them in court. Knowing that Jill likes to order fresh flowers each week from a local florist, the police arrange to place a hidden microphone inside the vase of flowers going to her house. Once the flowers are delivered by the florist, the police can hear and record conversations Jill is having with Jack inside their home. While inside their home, they discuss plans to place bombs at an elementary school. The police use these recordings to get a warrant to physically search their home where they find bomb-making materials and plans to execute the terrorist attack. IRAC if the judge should allow this evidence to be used at trial.

5. Defense attorney Roger Checkers is in court one day and he finishes early. He decides to go get some ice cream and when he leaves the court building, he forgets to take his suitcase with him. A deputy notices an unattended briefcase lying on the floor and checks it for a label which will identify the owner. She does not find one on the exterior, so she opens it to see if there is a nametag inside. Inside she does find a nametag identifying the briefcase as that of Roger Checkers. She also finds a small bag of cocaine. If Roger Checkers is prosecuted, is the cocaine found inside admissible?

6. Sarah is weighing and packaging cocaine for distribution. She is doing it in the window of her house. An officer who is walking down the public sidewalk observes this. He then proceeds to go up to her door, knock it down, arrest Sarah, and seize the cocaine. Is this arrest and seizure of the cocaine lawful?

The Third-Party Doctrine

The review questions touch on the "plain view" doctrine—the legal rule that, when something is left "in plain view," the authorities are not bound by Fourth Amendment requirements in searching or seizing evidence, no warrant is required, and the conduct is reasonable. This is because when you leave something out in plain view, you are clearly demonstrating you have no reasonable expectation of privacy and, without any such expectation of privacy, there is no Fourth Amendment interest to protect.

Using much the same logic, the courts have ruled that when you disclose something to a third party, you are giving up any expectation of privacy, at least in those cases where there has not been a long history of the law protecting the confidentiality of the disclosure. Some disclosures are protected by law—disclosures made to priest, pastor, or other clergy, disclosures made to a physician, and disclosures made to an attorney are those we are all most familiar with. Historically the law recognized that the need for a person to have open conversations with one's spiritual advisor, legal advisor, or medical care provider was of such importance that those conversations, so long as they were otherwise made with an effort to protect privacy (taking place, for example, in the doctor's office, the lawyer's office, or the confessional), the communication would be privileged.

But any communication made where others can overhear is not considered private, and so records or other material turned over to third party not enjoying one of these special statuses also is not considered private. This is a part of Fourth Amendment law that has a lot to do with electronic surveillance, and so we start by looking at the two cases that form the basis for this "Third-Party Doctrine."

United States v. Miller, 425 U.S. 435 (1976)[*]

Miller was convicted of possessing an unregistered still, carrying on the business of a distiller without giving bond and with intent to defraud the Government of whiskey tax, possessing 175 gallons of whiskey upon which no taxes had been paid, and conspiring to defraud the United States of tax revenues. Prior to trial, respondent moved to suppress copies of checks and other bank records obtained by means of allegedly defective subpoenas[1] served upon two banks at which he had accounts. The records had been maintained by the banks in compliance with the requirements of the Bank Secrecy Act of 1970. We find that respondent had no protectable Fourth Amendment interest in the subpoenaed documents.

On December 18, 1972, in response to an informant's tip, a deputy sheriff from Houston County, Ga., stopped a van-type truck occupied by two of respondent's alleged coconspirators. The truck contained distillery apparatus and raw material. On January 9, 1973, a fire broke out in a Kathleen, Ga., warehouse rented to respondent. During the blaze, firemen and sheriff department officials discovered a 7,500-gallon-capacity distillery, 175 gallons of non-tax-paid whiskey, and related paraphernalia.

Two weeks later, agents from the Treasury Department's Alcohol, Tobacco and Firearms Bureau presented subpoenas issued by the federal District Court (upon the request of the U.S. Attorney's office) to the presidents of the Citizens & Southern National Bank of Warner Robins and the Bank of Byron, where respondent maintained accounts. The subpoenas required the two presidents to appear on January 24, 1973, and to produce

---

[*] The case has been heavily edited and paraphrased by the authors for clarity. See disclaimer in introduction.

1. A subpoena is a court order for a third party to turn over relevant material in its possession.

"all records of accounts, i.e., savings, checking, loan or otherwise, in the name of Mr. Mitch Miller [respondent], 3859 Mathis Street, Macon, Ga. and/or Mitch Miller Associates, 100 Executive Terrace, Warner Robins, Ga. from October 1, 1972, through the present date [January 22, 1973, in the case of the Bank of Byron, and January 23, 1973, in the case of the Citizens & Southern National Bank of Warner Robins]."

The banks did not advise respondent that the subpoenas had been served, but ordered their employees to make the records available and to provide copies of any documents the agents desired. At the Bank of Byron, an agent was shown microfilm records of the relevant account and provided with copies of one deposit slip and one or two checks. At the Citizens & Southern National Bank, microfilm records also were shown to the agent, and he was given copies of the records of respondent's account during the applicable period. These included all checks, deposit slips, two financial statements, and three monthly statements. The bank presidents were then told that it would not be necessary to appear in person before the grand jury.

19 days after the return date on the subpoenas, respondent and four others were indicted. The overt acts alleged to have been committed in furtherance of the conspiracy included three financial transactions—the rental by respondent of the van-type truck, the purchase by respondent of radio equipment, and the purchase by respondent of a quantity of sheet metal and metal pipe. The bank records were used in the investigation and provided investigatory leads. Copies of the checks also were introduced at trial to establish the overt acts described above.

In his motion to suppress, respondent argued that the bank documents were illegally seized.

We find that there was no intrusion into any area in which respondent had a protected Fourth Amendment interest.

In *Hoffa v. United States* (1966), the Court said that "no interest legitimately protected by the Fourth Amendment" is implicated by governmental investigative activities unless there is an intrusion into a zone of privacy, into "the security a man relies upon when he places himself or his property within a constitutionally protected area." The subpoenaed documents do not fall within a protected zone of privacy.

On their face, the documents subpoenaed here are not respondent's "private papers." Respondent had neither ownership nor possession of those documents. Instead, these are the business records of the banks. Banks are not neutrals in transactions involving negotiable instruments, but parties to the instruments with a substantial stake in their continued availability and acceptance.

The records of respondent's bank accounts which the federal Bank Secrecy Act requires the bank to keep pertain to transactions to which the bank was itself a party.

Respondent argues, however, that because of the Bank Secrecy Act, the subpoena in this case was the functional equivalent of a search and seizure of the depositor's "private papers." This is an invalid argument as the mere maintenance of records pursuant to the Bank Secrecy Act invade no Fourth Amendment right of any depositor. But respondent contends that the combination of the recordkeeping of the Bank Secrecy Act and the issuance of a subpoena to obtain those records permits the Government to circumvent the requirements of the Fourth Amendment by allowing it to obtain a depositor's private records without complying with the legal requirements that would be applicable had it obtained a warrant against him, Miller, directly. Therefore, we must address the question whether this case creates a Fourth Amendment interest in the depositor's banking records which are held by the bank.

Respondent urges that he has a Fourth Amendment interest in the records kept by the banks because they are merely copies of personal records that were made available to the banks for a limited purpose and in which he has a reasonable expectation of privacy. He relies on this Court's statement in *Katz v. United States* (1967) that we have departed from the narrow view that property interests control the right of the Government to search and seize, and that a "search and seizure" become unreasonable when the Government's activities violate the privacy upon which a person justifiably relies. But in *Katz*, the Court also stressed that what a person knowingly exposes to the public is not a subject of Fourth Amendment protection. We must examine the nature of the particular documents sought to be protected in order to determine whether there is a legitimate "expectation of privacy" concerning their contents.

Even if we direct our attention to the original checks and deposit slips, rather than to the microfilm copies actually viewed and obtained by means of the subpoena, we perceive no legitimate "expectation of privacy" in their contents. The checks are not confidential communications, but negotiable instruments to be used in commercial transactions. All of the documents obtained, including financial statements and deposit slips, contain only information voluntarily conveyed to the banks and exposed to their employees in the ordinary course of business. The lack of any legitimate expectation of privacy concerning the information kept in bank records was assumed by Congress in enacting the Bank Secrecy Act, the expressed purpose of which is to require records to be maintained because they "have a high degree of usefulness in criminal, tax, and regulatory investigations and proceedings."

The depositor takes the risk, in revealing his affairs to another, that the information will be conveyed by that person to the Government. This Court has held repeatedly that the Fourth Amendment does not prohibit the obtaining of information revealed to a third party and conveyed by him to Government authorities, even if the information is revealed on the assumption that it will be used only for a limited purpose and the confidence placed in the third party will not be betrayed.

This analysis is not changed by the mandate in the Bank Secrecy Act that records of depositors' transactions be maintained by banks.

Since no Fourth Amendment interests of the depositor are implicated here, this case is governed by the general rule that the issuance of a subpoena to a third party to obtain the records of that party does not violate the rights of a defendant, even if a criminal prosecution is contemplated at the time the subpoena is issued. Under these principles, it was firmly settled, before the passage of the Bank Secrecy Act, that an Internal Revenue Service summons directed to a third-party bank does not violate the Fourth Amendment rights of a depositor under investigation.

Many banks traditionally kept permanent records of their depositors' accounts, although not all banks did so, and the practice was declining in recent years. By requiring that such records be kept by all banks, the Bank Secrecy Act is not a novel means designed to circumvent established Fourth Amendment rights. It is merely an attempt to facilitate the use of a proper and longstanding law enforcement technique by insuring that records are available when they are needed.

END OF OPINION

This case involved the loss of privacy that results when a person turns personal information over to a third party, such as a bank, even where there is an expectation that this receiving party (the bank) will protect the privacy of the records. Recall that, in this case, the argument that the Bank Records Act should protect the secrecy of the records was dismissed by the Court. Many times we expect those we turn our records or other personal information over to will respect the same level of privacy that we would if we kept the information ourselves. *Miller* stands for the proposition that, at least where law enforcement (and by extension, national security community) access to the information is concerned, this is not the case. *Miller* is paired with another case from the same decade, *Smith v. Maryland*, that involved police access to certain records maintained by the telephone company.

Smith v. Maryland, 442 U.S. 735 (1979)*

This case presents the question whether the installation and use of a pen register constitutes a "search" within the meaning of the Fourth Amendment, made applicable to the States through the Fourteenth Amendment. A pen register is a device which records the phone numbers dialed from a telephone line.

On March 5, 1976, in Baltimore, Md., Patricia McDonough was robbed. She gave the police a description of the robber and of a 1975 Monte Carlo automobile she had observed near the scene of the crime. After the robbery, McDonough began receiving threatening and obscene phone calls from a man identifying himself as the robber. On one occasion, the caller asked that she step out on her front porch; she did so, and saw the 1975 Monte Carlo she had earlier described to police moving slowly past her home. On March 16, police spotted a man who met McDonough's description driving a 1975 Monte Carlo in her neighborhood. By tracing the license plate number, police learned that the car was registered in the name of petitioner, Michael Lee Smith.

The next day, the telephone company, at police request, installed a pen register at its central offices to record the numbers dialed from the telephone at petitioner's home. The police did not get a warrant or court order before having the pen register installed. The register revealed that on March 17 a call was placed from petitioner's home to

---

* The case has been heavily edited and paraphrased by the authors for clarity. See disclaimer in introduction.

McDonough's phone. On the basis of this and other evidence, the police obtained a warrant to search petitioner's residence. The search revealed that a page in petitioner's phone book was turned down to the name and number of Patricia McDonough; the phone book was seized. Petitioner was arrested, and a six-man lineup was held on March 19. McDonough identified petitioner as the man who had robbed her.

Petitioner was indicted in the Criminal Court of Baltimore for robbery. By pretrial motion, he sought to suppress "all fruits derived from the pen register" on the ground that the police had failed to secure a warrant prior to its installation. The trial court denied the suppression motion, holding that the warrantless installation of the pen register did not violate the Fourth Amendment. Petitioner then waived a jury trial, and the case was submitted to the court on an agreed statement of facts. The pen register tape (evidencing the fact that a phone call had been made from petitioner's phone to McDonough's phone) and the phone book seized in the search of petitioner's residence were admitted into evidence against him. Petitioner was convicted and was sentenced to six years.

The Fourth Amendment guarantees "the right of the people to be secure in their persons, houses, papers, and effects, against unreasonable searches and seizures." In determining whether a particular form of government-initiated electronic surveillance is a "search" within the meaning of the Fourth Amendment, we refer to *Katz v. United States*. In *Katz*, Government agents had intercepted the contents of a telephone conversation by attaching an electronic listening device to the outside of a public phone booth. The Court rejected the argument that a "search" can occur only when there has been a "physical intrusion" into a "constitutionally protected area," noting that the Fourth Amendment "protects people, not places." Because the Government's monitoring of Katz' conversation "violated the privacy upon which he justifiably relied while using the telephone booth," the Court held that it "constituted a 'search and seizure' within the meaning of the Fourth Amendment."

Consistently with *Katz*, this Court uniformly has held that the application of the Fourth Amendment depends on whether the person invoking its protection can claim a justifiable, a reasonable, or a "legitimate expectation of privacy" that has been invaded by government action. This inquiry, as Mr. Justice Harlan aptly noted in his *Katz* concurrence, normally embraces two discrete questions. The first is whether the individual, by his conduct, has "exhibited an actual (subjective) expectation of privacy," in the words of the *Katz* majority, the individual has shown that "he seeks to preserve something as private." The second question is whether the individual's subjective expectation of privacy is "one that society is prepared to recognize as 'reasonable,'"—whether, in the words of the *Katz* majority, the individual's expectation, viewed objectively, is "justifiable" under the circumstances.

In applying the *Katz* analysis to this case, it is important to begin by specifying precisely the nature of the state activity that is challenged. The activity here took the form of installing and using a pen register. Since the pen register was installed on telephone company property at the telephone company's central offices, petitioner obviously cannot claim that his "property" was invaded or that police intruded into a "constitutionally protected area." Petitioner's claim, rather, is that, notwithstanding the absence of a trespass, the State, as did the Government in *Katz*, infringed a "legitimate expectation of privacy" that petitioner held. Yet a pen register differs significantly from the listening device employed in *Katz*, for pen registers do not acquire the contents of communications. This Court recently noted:

> "Indeed, a law enforcement official could not even determine from the use of a pen register whether a communication existed. These devices do not hear sound. They disclose only the telephone numbers that have been dialed—a means of establishing communication. Neither the purport of any communication between the caller and the recipient of the call, their identities, nor whether the call was even completed is disclosed by pen registers."

Given a pen register's limited capabilities, therefore, petitioner's argument that its installation and use constituted a "search" necessarily rests upon a claim that he had a "legitimate expectation of privacy" regarding the numbers he dialed on his phone. This claim must be rejected. First, we doubt that people in general entertain any actual expectation of privacy in the numbers they dial. All telephone users realize that they must "convey" phone numbers to the telephone company, since it is through telephone company switching equipment that their calls are completed. All subscribers realize, moreover, that the phone company has facilities for making permanent records of the numbers they dial, for they see a list of their long-distance (toll) calls on their monthly bills. In fact, pen registers and similar devices are routinely used by telephone companies for the purposes of checking billing operations, detecting fraud and preventing violations of law. Electronic equipment is used not only to keep billing records of toll calls, but also to keep a record of all calls dialed from a telephone which is subject to a special rate structure. Pen registers are regularly employed to determine whether a home phone is being used to conduct a business, to check for a defective dial, or to check for overbilling. Although most people may be oblivious to a pen register's esoteric functions, they presumably have some awareness of one common use: to aid in the identification of persons making annoying or obscene calls. Most phone books tell subscribers, on a page entitled "Consumer Information," that the company "can frequently help in identifying to the authorities the origin of unwelcome and troublesome calls." Telephone users, in sum, typically know that they must convey numerical information to the phone company; that the phone company has facilities for recording this information; and that the phone company does in fact record this information for a variety of legitimate business purposes. Although subjective expectations cannot be scientifically gauged, it is too much to believe that telephone subscribers, under these circumstances, harbor any general expectation that the numbers they dial will remain secret.

Petitioner argues, however, that, whatever the expectations of telephone users in general, he demonstrated an expectation of privacy by his own conduct here, since he "used the telephone in his house to the exclusion of all others." But the site of the call is immaterial for purposes of analysis in this case. Although petitioner's conduct may have been calculated to keep the contents of his conversation private, his conduct was not and could not have been calculated to preserve the privacy of the number he dialed. Regardless of his location, petitioner had to convey that number to the telephone company in precisely the same way if he wished to complete his call. The fact that he dialed the number on his home phone rather than on some other phone could make no conceivable difference, nor could any subscriber rationally think that it would.

Second, even if petitioner did harbor some subjective expectation that the phone numbers he dialed would remain private, this expectation is not "one that society is prepared to recognize as 'reasonable.'" This Court consistently has held that a person has no legitimate expectation of privacy in information he voluntarily turns over to third parties. In *Miller*, for example, the Court held that a bank depositor has no "legitimate 'expectation of privacy' in financial information voluntarily conveyed to banks and exposed to their employees in the ordinary course of business." The Court explained:

> The depositor takes the risk, in revealing his affairs to another, that the information will be conveyed by that person to the Government. This Court has held repeatedly that the Fourth Amendment does not prohibit the obtaining of information revealed to a third party and conveyed by him to Government authorities, even if the information is revealed on the assumption that it will be used only for a limited purpose and the confidence placed in the third party will not be betrayed.

Because the depositor "assumed the risk" of disclosure, the Court held that it would be unreasonable for him to expect his financial records to remain private.

This analysis dictates that petitioner can claim no legitimate expectation of privacy here. When he used his phone, petitioner voluntarily conveyed numerical information to the telephone company and "exposed" that information to its equipment in the ordinary course of business. In so doing, petitioner assumed the risk that the company would reveal to police the numbers he dialed. The switching equipment that processed those numbers is merely the modern counterpart of the operator who, in an earlier day, personally completed calls for the subscriber. Petitioner concedes that if he had placed his calls through an operator, he could claim no legitimate expectation of privacy. We are not inclined to hold that a different constitutional result is required because the telephone company has decided to automate.

Petitioner argues, however, that automatic switching equipment differs from a live operator in one pertinent respect. An operator, in theory at least, is capable of remembering every number that is conveyed to him by callers. Electronic equipment, by contrast can "remember" only those numbers it is programmed to record, and telephone companies, in view of their present billing practices, usually do not record local calls. Since petitioner, in calling McDonough, was making a local call, his expectation of privacy as to her number, on this theory, would be legitimate.

This argument does not withstand scrutiny. The fortuity of whether or not the phone company in fact elects to make a quasi-permanent record of a particular number dialed does not in our view, make any constitutional difference. Regardless of the phone company's election, petitioner voluntarily conveyed to it information that it had facilities for recording and that it was free to record. In these circumstances, petitioner assumed the risk that the information would be divulged to police. Under petitioner's theory, Fourth Amendment protection would exist, or not, depending on how the telephone company chose to define local-dialing zones, and depending on how it chose to bill its customers for local calls. Calls placed across town, or dialed directly, would be protected; calls placed across the river, or dialed with operator assistance, might not be. We are not inclined to make a crazy quilt of the Fourth Amendment, especially in circumstances where (as here) the pattern of protection would be dictated by billing practices of a private corporation.

We therefore conclude that petitioner in all probability entertained no actual expectation of privacy in the phone numbers he dialed, and that, even if he did, his expectation was not "legitimate." The installation and use of a pen register, consequently, was not a "search," and no warrant was required. The judgment of the Maryland Court of Appeals is affirmed.

END OF OPINION

Statutory Protections of Privacy

The Fourth Amendment is not the only source of protection of privacy. Many of the privacy protections we have now come from statutes that Congress has enacted to deal with areas of privacy rights that the Fourth Amendment might not have been able to cover. And, in many cases, these statutes came after disclosure of activity that the people felt violated privacy rights even though the action might not have been prohibited by the Constitution. In fact, recall that the Supreme Court in the *Olmstead* decision stated "Congress may, of course, protect the secrecy of telephone messages by making them, when intercepted, inadmissible in evidence in federal criminal trials by direct legislation, and thus depart from the common law of evidence." Congress has, in fact, added to the protections of the Fourth Amendment in a number of ways.

During the 1950s, 1960s and 1970s, there was a series of disclosures about federal and state law enforcement agencies, national security organizations, and military intelligence engaging in warrantless surveillance of members of the civil rights movement, members of academia, and even the press and members of Congress. These disclosures resulted in a series of hearings by Congress known as the Church Committee hearings.[2] In large measure because of these hearings, Congress enacted a series of statutes that provided added protection to the privacy of American citizens.

---

2. See, for example, Johnson, Loch K., *A Season Of Inquiry, Congress And Intelligence*, Chicago: Dorsey Press (1988).

The Freedom of Information Act,[3] the Privacy Act,[4] the Foreign Intelligence Surveillance Act,[5] the Wiretap Statute, the Electronic Communications Privacy Act, the Stored Communications Act,[6] the Right to Financial Privacy Act (RFPA),[7] and the Fair Credit Reporting Act[8] are all statutes that were enacted to provide protection to the privacy of records that might otherwise simply be considered to have been made public because they were shared with government, banks, and other businesses. These statutes provide a means for law enforcement and national security agencies to gain access to records, but also provide procedural and substantive limits on how and under what circumstances these records may be obtained and the purposes for which they can be used. We don't have the space to go into a great deal of detail, but will summarize some key points here.

For law enforcement purposes, the most significant regulation passed was the Wiretap Act. The Wiretap Act was first passed as Title III of the Omnibus Crime Control and Safe Streets Act of 1968. Most warrants for law enforcement related wiretaps and electronic surveillance are known as "Title III Warrants." The Wiretap Act regulates the collection of actual content of wire and electronic communications. Prior to the 1986 amendment by Title I of the Electronic Communications Privacy Act (ECPA), the Wiretap Act covered only wire and oral communications. Title I of the ECPA extended that coverage to electronic communications. The Wiretap Act broadly prohibits the intentional interception, use, or disclosure of wire and electronic communications unless a statutory exception applies. These prohibitions bar third parties (including the government) from wiretapping telephones and installing electronic "sniffers" that read Internet traffic without proper authority and basis.

When authorized by the Justice Department and signed by a United States District Court or Court of Appeals judge, a wiretap order permits law enforcement to intercept communications for up to thirty days. The law imposes several requirements that have to be satisfied before investigators can obtain a Title III order. Most importantly, the application for the order must show probable cause to believe that the interception will reveal evidence of a predicate felony offense. There is also a broad exception that permits "any person" to intercept an electronic communication that might be made through a system configured in a way to ensures the communication is readily accessible to the general public. Congress wanted to protect electronic communications that are configured to be private, such as email and private electronic bulletin boards, as opposed to publicly accessible communications.

Acquisition of the contents of stored electronic or wire communications is governed by the Stored Communications Act. So while the statutes mentioned above govern

---

3. 5 U.S.C. § 552.
4. 5 U.S.C. § 552a.
5. 50 U.S.C. Chapter 36.
6. These three are all found in 18 U.S.C. Chapter 119.
7. 12 U.S.C. Chapter 35.
8. 15 U.S.C. § 1681.

when law enforcement may intercept and record ongoing communications, this law regulates when an electronic communication service provider may disclose the contents of or other information about a customer's emails and other electronic communications to private parties that is now stored in the memory of a computer, network server, or other communications system. Congress passed the Stored Communications Act to prohibit a provider of an electronic communication service "from knowingly divulging the contents of any communication while in electronic storage by that service to any person other than the addressee or intended recipient."[9]

Congress had decided that computer and communication system users have a legitimate interest in the confidentiality of their communications in electronic storage at a communications facility. The law also generally forbids the disclosure of non-content records to the government, but allows non-content records to be disclosed to private parties. What is important about this law, though, is that any disclosure of the identity of a user may not be disclosed but is subject to constitutional protection.

Under the Stored Communications Act there are four categories of information, each with differing access requirements:

- contents of wire or electronic communications in electronic storage;
- contents of wire or electronic communications in a remote computing service;
- subscriber records concerning electronic communication service or remote computing service; and
- basic subscriber information.

Access to information in one of these categories requires a search warrant, which may be obtained by a court order upon proof of "specific and articulable facts showing . . . reasonable grounds to believe that . . . the records or other information sought, are relevant and material to an ongoing criminal investigation."[10]

Five federal statutes authorize intelligence officials to request certain business record information in connection with national security investigations. The authority to issue these national security letters (NSLs) is comparable to the authority to issue administrative subpoenas. The ancestor of the first NSL letter provision is an exception to privacy protections afforded by the Right to Financial Privacy Act (RFPA). It was neither an affirmative grant of authority to request information nor a command to financial institutions to provide information when asked, but simply the restrictions on the release of customer information imposed on financial institutions by the RFPA, but it left them free to decline to comply when asked to do so. The law gives the FBI access to financial institution records in certain foreign intelligence cases.

In the Electronic Communications Privacy Act, Congress afforded the FBI comparable access to telephone company and other communications service provider customer information. Together, the two NSL provisions afforded the FBI access to communications and financial business records under limited

---

9. S.Rep. No. 99-541, 97th Cong. 2nd Sess. 37, reprinted in 1986 U.S.C.C.A.N. 3555, 3591.
10. 18 U.S.C. § 2703(d).

circumstances—customer and customer transaction information held by telephone carriers and banks pertaining to a foreign power or its agents relevant to a foreign counterintelligence investigation. In the mid-1990s, Congress added two more NSL provisions—one permits NSL use in connection with the investigation of government employee leaks of classified information under the National Security Act; the other grants the FBI access to credit agency records pursuant to the Fair Credit Reporting Act, under much the same conditions as apply to the records of financial institutions. These provisions contained nondisclosure provisions and limitations on further dissemination, except pursuant to guidelines promulgated by the Attorney General. Neither had an express enforcement mechanism nor identified penalties for failure to comply with either the NSL or the nondisclosure instruction. Some of these procedures were expanded after the terrorist attacks of 9/11 in the USA PATRIOT Act[11] and its amendments. We'll discuss that law in more detail in the next chapter.

Expanding Technology and Privacy Implications

Electronic communications and financial records are not the only areas where technology is affecting privacy. Let's continue our exploration of the topic by starting with this hypothetical scenario:

> Sally and Marvin are relaxing in their living room watching television while having a conversation about the marijuana plants growing in their basement. Unknown to them, the FBI is parked across the street, in a public parking spot, in a van and using super-sensitive listening equipment—equipment that allows them to hear what is going on inside the home even without planting a bug, wiretap, or other listening device, is listening to and recording their conversation. Do the FBI need a warrant for this?

You will recall that Brandeis and Warren wrote their article on "The Right to Privacy" because new inventions, like the photograph, the recording of sound, and the telegraph, began interfering with previous concepts of privacy. Well, the issue of how new technology affects privacy continues to affect society and the law. In recent years, there have been incredible scientific advancements in surveillance technology. We now have devices and instruments which can literally look, listen, and even smell through walls. We have technology that can follow us wherever we go, watch us wherever we go, and digital records of this can be archived and easily searched. What is the law whenever law enforcement uses these devices?

While a number of cases through the years struggled with this question, the case of *Kyllo v. United States* established that the use of technology to gain access to information that is kept behind walls—real or electronic ones—would indeed count as an "invasion" of the area and thus a search.

---

11. Uniting and Strengthening America by Providing Appropriate Tools Required to Intercept and Obstruct Terrorism Act of 2001, Public Law 107-56, Statutes at Large 115 Stat. 272 (2001).

Kyllo v. United States, 533 U.S. 27 (2001)*

This case presents the question whether the use of a thermal-imaging device aimed at a private home from a public street to detect relative amounts of heat within the home constitutes a "search" within the meaning of the Fourth Amendment.

In 1991 Agent William Elliott of the United States Department of the Interior came to suspect that marijuana was being grown in the home belonging to petitioner Danny Kyllo, part of a triplex on Rhododendron Drive in Florence, Oregon. Indoor marijuana growth typically requires high-intensity lamps. In order to determine whether an amount of heat was emanating from petitioner's home consistent with the use of such lamps, at 3:20 a.m. on January 16, 1992, Agent Elliott and Dan Haas used an Agema Thermovision 210 thermal imager to scan the triplex. Thermal imagers detect infrared radiation, which virtually all objects emit but which is not visible to the naked eye. The imager converts radiation into images based on relative warmth—black is cool, white is hot, shades of gray connote relative differences; in that respect, it operates somewhat like a video camera showing heat images. The scan of Kyllo's home took only a few minutes and was performed from the passenger seat of Agent Elliott's vehicle across the street from the front of the house and also from the street in back of the house. The scan showed that the roof over the garage and a side wall of petitioner's home were relatively hot compared to the rest of the home and substantially warmer than neighboring homes in the triplex. Agent Elliott concluded that petitioner was using halide lights to grow marijuana in his house, which indeed he was. Based on tips from informants, utility bills, and the thermal imaging, a Federal Magistrate Judge issued a warrant authorizing a search of petitioner's home, and the agents found an indoor growing operation involving more than 100 plants. Petitioner was indicted on one count of manufacturing marijuana. He unsuccessfully moved to suppress the evidence seized from his home and then entered a conditional guilty plea.

The Court of Appeals for the Ninth Circuit remanded the case for an evidentiary hearing regarding the intrusiveness of thermal imaging. On remand the District Court found that the Agema Thermovision 210 thermal imager "is a non-intrusive device which emits no rays or beams and shows a crude visual image of the heat being radiated from the outside of the house"; it "did not show any people or activity within the walls of the structure"; "the device used cannot penetrate walls or windows to reveal conversations or human activities"; and "no intimate details of the home were observed." Based on these findings, the District Court upheld the validity of the warrant that relied in part upon the thermal imaging, and reaffirmed its denial of the motion to suppress. A divided Court of Appeals initially reversed, but that opinion was withdrawn and the panel (after a change in composition) affirmed. The court held that petitioner had shown no subjective expectation of privacy because he had made no attempt to conceal the heat escaping from his home, and even if he

---

* The case has been heavily edited and paraphrased by the authors for clarity. See disclaimer in introduction.

had, there was no objectively reasonable expectation of privacy because the imager "did not expose any intimate details of Kyllo's life," only "amorphous 'hot spots' on the roof and exterior wall."

II

The Fourth Amendment provides that "The right of the people to be secure in their persons, houses, papers, and effects, against unreasonable searches and seizures, shall not be violated." "At the very core" of the Fourth Amendment "stands the right of a man to retreat into his own home and there be free from unreasonable governmental intrusion." With few exceptions, the question whether a warrantless search of a home is reasonable and hence constitutional must be answered no.

On the other hand, the antecedent question of whether or not a Fourth Amendment "search" has occurred is not so simple under our precedent. The permissibility of ordinary visual surveillance of a home used to be clear because, well into the 20th century, our Fourth Amendment jurisprudence was tied to common-law trespass, as explained in *Olmstead*. Visual surveillance was unquestionably lawful because 'the eye cannot by the laws of England be guilty of a trespass.' However, there has been a slight change ever since in *Katz* we disassociated violation of a person's Fourth Amendment rights from a physical trespassory violation of his property, but the lawfulness of warrantless visual surveillance of a home has still been preserved. As we observed in *California v. Ciraolo* (1986), "the Fourth Amendment protection of the home has never been extended to require law enforcement officers to shield their eyes when passing by a home on public thoroughfares." It is from this idea where we have the plain view doctrine.

One might think that the new validating rationale would be that examining the portion of a house that is in plain public view, while it is a "search" despite the absence of trespass, is not an "unreasonable" one under the Fourth Amendment. But in fact we have held that visual observation is no "search" at all—perhaps in order to preserve somewhat more intact our doctrine that warrantless searches are presumptively unconstitutional. In assessing when a search is not a search, we have applied somewhat in reverse the principle first enunciated in *Katz v. United States*. *Katz* involved eavesdropping by means of an electronic listening device placed on the outside of a telephone booth—a location not within the catalog ("persons, houses, papers, and effects") that the Fourth Amendment protects against unreasonable searches. We held that the Fourth Amendment nonetheless protected Katz from the warrantless eavesdropping because he "justifiably relied" upon the privacy of the telephone booth. As Justice Harlan's oft-quoted concurrence described it, a Fourth Amendment search occurs when the government violates a subjective expectation of privacy that society recognizes as reasonable. We have subsequently applied this principle to hold that a Fourth Amendment search does not occur—even when the explicitly protected location of a house is concerned—unless "the individual manifested a subjective expectation of privacy in the object of the challenged search," and "society is willing to recognize that expectation as reasonable."

The present case involves officers on a public street engaged in more than naked-eye surveillance of a home. We have previously reserved judgment as to how much technological enhancement of ordinary perception from such a vantage point, if any, is too much. While we held aerial photography of an industrial complex in *Dow Chemical Co. v. U.S.* when an airplane was in the lawful public airspace, we noted that we found "it important that this is not an area immediately adjacent to a private home, where privacy expectations are most heightened."

III

It would be foolish to contend that the degree of privacy secured to citizens by the Fourth Amendment has been entirely unaffected by the advance of technology. For example, as the cases discussed above make clear, the technology enabling human flight has exposed to public view (and hence, we have said, to official observation) uncovered portions of the house and its curtilage that once were private. The question we confront today is what limits there are upon this power of technology to shrink the realm of guaranteed privacy.

The *Katz* test—whether the individual has an expectation of privacy that society is prepared to recognize as reasonable—has often been criticized as circular, and hence subjective and unpredictable. While it may be difficult to refine *Katz* when the search of areas such as telephone booths, automobiles, or even the curtilage and uncovered portions of residences are at issue, in the case of the search of the interior of homes—the prototypical and hence most commonly litigated area of protected privacy—there is a ready criterion, with roots deep in the common law, of the minimal expectation of privacy that exists, and that is acknowledged to be reasonable. To withdraw protection of this minimum expectation would be to permit police technology to erode the privacy guaranteed by the Fourth Amendment. We think that obtaining by sense-enhancing technology any information regarding the interior of the home that could not otherwise have been obtained without physical "intrusion into a constitutionally protected area," constitutes a search—at least where (as here) the technology in question is not in general public use. This assures preservation of that degree of privacy against government that existed when the Fourth Amendment was adopted. On the basis of this criterion, the information obtained by the thermal imager in this case was the product of a search.

The Government maintains, however, that the thermal imaging must be upheld because it detected "only heat radiating from the external surface of the house." The dissent makes this its leading point, contending that there is a fundamental difference between what it calls "off-the-wall" observations and "through-the-wall surveillance." But just as a thermal imager captures only heat emanating from a house, so also a powerful directional microphone picks up only sound emanating from a house—and a satellite capable of scanning from many miles away would pick up only visible light emanating from a house. We rejected such a mechanical interpretation of the Fourth Amendment in *Katz*, where the eavesdropping device picked up only sound waves that reached the exterior of the phone booth. Reversing that approach would leave the homeowner at the mercy of advancing technology—including imaging technology that could discern all human activity in the home. While the technology used in the present case was relatively crude, the rule we adopt must take account of more sophisticated systems that are already in use or in development. The dissent's reliance on the distinction between "off-the-wall" and "through-the-wall" observation is entirely incompatible with the dissent's belief, which we discuss below, that thermal-imaging observations of the intimate details of a home are impermissible. The most sophisticated thermal imaging devices continue to measure heat "off-the-wall" rather than "through-the-wall"; the dissent's disapproval of those more sophisticated thermal-imaging devices is an acknowledgment that there is no substance to this distinction. As for the dissent's extraordinary assertion that anything learned through "an inference" cannot be a search, that would validate even the "through-the-wall" technologies that the dissent purports to disapprove. Surely the dissent does not believe that the through-the-wall radar or ultrasound technology produces an 8-by-10 Kodak glossy that needs no analysis (i.e., the making of inferences). And, of course, the novel proposition that inference insulates a search is blatantly contrary to *United States v. Karo*, 468 U.S. 705 (1984), where the police "inferred" from the activation of a beeper (that had previously been clandestinely placed in a can of ether) that a certain can of ether was in the home. The police activity was held to be a search, and the search was held unlawful.

The Government also contends that the thermal imaging was constitutional because it did not "detect private activities occurring in private areas." It points out that in *Dow Chemical* we observed that the enhanced aerial photography did not reveal any "intimate details." However, this involved enhanced aerial photography of an industrial complex, which does not share the Fourth Amendment sanctity of the home. The Fourth Amendment's protection of the home has never been tied to measurement of the quality or quantity of information obtained. In *Silverman v. U.S.*, for example, we made clear that any physical invasion of the structure of the home, "by even a fraction of an inch," was too much, and there is certainly no exception to the warrant requirement for the officer who barely cracks open the front door and sees nothing but the nonintimate rug on the vestibule floor. In the home, our cases show, all details are intimate details, because the entire area is held safe from prying government eyes. Thus, in *Karo*, the only thing detected was a can of ether in the home; and in *Arizona v. Hicks*, 480 U.S. 321 (1987), the only thing detected by a physical search that went beyond what officers lawfully present could observe in "plain view" was the registration number of a phonograph turntable. These were intimate details because they were details of the home, just as was the detail of how warm—or even how relatively warm—Kyllo was heating his residence.

Limiting the prohibition of thermal imaging to "intimate details" would not only be wrong in principle; it would be impractical in application, failing to provide "a workable accommodation between the needs of law enforcement and the interests protected by the Fourth Amendment." To begin with, there is no necessary connection between the sophistication of the surveillance equipment and the "intimacy" of the details that it observes—which means that one cannot say (and the police cannot be assured) that use of the relatively crude equipment at issue here will always be lawful. The Agema Thermovision 210 might disclose, for example, at what hour each night the lady of the house takes her daily sauna and bath—a detail that many would consider "intimate"; and a much more sophisticated system might detect nothing more intimate than the fact that someone left a closet light on. We could not, in other words, develop a rule approving only that through-the-wall surveillance which identifies objects no smaller than 36 by 36 inches, but would have to develop a jurisprudence specifying which home activities are "intimate" and which are not. And even when (if ever) that jurisprudence were fully developed, no police officer would be able to know in advance whether his through-the-wall surveillance picks up "intimate" details—and thus would be unable to know in advance whether it is constitutional.

We have said that the Fourth Amendment draws "a firm line at the entrance to the house." That line, we think, must be not only firm but also bright—which requires clear specification of those methods of surveillance that require a warrant. While it is certainly possible to conclude from the videotape of the thermal imaging that occurred in this case that no "significant" compromise of the homeowner's privacy has occurred, we must take the long view, from the original meaning of the Fourth Amendment forward.

The Fourth Amendment is to be construed in the light of what was deemed an unreasonable search and seizure when it was adopted, and in a manner which will conserve public interests as well as the interests and rights of individual citizens. Where, as here, the Government uses a device that is not in general public use, to explore details of the home that would previously have been unknowable without physical intrusion, the surveillance is a "search" and is presumptively unreasonable without a warrant.

Since we hold the Thermovision imaging to have been an unlawful search, it will remain for the District Court to determine whether, without the evidence it provided, the search warrant issued in this case was supported by probable cause—and if not, whether there is any other basis for supporting admission of the evidence that the search pursuant to the warrant produced.

END OF OPINION

This is an important case, so let's review the finding and analysis once again. Here, government agents stood on public property while using a heat imaging device to look at the wall of a privately owned home. Based on the fact that the heat signature coming off the wall was similar to the heat signature one might expect of certain lights used to grow marijuana, the police had probable cause to believe that marijuana was being grown inside the house. Using that image, the police obtained a warrant from the magistrate to conduct a physical search inside the house. The defendant, Kyllo, challenged that even looking at a house with a thermal imager requires a warrant because the knowledge the police gained of the interior contents of his home violated his reasonable expectation of privacy.

In reviewing this case, the U.S. Supreme Court set forth the rule that whenever law enforcement use technology not in general public use to discover what otherwise could only be learned by a physical intrusion, which would require a warrant, the government must have a warrant. Here, thermal imagers are not in general public use. The government used one to observe a house, and in doing so learned that there was marijuana inside. Previously, the only way to have learned about the marijuana inside the house was to have conducted a physical search, which would have required a warrant. Because the government learned through the warrantless use of technology what previously could only have been learned by physically searching the house, which could only be lawfully done pursuant to a warrant, to maintain the meaning of the Fourth Amendment in an electronic era, the Supreme Court required that a warrant should have been obtained to use the thermal imager in the first place. The Court was very deliberate in using the broad and encompassing language of "device not in general public use." This way, its ruling would apply to other technologies besides thermal imagers such as highly sensitive microphones, backscatter x-rays, and other devices which might not yet even have been invented.

Review Questions

1. Officer Brown is playing with his department's newest toy, a highly sensitive microphone that was purchased for $4,400 off Amazon.com. He is having fun, listening to private conversations people are having in their homes. In one house, Officer Brown overhears people discussing their plans to detonate a bomb at the Super Bowl. Using a recording of this conversation, he goes to the magistrate to get a warrant for to search the home. While doing a warranted search of the home, he finds illegal bomb-making materials. With this evidence, he goes back to the magistrate and gets an arrest warrant. The defendants are arrested and their case goes to trial where the defense attorney argues that the evidence should be suppressed. Do an IRAC analysis and see how the judge should rule at trial.

2. The year is 2050, and Officer Waldo is bored so he is playing around with his Google Glass, version 40.7, which he had purchased from the Dollar Store. To pass the time on the lonely stake-out of the Sampson's residence, he activates the device's thermal imaging app. Using the thermal imaging app, Officer Waldo looks at a house and sees heat coming off the house which gives him probable cause that the house is being used to grow Tomacco, which is a popular illegal drug in 2050. Using the image captured by the thermal imager, Officer Waldo goes to the magistrate to get a search warrant of the house and finds Tomacco. He then gets an arrest warrant and arrests the owners of the house. At trial, the defendants raise *Kyllo* as their defense. IRAC what you think happens.

3. The year is 2030 and the newest and hottest piece of technology in law enforcement is the "Backscatter X-Ray Goggles." These work a lot like the machines at the airport, which give TSA screeners the ability to see through a person's clothing, except they are portable. Just by looking at a person, law enforcement can now see through an individual's clothing. However, only prototypes exist because this technology is

so new. Naturally, the NYPD is one of the first to obtain this technology to test it out. While Officer Dan is walking through Times Square, he activates the glasses. With the glasses activated, he is seeing through the clothes of everyone present. Suddenly, he sees a person wearing a trench coat that is being used to conceal an illegal sawed-off shotgun. Officer Dan instantly subdues and arrests the person. What will happen when the defendant's lawyer makes a motion for the shotgun to be suppressed at trial?

4. Smith is a nature enthusiast and enjoys listening to bird songs. To capture bird songs, he has a special microphone/recording device he purchased for $4,400 off Amazon.com. One day while trying to capture bird songs, his microphone overhears his neighbors discussing a plot to bomb the Super Bowl. Mr. Smith turns the recording over to the police. What happens at trial when the defense lawyer tries to get the evidence thrown out as being unlawfully acquired by invading the rights of his clients?

These last questions are intended to make sure you don't forget what you learned in the last chapter; the Fourth Amendment only applies to government action. Still, it raises an interesting thought. What happens when, or if, highly invasive surveillance technologies enter general public use? Could we someday face a future where smartphones have features such as thermal imaging, ultra-sensitive microphones, electronic noses, and other features? What about the increasing use of closed-circuit or other surveillance cameras in public places? Just about every smartphone, laptop computer, or tablet now has GPS capability built in. What does this do to the *Katz* standard? Can technology and a reality of constant monitoring in public eventually completely erase any expectation of privacy?

The Emerging "Mosaic Theory" of Surveillance Law

Your right to privacy is most highly protected when you are inside your own home. What privacy do you have when you drive around town or walk down the sidewalk? Generally, you do not have any. This is part of the plain view doctrine. What you expose to the plain view of the outside world, including yourself, is not protected. The police can lawfully follow you around when you walk down the sidewalk or drive on public roadways, recording each place you visit ranging from the grocery store to the gynecologist. Cameras can be installed on public streets and record people and the licenses of passing vehicles (to run against a database of stolen vehicles or vehicles owned by persons with warrants out on them). Police and other devices can read plainly visible serial numbers and registration on passing vehicles in addition to license plates. Your very face is exposed to the plain view of the world, and technologies are being developed to integrate facial recognition software with government cameras to help catch suspected criminals.

For hundreds of years, the key limiting factor for why people were not continuously tracked and monitored while out in public had nothing to do with privacy law, but with the practical limitations on the ability to conduct around-the-clock continuous surveillance. Until recently, for a person to be continuously tracked in real time, this meant that law enforcement had to devote an agent and possibly a vehicle to follow that person around all of the time. It is very expensive to devote an officer, a vehicle, and other resources to continually track and monitor all movements of a single individual for an extended period of time. In addition, the record-keeping would be tremendously difficult. Think of the days and days and days of notes—how could anyone piece together all that information? So, with the exception of very high value targets (for example, Al Capone), the continuous tracking of persons was rarely done.

In recent years, though, improvements in technology have made it easier and less expensive for the government to track its citizens in real-time. There are many possible ways this can now be conducted including cell phone signals, cameras, and other means. One such method is through various systems that use the Global Positioning System (GPS), a series of satellites in orbit which provide real-time data on the location of a GPS receiver. When a GPS receiver is attached to a vehicle or when that function is activated on a smartphone, it is possible for law enforcement (or parents) to continuously track a person's exact movements in real time. Once very expensive, around-the-clock tracking is now very cheap and accurate. An active GPS receiver on your vehicle or your cellular phone could tell the government (or your mother) everywhere you go and how long you are there. For example, it could report that on Monday you left your home at 9am and went to an address (later determined to be the grocery store) and were there until 9:45am, and from there you went to the gynecologist's office building, arriving at 10am and leaving at 11am, from where you proceeded to the pharmacy. Or for another person, it could show that he left his house at 11am on Tuesday and arrived at the home of a known crack dealer at 11:15am, left at 11:45am and arrived at a gay bar at noon. After three hours at the gay bar, the person then arrived at an hourly motel at 3pm and stayed there until 5pm, at which point the person returned to his house and arrived at 5:20pm. Using public records, the police can tell that this person is a man married to a woman and is raising a family with three kids. Now, there is no Fourth Amendment prohibition from the police following people around, staying out of the way and not interfering, but simply watching. After all, all of this activity took place "in plain view," so there's no Fourth Amendment issue—or is there?

As these examples suggest, merely tracking one's location can have huge ramifications as to one's privacy. This is what is called a "mosaic approach" to privacy— just as mosaic art uses many small pieces of tile to create a big picture, the government is able to piece together significant amounts of otherwise public information to provide a picture of one's personal life using the surveillance, data storage, and search capabilities afforded by modern technology.

It was inevitable then, that a case involving GPS would eventually make its way to the U.S. Supreme Court. In the case of *United States v. Jones*, the Supreme Court ruled that law enforcement need a warrant whenever they are going to track a person's vehicle using GPS. As you will read, though, their reasoning had nothing to do with expectations of privacy. Instead, the Supreme Court returned to the theme we read in *Olmstead*: the ancient property-based doctrine of common law trespass.

As previously explained, common law trespass is one of the oldest torts, going back hundreds of years before the U.S. Constitution. Trespass is the ancient doctrine that without a warrant or consent, neither the public nor the government may enter upon your property. For example, if children kick a soccer ball onto the yard of a grumpy neighbor, this is a trespass and the grumpy neighbor can sue them because the property of another (the kid's soccer ball) entered his property without permission. (However, the damages resulting from this particular trespass of a child's soccer ball would be minimal, and the cost of suing would exceed the rewards.)

In *Jones*, the Court used this same analysis as a kid's soccer ball entering a neighbor's lawn in holding that the continuous GPS monitoring of a vehicle was also unlawful. While the justices struggled with the privacy implications, they were not willing to take the law and declare a new concept of privacy based on a mosaic theory. Instead, their view was that the simple act of attaching a GPS receiver underneath the vehicle was a trespass, just like a soccer ball entering the grumpy neighbor's lawn. This is what implicated the Fourth Amendment—this simple invasion of the property of the car's owner. What the police attached to the vehicle was irrelevant; all that mattered was that something was attached to the personal property of another without permission.

Although the majority opinion did not consider these privacy concerns, a few of the justices, namely Justices Sotomayor and Alito, did address the privacy issues in concurring opinions. As you will read below, these justices (who rarely agree on anything) put forth an argument that the Fourth Amendment incorporates both the common law idea of trespass and the post-*Katz* idea of a reasonable expectation of privacy. The view of these two justices was that a Fourth Amendment violation could also be found through the violation of a reasonable expectation of privacy from the ability to have one's vehicle continuously tracked without a warrant for over a month.

United States v. Jones, 132 S. Ct. 945 (2012)*

In 2004, Antoine Jones, owner and operator of a nightclub in the District of Columbia, came under suspicion of trafficking in narcotics and was made the target of an investigation by a joint FBI and Metropolitan Police Department task force. Officers employed various investigative techniques, including visual surveillance of the nightclub, installation of a camera focused on the front door of the club, and a pen register and wiretap covering Jones's cellular phone.

Based in part on information gathered from these sources, in 2005 the Government applied for a warrant authorizing the use of an electronic tracking device on

---

* The case has been heavily edited and paraphrased by the authors for clarity. See disclaimer in introduction.

the Jeep Grand Cherokee registered to Jones's wife. A warrant issued, authorizing installation of the device in the District of Columbia within 10 days.

On the 11th day, and not in the District of Columbia but in Maryland, agents installed a GPS tracking device on the undercarriage of the Jeep while it was parked in a public parking lot. Over the next 28 days, the Government used the device to track the vehicle's movements, and once had to replace the device's battery when the vehicle was parked in a different public lot in Maryland. By means of signals from multiple satellites, the device established the vehicle's location within 50 to 100 feet, and communicated that location by cellular phone to a Government computer. It relayed more than 2,000 pages of data over the 4-week period.

The Government ultimately obtained a multiple-count indictment charging Jones with conspiracy to distribute and possess with intent to distribute five kilograms or more of cocaine and 50 grams or more of cocaine. Before trial, Jones filed a motion to suppress evidence obtained through the GPS device. The District Court held the data admissible, because "a person traveling in an automobile on public thoroughfares has no reasonable expectation of privacy in his movements from one place to another."

The Government introduced at trial the GPS-derived locational data which connected Jones to the alleged conspirators' stash house that contained $850,000 in cash, 97 kilograms of cocaine, and 1 kilogram of cocaine base. The jury returned a guilty verdict, and the District Court sentenced Jones to life imprisonment. The United States Court of Appeals for the District of Columbia Circuit reversed the conviction because of admission of the evidence obtained by warrantless use of the GPS device which, it said, violated the Fourth Amendment.

. . .

The Fourth Amendment provides in relevant part that "the right of the people to be secure in their persons, houses, papers, and effects, against unreasonable searches and seizures, shall not be violated." It is beyond dispute that a vehicle is an "effect" as that term is used in the Amendment. We hold that the Government's installation of a GPS device on a target's vehicle, and its use of that device to monitor the vehicle's movements, constitutes a "search."

It is important to be clear about what occurred in this case: The Government physically occupied private property for the purpose of obtaining information. We have no doubt that such a physical intrusion would have been considered a "search" within the meaning of the Fourth Amendment when it was adopted. The numerous lawyers who drafted the Fourth Amendment were familiar with the British case *Entick v. Carrington*, 95 Eng. Rep. 807 (C.P. 1765). In that case, Lord Camden expressed in plain terms the significance of property rights in search-and-seizure analysis:

> Our law holds the property of every man so sacred, that no man can set his foot upon his neighbour's close without his leave; if he does he is a trespasser, though he does no damage at all; if he will tread upon his neighbour's ground, he must justify it by law.

The text of the Fourth Amendment reflects its close connection to property, since otherwise it would have referred simply to "the right of the people to be secure against unreasonable searches and seizures"; the phrase "in their persons, houses, papers, and effects" would have been superfluous.

Consistent with this understanding, our Fourth Amendment jurisprudence was tied to common-law trespass, at least until the latter half of the 20th century. Thus, in *Olmstead v. U.S.*, we held that wiretaps attached to telephone wires on the public streets did not constitute a Fourth Amendment search because "there was no entry of the houses or offices of the defendants."

Our later cases, of course, have deviated from that exclusively property-based approach. In *Katz v. United States*, we said that "the Fourth Amendment protects people, not places," and found a violation in attachment of an eavesdropping device to a public telephone booth. Our later cases have applied the analysis of Justice Harlan's concurrence in that case, which said that a violation occurs when government officers violate a person's "reasonable expectation of privacy."

The Government contends that the Harlan standard shows that no search occurred here, since Jones had no "reasonable expectation of privacy" in the area of the Jeep accessed by Government agents (its underbody) and in the locations of the Jeep on the public roads, which were visible to all. But we need not address the Government's contentions, because Jones's Fourth Amendment rights do not rise or fall with the *Katz* formulation. Instead, here we are simply looking to preserve the same level of privacy against government intrusions that existed when the Fourth Amendment was written. For most of our history the Fourth Amendment was understood to protect against the government's trespass upon the areas ("persons, houses, papers, and effects") it specifies in the text of the Fourth Amendment itself. *Katz* did not repudiate that understanding, but merely expanded it. The *Katz* reasonable-expectation-of-privacy test has been added to, not substituted for, the common-law trespassory test.

Attempting to justify its actions, the Government points to *New York v. Class* (1986) where we stated that "the exterior of a car is thrust into the public eye, and thus to examine it does not constitute a 'search.'" That statement is of marginal relevance here since, as the Government acknowledges, "the officers in this case did more than conduct a visual inspection of respondent's vehicle." By attaching the device to the Jeep, officers encroached on a protected area. In Class itself we suggested that this would make a difference, for we concluded that an officer's momentary reaching into the interior of a vehicle did constitute a search. This Court has to date not deviated from the understanding that mere visual observation does not constitute a search. A person traveling in an automobile on public thoroughfares has no reasonable expectation of privacy in his movements from one place to another.

Justice Sotomayor, concurring.

I join the Court's opinion because I agree that a search within the meaning of the Fourth Amendment occurs, at a minimum, "where, as here, the Government obtains information by physically intruding on a constitutionally protected area." In this case, the Government installed a Global Positioning System (GPS) tracking device on respondent Antoine Jones' Jeep without a valid warrant and without Jones' consent, then used that device to monitor the Jeep's movements over the course of four weeks. The Government usurped Jones' property for the purpose of conducting surveillance on him, thereby invading privacy interests long afforded, and undoubtedly entitled to, Fourth Amendment protection.

Of course, the Fourth Amendment is not concerned only with trespassory intrusions on property. Rather, even in the absence of a trespass, "a Fourth Amendment search occurs when the government violates a subjective expectation of privacy that society recognizes as reasonable." In *Katz,* this Court enlarged its then-prevailing focus on property rights by announcing that the reach of the Fourth Amendment does not "turn upon the presence or absence of a physical intrusion." As the majority's opinion makes clear, however, *Katz*'s reasonable-expectation-of-privacy test augmented, but did not displace or diminish, the common-law trespassory test that preceded it. Thus, "when the Government does engage in physical intrusion of a constitutionally protected area in order to obtain information, that intrusion may constitute a violation of the Fourth Amendment."

The trespassory test applied in the majority's opinion reflects an irreducible constitutional minimum: When the Government physically invades personal property to gather information, a search occurs. The reaffirmation of that principle suffices to decide this case.

Nonetheless, as Justice Alito notes in his concurring opinion, physical intrusion is now unnecessary to many forms of surveillance. With increasing regularity, the Government will be capable of duplicating the monitoring undertaken in this case by enlisting factory- or owner-installed vehicle tracking devices or GPS-enabled smartphones. In cases of electronic or other novel modes of surveillance that do not depend upon a physical invasion on property, the majority opinion's trespassory test may provide little guidance. But "situations involving merely the transmission of electronic signals without trespass would remain subject to *Katz* analysis." As Justice Alito incisively observes, the same technological advances that have made possible nontrespassory surveillance techniques will also affect the *Katz* test by shaping the evolution of societal privacy expectations. Under that rubric, I agree with Justice Alito that, at the very least, "longer term GPS monitoring in investigations of most offenses impinges on expectations of privacy."

In cases involving even short-term monitoring, some unique attributes of GPS surveillance relevant to the *Katz* analysis will require particular attention. GPS monitoring generates a precise, comprehensive record of a person's public movements that reflects a wealth of detail about her familial, political, professional, religious, and sexual associations. Disclosed in GPS data will be trips the indisputably private nature of which takes little imagination to conjure: trips to the psychiatrist, the plastic surgeon, the abortion clinic, the AIDS treatment center, the strip club, the criminal defense attorney, the by-the-hour motel, the union meeting, the mosque, synagogue or church, the gay bar and on and on. The Government can store such records and efficiently mine them for information years into the future. And because GPS monitoring is cheap in comparison to conventional surveillance techniques and, by design, proceeds surreptitiously, it evades the ordinary checks that constrain abusive law enforcement practices: limited police resources and community hostility.

Awareness that the Government may be watching chills associational and expressive freedoms. And the Government's unrestrained power to assemble data that reveal private aspects of identity is susceptible to abuse. The net result is that GPS monitoring—by making available at a relatively low cost such a substantial quantum of intimate information about any person whom the Government, in its unfettered discretion, chooses to track—may alter the relationship between citizen and government in a way that is inimical to democratic society.

I would take these attributes of GPS monitoring into account when considering the existence of a reasonable societal expectation of privacy in the sum of one's public movements. I would ask whether people reasonably expect that their movements will be recorded and aggregated in a manner that enables the Government to ascertain, more or less at will, their political and religious beliefs, sexual habits, and so on. I do not regard as dispositive the fact that the Government might obtain the fruits of GPS monitoring through lawful conventional surveillance techniques. I would also consider the appropriateness of entrusting to the Executive, in the absence of any oversight from a coordinate branch, a tool so amenable to misuse, especially in light of the Fourth Amendment's goal to curb arbitrary exercises of police power to and prevent "a too permeating police surveillance."

Justice Alito, with whom Justice Ginsburg, Justice Breyer, and Justice Kagan join, concurring in the judgment.

This case requires us to apply the Fourth Amendment's prohibition of unreasonable searches and seizures to a 21st-century surveillance technique, the use of a Global Positioning System (GPS) device to monitor a vehicle's movements for an extended period of time. Ironically, the Court has chosen to decide this case based on 18th-century tort law. By attaching a small GPS device to the underside of the vehicle that respondent drove, the law enforcement officers in this case engaged in conduct that might have provided grounds in 1791 for a lawsuit for trespass to private property. And for this reason, the Court concludes, the installation and use of the GPS device constituted a search.

This holding, in my judgment, is unwise. It strains the language of the Fourth Amendment; it has little if any support in current Fourth Amendment case law; and it is highly artificial. I would analyze the question presented in this case by asking whether respondent's reasonable expectations of privacy were violated by the long-term monitoring of the movements of the vehicle he drove.

The Fourth Amendment prohibits "unreasonable searches and seizures," and the Court makes very little effort to explain how the attachment or use of the GPS device fits within these terms. The Court does not contend that there was a seizure. A seizure of property occurs when "there is some meaningful interference with an individual's possessory interests in that property," and here there was none. Indeed, the success of the surveillance technique that the officers employed was dependent on the fact that the GPS did not interfere in any way with the operation of the vehicle, for if any such interference had been detected, the device might have been discovered.

The Court does claim that the installation and use of the GPS constituted a search, but this conclusion is dependent on the questionable proposition that these two procedures cannot be separated for purposes of Fourth Amendment analysis. If these two procedures are analyzed separately, it is not at all clear from the Court's opinion why either should be regarded as a search. It is clear that the attachment of the GPS device was not itself a search; if the device had not functioned or if the officers had not used it, no information would have been obtained. And the Court does not contend that the use of the device constituted a search either. On the contrary, the Court accepts the holding in *United States v. Knotts*, 460 U.S. 276 (1983), that the use of a surreptitiously planted electronic device to monitor a vehicle's movements on public roads did not amount to a search.

The Court argues—and I agree—that "we must 'assure preservation of that degree of privacy against government that existed when the Fourth Amendment was adopted.'" But it is almost impossible to think of late-18th-century situations that are analogous to what took place in this case. Is it possible to imagine a case in which a constable secreted himself somewhere in a coach and remained there for a period of time in order to monitor the movements of the coach's owner? The Court's theory seems to be that the concept of a search, as originally understood, comprehended any technical trespass that led to the gathering of evidence, but we know that this is incorrect. At common law, any unauthorized intrusion on private property was actionable, but a trespass on open fields, as opposed to the "curtilage" of a home, does not fall within the scope of the Fourth Amendment because private property outside the curtilage is not part of a "house" within the meaning of the Fourth Amendment.

The Court's reasoning in this case is very similar to that in the Court's early decisions involving wiretapping and electronic eavesdropping, namely, that a technical trespass followed by the gathering of evidence constitutes a search. In the early electronic surveillance cases, the Court concluded that a Fourth Amendment search occurred when private conversations were monitored as a result of an "unauthorized physical penetration into the premises occupied" by the defendant. In *Silverman*, police officers listened to conversations in an attached home by inserting a "spike mike" through the wall that this house shared with the vacant house next door. This procedure was held to be a search because the mike made contact with a heating duct on the other side of the wall and thus "usurped an integral part of the premises."

By contrast, in cases in which there was no trespass, it was held that there was no search. Thus, in *Olmstead v. United States* (1928), the Court found that the Fourth Amendment did not apply because "the taps from house lines were made in the streets near the houses." Similarly, the Court concluded that no search occurred in *Goldman v. United States*, 316 U.S. 129 (1942), where a "detectaphone" was placed on the outer wall of defendant's office for the purpose of overhearing conversations held within the room.

This trespass-based rule was repeatedly criticized. In *Olmstead*, Justice Brandeis wrote a dissenting opinion stating that it was "immaterial where the physical connection with the telephone wires was made." Although a private conversation transmitted by wire did not fall within the literal words of the Fourth Amendment, he argued, the Amendment should be understood as prohibiting "every unjustifiable intrusion by the government upon the privacy of the individual." In *Silverman*, Justice Douglas wrote a concurring opinion stating that "The concept of 'an unauthorized physical penetration into the premises,' on which the present decision rests seems to me beside the point. Was not the wrong done when the intimacies of the home were tapped, recorded, or revealed? The depth of the penetration of the electronic device—even the degree of its remoteness from the inside of the house—is not the measure of the injury."

"The search of one's home or office no longer requires physical entry, for science has brought forth far more effective devices for the invasion of a person's privacy than the direct and obvious methods of oppression which were detested by our forebears and which inspired the Fourth Amendment."

Katz v. United States (1967) finally did away with the old approach, holding that a trespass was not required for a Fourth Amendment violation. *Katz* involved the use of a listening device that was attached to the outside of a public telephone booth and that allowed police officers to eavesdrop on one end of the target's phone conversation. This procedure did not physically intrude on the area occupied by the target, but the *Katz* Court "repudiated" the old doctrine and held that "the fact that the electronic device employed did not happen to penetrate the wall of the booth can have no constitutional significance," stating that "The reach of the Fourth Amendment cannot turn upon the presence or absence of a physical intrusion into any given enclosure." The capacity to claim the protection for the Fourth Amendment depends not upon a property right in the invaded place but upon whether the person who claims the protection of the Amendment has a legitimate expectation of privacy in the invaded place.

The majority opinion largely disregards what is really important, which is the use of a GPS for the purpose of long-term tracking, and instead attaches great significance to something that most would view as relatively minor, which is attaching to the bottom of a car a small, light object that does not interfere in any way with the car's operation. Attaching such an object is generally regarded as so trivial that it does not provide a basis for recovery under modern tort law. But under the Court's reasoning, this conduct may violate the Fourth Amendment. By contrast, if long-term monitoring can be accomplished without committing a technical trespass—suppose, for example, that the Federal Government required or persuaded auto manufacturers to include a GPS tracking device in every car—the Court's theory would provide no protection.

Second, the Court's approach leads to incongruous results. If the police attach a GPS device to a car and use the device to follow the car for even a brief time, under the Court's theory, the Fourth Amendment applies. But if the police follow the same car for a much longer period using unmarked cars and aerial assistance, this tracking is not subject to any Fourth Amendment constraints.

Finally, the Court's reliance on the law of trespass will present particularly vexing problems in cases involving surveillance that is carried out by making electronic, as opposed to physical, contact with the item to be tracked. For example, suppose that the officers in the present case had followed respondent by surreptitiously activating a stolen vehicle detection system that came with the car when it was purchased. Would the sending of a radio signal to activate this system constitute a trespass to personal property? Trespass to personal property has traditionally required a physical touching of the property. In recent years, courts have wrestled with the application of this old tort in cases involving unwanted electronic contact with computer systems, and some have held that even the transmission of electrons that occurs when a communication is sent from one computer to another is enough. But may such decisions be followed in applying the Court's trespass theory? Assuming that what matters under the Court's theory is the law of trespass as it existed at the time of the adoption of the Fourth Amendment, do these recent decisions represent a change in the law or simply the application of the old tort to new situations?

The *Katz* expectation-of-privacy test avoids the problems and complications noted above, but it is not without its own difficulties. It involves a degree of circularity and judges are apt to confuse their own expectations of privacy with those of the hypothetical reasonable person to which the *Katz* test looks. In addition, the *Katz* test rests on the assumption that this hypothetical reasonable person has a well-developed and stable set of privacy expectations. But technology can change those expectations. Dramatic technological change may lead to periods in which popular expectations are in flux and may ultimately produce significant changes in popular attitudes. New technology may provide increased convenience or security at the expense of privacy, and many people may find the tradeoff worthwhile. And even if the public does not welcome the diminution of privacy that new technology entails, they may eventually reconcile themselves to this development as inevitable.

On the other hand, concern about new intrusions on privacy may spur the enactment of legislation to protect against these intrusions. This is what ultimately happened with respect to wiretapping. After *Katz*, Congress did not leave it to the courts to develop a body of Fourth Amendment case law governing that complex subject. Instead, Congress promptly enacted a comprehensive statute called the Electronic Communications Privacy Act, and since that time, the regulation of wiretapping has been governed primarily by statute and not by case law.

Recent years have seen the emergence of many new devices that permit the monitoring of a person's movements. In some locales, closed-circuit television video monitoring is becoming ubiquitous. On toll roads, automatic toll collection systems create a precise record of the movements of motorists who choose to make use of that convenience. Many motorists purchase cars that are equipped with devices that permit a central station to ascertain the car's location at any time so that roadside assistance may be provided if needed and the car may be found if it is stolen.

Perhaps most significant, cell phones and other wireless devices now permit wireless carriers to track and record the location of users—and as of June 2011, it has been reported, there were more than 322 million wireless devices in use in the United States. For older phones, the accuracy of the location information depends on the density of the tower network, but new "smart phones," which are equipped with a GPS device, permit more precise tracking. For example, when a user activates the GPS on such a phone, a provider is able to monitor the phone's location and speed of movement and can then report back real-time traffic conditions after combining ("crowdsourcing") the speed of all such phones on any particular road. Similarly, phone-location-tracking services are offered as "social" tools, allowing consumers to find (or to avoid) others who enroll in these services. The availability and use of these and other new devices will continue to shape the average person's expectations about the privacy of his or her daily movements.

In the pre-computer age, the greatest protections of privacy were neither constitutional nor statutory, but practical. Traditional surveillance for any extended period of time was difficult and costly and therefore rarely undertaken. The surveillance at issue in this case—constant monitoring of the location of a vehicle for four weeks—would have required a large team of agents, multiple vehicles, and perhaps aerial assistance. Only an investigation of unusual importance could have justified such an expenditure of law enforcement resources. Devices like the one used in the present case, however, make long-term monitoring relatively easy and cheap. In circumstances involving dramatic technological change, the best solution to privacy concerns may be legislative. A legislative body is well situated to gauge changing public attitudes, to draw detailed lines, and to balance privacy and public safety in a comprehensive way.

To date, however, Congress and most States have not enacted statutes regulating the use of GPS tracking technology for law enforcement purposes. The best that we can do in this case is to apply existing Fourth Amendment doctrine and to ask whether the use of GPS tracking in a particular case involved a degree of intrusion that a reasonable person would not have anticipated.

Under this approach, relatively short-term monitoring of a person's movements on public streets accords with expectations of privacy that our society has recognized as reasonable. But the use of longer term GPS monitoring in investigations of most offenses impinges on expectations of privacy. For such offenses, society's expectation has been that law enforcement agents and others would not—and indeed, in the main, simply could not—secretly monitor and catalogue every single movement of an individual's car for a very long period. In this case, for four weeks, law enforcement agents tracked every movement that respondent made in the vehicle he was driving. We need not identify with precision the point at which the tracking of this vehicle became a search, for the line was surely crossed before the 4-week mark. Other cases may present more difficult questions. But where uncertainty exists with respect to whether a certain period of GPS surveillance is long enough to constitute a Fourth Amendment search, the police may always seek a warrant. We also need not consider whether prolonged GPS monitoring in the context of investigations involving extraordinary offenses would similarly intrude on a constitutionally protected sphere of privacy. In such cases, long-term tracking might have been mounted using previously available techniques.

END OF OPINIONS

The majority opinion and the concurrences in *Jones* raised a number of issues related to GPS monitoring and numerous other forms of electronic surveillance. The majority opinion completely avoided the question of whether or not there were privacy issues involved with people being constantly tracked and monitored. Instead, the majority relied on the ancient doctrine of common law trespass. The court held that attaching a GPS device to the undercarriage of a vehicle without consent was a trespass. It did not matter that the GPS device did not have any effect on the performance of the vehicle or was an act so trivial under the tort of trespass that no one could recover enough money for it to make it worth suing over; all that mattered was that contact was being made with property of another without having first gotten permission of the owner or a court.

The *Jones* decision has been criticized for avoiding the broader privacy issue. People, so goes the argument, are more concerned with the fact that their movements are being constantly monitored than the fact that an object was attached to their vehicle without consent. But taking this approach would be a very big deal.

Before *Jones*, Fourth Amendment decisions had always evaluated each step of an investigation individually. The concurring opinions in Jones introduced what might be called a "mosaic theory" of the Fourth Amendment, by which courts evaluate a collective sequence of government activity as an aggregated whole to consider whether the sequence amounts to a search. An article by one of the leading scholars of Fourth Amendment Law considers the implications of a mosaic theory of the Fourth Amendment and argues that the mosaic approach reflects legitimate concerns, but that implementing it would be exceedingly difficult in light of rapid technological change. Courts can better respond to the concerns animating the mosaic theory within the traditional parameters of the sequential approach to Fourth Amendment analysis.[12]

This desire to address new "technology" by relying on common law property remedies was used by the Court in another case that involving trained drug dogs. Again, the court relied on a common law property concept, in this case that of a license.

Trespass law has a concept known as a "license." A license is permission for a person to enter your property. For example, if you invite a friend over for dinner, you have granted your friend a license to come onto your property and inside your house. However, this license is freely revocable; without any reason or justification, you can

---

12. Kerr, Orin, *The Mosaic Theory of the Fourth Amendment*, 111 Mich. L. Rev. 311 (2012). Available at: http://repository.law.umich.edu/mlr/vol111/iss3/1.

tell your friend to leave. If your friend fails to leave in a reasonable amount of time, he is a trespasser and can be sued for trespass. In some jurisdictions, he could also be arrested for criminal trespass if he fails to leave in a reasonable time!

Not all licenses are explicit; some are implied. For example, when you go to the grocery store and park your vehicle in the grocery store's parking lot, you probably did not receive a direct invitation from the property owners to park your car in their parking lot in front of their grocery store. It is simply understood by society that there is a general invitation to the public to use that parking lot for the purposes of parking your car so you can shop in the store.

It is possible for a person to violate a direct or an implied license. A person who enters the property for a reason other than what is given by a direct license or reasonably understood by an implied license is a trespasser. If you invite your friend over for dinner and your friend goes into your bedroom and starts rooting through your underwear, that friend has become a trespasser. Your invitation for your friend to come over for dinner is generally understood by society to not include an invite to go rooting through private areas of the home. In another example, if you purchase a ticket to see one show at the movie theater, but then move from that show to watch a second show without buying another ticket, you will have become a trespasser.

Just as much as private individuals can violate a license and become trespassers, so too can the police. In *Florida v. Jardines*, known as the "dog sniff case," the Court looked at both the idea of a trespass like in *Jones* and the idea of devices not in general public use as in *Kyllo*. Obviously, dogs are not electronic devices, but the legal issues gleaned from this case are both pertinent to electronic surveillance and a great recap of the issues covered so far in this chapter.

Florida v. Jardines, 569 U.S. (2013)*

We consider whether using a drug-sniffing dog on a homeowner's porch to investigate the contents of the home is a "search" within the meaning of the Fourth Amendment.

In 2006, Detective William Pedraja of the Miami-Dade Police Department received an unverified tip that marijuana was being grown in the home of respondent Joelis Jardines. One month later, the Department and the Drug Enforcement Administration sent a joint surveillance team to Jardines' home. Detective Pedraja was part of that team. He watched the home for fifteen minutes and saw no vehicles in the driveway or activity around the home, and could not see inside because the blinds were drawn. Detective Pedraja then approached Jardines' home accompanied by Detective Douglas Bartelt, a trained canine handler who had just arrived at the scene with his drug-sniffing dog. The dog was trained to detect the scent of marijuana, cocaine,

---

* The case has been heavily edited and paraphrased by the authors for clarity. See disclaimer in introduction.

heroin, and several other drugs, indicating the presence of any of these substances through particular behavioral changes recognizable by his handler.

Detective Bartelt had the dog on a six-foot leash. As the dog approached Jardines' front porch, he apparently sensed one of the odors he had been trained to detect, and began energetically exploring the area for the strongest point source of that odor. As Detective Bartelt explained, the dog "began tracking that airborne odor by tracking back and forth," engaging in what is called "bracketing," "back and forth, back and forth." Detective Bartelt gave the dog "the full six feet of the leash plus whatever safe distance he could give him" to do this—he testified that he needed to give the dog "as much distance as I can." And Detective Pedraja stood back while this was occurring, so that he would not "get knocked over" when the dog was "spinning around trying to find" the source.

After sniffing the base of the front door, the dog sat, which is the trained behavior upon discovering the odor's strongest point. Detective Bartelt then pulled the dog away from the door and returned to his vehicle. He left the scene after informing Detective Pedraja that there had been a positive alert for narcotics.

On the basis of what he had learned at the home, Detective Pedraja applied for and received a warrant to search the residence. When the warrant was executed later that day, Jardines attempted to flee and was arrested; the search revealed marijuana plants, and he was charged with trafficking in cannabis.

At trial, Jardines moved to suppress the marijuana plants on the ground that the canine investigation was an unreasonable search. Here, we determine whether the officers' conducted a search within the meaning of the Fourth Amendment.

The Fourth Amendment provides that the "right of the people to be secure in their persons, houses, papers, and effects, against unreasonable searches and seizures, shall not be violated." The Amendment establishes a simple baseline, one that for much of our history formed the exclusive basis for its protections: When "the Government obtains information by physically intruding" on persons, houses, papers, or effects, "a 'search' within the original meaning of the Fourth Amendment" has "undoubtedly occurred." By reason of our decision in *Katz v. United States*, property rights "are not the sole measure of Fourth Amendment violations"—but though *Katz* may add to the baseline, it does not subtract anything from the Amendment's protections "when the Government does engage in a physical intrusion of a constitutionally protected area."

That principle renders this case a straightforward one. The officers were gathering information in an area belonging to Jardines and immediately surrounding his house—in the curtilage of the house, which we have held enjoys protection as part of the home itself. And they gathered that information by physically entering and occupying the area to engage in conduct not explicitly or implicitly permitted by the homeowner.

The Fourth Amendment "indicates with some precision the places and things encompassed by its protections": persons, houses, papers, and effects. The Fourth Amendment does not, therefore, prevent all investigations conducted on private property; for example, an officer may (subject to *Katz*) gather information in what we have called "open fields"—even if those fields are privately owned—because such fields are not enumerated in the Amendment's text.

But when it comes to the Fourth Amendment, the home is first among equals. At the Amendment's "very core" stands "the right of a man to retreat into his own home and there be free from unreasonable governmental intrusion." This right would be of little practical value if the State's agents could stand in a home's porch or side garden and trawl for evidence with impunity; the right to retreat would be significantly diminished if the police could enter a man's property to observe his repose from just outside the front window.

We therefore regard the area "immediately surrounding and associated with the home"—what our cases call the curtilage—as "part of the home itself for Fourth Amendment purposes." That principle has ancient and durable roots. Just as the distinction between the home and the open fields is "as old as the common law," so too is the identity of home and what Justice Blackstone called the "curtilage or homestall," for the "house protects and privileges all its branches and appurtenants." This area around the home is "intimately linked to the home, both physically and psychologically," and is where "privacy expectations are most heightened." While the boundaries of the curtilage are generally "clearly marked," the "conception defining the curtilage" is at any rate familiar enough that it is "easily understood from our daily experience." Here there is no doubt that the officers entered it: The front porch is the classic exemplar of an area adjacent to the home and "to which the activity of home life extends."

Since the officers' investigation took place in a constitutionally protected area, we turn to the question of whether it was accomplished through an unlicensed physical intrusion. While law enforcement officers need not "shield their eyes" when passing by the home "on public thoroughfares," an officer's leave to gather information is sharply circumscribed when he steps off those thoroughfares and enters the Fourth Amendment's protected areas. In permitting, for example, visual observation of the home from "public navigable airspace," we were careful to note that it was done "in a physically nonintrusive manner."

In *Entick v. Carrington*, 2 Wils. K. B. 275, 95 Eng. Rep. 807 (K. B. 1765), a case undoubtedly familiar to every American statesman at the time of the founding of the U.S., states the general rule clearly: "Our law holds the property of every man so sacred, that no man can set his foot upon his neighbour's close without his leave." As it is undisputed that the detectives had all of their feet and all four of their dog's paws firmly planted on the constitutionally protected extension of Jardines' home, the only question is whether he had given his leave (even implicitly) for them to do so. He had not.

A license may be implied from the habits of the country, notwithstanding the strict rule of the English common law as to entry upon a close. We have accordingly recognized that "the knocker on the front door is treated as an invitation or license to attempt an entry, justifying ingress to the home by solicitors, hawkers and peddlers of all kinds." This implicit license typically permits the visitor to approach the home by the front path, knock promptly, wait briefly to be received, and then, absent invitation to linger longer, leave. Complying with the terms of that traditional invitation does not require fine-grained legal knowledge; it is generally managed without incident by the Nation's Girl Scouts and trick-or-treaters. Thus, a police officer not armed with a warrant may approach a home and knock, precisely because that is "no more than any private citizen might do." But introducing a trained police dog to explore the area around the home in hopes of discovering incriminating evidence is something else. There is no customary invitation to do that. An invitation to engage in canine forensic investigation assuredly does not inhere in the very act of hanging a knocker. To find a visitor knocking on the door is routine (even if sometimes unwelcome); to spot that same visitor exploring the front path with a metal detector, or marching his bloodhound into the garden before saying hello and asking permission, would inspire most of us to — well, call the police. The scope of a license — express or implied — is limited not only to a particular area but also to a specific purpose. Consent at a traffic stop to an officer's checking out an anonymous tip that there is a body in the trunk does not permit the officer to rummage through the trunk for narcotics. Here, the background social norms that invite a visitor to the front door do not invite him there to conduct a search.

The question before the court is precisely whether the officer's conduct was an objectively reasonable search. As we have described, that depends upon whether the officers had an implied license to enter the porch, which in turn depends upon the purpose for which they entered. Here, their behavior objectively reveals a purpose to conduct a search, which is not what anyone would think he had license to do.

The State argues that investigation by a forensic narcotics dog by definition cannot implicate any legitimate privacy interest. The State cites for authority past decisions where canine inspection of luggage in an airport, chemical testing of a substance that had fallen from a parcel in transit, and canine inspection of an automobile during a lawful traffic stop, do not violate the "reasonable expectation of privacy" described in *Katz*.

Just last Term, we considered an argument much like this. *Jones* held that tracking an automobile's whereabouts using a physically-mounted GPS receiver is a Fourth Amendment search. The Government argued that the *Katz* standard "showed that no search occurred," as the defendant had "no 'reasonable expectation of privacy'" in his whereabouts on the public roads—a proposition with at least as much support in our case law as the one the State marshals here. But because the GPS receiver had been physically mounted on the defendant's automobile (thus intruding on his "effects"), we held that tracking the vehicle's movements was a search: a person's "Fourth Amendment rights do not rise or fall with the *Katz* formulation." The *Katz* reasonable-expectations test "has been added to, not substituted for," the traditional property-based understanding of the Fourth Amendment, and so is unnecessary to consider when the government gains evidence by physically intruding on constitutionally protected areas.

Thus, we need not decide whether the officers' investigation of Jardines' home violated his expectation of privacy under *Katz*. One virtue of the Fourth Amendment's property-rights baseline is that it keeps easy cases easy. That the officers learned what they learned only by physically intruding on Jardines' property to gather evidence is enough to establish that a search occurred.

The government's use of trained police dogs to investigate the home and its immediate surroundings is a "search" within the meaning of the Fourth Amendment. The judgment of the Supreme Court of Florida is therefore affirmed.

Justice Kagan, with whom Justice Ginsburg and Justice Sotomayor join, concurring.

For me, a simple analogy clinches this case—and does so on privacy as well as property grounds. A stranger comes to the front door of your home carrying super-high-powered binoculars. He doesn't knock or say hello. Instead, he stands on the porch and uses the binoculars to peer through your windows, into your home's furthest corners. It doesn't take long (the binoculars are really very fine): In just a couple of minutes, his uncommon behavior allows him to learn details of your life you disclose to no one. Has your "visitor" trespassed on your property, exceeding the license you have granted to members of the public to, say, drop off the mail or distribute campaign flyers? Yes, he has. And has he also invaded your "reasonable expectation of privacy," by nosing into intimacies you sensibly thought protected from disclosure? Yes, of course, he has done that too.

That case is this case in every way that matters. Here, police officers came to Joelis Jardines' door with a super-sensitive instrument, which they deployed to detect things inside that they could not perceive unassisted. The equipment they used was animal, not mineral. Although dogs are common creatures in America, this particular dog was not your neighbor's pet who had come to your porch on a leisurely stroll. Drug-detection dogs are highly trained tools of law enforcement, geared to respond in distinctive ways to specific scents so as to convey clear and reliable information to their human partners. They are to the poodle down the street as high-powered binoculars are to a piece of plain glass. Like the binoculars, a drug-detection dog is a specialized device for discovering objects not in plain view (or plain smell). And as in the hypothetical above, that device was aimed here at a home—the most private and inviolate (or so we expect) of all the places and things the Fourth Amendment protects. Was this activity a trespass? Yes, as the Court holds to-day. Was it also an invasion of privacy? Yes, that as well.

The Court today treats this case under a property rubric; I write separately to note that I could just as happily have decided it by looking to Jardines' privacy interests. A decision along those lines would have looked . . . well, much like this one. It would have talked about "the right of a man to retreat into his own home and there be free from unreasonable governmental intrusion." It would have insisted on maintaining the "practical value" of that right by preventing police officers from standing in an adjacent space and trawling for evidence with impunity. It would have explained that privacy expectations are most heightened in the home and the surrounding area. And it would have determined that police officers invade those shared expectations when they use trained canine assistants to reveal within the confines of a home what they could not otherwise have found there.

It is not surprising that in a case involving a search of a home, property concepts and privacy concepts should so align. The law of property "naturally enough influences" our "shared social expectations" of what places should be free from governmental incursions. And so the sentiment "my home is my own," while originating in property law, now also denotes a common understanding—extending even beyond that law's formal protections—about an especially private sphere. Jardines' home was his property; it was also his most intimate and familiar space. The analysis proceeding from each of those facts, as today's decision reveals, runs mostly along the same path.

I can think of only one divergence: If we had decided this case on privacy grounds, we would have realized that *Kyllo v. United States* already resolved it. The *Kyllo* Court held that police officers conducted a search when they used a thermal-imaging device to detect heat emanating from a private home, even though they committed no trespass. Highlighting our intention to draw both a "firm" and a "bright" line at "the entrance to the house," we announced the following rule: "Where, as here, the Government uses a device that is not in general public use, to explore details of the home that would previously have been unknowable without physical intrusion, the surveillance is a 'search' and is presumptively unreasonable without a warrant."

That "firm" and "bright" rule governs this case: The police officers here conducted a search because they used a "device not in general public use" (a trained drug-detection dog) to "explore details of the home" (the presence of certain substances) that they would not otherwise have discovered without entering the premises.

And again, the dissent's argument that the device is just a dog cannot change the equation. As *Kyllo* made clear, the "sense-enhancing" tool at issue may be "crude" or "sophisticated," may be old or new (drug-detection dogs actually go back not "12,000 years" or "centuries" but only a few decades), may be either smaller or bigger than a breadbox; still, "at least where (as here)" the device is not "in general public use," training it on a home violates our "minimal expectation of privacy"—an expectation "that exists, and that is acknowledged to be reasonable." That does not mean the device is off-limits; it just means police officers cannot use it to examine a home without a warrant or exigent circumstance.

END OF OPINION

Much like in *Jones*, the majority opinion was governed less by any idea of a reasonable expectation of privacy, but by trespass doctrine. The Court recognized that there is an implied license for persons without an invitation to go onto your property, approach your front door, and knock to make an inquiry. This implied license may be for the police to approach a door to knock and see if someone is home who will consent to answer questions or even consent to a search of the home itself. The implied license may be so that Girl Scouts can sell cookies or other neighborhood children can knock on the door to ask if one of their peers can come out and play. Unless there is a sign saying "no solicitations," there is an implied license for salespersons to knock on your door and try to entice you with an offer. In any of these cases, the person who either owns the property or is in possession of the property (such as a renter) can tell the visitor to "Get off my property" upon which, if the visitor does not comply in a reasonable and timely manner, the person is a trespasser.

In *Jones*, the Court held that this implied license for persons to knock at your door did not extend to the police to go on your property with a drug-sniffing dog to look for evidence of criminal conduct. Bringing a drug-sniffing dog onto the property for the specific purpose of smelling for illegal drugs exceeded the scope of the implied license for visitors to approach your front door. This is similar to how a friend you invite into your home for dinner becomes a trespasser when he goes into the bedroom to paw through your underwear; the scope of your license for him to enter your home did not include an invitation to also go through your underwear.

Three of the justices did address the privacy aspects of the drug dog smelling outside a home for drugs. Although a dog is not an <u>electronic</u> device, it is a highly sensitive instrument, not in general public use, which was being used to discover the inside contents of a home; a feat which previously, would only have been possible with a physical intrusion. These justices applied the *Kyllo* analysis and considered a person's reasonable expectation of privacy. The concurring opinion focused on how, regardless whether the police have a drug-sniffing dog, thermal imager, highly sensitive microphone, or some other instrument which has yet to be invented, people always have a reasonable expectation of privacy in the contents of their homes. Pursuant to the majority opinion, it would be a trespass for the police to enter your property without permission specifically to look around for criminal evidence because doing so would violate the implied license for persons to approach your door. Pursuant to the concurring opinion, the use of a device to discover the interior of your home, a place understood to be private, also violates the reasonable expectation of privacy.

Review Questions

In each of the problems below, consider whether there is either a Fourth Amendment or a statutory right to privacy, and whether the law permits the search. Use the IRAC process to help your analysis.

1. Scott works at Walmart. Walmart gives its workers storage racks for workers to leave personal belongings, like purses or backpacks, while they are working. Scott regularly zips his backpack shut, and then locks it with a combination lock. Scott is suspected by the police of dealing heroin from Walmart, so one day while he is working the floor, the police go to his backpack where it is lying on the rack in plain view. Using a special master key, the police open the lock and then proceed to unzip

the backpack and find heroin inside. Based on this evidence, the police get a warrant to arrest Scott.

2. Scott works at Walmart. While he is working, his I-phone falls from his pocket. Scott does not notice this, but a coworker does. The coworker pick up the phone and, correctly guessing that Scott is using his birthday as the password, starts browsing the contents of the phone. After reading Scott's personal text messages and emails, he starts looking through the pictures on Scott's phone. To his horror, he finds sexually explicit images of underage children. The coworker emails these images to the police and names Scott as the owner of the phone. The police receive the emails with the pictures of the underage children attached and take them to a magistrate who issues a warrant for the seizure of the phone and Scott's arrest. At trial, the defense attorney argues that Scott's privacy was violated by the coworker hacking his password and browsing the phone's contents.

3. Brian is an undercover police officer. He has positioned himself outside of Jeffry's home. Installed on his laptop is the Wifi Hacker 5000, a device that enables his computer to intercept wireless internet signals between a computer and its router, even if password-protected. Using this device Brian is intercepting and recording all wireless internet traffic that is passing from Jeffry's computer to his home's wireless router (and then on to cyberspace). Upon reviewing the web history, Brian sees that Jeffry is accessing websites containing sexually explicit images of children. Brian takes these records to the magistrate and uses them to get a warrant for a seizure of Jeffry's computer and Jeffry's arrest. At trial, the defense moves to suppress the results of the evidence.

4. The year is 2025, and the Smell-o-meter 1000 is being sold to law enforcement. It functions as an olfactory machine, or an "electronic nose." At a cost of $10,000, it is about the size of a hairdryer and works by sucking in the air, running the air through filters designed to catch certain molecular chains, and then displaying on a screen the chemical or common names of molecules it picks up. Officer Lance is excited to receive this device and immediately starts to play with it, pointing it at people's homes. The device appears to work very well, as its screen displays a list of all of the items it "smells" inside of each house. Sometimes the screen displays common names such as "peanuts" or "dog." Other times, it displays chemical names such as "Sildenafil citrate" (Viagra), "Malic acid" (common in many fruit drinks), and "Sodium Chloride" (table salt). At some homes, the monitor displays the chemical name "Tetrahydrocannabinol," which Officer Lance recognizes as an active ingredient in marijuana. At one house he gets some unexpected chemical names appearing on the monitor. One of those names is "Trinitrotoluene," the chemical name of TNT, an explosive which is generally illegal for private citizens to own. Upon cross-checking the government database for people with licenses to possess TNT against a public database to ascertain who lives in the home and finding no match, Officer Lance goes to the magistrate and receives a warrant to search the house for TNT. During the search, TNT is discovered in the basement. Upon further investigation, police learn the homeowner is a member of the KKK and was planning to blow up a black church. The homeowner is arrested and prosecuted.

5. The year is 2050, and Officer Robin is at Walmart to purchase groceries. As she stands in the checkout line, she notices on sale right next to the chewing gum a children's toy, the Smell-o-meter 1000. It functions as an olfactory machine, which is the formal name of an "electronic nose." At a cost of $10,000, it is about the size of a hairdryer and works by being pointed in a certain direction and turned on, sucking in the air, running it through filters designed to catch certain molecular chains, and then displaying the chemical or common names of molecules it picks up on a screen. Given that it only costs $5, she purchases one as a toy for her daughter. After she gets back home she opens the Smell-o-meter 1000 and activates it; she wants to make sure it works properly before she gives it to her daughter. She takes the device outside her house and while standing on her own property, points it at her neighbor's house. To her shock, on the device's screen she sees "Trinitrotoluene," which she recognizes as TNT. Officer Robin checks a government database and verifies that her neighbors do not have a license to possess TNT, then proceeds to get a warrant to arrest her neighbors and search their house. While executing the warrant, Officer Robin discovers TNT in the basement and plans to blow up her neighbor's child's school.

6. Police officers Mina and Emily receive a tip that Aaron is growing marijuana inside his house. They look up Aaron's criminal records and see from a prior arrest that he is 19 years old and never got past his freshman year of high school. The police believe they can talk their way into getting his consent to search his home. They drive over to his house and see that it is a very dilapidated building with small holes in the walls and a few broken windows. They also see a vehicle which is registered to Aaron. The officers park in front of the house on the public street, walk onto the driveway, onto the walkway which leads to the porch, and up the stairs of his porch. Standing at front door, they ring the doorbell. No one answers, so they ring it again and wait. No one answers.

"Huh," Emily says, "this is strange. His car is still parked in his driveway. Do you think he's not home, or maybe he's just not answering because we're cops?" "I don't know," Mina says, and she pressed her ear up against the door to listen better. "I can hear some noise inside, but maybe it's just a dog." Emily gets on her knee to try to look under the door, but is unable to see inside the house. She looks up to the top of the door and notices that there is a slight gap between the top of the door and the frame. She points out this gap to Mina. "There is a gap between the top of the door and door frame," Emily says. "If you boost me up, I should be able to look through it and get a glimpse inside the house." Mina drops to a knee so that Emily can stand on her thigh. This gives Emily just enough height for her eye to be at the same level as the gap above the door.

As she stands outside the house on the front porch, she can see the interior of the home and observes a couple marijuana plants sitting on table. Based on what she sees, Emily goes to the local magistrate's office and obtains a warrant to enter the house to conduct a search. During the search, Emily finds multiple marijuana plants. Aaron is arrested and prosecuted for drug distribution. At trial, the defense attorney objects to the marijuana plants being admitted into evidence.

Key Terms

Plain view doctrine—The Fourth Amendment doctrine that evidence can be seized without a warrant or probable cause when three criteria are present: First, the officer must be lawfully present at the place where the evidence can be plainly viewed. Second, the officer to must have a lawful right of access to the object. Third, the incriminating character of the object must be "immediately apparent" and readily visible to the naked eye, without use of any equipment.

Reasonable expectation of privacy—The concept that the Fourth Amendment protects persons from official intrusions so long as they have a subjective expectation of privacy that society is prepared to accept.

Third-party doctrine—The legal theory that holds that people who voluntarily give information to third parties—such as banks, phone companies, internet service providers (ISPs), and e-mail servers—have "no reasonable expectation of privacy."

Further Reading

Bedi, Monu Singh, *Social Networks, Government Surveillance, and the Fourth Amendment Mosaic Theory* (December 2, 2014). Boston University Law Review, Vol. 94, No. 1809, 2014. Available at SSRN: http://ssrn.com/abstract=2533099.

Donohue, Laura K., *Bulk Metadata Collection: Statutory and Constitutional Considerations*, 37 Harvard Journal of Law & Public Policy, 757–900 (2014).

Donohue, Laura, *The Fourth Amendment in a Digital World* (2016). NYU Annual Survey of American Law, Forthcoming. Available at SSRN: http://ssrn.com/abstract=2836647.

Kerr, Orin S., *Four Models of Fourth Amendment Protection*, 60 Stanford Law Review 503 (2007); GWU Law School Public Law Research Paper No. 246. Available at SSRN: http://ssrn.com/abstract=976296.

Solove, Daniel J., *Nothing to Hide: The False Tradeoff between Privacy and Security*. Yale University Press, 2011.

Chapter 5

Foreign Surveillance, Searches, and Seizure

Overview

So far, much of the case law we have examined involves more traditional criminal law involving U.S. citizens acting within the United States. Homeland and national security law involves more than that, though. It involves addressing more serious threats to the United States, such as espionage and terrorism, and it involves actions by citizens as well as non-U.S. citizens, both in the United States and outside. This chapter will address several of these issues. We'll start with the issue of surveillance generally as it involves homeland and national security.

No National Security Exception to the Constitution

It is very important at the outset of this chapter to make the point that there is no such thing as a "national security exception" to the Fourth Amendment or to any other part of the Constitution. There are areas where the special circumstances of national security mean that terms like "reasonableness" and "exigency" have a more direct importance, and the courts as well as Congress have sought over the years to address those.

Now, through our history, in response to serious threats to the nation, the law enforcement and national security agencies of the U.S. government argued that such a general national security exception applies—and in most circumstances that argument has arisen in terms of the Fourth Amendment's requirement for a warrant and prohibition of unreasonable searches and seizures. This argument was based on the recognition that threats to the nation are different than "normal" criminal behavior, and the nation must be more concerned with preventing attacks than capturing and trying those who commit crimes.

As we will see, there is the "foreign intelligence" exception to the warrant clause of the Fourth Amendment, and there are other exceptions in cases of emergency, such as the exigent circumstances exception to the warrant requirement and the *Quarles* exception to the *Miranda* requirement, as we've discussed in the past. But these exceptions are not the same as a broad and general exception for national security.

The following case is important because it discusses this tension between national security and the rights of citizens. Just as the *Katz* decision paved the way for much of the present law on search and seizure, the *Keith* case is important in the special areas of homeland and national security. This case involves the issue of domestic terrorist activity, undertaken within the United States by U.S. citizens, with no clear tie to a foreign nation or foreign/international terrorist organization.

When you read this case, keep in mind that it was part of the domestic turmoil covered by the Church Commission reports which also led to many of the statutory protections on privacy discussed earlier.

United States v. U.S. District Court (Keith), 407 U.S. 297 (1972)*

The issue before us is an important one for the people of our country and their Government. It involves the delicate question of the President's power, acting through the Attorney General, to authorize electronic surveillance in internal security matters without prior judicial approval. Successive Presidents for more than one-quarter of a century have authorized such surveillance in varying degrees, without guidance from the Congress or a definitive decision of this Court. This case brings the issue here for the first time. Its resolution is a matter of national concern, requiring sensitivity both to the Government's right to protect itself from unlawful subversion and attack and to the citizen's right to be secure in his privacy against unreasonable Government intrusion.

This case arises from a criminal proceeding in the United States District Court for the Eastern District of Michigan, in which the United States charged three defendants with conspiracy to destroy Government property. One of the defendants, Plamondon, was charged with the dynamite bombing of an office of the Central Intelligence Agency in Ann Arbor, Michigan.

During pretrial proceedings, the defendants moved to compel the United States to disclose certain electronic surveillance information and to conduct a hearing to determine whether this information "tainted" the evidence on which the indictment was based or which the Government intended to offer at trial. In response, the Government filed an affidavit of the Attorney General, acknowledging that its agents had overheard conversations in which Plamondon had participated. The affidavit also stated that the Attorney General approved the wiretaps to gather intelligence information deemed necessary to protect the nation from attempts of domestic organizations to attack and subvert the existing structure of the Government.

On the basis of the Attorney General's affidavit and the sealed exhibit, the Government asserted that the surveillance was lawful, though conducted without prior judicial approval, as a reasonable exercise of the President's power (exercised through the Attorney General) to protect the national security. The District Court held that

---

* The case has been heavily edited and paraphrased by the authors for clarity. See disclaimer in introduction.

the surveillance violated the Fourth Amendment, and ordered the Government to make full disclosure to Plamondon of his overheard conversations.

Title III of the Omnibus Crime Control and Safe Streets Act, authorizes the use of electronic surveillance for classes of crimes. The Act sets forth the detailed and particularized application necessary to obtain such an order, as well as carefully circumscribed conditions for its use. The Act represents a comprehensive attempt by Congress to promote more effective control of crime while protecting the privacy of individual thought and expression. Much of Title III was drawn to meet the constitutional requirements for electronic surveillance enunciated by this Court in prior cases.

Together with the elaborate surveillance requirements in Title III, there is the following proviso, 18 U.S.C. § 2511(3):

> Nothing contained in this chapter or in section 605 of the Communications Act of 1934 (48 Stat. 1143; 47 U.S.C. 605) shall limit the constitutional power of the President to take such measures as he deems necessary to protect the Nation against actual or potential attack or other hostile acts of a foreign power, to obtain foreign intelligence information deemed essential to the security of the United States, or to protect national security information against foreign intelligence activities. Nor shall anything contained in this chapter be deemed to limit the constitutional power of the President to take such measures as he deems necessary to protect the United States against the overthrow of the Government by force or other unlawful means, or against any other clear and present danger to the structure or existence of the Government. The contents of any wire or oral communication intercepted by authority of the President in the exercise of the foregoing powers may be received in evidence in any trial hearing, or other proceeding only where such interception was reasonable, and shall not be otherwise used or disclosed except as is necessary to implement that power.

The Government relies on this section in conducting warrantless surveillance upon Americans in the name of national security. The government argues that this is Congress giving the President the authority to conduct such warrantless surveillance on Americans who, like the defendants who bombed the CIA building in Michigan, lack any connection to a foreign power. For reasons explained in this opinion, we disagree. The Government may not, in the name of national security, conduct warrantless surveillance upon Americans who have no connection to a foreign power.

It is important at the outset to emphasize the limited nature of the question before the Court. This case raises no constitutional challenge to electronic surveillance as specifically authorized by Title III of the Omnibus Crime Control and Safe Streets Act of 1968. Nor is there any question or doubt as to the necessity of obtaining a warrant in the surveillance of crimes unrelated to the national security interest. Further, the instant case requires no judgment on the scope of the President's surveillance power with respect to the activities of foreign powers, within or without this country. The Attorney General's affidavit in this case states that the surveillances were "deemed necessary to protect the nation from attempts of domestic organizations to attack and subvert the existing structure of Government." There is no evidence of any involvement, directly or indirectly, of a foreign power.

Our present inquiry, though important, is therefore a narrow one. It addresses a question left open by *Katz*, which was whether safeguards other than prior authorization by a neutral magistrate or judicial officer would satisfy the warrant clause of the Fourth Amendment in a situation involving the national security?

The determination of this question requires the essential Fourth Amendment inquiry into the "reasonableness" of the search and seizure in question, and the way in which that "reasonableness" derives content and meaning through reference to the warrant clause.

We begin the inquiry by noting that the President of the United States has the fundamental duty, under Art. II, § 1, of the Constitution, to "preserve, protect and defend the Constitution of the United States." Implicit in that duty is the power to protect our Government against those who would subvert or overthrow it by unlawful means. In the discharge of this duty, the President—through the Attorney General—may find it necessary to employ electronic surveillance to obtain intelligence information on the plans of those who plot unlawful acts against the Government. The use of such surveillance in internal security cases has been sanctioned more or less continuously by various Presidents and Attorneys General since July, 1946. Herbert Brownell, Attorney General under President Eisenhower, urged the use of electronic surveillance both in internal and international security matters on the grounds that those acting against the Government turn to the telephone to carry on their intrigue. The success of their plans frequently rests upon piecing together shreds of information received from many sources and many nests. The participants in the conspiracy are often dispersed and stationed in various strategic positions in government and industry throughout the country.

Though the Government and respondents debate their seriousness and magnitude, threats and acts of sabotage against the Government exist in sufficient number to justify investigative powers with respect to them. The covertness and complexity of potential unlawful conduct against the Government and the necessary dependency of many conspirators upon the telephone make electronic surveillance an effective investigatory instrument in certain circumstances. The marked acceleration in technological developments and sophistication in their use have resulted in new techniques for the planning, commission, and concealment of criminal activities. It would be contrary to the public interest for Government to deny to itself the prudent and lawful employment of those very techniques which are employed against the Government and its law-abiding citizens.

It has been said that "the most basic function of any government is to provide for the security of the individual and of his property." Unless the Government safeguards its own capacity to function so that it can preserve the security of its people, society itself could become so disordered that all rights and liberties would be endangered. As Chief Justice Hughes reminded us in *Cox v. New Hampshire*, 312 U.S. 569, 574 (1941):

Civil liberties, as guaranteed by the Constitution, imply the existence of an organized society maintaining public order without which liberty itself would be lost in the excesses of unrestrained abuses.

But a recognition of these elementary truths does not make the employment by Government of electronic surveillance a welcome development—even when employed with restraint and under judicial supervision. There is, understandably, a deep-seated uneasiness and apprehension that this capability will be used to intrude upon cherished privacy of law-abiding citizens. We look to the Bill of Rights to safeguard this privacy. Though physical entry of the home is the chief evil against which the wording of the Fourth Amendment is directed, its broader spirit now shields private speech from unreasonable surveillance. Our decision in *Katz* refused to lock the Fourth Amendment into instances of actual physical trespass. Rather, the Amendment governs not only the seizure of tangible items, but extends as well to the recording of oral statements without any technical trespass under local property law.

That decision implicitly recognized that the broad and unsuspected governmental incursions into conversational privacy which electronic surveillance entails necessitate the application of Fourth Amendment safeguards. National security cases, moreover, often reflect a convergence of First and Fourth Amendment values not present in cases of "ordinary" crime. Though the investigative duty of the executive may be stronger in such cases, so also is there greater jeopardy to constitutionally protected speech.

Historically, the struggle for freedom of speech and press in England was bound up with the issue of the scope of the search and seizure power. History abundantly documents the tendency of Government—however benevolent and benign its motive—to view with suspicion those who most fervently dispute its policies. Fourth Amendment protections become the more necessary when the targets of official surveillance may be those suspected of unorthodoxy in their political beliefs. The danger to political dissent is acute where the Government attempts to act under so vague a concept as the power to protect "domestic security." Given the difficulty of defining the domestic security interest, the danger of abuse in acting to protect that interest becomes apparent. Senator Hart addressed this dilemma in the floor debate on § 2511(3):

> As I read it—and this is my fear—we are saying that the President, on his motion, could declare—name your favorite poison—draft dodgers, Black Muslims, the Ku Klux Klan, or civil rights activists to be a clear and present danger to the structure or existence of the Government. The price of lawful public dissent must not be a dread of subjection to an unchecked surveillance power. Nor must the fear of unauthorized official eavesdropping deter vigorous citizen dissent and discussion of Government action in private conversation. For private dissent, no less than open public discourse, is essential to our free society.

As the Fourth Amendment is not absolute in its terms, our task is to examine and balance the basic values at stake in this case: the duty of Government to protect the domestic security, and the potential danger posed by unreasonable surveillance to individual privacy and free expression. If the legitimate need of Government to safeguard domestic security requires the use of electronic surveillance, the question is whether the needs of citizens for privacy and free expression may not be better protected by requiring a warrant before such surveillance is undertaken. We must also ask whether a warrant requirement would unduly frustrate the efforts of Government to protect itself from acts of subversion and overthrow directed against it.

Though the Fourth Amendment speaks broadly of "unreasonable searches and seizures," the definition of "reasonableness" turns, at least in part, on the more specific commands of the warrant clause. Some have argued that "the relevant test is not whether it is reasonable to procure a search warrant, but whether the search was reasonable," *United States v. Rabinowitz*, 339 U.S. 56 (1950). This view, however, overlooks the second clause of the Amendment. The warrant clause of the Fourth Amendment is not dead language. Rather, it has been a valued part of our constitutional law for decades, and it has determined the result in scores and scores of cases in courts all over this country. It is not an inconvenience to be somehow "weighed" against the claims of police efficiency. It is, or should be, an important working part of our machinery of government, operating as a matter of course to check the "well-intentioned but mistakenly overzealous executive officers" who are a part of any system of law enforcement.

Over two centuries ago, Lord Mansfield held that common law principles prohibited warrants that ordered the arrest of unnamed individuals who the officer might conclude were guilty of seditious libel. "It is not fit," said Mansfield, "that the receiving or judging of the information should be left to the discretion of the officer. The magistrate ought to judge; and should give certain directions to the officer." Lord Mansfield's formulation touches the very heart of the Fourth Amendment directive: that, where practical, a governmental search and seizure should represent both the efforts of the officer to gather evidence of wrongful acts and the judgment of the magistrate that the collected evidence is sufficient to justify invasion of a citizen's private premises or conversation. Inherent in the concept of a warrant is its issuance by a "neutral and detached magistrate." The further requirement of "probable cause" instructs the magistrate that baseless searches shall not proceed.

These Fourth Amendment freedoms cannot properly be guaranteed if domestic security surveillances may be conducted solely within the discretion of the Executive Branch. The Fourth Amendment does not contemplate the executive officers of Government as neutral and disinterested magistrates. Their duty and responsibility are to enforce the laws, to investigate, and to prosecute. But those charged with this investigative and prosecutorial duty should not be the sole judges of when to utilize constitutionally sensitive means in pursuing their tasks. The historical judgment, which the Fourth Amendment accepts, is that unreviewed executive discretion may yield too readily to pressures to obtain incriminating evidence and overlook potential invasions of privacy and protected speech.

It may well be that, in the instant case, the Government's surveillance of Plamondon's conversations was a reasonable one which readily would have gained prior judicial approval. But this Court has never sustained a search upon the sole ground that officers reasonably expected to find evidence of a particular crime and voluntarily confined their activities to the least intrusive means consistent with that end. The Fourth Amendment contemplates a prior judicial judgment, not the risk that executive discretion may be reasonably exercised. This judicial role accords with our basic constitutional doctrine that individual freedoms will best be preserved through a separation of powers and division of functions among the different branches and levels of Government. The independent check upon executive discretion is not satisfied, as the Government argues, by "extremely limited" post-surveillance judicial review. Indeed, post-surveillance review would never reach the surveillances which failed to result in prosecutions. Prior review by a neutral and detached magistrate is the time-tested means of effectuating Fourth Amendment rights.

It is true that there have been some exceptions to the warrant requirement. *Chimel v. California* (1969) (search of the area within the immediate reach of a person who has been arrested); *Terry v. Ohio* (1968) (stop-and-frisk); *McDonald v. United States* (1948) (exigent circumstances); *Carroll v. United States*, 267 U.S. 132 (1925) (automobile exception). But those exceptions are few in number, and carefully delineated; in general, they serve the legitimate needs of law enforcement officers to protect their own wellbeing and preserve evidence from destruction. Even while carving out those exceptions, as it did in *Terry v. Ohio*, the Court has reaffirmed the principle that the "police must, whenever practicable, obtain advance judicial approval of searches and seizures through the warrant procedure."

The Government argues that the special circumstances applicable to domestic security surveillances necessitate a further exception to the warrant requirement. It is urged that the requirement of prior judicial review would obstruct the President in the discharge of his constitutional duty to protect domestic security. We are told further that these surveillances are directed primarily to the collecting and maintaining of intelligence with respect to subversive forces, and are not an attempt to gather evidence for specific criminal prosecutions. It is said that this type of surveillance should not be subject to traditional warrant requirements which were established to govern investigation of criminal activity, not ongoing intelligence gathering. The Government further insists that courts as a practical matter would have neither the knowledge nor the techniques necessary to determine whether there was probable cause to believe that surveillance was necessary to protect national security.

These security problems, the Government contends, involve "a large number of complex and subtle factors" beyond the competence of courts to evaluate. As a final reason for exemption from a warrant requirement, the Government believes that disclosure to a magistrate of all or even a significant portion of the information involved in domestic security surveillances would create serious potential dangers to the national security and to the lives of informants and agents. The Government also argues that secrecy is the essential ingredient in intelligence gathering; requiring prior judicial authorization would create a greater "danger of leaks because, in addition to the judge, you have the clerk, the stenographer and some other officer like a law assistant or bailiff who may be apprised of the nature" of the surveillance.

These contentions in behalf of a complete exemption from the warrant requirement, when urged on behalf of the President and the national security in its domestic implications, merit the most careful consideration. We certainly do not reject them lightly, especially at a time of worldwide ferment and when civil disorders in this country are more prevalent than in the less turbulent periods of our history. There is, no doubt, pragmatic force to the Government's position. But we do not think a case has been made for the requested departure from Fourth Amendment standards. The circumstances described do not justify complete exemption of domestic security surveillance from prior judicial scrutiny. Official surveillance, whether its purpose be criminal investigation or ongoing intelligence gathering, risks infringement of constitutionally protected privacy of speech. Security surveillances are especially sensitive because of the inherent vagueness of the domestic security concept, the necessarily broad and continuing nature of intelligence gathering, and the temptation to utilize such surveillances to oversee political dissent. We recognize, as we have before, the constitutional basis of the President's domestic security role, but we think it must be exercised in a manner compatible with the Fourth Amendment. In this case, we hold that this requires an appropriate prior warrant procedure.

We cannot accept the Government's argument that internal security matters are too subtle and complex for judicial evaluation. Courts regularly deal with the most difficult issues of our society. There is no reason to believe that federal judges will be insensitive to or uncomprehending of the issues involved in domestic security cases. Certainly courts can recognize that domestic security surveillance involves different considerations from the surveillance of "ordinary crime." If the threat is too subtle or complex for our senior law enforcement officers to convey its significance to a court, one may question whether there is probable cause for surveillance.

Nor do we believe prior judicial approval will fracture the secrecy essential to official intelligence gathering. The investigation of criminal activity has long involved imparting sensitive information to judicial officers who have respected the confidentialities involved. Judges may be counted upon to be especially conscious of security requirements in national security cases. Title III of the Omnibus Crime Control and Safe Streets Act already has imposed this responsibility on the judiciary in connection with such crimes as espionage, sabotage, and treason, §§ 2516(1)(a) and (c), each of which may involve domestic as well as foreign security threats. Moreover, a warrant application involves no public or adversary proceedings: it is an ex parte request before a magistrate or judge. Whatever security dangers clerical and secretarial personnel may pose can be minimized by proper administrative measures, possibly to the point of allowing the Government itself to provide the necessary clerical assistance.

Thus, we conclude that the Government's concerns do not justify departure in this case from the customary Fourth Amendment requirement of judicial approval prior to initiation of a search or surveillance. Although some added burden will be imposed upon the Attorney General, this inconvenience is justified in a free society to protect constitutional values. Nor do we think the Government's domestic surveillance powers will be impaired to any significant degree. A prior warrant establishes presumptive validity of the surveillance and will minimize the burden of justification in post-surveillance judicial review. By no means of least importance will be the reassurance of the public generally that indiscriminate wiretapping and bugging of law-abiding citizens cannot occur.

END OF OPINION

As explained in *Keith*, after anarchists bombed a CIA building in Michigan, the U.S. Attorney General ordered warrantless electronic surveillance on the suspects. The Attorney General claimed that recent legislation (the Omnibus Crime Control Act) had given the government the authority to, in the name of national security, conduct warrantless surveillance on subversive elements who wanted to overthrow the government or if there was a "clear and present danger to the structure or existence of the Government." The Supreme Court struck down this claim, clarifying that the government cannot make a blanket claim of national security to conduct warrantless surveillance. It was concerned that giving the President power to unilaterally declare anyone a "clear and present danger" would open the door to a flood of violations of the rights of the people.

As a practical matter, it is dangerous to create a broad and unlimited "national security exception" to the requirement of warrants because, let's face it, *everything* can be ultimately connected to national security. For example, rising gasoline prices could be linked to the U.S. dependence on foreign oil. Agriculture can be connected to homeland security because of the threat of terrorists poisoning the food supply or the potential of rioting in the streets if there is a food shortage. (Historically, inadequate food has been a prevalent cause of government instability.) As you may have seen with the anti-drug commercials on television, there is a link between high school students purchasing illegal drugs to the illegal narcotics trade in foreign countries and even Islamic terrorists in Afghanistan. In contrast to the all-encompassing nature of the generic term "national security," which can be applied to anything (and everything!), foreign intelligence is a very narrow and limited exception. So this exception poses less of a threat to civil rights and was understood by the founding fathers at the time the Constitution was written.

It is important to keep in mind that the decision in the *Keith* case did not arise either in a vacuum or because the government wanted to harm its citizens—quite the opposite. The effect of two World Wars and the threat of conflict with the Soviet Union—a threat that could have meant the end of all life through nuclear war—made protection of national security a high priority.

World War II was instrumental in the development of intelligence agencies and clandestine activities including espionage and sabotage. The present structure of national security, including the creation of the Central Intelligence Agency, the National Security Agency, as well as the counter-intelligence role of the Federal Bureau of Investigation, was created or restructured after World War II and played a large role during the Cold War. Although the FBI, CIA, and other intelligence and law enforcement agencies intended to protect "we the people," during the era of the Vietnam War, increasing leaks about clandestine activities revealed how the efforts of these agencies posed a threat to civil rights. Examples included reports of warrantless surveillance on Americans for purely political purposes. Another example was the leak of the classified "Pentagon Papers," which revealed how President Johnson and other leading government officials knowingly and blatantly lied to the American people in order to promote the war in Vietnam and attempted to discredit the leaker by breaking into the office of his psychiatrist and stealing medical records.

Leaked reports and documents exposed the abuses of governmental power and ultimately led to two official Congressional investigations. In the House of Representatives, the Pike Committee investigated the civil rights abuses of Americans by intelligence agencies and law enforcement. More famously, Senator Frank Church did the same thing in the U.S. Senate where he headed the "Church Committee." What they uncovered shocked and alarmed them. When their findings were publicized, it shocked and alarmed the American people as well. It was discovered that without the knowledge of Congress or any form of oversight, the CIA had, at its own discretion, been planning assassinations and orchestrating coup d'etats in other countries. It was also learned that without warrants, the FBI had opened and photographed over 215,000 items of mail, including the mail of famous Americans such as Nobel Laureate Linus Pauling, U.S. Senator and Vice President Hubert Humphrey, and civil rights activist Dr. Martin Luther King.

With this documented abuse of civil rights in the name of national security, the need for reform was recognized. Those reforms included the enactment of the Privacy Act, the Freedom of Information Act, and, as we will discuss later, the Foreign Intelligence Surveillance Act (FISA).

Let's turn to the difference between *domestic* intelligence surveillance, as dealt with by the *Keith* case, and *foreign* intelligence surveillance, which has had a different treatment under the law.

Foreign Intelligence Surveillance

The term "foreign intelligence" refers to efforts to discover and either prevent or stop espionage and counter espionage undertaken by other nations as well as to the operations to gather intelligence on foreign terrorist organizations such as Al-Qaeda. Foreign intelligence surveillance and searches, then, usually take place inside the U.S., but the target of the search is an agent of a foreign power or a foreign terrorist organization. Examples include the FBI searching the office of a suspected Chinese spy located in Washington, D.C., or of the home of an Al-Qaeda operative in NYC.

Many students get confused by the "foreign" part of "foreign intelligence." Be sure that you remember that the searches and surveillance are, for the most part, taking place <u>inside</u> the territory of the U.S. The "foreign" part of "foreign intelligence" refers to the TARGET of the search. The TARGET must be a foreign operative, or the place being searched must be owned (i.e., house) or possessed (i.e., apartment) by a foreign operative or foreign government. For example, if the Chinese government rented office-space in a regular office in downtown D.C., surveillance of the place would be considered foreign intelligence.

Because these searches for the purposes of foreign intelligence are being physically conducted inside the U.S., they are governed by the U.S. Constitution, specifically, the Fourth Amendment. The rules for conducting the searches, though, are very different when part of the motivation of conducting a search is foreign intelligence for intelligence gathering as opposed to solely a regular criminal investigation as traditionally practiced by regular law enforcement.

Recall from prior chapters that, although the Fourth Amendment was written as a single sentence, it should be read as two separate and distinct clauses addressing completely different topics:

- The right of the people to be secure in their persons, houses, papers, and effects, against unreasonable searches and seizures, shall not be violated.
- No Warrants shall issue, but upon probable cause, supported by Oath or affirmation, and particularly describing the place to be searched, and the persons or things to be seized.

What the *Keith* case noted about warrantless searches and surveillance was the fact that the absence of a warrant takes away what the founders believed to be a very important protection of liberty—the requirement of authorities to go to a member of the judiciary for permission to search. It's not just the standard of proof required, but also the independence that the judiciary provides that ensures protection of civil liberties.

Now, even though the warrant requirement is an important protection, the Fourth Amendment does not state that every search requires a warrant. All it states about searches is that they all must be reasonable, and only certain circumstances which were understood at the time of the founding of this country (which include intercepting mail, searching homes and offices, or arresting persons for misdemeanors not committed in the officer's presence) require a warrant to conduct a search or seizure.

For the purposes of foreign intelligence gathering (which is typically espionage and counter-espionage), it has always been understood that the Constitution does not require warrants issued upon probable cause to conduct searches or seizures. Instead, the Fourth Amendment merely requires that such actions be reasonable. And most of the case law involving search and seizure law has included some reference to the distinction made between domestic law enforcement and foreign intelligence/counter intelligence efforts.

The *Keith* decision, as well as the widespread abuses disclosed through the Church Commission, raised the question of what was, indeed, "reasonable" in conducting surveillance and searches of foreign intelligence targets. Even if the distinction between foreign and domestic national security surveillance was recognized in the past, did the *Keith* decision change that? Actually, it did not—the distinction between the law governing domestic and foreign intelligence operations persisted. This was addressed in the following case.

United States v. Truong Dinh Hung, 629 F.2d 908 (1980)*

Truong Dinh Hung, more familiarly known as David Truong, along with Ronald Humphrey, were convicted of espionage, conspiracy to commit espionage and several espionage-related offenses for transmitting classified United States government information to representatives of the government of the Socialist Republic of Vietnam. In these appeals, they seek reversal of their convictions because of warrantless surveillance and searches. We hold that the warrantless searches and surveillance did not violate the Fourth Amendment.

David Truong, a Vietnamese citizen and son of a prominent Vietnamese political figure, came to the United States in 1965. At least since his arrival in the United States, Truong has pursued an active scholarly and political interest in Vietnam and the relationship between Vietnam and the United States. In 1976, Truong met Dung Krall, a Vietnamese-American, the wife of an American Naval Officer, who had extensive contacts among the Vietnamese community in Paris. Truong persuaded Krall to carry packages for him to Vietnamese in Paris. The recipients were representatives of the Socialist Republic of Vietnam at the time of the 1977 Paris negotiations between that country and the United States. The packages contained copies of diplomatic cables and other classified papers of the United States government dealing with Southeast Asia. Truong procured the copies from Ronald Humphrey, an employee of the United States Information Agency, who obtained the documents surreptitiously, copied them, removed their classification markings and furnished the copies to Truong. In a statement given after his arrest, Humphrey said that his motive was to improve relations between the North Vietnamese government and the United States so that he could be reunited with a woman whom he loved who was a prisoner of the North Vietnamese government.

Unknown to Truong, Krall was a confidential informant employed by the CIA and the FBI. Krall kept these agencies fully informed of Truong's activities and presented the packages Truong had given her to the FBI for inspection, copying and approval before she carried the documents to Paris. The FBI permitted this operation to continue, while monitoring it closely, from approximately September, 1976, until January 31, 1978.

When the intelligence agencies first learned that Truong was transmitting classified documents to Paris, they were understandably extremely anxious to locate Truong's source for his data. Toward that end, the government conducted a massive surveillance of Truong. Truong's phone was tapped and his apartment was bugged from May, 1977 to January, 1978. The telephone interception continued for 268 days and every conversation, with possibly one exception, was monitored and virtually all were taped. The eavesdropping device was operative for approximately 255 days and it ran continuously. No court authorization was ever sought or obtained for the

---

* The case has been heavily edited and paraphrased by the authors for clarity. See disclaimer in introduction.

installation and maintenance of the telephone tap or the bug. The government thus ascertained that Humphrey was providing Truong with the copies of secret documents. This leak of sensitive information of course ceased when Truong and Humphrey were arrested on January 31, 1978.

After a protracted trial, Truong and Humphrey were both convicted of espionage and conspiracy to commit espionage in violation of 18 U.S.C. §§ 371 and 794(a) and (c) [as well as other related crimes].

A. Foreign Intelligence Exception to the Warrant Requirement

The defendants raise a substantial challenge to their convictions by urging that the surveillance conducted by the FBI violated the Fourth Amendment and that all the evidence uncovered through that surveillance must consequently be suppressed. As has been stated, the government did not seek a warrant for the eavesdropping on Truong's phone conversations or the bugging of his apartment. Instead, it relied upon a "foreign intelligence" exception to the Fourth Amendment's warrant requirement. In the area of foreign intelligence, the government contends, the President may authorize surveillance without seeking a judicial warrant because of his constitutional prerogatives in the area of foreign affairs. On this basis, the FBI sought and received approval for the surveillance from the President's delegate, the Attorney General. This approval alone, according to the government, is constitutionally sufficient to authorize foreign intelligence surveillance such as the surveillance of Truong.

The district court accepted the government's argument that there exists a foreign intelligence exception to the warrant requirement. The district court, however, also decided that the executive could proceed without a warrant only so long as the investigation was "primarily" a foreign intelligence investigation. The district court decided that the FBI investigation had become primarily a criminal investigation by July 20, 1977, and excluded all evidence secured through warrantless surveillance after that date. Conversely, all evidence secured before July 20 was not suppressed by the district court, because it determined that during that period the investigation primarily concerned foreign intelligence.

We agree with the district court that the Executive Branch need not always obtain a warrant for foreign intelligence surveillance. Although the Supreme Court has never decided the issue which is presented to us, it formulated the analytical approach which we employ here in an analogous case, *United States v. United States District Court (Keith)*, 407 U.S. 297 (1972). In *Keith*, the executive had conducted warrantless domestic security surveillance. The Court posited two inquiries to guide the Fourth Amendment determination of whether a warrant is required:

If the legitimate need of Government to safeguard domestic security requires the use of electronic surveillance, the question is whether the needs of citizens for privacy and free expression may not be better protected by requiring a warrant before such surveillance is undertaken. We must also ask whether a warrant would unduly frustrate the efforts of Government to protect itself from acts of subversion and overthrow directed against it.

Balancing individual privacy and government needs, the Supreme Court concluded that the executive must seek a warrant before it undertakes domestic security surveillance.

For several reasons, the needs of the executive are so compelling in the area of foreign intelligence, unlike the area of domestic security, that a uniform warrant requirement would, following *Keith*, "unduly frustrate" the President in carrying out his foreign affairs responsibilities. First of all, attempts to counter foreign threats to the national security require the utmost stealth, speed, and secrecy. A warrant requirement would add a procedural hurdle that would reduce the flexibility of executive foreign intelligence initiatives, in some cases delay executive response to foreign intelligence threats, and increase the chance of leaks regarding sensitive executive operations.

More importantly, the executive possesses unparalleled expertise to make the decision whether to conduct foreign intelligence surveillance, whereas the judiciary is largely inexperienced in making the delicate and complex decisions that lie behind foreign intelligence surveillance. The executive branch, containing the State Department, the intelligence agencies, and the military, is constantly aware of the nation's security needs and the magnitude of external threats posed by numerous foreign nations and organizations.

On the other hand, while the courts possess expertise in making the probable cause determination involved in surveillance of suspected criminals, the courts are unschooled in diplomacy and military affairs, a mastery of which would be essential to passing upon an executive branch request that a foreign intelligence wiretap be authorized. Few, if any, district courts would be truly competent to judge the importance of particular information to the security of the United States or the "probable cause" to demonstrate that the government in fact needs to recover that information from one particular source.

Perhaps most crucially, the executive branch not only has superior expertise in the area of foreign intelligence, it is also constitutionally designated as the preeminent authority in foreign affairs. The President and his deputies are charged by the constitution with the conduct of the foreign policy of the United States in times of war and peace. Just as the separation of powers in *Keith* forced the executive to recognize a judicial role when the President conducts domestic security surveillance, so the separation of powers requires us to acknowledge the principal responsibility of the President for foreign affairs and concomitantly for foreign intelligence surveillance.

In sum, because of the need of the executive branch for flexibility, its practical experience, and its constitutional competence, the courts should not require the executive to secure a warrant each time it conducts foreign intelligence surveillance. However, because individual privacy interests are severely compromised any time the government conducts surveillance without prior judicial approval, this foreign intelligence exception to the Fourth Amendment warrant requirement must be carefully limited to those situations in which the interests of the executive are paramount. First, the government should be relieved of seeking a warrant only when the object of the search or the surveillance is a foreign power, its agent or collaborators. In such cases, the government has the greatest need for speed, stealth, and secrecy, and the surveillance in such cases is most likely to call into play difficult and subtle judgments about foreign and military affairs. When there is no foreign connection, the executive's needs become less compelling; and the surveillance more closely resembles the surveillance of suspected criminals, which must be authorized by warrant. Thus, if the government wishes to wiretap the phone of a government employee who is stealing sensitive documents for his personal reading or to leak to a newspaper, for instance, the absence of a foreign connection and the importance of individual privacy concerns contained within the Fourth Amendment lead to a requirement that the executive secure advance judicial approval for surveillance.

The surveillance in this case clearly satisfied this limitation upon the foreign intelligence exception to the warrant requirement. Krall, the government agent, received a letter of introduction to Truong through Dong, the president of the Vietnamese Association in Paris. According to Krall, Truong gave her documents to carry back to Dong, who handed the documents to representatives of the Vietnamese government. In addition, Krall testified that the Vietnamese ambassador to the United Nations told her that Truong had volunteered to obtain documents for the Vietnamese government. Moreover, Krall stated that Truong gave her documents to deliver to Phan Thanh Nam, head of the Vietnamese mission in Paris, who in turn gave her a letter for Truong. Obviously, there was ample evidence that tended to show collaboration with Vietnam on the part of Truong.

Second, as the district court ruled, the executive should be excused from securing a warrant only when the surveillance is conducted "primarily" for foreign intelligence reasons. We think that the district court adopted the proper test, because once surveillance becomes primarily a criminal investigation, the courts are entirely competent to make the usual probable cause determination, and because, importantly, individual privacy interests come to the fore and government foreign policy concerns recede when the government is primarily attempting to form the basis for a criminal prosecution. We thus reject the government's assertion that, if surveillance is to any degree directed at gathering foreign intelligence, the executive may ignore the warrant requirement of the Fourth Amendment.

The defendants urge that the "primarily" test does not go far enough to protect privacy interests. They argue that the government should be able to avoid the warrant requirement only when the surveillance is conducted "solely" for foreign policy reasons. The proposed "solely" test is unacceptable, however, because almost all foreign intelligence investigations are in part criminal investigations. Although espionage prosecutions are rare, there is always the possibility that the targets of the investigation will be prosecuted for criminal violations. Thus, if the defendants' "solely" test were adopted, the executive would be required to obtain a warrant almost every time it undertakes foreign intelligence surveillance, and, as indicated above, such a requirement would fail to give adequate consideration to the needs and responsibilities of the executive in the foreign intelligence area.

In this case, the district court concluded that on July 20, 1977, the investigation of Truong had become primarily a criminal investigation. Although the Criminal Division of the Justice Department had been aware of the investigation from its inception, until summer the Criminal Division had not taken a central role in the investigation. On July 19 and July 20, however, several memoranda circulated between the Justice Department and the various intelligence and national security agencies indicating that the government had begun to assemble a criminal prosecution. On the facts of this case, the district court's finding that July 20 was the critical date when the investigation became primarily a criminal investigation was clearly correct.

Therefore, because there was more than enough evidence to indicate that Truong had collaborated with the Vietnamese government and because the district court did not err in choosing July 20 as the date when the investigation became primarily a criminal investigation, we do not disturb the decision of the district court to exclude all evidence obtained through the surveillance after July 20 but to permit the government to introduce evidence secured through the surveillance before July 20.

Because the Fourth Amendment warrant requirement is a critical constitutional protection of individual privacy, this discussion should conclude by underscoring the limited nature of this foreign intelligence exception to the warrant requirement which we recognize in the instant case. The exception applies only to foreign powers, their agents, and their collaborators. Moreover, even these actors receive the protection of the warrant requirement if the government is primarily attempting to put together a criminal prosecution. Thus, the executive can proceed without a warrant only if it is attempting primarily to obtain foreign intelligence from foreign powers or their assistants. We think that the unique role of the executive in foreign affairs and the separation of powers will not permit this court to allow the executive less on the facts of this case, but we also are convinced that the Fourth Amendment will not permit us to grant the executive branch more.

B. Reasonableness of the Surveillance

Even if a warrant is not required, the Fourth Amendment requires that the surveillance be "reasonable." The reasonableness of the surveillance is determined by examining the circumstances of the particular case.

For seventy days prior to July 20, FBI agents intercepted all of Truong's phone calls; and, for almost as long a period, the agents listened to Truong's conversations with visitors in his apartment. As the district court observed, the surveillance was nonetheless reasonable, and we agree.

The purpose of the surveillance was to determine Truong's source or sources for government documents. Thus, it was necessary to intercept all his calls, because the government agents could never be sure whether a particular caller would reveal that he was a source of the documents sometime during his conversation with Truong. As well, when the government eavesdrops on clandestine groups like this one, investigators often find it necessary to intercept all calls in order to record possible code language or oblique references to the illegal scheme. Thus, on the facts of this case, the surveillance conducted by the government agents was reasonable.

END OF OPINION

As this case illustrates, efforts by law enforcement and national security agencies to address foreign intelligence remain governed by a different standard than domestic intelligence cases.

Historically, this makes sense. The intent of the founders when writing the warrant clause of the Fourth Amendment was simply to continue a preexisting rule of common law that originated in Britain requiring warrants for regular law enforcement purposes to investigate ordinary crimes. Although espionage is a crime, it is extremely different from ordinary crimes like theft, assault, and other common law crimes frequently handled by law enforcement. Foreign affairs is a unique area with much broader, more complicated, and more compelling concerns than regular criminal law enforcement. The founding fathers understood this and would have been familiar with British law that warrants are not required for counter-espionage. In more recent times, the courts have recognized the "magnitude of external threats posed by numerous foreign nations and organizations" so it was important that the President have the "stealth, speed, and secrecy" as well as the flexibility to respond to such threats.

As the Court noted in the Truong opinion, having to get a warrant to respond to international threats would "unduly frustrate" the president's ability to defend this country or respond to issues in foreign affairs. Having to get a warrant to address foreign threats both delays the president's ability to act and, with each extra procedural hurdle, increases the chances of an intelligence leak. Furthermore, it is the executive branch of the government that has the experts in national security and not the courts, so it is prudent for judges to defer to the president in matters involving national security.

The court recognized the civil liberties and privacy concerns of such a rule governing searches and seizures for purposes of foreign intelligence, so it was careful to specify that this exception is limited to only foreign intelligence cases. The search itself is performed inside the U.S., and the person being searched can even be a U.S. citizen, but so long as that person is the agent or operative of a foreign government or foreign terror organization, the U.S. Constitution allows that person to be searched or surveilled without a warrant. We'll address the issue of searches that take place outside of the United States later.

The Foreign Intelligence Surveillance Act

As these cases illustrate, the tension between protecting the United States against foreign threats while maintaining the civil liberties guaranteed by Congress is a difficult one. What is "reasonable" under these circumstances? How do we determine that the case is one of foreign intelligence and not domestic law enforcement? What if U.S. citizens who are not foreign agents are subject to one of these searches or surveillance activities—how is the balance between national security, law enforcement, and civil liberties to be protected?

One of the reforms undertaken, which tries to help strike the proper balance among these and other concerns, was the Foreign Intelligence Surveillance Act (FISA). The FISA was written to provide the president with the aforementioned "stealth, speed, and secrecy" needed in foreign affairs while still protecting civil liberties.

FISA created a new system for which the government can conduct foreign surveillance while still providing for judicial oversight to prevent a reoccurrence of these past abuses of civil rights and privacy. The text of the law is found at Chapter 36 of Title 50 of the U.S. Code, sections 1801 and following. Here is a brief summary of the process:

Pursuant to FISA, foreign surveillance is initiated by the U.S. Attorney General unilaterally authorizing foreign surveillance on a person or place. While this order is made without any prior judicial approval as required by a regular warrant, within 72 hours of the Attorney General giving the order, the government must subsequently obtain judicial approval of this surveillance. If the government is unable to obtain judicial authorization within 72 hours after-the-fact, the surveillance must be terminated.

The way the government obtains judicial approval to conduct foreign surveillance is by presenting the matter to a federal judge who sits on the Foreign Intelligence Surveillance Court (FISC) and getting a FISA order from that judge. This must be done within 72 hours. The FISC is comprised of 11 federal judges who are appointed by the Chief Justice of the U.S. Supreme Court. Prior to appointment to the FISC, these judges already have been appointed to a federal judgeship by a U.S. president and confirmed by the U.S. Senate. All persons nominated by the president for a federal judgeship undergo a thorough background check to ensure their loyalty to the U.S. and their trustworthiness to access highly classified information. The judges selected by the Chief Justice to sit on the FISA Court are granted the necessary security clearances to do the job, and they take on the responsibilities of the FISC in addition to their preexisting judicial work.

To get a FISA order, government officials, usually from the Department of Justice, will present evidence to the judge in closed and highly classified proceedings. The judge will look over the evidence and make certain findings. The necessary findings required for a FISA order are as follows:

1. That the target of the search and/or surveillance is a foreign power, or the agent of a foreign power;

2. Any place where electronic surveillance is directed or used against is in the ownership/possession of a foreign power or agent of one;

3. For physical searches, the premises or property to be searched is owned, used, possessed by, or is in transit to or from an agent of a foreign power or a foreign power; and

4. That the government has taken steps to minimize the search to only what was required.

If the judge is satisfied, he or she issues the order permitting the search or surveillance. The process is then somewhat similar to the process for getting a regular "Title III" warrant, in that the authorities are required to provide their justification to a member of the judiciary, but the process is streamlined and sensitive information (like intelligence sources and methods) is protected by the nature of the proceedings.

While items 1, 2, and 3 of the criteria noted above are fairly self-explanatory, the fourth one, requiring minimization procedures, is both extremely important and often overlooked in public discussion about the subject.

The purpose of minimization procedures is to prevent innocent persons, especially U.S. persons with no involvement as foreign agents, from being caught in an intelligence-gathering web. The government must have specific procedures in place in an effort to ensure that only the suspected agent or operative of a foreign power is being searched or surveilled, and no one else. For example, let's say that there is a known Al-Qaeda operative living in just one of the units of a 300-unit apartment building in NYC. It would be unlawful for the FBI to tap the telephones of everyone in the building and then sift through the collected recordings to find the communications of the Al-Qaeda operative. Instead, they would have to try to minimize their wiretap to only the apartment unit containing the Al-Qaeda operative. One example of this is United States Signals Intelligence Directive 18, which details policies and procedures to ensure NSA's missions and functions are conducted in a manner that safeguards the constitutional rights of U.S. persons. That document, like most minimization procedures, was (and remains) classified but was released in a declassified form by the Director of National Intelligence on November 18, 2013.[2]

Who Can Be Targeted by a FISA Order?

For a suspect to be monitored pursuant to a FISA order, that person must be the "agent of a foreign power." Just what is a foreign power, and what makes a person its agent? A foreign power is any foreign country, international terrorist group, or organization comprised mostly of non-U.S. citizens. The "foreign power" can be a friend or foe — it does not matter. Examples of foreign powers would include other nations such as China, Israel, or Germany, international terrorist organizations such as Al-Qaeda, ISIS, the IRA, and Hezbollah, and political parties in other countries such as the British Labour Party or the Indian National Congress in India.

An "agent of a foreign power" is any person, including U.S. citizens, who are providing aid, support, and assistance to the illegal activities of a foreign power. For example, if a person sends money to Al-Qaeda, that person has supported Al-Qaeda, thus becoming its agent. If another person passes classified U.S. Army secrets to

---

2. DNI Clapper Declassifies Additional Intelligence Community Documents Regarding Collection Under Section 501 of the Foreign Intelligence Surveillance Act, November 18, 2013. http://icontherecord.tumblr.com/post/67419963949/dni-clapper-declassifies-additional-intelligence. Statement posted on "IC On The Record," a website maintained by the Office of the Director of National Intelligence to facilitate greater public awareness of legal and policy issues regarding the intelligence process. http://icontherecord.tumblr.com.

China, that person has become a Chinese agent. In both examples, it does not matter whether or not the person is a U.S. citizen or not. Any person can become the agent of a foreign power by offering aid, support, or assistance in violation of the law.

To determine whether or not a person is the agent of a foreign power, you should use this helpful two-part test by applying it to a fact pattern.

1. First, a person is engaged in illegal activity or clandestine intelligence gathering activities.
2. Second, these activities are done on behalf of a foreign power. The foreign power will typically be either another country or an international terrorist organization.

If, and only if, both parts of this test have been met, would a FISA order be appropriate. If either part is not met, then issuing a FISA order would not be lawful; instead, the government would have to get a regular warrant to lawfully conduct the surveillance.

For example, assume that Janice works for the Department of Defense and is passing U.S. military secrets to China. Part 1 is met as she is engaged in illegal conduct by disclosing classified materials to a party unauthorized to receive them, and Part 2 is met because she is doing it on behalf of China, who is a foreign power. However, let's change the facts a little and, instead of Janice passing the military secrets to China, she is instead suspected of giving information to the *New York Times* (and only to the *New York Times*) to be published. Part 1 would still be met as she is engaged in illegal conduct; however, Part 2 would not be met because the *New York Times* is not a foreign power. The mere fact that foreigners happen to read the *New York Times* would be insufficient to make Janice the agent of a foreign power.

This second example involving the *New York Times* actually happened when Daniel Ellsberg leaked the Pentagon Papers, classified Department of Defense documents, to American media outlets including the *New York Times*. When this happened, the courts ruled that it was unlawful for the government to conduct foreign surveillance on Ellsberg because there was no evidence that he was acting on behalf of a foreign power. Instead, the government would have had to get a warrant to lawfully conduct surveillance on him. In contrast, Truong was a U.S. citizen who was trying to illegally pass classified materials to Vietnam, so today he would qualify for FISA surveillance.

This next case provides a bit more detail on the FISA process, including discussion on how the balance between national security and civil liberties is sought to be protected by the process.

United States v. Steven J. Rosen, Keith Weissman, 447 F. Supp. 2d 538 (2006)*

Defendants, Steven J. Rosen and Keith Weissman, are charged in a superseding indictment with one count of conspiring to communicate national defense

---

* The case has been heavily edited and paraphrased by the authors for clarity. See disclaimer in introduction.

information to persons not entitled to receive it, in violation of 18 U.S.C. § 793(d), (e) and (g). More specifically, Count One of the superseding indictment alleges that between April 1999 and continuing until August 2004, Rosen and Weissman along with alleged co-conspirator Lawrence Franklin, then an employee of the Department of Defense (DOD), were engaged in a conspiracy to communicate information relating to the national defense to those not entitled to receive it. According to the superseding indictment, Franklin and certain other unnamed government officials with authorized possession of classified national defense information communicated that information to Rosen and Weissman, who were employed at the time as lobbyists for the American-Israel Public Affairs Committee (AIPAC). It is further alleged that Rosen and Weissman then communicated the information received from their government sources to members of the media, other foreign policy analysts, and certain foreign officials, none of whom were authorized to receive this information.

In the course of its investigation of the alleged conspiracy, the government sought and obtained orders issued by the Foreign Intelligence Surveillance Court (FISC) pursuant to the Foreign Intelligence Surveillance Act (FISA), authorizing certain physical searches and electronic surveillance. As the investigation pertained to national security, these applications and orders were classified. Because the government intends to offer evidence obtained or derived from physical searches and electronic surveillance authorized by these orders, defendants seek by motion (1) to obtain disclosure of the classified applications submitted to the FISC, the FISC's orders, and related materials, and/or (2) to suppress the evidence obtained or derived from any searches or surveillance conducted pursuant to the issued FISA orders.

Defendants' motion and the government's opposition raise a number of questions concerning the proper scope of, and procedure for, district court review of challenges to FISA orders, as well as specific questions concerning whether the FISA orders in issue in this case issued in conformity with that statute's requirements. This memorandum opinion addresses these questions, beginning with an overview of the FISA procedure.

FISA, enacted in 1978, was Congress's response to three related concerns: (1) the judicial confusion over the existence, nature and scope of a foreign intelligence exception to the Fourth Amendment's warrant requirement that arose in the wake of the Supreme Court's 1972 decision in *United States v. United States District Court* (1972); (2) the Congressional concern over perceived Executive Branch abuses of such an exception; and (3) the felt need to provide the Executive Branch with an appropriate means to investigate and counter foreign intelligence threats. FISA accommodates these concerns by establishing a detailed process the Executive Branch must follow to obtain orders allowing it to collect foreign intelligence information without violating the rights of citizens of the United States. Although originally limited to electronic surveillance, FISA's coverage has now been expanded to include physical searches, as well. Thus, the detailed FISA process applicable to electronic surveillance relating to foreign intelligence also applies now to physical searches.

FISA's detailed procedure for obtaining orders authorizing electronic surveillance or physical searches of a foreign power or an agent of a foreign power begins with the government's filing of an *ex parte*, under seal application with the FISC. Such an application must be approved by the Attorney General and must include certain specified information. A FISC judge considering the application may also require the submission of additional information necessary to make the requisite findings.

After review of the application, a single judge of the FISC must enter an *ex parte* Order granting the government's application for electronic surveillance or a physical search of a foreign power or an agent of a foreign power provided the judge makes certain specific findings, including most importantly, that on the basis of the facts submitted by the applicant there is probable cause to believe that—

1. the target of the electronic surveillance or physical search is a foreign power or an agent of a foreign power, except that no United States person may be considered a foreign power or an agent of a foreign power solely upon the basis of activities protected by the First Amendment to the Constitution of the United States; and
2. for electronic surveillance, each of the facilities or places at which the electronic surveillance is directed is being used, or is about to be used, by a foreign power or an agent of a foreign power; or
3. for physical searches, the premises or property to be searched is owned, used, possessed by, or is in transit to or from an agent of a foreign power or a foreign power.

If the FISC judge's findings reflect that the government has satisfied the statute's requirements, the judge must issue an order approving the surveillance or search. Such an order must describe the target, the information sought, and the means of acquiring such information. The order must also set forth the period of time during which the electronic surveillance or physical searches are approved, which is generally ninety days or until the objective of the electronic surveillance or physical search has been achieved. Applications for a renewal of the order must generally be made upon the same basis as the original application and require the same findings by the FISC.

Although FISA is chiefly directed to obtaining foreign intelligence information, the Act specifically contemplates cooperation between federal authorities conducting electronic surveillance and physical searches pursuant to FISA and federal law enforcement officers investigating clandestine intelligence activities. In this respect, FISA explicitly allows the use of evidence derived from FISA surveillance and searches in criminal prosecutions.

If the Attorney General approves the use of evidence collected pursuant to FISA in a criminal prosecution, and the government intends to use or disclose FISA evidence at the trial of an "aggrieved person," the government must first notify the aggrieved person and the district court that the government intends to disclose or use the FISA evidence. On receiving such notification, an aggrieved person may seek to suppress any evidence derived from FISA surveillance or searches on the grounds that: (1) the evidence was unlawfully acquired; or (2) the electronic surveillance or physical search was not conducted in conformity with the Order of authorization or approval. And, if an aggrieved person moves to suppress FISA evidence or to obtain FISA material, then upon the filing of an affidavit by the Attorney General stating under oath that disclosure of such material would harm national security, the district court must review the FISA warrant applications and related materials *in camera* and *ex parte* to determine whether the surveillance or search of the aggrieved person was lawfully authorized and conducted.

II.

At the threshold, defendants seek disclosure of the FISA applications, orders, and related materials at issue in this case so they may effectively participate in the review process. On this point FISA is clear: It allows a reviewing court to disclose such materials only where such disclosure is necessary to make an accurate determination of the legality of the surveillance. Defendants claim this condition is met, by arguing (1) that the FISC's determination that they were agents of a foreign power was surely wrong; and (2) that evidence of the government's evident failure to comply with FISA's minimization procedures requires disclosure. Neither argument is persuasive.

Review of the FISA applications, orders and other materials in this case presented none of the concerns that might warrant disclosure to defendants. The FISA dockets contained no facial inconsistencies, nor did they disclose any reason to doubt any of the representations made by the government in its applications. Likewise, the targets of the surveillance are precisely defined. Finally, although defendants claim that the discovery obtained from the government contains a significant amount of non-foreign intelligence information, this contention relies upon an inordinately narrow view of what constitutes foreign intelligence information, and therefore is unavailing. For these reasons, and given the government's legitimate national security interest in maintaining the secrecy of the information contained in the FISA applications, disclosure of the FISA materials to defendants is not warranted in this case.

It is next necessary to address the lawfulness of the FISC's authorization of the electronic surveillance and physical searches conducted by the government in this case. In this regard, a careful and searching review of the FISA dockets discloses that the government's applications and the resulting FISC orders meet all the statutory requirements. Specifically, the President has authorized the Attorney General to approve applications to the FISC and each of the applications reviewed was made by a federal officer and approved by the Attorney General or his authorized designate. In addition, (i) the proposed minimization procedures met the statutory requirements contained in § 1801(h), (ii) the applications contained all of the required statements and certifications, and (iii) those certifications were not clearly erroneous on the basis of the facts submitted pursuant to § 1804(a)(7)(E).

Defendants' attack on the lawfulness of the FISA surveillance in this case focuses chiefly on two issues: (1) whether the FISC had probable cause to believe that the targets of the sanctioned surveillance were "agents of a foreign power," as required by FISA, and (2) whether there was proper compliance with the minimization procedures subsequent to the surveillance. Review of the FISA material confirms that both of these issues must be resolved in favor of the lawfulness of the surveillance.

Defendants' necessarily speculative contention that the FISC must have erred when it found probable cause to believe that the targets are agents of a foreign power is without merit. An agent of a foreign power is defined by the statute, in pertinent part, as any person who—

(A) knowingly engages in clandestine intelligence gathering activities for or on behalf of a foreign power, which activities involve or may involve a violation of the criminal statutes of the United States; (B) pursuant to the direction of an intelligence service or network of a foreign power, knowingly engages in any other clandestine intelligence activities for or on behalf of such power, which activities involve or are about to involve a violation of the criminal statutes of the United States; . . . or (E) knowingly aids or abets any person in the conduct of activities described in [the subparagraphs above] or knowingly conspires with any person to engage in activities described in [the subparagraphs above].

Although the phrase "clandestine intelligence gathering activities" is not defined in FISA, the legislative history demonstrates that the drafters viewed these "activities" in light of the criminal espionage laws, including 18 U.S.C. §§ 793 and 794, and considered that such "activities" would include, for example, "collection or transmission of information or material that is not generally available to the public." In addition, with respect to paragraph (E) above, Congress added "knowingly" to ensure that the aider or abettor cannot be an unknowing dupe. The bill requires that he know that the person he is aiding is engaged in the described activities.

Importantly, FISA is clear that in determining whether there is probable cause to believe that a potential target of FISA surveillance or a FISA search is an agent of a foreign power, the FISC judge may not consider a United States person an agent of a foreign power *solely* upon the basis of activities protected by the First Amendment. From this plain language, it follows that the probable cause determination may rely in part on activities protected by the First Amendment, provided the determination also relies on activities not protected by the First Amendment. This issue received extensive treatment in the legislative history, which, consistent with the statute's plain language, makes clear that First Amendment activities cannot form the *sole* basis for concluding a U.S. person is an agent of a foreign power. The following excerpt from the legislative history illustrates this point:

> The Bill is not intended to authorize electronic surveillance when a United States person's activities, even though secret and conducted for a foreign power, consist entirely of lawful acts such as lobbying or the use of confidential contacts Lo influence public officials, directly or indirectly, through the dissemination of information. Individuals exercising their right to lobby public officials or to engage in political dissent from official policy may well be in contact with representatives of foreign governments and groups when the issues concern foreign affairs or international economic matters. They

must continue to be free to communicate about such issues and to obtain information or exchange views with representatives of foreign governments or with foreign groups, free from any fear that such contact might be the basis for probable cause to believe they are acting at the direction of a foreign power thus triggering the government's power to conduct electronic surveillance.

The legislative history makes equally clear, however, that this protection extends only to the *lawful* exercise of First Amendment rights of speech, petition, assembly and association. Similarly, the House Report (Intelligence Committee) emphasized that FISA would not authorize surveillance of ethnic Americans who *lawfully* gather political information and perhaps even *lawfully* share it with the foreign government of their national origin. For example, electronic surveillance might be appropriate if there is probable cause to believe that—

> foreign intelligence services are hiding behind the cover of some person or organization in order to influence American political events and deceive Americans into believing that the opinions or influence are of domestic origin and initiative and such deception is willfully maintained in violation of the Foreign Agents Registration Act.

Thus, if the FISC judge has probable cause to believe that the potential target is engaged in *unlawful* activities in addition to those protected by the First Amendment, the FISC may authorize surveillance of a U.S. person. *See In re Sealed Case,* 310 F.3d at 738 ("We have noted, however, that where a U.S. person is involved, an 'agent of a foreign power' is defined in terms of criminal activity.").

In this respect, it is important to emphasize the significant difference between FISA's probable cause requirement and the government's ultimate burden to prove the existence of criminal activity beyond a reasonable doubt. Indeed, the Fourth Circuit has described probable cause in this context as "a fluid concept—turning on the assessment of probabilities in particular factual contexts—not readily, or even usefully, reduced to a neat set of rule[s]." Furthermore, in evaluating whether probable cause exists, it is the task of the issuing judge to make a practical, common-sense decision, whether, given all the circumstances set forth in the affidavit, there is a fair probability that the search will be fruitful. Probable cause means more than bare suspicion but less than absolute certainty that a search will be fruitful. And, in making the probable cause determination, FISA permits a judge to consider past activities of the target, as well as facts and circumstances relating to current or future activities of the target. Furthermore, with respect to those U.S. persons suspected of involvement in clandestine intelligence activities, the probable cause determination does not necessarily require a showing of an imminent violation of criminal law because Congress clearly intended a lesser showing of probable cause for these activities than that applicable to ordinary cases. Illustrative of this intent is FISA's description of clandestine intelligence activities as those that involve or may involve a violation of the criminal statutes of the United States. As FISA's drafters made clear: The term 'may involve' not only requires less information regarding the crime involved, but also permits electronic surveillance at some point prior to the time when a crime sought to be prevented, as for example, the transfer of classified documents, actually occurs.

Thus, while the statute is intended to avoid permitting electronic surveillance solely on the basis of First Amendment activities, it plainly allows a FISC judge to issue an order allowing the surveillance or physical search if there is probable cause to believe that the target, even if engaged in First Amendment activities, may also be involved in unlawful clandestine intelligence activities, or in knowingly aiding and abetting such activities. In these circumstances, the fact that a target is also involved in protected First Amendment activities is no bar to electronic surveillance pursuant to FISA.

A thorough review of the FISA dockets in issue confirms that the FISC had ample probable cause to believe that the targets were agents of a foreign power quite apart from their First Amendment lobbying activities. While the defendants' lobbying activities are generally protected by the First Amendment, willful violations of espionage laws are not, and as is demonstrated by the allegations contained in the superseding indictment, the FISC had probable cause to believe that such violations had occurred in this case.

Defendants' second argument in support of their motion is that the government failed to follow the applicable minimization procedures. In this regard, it is true that once the electronic surveillance or the physical search has been approved, the government must apply the specific minimization procedures contained in the application to the FISC. These minimization procedures are designed to protect, as far as reasonable, against the acquisition, retention, and dissemination of nonpublic information which is not foreign intelligence information. While the specific minimization procedures for each application are classified, they must meet the definition of minimization procedures under § 1801(h) for electronic surveillance and § 1821(4) for physical searches. FISA minimization procedures include, in pertinent part—

(1) specific procedures adopted by the Attorney General that are reasonably designed in light of the purpose and technique of the particular surveillance or search, to minimize the acquisition and retention, and prohibit the dissemination, of nonpublicly available information concerning unconsenting United States persons consistent with the need of the United States to obtain, produce, and disseminate foreign intelligence information; (2) procedures that require that nonpublicly available information, which is not foreign intelligence information, shall not be disseminated in a manner that identifies any United States person, without such person's consent, unless such person's identity is necessary to understand foreign intelligence information or assess its importance; (3) notwithstanding paragraphs (1) and (2), procedures that allow for the retention and dissemination of information that is evidence of a crime which has been, is being, or is about to be committed and that is to be retained or disseminated for law enforcement purposes.

Congress intended these minimization procedures to act as a safeguard for U.S. persons at the acquisition, retention and dissemination phases of electronic surveillance and searches. Thus, for example, minimization at the acquisition stage is designed to insure that the communications of nontarget U.S. persons who happen to be using a FISA target's telephone, or who happen to converse with the target about non-foreign intelligence information, are not improperly disseminated. Similarly, minimization at the retention stage is intended to ensure that information acquired, which is not necessary for obtaining, producing, or disseminating foreign intelligence information, be destroyed where feasible. Finally, the dissemination of foreign intelligence information needed for an approved purpose should be restricted to those officials with a need for such information. As the Foreign Intelligence Surveillance Court of Review has recently made clear, these procedures do not prohibit the sharing of foreign intelligence information between FBI intelligence officials and criminal prosecutors when there is evidence of a crime.

FISA's minimization procedures are meant to parallel the minimization procedures, which courts have sensibly construed as not requiring the total elimination of innocent conversation. On the contrary, in assessing the minimization effort, the Court's role is to determine whether on the whole the agents have shown a high regard for the right of privacy and have done all they reasonably could to avoid unnecessary intrusion. Thus, absent a charge that the minimization procedures have been disregarded completely, the test of compliance is whether a good faith effort to minimize was attempted.

Obviously, the extent of the government's minimization will depend largely on its construction of the term "foreign intelligence information." And in this respect, "foreign intelligence information" includes, among other things, information that relates to, and if concerning a United States person is necessary to, the ability of the United States to protect against clandestine intelligence activities by an intelligence service or network of a foreign power or by an agent of a foreign power. Acknowledging the inherent difficulty in determining whether something is related to clandestine activity, courts have construed "foreign intelligence information" broadly and sensibly allowed the government some latitude in its determination of what is foreign intelligence information. As the Fourth Circuit pointed out, it is not always immediately clear whether a particular conversation must be minimized because a conversation that seems innocuous on one day may later turn out to be of great significance, particularly if the individuals involved are talking in code. For this reason, when the government eavesdrops on clandestine groups investigators often find it necessary to intercept all calls in order to record possible code language or oblique references to the illegal scheme. This latitude was intended by FISA's drafters who understood that it may be necessary to acquire, retain and disseminate information concerning the known contacts of a U.S. person engaged in clandestine intelligence activities even though some of those contacts will invariably be innocent of any wrong-doing.

Given the breadth of the term "foreign intelligence information" in the context of investigating clandestine intelligence activities and the rule of reason that applies to the government's obligation to minimize non-pertinent information, defendants' motion to suppress for failure to properly minimize must be denied. The *ex parte, in camera* review of the FISA dockets discloses that any failures to minimize properly the electronic surveillance of the defendants were (i) inadvertent, (ii) disclosed to the FISC on discovery, and (iii) promptly rectified.

Yet, this does not end the analysis as the defendants also point to certain publicly available materials bearing on the FBI's general compliance with FISA during the period of this investigation. Specifically, defendants refer to (1) certain previously classified FBI documents, obtained by the media via the Freedom of Information Act, detailing violations of minimization procedures in certain unrelated cases, and (2) a March 8, 2006 Department of Justice, Office of the Inspector General Report to Congress on Implementation of Section 1001 of the USA Patriot Act describing certain failures of the FBI to adhere to FISA's requirements. These documents are general assessments and do not specifically address the integrity of the minimization effort that occurred here. As such, they are no more probative of a failure of minimization in this case than a general study of errors committed over a period of years in baseball would be probative of whether errors occurred in a specific game . . .

END OF OPINION

Review Questions

We will return a bit later in this chapter to the case of Steven Rosen and Keith Weisman, but first, let's work on understanding the basic concepts behind the FISA process by working through some fact patterns. In considering each, apply this two-part test to determine if FISA surveillance would be appropriate, or if a Title III warrant would be required:

a. First, whether a person is engaged in illegal activity or clandestine intelligence gathering activities.

b. Second, whether these activities are being undertaken on behalf of a foreign power or international terrorist organization.

1. John is an American citizen, born and raised in Virginia. While in college, he converted to a radical form of Islam. Disgusted with U.S. policies overseas in Islamic countries, he steals a credit card and uses it to purchase illegal explosives. He plans to put the explosive in his underwear to get it through airport security, and once in the air, detonate it to bring down the plane. He keeps all evidence and records of his plan on his smartphone. If the government received a tip about this plan from John's roommate, would government officials need a Title III warrant to access his smartphone, or could they use a FISA order?

2. John is an American citizen, born and raised in Virginia. While in college, he converted to a radical form of Islam. He makes contact with a person affiliated with Al-Qaeda. With this person's assistance, John steals a credit card and uses it to purchase illegal explosives. He plans to put the explosive in his underwear to get it through airport security, and once in the air, detonate it to bring down the plane. He keeps all evidence and records of his plan on his smartphone, and his roommate

discovers this and tips off the authorities. Would government officials need a warrant to access his smartphone, or could they use a FISA order?

3. Naomi is an engineer working for airplane manufacturer Lockheed Martin, an American corporation. She is working on a project to design the next generation of stealth aircraft. She wants to make extra money, so she decides to steal classified information and sell it to Boeing, another American aircraft manufacturer. Her unauthorized copy and transfer of files has alerted the attention of the FBI. If the FBI is to access the records on her personal computer at home, may it conduct foreign surveillance on her, or must it obtain a warrant?

4. Naomi is an engineer working for airplane manufacturer Lockheed Martin, an American corporation. She is working on a project to design the next generation of stealth aircraft. She is having financial troubles and wants to make extra money, and there is evidence that she has decided to steal classified information and sell it to China. Her unauthorized copy and transfer of files has alerted the attention of her employer who has notified the FBI. If the FBI wants to access the records on her personal computer at home, should it get a FISA order or a Title III warrant?

5. Chang is a member of the Chinese government and works in the Chinese embassy in Washington, D.C., as a computer security expert. He is dissatisfied with his government salary, so from his home computer he hacks American computers to steal credit card numbers. With this scheme, he buys himself sports cars, a big-screen television, a penthouse apartment, and frequents high-class call girls. Eventually, the FBI is alerted to his criminal activities. To clandestinely investigate the extent of Chang's scheme, should the FBI get a FISA order or a Title III warrant?

6. Chang is a member of the Chinese government and works in the Chinese embassy in Washington, D.C., as a computer security expert. He is dissatisfied with his current government salary and wants to be promoted. He decides to prove his value to his superiors by hacking into U.S. government databases to steal classified information. Eventually, the FBI is alerted to his criminal activities. To clandestinely investigate the extent of Chang's scheme, should the FBI get a FISA order or a Title III warrant?

FISA and the First Amendment

In the cases you read above there was reference to whether or not the individuals suspected of passing information along to the foreign power may have been exercising their First Amendment rights. This is an important issue.

As you will recall, the First Amendment states:

> Congress shall make no law respecting an establishment of religion, or prohibiting the free exercise thereof; or abridging the freedom of speech, or of the press; or the right of the people peaceably to assemble, and to petition the Government for a redress of grievances.

Freedom to speak, to assemble, to petition the government, and to both practice one's religion and be free from any type of government-imposed religion — these are among the most important of our rights as Americans, but they are also rights that, when exercised, can get one in trouble with "the powers that be."

Throughout history, people who expressed unpopular political opinions were frequently persecuted. One example would be Socrates being sentenced to death by his fellow citizens in Athens. And, as was disclosed through the Pike and Church Committee hearings, many Americans who were perceived as holding Communist or Socialist political views during the Cold War were illegally wiretapped and investigated. Other Americans who advocated for civil rights for blacks in the 1950s and 1960s were also illegally investigated. Military intelligence and FBI agents "infiltrated" churches and civil rights organizations, reporting on the activities of members. These activities as well as warrantless wiretapping and opening of mail not only violated the Fourth Amendment's prohibition against unlawful search and seizure, but also violated the First Amendment's right to free speech and association when done for political purposes. The text of FISA and the required minimization procedures are intended to prevent this type of infringement of rights to assembly, speech, as well as privacy.

Legally, so long as a person is not breaking the law, the First Amendment prohibits the government from targeting people for investigation solely because of their political viewpoints. Accordingly, the government may not conduct FISA surveillance on individuals solely because of their political activities. This means that so long as a person is not suspected of breaking the law, the government may not obtain a FISA order or a warrant to investigate persons who advocate radical political Islam, white power, the murder of homosexuals, the persecution of the Jews, protests at the funerals of dead soldiers, the overthrow of the U.S. federal government, or any other ideology, no matter how hateful, repulsive, or offensive the ideology may be. Additionally, the mere fact that a person has unpopular views cannot be the sole basis of a suspicion that the person is also doing something illegal.

This concept, and its First Amendment implications, is explained in the *Rosen* case. We looked at one Memorandum Decision of the federal court in this case; now let's look at another decision in the same case.

United States v. Rosen, 445 F. Supp. 2d 602 (2006)*

FISA is clear that in determining whether there is probable cause to believe that a potential target of FISA surveillance or a FISA search is an agent of a foreign power, the FISC judge may not consider a United States person an agent of a foreign power "solely upon the basis of activities protected by the First Amendment." From this plain language, it follows that the probable cause determination may rely in part on activities protected by the First Amendment, provided the determination also relies on activities not protected by the First Amendment. It is clear that First Amendment activities cannot form the sole basis for concluding a U.S. person is an agent of a foreign power.

---

* The case has been heavily edited and paraphrased by the authors for clarity. See disclaimer in introduction.

FISA is not intended to authorize electronic surveillance when a United States person's activities, even though secret and conducted for a foreign power, consist entirely of lawful acts such as lobbying, or the use of confidential contacts or influence public officials, directly or indirectly, through the dissemination of information. Individuals exercising their right to lobby public officials or to engage in political dissent from official policy may well be in contact with representatives of foreign governments and groups when the issues concern foreign affairs or international economic matters.

They must continue to be free to communicate about such issues and to obtain information or exchange views with representatives of foreign governments or with foreign groups, free from any fear that such contact might be the basis for probable cause to believe they are acting at the direction of a foreign power thus triggering the government's power to conduct electronic surveillance.

This protection extends only to the "lawful exercise of First Amendment rights of speech, petition, assembly and association." FISA does not authorize surveillance of ethnic Americans who lawfully gather political information and perhaps even lawfully share it with the foreign government of their national origin. For example, electronic surveillance might be appropriate if there is probable cause to believe that—foreign intelligence services are hiding behind the cover of some person or organization in order to influence American political events and deceive Americans into believing that the opinions or influence are of domestic origin and initiative and such deception is willfully maintained in violation of the Foreign Agents Registration Act.

Thus, if the FISC judge has probable cause to believe that the potential target is engaged in unlawful activities in addition to those protected by the First Amendment, the FISC may authorize surveillance of a U.S. person. Past opinions have noted that where a U.S. person is involved, an 'agent of a foreign power' is defined in terms of criminal activity.

In making the probable cause determination, FISA permits a judge to "consider past activities of the target, as well as facts and circumstances relating to current or future activities of the target." Furthermore, with respect to those U.S. persons suspected of involvement in clandestine intelligence activities, the probable cause determination does not necessarily require a showing of an imminent violation of criminal law because Congress clearly intended a lesser showing of probable cause for these activities than that applicable to ordinary cases. Illustrative of this intent is FISA's description of clandestine intelligence activities as those that involve or may involve a violation of the criminal statutes of the United States. As FISA's drafters made clear: The term 'may involve' not only requires less information regarding the crime involved, but also permits electronic surveillance at some point prior to the time when a crime sought to be prevented, as for example, the transfer of classified documents, actually occurs. Thus, while the statute is intended to avoid permitting electronic surveillance solely on the basis of First Amendment activities, it plainly allows a FISC judge to issue an order allowing the surveillance or physical search if there is probable cause to believe that the target, even if engaged in First Amendment activities, may also be involved in unlawful clandestine intelligence activities, or in knowingly aiding and abetting such activities. In these circumstances, the fact that a target is also involved in protected First Amendment activities is no bar to electronic surveillance pursuant to FISA.

END OF OPINION

In this decision the court makes it clear that a person cannot be suspected as being the agent of a foreign power if that person is engaging in *lawful* activities, such as making speeches and lobbying. For example, let's say you have a radical Islamist marching down the street holding a sign saying "Death to Infidels" while wearing a shirt depicting the face of Osama bin Laden. While he walks, this radical openly prays out loud that Allah sends future terror attacks against the U.S. Although this is totally repugnant to American values, there is nothing illegal about it. He is not doing any violence himself, nor is he offering any support, aid, or assistance for a future terrorist attack. He is merely exercising his First Amendment right to free speech to advocate a political and religious belief in Islamic extremism. The fact he happens to have an ideology shared by Al-Qaeda cannot be the sole basis of the government suspecting he is an agent of Al-Qaeda who can be targeted by FISA surveillance. To believe that he is an agent of Al-Qaeda who can be monitored by FISA surveillance, the government would need some other evidence that he is engaged in activity that offers aid, support, or assistance to Al-Qaeda, such as fundraising or planning an attack. The mere fact that he has the same ideology as Al-Qaeda is not, by itself, evidence that he is illegally offering aid, support, or assistance to Al-Qaeda.

It is important to remember that for a FISA order to be issued, "the FISC judge [must have] probable cause to believe that the potential target is engaged in unlawful activities in addition to those protected by the First Amendment . . ." For example, because of the First Amendment guarantee of the freedom of speech, it is perfectly lawful for a Jewish and pro-Israeli American to lobby members of Congress to support Israel. It would also be lawful for that person to secretly inform the Israeli government about his lobbying efforts. This activity and communication is protected by the First Amendment. However if, in addition to the lobbying, this person hands an Israeli government official a classified document, then the agent has just engaged in unlawful clandestine intelligence activities (by violating the Espionage Act of 1917) and would be an agent of Israel and can be surveyed pursuant to a FISA order.

Review Questions

Examine the following situations to determine if FISA surveillance would be lawful in the following fact patterns. In each problem, make sure that (1) the person is engaged in an unlawful activity, and (2) is the agent of a foreign power.

1. Muhammad is a Muslim fundamentalist who dreams of an Islamic theocracy here in the U.S. He makes frequent appearances at rallies in downtown Richmond where he parades around with a sign that says, "Islam will rule America." He also

writes letters to lawmakers and newspapers about how America is the "Great Satan" which will succumb to its own internal weaknesses brought on by our decadent and overly sexualized culture. In public, he prays that Allah will send another terror attack on this sinful nation. His writings and activities have alarmed the FBI, who are worried that, due to his radical beliefs and activities, he may already be an agent of an international terror organization such as Al-Qaeda. Based on the facts, the FBI go to the FISC and apply for a FISA order for authorization to access Muhammad's Gmail account, phone records, bank records, and other communications to see if he has had any correspondence with terrorists. Should the FISC judge authorize the FISA surveillance?

2. Muhammad is a Muslim fundamentalist living in New York City who dreams of an Islamic theocracy here in the U.S. He makes frequent appearances at rallies downtown where he parades around with a sign that says, "Islam will rule America." He also writes letters to lawmakers and newspapers about how America is the "Great Satan" which will succumb to its own internal weaknesses brought on by our decadent and overly sexualized culture. In public, he prays that Allah will send another terror attack on this sinful nation. The NSA lawfully intercepts a cellular communication from a known Al-Qaeda operative in Yemen, which contains detailed plans of an upcoming terrorist attack in New York City. The NSA was able to tell that the communication went into the apartment building where Muhammad lives, but were unable to tell which apartment unit received the communication. Because of Muhammad's known radical philosophy, the FBI suspects that he was the recipient of the communication containing plans for a terror plot. A lawful background check on the other residents of the building reveals that Muhammad is the only Muslim in the building and no other information is uncovered suggesting any of the other residents might be involved. Based on these facts above, the FBI go to the FISC and apply for a FISA order for authorization to access Muhammad's Gmail account, phone records, bank records, and other communications to see if he has had any correspondence with terrorists. Should the FISC judge authorize the FISA surveillance?

Prosecuting with FISA Evidence

Although FISA was intended for counterintelligence to defend national security from spies and international terrorists and not to gather evidence for criminal prosecution, evidence obtained pursuant to a lawful FISA order can be used in criminal prosecution. There are civil rights concerns about the government using evidence obtained without a proper warrant in criminal prosecution, so whenever FISA evidence is to be used in a U.S. court for criminal prosecutions, the procedure set forth in the *Rosen* decision earlier in this chapter must be followed.

Basically, as set forth in that case, there is a three-step process required for the government to be able to use FISA evidence at trial:

a. The government must notify the accused that it intends to use evidence obtained from FISA surveillance at trial;

b. The accused then must be given the opportunity to try to keep the evidence out of court by claiming that (1) the evidence was obtained in violation of the law; or (2) that the government obtained the evidence by violating the conditions set by the FISC judge when it established the authority for the search; and finally,

c. If the accused asserts either of the two conditions as justification for banning the use of the FISA evidence, the federal judge must review both the application the government made to obtain the FISA order and all other relevant materials and information presented by the defense to determine if the government violated the law in the application or, in the alternative, violated any of the terms of the FISA order. If either is the case, the judge should prohibit the use of the evidence.

Review Questions

Based on the readings above, use the IRAC process to analyze the following fact patterns and determine whether or not the FISA evidence should be admissible at a criminal trial.

1. The FBI learns from an undercover agent who has infiltrated Al-Qaeda that there is an ongoing terror plot to be carried out by Al-Qaeda member Brian. The FISC judge authorizes a FISA order, which allows the FBI to wiretap Brian for 30 days. The 30 days of wiretapping reveal nothing, so the FBI continues wiretapping Brian for another 15 days. On day 45, they record a conversation where Brian discusses a terror plot with a member of Al-Qaeda. Based on that conversation, which was recorded on day 45, Brian is arrested and prosecuted.

2. The FBI learns that Morgan is an Al-Qaeda agent prom a reliable informant living in Kabul. With the authorization of the U.S. Attorney General, the FBI wiretaps Morgan's mobile phone. Two hours after the wiretap is initiated, the FBI records Morgan having a conversation where he discusses a plan to conduct a terrorist attack. Fifty hours after the Attorney General ordered the wiretapping of Morgan's phone, an application is made to a FISC judge for a FISA order to wiretap Morgan's phone. The judge issues a FISA order to allow the FBI to wiretap Morgan's phone. Morgan is eventually arrested and, at trial, the FBI plans to introduce into evidence the recording of where Morgan discusses the plan to conduct a terrorist attack.

The "Wall" between Intelligence and Law Enforcement

Following the events of 9/11, there were claims that better intelligence sharing between government agencies might have prevented the terrorist attacks. This was true. Ever since Congress uncovered the abuses during the Pike and Church Committee investigations, and in an effort to protect the civil liberties of Americans, extremely strict safeguards have been put in place against the sharing of information gathered by intelligence agencies (normally the CIA, NSA, or military intelligence) with law enforcement (usually the FBI). This was because intelligence gathering, given its mission of preventing attacks on the United States has less due process protection of civil liberties than law enforcement evidence gathering (compare the "warrant" standard of 'probable cause,' with the intelligence-gathering standard of "reasonable"). It was feared (with some justification, given the abuses of the past) that the government might use the pretext of gathering foreign intelligence as an opportunity to conduct criminal investigations without a warrant.

This prohibition on the routine exchange of information between intelligence agencies and law enforcement agencies is known as "The Wall." The Wall was intended to prevent the government from misusing intelligence capabilities and operations to gather evidence when their interest was a criminal investigation more so than counter intelligence.

As one example of this safeguard, under "the wall" prior to 9/11, a FISA order to conduct surveillance could be issued provided that the *primary purpose* of the operation was to obtain intelligence, and not criminal evidence. So long as this "primary purpose" was demonstrated, and all other minimization procedures intended to protect innocent U.S. persons from being surveilled were followed, information of any crime that was uncovered as a result of the FISA order could be used in any criminal prosecution—even those that had nothing to do with the original purpose of the FISA Court-authorized surveillance. Pursuant to this rule, so long as the government's *primary purpose* in getting a FISA order was gathering foreign intelligence and not criminal evidence, the FISA order should have been issued and any information of wrongdoing obtained could be admissible at a later trial.

After 9/11, many in both the law enforcement and national security communities argued that The Wall (more specifically, the various rules and regulations that created The Wall) were too restrictive, and had possibly thwarted U.S. agencies from preventing the attacks on 9/11. As explained in the 9/11 Commission hearings by then Attorney General John Ashcroft:

> The single greatest structural cause for September 11 was the wall that segregated criminal investigators and intelligence agents. Government erected this wall. Government buttressed this wall. And before September 11, government was blinded by this wall. In 1995, the Justice Department embraced flawed legal reasoning, imposing a series of restrictions on the FBI that went beyond what the law required. The 1995 Guidelines and the procedures developed around them imposed draconian barriers to communications between the law enforcement and intelligence communities. The wall "effectively excluded" prosecutors from intelligence investigations. The wall left intelligence agents afraid to talk with criminal prosecutors or agents. In 1995, the Justice Department designed a system destined to fail.

The 9/11 Commission Report details how, in the days before September 11, "The Wall" specifically impeded the investigation into Zacarias Moussaoui, Khalid al-Midhar and Nawaf al-Hazmi. After the FBI arrested Moussaoui, agents became suspicious of his interest in commercial aircraft and sought approval for a criminal warrant to search his computer. The warrant was rejected because FBI officials feared breaching "The Wall". When the CIA finally told the FBI that al-Midhar and al-Hazmi were in the country in late August, agents in New York searched for the suspects. But because of "The Wall", FBI Headquarters refused to allow criminal investigators who knew the most about the most recent Al-Qaeda attack to join the hunt for the suspected terrorists.

At that time, a frustrated FBI investigator wrote Headquarters, quote, "Whatever has happened to this—someday someone will die—and wall or not—the public will not understand why we were not more effective and throwing every resource we had at certain 'problems'. Let's hope the National Security Law Unit will stand behind their decision then, especially since the biggest threat to us, UBL, is getting the most protection."[3]

In response to the intelligence and law enforcement failures that might have prevented 9/11, "The Wall" was lowered to better enable the sharing of intelligence with law enforcement. The PATRIOT Act amended the "primary purpose" test to a lower standard, the "significant purpose" test.

The United States Foreign Intelligence Surveillance Court of Review (the court which reviews decisions of the FISA Court) explains here how the "significant purpose" test is controlling and how it relates to "The Wall."

In re: Sealed Cases Nos. 02-001, 02-002, 310 F.3d 717 (2002)*

The court ordered that law enforcement officials shall not make recommendations to intelligence officials concerning the initiation, operation, continuation, or expansion of FISA searches or surveillances. Additionally, the FBI and the Criminal Division of the Department of Justice shall ensure that law enforcement officials do not direct or control the use of the FISA procedures to enhance criminal prosecution, and that advice intended to preserve the option of a criminal prosecution does not inadvertently result in the Criminal Division's directing or controlling the investigation using FISA searches and surveillances toward law enforcement objectives.

These restrictions are not original to the order appealed. They were actually set forth in an opinion written by former Presiding Judge of the FISA court on May 17 of this year. The May 17 opinion of the FISA court appears to proceed from the assumption that FISA constructed a barrier between counterintelligence / intelligence officials and law enforcement officers in the Executive Branch—indeed, it uses the word "wall" popularized by certain commentators and journalists to describe that supposed barrier.

The "Wall" emerges from the court's implicit interpretation of FISA. The court apparently believes it can approve applications for electronic surveillance only if the

---

3. Testimony of Attorney General John Ashcroft, the National Commission on Terrorist Attacks Upon the United States, April 13, 2004. http://www.justice.gov/archive/ag/testimony/2004/041304terrorismtestimony.htm.

* The case has been heavily edited and paraphrased by the authors for clarity. See disclaimer in introduction.

government's objective is not primarily directed toward criminal prosecution of the foreign agents for their foreign intelligence activity. But the court neither refers to any FISA language supporting that view, nor does it reference the Patriot Act amendments, which the government contends specifically altered FISA to make clear than application could be obtained even if criminal prosecution is the primary counter mechanism.

The government makes two main arguments. The first is that the supposed pre-Patriot Act limitation in FISA that restricts the government's intention to use foreign intelligence information in criminal prosecutions is an illusion; it finds no support in either the language of FISA or its legislative history. The government does recognize that several courts of appeals, while upholding the use of FISA surveillances, have opined that FISA may be used only if the government's primary purpose in pursuing foreign intelligence information is not criminal prosecution, but the government argues that those decisions, which did not carefully analyze the statute, were incorrect in their statements, if not incorrect in their holdings.

Alternatively, the government contends that even if the primary purpose test was a legitimate construction of FISA prior to the passage of the Patriot Act, the Act's amendments to FISA eliminate that concept.

The 1978 FISA

We turn first to the statute as enacted in 1978 where, for some puzzling reason, the Justice Department, at some point in the 1980s, began to read the statute as limiting the Department's ability to obtain FISA orders if it intended to prosecute the targeted agents—even for foreign intelligence crimes. To be sure, section 1804, which sets forth the elements of an application for an order, required a national security official in the Executive Branch, typically the director of the FBI, to certify that the purpose of the surveillance is to obtain foreign intelligence information (amended by the Patriot Act to read "a significant purpose"). But as the government now argues, the definition of foreign intelligence information includes evidence of crimes such as espionage, sabotage, or terrorism. Indeed, it is virtually impossible to read the 1978 FISA to exclude from its purpose the prosecution of foreign intelligence crimes, most importantly because, as we have noted, the definition of an agent of a foreign power—if he or she is a U.S. person—is grounded on criminal conduct.

The origin of what the government refers to as the false dichotomy between foreign intelligence information that is evidence of foreign intelligence crimes and that which is not appears to have been a Fourth Circuit case decided in 1980, *U.S. v. Truong Dinh Hung*. That case, however, involved an electronic surveillance carried out prior to the passage of FISA and was predicated on the President's executive power. In approving the district court's exclusion of evidence obtained through warrantless surveillance subsequent to the point in time when the government's investigation became primarily driven by law enforcement objectives, the court held that the Executive Branch should be excused from securing a warrant only when "the object of the search or the for surveillance is a foreign power, its agents, or collaborators" and "the surveillance is conducted 'primarily' for foreign intelligence reasons."

Sometime in the 1980s; the exact moment is shrouded in historical mystery; the Department applied the *Truong* analysis to an interpretation of the FISA statute. What is clear is that in 1995 the Attorney General adopted "Procedures for Contacts Between the FBI and the Criminal Division Concerning Foreign Intelligence and Foreign Counterintelligence Investigations."

Apparently to avoid running afoul of the primary purpose test used by some courts, the 1995 Procedures limited contacts between the FBI and the Criminal Division in cases where FISA surveillance or searches were being conducted by the FBI for foreign intelligence (FI) or foreign counterintelligence (FCI) purposes. The procedures state that "the FBI and Criminal Division should ensure that advice intended to preserve the option of a criminal prosecution does not inadvertently result in either the fact or the appearance of the Criminal Division's directing or controlling the FI or FCI investigation toward law enforcement objectives." Although these procedures provided for significant information sharing and coordination between criminal and FI or FCI investigations, based at least in part on the "directing or controlling" language, they eventually came to be narrowly interpreted within the Department of Justice, and most particularly by OIPR, as requiring OIPR to act as a "wall" to prevent the FBI intelligence officials from communicating with the Criminal Division regarding ongoing FI or FCI investigations.

The Patriot Act and the FISA Court's Decisions

The passage of the Patriot Act altered and to some degree muddied the landscape. In October 2001, Congress amended FISA to change "the purpose" language in 1804(a)(7)(B) to "a significant purpose." It also added a provision allowing "Federal officers who conduct electronic surveillance to acquire foreign intelligence information" to "consult with Federal law enforcement officers to coordinate efforts to investigate or protect against" attack or other grave hostile acts, sabotage or international terrorism, or clandestine intelligence activities, by foreign powers or their agents. And such coordination "shall not preclude" the government's certification that a significant purpose of the surveillance is to obtain foreign intelligence information, or the issuance of an order authorizing the surveillance. Although the Patriot Act amendments to FISA expressly sanctioned consultation and coordination between intelligence and law enforcement officials, in response to the first applications filed by OIPR under those amendments, in November 2001, the FISA court for the first time adopted the 1995 Procedures, as augmented by the January 2000 and August 2001 Procedures, as "minimization procedures" to apply in all cases before the court.

The Attorney General interpreted the Patriot Act quite differently. On March 6, 2002, the Attorney General approved new "Intelligence Sharing Procedures" to implement the Act's amendments to FISA. The 2002 Procedures supersede prior procedures and were designed to permit the complete exchange of information and advice between intelligence and law enforcement officials. They eliminated the "direction and control" test and allowed the exchange of advice between the FBI, OIPR, and the Criminal Division regarding "the initiation, operation, continuation, or expansion of FISA searches or surveillance." On March 7, 2002, the government filed a motion with the FISA court, noting that the Department of Justice had adopted the 2002 Procedures and proposing to follow those procedures in all matters before the court. The government also asked the FISA court to vacate its orders adopting the prior procedures as minimization procedures in all cases and imposing special "wall" procedures in certain cases.

Unpersuaded by the Attorney General's interpretation of the Patriot Act, the court ordered that the 2002 Procedures be adopted, with modifications, as minimization procedures to apply in all cases. The court emphasized that the definition of minimization procedures had not been amended by the Patriot Act, and reasoned that the 2002 Procedures cannot be used by the government to amend the Act in ways Congress has not intended.

Undeterred, the government submitted the application at issue in this appeal on July 19, 2002, and expressly proposed using the 2002 Procedures without modification. In an order issued the same day, the FISA judge hearing the application granted an order for surveillance of the target but modified the 2002 Procedures consistent with the court's May 17, 2002, order. It is the July 19, 2002 order that the government appeals. It is our task to do our best to read the statute to honor congressional intent. The better reading, it seems to us, excludes from the purpose of gaining foreign intelligence information a sole objective of criminal prosecution. We therefore reject the government's argument to the contrary. Yet this may not make much practical difference. Because, as the government points out, when it commences an electronic surveillance of a foreign agent, typically it will not have decided whether to prosecute the agent (whatever may be the subjective intent of the investigators or lawyers who initiate an investigation). So long as the government entertains a realistic option of dealing with the agent other than through criminal prosecution, it satisfies the significant purpose test.

The important point is—and here we agree with the government—the Patriot Act amendment, by using the word "significant," eliminated any justification for the FISA court to balance the relative weight the government places on criminal prosecution as compared to other counterintelligence responses. If the certification of the application's purpose articulates a broader objective than criminal prosecution—such as stopping an ongoing conspiracy—and includes other potential non-prosecutorial responses, the government meets the statutory test. Of course, if the court concluded that the government's sole objective was merely to gain evidence of past criminal conduct—even foreign intelligence crimes—to punish the agent rather than halt ongoing espionage or terrorist activity, the application should be denied.

It can be argued, however, that by providing that an application is to be granted if the government has only a "significant purpose" of gaining foreign intelligence information, the Patriot Act allows the government to have a primary objective of prosecuting an agent for a non-foreign intelligence crime. Yet we think that would be an anomalous reading of the amendment. For we see not the slightest indication that Congress meant to give that power to the Executive Branch. Accordingly, the manifestation of such a purpose, it seems to us, would continue to disqualify an application. That is not to deny that ordinary crimes might be inextricably intertwined with foreign intelligence crimes. For example, if a group of international terrorists were to engage in bank robberies in order to finance the manufacture of a bomb, evidence of the bank robbery should be treated just as evidence of the terrorist act itself. But the FISA process cannot be used as a device to investigate wholly unrelated ordinary crimes.

The FISA court expressed concern that unless FISA were "construed" in the fashion that it did, the government could use a FISA order as an improper substitute for an ordinary criminal warrant under Title III. That concern seems to suggest that the FISA court thought Title III procedures are constitutionally mandated if the government has a prosecutorial objective regarding an agent of a foreign power. But in *United States v. United States District Court (Keith)*, in which the Supreme Court explicitly declined to consider foreign intelligence surveillance; the Court indicated that, even with respect to domestic national security intelligence gathering for prosecutorial purposes where a warrant was mandated, Title III procedures were not constitutionally required: "We do not hold that the same type of standards and procedures prescribed by Title III are necessarily applicable to this case. We recognize that domestic security surveillance may involve different policy and practical considerations from the surveillance of 'ordinary crime.'" Nevertheless, in asking whether FISA procedures can be regarded as reasonable under the Fourth Amendment, we think it is instructive to compare those procedures and requirements with their Title III counterparts. Obviously, the closer those FISA procedures are to Title III procedures, the lesser are our constitutional concerns.

While Title III contains some protections that are not in FISA, in many significant respects the two statutes are equivalent, and in some, FISA contains additional protections. Still, to the extent the two statutes diverge in constitutionally relevant areas; in particular, in their probable cause and particularity showings; a FISA order may not be a "warrant" contemplated by the Fourth Amendment. We do not decide the issue but note that to the extent a FISA order comes close to meeting Title III, that certainly bears on its reasonableness under the Fourth Amendment.

Ultimately, the question becomes whether FISA, as amended by the Patriot Act, is a reasonable response based on a balance of the legitimate need of the government for foreign intelligence information to protect against national security threats with the protected right of citizens.

It will be recalled that the case that set forth the primary purpose test as constitutionally required was *Truong*. The Fourth Circuit thought that *Keith*'s balancing standard implied the adoption of the primary purpose test. We reiterate that *Truong* dealt with a pre-FISA surveillance based on the President's constitutional responsibility to conduct the foreign affairs of the United States. Although *Truong* suggested the line it drew was a constitutional minimum that would apply to a FISA surveillance, it had no occasion to consider the application of the statute carefully. The *Truong* court, as did all the other courts to have decided the issue, held that the President did have inherent authority to conduct warrantless searches to obtain foreign intelligence information. It was incumbent upon the court, therefore, to determine the boundaries of that constitutional authority in the case before it. We take for granted that the President does have that authority and, assuming that is so, FISA could not encroach on the President's constitutional power. The question before us is the reverse, does FISA amplify the President's power by providing a mechanism that at least approaches a classic warrant and which therefore supports the government's contention that FISA searches are constitutionally reasonable.

The *Truong* analysis, in our view, rested on a false premise and the line the court sought to draw was inherently unstable, unrealistic, and confusing. The false premise was the assertion that once the government moves to criminal prosecution, its "foreign policy concerns" recede. As we have discussed in the first part of the opinion, that is simply not true as it relates to counterintelligence. In that field the government's primary purpose is to halt the espionage or terrorism efforts, and criminal prosecutions can be, and usually are, interrelated with other techniques used to frustrate a foreign power's efforts.

Conclusion

Even without taking into account the President's inherent constitutional authority to conduct warrantless foreign intelligence surveillance, we think that procedures and government showings required under FISA, if they do not meet the minimum Fourth Amendment warrant standards, certainly come close. We therefore, believe firmly, applying the balancing test drawn from *Keith*, that FISA as amended is constitutional because the surveillances it authorizes are reasonable.

END OF OPINION

In order to get a FISA order before the enactment of the PATRIOT Act, the government's primary purpose had to be obtaining foreign intelligence and not gathering evidence for a criminal prosecution. In practice, this was being interpreted in a way that meant if criminal prosecution was *any* part of the purpose of an investigation, the FISA application could not be issued or, if issued, FISA-based information could not be used *in any way* by law enforcement. However, after the passage of the Patriot Act, all that was required for the government to obtain a FISA order was that foreign intelligence be *a significant purpose* of the investigation. In fact, under today's law, gathering evidence for a criminal prosecution can be the primary purpose of a FISA order. So long as gathering foreign intelligence is still a significant purpose of the investigation, the FISC judge would normally still grant the FISA order, and the resulting information can be shared between intelligence and law enforcement agencies.

You might wonder just what level of purpose meets the standard of "significant"? There is no clear definition provided in the statute. As a practical matter, it is not too difficult to find almost anything involving foreign intelligence or international terrorism "significant." Examples include getting intelligence on terrorist plots, preventing intelligence leaks, uncovering spies, and other foreign intelligence concerns. You would have to see almost nothing involving foreign surveillance to argue against a FISA order; essentially, that would be just normal everyday street crime.

This is, in fact, one of the primary arguments being made by civil liberty advocates against this new standard—they are concerned that this new standard is so low that just about any potential involvement with or connection to terrorist organizations can be the basis for FISA surveillance, eliminating the protections offered by the normal warrant procedure.

Review Questions

Explore this concept by analyzing the following:

1. For years, the Drug Enforcement Agency (DEA) has been trying to break the Cranston drug cartel, which is an entirely domestic criminal organization involved in drug smuggling operations inside the U.S. and at the U.S. border. The DEA has been trying to bring them down for many years, but has never been able to get enough evidence to get a warrant to conduct invasive surveillance on any member of the group. However, one day the DEA discover that a man they have probable cause to believe is affiliated with the Cranston cartel is selling information on U.S. border security to a person he knows to be an Al-Qaeda operative. Armed with this information, the DEA calls the General Counsel's Office at the National Security Agency (the office responsible for applying for FISA warrants) to request a FISA order to conduct surveillance on this member of the Cranston cartel. A representative from the DEA accompanies the Counsel to the judge to request the order.

The FISC judge is very surprised to have the DEA present at this meeting. "What is the DEA doing here?" the FISC judge asks. "We really want to bust the Cranston drug cartel for all of their past criminal history," the DEA attorney explains. "We think this person we want to survey has a lot of criminal history in his records on his computer, which is why we want a FISA order to access it, intercept all of his email, phone calls, and text conversations, and various other forms of surveillance on him."

"And this member of the Cranston drug cartel is also a member of Al-Qaeda?" the confused judge asks. "No," the DEA tells the judge. "He's just an American citizen who happens to be selling them information."

"And your primary purpose in getting a FISA order is to gather evidence of past criminal history so you can prosecute members of the Cranston drug cartel?" the judge asks. "That's right," the DEA agent says. "It just so happens that one of them is selling information to Al-Qaeda."

"Anything else I should know?" the judge asks. "Not really," the DEA representative says. "Sure, preventing this information on U.S. border security from getting to Al-Qaeda is significant, but we do admit that it's not anyone's primary purpose here. We are mainly focused on busting the Cranston drug cartel."

Based on this fact pattern, perform an IRAC analysis to determine whether or not the judge should issue a FISA order on this member of the drug cartel.

2. 65 years ago, Sean Moore was a spy for the British intelligence agency MI-6. He broke into the FBI headquarters in D.C., accessed the safe of FBI Director J. Edgar Hoover, and stole documents and microfiche containing U.S. military secrets. For

many years, the identity of the person who stole these documents was unknown, until Moore, on his 90th birthday, published his memoirs where he talks about this. The U.S. wants to prosecute him for his past crime. The FBI applies to FISC to get a FISA order to access Sean Moore's email and tap his phone line to see if they can develop evidence against him for this crime. The statute of limitations has not run. Do an IRAC analysis and advise whether this is appropriate.

Foreign Searches and Seizures

Earlier in this book, when we covered criminal procedure, we learned about the laws concerning traditional searches and surveillance inside the U.S. against domestic criminals and domestic terrorists. In the section on foreign surveillance, we covered searches which are conducted inside the U.S. where the target of the search was a foreign operative or the agent of a foreign power. Now you will learn about the laws governing searches conducted by U.S. law enforcement and military operating outside the U.S. borders in other countries.

Frequently, the needs of homeland security require both the military and law enforcement to conduct operations outside U.S. jurisdiction in foreign countries. Sometimes this is with the permission and cooperation of a foreign country. You may occasionally hear stories in the news about joint operations overseas involving the U.S. and other friendly nations. Other times, as in the case of the mission to take down Osama bin Laden, searches and operations are conducted without the knowledge, let alone the permission, of the foreign country where a mission or search is being conducted.

In these operations and missions, members of U.S. law enforcement and the military will physically and electronically conduct searches of people's homes, offices, computers, mobile devices, email accounts, and other places and items which might hold valuable information for counterintelligence as well as evidence for criminal prosecution. When U.S. law enforcement and military operate outside of the country, what rights and protections do the targets of their searches have? As you know, the Fourth Amendment governs searches and seizures by U.S. law enforcement, but what are its extraterritorial limitations and allowances? As a related matter, the Fifth Amendment protects the U.S. government from depriving people of "life, liberty, or property" without "due process of law." Seizing property or seizing (by arresting or killing) a person thus has potential Fifth Amendment issues as well. Does this implicate law enforcement or national security operations overseas at all?

The answer depends entirely on whether or not the target of the search or seizure is a U.S. citizen. Don't forget the case from the first chapter of this book, *Reid v. Covert*, which states that the U.S. Constitution still applies to U.S. citizens outside the U.S. If the target of a search/seizure is a U.S. citizen, then the Fourth Amendment (and possibly the Fifth Amendment) does apply; but not the warrant clause of the Fourth Amendment, only the reasonableness clause.

On the other hand, if the target of the search/seizure outside the U.S. is not a U.S. citizen, then the U.S. Constitution does not apply at all. If you read the U.S. Constitution, it continually refers to the rights of "the people." By "the people" it means only U.S. citizens or anyone lawfully inside the U.S. With few exceptions, the U.S. Constitution, including the Fourth Amendment, does not offer any legal rights or protections to non-U.S. citizens outside the borders of the U.S.

Let's look at two recent court decisions that address the law governing foreign searches. The first case, *U.S. v. Verdugo-Urquidez*, represents the law governing searches outside the U.S. where the target is not a U.S. citizen. The case of *In re: Terrorist Bombings* involves searches outside the U.S. where the target *is* a U.S. citizen.

As you read the cases, remember what you previously learned about the Fourth Amendment's two completely different clauses: (1) the reasonableness clause and (2) the warrant clause. Let's start with *Verdugo-Urquidez*.

Foreign Searches of Non-Citizens

United States v. Verdugo-Urquidez, 494 U.S. 259 (1990)*

The question presented by this case is whether the Fourth Amendment applies to the search and seizure by United States agents of property that is owned by a non-resident alien and located in a foreign country. We hold that it does not.

Respondent Rene Martin Verdugo-Urquidez is a citizen and resident of Mexico. He is believed by the United States Drug Enforcement Agency (DEA) to be one of the leaders of a large and violent organization in Mexico that smuggles narcotics into the United States. Based on a complaint charging respondent with various narcotics-related offenses, the Government obtained a warrant for his arrest on August 3, 1985. In January 1986, Mexican police officers, after discussions with United States marshals, apprehended Verdugo-Urquidez in Mexico and transported him to the United States Border Patrol station in Calexico, California. There, United States marshals arrested respondent and eventually moved him to a correctional center in San Diego, California, where he remains incarcerated pending trial.

Following respondent's arrest, Terry Bowen, a DEA agent assigned to the Calexico DEA office, decided to arrange for searches of Verdugo-Urquidez's Mexican residences located in Mexicali and San Felipe. Bowen believed that the searches would reveal evidence related to respondent's alleged narcotics trafficking activities and his involvement in the kidnaping and torture-murder of DEA Special Agent Enrique Camarena Salazar (for which respondent subsequently has been convicted in a separate prosecution). Bowen telephoned Walter White, the Assistant Special Agent in charge of the DEA office in Mexico City, and asked him to seek authorization for the search from the Director General of the Mexican Federal Judicial Police (MFJP). After several attempts to reach high ranking Mexican officials, White eventually

---

* The case has been heavily edited and paraphrased by the authors for clarity. See disclaimer in introduction.

contacted the Director General, who authorized the searches and promised the cooperation of Mexican authorities. Thereafter, DEA agents working in concert with officers of the MFJP searched respondent's properties in Mexicali and San Felipe and seized certain documents. In particular, the search of the Mexicali residence uncovered a tally sheet, which the Government believes reflects the quantities of marijuana smuggled by Verdugo-Urquidez into the United States.

The Fourth Amendment provides: "The right of the people to be secure in their persons, houses, papers, and effects, against unreasonable searches and seizures, shall not be violated, and no Warrants shall issue, but upon probable cause, supported by Oath or affirmation, and particularly describing the place to be searched, and the persons or things to be seized."

That text, by contrast with the Fifth and Sixth Amendments, extends its reach only to "the people." Contrary to the suggestion that the Framers used this phrase "simply to avoid an awkward rhetorical redundancy," "the people" seems to have been a term of art employed in select parts of the Constitution. The Preamble declares that the Constitution is ordained and established by "the People of the United States." The Second Amendment protects "the right of the people to keep and bear Arms," and the Ninth and Tenth Amendments provide that certain rights and powers are retained by and reserved to "the people." See also the First Amendment of the U.S. Constitution stating that "Congress shall make no law . . . abridging . . . the right of the people peaceably to assemble." Other parts of the U.S. Constitution also emphasize "the people" as seen in Article I, §2, cl. 1 stating that "The House of Representatives shall be composed of Members chosen every second Year by the People of the several States." While this textual exegesis is by no means conclusive, it suggests that "the people" protected by the Fourth Amendment, and by the First and Second Amendments, and to whom rights and powers are reserved in the Ninth and Tenth Amendments, refers to a class of persons who are part of a national community or who have otherwise developed sufficient connection with this country to be considered part of that community. The language of these Amendments contrasts with the words "person" and "accused" used in the Fifth and Sixth Amendments regulating procedure in criminal cases.

What we know of the history of the drafting of the Fourth Amendment also suggests that its purpose was to restrict searches and seizures which might be conducted by the United States in domestic matters. The Framers originally decided not to include a provision like the Fourth Amendment, because they believed the National Government lacked power to conduct searches and seizures. Many disputed the original view that the Federal Government possessed only narrow delegated powers over domestic affairs, however, and ultimately felt an Amendment prohibiting unreasonable searches and seizures was necessary. Madison, for example, argued that "there is a clause granting to Congress the power to make all laws which shall be necessary and proper for carrying into execution all of the powers vested in the Government of the United States," and that general warrants might be considered "necessary" for the purpose of collecting revenue. The driving force behind the adoption of the Amendment, as suggested by Madison's advocacy, was widespread hostility among the former colonists to the issuance of writs of assistance empowering revenue officers to search suspected places for smuggled goods, and general search warrants permitting the search of private houses, often to uncover papers that might be used to convict persons of libel. The available historical data show, therefore, that the purpose of the Fourth Amendment was to protect the people of the United States against arbitrary action by their own Government; it was never suggested that the provision was intended to restrain the actions of the Federal Government against aliens outside of the United States territory.

There is likewise no indication that the Fourth Amendment was understood by contemporaries of the Framers to apply to activities of the United States directed against aliens in foreign territory or in international waters. Only seven years after the ratification of the Amendment, French interference with American commercial vessels engaged in neutral trade triggered what came to be known as the "undeclared war" with France. In an Act to "protect the Commerce of the United States" in 1798, Congress authorized President Adams to "instruct the commanders of the public armed vessels which are, or which shall be employed in the service of the United States, to subdue, seize and take any armed French vessel, which shall be found within the jurisdictional limits of the United States, or elsewhere, on the high seas." This public naval force consisted of only 45 vessels, so Congress also gave the President power to grant to the owners of private armed ships and vessels of the United States "special commissions," which would allow them "the same license and authority for the subduing, seizing and capturing any armed French vessel, and for the recapture of the vessels, goods and effects of the people of the United States, as the public armed vessels of the United States may by law have." Under the latter provision, 365 private armed vessels were commissioned before March 1, 1799; together, these enactments resulted in scores of seizures of foreign vessels under congressional authority. Some commanders were held liable by this Court for unlawful seizures because their actions were beyond the scope of the congressional grant of authority, but it was never suggested that the Fourth Amendment restrained the authority of Congress or of United States agents to conduct operations such as this.

The global view taken by the Court of Appeals of the application of the Constitution is also contrary to this Court's decisions in the Insular Cases, which held that not every constitutional provision applies to governmental activity even where the United States has sovereign power. There is the general rule that in an unincorporated territory—one not clearly destined for statehood—Congress is not required to adopt "a system of laws which shall include the right of trial by jury, and that the Constitution does not, without legislation and of its own force, carry such right to territory so situated." Only "fundamental" constitutional rights are guaranteed to inhabitants of those territories. If that is true with respect to territories ultimately governed by Congress, respondent's claim that the protections of the Fourth Amendment extend to aliens in foreign nations is even weaker. And certainly, it is not open to us in light of the Insular Cases to endorse the view that every constitutional provision applies wherever the United States Government exercises its power.

Indeed, we have rejected the claim that aliens are entitled to Fifth Amendment rights outside the sovereign territory of the United States. In *Johnson v. Eisentrager*, 339 U.S. 763 (1950), the Court held that enemy aliens arrested in China and imprisoned in Germany after World War II could not obtain writs of habeas corpus in our federal courts on the ground that their convictions for war crimes had violated the Fifth Amendment and other constitutional provisions. The *Eisentrager* opinion acknowledged that in some cases constitutional provisions extend beyond the citizenry; "the alien has been accorded a generous and ascending scale of rights as he increases his identity with our society." But our rejection of extraterritorial application of the Fifth Amendment was emphatic:

> Such extraterritorial application of organic law would have been so significant an innovation in the practice of governments that, if intended or apprehended, it could scarcely have failed to excite contemporary comment. Not one word can be cited. No decision of this Court supports such a view. None of the learned commentators on our Constitution has even hinted at it. The practice of every modern government is opposed to it.

If such is true of the Fifth Amendment, which speaks in the relatively universal term of "person," it would seem even more true with respect to the Fourth Amendment, which applies only to "the people."

To support his all-encompassing view of the Fourth Amendment, Verdugo-Urquidez points to language from the plurality opinion in *Reid v. Covert* (1957). *Reid* involved an attempt by Congress to subject the wives of American servicemen to trial by military tribunals without the protection of the Fifth and Sixth Amendments. The Court held that it was unconstitutional to apply the Uniform Code of Military Justice to the trials of the American women for capital crimes. Four Justices "rejected the idea that when the United States acts against citizens abroad it can do so free of the Bill of Rights." The plurality went on to say:

> The United States is entirely a creature of the Constitution. Its power and authority have no other source. It can only act in accordance with all the limitations imposed by the Constitution. When the Government reaches out to punish a citizen who is abroad, the shield which the Bill of Rights and other parts of the Constitution provide to protect his life and liberty should not be stripped away just because he happens to be in another land.

Verdugo-Urquidez urges that we interpret this discussion to mean that federal officials are constrained by the Fourth Amendment wherever and against whomever they act. But the holding of *Reid* stands for no such sweeping proposition: it decided that United States citizens stationed abroad could invoke the protection of the Fifth and Sixth Amendments. The concurrences by Justices Frankfurter and Harlan in *Reid* resolved the case on much narrower grounds than the plurality and declined even to hold that United States citizens were entitled to the full range of constitutional protections in all overseas criminal prosecutions.

In *Reid v. Covert*, Justice Harlan, commented "that we have before us a question analogous, ultimately, to issues of due process; one can say, in fact, that the question of which specific safeguards of the Constitution are appropriately to be applied in a particular context overseas can be reduced to the issue of what process is 'due' a defendant in the particular circumstances of a particular case." In Verdugo-Urquidez, the respondent is not a United States citizen, so he can derive no comfort from the *Reid* holding.

Verdugo-Urquidez also mistakenly relies on past decisions where we have indicated that aliens do enjoy certain Constitutional rights. For example, in *Plyler v. Doe* we held that under the Equal Protection Clause, the children of illegal aliens are entitled to a free education in the nation's public primary schools. In *Bridges v. Wixon* we held that resident aliens have First Amendment rights. In *Wong Wing v. U.S.* we held that resident aliens are also entitled to Fifth and Sixth Amendment Rights. However, these cases establish only that aliens receive constitutional protections when they have come within the territory of the United States and developed substantial connections with this country. This does not exist here, for in the case before us, Verdugo-Urquidez is an alien who has had no previous significant voluntary connection with the United States, so these cases avail him not.

Respondent also contends that to treat aliens differently from citizens with respect to the Fourth Amendment somehow violates the equal protection component of the Fifth Amendment to the United States Constitution. Not only are history and case law against respondent, but as pointed out in *Johnson v. Eisentrager* (1950), the result of accepting his claim would have significant and deleterious consequences for the United States in conducting activities beyond its boundaries. Such a rule if adopted would apply not only to law enforcement operations abroad, but also to other foreign policy operations which might result in "searches or seizures." The United States frequently employs Armed Forces outside this country—over 200 times in our history—for the protection of American citizens or national security. Application of the Fourth Amendment to those circumstances could significantly disrupt the ability of the political branches to respond to foreign situations involving our national interest. Were respondent to prevail, aliens with no attachment to this country might well bring actions for damages to remedy claimed violations of the Fourth Amendment in foreign countries or in international waters. There are numerous potential problems if the Fourth Amendment abroad applied to aliens. The Members of the Executive and Legislative Branches are sworn to uphold the Constitution, and they presumably desire to follow its commands. But the global view of its applicability would plunge them into a sea of uncertainty as to what might be reasonable in the way of searches and seizures conducted abroad. Indeed, absent exigent circumstances, United States agents could not effect a "search or seizure" for law enforcement purposes in a foreign country without first obtaining a warrant—which would be a dead letter outside the United States—from a magistrate in this country. Even if no warrant were required, American agents would have to articulate specific facts giving them probable cause to undertake a search or seizure if they wished to comply with the Fourth Amendment.

We think that the text of the Fourth Amendment, its history, and our cases discussing the application of the Constitution to aliens and extraterritorially require rejection of respondent's claim. At the time of the search, he was a citizen and resident of Mexico with no voluntary attachment to the United States, and the place searched was located in Mexico. Under these circumstances, the Fourth Amendment has no application.

For better or for worse, we live in a world of nation-states in which our Government must be able to "function effectively in the company of sovereign nations." Some who violate our laws may live outside our borders under a regime quite different from that which obtains in this country. Situations threatening to important American interests may arise half-way around the globe, situations which in the view of the political branches of our Government require an American response with armed force. If there are to be restrictions on searches and seizures which occur incident to such American action, they must be imposed by the political branches through diplomatic understanding, treaty, or legislation.

END OF OPINION.

The point of the *Verdugo-Urquidez* opinion is that the Fourth Amendment is completely inapplicable *overseas* to the persons and properties of *non-U.S. citizens* which are physically located overseas and *outside* of U.S. jurisdiction. Do not even concern yourself with determining whether or not there was a warrant or if the search was reasonable; in these kinds of cases, the Fourth Amendment does not even apply. Other laws might apply, such as statutes that govern use of force or otherwise regulate the behavior of U.S. law enforcement and military personnel, but it would be those statutes and regulations, not the requirements of the Fourth (or Fifth) Amendment.

There are many reasons for this. Let's start with why the warrant clause is irrelevant in this context. First, what legal power and authority does a U.S. search warrant have in another country? The answer is none. The legal authority of a search warrant is limited to within U.S. jurisdiction. Think about it; if a Venezuelan police officer left Venezuela and took an airplane into the U.S., rented a car and drove to your house, knocked on your door and showed you a piece of paper signed by some Venezuelan judge in Caracas which he claimed gave him legal authority to search your house here in the U.S., would you be inclined to let him search? A Venezuelan judge sitting in Caracas has no jurisdiction in the U.S., so he has no authority over you or your property. Similarly, an American judge in the U.S. cannot sign a document which has legal authority over a person or property physically located in Venezuela, or anywhere else in the world except within the U.S.

The Court also points out that requiring a warrant to conduct searches overseas would greatly impede U.S. operations. For example, let's consider the raid on Osama bin Laden's compound in Pakistan. We sent in U.S. Navy SEALs who stormed the place, killing combatants and seizing computer hardware and documents for intelligence purposes. Not only did they not have warrant, they did not even have the permission of Pakistan. It would make no sense to say that any information learned by seizing the documents during the raid on bin Laden's compound would be inadmissible against prosecuting terrorists. Such rules and policies would be extremely detrimental to U.S. counter-terrorism policies across the world. Although missions are highly classified, U.S. Special Operations Command frequently conducts raids on terrorists all over the world, gathering both intelligence and criminal evidence in the process. Would you really tell a squad of Army soldiers in Afghanistan that they cannot enter a cave believed to be used by the Taliban unless they first get a warrant from a judge back in the U.S.? Such thinking defies commonsense as it would interfere with their ability to safely and effectively do their jobs. Similarly, could you imagine General Eisenhower having to get a warrant to order in the D-Day invasion of Normandy? The idea is ridiculous.

Verdugo-Urquidez also explains why the "reasonableness" clause of the Fourth Amendment does not apply to non-citizens overseas. While the non-applicability of warrants abroad is grounded more on practical concerns, the non-applicability of the "reasonableness" clause is more historic. When the founding fathers wrote the U.S. Constitution, their focus on "the people" was intended to only apply to U.S. citizens. The founders used "the people" when intending to refer to citizens, and the broader term "persons" when intending to refer to anyone falling under the jurisdiction or control of U.S. authority. More specific to the Fourth Amendment, ever since the U.S. Constitution was ratified, there is a longstanding history of not applying the Fourth Amendment to non-citizens outside the country. The *Verdugo-Urquidez* opinion uses the example of the U.S. Navy searching ships of other nations on the high seas during the Quasi-War with France from 1798 to 1800. It also points out the much more recent and famous U.S. Supreme Court case, *Johnson v. Eisentrager*, 339 U.S. 763 (1950), where the Court specifically stated that the protections of the U.S. Constitution do not apply to aliens outside the U.S., even if they were being prosecuted by the U.S.[4]

Although the Fourth Amendment does not offer any protections to non-citizens who are searched outside the U.S., that does not mean that no law applies. There is a rule in U.S. courts which excludes some evidence obtained during foreign searches under very narrow, specific, and particular circumstances. The rule is that *if information or evidence is obtained in a manner which is so heinous that it "shocks the conscience," then that material will be inadmissible in U.S. Courts.* What is meant by this "*shocks the conscience doctrine*" is that if the conduct of U.S. soldiers or law enforcement is so vile, repugnant, and inhumane that it shocks the conscience, any evidence obtained in the process will not be admissible in U.S. courts.

Just what is conduct that "shocks the conscience"? There is no official definition, but there are some general guidelines you can use, and courts have from time to time used the phrase to describe certain behavior. Any use of degrading treatment, torture, severe beatings, sexual assault and humiliation, and even the threat of such actions all qualify as conduct that "shocks the conscience." For example, if an FBI agent threatened to shoot a suspect or threatened to rape the suspect's daughter unless that person confessed, this would "shock the conscience," and any information

---

4. This issue will be revisited later in this book when we look at the detainees at Guantanamo Bay, Cuba.

obtained this way would be inadmissible in U.S. courts to prosecute that person. Other forms of conduct will qualify if it is severely degrading and inhumane, even if it did not cause physical harm. An example would be smearing fecal matter on a prisoner who has a dog collar and leash around his neck. However, minor issues such as an agitated investigator losing his cool and punching a suspect does not shock the conscience, although it is inappropriate. The pictures of what leaked from Abu Ghraib are excellent examples of conduct that shocks the conscience, as is the description of CIA torture disclosed by recent Senate investigation reports.

Foreign Searches of U.S. Citizens

While *Verdugo-Urquidez* answers the question of whether or not the Fourth Amendment applies abroad to non-U.S. citizens, it does not answer the question of whether the Fourth Amendment applies abroad to U.S. citizens. Given the ruling from *Reid v. Covert*, which we read at the very beginning of this text, the answer is "yes," the general protection of the Fourth Amendment does apply to searches of U.S. citizens overseas by U.S. law enforcement.

But it is not fair to say that the entire Fourth Amendment applies to the searches of U.S. citizens abroad. As you should recall, although the Fourth Amendment is a single sentence, the case law we have already reviewed illustrates that it addresses two separate and distinct contexts; first, that all searches must be reasonable, and, second, that some searches require a warrant based on probable cause. The following case illustrates how, for foreign searches of U.S. citizens, the warrant clause of the Fourth Amendment does not apply but the "reasonable" clause does.

In re Terrorist Bombings of U.S. Embassies in East Africa, 552 F.3d 157 (2008)*

Defendant-appellant Wadih El-Hage, a citizen of the United States, challenges his conviction in the United States District Court on numerous charges arising from his involvement in the August 7, 1998 bombings of the American Embassies in Nairobi, Kenya and Dar es Salaam, Tanzania (the "August 7 bombings"). In this opinion we consider El-Hage's challenge to the District Court's denial of his motion to suppress evidence obtained by the government from an August 1997 search of his residence in Nairobi, Kenya and electronic surveillance of telephone lines—land-based and cellular—conducted in Kenya between August 1996 and August 1997.

The question this case raises is "whether an American citizen acting abroad on behalf of a foreign power may invoke the Fourth Amendment, and especially its warrant provision, to suppress evidence obtained by the United States in connection with intelligence gathering operations." Because we hold that the Fourth Amendment's requirement of reasonableness—and not the Warrant Clause—governs extraterritorial searches of U.S. citizens and that the searches challenged on this

---

* The case has been heavily edited and paraphrased by the authors for clarity. See disclaimer in introduction.

appeal were reasonable, we find no error. El-Hage's Fourth Amendment challenge to his conviction is therefore without merit.

. . .

American intelligence became aware of Al-Qaeda's presence in Kenya by mid–1996 and identified five telephone numbers used by suspected Al-Qaeda associates. From August 1996 through August 1997, American intelligence officials monitored these telephone lines, including two El-Hage used: a phone line in the building where El-Hage lived and his cell phone. The Attorney General of the United States then authorized intelligence operatives to target El-Hage in particular. This authorization, first issued on April 4, 1997, was renewed in July 1997. Working with Kenyan authorities, U.S. officials searched El-Hage's home in Nairobi on August 21, 1997, pursuant to a document shown to El-Hage's wife that was "identified as a Kenyan warrant authorizing a search for 'stolen property.'" It is uncontested that the agents did not apply for or obtain a warrant from a U.S. court.

We must first determine whether and to what extent the Fourth Amendment's safeguards apply to overseas searches involving U.S. citizens. In *United States v. Toscanino*, a case involving a Fourth Amendment challenge to overseas wiretapping of a non-U.S. citizen, we observed that it was "well settled" that "the Bill of Rights has extraterritorial application to the conduct abroad of federal agents directed against United States citizens." (*Rosado v. Civiletti* (2d Cir.1980) (considering a Fourth Amendment challenge to a search conducted abroad by foreign authorities and observing in dicta that "the Bill of Rights does apply extraterritorially to protect American citizens against the illegal conduct of United States agents" (citing *Reid v. Covert*))). Nevertheless, we have not yet determined the specific question of the applicability of the Fourth Amendment's Warrant Clause to overseas searches. Faced with that question now, we hold that the Fourth Amendment's warrant requirement does not govern searches conducted abroad by U.S. agents; such searches of U.S. citizens need only satisfy the Fourth Amendment's requirement of reasonableness.

The Fourth Amendment to the U.S. Constitution protects "the right of the people to be secure in their persons, houses, papers, and effects, against unreasonable searches and seizures." The Supreme Court has explained that "it is a basic principle of Fourth Amendment law that searches and seizures inside a home without a warrant are presumptively unreasonable." "Nevertheless, because the ultimate touchstone of the Fourth Amendment is 'reasonableness,' the warrant requirement is subject to certain exceptions." It is well established that warrant is not required to establish the reasonableness of *all* government searches. Familiar exceptions to the warrant requirement arise from exigent circumstances, such as the risk of imminent destruction of evidence or the "hot pursuit" of a fleeing suspect, search after a lawful arrest, and with consent.

Custodial "inventory searches" are also exempt from the warrant requirement. Exceptions have also been established for searches conducted outside of criminal investigations. For example, disciplinary procedures in public schools are not governed by a warrant requirement, neither are civil-service drug-testing programs, nor are searches conducted at international borders. Administrative searches, particularly those involving heavily regulated industries, such as restaurants which must give entry to the health inspector, may also be exempt from the warrant requirement under certain circumstances. In these contexts, when the government seeks to *prevent* the development of hazardous conditions or to detect violations that rarely generate articulable grounds for searching any particular place or person the probable cause and warrant requirements give way to an evaluation of reasonableness.

The question of whether a warrant is required for overseas searches of U.S. citizens has not been decided by the Supreme Court or any circuit court. While never addressing the question directly, the Supreme Court provided some guidance on the issue in *United States v. Verdugo-Urquidez,* where the Court examined whether an alien with no voluntary attachment to the United States could invoke the protections of the Fourth Amendment to suppress evidence obtained through a warrantless search conducted in Mexico. Relying on the text of the Fourth Amendment, its history, and the Court's cases discussing the application of the Constitution to aliens and extraterritorially, the Supreme Court held that the Fourth Amendment affords no protection to *aliens* searched by U.S. officials outside of our borders. With respect to the applicability of the Warrant Clause abroad, the Court expressed doubt that the clause governed any overseas searches conducted by U.S. agents, explaining that warrants issued to conduct overseas searches "would be a dead letter outside the United States." Elaborating on this observation in a concurring opinion, Justice Kennedy concluded:

> The absence of local judges or magistrates available to issue warrants, the differing and perhaps unascertainable conceptions of reasonableness and privacy that prevail abroad, and the need to cooperate with foreign officials all indicate that the Fourth Amendment's warrant requirement should not apply in Mexico as it does in this country.

Both Justice Stevens, in a concurring opinion, and Justice Blackmun, in dissent, also took a dim view of applying the Warrant Clause to searches conducted abroad, noting that U.S. judicial officers have no power to issue such warrants. Stevens stated, "I do not believe the Warrant Clause has any application to searches of noncitizens' homes in foreign jurisdictions because American magistrates have no power to authorize such searches."; Justice Blackman stated that "An American magistrate's lack of power to authorize a search abroad renders the Warrant Clause inapplicable to the search of a noncitizen's residence outside this country." Accordingly, in *Verdugo-Urquidez,* seven justices of the Supreme Court endorsed the view that U.S. courts are not empowered to issue warrants for foreign searches.

These observations and the following reasons weigh against imposing a warrant requirement on overseas searches. First, there is nothing in our history or our precedents suggesting that U.S. officials must first obtain a warrant before conducting an overseas search. El-Hage has pointed to no authority—and we are aware of none—directly supporting the proposition that warrants are necessary for searches conducted abroad by U.S. law enforcement officers or local agents acting in collaboration with them; nor has El-Hage identified any instances in our history where a foreign search was conducted pursuant to an American search warrant. This dearth of authority is not surprising in light of the history of the Fourth Amendment and its Warrant Clause as well as the history of international affairs. As the *Verdugo-Urquidez* Court explained, "what we know of the history of the drafting of the Fourth Amendment... suggests that its purpose was to restrict searches and seizures which might be conducted by the United States in domestic matters." In addition, the Warrant Clause appears to have been invested with a meaning at the time of the drafting that differs significantly from our modern view of the requirement. Justice White observed that "at the time of the Bill of Rights, the warrant functioned as a powerful tool of law enforcement rather than as a protection for the rights of criminal suspects," and "it was the abusive use of the warrant power, rather than any excessive zeal in the discharge of peace officers' inherent authority, that precipitated the Fourth Amendment." Accordingly, we agree with the Ninth Circuit's observation that "foreign searches have neither been historically subject to the warrant procedure, nor could they be as a practical matter."

Second, nothing in the history of the foreign relations of the United States would require that U.S. officials obtain warrants from foreign magistrates before conducting searches overseas or, indeed, to suppose that all other states have search and investigation rules akin to our own. As the Supreme Court explained in *Verdugo-Urquidez*:

> For better or for worse, we live in a world of nation-states in which our Government must be able to function effectively in the company of sovereign nations. Some who violate our laws may live outside our borders under a regime quite different from that which obtains in this country. Situations threatening to important American interests may arise halfway around the globe, situations which in the view of the political branches of our Government require an American response with armed force. If there are to be restrictions on searches and seizures which occur incident to such American action, they must be imposed by the political branches through diplomatic understanding, treaty, or legislation.

> The American procedure of issuing search warrants on a showing of probable cause simply does not extend throughout the globe and, pursuant to the Supreme Court's instructions, the Constitution does not condition our government's investigative powers on the practices of foreign legal regimes quite different from that which obtains in this country.

Third, if U.S. judicial officers were to issue search warrants intended to have extraterritorial effect, such warrants would have dubious legal significance, if any, in a foreign nation. As a District Court recently observed, "it takes little to imagine the diplomatic and legal complications that would arise if American government officials traveled to another sovereign country and attempted to carry out a search of any kind, professing the authority to do so based on an American-issued search warrant." We agree with that observation. A warrant issued by a U.S. court would neither empower a U.S. agent to conduct a search nor would it necessarily compel the intended target to comply. It would be a nullity, or in the words of the Supreme Court, "a dead letter."

Fourth and finally, it is by no means clear that U.S. judicial officers could be authorized to issue warrants for overseas searches. Statutes authorizing courts to issue search warrants are construed to limit authority to the court's territorial jurisdiction.

For these reasons, we hold that the Fourth Amendment's Warrant Clause has no extraterritorial application and that foreign searches of U.S. citizens conducted by U.S. agents are subject only to the Fourth Amendment's requirement of reasonableness.

3. The Kenyan Searches Were Reasonable and Therefore Did Not Violate the Fourth Amendment.

Turning to the question of whether the searches at issue in this appeal—the search of El-Hage's Nairobi home and the surveillance of his Kenyan telephone lines—were reasonable. The defendant claims that, in his view, the searches were unreasonable, largely for two reasons. First, El-Hage insists that his Nairobi home deserves special consideration in light of the home's status as "the most fundamental bastion of privacy protected by the Fourth Amendment." Second, he contends that the electronic surveillance was far broader than necessary because it encompassed "many calls, if not the predominant amount, that were related solely to legitimate commercial purposes, and/or purely family and social matters."

To determine whether a search is reasonable under the Fourth Amendment, we examine the "totality of the circumstances" to balance "on the one hand, the degree to which it intrudes upon an individual's privacy and, on the other, the degree to which it is needed for the promotion of legitimate governmental interests." As discussed in greater detail below, we conclude that the searches' intrusion on El-Hage's privacy was outweighed by the government's manifest need to monitor his activities as an operative of Al-Qaeda because of the extreme threat Al-Qaeda presented, and continues to present, to national security. In light of these circumstances, the Kenyan searches were reasonable, and therefore not prohibited by the Fourth Amendment.

a. The Search of El-Hage's Home in Nairobi Was Reasonable.

El-Hage's principal challenge to the reasonableness of the search of his Nairobi residence appears to derive from Supreme Court precedents applying rigorous scrutiny to searches of a suspect's home. In *Kyllo v. United States*, for example, the Court explained: "At the very core of the Fourth Amendment stands the right of a man to retreat into his own home and there be free from unreasonable governmental intrusion. With few exceptions, the question whether a warrantless search of a home is reasonable and hence constitutional must be answered no." "In terms that apply equally to seizures of property and to seizures of persons, the Fourth Amendment has drawn a firm line at the entrance to the house. Absent exigent circumstances, that threshold may not reasonably be crossed without a warrant."

Warrantless searches of homes abroad, while subject to special scrutiny, are subject to a balancing test—weighing an individual's expectation of privacy against the government's need for certain information—for determining reasonableness under the Fourth Amendment.

Applying that test to the facts of this case, we first examine the extent to which the search of El-Hage's Nairobi home intruded upon his privacy. The intrusion was minimized by the fact that the search was not covert; indeed, U.S. agents searched El-Hage's home with the assistance of Kenyan authorities, pursuant to what was identified as a "Kenyan warrant authorizing a search." The search occurred during the daytime, and in the presence of El-Hage's wife. At the conclusion of the search, an inventory listing the items seized during the search was prepared and given to El-Hage's wife. In addition, "the scope of the search was limited to those items which were believed to have foreign intelligence value and retention and dissemination of the evidence acquired during the search were minimized."

U.S. intelligence officers became aware of Al-Qaeda's presence in Kenya in the spring of 1996. At about that time, they identified five telephone lines used by suspected Al-Qaeda associates, one of which was located in the same building as El-Hage's Nairobi home; another was a cellular phone used by El-Hage. After these telephone lines had been monitored for several months, the Attorney General of the United States authorized surveillance specifically targeting El-Hage. That authorization was renewed four months later, and, one month after that, U.S. agents searched El-Hage's home in Nairobi. This sequence of events is indicative of a disciplined approach to gathering indisputably vital intelligence on the activities of a foreign terrorist organization. U.S. agents did not breach the privacy of El-Hage's home on a whim or on the basis of an unsubstantiated tip; rather, they monitored telephonic communications involving him for nearly a year and conducted surveillance of his activities for five months before concluding that it was necessary to search his home. In light of these findings of fact, which El-Hage has not contested as clearly erroneous, we conclude that the search, while undoubtedly intrusive on El-Hage's privacy, was restrained in execution and narrow in focus.

Balanced against this restrained and limited intrusion on El-Hage's privacy, we have the government's manifest need to investigate possible threats to national security. As the District Court noted, Al-Qaeda "declared a war of terrorism against all members of the United States military worldwide" in 1996 and later against American civilians. The government had evidence establishing that El-Hage was working with Al-Qaeda in Kenya. On the basis of these findings of fact, we agree with the District Court that, at the time of the search of El-Hage's home, the government had a powerful need to gather additional intelligence on Al-Qaeda's activities in Kenya, which it had linked to El-Hage.

Balancing the search's limited intrusion on El-Hage's privacy against the manifest need of the government to monitor the activities of Al-Qaeda, which had been connected to El-Hage through a year of surveillance, we hold that the search of El-Hage's Nairobi residence was reasonable under the Fourth Amendment.

END OF OPINION

What is the difference between *Verdugo-Urquidez* and *In re Terrorist Bombings*? Simple—although both cases involved the searches of properties located outside the U.S., in the second case the defendant was a U.S. citizen, while in the first case, the defendant was a Mexican citizen. Keep in mind that the Supreme Court ruled in *Reid v. Covert* that the U.S. Constitution applies abroad to U.S. citizens, but the U.S. Constitution does not apply abroad to non-U.S. citizens.

Although the Fourth Amendment does apply abroad to searches of U.S. citizens, it is not applied the same way as domestic searches. Remember how the Fourth Amendment has two separate and distinct clauses: (1) that all searches must be reasonable; and (2) only a select number of searches require a warrant. There are a number searches inside the U.S. where warrants are not needed, so long as the search is reasonable. Examples include searches involving exigent circumstances, airport checkpoints, drunk driving checkpoints, border searches, searching of public school children, searches incident to lawful arrest, searches of inmates, inventories of vehicles, and health inspectors entering restaurants, to name but a few. If the government can provide a reasonable justification for why a search should be performed without a warrant, then the courts have often (not always) upheld a warrantless search.

Following this reasoning, there is a reasonable justification to not apply the warrant clause abroad, because a warrant signed by a U.S. judge would have no legal power or influence outside the jurisdiction of the U.S. If a U.S. search warrant is legally meaningless in a foreign country, then it would be absurd to require law enforcement to have a warrant to conduct a foreign search. So the legal validity of such searches turns on the Fourth Amendment's requirement of reasonableness.

Reasonableness of Foreign Searches of U.S. Citizens

Determining whether or not an overseas search of a U.S. citizen is reasonable is not always easy. Courts have ruled that this determination must be made by looking at "the totality of the circumstances." This requires that you focus your attention on (1) the basis of the search, and (2) how the search is being conducted.

The basis of the search means that one must look at the evidence for why the search is being performed. There must be a valid and *reasonable* justification for entering and searching the property of a U.S. citizen. Maybe a reliable informant told soldiers that the U.S. citizen in a certain household in Baghdad was storing weapons for insurgents. This might not meet the high standard of probable cause which is required for a warrant for a domestic search, but so long as the search was reasonable, it should be lawful—because the "totality of circumstances" includes factors like the threat involved, the absence of other local (host nation) law enforcement, reliability of the informant, and so forth. On the other hand, it would be unlawful for the U.S. government to search U.S. citizens overseas without any basis. You do not shed your protections against the U.S. government just because you are physically outside the U.S.

The second part requires that the search be performed in a reasonable manner. To determine whether or not the search is performed in a reasonable manner, look at the conduct of the people conducting the search. If FBI agents are cooperating with local authorities who are abusing the suspect, or are needlessly destroying property, or detaining persons far longer than necessary under harsh conditions, or some other conduct which violates the FBI (or other U.S. agency) internal rules and procedures, then there is a likely chance that a U.S. court would conclude their conduct is unreasonable.

In the case we read above, the U.S. court found the search to have been reasonable in large part because it was conducted in a manner which complied with local Kenyan law, a law which was close in many ways to what U.S. law would require, with FBI agents working in cooperation with Kenyan law enforcement. If the search is a joint operation where U.S. law enforcement is working alongside foreign law enforcement in accord with the law of the foreign country, odds are that the courts will conclude that the search is reasonable.

Always consider whether or not the search is being conducted in compliance with the laws of the land where the search was taking place. If this is the case, then it is extremely helpful to argue that fact as evidence that the search was reasonable. However, it is not always required that a search is conducted in full compliance with the local law. There can be special or extenuating circumstances which would render a search reasonable without any knowledge or cooperation of the foreign government, even if the search violates numerous laws of the host country. The raid on Osama bin Laden's compound is one such example. That was a military operation, not a law enforcement one, but even if law enforcement had participated, the totality of the circumstances there would likely have allowed evidence obtained to be used against anyone captured and brought to the U.S. for criminal trial.

In another more common example, let's say that a U.S. citizen joined up with Al-Qaeda to help with the drug trade financing the insurgency and was hiding out in a rural village with minimal presence of Afghani authorities. It would be perfectly justified for U.S. soldiers and law enforcement on their own, without any involvement of Afghan authorities, to conduct an armed raid on the house containing the individual. In contrast, however, if the FBI were to search a home owned by a U.S. citizen in London, it is much more likely that the presence and of British law enforcement would be required, and the search would have to be in compliance with British law for a U.S. court to consider evidence obtained in the search to be admissible. Given the reliability of British intelligence and law enforcement, it would be unreasonable to send the U.S. Navy SEALs on a clandestine raid in London when British authorities could much more easily (and less dangerously) apprehend the suspect.

In conclusion, be aware that non-citizens outside the U.S. are not protected by the Fourth Amendment (*Verdugo-Urquidez*). However, remember that *Reid v. Covert* tells us that just because U.S. citizens go abroad, they do not lose their rights. U.S. citizens abroad still have their rights against unreasonable searches and seizures; it is simply the warrant requirement which does not apply to U.S. citizens overseas. Although law enforcement may not have a warrant, so long as the search is reasonable in its basis and scope, it is lawful (*In re Terrorist Bombings*).

Review Questions

1. Hassan is a citizen of Saudi Arabia, and in compliance with local Saudi Arabian law, the FBI conducts a joint operation with Saudi Arabian police on Hassan's house in Saudi Arabia. Hassan is subsequently arrested, extradited, and charged with terrorism in a U.S. court. His lawyer argues that the search violated the Fourth Amendment because there was no warrant to search the house. Is his lawyer right? IRAC your answer. As a follow-up, how would you respond if Hasan's lawyer points out that there was no warrant from a U.S. judge or magistrate authorizing this search by the FBI?

2. Hassan is a citizen of Saudi Arabia. In a manner that fails to comply with local law, the FBI and Saudi Arabian police search his home. The search is conducted in an unreasonable manner as law enforcement completely trash the house in a violent and unnecessarily destructive way. The FBI had no reasonable basis to suspect Hassan of any crime, so this search is completely unreasonable in both its scope and how it is being conducted. However, evidence is still found linking Hassan to Al-Qaeda. He is taken back to the U.S. to stand trial. At trial, his lawyer protests the admissibility of any evidence obtained by the search, claiming that the information was obtained in a completely unreasonable manner, thus violating the Fourth Amendment. IRAC whether or not the lawyer is right.

3. Hassan is a citizen of Saudi Arabia and has a house in Saudi Arabia. In a manner that fails to comply with local law, the FBI and Saudi Arabian police conduct a joint operation to search his home. The search is conducted in an unreasonable manner as law enforcement completely trash the house in a violent and irresponsible way. The FBI had no reasonable basis to suspect Hassan of any crime. Despite hours of highly destructive searching of the house, nothing is being found. A frustrated FBI agent, without any training in cavity searches, suddenly pulls down the pants of Hassan, inserts an unlubricated finger into Hassan's anus, and, unexpectedly, feels something unnatural inside the rectum. The FBI agent extracts it, and it turns out to be a USB drive containing invaluable intelligence on Al-Qaeda. IRAC if the intelligence on the USB drive can be used as evidence in the prosecution of Hassan.

4. Jake is a U.S. citizen studying in Yemen one summer. His former college roommate tells law enforcement that he has a gut feeling that Jake is secretly an agent of Al-Qaeda. Based on this gut feeling, in a joint operation with Yemen's law enforcement in a manner which complies with local law, the FBI executes a search of Jake's apartment in Yemen. It turns out the roommate was right, and evidence is found linking Jake to Al-Qaeda. Is this evidence admissible at trial?

5. Jake is a U.S. citizen studying in Yemen. A reliable informant tells the FBI that he has first-hand knowledge that Jake is an Al-Qaeda operative. In cooperating with the Yemeni police and in compliance with Yemeni law, the police search Jake's apartment. Is this a valid search?

6. Jake is a U.S. citizen studying in Yemen. A reliable informant tells the FBI that he has first-hand knowledge that Jake is an Al-Qaeda operative. The FBI search Jake's

apartment. The search is conducted in an unreasonable manner as the apartment is unnecessarily trashed, objects are destroyed without justification, the FBI does not get the proper authority of Yemeni officials, and overall, law enforcement simply fails to comply with local laws governing searches. Can anything found during the search be used to prosecute Jake?

7. Brad is an American citizen living in Egypt with his roommate Eddie. Eddie is not an American citizen, but instead is a citizen of Britain. There is a terrorist attack in Egypt, and Brad and Eddie fall under suspicion for having conducted the bombing. The FBI and Egyptian police conduct a joint operation where they detain Brad and Eddie and search their home. The operation is botched horribly, and Brad and Eddie find themselves detained for countless hours as their home is torn apart in violation of both American and Egyptian laws governing searches and seizures. The police conduct is not so bad that it shocks the conscience, but nothing about it is reasonable. However, the search uncovers evidence that Brad and Eddie helped build a bomb used in the terror attack. They are both taken back to the U.S. to stand criminal trial. At their trial, their defense attorney makes a motion to exclude all evidence found in the search of Brad and Eddie's home. He justifies this motion on the grounds that the FBI and Egyptian authorities did not have a warrant when they conducted the search. He further bolsters his argument by pointing out that the search was conducted in an entirely unreasonable manner which violated the laws of both the U.S. and Egypt. The government concedes these points, but still wants the evidence to be admitted despite the fact that the search was done without a warrant and was done in an unreasonable manner. You are the judge. Write one IRAC analysis for Brad and one IRAC analysis for Eddie as you decide whether or not the evidence is admissible.

Cross-Border Actions

To finish this chapter, we will take a brief look at another issue in homeland and national security that is increasingly coming into the courts—what is the role and effect of the protections of the Fourth Amendment when the actions of U.S. law enforcement and national security agencies cross borders? To recap our earlier discussion, if the search, surveillance, or seizure involves a non-U.S. person located outside the United States, the *Verdugo-Urquidez* decision ruled that the Fourth Amendment is completely inapplicable. Under FISA, in large part because these operations take place within the United States, authority to engage in surveillance, searches, and seizures is permitted in cases with a significant interest in or purpose of preventing foreign intelligence or international terrorism under FISA rules; cases that are simply traditional law enforcement require the Title III warrants, as determined in the *Keith* decision.

But where does a search or seizure occur when the U.S. authority is present and acting in the United States and the person or records being acted upon are located outside the United States? Two recent cases involving alleged excessive use of force by U.S. Border Patrol agents[5] raise the question, and how these cases turn out might have implications for other parts of homeland and national security law.

In both of these cases,[6] which at the time of writing are still ongoing, the allegations are similar — U.S. Border Patrol agents are alleged to have shot from the U.S. side of the U.S.-Mexican border and, in each case, killed an individual on the Mexican side of the border. In each case the next of kin of the individual killed has alleged that the shootings were not justified and have sought to bring a civil rights complaint against the Border Patrol officers.[7] In one case, relying on *Verdugo-Urquidez*, the District Court has ruled that the case has no validity, as the "seizure" occurred in Mexico where the bullet hit and killed the Mexican citizen. In the other case, the court has ruled that, since the border area, even on the Mexican side, is an area where the U.S. imposes some measure of presence and control, and the Border Patrol officer was in the United States when he fired his weapon, the Fourth Amendment should apply and the case may go forward. In both cases appeals of the decisions will go forward and it is likely that the Supreme Court will have to rule on the issue.

In both cases, the District Courts looked not just at the cases we've read in this chapter, but also the decision *Boumediene v. Bush*, 553 U.S. 723 (2008), one of the key cases involving Guantanamo detainees ruling that at least some parts of the Constitution do apply to treatment of foreign nationals affected by actions of the United States outside of the United States. We talk about this case in more detail later in the text, but for now, it is enough to consider that *Boumediene* elaborates a "functional approach" to the selective application of constitutional limitations to U.S. government action outside U.S. sovereign territory.

Now, because all of the cases involving alleged violations of the Constitution ultimately turn on the specific facts, the real importance of these Border Patrol cases is that, depending on how the Supreme Court ends up dealing with the matter, the cases may not ever get to a court for consideration of the fact. Instead the courts will say (as the court in *Hernandez* has), "Sorry, but our laws do not apply." What might be the implications of the decision when this case rises to the Supreme Court?

Review Questions

Consider and discuss the following concerns raised:

1. In a recent case, the U.S. used (and is still using) drones to attack key individuals located in other countries who have been identified as combatants in the

---

5. *Tennessee v. Garner*, 471 U.S. 1 (1985), held that the use of deadly force constitutes a seizure under the Fourth Amendment, and that whether or not the use of force violates the victim's rights requires a balancing of the totality of the circumstances in each case.

6. *Rodriques v. Swatrz*, Summary Order 4:14-CV-022251-RCC (U.S. Dist. Ct., District of Arizona, 9 July 2015); *Hernandez v. United States et al.*, 757 F.3d 249 (5th Cir. 2014).

7. Such suits are permitted when it is alleged that a federal officer has violated the civil rights of an individual. *Bivens v. Six Unnamed Agents of the Federal Bureau of Investigation*, 403 U.S. 388 (1971).

ongoing struggle against international terrorist organizations. One of these was a U.S. citizen, but the key issue relied upon thus far by the government has been the fact that these attacks take place in the context of an armed conflict. But what will be the effect if, as a result of a decision that the Fourth Amendment applies, the U.S. officer deploying the weapon is located in the U.S. (as is the case in many of these attacks)?

2. What about a more traditional law enforcement situation? The Rodrigues and Hernandez cases involve Border patrol agents who claim they used force in self-defense across the border, and the lower courts seem to be suggesting that their decisions to use force cannot be challenged. If an individual located in the United States can use deadly force that has its effect in another country, are there <u>any</u> rules would limit the government's actions? What if a DEA officer used a drone to kill a drug smuggler deeper in Mexico, or in another country, knowing that the issue of whether or not the use of force is justified would never come to court in the U.S.?

3. What effect might this have on other cases—such as remote searches of computer files? Again, if FISA procedures apply, there are some safeguards built in; but what about cases of fraud, of commercial trade secret theft, or any number of other types of law enforcement where the victim of the crime is in the U.S. but the subject of the electronic surveillance/search/seizure is in another country?

There are no definitive answers on many of these issues for now. So these are good subjects for you and your peers to discuss, and they might help you understand the cases and principles we cover.

Key Terms

Agent of a foreign power—Any person other than a United States person, who acts in the United States as a member of, or as an officer or employee, of a foreign power; engages in international terrorism or activities in preparation therefore; or knowingly conspires with any person to engage in such activities.

Foreign intelligence surveillance—Efforts to discover and either prevent or stop espionage and counter-espionage undertaken by other nations, as well as the operations to gather intelligence on foreign terrorist organizations.

Foreign power—a foreign government or component of a foreign government, or an entity that is directed and controlled by foreign government or governments; or a group engaged in or preparing to engage in international terrorism.

Shocks the conscience doctrine—if the conduct of U.S. law enforcement or other authorities is so vile, repugnant, and inhumane that it shocks the conscience, any evidence obtained in the process will not be admissible in U.S. courts.

Further Reading

Funk, William, "Electronic Surveillance of Terrorism: The Intelligence/Law Enforcement Dilemma: A History," *Lewis & Clark Law Review*, Vol. 11, No. 4, 2007; Lewis & Clark Law School Legal Studies Research Paper No. 2008-9.

Seamon, Richard H., Gardner, William Dylan. *The Patriot Act and the Wall between Foreign Intelligence and Law Enforcement*, 28 Harv. J. of L.& Pub. Policy 319 (Spring 2005).

Walsh, Patrick, *Stepping on (or Over) the Constitution's Line: Evaluating FISA Section 702 in a World of Changing 'Reasonableness' Under the Fourth Amendment* 18 N.Y.U. J. Legis. & Pub. Pol'y, 741 (2015).

Young, Stewart M., *Verdugo in Cyberspace: Boundaries of Fourth Amendment Rights for Foreign Nationals in Cybercrime Cases*. Michigan Telecommunications and Technology Law Review, Vol. 10, p. 139, 2004.

Chapter 6

National Security Information

Classified Information, State Secrets, and Other Issues of Litigating National Security

Overview

Information plays a big role in national and homeland security. We have seen how the rules regarding searches, seizures, and surveillance apply to the gathering of information. In this chapter we will touch on how information is protected and appropriately disclosed, and how sensitive national security information affects litigating civil and criminal cases.

Why do nations keep secrets? In issuing the most recent version of the Executive Order on Classified National Security Information, President Obama used much the same language as his predecessors in identifying the tension involved in government secrecy:

> Our democratic principles require that the American people be informed of the activities of their Government. Also, our Nation's progress depends on the free flow of information both within the Government and to the American people. Nevertheless, throughout our history, the national defense has required that certain information be maintained in confidence in order to protect our citizens, our democratic institutions, our homeland security, and our interactions with foreign nations. Protecting information critical to our Nation's security and demonstrating our commitment to open Government through accurate and accountable application of classification standards and routine, secure, and effective declassification are equally important priorities.[1]

This statement shows that the handling of information is not a simple matter in a democracy. On the one hand, the people have what is referred to as "the right to know." On the other, the government needs to keep some information secret. But there are other reasons for secrecy.

A good reason for a country to keep secrets is so that its enemies do not find out certain information which, if known, would be damaging to national security. For example, the U.S. wants to keep secret how to build sophisticated military

---

1. Executive Order 13526: Classified National Security Information (Dec. 29, 2009).

technology such as fighter airplanes and nuclear bombs. If other nations such as Iran learned these secrets, it would be damaging to U.S. national security. Similarly, we also do not want other nations to learn the identity of our spies. If an adversary nation discovered who the U.S. spies in their country are, those individuals would be arrested, and possibly tortured and executed. The U.S. would lose valuable sources of intelligence. Furthermore, if it becomes known that our nation is unable to protect its intelligence assets, not only would adversaries be bolder, but friends and allies would be less likely to help us. As much as we value transparency in our government, we recognize and accept the need to keep certain information out of the public knowledge.

Sometimes the reason why nations keep secrets is not legitimate. From time to time governments have historically kept secrets so that its own people do not learn certain information that is embarrassing or that would politically compromise government leaders. A government withholding information from its own people to avoid embarrassment or political consequences is dangerous to liberty and freedom.

One review of this subject puts it this way:

> In practice, it is possible to distinguish at least three categories of government secrecy. The first, "genuine national security" works to protect information that would pose an identifiable threat to the security of the nation by compromising its defense or the conduct of its foreign relations... Protection of such information is not controversial. These safeguards are the raison d'etre of the classification system and the public interest is served when this type of information remains secure.
>
> A second category that often masks itself as genuine national secrecy, however, is actually something quite different. One might deem this version "bureaucratic secrecy." It reflects that natural tendency of bureaucracies... to hoard information. Whether out of convenience or [from a] dim suspicion that disclosure is intrinsically riskier than non-disclosure, government agencies always seem to err on the side of secrecy even when there is no obvious advantage at all...
>
> The third category of secrecy, "political secrecy," uses classification authority for political advantage. While probably the smallest in quantitative terms, this form of secrecy is actually the most problematic and objectionable. It exploits the generally accepted legitimacy of genuine national security interests in order to advance a self-serving agenda, to evade controversy, or to thwart accountability. In extreme cases, political secrecy conceals violations of law and threatens the integrity of the political process itself.[2]

The author goes on to note several examples of this last category—the decision to hide the fact that the Atomic Energy Commission would conduct secret experiments on humans without their knowledge or permission, the engagement of the CIA

---

2. Aftergood, Steven, Reducing Government Secrecy: Finding What Works. 27 Yale L. & Policy Rev. 399 (2009) at 402.

in similar human experiments involving dangerous drugs including LSD, and the exposure of unwitting subjects to radiation during the Cold War. Was this information kept secret because it was necessary for national security, or, as is more likely the case, because of a concern that the subjects of the experiments would not agree, or that the American people would object?

Unfortunately, in evaluating the motives for keeping information secret, it is not always easy to tell whether the secrecy is for a valid or an invalid reason. Here is another example of the issue from U.S. history:

During the Vietnam War, the neighboring nation of Cambodia had declared themselves to neutral in the conflict. Despite this, Viet Cong forces were using parts of Cambodia as safe havens from which to launch attacks against U.S. forces in South Vietnam. The U.S. was well aware of the Viet Cong's presence and activities in Cambodia. But U.S. leaders also knew that the Cambodian government would not give permission for U.S. forces to go into Cambodia after these Viet Cong, and (more importantly for our purposes) the government believed that the American population would oppose expanding the war effort by bombing locations inside Cambodia. When the U.S. started bombing locations in Cambodia, it was never acknowledged and was considered a state secret. This "secret" bombing campaign lasted for over a year and killed an estimated 50,000 to 150,000 people.[3] However, this secret was a secret only from the American people; the Cambodian people were well aware that bombs were being dropped on them, and it was not hard to guess whose bombs they were. Now, keeping the bombing secret meant that Cambodia could remain neutral, as they could claim they had no official knowledge of the bombing, but in the end, it was only the American people who were truly kept unaware of the bombing. The military did not gain any strategic or tactical advantage by keeping this information from the American people. There was no national security advantage in keeping this secret from the American people either. The reasons for keeping this action secret were purely political. The White House knew that expanding the scope of the Vietnam War would be an unpopular decision among the American people, so it was classified, and the public and even Congress were unaware of the orders to begin bombing inside Cambodia.

It is wrong for the government to classify information to hide it from the public simply because the information is unpopular or politically embarrassing. The problem is that when something is classified, there is rarely any way for the public to find out if it is being classified for a good reason or a bad and unlawful reason.

Protection of Classified Information from Disclosure

In the United States, sensitive national security information is kept out of the public domain by requiring that the information be protected in proper storage, requiring

---

3. http://www.yale.edu/cgp/Walrus_CambodiaBombing_OCT06.pdf.

that those who access it have the proper security clearance, or authorization to access or receive the information, and a "need to know" the information for an official purpose. We provide excerpts from the rules on this below.

It is a federal crime for a person to purposefully pass classified information to another who is not authorized to receive it. When that happens there are penalties, including criminal charges in certain cases. Criminal prosecution is authorized under the Espionage Act of 1917.

18 U.S. Code § 798 — Disclosure of classified information

(a) Whoever knowingly and willfully communicates, furnishes, transmits, or otherwise makes available to an unauthorized person, or publishes, or uses in any manner prejudicial to the safety or interest of the United States or for the benefit of any foreign government to the detriment of the United States any classified information —

(1) concerning the nature, preparation, or use of any code, cipher, or cryptographic system of the United States or any foreign government; or

(2) concerning the design, construction, use, maintenance, or repair of any device, apparatus, or appliance used or prepared or planned for use by the United States or any foreign government for cryptographic or communication intelligence purposes; or

(3) concerning the communication intelligence activities of the United States or any foreign government; or

(4) obtained by the processes of communication intelligence from the communications of any foreign government, knowing the same to have been obtained by such processes —

Shall be fined under this title or imprisoned not more than ten years, or both.

In addition to this statute, there are regulations governing the handling of sensitive national security information. Every federal agency has such a regulation, based on executive orders issued by American presidents throughout our history. Here are some parts of an executive order — as you read it, look at how the balance is struck between keeping sensitive information safe from disclosure and allowing for proper transparency of government action.

Executive Order 13526: Classified National Security Information (Dec. 29, 2009)

PART 1 — ORIGINAL CLASSIFICATION

Section 1.1. Classification Standards.

(a) Information may be originally classified under the terms of this order only if . . . the original classification authority determines that the unauthorized disclosure of the information reasonably could be expected to result in damage to the national security, which includes defense against transnational terrorism, and the original classification authority is able to identify or describe the damage.

(b) If there is significant doubt about the need to classify information, it shall not be classified.

. . .

(c) Classified information shall not be declassified automatically as a result of any unauthorized disclosure of identical or similar information.

(d) The unauthorized disclosure of foreign government information is presumed to cause damage to the national security.

Sec. 1.2. Classification Levels. (a) Information may be classified at one of the following three levels:

(1) "Top Secret" shall be applied to information, the unauthorized disclosure of which reasonably could be expected to cause exceptionally grave damage to the national security that the original classification authority is able to identify or describe.

(2) "Secret" shall be applied to information, the unauthorized disclosure of which reasonably could be expected to cause serious damage to the national security that the original classification authority is able to identify or describe.

(3) "Confidential" shall be applied to information, the unauthorized disclosure of which reasonably could be expected to cause damage to the national security that the original classification authority is able to identify or describe.

(b) Except as otherwise provided by statute, no other terms shall be used to identify United States classified information.

(c) If there is significant doubt about the appropriate level of classification, it shall be classified at the lower level.

. . .

Sec. 1.4. Classification Categories. Information shall not be considered for classification unless its unauthorized disclosure could reasonably be expected to cause identifiable or describable damage to the national security in accordance with section 1.2 of this order, and it pertains to one or more of the following:

(a) military plans, weapons systems, or operations;

(b) foreign government information;

(c) intelligence activities (including covert action), intelligence sources or methods, or cryptology;

(d) foreign relations or foreign activities of the United States, including confidential sources;

(e) scientific, technological, or economic matters relating to the national security;

(f) United States Government programs for safeguarding nuclear materials or facilities;

(g) vulnerabilities or capabilities of systems, installations, infrastructures, projects, plans, or protection services relating to the national security; or

(h) the development, production, or use of weapons of mass destruction.

. . .

Sec. 1.7. Classification Prohibitions and Limitations.

(a) In no case shall information be classified, continue to be maintained as classified, or fail to be declassified in order to:

(1) conceal violations of law, inefficiency, or administrative error;

(2) prevent embarrassment to a person, organization, or agency;

(3) restrain competition; or

(4) prevent or delay the release of information that does not require protection in the interest of the national security.

. . .

(d) Information that has not previously been disclosed to the public under proper authority may be classified or reclassified after an agency has received a request for it under the Freedom of Information Act (5 U.S.C. 552), the Presidential Records Act, 44 U.S.C. 2204(c)(1), the Privacy Act of 1974 (5 U.S.C. 552a), or the mandatory review provisions of section 3.5 of this order only if such classification meets the requirements of this order and is accomplished on a document-by-document basis with the personal participation or under the direction of the agency head, the deputy agency head, or the senior agency official designated under section 5.4 of this order. The requirements in this paragraph also apply to those situations in which information has been declassified in accordance with a specific date or event determined by an original classification authority in accordance with section 1.5 of this order.

(e) Compilations of items of information that are individually unclassified may be classified if the compiled information reveals an additional association or relationship that: (1) meets the standards for classification under this order; and (2) is not otherwise revealed in the individual items of information.

. . .

PART 3—DECLASSIFICATION AND DOWNGRADING

Sec. 3.1. Authority for Declassification. (a) Information shall be declassified as soon as it no longer meets the standards for classification under this order.

. . .

(c) The Director of National Intelligence (or, if delegated by the Director of National Intelligence, the Principal Deputy Director of National Intelligence) may, with respect to the Intelligence Community, after consultation with the head of the originating Intelligence Community element or department, declassify, downgrade, or direct the declassification or downgrading of information or intelligence relating to intelligence sources, methods, or activities.

...

Sec. 3.6. Processing Requests and Reviews. Notwithstanding section 4.1(i) of this order, in response to a request for information under the Freedom of Information Act, the Presidential Records Act, the Privacy Act of 1974, or the mandatory review provisions of this order:

(a) An agency may refuse to confirm or deny the existence or nonexistence of requested records whenever the fact of their existence or nonexistence is itself classified under this order or its predecessors.

(b) When an agency receives any request for documents in its custody that contain classified information that originated with other agencies or the disclosure of which would affect the interests or activities of other agencies with respect to the classified information, or identifies such documents in the process of implementing sections 3.3 or 3.4 of this order, it shall refer copies of any request and the pertinent documents to the originating agency for processing and may, after consultation with the originating agency, inform any requester of the referral unless such association is itself classified under this order or its predecessors. In cases in which the originating agency determines in writing that a response under paragraph (a) of this section is required, the referring agency shall respond to the requester in accordance with that paragraph.

...

PART 4—SAFEGUARDING

Sec. 4.1. General Restrictions on Access. (a) A person may have access to classified information provided that:

(1) a favorable determination of eligibility for access has been made by an agency head or the agency head's designee;

(2) the person has signed an approved nondisclosure agreement; and

(3) the person has a need-to-know the information.

...

(d) Classified information may not be removed from official premises without proper authorization.

(e) Persons authorized to disseminate classified information outside the executive branch shall ensure the protection of the information in a manner equivalent to that provided within the executive branch.

(f) Consistent with law, executive orders, directives, and regulations, an agency head or senior agency official or, with respect to the Intelligence Community, the Director of National Intelligence, shall establish uniform procedures to ensure that automated information systems, including networks and telecommunications systems, that collect, create, communicate, compute, disseminate, process, or store classified information:

(1) prevent access by unauthorized persons;

(2) ensure the integrity of the information; and

(3) to the maximum extent practicable, use:

    (A) common information technology standards, protocols, and interfaces that maximize the availability of, and access to, the information in a form and manner that facilitates its authorized use; and

    (B) standardized electronic formats to maximize the accessibility of information to persons who meet the criteria set forth in section 4.1(a) of this order.

(g) Consistent with law, executive orders, directives, and regulations, each agency head or senior agency official, or with respect to the Intelligence Community, the Director of National Intelligence, shall establish controls to ensure that classified information is used, processed, stored, reproduced, transmitted, and destroyed under conditions that provide adequate protection and prevent access by unauthorized persons.

(h) Consistent with directives issued pursuant to this order, an agency shall safeguard foreign government information under standards that provide a degree of protection at least equivalent to that required by the government or international organization of governments that furnished the information. . . .

(i)(1) Classified information originating in one agency may be disseminated to another agency or U.S. entity by any agency to which it has been made available without the consent of the originating agency, as long as the criteria for access under section 4.1(a) of this order are met, unless the originating agency has determined that prior authorization is required for such dissemination and has marked or indicated such requirement on the medium containing the classified information in accordance with implementing directives issued pursuant to this order.

. . .

<u>Sec. 5.5. Sanctions.</u> (a) If the Director of the Information Security Oversight Office finds that a violation of this order or its implementing directives has occurred, the Director shall make a report to the head of the agency or to the senior agency official so that corrective steps, if appropriate, may be taken.

(b) Officers and employees of the United States Government, and its contractors, licensees, certificate holders, and grantees shall be subject to appropriate sanctions if they knowingly, willfully, or negligently:

    (1) disclose to unauthorized persons information properly classified under this order or predecessor orders;

    (2) classify or continue the classification of information in violation of this order or any implementing directive;

    (3) create or continue a special access program contrary to the requirements of this order; or

    (4) contravene any other provision of this order or its implementing directives.

(c) Sanctions may include reprimand, suspension without pay, removal, termination of classification authority, loss or denial of access to classified information, or other sanctions in accordance with applicable law and agency regulation.

. . .

COMMENT

A key aspect of our free society is the right of the people to know what their government is doing. Under the common law, this was referred to as "the right to know." The protection of the people's right to know has been one of the constitutional foundations for the First Amendment's guarantee of a free press. Now, just how does the right to free speech under the First Amendment interact with classification of information? The Supreme Court addressed this issue in *New York Times v. U.S.,* which you will read below. Following that decision, Congress passed the Freedom of Information Act and Privacy Act, statutes that also ensure a level of government transparency and protect the public's right to know what government is doing on their behalf.

Before you read it, remember the hierarchy of legal authority:

1. The U.S. Constitution (which includes the First Amendment
2. Federal statutes such as (in this context) the Espionage Act of 1917, the Privacy Act, and the Freedom of Information Act
3. Federal regulations (such as executive orders)

Statutes and regulations governing classification and safeguarding of information can, in appropriate circumstances, be overcome by the First Amendment right to freedom of speech and freedom of the press. As you will read in the case below, while it is generally a crime for any person to pass classified documents to a third party, the First Amendment protects the right of a third party who is a member of "the Press" to publish those documents once they have been obtained.

This is not to say that a third party *should* publish classified documents it receives. Certain information, if made public, could harm national security and even lead to persons being killed. There are ethical and moral considerations at play. During World War II, there were many occurrences where classified information was obtained by the media. Out of a sense of patriotism and duty, the media would generally not disclose that information.

The case below arose out of the Vietnam War. While World War II had the support of the American people, the Vietnam War, which initially did enjoy widespread support, was in its later stages viewed as unnecessary and a waste of lives and money. Part of the reason for this was that the American people came to believe that the government had deliberately and purposefully lied to the American people to try to get them to support the war. The American people learned of this from many sources, but one of them was from the Pentagon Papers. In 1971, Daniel Ellsberg, who worked in the Pentagon, unlawfully passed classified information about the Vietnam War to the *New York Times*. Ellsberg was prosecuted under the Espionage Act of 1917.

(Interestingly, the judge dismissed charges against him not because of the merits of his case, but because, in its zeal to prosecute him, government investigators broke numerous laws.) Once the *New York Times* and *Washington Post* had these classified documents, they published them. The U.S. government sued the *NYT* and *Washington Post* to prevent the publication of more classified documents, claiming that publication would impair national security. But as you will read here, the government ultimately failed because of overriding concerns of the First Amendment freedoms of speech and press.

New York Times Co. v. United States, 403 U.S. 713 (1971)*

The United States seeks to prevent the *New York Times* and the *Washington Post* from publishing the contents of a classified study entitled 'History of U.S. Decision-Making Process on Viet Nam Policy.' Any system of prior restraints of expression comes to this Court bearing a heavy presumption against its constitutional validity. The Government carries a heavy burden of showing justification for the imposition of such a restraint.

Our Government was launched in 1789 with the adoption of the Constitution. The Bill of Rights, including the First Amendment, followed in 1791. Now, for the first time in the 182 years since the founding of the Republic, the federal courts are asked to hold that the First Amendment does not mean what it says, but rather means that the Government can halt the publication of current news of vital importance to the people of this country.

In seeking injunctions against these newspapers and in its presentation to the Court, the Executive Branch seems to have forgotten the essential purpose and history of the First Amendment. When the Constitution was adopted, many people strongly opposed it because the document contained no Bill of Rights to safeguard certain basic freedoms. They especially feared that the new powers granted to a central government might be interpreted to permit the government to curtail freedom of religion, press, assembly, and speech. In response to an overwhelming public clamor, James Madison offered a series of amendments to satisfy citizens that these great liberties would remain safe and beyond the power of government to abridge. Madison proposed what later became the First Amendment in three parts, two of which are set out below, and one of which proclaimed: 'The people shall not be deprived or abridged of their right to speak, to write, or to publish their sentiments; and the freedom of the press, as one of the great bulwarks of liberty, shall be inviolable.' The amendments were offered to curtail and restrict the general powers granted to the Executive, Legislative, and Judicial Branches two years before in the original Constitution. The Bill of Rights changed the original Constitution into a new charter under which no branch of government could abridge the people's freedoms of press, speech, religion, and assembly. Yet the Government argues and some members of the Court appear to agree that the general powers of the Government

---

* The case has been heavily edited and paraphrased by the authors for clarity. See disclaimer in introduction.

adopted in the original Constitution should be interpreted to limit and restrict the specific and emphatic guarantees of the Bill of Rights adopted later. I can imagine no greater perversion of history. Madison and the other Framers of the First Amendment, able men that they were, wrote in language they earnestly believed could never be misunderstood: 'Congress shall make no law abridging the freedom of the press.' Both the history and language of the First Amendment support the view that the press must be left free to publish news, whatever the source, without censorship, injunctions, or prior restraints.

In the First Amendment the Founding Fathers gave the free press the protection it must have to fulfill its essential role in our democracy. The press was to serve the governed, not the governors. The Government's power to censor the press was abolished so that the press would remain forever free to censure the Government. The press was protected so that it could bare the secrets of government and inform the people. Only a free and unrestrained press can effectively expose deception in government. And paramount among the responsibilities of a free press is the duty to prevent any part of the government from deceiving the people and sending them off to distant lands to die of foreign fevers and foreign shot and shell. In my view, far from deserving condemnation for their courageous reporting, the *New York Times*, the *Washington Post*, and other newspapers should be commended for serving the purpose that the Founding Fathers saw so clearly. In revealing the workings of government that led to the Vietnam War, the newspapers nobly did precisely that which the Founders hoped and trusted they would do.

The Government's case here is based on premises entirely different from those that guided the Framers of the First Amendment. The Government argues in its brief that in spite of the First Amendment, 'the authority of the Executive Department to protect the nation against publication of information whose disclosure would endanger the national security stems from two interrelated sources: the constitutional power of the President over the conduct of foreign affairs and his authority as Commander-in-Chief.'

In other words, we are asked to hold that despite the First Amendment's emphatic command, the Executive Branch, the Congress, and the Judiciary can make laws enjoining publication of current news and abridging freedom of the press in the name of 'national security.' The Government does not even attempt to rely on any act of Congress. Instead it makes the bold and dangerously far-reaching contention that the courts should take it upon themselves to 'make' a law abridging freedom of the press in the name of equity, presidential power and national security, even when the representatives of the people in Congress have adhered to the command of the First Amendment and refused to make such a law. To find that the President has 'inherent power' to halt the publication of news by resort to the courts would wipe out the First Amendment and destroy the fundamental liberty and security of the very people the Government hopes to make 'secure.' No one can read the history of the adoption of the First Amendment without being convinced beyond any doubt that it was injunctions like those sought here that Madison and his collaborators intended to outlaw in this Nation for all time.

The word 'security' is a broad, vague generality whose contours should not be invoked to abrogate the fundamental law embodied in the First Amendment. The guarding of military and diplomatic secrets at the expense of informed representative government provides no real security for our Republic. The Framers of the First Amendment, fully aware of both the need to defend a new nation and the abuses of the English and Colonial Governments, sought to give this new society strength and security by providing that freedom of speech, press, religion, and assembly should not be abridged. This thought was eloquently expressed in 1937 by Mr. Chief Justice Hughes—great man and great Chief Justice that he was—when the Court held a man could not be punished for attending a meeting run by Communists.

'The greater the importance of safeguarding the community from incitements to the overthrow of our institutions by force and violence, the more imperative is the need to preserve inviolate the constitutional rights of free speech, free press and free assembly in order to maintain the opportunity for free political discussion, to the end that government may be responsive to the will of the people and that changes, if desired, may be obtained by peaceful means. Therein lies the security of the Republic, the very foundation of constitutional government.'

END OF OPINION

For the reasons detailed in this opinion, there are situations where it is legal for third parties who are members of "the press" to publish classified information they have received without fear of prosecution, and for other people to read what is published. This is why it is lawful for many news anchors to read and discuss on live television classified documents posted on Wikileaks, or for newspapers to publish the information about the National Security Agency (NSA) leaked by Edward Snowden. The illegal act was the initial passing of classified information in the first place by Edward Snowden and Private Manning, but it was not illegal for journalists to publish or for Americans to read the classified documents.

Here is a question for you to consider and discuss, though—in this day and age, who is "the press"? It is easy to recognize that the *New York Times*, an American newspaper, was intended to be covered by the First Amendment's guarantee of a free press. But what about Pravda, a news organization owned and controlled by the Russian government? What about Wikileaks, an online entity not formally credentialed in any nation? What about an independent person here in the United States who maintains a blog? As you can imagine, the concept of "the press" has changed with the advent of online media, but the principle remains—the government will usually prosecute the person who initially discloses information, but will generally not go after anyone who can plausibly maintain that they qualify as "the press."

There is another important exception to this rule. Even if classified documents have been made publicly available through an intelligence leak, that does not mean the information is now unclassified. Persons with a security clearance still cannot access them without permission. The government has asserted that it has the authority to bar access to those with clearances, even though the press may publish such information if it gets ahold of it.

Here is an example from the Department of Defense[4]:

OFFICE OF THE UNDER SECRETARY OF DEFENSE
5000 DEFENSE PENTAGON
WASHINGTON, DC 20301-5000

JUN 0 7 2013

INTELLIGENCE

MEMORANDUM FOR DOD SECURITY DIRECTORS

SUBJECT: Notice to DoD Employees and Contractors on Protecting Classified Information and the Integrity of Unclassified Government Information Technology Systems

Classified information, whether or not already posted on public websites, disclosed to the media, or otherwise in the public domain remains classified and must be treated as such until it is declassified by an appropriate U.S. government authority. It is the responsibility of every DoD employee and contractor to protect classified information and to follow established procedures for accessing classified information only through authorized means. Leadership must establish a vigilant command climate that underscores the critical importance of safeguarding classified material against compromise.

Accordingly, we request all DoD components send prompt notification to your employees and contractors reminding them of these obligations. Procedures for responding to classified information found in the public domain are attached. These procedures will be promulgated in future DoD issuances. My point of contact is Mr. Jeremy Bouchard at (703) 604-0217 or Jeremy.Bouchard@osd.mil.

For Timothy A. Davis
Director of Security

Attachment:
As stated

Review Questions

Let's test how well you understand the difference between the illegality of passing classified documents and the lawful act of publishing classified information with the following problems. In each case, look through the regulations provided earlier and the analysis presented by the Supreme Court to determine if a wrongful act has been committed, or if the activity is protected by the First Amendment.

1. Freddie Loden is a computer programmer with the NSA and has top-secret clearance. He passes classified information to a CNN reporter about the NSA accessing the emails of private individuals. The reporter publicly displays and reads the documents out loud on the evening news.

2. When not on active duty, Army Reserve Private Charles Fanning works as a journalist for the *Chicago Herald*. While on Reserve duty one weekend, he prints

---

4. Retrieved from https://www.fas.org/sgp/othergov/dod/notice.pdf on 1 May 2016.

classified documents off of his computer, and takes them to his office at the *Chicago Herald* the next day. From the computer in his office and with the authorization of his supervisor, he scans the documents to the website of the *Chicago Herald*, publishing them for the world to see.

3. Captain Lakum is an officer in the U.S. Army. Like all military officers, he has a security clearance. One day he is having drinks with civilian friends, and one of them says to him, "Did you know that you are mentioned by name in one of those documents on Wikileaks?" The friend pulls up the document on his smartphone and tries to hand the phone to Captain Lakum, who initially rejects it. "I can't look at that," he says. "That material is classified." "Dude," his friend says, "you already have a 'top secret' clearance, and this stuff was only classified as merely 'secret.' You're cleared for reading this stuff. Besides, it's publicly available where anyone can read it. It's in the public domain. Seriously, it's right here on CNN!" Upon hearing that the classified documents are in the public domain where anyone can read them, Captain Lakum takes the phone and reads the documents on CNN's website where the documents have already been read by over a million other people. Has Captain Lakum done anything wrong?

Open Government and Access to Government Information

Now, you will remember that the period of the 1970s resulted in a number of reforms intended to reign in government mishandling of national security powers—including information. The Foreign Intelligence Surveillance Act dealt with regulating how the government collected information. Two other statutes regulate how the government maintains information and must release it.

The Privacy Act

The Privacy Act[5] provides safeguards against invasion of personal privacy through the misuse of records by federal agencies. It was enacted in 1974 to establish controls over what personal information is collected, maintained, used, and disseminated by agencies in the executive branch of the federal government. It is important to remember that the Privacy Act only applies to records that are located in a "system of records," defined as "a group of any records under the control of any agency from which information is retrieved by the name of the individual or by some identifying number, symbol, or other identifying particular assigned to the individual."

The Privacy Act guarantees three primary rights:

a. The right to see records about oneself, subject to Privacy Act exemptions;

b. The right to request the amendment of records that are not accurate, relevant, timely, or complete; and

---

5. 5 U.S.C. § 552a.

c. The right of individuals to be protected against unwarranted invasion of their privacy resulting from the collection, maintenance, use, and disclosure of personal information.

There are specific exceptions allowing the use of personal records:

- For statistical purposes by the Census Bureau and the Bureau of Labor Statistics;
- For routine uses within a U.S. government agency;
- For archival purposes "as a record which has sufficient historical or other value to warrant its continued preservation by the United States Government";
- For law enforcement purposes;
- For congressional investigations; and
- Other administrative purposes.

The Freedom of Information Act

The Freedom of Information Act (FOIA) [6] was signed into law in 1966 and provides that any person has the right of access to federal agency records or information. The law carries a presumption of disclosure; the burden is on the government—not the public—to substantiate why information may not be released. Upon written request, agencies of the United States government are required to disclose those records, unless the records can be lawfully withheld from disclosure under specific exemptions in the FOIA.

There are nine categories of documents that are exempt from disclosure under FOIA:

a. classified documents;

b. documents related solely to the internal personnel rules and practices of an agency;

c. documents specifically exempted from disclosure by another statute;

d. trade secrets and privileged commercial or financial information;

e. inter-agency or intra-agency memos or letters that would be considered "privileged" for litigation purposes;

f. personnel and medical files (the "personal privacy" exemption);

g. records compiled for law enforcement purposes (but these are only exempt where they could reasonably be expected to interfere with enforcement proceedings, or would deprive a person of the right to a fair trial, or could reasonably be expected to endanger someone's life or physical safety, etc.);

h. reports made for regulatory purposes by financial institutions to the government; and

---

6. 5 U.S. Code section 552.

i. geological and geophysical information (including maps) related to oil and gas wells.

This right of access is ultimately enforceable by filing a complaint in federal court.

The federal FOIA does not provide access to records held by the U.S. Congress, nor that of the federal judiciary. Nor does it provide access to records of state or local government agencies, or those held by private businesses or individuals. Each state and the District of Columbia have statutes governing public access to their records. The 1996 Electronic Freedom of Information Act (EFOIA) Amendments to the Freedom of Information Act require each agency to post on their agency website guides to making requests under the FOIA to that agency. An agency can only respond to requests for records it has created.

Litigating Cases involving Classified Information

So far, the national security focus of this textbook has been on criminal law, and classified information does, in many situations, have to be handled in criminal cases, both as the substance of a crime itself (such as prosecution of someone for spying against the United States) but also because the case involves evidence that needs to be classified. But, as you can imagine, handling classified information in a criminal case involves balancing the need of the government to keep the information secret but also the ability to allow the defense to know the evidence against them and to be able to defend against allegations in open court.

As you can imagine, criminal prosecutions involving classified information create tension between the legitimate interest of the government in protecting sensitive national security information, and a criminal defendant's rights under the United States Constitution and federal law to be able to see the evidence that is to be used against him/her or to introduce evidence that will help their case—evidence that might be classified. Along the same lines, some criminal defendants might try to employ what is known as "graymail" to avoid being prosecuted. The term "graymail" refers to situations where a defendant may seek to introduce classified information solely to force the prosecution to dismiss the charges against him. In other cases, classified information may actually be material to the defense, and excluding it would violate the defendant's constitutional rights.

The constitutional issues related to withholding classified information from a criminal defendant arise during two distinct phases of criminal litigation. First, issues may arise during the discovery phase when the defendant requests and is entitled to classified information in the possession of the prosecution. Secondly, issues may arise during the trial phase, when classified information is presented to the trier-of-fact as evidence of the defendant's guilt.

In many cases, the executive branch may resolve this tension before any charges are formally brought by simply forgoing prosecution in order to safeguard overriding national security concerns. But, as you can imagine, this is not the preferred option. Most of the time the government, and the courts, would prefer to find a way to allow the case to go forward, and balance the rights of the defendant with the needs of the government.

Protecting Classified Information in Criminal Cases: The Classified Information Procedures Act

The way that this balance is struck is through procedures set out in the Classified Information Procedures Act (CIPA).[7] The CIPA provides pretrial procedures that will permit the trial judge to rule on questions of admissibility involving classified information before introduction of the evidence in open court. These procedures are intended to provide a means for the court to distinguish instances of graymail from cases in which classified information is actually material to the defense.

The CIPA provides criminal procedures that permit a trial judge to rule on the relevance or admissibility of classified information in a secure setting. It requires a defendant to notify the prosecution and the court of any classified information that the defendant may seek to discover or disclose during trial. During the discovery phase, CIPA authorizes courts to issue protective orders limiting disclosure to members of the defense team that have obtained adequate security clearances, and to permit the government to use unclassified redactions or summaries of classified information that the defendant would normally be entitled to receive.

If classified information is to be introduced at trial, the court may allow substitutes of classified information to be used, so long as they provide the defendant with substantially the same ability to present a defense and do not otherwise violate his constitutional rights. Among the rights that may be implicated by the application of CIPA in a criminal prosecution are the defendant's right to have a public trial, to be confronted with the witnesses against him, and to have the assistance of counsel. CIPA may also be implicated by the obligation of the prosecution to provide the defendant, under *Brady v. Maryland*,[8] with exculpatory evidence that it might have in its possession and, pursuant to the Jencks Act,[9] to provide the defendant with any prior written statements of government witnesses.

The CIPA is based on a presumption that the government has a legitimate privilege against disclosing classified information in criminal matters. Courts have agreed that CIPA does not create any new privilege against the disclosure of classified information, but merely establishes some standard procedures to allow the government and the courts to determine the materiality of classified information to the defense in a criminal proceeding.

Under CIPA, if the government objects to disclosure of classified information that is material to the defense, the court is required to simply accept that assertion without

---

7. This material is adapted from CRS Report R41742. *Protecting Classified Information and the Rights of Criminal Defendants: The Classified Information Procedures Act* by Edward C. Liu and Todd Garvey, April 2, 2012 by the Congressional Research Service.
8. 373 U.S. 83 (1963).
9. 18 U.S.C. § 3500.

scrutiny, and impose nondisclosure orders upon the defendant. In such cases, though, the court is also empowered to dismiss the indictment against the defendant, or to impose other sanctions that the court considers appropriate. As a result, once a court, using the procedures under CIPA, has concluded that classified information is material to the case, the government must choose between (1) permitting the disclosure of that information or (2) the sanctions the court may impose, including dismissal of charges against the defendant.

Now, the facts involved in prosecutions implicating classified information can vary, but an important distinction that should be kept in mind in all cases is *from whom* information is being kept. In cases where the defendant is already aware of some classified information, the government may be seeking to prevent disclosure to the general public. However, in the case of terrorism prosecutions, the more typical situation is likely to be the introduction of classified information, such as the identity of an intelligence source, or the method by which intelligence about the case was collected, as part of the prosecution's case against the defendant. In these cases, the government may see the need to ask for protective orders preventing disclosure to the defendant, as well as to the public.

In order to safeguard classified information that is disclosed, CIPA authorizes courts to issue protective orders prohibiting or restricting the disclosure of such classified information. In some cases, protective orders may limit disclosure to individuals or attorneys who have received a security clearance from the government. As you can imagine, though, some defendants may be ineligible for the necessary security clearances. When that happens, the courts may issue protective orders prohibiting cleared counsel from sharing any classified information with the defendant. In the event that the defendant's attorneys are also unable to obtain the necessary security clearances, courts have appointed counsel with the necessary security clearance to represent the defendant in matters where disclosure of classified information may be necessary. However, the cleared counsel may be prohibited from disclosing the classified information to the uncleared defendant or uncleared defense counsel.

Below is an excerpt from the United States Attorney's Manual, the official guidance from the Department of Justice to its attorneys who have to deal with situations like this. Don't try to memorize all of this material, but skim through it so you can see actual guidelines that apply the concepts we discussed above.

2054. Synopsis of Classified Information Procedures Act (CIPA)[10]

1. DEFINITIONS, PRETRIAL CONFERENCE, PROTECTIVE ORDERS AND DISCOVERY

After a criminal indictment becomes public, the prosecutor remains responsible for taking reasonable precautions against the unauthorized disclosure of

---

10. U.S. Attorneys' Manual, U.S. Department of Justice, retrieved from *http://www.justice.gov/usam/criminal-resource-manual-2054-synopsis-classified-information-procedures-act-cipa*. Some citations removed.

classified information during the case. This responsibility applies both when the government intends to use classified information in its case-in-chief as well as when the defendant seeks to use classified information in his/her defense. The tool with which the proper protection of classified information may be ensured in indicted cases is the . . . (CIPA).

CIPA is a procedural statute; it neither adds to nor detracts from the substantive rights of the defendant or the discovery obligations of the government. Rather, the procedure for making these determinations is different in that it balances the right of a criminal defendant with the right of the sovereign to know in advance of a potential threat from a criminal prosecution to its national security. . . . Each of CIPA's provisions is designed to achieve those dual goals: preventing unnecessary or inadvertent disclosures of classified information and advising the government of the national security "cost" of going forward.

. . .

A. *Pretrial Conference*

Section 2 provides that "[a]t any time after the filing of the indictment or information, any party may move for a pretrial conference to consider matters relating to classified information that may arise in connection with the prosecution." Following such a motion, the district court "shall promptly hold a pretrial conference to establish the timing of requests for discovery, the provision of notice required by Section 5 of this Act, and the initiation of the procedure established by Section 6 (to determine the use, relevance, or admissibility of classified information) of this Act."

B. *Protective Orders*

Of critical importance in any criminal case, once there exists any likelihood that classified information may be at issue, is the entering of a protective order by the district court. CIPA Section 3 requires the court, upon the request of the government, to issue an order "to protect against the disclosure of any classified information disclosed by the United States to any defendant in any criminal case." The government's motion for a protective order is an excellent opportunity to begin educating the Court, including the judge's staff, about CIPA and related issues. It is essential that the motion include a memorandum of law that provides the court with an overview on national security matters and sets forth the authority by which the government may protect matters of national security, including the general authority of the Intelligence Community (IC) pursuant to the National Security Act of 1947, the Central Intelligence Act of 1949, and various Executive orders issued by the President . . . The protective order must be sufficiently comprehensive to ensure that access to classified information is restricted to cleared persons and to provide for adequate procedures and facilities for proper handling and protection of classified information during the pre-trial litigation and trial of the case.

. . .

An essential provision of a protective order is the appointment by the court of a Court Security Officer (CSO). The CSO ... is responsible for assisting both parties and the court staff in obtaining security clearances (not required for the judge); in the proper handling and storage of classified information, and in operating the special communication equipment that must be used in dealing with classified information.

C. *Discovery of Classified Information by Defendant*

Section 4 provides in pertinent part that "[t]he court, upon a sufficient showing, may authorize the United States to delete specified items of classified information from documents to be made available to the defendant through discovery under the Federal Rules of Criminal Procedure, to substitute a summary of the information for such classified documents, or to substitute a statement admitting the relevant facts that classified information would tend to prove." Like Rule 16(d)(1) of the Federal Rules of Criminal Procedure, section 4 provides that the Government may demonstrate that the use of such alternatives is warranted in an *in camera, ex parte* submission to the court.

. . .

- SECTIONS 5 AND 6: NOTICE AND PRETRIAL EVIDENTIARY RULINGS
NOTICE OF INTENT TO USE CLASSIFIED INFORMATION

  Following the discovery process under section 4, there are three critical pretrial steps in the handling of classified information under sections 5 and 6 of CIPA. First, the defendant must specify in detail, in a written notice, the precise classified information he reasonably expects to disclose. Second, the Court, upon a motion of the Government, shall hold a hearing pursuant to section 6(a) to determine the use, relevance and admissibility of the proposed evidence. Third, following the 6(a) hearing and formal findings of admissibility by the Court, the Government may move to substitute redacted versions of classified documents from the originals or to prepare an admission of certain relevant facts or summaries for classified information that the Court has ruled admissible.

  A. The Section 5(a) Notice Requirement

    PRETRIAL EVIDENTIARY HEARING, SUBSTITUTIONS
    AND STIPULATIONS

    The linchpin of CIPA is section 5(a), which requires a defendant who reasonably intends to disclose (or cause the disclosure of) classified information to provide timely pretrial written notice of his intention to the Court and the Government. . . .

    If a defendant fails to provide a sufficiently detailed notice far enough in advance of trial to permit the implementation of CIPA procedures, section 5(b) provides for preclusion . . . Similarly, if the defendant attempts to disclose at trial classified information which is not described in his/her section 5(a) notice, preclusion is the appropriate remedy prescribed by section 5(b) of the statute. . . .

B. The Section 6(a) Hearing

The purpose of the hearing pursuant to section 6(a) of CIPA is for the court "to make all determinations concerning the use, relevance, or admissibility of classified information that would otherwise be made during the trial...." 18 U.S.C. App. III §6(a). The statute expressly provides that, after a pretrial section 6(a) hearing on the admissibility of evidence, the court shall enter its rulings *prior* to the commencement of trial. If the Attorney General or his/her designee certifies to the court in a petition that a public proceeding may result in the disclosure of classified information, then the hearing will be held *in camera*. CIPA does not change the "generally applicable evidentiary rules of admissibility," but rather alters the *timing* of rulings as to admissibility to require them to be made before the trial.

At the section 6(a) hearing, the court is to hear the defense proffer and the arguments of counsel, and then rule whether the classified information identified by the defense is relevant under the standards of Fed.R.Evid. 401. The court's inquiry does not end there, for under Fed.R.Evid. 402, not all relevant evidence is admissible at trial. The Court therefore must also determine whether the evidence is cumulative, prejudicial, confusing, or misleading, so that it should be excluded under Fed.R.Evid. 403.

...

C. *Substitution Pursuant to Section 6(c)*

If the court rules any classified information to be admissible, section 6(c) of CIPA permits the Government to propose unclassified "substitutes" for that information. Specifically, the Government may move to substitute either (1) a statement admitting relevant facts that the classified information would tend to prove or (2) a summary of the classified information instead of the classified information itself. In many cases, the government will propose a redacted version of a classified document as a substitute for the original, having deleted only non-relevant classified information. A motion for substitution shall be granted if the "statement or summary will provide the defendant with substantially the same ability to make his defense as would disclosure of the specified classified information."

...

- OTHER RELEVANT CIPA PROCEDURES

...

B. Introduction of Classified Information

Section 8(a) provides that "writings, recordings, and photographs containing classified information may be admitted into evidence without change in their classification status." This provision simply recognizes that classification is an executive, not a judicial, function. Thus, section 8(a) implicitly allows the classifying agency, upon completion of the trial, to decide whether the information has been so compromised during trial that it could no longer be regarded as classified.

In order to prevent "unnecessary disclosure" of classified information, section 8(b) permits the court to order admission into evidence of only a part of a writing, recording, or photograph. Alternatively, the court may order into evidence the whole writing, recordings, or photograph with excision of all or part of the classified information contained therein. However, the provision does not provide grounds for excluding or excising part of a writing or recorded statement which ought in fairness to be considered contemporaneously with it. Thus, the court may admit into evidence part of a writing, recording, or photograph only when fairness does not require the whole document to be considered.

Section 8(c) provides a procedure to address the problem presented during a pretrial or trial proceeding when the defendant's counsel asks a question or embarks on a line of inquiry that would require the witness to disclose classified information not previously found by the court to be admissible. If the defendant knew that a question or line of inquiry would result in disclosure of classified information, he/she presumably would have given the government notice under section 5 and the provisions of section 6(a) would have been used. Section 8(c) serves, in effect, as a supplement to the hearing provisions of section 6(a) to cope with situations which cannot be handled effectively under that section, e.g., where the defendant does not realize that the answer to a given question will reveal classified information. Upon the government's objection to such a question, the court is required to take suitable action to avoid the improper disclosure of classified information.

C. Security Procedures

Section 9 required the Chief Justice of the United States to prescribe security procedures for the protection of classified information in the custody of Federal courts. On February 12, 1981, Chief Justice Burger promulgated these procedures.

. . .

D. Public Testimony By Intelligence Officers

Although the IC is committed to assisting law enforcement where it is legally proper to do so, it must also remain vigilant in protecting classified national security information from unauthorized disclosure. Just as with law enforcement agencies, the successful functioning of the IC turns in significant part upon the ability of its intelligence officers covertly to obtain information from human sources. In carrying out that task, the intelligence officers must, when necessary, be able to operate anonymously, that is, without their connection to an intelligence agency of the United States being known to the persons with whom they come in contact. For that reason, an intelligence agency is authorized under Executive Order 12958 to classify the true name of an intelligence officer.

. . .

In any criminal case in which it becomes likely that an intelligence agency employee will testify, the Assistant United States Attorney (AUSA) assigned to the case shall immediately notify the Internal Security Section (ISS). That office, in consultation with the general counsel at the appropriate intelligence agency, will assist the AUSA during pretrial motion practice and litigation on the issue of whether the witness should testify in true name and other issues related to the testimony of intelligence agency personnel.

...

As you can tell, there is a lot of room for a court to both consider and simultaneously protect sensitive national security information in a criminal case. Using these procedures, a great many espionage and terrorism cases have been successfully prosecuted in federal court over the years.

Let's now take a look at a case involving CIPA. In this decision an individual is charged with providing classified information to a foreign power.

United States v. Richard Craig Smith, 780 F.2d 1102 (1985)[*]

Richard Craig Smith has been indicted on five counts of espionage under 18 U.S.C. Secs. 793(a), 794(a) and (c). Prior to trial, Smith gave notice to the government and to the court pursuant to 18 U.S.C.App. Sec. 5 that he intended to disclose classified information as part of his defense. Following the procedures set out in the Classified Information Procedures Act, the district court conducted a closed hearing to determine the use, relevance, or admissibility of the classified information the defendant proffered. At the conclusion of the hearing, the court ruled that part of the classified information Smith sought to introduce would be admissible at trial. The government sought a reversal of the district court's ruling allowing introduction of the classified information. We conclude that the district court applied an incorrect legal standard in ruling upon the introduction of the classified information, and accordingly vacate the order of the district court and remand.

Smith was employed by the Army Intelligence Security Command (INSCOM) between 1973 and 1980. He is here charged with unlawfully selling in 1982 and 1983 certain classified information to Victor I. Okunev, an agent of the Soviet Union. The indictment charges that Smith met with Okunev at the Soviet Commercial Compound in Tokyo, Japan, twice in November 1982 and once in February 1983. Smith allegedly gave Okunev classified information regarding five INSCOM double agent operations, for which he received $11,000 from Okunev.

In his defense, on account of the facts he relates just below, Smith argues that he believed he was working for the Central Intelligence Agency (CIA) when he turned over the information to Okunev. He claims that he was sought out by two men who claimed to be CIA agents, Ken White and Danny Ishida. White and Ishida sought Smith's help in setting up a double agent project directed toward the Russians in Japan. Smith was to gain the confidence of the Soviets by supplying them with the

---

[*] The case has been heavily edited and paraphrased by the authors for clarity. See disclaimer in introduction.

details of eight INSCOM double agent operations. White and Ishida told Smith that this information would be of no real value to the Russians because those eight operations had been discontinued. Smith became convinced that White and Ishida were indeed working for the CIA and agreed to help them by supplying the specified information to the Russians.

Smith seeks to introduce at trial several pieces of classified information to support his defense that he thought he was working for the CIA when he sold the information to the Russians. Such proof may negate an essential element of the crimes charged, intent or reason to believe the information sold would be used to injure the United States or to the advantage of a foreign country. After a lengthy hearing, the district court ruled that Smith could introduce part of the classified information he relied upon in his defense. It found that certain classified information was relevant to Smith's defense and therefore was admissible at trial. For example, in a ruling not appealed from, the court found that details of the INSCOM operations White and Ishida allegedly gave to Smith to pass on to the Soviets were admissible because such information made the existence of White and Ishida more probable than otherwise would be the case.

The district court further found that CIPA was not intended to change the existing law of evidence regarding admissibility; and Congress did not intend to allow exclusion of evidence relevant to the defense simply because that evidence was classified. Because the evidence proffered was found to be relevant, it reasoned, it could be introduced at trial.

A panel of this court affirmed the district court's finding that the evidence in question was admissible. It concluded that the district court correctly applied the standards for judging relevance. It rejected the government's argument that governmental privilege required that a balancing test similar to the one set out in *Roviaro v. United States* (1957) should be applied here. The *Roviaro* standard as we view it is one that calls for balancing the public interest in protecting the information against the individual's right to prepare his defense. Its application results in a more strict rule of admissibility, and we think that standard should have been applied here.

In order to properly understand the troubling issue before us, we should review CIPA and the legislative history surrounding it. CIPA was enacted by Congress in an effort to combat the growing problem of **graymail**, a practice whereby a criminal defendant threatens to reveal classified information during the course of his trial in the hope of forcing the government to drop the criminal charge against him. Prior to the enactment of CIPA, the government had no method of evaluating such disclosure claims before trial actually began. Oftentimes it would abandon prosecution rather than risk possible disclosure of classified information.

CIPA established a pretrial procedure for ruling upon the admissibility of classified information. A criminal defendant must notify the United States and the court if he reasonably expects to disclose classified information during his trial or during any pretrial proceeding. A defendant is forbidden from disclosing any such information absent the giving of notice. The notice must specifically set out the classified information the defendant believes he will rely upon in his defense. A general statement of the areas the evidence will cover is insufficient.

Once the defendant gives notice of his intention to introduce classified information, the United States may request a hearing at which the court shall determine the use, relevance, or admissibility of classified information that would otherwise be made during the trial or pretrial proceeding. Upon a determination by the court that the classified information is admissible, the United States may move to substitute either a statement admitting relevant facts that the classified information would tend to prove or a summary of the classified information instead of the classified information itself. The court shall grant the government's motion if the substitution will give the defendant substantially the same ability to make his defense as would the disclosure of the classified information. If the court denies a motion for a substitution, the Attorney General can submit an affidavit objecting to the disclosure of the classified information at issue.

Once such an affidavit is filed, the defendant is barred from disclosing the classified information. The court then can dismiss certain counts of the indictment, find against the United States on issues relating to the classified information, strike testimony, or as a last resort dismiss the indictment. The United States can take an appeal from an adverse district court decision with respect to the disclosure of classified information.

This appeal concerns the construction and meaning of Sec. 6 of CIPA as it sets out the district court's role in deciding the use, relevance or admissibility of classified information as evidence. The legislative history is clear that Congress did not intend to alter the existing law governing the admissibility of evidence. Thus, the Conference Report provided " . . . the conferees agree that, as noted in the report to accompany S.1482 and H.R. 4736, nothing in the conference substitute is intended to change the existing standards for determining relevance and admissibility." The circuits that have considered the matter agree with the legislative history cited that ordinary rules of evidence determine admissibility under CIPA. No new substantive law was created by the enactment of CIPA. Neither did the adoption of the Federal Rules of Evidence change the existing law on the subject where not addressed.

The district court correctly concluded that CIPA was merely a procedural tool requiring a pretrial court ruling on the admissibility of classified information. The court then looked at the two groups of classified information at a CIPA hearing and concluded that they were relevant to Smith's defense. We find no error in the district court's conclusion as to some of the classified information it held should be admitted which would make Smith's account of the events more probable than without that evidence and hence relevant.

The relevance of some of the information is apparent when reviewing Smith's defense. He does not deny that he gave the classified information to the Soviets. He defends the charges against him solely on the grounds that he did not have the necessary intent or reason to believe the information would be used to harm the United States or to give advantage to a foreign nation. Instead, he claims that he thought he was aiding the United States by working for the CIA in setting up a double agent operation.

Not all relevant evidence is admissible at trial, however. The government argues that even if the evidence in question is relevant it should be excluded under a privilege similar to the informer's privilege recognized by *Roviaro v. United States* (1957). We believe that the district court committed an error of law in not applying such a privilege before ruling the relevant classified information admissible. Although evidence may be relevant, it yet may be inadmissible because of common law privileges with respect to the testimony. Some such common law privileges include the attorney-client privilege, marital privilege, military or state secrets, and the informant's privilege.

Roviaro recognizes the existence of a qualified privilege to withhold the identity of persons who furnish information regarding criminal activity to law enforcement officials. Such a privilege is designed to protect and foster the interests of law enforcement by encouraging citizens to aid criminal justice without fear of public disclosure.

The privilege is a qualified one, however. The privilege ceases once the reasons for it cease, that is, once disclosure occurs to "those who would have cause to resent the communication." The privilege must also give way when the informant or the contents of his communication "is relevant and helpful to the defense of an accused, or is essential to a fair determination of a cause." The trial court is required to balance the public interest in nondisclosure against the defendant's right to prepare a defense. A decision on disclosure of such information must depend on the "particular circumstances of each case, taking into consideration the crime charged, the possible defenses, the possible significance of the informer's testimony, and other relevant factors."

The defendant in *Roviaro* was convicted of selling heroin to one John Doe and illegally transporting that heroin. *Roviaro* moved to learn the identity of John Doe. The motion was denied. At trial, prosecution witnesses described John Doe's part in the drug transaction but he was never produced or identified. The Court vacated the conviction after concluding that John Doe was a material witness to the defendant because of his participation in the crime. Because John Doe was the only other participant in the crimes charged, his testimony was "highly relevant and might have been helpful to the defense."

Dual interests arise from nondisclosure of informers and the information they possess. First, the public interest is served by nondisclosure because it encourages persons to come forward with information that can aid effective law enforcement. Second, the safety and security of the person supplying the information is best protected by nondisclosure of his identity to those who may cause him harm. Those interests must be balanced against a defendant's right to present his defense. The privilege must give way to the "fundamental requirements of fairness." The defendant must come forward with something more than speculation as to the usefulness of such disclosure. Disclosure is not required despite the fact that a criminal defendant may have no other means of determining what relevant information the informant possesses. Disclosure is only required after a court has determined that the informer's testimony is highly relevant. One of the most important factors to be considered is the materiality of the evidence to the defendant's particular defense. The decision of whether the testimony of the informer will be relevant and helpful is usually within the trial judge's discretion.

The government's privilege does not give way simply because the defendant knows the informant's name or identity. Protection of the informant can justify nondisclosure of his address or location. When the informant's identity is known to the defendant but his location is not, the same balancing of the public interest in nondisclosure against the defendant's need for disclosure must occur. Defendant must still show that disclosure will significantly aid his defense.

The District of Columbia Circuit followed *McCray v. Illinois* (1967), which followed *Roviaro*, as the basis for concluding that a privilege exists allowing the government to refuse to disclose the location of drug surveillance operations in *United States v. Green* (D.C.Cir.1981). The interests to be protected by nondisclosure are the same in both instances. Hidden surveillance operations can be useful law enforcement tools only if they remain hidden and secret. The safety of police officers manning such an operation may be endangered by public disclosure. The cooperation of the public in participating in such an operation could be compromised by disclosure. These harms must be balanced against the defendant's need for the information. And in *United States v. Harley* (D.C.Cir.1982), the court extended the privilege to trials.

We find the principles *of Roviaro, Green,* and *Harley* applicable here. The government interest protected by nondisclosure is analogous. The government has a substantial interest in protecting sensitive sources and methods of gathering information. The gathering of such information and the methods used resemble closely the gathering of law enforcement information. The confidentiality of sources and the methods used in both instances are critical. Persons who supply information to the government regarding matters taking place in foreign countries are likely to be located outside the United States. Their safety would immediately be placed in jeopardy if their identity were made public. Revealing such information absent an essential need by a defendant would also result in the drying up of a primary source of information to our intelligence community.

Law enforcement domestic informers generally know who their enemies are; intelligence agents often do not. To give the domestic informer of the police more protection than the foreign informer of the CIA seems to us to place the security of the nation from foreign danger on a lower plane than the security of the nation from the danger from domestic criminals. In our opinion the national interest is as well served by cooperation with the CIA as with the domestic police.

As the Supreme Court has reasoned,

> "The Government has a compelling interest in protecting both the secrecy of information to our national security and the appearance of confidentiality so essential to the effective operation of our foreign intelligence service." . . . If potentially valuable intelligence sources come to think that the Agency will be unable to maintain the confidentiality of its relationship to them, many could well refuse to supply information to the Agency in the first place.
>
> Even a small chance that some court will order disclosure of a source's identity could well impair intelligence gathering and cause sources to "close up like a clam." To induce some sources to cooperate, the Government must tender as absolute an assurance of confidentiality as it possibly can. "The continued availability of [intelligence] sources depends upon the CIA's ability to guarantee the security of information that might compromise them and even danger [their] personal safety."

CIA v. Sims, 105 S.Ct. 1881 (1985)

We find the privilege applicable here even though Smith has had access to the information he seeks to admit at trial. *Roviaro* speaks of protection from "those who would have cause to resent the communication." This is not the typical informant case where the criminal defendant is usually the one that would resent the communications. Here, a significant part of the risk of harm arises from disclosure to the public. The government's interest is still protectable although Smith may have had access to the information. The privilege is not extinguished by previous disclosure to the defendant alone. The government interest to be protected here includes disclosure of the information to the public. We therefore conclude that the privilege did not cease because Smith has had access to the information.

Smith argues that even if the government's *Roviaro* type privilege exists, in the government's exercise of that privilege it must follow the substitution procedure of Sec. 6(c) of CIPA rather than seek exclusion of the evidence altogether. Adoption of Smith's argument would result in a substantive change in the law of evidence, exactly what Congress said CIPA was not designed to do. Had CIPA not been enacted, the government could have raised its privilege at trial. The trial court then should have engaged in the balancing test of *Roviaro*. If it determined that the government's interest was superior, taking all proper factors into account, the evidence would not be disclosed. That is yet the law, but CIPA dictates that such a decision be made prior to trial.

The court decisions construing CIPA are consistent with our holding here. In *United States v. Pringle* (1st Cir.1984), the defendants were convicted of possession and conspiracy to possess marijuana with the intent to import after a ship full of marijuana in their charge was seized. The defendants sought to have the government produce information regarding the surveillance, boarding and seizure of their ship. Instead of supplying the information, the government moved for a hearing under CIPA to prevent release of the material. Following an examination of the material in a private hearing between the Government and the judge, the district court refused to require the release of the information to the defendants. The court of appeals affirmed after applying *Roviaro*. It agreed with the district court that the information "was not relevant to the determination of the guilt or innocence of the defendants, was not helpful to the defense and was not essential to a fair determination of the cause." The significance of *Pringle*, of course, is that it applied *Roviaro* as the standard in its construction of CIPA.

We find no CIPA case that has involved the issue now before us. We reject Smith's argument that several cases hold that relevancy is the only determination to be made by the trial court. In those cases, the trial court determined that the evidence was not relevant so that it did not need to go further and decide if that relevant evidence was admissible.

Our holding is also supported by the language used by Congress in Sec. 6 of CIPA, requiring the district court to rule upon the use, relevance, or admissibility of classified information. Such language is consistent with existing law. Had Congress wished to allow all relevant classified information to be automatically admissible at trial, it would have so provided. The error of the district court here was in doing just that. It did not go further with its analysis than determine that the evidence was relevant. It should still have determined whether any relevant evidence was admissible in light of the applicable government privilege.

Having held that the district court erred by its failure to consider the government's privilege in arriving at its conclusion that the evidence in question was admissible at trial, we think it is not out of order to call to that court's attention some of the principles the cases have established, although we do not lay down at this time any rigid rule, for *Roviaro* requires that "whether a proper balance renders nondisclosure erroneous must depend upon the particular circumstances of each case, taking into consideration the crime charged, the possible defense, the possible significance of the informer's testimony, and other relevant factors." A district court may order disclosure only when the information is at least "essential to the defense," "necessary to his defense," and neither merely cumulative nor corroborative. We do hold, however, that we equate the disclosure of the classified information sought in this case with the disclosure of the various kinds of information sought about informers in the cases construing *Roviaro*. The *Roviaro* standard of admissibility is at the least more restrictive than the ordinary rules of relevancy would indicate.

The judgment of the district court is vacated and the case is remanded for reconsideration not inconsistent with this opinion.

END OF OPINION

Now, the CIPA applies to *criminal cases* only. However, as you can imagine, there are many legal issues involving national security that have nothing to do with criminal law. As evidenced by the remaining chapters in this book, criminal law is only a small section of national security law. There are many civil law issues concerning national security.

Protecting Classified Information in Civil Cases: The State Secrets Doctrine

In the American legal system, the term "civil law" refers to any area of law that is not criminal law. This includes areas of legal practice such as family law, contracts, insurance litigation, personal injury, tax law, and almost every other area of law. When people have disputes over civil law, be it for ordinary issues or those involving national security, they frequently file lawsuits. For example, just as parents would sue a drunk driver who killed their child, if a man's son is killed by a U.S. drone strike, he might file a wrongful death lawsuit where he sues the government to demand money over the alleged wrongful death of his son. In another example, the American Civil Liberties Union (ACLU) may file a lawsuit against the NSA to ask a judge to issue an order that the NSA cease wiretapping Americans.

When people file lawsuits for matters involving national security, they face unique issues which are not faced in regular lawsuits. A common issue faced is that both information as well as the very subject of the suit may be classified, so there are issues about obtaining information or discussing the matter in open court. Unlike the situation with criminal cases, there is no civil law version of the CIPA to regulate the use of classified information in court. This raises the question, how do we have lawsuits over national security matters without revealing state secrets?

The answer lies in procedural rules that address how we litigate national security issues involving state secrets and other classified information. These are commonly referred to as "the *Totten* Bar" and "the *Reynolds* Privilege."

Before we go into these topics, here's a crash course in the basics of federal civil procedure so you understand how a lawsuit works.

1. The first step of a lawsuit is when a person, referred to as the Plaintiff, starts the lawsuit by filing a **PLEADING** with the court known as a **COMPLAINT**. A pleading is a document filed by a party to a lawsuit explaining their side of the matter, and the complaint is the pleading filed by the person initiating the lawsuit containing a simple statement of fact, which forms the basis of the lawsuit, and the remedy being sought. For example, the ACLU could file a complaint making a simple declaration that the NSA is illegally surveilling Americans, and, as a remedy, ask the court to order that the NSA stop the surveillance. The complaint alleges both the wrong and the remedy.

2. The next step in the process of a lawsuit is filing the pleading known as the **ANSWER**. This is the document that the person being sued, referred to as the defendant, files in response to the pleading. The defendant can admit the claims made in the pleading, deny the claims, admit some claims and deny others, state that he or she does not know enough at the time to answer part or all of the pleading, or assert an affirmative defense.[11] For example, the NSA could deny that it is surveilling

---

11. An affirmative defense is where a person admits that one did an act of which one is accused, but had a legally justifiable reason for doing so. For example, let's say someone sues you for breaking his nose. If you assert an affirmative defense in your answer, you would admit to breaking the nose, but assert you still don't owe him anything because you were acting in self-defense.

Americans in its answer. The NSA could also admit to spying on Americans but claim that it is not breaking any laws when it does.

Now, in national security cases, another possibility is that the NSA could neither admit nor deny it is spying on Americans, but instead simply say that it cannot address the issue because doing so would reveal a state secret. This last option will be covered in this chapter when we discuss the *Totten* Bar.

3. After the plaintiff has filed the complaint and the defendant has filed his or her answer, the case then goes into the third stage, which is **DISCOVERY**. In a civil lawsuit, there is an obligation for parties to turn over all information relevant to the case, regardless of whether it is helpful or harmful to their case. This is the opposite of criminal law where an accused has the Fifth Amendment right to remain silent. The purpose of discovery is to get all information out in the open so both the plaintiff and defendant get a fair and accurate assessment of the lawsuit. By getting the facts out, not only can the trial be better, but the discovery process also provides an opportunity for the parties to decide if is better to settle the case on their own rather than going to trial.

For example, let's say you are in a pet store that claims none of its animals are poisonous, and you are bitten by a snake. The area around the bite immediately swells up, and you are rushed to the emergency room and hospitalized for five days for what you learn is exposure to snake venom. You sue the pet store for your injuries. In this suit, during discovery, the pet store owner would have to turn over the documents and records he has about the snake, even if they reveal that the snake was in fact poisonous and the owner knew that it was poisonous when he put it on display and allowed it near customers. Other important facts would be disclosed as well—any warnings, behavior by the store employees (or by you!) that increased the danger of a bite, and so forth.

Each year, during the discovery stage of lawsuits across the country, many people are caught trying to hide information they believe to be harmful to their case. When they do this and are caught, they can be held in contempt of court, charged with obstruction of justice, have the case decided against them because of their bad action, or perhaps even forced to pay fines and possibly even go to jail.

Discovery is more than just turning over documents, but also involves procedures that involve one party to the lawsuit asking the opposing party questions. A list of questions can be sent on paper, and the opposing party is required to answer the questions truthfully and in writing. These are known as "interrogatories." For example, with the pet store, the plaintiff could ask, "Where did the snake come from?" and the pet store owner would be legally required to answer truthfully, even if the answer is "Poisonous Snakes, Inc." Individuals can also be forced to sit down and, while under oath, orally answer questions about a lawsuit. This is known as a "deposition." In a deposition, the pet store owner could be asked if he knew that the snake was poisonous. If a person lies during a deposition, that person can be prosecuted for the crime of perjury.

Now, in the context of this course, you may be wondering what happens in a lawsuit when the information being sought, such as documents, is classified. As you will learn, with the *Reynolds* privilege, the government does not have to reveal information that contains state secrets.

Cases where the Subject of the Case Is Classified—The Totten *Bar*

What happens if a lawsuit is filed where the very issue of contention is itself a state secret? For example, what if a person has a secret contract with the U.S. government to risk his life and conduct espionage for the U.S. in exchange for money, but the government subsequently refuses to pay up and, as a result, the person (once safely in the U.S.) sues? How would the courts handle it? The answer is very simple: they don't hear the case. When a lawsuit is raised and *the very issue of contention is a state secret*, our courts dismiss the matter without even hearing the merits of the case. This concept is known as the *Totten* bar, and it comes from the following case:

Totten v. United States, 92 U.S. 105 (1876)[*]

This case was brought to recover compensation for services alleged to have been rendered by William A. Lloyd, under a contract with President Lincoln, made in July, 1861, by which he was to proceed South and ascertain the number of troops stationed at different points in the insurrectionary States, procure plans of forts and fortifications, and gain such other information as might be beneficial to the government of the United States, and report the facts to the President; for which services he was to be paid $200 a month.

Lloyd proceeded, under the contract, within the rebel lines, and remained there during the entire period of the war, collecting, and from time to time transmitting, information to the President; and that, upon the close of the war, he was only reimbursed his expenses.

The service stipulated by the contract was a secret service; the information sought was to be obtained clandestinely, and was to be communicated privately; the employment and the service were to be equally concealed. Both employer and agent must have understood that the lips of the other were to be forever sealed respecting the relation of either to the matter. This condition of the engagement was implied from the nature of the employment, and is implied in all secret employments of the government in time of war, or upon matters affecting our foreign relations, where a disclosure of the service might compromise or embarrass our government in its public duties, or endanger the person or injure the character of the agent. If in contracts of such a nature an action against the government could be maintained in court, whenever an agent should deem himself entitled to greater or different compensation than that awarded to him, the whole service in any case, and the manner of its discharge, with the details of dealings with individuals and officers, might be exposed, to the serious detriment of the public. A secret service, with liability to publicity in this way, would be impossible; and, as such services are sometimes indispensable to the

---

[*] The case has been heavily edited and paraphrased by the authors for clarity. See disclaimer in introduction.

government, its agents in those services must look for their compensation to the contingent fund of the department employing them, and to such allowance from it as those who dispense that fund may award. The secrecy which such contracts impose precludes any action for their enforcement. The publicity produced by an action would itself be a breach of a contract of that kind, and thus defeat a recovery.

It may be stated as a general principle, that public policy forbids the maintenance of any suit in a court of justice, the trial of which would inevitably lead to the disclosure of matters which the law itself regards as confidential, and respecting which it will not allow the confidence to be violated. On this principle, suits cannot be maintained which would require a disclosure of the confidences of the confessional, or those between husband and wife, or of communications by a client to his counsel for professional advice, or of a patient to his physician for a similar purpose. Much greater reason exists for the application of the principle to cases of contract for secret services with the government, as the existence of a contract of that kind is itself a fact not to be disclosed.

END OF OPINION

In *Totten*, the Court explained that contracts for espionage are inherently a state secret, and in open courts we will not litigate who our spies are. Doing so would be disastrous for national security. This has, as we'll see in the other cases in this section, been extended to a more general rule that, where the very subject of the lawsuit is a state secret, the lawsuit can be dismissed on the pleadings without ever reaching the question of evidence or deciding the case on its merits. For this reason, when someone files a lawsuit where the very issue of contention is itself a state secret, the courts will likely dismiss it, regardless of how legitimate the claim is or the harm the person has suffered.

Review Questions

Let's have you analyze some practice problems using the IRAC process to develop your understanding of the *Totten* bar.

1. Greenpeace files a lawsuit against the U.S. Navy. They claim that the U.S. Navy is testing a brand new and top-secret type of sonar which is unfortunately killing an endangered species of whale off the coast of California. Greenpeace asks the court to issue an order forbidding the Navy from testing this new top-secret sonar. How should the judge rule?

2. The City of Norfolk is filing a lawsuit against the U.S. Navy. They claim that the U.S. Navy is secretly storing nuclear weapons at the Naval Weapons Station located in Yorktown, Virginia, and that radiation from those weapons has affected cancer rates in a nearby community. How should the judge rule?

3. Chang works in Chinese intelligence and is passing secrets to the Americans. He has an agreement with his handler that if he does this for three years, the CIA will smuggle him into the U.S. and pay him $100,000 per year for the rest of his life. After three years of Chang upholding his end of the bargain, he is smuggled

into the U.S., and for the first five years there, he receives his $100,000. However, after five years, the CIA is facing a budget short-fall and starts paying him only $50,000 per year, so Chang sues. How should the judge rule?

4. The ACLU files a lawsuit against the NSA, alleging that the NSA has a top-secret supercomputer and program that captures, stores, and reads every email sent in America. In their lawsuit, the ACLU asks the judge to order the NSA to stop using this computer. How should the judge rule?

When the government answers the pleadings of a plaintiff, the government simply asserts the *Totten* bar by claiming that this case cannot be litigated because doing so would reveal state secrets. If the judge believes the government, the judge should dismiss the case. This can be very unfair to plaintiffs who may have a legitimate issue; it would be unjust for them not to be able to sue because they deserve money. This is also a concern to American civil liberties because it would be very problematic if the government could engage in illegal activities under the shield of the *Totten* bar. We will explore this last concern later in this chapter.

Now, the *Totten* bar or *Totten* doctrine is itself fairly narrow — and really only applies where it is clear that the very consideration of a lawsuit would inevitably disclose secrets. There are other cases which, on the surface, do not appear to have anything involving state secrets, but as they proceed it can become apparent that parts of the case, or at least some of the evidence involved in the case, may involve state secrets which should not be admitted into evidence. Now, as a practical matter, this will likely preclude the suit, but not necessarily. This is the subject of the *Reynolds* privilege, which states that the government may not be forced to provide classified evidence or be faced with a decision to lose a case unless it discloses such evidence. Together, these rules are not unlike other forms of privilege, such as doctor/patient, priest/penitent, or attorney/client.

Protecting Classified Evidence in Civil Lawsuits — The Reynolds *Privilege*

Frequently, people file lawsuits over issues that have nothing to do with national security. The lawsuits can involve normal everyday concerns such as car accidents, contract disputes, property ownership, and other commonplace affairs. Nevertheless, even if the issue under dispute is commonplace and unrelated to national security, it is possible that some of the evidence relevant to the case might be classified. For example, let's say people are killed in a plane crash during a training mission. The fact that a military plane crashes is hardly a state secret; you hear about this a few times a year in the news and read about it in newspapers. The problem is that a plaintiff would need evidence as to why the plane crashed, and it is possible that information concerning the plane's characteristics and why it crashed might be classified. Certain aspects of how military airplanes are constructed are classified so that other countries cannot build them or develop countermeasures to defeat them. Also, the missions they go on and the tasks they perform are sometimes classified as well. So there is any number of pieces of an otherwise routine lawsuit that may involve highly sensitive secrets.

As you learned in the beginning of this chapter, during *discovery* parties are to turn over information relevant to the lawsuit, even if it is damaging. The USAF might have relevant information about a plane and why it crashed, but that information might be classified. Would the USAF have to turn over that classified information during discovery?

The answer is no. This is called the *Reynolds* privilege. The *Reynolds* privilege states that the government is lawfully allowed to withhold relevant information if releasing the information would risk revealing state secrets. Now, obviously this can be problematic to plaintiffs, who sometimes need that vital information in order for a lawsuit to pursue. Without this information, the plaintiffs are likely to lose their lawsuit as they would be unable to show a jury why the plane crashed or prove that the USAF was negligent. While we understand the needs of the USAF to keep secrets, it is also troubling, we must admit, that the *Reynolds* privilege can allow the government to avoid liability.

The term "*Reynolds* privilege" comes from a court case involving the crash of an Air Force plane and the government's refusal to turn over information in a subsequent lawsuit. The government claimed that the information, if made public in court, would damage national security. The government claimed a privilege to withhold such information during discovery, even if it was relevant to the case.

United States v. Reynolds, 345 U.S. 1 (1953)*

These lawsuits arise from the deaths of three civilians in the crash of a B-29 aircraft at Waycross, Georgia, on October 6, 1948. Because an important question of the Government's privilege to resist discovery is involved, we granted review. The aircraft had taken flight for the purpose of testing secret electronic equipment, with four civilian observers aboard. While aloft, a fire broke out in one of the bomber's engines. Six of the nine crew members, and three of the four civilian observers, were killed in the crash.

The widows of the three deceased civilian observers brought consolidated suits against the United States. During discovery, the plaintiffs moved for production of the Air Force's official accident investigation report and the statements of the three surviving crew members, taken in connection with the official investigation. The Government moved to quash the motion, claiming that these matters were privileged against disclosure because they involve state secrets. The District Judge sustained plaintiffs' motion, holding that good cause for production had been shown, rejecting the Air Force's request.

Shortly after this decision, the District Court received a letter from the Secretary of the Air Force stating that "it has been determined that it would not be in the public interest to furnish this report." The court allowed a rehearing on its earlier order, and, at the rehearing, the Secretary of the Air Force filed a formal "Claim of

---

* The case has been heavily edited and paraphrased by the authors for clarity. See disclaimer in introduction.

Privilege." This document repeated the prior claim that the Government further objected to production of the documents "for the reason that the aircraft in question, together with the personnel on board, were engaged in a highly secret mission of the Air Force." An affidavit of the Air Force's highest ranking attorney, the Judge Advocate General, United States Air Force, was also filed with the court, which asserted that the demanded material could not be furnished "without seriously hampering national security, flying safety and the development of highly technical and secret military equipment." The same affidavit offered to produce the three surviving crew members, without cost, for examination by the plaintiffs. The witnesses would be allowed to refresh their memories from any statement made by them to the Air Force, and authorized to testify as to all matters except those of a "classified nature."

We have had broad propositions pressed upon us for decision. On behalf of the Government, it has been urged that the executive department heads have power to withhold any documents in their custody from judicial view if they deem it to be in the public interest. When the Secretary of the Air Force lodged his formal "Claim of Privilege," he attempted therein to invoke the privilege against revealing military secrets, a privilege which is well established in the law of evidence. The existence of the privilege is conceded by the court below, and, indeed, by the most outspoken critics of governmental claims to privilege.

Judicial experience with the privilege which protects military and state secrets has been limited in this country. Nevertheless, the principles which control the application of the privilege emerge quite clearly from the available precedents. The privilege belongs to the Government, and must be asserted by it; it can neither be claimed nor waived by a private party. It is not to be lightly invoked. There must be formal claim of privilege, lodged by the head of the department which has control over the matter, after actual personal consideration by that officer. The court itself must determine whether the circumstances are appropriate for the claim of privilege, and yet do so without forcing a disclosure of the very thing the privilege is designed to protect. The latter requirement is the only one which presents real difficulty. As to it, we find it helpful to draw upon judicial experience in dealing with an analogous privilege, the privilege against self-incrimination.

The privilege against self-incrimination presented the courts with a similar sort of problem. Too much judicial inquiry into the claim of privilege would force disclosure of the thing the privilege was meant to protect, while a complete abandonment of judicial control would lead to intolerable abuses. Indeed, in the earlier stages of judicial experience with the problem, both extremes were advocated, some saying that the bare assertion by the witness must be taken as conclusive, and others saying that the witness should be required to reveal the matter behind his claim of privilege to the judge for verification. Neither extreme prevailed, and a sound formula of compromise was developed. This formula received authoritative expression in this country as early as the *Burr* trial. There are differences in phraseology, but, in substance, it is agreed that the court must be satisfied from all the evidence and circumstances, and "from the implications of the question, in the setting in which it is asked, that a responsive answer to the question or an explanation of why it cannot be answered might be dangerous because injurious disclosure could result." If the court is so satisfied, the claim of the privilege will be accepted without requiring further disclosure.

Regardless of how it is articulated, some formula of compromise must be applied here. Judicial control over the evidence in a case cannot be abdicated to the caprice of executive officers. Yet we will not go so far as to say that the court may automatically require a complete disclosure to the judge before the claim of privilege will be accepted in any case. It may be possible to satisfy the court, from all the circumstances of the case, that there is a reasonable danger that compulsion of the evidence will expose military matters which, in the interest of national security, should not be divulged. When this is the case, the occasion for the privilege is appropriate, and the court should not jeopardize the security which the privilege is meant to protect by insisting upon an examination of the evidence, even by the judge alone, in chambers.

In the instant case, we cannot escape judicial notice that this is a time of vigorous preparation for national defense. Experience in the past has made it common knowledge that air power is one of the most potent weapons in our scheme of defense, and that newly developing electronic devices have greatly enhanced the effective use of air power. It is equally apparent that these electronic devices must be kept secret if their full military advantage is to be exploited in the national interests. On the record before the trial court, it appeared that this accident occurred to a military plane which had gone aloft to test secret electronic equipment. Certainly there was a reasonable danger that the accident investigation report would contain references to the secret electronic equipment which was the primary concern of the mission.

When the formal claim of privilege to not disclose the accident report was filed by the Secretary of the Air Force, under circumstances indicating a reasonable possibility that military secrets were involved, there was certainly a sufficient showing of privilege to cut off further demand for the document. Where there is a strong showing of necessity for documents by a plaintiff suing the government, the claim of privilege should not be lightly accepted, but even the most compelling necessity cannot overcome the claim of privilege if the court is ultimately satisfied that military secrets are at stake.

Respondents have cited us to those cases in the criminal field, where it has been held that the Government can invoke its evidentiary privileges only at the price of letting the defendant go free rather than reveal state secrets. The rationale of the criminal cases is that, since the Government which prosecutes an accused also has the duty to see that justice is done, it is unconscionable to allow it to undertake prosecution and then invoke its governmental privileges to deprive the accused of anything which might be material to his defense. Such rationale has no application in a civil forum, where the Government is not the moving party, but is a defendant only on terms to which it has consented.

The decision of the Court of Appeals is reversed, and the case will be remanded to the District Court for further proceedings consistent with the views expressed in this opinion.

END OF OPINION

The *Reynolds* privilege allows the government to refuse to turn over classified evidence during discovery, which, if disclosed, would be harmful to national security, even if that information is very helpful, relevant, or even necessary to the plaintiff's case. When the government asserts the *Reynolds* privilege, the judge will review the classified evidence in private (the legal term is *in camera*). (Federal judges have all undergone thorough background checks and are allowed to look at classified information when their job requires it.) If the judge agrees with the government's claim that the release of this information would be harmful to national security, he will allow the government to withhold the information, no matter how helpful or necessary it would be to the plaintiff's case. However, if the judge disagrees with the government and does not believe that the information, if made public, would harm national security, then he will require the government to turn the information over.

Be careful not to confuse the *Totten* bar with the *Reynolds* privilege. Although both are core components of state secrets doctrine case law, each case addresses one of two different approaches. The *Totten* bar is an absolute prohibition of a lawsuit where the very issue of contention is a state secret, such as who our spies are or where America stores vital national security tools (submarines, nuclear weapons, etc.). In contrast, the *Reynolds* privilege merely allows the government to withhold specific evidence if that evidence is classified and its release would harm national security. The difference is that with the *Reynolds* privilege, the very issue of the lawsuit is not a state secret; it just so happens that some of the evidence involved in the case is classified. For example, in *U.S. v. Reynolds*, the fact that an airplane crashed and the civilian passengers died was not a state secret. In no way did it endanger national security for people to hear that an airplane crashed. However, it was maintained that the government having to reveal WHY the airplane crashed would disclose classified information that needed to remain classified[12]. If the airplane crashed because a top-secret piece of equipment malfunctioned, this piece of equipment should not be disclosed in open court.

Review Questions

In each of the following determine whether to apply the *Reynolds* privilege, the *Totten* bar, or neither.

1. Private Smith is operating the newest Army tank during a demonstration. The mechanics and engineering of this tank are all highly classified. Something goes wrong, and the tank veers off-course and into a crowd of observers, killing three of

---

12. Recent disclosures indicate, though, that there in fact were no actual state secrets involved in this case. See Fisher, Louis. *In the Name of National Security: Unchecked Presidential Power and the Reynolds Case* (2006) at 165–169. Nevertheless, the case remains good law for the legal doctrine.

the spectators and injuring dozens more. The families of the deceased sue the Army in a wrongful death action and demand that the Army turn over all documents it has on its investigation as to the accident.

2. A U.S. spy submarine is on a secret mission when it collides with the bottom of a Japanese whaling vessel, causing $100,000 in damage. The submarine does not stop or surface, but continues on its secret mission. The owner of the vessel knows that there is a U.S. Navy base nearby and, looking at the damage inflicted, suspects that his boat collided with a U.S. submarine. He sues the U.S. Navy for compensation for the damage to his vessel.

3. Pam is a secretary with the CIA. One day she receives a message: "Putin has invaded Ukraine. Deliver this message to CIA Director IMMEDIATELY!!!" Pam prints out the message and runs down the hall as fast as she can to the Director's office. As she runs, she bumps into Jim, a CIA analyst, who had stepped into the hall to get some more coffee. Pam knocks Jim to the ground, and he breaks his hip. Jim later sues Pam and the CIA for his injury.

4. An unmarked unmanned aerial vehicle (UAV) (drone) falls from the sky and lands in Tehran, Iran, damaging a government building. None of the components are marked, but the Iranian government suspects it is an American drone and sues the U.S. for the damage to the building.

What if the government asserts the state secrets privilege not to protect national security but rather to hide misconduct or avoid liability? This is a legitimate concern and has happened. In fact, the very case *U.S. v. Reynolds*, which gave rise to the *Reynolds* privilege, was an example of government abuse of the state secrets privilege.

In *U.S. v. Reynolds*, the government refused to turn over the accident report with information on why the plane crashed, claiming that it contained information which, if made public, would harm national security. Fifty years later, when that report was declassified, it was learned that the government had lied. There was nothing in that report which would harm national security. The Air Force had simply classified the report and refused to turn it over to avoid being held liable for the plane crash and paying money to the victims' families.

Ideally, when a person has been wronged, he should have his day in court where he'll have a fair chance to prove his case. However, in the greater interests of national security, we will sometimes deny this right. The *Totten* bar will prevent a plaintiff from even getting into the courtroom so that his case can be heard. Under the *Reynolds* privilege, a person can still bring the lawsuit, but might be severely handicapped by being unable to access key pieces of evidence. Sometimes, without certain evidence, a case cannot proceed and will have to be dismissed; this dismissal is not automatic in cases involving the *Reynolds* privilege, but it is automatic when the *Totten* bar is invoked.

To demonstrate the potential for gross injustices resulting from applying the state secrets doctrine, we'll now read the case of *Mohamed v. Jeppesen Dataplan*. Here, the plaintiff alleged that the U.S. government had forcibly extradited him to another country to be tortured. These claims, if true, would likely justify him suing the U.S. for a lot of money. However, because of the state secrets doctrine, he did not get this opportunity. As you will read, the court stated that even if his claims are true and he was tortured because of the CIA, he still could not file a lawsuit in the U.S. because litigating his case risks revealing state secrets. Whether or not his claims are true, we do not know and we may never find out. This case also provides a great summary of both the *Totten* bar and the *Reynolds* privilege to help cement your understanding of state secrets doctrine.

Mohamed v. Jeppesen Dataplan, 614 F.3d 1070 (2010)*

This case requires us to address the difficult balance the state secrets doctrine strikes between fundamental principles of our liberty, including justice, transparency, accountability and national security. Although as judges we strive to honor all of these principles, there are times when exceptional circumstances create an irreconcilable conflict between them. On those rare occasions, we are bound to follow the Supreme Court's admonition that "even the most compelling necessity cannot overcome the claim of privilege if the court is ultimately satisfied that [state] secrets are at stake." After much deliberation, we reluctantly conclude this is such a case, and the plaintiffs' action must be dismissed. Accordingly, we affirm the judgment of the district court.

I. BACKGROUND

We emphasize that this factual background is based only on the allegations of plaintiffs' complaint, which at this stage in the litigation we construe in the light most favorable to the plaintiff, taking all allegations as true and drawing all reasonable inferences from the complaint in his favor. Whether plaintiff's allegations are in fact true has not been decided in this litigation, and, given the sensitive nature of the allegations, nothing we say in this opinion should be understood otherwise.

A. Factual Background

1. The Extraordinary Rendition Program

Plaintiffs allege that the Central Intelligence Agency (CIA), working in concert with other government agencies and officials of foreign governments, operated an extraordinary rendition program to gather intelligence by apprehending foreign nationals suspected of involvement in terrorist activities and transferring them in secret to foreign countries for detention and interrogation by United States or foreign officials. According to plaintiffs, this program has allowed agents of the U.S. government to employ interrogation methods that would otherwise have been prohibited under federal or international law.

Relying on documents in the public domain, plaintiffs, all foreign nationals, claim they were each processed through the extraordinary rendition program. They also

---

* The case has been heavily edited and paraphrased by the authors for clarity. See disclaimer in introduction.

make the following individual allegations. Plaintiff Ahmed Agiza, an Egyptian national who had been seeking asylum in Sweden, was captured by Swedish authorities, allegedly transferred to American custody and flown to Egypt. In Egypt, he claims he was held for five weeks "in a squalid, windowless, and frigid cell," where he was "severely and repeatedly beaten" and subjected to electric shock through electrodes attached to his ear lobes, nipples and genitals. Agiza was held in detention for two and a half years, after which he was given a six-hour trial before a military court, convicted and sentenced to 15 years in Egyptian prison. According to plaintiffs, "virtually every aspect of Agiza's rendition, including his torture in Egypt, has been publicly acknowledged by the Swedish government."

Plaintiff Abou Elkassim Britel, a 40-year-old Italian citizen of Moroccan origin, was arrested and detained in Pakistan on immigration charges. After several months in Pakistani detention, Britel was allegedly transferred to the custody of American officials. These officials dressed Britel in a diaper and a torn t-shirt and shackled and blindfolded him for a flight to Morocco. Once in Morocco, he says he was detained incommunicado by Moroccan security services at the Temara prison, where he was beaten, deprived of sleep and food and threatened with sexual torture, including sodomy with a bottle and castration. After being released and re-detained, Britel says he was coerced into signing a false confession, convicted of terrorism-related charges and sentenced to 15 years in a Moroccan prison.

[Other Plaintiffs made similar allegations]

2. Jeppesen's Alleged Involvement in the Rendition Program

Plaintiffs contend that publicly available information establishes that defendant Jeppesen Dataplan, Inc., a U.S. corporation, provided flight planning and logistical support services to the aircraft and crew on all of the flights transporting each of the five plaintiffs among the various locations where they were detained and allegedly subjected to torture. The complaint asserts "Jeppesen played an integral role in the forced" abductions and detentions and "provided direct and substantial services to the United States for its so-called 'extraordinary rendition' program," thereby "enabling the clandestine and forcible transportation of terrorism suspects to secret overseas detention facilities." It also alleges that Jeppesen provided this assistance with actual or constructive "knowledge of the objectives of the rendition program," including knowledge that the plaintiffs "would be subjected to forced disappearance, detention, and torture" by U.S. and foreign government officials.

B. Summary of the Claims

Plaintiffs brought suit against Jeppesen under the Alien Tort Statute, 28 U.S.C. § 1350, alleging seven theories of liability marshaled under two claims, one for "forced disappearance" and another for "torture and other cruel, inhuman or degrading treatment."

With respect to the forced disappearance claim, plaintiffs assert four theories of liability: (1) direct liability for active participation, (2) conspiracy with agents of the United States, (3) aiding and abetting agents of the United States and (4) direct liability "because Jeppesen demonstrated a reckless disregard as to whether Plaintiffs would be subjected to forced disappearance through its participation in the extraordinary rendition program and specifically its provision of flight and logistical support services to aircraft and crew that it knew or reasonably should have known would be used to transport them to secret detention and interrogation."

On the torture and degrading treatment claim, plaintiffs assert three theories of liability: (1) conspiracy with agents of the U.S. in plaintiffs' torture and degrading treatment, (2) aiding and abetting agents of the U.S. in subjecting plaintiffs to torture and degrading treatment and (3) direct liability "because Jeppesen demonstrated a reckless disregard as to whether Plaintiffs would be subjected to torture or other cruel, inhuman, or degrading treatment by providing flight and logistical support to aircraft and crew it knew or reasonably should have known would be used in the extraordinary rendition program to transport them to detention and interrogation."

Regarding Jeppesen's alleged actual or constructive knowledge that its services were being used to facilitate "forced disappearances," plaintiffs allege that Jeppesen "knew or reasonably should have known that the flights involved the transportation of terror suspects pursuant to the extraordinary rendition program," that their "knowledge of the objectives of the rendition program" may be inferred from the fact that they allegedly "falsified flight plans submitted to European air traffic control authorities to avoid public scrutiny of CIA flights" and that a Jeppesen employee admitted actual knowledge that the company was performing extraordinary rendition flights for the U.S. government. Similarly, plaintiffs allege that Jeppesen knew or should have known that that torture would result because it should have known it was carrying terror suspects for the CIA and that "the governments of the destination countries routinely subject detainees to torture and other forms of cruel, inhuman, or degrading treatment." They also rely on U.S. State Department country reports describing torture as "routine" in some of the countries to which plaintiffs were allegedly rendered, and note that Jeppesen claims on its website that it "monitors political and security situations" as part of its trip planning services.

C. Procedural History

Before Jeppesen answered the complaint, the United States moved to intervene and to dismiss plaintiffs' complaint under the state secrets doctrine. The then-Director of the CIA, General Michael Hayden, filed two declarations in support of the motion to dismiss, one classified, the other redacted and unclassified. The public declaration states that "disclosure of the information covered by this privilege assertion reasonably could be expected to cause serious—and in some instances, exceptionally grave—damage to the national security of the United States and, therefore, the information should be excluded from any use in this case." It further asserts that "because highly classified information is central to the allegations and issues in this case, the risk is great that further litigation will lead to disclosures harmful to U.S. national security and, accordingly, this case should be dismissed."

The district court granted the motions to intervene and dismiss and entered judgment in favor of Jeppesen, stating that "at the core of Plaintiffs' case against

Defendant Jeppesen are 'allegations' of covert U.S. military or CIA operations in foreign countries against foreign nationals—clearly a subject matter which is a state secret." Plaintiffs appealed. A three-judge panel of this court reversed and remanded, holding that the government had failed to establish a basis for dismissal under the state secrets doctrine but permitting the government to reassert the doctrine at subsequent stages of the litigation. We took the case en banc to resolve questions of exceptional importance regarding the scope and application of the state secrets doctrine.

The government maintains its assertion of privilege on appeal, continuing to rely on General Hayden's two declarations. While the appeal was pending Barack Obama succeeded George W. Bush as President of the United States. On September 23, 2009, the Obama administration announced new policies for invoking the state secrets privilege, effective October 1, 2009, in a memorandum from the Attorney General. The government certified both in its briefs and at oral argument before the en banc court that officials at the "highest levels of the Department of Justice" of the new administration had reviewed the assertion of privilege in this case and determined that it was appropriate under the newly announced policies.

III. THE STATE SECRETS DOCTRINE

The Supreme Court has long recognized that in exceptional circumstances courts must act in the interest of the country's national security to prevent disclosure of state secrets, even to the point of dismissing a case entirely. The contemporary state secrets doctrine encompasses two applications of this principle. One completely bars adjudication of claims premised on state secrets (the "*Totten* bar"); the other is an evidentiary privilege ("the *Reynolds* privilege") that excludes privileged evidence from the case and *may* result in dismissal of the claims. We first address the nature of these applications and then apply them to the facts of this case.

A. The *Totten* Bar

In 1876 the Supreme Court stated "as a *general principle* that public policy forbids the maintenance of any suit in a court of justice, the trial of which would inevitably lead to the disclosure of matters which the law itself regards as confidential." The Court again invoked the principle in 1953, citing *Totten* for the proposition that "where the very subject matter of the action" is "a matter of state secret," an action may be "dismissed on the pleadings without ever reaching the question of evidence" because it is "so obvious that the action should never prevail over the privilege." This application of *Totten*'s general principle—which we refer to as the *Totten* bar—is "designed not merely to defeat the asserted claims, but to preclude judicial inquiry" entirely. The Court first applied this bar in *Totten* itself, where the estate of a Civil War spy sued the United States for breaching an alleged agreement to compensate the spy for his wartime espionage services. Setting forth the general principle quoted above, the Court held that the action was barred because it was premised on the existence of a "contract for secret services with the government," which was "a fact not to be disclosed." A century later, the Court applied the *Totten* bar in *Weinberger v. Catholic Action of Hawaii/Peace Education Project* (1981). There, the plaintiffs sued under the National Environmental Policy Act of 1969, to compel the Navy to prepare an environmental impact statement regarding a military facility where the Navy allegedly proposed to store nuclear weapons. The Court held that the allegations were "beyond judicial scrutiny" because, "due to national security reasons, the Navy can neither admit nor deny that it proposes to store nuclear weapons at the facility."

The Court [in *Tenet v. Doe* (2005)] more recently reaffirmed and explained the *Totten* bar in a case involving two former Cold War spies who accused the CIA of reneging on a commitment to provide financial support in exchange for their espionage services. Relying on "*Totten*'s core concern" of "preventing the existence of the plaintiffs' relationship with the Government from being revealed," the Court held that the action was, like *Totten* and *Weinberger*, incapable of judicial review . . .

Plaintiffs contend that the *Totten* bar applies *only* to a narrow category of cases they say are not implicated here, namely claims premised on a plaintiff's espionage relationship with the government. We disagree. We read the Court's discussion of *Totten* in *Reynolds* to mean that the *Totten* bar applies to cases in which "the very subject matter of the action" is "a matter of state secret." A contract to perform espionage is only an example. This conclusion is confirmed by *Weinberger*, which relied on the *Totten* bar to hold that a case involving nuclear weapons secrets, and having nothing to do with espionage contracts, was "beyond judicial scrutiny." Thus, although the claims in both *Totten* and *Tenet* were premised on the existence of espionage agreements, and even though the plaintiffs in both *Totten* and *Tenet* were themselves parties to the espionage agreements, the *Totten* bar rests on a general principle that extends beyond that specific context. We therefore reject plaintiffs' unduly narrow view of the *Totten* bar and reaffirm our holding in *Al-Haramain* that the bar "has evolved into the principle that where the very subject matter of a lawsuit is a matter of state secret, the action must be dismissed without reaching the question of evidence." As we explain below, the *Totten* bar is a narrow rule, but it is not as narrow as plaintiffs contend.

We also disagree with plaintiffs' related contention that the *Totten* bar cannot apply unless the *plaintiff* is a party to a secret agreement with the government. The environmental groups and individuals who were the plaintiffs in *Weinberger* were not parties to agreements with the United States, secret or otherwise. The purpose of the bar, moreover, is to prevent the revelation of state secrets harmful to national security, a concern no less pressing when the plaintiffs are strangers to the espionage agreement that their litigation threatens to reveal. Thus, even if plaintiffs were correct that the *Totten* bar is limited to cases premised on espionage agreements with the government, we would reject their contention that the bar is necessarily limited to cases in which the plaintiffs are themselves parties to those agreements.

B. The *Reynolds* Privilege

In addition to the *Totten* bar, the state secrets doctrine encompasses a rivilege against revealing military or state secrets, a privilege which is well established in the law of evidence. A successful assertion of privilege under *Reynolds* will remove the privileged evidence from the litigation. Unlike the *Totten* bar, a valid claim of privilege under *Reynolds* does not automatically require dismissal of the case. In some instances, however, the assertion of privilege will require dismissal because it will become apparent during the *Reynolds* analysis that the case cannot proceed without privileged evidence, or that litigating the case to a judgment on the merits would present an unacceptable risk of disclosing state secrets.

Reynolds involved a military aircraft carrying secret electronic equipment. After the plane crashed, the estates of three civilian observers killed in the accident brought tort claims against the government. In discovery, plaintiffs sought production of the Air Force's official accident investigation report and the statements of three surviving crew members. The Air Force refused to produce the materials, citing the need to protect national security and military secrets. The district court ordered the government to produce the documents in camera so the court could determine whether they contained privileged material. When the government refused, the court sanctioned the government by establishing the facts on the issue of negligence in plaintiffs' favor.

The Supreme Court reversed and sustained the government's claim of privilege because "there was a reasonable danger that the accident investigation report would contain references to the secret electronic equipment which was the primary concern of the mission." The Court also provided guidance on how claims of privilege should be analyzed and held that, under the circumstances, the district court should have sustained the privilege without even requiring the government to produce the report for in camera review. The Court did not, however, dismiss the case outright. Rather, given that the secret electronic equipment was unrelated to the cause of the accident, it remanded to the district court, affording plaintiffs the opportunity to try to establish their claims without the privileged accident report and witness statements.

Analyzing claims under the *Reynolds* privilege involves three steps:

First, we must "ascertain that the procedural requirements for invoking the state secrets privilege have been satisfied." Second, we must make an independent determination whether the information is privileged. Finally, "the ultimate question to be resolved is how the matter should proceed in light of the successful privilege claim."

We discuss these steps in turn.

1. Procedural Requirements

a. Assertion of the privilege. "The privilege belongs to the Government and must be asserted by it; it can neither be claimed nor waived by a private party. The privilege "is not to be lightly invoked." This is especially true when, as in this case, the government seeks not merely to preclude the production of particular items of evidence (as in *Reynolds*) but to obtain dismissal of the entire action.

To ensure that the privilege is invoked no more often or extensively than necessary, *Reynolds* held that "there must be a formal claim of privilege, lodged by the head of the department which has control over the matter, after actual personal consideration by that officer." This certification is fundamental to the government's claim of privilege. As we have observed in a different context, the decision to invoke the privilege must "be a serious, considered judgment, not simply an administrative formality." The formal claim must reflect the certifying official's *personal* judgment; responsibility for this task may not be delegated to lesser-ranked officials. The claim also must be presented in sufficient detail for the court to make an independent determination of the validity of the claim of privilege and the scope of the evidence subject to the privilege.

In the present case, General Michael Hayden, then-Director of the CIA, asserted the initial, formal claim of privilege and submitted detailed public and classified declarations. We were informed at oral argument that the current Attorney General, Eric Holder, has also reviewed and approved the ongoing claim of privilege. Although *Reynolds* does not require review and approval by the Attorney General when a different agency head has control of the matter, such additional review by the executive branch's chief lawyer is appropriate and to be encouraged.

b. Timing. Plaintiffs contend that the government's assertion of privilege was premature, urging that the *Reynolds* privilege cannot be raised before an obligation to produce specific evidence subject to a claim of privilege has actually arisen. We disagree. The privilege may be asserted at any time, even at the pleading stage.

The privilege indisputably may be raised with respect to discovery requests seeking information the government contends is privileged. Courts have repeatedly sustained claims of privilege under those circumstances. In addition, the government may raise the privilege to prevent the disclosure of privileged information in a responsive pleading.

We also conclude that the government may assert a *Reynolds* privilege claim prospectively, even at the pleading stage, rather than waiting for an evidentiary dispute to arise during discovery or trial. . . . In some cases, the court may be able to determine with certainty from the nature of the allegations and the government's declarations in support of its claim of secrecy that litigation must be limited or cut off in order to protect state secrets, even before any discovery or evidentiary requests have been made. In such cases, waiting for specific evidentiary disputes to arise would be both unnecessary and potentially dangerous. . . . The showing the government must make to prevail on a claim of state secrets privilege may be especially difficult when attempted before any request for specific information or evidence has actually been made, but foreclosing the government from even trying to make that showing would be inconsistent with the need to protect state secrets.

2. The Court's Independent Evaluation of the Claim of Privilege

When the privilege has been properly invoked, the court must make an independent determination whether the information is privileged. The court must sustain a claim of privilege when it is satisfied, "from all the circumstances of the case, that there is a reasonable danger that compulsion of the evidence will expose matters which, in the interest of national security, should not be divulged." If this standard is met, the evidence is absolutely privileged, irrespective of the plaintiffs' countervailing need for it. "Even the most compelling necessity cannot overcome the claim of privilege if the court is ultimately satisfied that state secrets are at stake."

This step in the *Reynolds* analysis places on the court a special burden to assure itself that an appropriate balance is struck between protecting national security matters and preserving an open court system. In evaluating the need for secrecy, we acknowledge the need to defer to the Executive on matters of foreign policy and national security and surely cannot legitimately find ourselves second guessing the Executive in this arena. But the state secrets doctrine does not represent a surrender of judicial control over access to the courts.

Rather, to ensure that the state secrets privilege is asserted no more frequently and sweepingly than necessary, it is essential that the courts continue critically to examine instances of its invocation. We take very seriously our obligation to review the government's claims with a very careful, indeed a skeptical, eye, and not to accept at face value the government's claim or justification of privilege, though we must do so without forcing a disclosure of the very thing the privilege is designed to protect. Too much judicial inquiry into the claim of privilege would force disclosure of the thing the privilege was meant to protect, while a complete abandonment of judicial control would lead to intolerable abuses.

We do not offer a detailed definition of what constitutes a state secret. The Supreme Court in *Reynolds* found it sufficient to say that the privilege covers "matters which, in the interest of national security, should not be divulged." We do note, however, that an executive decision to *classify* information is insufficient to establish that the information is privileged. The privilege may not be used to shield any material not strictly necessary to prevent injury to national security. Although classification may be an indication of the need for secrecy, treating it as conclusive would trivialize the court's role, which the Supreme Court has clearly admonished "cannot be abdicated to the caprice of executive officers."

3. How Should the Matter Proceed?

When a court sustains a claim of privilege, it must then resolve "how the matter should proceed in light of the successful privilege claim." The court must assess whether it is feasible for the litigation to proceed without the protected evidence and, if so, how.

When the government successfully invokes the state secrets privilege, "the evidence is completely removed from the case." "Whenever possible, sensitive information must be disentangled from nonsensitive information to allow for the release of the latter." However, there will be occasions when, as a practical matter, secret and nonsecret information cannot be separated. In some cases, therefore, "it is appropriate that the courts restrict the parties' access not only to evidence which itself risks the disclosure of a state secret, but also those pieces of evidence or areas of questioning which press so closely upon highly sensitive material that they create a high risk of inadvertent or indirect disclosures." "If seemingly innocuous information is part of a mosaic, the state secrets privilege may be invoked to bar its disclosure and the court cannot order the government to disentangle this information from other [i.e., secret] information."

Ordinarily, simply excluding or otherwise walling off the privileged information may suffice to protect the state secrets and "the case will proceed accordingly, with no consequences save those resulting from the loss of evidence." In some instances, however, application of the privilege may require dismissal of the action. When this point is reached, the *Reynolds* privilege converges with the *Totten* bar, because both require dismissal. There are three circumstances when the *Reynolds* privilege would justify terminating a case.

First, if the plaintiff cannot prove the essential parts of her claim with nonprivileged evidence, then the court may dismiss her claim as it would with any plaintiff who cannot prove her case. Second, if the privilege deprives the government (or other defendant responsible for maintaining state secrets<i.e., Lockheed Martin>) of information that would otherwise give the government a valid defense to the claim, then the court may rule in favor of the government to dismiss the claim.

Third, and relevant here, even if the claims and defenses might theoretically be established without relying on privileged evidence, it may be impossible to proceed with the litigation because—privileged evidence being inseparable from nonprivileged information that will be necessary to the claims or defenses—litigating the case to a judgment on the merits would present an unacceptable risk of disclosing state secrets.... Litigation should be entirely foreclosed at the outset by dismissal of the action if it appears that "the danger of inadvertent compromise of the protected state secrets outweighs the public and private interests in attempting formally to resolve the dispute while honoring the privilege." As we shall explain, this circumstance exists here and requires dismissal.

IV. APPLICATION

We therefore turn to the application of the state secrets doctrine in this case. The government contends that the lawsuits should be dismissed, whether under the *Totten* bar or the *Reynolds* privilege, because "state secrets are so central to this case that permitting further proceedings would create an intolerable risk of disclosure that would jeopardize national security."

In contrast, plaintiffs argue that the *Totten* bar does not apply and that, even if the government is entitled to some protection under the *Reynolds* privilege, at least some claims survive. The district court appears to have dismissed the action under the *Totten* bar, making a "threshold determination" that "the very subject matter of the case is a state secret." Having dismissed on that basis, the district court did not address whether application of the *Reynolds* privilege would require dismissal.

We do not find it quite so clear that the very subject matter of this case is a state secret. Nonetheless, having conducted our own detailed analysis, we conclude that the district court reached the correct result because dismissal is warranted even under *Reynolds*. Recognizing the serious consequences to plaintiffs of dismissal, we explain our ruling so far as possible within the considerable constraints imposed on us by the state secrets doctrine itself.

A. The *Totten* Bar

The categorical absolute protection the Court found necessary in enunciating the *Totten* rule is appropriate only in narrow circumstances. The *Totten* bar applies only when the "very subject matter" of the action is a state secret—i.e., when it is "obvious" without conducting the detailed analysis required by *Reynolds* "that the action could never prevail over the privilege." The Court has applied the *Totten* bar on just three occasions, involving two different kinds of state secrets: In *Tenet* and *Totten* the Court applied the *Totten* bar to the distinct class of cases that depend upon clandestine spy relationships, and in *Weinberger* the Court applied the *Totten* bar to a case that depended on whether the Navy proposed to store nuclear weapons at a particular facility. Although the Court has not limited the *Totten* bar to cases premised on secret espionage agreements or the location of nuclear weapons, neither has it offered much guidance on when the *Totten* bar applies beyond these limited circumstances. Because the *Totten* bar is rarely applied and not clearly defined, because it is a judge made doctrine with extremely harsh consequences and because conducting a more detailed analysis will tend to improve the accuracy, transparency and legitimacy of the proceedings, district courts presented with disputes about state secrets should ordinarily undertake a detailed *Reynolds* analysis before deciding whether dismissal on the pleadings is justified.

Here, some of the plaintiffs' claims might well fall within the *Totten* bar. In particular, their allegations that Jeppesen conspired with agents of the United States in plaintiffs' forced disappearance, torture and degrading treatment are premised on the existence of an alleged covert relationship between Jeppesen and the government—a matter that the Fourth Circuit Court of Appeals has concluded is "practically indistinguishable from that categorically barred by *Totten* and *Tenet*." On the other hand, allegations based on plaintiffs' theory that Jeppesen should be liable simply for what it "should have known" about the alleged unlawful extraordinary rendition program while participating in it are not so obviously tied to proof of a secret agreement between Jeppesen and the government.

We do not resolve the difficult question of precisely which claims may be barred under *Totten* because application of the *Reynolds* privilege leads us to conclude that this litigation cannot proceed further. We rely on the *Reynolds* privilege rather than the *Totten* bar for several reasons. First, the government has asserted the *Reynolds* privilege along with the *Totten* bar, inviting the further inquiry *Reynolds* requires and presenting a record that compels dismissal even on this alternate ground. Second, we have discretion to affirm on any basis supported by the record. Third, resolving this case under *Reynolds* avoids difficult questions about the precise scope of the *Totten* bar and permits us to conduct a searching judicial review, fulfilling our obligation under *Reynolds* "to review the government's claim with a very careful, indeed a skeptical, eye, and not to accept at face value the government's claim or justification of privilege."

B. The *Reynolds* Privilege

There is no dispute that the government has complied with *Reynolds*' procedural requirements for invoking the state secrets privilege by filing General Hayden's formal claim of privilege in his public declaration We therefore focus on the second and third steps in the *Reynolds* analysis: *First,* whether and to what extent the matters the government contends must be kept secret are in fact matters of state secret; and *second,* if they are, whether the action can be litigated without relying on evidence that would necessarily reveal those secrets or press so closely upon them as to create an unjustifiable risk that they would be revealed. In doing so, we explain our decision as much as we can without compromising the secrets we are required to protect.

1. Whether and to What Extent the Evidence Is Privileged

The government asserts the state secrets privilege over four categories of evidence. In particular, the government contends that neither it nor Jeppesen should be compelled, through a responsive pleading, discovery responses or otherwise, to disclose: "[1] information that would tend to confirm or deny whether Jeppesen or any other private entity assisted the CIA with clandestine intelligence activities; [2] information about whether any foreign government cooperated with the CIA in clandestine intelligence activities; [3] information about the scope or operation of the CIA terrorist detention and interrogation program; [or 4] any other information concerning CIA clandestine intelligence operations that would tend to reveal intelligence activities, sources, or methods." These indisputably are matters that the state secrets privilege may cover. As the U.S. Supreme Court made clear . . . state secrets doctrine affords an "absolute protection" against revealing espionage relationships.

. . .

We have thoroughly and critically reviewed the government's public and classified declarations and are convinced that at least some of the matters it seeks to protect from disclosure in this litigation are valid state secrets, which, in the interest of national security, should not be divulged. The government's classified disclosures to the court are persuasive that compelled or inadvertent disclosure of such information in the course of litigation would seriously harm legitimate national security interests. In fact, every judge who has reviewed the government's formal, classified claim of privilege in this case agrees that in this sense the claim of privilege is proper, although we have different views as to the scope of the privilege and its impact on plaintiffs' case. The plaintiffs themselves do not dispute that, during the course of litigation, there may well be relevant evidence that may be properly withheld pursuant to the privilege.

We are precluded from explaining precisely which matters the privilege covers lest we jeopardize the secrets we are bound to protect. We can say, however, that the secrets fall within one or more of the four categories identified by the government and that we have independently and critically confirmed that their disclosure could be expected to cause significant harm to national security.

2. Effect on the Proceedings

Having determined that the privilege applies, we next determine whether the case must be dismissed under the *Reynolds* privilege. We have thoroughly considered plaintiffs' claims, several possible defenses and the prospective path of this litigation. We also have carefully and skeptically reviewed the government's classified submissions, which include supplemental information not presented to the district court. We rely heavily on these submissions, which describe the state secrets implicated here, the harm to national security that the government believes would result from explicit or implicit disclosure and the reasons why, in the government's view, further litigation would risk that disclosure.

Given plaintiffs' extensive submission of public documents and the stage of the litigation, we do not rely on the first two circumstances in which the *Reynolds* privilege requires dismissal—that is, whether plaintiffs could prove the basics of their case without privileged evidence, or whether the privilege deprives Jeppesen of evidence that would otherwise give it a valid defense to plaintiffs' claims. Instead, we assume without deciding that plaintiffs' basic case and Jeppesen's defenses may not inevitably depend on privileged evidence. Proceeding on that assumption, we hold that dismissal is nonetheless required under *Reynolds* because there is no feasible way to litigate Jeppesen's alleged liability without creating an unjustifiable risk of divulging state secrets.

We reach this conclusion because all seven of plaintiffs' claims, even if taken as true, describe Jeppesen as providing logistical support in a broad, complex process, certain aspects of which, the government has persuaded us, are absolutely protected by the state secrets privilege. Notwithstanding that some information about that process has become public, Jeppesen's alleged role and its attendant liability cannot be isolated from aspects that are secret and protected. Because the facts underlying plaintiffs' claims are so infused with these secrets, *any* plausible effort by Jeppesen to defend against them would create an unjustifiable risk of revealing state secrets, even if plaintiffs could make a basic case on one or more claims with nonprivileged evidence.

Here, further litigation presents an unacceptable risk of disclosure of state secrets no matter what legal or factual theories Jeppesen would choose to advance during a defense. Whether or not Jeppesen provided logistical support in connection with the extraordinary rendition and interrogation programs, there is precious little Jeppesen could say about its relevant conduct and knowledge without revealing information about how the United States government does *or does not* conduct covert operations. Our conclusion holds no matter what protective procedures the district court might employ. Adversarial litigation, including pretrial discovery of documents and witnesses and the presentation of documents and testimony at trial, is inherently complex and unpredictable. Although district courts are well equipped to wall off isolated secrets from disclosure, the challenge is exponentially greater in exceptional cases like this one, where the relevant secrets are difficult or impossible to isolate and even efforts to define a boundary between privileged and unprivileged evidence would risk disclosure by implication. In these rare circumstances, the risk of disclosure that further proceedings would create cannot be averted through the use of devices such as protective orders or restrictions on testimony. Dismissal at the pleading stage under *Reynolds* is a drastic result and should not be readily granted.

A case may fall outside the *Totten* bar and yet it may become clear during the *Reynolds* analysis that dismissal is required at the outset. . . . Here, our detailed *Reynolds* analysis reveals that the claims and possible defenses are so infused with state secrets that the risk of disclosing them is both apparent and inevitable. Dismissal under these circumstances, like dismissal under the *Totten* bar, reflects the general principle that "public policy forbids the maintenance of any suit in a court of justice, the trial of which would inevitably lead to the disclosure of matters which the law itself regards as confidential, and respecting which it will not allow the confidence to be violated."

Although we are necessarily precluded from explaining precisely why this case cannot be litigated without risking disclosure of state secrets, or the nature of the harm to national security that we are convinced would result from further litigation, we are able to offer a few observations.

First, we recognize that plaintiffs have proffered hundreds of pages of publicly available documents that they say corroborate some of their allegations concerning Jeppesen's alleged participation in aspects of the extraordinary rendition program. As the government has acknowledged, its claim of privilege does not extend to public documents. Accordingly, we do not hold that any of the documents plaintiffs have submitted are subject to the privilege; rather, we conclude that even assuming plaintiffs could establish their entire case *solely* through nonprivileged evidence — unlikely as that may be — any effort by Jeppesen to defend would unjustifiably risk disclosure of state secrets.

. . .

Second, we do not hold that the existence of the extraordinary rendition program is itself a state secret. The program has been publicly acknowledged by numerous government officials including the President of the United States. Even if its mere existence may once have been a "matter which, in the interest of national security, should not be divulged," it is not a state secret now.

Third, we acknowledge the government's official certification of the assertion of the state secrets privilege comports with the revised standards set forth in the current administration's September 23, 2009 memorandum, adopted several years after the government first invoked the privilege in this case. Those standards require the responsible agency to show that "assertion of the privilege is necessary to protect information the unauthorized disclosure of which reasonably could be expected to cause significant harm to the national defense or foreign relations." They also mandate that the Department of Justice "will not defend an invocation of the privilege in order to: (i) conceal violations of the law, inefficiency, or administrative error; (ii) prevent embarrassment to a person, organization, or agency of the United States government; (iii) restrain competition; or (iv) prevent or delay the release of information the release of which would not reasonably be expected to cause significant harm to national security." That certification here is consistent with our independent conclusion, having reviewed the government's public and classified declarations, that the government is not invoking the privilege to avoid embarrassment or to escape scrutiny of its recent controversial transfer and interrogation policies, rather than to protect legitimate national security concerns.

VI. CONCLUSION

We emphasize that it should be a rare case when the state secrets doctrine leads to dismissal at the outset of a case. Nonetheless, there are such cases—not just those subject to *Totten*'s per se rule, but those where the mandate for dismissal is apparent even under the more searching examination required by *Reynolds*. This is one of those rare cases.

For all the reasons the dissent articulates—including the impact on human rights, the importance of constitutional protections and the constraints of a judge-made doctrine—we do not reach our decision lightly or without close and skeptical scrutiny of the record and the government's case for secrecy and dismissal. We expect our decision today to inform district courts that *Totten* has its limits, that every effort should be made to parse claims to salvage a case like this using the *Reynolds* approach, that the standards for peremptory dismissal are very high and it is the district court's role to use its fact-finding and other tools to full advantage before it concludes that the rare step of dismissal is justified. We also acknowledge that this case presents a painful conflict between human rights and national security. As judges, we have tried our best to evaluate the competing claims of plaintiffs and the government and resolve that conflict according to the principles governing the state secrets doctrine set forth by the United States Supreme Court.

For the reasons stated, we hold that the government's valid assertion of the state secrets privilege warrants dismissal of the litigation, and affirm the judgment of the district court. The government shall bear all parties' costs on appeal.

END OF OPINION.

This opinion's recap of the state secrets privilege, both *Totten* and *Reynolds*, emphasizes that we do recognize that certain information should absolutely be kept out of court. We do not want the identities of our spies or the designs of nuclear weapons being revealed. At the same time, we do not want to create a shield which enables the government to hide its own misconduct like it did in *Reynolds* (as we later learned), or possibly even get away with human rights abuses like torture, as *Mohamed* alleged. Striking this balance is very difficult, but when in doubt, courts tend to err on the side of national security. Here, you can read an edited memo from the U.S. Department of Justice about how it should handle state secrets.

Office of the Attorney General

Washington D.C.

September 23, 2009

MEMORANDUM FOR HEADS OF EXECUTIVE DEPARTMENTS AND AGENCIES MEMORANDUM FOR THE HEADS OF DEPARTMENT COMPONENTS

FROM: The ATTORNEY GENERAL

SUBJECT: Policies and Procedures Governing Invocation of the State Secrets Privilege

I am issuing today new Department of Justice policies and administrative procedures that will provide greater accountability and reliability in the invocation of the state secrets privilege in litigation. The Department is adopting these policies and procedures to strengthen public confidence that the U.S. Government will invoke the privilege in court only when genuine and significant harm to national defense or foreign relations is at stake and only to the extent necessary to safeguard those interests. The policies and procedures set forth in this Memorandum are effective as of October 1. 2009, and the Department shall apply them in all cases in which a government department or agency thereafter seeks to invoke the state secrets privilege in litigation.

1. Standards for Determination

A. Legal Standard. The Department will defend an assertion of the state secrets privilege ("privilege") in litigation when a government department or agency seeking to assert the privilege makes a sufficient showing that assertion of the privilege is necessary to protect information the unauthorized disclosure of which reasonably could be expected to cause significant harm to the national defense or foreign relations ("national security' ") of the United States. With respect to classified information, the Department will defend invocation of the privilege to protect information properly classified pursuant to Executive Order 12958, as amended, or any successor order, at any level of classification, so long as the unauthorized disclosure of such information reasonably could be expected to cause significant harm to the national security of the United States. With respect to information that is nonpublic but not classified, the Department will also defend invocation of the privilege so long as the disclosure of such information reasonably could be expected to cause significant harm to the national security of the United States.

B. Narrow Tailoring. The Department's policy is that the privilege should be invoked only to the extent necessary to protect against the risk of significant harm to national security. The Department will seek to dismiss a litigant's claim or case on the basis of the state secrets privilege only when doing so is necessary to protect against the risk of significant harm to national security.

C. Limitations. The Department will not defend an invocation of the privilege in order to: (i) conceal violations of the law, inefficiency, or administrative error; (ii) prevent embarrassment to a person, organization, or agency of the United States government; (iii) restrain competition; or (iv) prevent or delay the release of information the release of which would not reasonably be expected to cause significant harm to national security.

2. Initial Procedures for Invocation of the Privilege

A. Evidentiary Support. A government department or agency seeking invocation of the privilege in litigation must submit to the Division in the Department with responsibility for the litigation in question1 a detailed declaration based on personal knowledge that specifies in detail: (i) the nature of the information that must be protected from unauthorized disclosure; (ii) the significant harm to national security that disclosure can reasonably be expected to cause; (iii) the reason why unauthorized disclosure is reasonably likely to cause such harm; and (iv) any other information relevant to the decision whether the privilege should be invoked in litigation.

The assertion of the state secrets doctrine remains very controversial, as many argue that its broad application allows wrongdoing by the government or by government contractors to escape scrutiny.[13] Consider, for example, the following: Government contractors are brought in to advise the CIA on interrogations procedures. Later investigations disclose that the interrogation procedures designed by these contractors constitute torture under both U.S. and international law.

1. Should innocent victims of such interrogation procedures (meaning those who were interrogated but found to have no involvement at all in terrorist activities) be able to bring a lawsuit for their injury and suffering?
2. Does it matter whether the government has acknowledged the interrogations?
3. Should the government be forced to disclose the names of the contractors who developed the interrogation programs?

Key Terms

Classified Information Procedure Act (CIPA)—A statute that contains procedural protections against unnecessary disclosure of classified information in criminal trials. The primary purpose of CIPA was to limit the threat by a criminal defendant to disclose classified information during the course of a trial.

Graymail—A threat by a criminal defendant to disclose classified information during the course of a trial, presenting the government with a demand to either allow disclosure of the classified information or dismiss the indictment.

***Reynolds* privilege**—Application of the state secrets privilege that allows a civil case to go forward, but applies an evidentiary rule that results in exclusion of specific evidence from a legal case based on affidavits submitted by the government stating that introducing this evidence into court proceedings might disclose sensitive information which might endanger national security.

---

13. See, for example "Background on the State Secrets Privilege," American Civil Liberties Union, retrieved from https://www.aclu.org/background-state-secrets-privilege on 1 May 2016.

State secrets doctrine—The state secrets privilege, when properly invoked, permits the government to block the release of any information in a lawsuit that, if disclosed, would cause harm to national security.

Totten **bar**—The strongest application of the state secrets privilege in a civil lawsuit when the very issue of contention is a state secret, allowing the court to dismiss the matter without hearing the merits of the case.

Further Reading

Cassman, Daniel R., *Keep It Secret, Keep It Safe: An Empirical Analysis of the State Secrets Doctrine.* 67 Stan. L. Rev. 1173(2015).

Fisher, Louis, *In the Name of National Security: Unchecked Presidential Power and the Reynolds Case* (University Press of Kansas, 2006).

Radsan, Afsheen John, *Remodeling the Classified Information Procedures Act (CIPA)* William Mitchell Legal Studies Research Paper No. 2010-09 (2010); Cardozo Law Review, Forthcoming. Available at SSRN: http://ssrn.com/abstract=1580239 or http://dx.doi.org/10.2139/ssrn.1580239

Telman, D. A. Jeremy, *Our Very Privileged Executive: Why the Judiciary Can (and Should) Fix the State Secrets Privilege* (2007). Law Faculty Publications. Paper 5. Available at http://scholar.valpo.edu/law_fac_pubs/5

Telman, D. A. Jeremy, *Intolerable Abuses: Rendition for Torture and the State Secrets Privilege*, 63 Ala. L. Rev. 429 (2012).

Vladeck, Stephen I., *The New National Security Canon.* 61 Am. U. L. Rev. 1295 (2012).

Vladeck, Stephen I., *Terrorism Trials and the Article III Courts after Abu Ali.* Texas Law Review, Forthcoming; American University, WCL Research Paper No. 2010-09 (2010). Available at SSRN: http://ssrn.com/abstract=1591065

Chapter 7

Bars to Litigating National Security Matters

Overview

The previous chapter discussed the state secrets doctrine and how that makes it difficult to bring some cases involving national security issues to court for rulings. In addition to the state secrets doctrine, there are other procedural issues plaintiffs face when they sue the government involving matters of national security. A procedural issue is something which has nothing to do with the merits of the facts or the substance of a case, but instead is a rule which governs how a case can be litigated, or if it can even be litigated at all, regardless of its merits. The three that we now focus on are:

1. Political Question
2. Standing
3. Ripeness

All three of these are based on constitutional principles that we introduced back in Chapter 1. A *political question* is a matter the courts will not examine because it is considered to be within the purview of the political process—a matter to be decided between Congress and the president. It is a part of the underlying separation of powers that forms the basis of our constitutional system. *Standing* is the issue of who has the right to sue. Just because a perceived wrong has occurred does not mean that just anyone can file a lawsuit over an issue. Only a person who has been harmed can sue. *Ripeness* is when a party is allowed to sue. As a general rule, one can only sue *after* an injury has occurred and not before. *Standing* and *ripeness* come from the language in Article III that gives the judicial branch authority over cases and controversies. A person who lacks standing can't sue because that person is not involved in the underlying controversy. And, until actual harm is suffered (or is inevitable), a case or controversy does not yet arise, and the issues are not ripe for consideration by the courts.

We'll discuss each of these in turn, and, as you will see, we will also look at some of the issues that arise when these procedural issues are applied to national security cases.

Political Questions

As noted earlier, a *political question* is a matter the courts will not examine because the matter is considered to be within the purview of the political process—a matter to be decided between Congress and the president, perhaps through elections, but certainly not in the courts. This concept was raised as early as in the historic Supreme Court case of *Marbury v. Madison* (1803), which we read in Chapter 1. In that case, you will remember, Chief Justice John Marshall pointed out a difference between two distinct functions of the secretary of state. Marshall stated that when the secretary of state was performing a purely discretionary matter, such as advising the president on matters of policy, he was not held to any legally identifiable standards. Therefore, some of the secretary's actions are unable to be reviewed by a court of law. The act of transferring the commission was not discretionary but administrative, and so that aspect of the case was properly before the court. But no court would take a case that would evaluate whether or not the advice a secretary of state might give a president was proper.

Think of it this way; in life, people tend to have areas in which they work and perform a job, and there will be other areas where they don't work. For example, a lawyer will represent people in court, and no matter how good the lawyer is at trying cases, he absolutely will not and should not perform brain surgery. Performing brain surgery is beyond the skills, training, and experiences of a lawyer, although it is perfectly acceptable for a neurosurgeon to do so.

Similarly, when it comes to a political question, the courts have recognized that it is within their job description to decide legal questions (the Constitution refers to these as "cases and controversies") and determine what the law is, but they will not decide public policy matters such as, for example, who "the enemy of America" is or how to conduct a military operation. That is the job of the president and Congress, and not judges who should be limited to deciding only legal disputes. For example, it is the job of Congress and not a judge to write laws, while the judge's job is to merely interpret the law as it already exists. It is also the job of the president and not the judge to execute the laws that Congress has enacted.

The leading Supreme Court case in the area of political question doctrine is *Baker v. Carr*, 369 U.S. 186 (1962). That case is considered to be the best explanation of when the political question should and should not apply. In this opinion, the Supreme Court outlined six characteristics of a political question. These include:

- A "textually demonstrable constitutional commitment of the issue to a coordinate political department; or"
- A "lack of judicially discoverable and manageable standards for resolving it; or"
- The "impossibility for a court's independent resolution without expressing a lack of respect for a coordinate branch of the government; or"
- The "impossibility of deciding the issue without an initial policy decision, which is beyond the discretion of the court; or"
- An "unusual need for unquestioning adherence to a political decision already made; or"

- The "potentiality of embarrassment from multifarious pronouncements by various departments on one question."

There can obviously be a dispute over what is or is not a "political question," especially when it comes to the issues that arise in national security cases. Let's look at some decisions that involve the political question doctrine.

El-Shifa Pharmaceutical Industries Co. v. United States, 607 F.3d 836 (2010)*

The owners of a Sudanese pharmaceutical plant sued the United States for unjustifiably destroying the plant, failing to compensate them for its destruction, and defaming them by asserting they had ties to Osama bin Laden. The district court dismissed their complaint. A panel of this court affirmed, holding that the political question doctrine barred the plaintiffs' claims. After granting rehearing en banc, we now affirm the district court on the same ground.

On August 7, 1998, the terrorist network headed by Osama bin Laden bombed United States embassies in Kenya and Tanzania. Hundreds were killed and thousands injured. On August 20, the United States responded by launching nearly simultaneous missile strikes against two targets: a terrorist training camp in Afghanistan and a factory in Sudan believed to be "associated with the bin Laden network" and "involved in the production of materials for chemical weapons." President Clinton addressed the American people, explaining "the objective of this action and why it was necessary." "Our target was terror; our mission was clear: to strike at the network of radical groups affiliated with and funded by Usama bin Laden, perhaps the preeminent organizer and financier of international terrorism in the world today." "The risks from inaction, to America and the world, would be far greater than action," the President proclaimed, "for that would embolden our enemies, leaving their ability and their willingness to strike us intact."

In a letter to the Congress the President reported that the strikes "were a necessary and proportionate response to the imminent threat of further terrorist attacks against U.S. personnel and facilities" and "were intended to prevent and deter additional attacks by a clearly identified terrorist threat." The following day, in a radio address to the nation, President Clinton explained his decision to take military action, stating, "Our goals were to disrupt bin Laden's terrorist network and destroy elements of its infrastructure in Afghanistan and Sudan. And our goal was to destroy, in Sudan, the factory with which bin Laden's network is associated, which was producing an ingredient essential for nerve gas. Citing "compelling evidence that the bin Laden network was poised to strike at us again" and was seeking to acquire chemical weapons, the President declared that "we simply could not stand idly by."

Other government officials elaborated upon the President's justifications for the attack on the plant. On the day of the strike, the Secretary of Defense stated that bin

---

* The case has been heavily edited and paraphrased by the authors for clarity. See disclaimer in introduction.

Laden "had some financial interest in contributing to this particular facility." An unnamed "senior intelligence official" asserted at a press briefing, "We know that bin Laden has made financial contributions to the Sudanese Military Industrial Complex, of which, we believe, the Shifa pharmaceutical plant is part." And on August 23, the National Security Advisor maintained that "Osama bin Laden was providing key financial help for the plant."

The plaintiffs in this case are the El-Shifa Pharmaceutical Industries Company (El-Shifa), the owner of the plant, and Salah El Din Ahmed Mohammed Idris (Idris), the principal owner of El-Shifa. They allege that striking the plant was a mistake, that it "was not a chemical weapons facility, was not connected to bin Laden or to terrorism, and was not otherwise a danger to public health and safety." Instead, the plaintiffs contend, the plant was Sudan's largest manufacturer of medicinal products, responsible for producing over half the pharmaceuticals used in Sudan. Because the case comes to us on appeal from a dismissal for lack of subject-matter jurisdiction, we take the plaintiffs' allegations as true.

According to the plaintiffs, within days of the attack, the press debunked the President's assertions that the plant was involved with chemical weapons and associated with bin Laden. Confronted with their error, senior administration and intelligence officials backpedaled, issuing what the plaintiffs characterize as "revised" or "new justifications" for the strike and conceding that any relationship between bin Laden and the plant was "indirect." Although the United States attacked the plant without knowing who owned it, officials learned within three days of the strike that Idris was the owner. After that point, "unidentified U.S. government officials" began telling reporters that Idris maintained direct or indirect financial relations with bin Laden, purchased the plant on bin Laden's behalf, acted as a front man or agent for bin Laden in Sudan, and had "ties" to bin Laden. The plaintiffs contend that neither the contemporaneous nor post-hoc justifications for the attack were true: "All of the justifications for the attack advanced by the United States were based on false factual premises and were offered with reckless disregard of the truth based upon grossly incomplete research and unreasonable analysis of inconclusive intelligence."

It is emphatically the province and duty of the judicial department to say what the law is, but some questions, in their nature political, are beyond the power of the courts to resolve. The political question doctrine is essentially a function of the separation of powers, and excludes from judicial review those controversies which revolve around policy choices and value determinations constitutionally committed for resolution to the halls of Congress or the confines of the Executive Branch. The doctrine of political question is designed to restrain the Judiciary from inappropriate interference in the business of the other branches of Government.

It is that no justiciable 'controversy' exists when parties seek adjudication of a political question. In the seminal case of *Baker v. Carr*, the Supreme Court explained that a claim presents a political question if it involves:

> [1] a textually demonstrable constitutional commitment of the issue to a coordinate political department; or [2] a lack of judicially discoverable and

manageable standards for resolving it; or [3] the impossibility of deciding without an initial policy determination of a kind clearly for nonjudicial discretion; or [4] the impossibility of a court's undertaking independent resolution without expressing lack of the respect due coordinate branches of government; or [5] an unusual need for unquestioning adherence to a political decision already made; or [6] the potentiality of embarrassment from multifarious pronouncements by various departments on one question. To find a political question, we need only conclude that one of these factors is present, not all.

Disputes involving foreign relations, such as the one before us, are quintessential sources of political questions. Because these cases raise issues that frequently turn on standards that defy judicial application or involve the exercise of a discretion demonstrably committed to the executive or legislature. Matters intimately related to foreign policy and national security are rarely proper subjects for judicial intervention, yet it is error to suppose that every case or controversy which touches foreign relations lies beyond judicial cognizance. Even in the context of military action, the courts may sometimes have a role. Therefore, we must conduct "a discriminating analysis of the particular question posed" in the "specific case" before the court to determine whether the political question doctrine prevents a claim from going forward.

In undertaking this discriminating analysis, we note, for example, that the political question doctrine does not bar a claim that the government has violated the Constitution simply because the claim implicates foreign relations. Because the judiciary is the "ultimate interpreter of the Constitution," in most instances claims alleging its violation will rightly be heard by the courts. No policy underlying the political question doctrine suggests that Congress or the Executive, or both acting in concert and in compliance with Art. I, can decide the constitutionality of a statute; that is a decision for the courts. Similarly, that a case may involve the conduct of the nation's foreign affairs does not necessarily prevent a court from determining whether the Executive has exceeded the scope of prescribed statutory authority or failed to obey the prohibition of a statute or treaty. One of the Judiciary's characteristic roles is to interpret statutes, and we cannot shirk this responsibility merely because of the "interplay" between the statute and "the conduct of this Nation's foreign relations."

We have consistently held, however, that courts are not a forum for reconsidering the wisdom of discretionary decisions made by the political branches in the realm of foreign policy or national security. In this vein, we have distinguished between claims requiring us to decide whether taking military action was "wise"—"a policy choice and value determination constitutionally committed for resolution to the halls of Congress or the confines of the Executive Branch"—and claims "presenting purely legal issues" such as whether the government had legal authority to act. Accordingly, we have declined to adjudicate claims seeking only a "determination whether the alleged conduct should have occurred." The presence of a political question in these cases turns not on the nature of the government conduct under review but more precisely on the question the plaintiff raises about the challenged action.

The political question doctrine bars our review of claims that, regardless of how they are presented to the court, call into question the prudence of the political branches (meaning President and Congress), in matters of foreign policy or national security constitutionally committed to their discretion. A plaintiff may not, for instance, clear the political question bar simply by "recasting such foreign policy and national security questions in tort terms." ... For example, in reviewing the Secretary of State's designation of a group as a "foreign terrorist organization" under the Antiterrorism and Effective Death Penalty Act, 8 U.S.C. § 1189 (2006), we may decide whether the government has followed the proper procedures, whether the organization is foreign, and whether it has engaged in terrorist activity, but we may not determine whether "the terrorist activity of the organization threatens the security of United States nationals or the national security of the United States". Whether this last criterion has been met presents a nonjusticiable political question because the Secretary's assessments of whether the terrorist activities of foreign organizations constitute threats to the United States are political judgments, decisions of a kind for which the Judiciary has neither aptitude, facilities nor responsibility and have long been held to belong in the domain of political power not subject to judicial intrusion or inquiry. The court may not reassess policy choices and value determinations the Constitution entrusts to the political branches, which are the President and Congress.

The conclusion that the strategic choices directing the nation's foreign affairs are constitutionally committed to the political branches reflects the institutional limitations of the judiciary and the lack of manageable standards to channel any judicial inquiry into these matters. The concept of a textual commitment to a political branch is not completely separate from the concept of a lack of judicially discoverable and manageable standards for resolving it; the lack of judicially manageable standards may strengthen the conclusion that there is a textually demonstrable commitment to a coordinate branch. We must decline to reconsider what are essentially policy choices because "the Judiciary is particularly ill suited to make such decisions, as 'courts are fundamentally underequipped to formulate national policies or develop standards for matters not legal in nature.'" In military matters in particular, the courts lack the competence to assess the strategic decision to deploy force or to create standards to determine whether the use of force was justified or well-founded.

The complex, subtle, and professional decisions as to the control of a military force are essentially professional military judgments, subject always to civilian control of the Legislative and Executive Branches. The ultimate responsibility for these decisions is appropriately vested in branches of the government which are periodically subject to electoral accountability. It is not the role of judges to second-guess, with the benefit of hindsight, another branch's determination that the interests of the United States call for military action.

The case at hand involves the decision to launch a military strike abroad. Conducting the discriminating analysis of the particular question posed by the claims the plaintiffs press on appeal, we conclude that both raise nonjusticiable political questions. The law-of-nations claim asks the court to decide whether the United

States' attack on the plant was "mistaken and not justified." The defamation claim similarly requires us to determine the factual validity of the government's stated reasons for the strike. If the political question doctrine means anything in the arena of national security and foreign relations, it means the courts cannot assess the merits of the President's decision to launch an attack on a foreign target, and the plaintiffs ask us to do just that. Therefore, we affirm the district court's dismissal of the plaintiffs' law-of-nations and defamation claims.

The plaintiffs' complaint asserts that customary international law requires states to compensate foreign nationals for property destruction that is mistaken and not justified. We hold this claim barred by the political question doctrine. We begin our analysis with the rule we have already identified and upon which both parties agree: courts cannot reconsider the wisdom of discretionary foreign policy decisions. The plaintiffs' law-of-nations claim falls squarely within this prohibition because it would require us to declare that the bombing of the El-Shifa plant was "mistaken and not justified." Whether an attack on a foreign target is justified—that is whether it is warranted or well-grounded—is a quintessential "policy choice and value determination constitutionally committed for resolution to the halls of Congress or the confines of the Executive Branch."

By asserting the El-Shifa bombing was "mistaken," the plaintiffs apparently mean that the United States would not have launched the strike if the relevant decisionmakers knew at the time what they allegedly know now—that the plant was neither involved in producing chemical weapons nor associated with bin Laden. But the political question doctrine does not permit us to mimic the constitutional role of the political branches by guessing how they would have conducted the nation's foreign policy had they been better informed. Whether the circumstances warrant a military attack on a foreign target is a "substantive political judgment entrusted expressly to the coordinate branches of government," and using a judicial forum to reconsider its wisdom would be anathema to the separation of powers. Undertaking a counterfactual inquiry into how the political branches would have exercised their discretion had they known the facts alleged in the plaintiffs' complaint would be to make a political judgment, not a legal one.

Moreover, Baker's prudential considerations counsel judicial restraint as well. First, the court lacks judicially manageable standards to adjudicate whether the attack on the El-Shifa plant was "mistaken and not justified." Courts are "ill equipped to determine the authenticity and utterly unable to assess the adequacy" of the government's "reasons for deeming nationals of a particular country a special threat." We could not decide this question without first fashioning out of whole cloth some standard for when military action is justified. The judiciary lacks the capacity for such a task. As we once said of a claim that certain covert operations were "wrongful," there are no judicially discoverable and manageable standards for the resolution of such a claim.

Second, the decision to take military action is a "policy determination of a kind clearly for nonjudicial discretion." Such foreign policy decisions are "delicate, complex, and involve large elements of prophecy. They are decisions of a kind for which the Judiciary has neither aptitude, facilities nor responsibility." In short, the decision to launch the military attack on the El-Shifa plant was constitutionally committed to the political branches, and this court is neither an effective nor appropriate forum for reweighing its merits. Because the plaintiffs' law-of-nations claim requires the court to second-guess that decision, we conclude that it presents a nonjusticiable political question.

In refusing to declare the El-Shifa attack "mistaken and not justified," we do not mean to imply that the contrary is true. We simply decline to answer a question outside the scope of our authority. By requiring that we reserve judgment, the political question doctrine protects the Congress and the Executive from judicial "invasion of their sphere," and guards against "the reputation of the Judicial Branch being 'borrowed by the political Branches to cloak their work in the neutral colors of judicial action.'"

The plaintiffs also claim that anonymous government officials defamed them by making statements linking them to bin Laden and international terrorism. This claim fares no better than their law-of-nations claim. It too would require the court to reconsider the merits of the decision to strike the El-Shifa plant by determining whether the government's justifications for the attack were false.

We begin by noting that the court cannot judge the veracity of the President's initial public explanations for the attack for the same reasons we cannot examine whether the attack was "mistaken and not justified." The President's statements justifying the attack are "inextricably intertwined" with a foreign policy decision constitutionally committed to the political branches because determining whether the President's statements were true would require a determination whether the alleged conduct should have occurred. A decision in favor of the plaintiffs would unavoidably involve a rejection of the Clinton Administration's stated justifications for launching the missile strike. A decision against the plaintiffs would affirm the wisdom of the Administration's decision to attack.

The plaintiffs maintain, however, that even if the political question doctrine bars review of the President's initial justifications for the attack, the court may nevertheless judge the veracity of the subsequent justifications, as defamatory and slanderous claims against them. Their argument is that the President defamed them by falsely claiming that they were associated with Osama bin Laden and were producing biological and chemical weapons for him.

We disagree. The allegedly defamatory statements cannot be disassociated from the initial justifications for the attack. The court cannot adjudicate the truth of the government's later justifications because, despite the plaintiffs' arguments to the contrary, they are fundamentally the same as the initial justifications. Even if what the plaintiff is saying is true, we find no material difference between the allegedly defamatory statements and the President's contemporaneous explanation of his decision to take military action.

On the day the United States destroyed the El-Shifa plant, President Clinton told the American people that he ordered the strike in part because the plant was "associated with the bin Laden network" and was a "chemical weapons-related facility." In their prayer for relief, the plaintiffs describe the allegedly defamatory statements as "claims . . . that Mr. Idris or El-Shifa are connected to Osama bin Laden, terrorist groups or the production of chemical weapons." This characterization of the allegedly defamatory statements closely tracks the President's own description of his reasons for launching the attack.

All of the allegedly defamatory statements essentially repeat the President's initial justification for the strike. Each describes a connection between bin Laden and the plant through its owner, Salah Idris. For example, "U.S. intelligence officials" stated Idris dealt financially with members of Islamic Jihad, which had been "absorbed into bin Laden's terror network." And government officials claimed "the owner and manager of the plant were . . . front men for bin Laden." Contrary to the plaintiffs' contentions, these statements do not represent a break from the President's contemporaneous explanation of his reasons for launching the strike. At most, they elaborate upon the nature of the connection between the plant and bin Laden—a connection the President offered on the day of the attack as one reason for taking military action. Declaring these later statements true or false would require us to make the same judgment about the President's initial justification for the attack.

The plaintiffs contend that Idris's alleged ties to bin Laden—the factual issue at the heart of their defamation claim—could not have played any part in the decision to bomb the plant because, at the time of the strike, the United States thought the plant was owned by the Sudanese government and not by Idris. Therefore, they argue, the court could declare the government's allegations that Idris was connected to bin Laden false without undermining the government's actual justifications for the attack. To be sure, at least one anonymous official had previously suggested the plant belonged to the Sudanese Military Industrial Complex. But this is beside the point. The President explained that the United States targeted the plant because it was associated with bin Laden, and officials continued to assert that same rationale when they told reporters the plant's owner was financially linked to bin Laden's network. A court's pronouncement that the plant's owner had no financial ties to bin Laden would directly contradict the government's justification for the attack by disclaiming the asserted association between the plant and the bin Laden network.

Under the political question doctrine, the foreign target of a military strike cannot challenge in court the wisdom of retaliatory military action taken by the United States. Despite their efforts to characterize the case differently, that is just what the plaintiffs have asked us to do.

END OF OPINION

In *El-Shifa*, the government purposefully bombed a pharmaceutical plant in Sudan, mistakenly believing that the plant's owners were connected to Osama bin Laden and that the plant was going to produce biological & chemical weapons for Al-Qaeda. After the bombing, it was discovered that the government's intelligence was incorrect, and the plant was in no way connected to terrorism. This mistake had lethal consequences because, prior to the bombing, the pharmacy provided 50% of all medications in Sudan. It is estimated that because the plant was no longer able to produce medications in an area of the world where they are much needed, thousands of innocent Sudanese people died; without the plant, there were shortages for medications that treat deadly but maintainable diseases such as malaria and tuberculosis.

When the plant's owners sued the U.S., they were seeking compensation for the loss of their plant and for being defamed (slandered) by U.S. officials who had mistakenly linked them to murderous terrorists including Osama bin Laden and the Al-Qaeda network. Imagine how you would feel if the president of the United States publicly announced that you were connected to terrorists and then had your property destroyed, even though you were completely innocent. You would probably expect some form of justice in court.

Even though the government's basis for the attack had been completely mistaken, the court refused to hear the case. Instead, the court dismissed the case as a "political question." The court explained that it is up to the president and Congress, and not the courts, to evaluate the credibility of intelligence and decide who America's enemies are and who should be attacked in the name of national security. Furthermore, any review or reconsideration of whom the political branches decided to attack was inappropriate interference by the judiciary. There are certain issues, especially policy decisions and judgments in going after America's enemies, which are beyond the purview of the courts.

Review Questions

Work through these fact settings to explore how the concept of a political question relates to national security.

1. Ari is an American studying abroad in Yemen with zero ties to terrorists. He learns from leaked intelligence documents on Wikileaks that the CIA has put his name on a list that contains members of Al-Qaeda. The people on this list are being targeted for killing by Predator drones. Ari knows that he is not associated with terrorists and that the CIA has clearly made a mistake in putting his name on this "kill list." In a panic to get his name off the list, through his attorney, Ari petitions a federal district court in the U.S. to declare that the CIA is mistaken and that he is not a terrorist, so his name should not be on the list. How should the court decide?

2. U.S. Air Force General Myers, a member of the military and thus the executive (president's) branch of government, is in charge of the U.S. military response to Russia's invasion of Ukraine. He announces a plan to send F-22s to the area as a show of force to deter Russia from sending any major military technology into Ukraine. The human rights group Coalition for Peace is concerned that this overt show of force violates international law because it is a major act of aggression by the U.S. The Constitution states that declaring war is the role of Congress, and the Coalition for Peace believes General Myers might trigger a war with his plan. They file a lawsuit asking a judge to issue an injunction, a court order, to prohibit the General from deploying F-22s around Ukraine. IRAC the judge's response to the Coalition for Peace lawsuit.

In *El-Shifra*, the court stated "that the strategic choices directing the nation's foreign affairs are constitutionally committed to the political branches reflects the institutional limitations of the judiciary and the lack of manageable standards to channel any judicial inquiry into these matters." This means that there are no set rules on how certain the president must be or how good intelligence must be before the president can make life and death policy decisions.

Does this mean that the courts are powerless to prevent the president from making terrible decisions and committing what are arguably numerous military acts of aggression, as was alleged in *El-Shifa*, because these actions are deemed necessary for national security? Quite possibly, the answer is "yes." The court stated, "Courts cannot reconsider the wisdom of discretionary foreign policy decisions." Furthermore, "In military matters in particular, the courts lack the competence to assess the strategic decision to deploy force or to create standards to determine whether the use of force was justified or well founded."

It may be alarming to consider that the courts are relatively powerless to prevent unwise, mistaken, or even dangerous decisions or actions by the president or Congress before-the-fact or to provide remedy after-the-fact. This fear is not completely unfounded. In fact, history shows us that the political question has been used to prevent courts from hearing matters involving issues of grave importance to national security.

The case of *Lowry v. Reagan*, which we read next, is one example. In this case, the Supreme Court ruled that they are unable to decide whether a president's unilateral use of military force, without the prior authorization of Congress, is permissible or not.

Throughout our history there has been tension between the ability of the president to commit U.S. forces to combat and the authority of the Congress to declare war. Following the Vietnam conflict, Congress enacted, over the veto of the president, the War Powers Resolution (WPR) which purported to limit the ability of the president to commit the United States to military combat without congressional involvement. Now, it has to be noted that every president from Carter through Obama has asserted that the WPR is unconstitutional, an infringement on the president's obligations as commander-in-chief, and so presidents have always acted "consistent with" as opposed to "as required by" the Resolution.

In the events leading up to this case, President Ronald Reagan unilaterally directed the U.S. Navy to enter into a military engagement with Iran. The United States had been involved in escorting neutral oil tankers through the Persian Gulf during a war between Iraq and Iran. Iranian forces had attacked some of these vessels, launching attacks from oil platforms located in the Gulf. President Reagan authorized an operation to neutralize the forces conducting these attacks. The War Powers Resolution of 1973 contains a clause requiring the president to notify Congress within 48 hours whenever the military is entered into "hostilities." This is to prevent secret wars from being undertaken without congressional oversight, such as the secret bombing of Cambodia. In this situation, President Reagan did not notify Congress about the naval engagement within the 48-hour timeframe contained in the War Powers Resolution. As a result, 110 members of Congress filed suit.

We look at the War Powers Resolution in more detail in the next chapter. Here, though, focus on the issue of the political question doctrine and how it limits the power of courts.

Lowry v. Reagan, 676 F. Supp. 333 (1987)*

Plaintiffs, 110 members of the House of Representatives, contend that the reporting requirement of section 4(a)(1) of the War Powers Resolution was triggered by the July 22, 1987, initiation of United States escort operations in the Persian Gulf and by the September 21, 1987, attack on an Iranian Navy ship laying mines in the Persian Gulf. Specifically, plaintiffs contend that United States Armed Forces have been introduced, without a declaration of war, "into hostilities or into situations where imminent involvement in hostilities is clearly indicated by the circumstances." Plaintiffs petition this Court to declare that the President was required to file reports concerning both the July and September incidents and to order the President to submit a report concerning continued use of United States Armed Forces in the Persian Gulf within forty-eight hours of the order in this case. For the reasons stated below, the Court declines to accept jurisdiction and DISMISSES this action.

I. THE WAR POWERS RESOLUTION

The War Powers Resolution, enacted over a presidential veto on November 7, 1973, sets forth procedures intended to guarantee Congress, in the absence of a declaration of war, an active role in all decisions concerning the deployment of United States Armed Forces into hostilities abroad. The procedures set forth in the War Powers Resolution include the requirement that the President consult with Congress "in every possible instance" before introducing United States Armed Forces into hostilities and, in any event, that the President submit a written report to the Speaker of the House of Representatives and the President pro tempore of the Senate within forty-eight hours of introducing "United States Armed Forces . . . into hostilities or into situations where imminent involvement in hostilities is clearly indicated by the circumstances." Although the War Powers Resolution provides for two other circumstances in which presidential reports must be filed, it is only when a report is filed to reflect the introduction of troops "into hostilities or into situations where imminent involvement in hostilities is clearly indicated by the circumstances."

II. FACTS

The current case concerns the application of the War Powers Resolution to recent activities of United States Armed Forces in the Persian Gulf. The Persian Gulf, a body of water partly bounded by Iran and Iraq, has become the site of numerous military incidents in the ongoing war between these two belligerents. In response to an increase in attacks on commercial shipping during 1986, Kuwait requested the

---

* The case has been heavily edited and paraphrased by the authors for clarity. See disclaimer in introduction.

United States to provide protection for Kuwaiti petroleum tankers passing through the Persian Gulf. The United States responded affirmatively on March 7, 1987, and the first reflagged tankers, escorted by United States Navy warships, entered the Persian Gulf by way of the Strait of Hormuz on July 22, 1987. Two days later a reflagged tanker, the S.S. Bridgeton, was seriously damaged when it struck a mine. On September 21, 1987, United States naval forces fired at an Iranian Navy ship that was laying mines in the Persian Gulf.

The executive and legislative branches gave prompt consideration to the applicability of the War Powers Resolution to these events. The Administration has stated that the War Powers Resolution does not apply to the escort operation in the Persian Gulf. Legislative debate on this topic is reflected in the introduction of several bills to invoke the War Powers Resolution with regard to the situation in the Persian Gulf. Recently, the Senate rejected Senator Brock Adams' bill to authorize the escort operations under the War Powers Resolution but moved to set new rules for handling future war powers disputes. Congress also debated the question of whether the War Powers Resolution should be amended or even repealed. Last summer, 110 Members of the House of Representatives and 3 Senators filed the initial complaint in this action.

III. ANALYSIS

Plaintiffs seek to enforce the War Powers Resolution. Plaintiffs contend that they should prevail as a matter of law because these facts indicate the existence of "hostilities" and, therefore, trigger the section 4(a)(1) reporting requirement. Defendant, in contrast, maintains that this case should be dismissed because it does not present a justiciable controversy. Defendant argues that the doctrines of standing, political question and equitable discretion all preclude judicial review. Defendant also maintains that plaintiffs fail to state a claim for which relief may be granted because a private right of action cannot be implied under the War Powers Resolution. The parties do not present the constitutionality of the War Powers Resolution to this Court.

This Court declines to exercise jurisdiction over this case in light of constraints of the political question doctrine. If the Court were to decide whether the President is required to submit a report to Congress under section 4(a)(1) of the War Powers Resolution, the Court also would have to decide whether United States Armed Forces in the Persian Gulf either are engaged in "hostilities" or in "situations where imminent involvement in hostilities is clearly indicated by the circumstances." Because the Court concludes that the exercise of federal jurisdiction in these circumstances would be both inappropriate and imprudent, the Court GRANTS defendant's Motion and DISMISSES this case.

The Political Question Doctrine

The profusion of relevant congressional activity also indicates that this case must be dismissed as a prudential matter under the political question doctrine. In a now-classic catalogue of conditions to which the political question doctrine applies, Mr. Justice Brennan explained in *Baker v. Carr* that:

prominent on the surface of any case held to involve a political question is found a textually demonstrable constitutional commitment of the issue to a coordinate political department; or a lack of judicially discoverable and manageable standards for resolving it; or the impossibility of deciding without an initial policy determination of a kind clearly for non-judicial discretion; or the impossibility of a court's undertaking independent resolution without expressing lack of respect due coordinate branches of government; or an unusual need for unquestioning adherence to a political decision already made; or the potentiality of embarrassment from multifarious pronouncements by various departments on one question.

Mr. Justice Brennan also stated, with regard to cases concerning foreign relations, that these matters often lie beyond judicial cognizance due the need for a "single-voiced statement of the Government's views." Mr. Justice Brennan noted, however, that it would be error to presume that all such cases are nonjusticiable absent "a discriminating analysis of the question posed."

Having analyzed the question in this case, the Court concludes that plaintiffs' request for declaratory relief presents a nonjusticiable political question. If the Court were to grant or deny declaratory relief, and decide whether United States Armed Forces stationed in the Persian Gulf are engaged in "hostilities or in situations where imminent involvement in hostilities is clearly indicated by the circumstances," the Court would risk the potentiality of embarrassment that would result from multifarious pronouncements by various departments on one question. Indeed, such a declaration necessarily would contradict legislative pronouncements on one side or the other of this issue. Moreover, a declaration of "hostilities" by this Court could impact on statements by the Executive that the United States is neutral in the Iran-Iraq war and, moreover, might create doubts in the international community regarding the resolve of the United States to adhere to this position. Because this Court concludes that the volatile situation in the Persian Gulf demands, in the words of *Baker v. Carr*, a "single-voiced statement of the Government's views," the Court refrains from joining the debate on the question of whether "hostilities" exist in that region.

The Court nonetheless notes that, had the constitutionality of the War Powers Resolution been squarely presented, "these prudential considerations would not have been relevant." Indeed, if Congress had enacted a joint resolution stating that "hostilities" existed in the Persian Gulf for purposes of section 4(a)(1) of the War Powers Resolution, but if the President still refused to file a section 4(a) report, this Court would have been presented with an issue ripe for judicial review. The Court's task then would have been to analyze the constitutional division of powers rather than to evaluate the seriousness of military activities. The former is within the purview of the judiciary.

IV. CONCLUSION

This Court will not take jurisdiction of this suit to enforce the War Powers Resolution because of the constraints of the political question doctrine. The constitutionality of the War Powers Resolution is not before the Court. Although adjudication of constitutional questions should not be encouraged, the courts nonetheless would have the responsibility of resolving the constitutionality of this provision if it were properly presented.

Therefore, defendant's Motion to Dismiss is GRANTED and this case is DISMISSED.

END OF OPINION

In this case, members of Congress and the president were involved in a political dispute as to whether or not a series of naval military operations between the U.S. and Iran in the Persian Gulf was so large or of a nature so as to constitute "hostilities" as defined in the War Powers Resolution, so as to trigger the clause which requires the president to formally notify Congress. The court's view was that issuing a ruling as to the meaning of "hostilities" would be akin to making a military judgment as to the size and nature of a conflict. The court refused to do this.

Recall from our previous discussion, courts are reluctant to involve themselves in military affairs, and leave those decisions to the president and Congress. Additionally, the court also properly recognized that this issue was a political dispute between the president and Congress. Courts are generally reluctant to involve themselves in disputes between the political branches, and here the court noted how members of Congress were trying to enact legislation on the matter, and did not want the court to give an order in lieu of the proper political process.

Despite the rationale and good reasons for the judiciary not wanting to involve itself in a political dispute, there are obvious problems with this approach. If the court refuses to step in how can a dispute over these issues ever be decided? Who but a Court can rule on the legitimacy of a president's decision whether or not the U.S. is engaged in "hostilities?"[1] If the decision to use force is always deemed a "political question," preventing any court from ever enforcing the reporting clause of the War Powers Resolution, which is intended to limit the president's unilateral and sometimes secretive use of force, is there any meaningful "check and balance" involved?

Recall the discussion on constitutional authority from the early chapters of the book[2] and the importance placed on the ability of the president to exercise his Article II authority. Can Congress limit the power the Constitution gives the president? Can the courts? Presidents will argue that this power — to unilaterally decide that a declaration of war is not necessary, but still decide to direct forces into battle — is consistent with Article II authority, while Congress will argue it infringes on their Article I authority, and no resolution will be possible.

As the previous opinions have stated, the issue of a political question not only includes questioning the wisdom and prudence of military decisions, but also of other

---

1. While there is some truth to this statement concerning minor conflicts, a court has recognized that in hostilities on the scale of Vietnam where 50,000 Americans dies, there are clearly "hostilities." Crocket, 558 F. Supp. at 898-899.
2. Review the decisions of the Court in Baker v. Carr, Curtiss-Wright, and the Youngstown Steel cases.

foreign policy decisions. Over the years, many U.S. policy leaders have made highly questionable and arguably unethical decisions when it comes to foreign affairs. There have been instances, particularly in Latin America, where the U.S. supported dictatorships with atrocious human rights records because these despots were hostile to communism. At the time, communism was a greater threat to America and our national interests than these dictatorships. Protecting the United States from the spread of a Soviet-dominated movement was viewed as worth the potential cost to American values that supporting these dictators would represent. And real people were harmed in these countries but, as explained in the opinion below, those persons who believed themselves harmed by diplomatic decisions by U.S. leaders could not sue the U.S. government because doing so would require the courts to second guess decisions by political leaders, thus creating a non-judiciable political question.

This next case dealt with just that situation.

Schneider v. Kissinger, 412 F.3d 190 (2005)*

René and Raúl Schneider, surviving sons of deceased Chilean General René Schneider, brought this against the United States and Henry Kissinger, who at the time of the relevant events was the National Security Advisor to the President of the United States. The complaint alleged that Kissinger and the United States had caused, in conjunction with Chilean persons not named as defendants, the kidnapping, torture, and death of their father, General Schneider. Because we believe that the courts lack jurisdiction over nonjusticiable questions raised by the complaint, we dismiss the case.

I. Background

Appellants filed their original complaint on September 10, 2001, identifying their relationship to the deceased general and claiming against Kissinger, the United States, and Richard Helms (former Director of the CIA). That complaint alleged that in 1970 the leader of the Chilean leftist coalition, Dr. Salvador Allende, won a slight plurality of the vote (36.3%) in Chile's presidential election, and that this victory on his part created the expectation that he would, in the following months, be ratified by the Chilean congress as the first socialist president of the country. According to the complaint, "key United States policymakers" opposed the choice of Allende as president of Chile and on September 8, 1970, "policymakers" began the process of assessing "the pros and cons and problems and prospects involved should a Chilean military coup be organized . . . with U.S. assistance." After receiving further information, on September 15, 1970, defendants Kissinger, Helms, and Attorney General John Mitchell met with President Nixon. The President ordered that steps be taken to prevent Allende from becoming president, and specifically, that the CIA was to "play a direct role in organizing a military coup d'etat in Chile" and do quickly whatever was possible to prevent the seating of a possible socialist president. The President expressed that he was "not concerned" about any risks

---

* The case has been heavily edited and paraphrased by the authors for clarity. See disclaimer in introduction.

involved, authorized $10 million in funds to effect such a coup, and required a plan of action be drafted within 48 hours.

The complaint further alleged that efforts to prevent Allende from achieving the presidency proceeded on two tracks. "Track I" was a covert political, economic, and propaganda campaign approved by a subcabinet level body of the executive established to exercise political control over covert operations abroad. "Track II" activities were undertaken in direct response to the President's September 15 order and were directed "towards actively promoting and encouraging the Chilean military to move against Allende." In the following months, the tracks moved together. The United States Ambassador to Chile was authorized to encourage a military coup and to intensify contacts with Chilean military officers in order to ascertain their willingness to support such a coup. The Ambassador was also authorized to make contacts in the Chilean military aware that the military would receive no military assistance from the United States if Allende became president of Chile. The Ambassador reported back that General Schneider would be an impediment to achieving the goals outlined in the President's directive, and that he would have to be neutralized. The complaint went on to allege particular acts undertaken in furtherance of the goal of establishing a military coup and claims for relief based on those actions, including the kidnapping, torture, and killing of General Schneider. In all, the complaint alleged seven claims: (1) summary execution; (2) torture; (3) cruel, inhumane, or degrading treatment; (4) arbitrary detention; (5) wrongful death; (6) assault and battery; and (7) intentional infliction of emotional distress.

II. The Political Question Doctrine

The principle that the courts lack jurisdiction over political decisions that are by their nature "committed to the political branches to the exclusion of the judiciary" is as old as the fundamental principle of judicial review. In the venerable case of *Marbury v. Madison*, Chief Justice Marshall first expressed the recognition by the judiciary of the existence of a class of cases constituting "political acts, belonging to the executive department alone, for the performance of which entire confidence is placed by our Constitution in the supreme executive; and for any misconduct respecting which, the injured individual has no remedy." In a continuing line beginning with Chief Justice Marshall's analysis in *Marbury v. Madison*, this doctrine has evolved as a limitation of the jurisdiction of the courts particularly applicable to foreign relations. Chief Justice Marshall, writing again in *United States v. Palmer* (1818), described questions of foreign policy as "belonging more properly to those who can place the nation in such a position with respect to foreign powers as to their own judgment shall appear wise; to whom are entrusted all its foreign relations; then to that tribunal whose power as well as duty is confined to the application of the rule which the legislature may prescribe for it." Contemporary application of the Political Question Doctrine draws on the analysis set forth in *Baker v. Carr* (1962). The *Baker* Court first recognized that "the political question doctrine is 'primarily a function of the separation of powers.'" In *Baker*, the Supreme Court enumerated six factors that may render a case nonjusticiable under the Political Question Doctrine:

Prominent on the surface of any case held to involve a political question is found a [1] textually demonstrable constitutional commitment of the issue to a coordinate political department; or [2] a lack of judicially discoverable and manageable standards for resolving it; or [3] the impossibility of deciding without an initial policy determination of a kind clearly for nonjudicial discretion; or [4] the impossibility of a court's undertaking independent resolution without expressing lack of respect due coordinate branches of government; or [5] an unusual need for unquestioning adherence to a political decision already made; or [6] the potentiality of embarrassment of multifarious pronouncements by various departments on one question.

The *Baker* analysis lists the six factors in the disjunctive, not the conjunctive. To find a political question, we need only conclude that one factor is present, not all. Nonetheless, we note that most of the factors counsel against the exercise of jurisdiction over the controversy that Plaintiff-Appellants bring to the court.

1. Textually demonstrable constitutional commitment to other branches

First, the lawsuit raises policy questions that are textually committed to a coordinate branch of government. As the Supreme Court suggested in *Marbury* and made clear in later cases, "The conduct of the foreign relations of our Government is committed by the Constitution to the Executive and Legislative—'the political'—Departments of the Government, and the propriety of what may be done in the exercise of this political power is not subject to judicial inquiry or decision." Otherwise put, "foreign policy decisions are the subject of just such a textual commitment," as contemplated in *Baker v. Carr*.

Absent precedent, there could still be no doubt that decision-making in the fields of foreign policy and national security is textually committed to the political branches of government. Article I, Section 8 of the Constitution provides an enumeration of powers of the legislature. That article is richly laden with delegation of foreign policy and national security powers. Direct allocation of such power is found in Section 8, Clause 1, "the Congress shall have the Power To . . . provide for the Common Defense . . ."; Clause 3, "To regulate commerce with foreign nations"; Clause 10, "To define and punish Piracies and Felonies committed on the High Seas and Offenses against the Law of Nations"; Clause 11, "To declare War, grant Letters of Marque and Reprisal, and make Rules concerning Captures on Land and Water"; Clause 12, "To raise and support Armies . . ."; Clause 13, "To provide and maintain a Navy"; Clause 14, "to make Rules for the Government and Regulation of the land and naval Forces"; Clause 15, "To provide for calling forth the Militia to . . . repel Invasions"; Clause 16, "To provide for organizing, arming, and disciplining, the Militia, and for governing such Part of them as may be employed in the Service of the United States."

In addition to these direct allocations to the Congress of these foreign relations and national security powers, other sections and clauses of Article I bear on the subject to provide further weight to the conclusion of contextual allocation. For example, Section 9 of Article I provides for the suspension of the writ of habeas corpus "when in cases of . . . invasion the public safety may require it." Section 10 allocates to the Congress the authority to provide consent to individual states, without which they may not "enter into any Agreement or Compact with . . . a foreign Power, or engage in War. . . ." This is not to mention the perhaps less direct but undeniably real connection between national security and other powers of Congress, such as that under Article I, Section 8, Clause 1, to "lay and collect Taxes," and Clause 2, to "borrow money on the credit of the United States."

Just as Article I of the Constitution evinces a clear textual allocation to the legislative branch, Article II likewise provides allocation of foreign relations and national security powers to the President, the unitary chief executive. Article II, Section 2 provides, that "the President shall be Commander in Chief of the Army and Navy of the United States, and of the Militia of the several States, when called into the actual Service of the United States. . . ." That same section further provides that the President "shall have Power, by and with the Advice and Consent of the Senate, to make Treaties, [and to] appoint Ambassadors, other public Ministers and Consuls." Section 3 of Article II provides that "he shall receive Ambassadors and other public Ministers . . . and shall Commission all the Officers of the United States," including obviously the officers of the military.

While the language of textual commitment of the President is not as extensive as that relating to the legislative branch, nonetheless it is plain that that commitment is real. Indeed, the Supreme Court has described the President as possessing "plenary and exclusive power" in the international arena and "as the sole organ of the federal government in the field of international relations. . . ."

By contrast, in Article III defining the judicial power of the United States the closest there is to a reference to foreign relations is the extension of jurisdiction to "Cases affecting Ambassadors, other public Ministers and Consuls." U.S. CONST., Art. III, § 1. Obviously all this provides is jurisdiction for adjudication of cases against those officers. It provides no authority for policymaking in the realm of foreign relations or provision of national security. It cannot then be denied that decision-making in the areas of foreign policy and national security is textually committed to the political branches.

Neither can it be overlooked that the subject matter of the instant case involves the foreign policy decisions of the United States. In 1970, at the height of the Cold War, officials of the executive branch, performing their delegated functions concerning national security and foreign relations, determined that it was in the best interest of the United States to take such steps as they deemed necessary to prevent the establishment of a government in a Western Hemisphere nation that in the view of those officials could lead to the establishment or spread of communism as a governing force in the Americas. This decision may have been unwise, or it may have been wise. The political branches may have since rejected the approach, or not. In any event, that decision was classically within the province of the political branches, not the courts. As the Supreme Court has repeatedly reminded us, "the political question doctrine excludes from judicial review those controversies which revolve around policy choices and value determinations constitutionally committed for resolution to the halls of Congress or the confines of the Executive Branch." This is so because "the Judiciary is particularly ill suited to make such decisions, as 'courts are fundamentally underequipped to formulate national policies or develop standards for matters not legal in nature.'"

2. No judicially discoverable and manageable standards

The second criterion of the *Baker* six brings under the nonjusticiable umbrella of political question any case as to which there is "a lack of judicially discoverable and manageable standards for resolving it." This factor, even taken apart from the first factor, supports the conclusion that this case must be dismissed. As the court well understood, for a court to adjudicate this case would be for that court to undertake the determination of whether, 35 years ago, at the height of the Cold War between the United States and the western powers on the one hand and the expanding communist empire on the other, "it was proper for an Executive Branch official . . . to support covert actions against" a committed Marxist who was set to take power in a Latin American country. Unlike the executive, the judiciary has no covert agents, no intelligence sources, and no policy advisors. The courts are therefore ill-suited to displace the political branches in such decision-making.

As we have said before of other security considerations in another context, "it is within the role of the executive to acquire and exercise the expertise of protecting national security. It is not within the role of the courts to second-guess executive judgments made in furtherance of that branch's proper role."

Appellants claim that the court erred in holding that no standards exist for determining whether "it was proper for an Executive Branch official . . . to support covert actions against an undesirable figure who was set to take power in a foreign nation." They assert that the court "misconstrued Plaintiffs' claims by framing the issue as an attack on policy." However, it is not at all clear to us why Appellants believe their suit to be anything other than such an attack. They claim that "courts should not invoke the political question doctrine to avoid adjudication of a violation of basic rights." However, this is not supported by past decisions.

Appellants had urged that "'the standards for evaluating wrongful death are well established' . . . and that the 'Court need not depart from these in managing the instant action.'" This formulation of the issues is no help. As the court stated, "resolving the present lawsuit would compel the court, at a minimum, to determine whether actions or omissions by an Executive Branch officer in the area of foreign relations and national security were 'wrongful' under tort law."

Regardless of their arguments, recasting foreign policy and national security questions in tort terms does not provide standards for making or reviewing foreign policy judgments. In *Aktepe*, the Eleventh Circuit considered a case brought by Turkish sailors alleging injuries and wrongful death suffered as a result of missiles fired by a United States Navy vessel during North Atlantic Treaty Organization training exercises. In holding that the action was barred by the second *Baker* political question factor, that court noted that "in order to determine whether the Navy conducted the missile-firing drill in a negligent manner, a court would have to determine how a reasonable military force would have conducted the drill." The *Aktepe* court went on to observe "as the Supreme Court noted in a related context, 'it is difficult to conceive of an area of governmental activity in which the courts have less competence.'" Similarly here, in order to determine whether the covert operations which allegedly led to the tragic death of General Schneider were wrongful, the court would have to define the standard for the government's use of covert operations in conjunction with political turmoil in another country. There are no justiciably discoverable and manageable standards for the resolution of such a claim.

3. Judicial resolution would require an initial policy determination of a kind clearly for nonjudicial discretion

Without rehashing the constitutional separation of powers concerns raised by the two *Baker* factors already discussed, we note that the same sort of problems raise the third factor as well. The District Court well stated the matter:

> Plaintiffs contend that "the Court is not here asked to pass judgment on any perceived value or danger of the Allende government to United States interests and need not make any policy determination[.]" While the plaintiffs are correct that the Court might be able to avoid evaluating the merits of a potential Allende Government in 1970, it would nonetheless be forced to pass judgment on the means used by the United States to keep that government from taking power.

While we are not at all convinced that we would be able to avoid evaluating the merits of the potential Allende government in 1970, we are completely in agreement with the District Court that we would be forced to pass judgment on the policy-based decision of the executive to use covert action to prevent that government from taking power. Allying United States intelligence operatives with dissidents in another country to kidnap a national of that country may be a drastic measure. To determine whether drastic measures should be taken in matters of foreign policy and national security is not the stuff of adjudication, but of policymaking. As the Supreme Court has emphasized, "the 'nuances' of 'the foreign policy of the United States . . . are much more the province of the Executive Branch and Congress than of this Court.'" Thus, we agree with the District Court that the third *Baker* factor also counsels against jurisdiction over this case.

4. The court could not proceed without expressing a lack of respect to coordinate branches of government

From what we have concluded as to the first three *Baker* factors, it seems apparent to us that we could not determine Appellants' claims without passing judgment on the decision of the executive branch to participate in the alleged covert operations-participation in which, we note from the record, has already been the subject of congressional investigation. We therefore affirm the conclusion of the District Court that "a court should refrain from entertaining a suit if it would be unable to do so without expressing a lack of respect due to its coequal Branches of Government."

5. Summary

For the reasons set forth above, we conclude that at least the first four of the six *Baker* factors compel a determination that this case raises political questions committed to the political branches and therefore is beyond the jurisdiction of the courts.

We caution that the lack of judicial authority to oversee the conduct of the executive branch in political matters does not leave the executive power unbounded. Granted, it is true, as Chief Justice Marshall recognized in *Marbury v. Madison*, that "the injured individual has no remedy." Nonetheless, the nation has recompense, and the checks and balances of the Constitution have not failed. The political branches effectively exercise such checks and balances on each other in the area of political questions.

If the executive in fact has exceeded his appropriate role in the constitutional scheme, Congress enjoys a broad range of authorities with which to exercise restraint and balance. We catalogued above those authorities specifically related to international relations and national security, but as we also noted there, Congress wields the general power to lay and collect taxes and to borrow money on the credit of the United States. Without an appropriation from Congress to fund an undertaking, the President cannot conduct any such undertaking. Indeed, Congress has used its appropriations power to draw limits upon the executive's activity in the area of foreign affairs. For example, in the Boland Amendment to the Department of Defense Appropriations Act, (1982), Congress proscribed the CIA from funding or participating in efforts to overthrow the Nicaraguan government. The Boland Amendment example is particularly striking in that elements of the executive branch apparently violated these congressional restraints. Thereafter, Congress exercised one of its other powerful tools against executive overreaching: congressional oversight. The alleged breach of the Boland Amendment gave rise to the Iran/Contra proceedings, which in time gave rise to investigations by an Independent Counsel acting under authority conferred by Congress in the Ethics in Government Act of 1978.

In the extreme case, Congress can repair to its authority under Article I, Section 3 of the Constitution to bring impeachment proceedings against an overreaching President. In fact, with reference to the very administration (President Nixon) at issue in this case, Congress did just that.

In short, the allocation of political questions to the political branches is not inconsistent with our constitutional tradition of limited government and balance of powers. It is precisely consistent, for it embodies limits and balances between the political branches without the intrusion of the courts into areas beyond our proper authority and expertise.

IV. Conclusion

For the reasons set forth above, we affirm the judgment of the District Court dismissing this action.

END OF OPINION

No matter how much one disagrees with the course of action in foreign affairs as conducted by members of the U.S. government, it is improper for the courts to intervene and second guess policy decisions set by the president and Congress. Courts decide questions of law, and not the wisdom of discretionary policy decisions. Here, Secretary of State Henry Kissinger implemented policies supporting barbarous regimes because the United States viewed them as preferable to the likely alternative, which would have been a communist regime. Not only was it considered likely that a communist regime would be more hostile to U.S. interests than a non-communist authoritarian regime, but it's possible that a communist power might have had an even worse human rights record. These judgments concerning which foreign policy best furthers U.S. interests and defends human rights are to be made by the president and Congress, and not the courts. Even if, in retrospect, the president and Congress choose poorly, the courts will not go back and second guess them.

The court did not say that the president is unrestrained in foreign affairs. The court points out that Congress can vote on legislation to prohibit or authorize discretionary military actions and foreign policy decisions. This, the court states, is the way it should be — each branch of government using their authority to provide checks and balance. However, it is not up to the courts to get involved in the propriety of these actions, or question their appropriateness.

Standing

Another issue that arises in the course of litigating national security issues is **standing**. The Supreme Court has stated that "the question of standing is whether the litigant is entitled to have the court decide the merits of the dispute or of particular issues."

There are a number of requirements that a plaintiff must establish to have standing before a federal court. The requirement that a plaintiff have standing to sue is a limit on the role of the judiciary and the law of Article III; standing is built on the idea of separation of powers. In the United States, The doctrine of standing has its first origins in a case called *Fairchild v. Hughes*, 258 U.S. 126 (1922). In *Fairchild*, a citizen sued the secretary of state and the attorney general to challenge the procedures by which the Nineteenth Amendment (which gave women the right to vote) was ratified. Prior to this case, the rule in many courts was that all persons had a right to pursue a private prosecution of a public right.[3] Since the decision in *Fairchild*, the doctrine has been more broadly interpreted by the courts and has also been incorporated in some statutes and court rules.

So, standing is the issue of who has the right to sue. Just because a perceived wrong has occurred does not mean that anyone can file a lawsuit over an issue. As a general rule, only a person who has been harmed can sue. For example, if you are walking down the sidewalk and a drunk driver jumps the curb and hits you, you have

---

3. The Metaphor of Standing and the Problem of Self-Governance, by Steven L. Winter, 40 *Stan. L. Rev.* 1371, July, 1988.

standing to sue because you were injured. On the other hand, your best friend would not have standing to sue, even on your behalf, because he was not injured by the drunk driver. Another person who could not sue on your behalf would be the organization Mothers Against Drunk Driving (MADD). Even though MADD's reason for existing is to fight drunk driving, as MADD was not injured by this drunk driver, MADD could not sue.

There is a narrow exception to this rule that only the injured party may sue, and that is where there is a "special relationship" between the injured person and the one bringing the lawsuit. For example, let's say that the drunk driver has knocked you into a coma. Because you are physically unable to bring a lawsuit, the court would allow your parents or your adult child to bring it on your behalf. Members of the immediate family are recognized as having a special relationship, and are allowed to file a suit on behalf of a minor child or an adult who is physically incapable of suing. There are a small number of other special relationships beyond immediate family that can arise, but they are few and limited.

When it comes to national security, who has standing to sue? In the case above concerning U.S. foreign policy in South America, we can agree that a person whose immediate family died because of U.S. foreign policy would have standing to bring a lawsuit, even if the case would later be dismissed as a political question. On the other hand, a regular American who disagrees with American foreign policy but has not personally suffered an injury to himself or immediate family would not have standing to sue. The "injury" one must suffer to have standing can be physical, or it could be more conceptual such as a loss of rights.

The concept of standing arose in the case below, where a U.S. congressman was held not to have standing to sue the president because the court found that he had not suffered any personal injury. As you read this case, consider the explanation of the doctrine and see how you think it applies in our system of laws and government.

Campbell v. Clinton, 203 F.3d 19 (2000)*

A number of congressmen, led by Tom Campbell of California, filed suit claiming that the President violated the War Powers Resolution and the War Powers Clause of the Constitution by directing U.S. forces' participation in the recent NATO campaign in Yugoslavia. The district court dismissed for lack of standing. We agree with the district court and therefore affirm.

On March 24, 1999, President Clinton announced the commencement of NATO air and cruise missile attacks on Yugoslav targets. Two days later he submitted to Congress a report, "consistent with the War Powers Resolution," detailing the circumstances necessitating the use of armed forces, the deployment's scope and expected duration, and asserting that he had "taken these actions pursuant to his authority ... as Commander in Chief and Chief Executive." On April 28, Congress voted on four

---

* The case has been heavily edited and paraphrased by the authors for clarity. See disclaimer in introduction.

resolutions related to the Yugoslav conflict: It voted down a declaration of war 427 to 2 and an "authorization" of the air strikes 213 to 213, but it also voted against requiring the President to immediately end U.S. participation in the NATO operation and voted to fund that involvement. The conflict between NATO and Yugoslavia continued for 79 days, ending on June 10 with Yugoslavia's agreement to withdraw its forces from Kosovo and allow deployment of a NATO-led peacekeeping force.

Throughout this period Pentagon, State Department, and NATO spokesmen informed the public on a frequent basis of developments in the fighting.

Appellants, 31 congressmen opposed to U.S. involvement in the Kosovo intervention, filed suit prior to termination of that conflict seeking a declaratory judgment that the President's use of American forces against Yugoslavia was unlawful under both the War Powers Clause of the Constitution and the War Powers Resolution ("the WPR"). The WPR requires the President to submit a report within 48 hours "in any case in which United States Armed Forces are introduced . . . into hostilities or into situations where imminent involvement in hostilities is clearly indicated by the circumstances," and to "terminate any use of United States Armed Forces with respect to which a report was submitted (or required to be submitted), unless the Congress . . . has declared war or has enacted a specific authorization for such use of United States Armed Forces" within 60 days. Appellants claim that the President did submit a report sufficient to trigger the WPR on March 26, or in any event was required to submit a report by that date, but nonetheless failed to end U.S. involvement in the hostilities after 60 days.

The government does not respond to appellants' claim on the merits. Instead the government challenges the jurisdiction of the federal courts to adjudicate this claim on three separate grounds: the case is moot; appellants lack standing, as the district court concluded; and the case is nonjusticiable. We agree with the district court that the congressmen lack standing.

The question whether congressmen have standing in federal court to challenge the lawfulness of actions of the executive was answered, at least in large part, in the Supreme Court's recent decision in *Raines v. Byrd*, (1997). *Raines* involved a constitutional challenge to the President's authority under the short-lived Line Item Veto Act. Individual congressmen claimed that under that Act a President could veto (unconstitutionally) only part of a law and thereby diminish the institutional power of Congress. Observing it had never held that congressmen have standing to assert an institutional injury as against the executive, the Court held that petitioners in the case lacked "legislative standing" to challenge the Act. The Court noted that petitioners already possessed an adequate political remedy, since they could vote to have the Line Item Veto Act repealed, or to provide individual spending bills with a statutory exemption.

Thereafter in *Chenoweth v. Clinton* (D.C.Cir.1999), emphasizing the separation-of-powers problems inherent in legislative standing, we held that congressmen had no standing to challenge the President's introduction of a program through executive order rather than statute. As in *Raines*, appellants contended that the President's action inflicted an institutional injury upon Congress, in this case by circumventing its legislative authority, but, we said,

> It is uncontested that the Congress could terminate the [contested program] were a sufficient number in each House so inclined. Because the parties' dispute is therefore fully susceptible to political resolution, we would [under circuit precedent] dismiss the complaint to avoid "meddl[ing] in the internal affairs of the legislative branch.

Applying *Raines*, we would reach the same conclusion.

In this case, Congress certainly could have passed a law forbidding the use of U.S. forces in the Yugoslav campaign; indeed, there was a measure—albeit only a concurrent resolution—introduced to require the President to withdraw U.S. troops. Unfortunately, however, for those congressmen who, like appellants, desired an end to U.S. involvement in Yugoslavia, this measure was defeated by a 139 to 290 vote. Of course, Congress always retains appropriations authority and could have cut off funds for the American role in the conflict. Again there was an effort to do so but it failed; appropriations were authorized. And there always remains the possibility of impeachment should a President act in disregard of Congress' authority on these matters.

Appellants' constitutional claim stands on no firmer footing. Appellants argue that the War Powers Clause of the Constitution proscribes a President from using military force except as is necessary to repel a sudden attack. But they also argue that the WPR "implements" or channels congressional authority under the Constitution. It may well be then that since we have determined that appellants lack standing to enforce the WPR there is nothing left of their constitutional claim. Assuming, however, that appellants' constitutional claim should be considered separately, the same logic dictates they do not have standing to bring such a challenge. That is to say Congress has a broad range of legislative authority it can use to stop a President's war making, and therefore under Raines congressmen may not challenge the President's war-making powers in federal court.

Accordingly, the district court is affirmed; appellants lack standing.

END OF OPINION

So, in this case where a congressman alleges that the president is violating the war powers of Congress, the court decides that the congressman does not have standing to sue because he has not suffered any real injury. Again, this does not mean the congressman is powerless. The court points out that the congressman could still stop the president's military actions by introducing legislation which orders the cessation of hostilities or cuts funding to the military action, and getting the rest of Congress to vote for it. Because the congressman still has means to remedy the situation himself without the courts getting involved, the court is unwilling to voice its opinion whether a violation of the U.S. Constitution has occurred. Maybe a violation did occur, and maybe it didn't; the court is not going to step in and be a referee in a dispute between the president and Congress when they are in disagreement over the law. This is especially true when a congressman still has the means at his disposal (a congressional vote or control of funding) to stop the president.

What is important for you to take away from this opinion is that if a congressman alleging that war powers are being violated by the president does not have standing to sue the president, then who does? The answer is probably no one, including a service member who is going to be deployed in a position where he or she will be in danger. It is very unrealistic to get a court order to stop military action, even when it is possibly unlawful military action in that it was conducted in a manner violating international law or domestic law, for the courts do not like to intervene in foreign affairs or national security. "Standing" is just one more tool, in addition to "political question," courts have to remove themselves from litigation involving national security.

Often, you hear about the American Civil Liberties Union (ACLU) or some other organization suing the government. How do these organizations have standing? There are a few different ways. Sometimes the ACLU will find a person who has been personally injured, and then file a lawsuit on that individual's behalf with that individual's permission, assistance, and cooperation.

Other times, when there is a perceived injury to many possible persons and it would be difficult to find an actual individual who has been injured, then an organization such as the ACLU would be allowed to file a lawsuit. For example, let's say that the NSA is accused of illegally wiretapping millions of Americans and reading their emails. Here, it would be very difficult to identify a specific individual whose email was read, but a wrong is being alleged on a large scale and it could potentially encompass many Americans, so the court would allow the ACLU to sue on their behalf.

In the example above, the ACLU would be allowed to sue for a general claim without a particular injured individual, but not an organization such as MADD. The reason why the ACLU would be allowed to sue here is this type of case and the issues it raises are the very reason why the ACLU exists; to protect civil liberties. The issues of a case involving NSA wiretapping are beyond the scope of why MADD exists, so MADD would not be allowed to sue. It simply makes sense for the ACLU, an organization devoted to the defense of civil liberties, to have standing in general lawsuits against the government concerning civil rights.

It is much easier to file a lawsuit with a particular individual who has been harmed, and courts will generally only allow lawsuits, like the example above with the ACLU, if and only if finding an individual who has been harmed would be unreasonably difficult.

Ripeness

In addition to political questions and standing, **ripeness** is another issue. Ripeness refers to the readiness of a case for litigation; in the words of one legal text, "a claim is not ripe for adjudication if it rests upon contingent future events that may not occur as anticipated, or indeed may not occur at all."[4] For example, if an ambiguous law has been enacted but that law has not actually been applied, a case that a person brings seeking to challenge the law lacks the ripeness necessary for a decision.

The goal is to prevent cases from coming to court prematurely. Courts do not want to be pulled into ruling on situations where any potential injury or stake is still too speculative to warrant action. Ripeness issues most usually arise when a plaintiff seeks anticipatory relief, such as an injunction. The U.S. Supreme Court put into place a two-part test for assessing ripeness challenges to federal regulations, a test that is now often applied to constitutional challenges to federal and state statutes as well. The Court said in *Abbott Laboratories v. Gardner*, 387 U.S. 136 (1967):

> Without undertaking to survey the intricacies of the ripeness doctrine it is fair to say that its basic rationale is to prevent the courts, through avoidance of premature adjudication, from entangling themselves in abstract disagreements over administrative policies, and also to protect the agencies from judicial interference until an administrative decision has been formalized and its effects felt in a concrete way by the challenging parties. The problem is best seen in a twofold aspect, requiring us to evaluate both the fitness of the issues for judicial decision and the hardship to the parties of withholding court consideration.

So, as a general rule, one can only sue AFTER an injury has occurred, and not before. You may have heard the expression that an ounce of prevention is worth a pound of cure; this is not true in America's courts. In American law, there is a strong preference for giving money after an injury, rather than a court order in advance to prevent an injury. There are exceptions to this rule, such as when the chances are very high that an injury (which is either irreparable or highly damaging) will occur if the court does not intervene beforehand.

American courts are very reluctant to issue court orders over what MIGHT happen in the future, and instead prefer only to issue preventative orders if the chances of an injury are extremely certain and likely, and preventative measures would be much less costly and intrusive than post-injury remedies. When it comes to national security, when is an appropriate time to sue? In national security, there are very few certainties, making it very difficult to know what will happen in the future and unlikely for courts to issue orders to prevent possible harms.

Let's use a very ridiculous example to establish this idea; let's say that in the town of Imaginationburg the local police department has recently purchased a battering ram to be used by SWAT teams for knocking down doors while conducting raids. If the citizens of Imaginationburg are afraid that the police will use it illegally by knocking down doors and conducting raids on homes without a warrant, would they file a lawsuit in advance and get a court order which orders the police department to only use it when they have a warrant or other lawful circumstances? Even though they

---

4. *Thomas v. Union Carbide Agricultural Products Co.*, 473 U.S. 568, 581 (1985) (quoting 13A C. Wright, A. Miller, & E. Cooper, Federal Practice and Procedure § 3532, p. 112 (1984)).

are only asking the court to issue an order that the police follow the law, this case would be dismissed because it is not ripe. Rather than give an order in advance to prevent unlawful conduct or injury or a court order which orders someone to follow the law before breaking it, American courts would prefer to have a lawsuit after a violation of the law for money damages if the SWAT team does commit an illegal entry.

In another illustration, let's say there is a rumor that the NSA is building a supercomputer that, among other qualities, has the capability of reading everyone's emails. Could an individual citizen file a lawsuit and get a court order that the NSA not use the computer for that specific purpose without a warrant? Probably not. In addition to the existence of such a computer being a state secret, this case simply would not be ripe for adjudication. A court would prefer that an injury actually occur and there be some evidence that the NSA had actually read the complaining person's emails in violation of the law, and only then upon a lawsuit being filed might a court issue an order (known as an "injunction") that the NSA refrain from reading emails without a warrant.

In another example from the case below, assume that the president is building up a military presence in a region of the world, and it is possible that the president, without any authorization of Congress, plans to use military force in possible violation of the law. As happened in the case below, the court is not going to give an order to prohibit the president from unlawfully using force. Instead, the court would hold that the case is not ripe for adjudication, and only if the president breaks the law would the court then even consider hearing the case.

As a matter of fact, this is what happened with the first Gulf War (otherwise known as DESERT STORM in 1991/1992). The opinion below explains the concept of ripeness, in addition to providing a great recap of the concept of political question doctrine and standing. Interestingly, here the court found that there was no political question and the plaintiffs did have standing. However, the case was not yet ripe for adjudication.

Dellums v. Bush, 752 F. Supp. 1141 (1990)*

This is a lawsuit by a number of members of Congress who request an injunction directed to the President of the United States to prevent him from initiating an offensive attack against Iraq without first securing a declaration of war or other explicit congressional authorization for such action.

The factual background is, briefly, as follows. On August 2, 1990, Iraq invaded the neighboring country of Kuwait. President George Bush almost immediately sent United States military forces to the Persian Gulf area to deter Iraqi aggression and to preserve the integrity of Saudi Arabia. The United States, generally by presidential order and at times with congressional concurrence, also took other steps, including

---

* The case has been heavily edited and paraphrased by the authors for clarity. See disclaimer in introduction.

a blockade of Iraq, which were approved by the United Nations Security Council, and participated in by a great many other nations.

On November 8, 1990, President Bush announced a substantial increase in the Persian Gulf military deployment, raising the troop level significantly above the 230,000 then present in the area. At the same time, the President stated that the objective was to provide "an adequate offensive military option" should that be necessary to achieve such goals as the withdrawal of Iraqi forces from Kuwait. Secretary of Defense Richard Cheney likewise referred to the ability of the additional military forces "to conduct offensive military operations."

The House of Representatives and the Senate have in various ways expressed their support for the President's past and present actions in the Persian Gulf. However, the Congress was not asked for, and it did not take, action pursuant to Article I, Section 8, Clause 11 of the Constitution "to declare war" on Iraq. On November 19, 1990, the congressional plaintiffs brought this action, which proceeds on the premise that the initiation of offensive United States military action is imminent, that such action would be unlawful in the absence of a declaration of war by the Congress, and that a war without concurrence by the Congress would deprive the congressional plaintiffs of the voice to which they are entitled under the Constitution.

The President raises a number of defenses to the lawsuit—most particularly that the complaint presents a non-justiciable political question, that plaintiffs lack standing to maintain the action, and that the issue of the proper allocation of the war making powers between the branches is not ripe for decision. These will now be considered seriatim.

II. Political Question

It is appropriate first to sketch out briefly the constitutional and legal framework in which the current controversy arises. Article I, Section 8, Clause 11 of the Constitution grants to the Congress the power "To declare War." the founding fathers felt it to be unwise to entrust the momentous power to involve the nation in a war to the President alone; Jefferson explained that he desired "an effectual check to the Dog of war"; James Wilson similarly expressed the expectation that this system would guard against hostilities being initiated by a single man. Even Abraham Lincoln, while a Congressman, said more than half a century later that "no one man should hold the power of bringing" war upon us.

The congressional power to declare war does not stand alone, however, but it is accompanied by powers granted to the President. Article II, Section 1, Clause 1 and Section 2 provide that "the executive powers shall be vested in a President of the United States of America," and that "the President shall be Commander in Chief of the Army and Navy...."

It is the position of the President that the simultaneous existence of all these provisions renders it impossible to isolate the war-declaring power. The Department further argues that the design of the Constitution is to have the various war- and military-related provisions construed and acting together, and that their harmonization is a political rather than a legal question. In short, the President relies on the political question doctrine.

That doctrine is premised both upon the separation of powers and the inherent limits of judicial abilities. In relation to the issues involved in this case, the President expands on its basic theme, contending that by their very nature the determination whether certain types of military actions require a declaration of war is not justiciable, but depends instead upon delicate judgments by the political branches. On that view, the question whether an offensive action taken by American armed forces constitutes an act of war (to be initiated by a declaration of war) or an "offensive military attack" (presumably undertaken by the President in his capacity as commander-in-chief) is not one of objective fact but involves an exercise of judgment based upon all the vagaries of foreign affairs and national security. Indeed, the President contends that there are no judicially discoverable and manageable standards to apply, claiming that only the political branches are able to determine whether or not this country is at war. Such a determination, it is said, is based upon "a political judgment" about the significance of those facts. Under that rationale, a court cannot make an independent determination on this issue because it cannot take adequate account of these political considerations.

This claim on behalf of the Executive is far too sweeping to be accepted by the courts. If the Executive had the sole power to determine that any particular offensive military operation, no matter how vast, does not constitute war-making but only an offensive military attack, the congressional power to declare war will be at the mercy of a semantic decision by the Executive. Such an "interpretation" would evade the plain language of the Constitution, and it cannot stand.

That is not to say that, assuming that the issue is factually close or ambiguous or fraught with intricate technical military and diplomatic baggage, the courts would not defer to the political branches to determine whether or not particular hostilities might qualify as a "war." However, here the forces involved are of such magnitude and significance as to present no serious claim that a war would not ensue if they became engaged in combat, and it is therefore clear that congressional approval is required if Congress desires to become involved.

Mitchell v. Laird (D.C.Cir.1973) provides guidance on this issue. In Mitchell, the Court of Appeals ruled there is "no insuperable difficulty in a court determining" the truth of the factual allegations in the complaint: that many Americans had been killed and large amounts of money had been spent in military activity in Indo-China. In the view of the appellate court, by looking at those facts a court could determine "whether the hostilities in Indo-China constituted a 'war,' within the meaning of that term in Article I, Section 8, Clause 11." The Court stated:

> Here the critical question to be initially decided is whether the hostilities in Indo-China constitute in the Constitutional sense a "war." If the plaintiffs' allegations are true, then in our opinion, as apparently in the opinion of President Nixon, there has been a war in Indo-China. Nor do we see any difficulty in a court facing up to the question as to whether because of the

war's duration and magnitude the President is or was without power to continue the war without Congressional approval.

In short, *Mitchell* stands for the proposition that courts do not lack the power and the ability to make the factual and legal determination of whether this nation's military actions constitute war for purposes of the constitutional War Clause.

Notwithstanding these relatively straightforward propositions, the President goes on to suggest that the issue in this case is still political rather than legal, because in order to resolve the dispute the Court would have to inject itself into foreign affairs, a subject which the Constitution commits to the political branches. That argument, too, must fail.

While the Constitution grants to the political branches, and in particular to the Executive, responsibility for conducting the nation's foreign affairs, it does not follow that the judicial power is excluded from the resolution of cases merely because they may touch upon such affairs. The court must instead look at "the particular question posed" in the case. In fact, courts are routinely deciding cases that touch upon or even have a substantial impact on foreign and defense policy.

The President's argument also ignores the fact that courts have historically made determinations about whether this country was at war for many other purposes—the construction of treaties, statutes, and even insurance contracts. These judicial determinations of a de facto state of war have occurred even in the absence of a congressional declaration.

Plaintiffs allege in their complaint that 230,000 American troops are currently deployed in Saudi Arabia and the Persian Gulf area, and that by the end of this month the number of American troops in the region will reach 380,000. They also allege, in light of the President's obtaining the support of the United Nations Security Council in a resolution allowing for the use of force against Iraq, that he is planning for an offensive military attack on Iraqi forces.

Given these factual allegations and the legal principles outlined above, the Court has no hesitation in concluding that an offensive entry into Iraq by several hundred thousand United States servicemen under the conditions described above could be described as a "war" within the meaning of Article I, Section 8, Clause 11, of the Constitution. To put it another way: the Court is not prepared to read out of the Constitution the clause granting to the Congress, and to it alone, the authority "to declare war."

III. Standing

The President argues next that the plaintiffs lack "standing" to pursue this action.

The Supreme Court has established a two-part test for determining standing under Article III of the Constitution. The plaintiff must allege: (1) that he personally suffered actual or threatened injury, and (2) that the "injury 'fairly can be traced to the challenged action' and 'is likely to be redressed by a favorable decision.'" For the purpose of determining standing on a motion to dismiss, the Court must "accept as true all material allegations of the complaint, and must construe the complaint in favor of the complaining party." Accordingly, plaintiffs' allegations of an imminent danger of hostilities between the United States forces and Iraq must be accepted as true for this purpose.

Plaintiffs further claim that their interest guaranteed by the War Clause of the Constitution is in immediate danger of being harmed by military actions the President may take against Iraq. That claim states a legally-cognizable injury, for as the Court of Appeals for this Circuit stated in a leading case, members of Congress plainly have an interest in protecting their right to vote on matters entrusted to their respective chambers by the Constitution. *Moore v. United States House of Representatives* (D.C.Cir. 1984).

Indeed, *Moore* pointed out even more explicitly that where a congressional plaintiff suffers "unconstitutional deprivations of his constitutional duties or rights . . . if the injuries are specific and discernible," a finding of harm sufficient to support standing is justified. To be sure, *Moore* and other decisions have found standing by members of Congress to challenge the Executive for actions the latter had already taken, and the President argues that these precedents do not apply where, as here, the subject of the suit are Executive actions that are only threatened. Especially in view of the extraordinary fact situation that is before the Court, that is a distinction without a difference.

When future harm is alleged as injury-in-fact, the plaintiff must be able to allege harm that is "both 'real and immediate' not 'conjectural' or 'hypothetical.'" Yet that plaintiff does not have to wait for the threatened harm to occur before obtaining standing.

The right asserted by the plaintiffs in this case is the right to vote for or against a declaration of war. In view of that subject matter, the right must of necessity be asserted before the President acts; once the President has acted, the asserted right of the members of Congress—to render war action by the President contingent upon a prior congressional declaration of war—is of course lost.

The President also argues that the threat of injury in this case is not immediate because there is only a "possibility" that the President will initiate war against Iraq, and additionally, that there is no way of knowing before the occurrence of such a possibility whether he would seek a declaration of war from Congress.

That argument, too, must fail, for although it is not entirely fixed what actions the Executive will take towards Iraq and what procedures he will follow with regard to his consultations with Congress, it is clearly more than unadorned speculation that the President will go to war by initiating hostilities against Iraq without first obtaining a declaration of war from Congress.

With close to 400,000 United States troops stationed in Saudi Arabia, with all troop rotation and leave provisions suspended, and with the President having acted vigorously on his own as well as through the Secretary of State to obtain from the United Nations Security Council a resolution authorizing the use of all available means to remove Iraqi forces from Kuwait, including the use of force, it is disingenuous for the President to characterize plaintiffs' allegations as to the imminence of the threat of offensive military action for standing purposes as "remote and conjectural," for standing purposes. For these reasons, the Court concludes that the plaintiffs have adequately alleged a threat of injury in fact necessary to support standing.

V. Ripeness

Although, as discussed above, the Court rejects several of defendant's objections to the maintenance of this lawsuit, and concludes that, in principle, an injunction may issue at the request of Members of Congress to prevent the conduct of a war which is about to be carried on without congressional authorization, it does not follow that these plaintiffs are entitled to relief at this juncture. For the plaintiffs are met with a significant obstacle to such relief: the doctrine of ripeness.

It has long been held that, as a matter of the deference that is due to the other branches of government, the Judiciary will undertake to render decisions that compel action by the President or the Congress only if the dispute before the Court is truly ripe, in that all the factors necessary for a decision are present then and there. The need for ripeness as a prerequisite to judicial action has particular weight in a case such as this. The principle that the courts shall be prudent in the exercise of their authority is never more compelling than when they are called upon to adjudicate on such sensitive issues as those trenching upon military and foreign affairs. Judicial restraint must, of course, be even further enhanced when the issue is one—as here—on which the other two branches may be deeply divided. Hence the necessity for determining at the outset whether the controversy is truly "ripe" for decision or whether, on the other hand, the Judiciary should abstain from rendering a decision on ripeness grounds.

In the context of this case, there are two aspects to ripeness, which the Court will now explore.

A. Actions By the Congress

No one knows the position of the Legislative Branch on the issue of war or peace with Iraq; certainly no one, including this Court, is able to ascertain the congressional position on that issue on the basis of this lawsuit brought by fifty-three members of the House of Representatives and one member of the U.S. Senate. It would be both premature and presumptuous for the Court to render a decision on the issue of whether a declaration of war is required at this time or in the near future when the Congress itself has provided no indication whether it deems such a declaration either necessary, on the one hand, or imprudent, on the other.

For these reasons, this Court has elected to follow the course described by Justice Powell in his concurrence in *Goldwater v. Carter* (1979). In that opinion, Justice Powell provided a test for ripeness in cases involving a confrontation between the legislative and executive branches that is helpful here. In *Goldwater*, President Carter had informed Taiwan that the United States would terminate the mutual defense treaty between the two countries within one year. The President made this announcement without the ratification of the Congress, and members of Congress brought suit claiming that, just as the Constitution required the Senate's ratification of the

President's decision to enter into a treaty, so too, congressional ratification was necessary to terminate a treaty.

Justice Powell proposed that "a dispute between Congress and the President is not ready for judicial review unless and until each branch has taken action asserting its constitutional authority." He further explained that in *Goldwater* there had been no such confrontation because there had as yet been no vote in the Senate as to what to do in the face of the President's action to terminate the treaty with Taiwan, and he went on to say that the Judicial Branch should not decide issues affecting the allocation of power between the President and Congress until the political branches reach a constitutional impasse. Otherwise we would encourage small groups or even individual Members of Congress to seek judicial resolution of issues before the normal political process has the opportunity to resolve the conflict. It cannot be said that either the Senate or the House has rejected the President's claim. If the Congress chooses not to confront the President, it is not our task to do so.

Justice Powell's reasoning commends itself to this Court. The consequences of judicial action in the instant case with the facts in their present posture may be drastic, but unnecessarily so. What if the Court issued the injunction requested by the plaintiffs, but it subsequently turned out that a majority of the members of the Legislative Branch were of the view (a) that the President is free as a legal or constitutional matter to proceed with his plans toward Iraq without a congressional declaration of war, or (b) more broadly, that the majority of the members of this Branch, for whatever reason, are content to leave this diplomatically and politically delicate decision to the President?

It would hardly do to have the Court, in effect, force a choice upon the Congress by a blunt injunctive decision, called for by only about ten percent of its membership, to the effect that, unless the rest of the Congress votes in favor of a declaration of war, the President, and the several hundred thousand troops he has dispatched to the Saudi Arabian desert, must be immobilized. Similarly, the President is entitled to be protected from an injunctive order respecting a declaration of war when there is no evidence that this is what the Legislative Branch as such—as distinguished from a fraction thereof—regards as a necessary prerequisite to military moves in the Arabian desert.

All these difficulties are avoided by a requirement that the plaintiffs in an action of this kind be or represent a majority of the Members of the Congress: the majority of the body that under the Constitution is the only one competent to declare war, and therefore also the one with the ability to seek an order from the courts to prevent anyone else, i.e., the Executive, from in effect declaring war. In short, unless the Congress as a whole, or by a majority, is heard from, the controversy here cannot be deemed ripe; it is only if the majority of the Congress seeks relief from an infringement on its constitutional war-declaration power that it may be entitled to receive it.

B. Actions Taken By the Executive

The second half of the ripeness issue involves the question whether the Executive Branch of government is so clearly committed to immediate military operations that may be equated with a "war" within the meaning of Article I, Section 8, Clause 11, of the Constitution that a judicial decision may properly be rendered regarding the application of that constitutional provision to the current situation.

Plaintiffs assert that the matter is currently ripe for judicial action because the President himself has stated that the present troop build-up is to provide an adequate offensive military option in the area. His successful effort to secure passage of United Nations Resolution 678, which authorizes the use of "all available means" to oust Iraqi forces remaining in Kuwait after January 15, 1991, is said to be an additional fact pointing toward the Executive's intention to initiate military hostilities against Iraq in the near future.

The President, on the other hand, points to statements of the President that the troops already in Saudi Arabia are a peacekeeping force to prove that the President might not initiate more offensive military actions. In addition, and more realistically, it is possible that the meetings set for later this month and next between President Bush and the Foreign Minister of Iraq, Tariq Aziz, in Washington, and Secretary of State James Baker and Saddam Hussein in Baghdad, may result in a diplomatic solution to the present situation, and in any event under the U.N. Security Council resolution there will not be resort to force before January 15, 1991.

Given the facts currently available to this Court, it would seem that as of now the Executive Branch has not shown a commitment to a definitive course of action sufficient to support ripeness. In any event, however, a final decision on that issue is not necessary at this time.

Should the congressional ripeness issue discussed in Part V-A above be resolved in favor of a finding of ripeness as a consequence of actions taken by the Congress as a whole, there will still be time enough to determine whether, in view of the conditions as they are found to exist at that time, the Executive is so clearly committed to early military operations amounting to "war" in the constitutional sense that the Court would be justified in concluding that the remainder of the test of ripeness has been met. And of course an injunction will be issued only if, on both of the aspects of the doctrine discussed above, the Court could find that the controversy is ripe for judicial decision. That situation does not, or at least not yet, prevail, and plaintiffs' request for a preliminary injunction will therefore not be granted.

For the reasons stated, it is this 13th day of December, 1990

ORDERED that plaintiffs' motion for preliminary injunction be and it is hereby denied.

END OF OPINION

When the court discussed "ripeness" in this case, it observed that that the president was well within his rights to build up the military in a troubled region of the world and prepare for military action. However, unless the president had in fact acted and in so acting had violated the law, it would be inappropriate for the court to act.

The court stated that it would only be ripe to issue an injunction AFTER the president had in fact violated the law and illegally invaded Iraq.

Although the law here is simple, can you see the potential problems that can arise from this legal doctrine? As a practical matter, once a war has been started, it is very difficult to change course. Once a nation has sacrificed lives, there is a point of pride in seeing a fight through to completion. Despite these potential practical problems, we also value a limited judiciary that does not involve itself in political affairs.

Unfortunately, though, this means that these various legal doctrines work together to significantly limit the ability to impose checks and balances on national security powers.

After September 11, the NSA began a classified foreign intelligence program, known as the Terrorist Surveillance Program (TSP), to intercept the international telephone and internet communications of persons and organizations within the United States, without obtaining warrants and therefore outside the parameters of the Foreign Intelligence Surveillance Act of 1978. This was considered necessary to protect the United States from terrorist attacks. Information about the program leaked to the press, and on January 17, 2006, the American Civil Liberties Union (ACLU), on its own behalf and on the behalf of three other organizations and five individuals, sued the National Security Agency (NSA), arguing the TSP was a violation of federal law (FISA) and unconstitutional. The government argued that the lawsuit should be dismissed based on the state secrets privilege and the plaintiffs' lack of standing.

On August 17, 2006, the U.S. District Court ruled that the TSP specifically involving "international telephone and internet communications of numerous persons and organizations" within the United States of America was unconstitutional and illegal, and ordered that it be halted immediately. She did not rule on the alleged NSA database of domestic call detail records, citing the state secrets privilege. This is the language from her opinion, which raises important questions about the balance between liberty and security and the effect of the legal rules we have been discussing here on our nation's system of checks and balances:

> [I]t is important to note that if the court were to deny standing based on the unsubstantiated minor distinctions drawn by Defendants, the President's actions in warrantless wiretapping, in contravention of FISA, Title II, and the First and Fourth amendments, would be immunized from judicial scrutiny. It was never the intent of the Framers to give the President such unfettered control, particularly where his actions blatantly disregard the parameters clearly enumerated in the Bill of Rights. The three separate branches of government were developed as a check and balance for one another. It is within the court's duty to ensure that power is never condensed into a single branch of government.

The Sixth Circuit Court of Appeals reversed this district judge's decision, declining to rule on the legality of the program, and finding that the plaintiffs lacked standing to bring the suit.

Here are some excerpts of the Court's decision:

> The plaintiffs do not contend—nor could they—that the mere practice of wiretapping (i.e., eavesdropping) is, by itself, unconstitutional, illegal, or even improper. Rather, the plaintiffs object to the NSA's eavesdropping without warrants, specifically FISA warrants with their associated limitations and minimization requirements . . . But the plaintiffs do not—and because of the State Secrets Doctrine cannot—produce any evidence that any of their own communications have ever been intercepted by the NSA, under the TSP, or without warrants. Instead, they assert a mere belief, which they contend is reasonable and which they label a "well founded belief," . . . Notably, the plaintiffs do not allege as injury that they personally, either as individuals or associations, anticipate or fear any form of direct reprisal by the government (e.g., the NSA, the Justice Department, the Department of Homeland Security, etc.), such as criminal prosecution, deportation, administrative inquiry, civil litigation, or even public exposure. The injuries that these plaintiffs allege are not so direct; they are more amorphous . . . Implicit in each of the plaintiffs' alleged injuries is the underlying possibility—which the plaintiffs label a "well founded belief" and seek to treat as a probability or even a certainty—that the NSA is presently intercepting, or will eventually intercept, communications to or from one or more of these particular plaintiffs, and that such interception would be detrimental to the plaintiffs' clients, sources, or overseas contacts. This is the premise upon which the plaintiffs' entire theory is built. But even though the plaintiffs' beliefs—based on their superior knowledge of their contacts' activities—may be reasonable, the alternative possibility remains that the NSA might not be intercepting, and might never actually intercept, any communication by any of the plaintiffs named in this lawsuit.

On February 19, 2008, the United States Supreme Court, without comment, turned down an appeal from the ACLU to let it pursue the lawsuit.

Consider the language from both the District Court and from the Court of Appeals. Has the court adequately protected civil liberties? It took the Congress several years to pass any limits on the electronic surveillance programs, and many believe that Congress has still not acted effectively to limit the authority for these surveillance programs. So are there any effective checks or balances on the actions of the national security agencies?

There are no simple answers to these issues, no straightforward answers. But the debates are important ones that we must continue to have.

Review Questions

Apply the doctrines of political question, standing and ripeness to the following hypothetical fact patterns. Which, if any, should apply? Justify your response based on the cases read thus far.

1. An American citizen living in Yemen contacts the court by filing a complaint that he has been targeted by the U.S. government for attack without due process of law. Can he proceed with the lawsuit?

2. An Army captain deployed to Iraq to fight the so-called Islamic State alleges that the failure of the president to obtain a new Authorization for the Use of Military Force from Congress means that the decision to continue to deploy U.S. servicemembers to the conflict violates the War Powers Act. May the captain proceed with his lawsuit?

3. Based on evidence that the NSA collects vast amounts of telephone metadata from U.S. phone records as well as from non-U.S. sources, a citizen's group asks for an injunction against such collection unless an ordinary Title III (probable cause) warrant is issued. May their case proceed?

Key Terms

Political question—A matter the courts will not examine because it is considered to be within the purview of the political process—a matter to be decided between Congress and the president, perhaps through elections, but certainly not in the courts.

Ripeness—The readiness of a case for litigation. A claim is not ripe for adjudication if it rests upon contingent future events that may not occur as anticipated, or indeed may not occur at all.

Standing—The ability of a party to demonstrate to the court sufficient connection to and harm from the law or action challenged to support that party's participation in the case.

Further Reading

Cole, Jared P., *The Political Question Doctrine: Justiciability and the Separation of Powers* Congressional Research Service Report R 43834, December 23, 2014

Henkin, Louis, *Is There a "Political Question" Doctrine?*, The Yale Law Journal. Vol. 85, No. 5 (Apr., 1976), pp. 597–625

Slobogin, Christopher, *Standing and Covert Surveillance*, 42 Pepp. L. Rev. 517 (2014) Available at: http://digitalcommons.pepperdine.edu/plr/vol42/iss3/4

Chapter 8

National Emergencies and Domestic Preparedness

Overview

In Chapter 2 we discussed the Constitutional framework that allows the president, as chief executive and commander-in-chief, to take action in defense of the nation. We also discussed the checks and balances of power between the president and the Congress in the area of national security. In this chapter we will expand this discussion a bit to examine the authorities exercised by the president and Congress, as well as states, in the event of crisis, exigency, or emergency circumstances. Whether it is in the case of war or near war situations, natural disaster, or the outbreak of an epidemic, the government has undertaken the authority and power to act. Such powers may be stated explicitly or implied by the Constitution, assumed by the chief executive to be permissible constitutionally, or inferred from or specified by statute. Through legislation, Congress has made a great many delegations of authority in this regard over the past 200 years.

Until World War I, presidents used emergency powers at their own discretion. Proclamations announced the exercise of exigency authority. Both as a result of the nation's involvement in that war and as the result of changing circumstances and threats for much of the next half-century or so, chief executives had available to them a growing body of standby emergency authority which became operative upon the issuance of a proclamation declaring a condition of national emergency. Sometimes such proclamations confined the matter of crisis to a specific policy sphere, and sometimes they included no limitation at all. Sometimes the focus was on responding to an emergency or a threat, and at times the focus was on prevention and recovery.

In 1976, Congress passed the National Emergencies Act. This law eliminated or modified some statutory grants of emergency authority, requiring the president to declare formally the existence of a national emergency and to specify what statutory authority would be used. It provided a means for Congress to countermand the president's declaration and the activated authority being sought. And, over the thirty years since that law was passed, both natural and man-made emergencies and disasters caused periodic review and revision to the web of laws and regulations that address preparedness and response. The most recent set of reforms came with the terrorist attacks on September 11, 2001 and Hurricane Katrina in 2005.

This chapter will build on the material in Chapter 2 and address the statutes, regulations, and case law that regulate the preparedness and emergency response functions of the government. We'll first provide a bit of history, then discuss the states and regulations as well as some case law.

The Police Power of the Government

We start with a short description of what is called "the police power" of the government. The police power is simply the power of government to exercise control. In a representative democracy such as the United States, this power is exercised on behalf of, and in order to protect, the people. We see this most directly in the plain expression of policing — passing laws and holding people accountable to those laws. But the term "police power" refers to a broader responsibility and authority, extending to health and safety regulation as well as, in the context of this course, homeland and national security.

Much of the police power is exercised at the state and local level, and it was to protect that authority that the Tenth Amendment is intended. That similar power can be held at both the federal and at the state level has been part of the law of this nation since its inception. In the initial chapters of this text we discussed the separation of powers and shared responsibilities of Congress, the president, and the courts for national security. So, in this field of study we can see that responsibility for emergency preparedness and response is shared, not only between the president and Congress, but also between the federal government and the state and tribal governments.

Finding the proper balance between federal and state authority has not always been easy. In this first case, which focused on the power of Congress to regulate commerce, and whether "the police power" existed at all in the federal government, we also see language that discusses how power to address health and safety may need to be, and thus may appropriately be, regulated at both the state and federal level.

Gibbons v. Ogden, 22 U.S. 9 Wheat. 1 (1824)*

Mr. Chief Justice MARSHALL delivered the opinion of the Court ...

The appellant contends that this decree is erroneous because the laws which purport to give the exclusive privilege it sustains are repugnant to the Constitution and laws of the United States.

They are said to be repugnant:

1st. To that clause in the Constitution which authorizes Congress to regulate commerce.

2d. To that which authorizes Congress to promote the progress of science and useful arts.

---

* The case has been heavily edited and paraphrased by the authors for clarity. See disclaimer in introduction.

The State of New York maintains the Constitutionality of these laws, and their Legislature, their Council of Revision, and their Judges, have repeatedly concurred in this opinion....

As preliminary to the very able discussions of the Constitution which we have heard from the bar, and as having some influence on its construction, reference has been made to the political situation of these States anterior to its formation. It has been said that they were sovereign, were completely independent, and were connected with each other only by a league. This is true. But, when these allied sovereigns converted their league into a government, when they converted their Congress of Ambassadors, deputed to deliberate on their common concerns and to recommend measures of general utility, into a Legislature, empowered to enact laws on the most interesting subjects, the whole character in which the States appear underwent a change, the extent of which must be determined by a fair consideration of the instrument by which that change was effected.

This instrument contains an enumeration of powers expressly granted by the people to their government. It has been said that these powers ought to be construed strictly. But why ought they to be so construed? Is there one sentence in the Constitution which gives countenance to this rule? In the last of the enumerated powers, that which grants expressly the means for carrying all others into execution, Congress is authorized "to make all laws which shall be necessary and proper" for the purpose. Nor is there one sentence in the Constitution which has been pointed out by the gentlemen of the bar or which we have been able to discern that prescribes this rule. We do not, therefore, think ourselves justified in adopting it. That narrow construction which would cripple the government and render it unequal to the object for which it is declared to be instituted, and to which the powers given, as fairly understood, render it competent; then we cannot perceive the propriety of this strict construction, nor adopt it as the rule by which the Constitution is to be expounded. The grant does not convey power which might be beneficial to the grantor if retained by himself, or which can ensure solely to the benefit of the grantee, but is an investment of power for the general advantage, in the hands of agents selected for that purpose, which power can never be exercised by the people themselves, but must be placed in the hands of agents or lie dormant. We know of no rule for construing the extent of such powers other than is given by the language of the instrument which confers them, taken in connection with the purposes for which they were conferred.

The words are, "Congress shall have power to regulate commerce with foreign nations, and among the several States, and with the Indian tribes."

We are now arrived at the inquiry—What is this power?

It is the power to regulate, that is, to prescribe the rule by which commerce is to be governed. This power, like all others vested in Congress, is complete in itself, may be exercised to its utmost extent, and acknowledges no limitations other than are prescribed in the Constitution. These are expressed in plain terms, and do not affect the questions which arise in this case, or which have been discussed at the bar. If, as has always been understood, the sovereignty of Congress, though limited to specified objects, is plenary as to those objects, the power over commerce with foreign nations, and among the several States, is vested in Congress as absolutely as it would be in a single government, having in its Constitution the same restrictions on the exercise of the power as are found in the Constitution of the United States. The wisdom and the discretion of Congress, their identity with the people, and the influence which their constituents possess at elections are, in this, as in many other instances, as that, for example, of declaring war, the sole restraints on which they have relied, to secure them from its abuse. They are the restraints on which the people must often they solely, in all representative governments.

But it has been urged with great earnestness that, although the power of Congress to regulate commerce with foreign nations and among the several States be coextensive with the subject itself, and have no other limits than are prescribed in the Constitution, yet the States may severally exercise the same power, within their respective jurisdictions. In support of this argument, it is said that they possessed it as an inseparable attribute of sovereignty, before the formation of the Constitution, and still retain it except so far as they have surrendered it by that instrument; that this principle results from the nature of the government, and is secured by the tenth amendment; that an affirmative grant of power is not exclusive unless in its own nature it be such that the continued exercise of it by the former possessor is inconsistent with the grant, and that this is not of that description.

The appellant, conceding these postulates except the last, contends that full power to regulate a particular subject implies the whole power, and leaves no residuum; that a grant of the whole is incompatible with the existence of a right in another to any part of it.

Although many of the powers formerly exercised by the States are transferred to the government of the Union, yet the State governments remain, and constitute a most important part of our system. When, then, each government exercises the power of taxation, neither is exercising the power of the other.

Inspection laws are said to be regulations of commerce, and are certainly recognized in the Constitution as being passed in the exercise of a power remaining with the States . . .

They form a portion of that immense mass of legislation which embraces everything within the territory of a State not surrendered to the General Government; all which can be most advantageously exercised by the States themselves. Inspection laws, quarantine laws, health laws of every description, as well as laws for regulating the internal commerce of a State, and those which respect turnpike roads, ferries, &c., are component parts of this mass.

No direct general power over these objects is granted to Congress, and, consequently, they remain subject to State legislation. If the legislative power of the Union can reach them, it must be for national purposes, it must be where the power is expressly given for a special purpose or is clearly incidental to some power which is expressly given. It is obvious that the government of the Union, in the exercise of its express powers—that, for example, of regulating commerce with foreign nations and among the States—may use means that may also be employed by a State in the exercise of its acknowledged powers—that, for example, of regulating commerce within the State.

In our complex system, presenting the rare and difficult scheme of one General Government whose action extends over the whole but which possesses only certain enumerated powers, and of numerous State governments which retain and exercise all powers not delegated to the Union, contests respecting power must arise. Were it even otherwise, the measures taken by the respective governments to execute their acknowledged powers would often be of the same description, and might sometimes interfere. This, however, does not prove that the one is exercising, or has a right to exercise, the powers of the other.

The acts of Congress passed in 1796 and 1799, 2 U.S.L. 345, 3 U.S.L. 126, empowering and directing the officers of the General Government to conform to and assist in the execution of the quarantine and health laws of a State proceed, it is said, upon the idea that these laws are constitutional. It is undoubtedly true that they do proceed upon that idea, and the constitutionality of such laws has never, so far as we are informed, been denied. But they do not imply an acknowledgment that a State may rightfully regulate commerce with foreign nations or among the States, for they do not imply that such laws are an exercise of that power, or enacted with a view to it. On the contrary, they are treated as quarantine and health laws, are so denominated in the acts of Congress, and are considered as flowing from the acknowledged power of a State to provide for the health of its citizens.

Although Congress cannot enable a State to legislate, Congress may adopt the provisions of a State on any subject. When the government of the Union was brought into existence, it found a system for the regulation of its pilots in full force in every State. The act which has been mentioned adopts this system, and gives it the same validity as if its provisions had been specially made by Congress. But the act, it may be said, is prospective also, and the adoption of laws to be made in future presupposes the right in the maker to legislate on the subject.

It has been contended by the counsel for the appellant that, as the word "to regulate" implies in its nature full power over the thing to be regulated, it excludes necessarily the action of all others that would perform the same operation on the same thing. That regulation is designed for the entire result, applying to those parts which remain as they were, as well as to those which are altered. It produces a uniform whole which is as much disturbed and deranged by changing what the regulating power designs to leave untouched as that on which it has operated.

END OF OPINION

Government authority to regulate behavior, whether at the federal level or the state level, is part of "the police power" and has been ruled to extend to many areas where the good of the community may outweigh some liberty interests of individuals. One of the key Supreme Court decisions on this topic involved the subject of mandatory immunization. One of the most dangerous diseases in human history has been smallpox. Smallpox epidemics have killed millions, and at the beginning of the 20th century a number of communities required citizens to be immunized. Those requirements were argued to be in violation of personal liberty—an argument that some people continue to make even in present times. But the personal liberty of the individual can inevitably come into conflict with the potential safety of the community and so the question had to be asked whether a community could force an individual to be vaccinated against his or her will, or if such a requirement was an impermissible infringement on liberty.

In the case of *Jacobson v. Massachusetts*, the Supreme Court ruled that such laws did not violate the U.S. Constitution.

Jacobson v. Massachusetts, 197 U.S. 11 (1905)*

This case involves the validity, under the Constitution of the United States, of certain provisions in the statutes of Massachusetts relating to vaccination.

The Board of Health of the city of Cambridge, Massachusetts, on the twenty-seventh day of February, 1902, adopted the following regulation:

"Whereas, smallpox has been prevalent to some extent in the city of Cambridge and still continues to increase; and whereas it is necessary for the speedy extermination of the disease that all persons not protected by vaccination should be vaccinated, and whereas, in the opinion of the board, the public health and safety require the vaccination or revaccination of all the inhabitants of Cambridge; be it ordered, that all the inhabitants of the city who have not been successfully vaccinated since March 1, 1897, be vaccinated or revaccinated."

MR. JUSTICE HARLAN . . . delivered the opinion of the court.

The Supreme Judicial Court of Massachusetts said in the present case:

"Let us consider the offer of evidence which was made by the defendant Jacobson. The propositions which he offered to prove, as to what vaccination consists of, is nothing more than a fact of common knowledge, upon which the statute is founded, and proof of it was unnecessary and immaterial. Moreover, his views could not affect the validity of the statute, nor entitle him to be excepted from its provisions. The other eleven propositions all relate to alleged injurious or dangerous effects of vaccination. The defendant 'offered to prove and show by competent evidence' these so-called facts. Each of them, in its nature, is such that it cannot be stated as a truth, otherwise than as a matter of opinion. The only 'competent evidence' that could be presented to the court to prove these propositions was the testimony of experts, giving their opinions. It would not have been competent to introduce the medical history of individual cases.

Assuming that medical experts could have been found who would have testified in support of these propositions, and that it had become the duty of the judge to instruct the jury as to whether or not the statute is constitutional, he would have been

---

* The case has been heavily edited and paraphrased by the authors for clarity. See disclaimer in introduction.

obliged to consider the evidence in connection with facts of common knowledge, which the court will always regard in passing upon the constitutionality of a statute. He would have considered this testimony of experts in connection with the facts, that for nearly a century, most of the members of the medical profession have regarded vaccination, repeated after intervals, as a preventive of smallpox; that, while they have recognized the possibility of injury to an individual from carelessness in the performance of it, or even, in a conceivable case, without carelessness, they generally have considered the risk of such an injury too small to be seriously weighed as against the benefits coming from the discreet and proper use of the preventive, and that not only the medical profession and the people generally have for a long time entertained these opinions, but legislatures and courts have acted upon them with general unanimity. If the defendant had been permitted to introduce such expert testimony as he had in support of these several propositions, it could not have changed the result. It would not have justified the court in holding that the legislature had transcended its power in enacting this statute on their judgment of what the welfare of the people demands."

Taking the above observations of the state court as indicating the scope of the statute—and such is our duty—we assume for the purposes of the present inquiry that its provisions require, at least as a general rule, that adults not under guardianship and remaining within the limits of the city of Cambridge must submit to the regulation adopted by the Board of Health. Is the statute, so construed, therefore, inconsistent with the liberty which the Constitution of the United States secures to every person against deprivation by the State?

The authority of the State to enact this statute is to be referred to what is commonly called the police power—a power which the State did not surrender when becoming a member of the Union under the Constitution. Although this court has refrained from any attempt to define the limits of that power, yet it has distinctly recognized the authority of a State to enact quarantine laws and "health laws of every description;" indeed, all laws that relate to matters completely within its territory and which do not, by their necessary operation, affect the people of other States. According to settled principles, the police power of a State must be held to embrace, at least, such reasonable regulations established directly by legislative enactment as will protect the public health and the public safety. It is equally true that the State may invest local bodies called into existence for purposes of local administration with authority in some appropriate way to safeguard the public health and the public safety. The mode or manner in which those results are to be accomplished is within the discretion of the State, subject, of course, so far as Federal power is concerned, only to the condition that no rule prescribed by a State, nor any regulation adopted by a local governmental agency acting under the sanction of state legislation, shall contravene the Constitution of the United States or infringe any right granted or secured by that instrument. A local enactment or regulation, even if based on the acknowledged police powers of a State, must always yield in case of conflict with the exercise by the General Government of any power it possesses under the Constitution, or with any right which that instrument gives or secures.

We come, then, to inquire whether any right given or secured by the Constitution is invaded by the statute as interpreted by the state court. The defendant insists that his liberty is invaded when the State subjects him to fine or imprisonment for neglecting or refusing to submit to vaccination; that a compulsory vaccination law is unreasonable, arbitrary and oppressive, and, therefore, hostile to the inherent right of every freeman to care for his own body and health in such way as to him seems best, and that the execution of such a law against one who objects to vaccination, no matter for what reason, is nothing short of an assault upon his person.

But the liberty secured by the Constitution of the United States to every person within its jurisdiction does not import an absolute right in each person to be, at all times and in all circumstances, wholly freed from restraint. There are manifold restraints to which every person is necessarily subject for the common good. On any other basis, organized society could not exist with safety to its members.

Society based on the rule that each one is a law unto himself would soon be confronted with disorder and anarchy. Real liberty for all could not exist under the operation of a principle which recognizes the right of each individual person to use his own, whether in respect of his person or his property, regardless of the injury that may be done to others. This court has more than once recognized it as a fundamental principle that

> "persons and property are subjected to all kinds of restraints and burdens, in order to secure the general comfort, health, and prosperity of the State, of the perfect right of the legislature to do which no question ever was, or upon acknowledged general principles ever can be, made so far as natural persons are concerned."

In *Crowley v. Christensen*, 137 U.S. 86, 137 U.S. 89, we said:

> "The possession and enjoyment of all rights are subject to such reasonable conditions as may be deemed by the governing authority of the country essential to the safety, health, peace, good order and morals of the community. Even liberty itself, the greatest of all rights, is not unrestricted license to act according to one's own will. It is only freedom from restraint under conditions essential to the equal enjoyment of the same right by others. It is then liberty regulated by law."

In the constitution of Massachusetts adopted in 1780, it was laid down as a fundamental principle of the social compact that the whole people covenants with each citizen, and each citizen with the whole people, that all shall be governed by certain laws for "the common good," and that government is instituted

> "for the common good, for the protection, safety, prosperity and happiness of the people, and not for the profit, honor or private interests of anyone man, family or class of men."

Applying these principles to the present case, it is to be observed that the legislature of Massachusetts required the inhabitants of a city or town to be vaccinated only when, in the opinion of the Board of Health, that was necessary for the public health or the public safety. The authority to determine for all what ought to be done in such an emergency must have been lodged somewhere or in some body, and surely it was appropriate for the legislature to refer that question, in the first instance, to a Board of Health, composed of persons residing in the locality affected and appointed, presumably, because of their fitness to determine such questions.

To invest such a body with authority over such matters was not an unusual nor an unreasonable or arbitrary requirement. Upon the principle of self-defense, of paramount necessity, a community has the right to protect itself against an epidemic of disease which threatens the safety of its members. It is to be observed that, when the regulation in question was adopted, smallpox, according to the recitals in the regulation adopted by the Board of Health, was prevalent to some extent in the city of Cambridge, and the disease was increasing. If such was the situation—and nothing is asserted or appears in the record to the contrary—if we are to attach any value whatever to the knowledge which, it is safe to affirm, is common to all civilized peoples touching smallpox and the methods most usually employed to eradicate that disease, it cannot be adjudged that the present regulation of the Board of Health was not necessary in order to protect the public health and secure the public safety. Smallpox being prevalent and increasing at Cambridge, the court would usurp the functions of another branch of government if it adjudged, as matter of law, that the mode adopted under the sanction of the State, to protect the people at large was arbitrary and not justified by the necessities of the case. We say necessities of the case because it might be that an acknowledged power of a local community to protect itself against an epidemic threatening the safety of all, might be exercised in particular circumstances and in reference to particular persons in such an arbitrary, unreasonable manner, or might go so far beyond what was reasonably required for the safety of the public, as to authorize or compel the courts to interfere for the protection of such persons.

In *Railroad Company v. Husen*, 95 U.S. 465 (1878), this court recognized the right of a State to pass sanitary laws, laws for the protection of life, liberty, heath or property within its limits, laws to prevent persons and animals suffering under contagious or infectious diseases, or convicts, from coming within its borders. But as the laws there involved went beyond the necessity of the case and under the guise of exerting a police power invaded the domain of Federal authority, and violated rights secured by the Constitution, this court deemed it to be its duty to hold such laws invalid. If the mode adopted by the Commonwealth of Massachusetts for the protection of its local communities against smallpox proved to be distressing, inconvenient or objectionable to some—if nothing more could be reasonably affirmed of the statute in question—the answer is that it was the duty of the constituted authorities primarily to keep in view the welfare, comfort and safety of the many, and not permit the interests of the many to be subordinated to the wishes or convenience of the few.

There is, of course, a sphere within which the individual may assert the supremacy of his own will and rightfully dispute the authority of any human government, especially of any free government existing under a written constitution, to interfere with the exercise of that will. But it is equally true that, in every well-ordered society charged with the duty of conserving the safety of its members the rights of the individual in respect of his liberty may at times, under the pressure of great dangers, be subjected to such restraint, to be enforced by reasonable regulations, as the safety of the general public may demand. . . .

The liberty secured by the Fourteenth Amendment, this court has said, consists, in part, in the right of a person to live and work where he will, and yet he may be compelled, by force if need be, against his will and without regard to his personal wishes or his pecuniary interests, or even his religious or political convictions, to take his place in the ranks of the army of his country and risk the chance of being shot down in its defense. It is not, therefore, true that the power of the public to guard itself against imminent danger depends in every case involving the control of one's body upon his willingness to submit to reasonable regulations established by the constituted authorities, under the sanction of the State, for the purpose of protecting the public collectively against such danger.

Looking at the propositions embodied in the defendant's rejected offers of proof, it is clear that they are more formidable by their number than by their inherent value. Those offers, in the main, seem to have had no purpose except to state the general theory of those of the medical profession who attach little or no value to vaccination as a means of preventing the spread of smallpox, or who think that vaccination causes other diseases of the body. What everybody knows, the court must know, and therefore the state court judicially knew, as this court knows, that an opposite theory accords with the common belief and is maintained by high medical authority. We must assume that, when the statute in question was passed, the legislature of Massachusetts was not unaware of these opposing theories, and was compelled, of necessity, to choose between them. It was not compelled to commit a matter involving the public health and safety to the final decision of a court or jury. It is no part of the function of a court or a jury to determine which one of two modes was likely to be the most effective for the protection of the public against disease. That was for the legislative department to determine in the light of all the information it had or could obtain. It could not properly abdicate its function to guard the public health and safety.

The state legislature proceeded upon the theory which recognized vaccination as at least an effective, if not the best, known way in which to meet and suppress the evils of a smallpox epidemic that imperiled an entire population. Upon what sound principles as to the relations existing between the different departments of government can the court review this action of the legislature? If there is any such power in the judiciary to review legislative action in respect of a matter affecting the general welfare, it can only be when that which the legislature has done comes within the rule that,

> "if a statute purporting to have been enacted to protect the public health, the public morals, or the public safety has no real or substantial relation to those objects, or is, beyond all question, a plain, palpable invasion of rights secured by the fundamental law, it is the duty of the courts to so adjudge, and thereby give effect to the Constitution."

Whatever may be thought of the expediency of this statute, it cannot be affirmed to be, beyond question, in palpable conflict with the Constitution. Nor, in view of the methods employed to stamp out the disease of smallpox, can anyone confidently assert that the means prescribed by the State to that end has no real or substantial relation to the protection of the public health and the public safety. Such an assertion would not be consistent with the experience of this and other countries whose authorities have dealt with the disease of smallpox. And the principle of vaccination as a means to prevent the spread of smallpox has been enforced in many States by statutes making the vaccination of children a condition of their right to enter or remain in public schools.

The latest case upon the subject of which we are aware is *Viemeister v. White, President* decided very recently by the Court of Appeals of New York. That case involved the validity of a statute excluding from the public schools all children who had not been vaccinated. One contention was that the statute and the regulation adopted in exercise of its provisions was inconsistent with the rights, privileges and liberties of the citizen. The contention was overruled, the court saying, among other things:

> "Smallpox is known of all to be a dangerous and contagious disease. If vaccination strongly tends to prevent the transmission or spread of this disease, it logically follows that children may be refused admission to the public schools until they have been vaccinated. The appellant claims that vaccination does not tend to prevent smallpox, but tends to bring about other diseases, and that it does much harm, with no good."

> "It must be conceded that some laymen, both learned and unlearned, and some physicians of great skill and repute, do not believe that vaccination is a preventive of smallpox. The common belief, however, is that it has a decided tendency to prevent the spread of this fearful disease and to render it less dangerous to those who contract it. While not accepted by all, it is accepted by the mass of the people, as well as by most members of the medical profession. It has been general in our State and in most civilized nations for generations. It is generally accepted in theory and generally applied in practice, both by the voluntary action of the people and in obedience to the command of law. Nearly every State of the Union has statutes to encourage, or directly or indirectly to require, vaccination, and this is true of most nations of Europe."

> "A common belief, like common knowledge, does not require evidence to establish its existence, but may be acted upon without proof by the legislature and the courts."

> "The fact that the belief is not universal is not controlling, for there is scarcely any belief that is accepted by everyone. The possibility that the belief may be wrong, and that science may yet show it to be wrong, is not conclusive, for the legislature has the right to pass laws which, according to the common belief of the people, are adapted to prevent the spread of contagious diseases. In a free country, where the government is by the people, through their

chosen representatives, practical legislation admits of no other standard of action; for what the people believe is for the common welfare must be accepted as tending to promote the common welfare, whether it does, in fact, or not. Any other basis would conflict with the spirit of the Constitution, and would sanction measures opposed to a republican form of government. While we do not decide and cannot decide that vaccination is a preventive of smallpox, we take judicial notice of the fact that this is the common belief of the people of the State, and, with this fact as a foundation, we hold that the statute in question is a health law, enacted in a reasonable and proper exercise of the police power."

Since, then, vaccination, as a means of protecting a community against smallpox, finds strong support in the experience of this and other countries, no court, much less a jury, is justified in disregarding the action of the legislature simply because, in its or their opinion, that particular method was—perhaps or possibly—not the best either for children or adults.

The legislature assumed that some children, by reason of their condition at the time, might not be fit subjects of vaccination, and it is suggested—and we will not say without reason—that such is the case with some adults. But the defendant did not offer to prove that, by reason of his then condition, he was, in fact, not a fit subject of vaccination at the time he was informed of the requirement of the regulation adopted by the Board of Health. It is entirely consistent with his offer of proof that, after reaching full age, he had become, so far as medical skill could discover, and, when informed of the regulation of the Board of Health, was, a fit subject of vaccination, and that the vaccine matter to be used in his case was such as any medical practitioner of good standing would regard as proper to be used. The matured opinions of medical men everywhere, and the experience of mankind, as all must know, negative the suggestion that it is not possible in any case to determine whether vaccination is safe. Was defendant exempted from the operation of the statute simply because of his dread of the same evil results experienced by him when a child and had observed in the cases of his son and other children? Could he reasonably claim such an exemption because, "quite often" or "occasionally," injury had resulted from vaccination, or because it was impossible, in the opinion of some, by any practical test, to determine with absolute certainty whether a particular person could be safely vaccinated?

It seems to the court that an affirmative answer to these questions would practically strip the legislative department of its function to care for the public health and the public safety when endangered by epidemics of disease. Such an answer would mean that compulsory vaccination could not, in any conceivable case, be legally enforced in a community, even at the command of the legislature, however widespread the epidemic of smallpox, and however deep and universal was the belief of the community and of its medical advisers, that a system of general vaccination was vital to the safety of all.

We are not prepared to hold that a minority, residing or remaining in any city or town where smallpox is prevalent, and enjoying the general protection afforded by an organized local government, may thus defy the will of its constituted authorities, acting in good faith for all, under the legislative sanction of the State. If such be the privilege of a minority, then a like privilege would belong to each individual of the community, and the spectacle would be presented of the welfare and safety of an entire population being subordinated to the notions of a single individual who chooses to remain a part of that population. We are unwilling to hold it to be an element in the liberty secured by the Constitution of the United States that one person, or a minority of persons, residing in any community and enjoying the benefits of its local government, should have the power thus to dominate the majority when supported in their action by the authority of the State. While this court should guard with firmness every right appertaining to life, liberty or property as secured to the individual by the Supreme Law of the Land, it is of the last importance that it should not invade the domain of local authority except when it is plainly necessary to do so in order to enforce that law. The safety and the health of the people of Massachusetts are, in the first instance, for that Commonwealth to guard and protect. They are matters that do not ordinarily concern the National Government. So far as they can be reached by any government, they depend, primarily, upon such action as the State in its wisdom may take, and we do not perceive that this legislation has invaded any right secured by the Federal Constitution.

Before closing this opinion, we deem it appropriate, in order to prevent misapprehension as to our views, to observe—perhaps to repeat a thought already sufficiently expressed, namely—that the police power of a State, whether exercised by the legislature or by a local body acting under its authority, may be exerted in such circumstances or by regulations so arbitrary and oppressive in particular cases as to justify the interference of the courts to prevent wrong and oppression. Extreme cases can be readily suggested. Ordinarily such cases are not safe guides in the administration of the law. It is easy, for instance, to suppose the case of an adult who is embraced by the mere words of the act, but yet to subject whom to vaccination in a particular condition of his health or body, would be cruel and inhuman in the last degree. We are not to be understood as holding that the statute was intended to be applied to such a case, or, if it as so intended, that the judiciary would not be competent to interfere and protect the health and life of the individual concerned. "All laws," this court has said,

> "should receive a sensible construction. General terms should be so limited in their application as not to lead to injustice, oppression or absurd consequence. It will always, therefore, be presumed that the legislature intended exceptions to its language which would avoid results of that character. The reason of the law in such cases should prevail over its letter."

Until otherwise informed by the highest court of Massachusetts, we are not inclined to hold that the statute establishes the absolute rule that an adult must be vaccinated if it be apparent or can be shown with reasonable certainty that he is not at the time a fit subject of vaccination or that vaccination, by reason of his then condition, would seriously impair his health or probably cause his death. . . .

We now decide only that the statute covers the present case, and that nothing clearly appears that would justify this court in holding it to be unconstitutional and inoperative in its application to the plaintiff in error.

The judgment of the court below must be affirmed.

END OF OPINION

It's clear from this case, and other cases that arose around the nation, that the law permits federal, state, and local governments to take action such as requiring vaccination or quarantine in order to protect the broader society. In the United States, legislation authorizing quarantine has been enacted in every state, and these laws have been upheld by the Supreme Court. Especially when there is no vaccine or demonstrably effective treatment, officials may conclude that quarantine remains, not simply an important part of the strategy for containing infectious diseases, but a necessary step. But how are decisions like this to be made? Is the legality of the measure enough? The problems have been in identifying when quarantine is necessary and in implementation. The opinion we just read included an acknowledgment that medical opinion may differ, and disagreements over the necessity of measures are part of what elected officials as well as enforcement agencies must consider.

Such decisions are fraught with ethical challenges. Some have suggested that public health officials should consider ethical principles in deciding whether and how to impose a quarantine: (1) necessity, effectiveness, and scientific rationale; (2) proportionality and least infringement; (3) humane supportive services; and (4) public justification.[1] What are your thoughts?

How the police power is applied is important for legal as well as ethical reasons. From local police on up, there is a tremendous capacity for discretion to be exercised and this discretion can be used both properly as well as improperly.

The last case we will look at in this part of the chapter deals with the power of the governments to impose a curfew, and looks at the criteria that makes such impositions reasonable. This case arose after Hurricane Andrew hit the southern United States in the 1990s. After this case we will look at the history of disaster response and the key laws and regulations that have been adopted.

Smith v. Avino, 91 F.3d 105 (11th Cir. 1996)[*]

This is an official capacity suit against Metropolitan Dade County and its manager challenging the curfew that was imposed in the wake of Hurricane Andrew. The plaintiffs alleged the curfew was unconstitutionally vague and overly broad, both

---

1. Rothstein, Mark A., From SARS to Ebola: Legal and Ethical Considerations for Modern Quarantine (January 9, 2015). Indiana Health Law Review, vol.12, no.1, 2015; Available at SSRN: http://ssrn.com/abstract=2499701 or http://dx.doi.org/10.2139/ssrn.2499701

[*] The case has been heavily edited and paraphrased by the authors for clarity. See disclaimer in introduction.

facially and as applied, and sought a declaratory decree, damages, and attorneys fees pursuant to 42 U.S.C. § 1988.

Hurricane Andrew struck Dade County, Florida, on August 24, 1992. The storm's widespread destruction to homes, roads, power, and communication services is undisputed. The Governor of the State of Florida issued an Executive Order that declared a state of emergency and provided that Miami city and Metropolitan Dade County officials could impose curfews until December 21, 1992. The county manager issued a proclamation setting a curfew for the County from 7:00 pm to 7:00 am. The National Guard, as well as other law enforcement officials, was called in to assist local police. Over the next few weeks, the curfew was modified as to geographical area and time of enforcement. By October 2, 1992, the curfew was in effect from 10:00 pm through 5:00 am and covered a specified area of south county. Each proclamation required that persons in the affected area were to remain in their homes during the curfew hours, unless otherwise authorized. The curfew was lifted November 16, 1992, twenty-four hours after the National Guard departed.

The challenged curfew language required that "all persons residing in these areas are commanded to remain in their homes during the hours of the curfew, unless otherwise authorized by Dade County, State of Florida or federal officials."

The basic law concerning the vagueness and overbreadth of legislative authority has been established by the Supreme Court. A statute is void for vagueness when its prohibition is so vague as to leave an individual without knowledge of the nature of the activity that is prohibited. To pass constitutional muster, a statute must "give the person of ordinary intelligence a reasonable opportunity to know what is prohibited, and provide explicit standards for those who apply it" to avoid arbitrary and discriminatory enforcement. Even a clear, precise ordinance may be "overbroad" if it prohibits constitutionally protected conduct.

Once a law is determined to be constitutional as written, it may still be challenged if it was applied in an unconstitutional manner. The key to judicial consideration to the challenge in this instance lies in the circumstances under which the curfew was instituted. The plaintiffs do not argue, nor can there be any doubt, that the devastation and chaos created by Hurricane Andrew required the authorities to act, and act quickly, to protect the interests of the victims. In fact, the first prayer for relief in the plaintiffs' complaint asked the court to declare unconstitutional and unlawful the "failure of Defendants" to create and implement constitutionally valid ordinances. Police action was clearly required.

Cases have consistently held it is a proper exercise of police power to respond to emergency situations with temporary curfews that might curtail the movement of persons who otherwise would enjoy freedom from restriction. *Moorhead v. Farrelly* (D.V.I.1989) (ravages of Hurricane Hugo); *United States v. Chalk* (4th Cir.1971) (civil unrest after racial incident); *In re Juan C.* (1994) (widespread looting, violence during riots in Los Angeles).

In such circumstances, governing authorities must be granted the proper deference and wide latitude necessary for dealing with the emergency. From prior decisions involving natural disasters, both of the judges in the district court gleaned the proper approach in such matters: when a curfew is imposed as an emergency measure in response to a natural disaster, the scope of review in cases challenging its constitutionality "is limited to a determination whether the executive's actions were taken in good faith and whether there is some factual basis for the decision that the restrictions imposed were necessary to maintain order."

Plaintiffs concede a curfew was necessary when imposed. There has been no suggestion that the defendants acted in bad faith. The curfew was in direct response to the official emergency declared by the Governor of the State and the factual emergency conceded to exist. Flexibility in any such curfew is a key ingredient to provide the enforcing authorities with the practical ability to carry out the purposes for which it is instituted.

Plaintiffs complain that the curfew is unconstitutionally vague both on its face and as applied because it failed to advise residents of the parameters of their right to travel. Though the curfew allowed "authorized" travel, there was no criteria set forth in the curfew order itself for obtaining authorization; no stated exceptions for necessary travel to or from work, school, religious activities, or in connection with medical or personal emergencies for the residents; nor were there exceptions for emergency personnel, such as ambulance drivers or firefighters to enter the area during the curfew.

Contrary to plaintiffs' argument that this information was unavailable to residents, the district court made factual findings, unchallenged on this appeal, that the police were given guidelines in the exercise of discretion to permit travel for medical reasons, work, or school, and that the police trained the military in the application thereof. There was also testimony that during regular door-to-door visits by police officers, the community was advised of the possibilities for obtaining authorization for travel during curfew hours.

Basically, plaintiffs argue that the curfew is constitutionally flawed because it did not contain "built-in exceptions" for necessary activity. That court, in considering a curfew that was imposed to quell a riot, acknowledged that "under usual and normal circumstances and as a general proposition, this may be true. But the circumstances existing at the time were not usual, nor were they normal." While we would agree with plaintiffs that in a normal situation, the proclamation should be as informative as possible, under the emergency circumstances present in this case, the proclamation was not constitutionally flawed because it did not include exceptions. In an emergency situation, fundamental rights such as the right of travel and free speech may be temporarily limited or suspended. See *Korematsu v. United States* (1944).

The claims tried by Judge Mishler—that the curfew was overbroad because it impinged on plaintiffs' personal liberties and continued after the emergency ended and that it was void for vagueness as it was applied to plaintiffs because of selective enforcement—were denied because the findings of fact did not support the claims. Those findings are protected here by the clearly erroneous standard of review.

The district court properly held that it could not say that the curfew was so broad or vague that it unconstitutionally denied personal liberty without due process of law. The nature of the emergency and the exigency of the time warranted the imposition and length of the curfew.

It is significant that the parties have cited no cases, nor have we found any in which a curfew mandated because of a situation caused by a natural disaster was held unconstitutional so that affected persons could recover damages against the local authorities.

AFFIRMED.

END OF OPINION

These three cases provide you some insight into the key legal issues of disaster response and emergency preparedness. The laws governing this field are extensive, not just at the federal level, but also at the state and local level. We don't have the time or space in this course to go into all of those laws in any depth. What we will do, though, is look briefly at the history of federal emergency response as it developed throughout the 20th century. The period from 1915 (World War One) through 2005 (Hurricane Katrina) saw a lot of movement trying to balance national security programs with preparedness for natural disaster, health, and safety.

A Short History of Disaster and Emergency Preparedness[2]

The modern approach to disaster and emergency preparedness was first undertaken by the Council of National Defense, established on August 29, 1916, as a presidential advisory board that included the secretaries of War, Navy, Interior, Agriculture, Commerce, and Labor, who were supported by an Advisory Committee appointed by the president. Its responsibilities included "coordinating resources and industries for national defense" and "stimulating civilian morale." In 1933, President Franklin Roosevelt established the National Emergency Council (NEC), which consisted of the president, his cabinet members, and the head of nearly every major federal agency, commission, and board. The mission of the NEC included programs unrelated to civil defense but did address coordination of emergency programs among all agencies involved in national preparedness. States were asked to establish local counterpart councils.

Tensions among federal, state, and local governments began to rise about authority and resources. Federal funding was reserved primarily for preparedness against

---

2. This section is adapted from *Civil Defense and Homeland Security: A Short History of National Preparedness Efforts,* September 2006, prepared by the Director of the Department of Homeland Security's National Preparedness Task Force. Available at https://training.fema.gov/hiedu/docs/dhs%20civil%20defense-hs%20-%20short%20history.pdf

attack, while non-attack disaster preparedness remained almost entirely the responsibility of states. States asserted they were not given enough power to manage civil defense tasks, and local governments claimed that urban areas did not receive proper consideration and resources from atate governments.

Mayor Fiorello La Guardia of New York City wrote a letter to President Roosevelt stating:

> There is a need for a strong Federal Department to coordinate activities, and not only to coordinate but to initiate and get things going. Please bear in mind that up to this war and never in our history, has the civilian population been exposed to attack. The new technique of war has created the necessity for developing new techniques of civilian defense.

President Roosevelt responded to the increasing concern of the public and local officials by creating the Office of Civilian Defense (OCD) in 1941, which oversaw unprecedented federal involvement in attack preparedness. As with the Council of National Defense, the OCD created corresponding defense councils at the local level. While the OCD did not fulfill all of its ambitious goals, it did begin the development of concrete civil defense plans, including air raid drills, blackouts, and sandbag stockpiling. There was tension over whether efforts should emphasize protective services (typically done at that time by men), or social welfare services (typically undertaken at that time by women). There were those who considered the program's broad reach and social development programs to be socialist or communist. Others believed its tasks were better undertaken by the Department of War. This conflict over the meaning and purpose of civil defense continued for several decades.

Soon after taking office, President Harry Truman abolished the OCD. Civil defense was not a priority because many Americans believed that the immediate threat of war had receded. In 1947 the War Department's Civil Defense Board released a report recommending that the military focus on military missions, and that civil defense would be best implemented locally as "self-help" by civilians. The National Security Act of 1947, best known for the creation of the Central Intelligence Agency, also established the National Security Resources Board (NSRB), which would be responsible for mobilizing civilian and military support in time of emergency. As U.S.-Soviet relations became increasingly strained, the government established the Office of Civil Defense Planning (OCDP) and recommended creation of a permanent civil defense agency directly under the president or secretary of defense. Some in Congress and the public, though, feared the effort could lead to a "garrison state" by transferring what should be a civilian responsibility to the military.

ODCP recommended that the federal government provide guidance and assistance, but that state and local governments handle operational responsibilities. Even these recommendations were viewed by some as too far-reaching, making unrealistic demands on the public and government in terms of the cost and scope of civil defense. Truman assigned civil defense planning to the NSRB, a civilian agency, but the NSRB did not receive much in the way of resources or authority.

When the United States lost its monopoly on nuclear weapons with the successful Soviet test of a nuclear weapon in August of 1949, the climate changed dramatically. Local governments began to demand a clear outline of what to do in case of attack. In 1950, Congress enacted the Federal Civil Defense Act, keeping much of the civil defense burden on the states and creating the Federal Civil Defense Administration (FCDA) to formulate national policy to guide the states' efforts. The program sought to improve federal–state coordination, established an attack warning system, and stockpiled supplies. It also started a national civic education campaign specifically aimed to teach schoolchildren about preparedness, primarily through civil defense drills and movies that would be shown in classrooms across the nation—among them "Duck and Cover," a cartoon which, through its main character Bert the Turtle, showed children what to do when they saw "the flash of an atomic bomb." The public education campaign promoted the idea that, with preparation, a nuclear attack could be survivable.

Despite ambitious funding requests, actual appropriations to civil defense remained low. Nevertheless, the concept of civil defense as a purposeful approach to the protection of citizens from threats outside the nation's borders began to take shape. Though each presidential administration would focus on different programs and approaches, civil defense remained an important initiative during the coming decades.

President Dwight Eisenhower's approach to civil defense supported mass evacuation, proper training for civil defense officials, and regular public drills. The Eisenhower administration developed the massive federal interstate highway program, connecting major cities and in the process providing a means for evacuation. The FCDA presented a National Shelter Policy, which proposed "federally subsidized self-help" such as tax incentives or special mortgage rates to shelter-owning families.

In 1957, a government report concluded that the United States could not defend itself from a Soviet surprise attack on the homeland and recommended funding antiballistic missile (ABM) defense systems and adopting the FCDA shelter proposal. Eisenhower secretly commissioned the building of an underground bunker in West Virginia that would serve as a safe haven for top members of Congress in the event of a catastrophe. The public remained completely unaware of the West Virginia bunker, built under the five-star Greenbrier Resort until 1992, which was only placed on full alert once, during the Cuban Missile Crisis in 1962.

John F. Kennedy made civil defense more of a priority than at any previous time in U.S. history, dividing the Office of Civil Defense and Mobilization into two new organizations. The Office of Emergency Planning (OEP) was part of the president's executive office and tasked with advising and assisting the president in determining policy for all nonmilitary emergency preparedness, including civil defense. The Office of Civil Defense (OCD), part of the Office of the Secretary of Defense, was tasked with overseeing the nation's civil defense and fallout shelter programs.

The 1961 Berlin crisis gave renewed urgency to improve U.S. civil defense, especially to the shelter program. OCD sought more cost-effective protection by using existing buildings, and began a nationwide survey of all existing shelters, looking for facilities that would have space for at least 50 people, include one cubic foot of storage space per person, and provide some radiation protection. The Defense Supply Agency furnished supplies to local governments for stocking shelters in their regions. By 1963, 104 million individual shelter spaces had been identified, 46 million marked, and 9 million spaces had been stocked with supplies.

Earlier in the decade, Secretary of Defense Robert McNamara had begun to describe the concept of "mutual assured destruction" (MAD). Under this concept, the fact that the Soviet Union and the United States had the capacity to effectively annihilate one another with the weapons in their arsenals was considered an effective deterrent to offensive action. As this strategy was announced, a growing percentage of the population began to wonder if civil defense programs could ever adequately protect citizens from a largescale nuclear attack.

Kennedy's assassination in November 1963 marked the beginning of a drastic cutback in funding of the nation's civil defense program. In an ironic twist, attention to civil defense was also undermined by a series of major natural disasters that rattled the nation. Hurricanes Hilda and Betsy devastated the Southeast, an Alaskan earthquake caused a damaging tidal wave in California, and a lethal tornado swept through Indiana on Palm Sunday in 1965. Senator Birch Bayh of Indiana sponsored legislation that granted emergency federal loan assistance to disaster victims, and he urged Congress over the next few years to provide even more disaster assistance to citizens. The concept of all-hazards assistance was gaining adherents, at the expense of civil preparedness for nuclear attack. The Vietnam War struck a further blow to civil defense during the Johnson years, draining increasing amounts of time, money, and resources from other efforts.

By the time President Nixon entered office in 1969, public and government interest in civil defense had fallen precipitously. A series of natural disasters during Nixon's early tenure increased the pressure to expand civil defense to include preparation and response to natural disasters. In August 1969 Hurricane Camille wreaked havoc in the greater Gulf Coast region, exposing significant flaws in natural disaster preparedness at a time when no centralized system for disaster relief existed. In response, Congress passed the Disaster Relief Act of 1969, which included the concept of a Federal Coordinating Officer (FCO), an individual appointed by the president, who would manage federal disaster assistance on-the-spot at a given disaster area.

The administration responded by introducing two significant domestic policy changes: the establishment of a "dual-use approach" to federal citizen preparedness programs, and the replacement of the Office of Civil Defense with the Defense Civil Preparedness Agency (DCPA). Federal funds allocated for the exclusive purpose of preparing for military attacks could be shared with state and local governments for natural disaster preparedness. This dual-use initiative held that preparations for evacuation, communications, and survival are common to both natural disasters and enemy military strikes on the homeland. From a practical perspective, the dual-use approach allowed more efficient use of limited resources, allowing planners to address a wider range of scenarios.

President Nixon's decision to increase focus on preparedness against natural disaster aligned with U.S. foreign policy considerations. In order to reinforce the doctrine of MAD, the United States was involved in negotiations with the Soviet Union to limit defensive weapon capabilities, and the administration felt that these negotiations would be jeopardized if either side continued to build up nuclear attack-related civil defense programs. The "dual use" approach allowed protection without reflecting on the arms control efforts.

This "dual use" approach was also attractive to state and local authorities. The change also gained public support. While state and local officials had in the past been reluctant to participate in nuclear attack planning, this reluctance did not extend to preparedness in the context of a particular hazard in a specific area (e.g., floods in coastal or riverine areas, hurricanes in coastal areas, tornadoes in the Midwest and Plains states, and civil unrest in urban areas). Planning for natural disasters was viewed as more effective, less resource intensive, and better able to deliver tangible benefits at both the state and local level.

At first, the Ford administration supported this dual-use approach to preparedness, but soon civil defense was returned to the original Truman/Eisenhower focus on nuclear attack preparedness. There were several reasons for this. The Office of Management and Budget (OMB) limited DOD's ability to use civil defense funding for natural disaster mitigation and preparedness. Incoming Secretary of Defense Donald Rumsfeld strongly opposed the dual-use approach, believing that the federal government should address only attack preparedness, with peacetime disasters being designated a state and local responsibility. Ideas of flexible targeting and limited retaliation developed into the policy of "flexible response," based on the idea that both the Soviet Union and the United States had the capability for small-scale nuclear attacks against specific, highly-strategic sites by the other side. Since some of these sites could be civilian in nature, some level of civil defense and nuclear attack preparedness was necessary.

Upon taking office, President Carter began his own review of civil defense bureaucracies. On March 28, 1979, an accident unfolded at the nuclear energy plant on Three Mile Island, near Harrisburg, Pennsylvania. The slow response and poor local-federal coordination dramatically demonstrated the need for better disaster coordination and planning. On July 20, 1979 the Carter administration established the Federal Emergency Management Agency (FEMA) as the lead agency for coordinating federal disaster relief efforts. FEMA absorbed the Federal Insurance Administration, the National Fire Prevention and Control Administration, the National Weather Service Community Preparedness Program, the Federal Preparedness Agency of the General Services Administration, and the Federal Disaster Assistance Administration activities from HUD, combining them into a single independent agency, the single largest consolidation of civil defense efforts in U.S. history.

Despite the reorganization, though, civil defense planning did not dramatically change. Congressional leaders had little fear of public concern about keeping civil defense funding low. Most people by this time had little faith that any civil defense planning could lessen the impact of nuclear war. This public attitude would continue throughout the rest of the Cold War period, and so Congress felt it could safely ignore the issue.

Ronald Reagan entered office with the intention of building on the civil defense foundations set by his predecessors. Though Reagan favored the dual-use approach, his civil defense strategy was largely a continuation of Carter's and was designed to promote deterrence, improve natural disaster preparedness, and reduce the possibility of coercion by enemy forces.

In 1983, FEMA instituted plans for an Integrated Emergency Management System (IEMS) to develop full all-hazard preparedness plans at the federal level, under which state civil defense planners would develop multi-hazard preparedness plans based on threats faced by specific localities. Congress was not persuaded that the IEMS would effectively address the management of all-hazard preparedness, however, and so never provided funding at the levels FEMA requested. On November 23, 1988 the Disaster Relief Act of 1974 was amended to become what is now known as the Stafford Act. The Act defined the disaster declaration process and provided the statutory authority for Federal assistance during a disaster, resulting in a clearer definition of FEMA's role in emergency management.

A series of three significant natural disasters in the first year after George H.W. Bush took office challenged the nation's all-hazards preparedness. On March 24, 1989, 11 million gallons of crude oil spilled into Prince William Sound in the Gulf of Alaska from the Exxon Valdez oil tanker, the largest oil spill in U.S. history. Instead of using FEMA to coordinate the response, Bush invoked the Federal Water Pollution Control Act, under which the Environmental Protection Agency and Coast Guard managed the event. The administration was ill-prepared to manage an environmental crisis of such large scale and was widely criticized for the poor response. On September 13, 1989, Hurricane Hugo struck the Virgin Islands, Puerto Rico, and South Carolina, inflicting significant damage. This time Bush chose his secretary of the interior to provide executive oversight. FEMA's participation was plagued by shortages of properly trained personnel, communication problems, and a lack of coordination. Within a month of Hurricane Hugo, the Loma Prieta earthquake struck northern California causing an estimated $6 billion in damage. Already stretched thin from Hurricane Hugo, FEMA's response continued to be hindered by staffing and coordination problems. Again, President Bush appointed a cabinet-level representative, the secretary of transportation, to oversee recovery operations, and again FEMA's contribution to response and recovery was judged inadequate.

Dissatisfaction with FEMA's response to these events led the agency to begin developing the Federal Response Plan (FRP) in November 1990. Drawing from the Incident Command System and Incident Management System framework, the FRP defined how 27 different federal agencies and the American Red Cross would respond to the needs of state and local governments when overwhelmed by a disaster. The plan used a functional approach to identify the type of assistance, such as food, communications, and transportation, to be provided by the federal government.

By the second year of the administration, other significant political changes occurred. The Berlin Wall fell in 1989, followed shortly by the collapse of the Soviet Union and the fall of communist governments across Eastern Europe. The Cold War had come to a rapid and unanticipated end, the perceived threat of a strategic nuclear attack on the United States diminished almost overnight and, as a result, civil defense was no longer a priority for emergency planners or for Congress. With the recent natural and man-made disasters in mind, FEMA planners began to adopt the idea of a true all-hazards approach to disaster preparedness. In March of 1992 President Bush signed a National Security Directive instructing FEMA to develop a multi-hazard approach to emergency management, combining civil defense preparedness with natural and man-made disaster preparedness.

In August 1992, Hurricane Andrew hit south Florida and the central Louisiana coast. President Bush once again appointed a cabinet-level representative, the secretary of transportation, to coordinate federal relief efforts. Unfortunately, this did not improve performance as "government at all levels was slow to comprehend the scope of the disaster." And, despite the FRP, FEMA and other agencies involved in the response and recovery faced the same kinds of coordination and logistical problems they had three years prior. FEMA was again strongly criticized for its poor performance.

Upon taking office in 1993, President Bill Clinton appointed James Lee Witt director of FEMA. Witt immediately reorganized FEMA, creating functional directorates corresponding to the major phases of emergency management: Mitigation; Preparedness; Training and Exercise; and Response and Recovery. Clinton also elevated the FEMA directorship to cabinet-level status, improving the line of communication between the director and the president.

At the same time, a new recognition of the threat of terrorist attacks was beginning to emerge. This was in part a result of the World Trade Center bombing in 1993. The blast left a five-story-deep crater, caused $500 million in damages, killed 6 people and wounded 1,042. Congress responded by including a provision in the National Defense Authorization Act calling for FEMA to develop a capability for early detection and warning of and response to potential terrorist use of chemical or biological agents or weapons as well as natural disasters or emergencies involving industrial chemicals or widespread outbreak of disease.

In November 1994, the Federal Civil Defense Act of 1950 was repealed and all civil defense authority was transferred to Title VI of the Stafford Act, completing the evolution of civil defense into an all-hazards approach to preparedness. FEMA now had statutory responsibility for coordinating a comprehensive emergency preparedness system to deal with all types of disasters. This law also ended Armed Services Committee oversight over FEMA and significantly reduced the priority of national security programs within FEMA.

In 1995 and 1996 a series of major terrorist attacks launched domestically and abroad further influenced U.S. preparedness policies. In March 1995, the Japanese religious cult Aum Shinrikyo released Sarin nerve gas on five separate cars of three different subway lines in Tokyo, killing twelve and injuring thousands. One month later, Timothy McVeigh and Terry Nichols detonated a truck bomb at the Alfred P. Murrah Federal Building in Oklahoma City, killing 169 people. On June 25, 1996, the Khobar Towers, a U.S. military facility in Dhahran, Saudi Arabia, was bombed, killing 19 Americans. These events had a profound effect on U.S. lawmakers and the administration. Congress passed legislation requiring DOD to provide training and expert advice to civilian agencies at all levels of government on appropriate responses to the use of a weapon of mass destruction (WMD) against the American public. DOD established 10 National Guard Rapid Assessment and Initial Detection (RAID) teams, which served to provide technical expertise and equipment to deal with a WMD attack. WMD preparedness, though, was transferred from DOD to the Office of Domestic Preparedness (ODP) within the Department of Justice (DOJ). The result of these actions was a new fragmentation of responsibility.

As the century came to a close, a new concept of homeland security began to emerge. Presidential Decision Directive (PDD) 62, signed by President Clinton in May 1998, created the Office of the National Coordinator for Security, Infrastructure Protection, and Counter-Terrorism within the Executive Office of the President, designed to coordinate counter- terrorism policy, preparedness, and consequence management. Later that year President Clinton issued PDD 63 on Critical Infrastructure Protection. PDD 63 required the creation of a National Infrastructure Assurance Plan, establishing principles for protecting the nation against the threat of smaller-scale terrorist attacks against information technology and supply chains that could disrupt the economy. In the absence of a centralized authority for homeland security, different federal agencies were designated as lead agencies in their sector of expertise and directed to develop sector-specific Information Sharing and Analysis Centers to coordinate efforts with the private sector.

At the same time, the U.S. Commission on National Security in the 21st Century, known as the Hart-Rudman Commission, began to reexamine U.S. national security policies. One of its recommendations was the creation of a cabinet-level National Homeland Security Agency responsible for planning, coordinating, and integrating various U.S. government activities involved in "homeland security." The commission defined homeland security as "the protection of the territory, critical infrastructures, and citizens of the United States by Federal, State, and local government entities from the threat or use of chemical, biological, radiological, nuclear, cyber, or conventional weapons by military or other means." Another commission formed during the Clinton administration, the Advisory Panel to Assess Domestic Response Capabilities for Terrorism Involving Weapons of Mass Destruction, which was chaired by Virginia Governor Jim Gilmore, and developed and delivered a series of reports to the president and Congress between 1999 and 2003. Of the Gilmore Commission's 164 recommendations, 146 were adopted in whole or in part, including creation of a national fusion center to integrate and analyze all intelligence pertaining to terrorism and counterterrorism and the creation of a civil liberties oversight board. The impetus to implement many of these recommendations only occurred, however, following the series of devastating attacks on the U.S. homeland that occurred during the initial months of the next administration.

The initial months of George W. Bush's presidency saw a general continuation of existing policies, but also organizational changes that affected how national security and homeland security policies would be generated. With a goal to create a more formal structure, the Bush administration abolished ad hoc interagency working groups and replaced them with Policy Coordination Committees within the National Security Council. A Counterterrorism and National Preparedness Policy Coordinating Committee was established, composed of four working groups: Continuity of Federal Operations, Counterterrorism and Security, Preparedness and WMD, and Information Infrastructure Protection and Assurance.

In the wake of the September 11, 2001 terrorist attacks, there was near-universal agreement that homeland security required a major reassessment, increased funding, and administrative reorganization. In October 2001, the White House Office of Homeland Security was established by executive order to work with departments and agencies to develop and coordinate a comprehensive national strategy to secure the United States from terrorist threats or attacks. In March 2002 another executive order created the Homeland Security Advisory Council to advise the president. In his 2002 State of the Union address, the president announced the establishment of the USA Freedom Corps to promote a culture of service, citizenship, and responsibility in America. Under the Freedom Corps initiative, the White House established Citizen Corps within FEMA to engage individual citizens through education, training, and volunteer service to make communities better prepared to prevent, protect, respond, and recover from all-hazards. Citizen Corps involved Americans in programs such as Community Emergency Response Teams, Fire Corps, Neighborhood Watch, Medical Reserve Corps, and Volunteers in Police Service. On March 12, 2002, the Homeland Security Advisory System (HSAS) created a threat-based, color-coded system, so protective measures could be implemented to reduce the likelihood or impact of an attack on the homeland.

The Bush administration also began to develop strategic documents and statements, including the National Security Strategy, the National Strategy for Homeland Security (NSHS), and the National Strategy to Combat Weapons of Mass Destruction. As these were developed, Congress continued to push for more substantial reorganization of federal agencies involved in homeland security. The Homeland Security Act of 2002, the largest government reorganization since the creation of the Department of Defense in the late 1940s, created the Department of Homeland Security (DHS) with an initial budget of $37 billion as it inherited approximately 200,000 people from 22 federal agencies.

Understandably, much of DHS's initial work focused on addressing the threat of domestic terrorism. All-hazards preparedness soon became a top priority as well. Homeland Security Presidential Directive-8: National Preparedness (HSPD-8), issued in December 2003, defined preparedness as encompassing "threatened or actual domestic terrorist attacks, major disasters, and other emergencies." HSPD-8 tasked DHS to take lead in creating a National Preparedness Goal coordinating federal, state, local, and private sector efforts to encourage active citizen participation and developing a plan to provide accurate and timely information to the public.

The National Preparedness Goal was released in March, 2005, presenting preparedness as a coordinated, national effort involving every level of government, the private sector, non- governmental organizations, and individual citizens, and calling for the development and strengthening of capabilities that would address the full range of homeland security missions (prevention, protection, response and recovery). A new National Response Plan (NRP) was developed to replace the earlier Federal Response Plan, and the National Incident Management System (NIMS) was introduced to provide a common framework for incident management. A National Strategy for Physical Protection of Critical Infrastructures and Key Assets was also developed, officially recognizing the role of the private sector and the need for partnerships between government and the private sector in protecting the nation. The structure for such partnerships was detailed in the National Infrastructure Protection Plan, issued in June 2006.[3]

The nation's preparedness received another serious test when, on August 29, 2005, Hurricane Katrina made landfall along the Mississippi and Louisiana coasts. The storm was followed by levee failures in New Orleans, and unprecedented devastation. Virtually the entire Mississippi coast was leveled by storm surge, much of the city of New Orleans was under water, and the federal, state, and local response proved inadequate to the unprecedented catastrophic challenge. The new National Response Plan had not been fully trained or implemented across all agencies and levels of government and had never been tested in a major event. President Bush demanded a nationwide review of the status of catastrophic planning. DHS and the Department of Transportation were tasked to conduct the review in major urban areas across the country. The Review determined that disaster planning for catastrophic events in the United States suffers from failure to account for the full scope of catastrophic events; outmoded planning processes, products, and tools; and inadequate attention to coordination.

While recognizing the importance of federal leadership and coordination, DHS continues to stress that state, tribal, and local governments must be the first line of defense against disaster and attack. DHS administers grant programs, has provided counterterrorism training to emergency response personnel from across the country on a range of incident response issues such as incident management, unified command, and public works protection and response, and has conducted exercises at the federal, state, and local level to improve preparedness for and response to terrorist attacks and natural disasters.

Emergency Preparedness and Response Statutes

Statutory Provisions In General

As the previous overview indicates, the history of civil defense and disaster preparedness shows the programs have gone through significant shifts. Along the way

---

3. Documents referenced in this section can be found at http://www.dhs.gov/national-preparedness-guidelines

there have been a series of statutes, presidential directives, and regulations enacted. It would be impractical for us to include them all in this text, so here is a brief list and description of the key federal statutes.

- Homeland Security Act of 2002: This Act established the Department of Homeland Security and set forth the primary mission of the department.
- Intelligence Reform and Terrorism Prevention Act of 2004 (Public Law 108-458): Among other things, this Act addresses transportation security, border surveillance, alien detention, visa requirements, and alien smuggling.
- Implementing Recommendations of the 9-11 Commission Act of 2007 (Public Law 110-53): This Act addresses a wide range of the department's missions, including cargo security, critical infrastructure protection, grant administration, intelligence and information sharing, privacy, and transportation security.

Emergency Management

- Robert T. Stafford Disaster Relief and Emergency Assistance Act and Related Authorities: The Stafford Act prescribes circumstances for declaring disasters and emergencies and the types of assistance to be provided in such situations, among other things.
- Post-Katrina Emergency Management Reform Act of 2006 (Public Law 109-295): This Act revised a number of provisions in the Stafford Act and the Homeland Security Act to strengthen the nation's response to disasters and emergencies.

Immigration and Border Security

- Immigration and Nationality Act: The Immigration and Nationality Act includes many provisions relating to the admission of aliens, the removal of aliens, grants of asylum, and the investigation of human trafficking.

Maritime Security

- Maritime Transportation Security Act of 2002 (Public Law 107-295): In large part, this Act deals with port and waterway security.
- Coast Guard and Maritime Transportation Act of 2006 (Public Law 109-241): This Act deals with U.S. Coast Guard issues, shipping and navigation, hurricane response, and other related issues.
- Security and Accountability For Every Port Act of 2006 (SAFE Port Act) (Public Law 109-347): Many of this Act's provisions relate to programs designed to secure the United States' sea ports and shipping lanes.
- Coast Guard Authorization Act of 2010 (Public Law 111-281): In addition to other things, this Act reauthorized a number of U.S. Coast Guard programs, addresses acquisition and workforce matters, and deals with port security.

Transportation Security

- Aviation and Transportation Security Act (Public Law 107-71): This Act established the Transportation Security Administration (TSA) and vested security functions previously performed by the Federal Aviation Administration in TSA, among other things.

The most significant statutory provision for emergency response is contained in the Stafford Act and in the Presidential Directives promulgated since September 11, 2001. We provide excerpts from these in the next section of the chapter. Look through these laws and directives consider how they relate to the concepts discussed in the historical overview and in light of the Constitutional framework discussed in Chapter 2.

Excerpts from Title 42—Public Health and Welfare

CHAPTER 68—DISASTER RELIEF

§ 5121. Congressional findings and declarations

(a) The Congress hereby finds and declares that—

(1) because disasters often cause loss of life, human suffering, loss of income, and property loss and damage; and

(2) because disasters often disrupt the normal functioning of governments and communities, and adversely affect individuals and families with great severity;

special measures, designed to assist the efforts of the affected States in expediting the rendering of aid, assistance, and emergency services, and the reconstruction and rehabilitation of devastated areas, are necessary.

(b) It is the intent of the Congress, by this chapter, to provide an orderly and continuing means of assistance by the Federal Government to State and local governments in carrying out their responsibilities to alleviate the suffering and damage which result from such disasters by—

(1) revising and broadening the scope of existing disaster relief programs;

(2) encouraging the development of comprehensive disaster preparedness and assistance plans, programs, capabilities, and organizations by the States and by local governments;

(3) achieving greater coordination and responsiveness of disaster preparedness and relief programs;

(4) encouraging individuals, States, and local governments to protect themselves by obtaining insurance coverage to supplement or replace governmental assistance;

(5) encouraging hazard mitigation measures to reduce losses from disasters, including development of land use and construction regulations; and

(6) providing Federal assistance programs for both public and private losses sustained in disasters

§ 5122. Definitions

As used in this chapter—

(1) Emergency.—"Emergency" means any occasion or instance for which, in the determination of the President, Federal assistance is needed to supplement State and local efforts and capabilities to save lives and to protect property and public health and safety, or to lessen or avert the threat of a catastrophe in any part of the United States.

(2) Major disaster.—"Major disaster" means any natural catastrophe (including any hurricane, tornado, storm, high water, wind driven water, tidal wave, tsunami, earthquake, volcanic eruption, landslide, mudslide, snowstorm, or drought), or, regardless of cause, any fire, flood, or explosion, in any part of the United States, which in the determination of the President causes damage of sufficient severity and magnitude to warrant major disaster assistance under this chapter to supplement the efforts and available resources of States, local governments, and disaster relief organizations in alleviating the damage, loss, hardship, or suffering caused thereby.

(3) "United States" means the fifty States, the District of Columbia, Puerto Rico, the Virgin Islands, Guam, American Samoa, and the Commonwealth of the Northern Mariana Islands.

(4) "State" means any State of the United States, the District of Columbia, Puerto Rico, the Virgin Islands, Guam, American Samoa, and the Commonwealth of the Northern Mariana Islands.

. . .

(7) Local government.—The term "local government" means—

    (A) a county, municipality, city, town, township, local public authority, school district, special district, intrastate district, council of governments (regardless of whether the council of governments is incorporated as a nonprofit corporation under State law), regional or interstate government entity, or agency or instrumentality of a local government;

    (B) an Indian tribe or authorized tribal organization, or Alaska Native village or organization; and

    (C) a rural community, unincorporated town or village, or other public entity, for which an application for assistance is made by a State or political subdivision of a State.

(8) "Federal agency" means any department, independent establishment, Government corporation, or other agency of the executive branch of the Federal Government, including the United States Postal Service, but shall not include the American National Red Cross.

§ 5131. Federal and State disaster preparedness programs

(a) Utilization of services of other agencies

The President is authorized to establish a program of disaster preparedness that utilizes services of all appropriate agencies and includes—

1. preparation of disaster preparedness plans for mitigation, warning, emergency operations, rehabilitation, and recovery;
2. training and exercises;
3. postdisaster critiques and evaluations;
4. annual review of programs;
5. coordination of Federal, State, and local preparedness programs;
6. application of science and technology;
7. research.

...

§ 5133. Predisaster hazard mitigation

...

(b) Establishment of program

The President may establish a program to provide technical and financial assistance to States and local governments to assist in the implementation of predisaster hazard mitigation measures that are cost-effective and are designed to reduce injuries, loss of life, and damage and destruction of property, including damage to critical services and facilities under the jurisdiction of the States or local governments.

(c) Approval by President

If the President determines that a State or local government has identified natural disaster hazards in areas under its jurisdiction and has demonstrated the ability to form effective public-private natural disaster hazard mitigation partnerships, the President, using amounts in the National Predisaster Mitigation Fund established under subsection (i) of this section (referred to in this section as the "Fund"), may provide technical and financial assistance to the State or local government to be used in accordance with subsection (e) of this section.

(d) State recommendations

(1) In general

(A) Recommendations

The Governor of each State may recommend to the President not fewer than five local governments to receive assistance under this section.

...

§ 5134. Interagency task force

(a) In general

The President shall establish a Federal interagency task force for the purpose of coordinating the implementation of predisaster hazard mitigation programs administered by the Federal Government.

(b) Chairperson

The Administrator of the Federal Emergency Management Agency shall serve as the chairperson of the task force.

(c) Membership

The membership of the task force shall include representatives of—

1. relevant Federal agencies;
2. State and local government organizations (including Indian tribes); and
3. the American Red Cross.

§ 5141. Waiver of administrative conditions

Any Federal agency charged with the administration of a Federal assistance program may, if so requested by the applicant State or local authorities, modify or waive, for a major disaster, such administrative conditions for assistance as would otherwise prevent the giving of assistance under such programs if the inability to meet such conditions is a result of the major disaster.

§ 5143. Coordinating officers

(a) Appointment of Federal coordinating officer

Immediately upon his declaration of a major disaster or emergency, the President shall appoint a Federal coordinating officer to operate in the affected area.

(b) Functions of Federal coordinating officer

In order to effectuate the purposes of this chapter, the Federal coordinating officer, within the affected area, shall—

(1) make an initial appraisal of the types of relief most urgently needed;

(2) establish such field offices as he deems necessary and as are authorized by the President;

(3) coordinate the administration of relief, including activities of the State and local governments, the American National Red Cross, the Salvation Army, the Mennonite Disaster Service, and other relief or disaster assistance organizations, which agree to operate under his advice or direction, except that nothing contained in this chapter shall limit or in any way affect the responsibilities of the American National Red Cross under chapter 3001 of title 36; and

(4) take such other action, consistent with authority delegated to him by the President, and consistent with the provisions of this chapter, as he may deem necessary to assist local citizens and public officials in promptly obtaining assistance to which they are entitled.

(c) State coordinating officer

When the President determines assistance under this chapter is necessary, he shall request that the Governor of the affected State designate a State coordinating officer for the purpose of coordinating State and local disaster assistance efforts with those of the Federal Government.

(d) Single Federal coordinating officer for multistate area

Where the area affected by a major disaster or emergency includes parts of more than 1 State, the President, at the discretion of the President, may appoint a single Federal coordinating officer for the entire affected area, and may appoint such deputy Federal coordinating officers to assist the Federal coordinating officer as the President determines appropriate.

§ 5144. Emergency support and response teams

(a) Emergency support teams

The President shall form emergency support teams of Federal personnel to be deployed in an area affected by a major disaster or emergency. Such emergency support teams shall assist the Federal coordinating officer in carrying out his responsibilities pursuant to this chapter. Upon request of the President, the head of any Federal agency is directed to detail to temporary duty with the emergency support teams on either a reimbursable or nonreimbursable basis, as is determined necessary by the President, such personnel within the administrative jurisdiction of the head of the Federal agency as the President may need or believe to be useful for carrying out the functions of the emergency support teams, each such detail to be without loss of seniority, pay, or other employee status.

(b) Emergency response teams

(1) Establishment

In carrying out subsection (a), the President, acting through the Administrator of the Federal Emergency Management Agency, shall establish—

(A) at a minimum 3 national response teams; and

(B) sufficient regional response teams, including Regional Office strike teams under section 317 of title 6; and

(C) other response teams as may be necessary to meet the incident management responsibilities of the Federal Government.

. . .

§ 5147. Reimbursement of Federal agencies

Federal agencies may be reimbursed for expenditures under this chapter from funds appropriated for the purposes of this chapter. Any funds received by Federal agencies as reimbursement for services or supplies furnished under the authority of this chapter shall be deposited to the credit of the appropriation or appropriations currently available for such services or supplies.

§ 5148. Nonliability of Federal Government

The Federal Government shall not be liable for any claim based upon the exercise or performance of or the failure to exercise or perform a discretionary function or duty on the part of a Federal agency or an employee of the Federal Government in carrying out the provisions of this chapter.

§ 5149. Performance of services

(a) Utilization of services or facilities of State and local governments

In carrying out the purposes of this chapter, any Federal agency is authorized to accept and utilize the services or facilities of any State or local government, or of any agency, office, or employee thereof, with the consent of such government.

. . .

§ 5150. Use of local firms and individuals

(a) Contracts or agreements with private entities

(1) In general

In the expenditure of Federal funds for debris clearance, distribution of supplies, reconstruction, and other major disaster or emergency assistance activities which may be carried out by contract or agreement with private organizations, firms, or individuals, preference shall be given, to the extent feasible and practicable, to those organizations, firms, and individuals residing or doing business primarily in the area affected by such major disaster or emergency.

(2) Construction

This subsection shall not be considered to restrict the use of Department of Defense resources under this chapter in the provision of assistance in a major disaster.

. . .

§ 5152. Use and coordination of relief organizations

(a) In providing relief and assistance under this chapter, the President may utilize, with their consent, the personnel and facilities of the American National Red Cross, the Salvation Army, the Mennonite Disaster Service, and other relief or disaster assistance organizations, in the distribution of medicine, food, supplies, or other items, and in the restoration, rehabilitation, or reconstruction of community services housing and essential facilities, whenever the President finds that such utilization is necessary.

. . .

§ 5164. Rules and regulations

The President may prescribe such rules and regulations as may be necessary and proper to carry out the provisions of this chapter, and may exercise, either directly or through such Federal agency as the President may designate, any power or authority conferred to the President by this chapter.

§ 5165. Mitigation planning

(a) Requirement of mitigation plan

As a condition of receipt of an increased Federal share for hazard mitigation measures under subsection (e) of this section, a State, local, or tribal government shall develop and submit for approval to the President a mitigation plan that outlines processes for identifying the natural hazards, risks, and vulnerabilities of the area under the jurisdiction of the government.

(b) Local and tribal plans

Each mitigation plan developed by a local or tribal government shall—

(1) describe actions to mitigate hazards, risks, and vulnerabilities identified under the plan; and

(2) establish a strategy to implement those actions.

(c) State plans

The State process of development of a mitigation plan under this section shall—

(1) identify the natural hazards, risks, and vulnerabilities of areas in the State;

(2) support development of local mitigation plans;

(3) provide for technical assistance to local and tribal governments for mitigation planning; and

(4) identify and prioritize mitigation actions that the State will support, as resources become available.

§ 5170. Procedure for declaration

All requests for a declaration by the President that a major disaster exists shall be made by the Governor of the affected State. Such a request shall be based on a finding that the disaster is of such severity and magnitude that effective response is beyond the capabilities of the State and the affected local governments and that Federal assistance is necessary. As part of such request, and as a prerequisite to major disaster assistance under this chapter, the Governor shall take appropriate response action under State law and direct execution of the State's emergency plan. The Governor shall furnish information on the nature and amount of State and local resources which have been or will be committed to alleviating the results of the disaster, and shall certify that, for the current disaster, State and local government obligations and expenditures (of which State commitments must be a significant proportion) will comply with all applicable cost-sharing requirements of this chapter. Based on the request of a Governor under this section, the President may declare under this chapter that a major disaster or emergency exists.

§ 5170a. General Federal assistance

In any major disaster, the President may—

(1) direct any Federal agency, with or without reimbursement, to utilize its authorities and the resources granted to it under Federal law (including personnel, equipment, supplies, facilities, and managerial, technical, and

advisory services) in support of State and local assistance response or recovery efforts, including precautionary evacuations;

(2) coordinate all disaster relief assistance (including voluntary assistance) provided by Federal agencies, private organizations, and State and local governments, including precautionary evacuations and recovery;

(3) provide technical and advisory assistance to affected State and local governments for—

(A) the performance of essential community services;

(B) issuance of warnings of risks and hazards;

(C) public health and safety information, including dissemination of such information;

(D) provision of health and safety measures;

(E) management, control, and reduction of immediate threats to public health and safety; and

(F) recovery activities, including disaster impact assessments and planning;

(4) assist State and local governments in the distribution of medicine, food, and other consumable supplies, and emergency assistance; and

(5) provide accelerated Federal assistance and Federal support where necessary to save lives, prevent human suffering, or mitigate severe damage, which may be provided in the absence of a specific request and in which case the President—

(A) shall, to the fullest extent practicable, promptly notify and coordinate with officials in a State in which such assistance or support is provided; and

(B) shall not, in notifying and coordinating with a State under subparagraph (A), delay or impede the rapid deployment, use, and distribution of critical resources to victims of a major disaster.

§ 5170b. Essential assistance

(a) In general

Federal agencies may on the direction of the President, provide assistance essential to meeting immediate threats to life and property resulting from a major disaster, as follows:

(1) Federal resources, generally

Utilizing, lending, or donating to State and local governments Federal equipment, supplies, facilities, personnel, and other resources, other than the extension of credit, for use or distribution by such governments in accordance with the purposes of this chapter.

(2) Medicine, food, and other consumables

Distributing or rendering through State and local governments, the American National Red Cross, the Salvation Army, the Mennonite Disaster Service, and other relief and disaster assistance organizations medicine durable medical equipment, food, and other consumable supplies, and other services and assistance to disaster victims.

(3) Work and services to save lives and protect property

Performing on public or private lands or waters any work or services essential to saving lives and protecting and preserving property or public health and safety, including—

(A) debris removal;

(B) search and rescue, emergency medical care, emergency mass care, emergency shelter, and provision of food, water, medicine durable medical equipment, and other essential needs, including movement of supplies or persons;

(C) clearance of roads and construction of temporary bridges necessary to the performance of emergency tasks and essential community services;

(D) provision of temporary facilities for schools and other essential community services;

(E) demolition of unsafe structures which endanger the public;

(F) warning of further risks and hazards;

(G) dissemination of public information and assistance regarding health and safety measures;

(H) provision of technical advice to State and local governments on disaster management and control;

(I) reduction of immediate threats to life, property, and public health and safety; and

(J) provision of rescue, care, shelter, and essential needs—

    (i) to individuals with household pets and service animals; and

    (ii) to such pets and animals.

. . .

(c) Utilization of DOD resources

(1) General rule

During the immediate aftermath of an incident which may ultimately qualify for assistance under this subchapter or subchapter IV-A of this chapter, the Governor of the State in which such incident occurred may request the President to direct the Secretary of Defense to utilize the resources of the Department of Defense for the purpose of performing on public and private lands any emergency work which is made necessary by such incident and which is essential for the preservation of life and property. If the President determines that such work is essential for the preservation of life and property, the President shall grant such request to the extent the President determines practicable. Such emergency work may only be carried out for a period not to exceed 10 days.

...

(6) Definitions

For purposes of this section—

(A) Department of Defense

The term "Department of Defense" has the meaning the term "department" has under section 101 of title 10.

(B) Emergency work

The term "emergency work" includes clearance and removal of debris and wreckage and temporary restoration of essential public facilities and services.

...

§ 5174. Federal assistance to individuals and households

(a) In general

(1) Provision of assistance

In accordance with this section, the President, in consultation with the Governor of a State, may provide financial assistance, and, if necessary, direct services, to individuals and households in the State who, as a direct result of a major disaster, have necessary expenses and serious needs in cases in which the individuals and households are unable to meet such expenses or needs through other means.

...

§ 5177. Unemployment assistance

(a) Benefit assistance

The President is authorized to provide to any individual unemployed as a result of a major disaster such benefit assistance as he deems appropriate while such individual is unemployed for the weeks of such unemployment with respect to which the individual is not entitled to any other unemployment compensation (as that term is defined in section 85(b) of title 26) or waiting period credit. . . .

(b) Reemployment assistance

(1) State assistance

A State shall provide, without reimbursement from any funds provided under this chapter, reemployment assistance services under any other law administered by the State to individuals receiving benefits under this section.

(2) Federal assistance

The President may provide reemployment assistance services under other laws to individuals who are unemployed as a result of a major disaster and who reside in a State which does not provide such services.

...

§ 5180. Food commodities

(a) Emergency mass feeding

The President is authorized and directed to assure that adequate stocks of food will be ready and conveniently available for emergency mass feeding or distribution in any area of the United States which suffers a major disaster or emergency.

(b) Funds for purchase of food commodities

The Secretary of Agriculture shall utilize funds appropriated under section 612c of title 7, to purchase food commodities necessary to provide adequate supplies for use in any area of the United States in the event of a major disaster or emergency in such area.

...

§ 5187. Fire management assistance

(a) In general

The President is authorized to provide assistance, including grants, equipment, supplies, and personnel, to any State or local government for the mitigation, management, and control of any fire on public or private forest land or grassland that threatens such destruction as would constitute a major disaster.

(b) Coordination with State and tribal departments of forestry

In providing assistance under this section, the President shall coordinate with State and tribal departments of forestry.

(c) Essential assistance

In providing assistance under this section, the President may use the authority provided under section 5170b of this title.

(d) Rules and regulations

The President shall prescribe such rules and regulations as are necessary to carry out this section.

...

§ 5191. Procedure for declaration

(a) Request and declaration

All requests for a declaration by the President that an emergency exists shall be made by the Governor of the affected State. Such a request shall be based on a finding that the situation is of such severity and magnitude that effective response is beyond the capabilities of the State and the affected local governments and that Federal assistance is necessary. As a part of such request, and as a prerequisite to emergency assistance under this chapter, the Governor shall take appropriate action under State law and direct execution of the State's emergency plan. The Governor shall furnish information describing the State and local efforts and resources which have been or will be used to alleviate the emergency, and will define the type and extent of Federal aid required. Based upon such Governor's request, the President may declare that an emergency exists.

(b) Certain emergencies involving Federal primary responsibility

The President may exercise any authority vested in him by section 5192 of this title or section 5193 of this title with respect to an emergency when he determines that an emergency exists for which the primary responsibility for response rests with the United States because the emergency involves a subject area for which, under the Constitution or laws of the United States, the United States exercises exclusive or preeminent responsibility and authority. In determining whether or not such an emergency exists, the President shall consult the Governor of any affected State, if practicable. The President's determination may be made without regard to subsection (a) of this section.

§ 5192. Federal emergency assistance

(a) Specified

In any emergency, the President may—

(1) direct any Federal agency, with or without reimbursement, to utilize its authorities and the resources granted to it under Federal law (including personnel, equipment, supplies, facilities, and managerial, technical and advisory services) in support of State and local emergency assistance efforts to save lives, protect property and public health and safety, and lessen or avert the threat of a catastrophe, including precautionary evacuations;

(2) coordinate all disaster relief assistance (including voluntary assistance) provided by Federal agencies, private organizations, and State and local governments;

(3) provide technical and advisory assistance to affected State and local governments for—

   (A) the performance of essential community services;

   (B) issuance of warnings of risks or hazards;

   (C) public health and safety information, including dissemination of such information;

   (D) provision of health and safety measures; and

   (E) management, control, and reduction of immediate threats to public health and safety;

(4) provide emergency assistance through Federal agencies;

(5) remove debris in accordance with the terms and conditions of section 5173 of this title;

(6) provide assistance in accordance with section 5174 of this title;

(7) assist State and local governments in the distribution of medicine, food, and other consumable supplies, and emergency assistance; and

(8) provide accelerated Federal assistance and Federal support where necessary to save lives, prevent human suffering, or mitigate severe damage, which may be provided in the absence of a specific request and in which case the President—

   (A) shall, to the fullest extent practicable, promptly notify and coordinate with a State in which such assistance or support is provided; and

   (B) shall not, in notifying and coordinating with a State under subparagraph (A), delay or impede the rapid deployment, use, and distribution of critical resources to victims of an emergency.

. . .

§ 5195. Declaration of policy

The purpose of this subchapter is to provide a system of emergency preparedness for the protection of life and property in the United States from hazards and to vest responsibility for emergency preparedness jointly in the Federal Government and the States and their political subdivisions. The Congress recognizes that the organizational structure established jointly by the Federal Government and the States and their political subdivisions for emergency preparedness purposes can be effectively utilized to provide relief and assistance to people in areas of the United States struck by a hazard. The Federal Government shall provide necessary direction, coordination, and guidance, and shall provide necessary assistance, as authorized in this subchapter so that a comprehensive emergency preparedness system exists for all hazards.

§ 5196. Detailed functions of administration

(a) In general

In order to carry out the policy described in section 5195 of this title, the Administrator shall have the authorities provided in this section.

(b) Federal emergency response plans and programs

The Administrator may prepare Federal response plans and programs for the emergency preparedness of the United States and sponsor and direct such plans and programs. To prepare such plans and programs and coordinate such plans and programs with State efforts, the Administrator may request such reports on State plans and operations for emergency preparedness as may be necessary to keep the President, Congress, and the States advised of the status of emergency preparedness in the United States.

. . .

(d) Communications and warnings

The Administrator may make appropriate provision for necessary emergency preparedness communications and for dissemination of warnings to the civilian population of a hazard.

(e) Emergency preparedness measures

The Administrator may study and develop emergency preparedness measures designed to afford adequate protection of life and property, including—

(1) research and studies as to the best methods of treating the effects of hazards;

(2) developing shelter designs and materials for protective covering or construction;

(3) developing equipment or facilities and effecting the standardization thereof to meet emergency preparedness requirements; and

(4) plans that take into account the needs of individuals with pets and service animals prior to, during, and following a major disaster or emergency.

. . .

(h) Emergency preparedness compacts

(1) The Administrator shall establish a program supporting the development of emergency preparedness compacts for acts of terrorism, disasters, and emergencies throughout the Nation, by—

(A) identifying and cataloging existing emergency preparedness compacts for acts of terrorism, disasters, and emergencies at the State and local levels of government;

(B) disseminating to State and local governments examples of best practices in the development of emergency preparedness compacts and models of existing emergency preparedness compacts, including agreements involving interstate jurisdictions; and

(C) completing an inventory of Federal response capabilities for acts of terrorism, disasters, and emergencies, making such inventory available to appropriate Federal, State, and local government officials, and ensuring that such inventory is as current and accurate as practicable.

(2) The Administrator may—

(A) assist and encourage the States to negotiate and enter into interstate emergency preparedness compacts;

(B) review the terms and conditions of such proposed compacts in order to assist, to the extent feasible, in obtaining uniformity between such compacts and consistency with Federal emergency response plans and programs;

(C) assist and coordinate the activities under such compacts; and

(D) aid and assist in encouraging reciprocal emergency preparedness legislation by the States which will permit the furnishing of mutual aid for emergency preparedness purposes in the event of a hazard which cannot be adequately met or controlled by a State or political subdivision thereof threatened with or experiencing a hazard.

(3) A copy of each interstate emergency preparedness compact shall be transmitted promptly to the Senate and the House of Representatives. The consent of Congress is deemed to be granted to each such compact upon the expiration of the 60-day period beginning on the date on which the compact is transmitted to Congress.

(4) Nothing in this subsection shall be construed as preventing Congress from disapproving, or withdrawing at any time its consent to, any interstate emergency preparedness compact.

...

§ 5196a. Mutual aid pacts between States and neighboring countries

The Administrator shall give all practicable assistance to States in arranging, through the Department of State, mutual emergency preparedness aid between the States and neighboring countries.

...

§ 5201. Rules and regulations

(a)(1) The President may prescribe such rules and regulations as may be necessary and proper to carry out any of the provisions of this chapter, and he may exercise any power or authority conferred on him by any section of this chapter either directly or through such Federal agency or agencies as he may designate.

...

§ 5207. Firearms policies

(a) Prohibition on confiscation of firearms

No officer or employee of the United States (including any member of the uniformed services), or person operating pursuant to or under color of Federal law, or receiving Federal funds, or under control of any Federal official, or providing services to such an officer, employee, or other person, while acting in support of relief from a major disaster or emergency, may—

(1) temporarily or permanently seize, or authorize seizure of, any firearm the possession of which is not prohibited under Federal, State, or local law, other than for forfeiture in compliance with Federal law or as evidence in a criminal investigation;

(2) require registration of any firearm for which registration is not required by Federal, State, or local law;

(3) prohibit possession of any firearm, or promulgate any rule, regulation, or order prohibiting possession of any firearm, in any place or by any person where such possession is not otherwise prohibited by Federal, State, or local law; or

(4) prohibit the carrying of firearms by any person otherwise authorized to carry firearms under Federal, State, or local law, solely because such

person is operating under the direction, control, or supervision of a Federal agency in support of relief from the major disaster or emergency.

(b) Limitation

Nothing in this section shall be construed to prohibit any person in subsection (a) from requiring the temporary surrender of a firearm as a condition for entry into any mode of transportation used for rescue or evacuation during a major disaster or emergency, provided that such temporarily surrendered firearm is returned at the completion of such rescue or evacuation.

Presidential Directives Regarding Emergency Preparedness and Response

After the attacks on September 11, 2001, President Bush issued a series of presidential directives—"Homeland Security Policy Directives"—that provided direction and guidance to federal agencies. As presidential executive orders, these directives have the force of law when applied to federal agencies and their employees. The text of these are fairly extensive and so are not included here; rather, what follows is a summary of the key provisions of those directives.

HSPD-5 — Management of Domestic Incidents

HSPD-5 was issued by President Bush on February 28, 2003, to improve management of domestic incidents by establishing a single, comprehensive national incident management system. The Homeland Security Act of 2002 created the Department of Homeland Security (DHS) and assigned the Secretary of Homeland Security responsibility for coordinating federal emergency operations within the United States. Federal emergency operations include preparing for, responding to, and recovering from terrorist attacks, major disasters, and other emergencies. DHS coordinates federal resources when any one of several conditions occurs:

1. a federal department or agency requests their assistance,
2. the resources of state and local authorities are overwhelmed and they request federal assistance,
3. more than one federal department or agency is substantially involved in responding to an incident, and/or
4. the president directs the secretary to assume responsibility for managing the domestic incident.

HSPD-5 also recognizes the role that state, tribal, and local governments; nongovernmental organizations; and the private sector play in managing incidents. Initial responsibility for managing domestic incidents generally falls on state and local authorities. When their resources are overwhelmed, or when federal property is involved, the federal government provides assistance.

In order to provide a consistent, coordinated, nation-wide approach for emergency operations across all levels of government, HSPD-5 directed DHS to develop and administer a National Incident Management System (NIMS) and a National Response Plan. Together, NIMS and the NRP provide an approach for federal, state, and local governments to effectively prepare for, respond to, and recover from domestic incidents, regardless of cause, size, or complexity.

HSPD-7 — Critical Infrastructure Identification, Prioritization, and Protection

HSPD-7, issued by President George W. Bush on December 17, 2003, establishes a national policy for federal departments and agencies to identify and prioritize critical U.S. infrastructure and key resources and to protect them from terrorist attacks. Federal departments and agencies will work with state and local governments and the private sector to accomplish this objective. HSPD-7 also identifies Sector-Specific Agencies, which, under DHS' overall coordination, lead efforts to protect specific critical sectors and key resources.

In addition, HSPD-7 requires DHS to develop a comprehensive, integrated National Plan for Critical Infrastructure and Key Resources Protection (NPIP).

Sector-Specific Agencies: Sector-Specific Agencies are agencies responsible for ensuring the protection of a particular resource or part of the national infrastructure. For example, the Department of Energy is the Sector-Specific Agency for the energy sector of the economy.

Sector-Specific Agencies collaborate with other federal, state, and local governments and the private sector to assess and reduce vulnerabilities within the sector. They also encourage the use of risk-management strategies to protect against and mitigate the effects of attacks against the infrastructure and critical resources within the sector.

Nuclear Sector: HSPD-7 specifically requires DHS to work with the Nuclear Regulatory Commission and, as appropriate, the Department of Energy to protect elements of the nuclear sector:

- nuclear reactors used for generation, research, testing, and training,
- nuclear materials used in medical, industrial, and academic settings and facilities that fabricate nuclear fuel,
- the transportation, storage, and disposal of nuclear materials and waste.

General Critical Infrastructure Protection Responsibilities of All Agencies: In addition, HSPD-7 assigns federal agencies and departments a number of general responsibilities related to critical infrastructure protection:

- ensuring that homeland security programs do not diminish the overall economic security of the United States,
- appropriately protecting information associated with carrying out the directive, including voluntarily provided information and information that would facilitate terrorists' targeting critical infrastructure and key resources,

- cooperating with DHS to estimate the potential impact of terrorist attacks on critical infrastructure and key resources,
- submitting a plan for protecting the physical and cyber critical infrastructure and key resources owned or operated by the department or agency. These plans address identification, prioritization, protection, and contingency planning, including the recovery and rebuilding of essential capabilities. (EPA has completed and submitted the Agency's plan to DHS.)

HSPD-8 — National Preparedness

As a companion to HSPD-5, HSPD-8 requires DHS to establish a national domestic all-hazards preparedness goal and describes the way federal departments and agencies will prepare for a response to a national incident. The intent of the national preparedness goal is to ensure that all levels of government work together toward a common, measurable state of readiness and have adequate support to meet the goal. It includes a system for assessing the Nation's overall readiness to respond to major events, especially those involving acts of terrorism.

HSPD-8 names the Secretary of Homeland Security as the principal federal official for coordinating the implementation of all-hazards preparedness. DHS is undertaking a number of tasks to fulfill this role:

- developing plans to identify the research and development needs of national first responders based on current and future threats,
- establishing a national program and planning system for conducting homeland security preparedness-related exercises,
- identifying classes of homeland security-related information and appropriate means for transmitting them into the system,
- developing and maintaining a federal response capability inventory that includes the readiness for deployment of staff and equipment.

Citizen Involvement: HSPD-8 encourages citizen involvement in preparedness efforts. The Secretary of Homeland Security is responsible for working with appropriate federal, state, and local government organizations and the private sector to encourage active citizen participation in preparedness efforts. DHS will periodically identify best practices for integrating private citizen capabilities into local preparedness efforts. In addition, DHS will develop a comprehensive plan to coordinate and provide accurate and timely preparedness information to the general public, first responders, government organizations, the private sector, and other organizations as needed.

PPD-8: National Preparedness

In 2011 President Obama issued a new Presidential Policy Directive, repealing HSPD-5 and HSPD-8, but leaving intact the agency and state plans that had been developed:

Presidential Policy Directive / PPD-8: National Preparedness

March 30, 2011

This directive is aimed at strengthening the security and resilience of the United States through systematic preparation for the threats that pose the greatest risk to the security of the Nation, including acts of terrorism, cyber attacks, pandemics, and catastrophic natural disasters. Our national preparedness is the shared responsibility of all levels of government, the private and nonprofit sectors, and individual citizens. Everyone can contribute to safeguarding the Nation from harm. As such, while this directive is intended to galvanize action by the Federal Government, it is also aimed at facilitating an integrated, all-of-Nation, capabilities-based approach to preparedness.

Therefore, I hereby direct the development of a national preparedness goal that identifies the core capabilities necessary for preparedness and a national preparedness system to guide activities that will enable the Nation to achieve the goal. The system will allow the Nation to track the progress of our ability to build and improve the capabilities necessary to prevent, protect against, mitigate the effects of, respond to, and recover from those threats that pose the greatest risk to the security of the Nation.

The Assistant to the President for Homeland Security and Counterterrorism shall coordinate the interagency development of an implementation plan for completing the national preparedness goal and national preparedness system. The implementation plan shall be submitted to me within 60 days from the date of this directive, and shall assign departmental responsibilities and delivery timelines for the development of the national planning frameworks and associated interagency operational plans described below.

National Preparedness Goal

Within 180 days from the date of this directive, the Secretary of Homeland Security shall develop and submit the national preparedness goal to me, through the Assistant to the President for Homeland Security and Counterterrorism. The Secretary shall coordinate this effort with other executive departments and agencies, and consult with State, local, tribal, and territorial governments, the private and nonprofit sectors, and the public.

The national preparedness goal shall be informed by the risk of specific threats and vulnerabilities—taking into account regional variations—and include concrete, measurable, and prioritized objectives to mitigate that risk. The national preparedness goal shall define the core capabilities necessary to prepare for the specific types of incidents that pose the greatest risk to the security of the Nation, and shall emphasize actions aimed at achieving an integrated, layered, and all-of-Nation preparedness approach that optimizes the use of available resources. The national preparedness goal shall reflect the policy direction outlined in the National Security Strategy (May 2010), applicable Presidential Policy Directives, Homeland Security

Presidential Directives, National Security Presidential Directives, and national strategies, as well as guidance from the Interagency Policy Committee process. The goal shall be reviewed regularly to evaluate consistency with these policies, evolving conditions, and the National Incident Management System.

National Preparedness System

The national preparedness system shall be an integrated set of guidance, programs, and processes that will enable the Nation to meet the national preparedness goal. Within 240 days from the date of this directive, the Secretary of Homeland Security shall develop and submit a description of the national preparedness system to me, through the Assistant to the President for Homeland Security and Counterterrorism. The Secretary shall coordinate this effort with other executive departments and agencies, and consult with State, local, tribal, and territorial governments, the private and nonprofit sectors, and the public.

The national preparedness system shall be designed to help guide the domestic efforts of all levels of government, the private and nonprofit sectors, and the public to build and sustain the capabilities outlined in the national preparedness goal. The national preparedness system shall include guidance for planning, organization, equipment, training, and exercises to build and maintain domestic capabilities. It shall provide an all-of-Nation approach for building and sustaining a cycle of preparedness activities over time.

The national preparedness system shall include a series of integrated national planning frameworks, covering prevention, protection, mitigation, response, and recovery. The frameworks shall be built upon scalable, flexible, and adaptable coordinating structures to align key roles and responsibilities to deliver the necessary capabilities. The frameworks shall be coordinated under a unified system with a common terminology and approach, built around basic plans that support the all-hazards approach to preparedness and functional or incident annexes to describe any unique requirements for particular threats or scenarios, as needed. Each framework shall describe how actions taken in the framework are coordinated with relevant actions described in the other frameworks across the preparedness spectrum.

The national preparedness system shall include an interagency operational plan to support each national planning framework. Each interagency operational plan shall include a more detailed concept of operations; description of critical tasks and responsibilities; detailed resource, personnel, and sourcing requirements; and specific provisions for the rapid integration of resources and personnel.

All executive departments and agencies with roles in the national planning frameworks shall develop department-level operational plans to support the interagency operational plans, as needed. Each national planning framework shall include guidance to support corresponding planning for State, local, tribal, and territorial governments.

The national preparedness system shall include resource guidance, such as arrangements enabling the ability to share personnel. It shall provide equipment guidance aimed at nationwide interoperability; and shall provide guidance for national training and exercise programs, to facilitate our ability to build and sustain the capabilities defined in the national preparedness goal and evaluate progress toward meeting the goal.

The national preparedness system shall include recommendations and guidance to support preparedness planning for businesses, communities, families, and individuals.

The national preparedness system shall include a comprehensive approach to assess national preparedness that uses consistent methodology to measure the operational readiness of national capabilities at the time of assessment, with clear, objective and quantifiable performance measures, against the target capability levels identified in the national preparedness goal.

Building and Sustaining Preparedness

The Secretary of Homeland Security shall coordinate a comprehensive campaign to build and sustain national preparedness, including public outreach and community-based and private-sector programs to enhance national resilience, the provision of Federal financial assistance, preparedness efforts by the Federal Government, and national research and development efforts.

National Preparedness Report

Within 1 year from the date of this directive, the Secretary of Homeland Security shall submit the first national preparedness report based on the national preparedness goal to me, through the Assistant to the President for Homeland Security and Counterterrorism. The Secretary shall coordinate this effort with other executive departments and agencies and consult with State, local, tribal, and territorial governments, the private and nonprofit sectors, and the public. The Secretary shall submit the report annually in sufficient time to allow it to inform the preparation of my Administration's budget.

Roles and Responsibilities

The Assistant to the President for Homeland Security and Counterterrorism shall periodically review progress toward achieving the national preparedness goal.

The Secretary of Homeland Security is responsible for coordinating the domestic all-hazards preparedness efforts of all executive departments and agencies, in consultation with State, local, tribal, and territorial governments, nongovernmental organizations, private-sector partners, and the general public; and for developing the national preparedness goal.

The heads of all executive departments and agencies with roles in prevention, protection, mitigation, response, and recovery are responsible for national preparedness efforts, including department-specific operational plans, as needed, consistent with their statutory roles and responsibilities.

Nothing in this directive is intended to alter or impede the ability to carry out the authorities of executive departments and agencies to perform their responsibilities under law and consistent with applicable legal authorities and other Presidential guidance. This directive shall be implemented consistent with relevant authorities, including the Post-Katrina Emergency Management Reform Act of 2006 and its assignment of responsibilities with respect to the Administrator of the Federal Emergency Management Agency.

Nothing in this directive is intended to interfere with the authority of the Attorney General or Director of the Federal Bureau of Investigation with regard to the direction, conduct, control, planning, organization, equipment, training, exercises, or other activities concerning domestic counterterrorism, intelligence, and law enforcement activities.

Nothing in this directive shall limit the authority of the Secretary of Defense with regard to the command and control, planning, organization, equipment, training, exercises, employment, or other activities of Department of Defense forces, or the allocation of Department of Defense resources.

If resolution on a particular matter called for in this directive cannot be reached between or among executive departments and agencies, the matter shall be referred to me through the Assistant to the President for Homeland Security and Counterterrorism.

This directive replaces Homeland Security Presidential Directive (HSPD)-8 (National Preparedness), issued December 17, 2003, and HSPD-8 Annex I (National Planning), issued December 4, 2007, which are hereby rescinded, except for paragraph 44 of HSPD-8 Annex I. Individual plans developed under HSPD-8 and Annex I remain in effect until rescinded or otherwise replaced.

Definitions:

For the purposes of this directive:

(a) The term "national preparedness" refers to the actions taken to plan, organize, equip, train, and exercise to build and sustain the capabilities necessary to prevent, protect against, mitigate the effects of, respond to, and recover from those threats that pose the greatest risk to the security of the Nation.

(b) The term "security" refers to the protection of the Nation and its people, vital interests, and way of life.

(c) The term "resilience" refers to the ability to adapt to changing conditions and withstand and rapidly recover from disruption due to emergencies.

(d) The term "prevention" refers to those capabilities necessary to avoid, prevent, or stop a threatened or actual act of terrorism. Prevention capabilities include, but are not limited to, information sharing and warning; domestic counterterrorism; and preventing the acquisition or use of weapons of mass destruction (WMD). For purposes of the prevention framework called for in this directive, the term "prevention" refers to preventing imminent threats.

(e) The term "protection" refers to those capabilities necessary to secure the homeland against acts of terrorism and manmade or natural disasters. Protection capabilities include, but are not limited to, defense against WMD threats; defense of agriculture and food; critical infrastructure protection; protection of key leadership and events; border security; maritime security; transportation security; immigration security; and cybersecurity.

(f) The term "mitigation" refers to those capabilities necessary to reduce loss of life and property by lessening the impact of disasters. Mitigation capabilities include, but are not limited to, community-wide risk reduction projects; efforts to improve the resilience of critical infrastructure and key resource lifelines; risk reduction for specific vulnerabilities from natural hazards or acts of terrorism; and initiatives to reduce future risks after a disaster has occurred.

(g) The term "response" refers to those capabilities necessary to save lives, protect property and the environment, and meet basic human needs after an incident has occurred.

(h) The term "recovery" refers to those capabilities necessary to assist communities affected by an incident to recover effectively, including, but not limited to, rebuilding infrastructure systems; providing adequate interim and long-term housing for survivors; restoring health, social, and community services; promoting economic development; and restoring natural and cultural resources.

BARACK OBAMA
Last Published Date: June 24, 2015

Use of the Military in Disaster Response

Finally, let's take a brief look at the use of the military within the United States. We have become used to seeing members of the military, normally the National Guard, but also elements of the other services, involved in dealing with crises, providing additional airport security, and otherwise supporting response efforts. The legal authority for this is complex, though.

The first statute we'll look at is the Posse Comitatus Act, which limits the powers of the federal government in using military personnel as domestic law enforcement personnel. It was passed as an amendment to an Army appropriation bill following the end of Reconstruction. The Act only specifically applies to the Army and, as amended in 1956, the Air Force. While the Act does not explicitly mention the naval services, specifically the Navy and the Marine Corps, the Department of the Navy has regulations that give the Act force with respect to those services as well. The Act does not prevent the National Guard from acting in a law enforcement capacity when it is operating under state authority within its home state or in an adjacent state if invited by that state's governor. The United States Coast Guard, which operates under the Department of Homeland Security, is also not covered by the Posse Comitatus

Act. Although the Coast Guard is an armed service, it also has both a maritime law enforcement mission and a federal regulatory agency mission.

The Posse Comitatus Act provides the basic limitation, but other elements of law also govern when and how the military can be used to support civil authorities. The Insurrection Act of 1807 governs the ability of the president of the United States to deploy troops within the United States to put down lawlessness, insurrection, and rebellion. This authority was used to help enforce civil rights and to deal with riots in the 1950s, 1960s, and 1970s. Finally, there are a number of provisions of law that govern when and how certain capabilities and equipment that the military has may be used to support law enforcement and other civil authorities.

Title 18 U.S. Code—Crimes and Criminal Procedure

§ 1385 Use of the Army and Air Force as Posse Comitatus

Whoever, except in cases and under circumstances expressly authorized by the Constitution or Act of Congress, willfully uses any part of the Army or the Air Force as a posse comitatus or otherwise to execute the laws shall be fined under this title or imprisoned not more than two years, or both.

Title 10 U.S. Code—ARMED FORCES

CHAPTER 15—INSURRECTION

§ 331. Federal aid for State governments

Whenever there is an insurrections in any State against its government, the President may, upon the request of its legislature or of its governor if the legislature cannot be convened, call into Federal service such of the militia of the other States, in the number requested by that State, and use such of the armed forces, as he considers necessary to suppress the insurrection.

§ 332. Use of militia and armed forces to enforce Federal authority

Whenever the President considers that unlawful obstructions, combinations, or assemblages, or rebellion against the authority of the United States, make it impracticable to enforce the laws of the United States in any State by the ordinary course of judicial proceedings, he may call into Federal service such of the militia of any State, and use such of the armed forces, as he considers necessary to enforce those laws or to suppress the rebellion.

§ 333. Interference with State and Federal law

The President, by using the militia or the armed forces, or both, or by any other means, shall take such measures as he considers necessary to suppress, in a State, any insurrection, domestic violence, unlawful combination, or conspiracy, if it—

(1) so hinders the execution of the laws of that State, and of the United States within the State, that any part or class of its people is deprived of a right, privilege, immunity, or protection named in the Constitution and secured by law, and the constituted authorities of that State are unable, fail, or refuse to protect that right, privilege, or immunity, or to give that protection; or

(2) opposes or obstructs the execution of the laws of the United States or impedes the course of justice under those laws.

In any situation covered by clause (1), the State shall be considered to have denied the equal protection of the laws secured by the Constitution.

§ 334. Proclamation to disperse

Whenever the President considers it necessary to use the militia or the armed forces under this chapter, he shall, by proclamation, immediately order the insurgents or those obstructing the enforcement of the laws to disperse and retire peaceably to their abodes within a limited time.

§ 335. Guam and Virgin Islands included as "State"

For purposes of this chapter, the term "State" includes Guam and the Virgin Islands.

Excerpts from 10 U.S. Code Ch. 18 — Military Support for Civilian Law Enforcement Agencies

§ 371. Use of information collected during military operations

(a) The Secretary of Defense may, in accordance with other applicable law, provide to Federal, State, or local civilian law enforcement officials any information collected during the normal course of military training or operations that may be relevant to a violation of any Federal or State law within the jurisdiction of such officials.

(b) The needs of civilian law enforcement officials for information shall, to the maximum extent practicable, be taken into account in the planning and execution of military training or operations.

(c) The Secretary of Defense shall ensure, to the extent consistent with national security, that intelligence information held by the Department of Defense and relevant to drug interdiction or other civilian law enforcement matters is provided promptly to appropriate civilian law enforcement officials.

§ 372. Use of military equipment and facilities

(a) In General. — The Secretary of Defense may, in accordance with other applicable law, make available any equipment (including associated supplies or spare parts), base facility, or research facility of the Department of Defense to any Federal, State, or local civilian law enforcement official for law enforcement purposes.

. . .

§ 373. Training and advising civilian law enforcement officials

The Secretary of Defense may, in accordance with other applicable law, make Department of Defense personnel available —

(1) to train Federal, State, and local civilian law enforcement officials in the operation and maintenance of equipment, including equipment made available under section 372 of this title; and

(2) to provide such law enforcement officials with expert advice relevant to the purposes of this chapter.

§ 374. Maintenance and operation of equipment

(a) The Secretary of Defense may, in accordance with other applicable law, make Department of Defense personnel available for the maintenance of equipment for Federal, State, and local civilian law enforcement officials, including equipment made available under section 372 of this title.

(b)(1) Subject to paragraph (2) and in accordance with other applicable law, the Secretary of Defense may, upon request from the head of a Federal law enforcement agency, make Department of Defense personnel available to operate equipment (including equipment made available under section 372 of this title) . . .

(c) The Secretary of Defense may, in accordance with other applicable law, make Department of Defense personnel available to any Federal, State, or local civilian law enforcement agency to operate equipment for purposes other than described in subsection (b)(2) only to the extent that such support does not involve direct participation by such personnel in a civilian law enforcement operation unless such direct participation is otherwise authorized by law.

§ 375. Restriction on direct participation by military personnel

The Secretary of Defense shall prescribe such regulations as may be necessary to ensure that any activity (including the provision of any equipment or facility or the assignment or detail of any personnel) under this chapter does not include or permit direct participation by a member of the Army, Navy, Air Force, or Marine Corps in a search, seizure, arrest, or other similar activity unless participation in such activity by such member is otherwise authorized by law.

§ 382. Emergency situations involving weapons of mass destruction

(a) In General.—The Secretary of Defense, upon the request of the Attorney General, may provide assistance in support of Department of Justice activities relating to the enforcement of section 175, 229, or 2332a of title 18 during an emergency situation involving a weapon of mass destruction. Department of Defense resources, including personnel of the Department of Defense, may be used to provide such assistance if—

1. the Secretary of Defense and the Attorney General jointly determine that an emergency situation exists; and
2. the Secretary of Defense determines that the provision of such assistance will not adversely affect the military preparedness of the United States.

(b) Emergency Situations Covered.—In this section, the term "emergency situation involving a weapon of mass destruction" means a circumstance involving a weapon of mass destruction—

1. that poses a serious threat to the interests of the United States; and
2. in which—

(A) civilian expertise and capabilities are not readily available to provide the required assistance to counter the threat immediately posed by the weapon involved;

(B) special capabilities and expertise of the Department of Defense are necessary and critical to counter the threat posed by the weapon involved; and

(C) enforcement of section 175, 229, or 2332a of title 18 would be seriously impaired if the Department of Defense assistance were not provided.

(c) Forms of Assistance.—The assistance referred to in subsection (a) includes the operation of equipment (including equipment made available under section 372 of this title) to monitor, contain, disable, or dispose of the weapon involved or elements of the weapon.

(d) Regulations.—(1) The Secretary of Defense and the Attorney General shall jointly prescribe regulations concerning the types of assistance that may be provided under this section. Such regulations shall also describe the actions that Department of Defense personnel may take in circumstances incident to the provision of assistance under this section.

(2)(A) Except as provided in subparagraph (B), the regulations may not authorize the following actions:

(i) Arrest.

(ii) Any direct participation in conducting a search for or seizure of evidence related to a violation of section 175, 229, or 2332a of title 18.

(iii) Any direct participation in the collection of intelligence for law enforcement purposes.

(B) The regulations may authorize an action described in subparagraph (A) to be taken under the following conditions:

(i) The action is considered necessary for the immediate protection of human life, and civilian law enforcement officials are not capable of taking the action.

(ii) The action is otherwise authorized under subsection (c) or under otherwise applicable law.

The use of the military in responding to emergencies, especially cases of violence, is an extremely sensitive one. The general rule that the military cannot be used to enforce the law, contained in the Posse Comitatus Act, is subject to a number of exceptions, cases, as contemplated by the statute, "authorized by the Constitution or Act of Congress."

One case that addressed these issues took over ten years to litigate—and it involved the use of the military to support U.S. Marshals and FBI agents at the village of Wounded Knee, South Dakota. Look over this case, and consider how the arguments raised might apply in the present post-9/11 environment.

Bissonette v. Haig, 776 F.2d 1384 (1985), affirmed 485 U.S. 264 (1988)*

This is an action for damages caused by defendants' alleged violations of the Constitution of the United States. The complaint alleges, among other things, that the defendants seized and confined plaintiffs within an "armed perimeter" by the unlawful use of military force, and that this conduct violated not only a federal statute but also the Fourth Amendment. The use of federal military force, plaintiffs argue, without lawful authority and in violation of the Posse Comitatus Act, 18 U.S.C. § 1385, was an "unreasonable" seizure of their persons within the meaning of the Fourth Amendment. We hold that the complaint states a claim upon which relief may be granted. The judgment of the District Court, dismissing the complaint with prejudice for failure to state a claim, will therefore be reversed, and the cause remanded for further proceedings consistent with this opinion.

This case arises out of the occupation of the village of Wounded Knee, South Dakota, on the Pine Ridge Reservation by an armed group of Indians on February 27, 1973. On the evening when the occupation began, members of the Federal Bureau of Investigation, the United States Marshals Service, and the Bureau of Indian Affairs Police sealed off the village by establishing roadblocks at all major entry and exit roads. The standoff between the Indians and the law-enforcement authorities ended about ten weeks later with the surrender of the Indians occupying the village.

In February 1975, the plaintiffs, most of whom at the time of the occupation were residents of the Pine Ridge Indian Reservation, brought this action alleging that the defendants, who were military personnel or federal officials, conspired to seize and assault them and destroy their property in violation of several constitutional and statutory provisions. The plaintiffs relied exclusively on the theory that constitutional violations occurred because military personnel and equipment were used to accomplish various seizures, searches, and assaults.

Plaintiffs allege three sets of substantive claims. First, they claim that they were unreasonably seized and confined in the village of Wounded Knee contrary to the Fourth Amendment and their rights to free movement and travel. Second, they claim that they were unreasonably searched by ground and aerial surveillance. In both cases, plaintiffs assert that the seizures and searches were unreasonable because "Defendants accomplished or caused to be accomplished those actions by means of the unconstitutional and felonious use of parts of the United States Army or Air Force...." Third, plaintiffs claim they were assaulted, deprived of life in one instance, and deprived of property contrary to their rights under the Fifth and Eighth Amendments. Again, plaintiffs allege that these actions were unconstitutional "for the reason that the arms used in the force or threat of force were parts of the United States Army or Air Force...."

---

* The case has been heavily edited and paraphrased by the authors for clarity. See disclaimer in introduction.

These allegations must be viewed against the background of the Posse Comitatus Act of 1878, 18 U.S.C. § 1385, which plaintiffs claim was violated here. The statute provides:

§ 1385. Use of Army and Air Force as posse comitatus Whoever, except in cases and under circumstances expressly authorized by the Constitution or Act of Congress, willfully uses any part of the Army or the Air Force as a posse comitatus or otherwise to execute the laws shall be fined not more than $10,000 or imprisoned not more than two years, or both.

The first two sets of claims raise the question whether a search or seizure, otherwise permissible, can be rendered unreasonable under the Fourth Amendment because military personnel or equipment were used to accomplish those actions. We believe that the Constitution, certain acts of Congress, and the decisions of the Supreme Court embody certain limitations on the use of military personnel in enforcing the civil law, and that searches and seizures in circumstances which exceed those limits are unreasonable under the Fourth Amendment.

The Supreme Court has recently indicated that a seizure can be unreasonable even if it is supported by probable cause. *Tennessee v. Garner,* 471 U.S. 1 (1985) (seizure with deadly force of fleeing burglar who was apparently unarmed is unreasonable under the Fourth Amendment, whether or not probable cause exists to believe the fugitive has committed a crime). Reasonableness is determined by balancing the interests for and against the seizure. Usually, the interests arrayed against a seizure are those of the individual in privacy, freedom of movement, or, in the case of a seizure by deadly force, life. Here, however, the opposing interests are more societal and governmental than strictly individual in character. They concern the special threats to constitutional government inherent in military enforcement of civilian law. That these governmental interests should weigh in the Fourth Amendment balance is neither novel nor surprising. In the typical Fourth Amendment case, the interests of the individual are balanced against those of the government. That some of those governmental interests are on the other side of the Fourth Amendment balance does not make them any less relevant or important.

Civilian rule is basic to our system of government. The use of military forces to seize civilians can expose civilian government to the threat of military rule and the suspension of constitutional liberties. On a lesser scale, military enforcement of the civil law leaves the protection of vital Fourth and Fifth Amendment rights in the hands of persons who are not trained to uphold these rights. It may also chill the exercise of fundamental rights, such as the rights to speak freely and to vote, and create the atmosphere of fear and hostility which exists in territories occupied by enemy forces.

The interest in limiting military involvement in civilian affairs has a long tradition beginning with the Declaration of Independence and continued in the Constitution, certain acts of Congress, and decisions of the Supreme Court. The Declaration of Independence states among the grounds for severing ties with Great Britain that the King "has kept among us, in times of peace, Standing Armies without Consent of our Legislature . . . [and] has affected to render the Military independent of and superior to the Civil power." These concerns were later raised at the Constitutional Convention. Luther Martin of Maryland said, "when a government wishes to deprive its citizens of freedom, and reduce them to slavery, it generally makes use of a standing army."

The Constitution itself limits the role of the military in civilian affairs: it makes the President, the highest civilian official in the Executive Branch, Commander in Chief of the armed services (Art. II, § 2); it limits the appropriations for armed forces to two years and grants to the Congress the power to make rules to govern the armed forces (Art. I, § 8, cl. 14); and it forbids the involuntary quartering of soldiers in any house in time of peace (Third Amendment).

Congress has passed several statutes limiting the use of the military in enforcing the civil law. As already noted, 18 U.S.C. § 1385 makes it a crime for anyone, "except in cases and circumstances expressly authorized by the Constitution or Act of Congress . . . [to use] any part of the Army or Air Force as a posse comitatus or otherwise to execute the laws." Title 10 U.S.C. §§ 331–335 delimit the circumstances under which the President may call upon the national guard or military to suppress insurrection or domestic violence. See also 32 C.F.R. § 215 (1984).

The Supreme Court has also recognized the constitutional limitations placed on military involvement in civilian affairs. A leading case is *Ex parte Milligan*, 4 Wall. 2, 71 U.S. 2, (1866), a Civil War case where the Court held that military commissions had no authority to try civilians in States not engaged in rebellion, in which the civil courts were open. More recently, in *Laird v. Tatum*, 408 U.S. 1 (1972), statements the Court made in dicta reaffirm these limitations:

The concerns of the Executive and Legislative Branches reflect a traditional and strong resistance of Americans to any military intrusion into civilian affairs. That tradition has deep roots in our history and found early expression, for example, in the Third Amendment's explicit prohibition against quartering soldiers in private homes without consent and in the constitutional provisions for civilian control of the military. Those prohibitions are not directly presented by this case, but their philosophical underpinnings explain our traditional insistence on limitations on military operations in peacetime. Indeed, when presented with claims of judicially cognizable injury resulting from military intrusion into the civilian sector, federal courts are fully empowered to consider claims of those asserting such injury; there is nothing in our Nation's history or in this Court's decided cases, including our holding today, that can properly be seen as giving any indication that actual or threatened injury by reason of unlawful activities of the military would go unnoticed or unremedied.

The governmental interests favoring military assistance to civilian law enforcement are primarily twofold: first, to maintain order in times of domestic violence or rebellion; and second, to improve the efficiency of civilian law enforcement by giving it the benefit of military technologies, equipment, information, and training personnel. These interests can and have been accommodated by acts of Congress to the overriding interest of preserving civilian government and law enforcement. At the time of the Wounded Knee occupation, Congress had prohibited the use of the military to execute the civilian laws, except when expressly authorized. And it had placed specific limits on the President's power to use the national guard and military in emergency situations. For example, under 10 U.S.C. §332, the President may call upon the military only after having determined that domestic unrest makes it "impracticable to enforce the laws of the United States by the ordinary course of judicial proceedings," and under 10 U.S.C. §334, he may do so only after having issued a proclamation ordering the insurgents to disperse. Those steps were not taken here.

We believe that the limits established by Congress on the use of the military for civilian law enforcement provide a reliable guidepost by which to evaluate the reasonableness for Fourth Amendment purposes of the seizures and searches in question here. Congress has acted to establish reasonable limits on the President's use of military forces in emergency situations, and in doing so has circumscribed whatever, if any, inherent power the President may have had absent such legislation. This is the teaching of *Youngstown Sheet & Tube Co. v. Sawyer* (1952). There the President attempted to justify his seizure of the steel mills on grounds of inherent executive power to protect national security. Justice Black, writing for the Court, rejected this assertion of executive authority, and in addition four of the five judges concurring in the Court's opinion or judgment wrote separate opinions expressing the view that Congress had precluded the exercise of inherent executive authority by specifically refusing to give the President the power of seizure.

As will be seen shortly when we come to discuss plaintiff's allegations under the Due Process Clause of the Fifth Amendment, the essence of due process is that no governmental power, civilian or military, may be used to restrain the liberty of the citizen or seize his property otherwise than in accordance with the forms of law, including, in most instances, judicial proceedings. In the context of the Fourth Amendment, however, we believe plaintiffs' theory that the use of military force is in a class by itself has merit. The legal traditions which we have briefly summarized establish that the use of military force for domestic law-enforcement purposes is in a special category, and that both the courts and Congress have been alert to keep it there. In short, if the use of military personnel is both unauthorized by any statute, and contrary to a specific criminal prohibition, and if citizens are seized or searched by military means in such a case, we have no hesitation in declaring that such searches and seizures are constitutionally "unreasonable." We do not mean to say that every search or seizure that violates a statute of any kind is necessarily a violation of the Fourth Amendment. But the statute prohibiting the conduct engaged in by defendants here is, as we have attempted to explain, not just any act of Congress. It is the embodiment of a long tradition of suspicion and hostility towards the use of military force for domestic purposes.

Plaintiffs' Fourth Amendment case, therefore, must stand or fall on the proposition that military activity in connection with the occupation of Wounded Knee violated the Posse Comitatus Act.

In *United States v. Casper*, 541 F.2d 1275 (8th Cir.1976), we specifically held that military assistance given to civilian authorities at Wounded Knee did not violate this statute. In *Casper*, several defendants who were convicted of attempting to interfere with United States Marshals and FBI agents during the Wounded Knee disorder. They appealed their convictions on the grounds that the federal officials allegedly interfered with had been acting in violated of the Posse Comitatus Act. Specifically, the District Court had found on a stipulated record that the following activities did not violate the Act: the use of Air Force personnel, planes, and cameras to fly surveillance; the advice of military officers in dealing with the disorder; and the furnishing of equipment and supplies. We affirmed "on the basis of the trial court's thorough and well-reasoned opinion."

Plaintiffs in the present civil action were not parties in this prior criminal case, nor were defendants here, with perhaps one or two exceptions, among the federal officials with whom interference was charged in the criminal prosecution. Therefore, our judgment in *Casper* does not estop plaintiffs to relitigate the question whether a violation of the Posse Comitatus Act occurred at Wounded Knee. *Casper* does, however, stand as a binding precedent in this Circuit on the interpretation of the Act. Therefore, unless plaintiffs now allege that the defendants took actions that went beyond those alleged in the *Casper* case, the actions alleged in the complaint now before us cannot violate the Act.

In *Casper*, quoting from Judge VanSickle's opinion for the District Court, 419 F.Supp. at 194, we approved the following standard for determining whether a violation of the Posse Comitatus Act had occurred:

Were Army or Air Force personnel used by the civilian law enforcement officers at Wounded Knee in such a manner that the military personnel subjected the citizens to the exercise of military power which was regulatory, proscriptive, or compulsory in nature, either presently or prospectively?

This formulation is based on language found in the Supreme Court's opinion in *Laird v. Tatum* (1972). *Laird* involved a claim that First Amendment rights were chilled by the existence of a data-gathering system maintained by Army Intelligence, a system described by plaintiffs in that case as involving the surveillance of lawful civilian political activity. The Court rejected this claim on the ground that no justiciable controversy existed. It held that the mere existence of this challenged data-gathering system infringed no rights of plaintiffs, since there had been no showing of objective harm or threat of specific future harm.

When this concept is transplanted into the present legal context, we take it to mean that military involvement, even when not expressly authorized by the Constitution or a statute, does not violate the Posse Comitatus Act unless it actually regulates, forbids, or compels some conduct on the part of those claiming relief. A mere threat of some future injury would be insufficient. In addition, the mere furnishing of materials and supplies cannot violate the statute. The same thing is true, as we have previously noted, of the use of military personnel, planes, and cameras to fly surveillance and the advice of military officers in dealing with the disorder, advice, that is, as distinguished from active participation or direction.

The question becomes, then, whether the present complaint alleges more than these kinds of activities. The complaint goes well beyond an allegation that defendants simply furnished supplies, aerial surveillance, and advice. It specifically charges that "the several Defendants maintained or caused to be maintained roadblocks and armed patrols constituting an armed perimeter around the village of Wounded Knee. . . ." Defendants' actions, it is charged, "seized, confined, and made prisoners [of plaintiffs] against their will. . . ." These allegations amount to a claim that defendants' activities, allegedly in violation of the Posse Comitatus Act, were "regulatory, proscriptive, or compulsory," in the sense that these activities directly restrained plaintiffs' freedom of movement. No more is required to survive a motion to dismiss. We hold, therefore, that plaintiffs' first set of claims, alleging an unreasonable seizure in violation of the Fourth Amendment because of defendants' confinement of plaintiffs within an armed perimeter, does state a cause of action.

As to the second set of claims, we hold that they do not state a cause of action. In these claims, plaintiffs charge that they were searched and subjected to surveillance against their will by aerial photographic and visual search and surveillance. As we have already noted, *Casper* holds that this sort of activity does not violate the Posse Comitatus Act. It is therefore not "unreasonable" for Fourth Amendment purposes. In addition, there is no allegation that this aerial surveillance occurred "in the area immediately surrounding the home" or in an area where plaintiffs had a legitimate expectation of privacy. See *Oliver v. United States,* 466 U.S. 170 (1984) (no legitimate expectation of privacy for activities occurring in an open field; aerial surveillance of such an area, even if involving a trespass under state property law, is not an unreasonable search).

The third set of claims invokes the Due Process Clause of the Fifth Amendment. Plaintiffs argue that they were deprived of liberty, property, and, in the case of the son of one of the plaintiffs, life without due process of law. In the ordinary case, a claimed lack of due process relates to the absence of a notice and hearing or certain other procedural deficiencies. Plaintiffs' theory here is quite different. They claim a due-process violation by reason of the mere fact that the confinement and other deprivations inflicted upon them derived from military action instead of civilian. Plaintiffs cite a number of 19th-century cases which they say supports this view. We have carefully examined each of these authorities and find in them no clear support for the novel theory advocated by plaintiffs. In *Merryman,* for example, the Chief Justice did mention the Due Process Clause of the Fifth Amendment, and the petitioner in that habeas corpus proceeding was in military custody, but the result in the case would have been exactly the same had the custody been civilian, because Merryman was seized and imprisoned without any judicial process. It was the absence of that process, rather than the military character of Merryman's custodian, that caused the Chief Justice to take the view that the petitioner was unconstitutionally confined.

Most of the other cases relied on by plaintiffs are ordinary tort actions in which the defendants set up as a defense that they were acting pursuant to military authority. Plaintiffs then contested the validity of this defense, and the courts sided with plaintiffs, but these holdings seem to be based rather on the theory that under the circumstances of each case the assertion of military power was simply unauthorized, rather than on any limitation on military power stemming from the Due Process

Clause of the Fifth Amendment. To be sure, the proposition that a power delegated to an officer of the federal government cannot be exercised in such a way as to conflict with the Due Process Clause of the Fifth Amendment is not far removed from the proposition that no such power was ever delegated in the first place. The two legal theories, however, remain analytically distinct, and plaintiffs' complaint here is clearly grounded on the due-process theory that an action by a military officer can violate the Fifth Amendment even though exactly the same thing, if done by a civilian federal official, would not. With this proposition we do not agree, nor do we believe that plaintiffs, ten years after the filing of their complaint, should be allowed to espouse a new theory of constitutional relief.

Our decision to reject plaintiffs' due-process theory is reinforced by the knowledge that all of the proof relevant under such a theory will still come in if and when the Fourth Amendment search-and-seizure theory goes to trial. In other words, plaintiffs do not really need the due-process theory in order to secure relief here, the Court having already held that an unauthorized action by a military officer can be "unreasonable" under the Fourth Amendment even though the same thing, if done by a civilian official, would not.

In short, we hold that with one exception the complaint failed to state a claim. This exception relates to the allegation that defendants seized and confined plaintiffs within an armed perimeter, that these actions were not authorized by law and were a violation of the Posse Comitatus Act, and that, therefore, an "unreasonable" seizure within the meaning of the Fourth Amendment took place. As to this single theory, we hold that the complaint states a claim on which relief can be granted.

END OF OPINION

How does this opinion square with the current environment? What about use of the military for counter-terrorism within the United States? Has the situation changed with regard to the use of the military?

In an opinion for the President after the 9/11 attacks, the Justice department provided the following analysis:

> We conclude that the President has both constitutional and statutory authority to use the armed forces in military operations, against terrorists, within the United States. we believe that these operations generally would not be subject to the constraints of the Fourth Amendment, so long as the armed forces are undertaking a military function. Even if the Fourth Amendment were to apply, however, we believe that most military operations would satisfy the Constitution's reasonableness requirement and continue to be lawful.[4]

Recall in the *Youngstown Steel* decision that Justice Jackson noted three different levels of presidential authority—that the president had the greatest authority when

---

4. Memorandum—Authority for Use of Military Force to Combat Terrorist Activities Within the United States, Department of Justice Office of Legal Counsel, October 23, 2001.

acting in a way specifically authorized by Congress, that the next lowest level of authority existed when the President was acting and Congress had not acted, and the lowest level of Presidential authority that existed when the President was asserting the need to act even though Congress had said otherwise. The material in this chapter details how Congress and the president have worked to find a balance of authority that both protected essential liberties and allowed for effective response to emergencies. Keep these concepts in mind as we move on to other aspects of Homeland and National Security.

Review Questions

Based on the material in this chapter, how would you assess the legal issues in the following fact patterns?

1. Following an outbreak of the deadly Ebola virus in several West African nations, the governor of New Jersey orders that all medical personnel, including those assigned to active military or National Guard units, that return from duty in the affected areas are to be involuntarily quarantined until his office can be assured that none of the personnel are infected or in a position to infect others.

2. Following a series of severe storms and flooding in an area of central Pennsylvania, the Commanding General of an active U.S. Army base orders his military police to begin patrolling the county, with orders to detain anyone suspected of looting or any other unlawful activity until civilian authorities can be called in the take custody.

3. Following a serious hurricane, the federal on-scene commander (a U.S. Coast Guard admiral) advises that the area is still unsafe for habitation and that the area remains under a mandatory evacuation order and all residents who have evacuated must remain away from their homes. The governor and the mayor of the city hardest hit by the hurricane issue a press statement countermanding the federal evacuation order and asking residents to return as soon as possible.

Key Terms

Civil defense—An effort to protect the citizens of a state (generally non-combatants) from military attack. It uses the principles of emergency operations: prevention, mitigation, preparation, response, or emergency evacuation and recovery.

Disaster preparedness—A continuous cycle of planning, organizing, training, equipping, exercising, evaluating, and taking corrective action in an effort to ensure effective coordination during incident response.

Police power of the state—The capacity of the government (federal, state, or local) to regulate behavior and enforce order within their territory for the betterment of the health, safety, morals, and general welfare of their inhabitants.

Posse Comitatus—The common-law or statute law authority of a county sheriff, or other law officer, to conscript any able-bodied man to assist him in keeping the peace, or a group of citizens assembled by the authorities to deal with an emergency.

Under U.S. law, except where specifically authorized by federal statute, use of any part of the U.S. Army, Air Force, Navy, or Marine Corps (but not the National Guard) for civilian law enforcement purposes is illegal.

Further Reading

Banks, William and Stephen Dycus. *Soldiers on the Home Front: The Domestic Role of the American Military*. Harvard Univ. Press, 2016.

Civil Defense and Homeland Security: A Short History of National Preparedness Efforts, September 2006, prepared by the Director of the Department of Homeland Security's National Preparedness Task Force. Available at https://training.fema.gov/hiedu/docs/dhs%20civil%20defense-hs%20-%20short%20history.pdf

Powell, Tia and Hanfling, Dan and Gostin, Lawrence O., *Emergency Preparedness and Public Health: The Lessons of Hurricane Sandy* (November 16, 2012). JAMA Online, 2012; Georgetown Public Law Research Paper No. 12-189. Available at SSRN: http://ssrn.com/abstract=2184839

Price, Polly J., *Sovereignty, Citizenship and Public Health in the United States*. NYU J. of Legis. and Pub. Policy, Vol. 17, 919–988(2014); Emory Legal Studies Research Paper No. 14-272.

Chapter 9

War Powers

Overview

The ability to use military force is the ultimate power of any government, including ours. Under our constitutional system of checks and balances, this power is shared between the executive and legislative branches, and you can see, in reviewing the chapters on the constitutional framework and on domestic preparedness, some aspects of how that balance has been struck. In many cases, though, the exercise of war powers is governed by a form of common law, inferred from language and historic practice.

In the case of the legislative branch, we find most of the war powers of Congress among the enumerated powers listed in Article 1, Section 8 of the Constitution, including:

- "... and provide for the common Defence and general Welfare of the United States;"
- "To define and punish Piracies committed on the high Seas, and Offences against the Law of Nations;"
- "To declare War, grant Letters of Marque and Reprisal, and make Rules concerning Captures on Land and Water;"
- "To raise and support Armies..."
- "To provide and maintain a Navy;"
- "To make Rules for the Government and Regulation of the land and navy Forces;"
- "To provide for calling forth the Militia to execute the Laws of the Union, suppress Insurrections and repel Invasions;"
- "To provide for organizing, arming, and disciplining, the Militia, and for governing such Part of them as may be employed in the Service of the United States, reserving to the States respectively, the Appointment of the Officers, and the Authority of training the militia according to the discipline prescribed by Congress;"
- "... for the Erection of Forts, Magazines, Arsenals, dock-Yards, and other needful Buildings;"

and

- "To make all Laws which shall be necessary and proper for carrying into execution the foregoing Powers, and all other Powers vested by this Constitution in the Government of the United States or in any Department or Officer thereof."

As you can see, the Constitution gives Congress considerable authority that bears on the ability to use the military. Let's examine some of them:

- "To raise and support Armies . . ."
- "To provide and maintain a Navy;"

These clauses give Congress, not the president, the discretion to determine just how large and how small the U.S. military should be. Notice how the Congress is to "raise and support Armies," but "provide and maintain a Navy." Think about why this difference in language was chosen. The United States has been, since its beginning, a form of "island nation" dependent on ongoing maritime commerce for survival. Our founders saw the primary threat to national security as coming, not from elsewhere on the American continent, but from the European nations. So a permanent Navy was necessary to protect the nation and its commerce, and there would be time, if needed, to raise an Army. This Army would be formed from formal state militias and, if you look at war memorials around the country, this in the make-up of the Army is evident, even through the Second World War.

Although the Air Force and Coast Guard, as well as the rest of the Department of Defense and the Central Intelligence Agency, are not specifically mentioned in the Constitution, it is understood that they are included in the spirit of this clause. Based in large measure on this authority and the others we will discuss, Congress makes the important decisions regarding the structure of the military, such as the number and types of ships in the Navy, which airplanes should be developed, which military installations should be closed or expanded, whether tanks or helicopters should be purchased, and more. Although the executive branch, in the form of the president, his secretaries of defense and of the services, and the military's top generals and admirals, give Congress their expert opinions as to what exactly the military needs and make recommendations for how Congress should vote, the decision on these matters is ultimately the authority of Congress.

- "To make Rules for the Government and Regulation of the land and naval Forces;"

This clause gives Congress the authority to write and authorize the regulations by which the military operates. In this regard, we usually think of the Uniform Code of Military Justice (UCMJ), the legal code that regulates the conduct of servicemembers and provides the basis of the military justice system, which we will explore later in this book. The UCMJ includes laws such as prohibitions against common crimes like drug use, stealing, rape, and murder as well as uniquely military offenses such as cowardice, dereliction of duty, and conduct unbecoming of an officer and gentleman. This authority also provides for rules on how the military departments will be formed—the major commands such as the Pacific Command or Central Command—the organization of the Defense Department, and even the rules by which material is bought and buildings are constructed. This text also provides authority to the Congress to enact laws that guide how the president, as commander in chief, can use tools such as a military commission to try those suspected of war crimes against the United States and its people.

- "To declare War..."

As we will explore, this power to declare war, although a simple phrase, has been one of the most controversial aspects of the war powers because of its overlap with the war powers of the president. To some, this means that only Congress should decide when the nation uses the tools of war, or armed conflict, against others. Others believe that this was intended only to deal with the formal legal status of the nation, and not to interfere with the president's authority as commander in chief to decide when to use the military. We get into this in more detail later.

In addition to these powers listed above, there is one extremely important power that Congress has that affects every aspect of the federal government's actions, including during wartime. Contained in Article I, section 9, it is commonly referred to as "the power of the purse":

- "No Money shall be drawn from the Treasury, but in Consequence of Appropriations made by Law;"

It is this power, many believe, that provides the greatest check and balance against the powers that might be exercised by the president. Here is how that power has been described:

> The Framers were familiar with efforts by English kings to rely on extra-parliamentary sources of revenue for their military expeditions and other activities. Some of the payments came from foreign governments. Because of these transgressions, England lurched into a civil war and Charles I lost both his office and his head. The rise of democratic government is directly related to legislative control over all expenditures ... The U.S. Constitution attempted to avoid the British history of civil war and bloodshed by vesting the power of the purse squarely in Congress. ... This power of the purse, said Madison in Federalist No. 58, represents the "most compleat and effectual weapon with which any constitution can arm the immediate representatives of the people, for obtaining a redress of every grievance, and for carrying into effect every just and salutary measure." The Framers did more than place the power of the purse with Congress. They deliberately divided government by making the President the commander in chief and reserving to Congress the power to finance military expeditions. The Framers rejected a government in which a single branch could both make war and fund it.[1]

---

1. Louis Fisher, *Distribution of Constitutional Authority: How Tightly Can Congress Draw the Purse Strings?* 83 A.J.I.L 738 (1989). See also Kate Stith, *Congress' Power of the Purse*, 97 Yale L. J. 595 (1988).

Article II of the Constitution sets forth the powers of the president. The list of powers is not as expansive as in the case of the powers given to Congress. In contrast with the numerous specified war powers of Congress, the president's explicit war powers are contained in the following two clauses in Article II, section 2:

- "He shall have Power, by and with the Advice and Consent of the Senate, to make Treaties, provided two thirds of the Senators present concur; and he shall nominate, and by and with the Advice and Consent of the Senate, shall appoint Ambassadors . . ."

- "The President shall be Commander in Chief of the Army and Navy of the United States, and of the Militia of the several States, when called into the actual Service of the United States."

As well as this language from section 3:

- ". . . he shall take Care that the laws be faithfully executed . . ."

While the list of express authority is less, the history of the presidency shows that the language used has been interpreted to give the president broad authority to use the military forces (as well as associated capabilities like the intelligence community) in very expansive ways. This balance is often the source of legitimate debate in our nation, as you will see.

Recall from our earlier discussion that the language in Article I and Article II of the Constitution is very different—Article I vests the legislative powers "herein granted" in the Congress, while Article II simply vests "the Executive Power" in the president. The fact that the framers did not include the limiting language "herein granted" when describing the executive power is considered the basis for the power of the president to lead the nation in international affairs and as the legal basis for a president's unilateral use of military force. This difference in language has been the source of controversy since the beginning of the nation, but what is important to remember in this context is that every president in our history has taken the view that "the Executive Power" is to be interpreted as broadly as necessary to protect the nation, subject to the limitations contained elsewhere in the Constitution.

It is worth exploring what the founding fathers intended when they wrote the war powers of the U.S. Constitution. Unfortunately, it is difficult to determine what they intended because few records remain from the Constitutional Convention. What is known is that the delegates did engage in a debate as to whether or not the text should read that Congress has the power to "declare war" or to "make war." Ultimately, Congress decided on "declaring war"; there are a few leading theories as to why this is, and they are not mutually exclusive.

A popular theory is that the delegates did not want to give any single person, the president, the power to unilaterally enter the country into a war. The founding fathers had, after overthrowing the rule of a king, a fear of a strong chief executive, which was why they gave many of the most important powers to Congress, and not the president. It was also viewed that in many ways, simply "declaring war" is a legal technicality. If another country were to invade the U.S., the country would be at war, regardless of whether or not Congress took the time to declare it. This view ties into another understood power of the president to defend the country from sudden attacks. Assume that Canada were to invade the U.S. (a real fear at the time the Constitution was written). If this were to occur, the president would, as commander in chief, be able to lead the military in fending off the attack; however, once the initial attack has been fended off, it might then be up to Congress to decide whether or not any more should be done, such as an invasion of Canada to prevent future attacks.

Still, these are merely theories put together from the scant records remaining from the Constitutional Convention and other writings of the Founders,[2] and the actual answer is not certain. To quote Supreme Court Justice Jackson, "Just what our forefathers did envision, or would have envisioned had they foreseen modern conditions, must be divined from materials almost as enigmatic as the dreams Joseph was called upon to interpret for Pharaoh."

The use of congressional authority to declare war has been the exception, not the rule, throughout our history. Presidents have frequently acted without the authorization of Congress and introduced the U.S. military into combat. The U.S. military has undertaken over 300 significant military engagements since the creation of the nation. On only 12 of these occasions has Congress actually expressly voted its advance approval for military action. Of those 12, only five were formal declarations of war. The other seven were merely votes to authorize the president's use of military force, such as the "Gulf of Tonkin Resolution" that authorized the U.S. military action in Vietnam, or the more recent "Authorization for the Use of Military Force," one of which authorized military action in response to the attacks of September 11, 2001, and another which authorized the invasion if Iraq. In all cases other than those 12 exceptions, it has been the unilateral decision of the president to send American troops into combat.

This leads to the ultimate question of the war powers: When must the president have the authorization of Congress to send the military into combat, as opposed to authorizing the use of force based on the "inherent" powers of the president? There is no clear answer, as the examples of history do not follow any single pattern. For example, Congress declared war on Spain in 1898, and the Spanish-American War resulted in a total of 345 American combat deaths. In contrast, without any Congressional authorization, but instead relying just on a UN Resolution, President Truman entered the U.S. military in the Korean War, which resulted in 30,000 American casualties. When President Reagan ordered the invasion of Grenada in Operation Urgent Fury in 1983, and when President George H.W. Bush (the senior) ordered the invasion of Panama in Operation Just Cause in 1989, neither of these presidents had congressional authorization. More recently in 2011, President Obama did not have any congressional authorization when he ordered air strikes on Libya to assist NATO in its operation to overthrow Libya's dictator, Muammar Gaddafi.

---

2. As noted earlier, Alexander Hamilton and James Madison wrote in detail of this issue in the Pacificus and Helviticus debates, and Hamilton addressed the concerns in Federalist Papers 24, 25, and 69.

While recognizing that the president needs flexibility to deal with the numerous threats to American security, many people throughout our nation's history have found it troubling that, without congressional authorization, U.S. presidents unilaterally send the U.S. military into hostilities, including cases where the military ends up overthrowing foreign governments. The reasonable concern is that this unilateral action by the president encroaches on Congress's power to "declare war." This remains a hotly debated yet unanswered question, as no court has held that these presidential actions violate the U.S. Constitution, and, as we have seen, presidents can and do unilaterally enter the military into situations which have regional and global ramifications without ever facing legal consequences. Of course, there can be political consequences. Presidents realize that the process of getting congressional authority often helps build popular support for the action, and also ensures that Congress is politically "on the hook" for the decision along with the president. But these are political, not legal, considerations.

Instead of declaring war, Congress has occasionally passed a bill to allow for the use of military force, which is considered the legal equivalent to a declaration of war, although it does not call the bill a "declaration of war." For example, after 9/11 Congress never formally declared war on the Taliban or Al-Qaeda. Instead, Congress passed the Authorization for the Use of Military Force (AUMF),[3] which authorizes the use of United States Armed Forces against those responsible for the attacks:

Section 2—Authorization for Use of United States Armed Forces

(a) That the President is authorized to use all necessary and appropriate force against those nations, organizations, or persons he determines planned, authorized, committed, or aided the terrorist attacks that occurred on September 11, 2001, or harbored such organizations or persons, in order to prevent any future acts of international terrorism against the United States by such nations, organizations or persons.

It's pretty easy to see this as the equivalent of a declaration of war in that it gives the president what is almost unbridled authority to use the military in any means necessary to pursue those behind 9/11. Congress passed another AUMF in 2003 to grant President Bush the authority to go to war with Iraq.[4] Even the Vietnam War, which claimed over 50,000 American lives, was never formally declared. Instead, Congress passed the Gulf of Tonkin Resolution[5] to authorize the president "to take all necessary measures to repel any armed attack against the forces of the United States and to prevent further aggression."

There is no single answer to the question of why the U.S. does not formally declare war anymore. One explanation is that, since adopting the United Nations Charter,

---

3. Codified at 115 Stat. 224 and passed as S.J. Res. by the United States Congress on September 14, 2001.

4. Authorization for Use of Military Force Against Iraq Resolution of 2002, Pub.L. 107–243, 116 Stat. 1498, enacted October 16, 2002.

5. The Gulf of Tonkin Resolution or the Southeast Asia Resolution, Pub.L. 88–408, 78 Stat. 384, enacted August 10, 1964.

the use of military force is to be left to cases of self-defense or as authorized by the UN Security Council. "War" as a tool of politics is arguably outdated, even though it may was once commonly used to settle differences, gain territory, or obtain resources. Another related view is that it is simply a matter of public relations. In this modern era, war is looked upon as an uncivilized and dirty business. A nation that declares war takes on a connotation of aggression. It is much better for public relations to spin a military operation as a defensive measure, an act to protect human rights, or an act of liberation rather than a formal war. It helps if an action is viewed as defensive or as a liberation effort instead of a war waged for conquest. For example, the 2003 war with Iraq was referred to as "Operation Iraqi Freedom," not "Operation Iraqi Invasion."

Furthermore, a formal declaration of war grants the president significant powers under a wide variety of laws to control the economy, such as the price controls and rationing seen during World War II. It forces other nations to choose sides and has diplomatic and economic implications far beyond what the nation may want to undertake. So, for many reasons, it is better politically to label an action as something other than a war.

As a result of all this history, it is now generally agreed that it is legally irrelevant whether or not there is a formal "Declaration of War," titled as such, enacted by Congress. What ultimately matters in just about every aspect of homeland and national security law is that the president and Congress are in agreement as to whether or not the military should be used. This principle is addressed in a Vietnam-era case, *Orlando v. Laird*.

Orlando v. Laird, 443 F.2d 1039 (1971)*

Shortly after receiving orders to report for transfer to Vietnam, Private First Class Malcolm A. Berk and Specialist Salvatore Orlando, enlistees in the United States Army, commenced separate actions in June, 1970, seeking to enjoin the Secretary of Defense, the Secretary of the Army and the commanding officers, who signed their deployment orders, from enforcing them. The plaintiffs-appellants contended that these executive officers exceeded their constitutional authority by ordering them to participate in a war not properly authorized by Congress. They point out that Congress has not officially declared war in Vietnam.

In *Berk v. Laird* we held that the war declaring power of Congress, enumerated in Article I, section 8, of the Constitution, contains a "discoverable standard calling for some mutual participation by Congress..."

The district court denied Orlando's motion for a preliminary injunction on the ground that his deployment orders were constitutionally authorized, because Congress, by "appropriating the nation's treasure and conscripting its manpower," had "furnished forth the sinew of war" and because "the reality of the collaborative

---

* The case has been heavily edited and paraphrased by the authors for clarity. See disclaimer in introduction.

action of the executive and the legislative required by the Constitution has been present from the earliest stages." The district court ruled that there had been joint action by the President and Congress.

It is the appellants' position that the sufficiency of congressional authorization is a matter within judicial competence because that question can be resolved by "judicially discoverable and manageable standards" dictated by the congressional power "to declare War." They interpret the constitutional provision to require an express and explicit congressional authorization of the Vietnam hostilities though not necessarily in the words, "We declare that the United States of America is at war with North Vietnam." In support of this construction they point out that the original intent of the clause was to place responsibility for the initiation of war upon the body most responsive to popular will and argue that historical developments have not altered the need for significant congressional participation in such commitments of national resources. They further assert that, without a requirement of express and explicit congressional authorization, developments committing the nation to war became the inevitable adjuncts of presidential direction of foreign policy, and, because military appropriations and other war-implementing enactments lack an explicit authorization of particular hostilities, they cannot, as a matter of law, be considered sufficient.

The Government on the other hand takes the position that the military action in South Vietnam was authorized by Congress in the "Joint Resolution to Promote the Maintenance of Internal Peace and Security in Southeast Asia" (the Gulf of Tonkin Resolution); and that the military action was authorized and ratified by congressional appropriations expressly designated for use in support of the military operations in Vietnam.

As we see it, the test is whether there is any action by the Congress sufficient to authorize or ratify the military activity in question. The evidentiary materials produced at the hearings in the district court clearly disclose that this test is satisfied.

The Congress and the Executive have taken mutual and joint action in the prosecution and support of military operations in Southeast Asia from the beginning of those operations. The Tonkin Gulf Resolution, enacted August 10, 1964 (repealed December 31, 1970) was passed at the request of President Johnson and, though occasioned by specific naval incidents in the Gulf of Tonkin, was expressed in broad language which clearly showed the state of mind of the Congress and its intention fully to implement and support the military and naval actions taken by and planned to be taken by the President at that time in Southeast Asia, and as might be required in the future "to prevent further aggression." Congress has ratified the executive's initiatives by appropriating billions of dollars to carry out military operations in Southeast Asia and by extending the Military Selective Service Act with full knowledge that persons conscripted under that Act had been, and would continue to be, sent to Vietnam. Moreover, it specifically conscripted manpower to fill "the substantial induction calls necessitated by the current Vietnam buildup."

There is, therefore, no lack of clear evidence to support a conclusion that there was an abundance of continuing mutual participation in the prosecution of the war.

Both branches collaborated in the endeavor, and neither could long maintain such a war without the concurrence and cooperation of the other.

Although appellants do not contend that Congress can exercise its war-declaring power only through a formal declaration, they argue that congressional authorization cannot, as a matter of law, be inferred from military appropriations or other war-implementing legislation that does not contain an express and explicit authorization for the making of war by the President. Putting aside for a moment the explicit authorization of the Tonkin Gulf Resolution, we disagree with appellants' interpretation of the declaration clause for neither the language nor the purpose underlying that provision prohibits an inference of the fact of authorization from such legislative action as we have in this instance. The framers' intent to vest the war power in Congress is in no way defeated by permitting an inference of authorization from legislative action furnishing the manpower and materials of war for the protracted military operation in Southeast Asia.

The choice, for example, between an explicit declaration on the one hand and a resolution and war-implementing legislation, on the other, as the medium for expression of congressional consent involves the exercise of a discretion demonstrably committed to the legislature.

Such a choice involves an important area of decision making in which, through mutual influence and reciprocal action between the President and the Congress, policies governing the relationship between this country and other parts of the world are formulated in the best interests of the United States. If there can be nothing more than minor military operations conducted under any circumstances, short of an express and explicit declaration of war by Congress, then extended military operations could not be conducted even though both the Congress and the President were agreed that they were necessary and were also agreed that a formal declaration of war would place the nation in a posture in its international relations which would be against its best interests. For the judicial branch to enunciate and enforce such a standard would be not only extremely unwise but also would constitute a deep invasion of the role of the President and Congress. As the Government says, "... decisions regarding the form and substance of congressional enactments authorizing hostilities are determined by highly complex considerations of diplomacy, foreign policy and military strategy inappropriate to judicial inquiry." It would, indeed, destroy the flexibility of action which the executive and legislative branches must have in dealing with other sovereigns. What has been said and done by both the President and the Congress in their collaborative conduct of the military operations in Vietnam implies a consensus on the advisability of not making a formal declaration of war because it would be contrary to the interests of the United States to do so. The making of a policy decision of that kind is clearly within the constitutional domain of those two branches and is just as clearly not within the competency or power of the judiciary.

Beyond determining that there has been some mutual participation between the Congress and the President, which unquestionably exists here, with action by the Congress sufficient to authorize or ratify the military activity at issue, it is clear that the constitutional propriety of the means by which Congress has chosen to ratify and approve the protracted military operations in Southeast Asia is a political question. The form which congressional authorization should take is one of policy, committed to the discretion of the Congress and outside the power and competency of the judiciary, because there are no intelligible and objectively manageable standards by which to judge such actions.

The judgments of the district court are affirmed.

END OF OPINION

As the court explains, the one subject that is settled is that there is no legal requirement for a formal "declaration of war." What matters is the spirit of the text—that Congress and the president work together to fight a war, even if one has not been formally declared. Although Congress never voted to declare war in Vietnam, Congress still voted to pass the Gulf of Tonkin Resolution to authorize the president to send troops in Vietnam. Congress continued supporting the war effort by funding the war.

The government in this case had insisted that the president's authority, in the absence of a declaration of war, was the same with regard to the use of the military as in other aspects of foreign relations. The court did not go that far, but relied on the collaboration between the president and Congress in deciding that the conflict was properly authorized. Is this collaboration always necessary? And must the authority come before hostilities are undertaken? There is little doubt that if the country were to be invaded, the president could respond to address the threat without waiting on Congress. Even though Congress's job is to "declare war," as argued at the Constitutional Convention, war is a "state of things" and can exist, even if not declared.

A landmark case that looks at the war powers of the president and the significance of the phrase "declare war" was the *Prize Cases* decision. This case concerned several cases coming out of the American Civil War that involved the U.S. Navy seizing ships that transported goods for the Confederacy. During times of peace, the seizure of ships is unlawful. But during a time of war, such action is lawful, and the seized ship and its cargo can be claimed as a war prize.

When the Union captured ships transporting goods through the blockade of the Confederacy, claiming the ships as war prizes, the owners of the seized ships sued. The owners pointed out that there had never been a declaration of war against the Confederacy. They argued that the president's war powers were not activated because there was no declaration of war, so it was unlawful for him to blockade southern ports. They also argued that the Confederacy was not, at least according to the Union, an independent nation, but merely some states in rebellion, and, in accordance with recognized international law, a nation cannot declare war on itself. Furthermore, the owners argued that the president was unilaterally *declaring* war against the ship-owners' home nations by *committing an act of war*, blockading the south and seizing its ships. They argued that because the Constitution gives only Congress and not the president the power to declare war, the president's actions were unconstitutional.

The Prize Cases, 67 U.S. 635 (1863)[*]

It is well established that a ship captured during war may be kept as a prize. However, if there is not a war, such seizure of another's vessel is an act of piracy.

There are certain propositions of law which must necessarily affect the ultimate decision of these cases, and many others, which it will be proper to discuss and decide before we notice the special facts peculiar to each.

They are, first, did the President have a right to institute a blockade of ports in possession of persons in armed rebellion against the Government, on the principles of international law, as known and acknowledged among civilized States?

Second, was the property of persons domiciled or residing within those States a proper subject of capture on the sea as 'enemies' property?'

Neutrals have a right to challenge the existence of a blockade, and also the authority of the party exercising the right to institute it. They have a right to enter the ports of a friendly nation for the purposes of trade and commerce, but are bound to recognize the rights of a belligerent engaged in actual war, to use this mode of coercion, for the purpose of subduing the enemy.

That a blockade actually existed, and was formally declared and notified by the President on the 27th and 30th of April, 1861, is an admitted fact in these cases. That the President, as the Executive Chief of the Government and Commander-in-chief of the Army and Navy, was the proper person to make such notification, has not been, and cannot be disputed.

The right of prize and capture has its origin in customary international law and is governed and adjudged under the law of nations. To legitimate the capture of a neutral vessel or property on the high seas, a war must exist, and the neutral must have a knowledge or notice of the intention of one of the parties' belligerent to use this mode of coercion against a port, city, or territory, in possession of the other.

Let us enquire whether, at the time this blockade was instituted, a state of war existed which would justify a resort to these means of subduing the hostile force. War has been well defined to be, 'That state in which a nation prosecutes its right by force.' The parties belligerent in a public war are independent nations. But it is not necessary to constitute war, that both parties should be acknowledged as independent nations or sovereign States. A war may exist where one of the belligerents, claims sovereign rights as against the other.

Insurrection against a government may or may not culminate in an organized rebellion, but a civil war always begins by insurrection against the lawful authority of the Government. A civil war is never solemnly declared; it becomes such by its accidents-the number, power, and organization of the persons who originate and carry it on. When the party in rebellion occupy and hold in a hostile manner a certain portion of territory; have declared their independence; have cast off their

---

[*] The case has been heavily edited and paraphrased by the authors for clarity. See disclaimer in introduction.

allegiance; have organized armies; have commenced hostilities against their former sovereign, the world acknowledges them as belligerents, and the contest a war. They claim to be in arms to establish their liberty and independence, in order to become a sovereign State, while the sovereign party treats them as insurgents and rebels who owe allegiance, and who should be punished with death for their treason.

The laws of war, as established among nations, have their foundation in reason, and all tend to mitigate the cruelties and misery produced by the scourge of war. Hence the parties to a civil war usually concede to each other belligerent rights. They exchange prisoners, and adopt the other courtesies and rules common to public or national wars.

As a civil war is never publicly proclaimed, its actual existence is a fact in our domestic history which the Court is bound to notice and to know.

The true test of its existence, as found in the writings of the sages of the common law, may be thus summarily stated: 'When the regular course of justice is interrupted by revolt, rebellion, or insurrection, so that the Courts of Justice cannot be kept open, civil war exists and hostilities may be prosecuted on the same footing as if those opposing the Government were foreign enemies invading the land.'

By the Constitution, Congress alone has the power to declare a national or foreign war. The President cannot declare war against a State, or any number of States, by virtue of any clause in the Constitution. The Constitution confers on the President the whole Executive power. He is bound to take care that the laws be faithfully executed. He is Commander-in-chief of the Army and Navy of the United States, and of the militia of the several States when called into the actual service of the United States. He has no power to initiate or declare a war either against a foreign nation or a domestic State. But by the Acts of Congress of February 28th, 1795, and 3d of March, 1807, he is authorized to called out the militia and use the military and naval forces of the United States in case of invasion by foreign nations, and to suppress insurrection against the government of a State or of the United States.

If a war is made by invasion of a foreign nation, the President is not only authorized but bound to resist force by force. He does not initiate the war, but is bound to accept the challenge without waiting for any special legislative authority. And whether the hostile party be a foreign invader, or States organized in rebellion, it is none the less a war, although the declaration of it be 'unilateral.' Lord Stowell observes, 'It is not the less a war on that account, for war may exist without a declaration on either side. It is so laid down by the best writers on the law of nations. A declaration of war by one country only, is not a mere challenge to be accepted or refused at pleasure by the other.' . . .

The battles of Palo Alto and Resaca de la Palma had been fought before the passage of the Act of Congress of May 13th, 1846, which recognized 'a state of war as existing by the act of the Republic of Mexico.' This act not only provided for the future prosecution of the war, but was itself a vindication and ratification of the Act of the President in accepting the challenge without a previous formal declaration of war by Congress.

This greatest of civil wars was not gradually developed by popular commotion, tumultuous assemblies, or local unorganized insurrections. However long may have been its previous conception, it nevertheless sprung forth suddenly from the parent brain, a Minerva in the full panoply of war. The President was bound to meet it in the shape it presented itself, without waiting for Congress to baptize it with a name; and no name given to it by him or them could change the fact.

... It is not necessary that the independence of the revolted province or State be acknowledged in order to constitute it a party belligerent in a war according to the law of nations. Foreign nations acknowledge it as war by a declaration of neutrality. The condition of neutrality cannot exist unless there be two belligerent parties. In the case of the *Santissima Trinidad*, (7 Wheaton, 337) this Court said: 'The Government of the United States has recognized the existence of a civil war between Spain and her colonies, and has avowed her determination to remain neutral between the parties. Each party is therefore deemed by us a belligerent nation, having, so far as concerns us, the sovereign rights of war.'

As soon as the news of the attack on Fort Sumter, and the organization of a government by the seceding States, assuming to act as belligerents, could become known in Europe, on the 13th of May, 1861, the Queen of England issued her proclamation of neutrality, 'recognizing hostilities as existing between the Government of the United States of American and certain States styling themselves the Confederate States of America.' This was immediately followed by similar declarations or silent acquiescence by other nations.

After such an official recognition by the sovereign, a citizen of a foreign State is estopped to deny the existence of a war with all its consequences as regards neutrals. They cannot ask a Court to affect a technical ignorance of the existence of a war, which all the world acknowledges to be the greatest civil war known in the history of the human race, and thus cripple the arm of the Government and paralyze its power by subtle definitions and ingenious sophisms.

The law of nations is also called the law of nature; it is founded on the common consent as well as the common sense of the world. It contains no such anomalous doctrine as that which this Court are now for the first time desired to pronounce, to wit: That insurgents who have risen in rebellion against their sovereign, expelled her Courts, established a revolutionary government, organized armies, and commenced hostilities, are not enemies because they are traitors; and a war levied on the Government by traitors, in order to dismember and destroy it, is not a war because it is an 'insurrection.'

Whether the President in fulfilling his duties, as Commander-in-chief, in suppressing an insurrection, has met with such armed hostile resistance, and a civil war of such alarming proportions as will compel him to accord to them the character of belligerents, is a question to be decided by him, and this Court must be governed by the decisions and acts of the political department of the Government to which this power was entrusted. 'He must determine what degree of force the crisis demands.' The proclamation of blockade is itself official and conclusive evidence to the Court that a state of war existed which demanded and authorized a recourse to such a measure, under the circumstances peculiar to the case.

If it were necessary to the technical existence of a war, that it should have a legislative sanction, we find it in almost every act passed at the extraordinary session of the Legislature of 1861, which was wholly employed in enacting laws to enable the Government to prosecute the war with vigor and efficiency. And finally, in 1861, we find Congress did subsequently pass an act 'approving, legalizing, and making valid all the acts, proclamations, and orders of the President, as if they had been issued and done under the previous express authority and direction of the Congress of the United States.'

Without admitting that such an act was necessary under the circumstances, it is plain that if the President had in any manner assumed powers which it was necessary should have the authority or sanction of Congress, that on the well-known principle of law that retroactive ratification is permissible, this ratification has operated to perfectly cure the defect. In the case of Brown v. United States, Mr. Justice Story treats of this subject, and cites numerous authorities to which we may refer to prove this position, and concludes, 'I am perfectly satisfied that no subject can commence hostilities or capture property of an enemy, when the sovereign has prohibited it. But suppose he did, I would ask if the sovereign may not ratify his proceedings, and thus by a retroactive operation give validity to them?'

Although Mr. Justice Story dissented from the majority of the Court on the whole case, the doctrine stated by him on this point is correct and fully substantiated by authority. The objection made to this act of ratification, that it is *ex post facto* meaning "after the fact," and therefore unconstitutional and void, might possibly have some weight on the trial of an indictment in a criminal Court. But precedents from that source cannot be received as authoritative in a tribunal administering public and international law.

On this first question therefore we are of the opinion that the President had a right, under the customary law of war, to institute a blockade of ports in possession of the States in rebellion, which neutrals are bound to regard.

We come now to the consideration of the second question. What is included in the term 'enemies' property?'

The appellants contend that the term 'enemy' is properly applicable to those only who are subjects or citizens of a foreign State at war with our own. They quote from the pages of the common law, which say, 'that persons who wage war against the King may be of two kinds, subjects or citizens. The former are not proper enemies, but rebels and traitors; the latter are those that come properly under the name of enemies.'

They insist, moreover, that the President himself, in his proclamation, admits that great numbers of the persons residing within the territories in possession of the insurgent government, are loyal in their feelings, and forced by compulsion and the violence of the rebellious and revolutionary party and its 'de facto government' to submit to their laws and assist in their scheme of revolution; that the acts of the usurping government cannot legally sever the bond of their allegiance; they have, therefore, a co-relative right to claim the protection of the government for their persons and property, and to be treated as loyal citizens, till legally convicted of having renounced their allegiance and made war against the Government by treasonably resisting its laws.

They contend, also, that insurrection is the act of individuals and not of a government or sovereignty; that the individuals engaged are subjects of law. That confiscation of their property can be effected only under a municipal law. That by the law of the land such confiscation cannot take place without the conviction of the owner of some offence, and finally that the secession ordinances are nullities and ineffectual to release any citizen from his allegiance to the national Government, and consequently that the Constitution and Laws of the United States are still operative over persons in all the States for punishment as well as protection.

This argument rests on the assumption of two propositions, each of which is without foundation on the established law of nations. It assumes that where a civil war exists, the party belligerent claiming to be sovereign, cannot, for some unknown reason, exercise the rights of belligerents, although the revolutionary party may. Being sovereign, he can exercise only sovereign rights over the other party. The insurgent may be killed on the battle-field or by the executioner; his property on land may be confiscated under the municipal law; but the commerce on the ocean, which supplies the rebels with means to support the war, cannot be made the subject of capture under the laws of war, because it is 'unconstitutional!!!' Now, it is a proposition never doubted, that the belligerent party who claims to be sovereign, may exercise both belligerent and sovereign rights. Treating the other party as a belligerent and using only the milder modes of coercion which the law of nations has introduced to mitigate the rigors of war, cannot be a subject of complaint by the party to whom it is accorded as a grace or granted as a necessity. We have shown that a civil war such as that now waged between the Northern and Southern States is properly conducted according to the humane regulations of public law as regards capture on the ocean.

Under the very peculiar Constitution of this Government, although the citizens owe supreme allegiance to the Federal Government, they owe also a qualified allegiance to the State in which they are domiciled. Their persons and property are subject to its laws.

Hence, in organizing this rebellion, they have acted as States claiming to be sovereign over all persons and property within their respective limits, and asserting a right to absolve their citizens from their allegiance to the Federal Government. Several of these States have combined to form a new confederacy, claiming to be acknowledged by the world as a sovereign State. Their right to do so is now being decided by wager of battle. The ports and territory of each of these States are held in hostility to the General Government. It is no loose, unorganized insurrection, having no defined boundary or possession. It has a boundary marked by lines of bayonets, and which can be crossed only by force-south of this line is enemies' territory, because it is claimed and held in possession by an organized, hostile and belligerent power.

All persons residing within this territory whose property may be used to increase the revenues of the hostile power are, in this contest, liable to be treated as enemies, though not foreigners. They have cast off their allegiance and made war on their Government, and are none the less enemies because they are traitors.

But in defining the meaning of the term 'enemies' property,' we will be led into error if we refer to Fleta and Lord Coke for their definition of the word 'enemy.' It is a technical phrase peculiar to prize courts, and depends upon principles of public policy as distinguished from the common law.

Whether property be liable to capture as 'enemies' property' does not in any manner depend on the personal allegiance of the owner. 'It is the illegal traffic that stamps it as 'enemies' property.' It is of no consequence whether it belongs to an ally or a citizen. The owner, for now, is an enemy.'

The produce of the soil of the hostile territory, as well as other property engaged in the commerce of the hostile power, as the source of its wealth and strength, are always regarded as legitimate prize, without regard to the domicil of the owner, and much more so if he reside and trade within their territory.

We now proceed to notice the facts peculiar to the several cases submitted for our consideration. The principles which have just been stated apply alike to all of them.

The case of the brig Amy Warwick.

This vessel was captured upon the high seas by the United States gunboat Quaker City, and with her cargo was sent into the district of Massachusetts for condemnation. The brig was claimed by David Currie and others. The cargo consisted of coffee, and was claimed, four hundred bags by Edmund Davenport & Co., and four thousand seven hundred bags by Dunlap, Moncure & Co. The title of these parties as respectively claimed was conceded. All the claimants at the time of the capture, and for a long time before, were residents of Richmond, Va., and were engaged in business there. Consequently, their property was justly condemned as 'enemies' property.'

The decree below is affirmed with costs.

END OF OPINION

Here, the Court pointed out that it was irrelevant whether or not Congress had formally declared war. They pointed out that war is a "state of things." This means that the fact that Congress had not declared a war did not mean one did not exist; obviously the American Civil War was a war, even if it was never formally declared, or was a civil war, an insurrection, or a rebellion. A nation does not declare war on itself and, as a practical matter, a civil war is *never* declared. The fact that the Union refused to declare war on the southern states or recognize them as a sovereign nation did not mean that the laws of war, including the law of capture on the high seas, did not apply, because regardless of the terminology being used, there was a war going on.

The Constitution gives the president the power to suppress insurrection and rebellion, and it is understood that the president has inherent defensive powers, regardless of whether the war is declared or not. Furthermore, as commander in chief, he is empowered to decide just how the war is to be fought. If the president chooses to fight a war by putting up a blockade and seizing enemy ships, that action is well within his constitutional war powers, even if a war has not been formally declared. Lastly, Congress passed legislation after-the-fact, recognizing the president's earlier actions as lawful, so the president and Congress were working in concert.

Review Questions

1. Recall from a previous chapter the "political question" doctrine. Can you find language in this decision that suggests the Court was applying, at least by implication, that doctrine in refusing to second-guess the actions taken by the president and Congress?

2. The *Prize Cases* are recognized for the principle that a state of war can exist between a nation and a non-state actor—such as the Confederacy. How might this case have affected the decisions of the Congress and president in choosing how to respond to the attacks of September 11, 2001?[6]

Let's look at another case. In 1854, Captain George Hollins, commanding the U.S.S. Cyane, shelled the city of Greytown, Nicaragua, in response to the theft and destruction of American property and an attack upon a U.S. government official. Durand, an American citizen living in Nicaragua, had property destroyed by the bombardment and sued. Look at the language in this decision of the federal court in New York.

Durand v. Hollins, 8 F. Cas. 111 (C.C. S.D. N.Y. 1860)[*]

The argument is that neither the president nor the secretary of the navy had authority to give the orders relied on to the defendant, and, hence, that they afford no legal justification for the destruction of property.

The executive power, under the constitution, is vested in the president of the United States. He is commander-in-chief of the army and navy, and has imposed upon him the duty to "take care that the laws be faithfully executed."

As the executive head of the nation, the president is made the only legitimate organ of the general government, to open and carry on correspondence or negotiations with foreign nations, in matters concerning the interests of the country or of its citizens. It is to him, also, the citizens abroad must look for protection of person and of property, and for the faithful execution of the laws existing and intended for their protection. For this purpose, the whole executive power of the country is placed in his

---

6. An excellent book that examines both the laws of war as they applied to the American Civil War, but also draws parallels between the challenges facing the Lincoln and Bush administrations, is found in "Lincoln's Code: The Laws of War in American History" by John Fabian Witt (Simon and Schuster 2012).

* The case has been heavily edited and paraphrased by the authors for clarity. See disclaimer in introduction.

hands, under the constitution, and the laws passed in pursuance thereof; and different departments of government have been organized, through which this power may be most conveniently executed, whether by negotiation or by force—a department of state and a department of the navy.

Now, as it respects the interposition of the executive abroad, for the protection of the lives or property of the citizen, the duty must, of necessity, rest in the discretion of the president. Acts of lawless violence, or of threatened violence to the citizen or his property, cannot be anticipated and provided for; and the protection, to be effectual or of any avail, may, not unfrequently, require the most prompt and decided action. Under our system of government, the citizen abroad is as much entitled to protection as the citizen at home. The great object and duty of government is the protection of the lives, liberty, and property of the people composing it, whether abroad or at home; and any government failing in the accomplishment of the object, or the performance of the duty, is not worth preserving. I have said, that the interposition of the president abroad, for the protection of the citizen, must necessarily rest in his discretion; and it is quite clear that, in all cases where a public act or order rests in executive discretion neither he nor his authorized agent is personally civilly responsible for the consequences.

As was observed by Chief Justice Marshall, in *Marbury v. Madison*, "By the constitution of the United States, the president is invested with certain important political powers, in the exercise of which he is to use his own discretion, and is accountable only to his country in his political character, and to his own conscience. To aid him in the performance of these duties, he is authorized to appoint certain officers, who act by his authority, and in conformity with his orders. In such cases, their acts are his acts, and, whatever opinion may be entertained of the manner in which executive discretion may be used, still there exists, and can exist, no power to control that discretion. The subjects are political. They respect the nation, not individual rights, and, being entrusted to the executive, the decision of the executive is conclusive." This is a sound principle, and governs the present case.

The question whether it was the duty of the president to interpose for the protection of the citizens at Greytown against an irresponsible and marauding community that had established itself there, was a public political question, in which the government, as well as the citizens whose interests were involved, was concerned, and which belonged to the executive to determine; and his decision is final and conclusive, and justified the defendant in the execution of his orders given through the secretary of the navy.

END OF OPINION

Note the expansive interpretation of presidential authority described by the Court in this case. This goes to the point made earlier, that "the Executive Power" was often interpreted so as to give the president the broadest authority to act.

This case is also an illustration of the use of the military, outside the limits of a declared war, to protect American citizens and property overseas. This has tended to be the most frequent justification for the use of the military by a president—in

Grenada by President Reagan, in Panama by President George H.W. Bush, and at other times. As we discussed earlier, presidents of all political parties have used the military for a variety of reasons, often without any authorization by Congress.

It is worth noting that these unilateral military actions by the president are usually relatively minor military engagements. When we say that a military engagement is "minor," we mean that, for a nation as large and powerful as the U.S., the use of military force is minor. For example, when President Bush unilaterally ordered the invasion of Panama in 1989, the U.S. military force involved was under 30,000 troops, and there were fewer than 400 American casualties. To a nation the size of the U.S., relative to the war in Vietnam where there were half a million troops on the ground, this was a very minor fight. However, to the Panamanian forces who numbered fewer than 20,000 in their entirety, this was a large fight and massive invasion. Other military actions involved even fewer forces, in some cases consisting of airstrikes with only a few planes or, increasingly, with unmanned or remotely-piloted aircraft.

There is no official number in the terms of manpower or casualties at which point the president must have the approval of Congress. However, as a practical matter, there is a very clear and distinct point where the president must have the approval of Congress, and it ties into what may be Congress's most potent war power, its "power of the purse." The phrase "the power of the purse" refers to the fact that the Constitution grants Congress, not the president, control over the federal budget and spending.

Remember, Sections 8 and 9 of Article I of the U.S. Constitution include the language granting Congress the power to control spending for the military and for the rest of the federal government. Military operations are expensive. It is impossible for a president to wage a large-scale operation such as the Vietnam War or the ongoing war in Afghanistan without getting appropriations from Congress. If Congress wishes to prevent or even end a conflict, Congress can simply pass a spending bill to cut off funding.

That is exactly how the Vietnam War was ended; Congress passed the following language in several funding bills:

> Sec. 304. No funds appropriated in this Act shall be expended to aid or assist in the reconstruction of the Democratic Republic of Vietnam (North Vietnam).
>
> Sec. 307. None of the funds herein appropriated under this Act may be expended to support directly or indirectly combat activities in or over Cambodia, Laos, North Vietnam and South Vietnam or off the shores of Cambodia, Laos, North Vietnam and South Vietnam by United States forces, and after August 15, 1973, no other funds heretofore appropriated under any other Act may be expended for such purpose.[7]

The Vietnam War was never formally declared over by the president or Congress. Instead, Congress simply cut off funding. While this action by Congress was

---

7. Second Supplemental Appropriations Act, P.L. 93-50, H.R. 9055.

responsible for ending much of the U.S. involvement in Vietnam, it should be noted that even after this language was made law, President Gerald Ford unilaterally ordered a rescue mission when the American vessel MAYAGUEZ was captured by the Cambodian navy in 1975. An even more significant action taken by the executive in the face of Congressional prohibition took place during the Reagan Administration.

Upset with a series of disclosures about U.S.-supported insurgents in South America violating human rights during conflicts with Communist-backed forces in several countries, Congress passed the Boland Amendment, which prohibited any covert (secret) support. Congress insisted that they needed to know about any actions that might be taken to provide military support in these situations. Even though Congress had forbidden giving U.S. support to the anti-Communist forces in Nicaragua, members of the executive branch—members of the National Security Council staff and the intelligence community, in particular—did provide support. Further, to evade the funding restrictions that Congress had put into place, these members of the Reagan administration arranged for private funding of the effort by selling weapons to Iran. The incident, known as "The Iran-Contra Scandal," caused a constitutional crisis resulting in hearings and criminal trials for several government officials.[8] Many also sought the resignation or impeachment of President Reagan. It could never be conclusively established that President Reagan knew of, let alone authorized, the illegal activities of members of the executive branch, so nothing came of this.

One interpretation of the question of when the president must get the authorization of Congress is that he must get it for a large military operation that will require an additional appropriation of funds. As a matter of practicality, a minor operation, such as one on the scale of the invasion of Panama or isolated airstrikes against ISIS, can be covered by the regular military budget without extra funds having to be allocated by Congress. The president is arguably allowed to unilaterally engage in military actions which are so minor that he does not need extra funding from Congress to finance the operation. In contrast, if a military operation is going to be so expensive that it will take extra funding from Congress, then the president has no choice but to get the approval of Congress to conduct this operation. That approval might come in the form of an "authorization to use military force," or it might simply come in the form of specific appropriations by Congress for the purpose—after all, Congress wouldn't give the money for the purpose if approval weren't implied. In this way, we can analogize the president to a teenager, and Congress to the parent—if a teen says, "Dad, can I have $100 to go to a concert?" and the father hands the teen $100, the teen can safely assume that Dad approves of the way the money will be spent.

What if Congress does not want the president to go to war, or wants to limit the scope of a minor war conflict? Although the president, as commander in chief,

---

8. For more information, see "The Iran-Contra Affair" at http://www.pbs.org/wgbh/americanexperience/features/general-article/reagan-iran/, "Understanding the Iran-Cointra Affairs" at http://www.brown.edu/Research/Understanding_the_Iran_Contra_Affair/, the Report of the Congressional Committees Investigating the Iran-Contra Affair, available at http://nsarchive.gwu.edu/NSAEBB/NSAEBB40/19871117.pdf, and the "Final Report of the Independent Counsel for Iran-Contra Matters," available at http://fas.org/irp/offdocs/walsh/.

controls how a war is to be fought, Congress can still, in theory, place controls and limits on how wars are fought. The importance of this principle came to light during the case of *Little v. Barreme*. In the years 1798 to 1800, the U.S. was engaged in an undeclared and limited war against France, fought only at sea. It was referred to as "the Quasi-War." French privateers preyed on American merchant vessels, and the weak American Navy was largely ineffective at stopping them. Vessels seized by the opposing side would be taken as war prizes.

Little v. Barreme, 6 U.S. 170 (1804)*

The Flying-Fish a Danish vessel having on board Danish and neutral property, was captured on the 2d of December 1799, on a voyage from Jeremie to St. Thomas's, by the United States frigate Boston, commanded by Captain Little, and brought into the port of Boston, where she was libelled as an American vessel that had violated the non-intercourse law. The judge before whom the cause was tried, directed a restoration of the vessel and cargo as neutral property, but refused to award damages for the capture and detention, because in his opinion, there was probable cause to suspect the vessel to be American.

On an appeal to the circuit court this sentence was reversed, because the Flying-Fish was on a voyage from, not to, a French port, and was therefore, had she even been an American vessel, not liable to capture on the high seas.

During the hostilities between the United States and France, an act for the suspension of all intercourse between the two nations was annually passed. That under which the Flying-Fish was condemned, declared every vessel, owned, hired or employed wholly or in part by an American, which should be employed in any traffic or commerce with or for any person resident within the jurisdiction or under the authority of the French republic, to be forfeited together with her cargo; the one half to accrue to the United States, and the other to any person or persons, citizens of the United States, who will inform and prosecute for the same.

The 5th section of this act authorizes the president of the United States, to instruct the commanders of armed vessels, "to stop and examine any ship or vessel of the United States on the high sea, which there may be reason to suspect to be engaged in any traffic or commerce contrary to the true tenor of the act, and if upon examination it should appear that such ship or vessel is bound or sailing to any port or place within the territory of the French republic or her dependencies, it is rendered lawful to seize such vessel, and send her into the United States for adjudication."

It is by no means clear that the president of the United States whose high duty it is to "take care that the laws be faithfully executed," and who is commander in chief of the armies and navies of the United States, might not, without any special authority for that purpose, in the then existing state of things, have empowered the officers commanding the armed vessels of the United States, to seize and send into port for

---

* The case has been heavily edited and paraphrased by the authors for clarity. See disclaimer in introduction.

adjudication, American vessels which were forfeited by being engaged in this illicit commerce. But when it is observed that the general clause of the first section of the "act, which declares that such vessels may be seized, and may be prosecuted in any district or circuit court, which shall be holden within or for the district where the seizure shall be made," obviously contemplates a seizure within the United States; and that the 5th section gives a special authority to seize on the high seas, and limits that authority to the seizure of vessels bound or sailing to a French port, the legislature seem to have prescribed that the manner in which this law shall be carried into execution, was to exclude a seizure of any vessel not bound to a French port. Of consequence, however strong the circumstances might be, which induced Captain Little to suspect the Flying-Fish to be an American vessel, they could not excuse the detention of her, since he would not have been authorized to detain her had she been really American.

It was so obvious, that if only vessels sailing to a French port could be seized on the high seas, that the law would be very often evaded, that this act of congress appears to have received a different construction from the executive of the United States; a construction much better calculated to give it effect.

A copy of this act was transmitted by the secretary of the navy, to the captains of the armed vessels, who were ordered to consider [it] as a part of their instructions. The same letter contained the following clause.

> "A proper discharge of the important duties enjoined on you, arising out of this act, will require the exercise of a sound and an impartial judgment. You are not only to do all that in you lies, to prevent all intercourse, whether direct or circuitous, between the ports of the United States, and those of France or her dependencies, where the vessels are apparently as well as really American, and protected by American papers only, but you are to be vigilant that vessels or cargoes really American, but covered by Danish or other foreign papers, and bound to or from French ports, do not escape you."

These orders given by the executive under the construction of the act of congress made by the department to which its execution was assigned, enjoin the seizure of American vessels sailing from a French port. Is the officer who obeys them liable for damages sustained by this misconstruction of the act, or will his orders excuse him? If his instructions afford him no protection, then the law must take its course, and he must pay such damages as are legally awarded against him; if they excuse an act not otherwise excusable, it would then be necessary to inquire whether this is a case in which the probable cause which existed to induce a suspicion that the vessel was American, would excuse the captor from damages when the vessel appeared in fact to be neutral.

I confess the first bias of my mind was very strong in favor of the opinion that though the instructions of the executive could not give a right, they might yet excuse from damages. I was much inclined to think that a distinction ought to be taken between acts of civil and those of military officers; and between proceedings within the body of the country and those on the high seas. That implicit obedience which military men usually pay to the orders of their superiors, which indeed is indispensably necessary to every military system, appeared to me strongly to imply the principle that those orders, if not to perform a prohibited act, ought to justify the person whose general duty it is to obey them, and who is placed by the laws of his country in a situation which in general requires that he should obey them. I was strongly inclined to think that where, in consequence of orders from the legitimate authority, a vessel is seized with pure intention, the claim of the injured party for damages would be against that government from which the orders proceeded, and would be a proper subject for negotiation. But I have been convinced that I was mistaken, and I have receded from this first opinion. I acquiesce in that of my brethren, which is, that the instructions cannot change the nature of the transaction, or legalize an act which without those instructions would have been a plain trespass.

It becomes therefore unnecessary to inquire whether the probable cause afforded by the conduct of the Flying-Fish to suspect her of being an American, would excuse Captain Little from damages for having seized and sent her into port, since had she actually been an American, the seizure would have been unlawful?

Captain Little then must be answerable in damages to the owner of this neutral vessel, and as the account taken by order of the circuit court is not objectionable on its face, and has not been excepted to by council before the proper tribunal, this court can receive no objection to it.

There appears then to be no error in the judgment of the circuit court, and it must be affirmed with costs.

END OF OPINION

Here, Congress passed a law that authorized the president to seize vessels sailing <u>to</u> French ports. What President John Adams did was issued an executive order for the U.S. Navy to also seize vessels sailing <u>from</u> French ports. This was declared unconstitutional by the Court because the action amounted to the president making a law. According to the U.S. Constitution, only Congress is allowed to make law. Members of the military are to follow only lawful orders, and given that the order to seize ships sailing from French ports was unlawful because the president cannot make law, Captain Little was held personally liable for following an unlawful order. Although the president is the commander in chief, this case reinforces the idea that Congress can place considerable controls over just how wars are to be fought.

Review Questions

1. The U.S. decides to help Syrian rebels in its civil war against the Assad government. Congress passes legislation authorizing planes to fly over Syria and drop ordnance, or Navy vessels in the Mediterranean to fire missiles, but explicitly orders that no troops be "on the ground" in Syria and further states that no appropriated funds may be used to support ground troops in Syria. The president gives the U.S. military permission to place special operators on the ground to help pinpoint targets with lasers for the Air Force bombers. Is this lawful?

2. Individuals who are members of Hamas fly an airplane into the Empire State Building, killing 3,000 Americans. Congress passes legislation which authorizes the president to invade the Gaza Strip where Hamas is headquartered, specifying that the authority is to take action "within that territory of land known as 'the Gaza Strip.'" The American president, knowing that Hamas also has forces in the West Bank, also sends the military into the West Bank territory. Is this lawful? In this situation Congress specifically limited the fighting to a specific geographic area. In contrast, the AUMF passed after 9/11 simply authorized the president to go after Al-Qaeda without imposing any geographical limitation. Is the imposition of geographical limits a proper exercise of Congressional authority, or is it an unconstitutional limit on the president's authority as commander in chief?

The president always has his inherent Article II authorities, including the obligation to protect Americans. As a result, presidents have always reserved the right to act, even against the will of Congress, where they believe the congressional action violates the constitutional authority.

In the MAYAGUEZ case mentioned earlier, Congress specifically prohibited ANY form of military action in Southeast Asia—Vietnam, Cambodia, Laos, etc. But President Ford ordered a rescue operation for the crew of the MAYAGUEZ because of an understanding that Congress can never overrule the president's inherent constitutional obligations.

So, what can the president do on his own authority as commander in chief, and what requires the authorization of Congress?

Let's read *Youngstown v. Sawyer*, a case we mentioned at the beginning of this text, and probably the most famous and important Supreme Court case concerning the war powers of the president and Congress. This case takes place against the backdrop of the Korean War. Fighting a war involves more than just combat itself. To support a war requires extensive civilian support. This civilian support includes farming to feed the military, obtaining and continuously supplying fuel to support military vehicles, and the smooth operations of factories where military equipment are constructed. Do the president's war powers as commander in chief include the power to control these civilian networks and systems when they are being used to support a war? The famous opinion below suggests that they do not, but the case stands for much more than that.

Youngstown Sheet & Tube Co. v. Sawyer, 343 U.S. 579 (1952)[*]
(The Steel Seizure Case)

MR. JUSTICE BLACK delivered the opinion of the Court.

We are asked to decide whether the President was acting within his constitutional power when he issued an order directing the Secretary of Commerce to take possession of and operate most of the Nation's steel mills. The mill owners argue

---

[*] The case has been heavily edited and paraphrased by the authors for clarity. See disclaimer in introduction.

that the President's order amounts to lawmaking, a legislative function which the Constitution has expressly confided to the Congress, and not to the President. The Government's position is that the order was made on findings of the President that his action was necessary to avert a national catastrophe which would inevitably result from a stoppage of steel production, and that, in meeting this grave emergency, the President was acting within the aggregate of his constitutional powers as the Nation's Chief Executive and the Commander in Chief of the Armed Forces of the United States. The issue emerges here from the following series of events:

In the latter part of 1951, a dispute arose between the steel companies and their employees over terms and conditions that should be included in new collective bargaining agreements. Long-continued conferences failed to resolve the dispute. On December 18, 1951, the employees' representative, United Steelworkers of America, CIO, gave notice of an intention to strike when the existing bargaining agreements expired on December 31. The Federal Mediation and Conciliation Service then intervened in an effort to get labor and management to agree. This failing, the President on December 22, 1951, referred the dispute to the Federal Wage Stabilization Board to investigate and make recommendations for fair and equitable terms of settlement. This Board's report resulted in no settlement. On April 4, 1952, the Union gave notice of a nationwide strike called to begin at 12:01 a.m. April 9. The indispensability of steel as a component of substantially all weapons and other war materials led the President to believe that the proposed work stoppage would immediately jeopardize our national defense and that governmental seizure of the steel mills was necessary in order to assure the continued availability of steel. Reciting these considerations for his action, the President, a few hours before the strike was to begin, issued Executive Order 10340. The order directed the Secretary of Commerce to take possession of most of the steel mills and keep them running. The Secretary immediately issued his own possessory orders, calling upon the presidents of the various seized companies to serve as operating managers for the United States. They were directed to carry on their activities in accordance with regulations and directions of the Secretary. The next morning the President sent a message to Congress reporting his action. Twelve days later, he sent a second message. Congress has taken no action.

Obeying the Secretary's orders under protest, the companies brought proceedings against him in the District Court. Their complaints charged that the seizure was not authorized by an act of Congress or by any constitutional provisions. The District Court was asked to declare the orders of the President and the Secretary invalid and to issue preliminary and permanent injunctions restraining their enforcement. Opposing the motion for preliminary injunction, the United States asserted that a strike disrupting steel production for even a brief period would so endanger the well-being and safety of the Nation that the President had "inherent power" to do what he had done—power "supported by the Constitution, by historical precedent, and by court decisions." Holding against the President on all points, the District Court, on April 30, issued a preliminary injunction restraining the Secretary from "continuing the seizure and possession of the plants . . . and from acting under the purported authority of Executive Order No. 10340. On the same day, the Court of Appeals stayed the District Court's injunction. Deeming it best that the issues raised be promptly decided by this Court, we granted review.

Two crucial issues have developed: First. Should final determination of the constitutional validity of the President's order be made in this case which has proceeded no further than the preliminary injunction stage? Second. If so, is the seizure order within the constitutional power of the President?

I

The President's power, if any, to issue the order must stem either from an act of Congress or from the Constitution itself. There is no statute that expressly authorizes the President to take possession of property as he did here. Nor is there any act of Congress to which our attention has been directed from which such a power can fairly be implied. Indeed, we do not understand the Government to rely on statutory authorization for this seizure. There are two statutes which do authorize the President to take both personal and real property under certain conditions. However, the Government admits that these conditions were not met, and that the President's order was not rooted in either of the statutes. The Government refers to the seizure provisions of one of these statutes as "much too cumbersome, involved, and time-consuming for the crisis which was at hand."

Moreover, the use of the seizure technique to solve labor disputes in order to prevent work stoppages was not only unauthorized by any congressional enactment; prior to this controversy, Congress had refused to adopt that method of settling labor disputes. When the Taft-Hartley Act was under consideration in 1947, Congress rejected an amendment which would have authorized such governmental seizures in cases of emergency. Apparently it was thought that the technique of seizure, like that of compulsory arbitration, would interfere with the process of collective bargaining. Consequently, the plan Congress adopted in that Act did not provide for seizure under any circumstances. Instead, the plan sought to bring about settlements by use of the customary devices of mediation, conciliation, investigation by boards of inquiry, and public reports. In some instances, temporary injunctions were authorized to provide cooling-off periods. All this failing, unions were left free to strike after a secret vote by employees as to whether they wished to accept their employers' final settlement offer.

Given that there is no statute giving the President the authority to do what he did, it is clear that if the President had authority to issue the order he did, it must be found in some provision of the Constitution. This is a problem for the President, because there is no express constitutional language granting this power to the President. Instead, the contention is that presidential power should be implied from the aggregate of his powers under the Constitution.[9] Here, the President is claiming that this aggregate power to seize the mills can be implied by provisions in Article II which say that "The executive Power shall be vested in a President..."; that "he shall take

---

9. Authors' note: This "aggregate" idea is something courts do; as you read in *Griswold v. Connecticut*, a right to privacy was established from the aggregate of other rights.

Care that the Laws be faithfully executed", and that he "shall be Commander in Chief of the Army and Navy of the United States."

We disagree with the President. The order cannot properly be sustained as an exercise of the President's military power as Commander in Chief of the Armed Forces. The Government attempts to do so by citing a number of cases upholding broad powers in military commanders engaged in day-to-day fighting in a theater of war. Such cases need not concern us here, for we are not in the area where the war is taking place. Even though "theater of war" is an expanding concept and to some extent includes support efforts at home, we cannot with faithfulness to our constitutional system hold that the Commander in Chief of the Armed Forces has the ultimate power as such to take possession of private property in order to keep labor disputes from stopping production, even in times of war. This is a job for the Nation's lawmakers and not for the military authorities.

Nor can the seizure order be sustained because of the several constitutional provisions that grant executive power to the President. In the framework of our Constitution, the President's power to see that the laws are faithfully executed refutes the idea that he is to be a lawmaker. The Constitution limits his functions in the lawmaking process to the recommending of laws he thinks wise and the vetoing of laws he thinks bad. And the Constitution is neither silent nor equivocal about who shall make laws which the President is to execute. The first section of the first article says that "All legislative Powers herein granted shall be vested in a Congress of the United States. . . ." After granting many powers to the Congress, Article I goes on to provide that Congress may make all Laws which shall be necessary and proper for carrying into Execution the foregoing Powers, and all other Powers vested by this Constitution in the Government of the United States, or in any Department or Officer thereof.

The President's order does not direct that a congressional policy be executed in a manner prescribed by Congress—it directs that a presidential policy be executed in a manner prescribed by the President. The preamble of the order itself, like that of many statutes, sets out reasons why the President believes certain policies should be adopted, proclaims these policies as rules of conduct to be followed, and again, like a statute, authorizes a government official to promulgate additional rules and regulations consistent with the policy proclaimed and needed to carry that policy into execution. The power of Congress to adopt such public policies as those proclaimed by the order is beyond question. It can authorize the taking of private property for public use. It can make laws regulating the relationships between employers and employees, prescribing rules designed to settle labor disputes, and fixing wages and working conditions in certain fields of our economy. The Constitution does not subject this lawmaking power of Congress to presidential or military supervision or control.

It is said that other Presidents, without congressional authority, have taken possession of private business enterprises in order to settle labor disputes. But even if this be true, Congress has not thereby lost its exclusive constitutional authority to make laws necessary and proper to carry out the powers vested by the Constitution "in the Government of the United States, or any Department or Officer thereof."

The Founders of this Nation entrusted the lawmaking power to the Congress alone in both good and bad times. It would do no good to recall the historical events, the fears of power, and the hopes for freedom that lay behind their choice. Such a review would but confirm our holding that this seizure order cannot stand.

The judgment of the District Court is

Affirmed.

MR. JUSTICE JACKSON, concurring in the judgment and opinion of the Court.

That comprehensive and undefined presidential powers hold both practical advantages and grave dangers for the country which will impress anyone who has served as legal adviser to a President in time of transition and public anxiety. While an interval of detached reflection may temper teachings of that experience, they probably are a more realistic influence on my views than the conventional materials of judicial decision which seem unduly to accentuate doctrine and legal fiction. But, as we approach the question of presidential power, we half overcome mental hazards by recognizing them. The opinions of judges, no less than executives and publicists, often suffer the infirmity of confusing the issue of a power's validity with the cause it is invoked to promote, of confounding the permanent executive office with its temporary occupant. The tendency is strong to emphasize transient results upon policies—such as wages or stabilization—and lose sight of enduring consequences upon the balanced power structure of our Republic.

A judge, like an executive adviser, may be surprised at the poverty of really useful and unambiguous authority applicable to concrete problems of the President's war powers as they actually present themselves. Just what our forefathers did envision, or would have envisioned had they foreseen modern conditions, must be divined from materials almost as enigmatic as the dreams Joseph was called upon to interpret for Pharaoh. A century and a half of partisan debate and scholarly speculation yields no net result, but only supplies more or less apt quotations from respected sources on each side of any question. They largely cancel each other. And court decisions are indecisive because of the judicial practice of dealing with the largest questions in the most narrow way.

The actual art of governing under our Constitution does not, and cannot, conform to judicial definitions of the power of any of its branches based on isolated clauses, or even single Articles take out of context. While the Constitution diffuses power among three branches of government to secure liberty, it also contemplates that practice will integrate the dispersed powers into a workable government. It enjoins upon its branches separateness but interdependence, autonomy but reciprocity. Presidential powers are not fixed but fluctuate depending upon their disjunction or conjunction with those of Congress. We may well begin by a somewhat over-simplified grouping of practical situations in which a President may doubt, or others may challenge, his powers, and by distinguishing roughly the legal consequences of this factor of relativity.

1. When the President acts pursuant to an express or implied authorization of Congress, his authority is at its maximum, for it includes all that he possesses in his own

right plus all that Congress can delegate. In these circumstances, and in these only, may he be said (for what it may be worth) to personify the federal sovereignty. If his act is held unconstitutional under these circumstances, it usually means that the Federal Government, as an undivided whole, lacks power. A seizure executed by the President pursuant to an Act of Congress would be supported by the strongest of presumptions and the widest latitude of judicial interpretation, and the burden of persuasion would rest heavily upon any who might attack it.

2. When the President acts in absence of either a congressional grant or denial of authority, he can only rely upon his own independent powers, but there is a zone of twilight in which he and Congress may have concurrent authority, or in which its distribution is uncertain. Therefore, congressional inertia or indifference may sometimes, at least, as a practical matter, enable, if not invite, measures on independent presidential responsibility. In this area, any actual test of power is likely to depend on the imperatives of events and contemporary imponderables, rather than on abstract theories of law.

3. When the President takes measures incompatible with the expressed or implied will of Congress, his power is at its lowest ebb, for then he can rely only upon his own constitutional powers minus any constitutional powers of Congress over the matter. Courts can sustain exclusive presidential control in such a case only by disabling the Congress from acting upon the subject. Presidential claim to a power at once so conclusive and preclusive must be scrutinized with caution, for what is at stake is the equilibrium established by our constitutional system.

Into which of these classifications does this executive seizure of the steel industry fit? It is eliminated from the first category by admission, for it is conceded that no congressional authorization exists for this seizure. That takes away also the support of the many precedents and declarations which were made in relation, and must be confined, to this category.

Can it then be defended under flexible tests available to the second category? It seems clearly eliminated from that class, because Congress has not left seizure of private property an open field, but has covered it by three statutes which are inconsistent with this seizure.

This leaves the current seizure to be justified only by the severe tests under the third grouping, where it can be supported only by any remainder of executive power after subtraction of such powers as Congress may have over the subject. In short, we can sustain the President only by holding that seizure of such strike-bound industries is within his domain and beyond control by Congress. Thus, this Court's first review of such seizures occurs under circumstances which leave presidential power most vulnerable to attack and in the least favorable of possible constitutional postures.

I did not suppose, and I am not persuaded, that history leaves it open to question, at least in the courts, that the executive branch, like the Federal Government as a whole, possesses only delegated powers. The purpose of the Constitution was not only to grant power, but to keep it from getting out of hand. However, because the President does not enjoy unmentioned powers does not mean that the mentioned ones should be narrowed by an overly narrow construction. Some clauses could be made almost unworkable, as well as immutable, by refusal to indulge some flexibility of interpretation for changing times. I have in the past, and do now, give to the enumerated powers the scope and flexibility afforded by what seem to be reasonable, practical implications, instead of the rigidity dictated by strict adherence to the text.

The President seeks the power of seizure in three clauses of the Executive Article, the first reading, "The executive Power shall be vested in a President of the United States of America." Lest I be thought to exaggerate, I quote the interpretation which his brief puts upon it: "In our view, this clause constitutes a grant of all the executive powers of which the Government is capable." If that is true, it is difficult to see why the forefathers bothered to add several specific items, including some trifling ones.

The example of such unlimited executive power that must have most impressed the forefathers was the prerogative exercised by George III, and the description of its evils in the Declaration of Independence leads me to doubt that they were creating their new Executive in his image with the power to seize private property as presented here today. Continental European examples were no more appealing. And, if we seek instruction from our own times, we can match it only from the executive powers in those governments we disparagingly describe as totalitarian. I cannot accept the view that this clause is a grant in bulk of all conceivable executive power, but regard it as an allocation to the presidential office of the generic powers thereafter stated.

The clause on which the Government next relies is that "The President shall be Commander in Chief of the Army and Navy of the United States. . . ." These cryptic words have given rise to some of the most persistent controversies in our constitutional history. Of course, they imply something more than an empty title. But just what authority goes with the name has plagued presidential advisers who would not waive or narrow it, yet cannot say where it begins or ends. It undoubtedly puts the Nation's armed forces under presidential command. Consequently, this loose interpretation is sometimes advanced as support for any presidential action, internal or external, involving use of force, the idea being that it vests power to do anything, anywhere, that can be done with an army or navy.

That seems to be the logic of an argument tendered at our bar—that the President having, on his own responsibility, sent American troops abroad derives from that act "affirmative power" to seize the means of producing a supply of steel for them. To quote, "Perhaps the most forceful illustration of the scope of Presidential power in this connection is the fact that American troops in Korea, whose safety and effectiveness are so directly involved here, were sent to the field by an exercise of the President's constitutional powers."

Thus, it is said, he has invested himself with "war powers." I cannot foresee all that it might entail if the Court should indorse this argument, after all, almost anything can be somehow connected to the war effort. Nothing in our Constitution is plainer than that declaration of a war is entrusted only to Congress. Of course, a state of war may, in fact, exist without a formal declaration. But no doctrine that the Court could promulgate would seem to me more sinister and alarming than that a President whose conduct of foreign affairs is so largely uncontrolled, and often even is unknown, can vastly enlarge his mastery over the internal affairs of the country by his own commitment of the Nation's armed forces to some foreign venture.

Assuming that we are in a war, regardless whether it is declared by Congress or not declared by Congress, does either empower the Commander in Chief to seize industries he thinks necessary to supply our army? The Constitution expressly places in Congress power "to raise and support Armies" and "to provide and maintain a Navy." This certainly lays upon Congress primary responsibility for supplying the armed forces. Congress alone controls the raising of revenues and their appropriation, and may determine in what manner and by what means they shall be spent for military and naval procurement. I suppose no one would doubt that Congress can take over war supply as a Government enterprise. On the other hand, if Congress sees fit to rely on free private enterprise collectively bargaining with free labor for support and maintenance of our armed forces, can the Executive, because of lawful disagreements incidental to that process, seize the facility for operation upon Government-imposed terms?

There are indications that the Constitution did not contemplate that the title Commander in Chief of the Army and Navy will constitute him also Commander in Chief of the country, its industries, and its inhabitants. He has no monopoly of "war powers," whatever they are. While Congress cannot deprive the President of the command of the army and navy, only Congress can provide him an army or navy to command. It is also empowered to make rules for the "Government and Regulation of land and naval Forces," by which it may, to some unknown extent, impinge upon even command functions.

That military powers of the Commander in Chief were not to supersede representative government of internal affairs seems obvious from the Constitution and from elementary American history. Time out of mind, and even now, in many parts of the world, a military commander can seize private housing to shelter his troops. Not so, however, in the United States, for the Third Amendment says, "No Soldier shall, in time of peace be quartered in any house, without the consent of the Owner, nor in time of war, but in a manner to be prescribed by law."

Thus, even in war time, his seizure of needed military housing must be authorized by Congress. It also was expressly left to Congress to "provide for calling forth the Militia to execute the Laws of the Union, suppress Insurrections and repel Invasions. . . ." Such a limitation on the command power, written at a time when the militia, rather than a standing army, was contemplated as the military weapon of the Republic, underscores the Constitution's policy that Congress, not the Executive, should control utilization of the war power as an instrument of domestic policy. Congress, fulfilling that function, has authorized the President to use the army to enforce certain civil rights. On the other hand, Congress has forbidden him to use the army for the purpose of executing general laws except when expressly authorized by the Constitution or by Act of Congress.

While broad claims under this rubric often have been made, advice to the President in specific matters usually has carried overtones that powers, even under this head, are measured by the command functions usual to the topmost officer of the army and navy. Even then, heed has been taken of any efforts of Congress to negative his authority.

We should not use this occasion to circumscribe, much less to contract, the lawful role of the President as Commander in Chief. I should indulge the widest latitude of interpretation to sustain his exclusive function to command the instruments of national force, at least when turned against the outside world for the security of our society. But, when it is turned inward not because of rebellion, but because of a lawful economic struggle between industry and labor, it should have no such indulgence. His command power is not such an absolute as might be implied from that office in a militaristic system, but is subject to limitations consistent with a constitutional Republic whose law and policymaking branch is a representative Congress. The purpose of lodging dual titles in one man was to insure that the civilian would control the military, not to enable the military to subordinate the presidential office. No penance would ever expiate the sin against free government of holding that a President can escape control of executive powers by law through assuming his military role. What the power of command may include I do not try to envision, but I think it is not a military prerogative, without support of law, to seize persons or property because they are important or even essential for the military and naval establishment.

The third clause in which the President finds seizure powers is that "he shall take Care that the Laws be faithfully executed. . . . That authority must be matched against words of the Fifth Amendment that "No person shall be . . . deprived of life, liberty or property, without due process of law. . . ." One gives a governmental authority that reaches so far as there is law, the other gives a private right that authority shall go no farther. These signify about all there is of the principle that ours is a government of laws, not of men, and that we submit ourselves to rulers only if under rules.

The President lastly grounds support of the seizure upon nebulous, inherent powers never expressly granted, but said to have accrued to the office from the customs and claims of preceding administrations. The plea is for a resulting power to deal with a crisis or an emergency according to the necessities of the case, the unarticulated assumption being that necessity knows no law.

Loose and irresponsible use of adjectives colors all nonlegal and much legal discussion of presidential powers. "Inherent" powers, "implied" powers, "incidental" powers, "plenary" powers, "war" powers and "emergency" powers are used, often interchangeably and without fixed or ascertainable meanings.

The vagueness and generality of the clauses that set forth presidential powers afford a plausible basis for pressures within and without an administration for presidential action beyond that supported by those whose responsibility it is to defend his actions in court. The claim of inherent and unrestricted presidential powers has long been a persuasive dialectical weapon in political controversy. While it is not surprising that counsel should grasp support from such unadjudicated claims of power, a judge cannot accept self-serving press statements of the attorney for one of the interested parties as authority in answering a constitutional question, even if the advocate was himself. But prudence has counseled that actual reliance on such nebulous claims stop short of provoking a judicial test.

The President, acknowledging that Congress has never authorized the seizure here, says practice of prior Presidents has authorized it. He seeks color of legality from claimed executive precedents, chief of which is President Roosevelt's seizure, on June 9, 1941, of the California plant of the North American Aviation Company. Its superficial similarities with the present case, upon analysis, yield to distinctions so decisive that it cannot be regarded as even a precedent, much less an authority for the present seizure.

The appeal, however, that we declare the existence of inherent powers ex necessitate to meet an emergency asks us to do what many think would be wise, although it is something the forefathers omitted. They knew what emergencies were, knew the pressures they engender for authoritative action, knew, too, how they afford a ready pretext for usurpation. We may also suspect that they suspected that emergency powers would tend to kindle emergencies. Aside from suspension of the privilege of the writ of habeas corpus in time of rebellion or invasion, when the public safety may require it, they made no express provision for exercise of extraordinary authority because of a crisis. I do not think we rightfully may so amend their work, and, if we could, I am not convinced it would be wise to do so, although many modern nations have forthrightly recognized that war and economic crises may upset the normal balance between liberty and authority. Their experience with emergency powers may not be irrelevant to the argument here that we should say that the Executive, of his own volition, can invest himself with undefined emergency powers.

Germany, after the First World War, framed the Weimar Constitution, designed to secure her liberties in the Western tradition. However, the President of the Republic, without concurrence of the Reichstag, was empowered temporarily to suspend any or all individual rights if public safety and order were seriously disturbed or endangered. This proved a temptation to every government, whatever its shade of opinion, and, in 13 years, suspension of rights was invoked on more than 250 occasions. Finally, Hitler persuaded President Von Hindenberg to suspend all such rights, and they were never restored.

The French Republic provided for a very different kind of emergency government known as the "state of siege." It differed from the German emergency dictatorship, particularly in that emergency powers could not be assumed at will by the Executive, but could only be granted as a parliamentary measure. And it did not, as in Germany, result in a suspension or abrogation of law, but was a legal institution governed by special legal rules and terminable by parliamentary authority.

Great Britain also has fought both World Wars under a sort of temporary dictatorship created by legislation. As Parliament is not bound by written constitutional limitations, it established a crisis government simply by delegation to its Ministers of a larger measure than usual of its own unlimited power, which is exercised under its supervision by Ministers whom it may dismiss. This has been called the "high-water mark in the voluntary surrender of liberty," but, as Churchill put it, "Parliament stands custodian of these surrendered liberties, and its most sacred duty will be to restore them in their fullness when victory has crowned our exertions and our perseverance." Thus, parliamentary control made emergency powers compatible with freedom.

This contemporary foreign experience may be inconclusive as to the wisdom of lodging emergency powers somewhere in a modern government. But it suggests that emergency powers are consistent with free government only when their control is lodged elsewhere than in the Executive who exercises them. That is the safeguard that would be nullified by our adoption of the "inherent powers" formula. Nothing in my experience convinces me that such risks are warranted by any real necessity, although such powers would, of course, be an executive convenience.

In the practical working of our Government, we already have evolved a technique within the framework of the Constitution by which normal executive powers may be considerably expanded to meet an emergency. Congress may and has granted extraordinary authorities which lie dormant in normal times but may be called into play by the Executive in war or upon proclamation of a national emergency. In 1939, upon congressional request, the Attorney General listed ninety-nine such separate statutory grants by Congress of emergency or wartime executive powers. They were invoked from time to time as need appeared. Under this procedure, we retain Government by law—special, temporary law, perhaps, but law nonetheless. The public may know the extent and limitations of the powers that can be asserted, and persons affected may be informed from the statute of their rights and duties.

In view of the ease, expedition and safety with which Congress can grant and has granted large emergency powers, certainly ample to embrace this crisis, I am quite unimpressed with the argument that we should affirm possession of them without statute. Such power either has no beginning or it has no end. If it exists, it need submit to no legal restraint. I am not alarmed that it would plunge us straightway into dictatorship, but it is at least a step in that wrong direction.

As to whether there is imperative necessity for such powers, it is relevant to note the gap that exists between the President's paper powers and his real powers. The Constitution does not disclose the measure of the actual controls wielded by the modern presidential office. That instrument must be understood as an Eighteenth-Century sketch of a government hoped for, not as a blueprint of the Government that is. Vast accretions of federal power, eroded from that reserved by the States, have magnified the scope of presidential activity. Subtle shifts take place in the centers of real power that do not show on the face of the Constitution.

Executive power has the advantage of concentration in a single head in whose choice the whole Nation has a part, making him the focus of public hopes and expectations. In drama, magnitude and finality, his decisions so far overshadow any others that, almost alone, he fills the public eye and ear. No other personality in public life can begin to compete with him in access to the public mind through modern methods of communications. By his prestige as head of state and his influence upon public opinion, he exerts a leverage upon those who are supposed to check and balance his power which often cancels their effectiveness.

Moreover, rise of the party system has made a significant extraconstitutional supplement to real executive power. No appraisal of his necessities is realistic which overlooks that he heads a political system, as well as a legal system. Party loyalties and interests, sometimes more binding than law, extend his effective control into branches of government other than his own, and he often may win, as a political leader, what he cannot command under the Constitution. Indeed, Woodrow Wilson, commenting on the President as leader both of his party and of the Nation, observed, "If he rightly interpret the national thought and boldly insist upon it, he is irresistible.... His office is anything he has the sagacity and force to make it."

I cannot be brought to believe that this country will suffer if the Court refuses further to aggrandize the presidential office, already so potent and so relatively immune from judicial review, at the expense of Congress.

But I have no illusion that any decision by this Court can keep power in the hands of Congress if it is not wise and timely in meeting its problems. A crisis that challenges the President equally, or perhaps primarily, challenges Congress. If not good law, there was worldly wisdom in the maxim attributed to Napoleon that "The tools belong to the man who can use them." We may say that power to legislate for emergencies belongs in the hands of Congress, but only Congress itself can prevent power from slipping through its fingers.

The essence of our free Government is "leave to live by no man's leave, underneath the law"—to be governed by those impersonal forces which we call law. Our Government is fashioned to fulfill this concept so far as humanly possible. The Executive, except for recommendation and veto, has no legislative power. The executive action we have here originates in the individual will of the President, and represents an exercise of authority without law. No one, perhaps not even the President, knows the limits of the power he may seek to exert in this instance, and the parties affected cannot learn the limit of their rights. We do not know today what powers over labor or property would be claimed to flow from Government possession if we should legalize it, what rights to compensation would be claimed or recognized, or on what contingency it would end. With all its defects, delays and inconveniences, men have discovered no technique for long preserving free government except that the Executive be under the law, and that the law be made by parliamentary deliberations.

Such institutions may be destined to pass away. But it is the duty of the Court to be last, not first, to give them up.

END OF OPINION

Ultimately, what a divided Supreme Court said in *Youngstown v. Sawyer* is that the power of the president can only come from either the U.S. Constitution or from an act of Congress. We are a nation under the principle of a government of limited powers, so if there is nothing from Congress or in the Constitution giving the president the power to do something, then the president cannot lawfully do it. Here, there was nothing in the U.S. Constitution giving the president the power to seize privately owned property in the U.S., even when it was to support the war effort, nor had there been any legislation passed by Congress giving the president the power to seize privately owned property to support the war effort. Because of this, the U.S. Supreme Court found that the president could not lawfully seize the steel mill. The inherent authority of the president as commander in chief can go far, but in this case, the Court put limits on just how far.

In his concurring opinion, Justice Jackson divided the legitimacy of a president's actions into three possible categories:

1. Where the president is acting pursuant to both his constitutional power and an act of Congress. This is when the president's power is at its apex, and any action he makes is most likely to be lawful. An example of this would be where Congress explicitly votes to authorize military action, and, acting as commander in chief, the president orders the military into hostilities. Under these circumstances, there would be no doubt as to the authority of the president to wage war.

2. Where the president is acting without the express authorization of Congress, and instead is relying only on his own Constitutional powers. Here, there can be a presumption of legality in the president's authority, but the burden shifts to Congress. If it does not act to limit the president, the failure to act will suggest congressional acquiescence. An example of this would be in 2011 when President Obama, without a vote of approval or disapproval of Congress and relying only on his power as commander in chief, ordered the bombing of Libya to oust Gaddafi. Another example is when President Obama ordered air strikes on ISIS targets in Syria and Iraq. In both cases, although members of Congress complained about the president's actions, no laws were passed limiting the decision made. The result, unfortunately, is a "zone of twilight" where the distribution of the war powers of Congress and the president is uncertain.

3. The third level is where the president takes measures that are against the expressed or implied will of Congress. This is where the president's power is at his lowest, and his action is most likely to be declared illegal. He has to rely only on his own constitutional powers, minus the powers of Congress over the matter. This is what happened in *Youngstown v. Sawyer*. Congress had decided against a bill to authorize the president to seize private property for the Korean War effort, but President Truman went ahead and did it anyway. Consequently, the Court ruled his actions to be unlawful.

It's important to understand what Justice Jackson is saying in these three situations. Note that he never says that the president has NO power or even that the action of the president is illegal. Every president has his inherent Article II authorities to act and, as a matter of practice, presidents throughout history have chosen to act rather than stand by and do nothing when they saw what they believed was a crisis. But what Jackson emphasizes is that presidential power and legitimacy is strongest when acting together with Congress, and weakest when acting against

Congress—so weak that, in some cases (such as this one), a Court may rule against him. And when Congress is silent? Then the president will probably take the initiative to act, and it is up to Congress to agree, disagree, or remain silent. You can consider yourself (or discuss in class) situations where each of these three situations has arisen, and what the result has been.

Let's revisit *Little v. Barrame* under the framework of Jackson's three categories. In *Little v. Barrame*, the president gave an order which went against the explicit authorization of Congress that only ships sailing to French ports be seized. This seems to fall under Jackson's third category, where the president's power is weakest. Consequently, the executive order to seize ships sailing from French ports was held to be unlawful. However, in the *Prize Cases* the president acted where Congress was silent, relying on his constitutional powers, placing him in Jackson's second category. Then, after the fact, Congress gave its approval of the president's actions, placing them in Jackson's first category.

As you can see the power of the president, in the name of national security, including the ability to prepare for and wage war, is not absolute, but is heavily reliant upon and intertwined with Congress's war powers. In many cases, the president is dependent on Congress for the authority to take measures to protect national security. The president is prohibited from making law and rules on his own.

Review Questions

1. Assume that the U.S. and Iran are engaged in armed conflict. Congress has enacted an AUMF but did not formally "declare war." It is no easy task to send soldiers, equipment, supplies, and other materials for the conflict all the way to Iran. To do this requires reliable cargo airplanes built by Boeing, a civilian-owned airplane manufacturer. However, one day the Boeing workers at the factory, where these planes are built, go on strike, demanding an increase in pay. The president unilaterally declares that, pursuant to his war powers as commander in chief, he is taking control of this factory and orders the workers back to work manufacturing airplanes. His reasoning is that these planes are vital to the war effort. As with the situation in *Youngstown Steel*, there is nothing in the president's inherent constitutional authority specifically granting the president the authority to seize the Boeing factory (commander in chief does not equal supplier in chief). The AUMF passed by Congress granting the president authority to use military force does not include language authorizing seizure of industry.[10] Is this action by the president lawful?

2. Again, assume that the U.S. and Iran are "at war," following a formal declaration of war by Congress. It is no easy task to send soldiers, equipment, supplies, and

---

10. It should be noted that there is authority for the president, in times of national emergency (including but not limited to a time of war), to take a number of actions regarding, among other things, the priority of government contracts over other contracts businesses might have, in order to ensure that the needs of the government are met during the emergency. These authorities are contained in the Defense Production Act of 1950, U.S.C. App sec. 2061 et seq. and implemented through Executive Order 12919 of 1994.

other materials for the war effort all the way to Iran. To do this requires reliable cargo airplanes built by Boeing, a civilian-owned airplane manufacturer. However, one day the Boeing workers at the factory, where these planes are built, go on strike, demanding an increase in pay. Congress passes legislation nationalizing airplane manufacturers in America and giving the president control over the civilian labor forces necessary for the war effort. Pursuant to this legislation, the president declares that the government is taking control of this factory, and, in accord with his powers as commander in chief, he orders the workers back to work manufacturing airplanes. Is this lawful?

As you can see, the power of the president in the area of national security is not unlimited. Before moving on to the next section on the war powers, remember that the president's power to act can only come from the Constitution or from an act of Congress. The president is only allowed to pass binding rules and regulations on Americans if Congress has already passed legislation expressly granting him permission to do so. Any rules coming from an agency within the executive branch must be narrowly tailored so as to further the agency's very mission as established by Congress.

The War Powers Resolution

Over the years, particularly during the era of the Vietnam War, the public and members of Congress grew increasingly concerned by the history of the president's unilateral—and often secret—use of the military. Consequently, Congress took measures to address this when it passed the War Powers Resolution of 1973 (WPR). Prior to explaining the WPR, some history would be helpful for your understanding of the legal issues and the significance of the WPR.

Although Congress did authorize the war in Vietnam, many Americans felt that the White House had lied to both Congress and the American people about the war, the Gulf of Tonkin incident (which led to Congressional authorization of the war), casualties, chances of success, and other aspects of the war. On many other issues the White House did not lie, but instead simply withheld information about the war from Congress and the American people. Although Congress was funding the Vietnam War, they were misled about just what exactly it was they were funding. At the same time, disclosures about the use of the military and other intelligence services within the United States contributed to an increasing distrust of the presidency. The release of the Pentagon Papers, a classified analysis report on the Vietnam War that seemed to contradict what the government had been saying about the war, furthered this distrust.

In response, a number of measures were introduced to prevent the president from, in the eyes of the sponsors of the laws, ever again knowingly and intentionally misleading the American people and Congress into war, or from waging a war which was not known about by Congress. These measures, and others which would be enacted later in the 1970s and 1980s, were in large part to ensure that members of Congress would be informed of clandestine national security measures which were being conducted by the executive. We covered some of these measures when we talked about foreign surveillance and why FISA was introduced. In addition to providing better oversight of the president's intelligence gathering, Congress also wanted better oversight of the president's unilateral use of the war powers. For these reasons, Congress passed the WPR.

The WPR was a short bill with the most important parts included below for your reading. Key provisions of it are that within 48 hours of introducing the American military into hostilities, the president is required to inform key members of Congress of the military action. This is to prevent secret wars from occurring. For example, members of Congress claimed that they had been unaware that the president had expanded the Vietnam War to include operations in the neighboring nations of Laos and Cambodia. Requiring formal notification would ensure that Congress would be aware of future conflicts and other uses of the U.S. military. Another key provision of the WPR, while recognizing that the president does have the authority to unilaterally introduce the U.S. military into hostilities, requires that the president terminate the use of force after sixty days if Congress has not explicitly voted after-the-fact to continue the conflict. There is an exception to this rule, which allows a 30-day extension for the use of force to continue in the face of Congressional silence. Take time now to read the WPR.

Text of Public Law 93-148

Joint Resolution Concerning the War Powers of Congress and the President.

Resolved by the Senate and the House of Representatives of the United States of America in Congress assembled,

SHORT TITLE

SECTION 1. This joint resolution may be cited as the "War Powers Resolution".

PURPOSE AND POLICY

SEC. 2. (a) It is the purpose of this joint resolution to fulfill the intent of the framers of the Constitution of the United States and insure that the collective judgement of both the Congress and the President will apply to the introduction of United States Armed Forces into hostilities, or into situations where imminent involvement in hostilities is clearly indicated by the circumstances, and to the continued use of such forces in hostilities or in such situations.

(b) Under article I, section 8, of the Constitution, it is specifically provided that the Congress shall have the power to make all laws necessary and proper for carrying into execution, not only its own powers but also all other powers vested by the Constitution in the Government of the United States, or in any department or officer thereof.

(c) The constitutional powers of the President as Commander-in-Chief to introduce United States Armed Forces into hostilities, or into situations where imminent involvement in hostilities is clearly indicated by the circumstances, are exercised only pursuant to (1) a declaration of war, (2) specific statutory authorization, or (3) a national emergency created by attack upon the United States, its territories or possessions, or its armed forces.

CONSULTATION

SEC. 3. The President in every possible instance shall consult with Congress before introducing United States Armed Forces into hostilities or into situation where imminent involvement in hostilities is clearly indicated by the circumstances, and after every such introduction shall consult regularly with the Congress until United States Armed Forces are no longer engaged in hostilities or have been removed from such situations.

REPORTING

SEC. 4. (a) In the absence of a declaration of war, in any case in which United States Armed Forces are introduced—

(1) into hostilities or into situations where imminent involvement in hostilities is clearly indicated by the circumstances;

(2) into the territory, airspace or waters of a foreign nation, while equipped for combat, except for deployments which relate solely to supply, replacement, repair, or training of such forces; or

(3) in numbers which substantially enlarge United States Armed Forces equipped for combat already located in a foreign nation; the president shall submit within 48 hours to the Speaker of the House of Representatives and to the President pro tempore of the Senate a report, in writing, setting forth—

(A) the circumstances necessitating the introduction of United States Armed Forces;

(B) the constitutional and legislative authority under which such introduction took place; and

(C) the estimated scope and duration of the hostilities or involvement.

(b) The President shall provide such other information as the Congress may request in the fulfillment of its constitutional responsibilities with respect to committing the Nation to war and to the use of United States Armed Forces abroad.

(c) Whenever United States Armed Forces are introduced into hostilities or into any situation described in subsection (a) of this section, the President shall, so long as such armed forces continue to be engaged in such hostilities or situation, report to the Congress periodically on the status of such hostilities or situation as well as on the scope and duration of such hostilities or situation, but in no event shall he report to the Congress less often than once every six months.

CONGRESSIONAL ACTION

SEC. 5. (a) Each report submitted pursuant to section 4(a)(1) shall be transmitted to the Speaker of the House of Representatives and to the President pro tempore of the Senate on the same calendar day. Each report so transmitted shall be referred to the Committee on Foreign Affairs of the House of Representatives and to the Committee on Foreign Relations of the Senate for appropriate action. If, when the report is transmitted, the Congress has adjourned sine die or has adjourned for any period in excess of three calendar days, the Speaker of the House of Representatives and the President pro tempore of the Senate, if they deem it advisable (or if petitioned by at least 30 percent of the membership of their respective Houses) shall jointly request the President to convene Congress in order that it may consider the report and take appropriate action pursuant to this section.

(b) Within sixty calendar days after a report is submitted or is required to be submitted pursuant to section 4(a)(1), whichever is earlier, the President shall terminate any use of United States Armed Forces with respect to which such report was submitted (or required to be submitted), unless the Congress (1) has declared war or has enacted a specific authorization for such use of United States Armed Forces, (2) has extended by law such sixty-day period, or (3) is physically unable to meet as a result of an armed attack upon the United States. Such sixty-day period shall be extended for not more than an additional thirty days if the President determines and certifies to the Congress in writing that unavoidable military necessity respecting the safety of United States Armed Forces requires the continued use of such armed forces in the course of bringing about a prompt removal of such forces.

(c) Notwithstanding subsection (b), at any time that United States Armed Forces are engaged in hostilities outside the territory of the United States, its possessions and territories without a declaration of war or specific statutory authorization, such forces shall be removed by the President if the Congress so directs by concurrent resolution.

No sitting U.S. president—*not one*—has ever acknowledged the constitutionality of the WPR. While presidents generally follow the procedures of notification in the WPR, they do so noting they are providing the information "in a manner consistent with" and not "pursuant to" or other language that suggests they need to do this. In fact, there is a good argument against its constitutionality as there is a concern that it infringes upon the war powers of the president.

R.M. Nixon memorandum of 24 October 1973 to House of Representatives

When President Nixon vetoed the WPR, he wrote out his explanation of why he thought it was both a bad idea and unconstitutional. His analysis has generally been adopted by each president that followed him—Republicans as well as Democrats. You can read his explanation below.

To the House of Representatives:

I hereby return without my approval House Joint Resolution 542—the War Powers Resolution. While I am in accord with the desire of the Congress to assert its proper role in the conduct of our foreign affairs, the restrictions which this resolution would impose upon the authority of the President are both unconstitutional and dangerous to the best interests of our Nation.

The proper roles of the Congress and the Executive in the conduct of foreign affairs have been debated since the founding of our country. Only recently, however, has there been a serious challenge to the wisdom of the Founding Fathers in choosing not to draw a precise and detailed line of demarcation between the foreign policy powers of the two branches.

The Founding Fathers understood the impossibility of foreseeing every contingency that might arise in this complex area. They acknowledged the need for flexibility in responding to changing circumstances. They recognized that foreign policy decisions must be made through close cooperation between the two branches and not through rigidly codified procedures.

These principles remain as valid today as they were when our Constitution was written. Yet House Joint Resolution 542 would violate those principles by defining the President's powers in ways which would strictly limit his constitutional authority.

CLEARLY UNCONSTITUTIONAL

House Joint Resolution 542 would attempt to take away, by a mere legislative act, authorities which the President has properly exercised under the Constitution for almost 200 years. One of its provisions would automatically cut off certain authorities after sixty days unless the Congress extended them. Another would allow the Congress to eliminate certain authorities merely by the passage of a concurrent resolution—an action which does not normally have the force of law, since it denies the President his constitutional role in approving legislation.

I believe that both these provisions are unconstitutional. The only way in which the constitutional powers of a branch of the Government can be altered is by amending the Constitution—and any attempt to make such alterations by legislation alone is clearly without force.

UNDERMINING OUR FOREIGN POLICY

While I firmly believe that a veto of House Joint Resolution 542 is warranted solely on constitutional grounds, I am also deeply disturbed by the practical consequences of this resolution. For it would seriously undermine this Nation's ability to act decisively and convincingly in times of international crisis. As a result, the confidence of our allies in our ability to assist them could be diminished and the respect of our adversaries for our deterrent posture could decline. A permanent and substantial element of unpredictability would be injected into the world's assessment of American behavior, further increasing the likelihood of miscalculation and war.

If this resolution had been in operation, America's effective response to a variety of challenges in recent years would have been vastly complicated or even made impossible. We may well have been unable to respond in the way we did during the Berlin crisis of 1961, the Cuban missile crisis of 1962, the Congo rescue operation in 1964, and the Jordanian crisis of 1970—to mention just a few examples. In addition, our recent actions to bring about a peaceful settlement of the hostilities in the Middle East would have been seriously impaired if this resolution had been in force.

While all the specific consequences of House Joint Resolution 542 cannot yet be predicted, it is clear that it would undercut the ability of the United States to act as an effective influence for peace. For example, the provision automatically cutting off certain authorities after 60 days unless they are extended by the Congress could work to prolong or intensify a crisis. Until the Congress suspended the deadline, there would be at least a chance of United States withdrawal and an adversary would be tempted therefore to postpone serious negotiations until the 60 days were up. Only after the Congress acted would there be a strong incentive for an adversary to negotiate. In addition, the very existence of a deadline could lead to an escalation of hostilities in order to achieve certain objectives before the 60 days expired.

The measure would jeopardize our role as a force for peace in other ways as well.

It would, for example, strike from the President's hand a wide range of important peace-keeping tools by eliminating his ability to exercise quiet diplomacy backed by subtle shifts in our military deployments. It would also cast into doubt authorities which Presidents have used to undertake certain humanitarian relief missions in conflict areas, to protect fishing boats from seizure, to deal with ship or aircraft hijackings, and to respond to threats of attack. Not the least of the adverse consequences of this resolution would be the prohibition contained in section 8 against fulfilling our obligations under the NATO treaty as ratified by the Senate. Finally, since the bill is somewhat vague as to when the 60 day rule would apply, it could lead to extreme confusion and dangerous disagreements concerning the prerogatives of the two branches, seriously damaging our ability to respond to international crises.

FAILURE TO REQUIRE POSITIVE CONGRESSIONAL ACTION

I am particularly disturbed by the fact that certain of the President's constitutional powers as Commander in Chief of the Armed Forces would terminate automatically under this resolution. 60 days after they were invoked. No overt Congressional action would be required to cut off these powers—they would disappear automatically unless the Congress extended them. In effect, the Congress is here attempting to increase its policy-making role through a provision which requires it to take absolutely no action at all.

In my view, the proper way for the Congress to make known its will on such foreign policy questions is through a positive action, with full debate on the merits of the issue and with each member taking the responsibility of casting a yes or no vote after considering those merits. The authorization and appropriations process represents one of the ways in which such influence can be exercised. I do not, however, believe that the Congress can responsibly contribute its considered, collective judgment on such grave questions without full debate and without a yes or no vote. Yet this is precisely what the joint resolution would allow. It would give every future Congress the ability to handcuff every future President merely by doing nothing and sitting still. In my view, one cannot become a responsible partner unless one is prepared to take responsible action.

STRENGTHENING COOPERATION BETWEEN THE CONGRESS AND THE EXECUTIVE BRANCHES

The responsible and effective exercise of the war powers requires the fullest cooperation between the Congress and the Executive and the prudent fulfillment by each branch of its constitutional responsibilities. House Joint Resolution 542 includes certain constructive measures which would foster this process by enhancing the flow of information from the executive branch to the Congress. Section 3, for example, calls for consultations with the Congress before and during the involvement of the United States forces in hostilities abroad. This provision is consistent with the desire of this Administration for regularized consultations with the Congress in an even wider range of circumstances.

I believe that full and cooperative participation in foreign policy matters by both the executive and the legislative branches could be enhanced by a careful and dispassionate study of their constitutional roles. Helpful proposals for such a study have already been made in the Congress. I would welcome the establishment of a non-partisan commission on the constitutional roles of the Congress and the President in the conduct of foreign affairs. This commission could make a thorough review of the principal constitutional issues in Executive-Congressional relations, including the war powers, the international agreement powers, and the question of Executive privilege, and then submit its recommendations to the President and the Congress. The members of such a commission could be drawn from both parties — and could represent many perspectives including those of the Congress, the executive branch, the legal profession, and the academic community.

This Administration is dedicated to strengthening cooperation between the Congress and the President in the conduct of foreign affairs and to preserving the constitutional prerogatives of both branches of our Government. I know that the Congress shares that goal. A commission on the constitutional roles of the Congress and the President would provide a useful opportunity for both branches to work together toward that common objective.

RICHARD NIXON
The White House, October 24, 1973.

Congress was able to override President Nixon's veto, making the WPR law. Nevertheless, the constitutionality of the WPR remains a source of controversy,[11] and attempts by Congress to force the president to comply with the WPR are frequently ignored. This causes the effectiveness of the WPR to be very questionable as a matter of law.

As mentioned above, keep in mind that the president's responsibility under the Constitution to see that the laws are faithfully executed does not mean that the president is bound to follow every statute passed by Congress, nor does it mean that, by refusing to abide by a statute, the president is "making law." Remember that the highest law of the land is the United States Constitution. So a president has an obligation to follow the Constitution even if that means going against what the Congress has said.[12]

Office of Legal Counsel Opinion dated 1 April 2011 (Applicability of WPR to military operations in Libya)

The last reading for this chapter is a long one; the opinion of the Department of Justice's Office of Legal Counsel on the proposed use of military force in Libya in April 2011. Remember, this memorandum itself did not "make law," but expressed the views of the Department of Justice on what the law regarding the use of military force was in this case. We have removed the footnotes and most (but not all) of the citations to try and make the opinion easier to read. As you go through this opinion, consider how the combination of constitutional interpretation, other statutes and action by Congress, as well as historic practice are combined to provide the legal foundation for presidential action.

MEMORANDUM OPINION FOR THE ATTORNEY GENERAL, April 1, 2011[13]

This memorandum memorializes advice this Office provided to you, prior to the commencement of recent United States military operations in Libya, regarding the President's legal authority to conduct such operations. For the reasons explained below, we concluded that the President had the constitutional authority to direct the use of force in Libya because he could reasonably determine that such use of force was in the national interest. We also advised that prior congressional approval was not constitutionally required to use military force in the limited operations under consideration.

---

11. See, for example, Robert F. Turner, *The War Powers Resolution: Unconstitutional, Unnecessary, and Unhelpful*, 17 Loy.L.A.L.Rev. 683 (1984) Available at http://digitalcommons.edu/llr/vol17/iss3/5.

12. The foundation for this has been laid out by the Office of Legal Counsel of the Department of Justice in a legal opinion issued on November 2, 1994 entitled "Presidential Authority to decline to Execute Unconstitutional Statutes." http://www.justice.gov/olc/opinion/presidential-authority-decline-execute-unconstitutional-statutes.

13. The full opinion, with footnotes and references, is available at http://www.justice.gov/sites/default/files/olc/opinions/2011/04/31/authority-military-use-in-libya_0.pdf.

I.

In mid-February 2011, amid widespread popular demonstrations seeking governmental reform in the neighboring countries of Tunisia and Egypt, as well as elsewhere in the Middle East and North Africa, protests began in Libya against the autocratic government of Colonel Muammar Qadhafi, who has ruled Libya since taking power in a 1969 coup. Qadhafi moved swiftly in an attempt to end the protests using military force. Some Libyan government officials and elements of the Libyan military left the Qadhafi regime, and by early March, Qadhafi had lost control over much of the eastern part of the country, including the city of Benghazi. The Libyan government's operations against its opponents reportedly included strafing of protesters and shelling, bombing, and other violence deliberately targeting civilians. Many refugees fled to Egypt and other neighboring countries to escape the violence, creating a serious crisis in the region.

On February 26, 2011, the United Nations Security Council ("UNSC") unanimously adopted Resolution 1970, which "expressed grave concern at the situation in the Libyan Arab Jamahiriya," "condemn[ed] the violence and use of force against civilians," and "deplored the gross and systematic violation of human rights" in Libya. The resolution called upon member states, among other things, to take "the necessary measures" to prevent arms transfers "from or through their territories or by their nationals, or using their flag vessels or aircraft"; to freeze the assets of Qadhafi and certain other close associates of the regime; and to "facilitate and support the return of humanitarian agencies and make available humanitarian and related assistance" in Libya. The resolution did not, however, authorize members of the United Nations to use military force in Libya.

The Libyan government's violence against civilians continued, and even escalated, despite condemnation by the UNSC and strong expressions of disapproval from other regional and international bodies. See, e.g., African Union, Communique of the 265th Meeting of the Peace and Security Council (Mar. 10, 2011) (describing the "prevailing situation in Libya" as "posing a serious threat to peace and security in that country and in the region as a whole" and "reiterating AU's strong and unequivocal condemnation of the indiscriminate use of force and lethal weapons"). On March 1, 2011, the United States Senate passed by unanimous consent Senate Resolution 85. Among other things, the Resolution "strongly condemn[ed] the gross and systematic violations of human rights in Libya, including violent attacks on protesters demanding democratic reforms," "call[ed] on Muammar Gadhafi to desist from further violence," and "urge[d] the United Nations Security Council to take such further action as may be necessary to protect civilians in Libya from attack, including the possible imposition of a no-fly zone over Libyan territory." S. Res. 85, 112th Cong. §§ 2, 3, 7 (as passed by Senate, Mar. 1, 2011). On March 12, the Council of the League of Arab States similarly called on the UNSC "to take the necessary measures to impose immediately a no-fly zone on Libyan military aviation" and "to establish safe areas in places exposed to shelling as a precautionary measure that allows the protection of the Libyan people and foreign nationals residing in Libya, while respecting the sovereignty and territorial integrity of neighboring States." (Mar. 12, 2011).

By March 17, 2011, Qadhafi's forces were preparing to retake the city of Benghazi. Pledging that his forces would begin an assault on the city that night and show "no mercy and no pity" to those who would not give up resistance, Qadhafi stated in a radio address: "We will come house by house, room by room. It's over. The issue has been decided." Qadhafi, President Obama later noted, "compared [his people] to rats, and threatened to go door to door to inflict punishment. . . . We knew that if we . . . waited one more day, Benghazi, a city nearly the size of Charlotte, could suffer a massacre that would have reverberated across the region and stained the conscience of the world."

Later the same day, the UNSC addressed the situation in Libya again by adopting, by a vote of 10-0 (with five members abstaining), Resolution 1973, which imposed a no-fly zone and authorized the use of military force to protect civilians. In this resolution, the UNSC determined that the "situation" in Libya "continues to constitute a threat to international peace and security" and "demanded the immediate establishment of a cease-fire and a complete end to violence and all attacks against, and abuses of, civilians." Resolution 1973 authorized member states, acting individually or through regional organizations, "to take all necessary measures . . . to protect civilians and civilian populated areas under threat of attack in the Libyan Arab Jamahiriya, including Benghazi, while excluding a foreign occupation force of any form on any part of Libyan territory." The resolution also specifically authorized member states to enforce "a ban on all unauthorized flights in the airspace of the Libyan Arab Jamahiriya in order to help protect civilians" and to take "all measures commensurate to the specific circumstances" to inspect vessels on the high seas suspected of violating the arms embargo imposed on Libya by Resolution 1970.

In remarks on March 18, 2011, President Obama stated that, to avoid military intervention to enforce Resolution 1973, Qadhafi needed to: implement an immediate ceasefire, including by ending all attacks on civilians; halt his troops' advance on Benghazi; pull his troops back from three other cities; and establish water, electricity, and gas supplies to all areas. The President also identified several national interests supporting United States involvement in the planned operations:

Now, here is why this matters to us. Left unchecked, we have every reason to believe that Qaddafi would commit atrocities against his people. Many thousands could die. A humanitarian crisis would ensue. The entire region could be destabilized, endangering many of our allies and partners. The calls of the Libyan people for help would go unanswered. The democratic values that we stand for would be overrun. Moreover, the words of the international community would be rendered hollow.

President Obama further noted the broader context of the Libyan uprising, describing it as "just one more chapter in the change that is unfolding across the Middle East and North Africa."

Despite a statement from Libya's Foreign Minister that Libya would honor the requested ceasefire, the Libyan government continued to conduct offensive operations, including attacks on civilians and civilian-populated areas. Consistent with the reporting provisions of the War Powers Resolution, 50 U.S.C. § 1543(a) (2006), President Obama provided a report to Congress less than forty-eight hours later, on March 21, 2011. The President explained:

At approximately 3:00 p.m. Eastern Daylight Time, on March 19, 2011, at my direction, U.S. military forces commenced operations to assist an international effort authorized by the United Nations (U.N.) Security Council and undertaken with the support of European allies and Arab partners, to prevent a humanitarian catastrophe and address the threat posed to international peace and security by the crisis in Libya. As part of the multilateral response authorized under U.N. Security Council Resolution 1973, U.S. military forces, under the command of Commander, U.S. Africa Command, began a series of strikes against air defense systems and military airfields for the purposes of preparing a no-fly zone. These strikes will be limited in their nature, duration, and scope. Their purpose is to support an international coalition as it takes all necessary measures to enforce the terms of U.N. Security Council Resolution 1973. These limited U.S. actions will set the stage for further action by other coalition partners.

The report then described the background to the strikes, including UNSC Resolution 1973, the demand for a ceasefire, and Qadhafi's continued attacks.

The March 21 report also identified the risks to regional and international peace and security that, in the President's judgment, had justified military intervention:

Qadhafi's continued attacks and threats against civilians and civilian populated areas are of grave concern to neighboring Arab nations and, as expressly stated in U.N. Security Council Resolution 1973, constitute a threat to the region and to international peace and security. His illegitimate use of force not only is causing the deaths of substantial numbers of civilians among his own people, but also is forcing many others to flee to neighboring countries, thereby destabilizing the peace and security of the region. Left unaddressed, the growing instability in Libya could ignite wider instability in the Middle East, with dangerous consequences to the national security interests of the United States. Qadhafi's defiance of the Arab League, as well as the broader international community . . . represents a lawless challenge to the authority of the Security Council and its efforts to preserve stability in the region. Qadhafi has forfeited his responsibility to protect his own citizens and created a serious need for immediate humanitarian assistance and protection, with any delay only putting more civilians at risk.

Emphasizing that "[t]he United States has not deployed ground forces into Libya," the President explained that "United States forces are conducting a limited and well-defined mission in support of international efforts to protect civilians and prevent a humanitarian disaster" and thus had targeted only "the Qadhafi regime's air defense systems, command and control structures, and other capabilities of Qadhafi's armed forces used to attack civilians and civilian populated areas." The President also indicated that "[w]e will seek a rapid, but responsible, transition of operations to coalition, regional, or international organizations that are postured to continue activities as may be necessary to realize the objectives of U.N. Security Council Resolutions 1970 and 1973." As authority for the military operations in Libya, President Obama invoked his "constitutional authority to conduct U.S. foreign relations" and his authority "as Commander in Chief and Chief Executive."

Before the initiation of military operations in Libya, White House and other executive branch officials conducted multiple meetings and briefings on Libya with members of Congress and testified on the Administration's policy at congressional hearings. President Obama invited Republican and Democratic leaders of Congress to the White House for consultation on March 18, 2011 before launching United States military operations, and personally briefed members of Congress on the ongoing operations on March 25, 2011. Senior executive branch officials are continuing to brief Senators and members of Congress on U.S. operations and events in Libya as they develop.

On March 28, 2011, President Obama addressed the nation regarding the situation in Libya. The President stated that the coalition had succeeded in averting a massacre in Libya and that the United States was now transferring "the lead in enforcing the no-fly zone and protecting civilians on the ground . . . to our allies and partners." In future coalition operations in Libya, the President continued, "the United States will play a supporting role—including intelligence, logistical support, search and rescue assistance, and capabilities to jam regime communications." The President also reiterated the national interests supporting military action by the United States. "[G]iven the costs and risks of intervention," he explained, "we must always measure our interests against the need for action." But, "[i]n this particular country—Libya—at this particular moment, we were faced with the prospect of violence on a horrific scale," and "[w]e had a unique ability to stop that violence." Failure to prevent a slaughter would have disregarded America's "important strategic interest in preventing Qaddafi from overrunning those who oppose him":

> A massacre would have driven thousands of additional refugees across Libya's borders, putting enormous strains on the peaceful—yet fragile—transitions in Egypt and Tunisia. The democratic impulses that are dawning across the region would be eclipsed by the darkest form of dictatorship, as repressive leaders concluded that violence is the best strategy to cling to power. The writ of the United Nations Security Council would have been shown to be little more than empty words, crippling that institution's future credibility to uphold global peace and security. So while I will never minimize the costs involved in military action, I am convinced that a failure to act in Libya would have carried a far greater price for America.

As of March 31, 2011, the United States had transferred responsibility for all ongoing coalition military operations in Libya to the North Atlantic Treaty Alliance ("NATO").

II.

The President explained in his March 21, 2011 report to Congress that the use of military force in Libya serves important U.S. interests in preventing instability in the Middle East and preserving the credibility and effectiveness of the United Nations Security Council. The President also stated that he intended the anticipated United

States military operations in Libya to be limited in nature, scope, and duration. The goal of action by the United States was to "set the stage" for further action by coalition partners in implementing UNSC Resolution 1973, particularly through destruction of Libyan military assets that could either threaten coalition aircraft policing the UNSC-declared no-fly zone or engage in attacks on civilians and civilian-populated areas. In addition, no U.S. ground forces would be deployed, except possibly for any search and rescue missions, and the risk of substantial casualties for U.S. forces would be low.

As we advised you prior to the commencement of military operations, we believe that, under these circumstances, the President had constitutional authority, as Commander in Chief and Chief Executive and pursuant to his foreign affairs powers, to direct such limited military operations abroad, even without prior specific congressional approval.

A.

Earlier opinions of this Office and other historical precedents establish the framework for our analysis. As we explained in 1992, Attorneys General and this Office "have concluded that the President has the power to commit United States troops abroad," as well as to "take military action," "for the purpose of protecting important national interests," even without specific prior authorization from Congress. Authority to Use United States Military Forces in Somalia, 16 Op. O.L.C. 6 (1992). This independent authority of the President, which exists at least insofar as Congress has not specifically restricted it, see Deployment of United States Armed Forces into Haiti, 18 Op. O.L.C. 173, (1994), derives from the President's "unique responsibility," as Commander in Chief and Chief Executive, for "foreign and military affairs," as well as national security. Sale v. Haitian Centers Council, Inc., 509 U.S. 155 (1993); U.S. Const. art. II, § 1, cl. 1, § 2, cl. 2.

The Constitution, to be sure, divides authority over the military between the President and Congress, assigning to Congress the authority to "declare War," "raise and support Armies," and "provide and maintain a Navy," as well as general authority over the appropriations on which any military operation necessarily depends. U.S. Const. art. I, § 8, cl. 1, 11-14. Yet, under "the historical gloss on the 'executive Power' vested in Article II of the Constitution," the President bears the "'vast share of responsibility for the conduct of our foreign relations,'" Am. Ins. Ass'n v. Garamendi, 539 U.S. 396 (2003) (quoting Youngstown Sheet & Tube Co.v. Sawyer (1952) (Frankfurter, J., concurring)), and accordingly holds "independent authority 'in the areas of foreign policy and national security.'" Moreover, the President as Commander in Chief "superintend[s] the military," Loving v. United States, 517 U.S. 748 (1996), and "is authorized to direct the movements of the naval and military forces placed by law at his command." Fleming v. Page, 50 U.S. 603 (1850); see also Placing of United States Armed Forces Under United Nations Operational or Tactical Control, 20 Op. O.L.C. 182 (1996).

The President also holds "the implicit advantage ... over the legislature under our constitutional scheme in situations calling for immediate action," given that imminent national security threats and rapidly evolving military and diplomatic circumstances may require a swift response by the United States without the opportunity for congressional deliberation and action. Presidential Power to Use the Armed Forces Abroad Without Statutory Authorization, 4A Op.O.L.C. 185 (1980); see also Haig, 453 U.S. at 292 (noting "'the changeable and explosive nature of contemporary international relations, and the fact that the Executive is immediately privy to information which cannot be swiftly presented to, evaluated by, and acted upon by the legislature'". Accordingly, as Attorney General (later Justice) Robert Jackson observed over half a century ago, "the President's authority has long been recognized as extending to the dispatch of armed forces outside of the United States, either on missions of goodwill or rescue, or for the purpose of protecting American lives or property or American interests." Training of British Flying Students in the United States, 40 Op. Att'y Gen. 58 (1941).

This understanding of the President's constitutional authority reflects not only the express assignment of powers and responsibilities to the President and Congress in the Constitution, but also, as noted, the "historical gloss" placed on the Constitution by two centuries of practice. "Our history," this Office observed in 1980, "is replete with instances of presidential uses of military force abroad in the absence of prior congressional approval." Presidential Power, 4A Op. O.L.C. at 187; see generally Richard F. Grimmett, Cong. Research Serv., R41677, Instances of Use of United States Armed Forces Abroad, 1798–2010 (2011). Since then, instances of such presidential initiative have only multiplied, with Presidents ordering, to give just a few examples, bombing in Libya (1986), an intervention in Panama (1989), troop deployments to Somalia (1992), Bosnia (1995), and Haiti (twice, 1994 and 2004), air patrols and airstrikes in Bosnia (1993–1995), and a bombing campaign in Yugoslavia (1999), without specific prior authorizing legislation. See Grimmett, supra, at 13–31. This historical practice is an important indication of constitutional meaning, because it reflects the two political branches' practical understanding, developed since the founding of the Republic, of their respective roles and responsibilities with respect to national defense, and because "[m]atters intimately related to foreign policy and national security are rarely proper subjects for judicial intervention." In this context, the "pattern of executive conduct, made under claim of right, extended over many decades and engaged in by Presidents of both parties, 'evidences the existence of broad constitutional power.'" "The scope and limits" of Congress's power to declare war "are not well defined by constitutional text, case law, or statute," but the relationship between that power and the President's authority as Commander in Chief and Chief Executive has been instead "clarified by 200 years of practice."

Indeed, Congress itself has implicitly recognized this presidential authority. The War Powers Resolution ("WPR"), 50 U.S.C. §§ 1541–1548 (2006), a statute Congress described as intended "to fulfill the intent of the framers of the Constitution of the United States," provides that, in the absence of a declaration of war, the President must report to Congress within 48 hours of taking certain actions, including introduction of U.S. forces "into hostilities or into situations where imminent involvement in hostilities is clearly indicated by the circumstances." The Resolution further provides that the President generally must terminate such use of force within 60 days (or 90 days for military necessity) unless Congress extends this deadline, declares war, or "enact[s] a specific authorization."

As this Office has explained, although the WPR does not itself provide affirmative statutory authority for military operations, the Resolution's "structure . . . recognizes and presupposes the existence of unilateral presidential authority to deploy armed forces" into hostilities or circumstances presenting an imminent risk of hostilities. That structure—requiring a report within 48 hours after the start of hostilities and their termination within 60 days after that—"makes sense only if the President may introduce troops into hostilities or potential hostilities without prior authorization by the Congress."

We have acknowledged one possible constitutionally-based limit on this presidential authority to employ military force in defense of important national interests—a planned military engagement that constitutes a "war" within the meaning of the Declaration of War Clause may require prior congressional authorization. But the historical practice of presidential military action without congressional approval precludes any suggestion that Congress's authority to declare war covers every military engagement, however limited, that the President initiates.

In our view, determining whether a particular planned engagement constitutes a "war" for constitutional purposes instead requires a fact-specific assessment of the "anticipated nature, scope, and duration" of the planned military operations. This standard generally will be satisfied only by prolonged and substantial military engagements, typically involving exposure of U.S. military personnel to significant risk over a substantial period. Again, Congress's own key enactment on the subject reflects this understanding. By allowing United States involvement in hostilities to continue for 60 or 90 days, Congress signaled in the WPR that it considers congressional authorization most critical or "major, prolonged conflicts such as the wars in Vietnam and Korea," not more limited engagements.

Applying this fact-specific analysis, we concluded in 1994 that a planned deployment of up to 20,000 United States troops to Haiti to oust military leaders and reinstall Haiti's legitimate government was not a "war" requiring advance congressional approval.

"In deciding whether prior Congressional authorization for the Haitian deployment was constitutionally necessary," we observed, "the President was entitled to take into account the anticipated nature, scope, and duration of the planned deployment, and in particular the limited antecedent risk that United States forces would encounter significant armed resistance or suffer or inflict substantial casualties as a result of the deployment." Similarly, a year later we concluded that a proposed deployment of approximately 20,000 ground troops to enforce a peace agreement in Bosnia and Herzegovina also was not a "war," even though this deployment involved some "risk that the United States [would] incur (and inflict) casualties." For more than two years preceding this deployment, the United States had undertaken air operations over Bosnia to enforce a UNSC-declared "no-fly zone," protect United Nations peacekeeping forces, and secure "safe areas" for civilians, including one two-week operation in which NATO attacked hundreds of targets and the United States alone flew over 2300 sorties—all based on the President's "constitutional authority to conduct the foreign relations of the United States and as Commander in Chief and Chief Executive," without a declaration of war or other specific prior approval from Congress. This Office acknowledged that "deployment of 20,000 troops on the ground is an essentially different, and more problematic, type of intervention," than air or naval operations because of the increased risk of United States casualties and the far greater difficulty of withdrawing United States ground forces. But we nonetheless concluded that the anticipated risks were not sufficient to make the deployment a "'war' in any sense of the word." Proposed Bosnia Deployment, 19 Op. O.L.C. at 333–34.

B.

Under the framework of these precedents, the President's legal authority to direct military force in Libya turns on two questions: first, whether United States operations in Libya would serve sufficiently important national interests to permit the President's action as Commander in Chief and Chief Executive and pursuant to his authority to conduct U.S. foreign relations; and second, whether the military operations that the President anticipated ordering would be sufficiently extensive in "nature, scope, and duration" to constitute a "war" requiring prior specific congressional approval under the Declaration of War Clause.

In prior opinions, this Office has identified a variety of national interests that, alone or in combination, may justify use of military force by the President. In 2004, for example, we found adequate legal authority for the deployment of U.S. forces to Haiti based on national interests in protecting the lives and property of Americans in the country, preserving "regional stability," and maintaining the credibility of United Nations Security Council mandates. Memorandum for Alberto R. Gonzales, Counsel to the President, from Jack L. Goldsmith III, Assistant Attorney General, Office of Legal Counsel, Re: Deployment of United States Armed Forces to Haiti at 3–4 (Mar. 17, 2004) available at http://www.justice.gov/olc/ opinions.htm. In 1995, we similarly concluded that the President's authority to deploy approximately 20,000 ground troops to Bosnia, for purposes of enforcing a peace agreement ending the civil war there, rested on national interests in completing a "pattern of inter-allied cooperation and assistance" established by prior U.S. participation in NATO air and naval support for peacekeeping efforts, "preserving peace in the region and forestalling the threat of a wider conflict," and maintaining the credibility of the UNSC. And in 1992, we explained the President's authority to deploy troops in Somalia in terms of national interests in providing security for American civilians and military personnel involved in UNSC-supported humanitarian relief efforts and (once again) enforcing UNSC mandates.

In our view, the combination of at least two national interests that the President reasonably determined were at stake here—preserving regional stability and supporting the UNSC's credibility and effectiveness—provided a sufficient basis for the President's exercise of his constitutional authority to order the use of military force.

First, the United States has a strong national security and foreign policy interest in security and stability in the Middle East that was threatened by Qadhafi's actions in Libya. As noted, we recognized similar regional stability interests as justifications for presidential military actions in Haiti and Bosnia. With respect to Haiti, we found "an obvious interest in maintaining peace and stability," "[g]iven the proximity of Haiti to the United States," and particularly considering that "past instances of unrest in Haiti have led to the mass emigration of refugees attempting to reach the United States." In the case of Bosnia, we noted (quoting prior statements by President Clinton justifying military action) the longstanding commitment of the United States to the "'principle that the security and stability of Europe is of fundamental interest to the United States,'" and we identified, as justification for the military action, the President's determination that "[i]f the war in the former Yugoslavia resumes, 'there is a very real risk that it could spread beyond Bosnia, and involve Europe's new democracies as well as our NATO allies.'" In addition, in another important precedent, President Clinton justified extensive airstrikes in the Federal Republic of Yugoslavia ("FRY") in 1999—military action later ratified by Congress but initially conducted without specific authorization—based on concerns about the threat to regional security created by that government's repressive treatment of the ethnic Albanian population in Kosovo. "The FRY government's violence," President Clinton explained, "creates a conflict with no natural boundaries, pushing refugees across borders and potentially drawing in neighboring countries. The Kosovo region is a tinderbox that could ignite a wider European war with dangerous consequences to the United States.

As his statements make clear, President Obama determined in this case that the Libyan government's actions posed similar risks to regional peace and security. Much as violence in Bosnia and Kosovo in the 1990s risked creating large refugee movements, destabilizing neighboring countries, and inviting wider conflict, here the Libyan government's "illegitimate use of force . . . [was] forcing many [civilians] to flee to neighboring countries, thereby destabilizing the peace and security of the region." "Left unaddressed," the President noted in his report to Congress, "the growing instability in Libya could ignite wider instability in the Middle East, with dangerous consequences to the national security interests of the United States." Without outside intervention, Libya's civilian population faced a "humanitarian catastrophe," as the President put it on another occasion, "innocent people" in Libya were "being brutalized" and Qadhafi "threaten[ed] a bloodbath that could destabilize an entire region." The risk of regional destabilization in this case was also recognized by the UNSC, which determined in Resolution 1973 that the "situation" in Libya "constitute[d] a threat to international peace and security." S.C. Res. 1973. As this Office has previously observed, "[t]he President is entitled to rely on" such UNSC findings "in making his determination that the interests of the United States justify providing the military assistance that [the UNSC resolution] calls for."

Qadhafi's actions not only endangered regional stability by increasing refugee flows and creating a humanitarian crisis, but, if unchecked, also could have encouraged the repression of other democratic uprisings that were part of a larger movement in the Middle East, thereby further undermining United States foreign policy goals in the region. Against the background of widespread popular unrest in the region, events in Libya formed "just one more chapter in the change that is unfolding across the Middle East and North Africa." Qadhafi's campaign of violence against his own country's citizens thus might have set an example for others in the region, causing "[t]he democratic impulses that are dawning across the region [to] be eclipsed by the darkest form of dictatorship, as repressive leaders concluded that violence is the best strategy to cling to power." At a minimum, a massacre in Libya could have imperiled transitions to democratic government underway in neighboring Egypt and Tunisia by driving "thousands of additional refugees across Libya's borders." Based on these factors, we believe the President could reasonably find a significant national security interest in preventing Libyan instability from spreading elsewhere in this critical region.

The second important national interest implicated here, which reinforces the first, is the longstanding U.S. commitment to maintaining the credibility of the United Nations Security Council and the effectiveness of its actions to promote international peace and security. Since at least the Korean War, the United States government has recognized that "'[t]he continued existence of the United Nations as an effective international organization is a paramount United States interest.'" Accordingly, although of course the President is not required to direct the use of military force simply because the UNSC has authorized it, this Office has recognized that "'maintaining the credibility of United Nations Security Council decisions, protecting the security of United Nations and related relief efforts, and ensuring the effectiveness of United Nations peacekeeping operations can be considered a vital national interest'" on which the President may rely in determining that U.S. interests justify the use of military force. Here, the UNSC's credibility and effectiveness as an instrument of global peace and stability were at stake in Libya once the UNSC took action to impose a no-fly zone and ensure the safety of civilians—particularly after Qadhafi's forces ignored the UNSC's call for a cease fire and for the cessation of attacks on civilians. As President Obama noted, without military action to stop Qadhafi's repression, "[t]he writ of the United Nations Security Council would have been shown to be little more than empty words, crippling that institution's future credibility to uphold global peace and security." We think the President could legitimately find that military action by the United States to assist the international coalition in giving effect to UNSC Resolution 1973 was needed to secure "a substantial national foreign policy objective."

We conclude, therefore, that the use of military force in Libya was supported by sufficiently important national interests to fall within the President's constitutional power. At the same time, turning to the second element of the analysis, we do not believe that anticipated United States operations in Libya amounted to a "war" in the constitutional sense necessitating congressional approval under the Declaration of War Clause. This inquiry, as noted, is highly fact-specific and turns on no single factor. Here, considering all the relevant circumstances, we believe applicable historical precedents demonstrate that the limited military operations the President anticipated directing were not a "war" for constitutional purposes.

As in the case of the no-fly zone patrols and periodic airstrikes in Bosnia before the deployment of ground troops in 1995 and the NATO bombing campaign in connection with the Kosovo conflict in 1999—two military campaigns initiated without a prior declaration of war or other specific congressional authorization—President Obama determined that the use of force in Libya by the United States would be limited to airstrikes and associated support missions; the President made clear that "[t]he United States is not going to deploy ground troops in Libya." The planned operations thus avoided the difficulties of withdrawal and risks of escalation that may attend commitment of ground forces—two factors that this Office has identified as "arguably" indicating "a greater need for approval [from Congress] at the outset," to avoid creating a situation in which "Congress may be confronted with circumstances in which the exercise of its power to declare war is effectively foreclosed." Furthermore, also as in prior operations conducted without a declaration of war or other specific authorizing legislation, the anticipated operations here served a "limited mission" and did not "aim at the conquest or occupation of territory." President Obama directed United States forces to "conduct[] a limited and well-defined mission in support of international efforts to protect civilians and prevent a humanitarian disaster"; American airstrikes accordingly were to be "limited in their nature, duration, and scope." As the President explained, "we are not going to use force to go beyond [this] well-defined goal." And although it might not be true here that "the risk of sustained military conflict was negligible," the anticipated operations also did not involve a "preparatory bombardment" in anticipation of a ground invasion—a form of military operation we distinguished from the deployment (without preparatory bombing) of 20,000 U.S. troops to Haiti in concluding that the latter operation did not require advance congressional approval. Considering the historical practice of even intensive military action—such as the 17-day-long 1995 campaign of NATO airstrikes in Bosnia and some two months of bombing in Yugoslavia in 1999—without specific prior congressional approval, as well as the limited means, objectives, and intended duration of the anticipated operations in Libya, we do not think the "anticipated nature, scope, and duration" of the use of force by the United States in Libya rose to the level of a "war" in the constitutional sense, requiring the President to seek a declaration of war or other prior authorization from Congress.

Accordingly, we conclude that President Obama could rely on his constitutional power to safeguard the national interest by directing the anticipated military operations in Libya—which were limited in their nature, scope, and duration—without prior congressional authorization.

/s/ CAROLINE D. KRASS

Principal Deputy Assistant Attorney General

Key Terms

Authorization for the Use of Military Force—Under U.S. law, a congressional authorization to the president that military force may be used in a specific circumstance or set of circumstances. This can be against another nation or against a non-state actor, such as a terrorist organization.

Declaration of war—A formal declaration made by a nation's government that a formal state of war exists between two nations.

Power of the purse—The common reference to the ability of the Congress to control activity of the executive branch by limiting funding for certain actions.

Further Reading

Ely, John Hart. *War and Responsibility; Constitutional Lessons of Vietnam and Its Aftermath* (Princeton Univ. Press, 1973).

Fisher, Louis, *Distribution of Constitutional Authority: How Tightly Can Congress Draw the Purse Strings?* 83 A.J.I.L 738 (1989). See also Kate Stith, *Congress' Power of the Purse*, 97 Yale L. J. 595 (1988).

Turner, Robert F., *The War Powers Resolution: Unconstitutional, Unnecessary, and Unhelpful*, 17 Loy. L.A. L. Rev. 683 (1984).

Yoo, John, *Crisis and Command: A History of Executive Power from George Washington to George W. Bush* (Kaplan Publishing, 2010).

Chapter 10

International Law and National Security

Overview

Our homeland and national security depends on not just what our government does within the United States and involving our own citizens, but also how we interact with other nations, their citizens, and with various international organizations and non-state groups. Article VI of the Constitution provides

> "This Constitution, and the laws of the United States which shall be made in pursuance thereof; and all treaties made, or which shall be made, under the authority of the United States, shall be the supreme law of the land; and the judges in every state shall be bound thereby, anything in the Constitution or laws of any State to the contrary notwithstanding."

And one of the express powers of the Congress listed in Article I Section 8 is to

> "define and punish ... offenses against the laws of Nations."

We can see from this that international law—whether in the specific form of treaties (and other international agreements) or the more broadly stated "laws of Nations"—is a part of our legal system. This chapter looks at the ways international law affecting homeland and national security has been addressed in our courts.

International law, or the law of nations, is the collection of rules that are considered legally binding on nations in their interaction with each other. This seems like a repetition of words, but the point is an important one. Nations, like people, act for different reasons. Some of these are practical, or reflect a policy choice, and some are made because of a sense of legal obligation. Only the last of these would count as "law."

One of the earliest definitions used is that the law of nations consists of "the rights subsisting between nations or states and the obligations correspondent to those rights."[1] So international law is a body of law which principally applies between nations, as opposed to domestic law which applies between a nation and its citizens. There are a number of sources of international law, but the commonly accepted list

---

1. Emer de Vattel, *Essay on the Foundation of Natural Law and on the First principle of the Obligation Men Find Themselves Under to Observe Laws, 1797*, translated by T. J. Hochstrasser, from The Law of Nations (Liberty Fund, Indianapolis, 2008).

comes from the Statute of the International Court of Justice, agreed to by all of the world's nations at the formation of the United Nations in 1945:

   a. international conventions [agreements], whether general or particular, establishing rules expressly recognized by the [participating] states;

   b. international custom, as evidence of a general practice accepted as law; and

   c. the general principles of law recognized by civilized nations;

(1) The first source includes treaties and other agreements. Nations make agreements with one another about how to conduct themselves. These agreements can be very detailed, involving a number of different nations, or very simple and only between two nations. They can be formal, such as when nations sign treaties, or informal, as executive agreements between parts of the government. One example of a formal agreement between a number of nations would be the North Atlantic Treaty which formed the North Atlantic Treaty Organization (NATO) in 1949. This was a treaty formed in response to the threat of the Soviet Union and which, most significantly, required the twelve member states to all come to the aid of any other member state which was under attack.

(2) The second source is referred to as "customary international law" (CIL) and, as stated above, consists of evidence of a general practice accepted as law. Over the years, in a number of circumstances, various customs and traditions have arisen for how nations are expected to conduct themselves. Over time, these customs are relied on and are considered binding. Now, as a practical matter, in today's modern era almost every custom or tradition has been written down in a treaty. But this is not always the case. For example, much of the Law of War or the Law of the Sea developed over time, and only recently has been written down in international agreements.

(3) The third source of international law consists of the general principles of law recognized by all nations as binding. While this sounds much like customary international law, these general principles (or *jus cogens*) are much more fundamental—they are rules that form the foundation, so to speak, of international law. The right of a nation to its sovereign independence is one such rule, as is the expectation that a nation that signs a treaty is obligated to fulfill its terms. More recently, certain rules regarding "crimes against humanity" such as genocide and torture have been declared to constitute *jus cogens*. Probably the most important distinction between *jus cogens* and other forms of international law is that *jus cogens* are considered to be so important that no nation is ever excused from stating in advance that they refuse to recognize it. So, for example, there can never be a situation where a nation would be excused from committing genocide.

Is international law really even "law"? This question comes up because the nature and enforcement of international law is very different than what we are used to. In common understanding, "law" comes from a very structured development and is enforced in a very structured way. But international law operates differently. It operates as well, or as poorly, as the "international community" wants it to. And it operates well (or poorly) based on the degree to which nations, especially those nations most directly involved, see compliance and enforcement as being in their best interest. Where this is clear—for example, in the international agreements regarding mail delivery—compliance is standard. In trade agreements, enforcement is usually clear and straightforward. But in cases where the stakes are much higher, enforcing compliance may be much more difficult.

The most significant reason why nations are sometimes reluctant to comply with or enforce international law is the respect for national sovereignty. National (or Westphalian) sovereignty is based on three principles. First, that each nation state has ultimate authority over its territory and domestic affairs, to the exclusion of all external powers. Second, the principle of non-interference in another country's domestic affairs. The third is that each state (no matter how large or small) is equal in international law. This is not that different than how we see ourselves as individuals—there is a strong tendency, especially in American political culture, to want to limit the degree to which anyone else can tell us what to do or how to live our lives. Similarly, our system of federalism limits the degree to which the federal government can dictate to states. So these principles of equality and non-interference at the international level mean that it is difficult sometimes to get agreement on what the law should be to begin with, and then to enforce compliance even after the law is agreed on.

Even where nations agree on what the law should be, and have agreed to be bound by the law, there may still be disputes as to the facts involved in a particular situation—again, not unlike how we interact with each other as individuals. We might agree that there should be a law against killing another person, but allow for a defense in cases of using force in self-defense. So we have disputes over the fact of whether or not the situation justified the action. Or, where there is a dispute over a contract, rarely do people say "we reject the notion of contracts" but rather claim that the facts show *they* are in the right and it is the other person who is wrong. This same sort of issue plays out between nations.

Here again, the concept of sovereignty comes into play—while we have agreed to have governments at the local, county, state, and federal level resolve these disputes, the same has not happened at the international level. Instead, the community has to decide how—or if—to resolve disputes.

Finally, because of the existence of many different cultures, political systems, and legal systems around the country, there may be agreement on the broad principles of an issue but no agreement on specifics. For example, even when we can agree on the "right to a fair trial," we will still disagree as to just what exactly constitutes a "fair trial." In the American legal system, a "fair trial" includes a jury of one's peers, an independent judge who does not act in the case but simply referees, a right to counsel, a right against self-incrimination, the opportunity to confront accusers, and a burden of proof that is "beyond reasonable doubt." In other countries, a person's refusal to speak in his or her own defense is viewed as evidence of guilt. Many nations have trials where guilt is decided by a judge, and there is no option of a jury of one's peers. And in some cases the judge gets involved in the case very early and actually directs the investigation, telling the police what to investigate. With such disputes over details, it is difficult to agree upon international standards that are easily and universally recognized when violated.

For our purposes in this textbook, what is important is not so much what international law is, but how it applies to our national and homeland security. So our discussion here will focus on how international law affects the actions our leaders might take, how it limits the choices we can make, and, on a very practical level, whether the rules of international law can be enforced in U.S. courts. We'll deal with this in a number of ways—first by looking at just how and when international law is taken into account by, or enforced in, U.S. courts. Then we'll look at some specific situations—such as how international law might affect how we conduct investigations of crimes that involve people outside our country, how these crimes can be brought into our courts, or how violations of international law can be used as a basis for a lawsuit.

In the first case we examine, we look at the application of international law as a binding source of law in our courts. It involves a dispute over small, coastal, fishing vessels that were seized during the Spanish-American war. During the Spanish-American War, the U.S. Navy had enacted a blockade around Cuba. The purpose of a blockade is to hurt the enemy by cutting off its trade with other nations. Under the laws of war, a blockade can interfere with commerce related to the war effort, but it does allow for some exceptions, as we'll see in the decision. It is also a part of international law that, when a vessel tries to run the blockade but is captured, that ship and its cargo can be seized by the capturing nation as war prizes. (You should remember that from the case *The Prize Cases*, which was about President Lincoln's war powers without a formal declaration of war.) The capturing nation could then sell the vessel and its cargo and keep the money, sharing a part of the proceeds with the crew of the ship that did the capturing. In peacetime this behavior is unlawful as piracy, but in times of war this had been an internationally acceptable practice.

The reason why there was a dispute here is that the ships seized were not international merchant ships, but just small, coastal fishing vessels. All they and their crew of fishermen did was provide food for the local people, and their activities made no contribution to the Spanish war effort. As the Court explains in detail below, even though there was no domestic U.S. law governing the conduct of U.S. Navy ships in relation to the specific issue of how to treat these small fishing vessels, there is a long-standing international custom that a blockading navy will not molest, let alone capture as war prizes, small coastal fishing vessels. It is customary international law to grant these small coastal fishing vessels free passage and let them go about their daily business of fishing. What happened when the U.S. Navy did violate this customary international law?

The Paquete Habana, 175 U.S. 677 (1900)*

These are two appeals from decrees of the District Court of the United States for the Southern District of Florida condemning two fishing vessels [The Paquete Habana and The Lola] and their cargoes as prize of war.

---

* The case has been heavily edited and paraphrased by the authors for clarity. See disclaimer in introduction.

Each vessel was a fishing boat, running in and out of Havana, and regularly engaged in fishing on the coast of Cuba; sailed under the Spanish flag; was owned by a Spanish subject of Cuban birth, living in the City of Havana; was commanded by a subject of Spain, also residing in Havana, and her master and crew had no interest in the vessel, but were entitled to shares, amounting in all to two-thirds, of her catch, the other third belonging to her owner. Her cargo consisted of fresh fish, caught by her crew from the sea, put on board as they were caught, and kept and sold alive. Until stopped by the blockading squadron, she had no knowledge of the existence of the war or of any blockade. She had no arms or ammunition on board, and made no attempt to run the blockade after she knew of its existence, nor any resistance at the time of the capture.

Both the fishing vessels were brought by their captors into Key West as a prize of war. Each vessel was thereupon sold by auction; the Paquete Habana for the sum of $490 and the Lola for the sum of $800. There was no other evidence in the record of the value of either vessel or of her cargo.

We are then brought to the consideration of the question whether, upon the facts appearing in these records, the fishing vessels were subject to capture by the armed vessels of the United States during the recent war with Spain.

By an ancient usage among civilized nations, beginning centuries ago and gradually ripening into a rule of international law, coast fishing vessels pursuing their vocation of catching and bringing in fresh fish have been recognized as exempt, with their cargoes and crews, from capture as prize of war.

This doctrine, however, has been earnestly contested at the bar, and no complete collection of the instances illustrating it is to be found, so far as we are aware, in a single published work, although many are referred to and discussed by the writers on international law. It is therefore worth the while to trace the history of the rule from the earliest accessible sources through the increasing recognition of it, with occasional setbacks, to what we may now justly consider as its final establishment in our own country and generally throughout the civilized world.

> [The opinion provides an extensive historic overview documenting many examples of how, over the centuries, nations have taken care to not molest small, coastal fishing vessels.]

The doctrine which exempts coast fishermen, with their vessels and cargoes, from capture as prize of war, has been familiar to the United States from the time of the War of Independence...

> [Here the Court lists examples of past U.S. practice recognizing this rule of exempting small fishing vessels and similar property.]

More on point to the subject at hand are the words of former U.S. Supreme Court justice:

> "Undoubtedly no single nation can change the law of the sea. The law is of universal obligation, and no statute of one or two nations can create obligations for the world. Like all the laws of nations, it rests upon the common

consent of civilized communities. It is of force not because it was prescribed by any superior power, but because it has been generally accepted as a rule of conduct. Whatever may have been its origin, whether in the usages of navigation, or in the ordinances of maritime states, or in both, it has become the law of the sea only by the concurrent sanction of those nations who may be said to constitute the commercial world. Many of the usages which prevail, and which have the force of law, doubtless originated in the positive prescriptions of some single state, which were at first of limited effect, but which, when generally accepted, became of universal obligation."

"This is not giving to the statutes of any nation extraterritorial effect. It is not treating them as general maritime laws, but it is recognition of the historical fact that, by common consent of mankind these rules have been acquiesced in as of general obligation. Of that fact we think we may take judicial notice. Foreign municipal laws must indeed be proved as facts, but it is not so with the law of nations."

The position taken by the United States during the recent war with Spain was quite in accord with the rule of international law, now generally recognized by civilized nations, in regard to coast fishing vessels. On April 21, 1898, the Secretary of the Navy gave instructions to Admiral Sampson, commanding the North Atlantic Squadron, to "immediately institute a blockade of the north coast of Cuba, extending from Cardenas on the east to Bahia Honda on the west." The blockade was immediately instituted accordingly. On April 22, the President issued a proclamation declaring that the United States had instituted and would maintain that blockade "in pursuance of the laws of the United States, and the law of nations applicable to such cases." And by the act of Congress of April 25, 1898, it was declared that the war between the United States and Spain existed on that day, and had existed since and including April 21.

On April 26, 1898, the President issued another proclamation which, after reciting the existence of the war as declared by Congress, contained this further recital:

"It being desirable that such war should be conducted upon principles in harmony with the present views of nations and sanctioned by their recent practice."

This recital makes no mention of fishing vessels. But the proclamation clearly manifests the general policy of the government to conduct the war in accordance with the principles of international law sanctioned by the recent practice of nations.

On April 28, 1898 (after the capture of the two fishing vessels now in question), Admiral Sampson telegraphed to the Secretary of the Navy as follows:

"I find that a large number of fishing schooners are attempting to get into Havana from their fishing grounds near the Florida reefs and coasts. They are generally manned by excellent seamen, belonging to the maritime inscription of Spain, who have already served in the Spanish navy, and who are liable to further service. As these trained men are naval reserves, most valuable to the Spaniards as artillerymen, either afloat or ashore, I recommend that they should be detained prisoners of war, and that I should be authorized to deliver them to the commanding officer of the army at Key West."

To that communication the Secretary of the Navy, on April 30, 1898, guardedly answered:

> "'Spanish fishing vessels attempting to violate blockade are subject, with crew, to capture, and any such vessel or crew considered likely to aid enemy may be detained.' The admiral's dispatch assumed that he was not authorized, without express order, to arrest coast fishermen peaceably pursuing their calling, and the necessary implication and evident intent of the response of the Navy Department were that Spanish coast fishing vessels and their crews should not be interfered with so long as they neither attempted to violate the blockade nor were considered likely to aid the enemy..."

There was no evidence of either vessel having engaged in any activity to support hostilities. Each vessel was of a moderate size, such as is not unusual in coast fishing smacks, and was regularly engaged in fishing on the coast of Cuba. The crew of each were few in number, had no interest in the vessel, and received, in return for their toil and enterprise, two-thirds of her catch, the other third going to her owner by way of compensation for her use. Each vessel went out from Havana to her fishing ground and was captured when returning along the coast of Cuba. The cargo of each consisted of fresh fish, caught by her crew from the sea and kept alive on board. Although one of the vessels extended her fishing trip across the Yucatan channel and fished on the coast of Yucatan, we cannot doubt that each was engaged in the coast fishery, and not in a commercial adventure, within the rule of international law.

The two vessels and their cargoes were condemned by the district court as prize of war; the vessels were sold under its decrees, and it does not appear what became of the fresh fish of which their cargoes consisted.

Upon the facts proved in either case, it is the duty of this Court, sitting as the highest prize court of the United States and administering the law of nations, to declare and adjudge that the capture was unlawful and without probable cause, and it is therefore, in each case Ordered, that the decree of the district court be reversed, and the proceeds of the sale of the vessel, together with the proceeds of any sale of her cargo, be restored to the claimant, with damages and costs.

END OF OPINION

Across the nations of the civilized world and in the U.S., there has always been a longstanding principle of customary international law not to molest coastal fishing vessels during a blockade. Although the U.S. did not have a domestic law specifically on topic, the U.S. Supreme Court still recognized that unwritten customary international law is a part of domestic U.S. law enforceable in U.S. courts, even when Congress has not passed domestic legislation on the topic.

The case above involved a situation where the court relied only on customary international law. There was no governing domestic (U.S.) law on the issue. This is not often the case. In most situations these days, it is very likely that Congress will have passed legislation on an issue. For example, even though slavery is prohibited under international law, it is also illegal in the U.S. under the Thirteenth Amendment and the criminal statutes enacted to enforce that Amendment.[2] This means that if a person were prosecuted in the U.S. for forcing a woman into slavery, the prosecution would be based under domestic criminal law and not under international law.

Although treaties and the law of nations are part of the "law of the land" under the Constitution, this does not necessarily mean that all aspects of international law are enforceable in the U.S. legal system. The Constitution prevails, and, in most situations, federal statute will also prevail. While that seems to set up an endless series of situations where the U.S. has to ignore international law, or violate the Constitution or U.S. law, that's not necessarily the case.

First, as you have no doubt realized by now, in many cases laws can be open to differing interpretations. Depending on which interpretation you choose, there might be a conflict between two laws, while a different interpretation would not have a conflict. Now, there is a legal principle known as the *Charming Betsey* Canon, which comes from a decision of the U.S. Supreme Court in 1804.[3] This principle states that "an act of Congress ought never to be construed to violate the law of nations if any other possible construction remains." So long as it is possible to interpret domestic legislation so that it does not violate international law, then the U.S. courts should do so.

Now, in the case of the *Paquete Habana* cases and *The Charming Betsey*, international law was considered controlling. In one case this was because there was no applicable U.S. federal law, and in the other because the laws were read in a way that did not conflict. Most often, though, international law is not seen as necessarily *controlling* the decision of a court but rather as *informing* it—as persuasive authority only.

Let's look at an example. Very recently, international law was used to inform the Supreme Court in deciding a case of constitutional law. The Eighth Amendment to the Constitution reads:

> Excessive bail shall not be required, nor excessive fines imposed, nor cruel and unusual punishments inflicted.

Just what exactly constitutes "cruel and unusual punishments"? That term is not defined in the U.S. Constitution but is open to interpretation. A brief look at history shows that "cruel and unusual" has had many meanings over the years. When the United States was founded, punishments such as branding, public shaming, and the whipping of criminals were all very acceptable, as was hanging considered an appropriate form of execution. Today, if instead of giving a thief time in jail and a fine, a convict was instead ordered to be publicly whipped and permanently branded like cattle, many would say that the sentence was cruel and unusual.

---

2. 18 U.S. Code Ch. 77, sec. 1581–1597.
3. *Murray v. The Charming Betsey*, 6 U.S. (2 Cranch) 64 (1804).

So looking both at domestic law and international law, just what exactly is "cruel and unusual"? In *Roper v. Simmons*, the U.S. Supreme Court, in interpreting the meaning of the Eighth Amendment, looked to international law for assistance.

Roper v. Simmons, 543 U.S. 551 (2005)*

This case requires us to address whether it is permissible under the Eighth Amendment to the Constitution of the United States to execute a juvenile offender who was older than 15 but younger than 18 when he committed a capital crime.

Our determination that the death penalty is disproportionate punishment for offenders under 18 finds confirmation in the stark reality that the United States is the only country in the world that continues to give official sanction to the juvenile death penalty. This reality does not become controlling, for the task of interpreting the Eighth Amendment remains our responsibility. In the past, the Court has referred to the laws of other countries and to international authorities as instructive for its interpretation of the Eighth Amendment's prohibition of "cruel and unusual punishments." In *Trop v. Dulles* (1948) it was stated that "The civilized nations of the world are in virtual unanimity that statelessness is not to be imposed as punishment for crime"); In *Atkins v. Virginia* (2002) it was recognized that "within the world community, the imposition of the death penalty for crimes committed by mentally retarded offenders is overwhelmingly disapproved." (Atkins plurality opinion) (noting the abolition of the juvenile death penalty "by other nations that share our Anglo-American heritage, and by the leading members of the Western European community," and observing that "we have previously recognized the relevance of the views of the international community in determining whether a punishment is cruel and unusual"; In *Enmund v. Florida* (1982) it was observed that "the doctrine of felony murder has been abolished in England and India, severely restricted in Canada and a number of other Commonwealth countries, and is unknown in continental Europe"; In *Coker v. Georgia* (1977) the plurality opinion stated that "It is . . . not irrelevant here that out of 60 major nations in the world surveyed in 1965, only 3 retained the death penalty for rape where death did not ensue."

Article 37 of the United Nations Convention on the Rights of the Child, which every country in the world has ratified save for the United States and Somalia, contains an express prohibition on capital punishment for crimes committed by juveniles under 18. No ratifying country has entered a reservation to the provision prohibiting the execution of juvenile offenders. Parallel prohibitions are contained in other significant international covenants.

Only seven countries other than the United States have executed juvenile offenders since 1990: Iran, Pakistan, Saudi Arabia, Yemen, Nigeria, the Democratic Republic of Congo, and China. Since then each of these countries has either abolished capital punishment for juveniles or made public disavowal of the practice. In sum, it

---

* The case has been heavily edited and paraphrased by the authors for clarity. See disclaimer in introduction.

is fair to say that the United States now stands alone in a world that has turned its face against the juvenile death penalty.

Though the international covenants prohibiting the juvenile death penalty are of more recent date, it is instructive to note that the United Kingdom abolished the juvenile death penalty before these covenants came into being. The United Kingdom's experience bears particular relevance here in light of the historic ties between our countries and in light of the Eighth Amendment's own origins. The Amendment was modeled on a parallel provision in the English Declaration of Rights of 1689, which provided: "Excessive Bail ought not to be required nor excessive Fines imposed; nor cruel and unusuall Punishments inflicted." As of now, the United Kingdom has abolished the death penalty in its entirety; but, decades before it took this step, it recognized the disproportionate nature of the juvenile death penalty; and it abolished that penalty as a separate matter. In 1930 an official committee recommended that the minimum age for execution be raised to 21. Parliament then enacted the Children and Young Person's Act of 1933, which prevented execution of those aged 18 at the date of the sentence. And in 1948, Parliament enacted the Criminal Justice Act, prohibiting the execution of any person under 18 at the time of the offense. In the 56 years that have passed since the United Kingdom abolished the juvenile death penalty, the weight of authority against it there, and in the international community, has become well established.

It is proper that we acknowledge the overwhelming weight of international opinion against the juvenile death penalty, resting in large part on the understanding that the instability and emotional imbalance of young people may often be a factor in the crime. The opinion of the world community, while not controlling our outcome, does provide respected and significant confirmation for our own conclusions.

Over time, from one generation to the next, the Constitution has come to earn the high respect and even, as James Madison dared to hope, the veneration of the American people. The document sets forth, and rests upon, innovative principles original to the American experience, such as federalism; a proven balance in political mechanisms through separation of powers; specific guarantees for the accused in criminal cases; and broad provisions to secure individual freedom and preserve human dignity. These doctrines and guarantees are central to the American experience and remain essential to our present-day self-definition and national identity. Not the least of the reasons we honor the Constitution, then, is because we know it to be our own. It does not lessen our fidelity to the Constitution or our pride in its origins to acknowledge that the express affirmation of certain fundamental rights by other nations and peoples simply underscores the centrality of those same rights within our own heritage of freedom.

The Eighth Amendment forbids imposition of the death penalty on offenders who were under the age of 18 when their crimes were committed.

END OF OPINION

Here, the U.S. Supreme Court did not apply any international law, convention, or treaty as binding legal authority. Instead, it used international law and laws in other nations to help interpret the meaning of ambiguous terminology within the U.S. Constitution. It is worth noting that when this opinion was published, this idea of using international norms to define ambiguous terminology in the U.S. Constitution received widespread criticism, especially from more conservative elements of society.[4] However, this methodology comports with the *Charming Betsey* Canon by seeking an interpretation of U.S. law (the 8th Amendment) that did not contradict international law (the human rights treaties cited). *Roper v. Simmons* remains controlling law despite the criticism.

When Domestic Law Conflicts with International Law

The *Paquette Habana* applies when we do not have any domestic law on point and we are dealing with *customary international law*. *Roper v. Simmons* and the *Charming Betsey* Canon apply when we have *domestic law that is open to different interpretations or is ambiguous*. Other times we will have domestic legislation that is not ambiguous and clearly violates international law. So, what happens when unambiguous domestic law clearly conflicts and even violates international law? Will the courts impose the domestic law or the international law? Does one supersede the other as a higher authority? In fact, our courts have routinely held that properly enacted federal law takes precedence over applicable international law, even if the U.S. law contradicts international law.

Some argue that, much like how federal law supersedes state law, international law always supersedes federal law. This is not the case in our legal system. International law does not trump domestic law. At most, international law can be helpful for defining ambiguous terminology in domestic law, but if international law conflicts with domestic law, domestic law controls.

This legal principle is explained in the following case, a relatively recent one involving wartime detention.

Al-Bihani v. Obama, 590 F.3d 866 (2010)*

Al-Bihani, a Yemeni citizen, has been held at the U.S. naval base detention facility in Guantanamo Bay, Cuba since 2002. [H]e eventually accompanied and served a paramilitary group allied with the Taliban, known as the 55th Arab Brigade, which

---

4. For those interested in looking at this more deeply, see Waters, Melissa A., Justice Scalia on the Use of Foreign Law in Constitutional Interpretation: Unidirectional Monologue or Co-Constitutive Dialogue?. Tulsa Journal of Comparative & International Law, (Symposium Issue) Vol. 12, p. 149, 2004. Available at SSRN: http://ssrn.com/abstract=896838.

* The case has been heavily edited and paraphrased by the authors for clarity. See disclaimer in introduction.

included Al-Qaeda members within its command structure and which fought on the front lines against the Northern Alliance. He worked as the brigade's cook and carried a brigade-issued weapon, but never fired it in combat. Combat, however — in the form of bombing by the U.S.-led Coalition that invaded Afghanistan in response to the attacks of September 11, 2001 — forced the 55th to retreat from the front lines in October 2001. At the end of this protracted retreat, Al-Bihani and the rest of the brigade surrendered, under orders, to Northern Alliance forces, and they kept him in custody until his handover to U.S. Coalition forces in early 2002. The U.S. military sent Al-Bihani to Guantanamo for detention and interrogation.

Al-Bihani's many arguments present this court with two overarching questions regarding the detainees at the Guantanamo Bay naval base. The first concerns whom the President can lawfully detain pursuant to statutes passed by Congress. The second asks what procedure is due to detainees challenging their detention in habeas corpus proceedings. The Supreme Court has provided scant guidance on these questions, consciously leaving the contours of the substantive and procedural law of detention open for lower courts to shape in a common law fashion.

Al-Bihani challenges the statutory legitimacy of his detention by advancing a number of arguments based upon the international laws of war. . . . Al-Bihani interprets international law to mean anyone not belonging to an official state military is a civilian. He says that civilians must commit a direct hostile act, such as firing a weapon in combat, before they can be lawfully detained. Because Al-Bihani did not commit such an act, he reasons his detention is unlawful.

Next, he argues the members of the 55th Arab Brigade were not subject to attack or detention by U.S. Coalition forces under the laws of co-belligerency because the 55th, although allied with the Taliban against the Northern Alliance, did not have the required opportunity to declare its neutrality in the fight against the United States. His third argument is that the conflict in which he was detained, an international war between the United States and Taliban-controlled Afghanistan, officially ended when the Taliban lost control of the Afghan government. Thus, absent a determination of future dangerousness, he must be released. His basis for this is the Geneva Convention Relative to the Treatment of Prisoners of War (Third Geneva Convention) art. 118, Aug. 12, 1949) Lastly, Al-Bihani posits a type of "clean hands" theory by which any authority the government has to detain him is undermined by its failure to accord him the prisoner-of-war status to which he believes he is entitled by international law.

We note that all of Al-Bihani's arguments rely heavily on the premise that the war powers granted by the AUMF and other statutes are limited by the international laws of war. This premise is mistaken. There is no indication in the AUMF, the Detainee Treatment Act of 2005, or the Military Commissions Act of 2006 or 2009, that Congress intended the international laws of war to act as extra-textual limiting principles for the President's war powers under the AUMF. The international laws of war as a whole have not been implemented domestically by Congress and are therefore not a source of authority for U.S. courts. Even assuming Congress had at some earlier point implemented the laws of war as domestic law through appropriate legislation, Congress had the power to authorize the President (in the AUMF and other later statutes) to exceed those bounds set by international law. Further weakening their relevance to this case, the international laws of war are not a fixed code. Their dictates and application to actual events are by nature contestable and fluid. There is "no precise formula" to identify a practice as custom and that it is often difficult to determine when a custom's transformation into law has taken place. Therefore, while the international laws of war are helpful to courts when identifying the general set of war powers to which the AUMF speaks, their lack of controlling legal force and firm definition render their use both inapposite and inadvisable when courts seek to determine the limits of the President's war powers. Therefore, putting aside that we find Al-Bihani's reading of international law to be unpersuasive, we have no occasion here to quibble over the intricate application of vague treaty provisions and amorphous customary principles. The sources we look to for resolution of Al-Bihani's case are the sources courts always look to: the text of relevant statutes and controlling domestic case law.

The AUMF, DTA, and MCA of 2006 and 2009 do not hinge the government's detention authority on proper identification of P.O.W.s or compliance with international law in general. In fact, the MCA of 2006, in a provision not altered by the MCA of 2009, explicitly precludes detainees from claiming the Geneva conventions— which include criteria to determine who is entitled to P.O.W. status—as a source of rights.

END OF OPINION

In *Al-Bihani*, the court ruled that it does not matter whether or not domestic laws violate international law; the court will make its decision based on what the applicable statutes say. Here is some language from one of the concurring opinions[5] from the case:

> "There is in the scholarly community an intuition that domestic statutes do not stand on their own authority, but rather rest against the backdrop of international norms ... If that is their wish, it is a curious one. The idea that international norms hang over domestic law as a corrective force to be implemented by courts is not only alien to our case law, but an aggrandizement of the judicial role beyond the Constitution's conception of the separation of powers."

And this language from one of the other judges[6] is also important:

> "First, international-law norms are not domestic U.S. law in the absence of action by the political branches to codify those norms. Congress and the President can and often do incorporate international-law principles into domestic U.S. law by way of a statute (or executive regulations issued

---

5. Brown, Circuit Judge, concurring in the denial of rehearing en banc.
6. Kavanaugh, Circuit Judge, concurring in the denial of rehearing en banc.

pursuant to statutory authority) or a self-executing treaty. When that happens, the relevant international-law principles become part of the domestic U.S. law that federal courts must enforce, assuming there is a cognizable cause of action and the prerequisites for federal jurisdiction are satisfied. But in light of the Supreme Court's 1938 decision in *Erie Railroad Co. v. Tompkins* (1938), which established that there is no federal general common law, international-law norms are not enforceable in federal courts unless the political branches have incorporated the norms into domestic U.S. law. None of the international-law norms cited by Al-Bihani has been so incorporated into domestic U.S. law."

Remember the hierarchy of laws from the first chapter of this book? It reads as follows:

1. U.S. Constitution
2. Federal legislation (statutes and treaties) and opinions by federal courts
3. State law
4. Municipal law

Nowhere in this legal hierarchy is there mention of international law other than the reference to treaties. And even then, as the court explains, "International-law norms are not domestic U.S. law in the absence of action by the political branches [Congress or President] to codify those norms."

This means that if there is no domestic law on point, unless we are dealing with customary international law, then the international law is completely unenforceable in U.S. courts. On the other hand, if there is domestic law on point, then that domestic law takes precedence over international law. Let's explore this concept with a hypothetical:

Assume that, with the exception of the United States, every country on the face of the Earth has signed a treaty to ban the killing of baby seals by clubbing them. A body of the United Nations passes multiple resolutions purporting to ban the clubbing of baby seals. In the U.S., there is zero legislation on point about clubbing baby seals. A famous actor announces he is organizing a baby seal clubbing hunting party. The organization People for the Ethical treatment of Animals (PETA) goes to federal court and asks for a court order to stop him, arguing that the practice violates international law and norms.

As detestable as the killing of baby seals by clubbing may be, the mere fact that it may violate international law is not a source of legal authority to stop the practice here in the U.S. As the *Al-Bihani* court stated, "courts may not interfere with the President's ... powers based on international-law norms that [Congress and the President] have not seen fit to enact into domestic U.S. law." In addition, a ban on the clubbing of baby seals is not customary international law; it has nothing to do with gross violations of human rights, nor would such a ban be a historic international principle. (Perhaps in the future animal welfare laws could become customary international law, but we are not at that point today.) It's not clear that the "ban" even constitutes international law at all under these facts—but that's not the point. Recall that the judges in *Al-Bihani* disagreed with his interpretations of what international law was but said *even if he was correct* it would make no difference in their decision.

To be clear, the court is not saying that the President has no obligation at all to obey international law. In *Al-Bihani* the court pointed out how Congress and the president have already enacted domestic laws, which make certain violations of international law also violations of domestic law, so that persons who violate these laws can be sued or prosecuted for their conduct in U.S. courts. For example, if U.S. soldiers were to go out and commit murder, they would not be prosecuted for violating international law; instead, they would be prosecuted for violating domestic law, specifically Article 118 of the Uniform Code of Military Justice (UCMJ), which prohibits murder. The UCMJ is a piece of domestic legislation, a criminal statute enacted by Congress, which has incorporated many international law principles.

Many were upset by the *Al-Bihani* opinion because they believe that U.S. law must always comply with international law in the same way it complies with federal statutes. Although a political and public policy argument can be made that the U.S. should comply with international law, unless we have enacted domestic legislation to incorporate international law, as a matter of law the U.S. courts are not legally required to apply that law in their decisions.

However, the court still cautioned the U.S. to not be completely blind to international law. The court stated, "the limited authority of the Judiciary to rely on international law to restrict the American war effort does not imply that that the political branches should ignore or disregard international-law norms." Here, the court was giving public policy advice to the president and Congress. Even though international law might not be enforceable in U.S. courts, for reasons concerning public policy, it is still often advisable for the U.S. to follow it, even if we legally are not required to do so.

Let's reduce our discussion on whether international law will be binding in the U.S. to four points:

1. If there is a U.S. federal statute directly on point, it supersedes any international law or customary international law.

2. If there is no U.S. federal law on point and the issue involves a longstanding, traditional, and customary international principle, then we can apply the international law in U.S. courts. (*Paquette Habana*)

3. If you have international law on point and also a U.S. federal statute or other federal rule of law on point, courts are to try to interpret that federal law, as much as possible, so it does not violate international law. (*Charming Betsey*)

4. If there is no applicable domestic U.S. federal law, and we are dealing with a developing international principle that does not have the status of customary international law and is not due to a treaty obligation of the U.S., the international rule is unenforceable in U.S. courts.

Review Questions

1. With the exception of the U.S., just about every single country on the face of the Earth has signed onto a treaty banning landmines. Although the U.S. does not use permanent landmines, it also has some situations where certain landmines are believed useful, and so it has not signed this treaty. Accordingly, in funding the military, Congress passes legislation contrary to the treaty explicitly authorizing the purchase of landmines that never de-activate. Human Rights First sues the Department of Defense, seeking an injunction against the purchase of landmines by the U.S. military, claiming this violates international law. How should the judge decide?

2. By the year 2090, with the exception of the U.S., every single country on the face of the Earth has signed onto a treaty banning landmines. This treaty is ruled by the International Court of Justice to "reflect customary international law." Nevertheless, as it has in the past, Congress votes specifically to authorize the acquisition and use of landmines. When the U.S. Army purchases a number of these mines, Human Rights Watch sues the Army for violating international law. How should the judge decide?

Enforcing International Human Rights Law in U.S. Courts

Most international law, as we have seen, is focused on law between nations—borders, trade agreements, and the like. It was a long-standing rule of international law in general that it applied only to relations between nation-states and did not apply to people. How a government treated its own people was seen as a matter entirely within that nation's sovereignty. As one leading scholar put it: "There is general agreement that, by virtue of its personal and territorial supremacy, a State can treat its own nationals according to discretion."[7] In the United Nations Charter it states that "Nothing contained in the present Charter shall authorize the United Nations to intervene in matters which are essentially within the domestic jurisdiction of any state..."[8] And yet, the UN Charter also claims that one of the key purposes of the United Nations is "... solving international problems of a ... humanitarian character, and in promoting and encouraging respect for human rights and fundamental freedoms for all..." Dr. Lauterpacht's book, quoted above, goes on to say:

> But there is a substantial body of opinion and of practice in support of the view that there are limits to that discretion and that when a State renders itself guilty of cruelties against, and persecution of its nationals in such a way as to deny their fundamental human rights and to shock the conscience of mankind, intervention in the interest of humanity is legally permissible.[9]

---

7. Lauterpacht, *Oppenheim's International Law, Volume I: Peace,* Longmans, Green, and Co., London (3rd ed., 1955) at 312.
8. Charter of the United Nations, Article 2, section 7.
9. Supra, note 8.

Since the United Nation was formed, there have been a number of human rights treaties, beginning with what is considered "The International Bill of Rights," which consists of the Universal Declaration of Human Rights (adopted in 1948), the International Covenant on Civil and Political Rights (1966) with its two Optional Protocols, and the International Covenant on Economic, Social and Cultural Rights (1966). In addition, a number of more specific human rights treaties have been adopted outlawing genocide and torture, and protecting the rights of women and children.[10]

Now, the effort since World War II to address the problem of human rights does not mean that human rights are, in fact, protected. We see that there are cases of human rights abuses happening all over the world, all the time. Protecting human rights has been a stated goal of U.S. foreign policy since at least the administration of President Jimmy Carter and has been a part of the national security strategy of the United States since at least the George W. Bush administration; certainly concern over human rights has been a concern for a much longer period of U.S. national security history.[11]

So how does the United Sates seek to enforce human rights? There are any number of steps the U.S. might take. The key step taken by the Carter administration was to tie human rights compliance to all treaties and other international negotiations. Another action taken, on occasion, has been for the United States, either alone or with others, to launch a military operation targeting those who are abusing human rights. This justification was used for operations in Haiti in 1994, and a pattern of myriad human rights abuses undertaken by former Iraqi leader Saddam Hussein was one of many justifications made for the U.S. invasion of Iraq in 2003.

Nations sometimes try to convince rogue nations to cease their human rights violations through economic sanctions, such as a ban on trade. This was used in the 1980s to force the nation of South Africa to change its policy of apartheid. Although exceptions are generally made to allow for trade for food and medical supplies so as to prevent a humanitarian crisis, the lack of trade puts economic pressure on a nation's leaders, in hopes of making the leaders reconsider whether the offending policy is really in their best interest. Sanctions are generally only effective if everyone participates. It's important to remember that sanctions impose a cost on the ones doing the sanctioning (in our example, the businesses refusing to sell to you also lose the money they would make from you). Many governments, because of the pressure put on them by their people, may choose to not join sanctions but rather maintain their trade.

Another legal remedy for addressing violations of international human rights law is for those who have been victims of human rights abuses filing a lawsuit against

---

10. A list of these, as well as links to the text, can be found on the web page for the United Nations High Commission for Human Rights, http://www.ohchr.org/EN/ProfessionalInterest/Pages/CoreInstruments.aspx See also the United Nation Secretary-General's 2009 Report (A/63/677) on Implementing the Responsibility to Protect http://www.un.org/en/ga/search/view_doc.asp?symbol=A/63/677.

11. See, as but one example, President John F. Kennedy's Proclamation 3508—Bill of Rights Day Human Rights Day, November 28, 1962, available at http://www.presidency.ucsb.edu/ws/?pid=24051.

the persons and nations who harmed them. This is the same idea behind a common lawsuit where people sue other people asking for money because of an injury. If a person commits acts of rape, murder, torture, and other gross violations of human rights, then in addition to being prosecuted (if that option is available), that person can also, in theory, be sued.

Now, international human rights law is a body of law by which governments have agreed that their government officials will act in a certain way toward their citizens and others who fall under their jurisdiction. So, almost by definition, when human rights are violated it was some government official who did the violating. Normally, there is a prohibition against anyone suing governments or government officials for acts committed as a part of official duties. This concept is known as "sovereign immunity." However, Congress (acting as "the sovereign") has enacted some laws waiving this immunity, creating exceptions to this rule.[12] To allow people to sue for harm caused to them by violations of international law committed by individuals who are not members of the U.S. government, the first Congress enacted the Alien Tort Statute (ATS).[13] The ATS states:

> "The district courts shall have original jurisdiction of any civil action by an alien for a tort only, committed in violation of the law of nations or a treaty of the United States."

Before explaining what the ATS does for human rights, let's go over a little history. Shortly after the ratification of the U.S. Constitution, one of the first acts of Congress was the passage of the Judiciary Act which, pursuant to Congress's constitutional authority, created the federal courts other than the Supreme Court and gave those courts jurisdiction over a variety of issues — admiralty, patents, and cases where non-citizens have suffered a harm committed in violation of "the law of nations." Now, there are few records of why each provision was included in this early law, but one theory is that the newly created United States waived its sovereign immunity and opened itself up to potential lawsuits in order to encourage other nations to form both diplomatic and trade relations with the U.S. It was a sign that this newly formed nation was agreeing to abide by customary international law in its dealings with other nations. "The law of nations" referred to the body of international law that existed at the time the U.S. was founded because, quite simply, we had no treaties with anyone yet except for the peace treaty with Great Britain following our independence.

As a practical matter, though, this law was almost never used until well after the Second World War and after the acceptance by many nations of the various human rights treaties. Because the "law of nations" now includes human rights abuses, this meant, in theory, that the ATS could possibly be used as the basis to bring about a lawsuit in federal courts for human rights abuses.

---

12. See, for example 11 U.S. Code sec. 106.
13. 28 U.S. Code sec. 1350.

In the following case, this theory was the basis for a lawsuit involving human rights abuses in Paraguay. The plaintiff, Filartiga, alleged that Pena-Irala, who had been a senior official of the Paraguayan police, had tortured and murdered his son as a form of retaliation against him for his political activities against the Paraguayan government.

Filartiga v. Pena-Irala, 630 F.2d 876 (1980)*

Upon ratification of the Constitution, the thirteen former colonies were fused into a single nation, one which, in its relations with foreign states, was bound both to observe and construe the accepted norms of international law, formerly known as the law of nations. Under the Articles of Confederation, the several states had interpreted and applied this body of doctrine as a part of their common law, but with the founding of the "more perfect Union" of 1789, the law of nations became preeminently a federal concern.

Implementing the constitutional mandate for national control over foreign relations, the First Congress passed the Alien Tort Statute giving the federal district courts jurisdiction over "all causes where an alien sues for a tort only (committed) in violation of the law of nations." [W]e hold that deliberate torture perpetrated under color of official authority violates universally accepted norms of the international law of human rights, regardless of the nationality of the parties. Thus, whenever an alleged torturer is found and served with process by an alien within our borders, [this law] provides federal jurisdiction.

The appellants, plaintiffs below, are citizens of the Republic of Paraguay. Dr. Joel Filartiga, a physician, describes himself as a longstanding opponent of the government of President Alfredo Stroessner, which has held power in Paraguay since 1954. His daughter, Dolly Filartiga, arrived in the United States in 1978 under a visitor's visa, and has since applied for permanent political asylum. The Filartigas brought this action in federal district court against Amerigo Norberto Pena-Irala (Pena), also a citizen of Paraguay, for wrongfully causing the death of Dr. Filartiga's seventeen-year old son, Joelito. For the purposes of this appeal from the federal district court, we . . . accept as true the allegations by the Filartigas concerning the harm they allege to have suffered.

The appellants contend that on March 29, 1976, Joelito Filartiga was kidnapped and tortured to death by Pena, who was then Inspector General of Police in Asuncion, Paraguay. Later that day, the police brought Dolly Filartiga to Pena's home where she was confronted with the body of her brother, which evidenced marks of severe torture. . . . The Filartigas claim that Joelito was tortured and killed in retaliation for his father's political activities and beliefs against the government.

Shortly thereafter, Dr. Filartiga commenced a criminal action in the Paraguayan courts against Pena and the police for the murder of his son. As a result, Dr. Filartiga's attorney was arrested and brought to police headquarters where, shackled to a

---

* The case has been heavily edited and paraphrased by the authors for clarity. See disclaimer in introduction.

wall, Pena threatened him with death. This attorney, it is alleged, has since been disbarred without just cause.

In July of 1978, Pena sold his house in Paraguay and entered the United States under a visitor's visa. He was accompanied by Juana Bautista Fernandez Villalba, who had lived with him in Paraguay. The couple remained in the United States beyond the term of their visas, and were living in Brooklyn, New York, when Dolly Filartiga, who was then living in Washington, D.C., learned of their presence. Acting on information provided by Dolly the Immigration and Naturalization Service arrested Pena and his companion, both of whom were subsequently ordered deported . . .

Almost immediately, Dolly caused Pena to be served with a summons and civil complaint to initiate a lawsuit at the Brooklyn Navy Yard, where he was being held pending deportation. The complaint alleged that Pena had wrongfully caused Joelito's death by torture and sought compensatory and punitive damages of $10,000,000. The cause of action is stated as arising under "wrongful death statutes; the U.N. Charter; the Universal Declaration on Human Rights; the U.N. Declaration Against Torture; the American Declaration of the Rights and Duties of Man; and other pertinent declarations, documents and practices constituting the customary international law of human rights and the law of nations," as well as 28 U.S.C. § 1350, Article II, sec. 2 and the Supremacy Clause of the U. S. Constitution. Jurisdiction, which is the authority and right of the court to hear the claims of these alleged violations of customary international law, is claimed under the Alien Tort Statute.

Appellants rest their principal argument in support of federal jurisdiction upon the Alien Tort Statute, 28 U.S.C. § 1350, which provides:

> "The district courts shall have original jurisdiction of any civil action by an alien for a tort only, committed in violation of the law of nations or a treaty of the United States."

Since appellants do not contend that their action arises directly under a treaty of the United States, to even know if a U.S. federal district court has jurisdiction we must ask if the conduct alleged violates the law of nations. In light of the universal condemnation of torture in numerous international agreements, and the renunciation of torture as an instrument of official policy by virtually all of the nations of the world (in principle if not in practice), we find that an act of torture committed by a state official against one held in detention violates established norms of the international law of human rights, and hence the customary law of nations.

The Supreme Court has enumerated the appropriate sources of international law. The law of nations "may be ascertained by consulting the works of jurists, writing professedly on public law; or by the general usage and practice of nations; or by judicial decisions recognizing and enforcing that law." *The Paquete Habana* (1900) reaffirmed that

> where there is no treaty, and no controlling executive or legislative act or judicial decision, resort must be had to the customs and usages of civilized nations; and, as evidence of these, to the works of jurists and commentators,

who by years of labor, research and experience, have made themselves peculiarly well acquainted with the subjects of which they treat. Such works are resorted to by judicial tribunals, not for the speculations of their authors concerning what the law ought to be, but for trustworthy evidence of what the law really is.

Modern international sources confirm the propriety of this approach.

Habana is particularly instructive for present purposes, for it held that the traditional prohibition against seizure of an enemy's coastal fishing vessels during wartime, a standard that began as one of comity only, had ripened over the preceding century into "a settled rule of international law" by "the general assent of civilized nations." Thus it is clear that courts must interpret international law not as it was in 1789, but as it has evolved and exists among the nations of the world today.

The requirement that a rule command "the general assent of civilized nations" to become binding upon them all is a stringent one. Were this not so, the courts of one nation might feel free to impose idiosyncratic legal rules upon others, in the name of applying international law. [For this reason], in *Banco Nacional de Cuba v. Sabbatino* (1964), the U.S. Supreme Court declined to pass judgment on the legality of the Cuban government's nationalization of foreign-owned interests within Cuba, noting the sharply contrasting views on the issue [held by different nations]. This case [with Filartiga presents us with a situation which is different] than the conflicted state of law that confronted the *Sabbatino* Court [involving Cuba's nationalization of foreign-owned interests within Cuba]. Indeed, to paraphrase that Court's statement, there are few, if any, issues in international law today on which opinion seems to be so united as the limitations on a state's power to torture persons held in its custody.

The United Nations Charter (a treaty of the United States) makes it clear that in this modern age a state's treatment of its own citizens is a matter of international concern. It provides:

> With a view to the creation of conditions of stability and well-being which are necessary for peaceful and friendly relations among nations ... the United Nations shall promote ... universal respect for, and observance of, human rights and fundamental freedoms for all without distinctions as to race, sex, language or religion. Art. 55.

And further:

> All members pledge themselves to take joint and separate action in cooperation with the Organization for the achievement of the purposes set forth in Article 55. Art. 56.

Although there is no universal agreement as to the precise extent of the "human rights and fundamental freedoms" guaranteed to all by the Charter, there is at present no dissent from the view that the guaranties include, at a bare minimum, the right to be free from torture. This prohibition has become part of customary international law, as evidenced and defined by the Universal Declaration of Human Rights,

General Assembly Resolution 217(III)A (Dec. 10, 1948) which states, in the plainest of terms, "no one shall be subjected to torture."

The General Assembly has declared that the Charter precepts embodied in this Universal Declaration "constitute basic principles of international law." Particularly relevant is the [1975 UN General Assembly] Declaration on the Protection of All Persons from Being Subjected to Torture which expressly prohibits any state from permitting the dastardly and totally inhuman act of torture. Torture, in turn, is defined as "any act by which severe pain and suffering, whether physical or mental, is intentionally inflicted by or at the instigation of a public official on a person for such purposes as . . . intimidating him or other persons."

The Declaration goes on to provide that "where it is proved that an act of torture or other cruel, inhuman or degrading treatment or punishment has been committed by or at the instigation of a public official, the victim shall be afforded redress and compensation, in accordance with national law."

These U.N. declarations are significant because they specify with great precision the obligations of member nations under the Charter. Since their adoption, members can no longer contend that they do not know what human rights they promised in the Charter to promote. Moreover, a U.N. Declaration is, according to one authoritative definition, "a formal and solemn instrument, suitable for rare occasions when principles of great and lasting importance are being enunciated." Accordingly, it has been observed that the Universal Declaration of Human Rights "no longer fits into the dichotomy of 'binding treaty' against 'non-binding pronouncement,' but is rather an authoritative statement of the international community." Thus, a Declaration creates an expectation of adherence, and "insofar as the expectation is gradually justified by State practice, a declaration may by custom become recognized as laying down rules binding upon the States." Indeed, several commentators have concluded that the Universal Declaration has become a part of binding, customary international law.

Turning to the act of torture, we have little difficulty discerning its universal renunciation in the modern usage and practice of nations. The international consensus surrounding torture has found expression in numerous international treaties and accords . . . The substance of these international agreements is reflected in modern national law as well. Although torture was once a routine concomitant of criminal interrogations in many nations, during the modern and hopefully more enlightened era it has been universally renounced. According to one survey, torture is prohibited, expressly or implicitly, by the constitutions of over fifty-five nations, including both the United States and Paraguay . . . Our State Department reports a general recognition of this principle:

> There now exists an international consensus that recognizes basic human rights and obligations owed by all governments to their citizens. There is no doubt that these rights are often violated; but virtually all governments acknowledge their validity. We have been directed to no assertion by any contemporary state of a right to torture its own or another nation's citizens.

Indeed, United States diplomatic contacts confirm the universal abhorrence with which torture is viewed.

In exchanges between United States embassies and all foreign states with which the United States maintains relations, it has been the Department of State's general experience that no government has asserted a right to torture its own nationals. Where reports of torture elicit some credence, a state usually responds by denial or, less frequently, by asserting that the conduct was unauthorized or constituted rough treatment short of torture.

Having examined the sources from which customary international law is derived the usage of nations, judicial opinions and the works of jurists, we conclude that official torture is now prohibited by the law of nations. The prohibition is clear and unambiguous, and admits of no distinction between treatment of aliens and citizens. . . . The treaties and accords cited above, as well as the express foreign policy of our own government, all make it clear that international law confers fundamental rights upon all people vis-a-vis their own governments. While the ultimate scope of those rights will be a subject for continuing refinement and elaboration, we hold that the right to be free from torture is now among them . . .

In the twentieth century the international community has come to recognize the common danger posed by the flagrant disregard of basic human rights and particularly the right to be free of torture. Spurred first by the Great War, and then the Second World War, civilized nations have banded together to prescribe acceptable norms of international behavior. From the ashes of the Second World War arose the United Nations Organization, amid hopes that an era of peace and cooperation had at last begun. Though many of these aspirations have remained elusive goals, circumstances cannot diminish that in many areas, true progress that has been made in the field of human rights. In the modern age, humanitarian and practical considerations have combined to lead the nations of the world to recognize that respect for fundamental human rights is in their individual and collective interest.

Among the rights universally proclaimed by all nations, as we have noted, is the right to be free of physical torture. Indeed, for purposes of civil liability, the torturer has become like the pirate and slave trader before him an enemy of all mankind. Our holding today, giving effect to a jurisdictional provision enacted by our First Congress, is a small but important step in the fulfillment of the ageless dream to free all people from brutal violence.

END OF OPINION

Pursuant to the decision of this case, and others like it, relying on the Alien Tort Statute, the U.S. claimed global jurisdiction over human rights abuses and, we can presume, over all crimes against humanity. If gross violations of human rights take place in a foreign country by persons who have no legal connection to the U.S., the courts have subject-matter jurisdiction over their actions (of course, these people still need to be brought within the personal jurisdiction of the court).

Not all violations of international law give rise to a claim to sue under the Alien Tort Statute. Only gross violations of human rights (i.e., torture and murder) or long-standing and traditional violations of international law (i.e., piracy, free passage to diplomats) can be the basis of a lawsuit under the Alien Tort Statute. This is explained in the following case.

<u>Sosa v. Alvarez-Machain, 542 U.S. 692 (2004)</u>*

The two issues are whether respondent Alvarez-Machain's allegation that the Drug Enforcement Administration instigated his abduction from Mexico for criminal trial in the United States supports a claim against the Government under the Federal Tort Claims Act (FTCA) and whether he may recover under the Alien Tort Statute (ATS). We hold that he is not entitled to a remedy under either statute.

In 1985, an agent of the Drug Enforcement Administration (DEA), Enrique Camarena-Salazar, was captured on assignment in Mexico and taken to a house in Guadalajara, where he was tortured over the course of a 2-day interrogation, then murdered. Based in part on eyewitness testimony, DEA officials in the United States came to believe that respondent Humberto Alvarez-Machain (Alvarez), a Mexican physician, was present at the house and used his knowledge as a medical doctor to prolong the agent's life in order to extend the interrogation and torture.

In 1990, a federal grand jury indicted Alvarez for the torture and murder of Camarena-Salazar, and the United States District Court for the Central District of California issued a warrant for his arrest. The DEA asked the Mexican Government for help in getting Alvarez into the United States, but when the requests and negotiations proved fruitless, the DEA approved a plan to hire Mexican nationals to seize Alvarez and bring him to the United States for trial. As planned by the DEA, a group of Mexicans abducted Alvarez from his house, held him overnight in a motel, and brought him by private plane to El Paso, Texas, where he was arrested by federal officers.

Once in American custody, Alvarez moved to dismiss the charges on the ground that his seizure was "outrageous governmental conduct," and violated the extradition treaty between the United States and Mexico. [The courts hearing and reviewing the case held that it was irrelevant how he got into the custody of the U.S.; the fact remained he was in U.S. jurisdiction at the moment, so he could be prosecuted for his alleged crimes. He faced a trial for his role in the torture of the DEA agent, but was acquitted, and he returned to Mexico.]

In 1993, after returning to Mexico, Alvarez began the civil action before us here. He sued [those involved for his abduction into the U.S., including the DEA] . . . Alvarez sought damages from the United States . . . alleging false arrest and . . . for a violation of the law of nations. [The ATS] provides in its entirety that "the district courts shall have original jurisdiction of any civil action by an alien for a tort only, committed in violation of the law of nations or a treaty of the United States."

---

* The case has been heavily edited and paraphrased by the authors for clarity. See disclaimer in introduction.

The District Court ... awarded summary judgment and $25,000 in damages to Alvarez on the ATS claim. A three-judge panel of the Ninth Circuit then affirmed the ATS judgment ... As for the ATS claim, the court called on its own precedent, "that the ATS not only provides federal courts with subject matter jurisdiction, but also creates a cause of action for an alleged violation of the law of nations." The Circuit then relied upon what it called the "clear and universally recognized norm prohibiting arbitrary arrest and detention," to support the conclusion that Alvarez's arrest amounted to a tort in violation of international law.... [T]he Ninth Circuit held that, because "the DEA had no authority to effect Alvarez's arrest and detention in Mexico," the United States was liable to him under California law for the tort of false arrest.

We granted [review of these cases] to clarify the scope ... of the ATS. We now reverse.

At the time of its enactment, the ATS enabled federal courts to hear claims in a very limited category defined by the law of nations and recognized at common law. We do not believe that the ATS's authority to entertain only a handful of international law claims understood in 1789 should be taken as authority to recognize the claims asserted by Alvarez. As enacted in 1789, the ATS gave the district courts the power to hear certain causes of action. This was a limited power to hear only certain cases, and did not give them the power to mold the law to expand the cases which they could hear.

When the United States declared their independence, they were bound to receive the law of nations ... These were traditional practices governing the behavior of nations. [At the time of the ATS, they had in mind] specific offenses against the law of nations already addressed by the criminal law of England: violation of safe conducts, infringement of the rights of ambassadors, and piracy. An assault against an ambassador, for example, impinged upon the sovereignty of the foreign nation and if not adequately redressed could rise to an issue of war. It was this narrow set of violations of the law of nations, admitting of a judicial remedy and at the same time threatening serious consequences in international affairs, which was probably on minds of the men who drafted the ATS with its reference to tort.

Before there was any ATS ... the Continental Congress was hamstrung by its inability to "cause infractions of treaties, or of the law of nations to be punished." Appreciation of the Continental Congress's incapacity to deal with this class of cases was intensified by the so-called Marbois incident of May 1784, in which a French adventurer, Longchamps, verbally and physically assaulted the Secretary of the French Legion in Philadelphia. Congress called repeatedly for state legislation addressing such matters, and concern over the inadequate vindication of the law of nations persisted through the time of the constitutional convention ...

The Framers responded by writing the Constitution vesting the Supreme Court with original jurisdiction over "all Cases affecting Ambassadors, other public ministers and Consuls." U.S. Const., Art. III, § 2. The Judiciary Act reinforced this Court's original jurisdiction over suits brought by diplomats, created alienage jurisdiction, and, of course, included the ATS.

There is no record of congressional discussion about private actions that might be subject to the jurisdictional provision, or about any need for further legislation to create private remedies; there is no record even of debate on the section. Given the lack of drafting history to give us guidance as to exactly what they intended when they wrote the ATS, and despite considerable scholarly attention, it is fair to say that a consensus understanding of what Congress intended has proven elusive.

Still, the history does tend to support two propositions. First, there is every reason to suppose that the First Congress did not pass the ATS as a jurisdictional convenience to be placed on the shelf for use by a future Congress or state legislature that might, some day, authorize the creation of causes of action or itself decide to make some element of the law of nations actionable for the benefit of foreigners. The anxieties of the preconstitutional period cannot be ignored easily enough to think that the statute was not meant to have a practical effect . . . Consider . . . that the First Congress was attentive enough to the law of nations to recognize certain offenses expressly as criminal . . . murder, or robbery, or other capital crimes, punishable as piracy if committed on the high seas and violation of safe conducts and assaults against ambassadors punished by imprisonment and fines described as "infractions of the law of nations". It would have been passing strange for this very Congress to vest federal courts expressly with jurisdiction to entertain civil causes brought by aliens alleging violations of the law of nations, but to no effect whatever until the Congress should take further action to incorporate international law by passing additional domestic law. There is too much in the historical record to believe that Congress would have enacted the ATS only to leave it lying powerless indefinitely.

The second inference to be drawn from the history is that Congress intended the ATS to furnish jurisdiction for a limited set of actions alleging violations of the law of nations. Uppermost in the legislative mind appears to have been offenses against ambassadors, violations of safe conduct, and individual actions arising out of prize captures and piracy. These are violations which concern nations as a whole, rather than mere individuals seeking relief in court.

In sum, although the ATS is a jurisdictional statute creating no new causes of action, the reasonable inference from the historical materials is that the statute was intended to have practical effect the moment it became law. The jurisdictional grant is best read as having been enacted on the understanding that the common law would provide a cause of action for the modest number of international law violations with a potential for personal liability at the time.

We think it is correct, then, to assume that the First Congress understood that the district courts would recognize private causes of action for certain torts in violation of the law of nations, though we have found no basis to suspect Congress had any examples in mind beyond those torts corresponding to the following three primary offenses: violation of safe conducts, infringement of the rights of ambassadors, and piracy. We assume, too, that no development in the two centuries from the enactment of [the ATS] to the birth of the modern line of cases beginning with *Filartiga v. Pena-Irala* has categorically precluded federal courts from recognizing a claim under the law of nations as an element of common law; Congress has not in any relevant way amended the ATS. Still, there are good reasons for a restrained conception of the discretion a federal court should exercise in considering a new cause of action of this kind. Accordingly, we think courts should require any claim based on the present-day law of nations to rest on a norm of international character accepted by the civilized world and defined with a specificity comparable to the features of the 18th-century paradigms we have recognized, such as modern day prohibitions against torture, murder, or the use of weapons of mass destruction against innocent civilians. This requirement is fatal to Alvarez's claim.

We are very reluctant to create new private causes of action under the ATS. We have no congressional mandate to seek out and define new and debatable violations of the law of nations, and modern indications of congressional understanding of the judicial role in the field have not affirmatively encouraged greater judicial creativity. There are some exceptions; for example, there is a clear mandate which appears in the Torture Victim Protection Act of 1991, providing authority that "establishes an unambiguous and modern basis for" federal claims of torture and extrajudicial killing. But that affirmative authority is confined to specific subject matter, and although the legislative history includes the remark that § 1350 should "remain intact to permit suits based on other norms that already exist or may ripen in the future into rules of customary international law," Congress as a body has done nothing to promote such suits. Several times, indeed, the Senate has expressly declined to give the federal courts the task of interpreting and applying international human rights law, as when its ratification of the International Covenant on Civil and Political Rights declared that the substantive provisions of the document were not self-executing. These reasons argue for great caution in adapting the law of nations to private rights.

While we would welcome any congressional guidance in exercising jurisdiction with such obvious potential to affect foreign relations, nothing Congress has done is a reason for us to shut the door to the law of nations entirely. It is enough to say that Congress may do that at any time (explicitly, or implicitly by treaties or statutes that occupy the field) just as it may modify or cancel any judicial decision so far as it rests on recognizing an international norm as such.

We must [therefore], derive a standard or set of standards for assessing the particular claim Alvarez raises, and for this case it suffices to look to the historical antecedents. Whatever the ultimate criteria for accepting a cause of action subject to jurisdiction under the ATS, we are persuaded that federal courts should not recognize private claims under for violations of any international law norm with less definite content and acceptance among civilized nations than the historical paradigms familiar when the ATS was enacted. For example, *United States v. Smith*, illustrates the specificity with which the law of nations defined piracy. This limit upon judicial recognition is generally consistent with the reasoning of many of the courts and judges who faced the issue before it reached this Court. In *Filartiga v. Pena-Irala*, it was stated that "For purposes of civil liability, the torturer has become—like the pirate and slave trader before him—*hostis humani generis*, an enemy of all mankind."

In *Tel-Oren v. Libyan Arab Republic*, a concurring opinion suggests that the limits of the ATS's reach are defined by "a handful of heinous actions—each of which violates definable, universal and obligatory norms." Other opinions have reinforced this idea, such as *In re Estate of Marcos Human Rights Litigation*, where it was stated that "Actionable violations of international law must be of a norm that is specific, universal, and obligatory." T]he determination whether a norm is sufficiently definite to support a cause of action should (and, indeed, inevitably must) involve an element of judgment about the practical consequences of making that cause available to litigants in the federal courts.

Thus, Alvarez's detention claim must be gauged against the current state of international law, looking to those sources we have long, albeit cautiously, recognized. As stated in *The Paquete Habana*, "Where there is no treaty, and no controlling executive or legislative act or judicial decision, resort must be had to the customs and usages of civilized nations; and, as evidence of these, to the works of jurists and commentators, who by years of labor, research and experience, have made themselves peculiarly well acquainted with the subjects of which they treat. Such works are resorted to by judicial tribunals, not for the speculations of their authors concerning what the law ought to be, but for trustworthy evidence of what the law really is."

To begin with, Alvarez cites two well-known international agreements that, despite their moral authority, have little utility under the standard set out in this opinion. He says that his abduction by Sosa was an "arbitrary arrest" within the meaning of the Universal Declaration of Human Rights (Declaration). And he traces the rule against arbitrary arrest not only to the Declaration, but also to article nine of the International Covenant on Civil and Political Rights (Covenant), to which the United States is a party, and to various other conventions to which it is not. But the Declaration does not of its own force impose obligations as a matter of international law. As stated by Eleanor Roosevelt, the Universal Declaration of Human Rights is "a statement of principles . . . setting up a common standard of achievement for all peoples and all nations'" and "'not a treaty or international agreement . . . imposing legal obligations." And, although the Covenant does bind the United States as a matter of international law, the United States ratified the Covenant on the express understanding that it was not self-executing and so did not itself create obligations enforceable in the federal courts. Accordingly, Alvarez cannot say that the Declaration and Covenant themselves establish the relevant and applicable rule of international law. He instead attempts to show that prohibition of arbitrary arrest has attained the status of binding customary international law.

Here, it is useful to examine Alvarez's complaint in greater detail. As he presently argues it, the claim does not rest on the cross-border feature of his abduction. Although the lower court granted relief in part on finding a violation of international law in taking Alvarez across the border from Mexico to the United States, the Court of Appeals rejected that ground of liability for failure to identify a norm of requisite force prohibiting a forcible abduction across a border. Instead, it relied on the conclusion that the law of the United States did not authorize Alvarez's arrest, because the DEA lacked extraterritorial authority and because Federal Rule of Criminal Procedure 4(d)(2) limited the warrant for Alvarez's arrest to "the jurisdiction of the United States." It is this position that Alvarez takes now: that his arrest was arbitrary and as such forbidden by international law not because it infringed the prerogatives of Mexico, but because no applicable law authorized it.

Whether or not this is an accurate reading of the Covenant, Alvarez cites little authority that a rule so broad has the status of a binding customary norm today. He certainly cites nothing to justify the federal courts in taking his broad rule as the predicate for a federal lawsuit, for its implications would be breathtaking.... His rule would support a cause of action under the ATS for any arrest, anywhere in the world, unauthorized by the law of the jurisdiction in which it took place, replacing domestic laws such as the Fourth Amendment which already provide for such violation. It would create a cause of action in federal court for arrests by state officers who simply exceed their authority; and for the violation of any limit that the law of any country might place on the authority of its own officers to arrest.

Whatever may be said for the broad principle Alvarez advances, in the present, imperfect world, it expresses an aspiration that exceeds any binding customary rule having the specificity we require. Creating a private cause of action to further that aspiration would go beyond any residual discretion we think it appropriate to exercise. It is enough to hold that a single illegal detention of less than a day, followed by the transfer of custody to lawful authorities and a prompt arraignment, violates no norm of customary international law so well defined as to support the creation of a remedy under the ATS.

The judgment of the Court of Appeals is Reversed.

END OF OPINION

So, while *Filartiga* indicated that the ATS could be a useful tool for victims to seek a legal remedy, *Alvarez-Machain* limited that usefulness where the injury was not incurred in what was seen as a clear violation of the law of nations, applicable within the United States.

This next case in our inquiry further limited the application of the ATS. The Kiobels were Nigerian nationals residing in the United States, who filed suit in federal court under the Alien Tort Statute, alleging that respondents—certain Dutch, British, and Nigerian corporations—aided and abetted the Nigerian Government in committing violations of the law of nations in Nigeria. In dismissing the complaint, the Second Circuit Court of Appeals had reasoned that the law of nations does not recognize corporate liability. Instead of focusing on this issue, the Supreme Court, in hearing the case, examined instead the extra-territorial effect of the law, whether and under what circumstances U.S. courts may recognize a cause of action under the ATS for violations of the law of nations occurring within the territory of a sovereign other than the United States.

The ATS provides that "[t]he district courts shall have original jurisdiction of any civil action by an alien for a tort only, committed in violation of the law of nations or a treaty of the United States." The Supreme Court held that a presumption against extraterritoriality applies to all U.S. law, including claims under the ATS, and, since nothing in the language of the statute rebuts that presumption, the ATS would not apply to actions that arose outside of the United States.

Kiobel v. Royal Dutch Petroleum Co., 133 S.Ct. 1659 (2013)*

CHIEF JUSTICE ROBERTS delivered the opinion of the Court.

Petitioners, a group of Nigerian nationals residing in the United States, filed suit in federal court against certain Dutch, British, and Nigerian corporations. Petitioners sued under the Alien Tort Statute, 28 U. S. C. § 1350, alleging that the corporations aided and abetted the Nigerian Government in committing violations of the law of nations in Nigeria. The question presented is whether and under what circumstances courts may recognize a cause of action under the Alien Tort Statute, for violations of the law of nations occurring within the territory of a sovereign other than the United States.

Petitioners were residents of Ogoniland, an area of 250 square miles located in the Niger delta area of Nigeria and populated by roughly half a million people. When the complaint was filed, respondents Royal Dutch Petroleum Company and Shell Transport and Trading Company, p.l.c., were holding companies incorporated in the Netherlands and England, respectively. Their joint subsidiary, respondent Shell Petroleum Development Company of Nigeria, Ltd. (SPDC), was incorporated in Nigeria, and engaged in oil exploration and production in Ogoniland. According to the complaint, after concerned residents of Ogoniland began protesting the environmental effects of SPDC's practices, respondents enlisted the Nigerian Government to violently suppress the burgeoning demonstrations. Throughout the early 1990's, the complaint alleges, Nigerian military and police forces attacked Ogoni villages, beating, raping, killing, and arresting residents and destroying or looting property. Petitioners further allege that respondents aided and abetted these atrocities by, among other things, providing the Nigerian forces with food, transportation, and compensation, as well as by allowing the Nigerian military to use respondents' property as a staging ground for attacks.

Following the alleged atrocities, petitioners moved to the United States where they have been granted political asylum and now reside as legal residents. See Supp. Brief for Petitioners 3, and n. 2. They filed suit in the United States District Court for the Southern District of New York, alleging jurisdiction under the Alien Tort Statute and requesting relief under customary international law. The ATS provides, in full, that "[t]he district courts shall have original jurisdiction of any civil action by an alien for a tort only, committed in violation of the law of nations or a treaty of the United States." According to petitioners, respondents violated the law of nations by aiding and abetting the Nigerian Government in committing (1) extrajudicial killings;

---

* The case has been heavily edited and paraphrased by the authors for clarity. See disclaimer in introduction.

(2) crimes against humanity; (3) torture and cruel treatment; (4) arbitrary arrest and detention; (5) violations of the rights to life, liberty, security, and association; (6) forced exile; and (7) property destruction. The District Court dismissed the first, fifth, sixth, and seventh claims, reasoning that the facts alleged to support those claims did not give rise to a violation of the law of nations. The court denied respondents' motion to dismiss with respect to the remaining claims, but certified its order for interlocutory appeal.

The Second Circuit dismissed the entire complaint, reasoning that the law of nations does not recognize corporate liability. . . . After oral argument, we directed the parties to file supplemental briefs addressing an additional question: "Whether and under what circumstances the [ATS] allows courts to recognize a cause of action for violations of the law of nations occurring within the territory of a sovereign other than the United States." We heard oral argument again and now affirm the judgment below, based on our answer to the second question.

Passed as part of the Judiciary Act of 1789, the ATS was invoked twice in the late 18th century, but then only once more over the next 167 years. The statute provides district courts with jurisdiction to hear certain claims, but does not expressly provide any causes of action. We held in *Sosa v. Alvarez-Machain* (2004), however, that the First Congress did not intend the provision to be "stillborn." The grant of jurisdiction is instead "best read as having been enacted on the understanding that the common law would provide a cause of action for [a] modest number of international law violations." We thus held that federal courts may "recognize private claims [for such violations] under federal common law." The Court in *Sosa* rejected the plaintiff 's claim in that case for "arbitrary arrest and detention," on the ground that it failed to state a violation of the law of nations with the requisite "definite content and acceptance among civilized nations."

The question here is not whether petitioners have stated a proper claim under the ATS, but whether a claim may reach conduct occurring in the territory of a foreign sovereign. Respondents contend that claims under the ATS do not, relying primarily on a canon of statutory interpretation known as the presumption against extraterritorial application. That canon provides that "[w]hen a statute gives no clear indication of an extraterritorial application, it has none," and reflects the "presumption that United States law governs domestically but does not rule the world." This presumption "serves to protect against unintended clashes between our laws and those of other nations which could result in international discord." As this Court has explained:

> "For us to run interference in . . . a delicate field of international relations there must be present the affirmative intention of the Congress clearly expressed. It alone has the facilities necessary to make fairly such an important policy decision where the possibilities of international discord are so evident and retaliative action so certain." . . . The presumption against extraterritorial application helps ensure that the Judiciary does not erroneously adopt an interpretation of U.S. law that carries foreign policy consequences not clearly intended by the political branches.

We typically apply the presumption to discern whether an Act of Congress regulating conduct applies abroad. The ATS, on the other hand, is "strictly jurisdictional." It does not directly regulate conduct or afford relief. It instead allows federal courts to recognize certain causes of action based on sufficiently definite norms of international law. But we think the principles underlying the canon of interpretation similarly constrain courts considering causes of action that may be brought under the ATS.

Indeed, the danger of unwarranted judicial interference in the conduct of foreign policy is magnified in the context of the ATS, because the question is not what Congress has done but instead what courts may do. This Court in *Sosa* repeatedly stressed the need for judicial caution in considering which claims could be brought under the ATS, in light of foreign policy concerns. As the Court explained, "the potential [foreign policy] implications... of recognizing... causes [under the ATS] should make courts particularly wary of impinging on the discretion of the Legislative and Executive Branches in managing foreign affairs."... "Since many attempts by federal courts to craft remedies for the violation of new norms of international law would raise risks of adverse foreign policy consequences, they should be undertaken, if at all, with great caution. The possible collateral consequences of making international rules privately actionable argue for judicial caution". These concerns... are all the more pressing when the question is whether a cause of action under the ATS reaches conduct within the territory of another sovereign.

These concerns are not diminished by the fact that *Sosa* limited federal courts to recognizing causes of action only for alleged violations of international law norms that are "'specific, universal, and obligatory.'" As demonstrated by Congress's enactment of the Torture Victim Protection Act of 1991, identifying such a norm is only the beginning of defining a cause of action.... Each of these decisions carries with it significant foreign policy implications.

The principles underlying the presumption against extraterritoriality thus constrain courts exercising their power under the ATS.

Petitioners contend that even if the presumption applies, the text, history, and purposes of the ATS rebut it for causes of action brought under that statute. It is true that Congress, even in a jurisdictional provision, can indicate that it intends federal law to apply to conduct occurring abroad. See, e.g., 18 U. S. C. § 1091(e) (providing jurisdiction over the offense of genocide "regardless of where the offense is committed" if the alleged offender is, among other things, "present in the United States"). But to rebut the presumption, the ATS would need to evince a "clear indication of extraterritoriality." It does not.

To begin, nothing in the text of the statute suggests that Congress intended causes of action recognized under it to have extraterritorial reach. The ATS covers actions by aliens for violations of the law of nations, but that does not imply extraterritorial reach—such violations affecting aliens can occur either within or outside the United States. Nor does the fact that the text reaches "any civil action" suggest application to torts committed abroad; it is well established that generic terms like "any" or "every" do not rebut the presumption against extraterritoriality.

Petitioners make much of the fact that the ATS provides jurisdiction over civil actions for "torts" in violation of the law of nations. They claim that in using that word, the First Congress "necessarily meant to provide for jurisdiction over extraterritorial transitory torts that could arise on foreign soil." For support, they cite the common-law doctrine that allowed courts to assume jurisdiction over such "transitory torts," including actions for personal injury, arising abroad. Wherever, by either the common law or the statute law of a State, a right of action has become fixed and a legal liability incurred, that liability may be enforced and the right of action pursued in any court which has jurisdiction of such matters and can obtain jurisdiction of the parties.

The question under Sosa is not whether a federal court has jurisdiction to entertain a cause of action provided by foreign or even international law. The question is instead whether the court has authority to recognize a cause of action under U. S. law to enforce a norm of international law. The reference to "tort" does not demonstrate that the First Congress "necessarily meant" for those causes of action to reach conduct in the territory of a foreign sovereign. In the end, nothing in the text of the ATS evinces the requisite clear indication of extraterritoriality.

Nor does the historical background against which the ATS was enacted overcome the presumption against application to conduct in the territory of another sovereign. We explained in Sosa that when Congress passed the ATS, "three principal offenses against the law of nations" had been identified by Blackstone: violation of safe conducts, infringement of the rights of ambassadors, and piracy. The first two offenses have no necessary extraterritorial application. Indeed, Blackstone — in describing them — did so in terms of conduct occurring within the forum nation.

Two notorious episodes involving violations of the law of nations occurred in the United States shortly before passage of the ATS. Each concerned the rights of ambassadors, and each involved conduct within the Union. . . . The two cases in which the ATS was invoked shortly after its passage also concerned conduct within the territory of the United States. These prominent contemporary examples — immediately before and after passage of the ATS — provide no support for the proposition that Congress expected causes of action to be brought under the statute for violations of the law of nations occurring abroad.

The third example of a violation of the law of nations familiar to the Congress that enacted the ATS was piracy. Piracy typically occurs on the high seas, beyond the territorial jurisdiction of the United States or any other country. This Court has generally treated the high seas the same as foreign soil for purposes of the presumption against extraterritorial application. Petitioners contend that because Congress surely intended the ATS to provide jurisdiction for actions against pirates, it necessarily anticipated the statute would apply to all conduct occurring abroad.

Applying U.S. law to pirates, however, does not typically impose the sovereign will of the United States onto conduct occurring within the territorial jurisdiction of another sovereign, and therefore carries less direct foreign policy consequences. Pirates were fair game wherever found, by any nation, because they generally did not operate within any jurisdiction. We do not think that the existence of a cause of action against them is a sufficient basis for concluding that other causes of action under the ATS reach conduct that does occur within the territory of another sovereign; pirates may well be a category unto themselves.

Petitioners also point to a 1795 opinion authored by Attorney General William Bradford. In 1794, in the midst of war between France and Great Britain, and notwithstanding the American official policy of neutrality, several U.S. citizens joined a French privateer fleet and attacked and plundered the British colony of Sierra Leone. In response to a protest from the British Ambassador, Attorney General Bradford responded as follows:

> So far . . . as the transactions complained of originated or took place in a foreign country, they are not within the cognizance of our courts; nor can the actors be legally prosecuted or punished for them by the United States. But crimes committed on the high seas are within the jurisdiction of the . . . courts of the United States; and, so far as the offence was committed thereon, I am inclined to think that it may be legally prosecuted in . . . those courts. . . . But some doubt rests on this point, in consequence of the terms in which the [applicable criminal law] is expressed. But there can be no doubt that the company or individuals who have been injured by these acts of hostility have a remedy by a civil suit in the courts of the United States; jurisdiction being expressly given to these courts in all cases where an alien sues for a tort only, in violation of the laws of nations, or a treaty of the United States. . . ." Id., at 58–59.

Attorney General Bradford's opinion defies a definitive reading and we need not adopt one here. Whatever its precise meaning, it deals with U.S. citizens who, by participating in an attack taking place both on the high seas and on a foreign shore, violated a treaty between the United States and Great Britain. The opinion hardly suffices to counter the weighty concerns underlying the presumption against extraterritoriality.

Finally, there is no indication that the ATS was passed to make the United States a uniquely hospitable forum for the enforcement of international norms. As Justice Story put it, "No nation has ever yet pretended to be the *custos morum* of the whole world. . . ." It is implausible to suppose that the First Congress wanted their fledgling Republic — struggling to receive international recognition — to be the first. Indeed, the parties offer no evidence that any nation, meek or mighty, presumed to do such a thing.

The United States was, however, embarrassed by its potential inability to provide judicial relief to foreign officials injured in the United States. Such offenses against ambassadors violated the law of nations, "and if not adequately redressed could rise to an issue of war." . . . The ATS ensured that the United States could provide a forum for adjudicating such incidents. Nothing about this historical context suggests that Congress also intended federal common law under the ATS to provide a cause of action for conduct occurring in the territory of another sovereign.

Indeed, far from avoiding diplomatic strife, providing such a cause of action could have generated it. Recent experience bears this out. See *Doe v. Exxon Mobil Corp.* (CADC 2011) (Kavanaugh, J., dissenting in part) (listing recent objections to extraterritorial applications of the ATS by Canada, Germany, Indonesia, Papua New Guinea, South Africa, Switzerland, and the United Kingdom). Moreover, accepting petitioners' view would imply that other nations, also applying the law of nations, could hale our citizens into their courts for alleged violations of the law of nations occurring in the United States, or anywhere else in the world. The presumption against extraterritoriality guards against our courts triggering such serious foreign policy consequences, and instead defers such decisions, quite appropriately, to the political branches.

We therefore conclude that the presumption against extraterritoriality applies to claims under the ATS, and that nothing in the statute rebuts that presumption. "[T]here is no clear indication of extraterritoriality here," and petitioners' case seeking relief for violations of the law of nations occurring outside the United States is barred.

On these facts, all the relevant conduct took place outside the United States. And even where the claims touch and concern the territory of the United States, they must do so with sufficient force to displace the presumption against extraterritorial application. Corporations are often present in many countries, and it would reach too far to say that mere corporate presence suffices. If Congress were to determine otherwise, a statute more specific than the ATS would be required.

The judgment of the Court of Appeals is affirmed.

END OF OPINION

While *Filartiga v. Pena-Irala* stands for the idea that the Alien Tort Statute gives U.S. courts jurisdiction to hear violations of international law, *Sosa v. Alvarez-Machain* stands for the idea that the courts are limited as to just which violations of international law they can hear. *Kiobel* clearly holds that the ATS is a jurisdictional statute but that it does NOT provide the underlying cause of action. So, just which wrongs give rise to a claim that can be heard in U.S. courts? The answer, as explained by the court in *Alvarez-Machain*, is that the claims are "specific, universal, and obligatory." They are either:

1. Traditional violations of the laws of nations. These are historic laws that existed in 1789 at the time the ATS was written and would include violations of safe conduct, infringement of the rights of ambassadors, and piracy.

or

2. Gross violations of human rights. This term includes torture, genocide, slavery, prolonged and arbitrary detention, the use of weapons of mass destruction, and forced disappearances to name but a few. These are acts that are universally condemned by international consensus. Just as pirates were internationally reviled for violating customary norms back when the ATS was written in 1789, today persons who engage in torture, genocide, and other gross civil rights violations are internationally reviled as breaking modern norms.

While the murder of family members gave rise to an ATS claim in *Filartiga*, the relatively minor act of kidnapping a physician suspected of being party to torture and bringing him into the U.S. to stand trial did not give rise to an ATS claim.

Finally, *Kiobel* requires some connection between the wrong-doer, his actions, and the United States—and merely being a corporation that does business in the U.S. is not enough (recall that in the other cases there was physical presence in the U.S.).

After *Filartiga*, many human rights activists believed that the United States could be the place where human rights abusers could be brought to justice through civil lawsuits if not through criminal prosecution. After *Kiobel*, this is not at all certain. In a concurring opinion to the case, Justice Kennedy suggested that *Kiobel* "is careful to leave open a number of significant questions regarding the reach and interpretation of the Alien Tort Statute," and the opinions by Justices Alito and Thomas seem to suggest the same.

Contrast these Justices' view with the view of Justices Breyer, Sotomayor, Ginsberg, and Kagan, who would have instead relied on an approach which would recognize an ATS action if "(1) the alleged tort occurs on American soil, (2) the defendant is an American national, or (3) the defendant's conduct substantially and adversely affects an important American national interest." In one recent case, the Southern District of Ohio rejected a *Kiobel* challenge filed by an individual being sued under the ATS, holding that "as [the defendant is] a permanent resident of the United States, the presumption . . . against extraterritoriality has been overcome in this case." This may suggest that lower courts might be considering the merits of the approach taken by the more liberal wing of the Supreme Court.

Treaties in the U.S. Legal System

Most of the time, the international law that our courts deal with is treaty law—law that comes from a formal treaty or other international agreement. These can take the place of formal conventions or agreements between several nations, such as the United Nations Charter, the North Atlantic Treaty, or the Chemical Weapons Convention. These are referred to as "multilateral agreements." Agreements between the United States and only one other nation—such as an extradition treaty—are referred to as bilateral agreements.

Article II, Section 2 of the Constitution establishes the most commonly understood method for the United States to enter into a treaty:

> "He shall have Power, by and with the Advice and Consent of the Senate, to make Treaties, provided two thirds of the Senators present concur; . . ."

In practice, what happens is that representatives of the United States—usually from the State Department, but also at times people from other interested agencies (Justice, Commerce, Defense, and so on), negotiate the terms of a treaty with counterparts from the other country or countries involved. Once the language of the treaty is agreed to, the president (or his representative) will sign the treaty and then submit it to the Senate for "Advice and Consent." If 2/3 of the Senators (67) agree, they send a resolution saying so back to the president, who completes what are called "instruments of ratification." Once this is done, the treaty is "in force" for the United States.

There are exceptions to this. Some agreements are considered "executive agreements," and they can be concluded by an agency without sending them through the Advice and Consent process. The State Department has a procedure known as "Circular 175 Procedure," after the regulation that lays out the process.[14] Some international agreements are completed as "congressional-executive agreements," which are authorized by a simple majority of both houses of Congress either before the agreement is negotiated or after it is concluded.[15]

Part of the ratification process of an international agreement is also the issuance of what are referred to as "Reservations, Understandings, or Declarations" or "RUD." These are statements made by a nation that indicate issues the nation thinks need clarification before the treaty is fully agreed to. These might be simple clarifications of language, or they may be substantial exceptions to parts of the treaty. The rationale is that an imperfect treaty is better than no treaty at all. A treaty that contains agreement on most terms is still preferable to having no agreement.

Only certain kinds of reservations are permissible. Reservations should generally be very limited to only a very narrow part of a treaty. Reservations are invalid if they defeat the whole point of the treaty. Some treaties in their very text prohibit any reservations at all. The rules for all this are found in the Vienna Convention on the Law of Treaties (VCLT) (yes, there is a treaty on how to make treaties).[16] The drafters at this convention wanted to do as much as possible to promote the making of treaties, even imperfect ones. Although the U.S. has not formally ratified the VCLT, the United States has indicated an intention to abide by most of its terms, considering most of it to reflect customary international law.

The U.S. generally makes two kinds of reservations to treaties. The first declares that the treaty is "not self-executing." This means that the treaty alone is not enforceable in domestic courts unless Congress passes legislation to implement its provisions. If the United States fails to pass the necessary legislation to uphold its international obligations, people whose treaty rights are violated have no recourse in domestic courts. The second kind of RUD limits the scope of the treaty. The United States frequently makes reservations limiting the scope of the treaty so as to make clear that the treaty cannot be interpreted in a way that might violate the U.S. Constitution, stating that it will not enact any part of a treaty that conflicts with the U.S.

---

14. U.S. Department of State Foreign Affairs Manual Volume 11, 11 FAM 721 Circular 175 Procedure, available at http://www.state.gov/documents/organization/88317.pdf. See also http://www.state.gov/s/l/treaty/c175/.

15. See *International Agreements: An analysis of Executive regulations and Practices, A Study Prepared for the Senate Committee on Foreign Relations by the Congressional Research Service*, 95th Cong., 1st Sess. 22 (1977).

16. https://treaties.un.org/doc/Publication/UNTS/Volume%201155/volume-1155-I-18232-English.pdf.

Constitution, as interpreted by the United States. The RUD might protect a specific sovereign power that the U.S. does not want to limit through the treaty. For example, the United States added a reservation when it ratified the Convention on the Prevention and Punishment of the Crime of Genocide stipulating that the International Court of Justice (ICJ) would not have general jurisdiction against all claims filed against the U.S., but would only have jurisdiction if the U.S. consented to it in a specific case.[17]

As you may recall from the first chapter of this book, in the hierarchy of American legal authority, treaties come second only to the U.S. Constitution, legally the equivalent of a federal statute. Treaties and federal statutes are both federal law and, as such, are equal sources of authority as "the law of the supreme law of the land." This language, the Supremacy clause of Article VI, means that if a federal law conflicts with state law, the federal law takes supremacy. If two federal statutes conflict, or if a treaty conflicts with a federal statute, then whichever one was enacted most recently will be controlling. This is known as the "last in time rule."

Just because a treaty has been ratified by the U.S. Senate does not always automatically make it enforceable law in U.S. courts. Some treaties that are ratified require the passage of domestic legislation before their terms can be binding law in U.S. courts. These are known as "non-self-executing" treaties, and, as mentioned above, the U.S. commonly takes the position that treaties are non-self-executing. Whether or not a treaty is self-executing or not is an important one, as the next set of cases demonstrate.

Foster & Elam v. Neilson, 27 U.S. (2 Pet.) 253 (1829)*

Mr Chief Justice MARSHALL delivered the opinion of the Court.

This suit was brought by the plaintiffs in the Court of the United States for the Eastern District of Louisiana to recover a tract of land lying in that district, about thirty miles east of the Mississippi, and in the possession of the defendant. The plaintiffs claimed under a grant for 40,000 [acres] of land, made by the Spanish governor, on the 2d of January, 1804, to Jayme Joydra, and ratified by the King of Spain on the 29th of May, 1804.... The defendant objected to the petition of the plaintiffs, alleging that it does not show a title on which they can recover; that the territory within which the land claimed is situated had been ceded before the grant to France, and by France to the United States; and that the grant is void, being made by persons who had no authority to make it....

In a controversy between two nations concerning national boundary, it is scarcely possible that the courts of either should refuse to abide by the measures adopted by

---

17. For another example, see, U.S. Reservations, Declarations, and Understandings, Convention Against Torture and Other Cruel, Inhuman or Degrading Treatment or Punishment, Cong. Rec. S17486-01 (daily ed., Oct. 27, 1990), retrieved from https://www1.umn.edu/humanrts/usdocs/tortres.html (accessed 30 Sep .2015).

* The case has been heavily edited and paraphrased by the authors for clarity. See disclaimer in introduction.

its own government. There being no common tribunal to decide between them, each determines for itself on its own rights, and if they cannot adjust their differences peaceably, the right remains with the strongest. The judiciary is not that department of the government to which the assertion of its interests against foreign powers is confided, and its duty commonly is to decide upon individual rights according to those principles which the political departments of the nation have established.

A treaty is, in its nature, a contract between two nations, not a legislative act. It does not generally effect, of itself, the object to be accomplished, especially so far as its operation is infra-territorial, but is carried into execution by the sovereign power of the respective parties to the instrument.

In the United States, a different principle is established. Our Constitution declares a treaty to be the law of the land. It is consequently to be regarded in courts of justice as equivalent to an act of the Legislature whenever it operates of itself, without the aid of any legislative provision. But when the terms of the stipulation import a contract, when either of the parties engages to perform a particular act, the treaty addresses itself to the political, not the Judicial, Department, and the Legislature must execute the contract before it can become a rule for the Court.

We are of opinion then, that the court committed no error in dismissing the petition of the plaintiff, and that the judgment ought to be affirmed with costs.

Whitney v. Robertson, 124 U.S. 190 (1888)*

MR. JUSTICE FIELD delivered the opinion of the Court.

The plaintiffs imported a large quantity of "centrifugal and molasses sugars," the produce and manufacture of the Island of San Domingo. These goods were similar in kind to sugars produced in the Hawaiian Islands, which are admitted free of duty under the treaty with the King of those islands and the act of Congress passed to carry the treaty into effect. They were duly entered at the custom house at the port of New York, the plaintiffs claiming that by the treaty with the Republic of San Domingo, the goods should be admitted on the same terms—that is, free of duty—as similar articles the produce and manufacture of the Hawaiian Islands. The defendant, who was at the time collector of the port, refused to allow this claim, treated the goods as dutiable articles under the acts of Congress, and exacted duties on them to the amount of $21,936. The plaintiffs appealed from the collector's decision to the Secretary of the Treasury, by whom the appeal was denied.

. . .

The treaty with the King of the Hawaiian Islands provides for the importation into the United States, free of duty, of various articles, the produce and manufacture of those islands, in consideration, among other things, of like exemption from duty on the importation into that country of sundry specified articles which are the

---

* The case has been heavily edited and paraphrased by the authors for clarity. See disclaimer in introduction.

produce and manufacture of the United States. The language of the first two articles of the treaty, which recite the reciprocal engagements of the two countries, declares that they are made in consideration "of the rights and privileges," and "as an equivalent therefor," which one concedes to the other.

The plaintiffs rely for a like exemption of the sugars imported by them from San Domingo upon the ninth article of the treaty with the Dominican Republic, which is as follows:

> No higher or other duty shall be imposed on the importation into the United States of any article, the growth, produce, or manufacture of the Dominican Republic, or of her fisheries, and no higher or other duty shall be imposed on the importation into the Dominican Republic of any article, the growth, produce, or manufacture of the United States, or their fisheries, than are or shall be payable on the like articles, the growth, produce, or manufacture of any other foreign country, or its fisheries.

In *Bartram v. Robertson*, decided at the last term, we held that brown and unrefined sugars, the produce and manufacture of the Island of St. Croix, which is part of the dominions of the King of Denmark, were not exempt from duty by force of the treaty with that country, because similar goods from the Hawaiian Islands were thus exempt. . . . And we held in the case mentioned that

> Those stipulations, even if conceded to be self-executing by the way of a proviso or exception to the general law imposing the duties, do not cover concessions like those made to the Hawaiian Islands for a valuable consideration. They were pledges of the two contracting parties, the United States and the King of Denmark, to each other that, in the imposition of duties on goods imported into one of the countries which were the produce or manufacture of the other, there should be no discrimination against them in favor of goods of like character imported from any other country. They imposed an obligation upon both countries to avoid hostile legislation in that respect, but they were not intended to interfere with special arrangements with other countries founded upon a concession of special privileges.

The ninth article of the treaty with that republic, in the clause quoted, is substantially like the fourth article in the treaty with the King of Denmark, that it is a pledge of the contracting parties that there shall be no discriminating legislation, against the importation of articles which are the growth, produce, or manufacture of their respective countries, in favor of articles of like character imported from any other country. It has no greater extent. It was never designed to prevent special concessions, upon sufficient considerations, touching the importation of specific articles into the country of the other.

But independently of considerations of this nature, there is another and complete answer to the pretensions of the plaintiffs. The act of Congress under which the duties were collected authorized their exaction. It is of general application, making no exception in favor of goods of any country. It was passed after the treaty with the Dominican Republic, and, if there be any conflict between the stipulations of the treaty and the requirements of the law, the latter must control.

A treaty is primarily a contract between two or more independent nations, and is so regarded by writers on public law. For the infraction of its provisions, a remedy must be sought by the injured party through reclamations upon the other. When the stipulations are not self-executing, they can only be enforced pursuant to legislation to carry them into effect, and such legislation is as much subject to modification and repeal by Congress as legislation upon any other subject. If the treaty contains stipulations which are self-executing—that is, require no legislation to make them operative—to that extent they have the force and effect of a legislative enactment. Congress may modify such provisions so far as they bind the United States, or supersede them altogether. By the Constitution, a treaty is placed on the same footing, and made of like obligation, with an act of legislation. Both are declared by that instrument to be the supreme law of the land, and no superior efficacy is given to either over the other. When the two relate to the same subject, the courts will always endeavor to construe them so as to give effect to both, if that can be done without violating the language of either; but if the two are inconsistent, the one last in date will control the other, provided always the stipulation of the treaty on the subject is self-executing.

The duty of the courts is to construe and give effect to the latest expression of the sovereign will. In *Head Money Cases*, it was objected to an act of Congress that it violated provisions contained in treaties with foreign nations, but the Court replied that so far as the provisions of the act were in conflict with any treaty, they must prevail in all the courts of the country, and after a full and elaborate consideration of the subject it held that

> ... so far as a treaty made by the United States with any foreign nation can be the subject of judicial cognizance in the courts of this country, it is subject to such acts as Congress may pass for its enforcement, modification, or repeal.

Judgment affirmed.

END OF OPINIONS

So the decisions in *Foster* and in *Whitney* set forth the rule that whether treaties should be self-executing is a matter for Congress to legislate. In the next Chapter we'll come back to this, as we look at how that rule was applied in a recent case involving the U.S. criminal court system and international law.

Review Questions

1. As the cases above discuss, application of international law to U.S. courts can take place in one of three ways. First, a rule can be considered **binding** authority that the U.S. court must follow. The second form is where a U.S. court considers international law (or the law of another state) to be **persuasive** authority (if they

think this is a good rule, we should at least think about it, too). The third view is that U.S. courts should never consider international law in any fashion unless a U.S. Congress or state legislature expressly adopts the international law as U.S. domestic law. What would you see as the advantages and disadvantages of each of these three approaches?

2. Suppose the United States entered into a UN Treaty that was intended to reduce the illegal trafficking in small arms to places of high violence, such as Iraq or Syria. Identify and discuss the issues that would be implicated if a person apprehended in violation of the treaty was a U.S. citizen operating from within the United States.

3. An individual who alleges he was detained by the CIA, tortured, and questioned for information regarding Al-Qaeda activity seeks to sue the individuals who ran the questioning under the Alien Tort Statute for violation of the Torture Convention, an international treaty that outlawed the use of torture and which the United States ratified. The individual, who was cleared of any involvement in terrorist activity, now resides in the United States. What factors should govern whether he can bring the lawsuit? (This question only goes to the ability to have the case heard at trial, not whether he should win.)

Key Terms

Alien Tort Statute—A section of the United States Code that, since 1980, courts have interpreted to allow foreign citizens to seek remedies in U.S. courts for human rights violations for conduct committed outside the United States.

Executive agreement—An international agreement, usually regarding routine administrative matters not warranting a formal treaty, made by the executive branch of the U.S. government without ratification by the Senate.

Binding authority (or precedent)—A rule of law, usually a statute or court decision, that a court hearing a case is required to apply in reaching a decision.

Persuasive authority—A rule of law, such as a statute or court decision, that another court is not required to apply, but chooses to consider in order to inform its own views.

Self-executing treaty— A **treaty** that becomes judicially enforceable upon ratification. As opposed to a **non-self-executing treaty**, which becomes judicially enforceable only through the implementation of legislation.

Treaty—A formally concluded and ratified agreement between countries.

Further Reading

Bradley, Curtis J., *International Law in the U.S. Legal System*, 2d ed. (Oxford Univ. Press, 2015).

Breyer, Stephen, *The Court and the World, American Law and the New Global Realities* (Albert Knopf, N.Y., 2015).

Dodge, William S., *The Constitutionality of the Alien Tort Statute: Some Observations on Text and Context*. 42 Virginia Journal of International Law 687 (2002).

Koh, Harold Hongju, *International Law as Part of Our Law* (2004). Faculty Scholarship Series. Paper 1782. http://digitalcommons.law.yale.edu/fss_papers/1782.

Kolieb, Jonathan, *Kiobel vs. Royal Dutch Shell: A Challenge to Transitional Justice*. Macquarie Law Journal, Vol. 13 (2014).

Symeonides, Symeon C., *Choice of Law in the American Courts in 2015: Twenty-Ninth Annual Survey* (December 31, 2015). American Journal of Comparative Law, Vol. 64, No. 1 (2016).

Waters, Melissa A., *Justice Scalia on the Use of Foreign Law in Constitutional Interpretation: Unidirectional Monologue or Co-Constitutive Dialogue?* Tulsa Journal of Comparative & International Law, (Symposium Issue) Vol. 12, p. 149 (2004).

Chapter 11

International Law and Federalism

Overview

The last chapter introduced some of the ways that international law affects national security and foreign policy in our courts. But the United States is not a single legal jurisdiction with only one court system. As you recall from earlier chapters, our system is a federal one, with jurisdiction over a number of issues residing at the state level as well as, or instead of, at the federal level.

What happens when a state law or municipal ordinance conflicts with a treaty or other international law? The answer is simple: based on the Supremacy Clause in Article VI of the Constitution, treaties supersede state or local law. Now, this might seem like a simple and easy concept, but it is about to become much more complicated as we consider the language in the Tenth Amendment to the Constitution:

> "The powers not delegated to the United States by the Constitution, nor prohibited by it to the States, are reserved to the States respectively, or to the people."

The federal government is a limited government, and its powers are limited to only what is narrowly prescribed by the U.S. Constitution. If it does not have a power explicitly granted to it in the Constitution, then the federal government cannot act. The concept of federalism, the separation of authority between the state governments and the federal government, is part of the checks and balances under our Constitution. Although the federal government can certainly, at times, exert considerable influence over the states, this influence is limited. There are many actions that are illegal for the federal government to do, but perfectly legal for the states to do.

For example, in *Printz v. U.S.*, the Supreme Court held that the Brady Handgun Violence Prevention Act was illegal because it violated the Tenth Amendment. The Act had required state and local law enforcement to conduct background checks for handgun purchases. The problem was that this requirement violated the Tenth Amendment by having the federal government require states to do something that was considered to be a matter of state authority. It would be perfectly permissible for a state to enact its own laws through the state's legislature, which requires its own law enforcement to conduct a background check prior to the purchase of a hand gun. (In fact, many do just that already.) However, the Court ruled that it was unconstitutional for the federal government to "require" or "force" the states to perform background checks.

Although the federal government cannot force states to enact policies that are outside the limits set out in the Constitution, it can make the acceptance of federal funding contingent on the states adopting certain federal policies. For example, it would violate the Tenth Amendment for the federal government to impose a national alcohol drinking age of 21, or to order each state to set its drinking age at 21. Nevertheless, the drinking age everywhere in the U.S. is 21. This is because the federal government induced the states to raise the state drinking age from 18 to 21 by making the award of federal highway funds contingent on there being a drinking age of 21. States wanted this federal funding, so state legislatures raised their drinking ages from 18 to 21. Because states could have chosen to not raise the drinking ages (and as a result forgo the federal funding), this was not a violation of the Tenth Amendment.

Two clauses in the U.S. Constitution are relied on for much of the power that Congress has. Under Article I, section 8, Congress has express authority:

- "To regulate commerce with foreign Nations, and *among the several States*, and with the Indian Tribes." (Article 1, Section 8, Clause 3)
- "To make all Laws which shall be *necessary and proper* for carrying into Execution the foregoing Powers, and all other Powers vested by this Constitution in the Government of the United States, or in any Department or Officer thereof." (Article, 1, Section8, Clause 18)

The second clause, known as the "necessary and proper" clause of the U.S. Constitution, was highly controversial at the time it was written and remains controversial today. There was concern that it would give the federal government unlimited power simply by the government deciding that some action was "necessary." Supporters argued that it gave Congress only the power to do what was already authorized by other language in the Constitution. The meaning of the clause continues to be hotly contested.

The first clause is known as the "commerce clause" of the U.S. Constitution. It often works in conjunction with the "necessary and proper" clause. One thing the commerce clause does is give Congress the power to regulate inter-state commerce — in other words, any activity that has an effect across state lines. Now, in the 1780s this was not a lot of power, but as time went on, more and more activity became part of "interstate commerce." In *Wickard v. Filburn* (1942), for example, the Supreme Court held that a farmer growing wheat on his own land to feed to his own pigs was affecting interstate commerce because this meant that the farmer was not purchasing wheat from elsewhere.

There have been only a very limited number of instances where courts have found laws which relied on the commerce clause to instead be unrelated to interstate commerce and thus unconstitutional. One such case is *U.S. v. Lopez*, which held the Gun Free School Zones Act of 1990 to be unconstitutional. This law made it a federal crime for firearms to be brought into a school zone. The Court held that this action was unrelated to commerce, so it was unconstitutional. To fix this, Congress subsequently changed the language of the law to forbid the possession of guns near schools where the gun in question "has moved in or otherwise affects interstate commerce."

A federal prosecutor would then have to prove this element of the action in order to get a conviction. In another example, in *U.S. v. Morrison*, the Court ruled that the Violence Against Women Act (which gave victims of gender-motivated violence the right to sue their attackers in federal court) was unconstitutional. As reprehensible as gender-motivated violence may be, it is unrelated to interstate commerce, so it was not in the power of Congress to pass laws on it.

Now, you may be wondering why all of this information about the Tenth Amendment and federalism is in a chapter on treaties. This reason will become clear as you read the following case, *Missouri v. Holland*. This case involved the issues of treaties and the Tenth Amendment. Originally, Congress passed a statute to regulate the hunting of migratory birds that crossed both state and international borders. However, the Supreme Court held that such a statute violated the Constitution, specifically the Tenth Amendment, because there was no enumerated power in the Constitution giving Congress the power to regulate migratory birds. In response, the federal government made a treaty with Canada and Great Britain to regulate the hunting of migratory birds. The states challenged the constitutionality of the treaty, and this time, the Supreme Court held such a law, made by treaty and not by statute, was valid.

Missouri v. Holland, 252 U.S. 416 (1920)*

This is a [lawsuit] by the State of Missouri to prevent the a game warden of the United States from attempting to enforce the Migratory Bird Treaty Act, and the regulations made by the Secretary of Agriculture in pursuance of the same. [Missouri claims that the Treaty is an unconstitutional interference with the rights reserved to the States by the Tenth Amendment.]

On December 8, 1916, a treaty between the United States and Great Britain (the government in control of the foreign affairs of Canada), was proclaimed by the President. It recited that many species of birds in their annual migrations traversed certain parts of the United States and of Canada, that they were of great value as a source of food and in destroying insects injurious to vegetation, but were in danger of extermination through lack of adequate protection. It therefore provided for specified close seasons and protection in other forms, and agreed that the two powers would take or propose to their law-making bodies the necessary measures for carrying the treaty out. The treaty and related statute prohibited the killing, capturing or selling any of the migratory birds included in the terms of the treaty except as permitted by regulations compatible with those terms, to be made by the Secretary of Agriculture. The question raised is whether the treaty and statute are void as an interference with the Tenth Amendment rights reserved to the States.

To answer this question it is not enough to refer to the Tenth Amendment, reserving the powers not delegated to the United States, because by the U.S. Constitution Article II, §2, the power to make treaties is delegated expressly, and by Article VI

---

* The case has been heavily edited and paraphrased by the authors for clarity. See disclaimer in introduction.

treaties made under the authority of the United States, along with the Constitution and laws of the United States made in pursuance thereof, are declared the supreme law of the land. If the treaty is valid there can be no dispute about the validity of the statute under Article I, § 8, as a necessary and proper means to execute the powers of the Government. The language of the Constitution as to the supremacy of treaties being general, the question before us is narrowed to an inquiry into the ground upon which the present supposed exception is placed.

It is said that a treaty cannot be valid if it infringes the Constitution, that there are limits, therefore, to the treaty-making power, and that one such limit is that what an act of Congress could not do unaided, in derogation of the powers reserved to the States, a treaty cannot do. An earlier act of Congress that attempted by itself and not in pursuance of a treaty to regulate the killing of migratory birds within the States had been held unconstitutional.

Acts of Congress are the supreme law of the land only when made in pursuance of the Constitution, while treaties are declared to be so when made under the authority of the United States. It is open to question whether the authority of the United States means more than the formal acts prescribed to make the treaty. We do not mean to imply that there are no qualifications to the treaty-making power; but they must be ascertained in a different way. It is obvious that there may be matters of the sharpest exigency for the national well-being that an act of Congress could not deal with but that a treaty followed by such an act could, and it is not lightly to be assumed that, in matters requiring national action, "a power which must belong to and somewhere reside in every civilized government" is not to be found.

What was said in that case with regard to the powers of the States applies with equal force to the powers of the nation in cases where the States individually are incompetent to act. We are not yet discussing the particular case before us but only are considering the validity of the test proposed. With regard to that we may add that when we are dealing with words that also are a constituent act, like the Constitution of the United States, we must realize that they have called into life a being the development of which could not have been foreseen completely by the most gifted of its begetters. It was enough for them to realize or to hope that they had created an organism; it has taken a century and has cost their successors much sweat and blood to prove that they created a nation. The case before us must be considered in the light of our whole experience and not merely in that of what was said a hundred years ago. The treaty in question does not contravene any prohibitory words to be found in the Constitution. The only question is whether it is forbidden to accomplish by treaty what the general terms of the Tenth Amendment had declared forbidden to accomplish by statute.

The State as we have intimated founds its claim of exclusive authority upon an assertion of title to migratory birds, an assertion that is embodied in statute. No doubt it is true that as between a State and its inhabitants the State may regulate the killing and sale of such birds, but it does not follow that its authority is exclusive of paramount powers. To put the claim of the State upon title is to lean upon a slender reed. Wild birds are not in the possession of anyone; and possession is the beginning of ownership. The whole foundation of the State's rights is the presence within their jurisdiction of birds that yesterday had not arrived, tomorrow may be in another State and in a week a thousand miles away. If we are to be accurate we cannot put the case of the State upon higher ground than that the treaty deals with creatures that for the moment are within the state borders, that it must be carried out by officers of the United States within the same territory, and that but for the treaty the State would be free to regulate this subject itself.

As most of the laws of the United States are carried out within the States and as many of them deal with matters which in the silence of such laws the State might regulate, such general grounds are not enough to support Missouri's claim. Valid treaties of course "are as binding within the territorial limits of the States as they are elsewhere throughout the dominion of the United States." No doubt the great body of private relations usually fall within the control of the State, but a treaty may override its power. We do not have to invoke the later developments of constitutional law for this proposition.

Here a national interest of very nearly the first magnitude is involved. It can be protected only by national action in concert with that of another power. The subject-matter is only transitorily within the State and has no permanent habitat therein. But for the treaty and the statute there soon might be no birds for any powers to deal with. We see nothing in the Constitution that compels the Government to sit by while a food supply is cut off and the protectors of our forests and our crops are destroyed. It is not sufficient to rely upon the States. The reliance is vain, and were it otherwise, the question is whether the United States is forbidden to act. We are of opinion that the treaty and statute must be upheld.

END OF OPINION

Missouri v. Holland is typically referred to as "the migratory bird case." Even though a federal court had in a prior opinion declared a federal statute, which regulated migratory birds to be unconstitutional because it violated the Tenth Amendment, the Court subsequently held that a law containing similar language would be permissible if the statute was enacted in order to put a treaty into effect.

In the next case, *Asakura v. Seattle,* this same principle is applied to invalidate a local ordinance that was considered to violate a treaty. The city of Seattle passed a local ordinance specifically to discriminate against non-U.S. citizens. There was, however, a non-discrimination treaty between the U.S. and Japan. This case determined the supremacy of a treaty over a local ordinance.

Asakura v. Seattle, 265 U.S. 332 (1924)*

Plaintiff is a subject of Japan, and, since 1904, has resided in Seattle, Washington. Since July, 1915, he has been engaged in business there as a pawnbroker. The city

---

* The case has been heavily edited and paraphrased by the authors for clarity. See disclaimer in introduction.

passed an ordinance . . . , regulating the business of pawnbroker . . . [making] it unlawful for any person to engage in the business unless he shall have a license, and the ordinance provides "that no such license shall be granted unless the applicant be a citizen of the United States." Violations of the ordinance are punishable by fine or imprisonment or both.

Asakura brought this suit against Seattle to restrain it from enforcing the ordinance against him. He attacked the ordinance on the ground that it violates the treaty between the United States and the Empire of Japan, violates the constitution of the State of Washington, and also violates the due process and equal protection clauses of the Fourteenth Amendment of the Constitution of the United States. He declared his willingness to comply with any valid ordinance relating to the business of pawnbroker. It was shown that he had about $5,000 invested in his business, which would be broken up and destroyed by the enforcement of the ordinance.

Does the ordinance violate the treaty? Plaintiff in error invokes and relies upon the following provisions: "The citizens or subjects of each of the High Contracting Parties shall have liberty to enter, travel and reside in the territories of the other to carry on trade, wholesale and retail, to own or lease and occupy houses, manufactories, warehouses and shops, to employ agents of their choice, to lease land for residential and commercial purposes, and generally to do anything incident to or necessary for trade upon the same terms as native citizens or subjects, submitting themselves to the laws and regulations there established. . . . The citizens or subjects of each . . . shall receive, in the territories of the other, the most constant protection and security for their persons and property . . ."

A treaty made under the authority of the United States "shall be the supreme law of the land; and the judges in every State shall be bound thereby, any thing in the constitution or laws of any State to the contrary notwithstanding." Constitution, Art. VI, §2. The treaty-making power of the United States is not limited by any express provision of the Constitution, and, though it does not extend so far as to authorize what the Constitution forbids, it does extend to all proper subjects of negotiation between our government and other nations. The treaty was made to strengthen friendly relations between the two nations. As to the things covered by it, the provision quoted establishes the rule of equality between Japanese subjects while in this country and native citizens. Treaties for the protection of citizens of one country residing in the territory of another are numerous, and make for good understanding between nations. The treaty is binding within the State of Washington. The rule of equality established by it cannot be rendered nugatory in any part of the United States by municipal ordinances or state laws. It stands on the same footing of supremacy as do the provisions of the Constitution and laws of the United States. It operates of itself without the aid of any legislation, state or national; and it will be applied and given authoritative effect by the courts.

The purpose of the ordinance complained of is to regulate, not to prohibit, the business of pawnbroker. But it makes it impossible for aliens to carry on the business. It need not be considered whether the State, if it sees fit, may forbid and destroy the business generally. Such a law would apply equally to aliens and citizens, and no question of conflict with the treaty would arise. The grievance here alleged is that plaintiff in error, in violation of the treaty, is denied equal opportunity.

The ordinance violates the treaty. The question in the present case relates solely to Japanese subjects who have been admitted to this country.

END OF OPINION

The Tenth Amendment affects which laws can be enacted by the federal government and which laws remain within the power of the state. The decisions of these cases set the rule that the Treaty Power allows the federal government to, in effect, legislate even in areas that otherwise would be under the state's authority. Note that these cases do NOT stand for the proposition that a treaty can simply set aside a requirement of the Constitution, especially as it applies to fundamental civil rights. Remember the case of *Reid v. Covert*? That case and many others affirm that courts will not give legal effect to a treaty if doing so would contradict the civil rights protected by the U.S. Constitution.

Just as the Tenth Amendment of the Constitution limits the federal government, other clauses in the Constitution are understood to limit the power of the states, especially with regard to anything involving foreign relations. For example, Article 1, Section 10, provides that

- "No State shall enter into any Treaty, Alliance, or Confederation;"
- "enter into any Agreement or Compact with another State, or with a foreign Power"

There are additional clauses as well that further impart the idea that the founding fathers did not want the states to get involved in foreign affairs. In contrast, there is direct authorization in the U.S. Constitution for the president and Congress to engage in foreign affairs. For example, in Article I, Section 8, Congress is charged to:

- "regulate Commerce with foreign Nations,"
- "establish an uniform Rule of Naturalization,"
- "foreign Coin" (referenced in relation to Congress's power to regulate)
- "define and punish Piracies and Felonies committed on the high Seas, and Offences against the Law of Nations"

There are other clauses as well that further bolster this notion, such as Article II, Section 2, granting the president the power to appoint the U.S.'s ambassadors to the world, and in Section 3, to receive the ambassadors of other nations. What roles are the states to have in foreign affairs? The answer is simple: none, as is explained in the following case.

Crosby v. National Foreign Trade Council, 530 U.S. 363 (2000)*

The issue is whether the Burma law of the Commonwealth of Massachusetts, restricting the authority of its agencies to purchase goods or services from companies doing business with Burma, is invalid under the Supremacy Clause of the National Constitution owing to its threat of frustrating federal statutory objectives. We hold that it is.

In June 1996, Massachusetts adopted "An Act Regulating State Contracts with Companies Doing Business with or in Burma (Myanmar)." The statute generally bars state entities from buying goods or services from any person (defined to include a business organization) identified on a "restricted purchase list" of those doing business with Burma. Although the statute has no general provision for waiver or termination of its ban, it does exempt from boycott any entities present in Burma solely to report the news, or to provide international telecommunication goods or services, or medical supplies.

"Doing business with Burma" is broadly defined in the statute. To enforce the ban, the Act requires petitioner Secretary of Administration and Finance to maintain a "restricted purchase list" of all firms "doing business with Burma."

In September 1996, three months after the Massachusetts law was enacted, Congress passed a statute imposing a set of mandatory and conditional sanctions on Burma. The federal Act has five basic parts, three substantive and two procedural.

First, it imposes three sanctions directly on Burma. It bans all aid to the Burmese Government except for humanitarian assistance, counter narcotics efforts, and promotion of human rights and democracy. The statute instructs United States representatives to international financial institutions to vote against loans or other assistance to or for Burma, and it provides that no entry visa shall be issued to any Burmese Government official unless required by treaty or to staff the Burmese mission to the United Nations. These restrictions are to remain in effect "until such time as the President determines and certifies to Congress that Burma has made measurable and substantial progress in improving human rights practices and implementing democratic government."

Second, the federal Act authorizes the President to impose further sanctions subject to certain conditions. He may prohibit "United States persons" from "new investment" in Burma, and shall do so if he determines and certifies to Congress that the Burmese Government has physically harmed, rearrested, or exiled Daw Aung San Suu Kyi (the opposition leader selected to receive the Nobel Peace Prize), or has committed "large-scale repression of or violence against the Democratic opposition." "New investment" is defined as entry into a contract that would favor the "economical development of resources located in Burma," or would provide ownership interests in or benefits from such development, but the term specifically excludes

---

* The case has been heavily edited and paraphrased by the authors for clarity. See disclaimer in introduction.

(and thus excludes from any Presidential prohibition) "entry into, performance of, or financing of a contract to sell or purchase goods, services, or technology."

Third, the statute directs the President to work to develop "a comprehensive, multilateral strategy to bring democracy to and improve human rights practices and the quality of life in Burma." He is instructed to cooperate with members of the Association of Southeast Asian Nations (ASEAN) and with other countries having major trade and investment interests in Burma to devise such an approach, and to pursue the additional objective of fostering dialogue between the ruling State Law and Order Restoration Council (SLORC) and democratic opposition groups.

As for the procedural provisions of the federal statute, the fourth section requires the President to report periodically to certain congressional committee chairmen on the progress toward democratization and better living conditions in Burma as well as on the development of the required strategy. And the fifth part of the federal Act authorizes the President "to waive, temporarily or permanently, any sanction [under the federal Act] . . . if he determines and certifies to Congress that the application of such sanction would be contrary to the national security interests of the United States."

On May 20, 1997, the President issued the Burma Executive Order, Exec. Order No. 13047. . . . The order generally incorporated the exceptions and exemptions addressed in the statute. Finally, the President delegated to the Secretary of State the tasks of working with ASEAN and other countries to develop a strategy for democracy, human rights, and the quality of life in Burma, and of making the required congressional reports.

Respondent National Foreign Trade Council (Council) is a nonprofit corporation representing companies engaged in foreign commerce; 34 of its members were on the Massachusetts restricted purchase list in 1998. . . . In April 1998, the Council filed suit in the United States District Court for the District of Massachusetts . . . The Council argued that the [Massachusetts] state law unconstitutionally infringed on the federal foreign affairs power, violated the Foreign Commerce Clause, and was preempted by the federal Act.

After detailed stipulations, briefing, and argument, the District Court permanently enjoined enforcement of the state Act, holding that it "unconstitutionally impinged on the federal government's exclusive authority to regulate foreign affairs." The United States Court of Appeals for the First Circuit affirmed. We granted review and now affirm.

A fundamental principle of the Constitution is that Congress has the power to preempt state law. This is found in Art. VI, cl. 2 of the Constitution. Even without an express provision for preemption, we have found that state law must yield to a congressional Act in at least two circumstances. When Congress intends federal law to "occupy the field," state law in that area is preempted. And even if Congress has not occupied the field, state law is naturally preempted to the extent of any conflict with a federal statute. We will find preemption where it is impossible for a private party to comply with both state and federal law, and where "under the circumstances of a particular case, the challenged state law stands as an obstacle to the accomplishment and execution of the full purposes and objectives of Congress." What is a sufficient obstacle is a matter of judgment, to be informed by examining the federal statute as a whole and identifying its purpose and intended effects:

> For when the question is whether a Federal act overrides a state law, the entire scheme of the statute must of course be considered and that which needs must be implied is of no less force than that which is expressed. If the purpose of the act cannot otherwise be accomplished—if its operation within its chosen field else must be frustrated and its provisions be refused their natural effect—the state law must yield to the regulation of Congress within the sphere of its delegated power.

Applying this standard, we find that the state law undermines the intended purpose and "natural effect" of at least three provisions of the federal Act, that is, its delegation of effective discretion to the President to control economic sanctions against Burma, its limitation of sanctions solely to United States persons and new investment, and its directive to the President to proceed diplomatically in developing a comprehensive, multilateral strategy toward Burma.

First, Congress clearly intended the federal Act to provide the President with flexible and effective authority over economic sanctions against Burma. . . . [M]ost significantly, Congress empowered the President "to waive, temporarily or permanently, any sanction under the federal Act if he determines and certifies to Congress that the application of such sanction would be contrary to the national security interests of the United States."

This express investiture of the President with statutory authority to act for the United States in imposing sanctions with respect to the Government of Burma, augmented by the flexibility to respond to change by suspending sanctions in the interest of national security, recalls Justice Jackson's observation in *Youngstown Sheet & Tube Co. v. Sawyer* (1952): "When the President acts pursuant to an express or implied authorization of Congress, his authority is at its maximum, for it includes all that he possesses in his own right plus all that Congress can delegate." Within the sphere defined by Congress, then, the statute has placed the President in a position with as much discretion to exercise economic leverage against Burma, with an eye toward national security, as our law will admit. And it is just this plenitude of Executive authority that we think controls the issue of preemption here. . . . It is simply implausible that Congress would have gone to such lengths to empower the President if it had been willing to compromise his effectiveness by deference to every provision of state statute or local ordinance that might, if enforced, blunt the consequences of discretionary Presidential action.

And that is just what the Massachusetts Burma law would do in imposing a different, state system of economic pressure against the Burmese political regime. . . . This unyielding application undermines the President's intended statutory authority by making it impossible for him to restrain fully the coercive power of the national economy when he may choose to take the discretionary action open to him, whether he believes that the national interest requires sanctions to be lifted, or believes that the promise of lifting sanctions would move the Burmese regime in the democratic direction. Quite simply, if the Massachusetts law is enforceable the President has less to offer and less economic and diplomatic leverage as a consequence.... It thus "stands as an obstacle to the accomplishment and execution of the full purposes and objectives of Congress."

. . .

Finally, the state Act is at odds with the President's intended authority to speak for the United States among the world's nations in developing a "comprehensive, multilateral strategy to bring democracy to and improve human rights practices and the quality of life in Burma." Congress called for Presidential cooperation with members of ASEAN and other countries in developing such a strategy, directed the President to encourage a dialogue between the Government of Burma and the democratic opposition, and required him to report to the Congress on the progress of his diplomatic efforts. As with Congress's explicit delegation to the President of power over economic sanctions, Congress's express command to the President to take the initiative for the United States among the international community invested him with the maximum authority of the National Government . . . This clear mandate and invocation of exclusively national power belies any suggestion that Congress intended the President's effective voice to be obscured by state or local action.

. . . [T]he differences between the state and federal Acts in scope and type of sanctions . . . compromise the very capacity of the President to speak for the Nation with one voice in dealing with other governments. . . . [T]he President's maximum power to persuade rests on his capacity to bargain for the benefits of access to the entire national economy without exception for enclaves fenced off willy-nilly by inconsistent political tactics. When such exceptions do qualify his capacity to present a coherent position on behalf of the national economy, he is weakened . . . not only in dealing with the Burmese regime, but in working together with other nations in hopes of reaching common policy and "comprehensive" strategy.

While the threat to the President's power to speak and bargain effectively with other nations seems clear enough, the record is replete with evidence to answer any skeptics. First, in response to the passage of the state Act, a number of this country's allies and trading partners filed formal protests with the National Government. EU officials have warned that the state Act "could have a damaging effect on bilateral EU–US relations."

Second, the EU and Japan have gone a step further in lodging formal complaints against the United States in the World Trade Organization (WTO), claiming that the state Act violates certain provisions of the Agreement on Government Procurement, and the consequence has been to embroil the National Government for some time now in international dispute proceedings under the auspices of the WTO. In their brief before this Court, EU officials point to the WTO dispute as threatening relations with the United States, and note that the state Act has become the topic of "intensive discussions" with officials of the United States at the highest levels, those discussions including exchanges at the twice yearly EU–U.S. Summit.

Third, the Executive has consistently represented that the state Act has complicated its dealings with foreign sovereigns and proven an impediment to accomplishing objectives assigned it by Congress. [The] Assistant Secretary of State has directly addressed the mandate of the federal Burma law in saying that the imposition of unilateral state sanctions under the state Act "complicates efforts to build coalitions with our allies" to promote democracy and human rights in Burma. . . . This point has been consistently echoed in the State Department:

> While the Massachusetts sanctions on Burma were adopted in pursuit of a noble goal, the restoration of democracy in Burma, these measures also risk shifting the focus of the debate with our European Allies away from the best way to bring pressure against the State Law and Order Restoration Council (SLORC) to a potential WTO dispute over its consistency with our international obligations. Let me be clear. We are working with Massachusetts in the WTO dispute settlement process. But we must be honest in saying that the threatened WTO case risks diverting United States' and Europe's attention from focusing where it should be—on Burma.

This evidence in combination is more than sufficient to show that the state Act stands as an obstacle in addressing the congressional obligation to devise a comprehensive, multilateral strategy. . . . [R]epeated representations by the Executive Branch supported by formal diplomatic protests and concrete disputes are more than sufficient to demonstrate that the state Act stands in the way of Congress's diplomatic objectives.

The State's remaining argument . . . contends that the failure of Congress to preempt the state Act demonstrates implicit permission. The State points out that Congress has repeatedly declined to enact express preemption provisions aimed at state and local sanctions, and it calls our attention to the large number of such measures passed against South Africa in the 1980's, which various authorities cited have thought were not preempted. . . . The argument is unconvincing on more than one level. A failure to provide for preemption expressly may reflect nothing more than the settled character of implied preemption doctrine that courts will dependably apply, and in any event, the existence of conflict cognizable under the Supremacy Clause does not depend on express congressional recognition that federal and state law may conflict. The State's inference of congressional intent is unwarranted here, therefore, simply because the silence of Congress is ambiguous.

Because the state Act's provisions conflict with Congress's specific delegation to the President of flexible discretion, with limitation of sanctions to a limited scope of actions and actors, and with direction to develop a comprehensive, multilateral strategy under the federal Act, it is preempted, and its application is unconstitutional, under the Supremacy Clause.

END OF OPINION

Here, Massachusetts took a stand against the genocide and violence in Burma. Despite the good humanitarian intentions of Massachusetts, this state action was held to involve foreign affairs, a field reserved solely for the federal government. Consequently, the state law was struck down. This was not the first and only time where the courts limited state authority to act in areas of foreign affairs. In another example, *American Insurance Association v. Garamendi* (2003), California had required insurance companies in its state to publish information regarding insurance policies held by persons in Europe from 1920 through 1945. This was a response to allegations of insurance companies cheating holocaust survivors out of money owed to them as a result of losing their property and family. Despite the good intentions of California, this was still the impermissible involvement of a state in the field of foreign affairs. The law was struck down.

In this next case, we look at a different aspect of how international law does or does not affect legal processes in our courts, especially state courts. One concern that all nations have is how their citizens are treated when they visit other countries. Now, it should go without saying that when a citizen of one nation is in the territory of another, that person is subject to the laws of the nation where he or she is located. So, when you or I visit Canada or the Bahamas on vacation or work, we are subject to Canadian or Bahamian law and can be arrested and tried if we violate the law.

In the Vienna Convention on Consular Relations, nations agreed that they would notify the embassies of a person from that country who might be arrested and tried. This was to allow the home nation to observe the trial, to communicate with the person and his or her family and, if the home nation thought it necessary, to raise the treatment as a diplomatic issue.

In the case below, this did not happen. Texas authorities arrested a Mexican national who was accused of murder. That person was convicted and sentenced. He raised the failure to contact his home nation on appeal, saying that the violation of the treaty rendered his trial and conviction illegal.

Medellin v. Texas, 552 U.S. 491 (2008)*

Chief Justice Roberts delivered the opinion of the Court:

The International Court of Justice (ICJ), located in the Hague, is a tribunal established pursuant to the United Nations Charter to adjudicate disputes between member states. In *the Case Concerning Avena and Other Mexican Nationals (Mex. v. U.S.)*, that tribunal considered a claim brought by Mexico against the United States. The ICJ held that, based on violations by the US of the Vienna Convention, 51 named Mexican nationals were entitled to review and reconsideration of their state-court convictions and sentences in the United States.

Petitioner José Ernesto Medellin, who had been convicted and sentenced in Texas state court for murder, is one of the 51 Mexican nationals named in

---

* The case has been heavily edited and paraphrased by the authors for clarity. See disclaimer in introduction.

the *Avena* decision. Relying on the ICJ's decision and the President's Memorandum, Medellín filed an application for a writ of habeas corpus in state court. The Texas Court of Criminal Appeals dismissed Medellín's application as an abuse of the writ under state law, given Medellín's failure to raise his Vienna Convention claim in a timely manner under state law. We granted review to decide two questions.

First, is the ICJ's judgment in *Avena* directly enforceable as domestic law in a state court in the United States?

Second, does the President's Memorandum independently require the States to provide review and reconsideration of the claims of the 51 Mexican nationals named in *Avena* without regard to state procedural default rules?

We conclude that neither *Avena* nor the President's Memorandum constitutes directly enforceable federal law that pre-empts state limitations on the filing of successive habeas petitions. We therefore affirm the decision below.

In 1969, the United States, upon the advice and consent of the Senate, ratified the Vienna Convention on Consular Relations (Vienna Convention or Convention), and the Optional Protocol Concerning the Compulsory Settlement of Disputes to the Vienna Convention (Optional Protocol or Protocol). The preamble to the Convention provides that its purpose is to "contribute to the development of friendly relations among nations." Toward that end, Article 36 of the Convention was drafted to "facilitate the exercise of consular functions." It provides that if a person detained by a foreign country "so requests, the competent authorities of the receiving State shall, without delay, inform the consular post of the sending State" of such detention, and "inform the detainee of his right" to request assistance from the consul of his own state.

The Optional Protocol provides a venue for the resolution of disputes arising out of the interpretation or application of the Vienna Convention. Under the Protocol, such disputes "shall lie within the compulsory jurisdiction of the International Court of Justice" and "may accordingly be brought before the ICJ by any party to the dispute being a Party to the present Protocol."

According to the United Nations Charter Article 92, the ICJ is "the principal judicial organ of the United Nations." It was established in 1945 pursuant to the United Nations Charter. The ICJ Statute—annexed to the U.N. Charter—provides the organizational framework and governing procedures for cases brought before the ICJ.

Under Article 94(1) of the U.N. Charter, "each Member of the United Nations undertakes to comply with the decision of the ICJ in any case to which it is a party." The ICJ's jurisdiction in any particular case, however, is dependent upon the consent of the parties. The ICJ Statute delineates two ways in which a nation may consent to ICJ jurisdiction: It may consent generally to jurisdiction on any question arising under a treaty or general international law, or it may consent specifically to jurisdiction over a particular category of cases or disputes pursuant to a separate treaty. The United States originally consented to the general jurisdiction of the ICJ when it filed a declaration recognizing compulsory jurisdiction under Art. 36(2) in 1946. The

United States withdrew from general ICJ jurisdiction in 1985. By ratifying the Optional Protocol to the Vienna Convention, the United States consented to the specific jurisdiction of the ICJ with respect to claims arising out of the Vienna Convention. On March 7, 2005, subsequent to the ICJ's judgment in Avena, the United States gave notice of withdrawal from the Optional Protocol to the Vienna Convention.

Petitioner José Ernesto Medellin, a Mexican national, has lived in the United States since preschool. A member of the "Black and Whites" gang, Medellin was convicted of capital murder and sentenced to death in Texas for the gang rape and brutal murders of two Houston teenagers.

On June 24, 1993, 14-year-old Jennifer Ertman and 16-year-old Elizabeth Pena were walking home when they encountered Medellin and several fellow gang members. Medellin attempted to engage Elizabeth in conversation. When she tried to run, petitioner threw her to the ground. Jennifer was grabbed by other gang members when she, in response to her friend's cries, ran back to help. The gang members raped both girls for over an hour. Then, to prevent their victims from identifying them, Medellin and his fellow gang members murdered the girls and discarded their bodies in a wooded area. Medellin was personally responsible for strangling at least one of the girls with her own shoelace. Medellin was arrested at approximately 4 a.m. on June 29, 1993. A few hours later, between 5:54 and 7:23 a.m., Medellin was given Miranda warnings; he then signed a written waiver and gave a detailed written confession. Local law enforcement officers did not, however, inform Medellin of his Vienna Convention right to notify the Mexican consulate of his detention. Medellin was convicted of capital murder and sentenced to death; his conviction and sentence were affirmed on appeal.

Medellin first raised his Vienna Convention claim in his first application for state post-conviction relief. The state trial court held that the claim was procedurally defaulted because Medellin had failed to raise it at trial or on direct review. The trial court also rejected the Vienna Convention claim on the merits, finding that Medellin had "failed to show that any non-notification of the Mexican authorities impacted on the validity of his conviction or punishment." The Texas Court of Criminal Appeals affirmed.

Medellin then filed a habeas petition in Federal District Court. The District Court denied relief, holding that Medellin's Vienna Convention claim was procedurally defaulted and that Medellin had failed to show prejudice arising from the Vienna Convention violation.

While Medellin's application for a certificate of appealability was pending in the Fifth Circuit, the ICJ issued its decision in *Avena*. The ICJ held that the United States had violated Article 36(1)(b) of the Vienna Convention by failing to inform the 51 named Mexican nationals, including Medellin, of their Vienna Convention rights. In the ICJ's determination, the United States was obligated "to provide, by means of its own choosing, review and reconsideration of the convictions and sentences of the [affected] Mexican nationals." The ICJ indicated that such review was required without regard to state procedural default rules.

The Fifth Circuit... concluded that the Vienna Convention did not confer individually enforceable rights. The court further ruled that it was in any event bound by the Supreme Court's decision in *Breard v. Greene* (1998), which held that Vienna Convention claims are subject to procedural default rules, rather than by the ICJ's contrary decision in *Avena*.

This Court granted review. Before we heard oral argument, however, President George W. Bush issued his Memorandum to the United States Attorney General, providing:

> I have determined, pursuant to the authority vested in me as President by the Constitution and the laws of the United States of America, that the United States will discharge its international obligations under the decision of the International Court of Justice in *Avena*, by having State courts give effect to the decision in accordance with general principles of comity in cases filed by the 51 Mexican nationals addressed in that decision.

Medellin, relying on the President's Memorandum and the ICJ's decision in *Avena*, filed a second application for habeas relief in state court. Because the state-court proceedings might have provided Medellin with the review and reconsideration he requested, and because his claim for federal relief might otherwise have been barred, we dismissed his petition for certiorari as improvidently granted.

The Texas Court of Criminal Appeals subsequently dismissed Medellin's second state habeas application as an abuse of the writ. In the court's view, neither the *Avena* decision nor the President's Memorandum was "binding federal law" that could displace the State's limitations on the filing of successive habeas applications. We again granted review.

Medellin first contends that the ICJ's judgment in *Avena* constitutes a "binding" obligation on the state and federal courts of the United States. He argues that "by virtue of the Supremacy Clause, the treaties requiring compliance with the *Avena* judgment are already the 'Law of the Land' by which all state and federal courts in this country are 'bound.'" Accordingly, Medellin argues, *Avena* is a binding federal rule of decision that pre-empts contrary state limitations on successive habeas petitions.

No one disputes that the *Avena* decision—a decision that flows from the treaties through which the United States submitted to ICJ jurisdiction with respect to Vienna Convention disputes—constitutes an international law obligation on the part of the United States. But not all international law obligations automatically constitute binding federal law enforceable in United States courts. The question we confront here is whether the *Avena* judgment has automatic domestic legal effect such that the judgment of its own force applies in state and federal courts.

This Court has long recognized the distinction between treaties that automatically have effect as domestic law, and those that—while they constitute international law commitments—do not by themselves function as binding federal law. The distinction was well explained by Chief Justice Marshall's opinion in *Foster v. Neilson* (1829), which held that a treaty is "equivalent to an act of the legislature," and hence self-executing, when it "operates of itself without the aid of any legislative provision." When, in contrast, "treaty stipulations are not self-executing they can only be enforced pursuant to legislation to carry them into effect." In sum, while treaties "may comprise international commitments, they are not domestic law unless Congress has either enacted implementing statutes or the treaty itself conveys an intention that it be 'self-executing' and is ratified on these terms."

A treaty is, of course, primarily a compact between independent nations. It ordinarily depends for the enforcement of its provisions on the interest and the honor of the governments which are parties to it. Alexander Hamilton recognized this in The Federalist No. 33, where he compared laws that individuals are "bound to observe" as "the supreme law of the land" with "a mere treaty, dependent on the good faith of the parties." Alexander Hamilton stated that, "If these interests fail, its infraction becomes the subject of international negotiations and reclamations. It is obvious that with all this the judicial courts have nothing to do and can give no redress." Only "if the treaty contains stipulations which are self-executing, that is, require no legislation to make them operative, will they have the force and effect of a legislative enactment."

Medellin nonetheless contends that the Optional Protocol, United Nations Charter, and ICJ Statute supply the "relevant obligation" to give the *Avena* judgment binding effect in the domestic courts of the United States. Because none of these treaty sources creates binding federal law in the absence of implementing legislation, and because it is uncontested that no such legislation exists, we conclude that the *Avena* judgment is not automatically binding domestic law.

The interpretation of a treaty, like the interpretation of a statute, begins with its text. Because a treaty ratified by the United States is "an agreement among sovereign powers," we have also considered as "aids to its interpretation" the negotiation and drafting history of the treaty as well as "the post-ratification understanding" of signatory nations.

As a signatory to the Optional Protocol, the United States agreed to submit disputes arising out of the Vienna Convention to the ICJ. The Protocol provides: "Disputes arising out of the interpretation or application of the Vienna Convention shall lie within the compulsory jurisdiction of the International Court of Justice." Of course, submitting to jurisdiction and agreeing to be bound are two different things. A party could, for example, agree to compulsory nonbinding arbitration. Such an agreement would require the party to appear before the arbitral tribunal without obligating the party to treat the tribunal's decision as binding.

The most natural reading of the Optional Protocol is as a bare grant of jurisdiction. It provides only that "disputes arising out of the interpretation or application of the Vienna Convention shall lie within the compulsory jurisdiction of the International Court of Justice" and "may accordingly be brought before the ICJ by any party to the dispute being a Party to the present Protocol." The Protocol says nothing about the effect of an ICJ decision and does not itself commit signatories to comply with an ICJ judgment. The Protocol is similarly silent as to any enforcement mechanism.

The obligation on the part of signatory nations to comply with ICJ judgments derives not from the Optional Protocol, but rather from Article 94 of the United Nations Charter—the provision that specifically addresses the effect of ICJ decisions. Article 94(1) provides that "each Member of the United Nations undertakes to comply with the decision of the ICJ in any case to which it is a party." The Executive Branch contends that the phrase "undertakes to comply" is not "an acknowledgement that an ICJ decision will have immediate legal effect in the courts of U.N. members," but rather "a commitment on the part of U.N. Members to take future action through their political branches to comply with an ICJ decision."

We agree with this construction of Article 94. The Article is not a directive to domestic courts. It does not provide that the United States "shall" or "must" comply with an ICJ decision, nor indicate that the Senate that ratified the U.N. Charter intended to vest ICJ decisions with immediate legal effect in domestic courts. Instead, "the words of Article 94 call upon governments to take certain action. In other words, the U.N. Charter reads like "a compact between independent nations" that "depends for the enforcement of its provisions on the interest and the honor of the governments which are parties to it."

The remainder of Article 94 confirms that the U. N. Charter does not contemplate the automatic enforceability of ICJ decisions in domestic courts. Article 94(2)—the enforcement provision—provides the sole remedy for noncompliance: referral to the United Nations Security Council by an aggrieved state.

The U.N. Charter's provision of an express diplomatic—that is, nonjudicial—remedy is itself evidence that ICJ judgments were not meant to be enforceable in domestic courts. And even this "quintessentially international remedy," is not absolute. First, the Security Council must "deem necessary" the issuance of a recommendation or measure to effectuate the judgment. Art. 94(2). Second, as the President and Senate were undoubtedly aware in subscribing to the U. N. Charter and Optional Protocol, the United States retained the unqualified right to exercise its veto of any Security Council resolution.

This was the understanding of the Executive Branch when the President agreed to the U.N. Charter and the declaration accepting general compulsory ICJ jurisdiction. The Congressional record from the time the UN Charter was being debated for ratification reflects this understanding, for it was stated that "If a state fails to perform its obligations under a judgment of the ICJ, the other party may have recourse to the Security Council." When Congress debated whether or not to accept compulsory jurisdiction of the ICJ, it was stated that "When the Court has rendered a judgment and one of the parties refuses to accept it, then the dispute becomes political rather than legal. It is as a political dispute that the matter is referred to the Security Council." During these debates, the State Department's legal advisor stated that while parties that accept ICJ jurisdiction have "a moral obligation" to comply with ICJ decisions, Article 94(2) provides the exclusive means of enforcement.

If ICJ judgments were instead regarded as automatically enforceable domestic law, they would be immediately and directly binding on state and federal courts pursuant to the Supremacy Clause. Mexico or the ICJ would have no need to proceed to the Security Council to enforce the judgment in this case. Noncompliance with an ICJ judgment through exercise of the Security Council veto—always regarded as an option by the Executive and ratifying Senate during and after consideration of the U. N. Charter, Optional Protocol, and ICJ Statute—would no longer be a viable alternative. There would be nothing to veto. In light of the U.N. Charter's remedial scheme, there is no reason to believe that the President and Senate signed up for such a result.

In sum, Medellin's view that ICJ decisions are automatically enforceable as domestic law is fatally undermined by the enforcement structure established by Article 94. . . . The pertinent international agreements, therefore, do not provide for implementation of ICJ judgments through direct enforcement in domestic courts, and "where a treaty does not provide a particular remedy, either expressly or implicitly, it is not for the federal courts to impose one on the States through lawmaking of their own."

END OF OPINION

So, to summarize *Medellin*, just because the U.S. ratifies a treaty to make it "the law of the land," meaning that the U.S. is bound in its international relations, it does *not* automatically mean that a treaty will be enforceable in U.S. courts as binding law. Although the U.S. may have a moral obligation to the world to uphold a treaty it has ratified, this is not the same as a legally enforceable rule in U.S. courts. To know whether or not a treaty is enforceable or unenforceable in U.S. courts, we must determine whether the treaty is self-executing or non-self executing. A self-executing treaty will be judicially enforceable in U.S. courts immediately upon its ratification by the U.S. Senate. No further action by the federal or state legislatures is necessary. In contrast, a non-self-executing treaty is not enforceable in U.S. courts without additional action by the president or Congress.

As the Court in *Medellin* indicated, the beginning general presumption is that treaties are not self-executing. The clearest way for a treaty to overcome the presumption is if the text of the treaty itself states that it is self-executing. If the treaty includes very detailed, clear, and specific language on how the treaty, in practice, is to be executed, this could *suggest* it was intended to be self-executing, but it is very unlikely that U.S. courts would so decide. Explicit language is best.

Keep in mind that the purpose of a treaty is to impose obligations between nations—the governments, not the citizens and residents. So, even if the treaty is not legally binding on domestic courts, a treaty still imposes a political obligation upon a nation to find a way to uphold its international obligations. And, in most cases, a nation will seek to find a way, using the national legislative processes, to implement a treaty. Any nation that fails to abide by terms it establishes in a treaty loses credibility. So, for example, even though the decision in the *Medellin* case was not enforced by the courts, the United States had to deal with damaged relations with Mexico in other areas—such as cooperation on drug trafficking. As a result of the *Medellin* case, the

U.S. Justice and State Departments worked harder to make sure they knew about foreign nationals arrested so that the notifications could be made as the treaty requires.

Extradition

So now we come to a topic involving the role of international law and its effect on our court system that directly affects homeland and national security—extradition, the request of one jurisdiction that a person accused of criminal activity, who is presently located in another jurisdiction, be turned over in order to stand trial. The United States and law enforcement authorities at the federal and state levels are often in the position of dealing either with making such a request or responding to one. And, since most of the law enforcement in the United States takes place at the state and local level, this is another area where international law and our federal system of government come into tension—when state or local criminal justice agencies must deal with an international treaty (or practice) as part of "the law of the land."

As you read through these cases, consider the issues we have already discussed in this chapter and in previous chapters (such as the section on foreign searches). Consider how the principles and issues we have already discussed find expression in this circumstance.

Terlinden v. Ames, 184 U.S. 270 (1902)*

MR. CHIEF JUSTICE FULLER delivered the opinion of the Court.

The Treaty of June 16, 1852, between the United States and the Kingdom of Prussia and other states of the Germanic Confederation provided that the parties thereto should,

> "deliver up to justice all persons who, being charged with the crime of murder, or assault with intent to commit murder, or piracy, or arson, or robbery, or forgery, or the utterance of forged papers, or the fabrication or circulation of counterfeit money, whether coin or paper money, or the embezzlement of public moneys, committed within the jurisdiction of either party, shall seek an asylum, or shall be found within the territories of the other."

Pursuant to section 5270 of the Revised Statutes, complaint was duly made . . . to hear applications for extradition and to issue warrants therefor, charging Terlinden with having . . . committed the crimes of forgery, counterfeiting, and the utterance of forged instruments, and with being a fugitive from the justice of [Prussia].

The complaint charged the forging and uttering of forged stock certificates of the Gerhard Terlinden Stock Company; the forging of the revenue stamp of . . . the Royal Prussian Revenue Office, and the forging and uttering of several [documents]. Attached to the complaint were duly authenticated copies of certain depositions

---

* The case has been heavily edited and paraphrased by the authors for clarity. See disclaimer in introduction.

taken before the examining judge of the court of Duisburg, Prussia, in which an investigation against Terlinden, ... was pending, together with a copy of the warrant for the arrest of Terlinden issued by that court, and of the provisions of the Penal Code of the German Empire applicable to the crimes in question and providing punishment therefor. The commissioner issued his warrant, and Terlinden was apprehended, whereupon Terlinden obtained from the district court the writ of habeas corpus under consideration.

The settled rule is that, in extradition proceedings, if the committing magistrate has jurisdiction of the subject matter and of the accused, and the offense charged is within the terms of the treaty of extradition, and the magistrate, in arriving at a decision to hold the accused, has before him competent legal evidence on which to exercise his judgment as to whether the facts are sufficient to establish the criminality of the accused for the purposes of extradition, such decision cannot be reviewed on habeas corpus.

The statute in respect of extradition gives no right of review to be exercised by any court or judicial officer, and what cannot be done directly cannot be done indirectly through the writ of habeas corpus. The court issuing the writ may, however,

> "inquire and adjudge whether the commissioner acquired jurisdiction of the matter, by conforming to the requirements of the treaty and the statute; whether he exceeded his jurisdiction, and whether he had any legal or competent evidence of facts before him, on which to exercise a judgment as to the criminality of the accused. But such court is not to inquire whether the legal evidence of facts before the commissioner was sufficient or insufficient to warrant his conclusion."

Generally speaking, "whether an extraditable crime has been committed is a question of mixed law and fact," but chiefly of fact, and the judgment of the magistrate rendered in good faith on legal evidence that the accused is guilty of the act charged, and that it constitutes an extraditable crime, cannot be reviewed on the weight of evidence, and is final for the purposes of the preliminary examination unless palpably erroneous in law.

This treaty was entered into by His Majesty the King of Prussia in his own name and in the names of eighteen other states of the Germanic Confederation ... On February 22, 1868, a treaty relative to naturalization was concluded between the United States and His Majesty, the King of Prussia, on behalf of the North German Confederation, the third article of which read as follows: "The convention for the mutual delivery of criminals, fugitives from justice, in certain cases, concluded between the United States on the one part and Prussia and other states of Germany on the other part, the sixteenth day of June, one thousand eight hundred and fifty-two, is hereby extended to all the states of the North German Confederation." ... During the period from 1871 to the present day, extradition from this country to Germany, and from Germany to this country, has been frequently granted under the treaty, which has thus been repeatedly recognized by both governments as in force.

Thus it appears that the German government has officially recognized, and continues to recognize, the Treaty of June 16, 1852 as still in force... It is out of the question that a citizen of one of the German states charged with being a fugitive from its justice should be permitted to call on the courts of this country to adjudicate the correctness of the conclusions of the Empire as to its powers and the powers of its members, and especially as the Executive Department of our government has accepted these conclusions and proceeded accordingly.

[T]he question whether power remains in a foreign state to carry out its treaty obligations is in its nature political, and not judicial, and that the courts ought not to interfere with the conclusions of the political department in that regard.

Treaties of extradition are executory in their character, and fall within the rule laid down by Chief Justice Marshall in *Foster v. Neilson*, thus:

> "Our Constitution declares a treaty to be the law of the land. It is consequently to be regarded in courts of justice as equivalent to an act of the legislature whenever it operates of itself without the aid of any legislative provision. But when the terms of the stipulation import a contract, when either of the parties engages to perform a particular act, the treaty addresses itself to the political, not the judicial, department."

In *Doe v. Braden*... Mr. Chief Justice Taney said:

> "The treaty is therefore a law made by the proper authority, and the courts of justice have no right to annul or disregard any of its provisions unless they violate the Constitution of the United States. It is their duty to interpret it and administer it according to its terms. And it would be impossible for the Executive Department of the government to conduct our foreign relations with any advantage to the country, and fulfill the duties which the Constitution has imposed upon it, if every court in the country was authorized to inquire and decide whether the person who ratified the treaty on behalf of a foreign nation had the power, by its Constitution and laws, to make the engagements into which he entered."

Extradition may be sufficiently defined to be the surrender by one nation to another of an individual accused or convicted of an offense outside of its own territory, and within the territorial jurisdiction of the other, which, being competent to try and to punish him, demands the surrender. In the United States, the general opinion and practice have been that extradition should be declined in the absence of a conventional or legislative provision. The power to surrender is clearly included within the treatymaking power and the corresponding power of appointing and receiving ambassadors and other public ministers. Its exercise pertains to public policy and governmental administration, is devolved on the Executive authority, and the warrant of surrender is issued by the Secretary of State as the representative of the President in foreign affairs.

If it be assumed in the case before us—and the papers presented on the motion for a stay advise us that such is the fact—that the commissioner, on hearing, deemed the evidence sufficient to sustain the charges, and certified his findings and the testimony to the Secretary of State, and a warrant for the surrender of Terlinden on the proper requisition was duly issued, it cannot be successfully contended that the courts could properly intervene on the ground that the treaty under which both governments had proceeded, had terminated by reason of the adoption of the Constitution of the German Empire, notwithstanding the judgment of both governments to the contrary.

The decisions of the Executive Department in matters of extradition, within its own sphere and in accordance with the Constitution, are not open to judicial revision, and it results that, where proceedings for extradition, regularly and constitutionally taken under the acts of Congress, are pending, they cannot be put an end to by writs of habeas corpus.

The district court was right, and its final order is

Affirmed.

END OF OPINION

Extradition treaties are, indeed, part of "the law of the land," and the power of the courts to second-guess the matters on which a person may be facing trial is limited by the terms of the treaty—if the request for extradition meets the terms of the treaty, the U.S. court is bound by that. And this is necessary because of the principle of reciprocity—we in the United States want those accused of crimes to be turned over to us, so we must be willing to turn over those accused of crimes in the nations with whom we have such treaties.

But there are great differences between nations and their criminal justice systems. Just as the principle of reciprocity is important, there are other principles that ensure we are not forced to abandon our legal values in meeting extradition requests. One area where international law affects the interpretation of extradition treaties involves what is referred to as the "dual-criminality" rule.

Collins v. Loisel, 259 U.S. 309 (1922)*

Mr. Justice BRANDEIS delivered the opinion of the Court.

First. Collins contends that the affidavit of the British consul general does not charge an extraditable offense. The argument is that the affidavit charges cheating merely; that cheating is not among the offenses enumerated in the extradition treaties; that cheating is a different offense from obtaining property under false pretenses, which is expressly named in the treaty of December 13, 1900 (32 Stat. 1864); that to convict of cheating it is sufficient to prove a promise of future performance which the promisor does not intend to perform, while to convict of obtaining property by false pretense it is essential that there be a false representation of a

---

* The case has been heavily edited and paraphrased by the authors for clarity. See disclaimer in introduction.

state of things past or present. It is true that an offense is extraditable only if the acts charged are criminal by the laws of both countries. It is also true that the charge made in the court of India rests upon section 420 of its Penal Code, which declares:

> 'Whoever cheats and thereby dishonestly induces the person deceived to deliver any property to any person . . . shall be punished with imprisonment of either description for a term which may extend to seven years and shall also be liable to fine'

whereas section 813 of the Revised Statutes of Louisiana declares:

> 'Whoever, by any false pretense, shall obtain, or aid and assist another in obtaining, from any person, money or any property, with intent to defraud him of the same, he shall, on conviction, be punished by imprisonment at hard labor or otherwise, not exceeding twelve months.'

The law does not require that the name by which the crime is described in the two countries shall be the same; nor that the scope of the liability shall be coextensive, or, in other respects, the same in the two countries. It is enough if the particular act charged is criminal in both jurisdictions. . . . The offense charged was, therefore, clearly extraditable.

Second. Collins contends that the evidence introduced was wholly inadmissible. [P]articularly objected to on this ground is the warrant of arrest and copies of prima facie proceedings in the Court of the Chief Presidency Magistrate, Bombay, which accompanied the affidavit of the British consul general. The consul general for the United States in Calcutta had certified that these papers proposed to be used upon an application for the extradition of Collins 'charged with the crime of obtaining valuable property by false pretenses alleged to have been committed in Bombay' were 'properly and legally authenticated, so as to entitle them to be received in evidence for similar purposes by the tribunals of British India, as required by the Act of Congress of August 3, 1882.' That act declares that 'depositions, warrants, and other papers, or the copies thereof' so authenticated, shall be received and admitted as evidence for all purposes on hearings of an extradition case if they bear 'the certificate of the principal diplomatic or consular officer of the United States resident in such foreign country.' One argument of Collins is that the admissibility of evidence is determined, not by the above provision of the act of 1882, but by section 5271 of the Revised Statutes, which provided only that copies of foreign depositions shall be admitted when 'attested upon the oath of the party producing them to be true copies,' and which did not provide for the admission of 'warrants or other papers,' and that, on these grounds, copies both of the Indian documents and of certain London depositions should have been excluded, since neither the consul general at Calcutta, the Secretary of the Embassy at London, nor the British consul general at New Orleans, could attest that the papers were true copies. But section 6 of the act of 1882 expressly provides for the repeal of so much of section 5271 as is inconsistent with earlier provisions of that act; and under section 5 thereof the admissibility of papers is not so restricted.

Another argument of Collins is that the Indian documents were not properly authenticated, because they were certified to by the consul general at Calcutta, and not by the consul at Bombay, where the offense charged is alleged to have been committed. The 'foreign country' here in question is India, not Bombay; and we may, in this connection, take judicial notice of the fact that the consul general of the United States who is stationed at Calcutta is the principal diplomatic or consular officer resident in that country and who he is.

Third. Collins contends that the evidence introduced did not support the charge of obtaining property by false pretenses. The papers introduced tended to prove that Collins obtained the pearl button from the jewelers as a result of his representing that he was a wealthy man; that he was a partner in William Collins & Sons Company of Glasgow and London; that he was a colonel in the Howe Battalion of the Royal Naval Division and was then on six months' leave; that he had a right to draw on Messrs. E. Curtice & Co., 8 Clarges street, London, the draft of 1,700 which he gave the jewelers; and that this was a firm of bankers. The papers tended to prove also that all these representations were false to Collins' knowledge. It is clear that evidence to this effect, if competent and believed, would justify a conviction not only for cheating, but also of obtaining property under false pretenses. . . . It was not the function of the committing magistrate to determine whether Collins was guilty, but merely whether there was competent legal evidence which, according to the law of Louisiana, would justify his apprehension and commitment for trial if the crime had been committed in that state. If there was such evidence this court has no power to review his finding. The papers . . . according to the law of Louisiana . . . furnished 'such reasonable ground to suppose him guilty as to make it proper that he should be tried.'

Fourth. Finally Collins contends that the evidence of criminality was not such as under the law of Louisiana would have justified his apprehension and commitment for trial if the crime or offense had been committed there. The argument is that by the law of Louisiana a person charged with having committed an offense is entitled to make a voluntary declaration before the committing magistrate and also to present evidence in his own behalf; that this right to introduce such evidence is, therefore, secured to a prisoner by the treaty; and that this requirement as to evidence of criminality was not complied with, because Collins was not permitted to introduce evidence in his own behalf.

Collins was allowed to testify, and it was clearly the purpose of the committing magistrate to permit him to testify fully, to things which might have explained ambiguities or doubtful elements in the prima facie case made against him. In other words, he was permitted to introduce evidence bearing upon the issue of probable cause. The evidence excluded related strictly to the defense. It is clear that the mere wrongful exclusion of specific pieces of evidence, however important, does not render the detention illegal. The function of the committing magistrate is to determine whether there is competent evidence to justify holding the accused to await trial, and not to determine whether the evidence is sufficient to justify a conviction.

Whether evidence offered on an issue before the committing magistrate is relevant is a matter which the law leaves to his determination, unless his action is so clearly unjustified as to amount to a denial of the hearing prescribed by law.

The phrase 'such evidence of criminality,' as used in the treaty, refers to the scope of the evidence or its sufficiency to block out those elements essential to a conviction. It does not refer to the character of specific instruments of evidence or to the rules governing admissibility. Thus, unsworn statements of absent witnesses may be acted upon by the committing magistrate, although they could not have been received by him under the law of the state on a preliminary examination. And whether there is a variance between the evidence and the complaint is to be decided by the general law and not by that of the state. Here the evidence introduced was clearly sufficient to block out those elements essential to a conviction under the laws of Louisiana of the crime of obtaining property by false pretenses. The law of Louisiana could not, and does not attempt to, require more. It is true that the procedure to be followed in hearings on commitment is determined by the law of the state in which they are held. But no procedural rule of a state could give to the prisoner a right to introduce evidence made irrelevant by a treaty.

Affirmed.

END OF OPINION

What takes place under an extradition process is not a complete trial of the case, or even a preliminary hearing, but enough of a review of the facts and evidence to assure the United States that the criminal justice system of the requesting jurisdiction has cause to believe that a crime has been committed and that evidence exists both as to the existence of the crime and the identity of the suspect. The resolution is left to the discretion of the committing magistrate (the deciding official), "unless his action is so clearly unjustified as to amount to a denial of the hearing prescribed by law."

The process of extradition, though, is rather unique because it involves both the judicial branch in assessing the evidence and the executive branch (State Department) in actually approving extradition. In the next case, the constitutional "separation of powers" is addressed.

Lo Duca v. United States, 93 F.3d 1100 (2d Cir., 1996)[*]

This appeal presents a novel challenge to the constitutionality of the United States extradition statute, 18 U.S.C. § 3184 (1994), which has governed the extradition of fugitives found in this country for nearly 150 years. Petitioner-appellant Paolo Lo Duca appeals from the judgment of the United States District Court for the Eastern District of New York, dismissing his petition for a writ of habeas corpus. Lo Duca contends primarily that his extradition is unconstitutional because

---

[*] The case has been heavily edited and paraphrased by the authors for clarity. See disclaimer in introduction.

section 3184 violates the doctrine of separation of powers. Because we see no constitutional infirmity in the statute, we affirm the judgment of the District Court.

In March 1993, Paolo Lo Duca was convicted by the Court of Palermo in Italy for various narcotics-related offenses after being tried in absentia. Although Lo Duca, an Italian citizen residing in Sands Point, New York, refused to appear for trial, he was represented by his attorney in all proceedings. The evidence showed that Lo Duca, as a member of the Sicilian Mafia, had conspired to import cocaine from Colombia through the United States to Italy. Lo Duca was sentenced by the Court of Palermo to nineteen years in prison.

The Republic of Italy subsequently submitted an application, in accordance with Article XII of the Italian-American extradition treaty, requesting that the United States provisionally arrest Lo Duca In May 1994, the Government, acting on behalf of the Republic of Italy, filed a complaint in the Eastern District of New York seeking an arrest warrant for Lo Duca. Then-Magistrate Judge Allyne R. Ross granted the request, and Lo Duca was taken into custody.

The Republic of Italy then made a formal request to extradite Lo Duca pursuant to Article X of the Extradition Treaty. In November 1994, Magistrate Judge Steven M. Gold held a hearing to review the evidence of criminality and determine whether Lo Duca could be extradited by the Secretary of State. Magistrate Judge Gold examined the appropriate documents required under the Extradition Treaty, including a text of the relevant Italian laws and a summary of the evidence against Lo Duca. He found probable cause to extradite.

Magistrate Judge Gold also considered a legal challenge to the extradition of Lo Duca for the Italian offense of "association of mafia type." Lo Duca contended that the Italian statute criminalized conduct that was not punishable under the laws of the United States, and therefore failed to meet the dual-criminality requirement of the Extradition Treaty. Magistrate Judge Gold rejected this argument, finding that the offense of "association of mafia type" applied to conspirators who "avail themselves of the power of intimidation and of the condition of subjection and conspiracy of silence deriving therefrom for the purpose of committing crimes." He concluded that the Italian offense was similar to RICO and other conspiracy offenses that are well-recognized in the United States. Magistrate Judge Gold then certified Lo Duca to the Secretary of State for extradition.

Lo Duca subsequently sought a writ of habeas corpus from the District Court arguing (1) that the documents submitted to the extradition officer were insufficient to comply with Article X of the Extradition Treaty, and (2) that the Italian offense of "association of mafia type" failed to meet the dual-criminality requirement. Judge Trager denied his petition for a writ of habeas corpus. Lo Duca now appeals.

I. The Constitutionality of 18 U.S.C. § 3184

The federal extradition statute, 18 U.S.C. § 3184, was first enacted nearly 150 years ago to provide a legal framework for extradition proceedings involving fugitives found in the United States. Prior to 1848, extradition was largely a matter committed to the discretion of the Executive Branch. See *Austin v. Healey* (2d Cir.1993) ("Congress reacted, in part, to 'the public clamor for judicial involvement in the extradition process.'"). The primary function of section 3184 is to "[interpose] the judiciary between the executive and the individual." To that end, the extradition statute requires the Government to submit a formal complaint setting forth the legal and factual bases for extradition. The complaint must be brought before an extradition officer — "any justice or judge of the United States, or any magistrate authorized by a court of the United States, or any judge of a court of record of general jurisdiction of any State." The extradition officer is then directed to hear and consider the "evidence of criminality." Id. If the evidence is sufficient "to sustain the charge under the provisions of the proper treaty or convention," the extradition officer is instructed to issue a certificate of extraditability to the Secretary of State. At that point, the Secretary of State has final authority to extradite the fugitive, but is not required to do so. Pursuant to its authority to conduct foreign affairs, the Executive Branch retains plenary discretion to refuse extradition.

The extradition hearing conducted pursuant to section 3184 "is not . . . in the nature of a final trial by which the prisoner could be convicted or acquitted of the crime charged against him." Instead, it is "essentially a preliminary examination to determine whether a case is made out which will justify the holding of the accused and his surrender to the demanding nation." As the Supreme Court has stated, "The function of the committing magistrate is to determine whether there is competent evidence to justify holding the accused to await trial, and not to determine whether the evidence is sufficient to justify a conviction." "What is at issue in the proceeding, therefore, 'is not punishability but prosecutability.'"

If the extradition officer issues a certificate of extraditability, the Secretary of State "may" order the fugitive to be delivered to the extraditing nation. The Secretary of State, however, is under no legal duty to do so. On the other hand, if the extradition officer declines to issue a certificate of extraditability, the complaint is dismissed and the Secretary of State has no authority to order the surrender of the fugitive. While a new extradition complaint may be submitted, unless it leads to a certificate of extraditability, no extradition is allowed.

In this case, Lo Duca's primary contention is that the legal framework established by the extradition statute is unconstitutional. Since the argument proffered by Lo Duca involves constitutional notions of separation of powers . . . we think that the constitutional issues advanced by Lo Duca are sufficiently important that they should be assessed on their merits.

Lo Duca presents two alternative contentions, consideration of which depends upon our resolution of an initial question: do judicial officers acting pursuant to section 3184 exercise the "judicial power" of the United States under Article III of the Constitution? If an extradition officer does exercise Article III power, then Lo Duca contends that the statutory scheme is unconstitutional since it subjects Article III judgments to revision by the Executive Branch. On the other hand, if an extradition officer does not exercise Article III power, then Lo Duca contends that Congress has unconstitutionally authorized federal judges and magistrate judges to engage in extra-judicial activities.

This is not the first time that our Circuit has considered the question of whether extradition officers exercise Article III power. In *Austin*, we recently held that the function performed by an extradition officer is not an exercise of the judicial power of the United States. Our holding in *Austin* derives primarily from the Supreme Court's decision in *In re Metzger* (1870), which held that the Court lacked jurisdiction to review the judgment of an extradition officer.

The statement in Metzger that extradition officers exercise "a special authority" implies that their adjudicatory powers do not derive from Article III. Rather, extradition officers have been said to act in a "non-institutional capacity." Although Lo Duca asserts that *Metzger* was overruled when Congress enacted section 3184, this Court in Mackin reached a different conclusion. Judge Friendly wrote that "[n]othing on the face of the statute or in its legislative history shows an intention to alter the Supreme Court's ruling [in *Metzger*] with respect to appealability." . . . Thus, the rule in *Metzger* remains viable, and the fact that decisions of extradition officers are non-appealable strongly indicates that such officers do not exercise Article III power.

[W]e conclude that . . . extradition officers do not exercise judicial power under Article III of the Constitution. We therefore turn to Lo Duca's following arguments, which contend that section 3184 is unconstitutional precisely because it does not confer Article III power.

A. Tidewater Claim

Lo Duca first argues that section 3184 violates the doctrine of separation of powers insofar as it seeks to require Article III courts to conduct non-Article III extradition proceedings. See *National Mutual Insurance Co. v. Tidewater Transfer Co.* (1949). In three separate opinions, six Justices reaffirmed the traditional view that federal courts are courts of limited jurisdiction whose judicial powers are bounded by Article III.

In cases reaching as far back as *Marbury v. Madison*, the Supreme Court has held that Congress may not expand the jurisdiction of federal courts beyond the limits established by Article III. Most recently, in *Seminole Tribe of Florida v. Florida* (1996), the Supreme Court stated that "Congress could not expand the jurisdiction of the federal courts beyond the bounds of Article III." Lo Duca relies on these cases to contend that the Constitution prevents Congress from vesting federal courts with jurisdiction over non-Article III extradition complaints.

Without questioning these cases, the Government responds that federal courts are not the subject of section 3184. Rather, "§ 3184 vests individual judges with jurisdiction over extradition requests." This distinction between "courts" and "judges" is dispositive. As Judge Friendly noted, section 3184 forbids "courts" to issue certificates of extraditability. . . . Only individual justices, judges, and magistrate judges are authorized to act under the statute. . . .

B. Mistretta Claim

Lo Duca next argues that, insofar as section 3184 requires judges to act in an extra-judicial capacity.

For nearly 150 years, federal judges have adjudicated extradition complaints under section 3184 with no indication of any adverse consequences. Of course, this is hardly surprising since an extradition proceeding is "an essentially neutral endeavor and one in which judicial participation is peculiarly appropriate." We conclude that the extrajudicial duties authorized by section 3184 do not undermine the integrity of the Judicial Branch, and *Mistretta* does not prohibit federal judges from hearing extradition complaints.

C. Appointments Clause Claim

Lo Duca's final argument invokes the Appointments Clause of the Constitution. U.S. Const. art. II, §2, cl. 2. He contends that, insofar as judicial officers acting under section 3184 do not serve in their traditional capacity as "justice," "judge," or "magistrate," they must receive a second appointment to carry out their duties as "extradition officer." Where Congress provides additional duties that are "germane" to an already existing position, the Appointments Clause does not require a second appointment. The "germaneness" standard is fully met in this case. The duties performed by an extradition officer are virtually identical to those performed every day by judges and magistrate judges in the course of preliminary criminal proceedings. Since extradition proceedings are sufficiently germane to the traditional duties of judges and magistrate judges, under the Appointments Clause, these judicial officers do not require a second appointment to hear extradition complaints.

II. Remaining Issues

Lo Duca also presents two non-constitutional claims: (1) the Magistrate Judge failed to issue a proper extradition order in accordance with the Italian-American extradition treaty, and (2) the Italian crime of "association of mafia type" is not an extraditable offense. Both claims are unavailing.

Since the United States extradition statute does not violate the doctrine of separation of powers, and Lo Duca's other claims are not grounds for reversal, the judgment of the District Court is affirmed.

END OF OPINION

All of the cases we have looked at thus far dealt with requests from foreign nations to turn over individuals for criminal trial. Increasingly, though, grave crimes against international human rights norms are being addressed by international tribunals. You will remember that, after World War II, many of the German High Command were tried by a tribunal at Nuremberg for crimes against humanity. In much the same way, following the conflicts in the Former Yugoslavia, in Sierra Leone, and elsewhere, the United Nations established tribunals to hear cases against individuals accused of acts of genocide, torture, and other human rights violations. The International Criminal Court (ICC) is another such international criminal court and, while the

United States has not ratified the treaty governing the ICC, this is always a possibility. How do these bodies fit in our understanding of the law of extradition? The following case addresses that issue.

Ntakirutimana v. Reno, 184 F.3d 419 (5th Cir., 1999)*

Emilio M. Garza, Circuit Judge

Elizaphan Ntakirutimana appeals the district court's denial of his habeas corpus petition that challenged the district court's grant of a second request for surrender. He alleges that the district court erred because (1) the Constitution of the United States requires an Article II treaty for the surrender of a person to the International Criminal Tribunal for Rwanda ("ICTR" or "Tribunal"), (2) the request for surrender does not establish probable cause, (3) the United Nations ("U.N.") Charter does not authorize the Security Council to establish the ICTR, and (4) the ICTR is not capable of protecting fundamental rights guaranteed by the United States Constitution and international law. We affirm.

I

Rwanda has been the source of ongoing ethnic conflict between members of the majority Hutu and minority Tutsi tribes. In April 1994, President Juvenal Habyarimana of Rwanda, a Hutu, was killed when his aircraft crashed due to an artillery attack. The crash triggered a wave of violence by the Hutus against the Tutsis, which resulted in the deaths of between 500,000 and one-million persons. Tutsi rebels triumphed over the Hutus, and the Tutsi-dominated government then requested the U.N. to create an international war crimes tribunal. An investigation by the U.N. established that the mass exterminations of the Tutsis—motivated by ethnic hatred—had been planned for months. The Security Council adopted Resolution 955, which created the ICTR to prosecute and to punish the individuals responsible for the violations in Rwanda and its neighboring states between January 1 and December 31, 1994. The Resolution directed that "all States shall take any measures necessary under their domestic law to implement the provisions of the present resolution and the Statute [of the ICTR]."

In 1995, the President of the United States entered into an executive agreement with the ICTR, entitled the Agreement on Surrender of Persons Between the Government of the United States and the International Tribunal for the Prosecution of Persons Responsible for Genocide and Other Serious Violations of International Humanitarian Law Committed in the Territory of Rwanda and Rwandan Citizens Responsible for Genocide and Other Such Violations Committed in the Territory of Neighboring States ("Agreement"). The Agreement provided that the United States "agrees to surrender to the Tribunal persons found in its territory whom the Tribunal has charged with or found guilty of a violation or violations within the competence of the Tribunal." In 1996, Congress enacted Public Law 104-106 [The

---

* The case has been heavily edited and paraphrased by the authors for clarity. See disclaimer in introduction.

National Defense Authorization Act for that year] to implement the Agreement. Section 1342(a)(1) of this legislation provides that the federal extradition statutes shall apply to the surrender of persons to the ICTR. Among the statutory provisions made applicable is 18 U.S.C. § 3184. This section authorizes a judicial officer to hold a hearing to consider a request for surrender. If the judicial officer finds the evidence sufficient to sustain the charges under the treaty or convention, then the officer certifies to the Secretary of State that the individual may be surrendered.

In June and September 1996, the ICTR returned two indictments against Pastor Ntakirutimana, charging him with the crimes of genocide, complicity in genocide, conspiracy to commit genocide, crimes against humanity, and serious violations of Article 3 common to the Geneva Conventions and of Additional Protocol II thereto. At the time of the charges, Ntakirutimana, a Hutu, served as President of the Seventh Day Adventist Church for all of Rwanda. He was based in a church complex (the "Complex") in Mugonero, Gishyita Commune, Kibuye Prefecture, Rwanda, and was well known in the Complex and the community. The first indictment alleges that, following the beginning of the wave of violence in 1994, Ntakirutimana and other individuals prepared and executed a plan by which they encouraged large numbers of the local Tutsis population to seek refuge in the Complex. They separated the Hutus from the Tutsis and encouraged the Hutus to leave. Ntakirutimana then raised an armed mob of Hutus, led them to the Complex, and directed the slaughter of the Tutsis who had sought shelter there. A Tribunal Judge confirmed the indictment and issued a warrant for Ntakirutimana's arrest.

The second indictment charges Ntakirutimana with conduct that occurred after the massacre at the Complex. The survivors of the attack fled to the Bisesero area of Kibuye Prefecture, Rwanda. The indictment alleges that Ntakirutimana drove armed Hutu soldiers into the Bisesero region, hunted for hiding Tutsis, and ordered the soldiers to kill them. A Tribunal Judge confirmed the second indictment and issued another warrant for Ntakirutimana's arrest.

Ntakirutimana has legally resided in Laredo, Texas since he left Rwanda in 1994. The ICTR requested that the United States extradite Ntakirutimana to the ICTR pursuant to the Agreement. In September 1996, the Government filed a request for Ntakirutimana's surrender to the ICTR in the Southern District of Texas. A Magistrate Judge, serving as the judicial officer, denied the Government's request for surrender. He held that Public Law 104-106 is unconstitutional because, based on historical practice, extradition requires a treaty. . . . He held alternatively that the request for surrender, and the supporting documents, did not provide probable cause to support the charges.

The district court certified the surrender to the ICTR. The court held that the Agreement and Public Law 104-106 provide a constitutional basis for the extradition of Ntakirutimana. The court also held that the evidence sufficed to establish probable cause for the charges against Ntakirutimana. Ntakirutimana filed a petition for a writ of habeas corpus under 28 U.S.C. § 2241. The district court denied the petition, and Ntakirutimana has timely appealed.

The scope of habeas corpus review of the findings of a judicial officer that conducted an extradition hearing is extremely limited. We inquire only into (1) whether the committing court had jurisdiction, (2) whether the offense charged is within the treaty, and (3) whether the evidence shows a reasonable ground to believe the accused guilty. A writ of habeas corpus in a case of extradition is not a means for rehearing the findings of the committing court.

Ntakirutimana alleges that Article II of the Constitution of the United States requires that an extradition occur pursuant to a treaty. It is unconstitutional, he claims, to extradite him to the ICTR pursuant to a statute in the absence of a treaty. Accordingly, he claims it is unconstitutional to extradite him on the basis of the Agreement and Pub.Law 104-106 (the "Congressional-Executive Agreement"). The district court concluded that it is constitutional to surrender Ntakirutimana in the absence of an "extradition treaty," because a statute authorized extradition. . . .

To determine whether a treaty is required to extradite Ntakirutimana, we turn to the text of the Constitution. Ntakirutimana contends that Article II, Section 2, Clause 2 of the Constitution requires a treaty to extradite. The Supreme Court has [held] that "[t]he power to surrender is clearly included within the treaty-making power and the corresponding power of appointing and receiving ambassadors and other public ministers."

Yet, the Court has found that the Executive's power to surrender fugitives is not unlimited. In *Valentine v. United States* (1936), the Supreme Court considered whether an exception clause in the United States' extradition treaty with France implicitly granted to the Executive the discretionary power to surrender citizens. The Court first stated that the power to provide for extradition is a national power that "is not confided to the Executive in the absence of treaty or legislative provision." The Court explained:

> [The power to extradite] rests upon the fundamental consideration that the Constitution creates no executive prerogative to dispose of the liberty of the individual. Proceedings against him must be authorized by law. There is no executive discretion to surrender him to a foreign government, unless that discretion is granted by law. It necessarily follows that as the legal authority does not exist save as it is given by act of Congress or by the terms of a treaty, it is not enough that the statute or treaty does not deny the power to surrender. It must be found that statute or treaty confers the power.

The Court then considered whether any statute authorized the Executive's discretion to extradite. The Court commented that:

> Whatever may be the power of the Congress to provide for extradition independent of treaty, that power has not been exercised save in relation to a foreign country or territory "occupied by or under the control of the United States." Aside from that limited provision, the Act of Congress relating to extradition simply defines the procedure to carry out an existing extradition treaty or convention.

The Court concluded that no statutory basis conferred the power on the Executive to surrender a citizen to the foreign government. The Court subsequently addressed whether the treaty conferred the power to surrender, and found that it did not. The Court concluded that, "we are constrained to hold that [the President's] power, in the absence of statute conferring an independent power, must be found in the terms of the treaty and that, as the treaty with France fails to grant the necessary authority, the President is without the power to surrender the respondents. The Court added that the remedy for this lack of power "lies with the Congress, or with the treaty-making power wherever the parties are willing to provide for the surrender of citizens."

Valentine indicates that a court should look to whether a treaty or statute grants executive discretion to extradite. Hence, *Valentine* supports the constitutionality of using the Congressional-Executive Agreement to extradite Ntakirutimana.... Notwithstanding the Constitution's text or *Valentine*, Ntakirutimana argues that the intent of the drafters of the Constitution supports his interpretation. He alleges that the delegates to the Constitutional Convention intentionally placed the Treaty power exclusively in the President and the Senate.... We are unpersuaded by Ntakirutimana's extended discussion of the Constitution's history.... To the contrary, "[t]he Constitution, while expounding procedural requirements for treaties alone, apparently contemplates alternate modes of international agreements." "The Supreme Court has recognized that of necessity the President may enter into certain binding agreements with foreign nations not strictly congruent with the formalities required by the Constitution's Treaty Clause." More specifically, the Supreme Court has repeatedly stated that a treaty or statute may confer the power to extradite.

Ntakirutimana next argues that historical practice establishes that a treaty is required to extradite. According to Ntakirutimana, the United States has never surrendered a person except pursuant to an Article II treaty, and the only involuntary transfers without an extradition treaty have been to "a foreign country or territory 'occupied by or under the control of the United States.'" This argument fails for numerous reasons. First, *Valentine* did not suggest that this "historical practice" limited Congress's power. Second, the Supreme Court's statements that a statute may confer the power to extradite also reflect a historical understanding of the Constitution. Even if Congress has rarely exercised the power to extradite by statute, a historical understanding exists nonetheless that it may do so. Third, in some instances in which a fugitive would not have been extraditable under a treaty, a fugitive has been extradited pursuant to a statute that "filled the gap" in the treaty.... Thus, we are unconvinced that the President's practice of usually submitting a negotiated treaty to the Senate reflects a historical understanding that a treaty is required to extradite.

We are unpersuaded by Ntakirutimana's other arguments. First, he asserts that the failure to require a treaty violates the Constitution's separation of powers. He contends that if a treaty is not required, then "the President alone could make dangerous agreements with foreign governments" or "Congress could legislate foreign affairs." This argument is not relevant to an Executive-Congressional agreement, which involves neither the President acting unilaterally nor Congress negotiating with foreign countries. Second, Ntakirutimana argues that "statutes cannot usurp the Treaty making power of Article II." The Supreme Court, however, has held that statutes can usurp a treaty. This is confirmed by the "last in time" rule that, if a statute and treaty are inconsistent, then the last in time will prevail. This rule explicitly contemplates that a statute and a treaty may at times cover the same subject matter. Third, Ntakirutimana contends that not requiring a treaty reads the treaty-making power out of the Constitution. Yet, the treaty-making power remains unaffected, because the President may still elect to submit a negotiated treaty to the Senate, instead of submitting legislation to Congress. Thus, we conclude that it is not unconstitutional to surrender Ntakirutimana to the ICTR pursuant to the Executive-Congressional Agreement.

Ntakirutimana contends next that the district court erred in dismissing his habeas petition because the request for surrender fails to establish probable cause. The Agreement with the ICTR requires that the Tribunal present "information sufficient to establish that there is a reasonable basis to believe that the person sought has committed the violation or violations for which surrender is requested." This requirement is designed to meet our constitutional "probable cause" standard in reviewing the sufficiency of the evidence in extradition proceedings. In reviewing a request for surrender, the committing court must determine whether probable cause exists to sustain the charges against the accused. Our function on habeas review "is to determine whether there is any competent evidence tending to show probable cause. The weight and sufficiency of that evidence is for the determination of the committing court." The district court concluded that probable cause existed to sustain the charges against Ntakirutimana. We hold that, based on Mostert's and Prosper's declarations, there is competent evidence in the record to support the district court's finding that the evidence established probable cause to believe that Ntakirutimana committed the crimes charged.

Finally, we turn to Ntakirutimana's remaining arguments. Ntakirutimana argues that the U.N. Charter does not authorize the Security Council to establish the ICTR, and that the only method for the U.N. to create an international criminal tribunal is by a multinational treaty. This issue is beyond the scope of habeas review. [I]t would be impossible for the Executive Department to conduct foreign relations if every court in the country was authorized to inquire and decide whether the person who ratified the treaty on behalf of a foreign nation had the power, by its Constitution and laws, to make the engagements into which he entered. Ntakirutimana contends additionally that the ICTR is incapable of protecting his rights under the United States Constitution and international law. He contends, for example, that the ICTR is incapable of protecting his due process rights and that the ICTR denies the right to be represented by the counsel of one's choice. Due to the limited scope of habeas review, we will not inquire into the procedures that await Ntakirutimana. "Such matters, so far as they may be pertinent, are left to the State Department, which ultimately will determine whether the appellant will be surrendered to the [ICTR]."

For the foregoing reasons, we AFFIRM the order of the district court denying Ntakirutimana's petition for a writ of habeas corpus, and LIFT the stay of extradition.

END OF OPINION

The final case we'll examine in this chapter involves, again, the fact that international law has only limited effect in our courts. To restate a point we made earlier, international law affects relations between nations and does not have any effect on how a nation's laws affect its own citizens, residents, or others within their jurisdiction unless the domestic law makes it applicable. So a violation of a treaty may affect the relations between the two nations involved, but it will not affect an individual's rights unless the domestic law has made it applicable.

In the early 1990s, as you will recall, agents working on behalf of the United States went into Mexico and kidnapped a doctor who had been involved in the torture of a DEA agent. Earlier in this chapter, we saw, in the 2004 decision (*Sosa v. Alvarez-Machain*, 542 U.S. 692), how that doctor was unable to file a claim using the Alien Tort Statute. In the following case, litigated after his abduction, an earlier Supreme Court ruled that the failure of the United States to abide by the extradition treaty with Mexico might give rise to an international dispute with the government of Mexico, but would not affect the legitimacy of Alvarez-Machain's prosecution in U.S. federal court.

United States v. Alvarez-Machain, 504 U.S. 655 (1992)*

The Chief Justice delivered the opinion of the Court.

The issue in this case is whether a criminal defendant, abducted to the United States from a nation with which it has an extradition treaty, thereby acquires a defense to the jurisdiction of this country's courts. We hold that he does not, and that he may be tried in federal district court for violations of the criminal law of the United States. Respondent, Humberto Alvarez Machain, is a citizen and resident of Mexico. He was indicted for participating in the kidnap and murder of United States Drug Enforcement Administration (DEA) special agent Enrique Camarena Salazar and a Mexican pilot working with Camarena, Alfredo Zavala Avelar. The DEA believes that respondent, a medical doctor, participated in the murder by prolonging agent Camarena's life so that others could further torture and interrogate him. On April 2, 1990, respondent was forcibly kidnapped from his medical office in Guadalajara, Mexico, to be flown by private plane to El Paso, Texas, where he was arrested by DEA officials. The District Court concluded that DEA agents were responsible for respondent's abduction, although they were not personally involved in it.

Respondent moved to dismiss the indictment, claiming that his abduction constituted outrageous governmental conduct, and that the District Court lacked jurisdiction to try him because he was abducted in violation of the extradition treaty between the United States and Mexico. The District Court rejected the outrageous

---

* The case has been heavily edited and paraphrased by the authors for clarity. See disclaimer in introduction.

governmental conduct claim, but held that it lacked jurisdiction to try respondent because his abduction violated the Extradition Treaty. The district court discharged respondent and ordered that he be repatriated to Mexico.

The Court of Appeals affirmed the dismissal of the indictment and the repatriation of respondent, relying on its decision in *United States v. Verdugo Urquidez*, (CA9 1991), cert. pending. In *Verdugo*, the Court of Appeals held that the forcible abduction of a Mexican national with the authorization or participation of the United States violated the Extradition Treaty between the United States and Mexico. Although the Treaty does not expressly prohibit such abductions, the Court of Appeals held that the "purpose" of the Treaty was violated by a forcible abduction, which, along with a formal protest by the offended nation, would give a defendant the right to invoke the Treaty violation to defeat jurisdiction of the district court to try him. The Court of Appeals further held that the proper remedy for such a violation would be dismissal of the indictment and repatriation of the defendant to Mexico.

In the instant case, the Court of Appeals affirmed the district court's finding that the United States had authorized the abduction of respondent, and that letters from the Mexican government to the United States government served as an official protest of the Treaty violation. Therefore, the Court of Appeals ordered that the indictment against respondent be dismissed and that respondent be repatriated to Mexico. We granted certiorari, and now reverse.

Although we have never before addressed the precise issue raised in the present case, we have previously considered proceedings in claimed violation of an extradition treaty, and proceedings against a defendant brought before a court by means of a forcible abduction. We addressed the former issue in *United States v. Rauscher* (1886); Justice Miller delivered the opinion of the Court, which carefully examined the terms and history of the treaty; the practice of nations in regards to extradition treaties; the case law from the states; and the writings of commentators, and reached the following conclusion:

> "[A] person who has been brought within the jurisdiction of the court by virtue of proceedings under an extradition treaty, can only be tried for one of the offences described in that treaty, and for the offence with which he is charged in the proceedings for his extradition, until a reasonable time and opportunity have been given him, after his release or trial upon such charge, to return to the country from whose asylum he had been forcibly taken under those proceedings."

Unlike the case before us today, the defendant in *Rauscher* had been brought to the United States by way of an extradition treaty; there was no issue of a forcible abduction.

In *Ker v. Illinois* (1886) we addressed the issue of a defendant brought before the court by way of a forcible abduction. Frederick Ker had been tried and convicted in an Illinois court for larceny; his presence before the court was procured by means of forcible abduction from Peru. A messenger was sent to Lima with the proper warrant to demand Ker by virtue of the extradition treaty between Peru and the United States. The messenger, however, disdained reliance on the treaty processes, and instead forcibly kidnapped Ker and brought him to the United States. We distinguished Ker's case from *Rauscher*, on the basis that Ker was not brought into the United States by virtue of the extradition treaty between the United States and Peru, and rejected Ker's argument that he had a right under the extradition treaty to be returned to this country only in accordance with its terms. We rejected Ker's due process argument more broadly, holding in line with "the highest authorities" that "such forcible abduction is no sufficient reason why the party should not answer when brought within the jurisdiction of the court which has the right to try him for such an offence, and presents no valid objection to his trial in such court."

In *Frisbie v. Collins* (1952), we applied the rule in Ker to a case in which the defendant had been kidnapped in Chicago by Michigan officers and brought to trial in Michigan. We upheld the conviction over objections based on the due process clause and the Federal Kidnapping Act and stated:

> "This Court has never departed from the rule that the power of a court to try a person for crime is not impaired by the fact that he had been brought within the court's jurisdiction by reason of a 'forcible abduction.' No persuasive reasons are now presented to justify overruling this line of cases. [D]ue process of law is satisfied when one present in court is convicted of crime after having been fairly apprized of the charges against him and after a fair trial in accordance with constitutional procedural safeguards. There is nothing in the Constitution that requires a court to permit a guilty person rightfully convicted to escape justice because he was brought to trial against his will."

The only differences between *Ker* and the present case are that *Ker* was decided on the premise that there was no governmental involvement in the abduction; and Peru, from which Ker was abducted, did not object to his prosecution. . . . Therefore, our first inquiry must be whether the abduction of respondent from Mexico violated the extradition treaty between the United States and Mexico. . . . In construing a treaty, as in construing a statute, we first look to its terms to determine its meaning. The Treaty says nothing about the obligations of the United States and Mexico to refrain from forcible abductions of people from the territory of the other nation, or the consequences under the Treaty if such an abduction occurs.

More critical to respondent's argument is Article 9 of the Treaty which provides:

1. "Neither Contracting Party shall be bound to deliver up its own nationals, but the executive authority of the requested Party shall, if not prevented by the laws of that Party, have the power to deliver them up if, in its discretion, it be deemed proper to do so.

2. "If extradition is not granted pursuant to paragraph 1 of this Article, the requested Party shall submit the case to its competent authorities for the purpose of prosecution, provided that Party has jurisdiction over the offense."

According to respondent, Article 9 embodies the terms of the bargain which the United States struck: if the United States wishes to prosecute a Mexican national, it may request that individual's extradition. Upon a request from the United States, Mexico may either extradite the individual, or submit the case to the proper authorities for prosecution in Mexico. In this way, respondent reasons, each nation preserved its right to choose whether its nationals would be tried in its own courts or by the courts of the other nation. This preservation of rights would be frustrated if either nation were free to abduct nationals of the other nation for the purposes of prosecution. We do not read the Treaty in such a fashion.

The history of negotiation and practice under the Treaty ... fails to show that abductions outside of the Treaty constitute a violation of the Treaty. As the Solicitor General notes, the Mexican government was made aware, as early as 1906, of the *Ker* doctrine, and the United States' position that it applied to forcible abductions made outside of the terms of the United States Mexico extradition treaty. Nonetheless, the current version of the Treaty, signed in 1978, does not attempt to establish a rule that would in any way curtail the effect of *Ker*. Moreover, although language which would grant individuals exactly the right sought by respondent had been considered and drafted as early as 1935, no such clause appears in the current treaty. Thus, the language of the Treaty, in the context of its history, does not support the proposition that the Treaty prohibits abductions outside of its terms.

The remaining question, therefore, is whether the Treaty should be interpreted so as to include an implied term prohibiting prosecution where the defendant's presence is obtained by means other than those established by the Treaty. ... Respondent contends that the Treaty must be interpreted against the backdrop of customary international law, and that international abductions are "so clearly prohibited in international law" that there was no reason to include such a clause in the Treaty itself. ... Respondent does not argue that these sources of international law provide an independent basis for the right respondent asserts ... but rather that they should inform the interpretation of the Treaty terms.

[T]he difficulty with the support respondent garners from international law is that none of it relates to the practice of nations in relation to extradition treaties. ... Respondent would have us find that the Treaty acts as a prohibition against a violation of the general principle of international law that one government may not "exercise its police power in the territory of another state." There are many actions which could be taken by a nation that would violate this principle, including waging war, but it cannot seriously be contended an invasion of the United States by Mexico would violate the terms of the extradition treaty between the two nations.

In sum, to infer from this Treaty and its terms that it prohibits all means of gaining the presence of an individual outside of its terms goes beyond established precedent and practice. The general principles cited by respondent simply fail to persuade us that we should imply in the United States Mexico Extradition Treaty a term prohibiting international abductions.

Respondent may be correct that respondent's abduction was "shocking," and that it may be in violation of general international law principles. Mexico has protested the abduction of respondent through diplomatic notes, and the decision of whether respondent should be returned to Mexico, as a matter outside of the Treaty, is a matter for the Executive Branch. We conclude, however, that respondent's abduction was not in violation of the Extradition Treaty between the United States and Mexico, and therefore the rule of *Ker v. Illinois* is fully applicable to this case. The fact of respondent's forcible abduction does not therefore prohibit his trial in a court in the United States for violations of the criminal laws of the United States.

The judgment of the Court of Appeals is therefore reversed, and the case is remanded for further proceedings consistent with this opinion.

So ordered.

END OF OPINION

Review Questions

1. Based on the case law above, how would the courts respond to a request from the United Kingdom for extradition of an individual who was alleged to have engaged in giving speeches on behalf of the Irish Republican Army in the 1970s (when the Troubles were at their most violent) but not actually engaged in violent activity himself? What sort of evidence would be adequate?

2. The United States learns that a senior member of ISIS has been captured and is being held by Italian authorities. This person was accused of torturing NATO personnel, some U.S., some from other nations. Can the U.S. seek extradition, based on the case law we've read? Would a full showing of evidence necessary to convict in a U.S. court be required?

3. What about a request from Italian authorities that CIA personnel accused of kidnapping an Italian citizen suspected of terrorist activity, in violation of the Extradition Treaty between the U.S. and Italy? Would the U.S. be required to comply?

4. What practical and policy reasons, in addition to strictly legal rules, apply in each of the cases above?

Key Terms

Extradition—The official process whereby one country transfers a suspected or convicted criminal to another country.

Federal Supremacy—The Supremacy Clause, Article VI, Paragraph 2 of the Constitution establishes that the federal constitution and federal law generally, including treaties, take precedence over state laws, and even state constitutions.

Preemption.—Based on the Supremacy Clause, a rule of law that action by the federal government through Congress enacting legislation on a subject shall control over state laws and/or preclude the state from enacting laws on the same subject.

Further Reading

Berman, Paul Schiff, *Federalism and International Law Through the Lens of Legal Pluralism*, 73 Mo. L. Rev. 1151 (2008).

Gold, Martin E, *Non-Extradition for Political Offenses: The Communist Perspective.* Harvard International Law Journal, Vol. 11, No. 191 (1970).

Paust, Jordan J., *Cybercrimes and the Domestication of International Criminal Law* (Panel, June 12, 2014). 5 Santa Clara Journal of International Law 2 (2007); U of Houston Law Center No. 2014-A-41.

Saul, Ben, *Terrorism as a Transnational Crime.* HANDBOOK OF TRANSNATIONAL CRIMINAL LAW, N. Boister and R. Currie, eds., pp. 394–408, Routledge, 2015; Sydney Law School Research Paper No. 14/06.

U.S. Department of Justice, *United States Attorneys' Manual* (USAM). Title 9, Section 9-15.000—International Extradition And Related Matters.

U.S. Department of Justice, *United States Attorneys' Manual* (USAM). Criminal Resource Manual, sections 535, 536, 601–603.

Wood, Diane P., *International Law and Federalism: What Is the Reach of Regulation?*, 23 Harvard Journal of Law and Public Policy 97 (1999).

Chapter 12

Detention and National Security

Overview

As we have seen in discussing other subjects in this book, national security and homeland security use criminal law and procedures as well as other legal authorities to investigate and deal with threats. Detention is a subject where legal authority can be based in one of two very different approaches—a law enforcement approach or a war-fighting approach.

Any detention under a law enforcement approach requires some level of individualized suspicion of wrongdoing as well as some procedure to provide due process. These protections are guaranteed to us under the Fourth, Fifth, Sixth, and Eighth Amendments of the U.S. Constitution. A "*Terry* stop," you will remember, requires only reasonable suspicion of criminal activity, and a police officer is entitled to detain a person only for a brief time to either rule out criminal behavior or provide additional information—probable cause—that will justify an arrest. A person arrested for a crime may then be detained until trial, but the due process clause of the Fifth Amendment requires that there be some form of hearing to determine the justification for the detention—a bail hearing where issues like probable danger to the community and likelihood of flight to avoid trial are considered. The Eighth Amendment provides that "excessive bail shall not be required," and the Sixth Amendment guarantees the right to be represented by an attorney and the right to a speedy trial. At trial, the due process requirements of the Fifth Amendment have limited the kinds of evidence that can be used and the way the trials must be handled, the right to appeal, and so forth. Again, this is an over-simplification, but you get the idea. An important principle of this process is that many of these review decisions are made by a judge or magistrate, not by the police.

We will discuss below the specifics of wartime detention authority, but you probably have a basic understanding from watching popular movies or reading about wars. Very simply, any member of the military involved in a war can be captured and held by the opposition until the end of the war. It is not necessary that the person being detained did anything wrong, as he or she is not acting as a private individual, but as an agent for his or her home government. All that's necessary is that the person being detained is a member of the force involved in the war. Now, this is an over-simplification that we'll explore later, but we will leave it at that for now.

The attacks on September 11, 2001, the announcement of a "Global War on Terror" by the Bush Administration, and the continued struggle against the Taliban,

Al-Qaeda, and affiliated organizations brought to the forefront the issues concerning persons captured, and whether the processes used would be those normally applied in wartime, those used in law enforcement, or something different from either. Previously, terrorism had been handled as a crime (destruction of property and murder), but the scope of the attacks and the nature of activity undertaken by Al-Qaeda caused our government to reconsider how to handle what was seen as a threat that did not clearly fit our usual view of either war or of crime. This chapter will discuss how we approached the issues of detaining and, in some cases, trying those we believed to be involved in the attacks.

In most cases of armed conflict, a fighter who is detained by the opposing force is not subject to any form of trial and punishment. These detainees are being held, not because they have broken any laws, but simply to keep them out of the fight until it's over. Once the conflict ends, fighters detained by each side were permitted to go home. The only exception to this, under the traditional laws of war, was in cases where the detained fighter was suspected of committing a war crime—espionage, torture, or committing atrocities against innocents, something like that. In such cases, the detaining power was allowed to put the detainee on trial and punish him or her for this war crime. This was often done on or near the battlefield and using procedures different than a normal criminal trial. During the Revolutionary War, General George Washington famously convened a military commission to try British Major John Andre for the crime of espionage. Andre was found guilty and subsequently executed. He was tried by a military commission and not a court-martial because he was a British soldier, and not one of our own soldiers.

Let's go over some basic terminology. A **tribunal** is just another term for a hearing or judicial proceeding. A criminal trial is a form of tribunal, and a "military tribunal" is simply a judicial proceeding handled by military authorities. The most common type of military tribunal is a "court-martial." A court-martial is a criminal trial of a military against one of its own members, or someone subject to the authority of the military. If Private Jones commits a crime in, say, Baltimore, Maryland, he can be tried by the civilian court for the crime but also by the military in a court-martial. If he commits that crime while overseas on a U.S. military base, or while on a military vessel, he would most likely be tried by the military at a court-martial.

When a person hears about the use of military commissions to try members of the enemy force, we tend to compare the procedures used at those tribunals with the modern court processes, and come to the conclusion that military tribunals do not offer the same level of "due process" we are used to. This is not necessarily the case. Keep in mind that many of the due process rights we have now only developed in our civilian court system since the end of the Second World War; look at the dates of many of the Supreme Court decisions in the criminal procedure chapters. The cases we will read about in this chapter address how, if at all, these procedures apply to the detention and trial of enemy combatants now.

An **enemy combatant** is any person who fights for the enemy. As mentioned above, the international law of armed conflict provides that combatants can be detained until the end of the conflict. The purpose of this detention is not punishment, but merely to remove the person from the fight. When a person is captured in a time of war, an initial determination must be made if the person is an enemy combatant who may be detained, or a non-combatant who should be released. This simply makes sense—we want to detain those who might fight against us, but we don't want to detain innocents who have not participated in the fight and who are simply in the wrong place at the wrong time.

It's not always easy to tell the two apart. For example, let's say U.S. soldiers in a rural region of Afghanistan stumble upon a young male who has in his possession an AK-47 and a 2-way radio. Perhaps this individual is fighting for the Taliban, thus making him an enemy combatant. If this is the case, then the young man can be lawfully captured and detained. But on the other hand, perhaps he is merely a shepherd who carries a radio to communicate with his family, and the AK-47 to protect himself and his flock from bandits or predators. If this is the case, he should be released and left to resume his business. How does the detaining military member tell which is the case? Just as in a criminal context, a temporary detention is permitted until a determination can be made, and the expectation under the law of armed conflict was for some form of hearing or process to decide whether continued detention was authorized.

Combatants can be detained until the end of the conflict. Obviously, just when a conflict will end is an unknown variable until it actually happens. This means that enemy combatants may be detained indefinitely. When a German soldier was captured in 1942, the American forces had no way of knowing when the war would end. But those captured and held knew that they would be detained for the duration of the war. And this makes sense. If you release an enemy soldier while the war is still going on, you would expect that soldier to rejoin his force and get back in the fight (after all, that's what soldiers do). There are two ways to stop that—either kill everyone who surrenders, or capture and hold them until the war is over. A soldier who knows he will be killed if captured will not surrender but keep fighting and killing YOUR troops, since he feels he has no choice. Clearly the indefinite detention of captured soldiers is better for both sides.

The Law of Armed Conflict is contained in a series of treaties, most commonly referred to as the Geneva Conventions. These laws have existed in some form throughout history, and the four Geneva Conventions of 1949 and two Additional Protocols completed in 1977 are the most recent versions of the laws of war.

When a person is determined to be an enemy combatant who is to be detained, then a determination must be made as to just what type of enemy combatant the detainee is. There are two types of captured enemy combatants: (1) combatants who are entitled to the privileged status of Prisoner of War (POW) who are merely to be detained until the end of a conflict, and (2) combatants who are suspected war criminals and are not entitled to POW status and who can be tried and punished for their crimes. In recent years we have begun using the terms "lawful" or "privileged" combatant and "unlawful" or "unprivileged" combatant to describe these two categories.

Lawful combatants are persons who are allowed to use deadly force while engaged in the conflict. They are those who directly participate in hostilities by fighting or some other combat-support action (such as planning or command), and who, by their conduct, are entitled to claim the privileges of combatant status. Most importantly, while using deadly force, they respect the laws of war by wearing a uniform or taking other straps to distinguish themselves from the population, ensuring as best they can to try to kill only other combatants and not innocent civilians, and so forth. As lawful combatants, they earn the privileged status of Prisoner of War as detailed in the Third Geneva Convention. Prisoners of war are not war criminals, and they cannot be punished for having taken up arms against the nation that currently holds them prisoner. They are to be merely detained until the end of the conflict, whenever that may be.

Unlawful combatants is a term sometimes used to refer to those who are not members of a regular armed force and who, when directly participating in hostilities, do not attempt to follow the law of armed conflict or other rules set out for combatants. They might engage in terrorism, targeting innocent civilians. They might engage in atrocities such as torture or widespread stealing from the people. They might hide among civilians, using them as shields or otherwise pretending to be civilians (making it impossible for the opposing force to tell who is who and thus putting innocents at greater risk). As such, when detained, these combatants are not entitled to POW status.

While those given POW status have many rights and privileges, it is not correct to say that unlawful combatants receive none. All who might be detained have certain rights as human beings. This means that they are entitled to food, water, shelter, medical care, and religious icons. They also have rights against being tortured, abused, or maltreated.

Lawful combatants have extra rights, referred to as privileges. These are extensively outlined in the Third Geneva Convention of 1949. A key example of these privileges is that a capturing nation must give enemy prisoners of war the same quality of food, housing, and medical care that it provides its own troops. For example, during World War II, the U.S. gave German POWs the same food and living quarters it was providing American soldiers in the U.S. This involved building housing for German POWs to the same specifications concerning space per person as was used for American GI barracks. A selection of other privileges which are bestowed upon enemy Prisoners of War are that their military rank must be respected, they are to receive fair pay for any work performed, they are prohibited from engaging in any war which is dangerous or helps the war effort (such as working for the detaining power in an arms factory), and that officers cannot be forced to perform manual labor.

Many people may be surprised to learn that enemy soldiers are supposed to be treated so well. Remember that the purpose of detaining these individuals is not to punish them, but to merely keep them out of the fight. Furthermore, POW status is earned by soldiers choosing to respect the laws of war, often at risk of their own lives.

The laws of war are intended to decrease the unnecessary suffering of war, and so those who take care to do so should be rewarded. For example, one of the reasons why soldiers wear uniforms is to distinguish themselves from non-combatants. A soldier's uniform is a signal to an enemy essentially saying, "I am a lawful target. You may kill me." This allows the enemy to actually be in a position to tell who is a combatant and who is an innocent civilian entitled to be protected and not attacked. The promise that a soldier will be fairly treated if given the privileged status of POW if he abides by the law of armed conflict provides an incentive to follow the law of war, even at the risk of his own life. It is in the interests of all involved to do what they can to prevent unnecessary suffering in war.

Another reason why it is important to respect the laws of war is to protect one's own soldiers. For example, one reason why German POWs were treated well by the U.S. in World War II was to discourage any form of retribution by the Germans against American POWs they had captured. If Germany heard that Americans were mistreating captured German soldiers, they in turn might have retaliated by mistreating and even executing American soldiers. This situation of mutual bad treatment is exactly what happened between the Soviets and Germans; both had a reputation for mistreating prisoners of the other, and, as a result, if one of these nations captured soldiers of the other, there was retribution. The mortality rate of prisoners was extremely high on both sides. But because the American and British forces had a reputation to treat German POWs well, unlike the Soviets, many Germans went out of their way to surrender to British and Americans rather than Soviets. One of the most famous ones was Werner von Braun, a German rocket engineer who had led the Nazi V-2 program and went on to develop the American ballistic missiles and space program. Another advantage of the good American treatment of German POWs was that it made the healing of relations between the two nations much easier after the war ended.

In contrast to those combatants who comply with the laws of war and earn the privileged status of Prisoner of War, those combatants who do not comply with the laws of armed conflict are not entitled to these privileges and can be treated as criminals and punished accordingly, following a trial by a national court or other tribunal. Examples include human rights crimes such as torture, cruel or inhuman treatment, and sexual assaults, to more combat-specific offenses such as not wearing a uniform or faking surrender. In some cases it also need not be a human rights violation or war crime—a consequence of losing the privileged status of a belligerent is the possibility of being tried for murder. Remember though, even "unlawful combatants" retain basic human rights. They are entitled to food, shelter, and medical care. They may not be tortured, abused, or subjected to cruel, inhuman, or degrading treatment.

How do we choose which process (criminal or warfare) to use in the context of international terrorism undertaken by highly capable groups like Al-Qaeda—not a nation but still acting in many ways like a fighting military? Do any of our constitutional protections apply? These are the issues that we will now turn to.

We will start our exploration of this subject by reading the federal circuit court case *Ex parte Merryman* (1861). During the American Civil War, President Lincoln suspended the right to habeas corpus and ordered a great many people who supported the Confederacy, or in some cases who simply opposed the war, to be detained. As you should recall, habeas corpus is the doctrine that a person who is under arrest is brought to a court where a neutral judge can hear the reason for that person's detention. It is up to the judge to determine whether or not there is enough evidence and justification to continue holding a person.

When habeas corpus is suspended, the requirement that a person is brought to a judicial figure to determine whether or not the person can be charged or continued to be held is suspended. This reduces an important check on the power of the government. According to the U.S. Constitution, under the powers of Congress (and not the president), Article 1, Section 9 states that "The Privilege of the Writ of Habeas Corpus shall not be suspended, unless when in Cases of Rebellion or Invasion the public Safety may require it."

President Lincoln did not go to Congress to ask for a law suspending the right to habeas corpus—he simply ordered it as an exercise of his power as commander in chief. As you read the opinion, which is a great review of the powers of the president, take note of the caustic tone of the opinion. The author of the opinion was Supreme Court Chief Justice Roger B. Taney, sitting in this case as a Circuit Court judge. Taney was a southerner, a slave-owner, and an ardent believer in state's rights. He is most famously remembered for authoring the infamous pre-war and pro-slavery *Dred Scott* decision, which was a major contributing factor to the Civil War. Although he remained loyal to the Union during the Civil War, Justice Taney made no secret of the fact that he detested Abraham Lincoln.

Ex Parte Merryman, 17 F. Cas. 144 (C.C.D. Md., 1861)*

The application in this case for a writ of the constitutional privilege of habeas corpus which gives judges the power to inquire into the cause of confinement of a person being held by the government.

The petition presents the following case: The petitioner resides in Maryland, in Baltimore county. While peaceably in his own house, with his family, it was at two o'clock, on the morning of the 25th of May, 1861, entered by an armed force, professing to act under military orders. He was then compelled to rise from his bed, taken into custody, and conveyed to Fort McHenry, where he is imprisoned by the commanding officer, without warrant from any lawful authority. The commander of the fort, Gen. George Cadwalader, by whom he is detained in confinement, does not deny any of the facts alleged in the petition. He states that the prisoner was arrested by order of Gen. Keim, of Pennsylvania, and conducted as a prisoner to Fort McHenry by his order, and placed in his (Gen. Cadwalader's) custody, to be there detained by him as a prisoner.

---

* The case has been heavily edited and paraphrased by the authors for clarity. See disclaimer in introduction.

A copy of the warrant, or order, under which the prisoner was arrested, was demanded by his attorney, and refused. It is not alleged in the return that any specific act, constituting an offense against the laws of the United States, has been charged against him upon oath; but he appears to have been arrested upon general charges of treason and rebellion, without proof, and without giving the names of the witnesses, or specifying the acts, which, in the judgment of the military officer, constituted these crimes. And having the prisoner thus in custody upon these vague and unsupported accusations, he refuses to obey the writ of habeas corpus, upon the ground that he is duly authorized by the President to suspend it.

The case, then, is simply this: A military officer residing in Pennsylvania issues an order to arrest a citizen of Maryland, upon vague and indefinite charges, without any proof, so far as appears. Under this order his house is entered in the night; he is seized as a prisoner, and conveyed to Fort McHenry, and there kept in close confinement. And when a habeas corpus is served on the commanding officer, requiring him to produce the prisoner before a Justice of the Supreme Court, in order that he may examine into the legality of the imprisonment, the answer of the officer is that he is authorized by the President to suspend the writ of habeas corpus at his discretion, and, in the exercise of that discretion, suspends it in this case, and on that ground refuses obedience to the writ.

As the case comes before me, therefore, I understand that the President not only claims the right to suspend the writ of habeas corpus himself, at his discretion, but to delegate that discretionary power to suspend habeas corpus to a military officer, and to leave it to him to determine whether he will or will not obey judicial process that may be served upon him.

No official notice has been given to the courts of justice, or to the public, by proclamation or otherwise, that the President claimed this power, and had exercised it in the manner stated in the return. And I certainly listened to it with some surprise, for I had supposed it to be one of those points of constitutional law upon which there is no difference of opinion, and that it was admitted on all hands that the privilege of the writ could not be suspended except by act of Congress.

The clause in the Constitution which authorizes the suspension of the privilege of the writ of habeas corpus is in the ninth section of the first article. This article is devoted to the Legislative Department of the United States, and has not the slightest reference to the Executive Department. It begins by providing "that all legislative powers therein granted shall be vested in a Congress of the United States, which shall consist of a Senate and House of Representatives." And after prescribing the manner in which these two branches of the legislative department shall be chosen, it proceeds to enumerate specifically the legislative powers which it thereby grants, and legislative powers which it expressly prohibits, and, at the conclusion of this specification, a clause is inserted giving Congress "the power to make all laws which may be necessary and proper for carrying into execution the foregoing powers, and all other powers vested by this Constitution in the Government of the United States or in any department or office thereof."

The power of legislation granted by this latter clause is by its word carefully confined to the specific objects before enumerated. But as this limitation was unavoidably somewhat indefinite, it was deemed necessary to guard more effectually certain great cardinal principles essential to the liberty of the citizen and to the rights and equality of the States by denying to Congress, in express terms, any power of legislation over them. It was apprehended, it seems, that such legislation might be attempted under the pretext that it was necessary and proper to carry into execution the powers granted; and it was determined that there should be no room to doubt, where rights of such vital importance were concerned, and, accordingly this clause is immediately followed by an enumeration of certain subjects to which the powers of legislation shall not extend; and the great importance which the framers of the Constitution attached to the privilege of the writ of habeas corpus, to protect the liberty of the citizen, is proved by the fact that its suspension, except in cases of invasion and rebellion, is first in the list of prohibited powers; and even in these cases the power is denied and its exercise prohibited unless the public safety shall require it.

It is Article II of the Constitution that provides for the organization of the Executive Department, and enumerates the powers conferred on it, and prescribes its duties. And if the high power to suspend habeas corpus now claimed was intended to be conferred on the President, it would undoubtedly be found in plain words in this article. But there is not a word in it that can furnish the slightest ground to justify the exercise of the power.

Instead, the article begins by declaring that the Executive power shall be vested in a President of the United States of America, to hold his office during the term of four years, and then proceeds to prescribe the mode of election, and to specify in precise and plain words the powers delegated to him and the duties imposed upon him. And the short term for which he is elected, and the narrow limits to which his power is confined, show the jealousy and apprehensions of future danger which the framers of the Constitution felt in relation to that department of the Government, and how carefully they withheld from it many of the powers belonging to the executive branch of the English Government which were considered as dangerous to the liberty of the subject, and conferred (as that in clear and specific terms) those powers only which were deemed essential to secure the successful operation of the Government.

He is elected, as I have already said, for the brief term of four years, and is made personally responsible, by impeachment, for malfeasance in office. He is, from necessity, and the nature of his duties, the Commander-in-Chief of the army and navy, and of the militia, when called into actual service. But no appropriation for the support of the army can be made by Congress for a longer term than two years, so that it is in the power of the succeeding House of Representatives to withhold the appropriation for its support, and thus disband it, if, in their judgment, the President used or designed to use it for improper purposes.

So, too, his powers in relation to the civil duties and authority necessarily conferred on him are carefully restricted, as well as those belonging to his military character. He cannot appoint the ordinary officers of Government, nor make a treaty with a foreign nation or Indian tribe without the advice and consent of the Senate, and cannot appoint even inferior officers unless he is authorized by an act of Congress to do so. He is not empowered to arrest anyone charged with an offence against the United States, and whom he may, from the evidence before him, believe to be guilty; nor can he authorize any officer, civil or military, to exercise this power, for the fifth article of the amendments to the Constitution expressly provides that no person "shall be deprived of life, liberty, or property without due process of law;" that is, judicial process. And even if the privilege of the writ of habeas corpus was suspended by act of Congress, and a party not subject to the rules and articles of war was afterwards arrested and imprisoned by regular judicial process, he could not be detained in prison or brought to trial before a military tribunal, for the article in the Amendments to the Constitution immediately following the one above referred to–that is, the sixth article–provides that, "In all criminal prosecutions, the accused shall enjoy the right to a speedy and public trial by an impartial jury of the State and district wherein the crime shall have been committed, which district shall have been previously ascertained by law; and to be informed of the nature and cause of the accusation; to be confronted with the witnesses against him; to have compulsory process for obtaining witnesses in his favor, and to have the assistance of counsel for his defence."

And the only power, therefore, which the President possesses, where the "life, liberty, or property" of a private citizen is concerned, is the power and duty prescribed in the third section of the second article, which requires "that he shall take care that the laws be faithfully executed." He is not authorized to execute them himself, or through agents or officers, civil or military, appointed by himself, but he is to take care that they be faithfully carried into execution as they are expounded and adjudged by the coordinate branch of the Government to which that duty is assigned by the Constitution. It is thus made his duty to come in aid of the judicial authority, if it shall be resisted by a force too strong to be overcome without the assistance of the Executive arm. But in exercising this power, he acts in subordination to judicial authority, assisting it to execute its process and enforce its judgments.

With such provisions in the Constitution, expressed in language too clear to be misunderstood by any one, I can see no ground whatever for supposing that the President, in any emergency or in any state of things, can authorize the suspension of the privilege of the writ of habeas corpus, or arrest a citizen, except in aid of the judicial power. He certainly does not faithfully execute the laws if he takes upon himself legislative power by suspending the writ of habeas corpus—and the judicial power, also, by arresting and imprisoning a person without due process of law. Nor can any argument be drawn from the necessities of government for self-defense, in times of tumult and danger. The Government of the United States is one of delegated and limited powers. It derives its existence and authority altogether from the Constitution, and neither of its branches—executive, legislative or judicial—can exercise any of the powers of government beyond those specified and granted. For the Tenth Amendment to the Constitution, in express terms, provides that "the powers not delegated to the United States by the Constitution, nor prohibited by it to the States, are reserved to the States, respectively, or to the people."

Indeed, the security against imprisonment by Executive authority, provided for in the fifth article of the Amendments of the Constitution, which I have before quoted, is nothing more than a copy of a like provision in the English constitution, which had been firmly established before the Declaration of Independence.

The right of the subject to the benefit of the writ of habeas corpus . . . was one of the great points in controversy during the long struggle in England between arbitrary government and free institutions, and must therefore have strongly attracted the attention of statesmen engaged in framing a new and, as they supposed, a freer government than the one which they had thrown off by the Revolution.

Accordingly, no power in England short of that of Parliament, can suspend or authorize the suspension of the writ of habeas corpus. I quote again from Blackstone:

> "But the happiness of our Constitution is, that it is not left to the executive power to determine when the danger of the State is so great as to render this measure expedient. It is the Parliament only or legislative power that, whenever it sees proper, can authorize the Crown, by suspending the habeas corpus for a short and limited time, to imprison suspected persons without giving any reason for so doing."

And if the President of the United States may suspend the writ, then the Constitution of the United States has conferred upon him more regal and absolute power over the liberty of the citizen than the people of England have thought it safe to entrust to the Crown—a power which the Queen of England cannot exercise at this day, and which could not have been lawfully exercised by the sovereign even in the reign of Charles the First.

Mr. Justice Story, speaking in his Commentaries, of the habeas corpus clause in the Constitution, says:

> It is obvious that cases of a peculiar emergency may arise, which may justify, nay, even require, the temporary suspension of any right to the writ. But as it has frequently happened in foreign countries, and even in England, that the writ has, upon various pretexts and occasions, been suspended, whereby persons apprehended upon suspicion have suffered a long imprisonment, sometimes from design, and sometimes because they were forgotten, the right to suspend it is expressly confined to cases of rebellion or invasion, where the public safety may require it. A very just and wholesome restraint, which cuts down at a blow a fruitful means of oppression, capable of being abused in bad times to the worst of purposes. Hitherto no suspension of the writ has ever been authorized by Congress since the establishment of the Constitution. It would seem, as the power is given to Congress to suspend the writ of habeas corpus in cases of rebellion or invasion, that the right to judge whether the exigency had arisen must exclusively belong to that body.

And Chief Justice Marshall, in delivering the opinion of the Supreme Court in the case *ex parte* Bollman and Swartwout, uses this decisive language:

"If at any time the public safety should require the suspension of the powers vested by this act in the courts of the United States, it is for the Legislature to say so. That question depends on political considerations, on which the Legislature is to decide. Until the legislative will be expressed, this court can only see its duty, and must obey the laws."

I can add nothing to these clear and emphatic words of my great predecessor.

But the documents before me show that the military authority in this case has gone far beyond the mere suspension of the privilege of the writ of habeas corpus. It has, by force of arms, thrust aside the judicial authorities and officers to whom the Constitution has confided the power and duty of interpreting and administering the laws, and substituted a military government in its place, to be administered and executed by military officers. For at the time these proceedings were had against John Merryman, the District Judge of Maryland—the commissioner appointed under the act of Congress—the District Attorney and the Marshal, all resided in the city of Baltimore, a few miles only from the home of the prisoner. Up to that time there had never been the slightest resistance or obstruction to the process of any Court or judicial officer of the United States in Maryland, except by the military authority.

And if a military officer, or any other person, had reason to believe that the prisoner had committed any offence against the laws of the United States, it was his duty to give information of the fact and the evidence to support it to the District Attorney, and it would then have become the duty of that officer to bring the matter before the District Judge or Commissioner, and if there was sufficient legal evidence to justify his arrest, the Judge or Commissioner would have issued his warrant to the Marshal to arrest him, and, upon the hearing of the party, would have held him to bail, or committed him for trial, according to the character of the offense as it appeared in the testimony, or would have discharged him immediately if there was not sufficient evidence to support the accusation.

There was no danger of any obstruction or resistance to the action of the civil authorities, and therefore no reason whatever for the interposition of the military. And yet, under these circumstances, a military officer, stationed in Pennsylvania, without giving any information to the District Attorney, and without any application to the judicial authorities, assumes to himself the judicial power in the District of Maryland; undertakes to decide what constitutes the crime of treason or rebellion; what evidence (if, indeed, he required any) is sufficient to support the accusation and justify the commitment; and commits the party, without having a hearing even before himself, to close custody in a strongly garrisoned fort, to be there held, it would seem, during the pleasure of those who committed him.

The Constitution provides, as I have before said, that "no person shall be deprived of life, liberty, or property, without due process of law." It declares that "the right of the people to be secure in their persons, houses, papers, and effects against unreasonable searches and seizures shall not be violated, and no warrant shall issue but upon probable cause, supported by oath or affirmation, and particularly describing the place to be searched and the persons or things to be seized." It provides that the party accused shall be entitled to a speedy trial in a court of justice.

And these great and fundamental laws, which Congress itself could not suspend, have been disregarded and suspended, like the writ of habeas corpus, by a military order, supported by force of arms. Such is the case now before me; and I can only say that if the authority which the Constitution has confided to the judiciary department and judicial officers may thus upon any pretext or under any circumstances be usurped by the military power at its discretion, the people of the United States are no longer living under a Government of laws, but every citizen holds life, liberty, and property at the will and pleasure of the army officer in whose military district he may happen to be found.

In such a case my duty was too plain to be mistaken. I have exercised all the power which the Constitution and laws confer on me, but that power has been resisted by a force too strong for me to overcome. It is possible that the officer who has incurred this grave responsibility may have misunderstood his instructions, and exceeded the authority intended to be given him. I shall, therefore, order all the proceedings in this case, with my opinion, to be filed and recorded in the Circuit Court of the United States for the District of Maryland, and direct the clerk to transmit a copy, under seal, to the President of the United States. It will then remain for that high officer, in fulfillment of his constitutional obligation to "take care that the laws be faithfully executed," to determine what measures he will take to cause the civil process of the United States to be respected and enforced.

R. B. Taney, Chief Justice

END OF OPINION

The U.S. Constitution provision which states that "The privilege of the Writ of Habeas Corpus shall not be suspended, unless when in Cases of Rebellion or Invasion the public Safety may require it" is contained in Article I, the section for the powers of Congress, not Article II, the power of the executive. There is no question that during the American Civil War there was a rebellion. In this opinion, though, the Chief Justice clarified that only Congress, and not the president, has authority under the Constitution to suspend habeas corpus. Because the order to suspend habeas corpus had come from the president and not Congress, it was not lawful.

Initially, President Lincoln ignored Justice Taney's ruling. Lincoln defended this action in a speech to Congress where he asked the rhetorical question, "Are all the laws, but one, to go unexecuted, and the government itself go to pieces, lest that one be violated?" Lincoln knew the seriousness that the Confederacy and its supporters presented to the Union. So he did what he thought necessary.

It is important to note, though, that Lincoln did not entirely ignore Congress. After this decision, Lincoln did ask Congress to ratify his action, and when Congress failed to pass a measure to uphold the suspension of habeas corpus, Lincoln ordered all political prisoners to be released. Later, when riots broke out in response to forced conscription in the Army, President Lincoln again suspended habeas corpus, and this time Congress ratified Lincoln's actions in March of 1863 by passing the Habeas Corpus Suspension Act.

The next case we will examine involved an individual who was tried and sentenced to be executed for actions in support of the Confederacy. Lambdin Milligan was a resident of Indiana who publicly protested the Union's war against the Confederacy. It was widely believed that Milligan was involved in a conspiracy against the United States, and so Milligan was arrested by military authorities on October 5, 1864. No warrant or affidavit was given to show that Milligan's arrest was authorized, and the arresting officers were told to shoot Milligan if he resisted or made any noise. He was tried before a military tribunal starting on October 21, 1864, and told that he had to prove his innocence. While this took place during the Civil War, it all happened in Indiana, far from the battlefields.

Ex Parte Milligan, 71 U.S. 2 (1866)*

On the 10th day of May, 1865, Lambdin P. Milligan presented a petition to be released from an alleged unlawful imprisonment. The case made by the petition is this: Milligan is a citizen of the United States; has lived for twenty years in Indiana, and, at the time of the grievances complained of, was not, and never had been, in the military or naval service of the United States. On the 5th day of October, 1864, while at home, he was arrested by order of General Alvin P. Hovey, commanding the military district of Indiana, and has ever since been kept in close confinement.

On the 21st day of October, 1864, he was brought before a military commission, convened at Indianapolis by order of General Hovey, tried on certain charges and specifications, found guilty, and sentenced to be hanged, and the sentence ordered to be executed on Friday, the 19th day of May, 1865.

Milligan insists that said military commission had no jurisdiction to try him upon the charges preferred, or upon any charges whatever, because he was a citizen of the United States and the State of Indiana, and had not been, since the commencement of the late Rebellion, a resident of any of the States whose citizens were arrayed against the government, and that the right of trial by jury was guaranteed to him by the Constitution of the United States.

The question asked here is "Whether, upon the facts stated in said petition and exhibits, the military commission mentioned therein had jurisdiction legally to try and sentence said Milligan in manner and form as in said petition and exhibits is stated?"

Milligan, not a resident of one of the rebellious states or a prisoner of war, but a citizen of Indiana for twenty years past and never in the military or naval service, is, while at his home, arrested by the military power of the United States, imprisoned, and, on certain criminal charges preferred against him, tried, convicted, and sentenced to be hanged by a military commission, organized under the direction of the military

---

* The case has been heavily edited and paraphrased by the authors for clarity. See disclaimer in introduction.

commander of the military district of Indiana. Had this tribunal the legal power and authority to try and punish this man?

No graver question was ever considered by this court, nor one which more concerns the rights of the whole people, for it is the birthright of every American citizen when charged with crime to be tried and punished according to law. The power of punishment is alone through the means which the laws have provided for that purpose, and, if they are ineffectual, there is an immunity from punishment, no matter how great an offender the individual may be or how much his crimes may have shocked the sense of justice of the country or endangered its safety. By the protection of the law, human rights are secured; withdraw that protection and they are at the mercy of wicked rulers or the clamor of an excited people.

If there was law to justify this military trial, it is not our province to interfere; if there was not, it is our duty to declare the nullity of the whole proceedings. The decision of this question does not depend on argument or judicial precedents, numerous and highly illustrative as they are. These precedents inform us of the extent of the struggle to preserve liberty and to relieve those in civil life from military trials. The founders of our government were familiar with the history of that struggle, and secured in a written constitution every right which the people had wrested from power during a contest of ages. By that Constitution and the laws authorized by it, this question must be determined. The provisions of that instrument on the administration of criminal justice are too plain and direct to leave room for misconstruction or doubt of their true meaning. Those applicable to this case are found in that clause of the original Constitution which says "That the trial of all crimes, except in case of impeachment, shall be by jury," and in the fourth, fifth, and sixth articles of the amendments. The fourth proclaims the right to be secure in person and effects against unreasonable search and seizure, and directs that a judicial warrant shall not issue "without proof of probable cause supported by oath or affirmation." The fifth declares that no person shall be held to answer for a capital or otherwise infamous crime unless on presentment by a grand jury, except in cases arising in the land or naval forces, or in the militia, when in actual service in time of war or public danger, nor be deprived of life, liberty, or property without due process of law.

And the sixth guarantees the right of trial by jury, in such manner and with such regulations that, with upright judges, impartial juries, and an able bar, the innocent will be saved and the guilty punished. It is in these words:

> In all criminal prosecutions the accused shall enjoy the right to a speedy and public trial by an impartial jury of the state and district wherein the crime shall have been committed, which district shall have been previously ascertained by law, and to be informed of the nature and cause of the accusation, to be confronted with the witnesses against him, to have compulsory process for obtaining witnesses in his favor, and to have the assistance of counsel for his defence.

These securities for personal liberty thus embodied were such as wisdom and experience had demonstrated to be necessary for the protection of those accused of crime. And so strong was the sense of the country of their importance, and so jealous were the people that these rights, highly prized, might be denied them by implication, that, when the original Constitution was proposed for adoption, it encountered severe opposition, and, but for the belief that it would be so amended as to embrace them, it would never have been ratified.

Time has proven the discernment of our ancestors, for even these provisions, expressed in such plain English words that it would seem the ingenuity of man could not evade them, are now, after the lapse of more than seventy years, sought to be avoided. Those great and good men foresaw that troublous times would arise when rulers and people would become restive under restraint, and seek by sharp and decisive measures to accomplish ends deemed just and proper, and that the principles of constitutional liberty would be in peril unless established by irrepealable law. The history of the world had taught them that what was done in the past might be attempted in the future.

The Constitution of the United States is a law for rulers and people, equally in war and in peace, and covers with the shield of its protection all classes of men, at all times and under all circumstances. No doctrine involving more pernicious consequences was ever invented by the wit of man than that any of its provisions can be suspended during any of the great exigencies of government. Such a doctrine leads directly to anarchy or despotism, but the theory of necessity on which it is based is false, for the government, within the Constitution, has all the powers granted to it which are necessary to preserve its existence, as has been happily proved by the result of the great effort to throw off its just authority.

Have any of the rights guaranteed by the Constitution been violated in the case of Milligan?, and, if so, what are they?

Every trial involves the exercise of judicial power, and from what source did the military commission that tried him derive their authority? Certainly no part of judicial power of the country was conferred on them, because the Constitution expressly vests it "in one supreme court and such inferior courts as the Congress may from time to time ordain and establish," and the commission which tried and sentenced Milligan was not a court ordained and established by Congress. They cannot justify on the mandate of the President, because he is controlled by law, and has his appropriate sphere of duty, which is to execute, not to make, the laws.

In Indiana, the Federal authority of the Union was always unopposed by the Confederacy, and its courts always open to hear criminal accusations and redress grievances, and no usage of war could sanction a military trial there for any offence whatever of a citizen in civil life in nowise connected with the military service. Congress could grant no such power, and, to the honor of our national legislature be it said, it has never been provoked by the state of the country even to attempt its exercise. One of the plainest constitutional provisions was therefore infringed when Milligan was tried by a court not ordained and established by Congress and not composed of judges appointed during good behavior.

Why was he not delivered to the Circuit Court of Indiana to be prosecuted according to law in a civilian court, and instead tried by a military commission? No reason of necessity for a military commission exists because Congress had declared penalties against the offences charged, provided for their punishment, and directed that court to hear and determine them. And soon after this military tribunal was ended, the civilian Circuit Court which ordinarily would have tried Milligan did meet, peacefully transacted its business, and adjourned. It needed no bayonets to protect it, and required no military aid to execute its judgments. It was held in a state, eminently distinguished for patriotism, by judges commissioned during the Rebellion, who were provided with juries, upright, intelligent, and selected by a marshal appointed by the President. The government had no right to conclude that Milligan, if guilty, would not receive just punishment from that civilian court, for its records disclose that it was constantly engaged in the trial of similar offences, and was never interrupted in its administration of criminal justice. If it was dangerous, in the distracted condition of affairs, to leave Milligan unrestrained of his liberty because he "conspired against the government, afforded aid and comfort to rebels, and incited the people to insurrection," the law said arrest him, confine him closely, render him powerless to do further mischief, and then present his case to the grand jury of the district, with proofs of his guilt, and, if indicted, try him according to the course of the common law. If this had been done, the Constitution would have been vindicated, the law of 1863 enforced, and the securities for personal liberty preserved and defended.

Another guarantee of freedom was broken when Milligan was denied a trial by jury. Until recently, no one ever doubted that the right of trial by jury was fortified in the organic law against the power of attack. It is now assailed, but if ideas can be expressed in words and language has any meaning, this right—one of the most valuable in a free country—is preserved to everyone accused of crime who is not serving in the military. The Sixth Amendment affirms that, "in all criminal prosecutions, the accused shall enjoy the right to a speedy and public trial by an impartial jury," language broad enough to embrace all persons and cases; but the fifth, recognizing the necessity of an indictment or presentment before anyone can be held to answer for high crimes, "excepts cases arising in the land or naval forces, or in the militia, when in actual service, in time of war or public danger," and the framers of the Constitution doubtless meant to limit the right of trial by jury in the sixth amendment to those persons who were subject to indictment or presentment in the fifth, which would not include servicemembers.

The discipline necessary to the efficiency of the army and navy required other and swifter modes of trial than are furnished by the common law courts, and, in pursuance of the power conferred by the Constitution, Congress has declared the kinds of trial, and the manner in which they shall be conducted, for offences committed while the party is in the military or naval service. Everyone connected with these branches of the public service is amenable to the jurisdiction which Congress has created for their government, and, while thus serving, surrenders his right to be tried by the civil courts. All other persons, citizens of states where the courts are open, if charged with crime, are guaranteed the inestimable privilege of trial by jury. This privilege is a vital principle, underlying the whole administration of criminal justice; it is not held by sufferance, and cannot be frittered away on any plea of state or political necessity. When peace prevails, and the authority of the government is undisputed, there is no difficulty of preserving the safeguards of liberty, for the ordinary modes of trial are never neglected, and no one wishes it otherwise; but if society is disturbed by civil commotion—if the passions of men are aroused and the restraints of law weakened, if not disregarded—these safeguards need, and should receive, the watchful care of those entrusted with the guardianship of the Constitution and laws. In no other way can we transmit to posterity unimpaired the blessings of liberty, consecrated by the sacrifices of the Revolution.

It is claimed that martial law covers with its broad mantle the proceedings of this military commission. The proposition is this: that, in a time of war, the commander of an armed force (if, in his opinion, the exigencies of the country demand it, and of which he is to judge) has the power, within the lines of his military district, to suspend all civil rights and their remedies and subject citizens, as well as soldiers to the rule of his will, and, in the exercise of his lawful authority, cannot be restrained except by his superior officer or the President of the United States.

If this position is sound to the extent claimed, then, when war exists, foreign or domestic, and the country is subdivided into military departments for mere convenience, the commander of one of them can, if he chooses, within his limits, on the plea of necessity, substitute military force for and to the exclusion of the laws, and punish all persons as he thinks right and proper, without fixed or certain rules.

The statement of this proposition shows its importance, for, if true, republican government is a failure, and there is an end of liberty regulated by law. Martial law established on such a basis destroys every guarantee of the Constitution, and effectually renders the "military independent of and superior to the civil power"—the attempt to do which by the King of Great Britain was deemed by our fathers such an offence that they assigned it to the world as one of the causes which impelled them to declare their independence. Civil liberty and this kind of martial law cannot endure together; the antagonism is irreconcilable, and, in the conflict, one or the other must perish.

This nation, as experience has proved, cannot always remain at peace, and has no right to expect that it will always have wise and humane rulers sincerely attached to the principles of the Constitution. Wicked men, ambitious of power, with hatred of liberty and contempt of law, may fill the place once occupied by Washington and Lincoln, and if this right is conceded, and the calamities of war again befall us, the dangers to human liberty are frightful to contemplate. If our fathers had failed to provide for just such a contingency, they would have been false to the trust reposed in them. They knew—the history of the world told them—the nation they were founding, be its existence short or long, would be involved in war; how often or how long continued human foresight could not tell, and that unlimited power, wherever lodged at such a time, was especially hazardous to freemen. For this and other equally weighty reasons, they secured the inheritance they had fought to maintain by incorporating in a written constitution the safeguards which time had proved were essential to its preservation. Not one of these safeguards can the President or Congress or the Judiciary disturb, except the one concerning the writ of habeas corpus.

It is essential to the safety of every government that, in a great crisis like the one we have just passed through, there should be a power somewhere of suspending the writ of habeas corpus. In every war, there are men of previously good character wicked enough to counsel their fellow-citizens to resist the measures deemed necessary by a good government to sustain its just authority and overthrow its enemies, and their influence may lead to dangerous combinations. In the emergency of the times, an immediate public investigation according to law may not be possible, and yet the period to the country may be too imminent to suffer such persons to go at large. Unquestionably, there is then an exigency which demands that the government, if it should see fit in the exercise of a proper discretion to make arrests, should not be required to produce the persons arrested in answer to a writ of habeas corpus. The Constitution goes no further. It does not say, after a writ of habeas corpus is denied a citizen, that he shall be tried otherwise than by the course of the common law; if it had intended this result, it was easy, by the use of direct words, to have accomplished it. The illustrious men who framed that instrument were guarding the foundations of civil liberty against the abuses of unlimited power; they were full of wisdom, and the lessons of history informed them that a trial by an established court, assisted by an impartial jury, was the only sure way of protecting the citizen against oppression and wrong. Knowing this, they limited the suspension to one great right, and left the rest to remain forever inviolable. But it is insisted that the safety of the country in time of war demands that this broad claim for martial law shall be sustained. If this were true, it could be well said that a country, preserved at the sacrifice of all the cardinal principles of liberty, is not worth the cost of preservation. Happily, it is not so.

It will be borne in mind that this is not a question of the power to proclaim martial law when war exists in a community and the courts and civil authorities are overthrown. Nor is it a question what rule a military commander, at the head of his army, can impose on states in rebellion to cripple their resources and quell the insurrection. The jurisdiction claimed is much more extensive. The necessities of the service during the Civil War required that the loyal states should be placed within the limits of certain military districts and commanders appointed in them, and it is urged that this, in a military sense, constituted them the theater of military operations, and as, in this case, Indiana had been and was again threatened with invasion by the enemy, the occasion was furnished to establish martial law. The conclusion does not follow from the premises. If armies were collected in Indiana, they were to be employed in another locality, where the laws were obstructed and the national authority disputed. On her soil there was no hostile foot; if once invaded, that invasion was at an end, and, with it, all pretext for martial law. Martial law cannot arise from a threatened invasion. The necessity must be actual and present, the invasion real, such as effectually closes the courts and deposes the civil administration.

It is difficult to see how the safety for the country required martial law in Indiana. If any of her citizens were plotting treason, the power of arrest could secure them until the government was prepared for their trial, when the courts were open and ready to try them. It was as easy to protect witnesses before a civil as a military tribunal, and as there could be no wish to convict except on sufficient legal evidence, surely an ordained and establish court was better able to judge of this than a military tribunal composed of gentlemen not trained to the profession of the law.

It follows from what has been said on this subject that there are occasions when martial rule can be properly applied. If, in foreign invasion or civil war, the courts are actually closed, and it is impossible to administer criminal justice according to law, then, on the theatre of active military operations, where war really prevails, there is a necessity to furnish a substitute for the civil authority, thus overthrown, to preserve the safety of the army and society, and as no power is left but the military, it is allowed to govern by martial rule until the laws can have their free course. As necessity creates the rule, so it limits its duration, for, if this government is continued after the courts are reinstated, it is a gross usurpation of power. Martial rule can never exist where the courts are open and in the proper and unobstructed exercise of their jurisdiction. It is also confined to the locality of actual war. Because, during the late Rebellion, it could have been enforced in Virginia, where the national authority was overturned and the courts driven out, it does not follow that it should obtain in Indiana, where that authority was never disputed and justice was always administered. And so, in the case of a foreign invasion, martial rule may become a necessity in one state when, in another, it would be "mere lawless violence." We are not without precedents in English and American history illustrating our views of this question, but it is hardly necessary to make particular reference to them.

If the military trial of Milligan was contrary to law, then he was entitled, on the facts stated in his petition, to be discharged from custody. Milligan was a citizen of Indiana, not in the military or naval service, and was detained in close confinement, by order of the President, from the 5th day of October, 1864, until the 2d day of January, 1865, when the Circuit Court for the District of Indiana, with a grand jury, convened in session at Indianapolis, and afterwards, on the 27th day of the same month, adjourned without finding an indictment or presentment against him. With these facts, the court was required to liberate him.

But it is insisted that Milligan was a prisoner of war, and therefore excluded from the privileges of the statute. It is not easy to see how he can be treated as a prisoner of war when he lived in Indiana for the past twenty years, was arrested there, and had not been, during the late troubles, a resident of any of the states in rebellion. If in Indiana he conspired with bad men to assist the enemy, he is punishable for it in the courts of Indiana; but, when tried for the offence, he cannot plead the rights of war, for he was not engaged in legal acts of hostility against the government, and only such persons, when captured, are prisoners of war. If he cannot enjoy the immunities attaching to the character of a prisoner of war, how can he be subject to their pains and penalties?

END OF OPINION

The Court ruled in *Ex parte Milligan* that, as a general rule, civilians should not be tried by a military commission but are instead entitled to be arrested, held, and tried in a regular civilian court which affords all of the constitutional protections granted by the U.S. Constitution. Military commissions historically lacked many of these constitutional protections, such as the right to an indictment by a grand jury, or a trial by a jury of one's peers.

Civilians can be tried by a military commission if, and only if, civilian courts are not operational because of invasion, rebellion, Civil War, or some other extreme reason. Milligan lived in an area in Indiana where civilian courts were still operating, he was a citizen of the U.S., was not a member of the Confederate military, and, we can presume, had not directly engaged in any wartime combat. He may have been a traitor to his country, but that does not automatically strip him of his constitutional rights and protections. Consequently, the Court rules, he should not have been tried by a military commission. Now, had he been captured in Virginia or had he been actively involved in combat as a member of the Confederate military, the decision might have been different. But those factors did not apply.

With this in mind, let's consider a more recent event—the Boston Marathon bombing in 2013. Here, you may recall, brothers Tamerlan and Dzhokhar Tsarnaev set off two bombs made of pressure cookers during the Boston Marathon, killing and injuring a great many people. Tamerlan was killed in an exchange of gunfire with police, but Dzhokhar was captured. Could Dzhokhar Tsarnaev be tried by a military commission at Guantanamo Bay, as some politicians urged? Under the criteria set forth in the *Milligan* case, the answer is no. Although these two men were immigrants who supported the causes of Islamic terrorists such as Al-Qaeda and who wished to do violence to Americans, they were nevertheless naturalized American citizens living in Boston who themselves were not actually members of any terrorist organization. Furthermore, the police and judicial processes in Boston were fully functioning, and there was no reason why the court procedures used in any serious murder case would not apply. As we subsequently learned, the normal criminal procedure worked, as Dzhokhar Tsarnaev was found guilty on all charges on April 8, 2015, and the following month was sentenced to death.

Note that the *Milligan* court did assert that civilians can be tried by military commission if, and only if, civilian courts are not operational. This exception makes sense and goes to part of the justification for the use of any military commission. Given the destructive nature of war, in a warzone or the immediate aftermath of a war, it is very possible that civilian government and infrastructure can be destroyed and disorganized. In such situations, quite possibly the only entity left with the capability to uphold law and order would be the military. The only way to bring a semblance of justice to what would otherwise be a lawless area would then be the military.

Now, *Ex parte Milligan* was about the legality of using a military tribunal to try a U.S. citizen who is *not* affiliated with the enemy for criminal acts committed *inside* the U.S. Although Milligan tried to hurt the Union and help the Confederacy, he did not have any actual relationship to the Confederacy, and he did not engage in armed conflict as part of that force. This is different from other instances where formal members of the enemy have infiltrated the U.S. and set about causing terror attacks and other acts in violation of the law of war.

The attack on 9/11 is one example involving terrorists formally aligned with Al-Qaeda, but a similar event happened in World War II. During that war, members of the German Army, two of whom were also U.S. citizens, infiltrated the U.S., disguised themselves as civilians in violation of international law, and then tried to carry out acts of sabotage and terrorism. They were captured (in some cases turning themselves in to the FBI) and charged.

Can there be a trial by a military commission instead of a civilian court when an official member of the enemy force is caught violating the laws of war while inside sovereign U.S.? And does it make any difference if this official member of the enemy force is also a U.S. citizen? The argument against trying them by a military commission was that their crimes occurred on U.S. soil where civilian courts were fully operational, and that two of them were citizens entitled to all protections of the U.S. Constitution. The argument for trying them by a military commission was that this was the traditional means of trying members of the enemy for war crimes.

In *Ex Parte Quirin*, the U.S. Supreme Court ruled that, under certain circumstances, it is permissible to try an enemy combatant by a military commission instead of a civilian court, even when the acts occur in the United States, even when the accused is a citizen, and even when the normal court system is operating.

Ex Parte Quirin, 317 U.S. 1 (1942)*

The question is whether the trial by Military Commission, appointed by Order of the President of July 2, 1942, on charges for violations of the law of war, is in conformity to the laws and Constitution of the United States.

All the petitioners were born in Germany; all have lived in the United States. All returned to Germany between 1933 and 1941. All except petitioner Haupt are admittedly citizens of the German Reich, with which the United States is at war. Haupt came to this country with his parents when he was five years old; it is contended that he became a citizen of the United States by virtue of the naturalization of his parents during his minority, and that he has not since lost his citizenship.

After the declaration of war between the United States and the German Reich, petitioners received training at a sabotage school near Berlin, Germany, where they were instructed in the use of explosives and in methods of secret writing. Thereafter petitioners proceeded from Germany to a seaport in Occupied France, where petitioners Burger, Heinck and Quirin boarded a German submarine which proceeded across the Atlantic to Amagansett Beach on Long Island, New York. They landed from the submarine in the hours of darkness, on or about June 13, 1942, carrying with them a supply of explosives, fuses, and incendiary and timing devices. While

---

* The case has been heavily edited and paraphrased by the authors for clarity. See disclaimer in introduction.

landing, they wore German Marine Infantry uniforms or parts of uniforms. Immediately after landing, they buried their uniforms and the other articles mentioned and proceeded in civilian dress to New York City.

The remaining four petitioners at the same French port boarded another German submarine, which carried them across the Atlantic to Ponte Vedra Beach, Florida. On or about June 17, 1942, they came ashore during the hours of darkness, wearing caps of the German Marine Infantry and carrying with them a supply of explosives, fuses, and incendiary and timing devices. They immediately buried their caps and the other articles mentioned, and proceeded in civilian dress to Jacksonville, Florida, and thence to various points in the United States. All were taken into custody in New York or Chicago by agents of the Federal Bureau of Investigation. All had received instructions in Germany from an officer of the German High Command to destroy war industries and war facilities in the United States, for which they or their relatives in Germany were to receive salary payments from the German Government. They also had been paid by the German Government during their course of training at the sabotage school, and had received substantial sums in United States currency, which were in their possession when arrested. The currency had been handed to them by an officer of the German High Command, who had instructed them to wear their German uniforms while landing in the United States.

The President, as President and Commander in Chief of the Army and Navy, by Order of July 2, 1942, appointed a Military Commission and directed it to try petitioners for offenses against the law of war, and prescribed regulations for the procedure on the trial and for review of the record of the trial and of any judgment or sentence of the Commission. On the same day, by Proclamation, the President declared that "all persons who are subjects, citizens or residents of any nation at war with the United States or who give obedience to or act under the direction of any such nation, and who during time of war enter or attempt to enter the United States through coastal or boundary defenses, and are charged with committing or attempting or preparing to commit sabotage, espionage, hostile or warlike acts, or violations of the law of war, shall be subject to the law of war and to the jurisdiction of military tribunals."

The Proclamation also stated that all such persons were denied access to the courts. Pursuant to direction of the Attorney General, the Federal Bureau of Investigation (FBI) surrendered custody of petitioners to the Provost Marshal of the Military District of Washington, who was directed by the Secretary of War to receive and keep them in custody, and who thereafter held petitioners for trial before the Commission.

On July 3, 1942, the Army prepared and lodged with the Commission the following charges against petitioners, supported by specifications:

1. Violation of the law of war.
2. Violation of Article 81 of the Articles of War, defining the offense of relieving or attempting to relieve, or corresponding with or giving intelligence to, the enemy.

3. Violation of Article 82, defining the offense of spying.

4. Conspiracy to commit the offenses alleged in charges 1, 2 and 3.

The Commission met on July 8, 1942, and proceeded with the trial. At the same time the trial by military commission was progressing, so too did the causes which were pending in this civilian Court concerning the lawfulness of trying the petitioners by military commission. It is conceded that, ever since petitioners' arrest, the state and federal courts in Florida, New York, and the District of Columbia, and in the states in which each of the petitioners was arrested or detained, have been open and functioning normally.

Petitioners' main contention is that the President is without any statutory or constitutional authority to order the petitioners to be tried by military tribunal for offenses with which they are charged; that, in consequence, they are entitled to be tried in the civil courts with the safeguards, including trial by jury, which the Fifth and Sixth Amendments guarantee to all persons charged in such courts with criminal offenses. In any case, it is urged that the President's Order, in prescribing the procedure of the Commission and the method for review of its findings and sentence, and the proceedings of the Commission under the Order, conflict with Articles of War adopted by Congress—particularly Articles 38, 43, 46, 50 1/2 and 70—and are illegal and void.

The Government challenges each of these propositions. But regardless of their merits, it also insists that petitioners must be denied access to the civilian courts, both because they are enemy aliens or have entered our territory as enemy belligerents, and because the President's Proclamation undertakes in terms to deny such access to the class of persons defined by the Proclamation, which aptly describes the character and conduct of petitioners. It is urged that, if they are enemy aliens or if the Proclamation has force, no civilian court may afford the petitioners a hearing.

Although the U.S. Supreme Court is a civilian court, there is certainly nothing in the Proclamation to preclude access to the civilian courts for determining its applicability to the particular case. And neither the Proclamation nor the fact that they are enemy aliens forecloses consideration by the courts of petitioners' contentions that the Constitution and laws of the United States constitutionally enacted forbid their trial by military commission. As announced in our opinion, we have resolved those questions by our conclusion that the Commission has jurisdiction to try the charge preferred against petitioners. There is therefore no occasion to decide contentions of the parties unrelated to this issue. We pass at once to the consideration of the basis of the Commission's authority.

We are not here concerned with any question of the guilt or innocence of petitioners. But the detention and trial of petitioners by military commission—ordered by the President in the declared exercise of his powers as Commander in Chief of the Army in time of war and of grave public danger—are not to be set aside by the courts without the clear conviction that they are in conflict with the Constitution or laws of Congress constitutionally enacted.

Congress and the President, like the courts, possess no power not derived from the Constitution. But one of the objects of the Constitution, as declared by the

Constitution's preamble, is to "provide for the common defence." As a means to that end, the Constitution gives to Congress the power to "provide for the common Defence," "To raise and support Armies," "To provide and maintain a Navy," and "To make Rules for the Government and Regulation of the land and naval Forces" Congress is given authority "To declare War, grant Letters of Marque and Reprisal, and make Rules concerning Captures on Land and Water," and "To define and punish Piracies and Felonies committed on the high Seas, and Offences against the Law of Nations." And finally, the Constitution authorizes Congress "To make all Laws which shall be necessary and proper for carrying into Execution the foregoing Powers, and all other Powers vested by this Constitution in the Government of the United States, or in any Department or Officer thereof."

The Constitution confers on the President the "executive Power," and imposes on him the duty to "take Care that the Laws be faithfully executed." It makes him the Commander in Chief of the Army and Navy, and empowers him to appoint and commission officers of the United States.

The Constitution thus invests the President, as Commander in Chief, with the power to wage war which Congress has declared, and to carry into effect all laws passed by Congress for the conduct of war and for the government and regulation of the Armed Forces, and all laws defining and punishing offenses against the law of nations, including those which pertain to the conduct of war.

By the Articles of War,[1] Congress has provided rules for the government of the Army. It has provided for the trial and punishment, by courts martial, of violations of the Articles of War by members of the armed forces and by specified classes of persons associated or serving with the Army. [T]he Articles also recognize the "military commission" as an appropriate tribunal for the trial and punishment of offenses against the law of war not ordinarily tried by court martial. Articles 38 and 46 authorize the President, with certain limitations, to prescribe the procedure for military commissions. Articles 81 and 82 authorize trial, either by court martial or military commission, of those charged with relieving, harboring or corresponding with the enemy and those charged with spying. And Article 15 declares that the provisions of these articles conferring jurisdiction upon courts martial shall not be construed as depriving military commissions or other military tribunals of concurrent jurisdiction in respect of offenders or offenses that, by statute or by the law of war may be triable by such military commissions or other military tribunals.

Article 2 includes among those persons subject to military law the personnel of our own military establishment. But this, as Article 12 provides, does not exclude from that class "any other person who by the law of war is subject to trial by military tribunals" and who, under Article 12, may be tried by court martial or under Article 15 by military commission.

---

1. The Articles of War was the federal statute containing military law used prior to the enactment of the Uniform Code of Military Justice.

Similarly, the Espionage Act of 1917, which authorizes trial in the civilian courts of certain offenses that tend to interfere with the prosecution of war, provides that nothing contained in the act "shall be deemed to limit the jurisdiction of the general courts-martial, military commissions, or naval courts-martial."

From the very beginning of its history, the U.S. Supreme Court has recognized and applied the law of war as including that part of the law of nations which prescribes, for the conduct of war, the status, rights and duties of enemy nations, as well as of enemy individuals. By the Articles of War, and especially Article 15, Congress has explicitly provided that military tribunals shall have jurisdiction to try offenders or offenses against the law of war in appropriate cases. Congress, in addition to making rules for the government of our Armed Forces, has thus exercised its authority to define and punish offenses against the law of nations by sanctioning the jurisdiction of military commissions to try persons for offenses which, according to the rules and precepts of the law of nations, and more particularly the law of war, are cognizable by such tribunals. And the President, as Commander in Chief, by his Proclamation in time of war, has invoked that law. By his Order creating the present Commission, he has undertaken to exercise the authority conferred upon him by Congress, and also such authority as the Constitution itself gives the Commander in Chief, to direct the performance of those functions which may constitutionally be performed by the military arm of the nation in time of war.

An important incident to the conduct of war is the adoption of measures by the military command not only to repel and defeat the enemy, but to seize and subject to disciplinary measures those enemies who, in their attempt to thwart or impede our military effort, have violated the law of war. Here, Congress has authorized trial of offenses against the law of war before such commissions. We are concerned only with the question whether it is within the constitutional power of the National Government to place petitioners upon trial before a military commission instead of a civilian court for the offenses with which they are charged. We must therefore first inquire whether any of the acts charged is an offense against the law of war as recognized before a military tribunal, and, if so, whether the Constitution prohibits the trial. We may assume that there are acts regarded in other countries, or by some writers on international law, as offenses against the law of war which would not be triable by military tribunal here, either because they are not recognized by our courts as violations of the law of war or because they are of that class of offenses constitutionally triable only by a jury. It was upon such grounds that the Court denied the right to proceed by military tribunal in Ex parte Milligan, supra. But, as we shall show, these petitioners were charged with an offense against the law of war which the Constitution does not require to be tried by jury.

The U.S. Constitution specifically allows Congress to "define and punish Piracies, and Felonies committed on the high Seas, and Offenses against the Law of Nations." Similarly, by the reference in the 15th Article of War to "offenders or offenses that . . . by the law of war may be triable by such military commissions," Congress has incorporated by reference, as within the jurisdiction of military commissions, all offenses which are defined as such by the law of war and which may constitutionally be included within that jurisdiction. Congress had the choice of crystallizing in permanent form and in minute detail every offense against the law of war, or of adopting the system of common law applied by military tribunals so far as it should be recognized and deemed applicable by the courts. It chose the latter course.

By universal agreement and practice, the law of war draws a distinction between the armed forces and the peaceful populations of belligerent nations, and also between those who are lawful and unlawful combatants. Lawful combatants are subject to capture and detention as prisoners of war by opposing military forces. Unlawful combatants are likewise subject to capture and detention, but, in addition, they are subject to trial and punishment by military tribunals for acts which render their belligerency unlawful. The spy who secretly and without uniform passes the military lines of a belligerent in time of war, seeking to gather military information and communicate it to the enemy, or an enemy combatant who without uniform comes secretly through the lines for the purpose of waging war by destruction of life or property, are familiar examples of belligerents who are generally deemed not to be entitled to the status of prisoners of war, but to be offenders against the law of war subject to trial and punishment by military tribunals.

Such was the practice of our own military authorities before the adoption of the Constitution, and during the Mexican and Civil Wars. Paragraph 83 of General Order No. 100 of April 24, 1863, directed that:

> Scouts or single soldiers, if disguised in the dress of the country, or in the uniform of the army hostile to their own, employed in obtaining information, if found within or lurking about the lines of the captor, are treated as spies, and suffer death.

And Paragraph 84, that

> Armed prowlers, by whatever names they may be called, or persons of the enemy's territory, who steal within the lines of the hostile army for the purpose of robbing, killing, or of destroying bridges, roads, or canals, or of robbing or destroying the mail, or of cutting the telegraph wires, are not entitled to the privileges of the prisoner of war.

These and related provisions have been continued in substance by the Rules of Land Warfare promulgated by the War Department for the guidance of the Army. Paragraph 357 of the 1940 Rules provides that "All war crimes are subject to the death penalty, although a lesser penalty may be imposed." Paragraph 8 divides the enemy population into "armed forces" and "peaceful population," and Paragraph 9 names as distinguishing characteristics of lawful belligerents that they "carry arms openly" and "have a fixed distinctive emblem." Paragraph 348 declares that "persons who take up arms and commit hostilities" without having the means of identification prescribed for belligerents are punishable as "war criminals." Paragraph 351 provides that "men and bodies of men, who, without being lawful belligerents" "nevertheless commit hostile acts of any kind" are not entitled to the privileges of prisoners of war if captured, and may be tried by military commission and punished by death or lesser punishment.

The definition of lawful belligerents by Paragraph 9 is that adopted by Article 1, Annex to Hague Convention No. IV of October 18, 1907, to which the United States was a signatory and which was ratified by the Senate in 1909. The preamble to the Convention declares:

> Until a more complete code of the laws of war has been issued, the High Contracting Parties deem it expedient to declare that, in cases not included in the Regulations adopted by them, the inhabitants and the belligerents remain under the protection and the rule of the principles of the law of nations, as they result from the usages established among civilized peoples, from the laws of humanity, and the dictates of the public conscience.

Our Government, by thus defining lawful belligerents entitled to be treated as prisoners of war, has recognized that there is a class of unlawful belligerents not entitled to that privilege, including those who, though combatants, do not wear "fixed and distinctive emblems." And, by Article 15 of the Articles of War, Congress has made provision for their trial and punishment by military commission, according to "the law of war."

Our Government has recognized that those who, during time of war, pass surreptitiously from enemy territory into our own, discarding their uniforms upon entry, for the commission of hostile acts involving destruction of life or property, have the status of unlawful combatants punishable as such by military commission. This precept of the law of war has been so recognized in practice both here and abroad, and has so generally been accepted as valid by authorities on international law that we think it must be regarded as a rule or principle of the law of war recognized by this Government by its enactment of the Fifteenth Article of War.

Specification 1 of the first charge is sufficient to charge all the petitioners with the offense of unlawful belligerency, trial of which is within the jurisdiction of the Commission, and the admitted facts affirmatively show that the charge is not without foundation.

Specification 1 states that petitioners, "being enemies of the United States and acting for the German Reich, a belligerent enemy nation, secretly and covertly passed, in civilian dress, contrary to the law of war, through the military and naval lines and defenses of the United States . . . and went behind such lines, contrary to the law of war, in civilian dress . . . for the purpose of committing . . . hostile acts, and, in particular, to destroy certain war industries, war utilities and war materials within the United States."

This specification plainly alleges violations of the law of war. As we have seen, entry upon our territory in time of war by enemy belligerents, including those acting under the direction of the armed forces of the enemy, for the purpose of destroying property used or useful in prosecuting the war, is a hostile and warlike act. It subjects those who participate in it without uniform to the punishment prescribed by the law of war for unlawful belligerents. It is meaningless that petitioners were not alleged to have carried conventional weapons or that their proposed hostile acts did not necessarily contemplate collision with the Armed Forces of the United States. Paragraphs 351 and 352 of the Rules of Land Warfare, already referred to, plainly contemplate that the hostile acts and purposes for which unlawful belligerents may be punished are not limited to assaults on military targets. Modern warfare is directed at the destruction of enemy war supplies and the implements of their production and transportation, quite as much as at the armed forces. Every consideration which makes the unlawful belligerent punishable is equally applicable whether his objective is the one or the other. The law of war cannot rightly treat those agents of enemy armies who enter our territory, armed with explosives intended for the destruction of war industries and supplies, as any the less belligerent enemies than are agents similarly entering for the purpose of destroying fortified places or our Armed Forces. By passing our boundaries for such purposes without uniform or other emblem signifying their belligerent status, or by discarding that means of identification after entry, such enemies become unlawful belligerents subject to trial and punishment.

Citizenship in the United States of an enemy belligerent does not relieve him from the consequences of a belligerency which is unlawful because in violation of the law of war. Citizens who associate themselves with the military arm of the enemy government, and, with its aid, guidance and direction, enter this country bent on hostile acts, are enemy belligerents within the meaning of the Hague Convention and the law of war. It is as an enemy belligerent that petitioner Haupt (who is a US citizen) is charged with entering the United States, and unlawful belligerency is the gravamen of the offense of which he is accused.

Nor are petitioners any the less belligerents if, as they argue, they have not actually committed or attempted to commit any act of depredation or entered the theatre or zone of active military operations. The argument leaves out of account the nature of the offense which the Government charges and which the Articles of War, an act of Congress, incorporates and punishes the law of war. It is that each petitioner, in circumstances which gave him the status of an enemy belligerent, passed our military and naval lines and defenses or went behind those lines, in civilian dress and with hostile purpose. The offense was complete when, with that purpose, they entered our territory in time of war without uniform or other appropriate means of identification. For that reason, even when committed by a citizen, the offense is distinct from the crime of treason defined in Article III, § 3 of the Constitution, since the absence of uniform essential to one is irrelevant to the other.

But petitioners insist that, even if the offenses with which they are charged are offenses against the law of war, their trial is subject to the requirement of the Fifth Amendment that no person shall be held to answer for a capital or otherwise infamous crime unless on a presentment or indictment of a grand jury, and that such trials by Article III, § 2, and the Sixth Amendment must be by jury in a civil court. Before the Amendments, § 2 of Article III, the Judiciary Article, had provided, "The Trial of all Crimes, except in Cases of Impeachment, shall be by Jury," and had directed that "such Trial shall be held in the State where the said Crimes shall have been committed."

Presentment by a grand jury and trial by a jury of one's peers where the crime was committed were, at the time of the adoption of the Constitution, familiar parts of the machinery for criminal trials in the civil courts. But these are not and have never been procedures used for military tribunals. This Court is not charged with enlarging the right to a grand jury indictment or a jury of one's peers; we seek to merely preserve these rights as they were recognized at the time the Constitution was drafted, which precludes these rights from being applied to military commissions. In the light of this long-continued and consistent interpretation of the Constitution, we must conclude that the Fifth and Sixth Amendments cannot be interpreted to extend the right to a grand jury indictment or a jury of one's peers to apply in a military commission. In fact, "cases arising in the land or naval forces" are expressly excepted from the Fifth and Sixth Amendments.

We may assume, without deciding, that a trial prosecuted before a military commission created by military authority is not one "arising in the land . . . forces," when the accused is not a member of or associated with those forces. But even so, the exception cannot be taken to affect those trials before military commissions which are neither within the exception nor within the provisions of Article III, §2, whose guaranty the Amendments did not enlarge. No exception is necessary to exclude from the operation of these provisions cases never deemed to be within their terms. An express exception from Article III, §2, and from the Fifth and Sixth Amendments, of trials of petty offenses and of criminal contempts has not been found necessary in order to preserve the traditional practice of trying those offenses without a jury. It is no more so in order to continue the practice of trying, before military tribunals without a jury, offenses committed by enemy belligerents against the law of war.

Section 2 of the Act of Congress of April 10, 1806, derived from the Resolution of the Continental Congress of August 21, 1776, imposed the death penalty on alien spies "according to the law and usage of nations, by sentence of a general court martial." This enactment must be regarded as a contemporary construction of both Article III, §2, and the Amendments as not foreclosing trial by military tribunals, without a jury, of offenses against the law of war committed by enemies not in or associated with our Armed Forces. It is a construction of the Constitution which has been followed since the founding of our Government, and is now continued in the 82nd Article of War. Such a construction is entitled to the greatest respect. It has not hitherto been challenged, and, so far as we are advised, it has never been suggested in the very extensive literature of the subject that an alien spy, in time of war, could not be tried by military tribunal without a jury.

The exception from the Amendments of "cases arising in the land or naval forces" was not aimed at trials by military tribunals, without a jury, of such offenses against the law of war. Its objective was quite different—to authorize the trial by court martial of the members of our Armed Forces for all that class of crimes which, under the Fifth and Sixth Amendments, might otherwise have been deemed triable in the civil courts. The cases mentioned in the exception are not restricted to those involving offenses against the law of war alone, but extend to trial of all offenses, including crimes which were of the class traditionally triable by jury at common law.

Since the Amendments do not preclude all trials of offenses against the law of war by military commission without a jury when the offenders are aliens and not members of our Armed Forces, it is plain that they present no greater obstacle to the trial in like manner of citizen enemies who have violated the law of war applicable to enemies. Under the original statute authorizing trial of alien spies by military tribunals, the offenders were outside the constitutional guaranty of trial by jury not because they were aliens, but only because they had violated the law of war by committing offenses constitutionally triable by military tribunal.

We cannot say that Congress, in preparing the Fifth and Sixth Amendments, intended to extend trial by jury to the cases of alien or citizen offenders against the law of war otherwise triable by military commission, while withholding it from members of our own armed forces charged with infractions of the Articles of War punishable by death. It is equally absurd to construe the Amendments—whose primary purpose was to continue unimpaired presentment by grand jury and trial by petit jury in all those cases in which they had been customary—as either abolishing all trials by military tribunals, save those of the personnel of our own armed forces, or, what in effect comes to the same thing, as imposing on all such tribunals the necessity of proceeding against unlawful enemy belligerents only on presentment and trial by jury. We conclude that the Fifth and Sixth Amendments did not restrict whatever authority was conferred by the Constitution to try offenses against the law of war by military commission, and that petitioners, charged with such an offense not required to be tried by jury at common law, were lawfully placed on trial by the Commission without a jury.

Petitioners, and especially petitioner Haupt, stress the pronouncement of this Court in the Milligan case, that the law of war "can never be applied to citizens in states which have upheld the authority of the government, and where the courts are open, and their process unobstructed." The facts of Milligan are very different than the facts present today. Milligan was a citizen and twenty years resident in Indiana. He had never been a resident of any of the states in rebellion so he could not be an enemy belligerent either entitled to the status of a prisoner of war or subject to the penalties imposed upon unlawful belligerents. Milligan, not being a part of or associated with the armed forces of the enemy, was a nonbelligerent, not subject to the law of war save as—in circumstances found not there to be present, and not involved here—martial law might be constitutionally established.

We need not inquire whether Congress may restrict the power of the Commander in Chief to deal with enemy belligerents. For the Court is unanimous in its conclusion that the Articles in question could not at any stage of the proceedings afford any basis for issuing the writ.

Accordingly, we conclude that Charge I, on which petitioners were detained for trial by the Military Commission, alleged an offense which the President is authorized to order tried by military commission; that his Order convening the Commission was a lawful order, and that the Commission was lawfully constituted; that the petitioners were held in lawful custody, and did not show cause for their discharge.

It follows that the orders of the District Court should be affirmed, and that leave to file petitions for habeas corpus in this Court should be denied.

END OF OPINION

As the Court ruled, trying all these men — including the one American citizen — was constitutional because combatants *who are part of the enemy forces*, and who, because of their unlawful behavior are not entitled to the privileges of combatants under the laws of war, can be tried by military commission. This is a standard and traditional practice under the laws of war. The fact that a U.S. citizen was also a soldier in the German army does not grant him any special privileges, for U.S. citizenship is no bar to also being an official member of the recognized enemy who violates the law of war.

This case can be distinguished from *Ex parte Milligan* because the facts were different. Not only was Milligan a U.S. citizen, but he lacked any formal connections to the military of the Confederate States of America. He may have supported the Confederacy in terms of his views, but he had not undertaken any combatant activities and had not committed any violations of the laws of war. In contrast, all of the German soldiers in the *Quirin* case, including the ones who held U.S. citizenship, were official members of the Germany Army. They had been trained in German military facilities, received transport to America via the German Navy, and had entered the U.S. while wearing German Army uniforms. Because they were members of the enemy, they could be tried by military commission, regardless whether or not civilian courts were operating or whether they held U.S. citizenship.

Military Detention and Trial after 9/11

A month after the attacks of September 11, 2001, the United States invaded Afghanistan in operations against Al-Qaeda, the Taliban, and other associated forces. It was initially an operation involving a small number of American ground forces, relying in large measure on an air campaign and the Afghan forces known as the Northern Alliance. Many members of the Taliban and Al-Qaeda were taken prisoner, and a large number of these were being detained at Qala-i-Jangi, a 19th-century fortress in Afghanistan. The Northern Alliance soldiers sent to guard them were untrained in handling prisoners, prisoners were loosely guarded, the prison was insufficiently staffed, and weapons were easily smuggled into the prison. There was a prisoner uprising and attempted outbreak which led to many deaths, including that of CIA officer Michael Spann, making him the first American casualty of the war.

This incident at the prison in Afghanistan led American planners to look for alternatives. What they wanted was a secure facility where prisoners could not only be detained without fear of another breakout, but also questioned for intelligence. There was tremendous fear at this time that Al-Qaeda might have put plans for other 9/11-like attacks into play, and the leadership of Al-Qaeda was still free.

Many of these fighters were automatically classified as "unlawful combatants" based on the determination of President Bush that Al-Qaeda and most Taliban fighters, having acted in ways inconsistent with the laws of war (in particular by attacking the American civilian population and failing to wear uniforms when in combat), would not be afforded the privileges of Prisoners of War under the Third Geneva Conventions of 1949. In particular, Article 17 of that treaty significantly limits the ability of a detaining power to interrogate prisoners. By classifying the detainees as "unlawful combatants," the Bush administration determined that it would have the ability to conduct interrogations, and thus hopefully prevent future terrorist attacks.

The Bush administration was also concerned that if these unlawful combatants were brought onto U.S. soil, for example to a military or federal prison, they might receive certain due process rights such as the Fifth Amendment right to remain silent, which would interfere with the ability to interrogate them. The administration wanted to ensure that the military would retain control over the detainees and was concerned that on U.S. soil, the detainees would have the right of habeas corpus.

There was justification for this position. Following World War II, the U.S. Supreme Court had held that U.S. civilian courts did not have jurisdiction over a U.S.-operated prison in Germany. Based on this precedent, the administration believed that U.S. civilian courts would not have jurisdiction over a U.S. military detention facility operated in Cuba.

Johnson v. Eisentrager, 339 U.S. 763 (1950)*

The ultimate question in this case is one of jurisdiction of civil courts of the United States in relation to military authorities in dealing with enemy aliens overseas. The issues come here in this way:

Twenty-one German nationals petitioned the District Court of the District of Columbia for writs of habeas corpus. They alleged that, prior to May 8, 1945, they were in the service of German armed forces in China. They amended to allege that their employment there was by civilian agencies of the German Government. On May 8, 1945, the German High Command executed an act of unconditional surrender, expressly obligating all forces under German control at once to cease active hostilities. These prisoners have been convicted of violating laws of war, by engaging in, permitting or ordering continued military activity against the United States after surrender of Germany and before surrender of Japan. Their hostile operations consisted principally of collecting and furnishing intelligence concerning American forces and their movements to the Japanese armed forces. They, with six others who were acquitted, were taken into custody by the United States Army after the Japanese surrender and were tried and convicted by a Military Commission. The Commission sat in China, with express consent of the Chinese Government. The proceeding was conducted wholly by American military authorities and involved no

---

* The case has been heavily edited and paraphrased by the authors for clarity. See disclaimer in introduction.

international participation. After conviction, the sentences were duly reviewed and approved by military reviewing authority.

The prisoners were repatriated to Germany to serve their sentences. Their immediate custodian is Commandant of Landsberg Prison, an American Army officer under the Commanding General, Third United States Army, and the Commanding General, European Command. Respondents named in the petition are Secretary of Defense, Secretary of the Army, Chief of Staff of the Army, and the Joint Chiefs of Staff of the United States.

The petition alleges, and respondents denied, that the jailer is subject to their direction. The Court of Appeals assumed, and we do likewise, that, while prisoners are in immediate physical custody of an officer or officers not parties to the proceeding, respondents named in the petition have lawful authority to effect their release.

The petition prays an order that the prisoners be produced before the District Court, that it may inquire into their confinement and order them discharged from such offenses and confinement. It is claimed that their trial, conviction and imprisonment violate Articles I and III of the Constitution, and the Fifth Amendment thereto, and other provisions of the Constitution and laws of the United States and provisions of the Geneva Convention governing treatment of prisoners of war.

The Court of Appeals concluded that any person, including an enemy alien, deprived of his liberty anywhere under any purported authority of the United States is entitled to the writ if he can show that extension to his case of any constitutional rights or limitations would show his imprisonment illegal; that, although no statutory jurisdiction of such cases is given, courts must be held to possess jurisdiction as part of the judicial power of the United States; that where deprivation of liberty by an official act occurs outside the territorial jurisdiction of any District Court, the petition will lie in the District Court which has territorial jurisdiction over officials who have directive power over the immediate jailer.

The obvious importance of these holdings to both judicial administration and military operations impelled us to grant review. The case is before us only on issues of law. The writ of habeas corpus must be granted "unless it appears from the application" that the applicants are not entitled to it.

We are cited to no instance where a court, in this or any other country where the writ is known, has issued it on behalf of an alien enemy who, at no relevant time and in no stage of his captivity, has been within its territorial jurisdiction. Nothing in the text of the Constitution extends such a right, nor does anything in our statutes. Absence of support from legislative or juridical sources is implicit in the statement of the court below that "The answers stem directly from fundamentals. They cannot be found by casual reference to statutes or cases." The breadth of the court's premises and solution requires us to consider questions basic to alien enemy and kindred litigation which for some years have been beating upon our doors.

Modern American law has come a long way since the time when outbreak of war made every enemy national an outlaw, subject to both public and private slaughter, cruelty and plunder. But even by the most magnanimous view, our law does not abolish inherent distinctions recognized throughout the civilized world between citizens and aliens, nor between aliens of friendly and of enemy allegiance, nor between resident enemy aliens who have submitted themselves to our laws and non-resident enemy aliens who at all times have remained with, and adhered to, enemy governments.

With the citizen we are now little concerned, except to set his case apart as untouched by this decision and to take measure of the difference between his status and that of all categories of aliens. Because the Government's obligation of protection is correlative with the duty of loyal support inherent in the citizen's allegiance, Congress has directed the President to exert the full diplomatic and political power of the United States on behalf of any citizen, but of no other, in jeopardy abroad. When any citizen is deprived of his liberty by any foreign government, it is made the duty of the President to demand the reasons and, if the detention appears wrongful, to use means not amounting to acts of war to effectuate his release. It is neither sentimentality nor chauvinism to repeat that "Citizenship is a high privilege."

The alien, to whom the United States has been traditionally hospitable, has been accorded a generous and ascending scale of rights as he increases his identity with our society. Mere lawful presence in the country creates an implied assurance of safe conduct and gives him certain rights; they become more extensive and secure when he makes preliminary declaration of intention to become a citizen, and they expand to those of full citizenship upon naturalization. During his probationary residence, this Court has steadily enlarged his right against Executive deportation except upon full and fair hearing. And, at least since 1886, we have extended to the person and property of resident aliens important constitutional guarantees—such as the due process of law of the Fourteenth Amendment.

But, in extending constitutional protections beyond the citizenry, the Court has been at pains to point out that it was the alien's presence within its territorial jurisdiction that gave the Judiciary power to act. In the pioneer case of *Yick Wo v. Hopkins*, the Court said of the Fourteenth Amendment, "These provisions are universal in their application, to all persons within the territorial jurisdiction, without regard to any differences of race, of color, or of nationality." And in *The Japanese Immigrant Case*, the Court held its processes available to "an alien, who has entered the country, and has become subject in all respects to its jurisdiction, and a part of its population, although alleged to be illegally here."

It is war that exposes the relative vulnerability of the German soldiers' alien status. The security and protection he enjoyed when Germany was in friendship with the United States was greatly impaired when Germany took up arms against us. While his treatment in captivity by the Americans is more humane and endurable than the experience of American soldiers in German camps, his captivity is still not a happy one. But disabilities this country lays upon the alien who becomes also an enemy are imposed temporarily as an incident of war and not as an incident of alienage.

American doctrine as to effects of war upon the status of the nationals of nations we were fighting took permanent shape following our first foreign war. Chancellor

Kent, after considering the leading authorities of his time, declared the law to be that "... in war, the subjects of each country were enemies to each other, and bound to regard and treat each other as such." This historic statement has since been validated by the actualities of modern total warfare." ... The alien enemy is bound by an allegiance which commits him to lose no opportunity to forward the cause of our enemy; hence the United States, assuming him to be faithful to his allegiance, regards him as part of the enemy resources. It therefore takes measures to disable him from commission of hostile acts imputed as his intention because they are a duty to his sovereign.

Executive power over enemy aliens, undelayed and unhampered by litigation, has been deemed, throughout our history, essential to war-time security. This is in keeping with the practices of the most enlightened of nations and has resulted in treatment of alien enemies more considerate than that which has prevailed among any of our enemies and some of our allies.

The resident enemy alien is constitutionally subject to summary arrest, internment and deportation whenever a "declared war" exists. Courts will entertain his plea for freedom from Executive custody only to ascertain the existence of a state of war and whether he is an alien enemy and so subject to the Alien Enemy Act. Once these jurisdictional elements have been determined, courts will not inquire into any other issue as to his internment.

We are here confronted with a decision whose basic premise is that these prisoners are entitled, as a constitutional right, to sue in some court of the United States for a writ of habeas corpus. To support that assumption we must hold that a prisoner of our military authorities is constitutionally entitled to the writ, even though he (a) is an enemy alien; (b) has never been or resided in the United States; (c) was captured outside of our territory and there held in military custody as a prisoner of war; (d) was tried and convicted by a Military Commission sitting outside the United States; (e) for offenses against laws of war committed outside the United States; (f) and is at all times imprisoned outside the United States.

A basic consideration in habeas corpus practice is that the prisoner will be produced before the court. To grant the writ to these prisoners might mean that our army must transport them across the seas for hearing. This would require allocation of shipping space, guarding personnel, billeting and rations. It might also require transportation for whatever witnesses the prisoners desired to call as well as transportation for those necessary to defend legality of the sentence. The writ, since it is held to be a matter of right, would be equally available to enemies during active hostilities as in the present twilight between war and peace. Such trials would hamper the war effort and bring aid and comfort to the enemy. They would diminish the prestige of our commanders, not only with enemies but with wavering neutrals. It would be difficult to devise more effective fettering of a field commander than to allow the very enemies he is ordered to reduce to submission to call him to account in his own civil courts and divert his efforts and attention from the military offensive abroad to the legal defensive at home. Nor is it unlikely that the result of such enemy litigiousness would be a conflict between judicial and military opinion highly comforting to enemies of the United States.

The prisoners rely, however, upon two decisions of this Court to get them over the threshold—*Ex parte Quirin*, and *In re Yamashita*. Reliance on the *Quirin* case is clearly mistaken. Those prisoners were in custody in the District of Columbia. One was, or claimed to be, a citizen. They were tried by a Military Commission sitting in the District of Columbia at a time when civil courts were open and functioning normally. They were arrested by civil authorities and the prosecution was personally directed by the Attorney General, a civilian prosecutor, for acts committed in the United States. They waived arraignment before a civil court and it was contended that the civil courts thereby acquired jurisdiction and could not be ousted by the Military. None of the places where they were acting, arrested, tried or imprisoned were, it was contended, in a zone of active military operations or under martial law or any other military control, and no circumstances justified transferring them from civil to military jurisdiction. None of these grave grounds for challenging military jurisdiction can be urged in the case now before us.

Nor can the Court's decision in the *Yamashita* case aid the prisoners. Yamashita was the Japanese General whose troops engaged in many war-crimes in parts of the American territories in the Philippines during World War II. This Court refused to receive Yamashita's petition for a writ of habeas corpus. For hearing and opinion, it was consolidated with another application to review the refusal of habeas corpus by the Supreme Court of the Philippines over whose decisions the statute then gave this Court a right of review. By reason of our sovereignty at that time over these insular possessions, Yamashita stood much as did Quirin before American courts. Yamashita's offenses were committed on our territory, he was tried within the jurisdiction of our insular courts and he was imprisoned within territory of the United States. None of these heads of jurisdiction can be invoked by these prisoners.

Despite this, the doors of our courts have not been summarily closed upon these prisoners. Three courts have considered their application and have provided their counsel opportunity to advance every argument in their support and to show some reason in the petition why they should not be subject to the usual disabilities of nonresident enemy aliens. This is the same preliminary hearing as to sufficiency of application that was extended in *Quirin* and *Yamashita*. After hearing all contentions they have seen fit to advance and considering every contention we can base on their application and the holdings below, we arrive at the same conclusion the Court reached in each of those cases; that no right to the writ of habeas corpus appears.

The doctrine that the term "any person" in the Fifth Amendment spreads its protection over alien enemies anywhere in the world engaged in hostilities against us, should be weighed in light of the full text of that Amendment:

"No person shall be held to answer for a capital, or otherwise infamous crime, unless on a presentment or indictment of a Grand Jury, except in cases arising in the land or naval forces, or in the Militia, when in actual service in time of War or public danger; nor shall any person be subject for the same offense to be twice put in jeopardy of life or limb; nor shall be compelled in any criminal case to be a witness against himself, nor be deprived of life, liberty, or property, without due process of law; nor shall private property be taken for public use, without just compensation."

When we analyze the claim prisoners are asserting and the court below sustained, it amounts to a right not to be tried at all for an offense against our armed forces. If the Fifth Amendment protects them from military trial, the Sixth Amendment as clearly prohibits their trial by civil courts. The latter requires in all criminal prosecutions that "the accused" be tried "by an impartial jury of the State and district wherein the crime shall have been committed, which district shall have been previously ascertained by law." And if the Fifth be held to embrace these prisoners because it uses the inclusive term "no person," the Sixth must, for it applies to all "accused." No suggestion is advanced by the court below, or by prisoners, of any constitutional method by which any violations of the laws of war endangering the United States forces could be reached or punished, if it were not by a Military Commission in the theater where the offense was committed.

The Court of Appeals has cited no authority whatever for holding that the Fifth Amendment confers rights upon all persons, whatever their nationality, wherever they are located and whatever their offenses. If this Amendment invests enemy aliens in unlawful hostile action against us with immunity from military trial, it puts them in a more protected position than our own soldiers. American citizens conscripted into the military service are thereby stripped of their Fifth Amendment rights and as members of the military establishment are subject to its discipline, including military trials for offenses against aliens or Americans. Can there be any doubt that our foes would also have been excepted, but for the assumption "any person" would never be read to include those in arms against us? It would be a paradox indeed if what the Amendment denied to Americans it guaranteed to enemies. And, of course, it cannot be claimed that such shelter is due them as a matter of comity for any reciprocal rights conferred by enemy governments on American soldiers.

The decision below would extend coverage of our Constitution to nonresident alien enemies denied to resident alien enemies. The latter are entitled only to judicial hearing to determine what the petition of these prisoners admits: that they are really alien enemies. When that appears, those resident here may be deprived of liberty by Executive action without hearing. While this is preventive rather than punitive detention, no reason is apparent why an alien enemy charged with having committed a crime should have greater immunities from Executive action than one who it is only feared might at some future time commit a hostile act.

If the Fifth Amendment confers its rights on all the world except Americans engaged in defending it, the same must be true of the companion civil-rights Amendments, for none of them is limited by its express terms, territorially or as to persons. Such a construction would mean that during military occupation irreconcilable enemy elements, guerrilla fighters, and "werewolves" could require the American Judiciary to assure them freedoms of speech, press, and assembly as in the First

Amendment, right to bear arms as in the Second, security against "unreasonable" searches and seizures as in the Fourth, as well as rights to jury trial as in the Fifth and Sixth Amendments.

Such extraterritorial application of organic law would have been so significant an innovation in the practice of governments that, if intended or apprehended, it could scarcely have failed to excite contemporary comment. Not one word can be cited. No decision of this Court supports such a view. None of the learned commentators on our Constitution has even hinted at it. The practice of every modern government is opposed to it.

We hold that the Constitution does not confer a right of personal security or an immunity from military trial and punishment upon an alien enemy engaged in the hostile service of a government at war with the United States.

The jurisdiction of military authorities, during or following hostilities, to punish those guilty of offenses against the laws of war is long-established. By the Treaty of Versailles Article 228, "The German Government recognises the right of the Allied and Associated Powers to bring before military tribunals persons accused of having committed acts in violation of the laws and customs of war." This Court has characterized as "well-established" the "power of the military to exercise jurisdiction over members of the armed forces, those directly connected with such forces, or enemy belligerents, prisoners of war, or others charged with violating the laws of war." And we have held in the Quirin and Yamashita cases that the Military Commission is a lawful tribunal to adjudge enemy offenses against the laws of war.

It is not for us to say whether these prisoners were or were not guilty of a war crime, or whether if we were to retry the case we would agree to the findings of fact or the application of the laws of war made by the Military Commission. The petition shows that these prisoners were formally accused of violating the laws of war and fully informed of particulars of these charges. As we observed in the Yamashita case, "If the military tribunals have lawful authority to hear, decide and condemn, their action is not subject to judicial review merely because they have made a wrong decision on disputed facts. Correction of their errors of decision is not for the courts but for the military authorities which are alone authorized to review their decisions." "We consider here only the lawful power of the commission to try the petitioner for the offense charged."

These prisoners do not assert, and could not, that anything in the Geneva Convention makes them immune from prosecution or punishment for war crimes. Article 75 thereof expressly provides that a prisoner of war may be detained until the end of such proceedings and, if necessary, until the expiration of the punishment.

We are unable to find that the petition alleges any fact showing lack of jurisdiction in the military authorities to accuse, try and condemn these prisoners or that they acted in excess of their lawful powers.

END OF OPINION

In this decision, the Supreme Court ruled that individuals captured and held in a U.S.-controlled prison outside of the United States could not petition the U.S. courts for habeas corpus. This decision was a key factor in the decision to use the military facility at Guantanamo Bay to detain those captured in the conflict with the Taliban and Al-Qaeda.

It is important to look at the very practical reasons the Court sets out to justify its decision. Wartime is different than peacetime, and demands on a military deployed overseas are different than those that exist inside the U.S. in a normal criminal case. These differences are important.

How important might it have been that Guantanamo, while not within the United States, was nevertheless a place far from the battlefields of Iraq and Afghanistan?

How important was it that Guantanamo, while not U.S. territory, was nevertheless a U.S. Navy Base, on land held through a perpetual lease from Cuba for over a hundred years?

How important is it when cases come to the courts in the context of a "war" that looks much different than was the case with World War II, a conflict that may go on forever? These are some of the issues that the courts deal with in applying the cases we have read.

Eisentrager involved detainees who were not U.S. citizens or detainees. That turned out not to be the case with all of the fighters captured in Afghanistan. Yaser Esam Hamdi had been captured and turned over to the U.S. forces during these early stages of the conflict. During his initial processing, the United States discovered that, while Hamdi held Saudi citizenship and had lived most of his life in Saudi Arabia, he had in fact been born in Louisiana while his father was working there for an oil company. Hamdi thus held U.S citizenship as well. Now, other than the fact that he was caught while fighting as a civilian, not in uniform, and not as a member of any formal national military, there was no indication that Hamdi had committed any war crimes (in fact it was uncertain whether he had actually even had a chance to fight before being captured). So, in all likelihood, what was expected was that he would be detained, away from the battlefield, until the end of the conflict or some other time that his release might be authorized. But, because he was a U.S. citizen, it was not certain whether the courts would provide him any due process rights. The administration was certain they would win any challenge, based on the *Quirin* case, but also did not want to give the U.S. courts any excuse to exercise jurisdiction over any aspect of the facility at Guantanamo Bay, so Hamdi was brought to the United States where he was held in U.S. Navy confinement facilities, first in Norfolk, Virginia, and then in Charleston, South Carolina.

When the federal public defender assigned to the U.S. District Court in Virginia learned that Hamdi had been brought to the Navy Brig in Norfolk, he filed an action in habeas corpus. That case eventually went to the Supreme Court for decision.

As you will read below, the Court agreed that the president does have the authority to detain U.S. citizens who are enemy combatants. The Court relied on the language the Congress used in the 2001 Authorization for the Use of Military Force (AUMF), which essentially authorized the president to go to war with Al-Qaeda and the Taliban. The Court's opinion was that the act of taking prisoners is an inherent part of war, so even though the AUMF never specifically mentions prisoners, it is simply understood that the authorization for the president to use force when he uses "any and all means" against the perpetrators of the 9/11 attacks naturally included authorization for taking and holding enemy combatants, even if they were U.S. citizens.

Second, and most importantly, the Court held that Hamdi, as a U.S. citizen, did have a right to habeas corpus. Although citizens can be detained as enemy combatants, they must be granted a meaningful opportunity to challenge their classification as enemy combatants before a neutral decision-maker.

Hamdi v. Rumsfeld, 542 U.S. 507 (2004)*

At this difficult time in our Nation's history, we are called upon to consider the legality of the Government's detention of a United States citizen on United States soil as an "enemy combatant." We also address the constitutional process guaranteed to one who seeks to challenge his classification as an "enemy combatant." We hold that although Congress authorized the detention of combatants through the 2001 Authorization for the Use of Military Force (AUMF), due process requires that a U.S. citizen held in the United States as an enemy combatant is given a meaningful opportunity to contest the factual basis for that detention before a neutral decision-maker.

On September 11, 2001, the Al-Qaeda terrorist network used hijacked commercial airliners to attack prominent targets in the United States. Approximately 3,000 people were killed in those attacks. One week later, in response to these "acts of treacherous violence," Congress passed a resolution titled the Authorization for Use of Military Force ("the AUMF") which authorized the President to "use all necessary and appropriate force against those nations, organizations, or persons he determines planned, authorized, committed, or aided the terrorist attacks" or "harbored such organizations or persons, in order to prevent any future acts of international terrorism against the United States by such nations, organizations or persons." Soon thereafter, the President ordered United States Armed Forces to Afghanistan, with a mission to subdue Al-Qaeda and quell the Taliban regime that was known to support it.

This case arises out of the detention of a man whom the Government alleges took up arms with the Taliban during this conflict. His name is Yaser Esam Hamdi. Born an American citizen in Louisiana in 1980, Hamdi moved with his family to Saudi Arabia as a child. By 2001, he resided in Afghanistan. At some point that year, he was seized by members of the Northern Alliance, a coalition of military groups opposed to the Taliban government, and eventually was turned over to the United States military. The Government asserts that it initially detained and interrogated Hamdi in Afghanistan before transferring him to the United States Naval Base in

---

* The case has been heavily edited and paraphrased by the authors for clarity. See disclaimer in introduction.

Guantanamo Bay in January 2002. In April 2002, upon learning that Hamdi is an American citizen, authorities transferred him to a naval brig in Norfolk, Virginia, where he remained until a recent transfer to a brig in Charleston, South Carolina. The Government contends that Hamdi is an "enemy combatant," and that this status justifies holding him in the United States indefinitely—without formal charges or proceedings—unless and until it makes the determination that access to counsel or further process is warranted.

In June 2002, Hamdi's father filed the present petition for a writ of habeas corpus. He alleges that the Government has held his son "without access to legal counsel or notice of any charges pending against him." The petition contends that Hamdi's detention was not legally authorized. It argues that, "as an American citizen, Hamdi enjoys the full protections of the Constitution," and that Hamdi's detention in the United States without charges, access to an impartial tribunal, or assistance of counsel "violated and continues to violate the Fifth and Fourteenth Amendments to the United States Constitution." The habeas petition asks that the court, among other things, (1) appoint counsel for Hamdi; (2) order respondents to cease interrogating him; (3) declare that he is being held in violation of the Fifth and Fourteenth Amendments; (4) "to the extent Respondents contest any material factual allegations in this Petition, schedule an evidentiary hearing, at which Petitioners may adduce proof in support of their allegations"; and (5) order that Hamdi be released from his "unlawful custody."

The threshold question before us is whether the Executive has the authority to detain citizens who qualify as "enemy combatants." For purposes of this case, the "enemy combatant" that it is seeking to detain is an individual who, it alleges, was "'part of or supporting forces hostile to the United States or coalition partners'" in Afghanistan and who "'engaged in an armed conflict against the United States'" there. We therefore answer only the narrow question before us: whether the detention of citizens falling within that definition is authorized. It is our opinion that Congress has in fact authorized Hamdi's detention, through the AUMF.

The AUMF authorizes the President to use "all necessary and appropriate force" against "nations, organizations, or persons" associated with the September 11, 2001, terrorist attacks. There can be no doubt that individuals who fought against the United States in Afghanistan as part of the Taliban, an organization known to have supported the Al-Qaeda terrorist network responsible for those attacks, are individuals Congress sought to target in passing the AUMF. We conclude that detention of individuals falling into the limited category we are considering, for the duration of the particular conflict in which they were captured, is so fundamental and accepted an incident to war as to be an exercise of the "necessary and appropriate force" Congress has authorized the President to use.

We stated in Ex parte Quirin that the capture and detention of lawful combatants and the capture, detention, and trial of unlawful combatants, by "universal agreement and practice," are "important incidents of war." The purpose of detention is to prevent captured individuals from returning to the field of battle and taking up arms once again. It is established international law that "Captivity in war is 'neither revenge, nor punishment, but solely protective custody, the only purpose of which is to prevent the prisoners of war from further participation in the war. While inconvenient to one who is detained, it is merely a temporary detention which is devoid of all penal character.'" A prisoner of war is no convict; his imprisonment is a simple war measure. "The object of capture is to prevent the captured individual from serving the enemy. He is disarmed and from then on must be removed as completely as practicable from the front, treated humanely, and in time exchanged, repatriated, or otherwise released.

There is no bar to this Nation's holding one of its own citizens as an enemy combatant. In Quirin, one of the detainees, Haupt, was a United States citizen. We held that "citizens who associate themselves with the military arm of the enemy government, and with its aid, guidance and direction enter this country bent on hostile acts, are enemy belligerents within the meaning of the law of war." While Haupt was tried for violations of the law of war, nothing in Quirin suggests that his citizenship would have precluded his mere detention for the duration of the relevant hostilities. Nor can we see any reason for drawing such a line here. A citizen, no less than an alien, can be part of or supporting forces hostile to the United States or coalition partners" and "engaged in an armed conflict against the United States; such a citizen, if released, would pose the same threat of returning to the front during the ongoing conflict.

In light of these principles, it is of no moment that the AUMF does not use specific language of detention. Because detention to prevent a combatant's return to the battlefield is a fundamental incident of waging war, in permitting the use of "necessary and appropriate force," Congress has clearly and unmistakably authorized detention in the narrow circumstances considered here.

Hamdi objects, nevertheless, that Congress has not authorized the indefinite detention to which he is now subject. The Government responds that "the detention of enemy combatants during World War II was just as 'indefinite' while that war was being fought." We take Hamdi's objection to be not to the lack of certainty regarding the date on which the conflict will end, but to the substantial prospect of perpetual detention. We recognize that the national security underpinnings of the "war on terror," although crucially important, are broad and malleable. As the Government concedes, "given its unconventional nature, the current conflict is unlikely to end with a formal cease-fire agreement, which is the traditional method of ending a conflict." The prospect Hamdi raises is therefore not far-fetched. If the Government does not consider this unconventional war won for two generations, and if it maintains during that time that Hamdi might, if released, rejoin forces fighting against the United States, then the position it has taken throughout the litigation of this case suggests that Hamdi's detention could last for the rest of his life.

It is a clearly established principle of the law of war that detention may last no longer than active hostilities. The Third Geneva Convention states that "Prisoners of war shall be released and repatriated without delay after the cessation of active hostilities." The 1899 Hague Convention also indicates that prisoners should be repatriated upon the "conclusion of peace."

Hamdi contends that the AUMF does not authorize indefinite or perpetual detention. Certainly, we agree that indefinite detention for the purpose of interrogation is not authorized. Further, we understand Congress' grant of authority for the use of "necessary and appropriate force" to include the authority to detain for the duration of the relevant conflict, and our understanding is based on longstanding law-of-war principles. If the practical circumstances of a given conflict are entirely unlike those of the conflicts that informed the development of the law of war, that understanding may unravel. But that is not the situation we face as of this date. Active combat operations against Taliban fighters apparently are ongoing in Afghanistan. The United States may detain, for the duration of these hostilities, individuals legitimately determined to be Taliban combatants who engaged in an armed conflict against the United States. If the record establishes that United States troops are still involved in active combat in Afghanistan, those detentions are part of the exercise of "necessary and appropriate force," and therefore are authorized by the AUMF.

Ex parte Milligan does not undermine our holding about the Government's authority to seize enemy combatants, as we define that term today. In that case, the Court made repeated reference to the fact that its inquiry into whether the military tribunal had jurisdiction to try and punish Milligan turned in large part on the fact that Milligan was not a prisoner of war, but a resident of Indiana arrested while at home there. That fact was central to its conclusion. Had Milligan been captured while he was assisting Confederate soldiers by carrying a rifle against Union troops on a Confederate battlefield, the holding of the Court might well have been different. The Court's repeated explanations that Milligan was not a prisoner of war suggest that had these different circumstances been present he could have been detained under military authority for the duration of the conflict, whether or not he was a citizen.

Quirin was a unanimous opinion. It both postdates and clarifies Milligan, providing us with the most appropriate precedent that we have on the question of whether citizens may be detained in such circumstances. Brushing aside such precedent—particularly when doing so gives rise to a host of new questions never dealt with by this Court—is unjustified and unwise.

There is a precedent for Hamdi's detention, despite the fact that he is a U.S. citizen. In *In re Territo* (9th Cir. 1946), a United States citizen-POW (a member of the Italian army) from World War II was seized on the battlefield in Sicily and then held in the United States. The court in that case held that the military detention of that United States citizen was lawful. Similarly, here we have a United States citizen captured in a foreign combat zone.

Even in cases in which the detention of enemy combatants is legally authorized, there remains the question of what process is constitutionally due to a citizen who disputes his enemy-combatant status. Hamdi argues that he is owed a meaningful and timely hearing and that extra-judicial detention that begins and ends with the submission of an affidavit based on third-hand hearsay does not comport with the Fifth and Fourteenth Amendments. The Government counters that any more process than was provided below would be both unworkable and constitutionally intolerable. Our resolution of this dispute requires a careful examination both of the writ of habeas corpus, which Hamdi now seeks to employ as a mechanism of judicial review, and of the Due Process Clause, which informs the procedural contours of that mechanism in this instance.

Though they reach radically different conclusions on the process that ought to attend the present proceeding, the parties begin on common ground. All agree that, absent suspension, the writ of habeas corpus remains available to every individual detained within the United States. Only in the rarest of circumstances has Congress seen fit to suspend the writ. At all other times, it has remained a critical check on the Executive, ensuring that it does not detain individuals except in accordance with law. All agree suspension of the writ has not occurred here. Thus, it is undisputed that Hamdi was properly before an Article III court to challenge his detention under 28 U.S.C. § 2241. Further, all agree that § 2241 and its companion provisions provide at least a skeletal outline of the procedures to be afforded a petitioner in federal habeas review. Most notably, § 2243 provides that "the person detained may, under oath, deny any of the facts set forth in the return or allege any other material facts," and § 2246 allows the taking of evidence in habeas proceedings by deposition, affidavit, or interrogatories.

The simple outline of § 2241 makes clear both that Congress envisioned that habeas petitioners would have some opportunity to present and rebut facts and that courts in cases like this retain some ability to vary the ways in which they do so as mandated by due process. The Government suggests two separate reasons for its position that no further process is due.

First, the Government urges that because it is "undisputed" that Hamdi's seizure took place in a combat zone, the habeas determination can be made purely as a matter of law, with no further hearing or factfinding necessary. This argument is easily rejected. The circumstances surrounding Hamdi's seizure cannot in any way be characterized as "undisputed," as "those circumstances are neither conceded in fact, nor susceptible to concession in law, because Hamdi has not been permitted to speak for himself or even through counsel as to those circumstances." Further, the "facts" that constitute the alleged concession are insufficient to support Hamdi's detention. Under the definition of enemy combatant that we accept today as falling within the scope of Congress' authorization, Hamdi would need to be "part of or supporting forces hostile to the United States or coalition partners" and "engaged in an armed conflict against the United States" to justify his detention in the United States for the duration of the relevant conflict. The habeas petition states only that "when seized by the United States Government, Mr. Hamdi resided in Afghanistan." An assertion that one resided in a country in which combat operations are taking place is not a concession that one was "captured in a zone of active combat operations in a foreign theater of war," and certainly is not a concession that one was "part of or supporting forces hostile to the United States or coalition partners" and "engaged in an armed conflict against the United States." Accordingly, we reject any argument that Hamdi has made concessions that eliminate any right to further process.

The Government's second argument requires closer consideration. This is the argument that further factual exploration is unwarranted and inappropriate in light of the extraordinary constitutional interests at stake. Under the Government's most extreme rendition of this argument, "respect for separation of powers and the limited institutional capabilities of courts in matters of military decision-making in connection with an ongoing conflict" ought to eliminate entirely any individual process, restricting the courts to investigating only whether legal authorization exists for the broader detention scheme. At most, the Government argues, courts should review its determination that a citizen is an enemy combatant under a very deferential "some evidence" standard. This is where if the government puts forth any evidence, its decision is to be uphold, regardless of the weight of the evidence against it.

In response, Hamdi emphasizes that this Court consistently has recognized that an individual challenging his detention may not be held at the will of the Executive without recourse to some proceeding before a neutral tribunal. He argues that the Fourth Circuit Court of Appeals, whom we overrule in this matter, inappropriately "ceded power to the Executive during wartime to define the conduct for which a citizen may be detained, judge whether that citizen has engaged in the proscribed conduct, and imprison that citizen indefinitely," and that due process demands that he receive a hearing in which he may challenge the government's evidence and introduce his own counter evidence.

Both of these positions highlight legitimate concerns. And both emphasize the tension that often exists between the autonomy that the Government asserts is necessary in order to pursue effectively a particular goal and the process that a citizen contends he is due before he is deprived of a constitutional right. The ordinary mechanism that we use for balancing such serious competing interests, and for determining the procedures that are necessary to ensure that a citizen is not "deprived of life, liberty, or property, without due process of law," is the test that we articulated in *Mathews v. Eldridge*, 424 U.S. 319 (1976). *Mathews* dictates that the process due in any given instance is determined by weighing "the private interest that will be affected by the official action" against the Government's asserted interest, "including the function involved" and the burdens the Government would face in providing greater process. The *Mathews* calculus then contemplates a judicious balancing of these concerns, through an analysis of "the risk of an erroneous deprivation" of the private interest if the process were reduced and the "probable value, if any, of additional or substitute safeguards." We take each of these steps in turn.

Hamdi's private interest affected by the official action, is the most elemental of liberty interests—the interest in being free from physical detention by one's own government. Freedom from bodily restraint has always been at the core of the liberty protected by the Due Process Clause from arbitrary governmental action. In our society liberty is the norm, and detention without trial is the carefully limited exception. We have always been careful not to minimize the importance and fundamental nature of the individual's right to liberty, and we will not do so today.

Nor is the weight on this side of the *Mathews* scale offset by the circumstances of war or the accusation of treasonous behavior, for "it is clear that commitment for any purpose constitutes a significant deprivation of liberty that requires due process protection, and at this stage in the Mathews calculus, we consider the interest of the erroneously detained individual. Procedural due process rules are meant to protect persons not from the deprivation, but from the mistaken or unjustified deprivation of life, liberty, or property. The risk of erroneous deprivation of a citizen's liberty in the absence of sufficient process here is very real. The nature of humanitarian relief work and journalism present a significant risk of mistaken military detentions. Moreover, as critical as the Government's interest may be in detaining those who actually pose an immediate threat to the national security of the United States during ongoing international conflict, history and common sense teach us that an unchecked system of detention carries the potential to become a means for oppression and abuse of others who do not present that sort of threat. The Founders knew — the history of the world told them — the nation they were founding, be its existence short or long, would be involved in war; how often or how long continued, human foresight could not tell; and that unlimited power, wherever lodged at such a time, was especially hazardous to freemen". Because we live in a society in which mere public intolerance or animosity cannot constitutionally justify the deprivation of a person's physical liberty, our starting point for the *Mathews v. Eldridge* analysis is unaltered by the allegations surrounding the particular detainee or the organizations with which he is alleged to have associated. We reaffirm today the fundamental nature of a citizen's right to be free from involuntary confinement by his own government without due process of law, and we weigh the opposing governmental interests against the curtailment of liberty that such confinement entails.

On the other side of the scale are the weighty and sensitive governmental interests in ensuring that those who have in fact fought with the enemy during a war do not return to battle against the United States. As discussed above, the law of war and the realities of combat may render such detentions both necessary and appropriate, and our due process analysis need not blink at those realities. Without doubt, our Constitution recognizes that core strategic matters of warmaking belong in the hands of those who are best positioned and most politically accountable for making them. For this reason, the courts rare reluctant to intrude upon the authority of the Executive in military and national security affairs, and that military commanders engaged in day-to-day fighting in a theater of war should have broad powers.

The Government also argues at some length that its interests in reducing the process available to alleged enemy combatants are heightened by the practical difficulties that would accompany a system of trial-like process. In its view, military officers who are engaged in the serious work of waging battle would be unnecessarily and dangerously distracted by litigation half a world away, and discovery into military operations would both intrude on the sensitive secrets of national defense and result in a futile search for evidence buried under the rubble of war. To the extent that these burdens are triggered by heightened procedures, they are properly taken into account in our due process analysis.

Striking the proper constitutional balance here is of great importance to the Nation during this period of ongoing combat. But it is equally vital that our calculus not give short shrift to the values that this country holds dear or to the privilege that is American citizenship. It is during our most challenging and uncertain moments that our Nation's commitment to due process is most severely tested; and it is in those times that we must preserve our commitment at home to the principles for which we fight abroad. The imperative necessity for safeguarding these rights to procedural due process under the gravest of emergencies has existed throughout our constitutional history, for it is then, under the pressing exigencies of crisis, that there is the greatest temptation to dispense with guarantees which, it is feared, will inhibit government action. It would indeed be ironic if, in the name of national defense, we would sanction the subversion of one of those liberties which makes the defense of the Nation worthwhile.

We therefore hold that a citizen-detainee seeking to challenge his classification as an enemy combatant must receive notice of the factual basis for his classification, and a fair opportunity to rebut the Government's factual assertions before a neutral decision-maker. An essential principle of due process is that a deprivation of life, liberty, or property 'be preceded by notice and opportunity for hearing appropriate to the nature of the case. Due process requires a 'neutral and detached judge in the first instance'. "For more than a century the central meaning of procedural due process has been clear: 'Parties whose rights are to be affected are entitled to be heard; and in order that they may enjoy that right they must first be notified.' It is equally fundamental that the right to notice and an opportunity to be heard 'must be granted at a meaningful time and in a meaningful manner. These essential constitutional promises may not be eroded.

We think it unlikely that this basic process will have the dire impact on the central functions of warmaking that the Government forecasts. The parties agree that initial captures on the battlefield need not receive the process we have discussed here; that process is due only when the determination is made to continue to hold those who have been seized. The Government has made clear in its briefing that documentation regarding battlefield detainees already is kept in the ordinary course of military affairs. Any factfinding imposition created by requiring a knowledgeable affiant to summarize these records to an independent tribunal is a minimal one. Likewise, arguments that military officers ought not have to wage war under the threat of litigation lose much of their steam when factual disputes at enemy-combatant hearings are limited to the alleged combatant's acts. This focus meddles little, if at all, in the strategy or conduct of war, inquiring only into the appropriateness of continuing to detain an individual claimed to have taken up arms against the United States. While we accord the greatest respect and consideration to the judgments of military authorities in matters relating to the actual prosecution of a war, and recognize that the scope of that discretion necessarily is wide, it does not infringe on the core role of the military for the courts to exercise their own time-honored and constitutionally mandated roles of reviewing and resolving claims like those presented here.

Even before *Youngstown v. Sawyer*, we have long since made clear that a state of war is not a blank check for the President when it comes to the rights of the Nation's citizens. Whatever power the United States Constitution envisions for the Executive in its exchanges with other nations or with enemy organizations in times of conflict, it most assuredly envisions a role for all three branches when individual liberties are at stake. The war power "is a power to wage war successfully, and thus it permits the harnessing of the entire energies of the people in a supreme cooperative effort to preserve the nation. But even the war power does not remove constitutional limitations safeguarding essential liberties. Likewise, we have made clear that, unless Congress acts to suspend it, the Great Writ of habeas corpus allows the Judicial Branch to play a necessary role in maintaining this delicate balance of governance, serving as an important judicial check on the Executive's discretion in the realm of detentions.

At its historical core, the writ of habeas corpus has served as a means of reviewing the legality of Executive detention, and it is in that context that its protections have been strongest. Thus, while we do not question that our due process assessment must pay keen attention to the particular burdens faced by the Executive in the context of military action, it would turn our system of checks and balances on its head to suggest that a citizen could not make his way to court with a challenge to the factual basis for his detention by his government, simply because the Executive opposes making available such a challenge. Absent suspension of the writ by Congress, a citizen detained as an enemy combatant is entitled to this process.

Because we conclude that due process demands some system for a citizen detainee to refute his classification, the proposed "some evidence" standard is inadequate. Any process in which the Executive's factual assertions go wholly unchallenged or are simply presumed correct without any opportunity for the alleged combatant to demonstrate otherwise falls constitutionally short. As the Government itself has recognized, we have utilized the "some evidence" standard in the past as a standard of review, not as a standard of proof. That is, it primarily has been employed by courts in examining an administrative record developed after an adversarial proceeding — one with process at least of the sort that we today hold is constitutionally mandated in the citizen enemy-combatant setting. This standard therefore is ill suited to the situation in which a habeas petitioner has received no prior proceedings before any tribunal and had no prior opportunity to rebut the Executive's factual assertions before a neutral decisionmaker.

Aside from unspecified "screening" processes, and military interrogations in which the Government suggests Hamdi could have contested his classification, Hamdi has received no process. An interrogation by one's captor, however effective an intelligence-gathering tool, hardly constitutes a constitutionally adequate factfinding before a neutral decisionmaker. The "process" Hamdi has received is not that to which he is entitled under the Due Process Clause.

There remains the possibility that the standards we have articulated could be met by an appropriately authorized and properly constituted military tribunal.... [M]ilitary regulations already provide for such process in related instances, dictating that tribunals be made available to determine the status of enemy detainees who assert prisoner-of-war status under the Geneva Convention. In the absence of such process, however, a court that receives a petition for a writ of habeas corpus from an alleged enemy combatant must itself ensure that the minimum requirements of due process are achieved. Both courts below recognized as much, focusing their energies on the question of whether Hamdi was due an opportunity to rebut the Government's case against him. The Government, too, proceeded on this assumption, presenting its affidavit and then seeking that it be evaluated under a deferential standard of review based on burdens that it alleged would accompany any greater process. As we have discussed, a habeas court in a case such as this may accept affidavit evidence like that contained here, so long as it also permits the alleged combatant to present his own factual case to rebut the Government's return. We anticipate that a District Court would proceed with the caution that we have indicated is necessary in this setting, engaging in a factfinding process that is both prudent and incremental. We have no reason to doubt that courts faced with these sensitive matters will pay proper heed both to the matters of national security that might arise in an individual case and to the constitutional limitations safeguarding essential liberties that remain vibrant even in times of security concerns.

END OF OPINION

The Government is allowed to detain citizens who are enemy combatants. The government may detain them until the end of the conflict, whenever that is. However, U.S. citizens who are detained have the due process right under habeas corpus to challenge their classification and detention as enemy combatants. They have a right to appear before a neutral judicial officer and put forth evidence that they are not enemy combatants. At this same forum, the government will have to put forth sufficient evidence to establish that the detainee is in fact an enemy combatant who can lawfully be detained until the end of the conflict.

Hamdi was about the habeas corpus rights of a U.S. citizen. How about the rights of the non-citizens who are being detained as enemy combatants? Do they have the right to challenge the basis of their detention? In *Johnson v. Eisentrager,* the U.S. Supreme Court was of the opinion that non-resident aliens captured in a war theater in a foreign country as unlawful combatants in a time of war had no right to petition the U.S. civilian courts for habeas corpus. Even though they were held in a U.S.-controlled prison in a section of Germany controlled by U.S. military authorities, the view was that they were never on U.S. jurisdiction so they did not have the protections of the U.S. Constitution.

Similarly, when unlawful combatants were captured in Afghanistan, they were sent to a U.S. military prison at Guantanamo Bay, Cuba. For the reasons stated by the Court in *Eisentrager,* military authorities believed that the U.S. Constitution, including the right of habeas corpus, did not apply. However, their legal opinion was incorrect, as explained in the subsequent U.S. Supreme Court case *Rasul v. Bush*, which ruled that the detainees at Guantanamo Bay do have the right of habeas corpus.

Rasul v. Bush, 542 U.S. 466 (2004)*

These two cases present the narrow but important question whether United States courts lack jurisdiction to consider challenges to the legality of the detention of foreign nationals captured abroad in connection with hostilities and incarcerated at the Guantanamo Bay Naval Base, Cuba.

On September 11, 2001, agents of the Al-Qaeda terrorist network hijacked four commercial airliners and used them as missiles to attack American targets. While one of the four attacks was foiled by the heroism of the plane's passengers, the other three killed approximately 3,000 innocent civilians, destroyed hundreds of millions of dollars of property, and severely damaged the U.S. economy. In response to the attacks, Congress passed a joint resolution, the Authorization for the Use of Military Force, authorizing the President to use "all necessary and appropriate force against those nations, organizations, or persons he determines planned, authorized, committed, or aided the terrorist attacks . . . or harbored such organizations or persons." Acting pursuant to that authorization, the President sent U.S. Armed Forces into Afghanistan to wage a military campaign against Al-Qaeda and the Taliban regime that had supported it.

Petitioners in these cases are 2 Australian citizens and 12 Kuwaiti citizens who were captured abroad during hostilities between the United States and the Taliban. Since early 2002, the U.S. military has held them—along with, according to the Government's estimate, approximately 640 other non-Americans captured abroad—at the Naval Base at Guantanamo Bay. The United States occupies the Base, which comprises 45 square miles of land and water along the southeast coast of Cuba, pursuant to a 1903 Lease Agreement executed with the newly independent Republic of Cuba in the aftermath of the Spanish-American War. Under the Agreement, "the United States recognizes the continuance of the ultimate sovereignty of the Republic of Cuba over the leased areas," while "the Republic of Cuba consents that during the period of the occupation by the United States, the United States shall exercise complete jurisdiction and control over and within said areas." In 1934, the parties entered into a treaty providing that, absent an agreement to modify or abrogate the lease, the lease would remain in effect "so long as the United States of America shall not abandon the naval station of Guantanamo."

In 2002, petitioners filed various actions in the U.S. District Court for the District of Columbia challenging the legality of their detention at the Base. All alleged that none of the petitioners has ever been a combatant against the United States or has ever engaged in any terrorist acts. They also alleged that none has been charged

---

* The case has been heavily edited and paraphrased by the authors for clarity. See disclaimer in introduction.

with any wrongdoing, permitted to consult with counsel, or provided access to the courts or any other tribunal.

The two Australians, Mamdouh Habib and David Hicks, each filed a petition for writ of habeas corpus, seeking release from custody, access to counsel, freedom from interrogations, and other relief. Fawzi Khalid Abdullah Fahad Al Odah and the 11 other Kuwaiti detainees filed a complaint seeking to be informed of the charges against them, to be allowed to meet with their families and with counsel, and to have access to the courts or some other impartial tribunal. They claimed that denial of these rights violates the Constitution, international law, and treaties of the United States.

Construing all three actions as petitions for writs of habeas corpus, the District Court dismissed them for want of jurisdiction. The court held, in reliance on our opinion in *Johnson v. Eisentrager*, that "aliens detained outside the sovereign territory of the United States may not invoke a petition for a writ of habeas corpus." The Court of Appeals affirmed. Reading *Eisentrager* to hold that "the privilege of litigation does not extend to aliens in military custody who have no presence in 'any territory over which the United States is sovereign," it held that the District Court lacked jurisdiction over petitioners' habeas actions, as well as their remaining federal statutory claims that do not sound in habeas. We granted review, and now reverse.

Congress has granted federal district courts, within their respective jurisdictions, the authority to hear applications for habeas corpus by any person who claims to be held in custody in violation of the Constitution or laws or treaties of the United States. This law traces its ancestry to the first grant of federal court jurisdiction: Section 14 of the Judiciary Act of 1789 authorized federal courts to issue the writ of habeas corpus to prisoners "in custody, under or by colour of the authority of the United States, or committed for trial before some court of the same." In 1867, Congress extended the protections of the writ to "all cases where any person may be restrained of his or her liberty in violation of the constitution, or of any treaty or law of the United States."

Habeas corpus is, however, a writ which comes before any statute, throwing its root deep into the genius of our common law. The writ appeared in English law several centuries ago, became an integral part of our common-law heritage by the time the Colonies achieved independence, and received explicit recognition in the Constitution, which forbids suspension of "the Privilege of the Writ of Habeas Corpus . . . unless when in Cases of Rebellion or Invasion the public Safety may require it," Art. I, § 9, cl. 2.

As it has evolved over the past two centuries, the habeas statute clearly has expanded habeas corpus beyond the limits that obtained during the 17th and 18th centuries. But at its historical core, the writ of habeas corpus has served as a means of reviewing the legality of Executive detention, and it is in that context that its protections have been strongest. The historic purpose of the writ has been to relieve detention by executive authorities without judicial trial. As Justice Jackson wrote in an opinion respecting the availability of habeas corpus to aliens held in U.S. custody:

"Executive imprisonment has been considered oppressive and lawless since John, at Runnymede, pledged that no free man should be imprisoned, dispossessed, outlawed, or exiled save by the judgment of his peers or by the law of the land. The judges of England developed the writ of habeas corpus largely to preserve these immunities from executive restraint."

Consistent with the historic purpose of the writ, this Court has recognized the federal courts' power to review applications for habeas relief in a wide variety of cases involving Executive detention, in wartime as well as in times of peace. The Court has, for example, entertained the habeas petitions of an American citizen who plotted an attack on military installations during the Civil War, *Ex parte Milligan*, and of admitted enemy aliens convicted of war crimes during a declared war and held in the United States, *Ex parte Quirin*, and its insular possessions when its territories in the Philippines were occupied by Japan, *In re Yamashita*.

The question now before us is whether the habeas statute confers a right to judicial review of the legality of Executive detention of aliens in a territory over which the United States exercises plenary and exclusive jurisdiction, but not "ultimate sovereignty."

Respondents' primary submission is that the answer to the jurisdictional question is controlled by our decision in *Eisentrager*. In that case, we held that a Federal District Court lacked authority to issue a writ of habeas corpus to 21 German citizens who had been captured by U.S. forces in China, tried and convicted of war crimes by an American military commission headquartered in Nanking, and incarcerated in the Landsberg Prison in occupied Germany. The Court of Appeals in *Eisentrager* had incorrectly found jurisdiction, reasoning that "any person who is deprived of his liberty by officials of the United States, acting under purported authority of that Government, and who can show that his confinement is in violation of a prohibition of the Constitution, has a right to the writ." In reversing that determination, this Court summarized the six critical facts in the case:

> "We are here confronted with a decision whose basic premise is that these prisoners are entitled, as a constitutional right, to sue in some court of the United States for a writ of habeas corpus. To support that assumption we must hold that a prisoner of our military authorities is constitutionally entitled to the writ, even though he (a) is an enemy alien; (b) has never been or resided in the United States; (c) was captured outside of our territory and there held in military custody as a prisoner of war; (d) was tried and convicted by a Military Commission sitting outside the United States; (e) for offenses against laws of war committed outside the United States; (f) and is at all times imprisoned outside the United States."

On this set of facts, the Court concluded, "no right to the writ of habeas corpus appears."

Petitioners in these cases differ from the *Eisentrager* detainees in important respects: They are not nationals of countries at war with the United States, and they deny that they have engaged in or plotted acts of aggression against the United States;

they have never been afforded access to any tribunal, much less charged with and convicted of wrongdoing; and for more than two years they have been imprisoned in territory over which the United States exercises exclusive jurisdiction and control.

Not only are petitioners differently situated from the *Eisentrager* detainees, but the Court in Eisentrager made quite clear that all six of the facts critical to its disposition were relevant only to the question of the prisoners' constitutional entitlement to habeas corpus. The Court had far less to say on the question of the petitioners' statutory entitlement to habeas review. Its only statement on the subject was a passing reference to the absence of statutory authorization: "Nothing in the text of the Constitution extends such a right, nor does anything in our statutes."

By the express terms of its agreements with Cuba, the United States exercises "complete jurisdiction and control" over the Guantanamo Bay Naval Base, and may continue to exercise such control permanently if it so chooses. Respondents themselves concede that the habeas statute would create federal-court jurisdiction over the claims of an American citizen held at the base. Considering that the statute draws no distinction between Americans and aliens held in federal custody, there is little reason to think that Congress intended the geographical coverage of the statute to vary depending on the detainee's citizenship. Aliens held at the base, no less than American citizens, are entitled to invoke the federal courts' authority under § 2241.

Application of the habeas statute to persons detained at the base is consistent with the historical reach of the writ of habeas corpus. At common law, courts exercised habeas jurisdiction over the claims of aliens detained within sovereign territory of the realm, as well as the claims of persons detained in the so-called "exempt jurisdictions," where ordinary writs did not run, and all other dominions under the sovereign's control.

In the end, the answer to the question presented is clear. Petitioners contend that they are being held in federal custody in violation of the laws of the United States. No party questions the District Court's jurisdiction over petitioners' custodians. Section 2241, by its terms, requires nothing more. We therefore hold that § 2241 confers on the District Court jurisdiction to hear petitioners' habeas corpus challenges to the legality of their detention at the Guantanamo Bay Naval Base.

Nothing in *Eisentrager* or in any of our other cases categorically excludes aliens detained in military custody outside the United States from the "privilege of litigation" in U.S. courts. The courts of the United States have traditionally been open to nonresident aliens. Alien citizens, by the policy and practice of the courts of this country, are ordinarily permitted to resort to the courts for the redress of wrongs and the protection of their rights. And indeed, the Alien Tort Statute explicitly confers the privilege of suing for an actionable "tort committed in violation of the law of nations or a treaty of the United States" on aliens alone. The fact that petitioners in these cases are being held in military custody is immaterial to the question of the District Court's jurisdiction over their non-habeas statutory claims.

Whether and what further proceedings may become necessary after respondents make their response to the merits of petitioners' claims are matters that we need not address now. What is presently at stake is only whether the federal courts have jurisdiction to determine the legality of the Executive's potentially indefinite detention of individuals who claim to be wholly innocent of wrongdoing. Answering that question in the affirmative, we reverse the judgment of the Court of Appeals and remand for the District Court to consider in the first instance the merits of petitioners' claims.

END OF OPINION

Despite past rulings including *Johnson v. Eisentrager*, the Court decided that here the civilian federal district courts do have jurisdiction over the detainees in Guantanamo Bay, and thus could hear claims of habeas corpus. In 2005, Congress passed the Detainee Treatment Act (DTA). The DTA was Congress's attempt to address the problems the Court had pointed out in *Hamdi* and *Rasul*. It directed the Department of Defense to establish Combatant Status Review Tribunals (CSRTs) of Guantanamo Bay detainees to evaluate whether or not a person was an enemy combatant who could be detained, or was a noncombatant who should be released. It prohibited "cruel, inhuman, or degrading treatment or punishment" of prisoners at Guantanamo Bay, and required that all interrogations of detainees be performed in accord with the U.S. Army Field Manual. The act also said that the U.S. Supreme Court could not review decisions of the CSRTs, and only the D.C. Circuit Court could.

The Court was not satisfied that the DTA adequately met standards of due process required by the Constitution and by international law, as you see in the next opinion.

Hamdan v. Rumsfeld, 548 U.S. 557 (2006)*

Petitioner Salim Ahmed Hamdan, a Yemeni national, is in custody at an American prison in Guantanamo Bay, Cuba. In November 2001, during hostilities between the United States and the Taliban (which then governed Afghanistan), Hamdan was captured by militia forces and turned over to the U. S. military. In June 2002, he was transported to Guantanamo Bay. Over a year later, the President deemed him eligible for trial by military commission for then-unspecified crimes. After another year had passed, Hamdan was charged with one count of conspiracy "to commit offenses triable by military commission."

Hamdan filed petitions for writs of habeas corpus and to challenge the Executive Branch's intended means of prosecuting this charge. He concedes that a court-martial constituted in accordance with the Uniform Code of Military Justice (UCMJ) would have authority to try him. His objection is that the military commission the President has convened lacks such authority, for two principal reasons: First, neither congressional Act nor the common law of war supports trial by this commission for the crime of conspiracy—an offense that, Hamdan says, is not a violation of the law of war. Second, Hamdan contends, the procedures that the President has

---

* The case has been heavily edited and paraphrased by the authors for clarity. See disclaimer in introduction.

adopted to try him violate the most basic tenets of military and international law, including the principle that a defendant must be permitted to see and hear the evidence against him.

For the reasons that follow, we conclude that the military commission convened to try Hamdan lacks power to proceed because its structure and procedures violate both the UCMJ and the Geneva Conventions.

The procedures adopted to try Hamdan violate the Geneva Conventions. The Court of Appeals relied on *Johnson v. Eisentrager* to incorrectly hold that Hamdan could not invoke the Geneva Conventions to challenge the Government's plan to prosecute him in accordance with Commission Order No. 1. *Eisentrager* involved a challenge by 21 German nationals to their 1945 convictions for war crimes by a military tribunal convened in Nanking, China, and to their subsequent imprisonment in occupied Germany. The petitioners argued, that the 1929 Geneva Convention rendered illegal some of the procedures employed during their trials, which they said deviated impermissibly from the procedures used by courts-martial to try American soldiers. We rejected that claim on the merits because the petitioners (unlike Hamdan here) had failed to identify any prejudicial disparity "between the Commission that tried them and those that would try an offending soldier of the American forces of like rank," and in any event could claim no protection, under the 1929 Geneva Convention, during trials for crimes that occurred before their confinement as prisoners of war.

Buried in a footnote of the opinion, however, is this curious statement suggesting that the Court lacked power even to consider the merits of the Geneva Convention argument:

> "We are not holding that these prisoners have no right which the military authorities are bound to respect. The United States, by the Geneva Convention of July 27, 1929, concluded with forty-six other countries, including the German Reich, an agreement upon the treatment to be accorded captives. These prisoners claim to be and are entitled to its protection. It is, however, the obvious scheme of the Agreement that responsibility for observance and enforcement of these rights is upon political and military authorities. Rights of alien enemies are vindicated under it only through protests and intervention of protecting powers as the rights of our citizens against foreign governments are vindicated only by Presidential intervention." The Court of Appeals, on the strength of this footnote, held that "the 1949 Geneva Convention does not confer upon Hamdan a right to enforce its provisions in court."

Whatever else might be said about the *Eisentrager* footnote, it does not control this case. We may assume that "the obvious scheme" of the 1949 Conventions is identical in all relevant respects to that of the 1929 Geneva Convention, and even that that scheme would, absent some other provision of law, preclude Hamdan's invocation of the Convention's provisions as an independent source of law binding the Government's actions and furnishing petitioner with any enforceable right. For, regardless of the nature of the rights conferred on Hamdan, they are, as the Government does not dispute, part of the law of war. And compliance with the law of war is the condition upon which the authority set forth in Article 21 is granted.

As an alternative to its holding that Hamdan could not invoke the Geneva Conventions at all, the Court of Appeals concluded that the Conventions did not in any event apply to the armed conflict during which Hamdan was captured. The court accepted the Executive's assertions that Hamdan was captured in connection with the United States' war with Al-Qaeda and that that war is distinct from the war with the Taliban in Afghanistan. It further reasoned that the war with Al-Qaeda evades the reach of the Geneva Conventions. We, like Judge Williams, disagree with the latter conclusion.

The conflict with Al-Qaeda is not, according to the Government, a conflict to which the full protections afforded detainees under the 1949 Geneva Conventions apply because Article 2 of those Conventions (which appears in all four Conventions) renders the full protections applicable only to "all cases of declared war or of any other armed conflict which may arise between two or more of the High Contracting Parties." Since Hamdan was captured and detained incident to the conflict with Al-Qaeda and not the conflict with the Taliban, and since Al-Qaeda, unlike Afghanistan, is not a "High Contracting Party"—i. e., a signatory of the Conventions, the protections of those Conventions are not, it is argued, applicable to Hamdan.

We need not decide the merits of this argument because there is at least one provision of the Geneva Conventions that applies here even if the relevant conflict is not one between signatories. Article 3, often referred to as Common Article 3 because, like Article 2, it appears in all four Geneva Conventions, provides that in a "conflict not of an international character occurring in the territory of one of the High Contracting Parties, each Party to the conflict shall be bound to apply, as a minimum," certain provisions protecting "persons taking no active part in the hostilities, including members of armed forces who have laid down their arms and those placed outside the fight by detention." One such provision prohibits "the passing of sentences and the carrying out of executions without previous judgment pronounced by a regularly constituted court affording all the judicial guarantees which are recognized as indispensable by civilized peoples."

The Court of Appeals incorrectly thought, and the Government incorrectly asserts, that Common Article 3 does not apply to Hamdan because the conflict with Al-Qaeda, being "'international in scope,'" does not qualify as a "'conflict not of an international character.'" That reasoning is erroneous. The term "conflict not of an international character" is used here in contradistinction to a conflict between nations. So much is demonstrated by the "fundamental logic of the Convention's provisions on its application." Common Article 2 provides that "the present Convention shall apply to all cases of declared war or of any other armed conflict which may arise between two or more of the High Contracting Parties." High Contracting Parties (signatories) also must abide by all terms of the Conventions vis-à-vis one another even if one party to the conflict is a nonsignatory "Power," and must so abide vis-à-vis the nonsignatory if "the latter accepts and applies" those terms. Common Article 3, by contrast, affords some minimal protection, falling short of full protection under the Conventions, to individuals associated with neither a signatory nor even a nonsignatory "Power" who are involved in a conflict "in the territory of" a signatory. The latter kind of conflict is distinguishable from the conflict described in Common Article 2 chiefly because it does not involve a clash between nations (whether signatories or not). In context, then, the phrase "not of an international character" bears its literal meaning. The International Committee of the Red Cross, commenting on the Additional Protocols to the Geneva Conventions of 12 August 1949, stated that "A non-international armed conflict is distinct from an international armed conflict because of the legal status of the entities opposing each other."

Although the official commentaries accompanying Common Article 3 indicate that an important purpose of the provision was to furnish minimal protection to rebels involved in one kind of "conflict not of an international character," i. e., a civil war, the commentaries also make clear "that the scope of application of the Article must be as wide as possible." In fact, limiting language that would have rendered Common Article 3 applicable "especially to cases of civil war, colonial conflicts, or wars of religion" was omitted from the final version of the Article, which coupled broader scope of application with a narrower range of rights than did earlier proposed iterations.

Common Article 3, then, is applicable here and, as indicated above, requires that Hamdan be tried by a "regularly constituted court affording all the judicial guarantees which are recognized as indispensable by civilized peoples." While the term "regularly constituted court" is not specifically defined in either Common Article 3 or its accompanying commentary, other sources disclose its core meaning. The commentary accompanying a provision of the Fourth Geneva Convention, for example, defines "'regularly constituted'" tribunals to include "ordinary military courts" and "definitely exclude all special tribunals." And one of the Red Cross' own treatises defines "regularly constituted court" as used in Common Article 3 to mean "established and organised in accordance with the laws and procedures already in force in a country."

The Government offers only a cursory defense of Hamdan's military commission in light of Common Article 3. That defense fails because "the regular military courts in our system are the courts-martial established by congressional statutes." At a minimum, a military commission "can be 'regularly constituted' by the standards of our military justice system only if some practical need explains deviations from court-martial practice." As we have explained, no such need has been demonstrated here.

Inextricably intertwined with the question of regular constitution is the evaluation of the procedures governing the tribunal and whether they afford "all the judicial guarantees which are recognized as indispensable by civilized peoples." Like the phrase "regularly constituted court," this phrase is not defined in the text of the Geneva Conventions. But it must be understood to incorporate at least the barest of those trial protections that have been recognized by customary international law. Many of these are described in Article 75 of Protocol I to the Geneva Conventions of

1949, adopted in 1977. Although the United States declined to ratify Protocol I, its objections were not to Article 75 thereof. Indeed, it appears that the Government "regards the provisions of Article 75 as an articulation of safeguards to which all persons in the hands of an enemy are entitled." Among the rights set forth in Article 75 is the "right to be tried in one's presence."

We agree that the procedures adopted to try Hamdan deviate from those governing courts-martial in ways not justified by any "evident practical need," and for that reason, at least, fail to afford the requisite guarantees. We add only that various provisions of Commission Order No. 1 dispense with the principles, articulated in Article 75 and indisputably part of the customary international law, that an accused must, absent disruptive conduct or consent, be present for his trial and must be privy to the evidence against him. That the Government has a compelling interest in denying Hamdan access to certain sensitive information is not doubted. But, at least absent express statutory provision to the contrary, information used to convict a person of a crime must be disclosed to him.

Common Article 3 obviously tolerates a great degree of flexibility in trying individuals captured during armed conflict; its requirements are general ones, crafted to accommodate a wide variety of legal systems. But requirements they are nonetheless. The commission that the President has convened to try Hamdan does not meet those requirements.

We have assumed, as we must, that the allegations made in the Government's charge against Hamdan are true. We have assumed, moreover, the truth of the message implicit in that charge—that Hamdan is a dangerous individual whose beliefs, if acted upon, would cause great harm and even death to innocent civilians, and who would act upon those beliefs if given the opportunity. It bears emphasizing that Hamdan does not challenge, and we do not today address, the Government's power to detain him for the duration of active hostilities in order to prevent such harm. But in undertaking to try Hamdan and subject him to criminal punishment, the Executive is bound to comply with the rule of law that prevails in this jurisdiction.

The judgment of the Court of Appeals is reversed, and the case is remanded for further proceedings.

END OF OPINION

Unlawful combatants must be tried in a judicial system that affords them similar rights as regularly constituted courts. A regularly constituted court would be something such as a courts-martial used for our own servicemembers, or a civilian federal district court. Here, the tribunals used to try unlawful combatants had different rules that afforded unlawful combatants fewer protections. Consequently, this violated the Geneva Conventions, so these tribunals were unlawful.

The Bush administration had argued that the Geneva Conventions did not apply at all to those individuals detained as "unlawful combatants" at Guantanamo. It had also sought to avoid the application of habeas corpus to Guantanamo detainees. The Supreme Court has ruled against the president in all cases thus far. Now, in many of these situations the president had relied on his inherent commander in chief powers, much as Presidents Lincoln and Roosevelt had in the cases arising during the Civil War and World War II. If you look back at the early chapter on war powers, though, remember that, in the *Steel Seizure* cases, the Supreme Court had struck down President Truman's unilateral action and asserted that Congress should be involved in the decision process.

The last case we'll examine in this chapter considered a number of these issues, and the Court pulls together reasoning from the previous cases. It also addressed concerns with some of the congressional efforts to provide procedures for detention review and trial by military commission. As a summary of the issues involved on this topic, examine the analysis contained in the following case.

Boumediene v. Bush, 553 U.S. 723 (2008)*

Petitioners are aliens designated as enemy combatants and detained at the United States Naval Station at Guantanamo Bay, Cuba. . . . Petitioners present a question not resolved by our earlier cases relating to the detention of aliens at Guantanamo: whether they have the constitutional privilege of habeas corpus, a privilege not to be withdrawn except in conformance with the Suspension Clause, Art. I, §9, cl. 2. We hold these petitioners do have the habeas corpus privilege. Congress has enacted a statute, the Detainee Treatment Act of 2005 (DTA), that provides certain procedures for review of the detainees' status. We hold that those procedures are not an adequate and effective substitute for habeas corpus. Therefore §7 of the Military Commissions Act of 2006 (MCA) operates as an unconstitutional suspension of the writ.

Under the Authorization for Use of Military Force (AUMF), the President is authorized "to use all necessary and appropriate force against those nations, organizations, or persons he determines planned, authorized, committed, or aided the terrorist attacks that occurred on September 11, 2001, or harbored such organizations or persons, in order to prevent any future acts of international terrorism against the United States by such nations, organizations or persons."

In *Hamdi v. Rumsfeld,* five Members of the Court recognized that detention of individuals who fought against the United States in Afghanistan "for the duration of the particular conflict in which they were captured, is so fundamental and accepted an incident to war as to be an exercise of the 'necessary and appropriate force' Congress has authorized the President to use." After *Hamdi*, the Deputy Secretary of Defense established Combatant Status Review Tribunals (CSRTs) to determine whether individuals detained at Guantanamo were "enemy combatants," as the Department defines that term. A later memorandum established procedures to implement the CSRTs. The Government maintains these procedures were designed to comply with the due process requirements identified by the plurality in Hamdi.

---

* The case has been heavily edited and paraphrased by the authors for clarity. See disclaimer in introduction.

Interpreting the AUMF, the Department of Defense ordered the detention of these petitioners, and they were transferred to Guantanamo. Some of these individuals were apprehended on the battlefield in Afghanistan, others in places as far away from there as Bosnia and Gambia. All are foreign nationals, but none is a citizen of a nation at war with the United States. Each denies he is a member of the Al-Qaeda terrorist network that carried out the September 11 attacks or of the Taliban regime that provided sanctuary for Al-Qaeda. Each petitioner appeared before a separate CSRT; was determined to be an enemy combatant; and has sought a writ of habeas corpus in the United States District Court for the District of Columbia.

While appeals were pending from the District Court decisions, Congress passed the DTA. The DTA provides that "no court, justice, or judge shall have jurisdiction to hear or consider . . . an application for a writ of habeas corpus filed by or on behalf of an alien detained by the Department of Defense at Guantanamo Bay, Cuba." The DTA further provides that the Court of Appeals for the District of Columbia Circuit is the only court with "exclusive jurisdiction" to review decisions of the CSRTs.

In *Hamdan v. Rumsfeld*, the Court held this provision did not apply to cases (like Boumedine's) pending when the DTA was enacted. Congress responded by passing the Military Commissions Act (MCA). The authority to which the concurring opinion referred was the authority to "create military commissions of the kind at issue" in the case. Nothing in that opinion can be construed as an invitation for Congress to suspend the writ.

Following *Hamdan v. Rumsfeld*, in the lower court in Boumedine's case incorrectly ruled that the MCA must be read to strip from all federal courts the jurisdiction to consider detainee habeas corpus applications; that detainees are not entitled to the privilege of the writ or the protections of the Suspension Clause and, as a result, that it was unnecessary to consider whether Congress provided an adequate and effective substitute for habeas corpus in the DTA.

We granted review and overturn the lower court's ruling.

As a threshold matter, we must decide whether the MCA denies the federal courts jurisdiction to hear habeas corpus actions pending at the time of its enactment. We hold the statute does deny that jurisdiction, so that, if the statute is valid, petitioners' cases must be dismissed.

We now must determine whether petitioners are barred from federal courts because of their status, i.e., petitioners' designation by the Executive Branch as enemy combatants, or their physical location, i.e., their presence at Guantanamo Bay. The Government contends that noncitizens designated as enemy combatants and detained in territory located outside our Nation's borders have no constitutional rights and no privilege of habeas corpus. Petitioners contend they do have cognizable constitutional rights and that Congress, in seeking to eliminate habeas corpus in the Military Commissions Act, acted in violation of the Suspension Clause of the U.S. Constitution.

The Government says the right of habeas corpus through the Suspension Clause of the Constitution affords petitioners no rights because the United States does not claim sovereignty over the place of detention.

Guantanamo Bay is not formally part of the United States. And under the terms of the lease between the United States and Cuba, Cuba retains "ultimate sovereignty" over the territory while the United States exercises "complete jurisdiction and control." However, Cuba effectively has no rights as a sovereign, and at the same time the United States contends, that Guantanamo is not within its sovereign control.

We do not question the Government's position that Cuba, not the United States, maintains sovereignty, in the legal and technical sense of the term, over Guantanamo Bay. But this does not end the analysis as we inquire into the objective degree of control the U.S. asserts over foreign territory.

Indeed, it is not altogether uncommon for a territory to be under the sovereignty of one nation, while under the control, or practical sovereignty, of another. This condition can occur when the territory is seized during war, as Guantanamo was during the Spanish-American War. See, e.g., *Fleming v. Page* (1850) (noting that the port of Tampico, conquered by the United States during the war with Mexico, was "undoubtedly... subject to the sovereignty and dominion of the United States," but that it "does not follow that it was a part of the United States, or that it ceased to be a foreign country"). Accordingly, for purposes of our analysis here as in Rasul, we accept the Government's position that Cuba, and not the United States, retains rightful sovereignty over Guantanamo Bay, but at the same time we take notice of the obvious and uncontested fact that the United States, by virtue of its complete jurisdiction and control over the base, maintains de facto sovereignty over this territory.

The Court has discussed the issue of the Constitution's extraterritorial application on many occasions. These decisions undermine the Government's argument that the Constitution necessarily stops where de jure sovereignty ends.

In a series of opinions later known as *the Insular Cases*, the Court addressed whether the Constitution, by its own force, applies in any territory that is not a State. The Court held that the Constitution has independent force in these territories, a force not contingent upon acts of legislative grace. Yet noting the inherent practical difficulties of enforcing all constitutional provisions "always and everywhere," the Court devised in *the Insular Cases* a doctrine that allowed it to use its power sparingly and where it would be most needed. This century-old doctrine informs our analysis in the present matter.

Practical considerations likewise influenced the Court's analysis a half-century later in *Reid v. Covert*. The petitioners there, spouses of American servicemen, lived on American military bases in England and Japan. They were charged with crimes committed in those countries and tried before military courts, consistent with executive agreements the United States had entered into with the British and Japanese governments. Because the petitioners were not themselves military personnel, they argued they were entitled to trial by jury.

Justice Black, writing for the plurality, contrasted the cases before him with *the Insular Cases*, which involved territories "with wholly dissimilar traditions and institutions" that Congress intended to govern only "temporarily." Justice Frankfurter argued that the "specific circumstances of each particular case" are relevant in determining the geographic scope of the Constitution. Justice Harlan was the most explicit in rejecting a "rigid and abstract rule" for determining where constitutional guarantees extend. He read the Insular Cases to teach that whether a constitutional provision has extraterritorial effect depends upon the "particular circumstances, the practical necessities, and the possible alternatives which Congress had before it" and, in particular, whether judicial enforcement of the provision would be "impracticable and anomalous."

That the petitioners in *Reid* were American citizens was a key factor in the case and was central to the plurality's conclusion that the Fifth and Sixth Amendments apply to American civilians tried outside the United States. But practical considerations, related not to the petitioners' citizenship but to the place of their confinement and trial, were relevant to each Member of the *Reid* majority.

Practical considerations weighed heavily as well in *Johnson v. Eisentrager* (1950), where the Court addressed whether habeas corpus jurisdiction extended to enemy aliens who had been convicted of violating the laws of war. The prisoners were detained at Landsberg Prison in Germany during the Allied Powers' postwar occupation. The Court stressed the difficulties of ordering the Government to produce the prisoners in a habeas corpus proceeding. It "would require allocation of shipping space, guarding personnel, billeting and rations" and would damage the prestige of military commanders at a sensitive time. In considering these factors the Court sought to balance the constraints of military occupation with constitutional necessities.

True, the Court in *Eisentrager* denied access to the writ, and it noted the prisoners "at no relevant time were within any territory over which the United States is sovereign, and that the scenes of their offense, their capture, their trial and their punishment were all beyond the territorial jurisdiction of any court of the United States." The Government seizes upon this language as proof positive that the *Eisentrager* Court adopted a formalistic, sovereignty-based test for determining the reach of the Suspension Clause.

First, we do not accept the idea that the above-quoted passage from *Eisentrager* is the only authoritative language in the opinion. In that same case, the Court's further determinations, based on practical considerations, were integral in its opinion and came before the decision announced its holding.

Second, because the United States lacked both de jure sovereignty and plenary control over Landsberg Prison, it is far from clear that the *Eisentrager* Court used the term sovereignty only in the narrow technical sense and not to connote the degree of control the military asserted over the facility. . . . Even if we assume the *Eisentrager* Court considered the United States' lack of formal legal sovereignty over Landsberg Prison as the decisive factor in that case, its holding is not inconsistent with a functional approach to questions of extraterritoriality. The formal legal status of a given territory affects, at least to some extent, the political branches' control over that territory. De jure sovereignty is a factor that bears upon which constitutional guarantees apply there.

Third, if the Government's reading of *Eisentrager* were correct, the opinion would have marked not only a change in, but a complete repudiation of, *the Insular Cases'* (and later *Reid v. Covert's*) functional approach to questions of extraterritoriality. We cannot accept the Government's view. Nothing in *Eisentrager* says that de jure sovereignty is or has ever been the only relevant consideration in determining the geographic reach of the Constitution or of habeas corpus. Were that the case, there would be considerable tension between *Eisentrager*, on the one hand, and the *Insular Cases* and *Reid*, on the other. Our cases need not be read to conflict in this manner. A constricted reading of *Eisentrager* overlooks what we see as a common thread uniting the *Insular Cases*, *Eisentrager*, and *Reid*: the idea that questions of extraterritoriality turn on objective factors and practical concerns, not formalism.

The Government's formal sovereignty-based test raises troubling separation-of-powers concerns as well. The political history of Guantanamo illustrates the deficiencies of this approach. The United States has maintained complete and uninterrupted control of the bay for over 100 years. At the close of the Spanish-American War, Spain ceded control over the entire island of Cuba to the United States and specifically "relinquished all claims of sovereignty . . . and title." From the date the treaty with Spain was signed until the Cuban Republic was established on May 20, 1902, the United States governed the territory "in trust" for the benefit of the Cuban people. And although it recognized, by entering into the 1903 Lease Agreement, that Cuba retained "ultimate sovereignty" over Guantanamo, the United States continued to maintain the same plenary control it had enjoyed since 1898. Yet the Government's view is that the Constitution had no effect there, at least as to noncitizens, because the United States disclaimed sovereignty in the formal sense of the term. The necessary implication of the argument is that by surrendering formal sovereignty over any unincorporated territory to a third party, while at the same time entering into a lease that grants total control over the territory back to the United States, it would be possible for the political branches to govern without legal constraint.

Our basic charter cannot be contracted away like this. The Constitution grants Congress and the President the power to acquire, dispose of, and govern territory, not the power to decide when and where its terms apply. Even when the United States acts outside its borders, its powers are not absolute and unlimited but are subject to such restrictions as are expressed in the Constitution. Abstaining from questions involving formal sovereignty and territorial governance is one thing. To hold the political branches have the power to switch the Constitution on or off at will is quite another. The former position reflects this Court's recognition that certain matters requiring political judgments are best left to the political branches. The latter would permit a striking anomaly in our tripartite system of government, leading to a regime in which Congress and the President, not this Court, say "what the law is." *Marbury v. Madison* (1803).

These concerns have particular bearing upon the Suspension Clause question in the cases now before us, for the writ of habeas corpus is itself an indispensable mechanism for monitoring the separation of powers. The test for determining the scope of this provision must not be subject to manipulation by those whose power it is designed to restrain.

As we recognized in *Rasul*, the outlines of a framework for determining the reach of the Suspension Clause are suggested by the factors the Court relied upon in *Eisentrager*. In addition to the practical concerns discussed above, the *Eisentrager* Court found relevant that each petitioner:

> "(a) is an enemy alien; (b) has never been or resided in the United States; (c) was captured outside of our territory and there held in military custody as a prisoner of war; (d) was tried and convicted by a Military Commission sitting outside the United States; (e) for offenses against laws of war committed outside the United States; (f) and is at all times imprisoned outside the United States."

Based on this language from *Eisentrager*, and the reasoning in our other extraterritoriality opinions, we conclude that at least three factors are relevant in determining the reach of the Suspension Clause: (1) the citizenship and status of the detainee and the adequacy of the process through which that status determination was made; (2) the nature of the sites where apprehension and then detention took place; and (3) the practical obstacles inherent in resolving the prisoner's entitlement to the writ.

Applying this framework, we note at the onset that the status of these detainees is a matter of dispute. The petitioners, like those in *Eisentrager*, are not American citizens. But the petitioners in *Eisentrager* did not contest, it seems, the Court's assertion that they were "enemy aliens." In the instant cases, by contrast, the detainees deny they are enemy combatants. They have been afforded some process in CSRT proceedings to determine their status; but, unlike in *Eisentrager*, there has been no trial by military commission for violations of the laws of war. The difference is not trivial. The records from the *Eisentrager* trials suggest that, well before the petitioners brought their case to this Court, there had been a rigorous adversarial process to test the legality of their detention. The *Eisentrager* petitioners were charged by a bill of particulars that made detailed factual allegations against them. To rebut the accusations, they were entitled to representation by counsel, allowed to introduce evidence on their own behalf, and permitted to cross-examine the prosecution's witnesses.

In comparison, the procedural protections afforded to the detainees in the CSRT hearings are far more limited, and, we conclude, fall well short of the procedures and adversarial mechanisms that would eliminate the need for habeas corpus review. Although the detainee is assigned a "Personal Representative" to assist him during CSRT proceedings, the Secretary of the Navy's memorandum makes clear that person is not the detainee's lawyer or even his "advocate." The Government's evidence is accorded a presumption of validity. The detainee is allowed to present "reasonably available" evidence, but his ability to rebut the Government's evidence against him is limited by the circumstances of his confinement and his lack of counsel at this stage. And although the detainee can seek review of his status determination in the Court of Appeals, that review process cannot cure all defects in the earlier proceedings.

As to the second factor relevant to this analysis, the detainees here are similarly situated to the *Eisentrager* petitioners in that the sites of their apprehension and detention are technically outside the sovereign territory of the United States. As noted earlier, this is a factor that weighs against finding they have rights under the Suspension Clause. But there are critical differences between Landsberg Prison, circa 1950, and the United States Naval Station at Guantanamo Bay in 2008. Unlike its present control over the naval station, the United States' control over the prison in Germany was neither absolute nor indefinite. Like all parts of occupied Germany, the prison was under the jurisdiction of the combined Allied Forces. The United States was therefore answerable to its Allies for all activities occurring there. The Allies had not planned a long-term occupation of Germany, nor did they intend to displace all German institutions even during the period of occupation. . . . . Guantanamo Bay, on the other hand, is no transient possession. In every practical sense Guantanamo is not abroad; it is within the constant jurisdiction of the United States.

As to the third factor, we recognize, as the Court did in *Eisentrager*, that there are costs to holding the Suspension Clause applicable in a case of military detention abroad. Habeas corpus proceedings may require expenditure of funds by the Government and may divert the attention of military personnel from other pressing tasks. While we are sensitive to these concerns, we do not find them dispositive. Compliance with any judicial process requires some incremental expenditure of resources. Yet civilian courts and the Armed Forces have functioned alongside each other at various points in our history. The Government presents no credible arguments that the military mission at Guantanamo would be compromised if habeas corpus courts had jurisdiction to hear the detainees' claims. And in light of the plenary control the United States asserts over the base, none are apparent to us.

The situation in *Eisentrager* was far different, given the historical context and nature of the military's mission in post-War Germany. When hostilities in the European Theater came to an end, the United States became responsible for an occupation zone encompassing over 57,000 square miles with a population of 18 million. In addition to supervising massive reconstruction and aid efforts the American forces stationed in Germany faced potential security threats from a defeated enemy. In retrospect the post-War occupation may seem uneventful. But at the time Eisentrager was decided, the Court was right to be concerned about judicial interference with the military's efforts to contain "enemy elements, guerilla fighters, and 'were-wolves.'"

Similar threats are not apparent here; nor does the Government argue that they are. The United States Naval Station at Guantanamo Bay consists of 45 square miles of land and water. The base has been used, at various points, to house migrants and refugees temporarily. At present, however, other than the detainees themselves, the only long-term residents are American military personnel, their families, and a small number of workers. The detainees have been deemed enemies of the United States. At present, dangerous as they may be if released, they are contained in a secure prison facility located on an isolated and heavily fortified military base.

There is no indication, furthermore, that adjudicating a habeas corpus petition would cause friction with the host government. No Cuban court has jurisdiction over American military personnel at Guantanamo or the enemy combatants detained there. While obligated to abide by the terms of the lease, the United States is, for all practical purposes, answerable to no other sovereign for its acts on the base. Were that not the case, or if the detention facility were located in an active theater of war, arguments that issuing the writ would be "impracticable or anomalous" would have more weight. Under the facts presented here, however, there are few practical barriers to the running of the writ. To the extent barriers arise, habeas corpus procedures likely can be modified to address them.

It is true that before today the Court has never held that noncitizens detained by our Government in territory over which another country maintains de jure sovereignty have any rights under our Constitution. But the cases before us lack any precise historical parallel. They involve individuals detained by executive order for the duration of a conflict that, if measured from September 11, 2001, to the present, is already among the longest wars in American history. The detainees, moreover, are held in a territory that, while technically not part of the United States, is under the complete and total control of our Government. Under these circumstances the lack of a precedent on point is no barrier to our holding.

We hold that Art. I, §9, cl. 2, of the Constitution has full effect at Guantanamo Bay. If the privilege of habeas corpus is to be denied to the detainees now before us, Congress must act in accordance with the requirements of the Suspension Clause.

In light of this holding the question becomes whether the statute stripping jurisdiction to issue the writ avoids the Suspension Clause mandate because Congress has provided adequate substitute procedures for habeas corpus. The Government submits there has been compliance with the Suspension Clause because the DTA review process in the Court of Appeals provides an adequate substitute.

To the extent any doubt remains about Congress' intent, the legislative history confirms what the plain text strongly suggests: In passing the DTA and the MCA, Congress did not intend to create a process that differs from traditional habeas corpus process in name only. It intended to create a more limited procedure. It is against this background that we must interpret the DTA and assess its adequacy as a substitute for habeas corpus.

We do not try to offer a summary of what an adequate substitute for habeas corpus would look like. It is uncontroversial that the privilege of habeas corpus entitles the prisoner to a meaningful opportunity to demonstrate that he is being held pursuant to "the erroneous application or interpretation" of relevant law. And the habeas court must have the power to order the conditional release of an individual unlawfully detained—though release need not be the exclusive remedy and is not the appropriate one in every case in which the writ is granted. These are the easily identified attributes of any constitutionally adequate habeas corpus proceeding. But, depending on the circumstances, more may be required.

Accordingly, we will show great deference to the findings arising in the judgements of a court of record where a defendant has already had a fair, adversary proceeding and the prisoner already has had the opportunity to challenge the legality of his detention.... Habeas corpus proceedings need not resemble a criminal trial, even when the detention is by executive order. But the writ must be effective. The habeas court must have sufficient authority to conduct a meaningful review of both the cause for detention and the Executive's power to detain.

To determine the necessary scope of habeas corpus review, therefore, we must assess the CSRT process, the mechanism through which petitioners' designation as enemy combatants became final. Whether one characterizes the CSRT process as direct review of the Executive's battlefield determination that the detainee is an enemy combatant—as the parties have and as we do—or as the first step in the collateral review of a battlefield determination makes no difference in a proper analysis of whether the procedures Congress put in place are an adequate substitute for habeas corpus. What matters is the sum total of procedural protections afforded to the detainee at all stages, direct and collateral.

Petitioners identify what they see as myriad deficiencies in the CSRTs. The most relevant for our purposes are the constraints upon the detainee's ability to rebut the factual basis for the Government's assertion that he is an enemy combatant. As already noted, at the CSRT stage the detainee has limited means to find or present evidence to challenge the Government's case against him. He does not have the assistance of counsel and may not be aware of the most critical allegations that the Government relied upon to order his detention. The detainee can confront witnesses that testify during the CSRT proceedings. But given that there are in effect no limits on the admission of hearsay evidence—the only requirement is that the tribunal deem the evidence "relevant and helpful,"—the detainee's opportunity to question witnesses is likely to be more theoretical than real.

Although we make no judgment as to whether the CSRTs, as currently constituted, satisfy due process standards, we agree with petitioners that, even when all the parties involved in this process act with diligence and in good faith, there is considerable risk of error in the tribunal's findings of fact. This is a risk inherent in any process that is closed and accusatorial. And given that the consequence of error may be detention of persons for the duration of hostilities that may last a generation or more, this is a risk too significant to ignore.

For the writ of habeas corpus, or its substitute, to function as an effective and proper remedy in this context, the court that conducts the habeas proceeding must have the means to correct errors that occurred during the CSRT proceedings. This includes some authority to assess the sufficiency of the Government's evidence against the detainee. It also must have the authority to admit and consider relevant exculpatory evidence that was not introduced during the earlier proceeding. Federal habeas petitioners long have had the means to supplement the record on review, even in the post-conviction habeas setting. Here that opportunity is constitutionally required.

Consistent with the historic function and province of the writ, habeas corpus review may be more circumscribed if the underlying detention proceedings are more thorough than they were here. On their own terms, the proceedings in *Yamashita* and *Quirin*, like those in *Eisentrager*, had an adversarial structure that is lacking here. For example, in *Yamashita* the defendant was represented by six military lawyers and throughout the proceedings defense counsel demonstrated their professional skill and resourcefulness and their proper zeal for the defense with which they were charged.

The extent of the showing required of the Government in these cases is a matter to be determined. We need not explore it further at this stage. We do hold that when the judicial power to issue habeas corpus properly is invoked the judicial officer must have adequate authority to make a determination in light of the relevant law and facts and to formulate and issue appropriate orders for relief, including, if necessary, an order directing the prisoner's release . . . The DTA does not explicitly empower the Court of Appeals to order the applicant in a DTA review proceeding released should the court find that the standards and procedures used at his CSRT hearing were insufficient to justify detention. This is troubling.

The absence of a release remedy and specific language allowing AUMF challenges are not the only constitutional infirmities from which the statute potentially suffers, however. The more difficult question is whether the DTA permits the Court of Appeals to make requisite findings of fact. The DTA enables petitioners to request "review" of their CSRT determination in the Court of Appeals, but the "Scope of Review" provision confines the Court of Appeals' role to reviewing whether the CSRT followed the "standards and procedures" issued by the Department of Defense and assessing whether those "standards and procedures" are lawful. Among these standards is "the requirement that the conclusion of the Tribunal be supported by a preponderance of the evidence allowing a rebuttable presumption in favor of the Government's evidence."

Assuming the DTA can be construed to allow the Court of Appeals to review or correct the CSRT's factual determinations, as opposed to merely certifying that the tribunal applied the correct standard of proof, we see no way to construe the statute to allow what is also constitutionally required in this context: an opportunity for the detainee to present relevant exculpatory evidence that was not made part of the record in the earlier proceedings. Furthermore, even if the DTA allows introduction and consideration of relevant exculpatory evidence that was "reasonably available" to the Government at the time of the CSRT but not made part of the record, the DTA review proceeding falls short of being a constitutionally adequate substitute for habeas corpus because the detainee still would have no opportunity to present evidence discovered after the CSRT proceedings concluded. This is not a remote hypothetical. One of the petitioners, Mohamed Nechla, requested at his CSRT hearing that the Government contact his employer. The petitioner claimed the employer would corroborate Nechla's contention he had no affiliation with Al-Qaeda. Although the CSRT determined this testimony would be relevant, it also found the witness was not reasonably available to testify at the time of the hearing. Petitioner's counsel, however, now represents the witness is available to be heard. If a detainee can present reasonably available evidence demonstrating there is no basis for his continued detention, he must have the opportunity to present this evidence to a habeas corpus court. However, under the current rules of the DTA, the evidence identified by Nechla would be inadmissible in a DTA review proceeding. The role of an Article III court in the exercise of its habeas corpus function cannot be circumscribed in this manner.

By foreclosing consideration of evidence not presented or reasonably available to the detainee at the CSRT proceedings, the DTA disadvantages the detainee by limiting the scope of collateral review to a record that may not be accurate or complete. In other contexts, e.g., in post-trial habeas cases where the prisoner already has had a full and fair opportunity to develop the factual predicate of his claims, similar limitations on the scope of habeas review may be appropriate. In this context, however, where the underlying detention proceedings lack the necessary adversarial character, the detainee cannot be held responsible for all deficiencies in the record.

The real risks, the real threats, of terrorist attacks are constant and not likely soon to abate. The ways to disrupt our life and laws are so many and unforeseen that the Court should not attempt even some general catalogue of crises that might occur. Certain principles are apparent, however. Practical considerations and exigent circumstances inform the definition and reach of the law's writs, including habeas corpus. The cases and our tradition reflect this precept.

In cases involving foreign citizens detained abroad by the Executive, it likely would be both an impractical and unprecedented extension of judicial power to assume that habeas corpus would be available at the moment the prisoner is taken into custody. If and when habeas corpus jurisdiction applies, as it does in these cases, then proper deference can be accorded to reasonable procedures for screening and initial detention under lawful and proper conditions of confinement and treatment for a reasonable period of time. Domestic exigencies, furthermore, might also impose such onerous burdens on the Government that here, too, the Judicial Branch would be required to devise sensible rules for staying habeas corpus proceedings until the Government can comply with its requirements in a responsible way. . . . Here, as is true with detainees apprehended abroad, a relevant consideration in determining the courts' role is whether there are suitable alternative processes in place to protect against the arbitrary exercise of governmental power.

The cases before us, however, do not involve detainees who have been held for a short period of time while awaiting their CSRT determinations. In some of these cases six years have elapsed without the judicial oversight that habeas corpus or an adequate substitute demands. And there has been no showing that the Executive faces such onerous burdens that it cannot respond to habeas corpus actions. To require these detainees to complete DTA review before proceeding with their habeas corpus actions would be to require additional months, if not years, of delay. The first DTA review applications were filed over a year ago, but no decisions on the merits have been issued. While some delay in fashioning new procedures is unavoidable, the costs of delay can no longer be borne by those who are held in custody. The detainees in these cases are entitled to a prompt habeas corpus hearing.

Our decision today holds only that the petitioners before us are entitled to seek the writ, and that the DTA review procedures are an inadequate substitute for habeas corpus.

END OF OPINION

Since the Court ruled in *Boumediene*, detainees have won 35 out of 48 habeas hearings on the ground that there was insufficient evidence to justify their detention. Many others lost at those hearings and had their detention continued.

Immediately following *Boumediene*, the Bush administration argued that the decision was inapplicable to detainees being held at a U.S. detention facility at Bagram, Afghanistan, including detainees who had been captured outside of Afghanistan but then flown to Afghanistan to be held. The Bush and later Obama administrations relied on the unique nature of Guantanamo in arguing that the decision in *Boumediene* did not apply, but that *Eisentrager* continued to be the governing precedent. In January 2010, a three-judge panel of the D.C. Circuit Court of Appeals adopted the Bush/Obama position, holding that even detainees abducted outside of Afghanistan and then shipped to Bagram have no right to contest the legitimacy of their detention in a U.S. federal court, because *Boumediene* does not apply to prisons located within war zones (such as Afghanistan).[2]

What do these series of cases mean for the future of military detention of enemy combatants? It is important to keep a few things in mind.

First, while the procedures used at the military tribunals in the early cases differs significantly from what we now think of as adequate due process, many of the criminal procedures we are used to only came into being since the end of World War II. Also fairly recent, but effective, are the regulations and laws that developed during the 1970s–1990s to prosecute spies, organized crime, and drug kingpins, cases which deal with many of the same kinds of concerns as arise in terrorism-related cases.

Second, the entire subject of human rights is also very much a post-WWII construct. All of these treaties came into existence <u>after</u> the Second World War and the cases in *Quirin* and *Eisentrager*.

Finally, the ability of the government to gather evidence and present that evidence in hearings is much greater now than it used to be. Electronic surveillance now provides much more information than used to be the case. Think about how videoteleconferencing, cellphones, and even the availability of air travel has changed since the 1940s.

---

2. *Fadi Maqaleh, et al. v. Robert Gates, et al.*, No. 09-5265 (D.C. Cir. 2010).

There is almost always a great deal of deference to the president and executive branch early in any emergency, but that deference has always tended to subside as the emergency gave way to a "new normal." If all of the cases above had been raised within the first two years of the conflict in Afghanistan, might the courts have ruled differently? Consider how the issue of deference to the judgment of the executive branch might have shifted as the detainees were held without hearings, year after year.

There is no question, though, that military detention and military tribunals will continue to be one tool used by the government to address national security concerns.

Review Questions

1. Consider a case where an individual associated with Al-Qaeda or ISIS is captured in Belgium or France and transported to a U.S. military detention facility in Iraq. Does the fact that there are working judicial systems in the nations where the individual was captured, even though not the U.S., bear on whether the individual should be detained and what procedures apply?

2. What are the implications of a "war on terror" that cannot be ended by a peace treaty between two governments? Release of POWs at the end of a conflict was always premised on the belief that the combatants would follow the direction of their government that the war was over. How does this work if there is no "government" that can make this assurance on behalf of the detainees? Does this mean that individuals who are captured as combatants may be held in that status forever?

3. At the time of writing this book, there have been less than a dozen successful trials of Guantanamo detainees for the war crimes they are alleged to have committed; in the past decade, more than 200 individuals have been successfully prosecuted in U.S. federal district courts in the United States for terrorism-related offenses. Given that Guantanamo detainees enjoy the same due process rights in terms of access to counsel and the proceedings that take place at tribunal trials, why not simply try the rest of these cases in federal district court and be done with it? Consider the arguments for and against such a proposal.

Key Terms

Combatant—All members of the armed forces of a party to the conflict are combatants, except medical and religious personnel. As to the situation of members of armed opposition groups, persons do not enjoy the protection against attack accorded to civilians when they take a direct part in hostilities.

Common Article 3—Common to the four Geneva Conventions of 1949, it contains the essential rules of the Geneva Conventions in a condensed format and makes them applicable to all armed conflicts, whether international armed conflicts or conflicts not of an international character:

- It requires humane treatment for all persons in enemy hands, without any adverse distinction. It specifically prohibits murder, mutilation, torture, cruel, humiliating and degrading treatment, the taking of hostages and unfair trial.

- It requires that the wounded, sick and shipwrecked be collected and cared for.
- It grants the ICRC the right to offer its services to the parties to the conflict.
- It calls on the parties to the conflict to bring all or parts of the Geneva Conventions into force through so-called special agreements.
- It recognizes that the application of these rules does not affect the legal status of the parties to the conflict.

Habeas corpus—A writ of habeas corpus is used to bring a prisoner or other detainee before the court to determine if the person's imprisonment or detention is lawful. A *habeas* petition proceeds as a civil action against the agent who holds the defendant in custody. It can also be used to examine any extradition processes used, amount of bail, and the jurisdiction of the court.

Further Reading

Chesney, Robert and Goldsmith, Jack Landman, *Terrorism and the Convergence of Criminal and Military Detention Models.* Stanford Law Review, Vol. 60, 2008; Wake Forest Univ. Legal Studies Paper No. 1055501. Available at SSRN: http://ssrn.com/abstract=1055501.

Hafetz, Jonathan, *Military Detention in the 'War on Terrorism': Normalizing the Exceptional After 9/11* (March 16, 2012). Columbia Law Review Sidebar, Vol. 112, 2012.

Elsea, Jennifer K. *Detention of U.S. Persons as Enemy Belligerents.* Congressional Research Service Report R42337 (March 18, 2014).

Wittes, Benjamin, Chesney Robert M., and Reynolds, Larkin, The Harvard Law School National Security Research Committee. *The Emerging Law of Detention 2.0 The Guantánamo Habeas Cases as Lawmaking* (Brookings, April 2012) available at https://www.brookings.edu/research/the-emerging-law-of-detention-2-0-the-guantanamo-habeas-cases-as-lawmaking/.

Chapter 13

Military Justice

Overview

One of the most important components of our national security system is the military. The military acts in support of national security in many ways. Just a small list includes the active military serving overseas in different combat, training or forward presence operations, the National Guard working as part of the active forces or here in the United States as part of our disaster and emergency response strategies, military acting in support of civil authorities in areas like anti-terrorism, counter drug operations, or security, as well as the involvement of military capabilities and organizations like the National Security Agency providing support to other agencies like the FBI and the Drug Enforcement Agency. All of these activities are bounded by law and, in many cases, we have already talked about this, such as the laws involving support to disaster and emergency response, electronic surveillance, and the use of force against terrorist organizations and other adversaries.

Similarly, the laws and regulations governing the military have a constitutional basis. While Article 2 of the Constitution established the president as the commander in chief of the Army and Navy and their state militias when they are called into service of the United States, that power is shared with Congress. Article 1, section 8 includes in the express powers of Congress the authority:

- To constitute Tribunals inferior to the supreme Court;
- To define and punish Piracies and Felonies committed on the high Seas, and Offences against the Law of Nations;
- To declare War, grant Letters of Marque and Reprisal, and make Rules concerning Captures on Land and Water;
- To raise and support Armies, but no Appropriation of Money to that Use shall be for a longer Term than two Years;
- To provide and maintain a Navy;
- To make Rules for the Government and Regulation of the land and naval Forces;
- To provide for calling forth the Militia to execute the Laws of the Union, suppress Insurrections and repel Invasions;
- To provide for organizing, arming, and disciplining, the Militia, and for governing such Part of them as may be employed in the Service of the United States, reserving to the States respectively, the Appointment of the Officers, and the

Authority of training the Militia according to the discipline prescribed by Congress;

Most of the laws that Congress has passed under these authorities are contained in Title 10 of the United States Code, and those statutes cover everything from how the military is structured (including the creation of the U.S. Air Force) to how servicemembers and officers will be trained, to how decisions will be made on what equipment to buy and how facilities and bases will be run. Also included in these laws and regulations are the laws concerning military justice, and it is those laws that we will cover in this chapter.

Just as each state has its own set of laws, penal code, and criminal justice system, so too does the military. This set of laws is referred to as "the Uniform Code of Military Justice" (UCMJ) and is found in sections 801–946 of Title 10 of the U.S. Code. It provides the legal basis for the military justice system, including the rights of servicemembers under this system, the crimes and offenses of which servicemembers can be tried and convicted, establishment and structure of military courts and judges, and the legal procedures that govern this system of justice.

You will recall that, in the introductory chapter of this text, we read the case *Reid v. Covert*, and you will remember the ruling that, as a general rule of law, civilians (in this case, wives who are living with their spouses at a base overseas) cannot be tried by court-martial. After you review the facts of the case again, read the following discussion from the opinion, discussing aspects of the military justice system important for our consideration.

Reid v. Covert, 354 U.S. 1, 1957*

[The facts and holding of the case are contained at pages "x-ref" of this text.]

. . .

There have been a number of decisions in the lower federal courts which have upheld military trial of civilians performing services for the armed forces "in the field" during time of war. To the extent that these cases can be justified, insofar as they involved trial of persons who were not "members" of the armed forces, they must rest on the Government's "war powers." In the face of an actively hostile enemy, military commanders necessarily have broad power over persons on the battlefront. From a time prior to the adoption of the Constitution, the extraordinary circumstances present in an area of actual fighting have been considered sufficient to permit punishment of some civilians in that area by military courts under military rules. But neither Japan nor Great Britain could properly be said to be an area where active hostilities were under way at the time Mrs. Smith and Mrs. Covert committed their offenses or at the time they were tried.

. . .

---

* The case has been heavily edited and paraphrased by the authors for clarity. See disclaimer in introduction.

While we recognize that the "war powers" of the Congress and the Executive are broad, we reject the Government's argument that present threats to peace permit military trial of civilians accompanying the armed forces overseas in an area where no actual hostilities are under way. The exigencies which have required military rule on the battlefront are not present in areas where no conflict exists. Military trial of civilians "in the field" is an extraordinary jurisdiction, and it should not be expanded at the expense of the Bill of Rights. We agree with Colonel Winthrop, an expert on military jurisdiction, who declared: "a statute cannot be framed by which a civilian can lawfully be made amenable to the military jurisdiction in time of peace." (Emphasis not supplied.)

As this Court stated in *United States ex rel. Toth v. Quarles,* 350 U.S. 11, the business of soldiers is to fight and prepare to fight wars, not to try civilians for their alleged crimes. Traditionally, military justice has been a rough form of justice emphasizing summary procedures, speedy convictions and stern penalties with a view to maintaining obedience and fighting fitness in the ranks. Because of its very nature and purpose, the military must place great emphasis on discipline and efficiency. Correspondingly, there has always been less emphasis in the military on protecting the rights of the individual than in civilian society and in civilian courts.

Courts-martial are typically ad hoc bodies appointed by a military officer from among his subordinates. They have always been subject to varying degrees of "command influence." In essence, these tribunals are simply executive tribunals whose personnel are in the executive chain of command. Frequently, the members of the court-martial must look to the appointing officer for promotions, advantageous assignments and efficiency ratings—in short, for their future progress in the service. Conceding to military personnel that high degree of honesty and sense of justice which nearly all of them undoubtedly have, the members of a court-martial, in the nature of things, do not and cannot have the independence of jurors drawn from the general public or of civilian judges.

We recognize that a number of improvements have been made in military justice recently by engrafting more and more of the methods of civilian courts on courts-martial. In large part, these ameliorations stem from the reaction of civilians, who were inducted during the two World Wars, to their experience with military justice. Notwithstanding the recent reforms, military trial does not give an accused the same protection which exists in the civil courts. Looming far above all other deficiencies of the military trial, of course, is the absence of trial by jury before an independent judge after an indictment by a grand jury. Moreover the reforms are merely statutory; Congress—and perhaps the President—can reinstate former practices, subject to any limitations imposed by the Constitution, whenever it desires. As yet, it has not been clearly settled to what extent the Bill of Rights and other protective parts of the Constitution apply to military trials.

It must be emphasized that every person who comes within the jurisdiction of courts-martial is subject to military law—law that is substantially different from the law which governs civilian society. Military law is, in many respects, harsh law which is frequently cast in very sweeping and vague terms. It emphasizes the iron hand of discipline more that it does the even scales of justice. Moreover, it has not yet been definitely established to what extent the President, as Commander-in-Chief of the armed forces, or his delegates, can promulgate, supplement or change substantive military law as well as the procedures of military courts in time of peace, or in time of war. In any event, Congress has given the President broad discretion to provide the rules governing military trials.... If the President can provide rules of substantive law as well as procedure, then he and his military subordinates exercise legislative, executive and judicial powers with respect to those subject to military trials. Such blending of functions in one branch of the Government is the objectionable thing which the draftsmen of the Constitution endeavored to prevent by providing for the separation of governmental powers.

In summary, it still remains true that military tribunals have not been, and probably never can be, constituted in such way that they can have the same kind of qualifications that the Constitution has deemed essential to fair trials of civilians in federal courts. In part, this is attributable to the inherent differences in values and attitudes that separate the military establishment from civilian society. In the military, by necessity, emphasis must be placed on the security and order of the group, rather than on the value and integrity of the individual.

It is urged that the expansion of military jurisdiction over civilians claimed here is only slight, and that the practical necessity for it is very great. The attitude appears to be that a slight encroachment on the Bill of Rights and other safeguards in the Constitution need cause little concern. But to hold that these wives could be tried by the military would be a tempting precedent. Slight encroachments create new boundaries from which legions of power can seek new territory to capture ... [W]e cannot consider this encroachment a slight one. Throughout history, many transgressions by the military have been called "slight" and have been justified as "reasonable" in light of the "uniqueness" of the times. We cannot close our eyes to the fact that, today, the peoples of many nations are ruled by the military.

We should not break faith with this Nation's tradition of keeping military power subservient to civilian authority, a tradition which we believe is firmly embodied in the Constitution. The country has remained true to that faith for almost one hundred seventy years. Perhaps no group in the Nation has been truer than military men themselves. Unlike the soldiers of many other nations, they have been content to perform their military duties in defense of the Nation in every period of need, and to perform those duties well without attempting to usurp power which is not theirs under our system of constitutional government.

Ours is a government of divided authority on the assumption that in division there is not only strength but freedom from tyranny. And, under our Constitution, courts of law alone are given power to try civilians for their offenses against the United States.

. . .

In No. 701, *Reid v. Covert*, the judgment of the District Court directing that Mrs. Covert be released from custody is

Affirmed.

END OF CASE

Although the military justice system and the laws contained in the UCMJ do not apply to civilians, as this case demonstrates, they do apply to active duty servicemembers, members in the Reserves when called to active duty, members of the National Guard when called into the federal service, contractors serving in combat alongside the military (like analysts, supply personnel, and translators), and retirees. The crimes and offenses set forth in the UCMJ apply, and those subject to the UCMJ can be prosecuted for violating them, at any time and wherever the offense is committed, including crimes committed off-base within the United States. The military justice system is a system that operates parallel to our state and federal civilian criminal justice systems. It addresses both what we would refer to as "common-law" crimes such as murder, rape, and theft, as well as distinctly military offenses such as being absent without leave from one's place of duty, disobedience of orders, and disrespect.

Purpose of the Military Justice System

The need for a separate military justice system has been a part of our society since well before the United States was founded. As early as 1689, the English Parliament assumed the power to issue laws for the Army and Navy.[1] One of the first actions of General George Washington was to call upon the Continental Congress to adopt the British Articles of War to govern the Continental Army, which they did in June 1775, a full week before adopting the Declaration of Independence. The first Judge Advocate General (JAG) of the Army was appointed by the Continental Congress on July 29, 1775, and our military justice system was born.

The purpose of military law is, as a recent report affirmed, "to promote justice, to assist in maintaining good order and discipline in the armed forces, to promote efficiency and effectiveness in the military establishment, and thereby to strengthen the national security of the United States. These three major recurring themes—justice, discipline, and efficiency—are set forth in complementary clauses of the Preamble to the Manual for Courts-Martial and are woven throughout the structure and provisions of the UCMJ and the Manual. Since its inception in 1775, military law in the United States has evolved to recognize that all three components are essential to ensure that our national security is protected and strengthened by an effective, highly disciplined military force."[2]

And, as the Supreme Court has recognized in any number of cases, the need for military discipline administered through a separate military justice system is

---

1. The Army Lawyer, *A History of the Judge Advocate General's Corps*, 1775–1975 at p. 3.
2. U.S. Department of Defense, *Report of the Military Justice Review Group*, 22 December 2015, p. 16.

needed because the military is a unique part of society. It is, in the words of one decision,

> "a specialized society separate from civilian society" with "laws and traditions of its own [developed] during its long history." *Parker v. Levy* (1973). Moreover, "it is the primary business of armies and navies to fight or be ready to fight wars should the occasion arise." *Toth v. Quarles* (1955). To prepare for and perform its vital role, the military must insist upon a respect for duty and a discipline without counterpart in civilian life. The laws and traditions governing that discipline have a long history, but they are founded on unique military exigencies as powerful now as in the past. Their contemporary vitality repeatedly has been recognized by Congress.

The ultimate objective of a military is to fight and win wars. Fighting and winning wars is how the military protects and defends this country, and this is difficult to do if the military lacks good order and discipline. If a military fails to maintain good order and discipline, missions will fail, people will die, and the nation's safety will be at risk.

Another important reason to ensure commanders can maintain "good order and discipline" is the historic threat to liberty posed by militaries, especially standing armies. Throughout much of history the common soldier was not a source of inspiration and admiration but instead was a source of fear because soldiers frequently terrorized the defenseless. For commanders to prevent this, they must have the authority and means to keep their soldiers in check. The military justice system gives commanders the ability to punish soldiers who stray out of place or engage in forms of misconduct, even if those offenses occur far from the American civilian criminal courts.

And, as much as we would like to believe that our military is above such atrocity, the nature of war and its effect on people is the same across all societies. In 1968 in Vietnam, LT William Calley led his troops in destroying a village, deliberately killing women and children in the process. For his acts, including both the murders he personally committed as well as his failure to control the soldiers under his command and prevent them from committing murder, LT Calley was criminally charged and convicted to life in prison.[3] In another example from World War II, Japanese General Yamashita allowed troops under his command to plunder the Philippines, committing acts of rape, torture, theft, and murder. General Yamashita himself had not committed any unlawful acts but had simply refused to control his troops to prevent them from committing such acts. For his failure to maintain "good order and discipline" over his troops, a failure which resulted in the murder of civilians, he was tried by a military tribunal, convicted, and executed. Prior to his execution, the U.S. Supreme Court reviewed his case and, in affirming the conviction and sentence, stated:

---

3. This sentence was reduced to house arrest, and, after three years, LT Calley received a pardon from President Nixon. A good account of the event, as well as the discipline problems and culture that led to the atrocities can be found in any number of sources, such as the essay "MY LAI: AN AMERICAN TRAGEDY" by William George Eckhardt (© William George Eckhardt 2000), http://law2.umkc.edu/faculty/projects/ftrials/mylai/ecktragedy.html#_ftn1.

The question, then, is whether the law of war imposes on an army commander a duty to take such appropriate measures as are within his power to control the troops under his command for the prevention of the specified acts which are violations of the law of war and which are likely to attend the occupation of hostile territory by an uncontrolled soldiery, and whether he may be charged with personal responsibility for his failure to take such measures when violations result. That this was the precise issue to be tried was made clear by the statement of the prosecution at the opening of the trial.

It is evident that the conduct of military operations by troops whose excesses are unrestrained by the orders or efforts of their commander would almost certainly result in violations which it is the purpose of the law of war to prevent. Its purpose to protect civilian populations and prisoners of war from brutality would largely be defeated if the commander of an invading army could, with impunity, neglect to take reasonable measures for their protection. Hence, the law of war presupposes that its violation is to be avoided through the control of the operations of war by commanders who are to some extent responsible for their subordinates.[4]

When people hear the term "military justice," they frequently imagine unfair proceedings where the "normal" rules of due process do not apply, where everyone is found guilty and issued an extremely harsh sentence. There was a great deal of truth to this view in the past, but following World War II the U.S. military and Congress conducted an overhaul of the system. Today, the rules at a court-martial are very similar to those found in any federal criminal court.[5] Additionally, in some ways, members of the military enjoy more protections than civilians as recognized by the Court of Appeals of the Armed Forces, which has stated:

"In defining the rights of military personnel, Congress was not limited to the minimum requirements established by the Constitution, and in many instances, it has provided safeguards unparalleled in the civilian sector."
United States v. Mapes, 59 M.J. 60, 65 (C.A.A.F. 2003).

The rights discussed in this book that are provided in broader form to servicemembers include warnings of their right to remain silent and to an attorney, free counsel at all adverse proceedings (criminal, appeal, and administrative) regardless of ability to pay, a more robust appellate system, much more lenient sentences, and a much stronger aversion to pretrial confinement than in civilian justice.

Prior to the adoption of the Uniform Code of Military Justice, the military justice system did still differ in some significant ways from the civilian court system. While those accused of crimes normally faced a grand jury and then trial jury made up of other citizens chosen from the community, at a court-martial the accused would appear before a panel of military officers who had been appointed by a senior

---

4. *In re Yamashita*, 327 U.S. 1 (1946).
5. George S. Prugh, *Observations on the Uniform Code of Military Justice: 1954 and 2000*, 165 Mil.L.Rev. 21 (2000).

commanding officer (usually a general or admiral) known as the "convening authority." The panel would look at the evidence, hear from witnesses, and decide the fate of an accused. The officers who comprised the panel at courts-martial sat as both judge and jury, despite the fact that usually no one involved in the proceedings had any legal training. Almost everyone was found guilty and sentences were exceptionally harsh. After the panel had imposed its judgment, the high ranking general or admiral who had convened the panel for the courts-martial in the first place would come along and modify the sentence to whatever he believed appropriate.

There were tens of thousands of courts-martial held during World War II, and by the end of the conflict, more people were in the military prisons than in all the civilian prisons in the United States. Congress began looking into the matter and discovered just how unfair the military justice system had become. The main problem they identified lay in what was referred to as command influence. This was where Convening Authority or a senior commander would put pressure on the members of the panel for findings of guilt, which were often against the weight of the evidence. They would also pressure members of the panel to impose harsh sentences, even when the circumstances did not warrant it.

Here is a quote from one former military officer that is representative of what Congress heard:

> "[W]e were advised, not once but many times on the Courts that I sat on, that if we adjudged a person guilty we should inflict the maximum sentence and leave it to the Commanding General to make any reduction.... I was dismissed as a Law Officer and Member of a General Court-Martial because our General Court acquitted a colored man on a moral charge when the Commanding General wanted him convicted-yet the evidence didn't warrant it. I was called down and told that if I didn't convict in a greater number of cases I would be marked down in my Efficiency Rating; and I squared right off and said that wasn't my conception of justice and that they had better remove me, which was done forthwith." Vermont Governor Ernest Gibson

Now, the commanders who convened the courts-martial believed they had very rational reasons for finding everyone guilty, passing the harshest sentence possible, and then leaving it to the commander to modify the sentence to what he personally believed to be appropriate. Commanders believed that word of extremely harsh sentences being passed at courts-martial would spread among the troops, who then would be discouraged from committing criminal acts themselves. At the same time, word of the commander reducing the sentence to something reasonable and fair would also spread among his troops. The court-martial panel would be viewed by the troops as the "bad guys" while the commander was the "good guy" and would gain the respect and love of his troopers through such acts of mercy.[6]

---

6. "Background of the Uniform Code of Military Justice," Judge Advocate General's School, U.S. Army (1959), available at https://www.loc.gov/rr/frd/Military_Law/pdf/background-UCMJ.pdf' and George S. Prugh, *Observations on the Uniform Code of Military Justice: 1954 and 2000*, 165 Mil.L.Rev. 21 (2000).

For these reasons, Congress decided it was time to fix the problems stemming from command influence and the lack of professionalism in military justice by doing away with the Articles of War and replace it with the Uniform Code of Military Justice (UCMJ) in 1950. This was an important step to modernizing military justice and bringing it in line with the standards of fairness and due process we expect in civilian trials today. The UCMJ has been amended over the years to make military justice a very fair process that is modeled after and in many ways resembles the civilian criminal justice system in federal district courts. Today, if you were to observe an actual court-martial, you would be amazed how much it is like a civilian trial; there is a prosecutor (referred to in the military as "trial counsel"), a defense attorney representing the accused, and a military judge wearing a black robe presiding over the trial, and trials can be heard by a jury (referred to as a "panel"). In fact, were it not for the fact that everyone present is in a military uniform and the occasional mentions of military rules, ranks, and protocols, you might not even realize it was a military trial; you'd think you were in a civilian court. In fact, a famous civilian criminal defense attorney, F. Lee Bailey, who had served as a defense counsel in the U.S. Marine Corps before he became a lawyer, was fond of saying that if he were accused of a crime he would rather be tried in a military court than in any other system of justice because of the protections afforded the military accused.

Each branch of the military maintains a group of uniformed attorneys, referred to as "judge advocates." The term was taken from the British Army, and, as recounted earlier, the first judge advocate in the U.S. military was William Tudor who was requested by General George Washington and appointed to that position by Congress in 1775. Judge advocates serve as prosecutors, defense attorneys, military judges, and legal assistance attorneys who assist servicemembers who need help in common matters such as writing wills or settling a dispute with a landlord. Increasingly, judge advocates serve as key advisers to commanders on all aspects of the military, from laws concerning lawful expenditure of funds appropriated by Congress, Department of Defense contracts on everything from food to weapons systems, and advice to military commanders on the law of war and rules of engagement so as to ensure that our military complies with both domestic and international law in combat. Each service has, in addition to uniformed judge advocates, a group of civilian attorneys known as "general counsel" who also provide legal support to the military in partnership with the judge advocates.

Criminal and Disciplinary Processes

Before we talk about specific crimes under the UCMJ, let's talk about the various stages of criminal procedure in the military from the initial report of a crime through conviction and appeals. In many ways, it is very similar to most civilian jurisdictions, although there are some very important differences. At the beginning of the criminal process, it closely resembles civilian justice as it starts with a report of a crime and evidence being gathered. Before a person can be criminally charged with an offense, there must be a finding of "probable cause" that the accused committed the offense. Also important, for the military to legally search a place where a servicemember has a reasonable expectation of privacy, investigators must first procure a warrant or "search order," which is issued upon a finding of probable cause.

What happens next is the first divergence from civilian justice. In civilian justice, if a person commits a minor offense known as a "misdemeanor," that civilian can be convicted of that offense and will have a criminal record. Examples of misdemeanors in most states would be drunk driving, petty larceny, and hitting another person (simple assault). Although a misdemeanor conviction is nowhere near as serious as a felony conviction, it is still a blemish on one's permanent record. This means that on future job applications, housing applications, and many other background checks, a person would have to admit to having been convicted of a crime. In contrast, for many offenses in the military for which a civilian would face a criminal conviction, a servicemember would not face any criminal conviction. Instead, the servicemember would be punished through what is known as "non-judicial punishment" and, though punished, would not face the consequences of having a criminal conviction on one's record.

Non-judicial punishment is commonly referred to as an Article 15 after its code in the UCMJ.[7] In the Navy, it is referred to as a Captain's Mast. Although it does not result in a criminal conviction, it can result in a demotion in rank, loss of pay, brief confinement, extra work, and various restrictions. While junior enlisted members of the military can occasionally still go on to have successful careers with an Article 15 on their records, for officers, it is a career killer. An officer who has an Article 15 on his permanent record is unlikely to ever be promoted and will be forced out of the military once his or her term of service expires. You can read the full text of UCMJ Article 15 here, as it details many of the possible maximum punishments.

For cases considered too serious to be handled as non-judicial punishment under Article 15, a commander can refer the case to a "summary court-martial," which is, again, not a full criminal proceeding. For a summary court-martial, the commander appoints an officer, who can be but is not required to be a lawyer, to sit as a judge. The summary court-martial officer calls witnesses and considers evidence, but the accused has the right to present evidence and cross-examine any witnesses. Although the military provides a free attorney with whom the defendant can consult, the attorney is not allowed to represent the defendant during the summary courts-martial. If a servicemember chooses to retain his own private civilian attorney, however, that attorney may be present and represent the accused. Like an Article 15, punishment at summary courts-martial is very limited to no more than one month of confinement, hard labor for no more than 45 days, restrictions for no less than two months, forfeiture of no more than 2/3 pay for no more than one month, and reduction to the lowest enlisted rank.

With both an Article 15 non-judicial punishment and a summary court-martial, the combination of strict limits on what punishment can be awarded, and the fact that the results, though a part of the military record, are not considered "criminal"

---

7. Article 15, UCMJ is found at 10 U.S. Code sec. 815.

records balances off the lesser level of due process afforded. In addition, a servicemember accused of a crime always has the right to refuse an Article 15 or summary courts-martial and demand a real court-martial, where full due process rights and rules of evidence apply, as would a permanent criminal record if the servicemember is convicted. These proceedings are generally used only for minor violations of military discipline rules, such as disrespect to seniors or minor cases of absence without leave.

For more serious cases, including most of what we would all consider criminal activity, the matter is referred on to the "Convening Authority," the senior officer (often but not always a general officer or admiral) in command. The Convening Authority will decide whether or not he or she should "convene" a court-martial to try the servicemember for the alleged offense. It is from this "convening" of the courts-martial from which we get the designation of this senior general or admiral as the "Convening Authority."

When the Convening Authority decides whether or not to convene a court-martial, he or she will be advised by a military attorney known as the Staff Judge Advocate (SJA). The SJA will advise the commander on the applicable legal issues and whether there is enough evidence to go forward with a trial. The commander is free to disregard the advice of the SJA, but they rarely do so. This function of the Convening Authority is unique to the military—the combination of the commander and the SJA serve much like a District Attorney who decides whether or not to press charges against a suspect. However, once the decision is made to send a case to court-martial, the commander and the SJA (seen as the commander's representative) are absolutely prohibited from making any statements or taking any actions that indicate opinion in the matter of guilt, an appropriate sentence if convicted, or anything else which might influence the outcome of the case. This is a significant change from World War II.

There are two formal types of courts-martials. The less serious one is a Special Court-Martial, typically reserved for extremely serious misdemeanors or less serious felonies. The maximum penalty of a Special Court-Martial is one year of incarceration and a bad conduct discharge. All Special Courts-Martial are presided over by a military judge, and lawyers are present as prosecutors and defense attorneys. Just as in many civilian courts, the accused has the option to be tried by a judge or by a jury (referred to as a "panel") of at least three officers or senior enlisted personnel.

A General Court-Martial is the more serious type of courts-martial, authorized to award sentences up to a total forfeiture of all pay and allowances, a Dishonorable Discharge, confinement up to the maximum allowed for a crime (including life in prison), and even the death penalty. A trial can be before a judge alone (if requested by the accused) or a panel of servicemembers who must be of greater rank than the accused.

In the civilian criminal justice system, serious crimes must go to a grand jury before they can be sent to trial. A similar process exists in the military. Serious allegations are sent to what is known as an Article 32[8] hearing, where the prosecution must establish probable cause that the accused is guilty. The prosecution will have witnesses testify and introduce evidence to show that the accused is guilty. Unlike at a civilian grand jury, the accused is present and is represented by counsel. The defense counsel is allowed to cross-examine the prosecution's witnesses and challenge the evidence, as well as put on its own witnesses and introduce evidence showing innocence. The Article 32 officer is normally a military attorney, often a military judge assigned for the specific purpose of this hearing. In a sense, an Article 32 hearing is like a mini-trial. If, and only if, the military judge finds probable cause that the accused committed the crime will the matter go on to courts-martial.

With a military judge presiding, both special and general courts-martials are very much like a civilian trial; the prosecution presents its case and its witnesses and evidence, which are cross-examined by the defense. The defense then presents its case, if it has one, which will be cross-examined by the prosecutor. The Military Rules of Evidence were modeled after the Federal Rules of Evidence used during civilian criminal trials. An accused can choose to be tried by judge alone, or by a jury. In the military, the term for a "jury" is a "panel." A panel is a selection of officers chosen by the Convening Authority. The Convening Authority is expected to select panel members who have the good judgment, intelligence, and maturity to fairly decide a case, rather than selecting members who have a particular bias in an issue. There are strict rules concerning Command Influence, which prohibit the Convening Authority from selecting jurors based on how he thinks they are likely to decide a case or feel on the issues.

To further prevent any bias from seeping into the panel, which has been handpicked by the Convening Authority, just like in civilian court, there is voir dire where the prosecution and defense can remove members of the panel who might have a bias.

After a person is convicted and before any appellate court looks at the case, pursuant to UCMJ Article 60,[9] the Convening Authority must review the entire record of the court-martial, including transcripts from all trial proceedings, the police report, witness statements, the evidence, the accused's service record, and other materials. Upon completing the review of the record, the Convening Authority has some limited authority to modify the findings and sentence of a court-martial. Until recently, the power of a commander to overturn a conviction or change a sentence was very broad, but concerns over military commanders misusing the authority have led to Congressional action limiting this power.[10]

After the Convening Authority has reviewed the record of trial, the accused has a right to appeal. In most cases, the military's appellate system is more generous than

---

8. The specifics are found at Article 32, UCMJ, 10 U.S. Code sec. 832.
9. 10 U.S. Code sec. 860.
10. Discussion of this can be found in U.S. Department of Defense, *Report of the Military Justice Review Group*, 22 December 2015, found at www.dod.gov/dodgc/mcrg.html. At the time of this writing, the most recent reforms were still under Congressional review and had not yet been enacted into law.

the civilian appeals process and gives convicted servicemembers several different opportunities to have their sentences and convictions challenged, reduced, and overturned. For convictions that result in either a sentence of at least one year of confinement or a punitive (bad conduct or dishonorable) discharge, appeals are automatic, and the record of trial, conviction, and sentence must be reviewed and affirmed by a court of criminal appeals. Each branch of the military has its own appellate court. There is the Army Court of Criminal Appeals, Air Force Court of Criminal Appeals, Navy Marine Court of Criminal Appeals, and the Coast Guard Court of Criminal Appeals. These Courts of Criminal Appeals used to be called "Boards of Review" and "Courts of Military Review." You may see them referred to as such in upcoming cases. The judges who sit on these courts are senior judge advocates specifically appointed by the Judge Advocate General of their service.

For a court of criminal appeals to uphold a sentence, the majority of the judges must be convinced beyond reasonable doubt that the appellant is in fact guilty. If the judges are not convinced beyond reasonable doubt that the person is guilty, they are legally required to overturn the verdict. This is an extremely important due process protection to servicemembers and a critical distinction from civilian courts. In civilian courts, except for cases where the findings were clearly erroneous, appellate judges will not question any findings of fact made by a jury or alter a sentence. Civilian appellate judges typically limit their focus and attention to procedural rules, evidentiary matters, and legal interpretations by the trial judge. It is extremely rare for them to reconsider the wisdom of a jury's finding of guilt. This makes it extremely difficult for a civilian appellant to win a case on appeal. In contrast, in the military's appellate courts, a person who is convicted gets what is essentially the opportunity to retry the case through appellate briefs and oral arguments.

The military appellate courts can reduce any sentence they find excessive, but may not increase a sentence. In contrast, civilian appellate courts may not revise a sentence but must send the case back to the court that heard the case for reconsideration.

The highest level of appellate justice in the military is the Court of Appeals of the Armed Forces (CAAF), formerly referred to as the Court of Military Appeals (COMA). In keeping with the tradition of civilian oversight of the U.S. military, these judges must all be civilians. Most cases end review at this level, just as a state court decision would. But, just as in state or other federal court, a case from the military can ultimately find its way to the Supreme Court.

It is important to remember that the military courts are a type of federal court. This means that if a person is tried and acquitted in a court-martial, that person cannot be tried again for the same crime at another courts-martial or in a federal district court. However, that servicemember can be tried a second time in a civilian state court.

You might have heard of "double jeopardy" as meaning that a person can't be tried twice for the same crime. This is not completely correct. What double jeopardy prohibits is a person being tried twice by the same "sovereign." In our justice system, the federal government is one "sovereign," and the states are the other "sovereign." This means that a person can be tried for a crime in a federal court and acquitted, then tried for the exact same crime in a state court, and vice-versa. So a case can, in theory, be heard by both a military and a state criminal court, but not by a federal criminal court. This is rare though; even if legal, it is seen as a waste of resources and unfair.

Due Process and Civil Rights of Service Members

Now that we've established a foundation of the criminal procedure in the military, let's turn to the civil rights and liberties of servicemembers. A common question is, "Does the U.S. Constitution apply to members of the military?" This is hard to answer because the U.S. Supreme Court has never held that it does apply to members of the military, nor has it explicitly ruled it does not apply. What courts generally try to do is apply the U.S. Constitution to service members so long as it does not interfere with the special purpose of the military, which is fighting and winning wars. Over the years, the courts have developed a special balance to uphold the rights of servicemembers while ensuring the military can carry out its responsibilities.

Improper Command Influence

One of the elemental due process rights is the right to a fair trial. This has been a challenge in the military because everyone, including judges and military juries, are subject to military command authority. As referenced in the introduction of this chapter, command influence was once the greatest threat to fairness in military justice. The main reason why the Articles of War were discarded and the Uniform Code of Military Justice was written was to prevent command influence. Loosely defined, command influence is any action by the person convening the courts-martial, referred to as the Convening Authority, which could affect the outcome of military judicial proceedings. This means that commanders cannot ask for findings of guilt, certain sentences, or go out of their way to put on a panel officers they know are predisposed to vote a certain way. Prior to the UCMJ, it was routine for commanders to retaliate against or punish panel members who did not make decisions at courts-martial in accord with the wishes of the Convening Authority. Today, such direct or indirect action by the convening authority is strictly illegal. Even words or actions by commanders and other senior military leaders, which are not intended to influence a court-martial but just might have that effect anyway, are considered unlawful command influence.

There are two sections of the UCMJ addressing command influence—Articles 37 and 98.[11] UCMJ Article 37 prohibits commanders from intentionally or unintentionally doing anything that might affect the outcome of judicial proceedings. Article 98 makes purposeful violations of Article 37 a criminal act. No commander has ever been convicted of violating Article 98, although there have been numerous instances over the years of commanders violating Article 37. There are two reasons

---

11. 10 U.S. Code 837 and 10 U.S. Code 898, respectively.

for this. First, command influence can be very hard to prove in court. Second, when command influence does occur, it is rarely a commander purposefully trying to influence a court-martial. They are typically just off the cuff remarks or some act normally taken by a commander, but they just so happens to coincide with a court-martial so as to raise the possibility of command influence. For example, it can be expected for today's military leaders to speak out against sexual assault. It is an important issue and society wants its leaders to take meaningful action and lead in the fight against sexual assault. However, military leaders must be extremely careful in doing so, otherwise, like President Obama, they risk being accused of influencing courts-martial proceedings.

The following case is one example of a finding of unlawful command influence.

U.S. v. Baldwin, 54 M.J. 308 (2001)*

During the fall of 1997 and in February of 1998, Baldwin was tried by a general court-martial composed of officer members at Fort Bliss, Texas. She was found guilty of larceny, conduct unbecoming an officer, and of service-discrediting conduct (mail tampering and obstruction of justice). The members sentenced Baldwin to a dismissal from the military, 1 year of confinement, and total forfeiture of pay on February 6, 1998. The convening authority on May 19, 1998, approved this sentence, and the Court of Criminal Appeals affirmed on October 1, 1999.

On May 19, 2000, this Court granted review on the following issue of law:

I. WHETHER THE CONVENING AUTHORITY EXERCISED UNLAWFUL COMMAND INFLUENCE OVER THE PROCEEDINGS BY REQUIRING THE COURT MEMBERS, IN THE MIDDLE OF THE TRIAL, TO ATTEND AN OFFICER PROFESSIONAL DEVELOPMENT PROGRAM WHERE "APPROPRIATE" PUNISHMENTS FOR OFFICER COURT-MARTIAL DEFENDANTS WAS DISCUSSED.

[We find that there may have been command influence, for which reason we] remand this case for a hearing on the issue of unlawful command influence.

Nine months after her court-martial, Baldwin signed a statement and later filed it with the Court of Criminal Appeals. It said:

> November 20, 1998
>
> I, Holly M. Baldwin, would like to make the following statement. Shortly after I was transferred from Fort Lewis to Fort Bliss (fall 1997), Ft. Bliss was having a Family Values Week. One of the Officer Professional Development programs mandated by Commanding General Costello was one directed at Ethics. At that particular OPD, one of the topics discussed was an incident that happened with three of the Officers in the 31st ADA BDE that were being court-martialed. The address included comments that the court-martial

---

* The case has been heavily edited and paraphrased by the authors for clarity. See disclaimer in introduction.

sentences were too lenient and that the minimum sentence should be at least one year and that Officers should be punished harsher than enlisted soldiers because Officers should always set the example and be above reproach.

On the day of my conviction and sentencing, the final part of the trial was delayed for another OPD that was mandatory for all Officers on post. That afternoon after the officers on my panel went to the OPD, I was convicted and sentenced to 1 year at Ft. Leavenworth

Baldwin argued that "her sentence to one year in confinement and the rejection of her request for Resignation for the Good of the Service was the result of these actions, which clearly constitute unlawful command influence in this case."

Article 37, UCMJ, 10 USC § 837, states:

Art. 37. Unlawfully influencing action of court

> (a) No authority convening a general, special, or summary court-martial, nor any other commanding officer, may censure, reprimand, or admonish the court or any member, military judge, or counsel thereof, with respect to the findings or sentence adjudged by the court, or with respect to any other exercises of its or his functions in the conduct of the proceedings. No person subject to this chapter may attempt to coerce or, by any unauthorized means, influence the action of a court-martial or any other military tribunal or any member thereof, in reaching the findings or sentence in any case, or the action of any convening, approving, or reviewing authority with respect to his judicial acts. The foregoing provisions of the subsection shall not apply with respect to (1) general instructional or informational courses in military justice if such courses are designed solely for the purpose of instructing members of a command in the substantive and procedural aspects of courts-martial, or (2) to statements and instructions given in open court by the military judge, president of a special court-martial, or counsel.

We have long held that the use of command meetings to purposefully influence the members in determining a court-martial sentence violates Article 37, UCMJ. Moreover, we have also held that the mere "confluence" of the timing of such meetings with members during ongoing courts-martials and their subject matter dealing with court-martial sentences can require a sentence rehearing.

Here, [Baldwin claims] that there were two command officer meetings before and during her court-martial, which she and the officers of her panel attended. She also [claims] that various court-martial situations on base and in the Air Force at large were discussed. Furthermore, she asserts that comments were made that court-martial sentences were too lenient; that officers should always be punished more harshly than enlisted persons; and that the minimum sentences should be 1 year. Finally, appellant points out that she, an officer, subsequently received a 1-year sentence at her court-martial. If appellant's averments are true, then a confluence of timing and subject matter would exist.

The decision of the United States army Court of Criminal Appeals is set aside. The record of trial is returned to the Judge Advocate General of the Army for submission to the convening authority for a limited hearing on the issue of command influence. At the conclusion of the hearing, the judge will make specific findings of fact on that issue.

END OF CASE

In this case, a commander scheduling a meeting to discuss proper sentences at courts-martial for drug cases at the very same time his unit had a courts-martial for a servicemember accused of a drug offense was considered command influence because it may have influenced the way the members of the panel voted.

Review Questions

1. Major Charles Burns is accused of raping Captain Loretta Swift. His case moves through the courts-martial process, and a trial is scheduled to begin the next month. A month before the trial, the wife of the General who convened the courts-martial (meaning the convening authority) threw a surprise birthday party for her husband. The General was in attendance, and so too were many of his subordinates who he had selected to serve on the panel of the courts-martial. The conversation at the birthday party turns to the national debate of sexual assault in the military, and everyone is voicing their opinion. The General joins the casual conversation and, not realizing that the conversation is about the case in his unit, says "Personally, I think anyone in the military who has committed any sexual offense should be kicked out of the military." Spot the issue and write an IRAC.

2. After the death of his son from a heroin overdose, Admiral Harry goes out of his way to talk to sailors about the dangers of drug abuse and addiction. He frequently makes appearances at events at his unit where, as part of his address to sailors, he warns them to stay away from drugs. This tendency of his has given him the reputation and nickname "Heroin Harry." One day on his base, a sailor is arrested for using heroin. The matter goes to courts-martial and Admiral Harry selects the panel members. The defense attorney challenges the panel, raising the issue of command influence. How should the judge rule?

Miranda Rights and the Military

You may be wondering, when members of the military are arrested, do they have the right to remain silent? If so, are they told they have the right to remain silent? Are they told that they have a right to an attorney? The answer may surprise you, for it is a strong and definite "Yes." In fact, the concept and protections of what you call *Miranda* rights are even stronger in the military than in civilian justice. You probably are completely unaware that in *Miranda v. Arizona*, when the U.S. Supreme Court created the rule that civilians must be read their "rights," they were strongly influenced by the fact that for many years the military already had this requirement. Read this excerpt from *Miranda v. Arizona*:

> "Similarly, in our country, the Uniform Code of Military Justice has long provided that no suspect may be interrogated without first being warned of his right not to make a statement, and that any statement he makes may be used against him. Denial of the right to consult counsel during interrogation has also been proscribed by military tribunals. There appears to have been no marked detrimental effect on criminal law enforcement in these jurisdictions as a result of these rules."

The requirement of a reading of rights is found in UCMJ Article 31:

UCMJ Article 31: Compulsory Self-Incrimination Prohibited

a) No person subject to this chapter may compel any person to incriminate himself or to answer any questions the answer to which may tend to incriminate him.

b) No person subject to this chapter may interrogate, or request any statement from an accused or a person suspected of an offense without first informing him of the nature of the accusation and advising him that he does not have to make any statement regarding the offense of which he is accused or suspected and that any statement made by him may be used as evidence against him in a trial by court-martial.

c) No person subject to this chapter may compel any person to make a statement or produce evidence before any military tribunal if the statement or evidence in not material to the issue and may tend to degrade him.

d) No statement obtained from any person in violation of this article, or through the use of coercion, unlawful influence, or unlawful inducement may be received in evidence against him in a trial by court-martial.

As you learned in Chapter 2, civilian law enforcement must only give a *Miranda* warning to a person who is (1) in custody, and (2) being interrogated. However, as you can read in UCMJ Article 31, there is no requirement about custody. If someone in the military is being questioned by a superior or law enforcement about criminal activity, that person must be informed of his or her rights, regardless of whether or not he or she is in custody. Here's another way to look at it.

Civilian *Miranda* Rights Warning = Custody + Interrogation

Military Art 31(b) Rights Warning = Interrogation

Law enforcement are required to stop an interrogation, read the individual his/her rights, and ask the individual if they want to continue or to stop to prevent undue coercion by law enforcement. According to the Supreme Court, merely questioning a civilian is not coercive, but questioning a civilian who is in custody, not free to leave, is inherently coercive.

Now compare this concern with the very nature of the military. Servicemembers are trained to follow and obey orders, and can be punished for disobeying seniors.

Failure to show proper respect is itself a criminal offense under the UCMJ. A servicemember being questioned by a superior is already in a type of custody, because he or she is not free to leave without the permission of the superior. So the military understood that any questioning in the military is inherently coercive and could easily result in a servicemember feeling they are being compelled to incriminate him/herself in violation of the 5th Amendment. So the military has long applied what later became the *Miranda* rule to all questioning of suspects.

The following case provides a good example of the reasons behind this rule and when it applies.

U.S. v. Loukas, 29 M.J. 385 (1990)*

During August of 1987, Loukas was tried by a general court-martial composed of a military judge sitting alone at Pope Air Force Base, North Carolina. He was found guilty of wrongfully using cocaine and being incapacitated for duty, in violation of Articles 112a and 134 of the Uniform Code of Military Justice. He was sentenced to a dishonorable discharge, confinement for 8 months, total forfeitures, and reduction to the lowest enlisted grade. On December 7, 1987, the convening authority approved the findings and sentence as adjudged.

On appeal, defense counsel claimed that at trial, incriminating statements made by Loukas should not have been admitted into evidence. It is the holding of this court that the admission of statements made by the defendant were not barred by the Fifth Amendment or by Article 31.

Loukas' admissions were made during the course of a C–130 aircraft mission in support of drug suppression efforts in South America.

The evidence developed during the suppression hearing was that Loukas was on temporary duty from Pope Air Force Base, North Carolina, along with other crew members. Loukas was the loadmaster. Following an overnight stay at Panama City, Panama, Loukas' crew was scheduled to depart Howard Air Force Base for an early morning flight to Trinidad, Bolivia, where they were to receive a load of unspecified cargo. Loukas was not present at the scheduled crew show time. When he finally arrived at the aircraft he was two hours late. The record, surprisingly, does not reflect that he received a particularly unfriendly or otherwise negative greeting from his fellow crew members, all of whom were senior in grade to him. The co-pilot kidded him about the number of ladies he had been with the evening before. SSgt Dryer recalled in his testimony that he teased Loukas about his lateness. Apparently none of the crew members, at that point, noted anything in Loukas' appearance or demeanor that was alarming.

After the aircraft had been in flight for four or more hours the assistant crew chief, an Airman First Class Taranto, stepped into the cargo section. Loukas was the only other person present in that portion of the plane. There was no cargo or equipment on board at that time. Airman Taranto testified that he observed that Loukas was acting

---

* The case has been heavily edited and paraphrased by the authors for clarity. See disclaimer in introduction.

in an irrational manner. He pointed in the direction of the flight deck and inquired of Airman Taranto, "Do you see them?" and, "Do you see her?" Airman Taranto did not see anyone. It was apparent to him that Loukas was experiencing a hallucination. Loukas handed Airman Taranto his survival vest and .38 calibre pistol and told him to take it (apparently referring to the firearm) and that he didn't want it. The witness reported the incident to his immediate superior, SSgt Dryer, the crew chief.

SSgt Dryer went to the back of the aircraft and confronted Loukas. He testified during the hearing on the motion to suppress that he noted he Loukas appeared to be nervous and that he was perspiring profusely even though it was cool in that portion of the plane. Loukas continued to hallucinate. Gesturing in the direction of the flight deck, he inquired why "those people" were there and wondered why "they" didn't just come down and get him. The witness stated that he asked Loukas if he had taken any drugs. Loukas responded that he had not. SSgt Dryer leaned over close to where Loukas was sitting so that he could observe his eyes and asked in a more insistent manner, "Come on, what have you taken?" or, "What are you on?" or words to that effect. Loukas replied that he had taken some cocaine the night before. SSgt Dryer asked, "Is that all?" He received an affirmative answer. SSgt Dryer advised Loukas to secure his seatbelt and relax. According to his testimony he was somewhat concerned for the safety of the aircraft and its flight crew, particularly if Loukas started "freaking out."

SSgt Dryer reported his observations of Loukas to the flight engineer, a Technical Sergeant Drummond. The latter went to the back of the aircraft and observed Loukas. He retrieved bullets that Loukas had on his person. He returned to the flight deck area and consulted with SSgt Dryer. They concluded that the situation was under control and that it would not be necessary to alert the aircraft commander, Captain Cottam. It was agreed that someone would maintain direct observation of Loukas during the remainder of the flight.

The stated premise of the Court of Military Review majority opinions, both panel and en banc, (6–3), was that Sergeant Dryer was obligated by Article 31(b) to warn the accused of his rights before questioning him about possible drug use. This legal conclusion was drawn on a finding of fact that Sergeant Dryer was acting officially and not simply out of "idle curiosity." We disagree as a matter of law because the crew chief's inquiry was not a law-enforcement or disciplinary investigation which is also required before Article 31(b) becomes applicable.

In reaching this conclusion we first note the statutory language of Article 31, which states:

a) No person subject to this chapter may compel any person to incriminate himself or to answer any question the answer to which may tend to incriminate him.

b) No person subject to this chapter may interrogate, or request any statement from an accused or a person suspected of an offense without first informing him of the nature of the accusation and advising him that he does not have to make any statement regarding the offense of which he is accused or suspected and that any statement made by him may be used as evidence against him in a trial by court-martial.

c) No person subject to this chapter may compel any person to make a statement or produce evidence before any military tribunal if the statement or evidence is not material to the issue and may tend to degrade him.

d) No statement obtained from any person in violation of this article, or through the use of coercion, unlawful influence, or unlawful inducement may be received in evidence against him in a trial by court-martial.

This Court has long intimated that this statute requires warnings only when questioning is done during an official law-enforcement investigation or disciplinary inquiry. This rationale has been articulated for our construction of this important codal provision:

Article 31(b) extends the provisions of its predecessor, Article of War 24, . . . to persons "suspected" as well as "accused," but no intention to extend the requirement to other than "official investigation" is found in the legislative history of the Uniform Code.

Taken literally, this Article is applicable to interrogation by all persons included within the term "persons subject to the code" as defined by Article 2 of the Code, or any other who is suspected or accused of an offense. However, this phrase was used in a limited sense. In our opinion, in addition to the limitation referred to in the legislative history of the requirement, there is a definitely restrictive element of officiality in the choice of the language "interrogate or request any statement," wholly absent from the relatively loose phrase "person subject to this code," for military persons not assigned to investigate offenses, do not ordinarily interrogate nor do they request statements from others accused or suspected of crime. This is not the sole limitation upon the Article's applicability, however. Judicial discretion indicates a necessity for denying its application to a situation not considered by its framers, and wholly unrelated to the reasons for its creation.

Judge Latimer opined similarly in his opinion:

". . . Accordingly, I believe before the advice required by the Article need be given, three conditions should be fulfilled: first, the party asking the question should occupy some official position in connection with law enforcement or crime detection; second, that the inquiry be in furtherance of some official investigation; and third, the facts be developed far enough that the party conducting the investigation has reasonable grounds to suspect the person interrogated has committed an offense."

Collectively, all three conditions suggest that the interrogation be surrounded with an air of some officiality. Congress could not have intended Article 31(b) to cover casual conversations, because the language used compels the conclusion that the interrogator is pursuing some official inquiry as he must know that the person to whom he is talking is suspected of a crime; he must inform him of the nature of the accusation; and he must explain to him that what he says may be used against him in a court-martial.

An example of official, but not law-enforcement or disciplinary, questioning which is permitted without warnings under Article 31 is found in *United States v. Fisher*, 21 USCMA 223, 44 CMR 277 (1972). In that case, we held that a military doctor, not performing an investigative or disciplinary function or engaged in perfecting a criminal case, was not required to preface his medical diagnostic questions to a military subordinate with Article 31 warnings.

In the case before us, Sergeant Dryer was the crew chief of an operational military aircraft who was similarly responsible for the plane's safety and that of its crew, including the accused, his military subordinate. In addition, his questioning of the accused was limited to that required to fulfill his operational responsibilities, and there was no evidence suggesting his inquiries were designed to evade constitutional or codal rights. Finally, the unquestionable urgency of the threat and the immediacy of the crew chief's response underscore the legitimate operational nature of his queries. Under our precedents, the prosecution satisfactorily showed that Article 31 warnings were not required in this operational context.

This Court has implicitly held that a superior in the immediate chain of command of the suspect subordinate will normally be presumed to be acting in a command disciplinary function. However, this presumption is not so broad or inflexible as to preclude a limited exception where clearly justified.

As far as the so-called "public safety exception" in this case is concerned, we note that, strictly speaking, this is an exception to the Miranda warning requirements established by the Supreme Court to preserve Fifth-Amendment rights. *New York v. Quarles*, 467 U.S. 649, 655–56 (1984). These warnings apply to a suspect in custody and his interrogation by law-enforcement officials. There is no contention in this case that the accused was a suspect in custody or that Sergeant Dryer was a law-enforcement official, so *New York v. Quarles*, is not readily applicable.

END OF OPINION

Sergeant Dryer's questioning of the witnesses was not in the official capacity of a law enforcement officer, nor was it for the purpose of discovering criminal behavior. His concerns were more operational and for the safety of everyone on board the plane, including the defendant. In what was essentially the military's "public safety exception," the court held that this was permissible questioning of the servicemember about suspected criminal conduct without a preceding rights warning.

Review Questions

1. Colonel Mitchel hates his junior officer, LT Billy, and is looking for a way to get him out of the Air Force, or at least out of his office. One morning he learns that LT Billy had been arrested the previous evening for drunk driving. Seeing this as his opportunity, he goes over to LT Billy and acts concerned. "I am so sorry about what happened last night. Are you doing okay?"

"I'm fine," LT Billy says. "The charges won't stick."

"Why's that?" COL Mitchel asks.

"The arresting officer messed up the official breathalyzer down at the station," LT Billy explains. "Even though I was drunk off my ass from pounding a dozen shots of Jack Daniels whiskey, they couldn't get an official BAC. I'm sure my lawyer can plea bargain this DUI down into a reckless driving."

COL Mitchel suddenly smiles. "You are so getting kicked out of the Air Force," he says to a shocked LT Billy as he turns and walks out of the office. He then proceeds to draw up the paperwork to refer LT Billy for a Special-Courts Martial. At trial, COL Mitchel is called to testify about LT Billy's admission to him about drinking. If you are LT Billy's defense attorney, IRAC how you would keep his statements to COL Mitchel out of evidence.

2. 21-year-old Private Bailey and 22-year-old Specialist Hanks are watching an MMA match at Specialist Hank's house. They are talking, eating pizza, and drinking beer. Their conversation turns to the recent vandalism incidents at Fort Bragg where they are stationed. Someone has been spray-painting "Sergeant Sex-Machine" all over the barracks. "Do you know who's behind this 'Sergeant Sex-Machine' in our barracks?" SPC Hanks asks PVT Bailey. "Yeah," PVT Bailey says. "It's me!" The next day, SPC Hanks sees an opportunity to get in the good graces of his Sergeant, so he tells the Sergeant, "Last night PVT Bailey told me that he's the one behind the vandalism." This leads to PVT Bailey's arrest and charges against him. At courts-martial, PVT Bailey's defense attorney wants PVT Bailey's statements to SPC Hanks suppressed pursuant to UCMJ Article 31. How should the judge rule?

3. A platoon of elite Army soldiers are undergoing jungle training in the Amazon rainforest. In the third week of training, PVT Newman collapses, shaking and shivering. As the medic attends to PVT Newman, LT Seinfeld stands over him with a look of concern on his face. "What's going on, Newman?" LT Seinfeld asks. "What's wrong?" "I'm sorry, LT," PVT Newman says. "I haven't been following your orders to take those anti-malaria medicines. They were giving me an upset stomach." A helicopter is called in to evacuate PVT Newman from the rainforest so he can be given proper medical attention. Some weeks later after the training is completed, charges are brought against PVT Newman for disobeying a lawful order by not taking his anti-malaria medicines. His lawyer argues that his statement to LT Seinfeld be suppressed. If you are the military judge, how should you rule?

4. Private Jessica Williams reports that she was raped by Sergeant James Moore last night in the barracks. Army investigators invite SGT Moore to come down to the station and share with them his version of events that night. They start asking him about how much he had to drink, how much contact he had with Private Williams, and other related questions to the rape investigation. Prior to asking questions, they told him he was not in custody and free to leave at any time, but did not give him a rights warning. Are his statements admissible?

Searches and Inspections

Members of the military have many of the same Fourth Amendment rights as regular civilians when it comes to searches and seizures. Generally, a warrant (known as a "search authorization" or a "search order" in the military) must be issued upon a finding of probable cause by either a neutral judicial figure (military judge or magistrate) or a base's commander. Failure to obtain proper authority to do a search has the same potential outcome as in civilian justice, which is the suppression of the evidence. These rules are found in the Military Rules of Evidence, regulations authorized by Congress and approved by the president.[12]

There is one important difference in military justice concerning searches, and that is "inspections." In practice, an "inspection" is the exact same thing as a "search" — one person looking through another person's belongings, or digging around a person's living quarters, or even forcing a urinalysis. These inspections range from checking a helicopter for problems to checking military personnel and their living quarters for problems.

Earlier we discussed the general distinction between an "inspection" and a "search" in the chapter on search and seizure. What legally distinguishes an "inspection" from a "search" is that, in an inspection, no one is looking for or has any suspicion of criminal conduct or activity. The purpose of an inspection is to ensure the security, military fitness, or good order and discipline of the unit, organization, installation, vessel, aircraft, or vehicle. Can you imagine the problems which might arise if senior military leaders could not check to ensure that their soldiers are not unfit for combat by having drugs in their system? Or if military leaders could not ensure that nothing potentially hazardous, like a forgotten grenade or rotting food, was buried in the bottom of a footlocker? Remember, the military is expected to fight and win wars, so leaders must be able to conduct inspections to ensure that there is nothing wrong with equipment or people that would interfere with this duty.

Under an "inspection," so long as military leaders have zero suspicion of any criminal conduct, they can force soldiers to give urine samples for drug tests and look through their personal belongings. The primary purpose of an inspection is to ensure that everything and everyone is healthy and in good working order. They are checking to ensure that there is nothing that could interfere with the military's readiness to fight and win wars. However, the very second that the military has any suspicion, no matter how remote, that there is criminal activity or unlawful conduct, then this "inspection" is no longer an "inspection" but a "search," which requires a "search authorization" (the military term for a "warrant") that can only be issued upon a finding of "probable cause," just like in civilian justice.

It is an inspection to order random soldiers to urinate into a cup to make sure they are drug free, because having soldiers under the influence of drugs weakens the military's ability to fight and win wars. However, if a soldier is asked to urinate into

---

12. Military Rules of Evidence 311–313, contained in Exec. Order 13643, May 15, 2013, and found at http://armypubs.army.mil/epubs/pdf/mre2012.pdf.

a cup because there is a specific suspicion that he himself or someone in the unit is using drugs, then this is a "search" because it is being conducted to learn of criminal conduct. In this case, the commander is required to obtain and use the military version of a warrant, just as the police would.

Likewise, if a private is ordered to overturn his footlocker for a sergeant to go through it just to ensure there is nothing hazardous or contraband in it, such as a weapon or unsanitary conditions that might affect someone's health, then no search authorization is needed. However, if the sergeant is going through a soldier's footlocker because the sergeant suspects this individual soldier has something inappropriate in it (such as drugs), or because the sergeant suspects someone in the unit might have something inappropriate (perhaps unused ammo is missing from the firing range), then this is a search because the sergeant is looking for evidence of a crime. Such a search would only be lawful by the sergeant if the sergeant first recieved a search authorization from the base's commander or from a military judge or magistrate. The commander, military judge, or magistrate can only lawfully issue a search authorization if he or she makes the same finding of probable cause that a civilian judge or magistrate would make.

Here is a case looking at the difference between searches and inspections.

U.S. v. Campbell, 41 M.J. 177 (1994)*

In October of 1991, Campbell was tried at a general court-martial at Fort Bragg, North Carolina. He was found guilty of wrongful use of cocaine, in violation of Article 112a, UCMJ. He was sentenced to a bad-conduct discharge, confinement for 18 months, total forfeitures, and reduction to Private E1.

On May 4, 1993, this Court granted Campbell's petition for grant of review on the following issue:

WHETHER THE MILITARY JUDGE ERRED BY ADMITTING THE RESULTS OF CAMBELL'S URINALYSIS OVER DEFENSE OBJECTION.

We hold that Campbell's positive urinalysis test results and his subsequent confessions were improperly admitted in evidence at his court-martial. Furthermore, we hold that Campbell was prejudiced by admission of this evidence with respect to his conviction for wrongful use of cocaine.

The military judge in this case held an evidentiary hearing on a defense motion to suppress government evidence of Campbell's positive urinalysis test and his subsequent confessions. Defense counsel made the following argument:

> The urinalysis in question, sir, was ordered on the 15th. The primary factor behind this urinalysis was the first sergeant, First Sergeant Sharp of Alpha Company.

---

* The case has been heavily edited and paraphrased by the authors for clarity. See disclaimer in introduction.

First Sergeant Sharp heard rumors of suspected drug use in the company. He has no other concrete facts, but he does hear rumors. He eventually boils it down to that it is someone or some people in either Headquarters Platoon or 1st Platoon. The first sergeant then takes a look at both platoons, handpicks those people who he wants to be tested. He does this partially based upon who somebody would have associated with drug use. For instance, somebody in Headquarters Platoon who hangs out with somebody in 1st Platoon would then become, in the first sergeant's eyes, a suspect. He then compiles this list of twelve, fifteen suspects, gives it to the Company Commander, Captain Bangs, and then the test is ordered.

There's no independent basis for probable cause. My interviews with the first sergeant reveal that he did not suspect Sergeant Campbell at all of being involved in drugs. But still, the way he selected this list is a subterfuge. It certainly was an invalid inspection. On the fact that it's coming on the heel of rumors makes it highly suspect, Your Honor, and I think it should be suppressed.

The military judge then prompted defense counsel to state the specific grounds for the defense motion to suppress:

MJ: So, based upon your motion to suppress, your written motion to suppress, and what you've represented here in court today, the basis of your motion is-am I correct-that the urinalysis test that the accused was subjected to on the 15th of May, was not a valid military inspection?

DC: Yes, sir.

MJ: Under M.R.E. [Military Rules of Evidence] 313?

DC: Yes, sir.

MJ: And it was not because it was just a subterfuge for an illegal search.

DC: Yes, sir.

MJ: And it was just a subterfuge because the first sergeant just heard these generalized rumors.

DC: Yes, sir, involving unknown members of certain platoons. Rather than testing Headquarters Platoon entirely or 1st Platoon entirely, he subjectively starts to compile a list of those people who he feels should be tested.

MJ: And it's your further contention then that but for the positive urinalysis test, the accused would never have landed in the CID [Criminal Investigation Command] office on the 5th and 6th of June and would never have rendered statements which were incriminating.

DC: Yes, sir.

As its first witness, and the only witness to testify to the circumstances leading to the command-directed urinalysis, the prosecution called Campbell's first sergeant, First Sergeant (1SG) Sharp. 1SG Sharp testified that "there were rumors that there were drugs being used, consumed and distributed within the barracks." He further testified that he had been specifically informed by one soldier in his command, Sergeant (SGT) Rouse, that the drug problem was in the Headquarters and 1st Platoons. 1SG Sharp testified, "I was looking at every soldier in the headquarters element and trying to figure out who was actually dealing with guys in the 1st Platoon or what guys in the 1st Platoon were interacting with guys in Headquarters Platoon." 1SG Sharp stated that appellant associated with a soldier, SGT Anderson, who "had previously come up hot" on a urinalysis. Prior to appellant's urinalysis, 1SG Sharp observed appellant in the presence of SGT Anderson, and he characterized their presence in the barracks area as "suspicious." Finally, when asked by prosecution if he had "probable cause to conduct the urinalysis," 1SG Sharp responded, "Yes, sir. The indication was that we already had a guy that came up positive on a urinalysis and that my concern was the health and welfare of the soldiers that are in the unit."

During questioning by the military judge, 1SG Sharp testified that he had specifically asked SGT Rouse to identify those soldiers who SGT Rouse knew were using drugs. 1SG Sharp told the military judge that when SGT Rouse declined to provide that information, 1SG Sharp stated to SGT Rouse, "Just kind of give me an idea of which platoon I should be looking at." Prior to questioning SGT Rouse, 1SG Sharp "read him his rights so there wouldn't be any violation of his rights, and began to ask him questions." The first sergeant also questioned another soldier, Private First Class (PFC) Gochenaur, after reading him his rights. The first sergeant decided to take PFC Gochenaur's name off the list because he was personally "satisfied" with PFC Gochenaur's answers during the interview. Finally, when asked by the military judge who ordered the urinalysis, 1SG Sharp responded, "The company commander, sir. I advised him. He directed it."

The military judge denied the defense motion to suppress the results of the urinalysis and any evidence derived from that scientific test.

INVALID INSPECTION

Mil.R.Evid. 313(b) provides, in pertinent part, that "an 'inspection' is an examination of the whole or part of a unit, . . . conducted as an incident of command the primary purpose of which is to determine and to ensure the security, military fitness, or good order and discipline of the unit. . . ." It also states that "an order to produce body fluids, such as urine, is permissible in accordance with this rule." Moreover, this Court, in construing Mil.R.Evid. 313(b), has generally held that, "like other lawful inspections, a urinalysis must be ordered for a legitimate purpose and be conducted in a lawful manner. In accord, Mil.R.Evid. 313(b) provides that a urinalysis conducted "for the primary purpose of obtaining evidence for use in a trial by court-martial" or in an unreasonable fashion is "not an inspection within the meaning of this rule."

Mil.R.Evid. 313(b) expressly permits inspections to "locate . . . unlawful weapons and other contraband." However, if "specific individuals are selected for examination," Mil.R.Evid. 313(b) requires a showing "that the examination was an inspection" and not conducted for the primary purpose of "obtain[ing] a criminal conviction." Neither Mil.R.Evid. 313 nor the Fourth Amendment permits a military commander to pick and choose the members of his unit who will be tested for drugs and then to use the resulting evidence to obtain a criminal conviction. Instead, the testing must be performed on a nondiscriminatory basis pursuant to an established policy or guideline that will eliminate the opportunity for arbitrariness by the person performing the tests.

Proof of selection based on standard criteria or routine practice is well recognized as evidence that the persons inspected were not principally chosen on the basis of suspicion of criminal activity amounting to less than probable cause.

In this case, there was no evidence whatsoever that 1SG Sharp used anything but his suspicion of criminal activity to select appellant for this urinalysis test. As noted above, 1SG Sharp testified that he began compiling a list of soldiers to be tested after SGT Rouse informed him of a "drug problem" in the Headquarters and 1st Platoons. Appellant was assigned to 1st Platoon. 1SG Sharp also had information that SGT Anderson, a soldier in Headquarters Platoon, had recently tested positive on a urinalysis. Furthermore, he testified that on one occasion he observed appellant "associating" with SGT Anderson in the vicinity of the barracks and opined that it "looked suspicious." Finally, while he was compiling the list of names to present to the unit commander for urinalysis, 1SG Sharp found it necessary to advise two soldiers, SGT Rouse and PFC Gochenaur, of their "rights, and began to ask them questions." In such circumstances, we conclude that the military judge legally erred in holding the challenged urinalysis was shown by clear and convincing evidence to be a valid "inspection" within the meaning of Mil.R.Evid. 313(b).

INSUFFICIENT PROBABLE CAUSE SEARCH

The 1SG Sharpe mistakenly believed that he had probable cause to conduct the urinalysis, or more accurately, to advise the commander to direct the urinalysis. In the context of a search of an accused's quarters, probable cause to search exists when there is a reasonable belief that the person, property, or evidence sought is located in the place or on the person to be searched. In determining whether the base commander had probable cause to authorize the search of appellant's quarters, the question is whether, given all the circumstances set forth in the affidavit before him, a fair probability exists that the contraband would be found in appellant's quarters.

Examination of the record in this case fails to meet the above standard. Merely claiming to have probable cause is not sufficient to meet this test. Moreover, a general suspicion of criminal activity based on an unspecific hearsay report coupled with speculation based on association with known criminal offenders is also an insufficient basis to establish probable cause. Such a showing did not provide a substantial basis for anyone to conclude that there was a "fair probability" that metabolites of cocaine were in appellant's urine. Therefore, the urinalysis test in this case and evidence of its results should not have been admitted at appellant's court-martial.

The challenged urinalysis in this case was ordered by appellant's company commander on the advice of 1SG Sharp. Our conclusion that 1SG Sharp had no substantial basis for finding probable cause applies as well to the commander he advised.

DECISION

The decision of the United States Army Court of Military Review is reversed as to specification 1 of Charge III. The findings of guilty thereon are set aside and that specification and Charge are dismissed. The record of trial is returned to the Judge Advocate General of the Army for remand to that court for reassessment of the sentence based on the remaining findings of guilty.

END OF OPINION

In this case, Campbell was not randomly selected for a urinalysis, which is typically what is required for a lawful inspection. Instead, he was selected for a urinalysis based on his being associated with persons who might be using drugs. This means that there was a suspicion that he was doing drugs. This made his selection for a urinalysis not a lawful inspection, but an unlawful search because it lacked a finding of probable cause which is required for there to be proper authorization for a search coming from the commander, a military judge, or a magistrate. Some factors you can consider in whether or not you are dealing with a search or an inspection include:

Suspicion—If an "inspection" is being performed because someone made a report of criminal conduct, or someone else has a suspicion of criminal conduct, then it is not an "inspection" but a "search," which requires a finding of probable cause by the commander or judicial authority.

Randomness—If the people selected for an inspection are chosen randomly, as long as the purpose of inspection isn't a suspicion of criminal conduct, then there is a good chance this is a lawful inspection. However, if there is suspicion that a unit is having a problem, then even a randomized selection might be considered an unlawful search.

Everyone is being inspected—If an entire unit has to provide a urinalysis or open their footlockers, then there is a fair chance that it is a lawful inspection. However, if the rationale for inspecting everyone is based on a suspicion that at least one of them might have contraband, then this "inspection" would legally be a "search."

Review Questions

1. Sergeant Snork believes that a war is coming between the U.S. and Iran, and he wants to be sure that his men are prepared for combat. He starts a new training regimen, working them hard each day to teach them the skills they need to be good soldiers. He also wants to make sure that his men have all the equipment they need. So one day, he has all of the men line up by their bunk in the barracks and orders every soldier to completely empty the contents of his footlocker onto the floor. He wants to make sure that each soldier has all of the equipment he has been issued.

Much to Sergeant Snork's shock, one of the randomly selected soldiers, Private Bailey, has a large bag of marijuana among his belongings. SGT Snork calls the military police, and Private Bailey is arrested for possession with intent to distribute, a very serious felony. Private Bailey turns down his free court-appointed judge advocate as his defense attorney and instead hires a civilian to represent him with his own money.

At his court-martial, his lawyer tries to keep out of evidence the marijuana, claiming that it was found by an illegal search as it was discovered without a warrant issued by a neutral judicial figure or the base commander without any type of probable cause. Perform an IRAC analysis to determine whether or not the lawyer is right.

2. Upon discovering the large quantity of marijuana among Private Bailey's belongings, Sergeant Snork becomes suspicious that Private Bailey has been dealing drugs to the men in the platoon. Sergeant Snork would like to drug test everyone in his platoon, but, because of budget cuts, cannot afford to do so. Instead, Sergeant Snork selects the six men in his platoon who are known to eat the most junk food, believing that these are the people who are likely to have the "munchies" from marijuana use. A military judge finds probable cause and grants a search authorization, and the six soldiers are given a urinalysis. Sergeant Snork is right, and all six test positive for marijuana. At courts-martial, the attorneys for the six men argue that this was a search performed without a warrant issued by a neutral figure or base commander upon a finding of probable cause. They further argue that the men tested positive only because of the illegal search, and the results should be excluded. Are they right?

3. After the urinalysis of the six soldiers was found to be inadmissible, SGT Snork learned the importance of getting a search authorization, rather than conducting an inspection, when he had a suspicion that any of his soldiers were using drugs. For this reason, at a later date when SGT Snork caught many of his soldiers eating a suspicious amount of junk food in the future, he went to the base commander to get a search authorization. Should such a search authorization be issued?

4. The president of the United States is scheduled to appear at the USAF Academy in Colorado to address the cadets. The new commandant of the Academy does not want any cadets to do anything embarrassing, so he orders the instructors to go through the dorm room of each cadet and look for contraband such as stink bombs and firecrackers. In the room of Cadet April O'Neil, a bag of heroin is found. Is that heroin the product of a lawful inspection that will be admissible at trial, or an illegal search and inadmissible at trial?

5. Following the legalization of marijuana in Colorado, the commandant of the USAF Academy notices that sales of snack foods from the Academy's vending machines has skyrocketed. This makes him concerned that some of the cadets are using marijuana, which, regardless of Colorado state law, is still against military regulations. Consequently, he orders that every dorm room on campus be checked. Cadet Mary Jane is found with a small bag of marijuana in her sock drawer. Was this a lawful inspection or an unlawful search?

Free Speech in the Military

As a general rule, members of the military have the same First Amendment right to free speech as civilians, but there are exceptions. *Parker v. Levy,* discussed below, looks at some of those exceptions through the limitations imposed by Articles 133 and 134. But first, let's look at a case involving a crime unique to the Military.

Article 88 of the UCMJ forbids military officers (and *only* officers) from insulting the president and other senior political leaders:

UCMJ Article 88: Contempt Towards Officials

> Any commissioned officer who uses contemptuous words against the President, the Vice President, Congress, the Secretary of Defense, the Secretary of a military department, the Secretary of Transportation, or the Governor or legislature of any State, Territory, Commonwealth, or possession in which he is on duty or present shall be punished as a court-martial may direct.

This article places a seemingly un-constitutional prohibition on commissioned officers (but not, it should be noted, on enlisted personnel) by forbidding them from criticizing political leaders in a manner that could be considered "contemptuous." The right of Americans to insult, ridicule, and otherwise poke fun at their government officials is held sacrosanct. Note, however, that the statute does not prevent military officers from disagreeing with or criticizing the leadership. It merely prohibits "contemptuous words." The statute still permits criticism, as long as the criticism is offered in a manner that is consistent with the respect we would expect toward the civilian leadership. An attitude of "contempt" is one that might lead to disregarding orders, and if contempt is displayed by the officer corps towards the civilian leadership, how are the troops to act? This could interfere with their willingness and ability to accomplish the missions given to them by the civilian leadership.

The principles behind UCMJ Article 88 are explained in *U.S. v. Howe*.

U.S. v. Howe, 37 C.M.R. 429 (1967)*

Howe was arraigned before a general court-martial. He was charged with using contemptuous words against the President of the United States and conduct unbecoming an officer and a gentleman, in violation of Articles 88 and 133, Uniform Code of Military Justice. . . . He was convicted . . . and sentenced to dismissal, total forfeitures, and confinement at hard labor for two years.

The specification under the charge of violation of Article 88, supra, reads as follows: "In that Second Lieutenant Henry H. Howe, Junior, U. S. Army, Headquarters Company, 31st Engineer Battalion, Fort Bliss, Texas, did, in the vicinity of San Jacinto Plaza, El Paso, Texas, on or about 6 November 1965, wrongfully and publicly use contemptuous words against the President of the United States, Lyndon B. Johnson, by carrying and displaying to the public a sign reading as follows, to wit: 'LET'S HAVE MORE THAN A CHOICE BETWEEN PETTY IGNORANT FACISTS IN 1968' and on the other side of the sign the words 'END JOHNSON'S FACIST AGRESSION IN VIET NAM,' or words to that effect."

The specification under the charge of violation of Article 133, supra, reads as follows: "In that Second Lieutenant Henry H. Howe, Junior, U. S. Army, Headquarters

---

* The case has been heavily edited and paraphrased by the authors for clarity. See disclaimer in introduction.

Company, 31st Engineer Battalion, Fort Bliss, Texas, did in the vicinity of San Jacinto Plaza, El Paso, Texas, on or about 6 November 1965, wrongfully take part in a public demonstration by carrying and displaying to the public a sign reading as follows, to wit: 'LET'S HAVE MORE THAN A CHOICE BETWEEN PETTY IGNORANT FACISTS IN 1968' and on the other side the words 'END JOHNSON'S FACIST AGRESSION IN VIET NAM,' or words to that effect, his acts constituting conduct unbecoming an officer and gentleman in the United States Army."

In his initial petition for review, petitioner assigned the following as errors:

1. The charges against appellant violate the First Amendment to the Constitution.
2. Articles 88 and 133 are so vague and uncertain that they violate the Due Process clause of the Fifth Amendment.

Article 88, Uniform Code of Military Justice, reads as follows:

"Any commissioned officer who uses contemptuous words against the President, the Vice President, Congress, the Secretary of Defense, the Secretary of a military department, the Secretary of the Treasury, or the Governor or legislature of any State, Territory, Commonwealth, or possession in which he is on duty or present shall be punished as a court-martial may direct."

The petitioner contends that this Article and the charge laid under it violate the Bill of Rights and the First Amendment thereof.

We note that this provision was not new to military law when it was adopted as a part of the Uniform Code of Military Justice. Actually, this provision is older than the Bill of Rights, older than the Constitution, and older than the Republic itself.

The British Articles of War of 1765, in force at the beginning of our Revolutionary War, provided for the court-martial of any officer or soldier who presumed to use traitorous or disrespectful words against "the Sacred Person of his Majesty, or any of the Royal Family"; and of any officer or soldier who should "behave himself with Contempt or Disrespect towards the General, or other Commander in Chief of Our Forces, or shall speak Words tending to his Hurt or Dishonour."

The Articles of War adopted by the Continental Congress on June 30, 1775, revised the British language to adjust the same to the new concept of "Continental Forces" and made punishable by court-martial the act of any officer or soldier who behaved himself with "contempt or disrespect toward the general or generals, or commanders in chief of the continental forces, or shall speak false words, tending to his or their hurt or dishonor."

[This language has been kept through different versions of military law from then until now.] And, finally, it was reenacted in 1950 as Article 88 of the Uniform Code of Military Justice. Now, however, it applies to officers only; that portion of previous Articles relating to "other persons subject to military law" having been deleted.

The First Amendment to the Constitution of the United States provides:

"Congress shall make no law respecting an establishment of religion, or prohibiting the free exercise thereof; or abridging the freedom of speech, or of the press; or the right of the people peaceably to assemble, and to petition the Government for a redress of grievances."

Of it, the Supreme Court has said:

"At the outset we reject the view that freedom of speech and association . . . as protected by the First and Fourteenth Amendments, are 'absolutes,' not only in the undoubted sense that where the constitutional protection exists it must prevail, but also in the sense that the scope of that protection must be gathered solely from a literal reading of the First Amendment." We . . . believe that neither Hamilton nor Madison, nor any other competent person then or later, ever supposed that to make criminal the counseling of a murder within the jurisdiction of Congress would be an unconstitutional interference with free speech. . . .

[T]he character of every act depends upon the circumstances in which it is done. The most stringent protection of free speech would not protect a man in falsely shouting fire in a theatre, and causing a panic. The question in every case is whether the words used are used in such circumstances and are not such a nature as to create a clear and present danger that they will bring about the substantive evils that Congress has a right to prevent. It is a question of proximity and degree.

Speech is not an absolute, above and beyond control of the legislature when its judgment, subject to review here, is that certain kinds of speech are so undesirable as to warrant criminal sanction. Nothing is more certain in modern society than the principle that there are no absolutes, that a name, a phrase, a standard has meaning only when associated with the considerations which gave birth to the nomenclature. To those who would paralyze our Government in the face of impending threat by encasing it in a semantic straightjacket we must reply that all concepts are relative."

The evil which Article 88 of the Uniform Code, seeks to avoid is the impairment of discipline and the promotion of insubordination by an officer of the military service in using contemptuous words toward the Chief of State and the Commander-in-Chief of the Land and Naval Forces of the United States. Under the British Articles of War of 1765, the precursor to Article 88, Uniform Code of Military Justice, was included with the offense of sedition under Section II thereof, entitled, "Mutiny." It is similarly separated in the American Articles of War 1776, being grouped with the offenses of sedition and mutiny.

We know that hundreds of thousands of members of our military forces are committed to combat in Vietnam, casualties among our forces are heavy, and thousands are being recruited, or drafted, into our armed forces. That in the present times and circumstances such conduct by an officer constitutes a clear and present danger to discipline within our armed services, under the precedents established by the Supreme Court, seems to require no argument.

That Article 88 does not violate the First Amendment is clear.

END OF CASE

Review Questions

1. Captain Hurd has spent the past year in combat in Afghanistan. He finally finishes his long tour of duty and flies home where he has 30 days with his family before he has to fly back to Afghanistan. His father had been a Sergeant in Vietnam and today is an active member of Veterans for Peace. While Captain Hurd is home, he tries to spend as much time as possible with his father, and this includes going to a Veterans for Peace meeting. At the meeting, his father proudly introduces his son to his friends who invite Captain Hurd up to the podium to say a few words. Captain Hurd had not planned to say anything, but he does his best to come up with a few remarks. He says, "Well, I am proud to be over there fighting. I just think it's a shame what is going on over there. The soldiers fight and die, and the fat cat politicians get rich off our blood. People like President Obama disgust me. He's the biggest crook of them all, and completely without honor. Hopefully, next time, the American people will elect someone who is not a complete liar and dictator." The veterans cheer Captain Hurd's speech, and one of them, who happened to record it on his smart phone, uploads it to YouTube. Eventually, commanders learn of this speech and decide to file criminal charges against Captain Hurd. IRAC your answer.

2. Does it matter that he is not currently in uniform or on duty when he utters the speech?

3. The courts have held that Article 88 does not violate the First Amendment. Does this mean that officers may never express any opinion that is critical of the president or others listed in the article? What specific factors distinguish reasonable expression from a violation of this article?

Uniquely Military Offenses

The criminal code of the military is contained in Articles 77–134 of the UCMJ, Sections 877–934 of the U.S. Code.[13] Some crimes closely resemble those found in civilian criminal codes (such as larceny, assault, and murder), while others are "uniquely military offenses," such as absence without leave, disrespect, and dereliction of duty. Let's take a brief look at these types of offenses and why they exist in a military criminal code.

AWOL and Desertion

If you are a civilian and do not show up to work, you might get fired. In the military if you don't show up for work, you can be convicted of a federal crime and sent to jail. The two crimes most relevant to this are Absent Without Leave (AWOL) under UCMJ Article 86 and Desertion under UCMJ Article 85.

---

13. Note that, at the time of this writing, these sections are under review by Congress and may change in 2016 or 2017.

Being AWOL simply means that a person has failed to be where he or she should be. For example, if soldiers are supposed to be at Physical Training at 6am, and Private Sleepy shows up at 6:15am because he overslept, that means Private Sleepy was AWOL from 6:00am to 6:15am. He was not where he was supposed to be when he was supposed to be there. Soldiers who are AWOL do intend to return to rejoin their unit; it is simply that, for whatever reason, they are not where they are supposed to be. Now, given that it is not uncommon for someone to be late or make bad choices, soldiers who are AWOL for a short amount of time, who are not in a combat zone or other high-threat environment, and who otherwise have a good record typically receive some form of warning or non-judicial punishment. In more serious cases, though, a court-martial is a real possibility.

Desertion is similar to being AWOL, but much more serious. A deserter is someone who is AWOL and plans to remain AWOL permanently. The intent to remain away permanently is what makes someone a deserter, and not merely AWOL. Desertion is also the appropriate charge when the individual goes AWOL with the express intention of avoiding hazardous duty. Because the stakes are higher, the punishment is more severe in the case of desertion and could include the death penalty. In the American Civil War, for example, soldiers convicted of desertion were often shot, but the last American to be executed for desertion was Eddie Slovik, a soldier convicted of desertion during World War II. Normally, a deserter can expect to be sentenced to several years of confinement.

As a practical matter it is difficult to determine whether or not someone is merely AWOL or in fact intends to remain away permanently and should instead be charged with Desertion. There are a few factors the military courts consider in making this determination. Those factors include:

How long has the person been away from his unit?

How far away from his unit did the person travel?

Did the person get rid of his uniform or keep it?

Did the person get rid of his military records or keep them?

Did the person go AWOL when his unit was scheduled to deploy?

Did the person leave the country?

In many cases there will be a mix of the factors, some suggesting the person is AWOL and others suggesting the person is a deserter. Keeping in mind that, just as in the civilian court system, each element of a crime must be proved "beyond a reasonable doubt," it is common for individuals accused of Desertion to be convicted of the lesser crime of being AWOL, unless the intention to avoid hazardous duty or remain away permanently is clear. Here is a case that considers some of those factors.

U.S. v. Mackey, 46 C.M.R. 754 (1972)*

Mackey was tried by general court-martial . . . on a charge and specification alleging desertion in violation of Article 85, UCMJ. The appellant pleaded not guilty to the charge of desertion, but did plead guilty to the lesser included offense of unauthorized absence for approximately twenty-six months. However, after trial upon the merits, he was found guilty of desertion as charged. The military judge sentenced the appellant to be confined at hard labor for a period of one year and six months, to forfeit all pay and allowances, to be reduced to the grade of private, pay grade E-1, and to be discharged from the service with a dishonorable discharge.

It appears that the appellant was to have reported to Camp Pendleton, California, by 27 July 1969; he failed to do so, and eventually was apprehended by the Federal Bureau of Investigation in New York on 22 September 1971, whereupon he was confined by civil authorities, and turned over to military authorities on 5 October 1971. . . . On 7 October 1971, the appellant was confined in the brig at Camp Lejeune, and advised that he was suspected of an extended period of unauthorized absence. . . . The charges were referred to trial on 3 February 1972 and trial was held on 15 February 1972.

[On appeal, Mackey is arguing that the evidence does not establish beyond a reasonable doubt that he intended to remain away permanently. For this reason, he is arguing he should have been found guilty of the lesser charge of AWOL, and not the more serious charge of desertion.]

The thrust of Mackey's argument is that the inferences to be derived from the evidence that appellant lived at his home of record during his unauthorized absence, that he had retained his summer service uniform, service records, identification card and tags are sufficient to raise a reasonable doubt that the appellant intended to remain away permanently.

The government's case evidenced a period of about 26 months unauthorized absence, an absence which commenced while the appellant was under orders to eventually report to the ground forces in the Western Pacific while some of these forces were engaged in hostilities, and an absence which was terminated by apprehension at a place far removed from his place of duty.

Under the circumstances evidenced in this case, we are of the opinion that the evidence is sufficient to prove beyond reasonable doubt the element of intent away permanently. The assignment of error is denied.

END OF OPINION

In this case, although the person maintained his military uniforms and records and had continued to live in his home during his absence, he was still found guilty

---

* The case has been heavily edited and paraphrased by the authors for clarity. See disclaimer in introduction.

of desertion because he had been gone for over two years and that absence had started when his unit was supposed to head to Vietnam, an area where they would likely face hostilities. Based on the totality of the circumstances, the court found there was adequate evidence that he never intended to return to his unit.

Review Questions

Consider, in the following fact patterns, whether the facts alleged indicate the defendant is merely AWOL or a deserter.

1. Private Benson is not at formation Monday morning. He was arrested later that day in a motel room two hours from his base with his girlfriend. Also found in his room was a box of condoms.

2. Private O'Conner failed to report to formation Monday morning. He was arrested Wednesday at his parent's house. His mother had died over the weekend.

3. Private Harrison failed to report to formation Monday morning. He was arrested in Canada one week later living under an alias and holding a counterfeit Canadian passport.

4. Private Jackson failed to report to formation Monday morning at Fort Bragg. Five years later he was arrested in his home, which is located only two miles from Fort Bragg. In his home he had his uniforms, dog tags, and military papers.

The General Article[14]

In the military and in civilian life, most possible crimes that can be committed are clearly written and known in advance. For example, both state and military justice have clear laws prohibiting stealing. What makes the military more unique is that, given the special need of the military for flexibility to maintain good order and discipline, it has been granted the flexibility to invent crimes as needed, as well as hold its officer corps to a higher standard. This unusual legal measure is found in UCMJ Articles 134, the General Article, and UCMJ Article 133, punishing conduct unbecoming of an officer.

UCMJ Article 134, the General Article, states:

> Though not specifically mentioned in this chapter, all disorders and neglects to the prejudice of good order and discipline in the armed forces, all conduct of a nature to bring discredit upon the armed forces, and crimes and offenses not capital, of which persons subject to this chapter may be guilty, shall be taken cognizance of by a general, special, or summary court-martial, according to the nature and degree of the offense, and shall be punished at the discretion of that court.

What this means is that any conduct that is "prejudicial to good order and discipline" or is "service discrediting" can be criminally punished.

---

14. Note that, at the time of this writing, this specific section of the UCMJ was under review by Congress and may be significantly amended in 2016 or 2017.

"Prejudicial to good order and discipline" is any conduct or speech that interferes with unit cohesion, discipline, or job performance. The military is the ultimate team activity, and anything that interferes with how well the team gets along can have lethal consequences as well as endanger national security. It is impossible to think of every possible activity that might prejudice good order and discipline, which is why there is a general article banning this conduct outright.

Here are some examples of that conduct:

- "Upon hearing that Private White had slept with Private Black's wife, he was shunned and no one would speak to him."
  - Adultery is a crime itself in military justice. But sleeping with the spouse of someone in your own unit—when lives depend on being able to trust each other—is significantly prejudicial to good order and discipline.
- "People were talking about Corporal Klinger's cross-dressing so much that it interfered with their ability to get their job done."
- "That Corporal Heinz kept calling Private Goldberg a 'Jew-boy' and singling him out for being Jewish made it difficult for Private Goldberg to get his work done or fit in with the rest of his unit."
- "When learning that Private Jack had been arrested for allegedly raping Private Jill, half the unit thought she was lying to cover up her cheating on her husband and the other half believed she was telling the truth. This caused a lot of tension as people took sides."
  - Private Jack could be prosecuted for rape under Article 120, as well as for violating General Article 134 by causing tension and division in his unit.

"Service discrediting" is conduct that lowers public opinion of the military. The military holds a position of special trust and responsibility in society. It is important to the stability of society that the public trust the military will act honorably and decently. When someone betrays that trust, the military needs a way to punish that behavior. Some examples include:

- 20-year-old Private Nash is trying to arrange to meet with a 12-year-old girl he met online for a sexual encounter. Pedophiles are among the most reviled in society, and it is a negative reflection upon the entire Army if one of its own tries to do that.
  - The Private could be prosecuted for the crime of trying to arrange a sexual liaison with a minor, and under Article 134 for conduct that was service discrediting.
- 40-year-old Marine Corps Major Reid is caught trying to shoplift from a Walmart. The manager at Walmart, as well as the general population, may be shocked that an officer of the Marines is acting like a thug and lose respect for the entire Marine Corps.
  - The Marine can be charged with violating UCMJ Article 134 as well as larceny.

Sometimes a servicemember can only be charged with Article 134 if the crime does not otherwise appear in the UCMJ. For this reason, the Article is considered a "catch-all" offense. Other times, such as in cases of attempted shoplifting or sexual misconduct, the person can also be charged with the underlying criminal offense in addition to Article 134.

For someone to be convicted of Article 134, the prosecution must put on specific evidence of how the conduct was service discrediting or how the speech was prejudicial to good order and discipline. (They do not have to present evidence of both; just one or the other.) Even though it is commonsense that one soldier raping another soldier in a unit is prejudicial to good order and discipline, there must still be evidence put forward at trial to establish this; it cannot merely be assumed that it did. Consequently, to prove that conduct was prejudicial to good order and discipline, the prosecution will put forward a member of the military as a witness to testify how the alleged conduct interfered with good order and discipline. Similarly, to prove that conduct or speech was service discrediting, the prosecution would put forward a non-servicemember as a witness to testify how that individual lost some respect for the military upon hearing of the crime.

To determine whether a soldier can be charged under Article 134, ask the following question: Is his conduct going to lower public opinion of the military, or will it interfere with his unit's cohesion and discipline? If the answer is "yes" to either, then the military can charge the person for violating UCMJ Article 134.

Conduct Unbecoming

Officers are the leaders of the military. They hold a position of special trust and responsibility. If they engage in conduct or actions that betray that trust, they can be criminally punished for that betrayal through UCMJ Article 133.

Conduct Unbecoming, Article 133

"Any commissioned officer, cadet, or midshipman who is convicted of conduct unbecoming an officer and a gentleman shall be punished as a court-martial may direct."

The term "gentleman" dates back from the days when the military was comprised entirely of men, but refers more to the expected standard of behavior of an officer than to gender. Generally, almost all illegal or dishonest behavior committed by an officer is considered adequate for charging this offense in addition to charging the officer for the underlying conduct.

The Supreme Court addressed offenses under Articles 133 and 134 in the following case.

Parker v. Levy, 417 U.S. 733 (1974)*

Howard Levy, a physician, was a captain in the Army stationed at Fort Jackson, South Carolina. From the time he entered on active duty in July 1965 until his trial

---

* The case has been heavily edited and paraphrased by the authors for clarity. See disclaimer in introduction.

by court-martial, he was assigned as Chief of the Dermatological Service of the United States Army Hospital at Fort Jackson. On June 2, 1967, [CPT Levy] was convicted by a general court-martial of violations of Arts. 90, 133, and 134 of the Uniform Code of Military Justice, and sentenced to dismissal from the service, forfeiture of all pay and allowances, and confinement for three years at hard labor.

The facts upon which his conviction rests are virtually undisputed. The evidence admitted at his court-martial trial showed that one of the functions of the hospital to which CPT Levy was assigned was that of training Special Forces aide men. As Chief of the Dermatological Service, CPT Levy was to conduct a clinic for those aide men. In the late summer of 1966, it came to the attention of the hospital commander that the dermatology training of the students was unsatisfactory. After investigating the program and determining that appellee had totally neglected his duties, the commander called appellee to his office and personally handed him a written order to conduct the training. Appellee read the order, said that he understood it, but declared that he would not obey it because of his medical ethics. Appellee persisted in his refusal to obey the order, and later reviews of the program established that the training was still not being carried out.

During the same period of time, appellee made several public statements to enlisted personnel at the post, of which the following is representative:

> 'The United States is wrong in being involved in the Viet Nam War. I would refuse to go to Viet Nam if ordered to do so. I don't see why any colored soldier would go to Viet Nam: they should refuse to go to Viet Nam and if sent should refuse to fight because they are discriminated against and denied their freedom in the United States, and they are sacrificed and discriminated against in Viet Nam by being given all the hazardous duty and they are suffering the majority of casualties. If I were a colored soldier I would refuse to go to Viet Nam and if I were a colored soldier and were sent I would refuse to fight. Special Forces personnel are liars and thieves and killers of peasants and murderers of women and children.'

Appellee's military superiors originally contemplated nonjudicial proceedings against him under Art. 15 of the Uniform Code of Military Justice, but later determined that court-martial proceedings were appropriate. The specification under Art. 90 alleged that appellee willfully disobeyed the hospital commandant's order to establish the training program, in violation of that article, which punishes anyone subject to the Uniform Code of Military Justice who 'willfully disobeys a lawful command of his superior commissioned officer.' Statements to enlisted personnel were listed as specifications under the charges of violating Arts. 133 and 134 of the Code. Article 133 provides for the punishment of 'conduct unbecoming an officer and a gentleman,' while Art. 134 proscribes, inter alia, 'all disorders and neglects to the prejudice of good order and discipline in the armed forces.'

The specification under Art. 134 alleged that appellee 'did, at Fort Jackson, South Carolina, with design to promote disloyalty and disaffection among the troops, publicly utter (certain) statements to divers enlisted personnel at divers times . . .' The specification under Art. 133 alleged that appellee did 'while in the performance of his duties at the United States Army Hospital . . . wrongfully and dishonorably' make statements variously described as intemperate, defamatory, provoking, disloyal, contemptuous, and disrespectful to Special Forces personnel and to enlisted personnel who were patients or under his supervision.

Appellee was convicted by the court-martial, and his conviction was sustained on his appeals within the military.

This Court has long recognized that the military is, by necessity, a specialized society separate from civilian society. We have also recognized that the military has, again by necessity, developed laws and traditions of its own during its long history. The differences between the military and civilian communities result from the fact that 'it is the primary business of armies and navies to fight or ready to fight wars should the occasion arise.' In 1890 the U.S. Supreme Court observed: 'An army is not a deliberative body. It is the executive arm. Its law is that of obedience. No question can be left open as to the right to command in the officer, or the duty of obedience in the soldier.' More recently we noted that 'the military constitutes a specialized community governed by a separate discipline from that of the civilian,' and that 'the rights of men in the armed forces must perforce be conditioned to meet certain overriding demands of discipline and duty. We have also recognized that a military officer holds a particular position of responsibility and command in the Armed Forces; the President's commission recites that reposing special trust and confidence in the patriotism, valor, fidelity and abilities' of the appointee he is named to the specified rank during the pleasure of the President.

Just as military society has been a society apart from civilian society, so "[m]ilitary law . . . is a jurisprudence which exists separate and apart from the law which governs in our federal judicial establishment." And to maintain the discipline essential to perform its mission effectively, the military has developed what "may not unfitly be called the customary military law" or "general usage of the military service." The Court has approved the enforcement of those military customs and usages by courts-martial from the early days of this Nation.

[A look at history demonstrates that there is a long military tradition of codes, such as Articles 133 and 134, which grant military authorities flexibility to maintain good order and discipline and holding officers to a higher standard as the leaders within the military.] . . . One of the British Articles of War of 1765 made punishable 'all Disorders or Neglects . . . to the Prejudice of good Order and Military Discipline . . .' that were not mentioned in the other articles. Another of those articles provided:

> 'Whatsoever Commissioned Officer shall be convicted before a General Court-martial, of behaving in a scandalous infamous Manner, such as is unbecoming the Character of an Officer and a Gentleman, shall be discharged from Our Service.

In 1775 in the Revolution War the Continental Congress copied this last article for the American forces. In 1806, this was modified by Congress to read: "Any commissioned officer convicted before a general court-martial of conduct unbecoming an officer and a gentleman, shall be dismissed (from) the service." From 1806, it remained basically unchanged through numerous congressional reenactments until it was enacted as Art. 133 of the Uniform Code of Military Justice in 1951.

The British articles punishing "all Disorders and Neglects . . ." was also adopted by the Continental Congress in 1775 and reenacted in 1776. Except for a revision in 1916 which added the clause punishing "all conduct of a nature to bring discredit upon the military service," substantially the same language was preserved throughout the various reenactments of this article too, until, in 1951, it was enacted as Article 134 of the Uniform Code of Military Justice.

Decisions of the U.S. Supreme Court have recognized that the longstanding customs and usages of the services impart accepted meaning to the seemingly imprecise standards of Arts. 133 and 134. In *Dynes v. Hoover*, 20 How. 65 (1857), this Court upheld the Navy's general article, which provided that '(a)ll crimes committed by persons belonging to the navy, which are not specified in the foregoing articles, shall be punished according to the laws and customs in such cases at sea.'

The Court reasoned:

> 'When offences and crimes are not given in terms or by definition, the want of it may be supplied by a comprehensive enactment, such as the 32d article of the rules for the government of the navy, which means that courts martial have jurisdiction of such crimes as are not specified, but which have been recognised to be crimes and offences by the usages in the navy of all nations, and that they shall be punished according to the laws and customs of the sea. Notwithstanding the apparent indeterminateness of such a provision, it is not liable to abuse; for what those crimes are, and how they are to be punished, is well known by practical men in the navy and army, and by those who have studied the law of courts martial, and the offences of which the different courts martial have cognizance.'

In *Smith v. Whitney* (1886), this Court refused to issue a writ of prohibition against Smith's court-martial trial on charges of 'scandalous conduct tending to the destruction of good morals' and 'culpable inefficiency in the performance of duty.' The Court again recognized the role of 'the usages and customs of war' and 'old practice in the army' in the interpretation of military law by military tribunals.

In *United States v. Fletcher* (1893), the Court considered a court-martial conviction under what is now Art. 133, rejecting Captain Fletcher's claim that the court-martial could not properly have held that his refusal to pay a debt was 'conduct unbecoming an officer and a gentleman.' . . . [The decision] stressed the military's 'higher code termed honor, which holds its society to stricter accountability' and with which those trained only in civilian law are unfamiliar. In *Swaim v. United States* (1897), the Court affirmed another decision, this time refusing to disturb a court-martial conviction for conduct 'to the prejudice of good order and military discipline' in violation of the Articles of War. The Court recognized the role of 'unwritten law or usage' in giving meaning to the language of what is now Art. 134. In rejecting Swaim's argument that the evidence failed to establish an offense under the article, the Court said:

> "This is the very matter that falls within the province of courts-martial, and in respect to which their conclusions cannot be controlled or reviewed by the civil courts. As was said in *Smith v.Whitney*, 116 U.S. 178. 'Of questions not depending upon the construction of the statutes, but upon unwritten military law or usage, within the jurisdiction of courts-martial, military or naval officers, from their training and experience in the service, are more competent judges than the courts of common law.'"

Cases involving 'conduct to the prejudice of good order and military discipline,' as opposed to conduct unbecoming an officer, 'are still further beyond the bounds of ordinary judicial judgment, for they are not measurable by our innate sense of right and wrong, of honor and dishonor, but must be gauged by an actual knowledge and experience of military life, its usages and duties.'

The differences noted by this settled line of authority, first between the military community and the civilian community, and second between military law and civilian law, continue in the present day under the Uniform Code of Military Justice. That Code cannot be equated to a civilian criminal code. It, and the various versions of the Articles of War which have preceded it, regulate aspects of the conduct of members of the military which in the civilian sphere are left unregulated. While a civilian criminal code carves out a relatively small segment of potential conduct and declares it criminal, the Uniform Code of Military Justice essays more varied regulation of a much larger segment of the activities of the more tightly knit military community. In civilian life there is no legal sanction—civil or criminal—for failure to behave as an officer and a gentleman; in the military world, Art. 133 imposes such a sanction on a commissioned officer. The Code likewise imposes other sanctions for conduct that in civilian life is not subject to criminal penalties: disrespect toward superior commissioned officers, Art. 89; cruelty toward, or oppression or maltreatment of subordinates, Art. 93; negligent damaging, destruction, or wrongful disposition of military property of the United States, Art. 108; improper hazarding of a vessel, Art. 110; drunkenness on duty, Art. 112; and malingering, Art. 115.

But the other side of the coin is that the penalties provided in the Code vary from death and substantial penal confinement at one extreme to forms of administrative discipline which are below the threshold of what would normally be considered a criminal sanction at the other. Though all of the offenses described in the Code are punishable 'as a court-martial may direct,' and the accused may demand a trial by court-martial, Art. 15 of the Code also provides for the imposition of nonjudicial 'disciplinary punishments' for minor offenses without the intervention of a court-martial. The punishments imposable under that article are of a limited nature. With respect to officers, punishment may encompass suspension of duty, arrest in quarters for not more than 30 days, restriction for not more than 60 days, and forfeiture of pay for a limited period of time. In the case of enlisted men, such punishment may additionally include, among other things, reduction to the next inferior pay grade, extra fatigue duty, and correctional custody for not more than seven consecutive days. Thus, while legal proceedings actually brought before a court-martial are prosecuted in the name of the Government, and the accused has the right to demand that he be proceeded against in this manner before any sanctions may be imposed upon him, a range of minor sanctions for lesser infractions are often imposed administratively. Forfeiture of pay, reduction in rank, and even dismissal from the service bring to mind the law of labor-management relations as much as the civilian criminal law.

In short, the Uniform Code of Military Justice regulates a far broader range of the conduct of military personnel than a typical state criminal code regulates of the conduct of civilians; but at the same time the enforcement of that Code in the area of minor offenses is often by sanctions which are more akin to administrative or civil sanctions than to civilian criminal ones.

The availability of these lesser sanctions is not surprising in view of the different relationship of the Government to members of the military. It is not only that of lawgiver to citizen, but also that of employer to employee. Indeed, unlike the civilian situation, the Government is often employer, landlord, provisioner, and lawgiver rolled into one. That relationship also reflects the different purposes of the two communities. The military 'is the executive arm' whose 'law is that of obedience.' While members of the military community enjoy many of the same rights and bear many of the same burdens as do members of the civilian community, within the military community there is simply not the same autonomy as there is in the larger civilian community. The military establishment is subject to the control of the civilian Commander in Chief and the civilian departmental heads under him, and its function is to carry out the policies made by those civilian superiors.

Perhaps because of the broader sweep of the Uniform Code, the military makes an effort to advise its personnel of the contents of the Uniform Code, rather than depending on the ancient doctrine that everyone is presumed to know the law. Article 137 of the UCMJ requires that the provisions of the Code be 'carefully explained to each enlisted member at the time of his entrance on active duty, or within six days thereafter' and that they be 'explained again after he has completed six months of active duty.' Thus the numerically largest component of the services, the enlisted personnel, who might be expected to be a good deal less familiar with the UCMJ than commissioned officers, are required by its terms to receive instructions in its provisions. Article 137 further provides that a complete text of the Code and of the regulations prescribed by the President 'shall be made available to any person on active duty, upon his request, for his personal examination.'

With these very significant differences between military law and civilian law and between the military community and the civilian community in mind, we turn to CPT Levy's challenges to the constitutionality of Arts. 133 and 134.

[CPT Levy] urges that both Art. 133 and Art. 134 (the general article) are "void for vagueness" under the Due Process Clause of the Fifth Amendment and overbroad in violation of the First Amendment. We have recently said of the vagueness doctrine:

> "The doctrine incorporates notions of fair notice or warning. Moreover, it requires legislatures to set reasonably clear guidelines for law enforcement officials and triers of fact in order to prevent 'arbitrary and discriminatory enforcement.' Where a statute's literal scope, unaided by a narrowing state court interpretation, is capable of reaching expression sheltered by the First Amendment, the doctrine demands a greater degree of specificity than in other contexts."

Each of these articles has been construed by the United States Court of Military Appeals or by other military authorities in such a manner as to at least partially narrow its otherwise broad scope. The United States Court of Military Appeals has stated that Art. 134 should not be judged [in a vacuum], but in the context [as established by military legal history]. Article 134 "does not make every irregular, mischievous, or improper act a court-martial offense," . . . but its reach is limited to conduct that is "directly and palpably—as distinguished from indirectly and remotely—prejudicial to good order and discipline." "It applies only to calls for active opposition to the military policy of the United States, and does not criminalize all disagreement with, or objection to, a policy of the Government."

The Manual for Courts-Martial restates these limitations on the scope of Art. 134. It goes on to say that "[c]ertain disloyal statements by military personnel" may be punishable under Art. 134. "Examples are utterances designed to promote disloyalty or disaffection among troops, as praising the enemy, attacking the war aims of the United States, or denouncing our form of government."

UCMJ Art. 133 has similar limitations as Article 134. For an officer to be punished under Article 133, his conduct must offend so seriously against law, justice, morality or decorum as to expose to disgrace, socially or as a man, the offender, and at the same time must be of such a nature or committed under such circumstances as to bring dishonor or disrepute upon the military profession which he represents.

The effect of these constructions of Arts. 133 and 134 by the Court of Military Appeals and by other military authorities has been twofold: It has narrowed the very broad reach of the literal language of the articles, and at the same time has supplied considerable specificity by way of examples of the conduct which they cover. It would be idle to pretend that there are not areas within the general confines of the articles' language which have been left vague despite these narrowing constructions. But even though sizable areas of uncertainty as to the coverage of the articles may remain after their official interpretation by authoritative military sources, further content may be supplied even in these areas by less formalized custom and usage. And there also cannot be the slightest doubt under the military precedents that there is a substantial range of conduct to which both articles clearly apply without vagueness or imprecision. It is within that range that CPT Levy's conduct squarely falls.

Levy had fair notice from the language of each article that the particular conduct which he engaged in was punishable. For the reasons which differentiate military society from civilian society, we think Congress is permitted to legislate both with greater breadth and with greater flexibility when prescribing the rules by which the military shall be governed than it is when prescribing rules for the civilian sector. None of them suggests that one who has received fair warning of the criminality of his own conduct from the statute in question is nonetheless entitled to attack it because the language would not give similar fair warning with respect to other conduct which might be within its broad and literal ambit. One to whose conduct a statute clearly applies may not successfully challenge it for vagueness.

While the members of the military are not excluded from the protection granted by the First Amendment, the different character of the military community and of the military mission requires a different application of those protections. The fundamental necessity for obedience, and the consequent necessity for imposition of discipline, may render permissible within the military that which would be constitutionally impermissible outside it. Doctrines of First Amendment overbreadth asserted in support of challenges to imprecise language like that contained in Arts. 133 and 134 are not exempt from the operation of these principles. The United States Court of Military Appeals has sensibly expounded the reason for this different application of First Amendment doctrines in its opinion in *United States v. Priest*:

> 'In the armed forces some restrictions exist for reasons that have no counterpart in the civilian community. Disrespectful and contemptuous speech, even advocacy of violent change, is tolerable in the civilian community, for it does not directly affect the capacity of the Government to discharge its responsibilities unless it both is directed to inciting imminent lawless action and is likely to produce such action. In military life, however, other considerations must be weighed. The armed forces depend on a command structure that at times must commit men to combat, not only hazarding their lives but ultimately involving the security of the Nation itself. Speech that is protected in the civil population may nonetheless undermine the effectiveness of response to command. If it does, it is constitutionally unprotected.'

There is a wide range of the conduct of military personnel to which Arts. 133 and 134 may be applied without infringement of the First Amendment. While there may lurk at the fringes of the articles, even in the light of their narrowing construction by the United States Court of Military Appeals, some possibility that conduct which would be ultimately held to be protected by the First Amendment could be included within their prohibition, we deem this insufficient to invalidate either of them at the behest of [CPT Levy]. His conduct, that of a commissioned officer publicly urging enlisted personnel to refuse to obey orders which might send them into combat, was unprotected under the most expansive notions of the First Amendment. Articles 133 and 134 may constitutionally prohibit that conduct and a sufficiently large number of similar or related types of conduct so as to preclude their invalidation for overbreadth.

END OF OPINION

The U.S. Supreme Court recognized that special limitations and rules can be imposed on members of the military, especially the officers, to ensure that the military can perform its special mission of fighting and winning wars, and that officers do not betray the special trust they have been given by the president and Congress. For these reasons, conduct and speech that are lawful and constitutionally protected by civilians may be unlawful if uttered by members of the military.

Dereliction of Duty

If a civilian does a job poorly, he or she might be fired but would not be charged with a crime. In fact, in your life you do not have any legal obligation to do anything for anyone. In the military, though, the consequences of failing to do one's duty can have disastrous consequences. In the military, everyone has a special relationship to each other, to their jobs, and to the American people. So, in the military, if someone fails to do their job or follow orders, they can be criminally charged under UCMJ Article 92 for "dereliction of duty." That dereliction might be due to negligence, carelessness, or willful behavior, standards that might in the civilian world open one up to a lawsuit but not to criminal punishment. As you will read in the following case, in the military failing to do one's duty to the best of one's ability can be cause for punishment.

U.S. v. Allen Lawson, 33 M.J. 946 (1988)*

Appellant, a Marine Lieutenant and platoon leader, stands convicted by members at a contested general court-martial of failure to obey the lawful order of a superior officer to submit a roster of checkpoint Marines before posting them, dereliction of duty by failing to post as a pair Lance Corporals Rother and Key at a tactical exercise road checkpoint. The dereliction of duty and order offenses arose during a tactical Combined Arms Exercise (CAX) conducted in the California desert. The approved sentence extends to a dismissal, forty-nine days confinement, and forfeiture of all pay and allowances.

During the ill-fated CAX, appellant participated in mock tactical operations. Toward the end of training, he was assigned uncomplicated duties of (1) posting road guards in pairs along a route designated for a battalion-sized motorized night movement, (2) obtaining a roster of Marines posted as road guides, and (3) providing the roster to Captain Edwards, the appellant's superior coordinator for this movement.

Summarizing the Facts: The Commanding Officer had stressed personnel accountability at all times because of harsh desert conditions. For example, road guides all had to be posted in pairs, utilizing the buddy system. A list of all road guides and where they were posted was to be compiled in a list. This list was to be turned in to Captain Edwards. This was consistent with established battalion policy and, at the moment, driven by darkness and desert safety concerns. Lawson understood these

---

* The case has been heavily edited and paraphrased by the authors for clarity. See disclaimer in introduction.

leadership obligations but did not discharge them. He did not utilize the buddy system. He posted guards, not in pairs, but individually at distances of 300 to 400 meters apart. He did not make a list of road guides and their posts, nor did he provide any guide list to Captain Edwards. Upon the completion of the desert exercises, Lawson did not personally account for the men he had detailed as guards. Instead, he relied on the word of a Sergeant who mistakenly believed that all persons had been picked up. There was no list to be cross-checked to ensure that all guards had been picked up. Back at the barracks, it was noticed at weapon turn-in that Lance Corporal Rother's rifle card had not been turned in at the completion of the exercise. This was reported, but not acted upon. The commander later met with his officers, including the Appellant, and stressed that three things were to be accounted for — people, weapons and communication security material system gear. The next day, Lance Corporal Rother had still not turned in his weapon. Suspecting that he was still out in the desert, a search commenced. Lance Corporal Rother was later found dead.

The circumstances in which the appellant found himself on movement night, while a somewhat pressured, fast-moving and confusing situation, are common to tactical operations and exercises of this size and kind. Some of appellant's difficulties were of his own creation. particularly his failure to pick two of his own men and mount out with a complete unit on time. The circumstances of this exercise were not, as the court members also decided by their findings, of such magnitude as to excuse appellant from responsibility for his failures to follow his orders. Likewise, without regard to the derelictions, criminal or otherwise, of other officers, staff noncommissioned officers and other Marines involved in the fatal tactical movement, we are convinced, as were the court members, that appellant's failure to follow his orders with a good measure of plain common sense, was a key failure in a chain of events that could have been expected to and did result in leaving a Marine in the desert, alone, at night, with no apparent capacity to link up to his own or any other command.

While not a certainty, it was foreseeable that if the appellant did not follow his orders, a Marine could be left behind at night in a harsh environment, get lost, become disoriented, and die. The obedience to the orders and the application of due care were especially important [given the harsh environment]. Command safety policies and pairing guidance were more than adequate to alert appellant to the importance of following orders and the dangers of a failure to comply with them and exercise good judgment in the process. Common sense had to tell him that without a roster in the hands of the recovery detail and without proper guard posting, recovery operations would be haphazard and uncontrolled. No one was in a position to verify who was posted as guards and who was recovered. A detailed roster would have been mandated as a matter of judgment without regard to specific features of the fragmentary order.

We conclude that the evidence is legally sufficient to sustain the findings of guilty.
END OF OPINION

In the case above, a Marine officer had orders concerning how he posted and accounted for his men during a desert training exercise. Because he failed to follow his orders and posted his men with inadequate safety measures, a member of his platoon and a Marine under his command died. This is a tangible and deadly example of why in the military the failure to follow orders or to properly do one's job is not a mere administrative matter that can get someone fired, but a criminal offense that can get an offender incarcerated.

Abu Ghraib, Dereliction of Duty, and Maltreatment

Following the overthrow of Saddam Hussein, American military forces used many facilities previously operated by the Iraqi government. This included Iraqi prisons. At one of these prisons, a number of American soldiers behaved cruelly and inexcusably in their treatment of the prisoners under their guard. Photographs of the way they were treating prisoners made their way to the media and were published for the world public to view, shocking military and civilian leaders, the American public, and the world in general. Many individuals were horrified that American men and women were capable of committing such heinous acts to other human beings. It is thought that no one event contributed more to the support for the Iraqi insurgency and the rise of terrorism in the Middle East after 2003 than the events at Abu Ghraib.

These acts did not go unpunished. Many who participated in the abuse of the prisoners were court-martialed and served time in federal prison. Those servicemembers were prosecuted for Dereliction of Duty as well as for violations of the following:

UCMJ Article 93: Cruelty and Maltreatment

> "Any person subject to this chapter who is guilty of cruelty toward, or oppression or maltreatment of, any person subject to his orders shall be punished as a court-martial may direct."

Cruelty and maltreatment are not necessarily the result of people being sadistic (although it can be), but sometimes come about in people going overboard in having too much fun and hazing new members. Other times, maltreatment is much more obvious. There are times where people are cruel and push soldiers for reasons that have nothing to do with their training.

U.S. v. Harmon, 66 M.J. 710 (2008)*

SPC Harmon was convicted of conspiracy to maltreat detainees, dereliction of duty by willfully failing to protect detainees from abuse, and maltreatment of detainees (four specifications), in violation of Articles 81, 92, and 93, Uniform Code of Military Justice. The panel sentenced Harmon to reduction to Private, forfeiture of all pay and allowances, confinement for six months, and a bad-conduct discharge.

Appellant was a member of the 372nd Military Police Company, a reserve unit headquartered in Maryland. In May 2003, she deployed with the 372nd to Iraq. In August 2003, her unit assumed duties at the Baghdad Central Confinement Facility

---

* The case has been heavily edited and paraphrased by the authors for clarity. See disclaimer in introduction.

at Abu Ghraib, Iraq. At Abu Ghraib, appellant served as a guard in a prison structure called "Tier 1" (also known as "the hard site," to distinguish it from tent encampments holding other prisoners).

The charges in this case arise out of three incidents that occurred in Tier 1 during the fall of 2003. Evidence concerning these incidents comes principally from the testimony of the soldiers involved, from witnesses not implicated in the incidents, from photographs and video recordings made during the incidents, from two sworn statements that appellant made to investigators, and from a letter that appellant wrote on 20 October 2003 to her former roommate in the United States.

The Incident of 4 November 2003

On 4 November 2003, an incident took place in Tier 1 involving a detainee whom the MPs called "Gilligan." Photographs taken by Staff Sergeant (SSG) IF show the detainee wearing what appears to be a poncho, with his head and face hooded by an empty sandbag. The detainee is standing on a box. Wires are attached to his hands. When asked about the detainee, appellant said in a sworn statement to investigators:

> "He is nicknamed Gilligan. . . . He was just standing on the box with the sandbag over his head for about an hour. I put the wire on his hands. I do not recall how. I was joking with him and told him if he fell off he would get electrocuted."

The Incident of 7 November 2003

On 7 November 2003, some detainees in a tent encampment outside Tier 1 participated in a riot. For greater security, soldiers transferred seven of the suspected leaders of the riot onto Tier 1. These detainees were suspected of various serious street crimes, including rape. When the prisoners arrived at Tier 1, they were hooded and handcuffed. Acting without any claim of authority, MPs from the 372nd took it upon themselves to "discipline" these seven detainees. Appellant admitted in her sworn statement that she saw what was taking place, retrieved a digital camera, and then went to join the soldiers.

Shortly after their arrival at the prison, the MPs forced the detainees to sit or lie down on the floor in a pile. While they were on the ground, Sergeant (SGT) JD stomped on their fingers and toes and Corporal (CPL) CG kneeled on the top of the pile. Shortly afterward, SSG IF and CPL CG punched two of the hooded and handcuffed detainees. Appellant witnessed these actions but took no steps to prevent them. On the contrary, Appellant took a picture of CPL CG posing with his armed cocked, ready to punch a hooded detainee. Other soldiers also took photographs and videos throughout the evening.

The MPs subsequently stripped the detainees of their clothes. In her sworn statement, appellant admitted that she used a marker to write "I'm a rapeist (sic)" on the leg of a naked detainee accused of rape. Photographs admitted into evidence show these words starting on or near the detainee's buttocks and running down the back of his thigh.

When the detainees were naked and handcuffed, CPL CG arranged them to form a human pyramid. Appellant witnessed this misconduct and did not report it. Instead, she took a picture of CPL CG and Private First Class (PFC) LE posing with the pyramid of detainees. Appellant then posed for a picture with CPL CG. In the picture, they are smiling and a giving a "thumbs up" symbol with their hands, with appellant leaning over the detainee pyramid. Other forms of misconduct allegedly occurred later in the evening, but the evidence did not implicate appellant.

Appellant did not report the incidents of 4 November or 7 November to her chain of command or to anyone else in authority. In her letter of 20 October 2003 to her former roommate, appellant expressed concern about mistreatment of detainees prior to these three incidents. She wrote: "Again, I thought, okay, that's funny, then it hit me, that's a form of molestation. You can't do that. . . . The only reason I want to be there is to get the pictures that prove that the U.S. is not what they think." At no time, however, did appellant turn over any photographs until she came under investigation in January 2004.

Charge II—Dereliction of Duty

The charge alleges that appellant committed the offense of dereliction of duty in violation of Article 92. The specification asserts that appellant "who knew, of her duties at or near Baghdad Central Correctional Facility, Abu Ghraib, Iraq, from on or about 20 October 2003 to about 1 December 2003, was derelict in the performance of those duties in that she willfully failed to protect Iraqi detainees from abuse, cruelty and maltreatment, as it was her duty to do."

To obtain a conviction for willful dereliction of duty, the Government must prove beyond a reasonable doubt; "(1) That the accused had certain duties; (2) That the accused knew or reasonably should have known of the duties; and (3) That the accused was willfully derelict in the performance of those duties." The government's theory, accepted by the court-martial, was that appellant violated these elements through the conduct detailed above.

Appellant argues that the evidence is insufficient to sustain her conviction for two principal reasons. First, she contends that the evidence does not show that she knew or reasonably should have known of her duties to protect the detainees. She asserts that she was not adequately trained to serve as a prison guard and was not adequately trained in the law of armed conflict. She emphasizes that her company commander testified that her unit was unprepared to perform the mission they were assigned at Abu Ghraib. In addition, given that nudity and handcuffing detainees was common in the prison, she asserts that it was not clear which acts were permissible and which ones were not.

We disagree. Appellant may not have had the ideal training, or even good training, for serving in the prison. Her unit certainly did not behave as a well-trained military police company should. But the facts and reasonable inferences from the facts establish beyond a reasonable doubt that appellant knew that her duties included protecting Iraqi detainees from the kinds of abuse, cruelty, and maltreatment alleged in the specification and in the portions of the bill of particulars of which she was found guilty. On a previous occasion, appellant and another member of her company, SPC MA, removed the handcuffs from a detainee who had been handcuffed for six hours and reported the incident to a non-commissioned officer, an action which resulted in the removal of the responsible MP from duties at the location. In addition, SSG IF testified that prison guards knew that they had a duty to protect and care for the detainees. Finally, in her own letter of 20 October 2003, appellant recognized the wrongfulness of the misconduct. This evidence supports the conclusion that she knew her duties.

Second, appellant argues that she was not derelict in her duties because she was in fact taking steps to expose the abuse, as her letter of 20 October 2003 indicates. She asserts that she was taking photographs to document her company's misconduct, which she was planning to report. We disagree with this argument. Even if we credit what she said in her letter, she was still derelict when she committed the acts above. She was derelict in her duties when she attached the wires to the hands of the detainee nicknamed "Gilligan" and threatened him with electrocution. She was also derelict in her duties when she posed in a "thumbs up" photograph. She did not take these actions to reveal the wrongdoing of others. In addition, when she witnessed the misconduct of others alleged, she did nothing to stop it. Although she did take pictures, she did not contact any person in authority to report the misconduct or to turn over the pictures.

Charge III — Maltreatment

Charge III accuses appellant of cruelty and maltreatment in violation of Article 93. To obtain a conviction of this offense, the government must prove beyond a reasonable doubt: "(1) That a certain person was subject to the orders of the accused; and (2) That the accused was cruel toward, or oppressed, or maltreated that person." Our Manual for Courts Martial does not define cruelty, oppression, or maltreatment, other than to say that the offending conduct is "not necessarily physical" and that it "must be measured by an objective standard." Our superior court, however, clarified the offense in *United States v. Carson*, 57 M.J. 410, 415 (C.A.A.F.2002).

"The essence of the offense is abuse of authority. Whether conduct constitutes maltreatment within the meaning of Article 93, UCMJ, in a particular case requires consideration of the specific facts and circumstances of that case." Maltreatment is 'unwarranted, harmful, abusive, rough, or other unjustifiable treatment which, under all the circumstances . . . results in mental or physical pain or suffering.'" The court did not say that the government must prove that the victim actually suffered harm, as the model instruction indicated. Instead, in a prosecution for maltreatment under Article 93, UCMJ, it is not necessary to prove physical or mental harm or suffering on the part of the victim, although proof of such harm or suffering may be an important aspect of proving that the conduct meets the objective standard. It is only necessary to show, as measured from an objective viewpoint in light of the totality of the circumstances, that the accused's actions reasonably could have caused physical or mental harm or suffering.

Specifications 1 and 2

It is alleged that appellant "at or near Baghdad Central Correctional Facility, Abu Ghraib, Iraq, on or about 8 November 2003 did maltreat several detainees, persons subject to her orders, by taking two or more photographs of the naked detainees in a pyramid of human bodies." Specification 2 alleges that appellant "at or near Baghdad Central Correctional Facility, Abu Ghraib, Iraq, on or about 8 November 2003, did maltreat a detainee, a person subject to her orders, by photographing another guard, Corporal CG, with one arm cocked back as if he was going to hit the detainee in the neck or back."

Appellant argues that the evidence is insufficient to support her conviction of these two specifications because no detainee testified during the findings portion of the trial that he felt maltreated by appellant or that he was even aware that she took photographs of him. We disagree. As explained above, in Carson, our superior court specifically held that the government need not prove that the victims of maltreatment actually suffered harm.

In the totality of the circumstances, we conclude that appellant's actions described in Specifications 1 and 2 constitute maltreatment. Taking the photographs reasonably could have caused the detainees mental suffering. No reasonable detainee would want to be abused and, more importantly here, would wish his abusers to record this pointless, humiliating conduct. The detainees, in addition, had no ability to leave or to object or to do anything but what they were told. Appellant abused her authority as a guard in photographing the detainees.

Specification 3

Specification 3 alleges that appellant "at or near Baghdad Central Correctional Facility, Abu Ghraib, Iraq, on or about 6 November 2003, did maltreat a detainee, a person subject to her orders, by placing wires on the detainee's hands while he stood on a box with his head covered and then telling him if he fell off the box he would be electrocuted." Appellant contests the legal and factual sufficiency of the evidence on this specification on several grounds.

First, appellant argues that placing wires on a detainee's hands and telling him that he would be electrocuted, when the wires were not, in fact, connected to any electrical outlet, does not constitute maltreatment. We disagree. The evidence shows that the detainee had an empty sandbag over his head as a hood. A reasonable inference is that he was limited in his ability to see whether the wires actually were connected to an electrical outlet. Indeed, the photographs themselves do not show where the wires lead. In addition, the panel could infer, as do we, that appellant would not have told the detainee that he would be electrocuted, and the detainee would not have stood on the box for over an hour, if the threat of electrocution was not credible in the mind of the detainee. This conduct was abusive and constitutes maltreatment.

Second, appellant asserts that the detainee did not testify and there was no evidence that he was traumatized by these acts in any way. Again, we conclude that a reasonable person would feel frightened and threatened. The detainee's actual testimony was not necessary.

Finally, appellant argues, consistent with her sworn statement, that she believed they were joking when they put the wires on the detainee and that she did not believe he suffered any harm. This argument also has no merit. Under Carson, the focus is not on the subjective views of the oppressor or of the victim, but on whether the conduct is objectively abusive. Any reasonable observer would conclude that the conduct was so abusive that it constitutes maltreatment in violation of Article 93.

END OF OPINION

Clearly, SPC Harmon's cruelty was nothing more than the abuse of prisoners. Although she tried to justify her conduct, the Court found her reasoning to be insufficient, and she was convicted under UCMJ Article 93 for maltreatment. Even had SPC Harmon not touched or photographed the detainees herself, she still would be guilty of dereliction of duty because, as a prison guard, she had an affirmative action to uphold standards of honor and integrity by protecting the prisoners. Her failure to do so left her derelict in her duty as an American soldier.

Many of the concepts covered in this chapter may not be ones that the average law enforcement officer or someone assigned to the Department of Homeland Security or other part of the national security process encounter. But increasingly, as the struggle against violent extremists, international terrorism, and other threats to our nation are encountered, the principles we have addressed become increasingly important. Having a basic awareness of some of the concepts of military law and the military justice system is a critical piece of this profession.

Review Questions

1. Consider how social media (Facebook, Twitter, etc.) affects the military. Based on the case law in this chapter, what would you say are the limits of speech permitted to members of the military when engaging with social media? Are the rules different for officers than for enlisted?

2. Many nations, including most of NATO, use civilian criminal courts for crimes and a military discipline system only for uniquely military offenses (such as AWOL, disobedience of orders, etc.). Given advances in technology, communications, and transportation, are there still reasons for the U.S. military to use a completely separate system for all crimes committed by servicemembers? Discuss the pros and cons of moving to a system that tries all cases in civilian courts.

Key Terms

Court-martial (plural **courts-martial**)—A military court. A court-martial is empowered to determine the guilt of members of the armed forces subject to military law, and, if the defendant is found guilty, to decide upon punishment.

Non-judicial punishment—A form of military justice authorized by Article 15 of the Uniform Code of Military Justice (10 U.S. Code § 815). Non-judicial punishment or "NJP" permits commanders to administratively discipline troops without a court-martial.

Uniform Code of Military Justice (UCMJ) — Federal statutes found at 10 U.S.C. §§ 801–946, the foundation of U.S. military law. It was established by Congress in accordance with Article I, Section 8 of the Constitution, which provides that "The Congress shall have Power. . . . To make Rules for the Government and Regulation of the land and naval forces."

Further Reading

Bray, Chris, *Court-Martial: How Military Justice Has Shaped America from the Revolution to 9/11 and Beyond*, 1st Ed. (Norton 2016).

Shanor, Charles and Hogue, L., *Military Law in a Nutshell*, 4th Ed. (West 2013).

Office of the General Counsel, U.S. Department of Defense, *Military Justice System's Response to Unrestricted Reports of Sexual Assault*, 30 October 2013, available at http://www.sapr.mil/public/docs/reports/FY14_POTUS/FY14_DoD_Report_to_POTUS_Annex_4_OGC.pdf.

U.S. Department of Defense, *The Joint Service Committee on Military Justice*, http://jsc.defense.gov/.

Chapter 14

Other Civil Rights Issues in Homeland and National Security Law

Overview

Throughout this text we have been looking at the intersection of civil liberties and the need for security. The powers of the government to conduct searches, to engage in surveillance, to detain those suspected of national security crimes, and to otherwise defend the nation all are bounded by the rights protected under the Constitution. This final chapter is reserved for examining some civil rights issues that did not fit neatly into the other chapters, but which have nonetheless arisen throughout the nation's history of addressing homeland and national security.

National Security and the First Amendment

The first and most prominent of the original amendments to the Constitution is the First Amendment. If we look back through history at those places where the interests of a government and the interests of its people most often come into conflict, it is in the freedom of a people to gather together and to express political opinions critical of their government. Freedom of conscience and freedom of speech are, in so many ways, the foundation on which all other freedoms stand. Think about it—if people were not free to believe as they saw fit, how could the ideas of a government be challenged? If they could not gather with others to discuss those beliefs and ideas, or share those ideas through a free press, how could they test those ideas against others in a search for truth? And if they were not able to present those ideas to the government, how could any changes be made except through violence? If we look at those societies that we consider to lack freedom, where is the government oppression most obvious? In dictating what the people must believe, what they can and cannot say, in denying them the ability to gather in association and to present disputes to the government for resolution.

To truly appreciate all that is incorporated in the First Amendment, it is important to read it word for word, looking at each of its multiple parts.

Congress shall make no law respecting an establishment of religion, or prohibiting the free exercise thereof, or abridging the freedom of speech, or of the press; or the right of the people peaceably to assemble, and to petition the Government for a redress of grievances.

Given the context of this textbook, we will look most closely at the First Amendment freedoms of speech, the press, and of association as they have intersected with homeland and national security interests.

So just what does "the freedom of speech" actually mean? It obviously does not mean that any and all speech is legal, because we know that is not the case. Many forms of speech are against the law. Here is just a short list:

1. Threats of bodily harm to others and oneself;
2. Publication of knowingly false statements, often referred to as defamation, slander, or libel;
3. Publication of private information of a non-public figure, such as medical information, banking records, and so forth;
4. Making false statements as part of an effort to commit fraud;
5. Lying under oath in a court proceeding, often referred to as "perjury";
6. Knowingly making false statements to the police in a deliberate effort to hinder an investigation;
7. Disclosure of classified information to a source not allowed to receive it;
8. Making statement or words in a way deliberately intended to provoke violence, often referred to as "fighting words";
9. Asking another to commit a crime, or talking with others about a plan to commit a crime, referred to as solicitation and conspiracy.

So the government may, in some cases, outlaw or punish certain kinds of speech. Now, there may still be disputes over the limits of each of these restrictions — when does speech rise to "fighting words," or what is the boundary between one's right against self-incrimination and obstruction of justice? First Amendment law tests the balance between the need of a free society to allow certain forms of speech against the government interest in security and safety to determine where exactly government action is permitted and where it is considered to abridge the freedom of speech. We will look at some (not all) of those considerations in the following part of the chapter.

Before we go forward, we must point out an important concept concerning the First Amendment. The Bill of Rights (the first ten amendments to the Constitution) place limits on what the government is permitted to do, not what other individuals may do. So, just as the Fourth Amendment does not limit the right of a landlord to enter an apartment (that would be governed by the lease, not the Constitution), the First Amendment only protects against government action, not private actors. There can only be a First Amendment violation if the government does anything to a person as a response to political speech.

Private actors are perfectly free to ostracize, boycott, shun, or engage in other hostile (but non-violent) action in response to the speech of another. This, itself, is an example of First Amendment protections. If people were not allowed to express their disapproval and criticize the speech of others, then the act of interfering with or not allowing the criticism would itself violate the right to free speech. Inherent in the First Amendment right to say what you want and associate with whom you want is also a right to refuse to associate or have anything to do with others. The freedom to associate includes the implicit right also to refuse to associate.

Consider the following hypothetical situations and whether the First Amendment is implicated. If so, how? If not, why not?

1. An ESPN commentator states during a football game, "I think we should not allow so many Muslims into the U.S." He is immediately fired by ESPN. He sues ESPN, alleging they are violating his First Amendment right to free speech.

2. Dave is going through the airport security, and as he does, he strips down to a speedo and has written on his torso the Fourth Amendment as a form of political protest against airport screenings. He is arrested and charged with disorderly conduct.

3. The NRA plans to hold a convention at the Hilton Hotel. Mr. Hilton, because he disagrees with the NRA's stance on gun control, tells the group that they may not have their convention in his hotel. The NRA sues, alleging that Mr. Hilton is violating their First Amendment rights.

4. The IRS is accused of targeting and auditing the financial records of conservative organizations.

5. At a public university, the Dean of Student Conduct goes around the school, tearing down a pro-life group's fliers on the bulletin boards, which exist for public posting.

6. At a large, privately owned Christian school, the Dean of Student Conduct goes around campus tearing down pro-choice fliers on its bulletin boards.

Now, again, the issue of whether or not speech is constitutionally protected does not end the discussion. There are still issues of ethics, and there may be other interests that offset the free speech rights. Under certain circumstances, even speech that you might think would normally be constitutionally protected may be held to be unlawful. This can be seen in the following U.S. Supreme Court opinion.

Brandenburg v. Ohio, 395 U.S. 444 (1969)*

The appellant, a leader of a Ku Klux Klan group, was convicted under Ohio law for "advocating the duty, necessity, or propriety of crime, sabotage, violence, or unlawful methods of terrorism as a means of accomplishing industrial or political reform" and for "voluntarily assembling with any society, group, or assemblage of

---

* The case has been heavily edited and paraphrased by the authors for clarity. See disclaimer in introduction.

persons formed to teach or advocate the doctrines of criminal syndicalism." Criminal syndicalism is the doctrine of using criminal acts to accomplish social or political change. He was fined $1,000 and sentenced to one to 10 years' imprisonment. The appellant challenged the constitutionality of the criminal syndicalism statute under the First and Fourteenth Amendments to the United States Constitution, but the intermediate appellate court of Ohio affirmed his conviction without opinion. The Supreme Court of Ohio dismissed his appeal for the stated reason that "no substantial constitutional question exists." It did not file an opinion or explain its conclusions. We reverse.

The record shows that a man, identified at trial as the appellant, telephoned an announcer-reporter on the staff of a Cincinnati television station and invited him to come to a Ku Klux Klan "rally" to be held at a farm in Hamilton County. With the cooperation of the organizers, the reporter and a cameraman attended the meeting and filmed the events. Portions of the films were later broadcast on the local station and on a national network.

The prosecution's case rested on the films and on testimony identifying the appellant as the person who communicated with the reporter and who spoke at the rally. The State also introduced into evidence several articles appearing in the film, including a pistol, a rifle, a shotgun, ammunition, a Bible, and a red hood worn by the speaker in the films.

One film showed 12 hooded figures, some of whom carried firearms. They were gathered around a large wooden cross, which they burned. No one was present other than the participants and the newsmen who made the film. Most of the words uttered during the scene were incomprehensible when the film was projected, but scattered phrases could be understood that were derogatory of Negroes and, in one instance, of Jews. Another scene on the same film showed the appellant, in Klan regalia, making a speech. The speech, in full, was as follows:

> This is an organizers' meeting. We have had quite a few members here today which are—we have hundreds, hundreds of members throughout the State of Ohio. I can quote from a newspaper clipping from the Columbus, Ohio Dispatch, five weeks ago Sunday morning. The Klan has more members in the State of Ohio than does any other organization. We're not a revengent organization, but if our President, our Congress, our Supreme Court, continues to suppress the white, Caucasian race, it's possible that there might have to be some revengeance taken.

> We are marching on Congress July the Fourth, four hundred thousand strong. From there we are dividing into two groups, one group to march on St. Augustine, Florida, the other group to march into Mississippi. Thank you.

The second film showed six hooded figures one of whom, later identified as the appellant, repeated a speech very similar to that recorded on the first film. The reference to the possibility of "revengeance" was omitted, and one sentence was added: "Personally, I believe the nigger should be returned to Africa, the Jew returned to Israel." Though some of the figures in the films carried weapons, the speaker did not.

The Ohio Criminal Syndicalism Statute was enacted in 1919. From 1917 to 1920, identical or quite similar laws were adopted by 20 States and two territories. In 1927, this Court sustained the constitutionality of California's Criminal Syndicalism Act, the text of which is quite similar to that of the laws of Ohio. *Whitney v. California* (1927). The Court upheld the statute on the ground that, without more, "advocating" violent means to effect political and economic change involves such danger to the security of the State that the State may outlaw it. But *Whitney* has been thoroughly discredited by later decisions. These later decisions have fashioned the principle that the constitutional guarantees of free speech and free press do not permit a State to forbid or proscribe advocacy of the use of force or of law violation except where such advocacy is directed to inciting or producing imminent lawless action and is likely to incite or produce such action. As we said in *Noto v. United States*, (1961), "the mere abstract teaching ... of the moral propriety or even moral necessity for a resort to force and violence, is not the same as preparing a group for violent action and steeling it to such action." A statute which fails to draw this distinction impermissibly intrudes upon the freedoms guaranteed by the First Amendment. It sweeps within its condemnation speech which our Constitution has protected from governmental control.

Measured by this test, Ohio's Criminal Syndicalism Act cannot be sustained. The Act punishes persons who "advocate or teach the duty, necessity, or propriety" of violence "as a means of accomplishing industrial or political reform"; or who publish or circulate or display any book or paper containing such advocacy; or who "justify" the commission of violent acts "with intent to exemplify, spread or advocate the propriety of the doctrines of criminal syndicalism"; or who "voluntarily assemble" with a group formed "to teach or advocate the doctrines of criminal syndicalism." The statute's bald definition of the crime in terms of mere advocacy not distinguished from incitement to imminent lawless action

Accordingly, we are here confronted with a statute which, by its own words and as applied, purports to punish mere advocacy and to forbid, on pain of criminal punishment, assembly with others merely to advocate the described type of action. Such a statute falls within the condemnation of the First and Fourteenth Amendments. The contrary teaching of *Whitney v. California*, supra, cannot be supported, and that decision is therefore overruled.

END OF OPINION

Generally, political speech is protected, even if the speech advocates illegal activity. Otherwise it would be too easy for governments to limit dissent. But there needs to be a limit, so this case stands for the rule that speech, especially political speech, can be criminalized only when the speech is advocating or could lead to "imminent lawless action." What is meant by "imminent lawless action"? The Court limits this to "preparing a group for violent action and steeling it to such action." The threat should be immediate—perhaps within seconds, minutes, even hours. How to tell whether or not imminent lawless action will result? The location where the speech is being uttered, who is present within earshot of the speech, what else may have been going on, and other criteria such as this should be used.

Solicitation and Conspiracy

Now, the case above referred to the making of speech that carried with it the danger of imminent lawless activity. In some circumstances speech that is connected to unlawful behavior can be the basis for criminal prosecution even if the contemplated illegal activity is not "imminent." And, further, this speech could include religious and political overtones and still not be protected. This takes us into the concepts of solicitation and conspiracy.

What is solicitation? Solicitation is the act of asking, inducing, or otherwise encouraging someone to commit a crime. Here are some examples:

- "For $5,000, will you kill my husband?"
- "If you help me break into the Smith's home while they are on vacation, half of the loot is yours."

Your right to free speech does not include a right to ask or encourage people to commit crimes. Imminence is not a requirement for the crime of solicitation. Any request, inducement, or encouragement of a crime is illegal, regardless of whether or not it is imminent.

Where this runs into shades of grey is when it crosses into religious ideology. A Muslim cleric telling a congregation inside a mosque, "Loyal Muslims should behead non-believers," or a Christian preacher who quotes Christian text calling for adulterers to be stoned are both generally recognized as engaging in protected speech, advocating a religious belief. However, if a Muslim cleric tells a follower to behead the Jewish owner of a nearby kosher butcher shop, or a Christian leader tells his congregants to stone a woman suspected of being a prostitute, then we have each of these encouraging someone to commit a specific crime, unlawful even though also consisting of religious belief. What is the difference here? The first examples are merely advocating belief, while the latter are encouraging an actual and specific criminal act.

What is criminal conspiracy? Simply defined, conspiracy is an agreement between two or more people to commit a crime. If we look at it like a math problem,

$$\text{Conspiracy} = \text{Solicitation} + \text{Agreement}$$

First, one person asks another person to commit a crime. That is solicitation. Once another person agrees to commit a crime, you have the crime of conspiracy. Examples of criminal conspiracy include a terrorist cell plotting to blow up a building, two underage college freshmen pooling their money together to purchase beer, or a group of 11 persons planning to rob a casino.

Now, in most cases, for a person to be convicted of criminal conspiracy requires not only there be "solicitation + agreement," but also an overt act in furtherance of the conspiracy.

$$\text{Conspiracy} = \text{Solicitation} + \text{Agreement} + \text{Overt Act in Furtherance of the Conspiracy}$$

For example, a terrorist cell would not only have had to agree to blow up a building, but would have had to do something to actually accomplish this objective. This might include looking online for possible targets, or going to Home Depot to purchase bomb-making materials such as fertilizer, diesel fuel, and so forth.

In some states no overt action is required, just the agreement to commit a crime. As a practical matter, though, it can be very difficult in court for a prosecutor to prove the existence of an agreement to commit a crime without evidence of some overt action to further a conspiracy.

The federal law relating to conspiracy (which has been challenged as infringing the First Amendment right to free speech) is as follows:

Seditious Conspiracy: 18 USC 3284

> If two or more persons in any State or Territory, or in any place subject to the jurisdiction of the United States, conspire to overthrow, put down, or to destroy by force the Government of the United States, or to levy war against them, or to oppose by force the authority thereof, or by force to prevent, hinder, or delay the execution of any law of the United States, or by force to seize, take, or possess any property of the United States contrary to the authority thereof, they shall each be fined under this title or imprisoned not more than twenty years, or both.

So, while it is perfectly lawful for a person to advocate the idea that the U.S. government should be overthrown by force or violence, it is illegal for any person to actually plan such action. This takes us to the following case, a national security prosecution of terrorist activity.

U.S. v. Rahman, 189 F.3d 88 (1999)[*]

These are appeals by ten defendants convicted of seditious conspiracy and other offenses arising out of a wide-ranging plot to conduct a campaign of urban terrorism. Among the activities of some or all of the defendants were rendering assistance to those who bombed the World Trade Center, planning to bomb bridges and tunnels in New York City, murdering Rabbi Meir Kahane, and planning to murder the President of Egypt.

I. The Government's Case

At trial, the Government sought to prove that the defendants and others joined in a seditious conspiracy to wage a war of urban terrorism against the United States and forcibly to oppose its authority. The Government also sought to prove various other counts against the defendants, all of which broadly relate to the seditious conspiracy. The Government alleged that members of the conspiracy (acting alone or in concert) took the following actions, among others, in furtherance of the group's objectives: the

---

[*] The case has been heavily edited and paraphrased by the authors for clarity. See disclaimer in introduction.

attempted murder of Hosni Mubarak, the provision of assistance to the bombing of the World Trade Center in New York City on February 26, 1993, and the Spring 1993 campaign of attempted bombings of buildings and tunnels in New York City. In addition, some members of the group were allegedly involved in the murder of Rabbi Meir Kahane.

The Government adduced evidence at trial showing the following: Abdel Rahman, a blind Islamic scholar and cleric, was the leader of the seditious conspiracy, the purpose of which was "jihad," in the sense of a struggle against the enemies of Islam. Indicative of this purpose, in a speech to his followers Abdel Rahman instructed that they were to "do jihad with the sword, with the cannon, with the grenades, with the missile against God's enemies." Abdel Rahman's role in the conspiracy was generally limited to overall supervision and direction of the membership, as he made efforts to remain a level above the details of individual operations. However, as a cleric and the group's leader, Abdel Rahman was entitled to dispense "fatwas," religious opinions on the holiness of an act, to members of the group sanctioning proposed courses of conduct and advising them whether the acts would be in furtherance of jihad.

According to his speeches and writings, Abdel Rahman perceives the United States as the primary oppressor of Muslims worldwide, active in assisting Israel to gain power in the Middle East, and largely under the control of the Jewish lobby. Abdel Rahman also considers the secular Egyptian government of Mubarak to be an oppressor because it has abided Jewish migration to Israel while seeking to decrease Muslim births. Holding these views, Abdel Rahman believes that jihad against Egypt and the United States is mandated by the Qur'an. Formation of a jihad army made up of small "divisions" and "battalions" to carry out this jihad was therefore necessary, according to Abdel Rahman, in order to beat back these oppressors of Islam including the United States.

Although Abdel Rahman did not arrive in the United States until 1990, a group of his followers began to organize the jihad army in New York beginning in 1989. At that time, law enforcement had several of the members of the group under surveillance. In July 1989, on three successive weekends, FBI agents observed and photographed members of the jihad organization, including (at different times), Nosair, Hampton-El, Mahmoud Abouhalima, Mohammad Salameh, and Nidal Ayyad (the latter three of whom were later convicted of the World Trade Center bombing, see *Salameh*, 152 F.3d at 161), shooting weapons, including AK-47's, at a public rifle range on Long Island. Although Abdel Rahman was in Egypt at the time, Nosair and Abouhalima called him there to discuss various issues including the progress of their military training, tape-recording these conversations for distribution among Abdel Rahman's followers. Nosair told Abdel Rahman "we have organized an encampment, we are concentrating here."

[The original opinion goes on at length detailing the activities of the different accused individuals.]

DISCUSSION

I. Constitutional Challenges

A. Seditious Conspiracy Statute and the Treason Clause

Defendant Nosair (joined by other defendants) contends that his conviction for seditious conspiracy, in violation of 18 U.S.C. § 2384, was illegal because it failed to satisfy the requirements of the Treason Clause of the U.S. Constitution, Art. III, § 3.

Article III, Section 3 provides, in relevant part:

> Treason against the United States, shall consist only in levying War against them, or in adhering to their Enemies, giving them Aid and Comfort. No Person shall be convicted of Treason unless on the Testimony of two Witnesses to the same overt Act, or on Confession in open Court.

The seditious conspiracy statute, 18 U.S.C. § 2384, provides:

> If two or more persons in any State or Territory, or in any place subject to the jurisdiction of the United States, conspire to overthrow, put down or to destroy by force the Government of the United States, or to levy war against them, or to oppose by force the authority thereof, or by force to prevent, hinder or delay the execution of any law of the United States, or by force to seize, take, or possess any property of the United States contrary to the authority thereof, they shall each be fined under this title or imprisoned not more than twenty years, or both.

B. Seditious Conspiracy Statute and the First Amendment

Rahman, joined by the other appellants, contends that the seditious conspiracy statute, 18 U.S.C. § 2384, is an unconstitutional burden on free speech and the free exercise of religion in violation of the First Amendment. First, Rahman argues that the statute is facially invalid because it criminalizes protected expression and that it is overbroad and unconstitutionally vague. Second, Abdel Rahman contends that his conviction violated the First Amendment because it rested solely on his political views and religious practices.

1. Facial Challenge

a. Restraint on Speech. 18 U.S.C. § 2384 provides:

> If two or more persons in any State or Territory, or in any place subject to the jurisdiction of the United States, conspire to overthrow, put down, or destroy by force the Government of the United States, or to levy war against them, or to oppose by force the authority thereof, or by force to prevent, hinder, or delay the execution of any law of the United States, or by force to seize, take, or possess any property of the United States contrary to the authority thereof, they shall be fined under this title or imprisoned not more than twenty years, or both.

As Section 2384 proscribes "speech" only when it constitutes an agreement to use force against the United States, Rahman's generalized First Amendment challenge to the statute is without merit.

It remains fundamental that while the state may not criminalize the expression of views—even including the view that violent overthrow of the government is desirable—it may nonetheless outlaw encouragement, inducement, or conspiracy to take violent action.... [I]n *Brandenburg v. Ohio* the Court held that a state may proscribe subversive advocacy only when such advocacy is directed towards, and is likely to result in, "imminent lawless action."

To be convicted under Section 2384, one must conspire to use force, not just to advocate the use of force. We have no doubt that this passes the test of constitutionality.

Our view of Section 2384's constitutionality also finds support in a number of the Supreme Court's more recent First Amendment decisions. As evidenced by the following selected quotations, these cases make clear that a line exists between expressions of belief, which are protected by the First Amendment, and threatened or actual uses of force, which are not.

"A physical assault is not expressive conduct protected by the First Amendment";

"Threats of violence are outside the First Amendment";

"The First Amendment does not protect violence";

"Congress may outlaw threats against President, provided that what is a threat is distinguished from what is constitutionally protected speech."

b. Vagueness and Overbreadth. Abdel Rahman also contends that Section 2384 is overbroad and void for vagueness.

(i) Overbreadth. A law is overbroad, and hence void, if it "does not aim specifically at evils within the allowable area of State control, but, on the contrary, sweeps within its ambit other activities that constitute an exercise of freedom of speech or of the press." Particularly when conduct and not speech is involved, to void the statute the overbreadth must be "real and substantial judged in relation to the statute's plainly legitimate sweep."

We recognize that laws targeting "sedition" must be scrutinized with care to assure that the threat of prosecution will not deter expression of unpopular viewpoints by persons ideologically opposed to the government. But Section 2384 is drawn sufficiently narrowly that we perceive no unacceptable risk of such abuse.

Rahman argues that Section 2384 is overbroad because Congress could have achieved its public safety aims "without chilling First Amendment rights" by punishing only "substantive acts involving bombs, weapons, or other violent acts." One of the beneficial purposes of the conspiracy law is to permit arrest and prosecution before the substantive crime has been accomplished. The Government, possessed of evidence of conspiratorial planning, need not wait until buildings and tunnels have been bombed and people killed before arresting the conspirators. Accordingly, it is well established that the Government may criminalize certain preparatory steps towards criminal action, even when the crime consists of the use of conspiratorial or exhortatory words. Because Section 2384 prohibits only conspiratorial agreement, we are satisfied that the statute is not constitutionally overbroad.

(ii) Vagueness. Abdel Rahman also challenges the statute for vagueness. A criminal statute, particularly one regulating speech, must "define the criminal offense with sufficient definiteness that ordinary people can understand what conduct is prohibited and in a manner that does not encourage arbitrary and discriminatory enforcement. Abdel Rahman argues that Section 2384 does not provide "fair warning" about what acts are unlawful, leaving constitutionally protected speech vulnerable to criminal prosecution.

There is indeed authority suggesting that the word "seditious" does not sufficiently convey what conduct it forbids to serve as an essential element of a crime. But the word "seditious" does not appear in the prohibitory text of the statute; it appears only in the caption. The terms of the statute are far more precise. The portions charged against Rahman and his co-defendants—conspiracy to levy war against the United States and to oppose by force the authority thereof—do not involve terms of such vague meaning. Furthermore, they unquestionably specify that agreement to use force is an essential element of the crime. Rahman therefore cannot prevail on the claim that the portions of Section 2384 charged against him criminalize mere expressions of opinion, or are unduly vague.

2. Application of Section 2384 to Rahman's Case

Rahman also argues that he was convicted not for entering into any conspiratorial agreement that Congress may properly forbid, but "solely for his religious words and deeds" which, he contends, are protected by the First Amendment. In support of this claim, Rahman cites the Government's use in evidence of his speeches and writings.

There are two answers to Rahman's contention. The first is that freedom of speech and of religion do not extend so far as to prevent prosecution of one who uses a public speech or a religious ministry to commit crimes. Numerous crimes under the federal criminal code are, or can be, committed by speech alone. As examples: Section 2 makes it an offense to "counsel," "command," "induce" or "procure" the commission of an offense against the United States. Section 371 makes it a crime to "conspire . . . to commit any offense against the United States." Section 373, with which Rahman was charged, makes it a crime to "solicit, command, induce, or otherwise endeavor to persuade" another person to commit a crime of violence. Various other statutes, like Section 2384, criminalize conspiracies of specified objectives, see, e.g., 18 U.S.C. § 1751(d) (conspiracy to kidnap); 18 U.S.C. § 1951 (conspiracy to interfere with commerce through robbery, extortion, or violence); 21 U.S.C. § 846 (conspiracy to violate drug laws). All of these offenses are characteristically committed through speech. Notwithstanding that political speech and religious exercise are among the activities most jealously guarded by the First Amendment, one is not immunized from prosecution for such speech-based offenses merely because one commits them through the medium of political speech or religious preaching. Of course, courts must be vigilant to insure that prosecutions are not improperly based on the mere expression of unpopular ideas. But if the evidence shows that the speeches crossed the line into criminal solicitation, procurement of criminal activity, or conspiracy to violate the laws, the prosecution is permissible.

The evidence justifying Rahman's conviction for conspiracy and solicitation showed beyond a reasonable doubt that he crossed this line. His speeches were not simply the expression of ideas; in some instances they constituted the crime of conspiracy to wage war on the United States under Section 2384 and solicitation of attack on the United States military installations, as well as of the murder of Egyptian President Hosni Mubarak under Section 373.

For example, Abdel Rahman told Salem he "should make up with God by turning his rifle's barrel to President Mubarak's chest, and killing him." On another occasion, speaking to Abdo Mohammed Haggag about murdering President Mubarak during his visit to the United States, Abdel Rahman told Haggag, "Depend on God. Carry out this operation. It does not require a fatwa. You are ready in training, but do it. Go ahead." The evidence further showed that Siddig Ali consulted with Abdel Rahman about the bombing of the United Nations Headquarters, and Abdel Rahman told him, "Yes, it's a must, it's a duty." On another occasion, when Abdel Rahman was asked by Salem about bombing the United Nations, he counseled against it on the ground that it would be "bad for Muslims," but added that Salem should "find a plan to destroy or to bomb or to inflict damage to the American Army."

Words of this nature—ones that instruct, solicit, or persuade others to commit crimes of violence—violate the law and may be properly prosecuted regardless of whether they are uttered in private, or in a public speech, or in administering the duties of a religious ministry. The fact that his speech or conduct was "religious" does not immunize him from prosecution under generally-applicable criminal statutes.

Rahman also protests the Government's use in evidence of his speeches, writings, and preachings that did not in themselves constitute the crimes of solicitation or conspiracy. He is correct that the Government placed in evidence many instances of Rahman's writings and speeches in which Rahman expressed his opinions within the protection of the First Amendment. However, while the First Amendment fully protects Rahman's right to express hostility against the United States, and he may not be prosecuted for so speaking, it does not prevent the use of such speeches or writings in evidence when relevant to prove a pertinent fact in a criminal prosecution. The Government was free to demonstrate Rahman's resentment and hostility toward the United States in order to show his motive for soliciting and procuring illegal attacks against the United States and against President Mubarak of Egypt.... The First Amendment does not prohibit the evidentiary use of speech to establish the elements of a crime or to prove motive or intent ...

Furthermore, [the trial judge] properly protected against the danger that Rahman might be convicted because of his unpopular religious beliefs that were hostile to the United States. He explained to the jury the limited use it was entitled to make of the material received as evidence of motive. He instructed that a defendant could not be convicted on the basis of his beliefs or the expression of them—even if those beliefs favored violence. He properly instructed the jury that it could find a defendant guilty only if the evidence proved he committed a crime charged in the indictment.

We reject Rahman's claim that his conviction violated his rights under the First Amendment.

END OF OPINION

As you read in the excerpt from the Court's opinion, Rahman was not convicted merely because he advocated the belief that the U.S. government should be overthrown through force or violence. He was convicted because he was encouraging individuals to go out and commit specific criminal acts. It just so happened that the reason he was encouraging people to go out and commit criminal acts was because of his belief the government should be overthrown. As a matter of law, it does not matter if a person encourages another person to commit a crime in the name of religion, to get money, for revenge, or any other reason; all that matters is that a crime is being encouraged. It just so happened that in this instance, the motivating principle to encourage the crime was a religious philosophy.

When faced with the question of criminal sedition, remember the following quote from *Rahman*: "Words of this nature—ones that instruct, solicit, or persuade others to commit crimes of violence—violate the law and may be properly prosecuted regardless of whether they are uttered in private, or in a public speech, or in administering the duties of a religious ministry."

Material Support of Terrorism

The issue of whether speech otherwise protected under the First Amendment can nevertheless be criminalized arose in the case of a group that actually sought to teach and counsel foreign groups on how to obtain political objectives *without* resorting to violence. The crime of "Material Support to Terrorism" has implicated the same issue—does speech that argues in favor of peaceful means of resolving disputes even violate the law prohibiting materials support to terrorism in a way that can be punished without going against the First Amendment? Take a look at the way the issue is addressed in the following case.

Holder v. Humanitarian Law Project, 561 U.S. 1 (2010)*

Congress has prohibited the provision of "material support or resources" to certain foreign organizations that engage in terrorist activity. 18 U. S. C. § 2339B(a)(1). That prohibition is based on a finding that the specified organizations "are so tainted by their criminal conduct that any contribution to such an organization facilitates that conduct." The plaintiffs in this litigation seek to provide support to two such organizations. Plaintiffs claim that they seek to facilitate only the lawful, nonviolent purposes of those groups, and that applying the material-support law to

---

* The case has been heavily edited and paraphrased by the authors for clarity. See disclaimer in introduction.

prevent them from doing so violates the Constitution. In particular, they claim that the statute is too vague, in violation of the Fifth Amendment, and that it infringes their rights to freedom of speech and association, in violation of the First Amendment. We conclude that the material-support statute is constitutional as applied to the particular activities plaintiffs have told us they wish to pursue. We do not, however, address the resolution of more difficult cases that may arise under the statute in the future.

This litigation concerns 18 U. S. C. § 2339B, which makes it a federal crime to "knowingly provid[e] material support or resources to a foreign terrorist organization." Congress has amended the definition of "material support or resources" periodically, but at present it is defined as follows:

> "[T]he term 'material support or resources' means any property, tangible or intangible, or service, including currency or monetary instruments or financial securities, financial services, lodging, training, expert advice or assistance, safehouses, false documentation or identification, communications equipment, facilities, weapons, lethal substances, explosives, personnel (1 or more individuals who may be or include oneself), and transportation, except medicine or religious materials."

The authority to designate an entity a "foreign terrorist organization" rests with the Secretary of State. She may, in consultation with the Secretary of the Treasury and the Attorney General, so designate an organization upon finding that it is foreign, engages in "terrorist activity" or "terrorism," and thereby "threatens the security of United States nationals or the national security of the United States." "'[N]ational security' means the national defense, foreign relations, or economic interests of the United States." An entity designated a foreign terrorist organization may seek review of that designation before the D. C. Circuit within 30 days of that designation.

In 1997, the Secretary of State designated 30 groups as foreign terrorist organizations. Two of those groups are the Kurdistan Workers' Party (also known as the Partiya Karkeran Kurdistan, or PKK) and the Liberation Tigers of Tamil Eelam (LTTE). The PKK is an organization founded in 1974 with the aim of establishing an independent Kurdish state in southeastern Turkey. The LTTE is an organization founded in 1976 for the purpose of creating an independent Tamil state in Sri Lanka.

Plaintiffs in this litigation are two U. S. citizens and six domestic organizations: the Humanitarian Law Project (HLP) (a human rights organization with consultative status to the United Nations); Ralph Fertig (the HLP's president, and a retired administrative law judge); Nagalingam Jeyalingam (a Tamil physician, born in Sri Lanka and a naturalized U. S. citizen); and five nonprofit groups dedicated to the interests of persons of Tamil descent.

As relevant here, plaintiffs claimed that the material-support statute was unconstitutional on two grounds: First, it violated their freedom of speech and freedom of association under the First Amendment, because it criminalized their provision of material support to the PKK and the LTTE, without requiring the Government to prove that plaintiffs had a specific intent to further the unlawful ends of those organizations. Second, plaintiffs argued that the statute was unconstitutionally vague.

Given the complicated 12-year history of this litigation, we pause to clarify the questions before us. Plaintiffs challenge § 2339B's prohibition on four types of material support—"training," "expert advice or assistance," "service," and "personnel." They raise three constitutional claims. First, plaintiffs claim that § 2339B violates the Due Process Clause of the Fifth Amendment because these four statutory terms are impermissibly vague. Second, plaintiffs claim that § 2339B violates their freedom of speech under the First Amendment. Third, plaintiffs claim that § 2339B violates their First Amendment freedom of association.

Plaintiffs do not challenge the above statutory terms in all their applications. Rather, plaintiffs claim that § 2339B is invalid to the extent it prohibits them from engaging in certain specified activities. . . . [T]hose activities are: (1) "train[ing] members of [the] PKK on how to use humanitarian and international law to peacefully resolve disputes"; (2) "engag[ing] in political advocacy on behalf of Kurds who live in Turkey"; and (3) "teach[ing] PKK members how to petition various representative bodies such as the United Nations for relief." With respect to the other plaintiffs, those activities are: (1) "train[ing] members of [the] LTTE to present claims for tsunami-related aid to mediators and international bodies"; (2) "offer[ing] their legal expertise in negotiating peace agreements between the LTTE and the Sri Lankan government"; and (3) "engag[ing] in political advocacy on behalf of Tamils who live in Sri Lanka."

Plaintiffs claim, as a threshold matter, that we should affirm the Court of Appeals without reaching any issues of constitutional law. They contend that we should interpret the material-support statute, when applied to speech, to require proof that a defendant intended to further a foreign terrorist organization's illegal activities. That interpretation, they say, would end the litigation because plaintiffs' proposed activities consist of speech, but plaintiffs do not intend to further unlawful conduct by the PKK or the LTTE.

We cannot avoid the constitutional issues in this litigation through plaintiffs' proposed interpretation of § 2339B.

We turn to the question whether the material-support statute, as applied to plaintiffs, is impermissibly vague under the Due Process Clause of the Fifth Amendment. . . . We have said that when a statute "interferes with the right of free speech or of association, a more stringent vagueness test should apply." "But 'perfect clarity and precise guidance have never been required even of regulations that restrict expressive activity.'"

Most of the activities in which plaintiffs seek to engage readily fall within the scope of the terms "training" and "expert advice or assistance." Plaintiffs want to "train members of [the] PKK on how to use humanitarian and international law to peacefully resolve disputes," and "teach PKK members how to petition various representative bodies such as the United Nations for relief." A person of ordinary intelligence would understand that instruction on resolving disputes through international law falls within the statute's definition of "training" because it imparts a "specific skill," not "general knowledge." Plaintiffs' activities also fall comfortably within the scope of "expert advice or assistance": A reasonable person would recognize that teaching the PKK how to petition for humanitarian relief before the United Nations involves advice derived from, as the statute puts it, "specialized knowledge." In fact, plaintiffs themselves have repeatedly used the terms "training" and "expert advice" throughout this litigation to describe their own proposed activities, demonstrating that these common terms readily and naturally cover plaintiffs' conduct.

We next consider whether the material-support statute, as applied to plaintiffs, violates the freedom of speech guaranteed by the First Amendment. Both plaintiffs and the Government take extreme positions on this question. Plaintiffs claim that Congress has banned their "pure political speech." It has not. Under the material-support statute, plaintiffs may say anything they wish on any topic. They may speak and write freely about the PKK and LTTE, the governments of Turkey and Sri Lanka, human rights, and international law. They may advocate before the United Nations. As the Government states: "The statute does not prohibit independent advocacy or expression of any kind." Congress has not, therefore, sought to suppress ideas or opinions in the form of "pure political speech." Rather, Congress has prohibited "material support," which most often does not take the form of speech at all. And when it does, the statute is carefully drawn to cover only a narrow category of speech to, under the direction of, or in coordination with foreign groups that the speaker knows to be terrorist organizations.

For its part, the Government takes the foregoing too far, claiming that the only thing truly at issue in this litigation is conduct, not speech. Section 2339B is directed at the fact of plaintiffs' interaction with the PKK and LTTE, the Government contends, and only incidentally burdens their expression. The Government argues that the proper standard of review is therefore the one set out in *United States v. O'Brien*, (1968). In that case, the Court rejected a First Amendment challenge to a conviction under a generally applicable prohibition on destroying draft cards, even though O'Brien had burned his card in protest against the draft. In so doing, we applied what we have since called "intermediate scrutiny," under which a "content-neutral regulation will be sustained under the First Amendment if it advances important governmental interests unrelated to the suppression of free speech and does not burden substantially more speech than necessary to further those interests."

The Government is wrong that the only thing actually at issue in this litigation is conduct, and therefore wrong to argue that *O'Brien* provides the correct standard of review. *O'Brien* does not provide the applicable standard for reviewing a content-based regulation of speech, and § 2339B regulates speech on the basis of its content. Plaintiffs want to speak to the PKK and the LTTE, and whether they may do so under § 2339B depends on what they say. If plaintiffs' speech to those groups imparts a "specific skill" or communicates advice derived from "specialized knowledge"—for example, training on the use of international law or advice on petitioning the United

Nations — then it is barred. On the other hand, plaintiffs' speech is not barred if it imparts only general or unspecialized knowledge.

Everyone agrees that the Government's interest in combating terrorism is an urgent objective of the highest order. Plaintiffs' complaint is that the ban on material support, applied to what they wish to do, is not "necessary to further that interest." The objective of combating terrorism does not justify prohibiting their speech, plaintiffs argue, because their support will advance only the legitimate activities of the designated terrorist organizations, not their terrorism.

Whether foreign terrorist organizations meaningfully segregate support of their legitimate activities from support of terrorism is an empirical question. When it enacted § 2339B in 1996, Congress made specific findings regarding the serious threat posed by international terrorism. One of those findings explicitly rejects plaintiffs' contention that their support would not further the terrorist activities of the PKK and LTTE: "[F]oreign organizations that engage in terrorist activity are so tainted by their criminal conduct that any contribution to such an organization facilitates that conduct."

Plaintiffs argue that the reference to "any contribution" in this finding meant only monetary support. There is no reason to read the finding to be so limited, particularly because Congress expressly prohibited so much more than monetary support in § 2339B. Congress's use of the term "contribution" is best read to reflect a determination that any form of material support furnished "to" a foreign terrorist organization should be barred, which is precisely what the material-support statute does. Indeed, when Congress enacted § 2339B, Congress simultaneously removed an exception . . . for the provision of material support in the form of "humanitarian assistance to persons not directly involved in" terrorist activity. That repeal demonstrates that Congress considered and rejected the view that ostensibly peaceful aid would have no harmful effects.

Material support meant to "promot[e] peaceable, lawful conduct," can further terrorism by foreign groups in multiple ways. "Material support" is a valuable resource by definition. Such support frees up other resources within the organization that may be put to violent ends. It also importantly helps lend legitimacy to foreign terrorist groups — legitimacy that makes it easier for those groups to persist, to recruit members, and to raise funds — all of which facilitate more terrorist attacks. "Terrorist organizations do not maintain organizational 'firewalls' that would prevent or deter . . . sharing and commingling of support and benefits." "[I]nvestigators have revealed how terrorist groups systematically conceal their activities behind charitable, social, and political fronts." "Indeed, some designated foreign terrorist organizations use social and political components to recruit personnel to carry out terrorist operations, and to provide support to criminal terrorists and their families in aid of such operations."

Providing foreign terrorist groups with material support in any form also furthers terrorism by straining the United States' relationships with its allies and undermining cooperative efforts between nations to prevent terrorist attacks. We see no reason to question Congress's finding that "international cooperation is required for an effective response to terrorism, as demonstrated by the numerous multilateral conventions in force providing universal prosecutive jurisdiction over persons involved in a variety of terrorist acts, including hostage taking, murder of an internationally protected person, and aircraft piracy and sabotage." The material-support statute furthers this international effort by prohibiting aid for foreign terrorist groups that harm the United States' partners abroad: "A number of designated foreign terrorist organizations have attacked moderate governments with which the United States has vigorously endeavored to maintain close and friendly relations," and those attacks "threaten [the] social, economic and political stability" of such governments.

At bottom, plaintiffs simply disagree with the considered judgment of Congress and the Executive that providing material support to a designated foreign terrorist organization—even seemingly benign support—bolsters the terrorist activities of that organization. That judgment, however, is entitled to significant weight, and we have persuasive evidence before us to sustain it. Given the sensitive interests in national security and foreign affairs at stake, the political branches have adequately substantiated their determination that, to serve the Government's interest in preventing terrorism, it was necessary to prohibit providing material support in the form of training, expert advice, personnel, and services to foreign terrorist groups, even if the supporters meant to promote only the groups' nonviolent ends.

We turn to the particular speech plaintiffs propose to undertake. First, plaintiffs propose to "train members of [the] PKK on how to use humanitarian and international law to peacefully resolve disputes." Congress can, consistent with the First Amendment, prohibit this direct training. It is wholly foreseeable that the PKK could use the "specific skill[s]" that plaintiffs propose to impart, as part of a broader strategy to promote terrorism. The PKK could, for example, pursue peaceful negotiation as a means of buying time to recover from short-term setbacks, lulling opponents into complacency, and ultimately preparing for renewed attacks. A foreign terrorist organization introduced to the structures of the international legal system might use the information to threaten, manipulate, and disrupt. This possibility is real, not remote.

Second, plaintiffs propose to "teach PKK members how to petition various representative bodies such as the United Nations for relief." The Government acts within First Amendment strictures in banning this proposed speech because it teaches the organization how to acquire "relief," which plaintiffs never define with any specificity, and which could readily include monetary aid. . . . Money is fungible, and Congress logically concluded that money a terrorist group such as the PKK obtains using the techniques plaintiffs propose to teach could be redirected to funding the group's violent activities.

Finally, plaintiffs propose to "engage in political advocacy on behalf of Kurds who live in Turkey," and "engage in political advocacy on behalf of Tamils who live in Sri Lanka." As explained above, plaintiffs do not specify their expected level of coordination with the PKK or LTTE or suggest what exactly their "advocacy" would consist of. Plaintiffs' proposals are phrased at such a high level of generality that they cannot prevail in this preenforcement challenge.

If only good can come from training our adversaries in international dispute resolution, presumably it would have been unconstitutional to prevent American citizens from training the Japanese Government on using international organizations and mechanisms to resolve disputes during World War II.... That view is not one the First Amendment requires us to embrace.

All this is not to say that any future applications of the material-support statute to speech or advocacy will survive First Amendment scrutiny. It is also not to say that any other statute relating to speech and terrorism would satisfy the First Amendment. In particular, we in no way suggest that a regulation of independent speech would pass constitutional muster, even if the Government were to show that such speech benefits foreign terrorist organizations. We also do not suggest that Congress could extend the same prohibition on material support at issue here to domestic organizations. We simply hold that, in prohibiting the particular forms of support that plaintiffs seek to provide to foreign terrorist groups, § 2339B does not violate the freedom of speech.

Plaintiffs' final claim is that the material-support statute violates their freedom of association under the First Amendment. Plaintiffs argue that the statute criminalizes the mere fact of their associating with the PKK and the LTTE, thereby running afoul of decisions like *De Jonge v. Oregon* (1937), and cases in which we have overturned sanctions for joining the Communist Party.

The Court of Appeals correctly rejected this claim because the statute does not penalize mere association with a foreign terrorist organization. As the Ninth Circuit put it: "The statute does not prohibit being a member of one of the designated groups or vigorously promoting and supporting the political goals of the group.... What [§ 2339B] prohibits is the act of giving material support...." Plaintiffs want to do the latter. Our decisions scrutinizing penalties on simple association or assembly are therefore inapposite.

The judgment of the United States Court of Appeals for the Ninth Circuit is affirmed in part and reversed in part, and the cases are remanded for further proceedings consistent with this opinion.

It is so ordered.

END OF OPINION

So, while the Court in *Rahman* said, "Words of this nature—ones that instruct, solicit, or persuade others to commit crimes of violence—violate the law and may be properly prosecuted regardless of whether they are uttered in private, or in a public speech, or in administering the duties of a religious ministry," the decision in *Humanitarian Law Project* holds that even words that seek to instruct or persuade others **not** to commit crimes of violence can still be lawfully criminalized if the audience is a terrorist organization.

Review Questions

1. Pastor Dan, leader of the KKK, gives a speech where he advocates the torture and murder of every Jew, black, and Muslim in America. His exact words are, "Our white race is under attack. Those sand monkeys, those kikes, those chinks, those niggers . . . they are the filth destroying this white Christian nation. Those animals should be tortured. They should be murdered. They should be exterminated until there isn't a single one left in this country." A police officer overhears his speech and arrests Pastor Dan. IRAC if Pastor Dan's First Amendment rights have been violated.

2. Pastor Dan is leading a KKK rally on a public street, and a black man walks past the sidewalk. Pastor Dan points at a black man and shouts at his Klan, "It is our duty to kill niggers like that one!" He is arrested and charged. He protests, claiming that he was just expressing his personal, deeply felt philosophy. IRAC this.

3. One morning at a mosque there is a guest speaker. He says to the crowd, "My brothers and sisters, we are at war with infidels. They want to destroy us and replace Islam with Christianity. This is a new crusade, and for our survival, we must fight back. You have a duty; to rise up and fight back against the infidels. As a good Muslim, you have a duty to kill non-believers." One of the congregation happens to be an off-duty police officer and in the middle of the speech, he arrests the speaker. IRAC if this arrest was lawful, or a violation of the First Amendment.

4. Steve is a member of the KKK. He has been planning on bombing a black church. He spends a lot of time and money in building a bomb. On the day in question, he gets cold feet and is unable to carry through with the bombing. He is having doubts whether or not this murder is the right thing to do. He goes to his Church to get some spiritual guidance from its leader, Pastor David Puke. He says, "Pastor Puke, for the past few months I've been building a bomb to blow up that nigger church in town. I was going to do it today, but now I'm not so sure this is the right thing to do." Pastor Puke replies, "Steve, it is the right thing to do. The white race is under attack and we need soldiers like yourself to go forth and do God's work." This gives Steve the confidence he needs to go out and carry out his bombing. It is a success and 28 people are killed. Steve is quickly arrested for murder. Pastor Puke is also under suspicion, but prosecutors are unsure if they can charge him with anything. What do you think? IRAC your answer.

Civil Liberties Issues and Profiling

The threat of terrorism raised another aspect of a concern that has challenged law enforcement and civil liberties advocates alike—to what degree is it proper to take an individual's (or a group's) racial and ethnic characteristics into consideration in an investigation? This practice is often referred to as "racial profiling."

For example, let's say a police officer sees a black man hanging around outside a 7/11. The police officer, believing blacks to be statistically more likely to commit crimes than whites, then decides to approach the black man and ask him why he is hanging around outside a 7/11. Here, the police officer used the person's race to consider whether or not the person might be a criminal. Another example involves airport security screenings. On occasion, airline passengers who "look Arab" are pulled aside for extra scrutiny during screenings.

Using race as one part of the description of a suspect, as simply one of several physical attributes, can be perfectly legal.

A description of a suspect is where the police believe that a crime has occurred and there is a description of a suspect that may include gender, height, clothes, and among other identifying characteristics, race or ethnicity. For example, let's say the police get a report that a 7/11 was robbed by a 20-year-old black man, six feet tall, wearing blue jeans and a white t-shirt. If the police spot an individual who fits this description, they could detain that individual. Or let's say there is an intelligence report that a 30-year-old Arab male affiliated with Al-Qaeda is going to pass through an airport. The police could then be on the lookout for a person matching this description.

What distinguishes description of a suspect from racial profiling is that in the former, a crime is already believed to have occurred, and there is information indicating who did it, which includes race. In cases of unlawful racial profiling, there is generally no other evidence that any crime has occurred. The police are simply using a racial identity to assume that this person fits a stereotype and, because of that, can commit a crime.

Racial profiling is illegal, in large measure, because of the equal protection clause of the Fourteenth Amendment of the U.S. Constitution:

> Section 1. All persons born or naturalized in the United States, and subject to the jurisdiction thereof, are citizens of the United States and of the State wherein they reside. No State shall make or enforce any law which shall abridge the privileges or immunities of citizens of the United States; nor shall any State deprive any person of life, liberty, or property, without due process of law; nor deny to any person within its jurisdiction the equal protection of the laws.

When racial profiling serves, not as one of many tools in an investigation, but as a basis or even substitute for investigation, those profiled have been denied due process and equal protection of the law. The following case demonstrates this principle.

Farag v. U.S., 587 F. Supp. 2d 436 (2008)*

On August 22, 2004, weeks away from the third anniversary of 9/11, plaintiffs Tarik Farag ("Farag") and Amro Elmasry ("Elmasry"), both Arabs, flew from San Diego to New York's John F. Kennedy Airport ("JFK") on American Airlines Flight 236. They

---

* The case has been heavily edited and paraphrased by the authors for clarity. See disclaimer in introduction.

claim that when they deplaned they were met by at least ten armed police officers in SWAT gear with shotguns and police dogs, ordered to raise their hands, frisked, handcuffed and taken to a police station, where they were placed in jail cells; they were not released until about four hours later, after having been interrogated at length during their imprisonment regarding suspected terrorist surveillance activity aboard the plane. The investigation yielded absolutely no evidence of wrongdoing.

Alleging that they were unlawfully seized and imprisoned, Farag and Elmasry have each [sued] FBI Special Agent William Ryan Plunkett ("Plunkett") and New York City Police Department Detective Thomas P. Smith ("Smith"), two counterterrorism agents responsible for plaintiffs' seizures, detentions and interrogations. Plaintiffs also sue the United States . . . for Plunkett's and Smith's allegedly tortious conduct. . . .

The Government considers this a case of first impression for the federal courts because it presents important questions concerning the scope of legitimate law enforcement activity in response to suspected terrorism-related conduct by passengers on board a domestic commercial aircraft. It contends (1) that the agents merely conducted a valid Terry stop when they seized, detained and questioned plaintiffs for approximately four hours, or (2) alternatively, if the Court determines that the agents arrested plaintiffs, that there was probable cause to do so. In either case, the Government takes the position that the Arabic ethnicity of the plaintiffs is and was a relevant factor in the Fourth Amendment analysis.

The Court rejects the Government's contention that plaintiffs' ethnicity can be a factor in determining the validity of plaintiffs' seizures and detentions . . .

I. Events at San Diego International Airport

Farag and Elmasry, long-time friends, were flying from San Diego International Airport to JFK after vacationing in California. Both were born in Egypt, but Farag, 36, had moved to the United States in 1971 at age five and later became an American citizen. He was a retired New York City police officer, and was then employed by the United States Bureau of Prisons as a corrections officer. Elmasry, 37, was an Egyptian citizen; he was employed in Egypt by General Electric as an area sales manager for its Africa-East Mediterranean region, and had a valid United States visa.

After plaintiffs boarded the plane, they took neighboring but non-adjacent seats: Farag was seated in 17E, a middle seat on the right side of the aisle, and Elmasry was seated in 18A, a window seat on the left side, one row behind Farag. Smith and Plunkett were seated nearby: Smith was in seat 17A, a window seat immediately in front of Elmasry and in the same row as Farag, but on the other side of the aisle, and Plunkett was one seat away in 17C, the aisle seat. The seat between Smith and Plunkett, 17B, was vacant. Plaintiffs did not know that Smith and Plunkett were counterterrorism agents.

Plaintiffs placed their carry-on luggage in the overhead compartments above their respective seats, and, once seated, "talked to each other, over the heads of the other passengers, in a mixture of Arabic and English." While the plane was at the gate, Elmasry entered the aisle and asked Plunkett if he would be willing to shift over one seat to 17B, the center seat, and let Elmasry sit in 17C, the aisle seat. Plunkett declined.

After Elmasry left his seat to speak to Plunkett, a female passenger seated next to Elmasry in 18B had stretched her legs across Elmasry's seat. After Plunkett refused Elmasry's request, Elmasry, rather than returning to his seat, asked Smith and Plunkett if he could sit between them, in the vacant seat 17B. Smith and Plunkett agreed. According to the agents' contemporaneous incident report, Plunkett thought it "unusual that anyone would move from an exit row window seat to an exit row middle seatin between two large men," but the report also acknowledges that Elmasry had explained that he wanted to change seats "so he could be 'close to his friend.'"

Even after Elmasry moved to 17B, he and Farag still "were only able to converse with each other over the heads of other passengers." Once again, they spoke "in a mixture of Arabic and English," but were now "speaking loudly." At some unspecified point, Farag fell asleep.

II. Events During the Flight

As the plane took off—as well as at various other times throughout the flight—Smith and Plunkett noticed Elmasry looking at his watch. According to the two agents, Elmasry appeared to be "timing" various events during the flight, such as takeoff, attainment of level flight, and the commencement of the meal service.

About half an hour after takeoff, Elmasry left his seat to go to the lavatory at the rear of the plane. On his way back, Elmasry spoke with a flight attendant, asking if there were two adjacent empty seats to which he and Farag might move. Elmasry then returned to the seat between Smith and Plunkett and fell asleep. He awoke during the meal service; Farag had already awakened some time earlier. Once the meal had been served and plaintiffs had eaten, the flight attendant with whom Elmasry had spoken approached him in his seat between the agents and "told him that there were two empty seats at the back of the plane for him and Farag." Elmasry entered the aisle, leaned over to Farag, and spoke a "very short sentence" in a mixture of Arabic and English. Plaintiffs moved to the two seats at the rear of the plane but did not take their carry-on bags with them.

About an hour and a half before landing, Smith and Plunkett decided that Farag and Elmasry should be detained and questioned when the plane landed because the agents were concerned that plaintiffs may be conducting terrorist surveillance or probing operations. Plunkett explained to the flight's captain that "two men of Middle Eastern descent" were "acting suspicious" in that "they were talking back and forth in Arabic" and that "one of them got up from his assigned seat and sat between Smith and Plunkett." Although the agents "did not feel that these two individuals posed an immediate threat to the flight," they nonetheless asked the captain to "request a team of officers to meet the approaching aircraft at the gate and to inform them that two Middle Eastern males will be stopped and questioned about their actions during the flight."

Elmasry and Farag remained at the back of the plane until shortly before landing. After an announcement was made that landing was imminent and the passengers were told to fasten their seat belts, Elmasry returned to seat 17B, between Smith and Plunkett, where he had previously been sitting; Farag sat in Elmasry's original seat, 18A, directly behind Smith.

Once the plane landed, at approximately 11:30 p.m. local time, Smith and Plunkett again saw Elmasry check his watch. The plane took between thirty and forty-five minutes to reach the gate. At some point during that interval, Elmasry took out his cellular phone and paged through his address book, deleting five or six entries. Meanwhile, Farag made two or three "short" calls on his cellular phone; he spoke in English.

While the plane was taxiing, Smith asked Elmasry, who was seated beside him, where he was from and what he did for a living. Elmasry truthfully told Smith that he was from Egypt, that he was employed by General Electric, and that he was in the United States on vacation. Elmasry then asked Smith what he did for a living; Smith falsely told Elmasry that he worked for the delivery company DHL. Elmasry remarked that Smith's job must involve a lot of traveling; Smith said that it did. Elmasry then told Smith that in his own job, he, too, "was always traveling."

III. Events at JFK

Once the plane reached the gate, Plunkett went to the front of the aircraft; soon thereafter, the passengers began deplaning. According to the agents, "Plaintiffs were detained as they exited the aircraft." As Elmasry recalled events, he retrieved his carry-on bag from the overhead bin and began to deplane, with Farag close behind. Smith and Plunkett had already deplaned. Upon exiting the aircraft, Elmasry saw uniformed police officers standing in the jetway. Plunkett was signaling toward him and Farag. One of the uniformed officers took hold of Elmasry and escorted him into the terminal; another officer did the same to Farag. No one pointed a gun at either plaintiff.

According to Farag, on the other hand, after the passengers had begun deplaning, five or six plainclothes Port Authority police officers boarded and identified themselves, speaking in a "conversational tone"; their badges were displayed on their jacket pockets. The Port Authority officers seized plaintiffs at their seats, grabbing them by their arms; they did not have their guns drawn and did not tell plaintiffs that they were under arrest. The officers asked for plaintiffs' carry-on bags and escorted them off the aircraft while Smith and Plunkett "were standing there."

Upon entering the terminal, plaintiffs saw a team of uniformed Port Authority police officers "in SWAT gear"; some had police dogs. The officers were "carrying shotguns," but no officer pointed a gun at either plaintiff. According to Farag, these officers formed a perimeter around the gate area. Farag and Elmasry were separated and taken to locations thirty-five to forty feet apart. Each was accompanied by two officers (Farag by Smith and Plunkett, and Elmasry by two Port Authority officers); a fifth officer walked back and forth between Farag and Elmasry. While at these two locations, Farag and Elmasry were ordered to raise their hands and were frisked.

Smith then began questioning Farag, who provided Smith with identification and told him truthfully that he was a retired New York City police officer and a federal corrections officer employed by the Bureau of Prisons. Farag mentioned to Smith that "after 9/11, when the CIA had come into the Federal Bureau of Prisons, Farag's supervisors had asked him to translate documents, to translate tapes." He also told Smith that he had "had guns pointed at him as a police officer" with the NYPD. Farag explained that during this conversation with Smith he was "scared, frightened, paranoid, and his mind was racing," that he was "jittery" and "shaking" and "his speech was not calm," and that he was in "a complete state of shock" and was "totally confused." Elmasry, who could see Farag at that time, observed that Farag was "nervous," that he looked agitated and jumpy, and that Farag raised his voice at times.

"At some point thereafter," the police officers handcuffed Farag and then Elmasry. Although Elmasry recalls being handcuffed "approximately fifteen minutes after being brought into the terminal," Plunkett, in his contemporaneous report, stated that plaintiffs were "handcuffed upon exiting the aircraft."

During this time in the terminal, none of the officers pointed their guns at plaintiffs, struck them, or called them any derogatory names. Farag testified that "all of the law enforcement officers who were on the scene acted in a professional manner."

IV. Events at the Port Authority Police Station

After they were handcuffed, Farag and Elmasry were taken in separate police cars to a Port Authority police station between five and fifteen minutes away. Upon their arrival, they were placed in separate holding cells. Elmasry's handcuffs were removed as soon as he was placed in the cell; Farag spent "a little while" inside his cell before his handcuffs were removed.

After thirty to forty-five minutes in his cell, Elmasry was taken to an interrogation room for questioning by Plunkett and a plainclothes Port Authority officer. The questioning lasted approximately two-and-a-half to three hours. "They would question him for fifteen to twenty minutes, then leave the room for twenty minutes, then question him again, then leave the room, again, several times," and "one time they questioned him for forty-five minutes to one hour." The Port Authority officer spoke "loudly" and in an "aggressive" manner. Elmasry was asked not just about his relationship with Farag, his seat changes, his glancing at his watch and his deletion of numbers from his cellular phone, but also about his religious beliefs, items in his luggage, his employment with General Electric, the stamps in his passport and various names and notes in his address book. Plunkett also viewed photographs stored in Elmasry's digital camera. At the end of the questioning, Plunkett told Elmasry that he had not been arrested, but merely "stopped for interrogation." Plunkett's contemporaneous notes state that Elmasry was "cooperative during the entire interview and showed no signs of hostility."

Farag remained in his cell for more than an hour. While he waited, Farag asked Smith twice if he could call a lawyer; "Smith said Farag could if he wanted to, but did not arrange for him to do so." Farag was then removed from his cell; he did not ask again to contact a lawyer. He was taken to an interrogation room where he was questioned by Smith for about two hours. He was asked not just about his relationship with Elmasry, their vacation together, and his seat changes on the airplane, but also about his religious practices, his employment background, whether he had any connections with anti-American groups, and whether he "could get close to the terrorists that he translated for at the Bureau of Prisons." Smith also examined photographs on Farag's digital camera.

In their report, the agents wrote that "during their questioning of Farag and Elmasry" they requested various background checks from the FBI, the CIA and the Bureau of Immigration and Customs Enforcement; these background checks confirmed that Farag had indeed been a New York City police officer and was then employed as a corrections officer with the Federal Bureau of Prisons. The record does not reflect whether these requests were made while plaintiffs were being questioned at the terminal or at some specific time during their jailhouse interrogation; nor does it reflect how long it took to get responses.

Farag and Elmasry were released at approximately 4:00 a.m., about four and a half hours after they had been taken off the plane. At no point during their detentions or interrogations did any officer strike or threaten them; nor did any officer use profanity or ethnic slurs.

The Commencement of the Litigation

The Government lists the following actions of Farag and Elmasry on the aircraft, which, they argue, supported the agents' "concern that plaintiffs may have been conducting terrorist surveillance or probing operations," and justified the agents' seizures, detentions, and interrogations of plaintiffs:

- At the beginning of the flight, despite sitting on opposite sides of the aisle, plaintiffs spoke to each other over the heads of other passengers in a mixture of Arabic and English;

- Elmasry made an allegedly "unusual" initial seat change "from a window seat to a middle seat between two other male passengers";

- After Elmasry changed seats, he and Farag talked to each other "loudly" over the heads of other passengers in a mixture of Arabic and English;

- Elmasry looked at his watch when the plane took off, when the plane landed, and at other points during the flight;

- After the meal service, Elmasry "got out of his seat, went into the aisle, leaned over to Farag, and spoke a 'very short sentence' to Farag in a mixture of Arabic and English";

- Immediately thereafter, plaintiffs moved together to the back of the plane, and did not take their carry-on luggage with them;

- Plaintiffs got up to return to the front of the cabin at the very end of the flight, after the "fasten seatbelt" indicator was lit;

- Upon returning to the front of the plane, Farag did not sit in his original seat (17E), but rather, in Elmasry's original seat (18A), which was located directly behind Smith;

- After the plane landed, Elmasry took out his cellular phone and deleted five or six numbers;

- While the plane was taxiing to the gate, Elmasry told Smith that "he is from Egypt, that he works for GE, and that 'his work is always traveling.'"

- See Gov't Br. at 14-16.

- The Government lists the following events that took place in the terminal at JFK, after plaintiffs were first detained, as further support for the agents' actions:

- Farag told Smith that "after 9/11, when the CIA had c[o]me into the Federal Bureau of Prisons, my supervisors had asked me to translate documents, to translate tapes, [and] in fact I did translate tapes";

- Farag told Smith that "I had guns pointed at me as a police officer";

- While Farag was telling these things to Smith, Farag was "jittery" and "shaking" and "his speech was not calm." He appeared "nervous" and seemed "jumpy and agitated," and he raised his voice.

DISCUSSION

II. Analysis

A. Were Plaintiffs Arrested?

Preliminarily, a plaintiff asserting a violation of the Fourth Amendment "must... show some deprivation of liberty consistent with the concept of 'seizure.'" *Singer v. Fulton County Sheriff* (2d Cir.1995). There is no question but that plaintiffs were subjected to a "seizure" cognizable under the Fourth Amendment, since Smith, Plunkett and the Port Authority officers (acting under Smith and Plunkett's authorization) "by means of physical force or show of authority... restrained the liberty" of plaintiffs, *Florida v. Bostick* (1991) (quoting *Terry*), and because under these circumstances, "a reasonable person would [not] feel free to decline the officers' requests or otherwise terminate the encounter...."

Nor can there be a serious question but that the plaintiffs were subject to a de facto arrest, notwithstanding the Government's contention that the entire episode was nothing more than a *Terry* stop. Each of three sets of factors standing alone — not to mention collectively — sufficed to convert the seizures into de facto arrests: (1) the officers' show of force and restraint of plaintiffs' movement at the terminal; (2) the transportation of plaintiffs to the police station, the confinement of plaintiffs in jail cells, and the custodial interrogation of plaintiffs; and (3) the duration of plaintiffs' confinements and interrogations.

B. Was There Probable Cause for the Arrests?

Probable cause to arrest exists "where the arresting officer has 'knowledge or reasonably trustworthy information of facts and circumstances that are sufficient to warrant a person of reasonable caution in the belief that the person to be arrested has committed or is committing a crime.'" Only "those facts available to the officer at the time of the arrest and immediately before it" may be considered. Moreover, probable cause is to be assessed on an objective basis; thus, "an arresting officer's state of mind (except for the facts that he knows) is irrelevant." The standard is a "fluid and contextual" one, requiring "examination of the totality of the circumstances of a given arrest."

"The Supreme Court has repeatedly stated that the probable-cause standard is 'a practical, nontechnical conception that deals with the factual and practical considerations of everyday life on which reasonable and prudent men, not legal technicians, act.'" A court must make its evaluation "from the perspective of a reasonable police officer in light of his training and experience."

1. Was There Probable Cause Based on Non-Ethnic Factors Alone?

The Government contends that even if the Court does not consider that plaintiffs were Arabs and that they were at times conversing in Arabic, the other factors relied upon by the Government constitute probable cause. The Court disagrees. The Government tacks together a number of benign circumstances in the apparent belief that their numerosity will carry the day . . . Yet, even viewing all of these circumstances as a whole, it cannot rationally be held that if, hypothetically, the plaintiffs were two Caucasian traveling companions speaking French, or another non-Arabic language which the agents did not understand, "a person of reasonable caution" would have believed that they were engaged in terrorist surveillance.

Principally, the Government relies on the agents' observations of plaintiffs' seat-changing and Elmasry's "timing" events with his watch. But the agents acknowledged in their incident report that they knew the plaintiffs were friends; quite logically, friends would want to sit as close to each other as possible, and they would also logically return to the vicinity of their original seats when the plane was landing to retrieve their carry-on luggage. As for Elmasry looking at his watch upon takeoff, landing, and at various other times during the flight, the proportion of airline passengers who do this is probably higher than the proportion who do not. A factual condition which is consistent with criminal activity will not predicate reasonable suspicion, if that factual condition occurs even more frequently among the law abiding public.

The Government also argues that Elmasry's deletion of five or six telephone numbers from his cellular phone while he waited for the plane to reach the gate "could have been interpreted as destroying evidence. This conclusion, however, is utter speculation; the Government does not assert that Elmasry made any telephone calls during or after the flight, and the record gives no indication that Elmasry suspected he was about to be caught sufficient to imbue his acts with a suggestion of guilt.

Most troubling, the heavy reliance which the Government places on the plaintiffs' speaking "loudly" to each other over the heads of other passengers and otherwise drawing attention to themselves is counterintuitive: it simply makes no sense that if Elmasry were a terrorist on a surveillance mission, he would speak "loudly" across the aisle to his companion before takeoff, seek out and converse with the flight attendant, relocate to a seat "between two large men," or volunteer to one of those "large men" that he was from Egypt. What terrorist engaged in surveillance activity would behave so conspicuously? One would expect that such activity would be characterized by secrecy.

Nor could plaintiffs' conduct in the terminal be reasonably viewed as an escalation of events that would then have given rise to probable cause. The Court fails to grasp the significance of Farag telling Smith that because he spoke Arabic he had been asked by the Bureau of Prisons to translate tapes, and that guns had been pointed at him as a police officer—both logical consequences of his past and present employments.

Reliance on Farag's nervousness and raised voice is also problematic . . . [A]pparent nervousness is of minimal probative value, given that many, if not most, individuals can become nervous or agitated when detained by police officers . . . [I]t is common for most people to exhibit signs of nervousness when confronted by a law enforcement officer whether or not the person is currently engaged in criminal activity. The fact that a person was acting 'a little nervous' has limited significance since most citizens, whether innocent or guilty, are likely to exhibit some signs of nervousness when confronted by the police. Moreover, Farag's "nervous" response to an unlawful show of force could not retroactively justify plaintiffs' arrests. While the government argues that the arrest was supported by the defendant's nervous behavior, this behavior occurred after he was illegally seized . . . In sum, viewed in the light most favorable to plaintiffs, the non-ethnic factors cited by the Government do not constitute probable cause.

3. Can Plaintiffs' Arab Ethnicity Serve as a Probable Cause Factor?

The Government argues that plaintiffs' Arab ethnicity and use of the Arabic language are relevant factors in the probable-cause, as well as the reasonable-suspicion, calculus because "all of the persons who participated in the 9/11 terrorist attacks were Middle Eastern males," . . . and "the United States continues to face a very real threat of domestic terrorism from Islamic terrorists."

The Government's position has some superficial appeal. After all, probable cause, and undoubtedly reasonable suspicion as well, is, once again, "a practical, nontechnical conception that deals with the factual and practical considerations of everyday life,'" and what American would not acknowledge that everyday life has changed in myriad ways, both great and small, since 9/11? Indeed, earlier this fall, the Second Circuit upheld a government program "that singled out male immigrants from two dozen predominantly Arab and Muslim countries for accelerated deportation after the Sept. 11, 2001, terrorist attacks" finding it a "plainly rational attempt to enhance national security." *Rajah v. Mukasey* (2d Cir. Sept. 24, 2008).

Rajah, however, did not deal with ethnicity in the context of probable cause or reasonable suspicion. Indeed, the Government recognizes that "there is no single precedent that resolves this case," which presumably accounts for its view of the case as one of first impression. Nevertheless, the interplay between race and the Fourth Amendment is not a recent phenomenon; courts and commentators have long struggled with the issue of whether and to what extent race can be a relevant consideration in the decision to detain an individual. That legal backdrop obviously bears on the Court's analysis here.

At the outset, it should be understood that the Fourth Amendment—unlike the Equal Protection Clause—imposes no a priori restriction on race-based governmental action. As the Supreme Court noted:

> The Constitution prohibits selective enforcement of the law based on considerations such as race. But the constitutional basis for objecting to intentionally discriminatory application of laws is the Equal Protection Clause, not the Fourth Amendment. Subjective intentions play no role in ordinary, probable-cause Fourth Amendment analysis.

Though the Fourth Amendment permits a pretext arrest, if otherwise supported by probable cause, the Equal Protection Clause still imposes restraint on impermissibly class-based discriminations.

Although the Fourth Amendment does not single out race as a matter of special concern, it does impose a general requirement that any factor considered in a decision to detain must contribute to "a particularized and objective basis for suspecting the particular person stopped of criminal activity." Race cannot affect probable cause or reasonable suspicion calculations unless it is statistically related to suspected criminal activity. Whether such a relationship exists in a given case is necessarily a fact-specific inquiry; nevertheless, the case law reveals some recurring themes.

Perhaps the least controversial use of race in the context of the Fourth Amendment is its use as an identifying factor. If the victim of, or witness to, a crime describes the perpetrator as a young white male wearing a white shirt and black pants, there can be little doubt that law enforcement officials may consider that description in deciding whom to detain, even though the description is based, in part, on race. Witnesses and victims frequently describe criminal perpetrators by the color of their skin. Where a suspect has been described by his race, it is a characteristic which may properly be used as one element of identification.

Courts have also confronted the so-called "racial incongruity" argument—i.e., that race is indicative of criminality when members of a particular race seem "out of place" in a particular location. Some courts—including the Second Circuit—have sidestepped the issue by finding probable cause or reasonable suspicion based on other, non-racial factors. For example, in *United States v. Magda* (S.D.N.Y.1976), the district court found reasonable suspicion lacking where "the reason for the stop was primarily because of an observed exchange between a young black man and a young white man in an area of the city defined as 'narcotics prone.'" The Second Circuit reversed, concluding that the circumstances and location of the transaction were sufficient to create reasonable suspicion; the circuit court made no mention of the race of the participants. see also *United States v. Richard* (3d Cir.1976) (noting that "the presence of two black males cruising in a car in a predominately white neighborhood is, by itself, insufficient cause for a belief that those persons have participated in a recent crime in the neighborhood," but reversing suppression order based on other factors); *State v. Wilson* (La. 2000) ("The officer made clear that while racial incongruity 'did factor in,' he considered other circumstances more important in his decision to make an investigatory stop.").

Those courts that have squarely addressed the incongruity argument have uniformly rejected it. The presence of an individual of one race in an area inhabited primarily by members of another race is not a sufficient basis to suggest that crime is afoot . . . It is the law that racial incongruity, i.e., a person of any race being allegedly 'out of place' in a particular geographic area, should never constitute a finding of reasonable suspicion of criminal activity . . . The fact that a black person is merely walking in a predominantly white neighborhood does not indicate that he has committed, is committing, or is about to commit a crime . . .

But this case involves neither identification nor racial incongruity. Rather, defendants' argument that plaintiffs' Arab ethnicity is a relevant consideration is premised on the notion that Arabs have a greater propensity than non-Arabs toward criminal activity—namely, terrorism.

Even granting that all of the participants in the 9/11 attacks were Arabs, and even assuming arguendo that a large proportion of would-be anti-American terrorists are Arabs, the likelihood that any given airline passenger of Arab ethnicity is a terrorist is so negligible that Arab ethnicity has no probative value in a particularized reasonable-suspicion or probable-cause determination . . . Reasonable suspicion requires particularized suspicion, and in an area in which a large number of people share a specific characteristic, that characteristic casts too wide a net to play any part in a particularized reasonable suspicion determination.

In *United States v. Swindle*, a drug-possession case, the circuit court held that an African-American defendant's Fourth Amendment rights were violated when he was stopped by the police "simply for being a black man in a high-crime area driving a car that the wanted fugitive had previously been seen 'near.'" The circuit court noted that the defendant's race matched the fugitive's, but stated that race was "the only obvious physical characteristic the men shared," suggesting that race—while a valid identifying factor—cannot serve as the only identifying factor. The court then stated: "courts agree that race, when considered by itself and sometimes even in tandem with other factors, does not generate reasonable suspicion for a stop." This use of the qualifier "sometimes even in tandem with other factors," is unexplained; it may or may not simply be that the court intended to signify that the use of race in the reasonable-suspicion calculus is prohibited except when it serves as one of several identifying factors.

In *Almeida-Amaral v. Gonzales*, the Second Circuit, discussing when a Fourth Amendment violation based on an illegal border-patrol stop would justify suppression of evidence obtained as a result of the stop in a civil deportation proceeding, noted that, "were there evidence that the stop was based on race, the violation would be egregious, and the exclusionary rule would apply." "A seizure may qualify as an egregious violation if the stop was based on race (or some other grossly improper consideration)." While the circuit court did not discuss stops based partially on race, this sweeping condemnation of racial considerations may well be taken as an indication that the Second Circuit would reject the Government's contention that plaintiffs' ethnicity could be considered as one factor in the Fourth Amendment calculus.

Although the question whether race or ethnicity may be used as one factor among others in evaluating reasonable suspicion or probable cause (outside of the identification scenario, and absent any compelling statistical evidence) remains unresolved by either the Supreme Court or the Second Circuit, there is a significant body of pre-9/11 precedent concluding that race is not indicative of criminal propensity. The Ninth Circuit's decision in *Montero-Camargo* is one example; although the court held that there were sufficient non-ethnic factors to constitute reasonable suspicion to stop the defendants, the majority rejected the notion that "reliance in part upon the Hispanic appearance of the three defendants," concluding that "Hispanic appearance is, in general, of such little probative value that it may not be considered as a relevant factor where particularized or individualized suspicion is required." Similarly, in *United States v. Clay*, the Eighth Circuit held that the defendant's race, considered together with several other factors, did not create reasonable suspicion for a *Terry* stop, stating that "although color of skin is an identifying factor, this court has consistently rejected the use of race in combination with other factors to justify investigative searches and seizures."

In *United States v. Ruiz*, a Utah district court held that no seizure cognizable under the Fourth Amendment had occurred, but nevertheless stated that, while race may be used to identify a suspect, "general circumstances of a person's race or ethnicity are not a proper factor in determining reasonable suspicion or probable cause," noting that "the overwhelming majority of Hispanics are not involved in drug trafficking or any other criminal endeavor." Various state courts have come to similar conclusions.

The federal and state-court precedent cited above clearly evidences what has been described as an increasing "hostility to the use of race as a basis for police action under the Fourth Amendment."

There is no doubt that the specter of 9/11 looms large over this case. Although this is the first post-9/11 case to address whether race may be used to establish criminal propensity under the Fourth Amendment, the Court cannot subscribe to the notion that in the wake of 9/11 this may now be permissible. As the Second Circuit recently admonished, "the strength of our system of constitutional rights derives from the steadfast protection of those rights in both normal and unusual times."

The Court fully recognizes the gravity of the situation that confronts investigative officials of the United States as a consequence of the 9/11 attack, and that the mindset of airline travelers has understandably been altered by 9/11. This justifiable apprehension must be assuaged by ensuring that security is strictly enforced, and by the passage of time without, hopefully, other episodic affronts to our country; but fear cannot be a factor to allow for the evisceration of the bedrock principle of our Constitution that no one can be arrested without probable cause that a crime has been committed.

END OF OPINION

In the opinion, the court suggested that had anyone except "Arabs" conducted themselves on an airplane the way Farag and his companion did, no one would have batted an eye. However, given the stereotype of the Arab terrorist, when these law enforcement officers saw "Arabs" acting the way they did on the plane, they presumed the two were engaged in unlawful behavior. Attributing suspicion of a crime to a person merely because of an identification with a certain racial or ethnic group is unlawful racial profiling, violating the equal protection clause of the Fourteenth Amendment.

Racial profiling most frequently comes up under the context of "stop-and-frisk" policies. As you should recall from Chapter 2, under the law announced by the Supreme Court in *Terry v. Ohio*, where the police have reasonable suspicion that a person is involved in criminal conduct and might be armed, it is lawful for police to frisk a person. Although this basis for a stop is lawful, in practice it has often been used as a substitute for evidence, not a basis for further inquiry based on evidence. It is often claimed (and, unfortunately, often proven) that police disproportionately engage in stop-and-frisk with minorities more than whites, implying a wrongful perception that persons can be suspected of engaging in criminal conduct just because they are black or Hispanic.

Review Questions

Use an IRAC analysis to consider whether the actions of the police are appropriate in each set of facts.

1. A bomb explodes in NYC, and people are running around screaming. A police officer develops a suspicion that a nearby Arab-looking male is responsible. The police officer calculates in his head: 12.5% chance the man committed the terrorist act by his presence at the scene, plus 12.5% chance the man committed the crime because of his body language which looks not completely shocked by the mayhem. Still, this isn't much to go on. The office then adds another 25% chance the man committed the crime based on the fact that this is an Arab in a neighborhood with few Arabs, and, statistically speaking, the enemy in the Global War on Terror are mostly Arabs. By taking the man's ethnic identity into account, the police officer reaches 50% probability in his head that the man took part in the terror attack and arrests him based on probable cause.

2. In an area of NYC with very few Muslims, a bomb explodes in a hotel lobby. Immediately afterward, a clerk reports having witnessed an individual who looked "Muslim" wearing blue jeans and a polo shirt leave a package in the lobby. An All Points Bulletin (APB) is immediately put out to be on the lookout for a Muslim male in blue jeans and a polo shirt. Fifteen minutes after the explosion, a police officer spots a man who looks Muslim wearing blue jeans and a polo shirt a few blocks from the scene. Taking into account the jeans at 12.5%, the polo shirt at 12.5%, and the fact that he looks "Muslim" at 25%, the officer gets to 50% and arrests this individual. At trial, the officer is asked, "Did you notice that this man is Muslim?" The officer responds, "I did. That's half the reason why I arrested him." The defense makes

a motion that evidence found subsequent to arrest be dismissed because this was racial profiling.

The policy of "stop and frisk" involves a relatively brief detention so the police can perform a very specific investigation—one based on the safety of the officer. The unlawful arrest and detention in the *Farang* case, while more egregious, was still relatively brief. What about a longer detention, again based not on evidence of actual wrongdoing but on ethnic and racial considerations alone? Our country faced this issue in the early days of WWII.

Internment of Japanese-Americans during World War II

During World War II, President Roosevelt ordered all persons of Japanese ancestry who resided near the Pacific coast to be interred for the duration of the war. These people were never charged of any crime, nor were they even alleged to have committed a crime. It was simply asserted by the government that there were some among the population who might have held loyalties to Japan and presumably would try to harm the U.S. war effort. Since it would be difficult, if not impossible, to tell exactly who of the many Japanese-Americans would actually be subversive, all Japanese people would have to be interred. As a result, roughly 100,000 Japanese-Americans were taken from their homes and detained in rudimentary camps for the duration of the war. Although a large number (approximately 10,000) of German- and Italian-Americans were also detained, these detainees were given a hearing and some due process prior to their detention. Japanese-Americans were given no such due process.

The legality of interring all people of Japanese origin—including citizens—was considered by the U.S. Supreme Court in 1944 (during the war), which held that the action was a lawful exercise of the president's war powers. In retrospect, the decision is considered among the most shameful ever released by the court. It is an important opinion in American legal history, and one which demonstrates how ideals of justice and the law can be cast aside in times of emergency.

<u>Korematsu v. United States, 323 U.S. 214 (1944)</u>*

The petitioner, an American citizen of Japanese descent, was convicted in a federal district court for remaining in San Leandro, California, a "Military Area," contrary to Civilian Exclusion Order No. 34 of the Commanding General of the Western Command, U.S. Army, which directed that, after May 9, 1942, all persons of Japanese ancestry should be excluded from that area. No question was raised as to petitioner's loyalty to the United States.

It should be noted, to begin with, that all legal restrictions which curtail the civil rights of a single racial group are immediately suspect. That is not to say that all such restrictions are unconstitutional. It is to say that courts must subject them to the

---

* The case has been heavily edited and paraphrased by the authors for clarity. See disclaimer in introduction.

most rigid scrutiny. Pressing public necessity may sometimes justify the existence of such restrictions; racial antagonism never can.

In the instant case, prosecution of the petitioner was begun by information charging violation of an Act of Congress, of March 21, 1942, 56 Stat. 173, which provides that

> ... whoever shall enter, remain in, leave, or commit any act in any military area or military zone prescribed, under the authority of an Executive order of the President, by the Secretary of War, or by any military commander designated by the Secretary of War, contrary to the restrictions applicable to any such area or zone or contrary to the order of the Secretary of War or any such military commander, shall, if it appears that he knew or should have known of the existence and extent of the restrictions or order and that his act was in violation thereof, be guilty of a misdemeanor and upon conviction shall be liable to a fine of not to exceed $5,000 or to imprisonment for not more than one year, or both, for each offense.

Exclusion Order No. 34, which the petitioner knowingly and admittedly violated, was one of a number of military orders and proclamations, all of which were substantially based upon Executive Order No. 9066. That order, issued after we were at war with Japan, declared that

> "the successful prosecution of the war requires every possible protection against espionage and against sabotage to national defense material, national defense premises, and national defense utilities..."

One of the series of orders and proclamations, a curfew order, which, like the exclusion order here, was promulgated pursuant to Executive Order 9066, subjected all persons of Japanese ancestry in prescribed West Coast military areas to remain in their residences from 8 p.m. to 6 a.m. As is the case with the exclusion order here, that prior curfew order was designed as a "protection against espionage and against sabotage." In *Hirabayashi v. United States*, we sustained a conviction obtained for violation of the curfew order imposed on persons of Japanese origin living in the US. The *Hirabayashi* conviction and this one thus rest on the same 1942 Congressional Act and the same basic executive and military orders, all of which orders were aimed at the twin dangers of espionage and sabotage.

The 1942 Act was attacked in the *Hirabayashi* case as an unconstitutional delegation of power; it was contended that the curfew order and other orders on which it rested were beyond the war powers of the Congress, the military authorities, and of the President, as Commander in Chief of the Army, and, finally, that to apply the curfew order against none but citizens of Japanese ancestry amounted to a constitutionally prohibited discrimination solely on account of race. To these questions, we gave the serious consideration which their importance justified. We upheld the curfew order as an exercise of the power of the government to take steps necessary to prevent espionage and sabotage in an area threatened by Japanese attack.

In the light of the principles we announced in the *Hirabayashi* case, we disagree with the claim that it was beyond the war power of Congress and the Executive to exclude those of Japanese ancestry from the West Coast war area at the time they did. True, exclusion from the area in which one's home is located is a far greater deprivation than constant confinement to the home from 8 p.m. to 6 a.m. Nothing short of apprehension by the proper military authorities of the gravest imminent danger to the public safety can constitutionally justify either. But exclusion from a threatened area, no less than curfew, has a definite and close relationship to the prevention of espionage and sabotage. The military authorities, charged with the primary responsibility of defending our shores, concluded that curfew provided inadequate protection and ordered exclusion. They did so, as pointed out in our *Hirabayashi* opinion, in accordance with Congressional authority to the military to say who should, and who should not, remain in the threatened areas.

In this case, petitioner Korematsu challenges the assumptions upon which we rested our conclusions in the Hirabayashi case. He also urges that, by May, 1942, when Order No. 34 was promulgated, all danger of Japanese invasion of the West Coast had disappeared. After careful consideration of these contentions, we are compelled to reject them.

Here, as in the *Hirabayashi* case,

> "... we cannot reject as unfounded the judgment of the military authorities and of Congress that there were disloyal members of that population, whose number and strength could not be precisely and quickly ascertained. We cannot say that the war-making branches of the Government did not have ground for believing that, in a critical hour, such persons could not readily be isolated and separately dealt with, and constituted a menace to the national defense and safety which demanded that prompt and adequate measures be taken to guard against it."

Like curfew, exclusion of those of Japanese origin was deemed necessary because of the presence of an unascertained number of disloyal members of the group, most of whom we have no doubt were loyal to this country. It was because we could not reject the finding of the military authorities that it was impossible to bring about an immediate segregation of the disloyal from the loyal that we sustained the validity of the curfew order as applying to the whole group. In the instant case, temporary exclusion of the entire group was rested by the military on the same ground. The judgment that exclusion of the whole group was, for the same reason, a military imperative answers the contention that the exclusion was in the nature of group punishment based on antagonism to those of Japanese origin. That there were members of the group who retained loyalties to Japan has been confirmed by investigations made subsequent to the exclusion. Approximately five thousand American citizens of Japanese ancestry refused to swear unqualified allegiance to the United States and to renounce allegiance to the Japanese Emperor, and several thousand evacuees requested repatriation to Japan.

We uphold the exclusion order as of the time it was made and when the petitioner violated it. In doing so, we are not unmindful of the hardships imposed by it upon a large group of American citizens. But hardships are part of war, and war is an aggregation of hardships. All citizens alike, both in and out of uniform, feel the impact of war in greater or lesser measure. Citizenship has its responsibilities, as well as its privileges, and, in time of war, the burden is always heavier. Compulsory exclusion of large groups of citizens from their homes, except under circumstances of direst emergency and peril, is inconsistent with our basic governmental institutions. But when, under conditions of modern warfare, our shores are threatened by hostile forces, the power to protect must be commensurate with the threatened danger.

It is said that we are dealing here with the case of imprisonment of a citizen in a concentration camp solely because of his ancestry, without evidence or inquiry concerning his loyalty and good disposition towards the United States. Our task would be simple, our duty clear, were this a case involving the imprisonment of a loyal citizen in a concentration camp because of racial prejudice. Regardless of the true nature of the assembly and relocation centers—and we deem it unjustifiable to call them concentration camps, with all the ugly connotations that term implies—we are dealing specifically with nothing but an exclusion order. To cast this case into outlines of racial prejudice, without reference to the real military dangers which were presented, merely confuses the issue. Korematsu was not excluded from the Military Area because of hostility to him or his race. He was excluded because we are at war with the Japanese Empire, because the properly constituted military authorities feared an invasion of our West Coast and felt constrained to take proper security measures, because they decided that the military urgency of the situation demanded that all citizens of Japanese ancestry be segregated from the West Coast temporarily, and, finally, because Congress, reposing its confidence in this time of war in our military leaders—as inevitably it must—determined that they should have the power to do just this. There was evidence of disloyalty on the part of some, the military authorities considered that the need for action was great, and time was short. We cannot—by availing ourselves of the calm perspective of hindsight—now say that, at that time, these actions were unjustified.

END OF OPINION

The majority of the Court upheld, for reasons of claimed military necessity, what our society look back on as a heinous act. But there was significant dissent from the policy, not just on the Court, but within the government and around the nation. The principles for this are best set forth in the dissenting opinion.

MURPHY, J., Dissenting Opinion

This exclusion of "all persons of Japanese ancestry, both alien and non-alien," from the Pacific Coast area on a plea of military necessity in the absence of martial law ought not to be approved. Such exclusion goes over "the very brink of constitutional power," and falls into the ugly abyss of racism.

In dealing with matters relating to the prosecution and progress of a war, we must accord great respect and consideration to the judgments of the military authorities who are on the scene and who have full knowledge of the military facts. The scope of their discretion must, as a matter of necessity and common sense, be wide. And their judgments ought not to be overruled lightly by judges whose training and duties ill-equip them to deal intelligently with matters so vital to the physical security of the nation.

At the same time, however, it is essential that there be definite limits to military discretion, especially where martial law has not been declared. Individuals must not be left impoverished of their constitutional rights on a plea of military necessity that has neither substance nor support. Thus, like other claims conflicting with the asserted constitutional rights of the individual, the military claim must subject itself to the judicial process of having its reasonableness determined and its conflicts with other interests reconciled.

What are the allowable limits of military discretion, and whether or not they have been overstepped in a particular case, are judicial questions.

The judicial test of whether the Government, on a plea of military necessity, can validly deprive an individual of any of his constitutional rights is whether the deprivation is reasonably related to a public danger that is so "immediate, imminent, and impending" as not to admit of delay and not to permit the intervention of ordinary constitutional processes to alleviate the danger. Civilian Exclusion Order No. 34, banishing from a prescribed area of the Pacific Coast "all persons of Japanese ancestry, both alien and non-alien," clearly does not meet that test. Being an obvious racial discrimination, the order deprives all those within its scope of the equal protection of the laws as guaranteed by the Fifth Amendment. It further deprives these individuals of their constitutional rights to live and work where they will, to establish a home where they choose and to move about freely. In excommunicating them without benefit of hearings, this order also deprives them of all their constitutional rights to procedural due process. Yet no reasonable relation to an "immediate, imminent, and impending" public danger is evident to support this racial restriction, which is one of the most sweeping and complete deprivations of constitutional rights in the history of this nation in the absence of martial law.

It must be conceded that the military and naval situation in the spring of 1942 was such as to generate a very real fear of invasion of the Pacific Coast, accompanied by fears of sabotage and espionage in that area. The military command was therefore justified in adopting all reasonable means necessary to combat these dangers. In adjudging the military action taken in light of the then apparent dangers, we must not erect too high or too meticulous standards; it is necessary only that the action have some reasonable relation to the removal of the dangers of invasion, sabotage and espionage. But the exclusion, either temporarily or permanently, of all persons with Japanese blood in their veins has no such reasonable relation. And that relation is lacking because the exclusion order necessarily must rely for its reasonableness upon the assumption that all persons of Japanese ancestry may have a dangerous tendency to commit sabotage and espionage and to aid our Japanese enemy in other ways. It is difficult to believe that reason, logic, or experience could be marshalled in support of such an assumption.

That this forced exclusion was the result in good measure of this erroneous assumption of racial guilt, rather than bona fide military necessity is evidenced by the Commanding General's Final Report on the evacuation from the Pacific Coast area. In it, he refers to all individuals of Japanese descent as "subversive," as belonging to "an enemy race" whose "racial strains are undiluted," and as constituting "over 112,000 potential enemies . . . at large today" along the Pacific Coast. In support of this blanket condemnation of all persons of Japanese descent, however, no reliable evidence is cited to show that such individuals were generally disloyal, or had generally so conducted themselves in this area as to constitute a special menace to defense installations or war industries, or had otherwise, by their behavior, furnished reasonable ground for their exclusion as a group.

Justification for the exclusion is sought, instead, mainly upon questionable racial and sociological grounds not ordinarily within the realm of expert military judgment, supplemented by certain semi-military conclusions drawn from an unwarranted use of circumstantial evidence. Individuals of Japanese ancestry are condemned because they are said to be "a large, unassimilated, tightly knit racial group, bound to an enemy nation by strong ties of race, culture, custom and religion." They are claimed to be given to "emperor worshipping ceremonies," and to "dual citizenship." Japanese language schools and allegedly pro-Japanese organizations are cited as evidence of possible group disloyalty, together with facts as to certain persons being educated and residing at length in Japan. It is intimated that many of these individuals deliberately resided "adjacent to strategic points," thus enabling them to carry into execution a tremendous program of sabotage on a mass scale should any considerable number of them have been inclined to do so.

The need for protective custody is also asserted. The report refers, without identity, to "numerous incidents of violence," as well as to other admittedly unverified or cumulative incidents. From this, plus certain other events not shown to have been connected with the Japanese Americans, it is concluded that the "situation was fraught with danger to the Japanese population itself," and that the general public "was ready to take matters into its own hands." Finally, it is intimated, though not directly charged or proved, that persons of Japanese ancestry were responsible for three minor isolated shellings and bombings of the Pacific Coast area, as well as for unidentified radio transmissions and night signaling.

The main reasons relied upon by those responsible for the forced evacuation, therefore, do not prove a reasonable relation between the group characteristics of Japanese Americans and the dangers of invasion, sabotage and espionage. The reasons appear, instead, to be largely an accumulation of much of the misinformation, half-truths and insinuations that for years have been directed against Japanese Americans by people with racial and economic prejudices—the same people who have been among the foremost advocates of the evacuation. A military judgment based upon such racial and sociological considerations is not entitled to the great weight ordinarily given the judgments based upon strictly military considerations. Especially is this so when every charge relative to race, religion, culture, geographical location, and legal and economic status has been substantially discredited by independent studies made by experts in these matters.

The military necessity which is essential to the validity of the evacuation order thus resolves itself into a few intimations that certain individuals actively aided the enemy, from which it is inferred that the entire group of Japanese Americans could not be trusted to be or remain loyal to the United States. No one denies, of course, that there were some disloyal persons of Japanese descent on the Pacific Coast who did all in their power to aid their ancestral land. Similar disloyal activities have been engaged in by many persons of German, Italian and even more pioneer stock in our country. But to infer that examples of individual disloyalty prove group disloyalty and justify discriminatory action against the entire group is to deny that, under our system of law, individual guilt is the sole basis for deprivation of rights. Moreover, this inference, which is at the very heart of the evacuation orders, has been used in support of the abhorrent and despicable treatment of minority groups by the dictatorial tyrannies which this nation is now pledged to destroy. To give constitutional sanction to that inference in this case, however well intentioned may have been the military command on the Pacific Coast, is to adopt one of the cruelest of the rationales used by our enemies to destroy the dignity of the individual and to encourage and open the door to discriminatory actions against other minority groups in the passions of tomorrow.

No adequate reason is given for the failure to treat these Japanese Americans on an individual basis by holding investigations and hearings to separate the loyal from the disloyal, as was done in the case of persons of German and Italian ancestry. It is asserted merely that the loyalties of this group "were unknown and time was of the essence." Yet nearly four months elapsed after Pearl Harbor before the first exclusion order was issued; nearly eight months went by until the last order was issued, and the last of these "subversive" persons was not actually removed until almost eleven months had elapsed. Leisure and deliberation seem to have been more of the essence than speed. And the fact that conditions were not such as to warrant a declaration of martial law adds strength to the belief that the factors of time and military necessity were not as urgent as they have been represented to be.

Moreover, there was no adequate proof that the Federal Bureau of Investigation and the military and naval intelligence services did not have the espionage and sabotage situation well in hand during this long period. Nor is there any denial of the fact that not one person of Japanese ancestry was accused or convicted of espionage or sabotage after Pearl Harbor while they were still free, a fact which is some evidence of the loyalty of the vast majority of these individuals and of the effectiveness of the established methods of combatting these evils. It seems incredible that, under these circumstances, it would have been impossible to hold loyalty hearings for the mere 112,000 persons involved—or at least for the 70,000 American citizens—especially when a large part of this number represented children and elderly men and women. Any inconvenience that may have accompanied an attempt to conform to procedural due process cannot be said to justify violations of constitutional rights of individuals.

I dissent, therefore, from this legalization of racism. Racial discrimination in any form and in any degree has no justifiable part whatever in our democratic way of life. It is unattractive in any setting, but it is utterly revolting among a free people who have embraced the principles set forth in the Constitution of the United States. All residents of this nation are kin in some way by blood or culture to a foreign land. Yet they are primarily and necessarily a part of the new and distinct civilization of the United States. They must, accordingly, be treated at all times as the heirs of the American experiment, and as entitled to all the rights and freedoms guaranteed by the Constitution.

END OF DISSENT

Interestingly, the same day *Korematsu v. U.S.* decision was released upholding the internment of all Japanese-American, the Court decided another case ordering the government to release a particular Japanese-American. In *Ex Parte Endo*, 323 U.S. 283 (1944), Endo was a Japanese-American who had sued for her release. The government conceded that the facts in that case demonstrated that Endo herself was a loyal American, but argued that it had to continue holding her along with all other Japanese-Americans. Here, the Court ruled that, once the government had conceded that someone was a loyal American, the government could not continue her detention.

Finally, to highlight further how justice can fall prey to fear, it has been determined that the cases were decided on false testimony. In May of 2011, the Acting Solicitor General of the United Stated (the chief prosecutor) issued a public apology because declassified documents showed that the Solicitor general at the time had misled the Supreme Court. By the time the cases of Gordon Hirabayashi and Fred Korematsu reached the Supreme Court, the Solicitor General had learned of a key intelligence report that undermined the rationale behind the internment. The Ringle Report, from the Office of Naval Intelligence, found that only a small percentage of Japanese Americans posed a potential security threat, and that the most dangerous were already known or in custody. But the Solicitor General did not inform the Court of the report, despite warnings from Department of Justice attorneys that failing to alert the Court "might approximate the suppression of evidence." Nor did he inform the Court that a key set of allegations used to justify the internment, that Japanese Americans were using radio transmitters to communicate with enemy submarines off the West Coast, had been discredited by the FBI and the FCC.[1]

---

1. See CONFESSION OF ERROR: THE SOLICITOR GENERAL'S MISTAKES DURING THE JAPANESE-AMERICAN INTERNMENT CASES, archived at https://www.justice.gov/archives/opa/blog/confession-error-solicitor-generals-mistakes-during-japanese-american-internment-cases

Extrajudicial Killings

As we have already read, the constitutional protections of equal protection under the law, the reasonableness of search and seizure law, and the protection that life, liberty, and property can be abridged only after a person is afforded due process of law comes under stress when the nation is in a wartime footing rather than peace. We now see that the detention of Japanese-Americans was a wrongful act of our government, and, while there were those who called for Arab-Americans to be detained after the attacks of 9/11, this was never a policy that the United States seriously considered.

But the consequences of a world-wide conflict against extremist terrorist organizations like Al-Qaeda and the so-called Islamic State (also known as Daesh or ISIS) have raised the questions of when, where, and how wartime rules apply. One area where this has been of particular consequence is in the area of "targeted killing," often using remotely piloted aircraft (or "drones"). Drones are flown over troubled areas of the world such as Afghanistan, Iraq, Yemen, and Pakistan where there is ongoing terrorist and insurgent activity and targets, including suspected insurgents or terrorists who are fired upon by missiles from the aircraft. This has taken place, not just in areas considered active battlefields such as Iraq or Afghanistan, but also in remote areas outside of the active battlefield.

Is this practice legal, or does it violate international and domestic law? Arguably the overall practice is legal, but there are a number of very serious concerns and issues, some legal, more often issues of ethics and morality. With any military attack, including those by missile strike, there is a risk of collateral damage as innocent bystanders may be killed, and there is a principle of warfare that nations are under an obligation to avoid collateral damage as much as possible, balancing the risk of such incidental injury to the innocent against the military value of the target. If a single insurgent or terrorist, even a very high-level one, is killed but so too are innocent bystanders, then the attack may create even more enemies as the family members of the deceased swear vengeance against America. Critics allege that drone strikes often pose too much of a risk to innocent bystanders. Alternatively, others argue that drones are highly effective at crippling insurgent and terrorist organizations in these conflicts by removing their leadership, that the strikes are at least as precise, and in many cases more precise, than any alternatives, and that the operations can take place without directly endangering the lives of U.S. servicemembers.

Another argument often made is that, because these drone strikes target specific individuals, they are assassinations, generally considered to be illegal. But the concept of an assassination refers to a killing made during peacetime for a political purpose, not a killing undertaken during an armed conflict against one considered to be part of the enemy force.

We have earlier discussed the reforms of the intelligence community undertaken as a result of the findings of the Church Committee. Those hearings revealed the U.S. intelligence communities had planned assassinations of foreign leaders such as Fidel

Castro. As a result, President Ford clearly and unequivocally banned assassinations through his issuance of an Executive Order, and every president since that time has included the ban in Executive Order 12333, the document by which the president directs the different agencies making up the intelligence community, giving them their authorities and restrictions. With regard to assassination, Executive Order 12333 states, "No person employed by or acting on behalf of the United States government shall engage in, or conspire to engage in, assassination."

Let's compare the targeted killing of a terrorist by a drone attack with the targeted killing of Admiral Yamamoto of the Japanese Imperial Navy. Admiral Yamamoto was the Japanese military leader who planned and led the attack on Pearl Harbor. He is generally acknowledged as being one of the greatest military minds of his generation, one of the few persons to have foreseen the importance of Naval aviation and the role of the aircraft carrier. Even though he planned the attack on Pearl Harbor, he had actually advised against the action; having studied in the U.S., he knew of America's character as well as its industrial might and ability to rebuild. When asked to attack Pearl Harbor, he famously and prophetically stated, "I shall run wild considerably for the first six months or a year if I destroy the American navy at Pearl Harbor, but I have utterly no confidence of the second and third years."

The success of the attack on Pearl Harbor made Yamamoto a hero in the eyes of the Japanese people as a military genius. When the U.S. started make advances in the South Pacific, Admiral Yamamoto was sent on a tour to raise the morale of Japanese troops. U.S. code-breakers learned that he would be touring the South Pacific and where he would be located at a certain time. On April 18, 1943, in what was called Operation Vengeance, American pilots found and shot down his plane.

This targeted killing of Yamamoto was not at all controversial. As a uniformed member of the Japanese Navy, he was self-identifying himself as a valid military target. Just as important, his killing deprived the Japanese of a valued war asset, which is a valid military objective. Even though, as a high-ranking Admiral, Yamamoto was not shooting at the U.S. himself, or even commanding a ship in combat, he was controlling and directing the actions of those who were.

Using the same rationale, the United States today considers that it may target, not just insurgents and terrorists actually involved in operations when they are hit, but those who play a key role in planning and directing others, just as a military staff could be attacked in previous wars.

Under the international law of armed conflict, it is perfectly lawful in times of war to kill members of the enemy who are actually engaged in hostilities. As we have seen, hostilities in present-day conflicts often extend beyond the battlefield, and civilians have been increasingly involved in activities more closely related to the conduct of hostilities, thus blurring the distinction between civilian and military functions. Some have argued that only direct combat activity should matter, while others argue that the concept of "direct participation in hostilities" should include persons offering aid, support, or comfort to the enemy. A valid criticism of this approach is that the decision of who is a permissible target begins to look less like warfare and more like the government executing criminal suspects (terrorists) without the judicial due process of a trial.

Now, no judicial due process is required just because the target of a killing is a U.S. citizen. Remember from *Ex Part Quirin* that being a U.S. citizen is no bar to one being classified as an enemy combatant subject to wartime (as opposed to criminal) sanction. "Citizens who associate themselves with the military arm of the enemy government, and with its aid, guidance and direction enter this country bent on hostile acts, are enemy belligerents within the meaning of . . . the law of war."

The issue has already come up in the case of one senior Al-Qaeda leader who happened to be an American citizen.

Al-Aulaqi v. Obama, 727 F. Supp. 2d 1 (2010)*

On August 30, 2010, plaintiff Nasser Al-Aulaqi ("plaintiff") filed this action, claiming that the President, the Secretary of Defense, and the Director of the CIA (collectively, "defendants") have unlawfully authorized the targeted killing of plaintiff's son, Anwar Al-Aulaqi, a dual U.S.-Yemeni citizen currently hiding in Yemen who has alleged ties to Al-Qaeda in the Arabian Peninsula ("AQAP"). Plaintiff seeks an injunction prohibiting defendants from intentionally killing Anwar Al-Aulaqi "unless he presents a concrete, specific, and imminent threat to life or physical safety, and there are no means other than lethal force that could reasonably be employed to neutralize the threat." Defendants have responded with a motion to dismiss plaintiff's complaint on five threshold grounds: standing, the political question doctrine, the Court's exercise of its "equitable discretion," the absence of a cause of action under the Alien Tort Statute ("ATS"), and the state secrets privilege.

This is a unique and extraordinary case. Both the threshold and merits issues present fundamental questions of separation of powers involving the proper role of the courts in our constitutional structure. Vital considerations of national security and of military and foreign affairs (and hence potentially of state secrets) are at play.

Stark, and perplexing, questions readily come to mind, including the following: How is it that judicial approval is required when the United States decides to target a U.S. citizen overseas for electronic surveillance, but that, according to defendants, judicial scrutiny is prohibited when the United States decides to target a U.S. citizen overseas for death? Can a U.S. citizen — himself or through another — use the U.S. judicial system to vindicate his constitutional rights while simultaneously evading U.S. law enforcement authorities, calling for "jihad against the West," and engaging in operational planning for an organization that has already carried out numerous terrorist attacks against the United States? Can the Executive order the assassination of a U.S. citizen without first affording him any form of judicial process whatsoever, based on the mere assertion that he is a dangerous member of a terrorist organization? How can the courts, as plaintiff proposes, make real-time assessments of the nature

---

* The case has been heavily edited and paraphrased by the authors for clarity. See disclaimer in introduction.

and severity of alleged threats to national security, determine the imminence of those threats, weigh the benefits and costs of possible diplomatic and military responses, and ultimately decide whether, and under what circumstances, the use of military force against such threats is justified? When would it ever make sense for the United States to disclose in advance to the "target" of contemplated military action the precise standards under which it will take that military action? And how does the evolving AQAP relate to core Al-Qaeda for purposes of assessing the legality of targeting AQAP (or its principals) under the September 18, 2001 Authorization for the Use of Military Force?

These and other legal and policy questions posed by this case are controversial and of great public interest. "Unfortunately, however, no matter how interesting and no matter how important this case may be . . . we cannot address it unless we have jurisdiction." Before reaching the merits of plaintiff's claims, then, this Court must decide whether plaintiff is the proper person to bring the constitutional and statutory challenges he asserts, and whether plaintiff's challenges, as framed, state claims within the ambit of the Judiciary to resolve. These jurisdictional issues pose "distinct and separate limitations, so that either the absence of standing or the presence of a political question suffices to prevent the power of the federal judiciary from being invoked by the complaining party."

Although these threshold questions of jurisdiction may seem less significant than the questions posed by the merits of plaintiff's claims, "much more than legal niceties are at stake here"—the "constitutional elements of jurisdiction are an essential ingredient of separation and equilibration of powers, restraining the courts from acting at certain times, and even restraining them from acting permanently regarding certain subjects." Here, the jurisdictional hurdles that plaintiff must surmount are both complex and at the heart of the intriguing nature of this case. But "a court without jurisdiction is a court without power, no matter how appealing the case for exceptions may be," and hence it is these threshold obstacles to reaching the merits of plaintiff's constitutional and statutory challenges that must be the initial focus of this Court's attention. Because these questions of justiciability require dismissal of this case at the outset, the serious issues regarding the merits of the alleged authorization of the targeted killing of a U.S. citizen overseas must await another day or another (non-judicial) forum.

BACKGROUND

This case arises from the United States's alleged policy of "authorizing, planning, and carrying out targeted killings, including of U.S. citizens, outside the context of armed conflict." Specifically, plaintiff, a Yemeni citizen, claims that the United States has authorized the targeted killing of plaintiff's son, Anwar Al-Aulaqi, in violation of the Constitution and international law.

Anwar Al-Aulaqi is a Muslim cleric with dual U.S.-Yemeni citizenship, who is currently believed to be in hiding in Yemen. Anwar Al-Aulaqi was born in New Mexico in 1971, and spent much of his early life in the United States, attending college at Colorado State University and receiving his master's degree from San

Diego State University before moving to Yemen in 2004. In 2010, the U.S. designated Anwar Al-Aulaqi as a terrorist in light of evidence that he was acting for or on behalf of al Queda and providing financial, material or technological support for, or other services to or in support of, acts of terrorism. In its designation of Al-Aulaqi as a terrorist, the US explained that he had taken on an increasingly operational role in al Queda since late 2009, as he "facilitated training camps in Yemen in support of acts of terrorism" and provided "instructions" to Umar Farouk Abdulmutallab, the man accused of attempting to detonate a bomb aboard a Detroit-bound Northwest Airlines flight on Christmas Day 2009. Media sources have also reported ties between Anwar Al-Aulaqi and Nidal Malik Hasan, the U.S. Army Major suspected of killing 13 people in a November 2009 shooting at Fort Hood, Texas. According to a January 2010 Los Angeles Times article, U.S. officials have discovered that Anwar Al-Aulaqi and Hasan exchanged as many as eighteen e-mails prior to the Fort Hood shootings.

Recently, Anwar Al-Aulaqi has made numerous public statements calling for "jihad against the West," praising the actions of "his students" Abdulmutallab and Hasan, and asking others to "follow suit." Public officials have explained that Al-Aulaqi's personal knowledge of the US and English make him very dangerous and effective as a terrorist recruiter. The United States has not yet publicly charged Anwar Al-Aulaqi with any crime. For his part, Anwar Al-Aulaqi has made clear that he has no intention of making himself available for criminal prosecution in U.S. courts, remarking in a May 2010 Al Queda video interview that he "will never surrender" to the United States, and that "if the Americans want me, they can come look for me."

Plaintiff does not deny his son's affiliation with Al-Qaeda or his designation as a terrorist. Rather, plaintiff challenges his son's alleged unlawful inclusion on so-called "kill lists" that he contends are maintained by the CIA and the military. In support of his claim that the United States has placed Anwar Al-Aulaqi on "kill lists," plaintiff cites a number of media reports, which attribute their information to anonymous U.S. military and intelligence sources. For example, in January 2010, The Washington Post reported that, according to unnamed military officials, Anwar Al-Aulaqi was on "a shortlist of U.S. citizens" that the military was authorized to kill or capture. A few months later, The Washington Post cited an anonymous U.S. official as stating that Anwar Al-Aulaqi had become "the first U.S. citizen added to a list of suspected terrorists the CIA is authorized to kill." And in July 2010, National Public Radio announced—on the basis of unidentified "intelligence sources"—that the United States had already ordered "almost a dozen" unsuccessful drone and airstrikes targeting Anwar Al-Aulaqi in Yemen.

Based on these news reports, plaintiff claims that the United States has placed Anwar Al-Aulaqi on the CIA and military "kill lists" without "charge, trial, or conviction." Plaintiff alleges that individuals like his son are placed on "kill lists" after a "closed executive process" in which defendants and other executive officials determine that "secret criteria" have been satisfied. Plaintiff further claims "upon information and belief" that once an individual is placed on a "kill list," he remains there for "months at a time." To support this claim, plaintiff quotes unnamed U.S. officials as stating that "kill lists" are reviewed every six months and names are removed from the list if there is no longer intelligence linking the person to "known terrorists or terrorist plans." Consequently, plaintiff argues, Anwar Al-Aulaqi is "now subject to a standing order that permits the CIA and the military to kill him without regard to whether, at the time lethal force will be used, he presents a concrete, specific, and imminent threat to life, or whether there are reasonable means short of lethal force that could be used to address any such threat."

The United States has neither confirmed nor denied the allegation that it has issued a "standing order" authorizing the CIA and JSOC to kill plaintiff's son. Additionally, the United States has neither confirmed nor denied whether—if it has, in fact, authorized the use of lethal force against plaintiff's son—the authorization was made with regard to whether Anwar Al-Aulaqi presents a concrete, specific, and imminent threat to life, or whether there were reasonable means short of lethal force that could be used to address any such threat. The United States has, however, repeatedly stated that if Anwar Al-Aulaqi "were to surrender or otherwise present himself to the proper authorities in a peaceful and appropriate manner, legal principles with which the United States has traditionally and uniformly complied would prohibit using lethal force or other violence against him in such circumstances."

Nevertheless, plaintiff alleges that due to his son's inclusion on the CIA and the military's "kill lists," Anwar Al-Aulaqi is in "hiding under threat of death and cannot access counsel or the courts to assert his constitutional rights without disclosing his whereabouts and exposing himself to possible attack by Defendants." Plaintiff therefore brings four claims—three constitutional, and one statutory—on his son's behalf. He asserts that the United States's alleged policy of authorizing the targeted killing of U.S. citizens, including plaintiff's son, outside of armed conflict, "in circumstances in which they do not present concrete, specific, and imminent threats to life or physical safety, and where there are means other than lethal force that could reasonably be employed to neutralize any such threat," violates (1) Anwar Al-Aulaqi Fourth Amendment right to be free from unreasonable seizures and (2) his Fifth Amendment right not to be deprived of life without due process of law. Plaintiff further claims that (3) the United States's refusal to disclose the criteria by which it selects U.S. citizens like plaintiff's son for targeted killing independently violates the notice requirement of the Fifth Amendment Due Process Clause. Finally, plaintiff brings (4) a statutory claim under the Alien Tort Statute ("ATS"), alleging that the United States's "policy of targeted killings violates treaty and customary international law."

Plaintiff seeks a declaration that, outside of armed conflict, the Constitution prohibits defendants "from carrying out the targeted killing of U.S. citizens," including Anwar Al-Aulaqi, "except in circumstances in which they present a concrete, specific, and imminent threat to life or physical safety, and there are no means other than lethal force that could reasonably be employed to neutralize the threat." Second, plaintiff requests a declaration that, outside of armed conflict, "treaty and customary international law" prohibit the targeted killing of all individuals—regardless of their citizenship—except in those same, limited circumstances. Third, plaintiff requests a court order prohibiting defendants from intentionally killing Anwar Al-Aulaqi "unless he presents a concrete, specific, and imminent threat to life or physical safety, and there are no means other than lethal force that could reasonably be employed to neutralize the threat." Finally, plaintiff seeks a court order ordering the Government to disclose the criteria that the United States uses to determine whether a U.S. citizen will be targeted for killing.

Presently before the Court is the US Government's motion to dismiss plaintiff's complaint on five distinct grounds: (1) standing; (2) political question; (3) "equitable discretion"; (4) lack of a cause of action under the ATS; and (5) the state secrets privilege.

DISCUSSION

I. Standing

Before this Court may consider the merits of the case, we must first check to see if the plaintiff has standing to sue. A plaintiff must suffer a "personal" injury to establish standing. Furthermore, a plaintiff generally must assert his own legal rights and interests, and cannot rest his claim to relief on the legal rights or interests of third parties. The court may recognize exceptions to this general rule, and it has done so in narrowly limited circumstances, The doctrines of "next friend" and "third party" standing constitute two such limited exceptions to the general rule that a party may not bring suit to vindicate the legal rights of another.

[The Court discussed and rejected the ability of al-Aulaqi's father to file suit on his son's behalf as "next friend." The Court also ruled that the Alien Tort Statute did not apply because the harm alleged would accrue to al-Aulaqi alone, who is a citizen.]

III. The Political Question Doctrine

Petitioner's claims should still be dismissed because they raise non-justiciable political questions. Like standing, the political question doctrine is an aspect of "the concept of justiciability, which expresses the jurisdictional limitations imposed on the federal courts by the 'case or controversy' requirement of Article III of the Constitution." The political question doctrine "is 'essentially a function of the separation of powers,'" and "excludes from judicial review those controversies which revolve around policy choices and value determinations constitutionally committed for resolution to the halls of Congress or the confines of the Executive Branch. The precise "contours" of the political question doctrine remain murky and unsettled, but the Supreme Court has articulated six factors which are said to be prominent on the surface of cases involving non-justiciable political questions:

> [1] a textually demonstrable constitutional commitment of the issue to a coordinate political department; or [2] a lack of judicially discoverable and manageable standards for resolving it; or [3] the impossibility of deciding without an initial policy determination of a kind clearly for nonjudicial discretion; or [4] the impossibility of a court's undertaking independent

resolution without expressing lack of respect due coordinate branches of government; or [5] an unusual need for unquestioning adherence to a political decision already made; or [6] the potentiality of embarrassment from multifarious pronouncements by various departments on one question.

The first two factors—a textual commitment to another branch of government and a lack of judicially manageable standards—are considered the most important, but in order for a case to be non-justiciable, the court need only conclude that one factor is present, not all.

An examination of the specific areas in which courts have invoked the political question doctrine reveals that national security, military matters and foreign relations are typical sources of political questions. Matters intimately related to foreign policy and national security are rarely proper subjects for judicial intervention. As the D.C. Circuit recently explained, cases involving national security and foreign relations "raise issues that frequently turn on standards that defy judicial application or involve the exercise of a discretion demonstrably committed to the executive or legislature." Unlike the political branches, the Judiciary has "no covert agents, no intelligence sources, and no policy advisors." Courts are thus institutionally ill-equipped "to assess the nature of battlefield decisions," or to "define the standard for the government's use of covert operations in conjunction with political turmoil in another country." These types of decisions involve delicate and complex policy judgments with "large elements of prophecy," and "are decisions of a kind for which the Judiciary has neither aptitude, facilities, nor responsibility." The difficulty that U.S. courts would encounter if they were tasked with ascertaining the 'facts' of military decisions exercised thousands of miles from the forum, lies at the heart of the determination whether the question posed is a 'political' one.

At the same time, the Supreme Court has also made clear that "it is error to suppose that every case or controversy which touches foreign relations lies beyond judicial cognizance." Although attacks on foreign policymaking are nonjusticiable, claims alleging non-compliance with the law are justiciable, even if they do have an effect on foreign affairs. The political question doctrine, the Supreme Court has warned, was only designed to cover a narrow category of carefully defined cases. In order to decide whether a particular legal challenge constitutes an impermissible "attack on foreign policymaking" or is instead a justiciable claim with a permissible effect on foreign affairs, a court must conduct a careful analysis of the particular question posed in the "specific" case.

Judicial resolution of the "particular questions" posed by plaintiff in this case would require this Court to decide: (1) the precise nature and extent of Anwar Al-Aulaqi's affiliation with Al Queda; (2) whether the branch of Al Queda with whom Anwar Al-Aulaqi is allegedly associated with is so closely linked to the Al Queda that the US is currently in conflict with so as to justify the Government's targeted killing of Anwar Al-Aulaqi; (3) whether Anwar Al-Aulaqi's alleged terrorist activity renders him a "concrete, specific, and imminent threat to life or physical safety,"; and (4) whether there are "means short of lethal force" that the United States could "reasonably" employ to address any threat that Anwar Al-Aulaqi poses to U.S. national security interests. Such determinations, in turn, would require this Court, in defendants' view, to understand and assess the capabilities of the alleged terrorist operative to carry out a threatened attack, what response would be sufficient to address that threat, possible diplomatic considerations that may bear on such responses, the vulnerability of potential targets that the alleged terrorist may strike, the availability of military and nonmilitary options, and the risks to military and nonmilitary personnel in attempting application of non-lethal force. Viewed through these prisms, it becomes clear that plaintiff's claims pose precisely the types of complex policy questions that the D.C. Circuit has historically held non-justiciable under the political question doctrine.

Most recently, in *El-Shifa v. United States* the D.C. Circuit Court examined whether the political question doctrine barred judicial resolution of claims by owners of a Sudanese pharmaceutical plant who brought suit seeking to recover damages after their plant was destroyed by an American cruise missile. President Clinton had ordered the missile strike in light of intelligence indicating that the plant was associated with the Osama bin Ladin network and involved in the production of materials for chemical weapons. The plaintiffs maintained that the U.S. government had been negligent in determining that the plant was tied to chemical weapons and Osama bin Laden and therefore sought a declaration that the government's failure to compensate them for the destruction of the plant violated customary international law, a declaration that statements government officials made about them were defamatory, and an injunction requiring the government to retract those statements. Dismissing the plaintiffs' claims as non-justiciable under the political question doctrine, the D.C. Circuit explained that "in military matters . . . the courts lack the competence to assess the strategic decision to employ force or to create standards to determine whether the use of force was justified or well-founded." Rather than endeavor to resolve questions beyond the Judiciary's institutional competence, the court held that "if the political question doctrine means anything in the arena of national security and foreign relations, it means the courts cannot assess the merits of the President's decision to launch an attack on a foreign target."

Here, plaintiff asks this Court to do exactly what the D.C. Circuit forbid in *El-Shifa*—assess the merits of the President's (alleged) decision to launch an attack on a foreign target. Although the "foreign target" happens to be a U.S. citizen, the same reasons that counseled against judicial resolution of the plaintiffs' claims in *El-Shifa* apply with equal force here. Just as in *El-Shifa*, any judicial determination as to the propriety of a military attack on Anwar Al-Aulaqi would require this court to review and second guess the standards that are to guide a President when he evaluates the veracity of military intelligence. Indeed, that is just what plaintiff has asked this Court to do. But there are no judicially manageable standards by which courts can endeavor to assess the President's interpretation of military intelligence and his resulting decision—based on that intelligence—whether to use military force against a terrorist target overseas. It would be difficult, if not extraordinary, for the federal courts to discover and announce the threshold standard by which the United

States government evaluates intelligence in making a decision to commit military force in an effort to thwart an imminent terrorist attack on Americans. Nor are there judicially manageable standards by which courts may determine the nature and magnitude of the national security threat posed by a particular individual. In fact, the D.C. Circuit has expressly held that the question whether an organization's alleged "terrorist activity" threatens "the national security of the United States" is "nonjusticiable." Given that courts may not undertake to assess whether a particular organization's alleged terrorist activities threaten national security, it would seem obvious that courts must also decline to assess whether a particular individual's alleged terrorist activities threaten national security. But absent such a judicial determination as to the nature and extent of the alleged national security threat that Anwar Al-Aulaqi poses to the United States, this Court cannot possibly determine whether the government's alleged use of lethal force against Anwar Al-Aulaqi would be "justified or well-founded." Thus, the second Baker factor—a "lack of judicially discoverable and manageable standards" for resolving the dispute—strongly counsels against judicial review of plaintiff's claims.

As the D.C. Circuit has explained, "it is not the role of judges to second-guess, with the benefit of hindsight, another branch's determination that the interests of the United States call for military action." Such military determinations are textually committed to the political branches. Article I, Section 8 of the Constitution is richly laden with the delegation of foreign policy and national security powers to Congress while Article II likewise provides allocation of foreign relations and national security powers to the President, the unitary chief executive and Commander in Chief of the Army and Navy. Moreover, any after-the-fact judicial assessment as to the propriety of the Executive's decision to employ military force abroad would run in opposition to the principle of the separation of powers.

The mere fact that the "foreign target" of military action in this case is an individual—rather than alleged enemy property—does not distinguish plaintiff's claims from those raised in *El-Shifa* for purposes of the political question doctrine. This court does not hold that the Executive possesses "unreviewable authority to order the assassination of any American whom he labels an enemy of the state." Rather, the Court only concludes that it lacks the capacity to determine whether a specific individual in hiding overseas, whom the Director of National Intelligence has stated is an "operational" member of Al-Qaeda, presents such a threat to national security that the United States may authorize the use of lethal force against him. This Court readily acknowledges that it is a "drastic measure" for the United States to employ lethal force against one of its own citizens abroad, even if that citizen is currently playing an operational role in a terrorist group that has claimed responsibility for numerous attacks against Saudi, Korean, Yemeni, and U.S. targets since January 2009. But a determination as to whether drastic measures should be taken in matters of foreign policy and national security is not the stuff of adjudication, but of policymaking. Because decision-making in the realm of military and foreign affairs is textually committed to the political branches, and because courts are functionally ill-equipped to make the types of complex policy judgments that would be required to adjudicate the merits of plaintiff's claims, the Court finds that the political question doctrine bars judicial resolution of this case.

IV. The Military and State Secrets Privilege

Defendants invoke the military and state secrets privilege as the final basis for dismissal of plaintiff's complaint. The state secrets privilege is premised on the recognition that "in exceptional circumstances courts must act in the interest of the country's national security to prevent disclosure of state secrets, even to the point of dismissing a case entirely." Contemporary state secrets doctrine encompasses two applications of this principle. One completely bars adjudication of claims premised on state secrets (the *Totten* bar); the other is an evidentiary privilege (the *Reynolds* privilege) that excludes privileged evidence from the case and may result in dismissal of the claims.

The *Totten* bar only applies where the very subject matter of the action' is itself a matter of state secret. In contrast, successful invocation of the *Reynolds* privilege removes the privileged evidence from the litigation, but does not necessarily require the plaintiffs' claims to be dismissed. Nevertheless, in some instances, the *Reynolds* privilege converges with the *Totten* bar and then the assertion of the privilege will require dismissal because it will become apparent during the *Reynolds* analysis that the case cannot proceed without privileged evidence, or that litigating the case to a judgment on the merits would present an unacceptable risk of disclosing state secrets.

Here, the Government does not argue that the very subject matter of this case is itself a state secret. Rather, they contend that this case is one in which the *Reynolds* privilege converges with the Totten bar because specific categories of information properly protected against disclosure by the privilege would be necessary to litigate each of plaintiff's claims. The Government correctly notes that the privilege protects information from disclosure "where there is a reasonable danger that disclosure would expose military matters which, in the interests of national security, should not be divulged." They argue that "where the claims and possible defenses are so infused with state secrets that the risk of disclosing them is both apparent and inevitable,' dismissal is required." And here, according to defendants, that is most certainly the case because in unclassified terms, the disclosure harmful to national security includes information needed to address whether or not, or under what circumstances, the United States may target a particular foreign terrorist organization and its senior leadership, the specific threat posed by Al-Qaeda or Anwar Al-Aulaqi, and other matters that plaintiff has put at issue, including any criteria governing the use of lethal force.

But defendants also correctly and forcefully observe that this Court need not, and should not, reach their claim of state secrets privilege because the case can be resolved on the other grounds they have presented. It is certainly true that the state secrets privilege should be invoked no more often or extensively than necessary. Indeed, last year the Attorney General promulgated a policy confirming that the state secrets privilege will only be invoked in limited circumstances involving a significant risk of harm to national security and after detailed procedures are followed (including personal approval of the Attorney General). And here, defendants have confirmed that the privilege has been invoked only after that careful review and adherence to the mandated procedures under the Attorney General's policy.

Under the circumstances, and particularly given both the extraordinary nature of this case and the other clear grounds for resolving it, the Court will not reach defendants' state secrets privilege claim. That is consistent with the request of the Executive Branch and with the law, and plaintiff does not contest that approach. Indeed, given the nature of the state secrets assessment here based on careful judicial review of classified submissions to which neither plaintiff nor his counsel have access, there is little that plaintiff can offer with respect to this issue. But in any event, because plaintiff lacks standing and his claims are non-justiciable, and because the state secrets privilege should not be invoked "more often or extensively than necessary," this Court will not reach defendants' invocation of the state secrets privilege.

For the foregoing reasons, the Court will grant defendants' motion to dismiss.

END OF OPINION

This case, then, did not directly address the legality of the policy but rather on the doctrine of the political question and state secrets doctrine. Just as we have seen in the earlier chapter on litigating national security cases, the Court simply decided that the matter was not one the Court could address.

Now, since this decision, the Justice Department has released a memo on the criteria for such attacks,[2] the Attorney General has made a formal statement,[3] and the president[4] also made an address discussing that criteria. At that speech, the president summed up the policy as follows:

> But when a U.S. citizen goes abroad to wage war against America and is actively plotting to kill U.S. citizens, and when neither the United States, nor our partners are in a position to capture him before he carries out a plot, his citizenship should no more serve as a shield than a sniper shooting down on an innocent crowd should be protected from a SWAT team.

Needless to say, the policy remains controversial. This controversy does not simply revolve around whether this is the correct approach to take against those who are proven to be legitimate targets—because remember that there has been no

---

2. The White Paper was first released by NBC News, and a full copy of it is available on the NBC website at http://msnbcmedia.msn.com/i/msnbc/sections/news/020413_DOJ_White_Paper.pdf, as well as a number of other online locations.

3. Attorney General Eric Holder Speaks at Northwestern University School of Law, March 5, 2012, available at https://www.justice.gov/opa/speech/attorney-general-eric-holder-speaks-northwestern-university-school-law.

4. Remarks by the President at National Defense University, May 23, 2013, available at https://www.whitehouse.gov/the-press-office/2013/05/23/remarks-president-national-defense-university.

formal trial to prove anything but rather a conclusion by the intelligence community and national leadership that adequate proof exists. What if they are wrong?

Imagine that you are studying abroad in Yemen and you learn that your name is on a kill list. Your options are quite limited. For reasons concerning standing, a friend or family member could not file a suit on your behalf to try to get your name off that list. Even if they were granted standing, the lawsuit would be dismissed as a political question. Whether it is a pharmaceutical plant in Sudan or a suspected terrorist, the courts will not question who or what the president considers to be a part of the enemy. Furthermore, your lawsuit to save your life would also be dismissed under state secrets doctrine. The only real option a person on the list for targeted killing always has is that of surrendering or turning oneself in to an American embassy. As the court pointed out, the international law of armed conflict prohibits the killing (without judicial due process) of an enemy combatant who has laid down his weapons and surrendered.

Voluntary Searches and the Right to Travel

Whenever you enter an amusement park or a stadium and a security guard requires you to open your bag so she can look through it, there is no Fourth Amendment issue, let alone a civil rights violation. Why? Because the Fourth Amendment only protects you from government actors, and not from the action of private parties, such as those who own the park or stadium. Now, what about at airports and an increasing number of subway stations where passengers are required to open their bags and submit them for inspection or be turned away?

There are two ways to approach these inspections. One is to view them, not as a criminal search for evidence, which requires a warrant issued upon probable cause, but instead as a public health and safety inspection, which must merely be reasonable. These checkpoints are not set up to catch criminals, so they are not criminal searches. Persons are selected at these checkpoints to be "inspected," not at the whim of the inspection officers, but by some preset criteria. The criteria might be that all persons are inspected, or it might be based on a formula (such as "every fourth person"). This criteria that these inspections eliminate any discretion on the part of inspection officers and the public safety justification are the same criteria used to uphold DWI checkpoints.

Another rationale supporting the legality of these inspections at subways is that they are voluntary, so no one is actually being "seized." Although in the U.S. one does have a right to travel, there is no constitutional right to travel by a certain method. A person does not have to choose to travel via mass transit or airline; one could choose to travel by automobile, horse, or foot. By choosing to use rail or airline to travel, one is also agreeing to the conditions for travel, including inspection. The legality of such inspections was upheld in the following opinion.

MacWade v. Kelly, 460 F.3d 260 (2006)*

We consider whether the government may employ random, suspicionless container searches in order to safeguard mass transportation facilities from terrorist attack. The precise issue before us is whether one such search regime, implemented on the New York City subway system, satisfies the special needs exception to the Fourth Amendment's usual requirement of individualized suspicion. We hold that it does.

Shortly after New York City implemented its search program, plaintiffs-appellants Brendan MacWade, Andrew Schonebaum, Joseph E. Gehring, Jr., Partha Banerjee, and Norman Murphy each attempted to enter the subway system. Each plaintiff either submitted to a baggage search and entered the subway or refused the search and consequently was required to exit the subway system. Disturbed by their treatment, they sued defendants-appellees New York City and Police Commissioner Raymond Kelly, asserting that the search regime violated the Fourth and Fourteenth Amendments. They sought a declaratory judgment, preliminary and permanent injunctive relief, and attorney's fees. After a two-day bench trial, the federal District Court found the search program constitutional pursuant to the special needs exception and dismissed the complaint with prejudice.

Plaintiffs appealed, raising three claims: (1) the special needs doctrine applies only in scenarios where the subject of a search possesses a diminished expectation of privacy, and because subway riders enjoy a full expectation of privacy in their bags, the District Court erred in applying the special needs exception here; (2) the District Court erred in finding that the search program serves a "special need" in the first instance; and (3) even if the search program serves a special need, the District Court erred in balancing the relevant factors because (a) the searches are intrusive; (b) there is no immediate terrorist threat; and (c) the City's evidence fails as a matter of law to establish that the Program is effective.

As set forth more fully below, we hold that the special needs doctrine may apply where, as here, the subject of a search possesses a full privacy expectation. Further, we hold that preventing a terrorist attack on the subway is a "special" need within the meaning of the doctrine. Finally, we hold that the search program is reasonable because it serves a paramount government interest and, under the circumstances, is narrowly tailored and sufficiently effective.

BACKGROUND

I. The Subway System and the Container Inspection Program

The New York City subway system is a singular component of America's urban infrastructure. The subway is an icon of the City's culture and history, an engine of its colossal economy, a subterranean repository of its art and music, and, most often, the place where millions of diverse New Yorkers and visitors stand elbow to elbow as they traverse the metropolis. Quantified, the subway system is staggering. It comprises 26

---

* The case has been heavily edited and paraphrased by the authors for clarity. See disclaimer in introduction.

interconnected train lines and 468 far-flung passenger stations. It operates every hour of every day. On an average weekday, it carries more than 4.7 million passengers and, over the course of a year, it transports approximately 1.4 billion riders. By any measure, the New York City subway system is America's largest and busiest.

Given the subway's enclosed spaces, extraordinary passenger volume, and cultural and economic importance, it is unsurprising—and undisputed—that terrorists view it as a prime target. In fact, terrorists have targeted it before. In 1997, police uncovered a plot to bomb Brooklyn's Atlantic Avenue subway station—a massive commuter hub that joins 10 different subway lines and the Long Island Railroad. In 2004, police thwarted another plot to bomb the Herald Square subway station, which networks eight different subway lines in midtown Manhattan.

Other cities have not been so fortunate in protecting their mass transportation systems. In 2004, terrorists killed over 240 people by using concealed explosives to bomb commuter trains in Madrid and Moscow. On July 7, 2005, terrorists—again using concealed explosives—killed more than 56 people and wounded another 700 individuals by launching a coordinated series of attacks on the London subway and bus systems. Two weeks later, on July 21, 2005, terrorists launched a second but unsuccessful wave of concealed explosive attacks on the London subway system.

That same day, the New York City Police Department ("NYPD") announced the Container Inspection Program (the "Program") that is the subject of this litigation. The NYPD designed the Program chiefly to deter terrorists from carrying concealed explosives onto the subway system and, to a lesser extent, to uncover any such attempt. Pursuant to the Program, the NYPD establishes daily inspection checkpoints at selected subway facilities. A "checkpoint" consists of a group of uniformed police officers standing at a folding table near the row of turnstiles disgorging onto the train platform. At the table, officers search the bags of a portion of subway riders entering the station.

In order to enhance the Program's deterrent effect, the NYPD selects the checkpoint locations "in a deliberative manner that may appear random, undefined, and unpredictable." In addition to switching checkpoint locations, the NYPD also varies their number, staffing, and scheduling so that the "deployment patterns ... are constantly shifting." While striving to maintain the veneer of random deployment, the NYPD bases its decisions on a sophisticated host of criteria, such as fluctuations in passenger volume and threat level, overlapping coverage provided by its other counterterrorism initiatives, and available manpower.

The officers assigned to each checkpoint give notice of the searches and make clear that they are voluntary. Close to their table they display a large poster notifying passengers that "backpacks and other containers [are] subject to inspection." The Metropolitan Transportation Authority, which operates the subway system, makes similar audio announcements in subway stations and on trains. A supervising sergeant at the checkpoint announces through a bullhorn that all persons wishing to enter the station are subject to a container search and those wishing to avoid the search must leave the station. Although declining the search is not by itself a basis for arrest, the police may arrest anyone who refuses to be searched and later attempts to reenter the subway system with the uninspected container.

Officers exercise virtually no discretion in determining whom to search. The supervising sergeant establishes a selection rate, such as every fifth or tenth person, based upon considerations such as the number of officers and the passenger volume at that particular checkpoint. The officers then search individuals in accordance with the established rate only.

Once the officers select a person to search, they limit their search as to scope, method, and duration. As to scope, officers search only those containers large enough to carry an explosive device, which means, for example, that they may not inspect wallets and small purses. Further, once they identify a container of eligible size, they must limit their inspection "to what is minimally necessary to ensure that the . . . item does not contain an explosive device," which they have been trained to recognize in various forms. They may not intentionally look for other contraband, although if officers incidentally discover such contraband, they may arrest the individual carrying it. Officers may not attempt to read any written or printed material. Nor may they request or record a passenger's personal information, such as his name, address, or demographic data.

The preferred inspection method is to ask the passenger to open his bag and manipulate his possessions himself so that the officer may determine, on a purely visual basis, if the bag contains an explosive device. If necessary, the officer may open the container and manipulate its contents himself. Finally, because officers must conduct the inspection for no "longer than necessary to ensure that the individual is not carrying an explosive device," a typical inspection lasts for a matter of seconds.

II. The Bench Trial and the District Court's Decision

Two weeks after the Program commenced, plaintiffs sued to halt it. During discovery, plaintiffs requested that the NYPD produce confidential data reflecting the number and location of checkpoints deployed since the Program's inception. The bench trial lasted two days. Of the evidence elicited, most relevant to this appeal is the testimony of three defense expert witnesses: David Cohen, the NYPD's Deputy Commissioner for Intelligence, Michael Sheehan, the NYPD's Deputy Commissioner for Counter-Terrorism, and Richard C. Clarke, former Chair of the Counter-Terrorism Security Group of the National Security Council. Each witness offered nearly identical opinions as to the Program's efficacy, and supported their opinions with nearly identical reasons.

The expert testimony established that terrorists "place a premium" on success. Accordingly, they seek out targets that are predictable and vulnerable—traits they ascertain through surveillance and a careful assessment of existing security measures. They also plan their operations carefully: they "rehearse the attack, they train it, they do dry runs." In light of these priorities, the Al-Qaeda Manual advises that terrorists "traveling on a mission" should avoid security "check points along the way."

The witnesses also testified that the Program's flexible and shifting deployment of checkpoints deters a terrorist attack because it introduces the variable of an unplanned checkpoint inspection and thus "throws uncertainty into every aspect of terrorist operations—from planning to implementation." Terrorists "don't want to be in a situation where one of their bombs doesn't go off, because on the day that they chose to go in subway station X, there were police doing searches." That unpredictability deters both a single-bomb attack and an attack consisting of multiple, synchronized bombings, such as those in London and Madrid.

Because the Program deters a terrorist from planning to attack the subway in the first place, the witnesses testified, the fact that a terrorist could decline a search and leave the subway system makes little difference in assessing the Program's efficacy. Similarly, the precise number of checkpoints employed on any given day is relatively unimportant because the critical aspects of the Program are that it is "random" and "routine," the combination of which "creates an incentive for terrorists to choose . . . an easier target." Finally, the testimony established that each of the City's counter-terrorism programs incrementally increases security and that taken together, the programs "address the broad range of concerns related to terrorist activity" and "have created an environment in New York City that has made it more difficult for terrorists to operate."

Upon the conclusion of closing arguments, the District Court issued an opinion in which it concluded that the Program was constitutional pursuant to the special needs exception. In its analysis, the District Court determined that the Program served a special need because it aimed to prevent, through deterrence and detection, "a terrorist attack on the subways."

Having established that the Program served a special need, the District Court proceeded to balance several factors. It concluded that the government interest in preventing a terrorist attack on the subway was of the very highest order as to the Program's efficacy, the District Court credited the expert testimony in concluding that the Program was a reasonable method of deterring (and detecting) a terrorist bombing on the subway.

Finally, the District Court resolved that the searches were "narrowly tailored and only minimally intrude upon privacy interests." Accordingly, the Court concluded that on balance the Program was constitutional, denied plaintiffs' application for declaratory and injunctive relief, and dismissed the complaint. This appeal promptly ensued.

DISCUSSION

II. The Special Needs Doctrine

The Fourth Amendment to the Constitution provides that, "The right of the people to be secure in their persons, houses, papers, and effects, against unreasonable searches and seizures, shall not be violated, and no Warrants shall issue, but upon probable cause. . . ." As the Fourth Amendment's text makes clear, the concept of reasonableness is the touchstone of the constitutionality of a governmental search. What is reasonable, of course, depends on all of the circumstances surrounding the search or seizure and the nature of the search or seizure itself. As a general matter, a search is unreasonable unless supported by a warrant issued upon probable cause. However, neither a warrant nor probable cause, nor, indeed, any measure of individualized suspicion, is an indispensable component of reasonableness in every circumstance.

In light of those longstanding principles, we upheld a program employing metal detectors and hand searches of carry-on baggage at airports. We determined that the purpose of the search program was not to serve as a general means for enforcing the criminal laws but rather to prevent airplane hijacking by terrorists. We then dispensed with the traditional warrant and probable cause requirements and instead balanced "the need for a search against the offensiveness of the intrusion." We concluded that, when the risk is the jeopardy to hundreds of human lives and millions of dollars of property inherent in the pirating or blowing up of a large airplane, the danger alone meets the test of reasonableness, so long as the search is conducted in good faith for the purpose of preventing hijacking or like damage and with reasonable scope and the passenger has been given advance notice of his liability to such a search so that he can avoid it by choosing not to travel by air.

Although at the time we lodged our decision within the broad rubric of reasonableness, our reasoning came to be known as the "special needs exception" roughly one decade later. Only in those exceptional circumstances in which special needs, beyond the need for normal law enforcement, make the warrant and probable-cause requirement impracticable, is a court entitled to substitute its balancing of interests for that of the Framers. Both before and after the doctrine's formal denomination, courts have applied it in a variety of contexts relevant here, including random airport searches, and highway sobriety checkpoints, highway information-gathering checkpoints, border patrol checkpoints; and random checkpoint stops near military installation.

The doctrine's central aspects are as follows. First, as a threshold matter, the search must "serve as its immediate purpose an objective distinct from the ordinary evidence gathering associated with crime investigation." Second, once the government satisfies that threshold requirement, the court determines whether the search is reasonable by balancing several competing considerations. These balancing factors include (1) the weight and immediacy of the government interest, (2) the nature of the privacy interest allegedly compromised by the search, (3) the character of the intrusion imposed by the search, and (4) the efficacy of the search in advancing the government interest.

III. The Program Is Constitutional

We address in turn each of plaintiffs' arguments as delineated in the introduction.

A. The special needs doctrine does not require that the subject of the search possess a diminished privacy interest

Plaintiffs first raise the purely legal contention that, as a threshold matter, the special needs doctrine applies only where the subject of the search possesses a reduced privacy interest. While it is true that in most special needs cases the relevant privacy interest is somewhat "limited," the Supreme Court never has implied—much less actually held—that a reduced privacy expectation is an essential condition of special needs analysis. For example, in *Ferguson v. Charleston*, (2001) the Court struck down a warrantless, suspicionless search regime in which a hospital subjected prenatal care patients to drug tests and then disclosed the test results to the police for law enforcement purposes. The Court expressly noted that the patients had a full privacy expectation in their medical test results but that the existence of such a privacy expectation was not "critical." Instead, the "critical difference" upon which the decision turned was that the policy failed to serve a special need "divorced from the State's generalized interest in law enforcement."

That approach comports with our long-standing view that the nature of the relevant privacy interest must not be treated in isolation or accorded dispositive weight, but rather must be balanced against other fact-specific considerations. In *United States v. Albarado*, we dismissed the notion that a full expectation of privacy, by itself, rendered unconstitutional warrantless, suspicionless magnetometer searches:

> It has been suggested that those who seek to travel on a common carrier have a lower "expectation of privacy" regarding their person and the bags they carry.... Such a suggestion has little analytical significance; if it were announced that all telephone lines would be tapped, it could be claimed that the public had no expectation of privacy on the telephone. What is clear is that the public does have the expectation, or at least under our Constitution has the right to expect, that no matter the threat, the search to counter it will be as limited as possible, consistent with meeting the threat.

Accordingly, to the extent that the principle needs clarification, we expressly hold that the special needs doctrine does not require, as a threshold matter, that the subject of the search possess a reduced privacy interest. Instead, once the government establishes a special need, the nature of the privacy interest is a factor to be weighed in the balance.

B. The container inspection program serves a special need

Plaintiffs next maintain that the District Court erred in concluding that the Program serves the special need of preventing a terrorist attack on the subway. Plaintiffs contend that the Program's immediate objective is merely to gather evidence for the purpose of enforcing the criminal law.

As a factual matter, we agree with the District Court's conclusion that the Program aims to prevent a terrorist attack on the subway. Defendants implemented the Program in response to a string of bombings on commuter trains and subway systems abroad, which indicates that its purpose is to prevent similar occurrences in New York City. In its particulars, the Program seeks out explosives only: officers are trained to recognize different explosives, they search only those containers capable of carrying explosive devices, and they may not intentionally search for other contraband, read written or printed material, or request personal information.

Additionally, the Program's voluntary nature illuminates its purpose: that an individual may refuse the search provided he leaves the subway establishes that the Program seeks to prevent a terrorist, laden with concealed explosives, from boarding a subway train in the first place.

As a legal matter, courts traditionally have considered special the government's need to prevent and discover latent or hidden hazards in order to ensure the safety of mass transportation mediums, such as trains, airplanes, and highways. We have no doubt that concealed explosives are a hidden hazard, that the Program's purpose is prophylactic, and that the nation's busiest subway system implicates the public's safety. Accordingly, preventing a terrorist from bombing the subways constitutes a special need that is distinct from ordinary post hoc criminal investigation. Further, the fact that an officer incidentally may discover a different kind of contraband and arrest its possessor does not alter the Program's intended purpose.

C. On balance, the Program is constitutional

Having concluded that the Program serves a special need, we next balance the factors set forth above to determine whether the search is reasonable and thus constitutional.

(i) The government interest is immediate and substantial

Given the enormous dangers to life and property from terrorists bombing the subway, we need not labor the point with respect to need. As they must, plaintiffs concede that the interest in preventing such an attack is paramount but contend that the lack of any specific threat to the subway system weakens that interest by depriving it of immediacy. Plaintiffs again overstate the relevance of a specific, extant threat.

No express threat or special imminence is required before we may accord great weight to the government's interest in staving off considerable harm. A demonstration of danger as to any particular airport or airline is not required since it is sufficient that the Government have a compelling interest in preventing an otherwise pervasive societal problem from spreading. All that is required is that the risk to public safety be substantial and real instead of merely symbolic. Where the risk to public safety is substantial and real, blanket suspicionless searches calibrated to the risk may rank as reasonable—for example, searches now routine at airports and at entrances to courts and other official buildings.

Pursuant to this standard, the threat in this case is sufficiently immediate. In light of the thwarted plots to bomb New York City's subway system, its continued desirability as a target, and the recent bombings of public transportation systems in Madrid, Moscow, and London, the risk to public safety is substantial and real. This is very analogous to the legality of searches at airports. There can be no doubt that preventing terrorist attacks on airplanes is of paramount importance. It is hard to overestimate the need to search air travelers for weapons and explosives before they are allowed to board the aircraft. As illustrated over the last three decades, the potential damage and destruction from air terrorism is horrifically enormous.

(ii) A subway rider has a full expectation of privacy in his containers

The nature of the privacy interest compromised by the search remains an important balancing factor. Whether an expectation of privacy exists for Fourth Amendment purposes depends upon two questions. First, we ask whether the individual, by his conduct, has exhibited an actual expectation of privacy. Second, we inquire whether the individual's expectation of privacy is one that society is prepared to recognize as reasonable.

As to the first question, a person carrying items in a closed, opaque bag has manifested his subjective expectation of privacy by keeping his belongings from plain view and indicating that, for whatever reason, he prefers to keep them close at hand. Further, the Supreme Court has recognized as objectively reasonable a bus rider's expectation that his bag will not be felt in an exploratory manner from the outside, let alone opened and its contents visually inspected or physically manipulated. The Fourth Amendment provides protection to the owner of every container that conceals its contents from plain view." Accordingly, a subway rider who keeps his bags on his person possesses an undiminished expectation of privacy therein. We therefore weigh this factor in favor of plaintiffs.

(iii) The search is minimally intrusive

Although a subway rider enjoys a full privacy expectation in the contents of his baggage, the kind of search at issue here minimally intrudes upon that interest. Several uncontested facts establish that the Program is narrowly tailored to achieve its purpose: (1) passengers receive notice of the searches and may decline to be searched so long as they leave the subway, (2) police search only those containers capable of concealing explosives, inspect eligible containers only to determine whether they contain explosives, inspect the containers visually unless it is necessary to manipulate their contents, and do not read printed or written material or request personal information, (3) a typical search lasts only for a matter of seconds, (4) uniformed personnel conduct the searches out in the open, which reduces the fear and stigma that removal to a hidden area can cause; and (5) police exercise no discretion in selecting whom to search, but rather employ a formula that ensures they do not arbitrarily exercise their authority. Although defendants need not employ "the least intrusive means," to serve the state interest, it appears they have approximated that model. Given the narrow tailoring that the Program achieves, this factor weighs strongly in favor of defendants, as the District Court properly concluded.

(iv) The Program is reasonably effective

In considering the degree to which the seizure advances the public interest, we must remember not to take away from politically accountable officials the decision as to which among reasonable alternative law enforcement techniques should be employed to deal with a serious public danger. That decision is best left to those with a unique understanding of, and responsibility for, limited public resources, including a finite number of police officers. Accordingly, we ought not conduct a searching examination of effectiveness. Instead, we need only determine whether the Program is a reasonably effective means of addressing the government interest in deterring and detecting a terrorist attack on the subway system.

The District Court credited the expert testimony of the government's witnesses concerning the Program's deterrent effect. Plaintiffs neither contest their expertise nor directly attack the substance of their testimony. Instead, plaintiffs claim that the Program can have no meaningful deterrent effect because the NYPD employs too few checkpoints. In support of that claim, plaintiffs rely upon various statistical manipulations of the sealed checkpoint data.

We will not peruse, parse, or extrapolate four months' worth of data in an attempt to divine how many checkpoints the City ought to deploy in the exercise of its day-to-day police power. Counter-terrorism experts and politically accountable officials have undertaken the delicate and esoteric task of deciding how best to marshal their available resources in light of the conditions prevailing on any given day. We will not—and may not—second-guess the minutiae of their considered decisions.

Instead, we must consider the Program at the level of its design. From that vantage, the expert testimony established that terrorists seek predictable and vulnerable targets, and the Program generates uncertainty that frustrates that goal, which, in turn, deters an attack. The randomness of the searches arguably increases the deterrent effects of airport screening procedures.

Plaintiffs next contend that because defendants' experts could not quantify the Program's deterrent effect, their testimony fails as a matter of law to establish efficacy. The concept of deterrence need not be reduced to a quotient before a court may recognize a search program as effective. Indeed, expressing the phenomena in numeric terms often is impossible because deterrence by definition results in an absence of data. Nor would we think, in view of the obvious deterrent purpose of these searches, that the validity of the Government's airport screening program necessarily turns on whether significant numbers of putative air pirates are actually discovered by the searches conducted under the program. For that same reason, the absence of a formal study of the Program's deterrent effect does not concern us.

Plaintiffs further claim that the Program is ineffective because police notify passengers of the searches, and passengers are free to walk away and attempt to reenter the subway at another point or time. Yet we always have viewed notice and the opportunity to decline as beneficial aspects of a suspicionless search regime because those features minimize intrusiveness. For example, in Edwards, we upheld suspicionless airport searches as reasonable "so long as the passenger has been given advance notice of his liability to such a search so that he can avoid it by choosing not to travel by air."

Importantly, if a would-be bomber declines a search, he must leave the subway or be arrested—an outcome that, for the purpose of preventing subway bombings, we consider reasonably effective, especially since the record establishes that terrorists prize predictability. Such "avoidance techniques" can be fraught with uncertainty because a random search program cannot be predicted and its machinations are not likely to be known or available. An unexpected change of plans might well stymie the attack, disrupt the synchronicity of multiple bombings, or at least reduce casualties by forcing the terrorist to detonate in a less populated location.

CONCLUSION

In sum, we hold that the Program is reasonable, and therefore constitutional, because (1) preventing a terrorist attack on the subway is a special need; (2) that need is weighty; (3) the Program is a reasonably effective deterrent; and (4) even though the searches intrude on a full privacy interest, they do so to a minimal degree. We thus AFFIRM the judgment of the District Court.

END OF DECISION

Another recent change affecting the right to travel has been the requirement that all those who seek to use mass transit have with them an approved form of government-issued identification. Now, the issue of having to carry government-issued identification has come up with regard to voting rights. While it is true that there are many situations in the nation that require a person to show identification, the controversy over "Voter ID" laws includes not simply the need to prove identity, but also whether the requirement is based on a desire to put barriers in front of certain groups when it comes to exercising their voting rights.[5] While a discussion of this issue is beyond the scope of this text, it does relate to the right to travel, as illustrated by the following case.

Gilmore v. Gonzales, 435 F.3d 1125 (2006)*

John Gilmore ("Gilmore") sued Southwest Airlines and the United States Attorney General, Alberto R. Gonzales, among other defendants, alleging that the enactment and enforcement of the Government's civilian airline passenger identification policy is unconstitutional. The identification policy requires airline passengers to present identification to airline personnel before boarding or be subjected to a search that is more exacting than the routine search that passengers who present identification encounter. Gilmore alleges that when he refused to present identification or be subjected to a more thorough search, he was not allowed to board his flights to Washington, D.C. Gilmore asserts that because the Government refuses to disclose the content of the identification policy, it is vague and uncertain and therefore violated his right to due process. He also alleges that when he was not allowed to board the airplanes, Defendants violated his right to travel, right to be free from unreasonable searches and seizures, right to freely associate, and right to petition the government for redress of grievances. We hold that neither the identification policy nor its

---

5. One useful discussion of the Voter ID issue can be found on the website of the National Conference of State Legislatures at http://www.ncsl.org/research/elections-and-campaigns/voter-id.aspx.

* The case has been heavily edited and paraphrased by the authors for clarity. See disclaimer in introduction.

application to Gilmore violated Gilmore's constitutional rights, and therefore we deny the petition.

Background

On July 4, 2002, Gilmore, a California resident and United States citizen, attempted to fly from Oakland International Airport to Baltimore-Washington International Airport on a Southwest Airlines flight. Gilmore intended to travel to Washington, D.C. to "petition the government for redress of grievances and to associate with others for that purpose." He was not allowed to fly, however, because he refused to present identification to Southwest Airlines when asked to do so.

Gilmore approached the Southwest ticketing counter with paper tickets that he already had purchased. When a Southwest ticketing clerk asked to see his identification, Gilmore refused. Although the clerk informed Gilmore that identification was required, he refused again. Gilmore asked whether the requirement was a government or Southwest rule, and whether there was any way that he could board the plane without presenting his identification. The clerk was unsure, but posited that the rule was an FAA security requirement. The clerk informed Gilmore that he could opt to be screened at the gate in lieu of presenting the requisite identification. The clerk then issued Gilmore a new boarding pass, which indicated that he was to be searched before boarding the airplane. At the gate, Gilmore again refused to show identification. In response to his question about the source of the identification rule, a Southwest employee stated that it was a government law. Gilmore then met with a Southwest customer service supervisor, who told him that the identification requirement was an airline policy. Gilmore left the airport, without being searched at the gate.

Gilmore filed a complaint against Defendants, challenging the constitutionality of several security measures, which he collectively referred to as "the Scheme," including the identification policy, CAPPS and CAPPS II, and No-Fly and Selectee lists. Gilmore alleged that these government security policies and provisions violated his right to due process, right to travel, right to be free from unreasonable searches and seizures, right to freely associate, and right to petition the government for redress of grievances. Gilmore also alleged that "similar requirements have been placed on travelers who use government-regulated passenger trains, and that similar requirements are being instituted for interstate bus travel."

Discussion

III. Right To Travel

Gilmore alleges that the identification policy violates his constitutional right to travel because he cannot travel by commercial airlines without presenting identification, which is an impermissible federal condition. We reject Gilmore's right to travel argument because the Constitution does not guarantee the right to travel by any particular form of transportation. Defendant's right to travel was not violated given that other forms of travel remained possible, even if they were not what were most convenient.

This court's earlier decision in *Miller v. Reed* (9th Cir.1999) is on point. In *Miller*, the plaintiff challenged California's requirement that applicants submit their social security numbers to the DMV in order to obtain valid drivers licenses. The plaintiff alleged that this policy violated his fundamental right to interstate travel and his right to freely exercise his religion. In affirming the district court's dismissal, we concluded that "by denying Miller a single mode of transportation—in a car driven by himself—the DMV did not unconstitutionally impede Miller's right to interstate travel." Although we recognized the fundamental right to interstate travel, we also acknowledged that burdens on a single mode of transportation do not implicate the right to interstate travel.

Like the plaintiff in *Miller*, Gilmore does not possess a fundamental right to travel by airplane even though it is the most convenient mode of travel for him. Moreover, the identification policy's "burden" is not unreasonable. The right of all citizens to be "free to travel throughout the length and breadth of our land uninhibited by statutes, rules, or regulations which unreasonably burden or restrict this movement. The identification policy requires that airline passengers either present identification or be subjected to a more extensive search. The more extensive search is similar to searches that we have determined were reasonable and "consistent with a full recognition of appellant's constitutional right to travel.

In *Davis*, an airline employee searched the defendant's briefcase as part of the airport's preboarding screening procedure. We held that airport screening searches of potential passengers and their immediate possessions for weapons and explosives is reasonable so long as each potential passenger maintains the right to leave the airport instead of submitting to the search. In so holding, we considered several airport screening procedures, including behavioral profiling, magnetometer screening, identification check, and physical search of the passenger's person and carry-on baggage. We see little difference between the search measures discussed in *Davis* and those that comprise the "selectee" search option of the passenger identification policy at hand. Additionally, Gilmore was free to decline both options and use a different mode of transportation. In sum, by requiring Gilmore to comply with the identification policy, Defendants did not violate his right to travel.

IV. Fourth Amendment

Gilmore next alleges that both options under the identification policy—presenting identification or undergoing a more intrusive search—are subject to Fourth Amendment limitations and violated his right to be free from unreasonable searches and seizures.

Request For Identification

Gilmore argues that the request for identification implicates the Fourth Amendment because "the government imposes a severe penalty on citizens who do not comply." Gilmore argues that the request for identification violates the Fourth Amendment because it constitutes "a warrantless general search for identification" that is unrelated to the goals of detecting weapons or explosives.

The request for identification, however, does not implicate the Fourth Amendment. A request for identification by the police does not, by itself, constitute a Fourth Amendment seizure. Rather, an individual is seized within the meaning of the Fourth Amendment only if, in view of all of the circumstances surrounding the incident, a reasonable person would have believed that he was not free to leave. In Delgado, the Supreme Court held that INS agents' questioning of factory workers about their citizenship status did not constitute a Fourth Amendment seizure. In $25,000 U.S. Currency, we held that a DEA agent's request for identification from a person waiting to board a flight was not a Fourth Amendment seizure.

Similarly, an airline personnel's request for Gilmore's identification was not a seizure within the meaning of the Fourth Amendment. Gilmore's experiences at the airport provides the best rebuttal to his argument that the requests for identification imposed a risk of arrest and were therefore seizures. Gilmore twice tried to board a plane without presenting identification, and twice left the airport when he was unsuccessful. He was not threatened with arrest or some other form of punishment; rather he simply was told that unless he complied with the policy, he would not be permitted to board the plane. There was no penalty for noncompliance.

Request To Search

Gilmore argues that the selectee option is also unconstitutional because the degree of intrusion is unreasonable. We reject this argument because it is foreclosed by prior decisions holding otherwise. The identification policy's search option implicates the Fourth Amendment. The government's participation in airport search programs brings any search conducted pursuant to those programs within the reach of the Fourth Amendment. Airport screening searches, however, do not per se violate a traveler's Fourth Amendment rights, and therefore must be analyzed for reasonableness. To meet the test of reasonableness, an administrative screening search must be as limited in its intrusiveness as is consistent with satisfaction of the administrative need that justifies it. It follows that airport screening searches are valid only if they recognize the right of a person to avoid search by electing not to board the aircraft.

Gilmore was free to reject either option under the identification policy, and leave the airport. In fact, Gilmore did just that. United Airlines presented him with the "selectee" option, which included walking through a magnetometer screening device, being subjected to a handheld magnetometer scan, having a light body patdown, removing his shoes, and having his bags hand searched and put through a CAT-scan machine. Gilmore declined and instead left the airport.

Additionally, the search option is no more extensive or intensive than necessary, in light of current technology, to detect weapons or explosives and is confined in good faith to prevent the carrying of weapons or explosives aboard aircrafts. Passengers may avoid the search by electing not to fly. Therefore, the search option was reasonable and did not violate Gilmore's Fourth Amendment rights.

Gilmore also suggests that the identification policy did not present a meaningful choice, but rather a "Hobson's Choice," in violation of the unconstitutional conditions doctrine. We have held, as a matter of constitutional law, that an airline passenger has a choice regarding searches:

> He may submit to a search of his person and immediate possessions as a condition to boarding; or he may turn around and leave. If he chooses to proceed, that choice, whether viewed as a relinquishment of an option to leave or an election to submit to the search, is essentially a "consent," granting the government a license to do what it would otherwise be barred from doing by the Fourth Amendment.

Gilmore had a meaningful choice. He could have presented identification, submitted to a search, or left the airport. That he chose the latter does not detract from the fact that he could have boarded the airplane had he chosen one of the other two options. Thus, we reject Gilmore's Fourth Amendment arguments.

In sum, we conclude that Defendants did not violate Gilmore's constitutional rights by adopting and implementing the airline identification policy. Therefore, his claims fail on the merits and we deny his petition for review.

END OF OPINION

As in the case of bag searches, the ability to choose the means of travel bears on the legal legitimacy of the identification requirement, tilting the balance in favor of the government's duty to protect the citizenry from potential harm. This balance also comes into play at the border. When choosing to enter the country, as this next case discloses, the ability of the government to condition that choice on insisting on the ability to search is great.

U.S. v. Arnold, 533 F.3d 1003 (2008)*

We must decide whether customs officers at Los Angeles International Airport may examine the electronic contents of a passenger's laptop computer without reasonable suspicion.

On July 17, 2005, forty-three-year-old Michael Arnold arrived at Los Angeles International Airport ("LAX") after a nearly twenty-hour flight from the Philippines. After retrieving his luggage from the baggage claim, Arnold proceeded to customs. U.S. Customs and Border Patrol ("CBP") Officer Laura Peng first saw Arnold while he was in line waiting to go through the checkpoint and selected him for secondary questioning. She asked Arnold where he had traveled, the purpose of his travel, and the length of his trip. Arnold stated that he had been on vacation for three weeks visiting friends in the Philippines.

Peng then inspected Arnold's luggage, which contained his laptop computer, a separate hard drive, a computer memory stick (also called a flash drive or USB

---

* The case has been heavily edited and paraphrased by the authors for clarity. See disclaimer in introduction.

drive), and six compact discs. Peng instructed Arnold to turn on the computer so she could see if it was functioning. While the computer was booting up, Peng turned it over to her colleague, CBP Officer John Roberts, and continued to inspect Arnold's luggage.

When the computer had booted up, its desktop displayed numerous icons and folders. Two folders were entitled "Kodak Pictures" and one was entitled "Kodak Memories." Peng and Roberts clicked on the Kodak folders, opened the files, and viewed the photos on Arnold's computer including one that depicted two nude women. Roberts called in supervisors, who in turn called in special agents with the United States Department of Homeland Security, Immigration and Customs Enforcement ("ICE"). The ICE agents questioned Arnold about the contents of his computer and detained him for several hours. They examined the computer equipment and found numerous images depicting what they believed to be child pornography. The officers seized the computer and storage devices but released Arnold. Two weeks later, federal agents obtained a warrant. Arnold was subsequently charged with crimes stemming from his possession and transportation of child pornography.

Arnold filed a motion to suppress arguing that the government conducted the search without reasonable suspicion. The government countered that: (1) reasonable suspicion was not required under the Fourth Amendment because of the border-search doctrine; and (2) if reasonable suspicion were necessary, that it was present in this case.

Arnold argues that the district court was correct in concluding that reasonable suspicion was required to search his laptop at the border because it is distinguishable from other containers of documents based on its ability to store greater amounts of information and its unique role in modern life.

Arnold argues that "laptop computers are fundamentally different from traditional closed containers," and analogizes them to "homes" and the "human mind." Arnold's analogy of a laptop to a home is based on his conclusion that a laptop's capacity allows for the storage of personal documents in an amount equivalent to that stored in one's home. He argues that a laptop is like the "human mind" because of its ability to record ideas, e-mail, internet chats and web-surfing habits.

The Fourth Amendment states that "the right of the people to be secure in their persons, houses, papers, and effects, against unreasonable searches and seizures, shall not be violated. . . ." Searches of international passengers at American airports are considered border searches because they occur at the "functional equivalent of a border." For example, a search of the passengers and cargo of an airplane arriving at a St. Louis airport after a non-stop flight from Mexico City would clearly be the functional equivalent of a border search. It is a given that the United States, as sovereign, has the inherent authority to protect, and a paramount interest in protecting, its territorial integrity. Generally, "searches made at the border are reasonable simply by virtue of the fact that they occur at the border."

The Supreme Court has stated that:

> The authority of the United States to search the baggage of arriving international travelers is based on its inherent sovereign authority to protect its territorial integrity. By reason of that authority, it is entitled to require that whoever seeks entry must establish the right to enter and to bring into the country whatever he may carry. In other words, the "Government's interest in preventing the entry of unwanted persons and effects is at its zenith at the international border." Therefore, "the luggage carried by a traveler entering the country may be searched at random by a customs officer no matter how great the traveler's desire to conceal the contents may be." Furthermore, "a traveler who carries a toothbrush and a few articles of clothing in a paper bag or knotted scarf may claim an equal right to conceal his possessions from official inspection as the sophisticated executive with the locked attaché case.

Courts have long held that searches of closed containers and their contents can be conducted at the border without particularized suspicion under the Fourth Amendment. Searches of the following specific items have been upheld without particularized suspicion: (1) the contents of a traveler's briefcase and luggage; (2) a traveler's "purse, wallet, or pockets,"; (3) papers found in containers such as pockets; and (4) pictures, films and other graphic materials. Import restrictions and searches of persons or packages at the national borders rest on different considerations and different rules of constitutional law from domestic regulations.

Nevertheless, the Supreme Court has drawn some limits on the border search power. Specifically, the Supreme Court has held that reasonable suspicion is required to search a traveler's anus because "the interests in human dignity and privacy which the Fourth Amendment protects forbid any such intrusion beyond the body's surface on the mere chance that desired evidence might be obtained. However, it has expressly declined to decide "what level of suspicion, if any, is required for non-routine border searches such as strip, body cavity, or involuntary x-ray searches." Furthermore, the Supreme Court has rejected creating a balancing test based on a "routine" and "non-routine" search framework, and has treated the terms as purely descriptive.

Other than when intrusive searches of the person are at issue, the Supreme Court has held open the possibility, "that some searches of property are so destructive as to require" particularized suspicion. (Complete disassembly and reassembly of a car gas tank did not require particularized suspicion). Indeed, the Supreme Court has left open the question of "whether, and under what circumstances, a border search might be deemed 'unreasonable' because of the particularly offensive manner in which it is carried out."

In any event, the district court's holding that particularized suspicion is required to search a laptop, based on cases involving the search of the person, was erroneous. Its reliance on such cases as *United States v. Vance* (9th Cir.1995) (holding that "as the search becomes more intrusive, more suspicion is needed" in the context of a search of the human body), to support its use of a sliding intrusiveness scale to determine when reasonable suspicion is needed to search property at the border is misplaced.

The Supreme Court has stated that complex balancing tests to determine what is a 'routine' search of a vehicle, as opposed to a more 'intrusive' search of a person, have no place in border searches of vehicles. The Supreme Court's analysis determining what protection to give a vehicle was not based on the unique characteristics of vehicles with respect to other property, but was based on the fact that a vehicle, as a piece of property, simply does not implicate the same "dignity and privacy" concerns as "highly intrusive searches of the person."

Therefore, we are satisfied that reasonable suspicion is not needed for customs officials to search a laptop or other personal electronic storage devices at the border.

For the foregoing reasons, the district court's decision to grant Arnold's motion to suppress must be **REVERSED**.

END OF OPINION

Now, not just in terms of U.S. domestic law, but also as a matter of customary international law, the right of a nation to control its borders is considered an essential element of state sovereignty. Based on this, any nation can, if it chooses, conduct a very thorough inspection of everything and everyone passing over their borders. As the preceding case indicates, only if a search is going to be particularly offensive due to its invasiveness, must there be any suspicion of wrongful activity. Although people might hold very personal and sensitive information on electronic devices, a computer or smart phone has no more legal protection at the border than a suitcase.

Now, for more practical reasons a government may choose not to conduct an extremely invasive search of everyone and everything at all times. To do so would require immense expenditure of time and money and would seriously impede commerce and legitimate travel. So nations seek to strike a balance between what they are legally permitted to do and what makes sense at the time. But from both an international law and a constitutional law perspective, the nation has almost unlimited discretion in striking that balance.

Review Questions

1. Consider the following hypothetical set of facts:

Angelina and Brad are driving back to the U.S. after vacationing in Cabo, Mexico. At the border they are stopped by a border patrol agent. The border patrol agent has been on high alert all day looking for drugs. He has no suspicion that Brad and Angelina have any contraband, but he still decides to go through every bag, container, and suitcase in the vehicle to search for contraband. He does this, but does not find anything.

The agent still does not have any particular suspicion that these specific individuals have contraband, but still decides to strip search Brad and Angelina and perform a cavity search on them to see if either is hiding drugs or other contraband in his or her rectum.

Conduct IRAC analyses of these facts.

   a. In the first, evaluate whether or not the search of their personal belongings was permissible.

   b. In the second, evaluate whether or not the cavity search was permissible.

   c. Finally, ask if the results of your analysis in (1) or (2) matter whether the decision to conduct the search in this manner was (a) up to the inspecting officer or (b) subject to some other policy that did not leave the officer any discretion.

2. Discuss the legal implications of the following proposals:

   a. An executive order is issued by the president, directing that no tourist visas can be issued to anyone claiming Islam as their religion.

   b. An executive order is issued to the Department of Justice to withhold federal funding for police departments unless the local police departments double the police presence in "predominantly Muslim" communities.

3. The police departments of several cities begin using commercial data-mining services commonly used by department stores to track potential buyers based on posts on social media that suggest the individuals might be interested in buying products sold by the stores. The police departments use the software to identify individuals who, based on their social media posts, might be susceptible to recruitment by terrorist organizations and bring these individuals in for questioning. Discuss the legal issues connected with such a policy and the pros and cons from a policy perspective.

4. Identify and discuss the legal issues connected with actions to increase border security such as requiring all travelers (citizens as well as non-citizens) entering the United States to allow law enforcement authorities to access any laptops, tablets, or cell phones in the traveler's possession.

Key terms

Border search exception—The **border search exception** is a doctrine that allows searches and seizures at international borders and their functional equivalent without a warrant or probable cause. Balanced against the sovereign's interests at the border are the Fourth Amendment rights of entrants. This balance at international borders means that routine searches are "reasonable" there, and therefore do not violate the Fourth Amendment's proscription against "unreasonable searches and seizures."

Imminent lawless action—Under the imminent lawless action test, speech is not protected by the First Amendment if the speaker intends to incite a violation of the law that is both imminent and likely.

Material support to terrorism—Any property, tangible or intangible, or service, including currency or monetary instruments or financial securities, financial services, lodging, training, expert advice or assistance, safehouses, false documentation or identification, communications equipment, facilities, weapons, lethal substances, explosives, personnel (one or more individuals who may be or include oneself), and transportation, except medicine or religious materials.

Profiling—The act or process of extrapolating information about a person based on known traits or tendencies. "**Racial profiling**" refers to the discriminatory practice by law enforcement officials of targeting individuals for suspicion of crime based on the individual's race, ethnicity, religion, or national origin.

Further Reading

Abel, Nikolas, *U.S. v. Mehanna, the First Amendment, and Material Support in the War on Terror.* Boston College Law Review (August, 2012). Available at SSRN: http://ssrn.com/abstract=2123407.

McDonnell, Thomas M., *Targeting the Foreign Born by Race and Nationality: Counter-Productive in the 'War on Terrorism'?* Pace International Law Review, Vol. 16, 2004. Available at SSRN: http://ssrn.com/abstract=2798700.

Powell, H. Jefferson. *Targeting Americans: The Constitutionality of the U.S. Drone War*, 1st Ed. (Oxford, 2016).

Smith, Brandon J., *Protecting Citizens and Their Speech: Balancing National Security and Free Speech When Prosecuting the Material Support of Terrorism* (March 13, 2012). Available at SSRN: http://ssrn.com/abstract=2021415.

Concluding Thoughts

In this textbook, we have provided you some cases that illustrate the ever-changing nature of the threats to national security both in terms of how those threats relate to our security but also how those threats will continue to raise new questions about our civil liberties.

It is the judgment of the authors that the inter-play between criminal law and national security law will continue to become more closely intertwined as technology relating to transportation and communication continues to bring our global world into our neighborhoods. Whether the field of homeland security law evolves as a new branch of the law, or whether it continues to develop as a bridging mechanism across many different areas of domestic and international law, remains to be seen.

No textbook in this field will ever be able to provide information that is completely up-to-date. In large part, that is why the authors of this text chose to provide actual text of court decisions and not simply an analysis of the final rules that come from those judgments. Contained in the opinions, as you have seen, is the analysis of the best legal minds our nation has had the privilege to enjoy. In this analysis you can find discussions of many of the issues that, in many cases, foreshadow the issues that we deal with today and those that will challenge us tomorrow.

Whether your future studies and career are in law enforcement, politics, the military, the intelligence community, or even business, the issues raised in this text will be among the most important you will have to face. It has been our hope to bring these issues to your attention in a manner that allows, not just for the learning of facts and rules, but also of critical analysis. In the end, this capacity for analysis is the most important aspect of homeland and national security law.

R. James Orr, JD, LL.M   Matt C. Pinsker, JD, LL.M.

Glossary

Administrative Search: A search not performed to look for evidence of criminal activity, but to protect the health and safety of the public.

Alien Tort Statute: A waiver of sovereign immunity which allows aliens to sue the U.S. for violations of the laws of nations.

Article I: Refers to the U.S. Constitution's section on the powers of Congress.

Article II: Refers to the U.S. Constitution's section on the powers of the president.

Article III: Refers to the U.S. Constitution's section on the powers of the judiciary.

Authorization for the Use of Military Force: Under U.S. law, a Congressional authorization to the president that military force may be used in a specific circumstance or set of circumstances. This can be against another nation or against a non-state actor, such as a terrorist organization.

Case law: Opinions written by judges that decide legal issues.

Central Intelligence Agency (CIA): Federal agency devoted to intelligence gathering and analysis to address foreign threats.

Church Committee: The Senate committee in 1976 that investigated civil rights violations by the U.S. intelligence community.

Civil defense: An effort to protect the citizens of a state (generally non-combatants) from military attack. It uses the principles of emergency operations: prevention, mitigation, preparation, response, or emergency evacuation and recovery.

Civil law: Any type of law that is not criminal. Is typically a lawsuit where a person is seeking either money or an injunction.

Classified Information Procedure Act (CIPA): A statute that contains procedural protections against unnecessary disclosure of classified information in criminal trials. The primary purpose of CIPA was to limit the threat by a criminal defendant to disclose classified information during the course of a trial.

Combatant: All members of the armed forces of a party to the conflict are combatants, except medical and religious personnel. As to the situation of members of armed opposition groups, persons do not enjoy the protection against attack accorded to civilians when they take a direct part in hostilities.

Commander in chief: This is the President of the United States, typically used in reference to the individual's supremacy of the military hierarchy.

Common Article 3: Common to the four Geneva Conventions of 1949, it contains the essential rules of the Geneva Conventions in a condensed format and makes them applicable to all armed conflicts.

Common law: Law crafted by tradition and judicial decisions rather than legislation.

Conspiracy: When two or more persons plot to commit a crime.

Constitution (U.S.): The highest law of the land that includes how the U.S. federal government will operate, the powers of the branches of government, and your basic civil rights.

Constitutional Convention: Where the founding fathers drafted the U.S. Constitution. There was extensive discussion over what the powers and duties of the federal government would be.

Criminal law: Relating to the prosecution of an individual for a crime or offense.

Custody: Where a reasonable person would not feel free to leave.

Declaration of War: A formal declaration made by a nation's government that a formal state of war exists between two nations.

Department of Defense: Executive department overseeing the Army, Navy, Air Force, and Marine Corp.

Disaster Preparedness: A continuous cycle of planning, organizing, training, equipping, exercising, evaluating, and taking corrective action in an effort to ensure effective coordination during incident response.

Electronic Communications Privacy Act- Statute which aims to increase privacy protections in the digital age above the bare minimum set by the Fourth Amendment.

Enemy combatant: Any person who fights for the enemy.

Exclusionary Rule- when evidence is taken in violation of an individual's rights by the government, that evidence may not be used against that individual. Exceptions to this rule include if the evidence would have been inevitably discovered or good faith reliance by law enforcement.

Executive agreement: An international agreement, usually regarding routine administrative matters not warranting a formal treaty, made by the executive branch of the U.S. government without ratification by the Senate.

Exigent circumstances: An emergency situation where a delay to get a warrant would likely result in either a loss of the evidence, a loss of life, or serious bodily injury.

Extradition: the official process whereby one country transfers a suspected or convicted criminal to another country.

Federal circuit court: The intermediate appellate courts of the U.S. government that hear appeals from the Federal district courts.

Federal district court: The trial courts of the federal government.

Federal Emergency Management Agency (FEMA): Responds to natural and man-made disasters.

Foreign Intelligence Surveillance Act: Legislation that provides judicial oversight to counter-intelligence activities.

Foreign surveillance: Investigations of the agent of a foreign power.

Fourth Amendment: From the Bill of Rights and regulating the government's powers to search and seize persons and property.

Freedom of Information Act (FOIA): Requires government agencies to turn over certain information to the public.

Graymail: A threat by a criminal defendant to disclose classified information during the course of a trial, presented to the government with a demand to either allow disclosure of the classified information or dismiss the indictment.

Habeas corpus: A writ of habeas corpus is used to bring a prisoner or other detainee before the court to determine if the person's imprisonment or detention is lawful. A *habeas* petition proceeds as a civil action against the agent who holds the defendant in custody. It can also be used to examine any extradition processes used, amount of bail, and the jurisdiction of the court.

Injunction: An order from a court that a person stops an action or starts an action.

International Court of Justice (ICJ): The court of the United Nations that rules on international matters.

International law: A framework of how nations will conduct themselves in their interactions with one another.

Interrogation: Any effort to extract information from a person.

Investigatory detention: Where the police have reasonable suspicion of unlawful conduct and do not allow a person to leave while they investigates.

Judicial review: The power of the courts to review a law and decide if it is constitutional, or if it is unconstitutional and will be struck down.

Lawful combatant: A person allowed to use deadly force in a conflict.

Misdemeanor: A minor criminal offense that typically carries the possibility of no more than a year in jail.

Non-judicial punishment: A form of military justice authorized by Article 15 of the Uniform Code of Military Justice (10 U.S. Code § 815). Non-judicial punishment or "NJP" permits commanders to administratively discipline troops without a court-martial.

PATRIOT ACT: Stands for "Providing Appropriate Tools Required to Intercept and Obstruct Terrorism." Amended the law to enable law enforcement and intelligence to share information and have more ready access to information.

Pike Committee: Investigations through the House of Representatives into the violations of American civil liberties by America's intelligence communities.

Plain view doctrine: What an individual voluntarily exposes to the public eye, that individual will not have any reasonable expectation of privacy in.

Police power of the state: The capacity of the government (federal, state, or local) to regulate behavior and enforce order within their territory for the betterment of the health, safety, morals, and general welfare of their inhabitants.

Political question: A matter the courts will not examine because it is considered to be within the purview of the political process—a matter to be decided between Congress and the president, perhaps through elections, but certainly not in the courts.

Posse Comitatus: The common-law or statute law authority of a county sheriff, or other law officer, to conscript any able-bodied man to assist him in keeping the peace, or a group of citizens assembled by the authorities to deal with an emergency. Under U.S. law, except where specifically authorized by federal statute, use of any part of the U.S. Army, Air Force, Navy, or Marine Corps (but not the National Guard) for civilian law enforcement purposes is illegal.

Power of the purse: The common reference to the ability of the Congress to control activity of the executive branch by limiting funding for certain actions.

Precedent: Because a legal issue was decided a certain way in the past, there is a strong inclination to decide that issue the same way in the future.

Prisoner of war: Legal status bestowed upon captured enemy combatants who were legally allowed to use force and, while using force, followed international law.

Probable cause: A reasonable ground for belief in certain facts—that a crime may have been committed (for an arrest) or when evidence of the crime is present in the place to be searched (for a search).

Public Safety Exception: A situation where the interests of public safety are so compelling that the courts have determined that police can interrogate a person without first issuing a *Miranda* warning, even if the facts and circumstances otherwise would clearly meet the *Miranda* threshold of a custodial interrogation.

Reasonableness standard: In the case of a search or seizure conducted without a warrant, a two-part test that determines, first, whether there was a reasonable basis for doing a search, and second, whether the search was conducted in a reasonable manner.

Reynolds privilege: Application of the state secrets privilege that allows a civil case to go forward, but applies an evidentiary rule that results in exclusion of specific evidence from a legal case based on affidavits submitted by the government stating that introducing this evidence into court proceedings might disclose sensitive information, which might endanger national security.

Ripeness: The readiness of a case for litigation. A claim is not ripe for adjudication if it rests upon contingent future events that may not occur as anticipated, or indeed may not occur at all.

Self-executing treaty: A treaty that becomes judicially enforceable upon ratification. As opposed to a non-self-executing treaty, which becomes judicially enforceable only through the implementation of legislation.

Shocks the conscience doctrine: If the conduct of U.S. law enforcement or other authorities is so vile, repugnant, and inhumane that it shocks the conscience, any evidence obtained in the process will not be admissible in U.S. courts.

Solicitation: The crime of trying to coerce or induce another person into committing a crime.

Standing: The ability of a party to demonstrate to the court sufficient connection to and harm from the law or action challenged to support that party's participation in the case.

State secrets doctrine: The state secrets privilege, when properly invoked, permits the government to block the release of any information in a lawsuit that, if disclosed, would cause harm to national security.

Status of Forces Agreement (SOFA): An agreement between the U.S. and a foreign country in which a U.S. military base resides. These agreements are to prevent problems from arising or address problems should they arise.

Statute: A law created by the passage of a bill by Congress and it being signed by the president. Or if vetoed by the president, then passed by 2/3 supermajority of Congress to override the president's veto.

Stop-and-Frisk: The law enforcement practice of detaining a person based on reasonable suspicion of unlawful conduct and then, based on a reasonable belief the person is armed and dangerous, frisking the individual for a weapon.

Stored Communications Act: Regulates government monitoring of information persons provide to third parties.

Terrorism: The use of violence or threat to achieve a political objective.

Third party doctrine: What a person voluntarily gives to a third party, one will not have any reasonable expectation of privacy in.

Totten bar: The strongest application of the state secrets privilege when a civil lawsuit is such that the very issue of contention is a state secret, allowing the court to dismiss the matter without hearing the merits of the case.

Treaty: An executive agreement between the U.S. and another country (or countries) that is ratified by 2/3 of the U.S. Senate.

Trespass: Property owners and possessors have the right to exclude the persons and property from entering upon their property. Persons who unlawfully place themselves or their property onto the property of others are trespassers.

Tribunal: Any judicial proceeding.

Uniform Code of Military Justice (UCMJ): Federal statutes found at 10 U.S.C. §§ 801–946, the foundation of U.S. military law. It was established by Congress in accordance with Article I, Section 8 of the Constitution, which provides that "The Congress shall have Power. . . . To make Rules for the Government and Regulation of the land and naval forces."

Unlawful combatant: Persons not allowed to use deadly force in a military conflict. Typically persons not part of regular armed force who are engaged in hostilities.

"The Wall": The division between intelligence gathering and law enforcement which can limit the sharing of information.

War powers: Refers to how the U.S. Constitution has divided the powers between the president and Congress to decide when and how the military should be used.

War Powers Resolution: Act passed by Congress and overrode President Nixon's veto requiring presidential notification of the use of military force and time limits on the president's unilateral use of military force.

Warrant: An authorization from a judicial officer (judge or magistrate), based upon probable cause, that allows the government to search for evidence or to seize and hold evidence or a suspect.

Index

Agent of a Foreign Power, *See* Terrorism
Al-Qaeda
   "Global War on Terrorism," announcement of by Bush administration, 535–536
   Al-Aulaqi case, 706
   Al-Bihani case, 460
   AUMF, in relation to, 574
      Taliban, 575
   Boston marathon bombing, in relation to, 554
   Common Article 3, 590
   criminal versus warfare process, 539
   declaration of war, congressional, 396
   el-Hage, in relation to, 222
   FISA order, target of, 185
      surveillance of, 198
   foreign intelligence surveillance of, 176
   in Kenya, 218, 222
   military detention, 565
   Quarles exception, 101
   racial profiling, 683
   September 11th, 2001, 574
   unlawful combatants, Bush administration classification of, 566
   wartime rules, application of, 704
Alien Tort Statute (ATS), 466–467, 490
   Al-Aulaqi case, 708–710
   Alvarez-Machain case, 472
   claims, justification for, 483
   Filartiga case, 468, 471
   human rights, gross violations of, 472, 484
   Jeppesen case, 271
   jurisdiction, district court, 477, 479
   Kiobel case, 478–484
   Law of nations, suing for violation of, 587
   Ntakirutimana case, 528
Anwar al-Aulaqi, 708
Article I, *See* Congress
Article II, *See* President
Article III, *See* Judiciary
Authorization for the Use of Military Force, 446
   attacks on September 11th, in response to, 396, 574
   declare war, Congressional authority to, 395 (*See also* Congress, War Powers)
   Hamdi case, 574
   Rasul case, 584
   targeting AQAP, purposes of assessing the legality of, 707
   War Powers Act, in relation to, 325

Case Law, xiii
   Al-Bihani case, 461
   confession, compulsion of, 79
   declare war, Congress' power to, 441
   extradition treaties, regarding, 529, 532
   Fourth Amendment, 150, 153, 159
      foreign search and seizure, 177
      of U.S. citizens, foreign search, 217
      race, 692
      search and seizure, 150, 159

government surveillance, 29
IRAC approach, application of, xxii
law, hierarchical sources of, xviii
legislative and executive power, balance between, 5
preparedness, emergency response functions of the government, 328
states secret doctrine, 268
Verdugo-Urquidez case, 214
Central Intelligence Agency (CIA)
  Abu Ghraib, 217
  after World War II, creation of, 175
  Aulaqi case, 706, 708–709
  Boland Agreement, 308
  casualty, war 565
  civil rights abuses (*See also* Church Committee) 176
  Craig Smith case, 253–254, 256
  domestic informers, 257
  domestic terrorism, 168
  extradition treaties, 532
  extraordinary rendition program, 270
  Kissinger case, 302
    political secrecy, 232
  safeguards, sharing of information against, 200
  Sims case, 258
  state secrets doctrine, 285 (*See* also State Secrets Doctrine)
    Jeppesen case, 272–273
    Reynolds Privilege, 276, 280
    Totten Bar, 274 (*See* also Totten Bar)
  Truong case, 178
  war powers clause, Article 1 section 8, 392
  warrantless surveillance, 168, 175
  mentioned in, 201, 264, 269, 296, 344, 490, 687–689
CIA. *See* Central Intelligence Agency.
Church Committee, 176, 200
  assassinations, alleged planned, 704
  persecution, domestic, 196
  privacy, statutory protection of, 134
CIPA, *See* Classified Information Protections Act
Civil Defense, 388–389
  Act, Federal, 345
  history of, 345–349
  National Emergency Council, mission of, 343–344
  Office of, 344
  Planning, Office of, 344
  statutory provisions, 352
Civil Law, xix
  civil law, military enforcement of, 383
  exclusionary rule, 63
  national security law, 259
  search and seizure, 382
  state secrets doctrine, in relation to, 260
Classified Information Procedures Act (CIPA), 247–251, 285
  classified information, 248
  Craig Smith case, 253–255, 258–259
  criminal law, 259
  definition of and authorizations, 285, 347
  evidence, admissibility of, 254
  graymail, 246–247, 254, 285
  procedure, substitution, 258
  state secrets doctrine, 260
Combatant, 215, 227, 536, 605, 706, 716
  Boumediene case, 593–594, 598, 600, 604
  combatant, enemy, 536
    classification of, 581
    detainment of, 536–537
    lawful vs. unlawful, 537–538, 560, 566
    Prisoner of War (POW) detention of, 576
    enemy combatants, types of, 537
      laws of war, and, 538–539
      rights of, 538

habeas corpus, resident enemy aliens suing for, 569
combatant, non, 388, 539
Ex Parte Quirin case, 555, 575
Guantanamo Bay, Combatant Status Review Tribunals (CSRT), 588, 592–594, 601
Hamdi case, 574
military commission, tried by, 565
privilege, Prisoner of War, 539
right to habeas corpus, 582–583
U.S. citizens, presidential authority to detain, 573
Combatant Status Review Tribunals (CSRT), *See* Combatant, *See* Department of Defense
Commander in Chief, xvi
Article II, enumeration of powers in, 305, 316, 383, 394, 713
"unique responsibility clause," 440
powers, constitutionally-delegated, 552
war powers clause, controversies concerning, 420
Department of Defense (*See* also Department of Defense)
executive order to, 16
disaster preparedness, 356
Libya, Obama administration's actions in, 439
conduct operations, legal authority to, 443
military establishment, civilian control over, 650
petitioners, detention of, 557
Youngstown Sheet case, question of misuse of powers concerning, 415, 417
war powers, monopoly over, 421
war powers, historical precedent concerning use of, 441
Common Article 3. *See* Geneva Conventions of 1949

Common Law, xxvii–xxviii, 113–114, 402
"right to know," 239
Alien Tort Statute, 473–475, 479
Sosa case, 481–482
court martial, trial by, 563
criminal procedure law, 35
decisions of the President, 6
detainees, Guantanamo Bay, 460
enemies' property, in relation to, 406
espionage, 183
habeus corpus, 585, 587–588
Katz test, 140
military justice, 649
necessity to prove guilt, 70
policing and, 40,
possession of one's person, right to, 48, 114,
property-based doctrine, 146, 151, 155, 158,
sources of law, hierarchical structure of, xviii
trial, admissible evidence at, 256
war powers, 391
Congress
Article I, xxvii, 4
"necessary and proper" clause, 494
Article II, differences between, 394
collect taxes, power to, 305
congressional power, enumeration of, 304
declaration of war, questions concerning, 301
express powers, 33
foreign affairs, 499
Gulf War, declaration of war, 316
habeas corpus, suspension of, 304, 546
impeachment proceedings, ability to bring forward, 308
international law, relation to, 449
legislative authority, 5
political question doctrine, 316
power of the purse, 6, 393

UCMJ, in relation to, 661
war power, enumerated powers of, 391–392
  "declare war," controversy over, 393
  constitutional convention, 394
  declare war, presidential inability to, 402
  declare war, use of congressional authority to, 395
    conflict between presidential use of force and, 396
  Gulf of Tonkin Resolution, 400
  political question, 316
  Prize Cases, 400, 406
power of the purse
  Article I, Section 9, 6, 393
  federalist papers, 393
  framer's intent, 393
  war power, ultimate, 409
Conspiracy, 668
  Hamdan case, 588
  liability, theories of, 271–272
  sedition, 669
    treason clause, in relation to, 671
  solicitation, 668
  speech, freedom of, 664
  statutory test, 205
  U.S. Code, Title 10, 377
Constitutional Convention
  infractions of treaties, punishment for, 473
  military versus civilian authority, relations between, 383
  Ntakirutimana case, in relation to, 526
  war powers, relation to, 394–395, 400 (*See* also Declaration of War)
Criminal Law, xix
  Alvarez-Machain case, 528
  basis of, 35
  civil law, relation to, 260 (*See* Civil Law)
  determination, probable cause, 191

foreign affairs, relation to, 183
law, domestic versus international, 456
laws, observance of, 60
Right to Privacy, 118
silence, Fifth Amendment right to, 261
Special Needs Doctrine, relation to, 722 (*See* also Special Needs Doctrine)
UCMJ, relation to, 624 (*See* also Uniformed Code of Military Justice)

Declaration of War
  authorization for the use of force, legal equivalent to, 396
  Commander in Chief, powers of, 430–431
  Dellums case, 315–317, 319–321
  economy, presidential powers over, 397
  legal requirement, necessity for, 400
  limit, constitutionally-based, 442
  president and congress, tensions between, 301
  U.S. interests, relation to, 399
  War Powers Resolution, 298, 441
  war prizes, 452
Department of Defense (DOD), 363
  advocates, judge, 615
  assistance, resources for, 362
  Boland Agreement, 308
  civilian law enforcement, use of military in support of, 378
  Combatant Status Review Tribunals (CSRT), 588, 602
    classification, combatant versus noncombatant, 588
  Commander in Chief, executive order from, 16
  Hamdi case, 594
  homeland security definition, xii
  Secretary of Defense, 375, 378–380

war powers, congressional, 392
WMD attack, preparedness for, 350
Disaster Preparedness
   Defense Civil Preparedness Agency, 346
   definition of, 388
   Federal Emergency Management Agency, 347
   government, police power of, 328 (*See* also Police Power)
   history of, 352, 354, 356
   presidential directives concerning, 369
   Stafford Act, 29
   states, responsibility of, 344
   use of military for, 376 (*See* also Posse Comitatus Act)

Electronic Communications Privacy Act, 135, 153
   Customer information, FBI access to, 136
Exclusionary Rule, 57, 60, 67
   evidence, suppression of, 693
   exceptions, 64
   interrogation techniques, improper, 70
   limitations, 61–63
   Miranda rights, 85
Executive Agreement. *See* President
Exigent Circumstances, 44–45, 67
   Fourth Amendment, restriction by, 221
   search and seizure, warrantless, 214
   warrant requirement, exception to, 123, 167, 173
      government searches, exceptions to, 218, 223
   warrantless entry, 64
Extradition Treaty
   absence of, 525–526
   Alvarez-Machain case, 472, 528
   bilateral agreements, 484
   treaty, Italian-American, 519, 522
   violation, questions of, 529–532
   extradition, questions concerning presidential authority over, 525–526

Federal District Court, xix
   Alien Tort Statute, in relation to, 467
   Alvarez-Machain case, violation of criminal law, 528
   combatants, unlawful trial of, 592, 605
   court martial, xxx
   Fourth Amendment, special needs exception to, 717
   Habeus corpus, authority to hear questions regarding, 585–586, 588
   Korematsu case, 696
   Law of Nations, related to, 468
   Medellin case, habeus petition for, 507
   Miller case, subpoenas for, 127
   political question, regarding, 296
   Reid case, xxiv
   servicemembers, trial of, 619
   UCMJ, relation to, 615
Federal Emergency Management Agency (FEMA).
   administration, second Bush, 348–349
   administrator, duties of, 357–358
   all-hazards approach, Bush administration's, 349
   establishment of, 347
   Freedom Corps Initiative, 351
FEMA. *See* Federal Emergency Management Agency
Foreign Intelligence Surveillance Act, 135, 176, 183, 244
   "the Wall," in relation to, 202–203 (*See* also The Wall)
   clandestine activities, relation between electronic surveillance and, 188

congressional concerns, response to, 187
content of, 183–195
cross-border actions, 226
first amendment and, 195–196
FISA order, acquisition of, 184
foreign Intelligence Surveillance Court, 187
foreign intelligence, maintaining civil liberties and, 184
Patriot Act, related to, 204–209
prosecution, use of evidence for, 199–202
Rosen case, 196–199
surveillance, foreign, 184, 429
targeting, requirements for, 185–186
TSP, in relation to, 323 (*See* Terrorist Surveillance Program)
FISA. *See* Foreign Intelligence Surveillance Act.
Freedom of Information Act (FOIA), 135, 245–246
"right to know," 239
civil rights abuses, reforms due to, 176
FOIA, documents exempted from, 245
information, classification and declassification of, 236–237
Rosen case, 194

Graymail, *See* Classified Information Procedures Act)
Geneva Conventions of 1949
Al-Bihani case, 461
Common Article 3, 605–606
Hamdan case, 589
declared vs. undeclared war, 590
international vs. non-international conflict, 591
Law of Armed Conflict, 537
POW's, privileges of, 566 (*See* also Prisoner of War)
regular constitution, question of, 591
unlawful combatants, trial of, 592

Habeas Corpus
adequate substitute for, 591–601
Al-Aulaqi case, challenging detention under, 460
balance of government, judiciary's role in, 582
Civil War, President Lincoln and, 540–541
Ex Parte Merriman case, executive authority to suspend habeas corpus, 541–547
definition of, 540, 606
extradition proceedings, 513
laws of war, enemy aliens' violation of, 596
Military Commissions Act, in relation to, 594
regarding extradition, right of review, 513, 515
review of findings, limits of, 525
right to, foreign detainees, 566–567, 573
citizens vs. non-citizens, 574, 583
suspension clause, 540, 598
historical inability to, 544
CSRT, in relation to, 598
suspension of, examples of, 304, 423

Injunction, xix
Al-Aulaqi case, 706
Dellums case, 315
conduct of war, prevention of, 320
Orlando case, 397
private companies, against unlawful seizure of, 416–417
Ripeness issues, 314
against President Bush, in Iraq, 323
International Court of Justice
international law, sources of, 450
jurisdiction, U.S. consent of, 486
Medellin case, 505
Optional Protocol, 506–507, 509

INDEX

Article 94, 510–511
International Law, 449
   self-executing treaty, in relation to, 462, 508–509
      versus non-self-executing, 475–476 judicially enforceable, 511
      definition of, 486
      treaties, U.S. reservations to, 485
      versus non-self-executing, stipulation differences between, 489, 511
   customary international law, 450
   domestic versus, 459
   extradition and, 512
   human rights law, 30, 464
      addressing violations of, legal remedies for, 465
      definition of, 466
      ratify, congress failure to, 475
   jus cogens, 30, 449
   political question doctrine, 293
   prize and capture, right of, 401
   warrant requirement, overseas exemptions from, 219
Investigatory Detention, 85
Islamic State (ISIS)
   FISA order, target of, 185
   operations against, congressional, 410
   Quarles exception to, 101
   wartime rules, application of, 704

Judicial Review, 6–7
   Al-Aulaqi case, 713, 715
   congressional authority, assertion of, 321
   defined, 33
   exclusions from, and political question doctrine, 290
   executive detention of aliens, legality of, 586
   Hamdi case, 578
   Lowry case, and doctrines excluded from, 299–300
   Marbury case, 7
   military tribunals, 572
   political question doctrine, in relation to, 303, 305, 710
   post-surveillance, exceptions to the warrant requirement, 173, 175
   Reynolds case, 279
Judiciary
   Article III, 18
      fifth and sixth Amendments, 24
      foreign relations, reference to, 305
         extradition, questions concerning, 520–521
      independent judiciary, provision of, 4
      judicial review, 6, 33
      section 2, 6, 24
         standing and ripeness, 287 (*See also* Standing, *See also* Ripeness)
         standing, 309
         two-part test, 318
   "case or controversy" requirement, 710
   civil court, necessity of trials and jury in a, 562
   enemy prisoners, right of habeas corpus to, 585
   foreign aliens, authority concerning domestic detention of, 568
   international law, in relation to, 463
   Judiciary Act, 466, 473
      Alien Tort Statute, in relation to, 479
      enemy prisoners, right of habeas corpus to, 585
   jurisdiction, questions of, 707
   national security, relating to, 241
      cases, national security, 711
   political question, doctrine of, 290
   ripeness, necessity of, 320
   treason clause, 671
   treason, crime of, 562

Lawful combatant, *See* Combatant
Law of Armed Conflict, 536
   combatant, unlawful, 538
   enemy combatant, killing of, 716
   POW, status of, 539 (*See* also Prisoner of War)

Mutual-Assured Destruction (MAD), 346

Non-Judicial Punishment, *See* Uniform Code of Military Justice
Non-self-executing Treaty, *See* International Law

Osama Bin-Laden
   El-Shifa case, question of political doctrine, related to, 712
   raid against, U.S. Navy seals, 215, 224
   searches and seizures, foreign, 209

PATRIOT Act
   "significant purpose," requirement, 207
   "The Wall," lowering of, 202, 204 (*See* also The Wall)
   FISA, in relation to, 203–204, 206
   minimization procedures, 205,
   Rosen case, 194
   unlawful prosecution, risk of, 205
Pike Committee, 176
Plain View Doctrine, 124–125, 144, 165
   home, warrantless visual surveillance of, 139
Police Power, 31
   application of, 340
   constitution, state right under the, 35
   international law, in relation to, 531
   of the state, 333
      extreme cases, 339
      reasonable regulations, necessity of embracing, 333
   of the government, 328
   Tenth Amendment, in relation to, 328
   regulate behavior, government authority to, 331
   temporary curfews, necessity of, 341
Political Question Doctrine, 287–288
   Al-Aulaqi case, 710, 714
      political questions, typical sources of, 711
   conditions of application, 299–300
   Dellums case, First Gulf War, 315
   El-Shifa case, 289–294
   foreign relations, disputes involving, 291–292, 712
   judicial review, exclusion of controversies from, 290
   nonjusticiable, factors to render a case, 303–304
Posse Comitatus, 376–377
   exceptions to, 380
   Title 18 U.S. Code, in relation to, 377, 382–383
   U.S. military, legal involvement of, 385
Power of the Purse, *See* Congress
President
   Article II, 305, 394, 713
      appoint ambassadors, power to, 305, 499
      conduct of foreign affairs, power over U.S., 440
      constitutional authority, inherent, 28
      framer's intent concerning, 305
      make treaties, power to, 305, 499
      vested powers, 4–5
      wage war, questions concerning presidential ability to, 301
      Youngstown Sheet case, power to seize commercial industries, 416
   commander in chief, *See* Commander in Chief
   executive agreement, 490

congressional authority, superseded by, xxx
Ntakirutimana case, 525–526
suspend habeas corpus, inability to, 546
treaties, power to make, 484
    extradition, questions concerning, 525–526
war powers, 316, 394
    congressional authorization, necessity of, 395
    internment of Japanese-American nationals, 696
    military forces, direction of, 440
    presidential versus congressional war powers, conflict between, 393
    Prize Cases, 400
    War Powers Resolution, 429
        infringement on presidential powers, questions over, 431
Prisoner of War, *See* Combatant
Public Safety Exception, 95
    Quarles case, 99
    Loukas case, 628

Reasonableness Standard, 39
    El-Hage case, searches of foreign citizens, 217–219, 222
    Fourth Amendment, reasonableness clause of, 39
    search and seizure, 40
    Terry case, 50
    two-part test,
    law enforcement, use of the military for, 384
    special needs doctrine, 720 (*See* also Special Needs Doctrine)
    stop-and-frisk, relation to, 56 (*See* also Stop-and-frisk)
    surveillance, 182
    U.S. citizen, question of stop-and-frisk- target, 209
    versus warrant requirement, 216
Reynolds Privilege, 264–265
    claims, steps to analyzing, 275–278
    definition of, 285
    dismissal, steps requiring, 281
    evidentiary privilege, 273, 714 (*See* also State Secrets Doctrine)
    in camera review, 268
    Jeppesen case, 278–280
    Reynolds case, 265, 268–269
    Totten Bar, in contrast to, 268–269, 714 (*See* also Totten Bar)
Ripeness, 287, 313
    two-part test, 314
    premature adjudication, prevention of, 314
    Dellums case, 320–322

Search
    administrative, 42–43, 219
        warrant requirement, exemption from, 219 (*See* also Warrant Requirement)
    search and seizure, (*See* Search and Seizure)
    warrantless, 40
        Fourth Amendment, 139
        U.S. citizens, domestic searches of, 223
        U.S. citizens, overseas searches of, 219
Search and Seizure
    "trespass" approach, 114
    foreign intelligence gathering, 177
    Fourth Amendment, in relation to, 142, 172, 548
        reasonableness, 39, 170 (*See* also Reasonableness)
    search vs. inspection, 630, 148
    Katz case, 119–120
    non-citizens, foreign searches of, 210
    property -based view, 124
    technology's impact on, 109
    unlawful, 59, 196
Self-executing Treaty, *See* International Law

Shocks the Conscience Doctrine, 216
   definition of, 228
   international human rights law, 464
     (*See* also International Law)
Solicitation, 668
   freedom of speech, 664
   Rahman case, 674
   requirements for, 668
Standing, 309
   definition of, 325
   requirement for, 287
     Article III, judiciary power under, 287 (*See* also Judiciary)
State Secrets Doctrine, 273
   controversial application of, 285
   dismissal of case under, 283
   evidence, required categories of, 280
   Jeppesen case, 270–272
   military secrets, privilege against revealing, 274
   national security, balance between principles and, 270
   Totten Bar vs. *Reynolds* Privilege, 268, 273, 278, 714
Stop-and-Frisk, 49, 696
   "*Terry* stop," 45
   racial profiling and, 55, 695
   reasonableness, 49, 55–56
   Terry case, 46
     distinctions of, 48
   versus search and seizure, 49
   warrant requirement, exceptions to, 173
Stored Communications Act, 135
   categories of information, access requirements for, 136
   congressional passage of, 136
   Stored electronic communications, acquisition of contents of, 135

Terrorism
   Abu Ghraib, scandal concerning, 655
   Al-Qaeda and, 222 (*See* also Al-Qaeda)
   AUMF, authorization for presidential use of force, 396, 574, 593
   Department of Homeland Security, initial focus of, 351
     public health statues, 367
     PPD-8, national preparedness, 371–272
   FISA, evidence of crimes, related to, 203
     cross-border actions, 226
   foreign power, agent of, 228
   Gillman Commission, 350
   homeland security, definition of, xii
   national security information, classification of, 235
     cases involving, 248
   material support of, 675, 734
   overseas searches, warrant requirement and, 216
   PATRIOT Act, 204
   PDD 62, counterterrorism coordination, 350
   Quarles exception, 101
   racial profiling, in relation to, 682
   secretary of state
     authority to designate a terrorist group, 676
   transnational aspect of, 35
   unlawful combatants, 538
   WWII, incident of domestic terrorism, 555
Terrorist Surveillance Program (TSP), 323–324
The Wall, 201
   9/11, prior to, 201
   PATRIOT Act, relation to, 202 (*See* PATRIOT Act)
Third-Party Doctrine, 127
   Miller case, 127
     Fourth Amendment, in relation to, 129
   Smith case, 133
     the Press, First Amendment protection of rights, 239

Timothy McVeigh, 350
Totten Bar, 260, 286
    definition of, 262, 264
    dismissal under, 282
    Jeppesen case, adjudication of claims, 273–275
        appropriate use of, 279
    military, state secrets privilege and, 714
    Totten case, state secrets doctrine, 273, 279 (*See* also State Secrets Doctrine)
    versus *Reynolds* privilege, 268–269, 273–275, 278, 714

Treaty
    "last in time" rule, 527
    Alien Tort Statue, in relation to, 587
    Alvarez-Machain case, 528
    constitutional power over, xxvi
    customary international law, 450 (*See* also International Law)
    detainees, Bush administration classification of combatants, 566
    extradition, 512, 515, 526
    habeas corpus, in relation to, 513
    making treaties, state's limits on, 499
    nations, contract between, 487, 509
    Ntakirutimana case, in relation to, 525
    presidential power to create, 542 (*See* also President)
    punishment for infractions of, 473
    self vs. non-self-executing, *See* International Law

Trespass
    "technical" trespass, 151
        surveillance, 153
    common-law, 146
    Fourth Amendment, 113, 139, 171
    Katz case, 152
    unreasonable search, 386
Tribunal, 536
    "some evidence" standard, 582
    Articles of War, in relation to, 558
    court, unlawful influence of, 622 (*See* also Uniform Code of Military Justice)
    Ex parte Milligan case, 554, 577
    Geneva Conventions 591
    Hamdi case, 575, 579
    hearsay evidence, admission in court of, 601
    human rights, violations of, 522
        Rwandan genocide, 523
    ICJ, 505 (*See* also International Court of Justice)
    law of war, offenses against, 559, 564
    Optional Protocol, in relation to, 509
    prisoners of war, 539
    reading of rights, 624

UCMJ, *See* Inform Code of Military Justice
Uniform Code of Military Justice (UCMJ), 392
    article 118, against murder, 463
    Article 60, Convening Authority, 618
    Article 88, insulting senior leaders, 637
    Campbell case, 631
    command influence, 620
    court martial, 536
    criminal procedure, stages of, 615
    criminal code, Articles 77–134, 640
        "General Article," 643–645
        AWOL, desertion, 640
        dereliction of duty, 653
        Abu Ghraib, 655
            maltreatment, 658
        Mackey case, desertion, 642
        officer, conduct unbecoming of, 645
            serious behavior, Article 133, 651
    definition of, 661
    military justice system, legal basis for, 608

military justice, modernization of, 615
military servicemembers, application of laws to, 611
non-judicial punishment, 616
purpose of, 611
reading of rights requirement, 624–625
unlawful command influence, 622
Unlawful Combatant, *See* Combatant

War Powers, 391
AUMF, relation to, 461
congress, enumerated powers of, 391–392
declaration of war, authorization for use of force *versus*, 395
essential liberties, removal of, 582
framer's intent, 394, 399
Japanese-Americans, internment of, 696
military trail of civilians, 609
power of the purse, 393, 409
president, enumerated powers of, 394
Prize Cases, 400, 407
war powers, congressional, 441
war powers, joint resolution concerning, 429
Youngstown Sheet case, 414
war powers, presidential limits on, 421
War Powers Resolution, 297, 428
Campbell case, 310–311
presidential war powers, infringement upon, 431
reporting clause, 301
role of Congress, 298
Warrant Requirement
custodial inventory searches, 218
exceptions to, 173–174
administrative searches, 219
exigent circumstances, 167
foreign intelligence, 179–181
executive, needs of the, 180
FISA, in relation to, 187
Fourth Amendment, in relation to, 177
overseas searches, 219
overseas, U.S. citizens, 224
plain view doctrine, in relation to, 124
privacy, reasonable expectation to, 123
U.S. agents, searches abroad by, 218